Marketing Planning
and Strategy

Marketing Planning and Strategy

Eighth Edition

Subhash C. Jain
University of Connecticut
George T. Haley
University of New Haven

CENGAGE
Learning™

Australia • Brazil • Japan • Korea • Mexico • Singapore • Spain • United Kingdom • United States

Marketing Planning and Strategy
Eighth Edition

Subhash C. Jain and George T. Haley

Executive Editors: Michele Baird, Maureen Staudt, and Michael Stranz

Marketing Manager: Lydia Lester

Managing Editor: Greg Albert

Sr. Marketing Coordinators: Lindsay Annett and Sara Mercurio

Production/Manufacturing Manager: Donna M. Brown

Premedia Supervisor: Becki Walker

Rights and Permissions Specialist: Kalina Ingham Hintz

Production Editor: K.A. Espy

Cover Image: © 2007 Getty

Composition House: Cadmus/KGL

For product information and technology assistance, contact us at **Cengage Learning Customer & Sales Support, 1-800-354-9706**

For permission to use material from this text or product, submit all requests online at **www.cengage.com/permissions** Further permissions questions can be emailed to **permissionrequest@cengage.com**

Library of Congress Control Number: 2008941127
Student Edition ISBN 13: 978-1-4266-3907-4
Student Edition ISBN 10: 1-4266-3907-4

Cengage Learning
5191 Natorp Boulevard
Mason, OH 45040
USA

Cengage Learning products are represented in Canada by Nelson Education, Ltd.

For your course and learning solutions, visit **academic.cengage.com** Purchase any of our products at your local college store or at our preferred online store **www.ichapters.com**

Printed in the United States of America
1 2 3 4 5 6 7 12 11 10 09

Special gratitude goes to my wife, Sadhna, and our children, Aveti and Amit, who played a key role in the completion of this work. Their ideas, human values, and commitment to creating the highest customer value made it possible.

Brief Contents

PREFACE xv

PART I   INTRODUCTION 1

    1   Marketing and the Concept of Planning and Strategy 3
    2   Strategic Marketing 19

PART II   STRATEGIC ANALYSIS 35

    3   Corporate Appraisal 37
    4   Understanding Competition 58
    5   Focusing on the Customer 80
    6   Scanning the Environment 96

PART III   STRATEGIC CAPABILITIES AND DIRECTION 119

    7   Measuring Strengths and Weaknesses 121
    8   Developing Marketing Objectives and Goals 139

PART IV   STRATEGY FORMULATION 159

    9   Strategy Selection 161
   10   Portfolio Analysis 181

PART V   STRATEGY IMPLEMENTATION AND CONTROL 205

   11   Organizational Structure 207
   12   Strategic Tools 225

PART VI   MARKETING STRATEGIES 251

   13   Market Strategies 253
   14   Product Strategies 271
   15   Pricing Strategies 306
   16   Distribution Strategies 330
   17   Promotion Strategies 355
   18   Global Market Strategies 380

     Cases 405

     Name Index 635

     Subject Index 639

Contents

PREFACE   XV

PART I   INTRODUCTION   1

1   Marketing and the Concept of Planning and Strategy   3
1.1   Concept of Planning   4
1.2   Concept of Strategy   8
1.3   Concept of Strategic Planning   9
1.4   Strategic Business Units (SBUs)   14
Summary   17
Discussion Questions   17
Notes   17

2   Strategic Marketing   19
2.1   Concept of Strategic Marketing   19
2.2   Aspects of Strategic Marketing   22
2.3   Strategic Marketing and Marketing Management   26
2.4   The Process of Strategic Marketing: An Example   27
2.5   Strategic Marketing Implementation   30
2.6   Plan of the Book   31
Summary   32
Discussion Questions   32
Notes   33

PART II   STRATEGIC ANALYSIS   35

3   Corporate Appraisal   37
3.1   Meaning of Corporate Appraisal   37
3.2   Factors in Appraisal: Corporate Publics   38
3.3   Factors in Appraisal: Value Orientation of Top Management   45
3.4   Factors in Appraisal: Corporate Resources   50
3.5   Past Performance of Business Units   55
Summary   56
Discussion Questions   56
Notes   57

4   Understanding Competition   58
4.1   Meaning of Competition   58
4.2   Theory of Competition   59
4.3   Classifying Competitors   60
4.4   Intensity, or Degree, of Competition   61
4.5   Competitive Intelligence   64
4.6   Seeking Competitive Advantage   70
4.7   Sustaining Competitive Advantage   76

	Summary	77
	Discussion Questions	78
	Notes	78

5	**Focusing on the Customer**	**80**
	5.1 Identifying Markets	80
	5.2 Customer Need	81
	5.3 Market Emergence	83
	5.4 Defining Market Boundaries	83
	5.5 Served Market	87
	5.6 Customer Segmentation	90
	Summary	94
	Discussion Questions	95
	Notes	95

6	**Scanning the Environment**	**96**
	6.1 Importance of Environmental Scanning	96
	6.2 What Scanning Can Accomplish	97
	6.3 The Concept of Environment	98
	6.4 State of the Art	98
	6.5 Types of Environment	101
	6.6 Environmental Scanning and Marketing Strategy	108
	6.7 Environmental Scanning Procedure	109
	6.8 Conducting Environmental Scanning: An Example	111
	6.9 Organizational Arrangements and Problems	113
	Summary	115
	Discussion Questions	116
	Notes	116
	Appendix: Scanning Techniques	117

PART III	**STRATEGIC CAPABILITIES AND DIRECTION**	**119**

7	**Measuring Strengths and Weaknesses**	**121**
	7.1 Meaning of Strengths and Weaknesses	121
	7.2 Studying Strengths and Weaknesses: State of the Art	122
	7.3 Systematic Measurement of Strengths and Weaknesses	124
	7.4 Analyzing Strengths and Weaknesses	131
	7.5 Concept of Synergy	136
	Summary	137
	Discussion Questions	137
	Notes	137

8	**Developing Marketing Objectives and Goals**	**139**
	8.1 Framework for Defining Objectives	140
	8.2 Corporate Strategic Direction	140
	8.3 SBU Objectives	144
	8.4 Business Mission	145
	8.5 SBU Objectives and Goals	149
	8.6 Product/Market Objectives	150
	8.7 Process of Setting Objectives	154
	Summary	157
	Discussion Questions	157
	Notes	157

PART IV		STRATEGY FORMULATION	159

	9	Strategy Selection	161
	9.1	Conceptual Scheme	161
	9.2	Product/Market Strategy	161
	9.3	Determining SBU Strategy	170
	9.4	Strategy Evaluation	174
		Summary	176
		Discussion Questions	176
		Notes	177
		Appendix: Perspectives on Strategic Thrusts	177

	10	Portfolio Analysis	181
	10.1	Product Life Cycle (PLC)	181
	10.2	Portfolio Matrix	186
	10.3	Multifactor Portfolio Matrix	194
	10.4	Portfolio Matrix: Critical Analysis	198
	10.5	A New Product Portfolio Approach: Porter's Generic Strategies Framework	202
	10.6	Portfolio Analysis Conclusion	202
		Summary	203
		Discussion Questions	203
		Notes	204

PART V		STRATEGY IMPLEMENTATION AND CONTROL	205

	11	Organizational Structure	207
	11.1	The Traditional Organization	207
	11.2	Creating Market-Responsive Organizations	208
	11.3	Role of Systems in Implementing Strategy	213
	11.4	Executive Reward Systems	214
	11.5	Leadership Style	216
	11.6	Measuring Strategic Performance	219
	11.7	Achieving Strategic Planning Effectiveness	219
	11.8	Strategic Planning and Marketing Organization	221
		Summary	222
		Discussion Questions	223
		Notes	223

	12	Strategic Tools	225
	12.1	Experience Curve Concept	225
	12.2	Profit Impact of Marketing Strategy (PIMS)	229
	12.3	Measuring the Value of Marketing Strategies	231
	12.4	Game Theory	233
	12.5	Delphi Technique	234
	12.6	Trend-Impact Analysis	236
	12.7	Cross-Impact Analysis	237
	12.8	Scenario Building	240
	12.9	Other Tools	241
		Summary	244
		Discussion Questions	244
		Notes	244
		Appendix: Experience Curve Construction	245

PART VI   MARKETING STRATEGIES   251

13   Market Strategies   253
13.1   Dimensions of Market Strategies   253
13.2   Market-Scope Strategy   253
13.3   Market-Geography Strategy   257
13.4   Market-Entry Strategy   259
13.5   Market-Commitment Strategy   262
13.6   Market-Dilution Strategy   264
Summary   266
Discussion Questions   266
Notes   267
Appendix: Perspectives of Market Strategies   268

14   Product Strategies   271
14.1   Dimensions of Product Strategies   271
14.2   Product-Positioning Strategy   271
14.3   Product-Repositioning Strategy   275
14.4   Product-Overlap Strategy   277
14.5   Product-Scope Strategy   279
14.6   Product-Design Strategy   281
14.7   Product-Elimination Strategy   283
14.8   New-Product Strategy   286
14.9   Diversification Strategy   292
14.10   Value-Marketing Strategy   294
Summary   300
Discussion Questions   301
Notes   301
Appendix: Perspectives of Product Strategies   303

15   Pricing Strategies   306
15.1   Review of Pricing Factors   306
15.2   Pricing Strategy for New Products   313
15.3   Pricing Strategies for Established Products   315
15.4   Price-Flexibility Strategy   319
15.5   Product Line-Pricing Strategy   320
15.6   Leasing Strategy   322
15.7   Bundling-Pricing Strategy   323
15.8   Price-Leadership Strategy   323
15.9   Pricing Strategy to Build Market Share   324
Summary   325
Discussion Questions   326
Notes   326
Appendix: Perspectives of Pricing Strategies   327

16   Distribution Strategies   330
16.1   Channel-Structure Strategy   330
16.2   Distribution-Scope Strategy   335
16.3   Multiple-Channel Strategy   338
16.4   Channel-Modification Strategy   342
16.5   Channel-Control Strategy   347
16.6   Conflict-Management Strategy   350

Summary   351
Discussion Questions   351
Notes   352
Appendix: Perspectives on Distribution Strategies   353

17   Promotion Strategies   **355**
17.1   Strategies for Developing Promotional Perspectives   356
17.2   Advertising Strategies   363
17.3   Personal Selling Strategies   371
Summary   376
Discussion Questions   377
Notes   377
Appendix: Perspectives on Promotion Strategies   378

18   Global Market Strategies   **380**
18.1   Identifying Target Markets   381
18.2   Entry Strategies   386
18.3   Global Market Environment   389
18.4   Strategy for Global Marketing Programs   392
18.5   Marketing in Global Business Strategy   394
18.6   Developing Global Market Strategy: An Example   396
Summary   401
Discussion Questions   402
Notes   402

CASES

1   The Lipitor Market   405

2   UPS vs. FedEx   409

3   Loblaws   414

4   CIBC: Introduction   421

5   NACSW's Growth Endeavors   433

6   The Nottoway Plantation, Restaurant, and Inn:
     The White Castle of Louisiana   441

7   Farggi   450

8   Revolution in the Jumbo Jet Market: Airbus – Boeing in 2001   465

9   SR Corp: Decisions for an Emerging Technology: Introduction   471

10   SpainSko   485

11   L'Oréal Netherlands B.V.: Product Introduction   502

12   Fast-Food Industry Woes   509

13   Lonetown Press   514

14   Wal-Mart, Inc.   519

15   Mickey Comes to the Rescue! Disneyland in Hong Kong   525

16   Kortec and Wrenware Architectural Hardware   529

17   Capital Insurance Company's Foray into Financial Services   535

18   Reinventing the Saturn Brand   540

19   Excelerite Integrated Systems, Inc. (EIS)   547

20   Lion Nathan China   549

21   IKEA   572

22   Bicycles for India   575

23   Hewlett-Packard Company in Vietnam   582

24   Cognex Corporation: Time for a New Vision?   595

25   Kentucky Fried Chicken and the Global Fast-Food Industry   608

26   Nestlé (Ghana) Ltd.   624

27   Planet Starbucks   631

Name Index   635

Subject Index   639

Preface

In an era marked by the challenges of global competition, rapidly changing technology, new consumer needs, and shifting demographics, the development of strategic marketing skills is essential if companies are to survive, let alone prosper. Because unique strategic marketing moves are not often as transparent to competitors and are nearly always difficult and time-consuming to copy, a focus on marketing strategy often yields significant advantage.

Marketing Planning and Strategy is a primer on strategic marketing. The book is intended for use in capstone marketing courses. The eighth edition contains two principle parts: text and cases. The text reviews the state of the art in marketing strategy, focusing on both research and concepts. The cases are comprehensive and integrative, most dealing with a broad range of marketing issues across varying strategic circumstances.

Today each company shares with all other companies the challenge of identifying and understanding the markets unfolding around it. Success will depend on the ability to perceive and understand these markets in all their subtlety, inconsistency, and rationality—in other words, in all their complexity. By choice, *Marketing Planning and Strategy* tries to illustrate and enrich this complexity so that students will approach the subject with the sophistication it deserves.

The book offers new ideas, new insights, and a reliable perspective on marketing strategy formulation. Topics of special interest include:

• Determining what marketing strategy can realistically accomplish for a business
• Determining when a business needs to reformulate its marketing strategy
• Distinguishing marketing strategy from marketing management
• Identifying underlying factors that must be considered in developing marketing strategy
• Analyzing corporate perspective and measuring strengths and weaknesses
• Examining basic changes in America's social and industrial environments that have led to the new emphasis on marketing strategy
• Developing a mission statement that can advance marketing efforts
• Setting realistic marketing objectives
• Determining roles for different products of a business unit
• Employing portfolio techniques in strategy determination and resource allocation
• Organizing for successful strategy implementation
• Identifying the latest techniques for gathering information, undertaking strategic analysis, and formulating strategies

In recent years, to clearly delineate the role of marketing in strategy development, a new term, strategic marketing, has been coined. Marketing may be viewed in three ways: as marketing management, as marketing strategy or strategic marketing, and as corporate marketing. Marketing management deals with strategy implementation, usually at the product/market or brand level. Strategic marketing focuses on strategy formulation, whereas corporate marketing provides inputs for corporate-wide strategy.

Strategy is commonly considered at the business unit level. At the heart of business unit strategy is marketing strategy, which becomes the basis of strategy in other functional areas. Integration of all functional strategies represents the business unit strategy. *Marketing Planning and Strategy* focuses on marketing strategy from the viewpoint of the business unit. The principles and concepts discussed in the book are universally applicable to organizations of all types: manufacturing and service, profit and nonprofit, domestic and foreign, small and large, low- and high-tech, and consumer and industrial products organizations. The book is analytical in approach and managerial in orientation.

HALLMARKS OF THE EIGHTH EDITION

This eighth edition presents a much more comprehensive treatment of the subject than previous editions. Developments in the field as evidenced by numerous journal articles, reports, and books on strategic marking and extension of my own thinking on the subject have enabled me to provide state-of-the-art coverage of the discipline.

Preparation of this new edition was guided by the following objectives:

- To provide emerging perspectives on strategic marketing
- To emphasize the emerging role of the Internet media on marketing strategy
- To add material on global market strategies
- To bring in the international focus in developing marketing strategy
- To examine such emerging topics as product quality and service
- To strengthen the discussion on strategy implementation
- To include new cases reflecting a variety of strategic marketing situations
- To update concepts, illustrations, and statistics throughout

Accomplishment of these objects led to a number of this edition's distinguishing features.

THE TEXT

Like the previous editions, the eighth edition is based on current conceptual and research literature. The text follows a basic model to explain marketing strategy formulation. The text is organized according to this model, which focuses on company, competition, customer, environment, strengths and weaknesses, objectives and goals, strategy development, and strategy implementation. The eighth edition also contains several significant improvements:

- Current thoughts and concepts in marketing strategy formulation, based on constructs that have taken place in the field
- Incorporation of global focus throughout the book
- Discussion of problems and their solution for successful marketing strategy implementation
- Substantial revision of the chapters on market, product, pricing, distribution, and promotion strategies as well as those on strategic implementation
- Updating of references to provide the most current perspectives on the subject
- Emphasis on the importance of emerging technologies in formulating marketing strategy
- Importance of ethical and social issues

THE CASES

This edition includes 30 cases, of which 10 are new. The cases have been used at such schools as Harvard Business School, Stanford University, E.M. Lyon, IESE, Graduate School of Business Administration Zurich, and the University of Connecticut. The cases deal with companies that students will recognize. Cases to illustrate each aspect of marketing strategy are included. Important improvements in cases include the following:

- An increased emphasis has been placed on including comprehensive and integrative cases that involve as many major strategy components as possible.
- New cases have been included, although the total number of cases has been kept to a manageable size
- A concentrated effort has been made to include cases that cover the full spectrum of organizational size
- The number of international cases has been increased to 15
- Five cases about service organizations—insurance, banking, entertainment, airlines, and Web-based business have been added

INSTRUCTOR'S MANUAL

The instructor's manual has been completely revised to provide in-depth analysis with a variety of new pedagogical aids: answers to the end-of-chapter discussion questions in the text; true/false, multiple choice, and fill-in exam questions; suggested syllabi; solutions to cases; suggestions for further reading; and a list of additional cases. Significant improvements in the manual include the following:

- Careful revision of seventh edition test bank questions and the addition of new questions for each chapter
- Chapter outlines providing quick chapter reviews
- Comprehensive case notes
- PowerPoint transparency masters software

Assumptions about the audience significantly affect the style and content of a book. This book is intended primarily for advanced undergraduates and graduate students. Thus, the material has been developed from a classroom-tested conceptual framework. Many of the conceptual schemes included in the book have been reshaped and modified, based on feedback provided by many distinguished marketers. The experiences of a large number of companies have been drawn upon and are cited throughout the book as illustrations.

This book concentrates on areas of strategic importance only, especially those having significant implications and particular relevance for the making of policy decisions in competitive situations. Discussion of routine day-to-day decisions is intentionally avoided to keep focus intact. The overall approach of this book is analytic rather than normative. This approach is necessary because strategy development is more an art than a science. In addition, strategy formulation is a highly complex process for which neat models and econometric equations, no matter how diligently worked out, do not suffice.

ACKNOWLEDGMENTS

A project of this nature cannot be completed without active support from different sources. I have been lucky in this respect to have received advice and assistance from many sources. I acknowledge the valuable feedback provided by students at the University of Connecticut and Graduate School of Business Administration Zurich, who read early drafts of the text as part of their assignments.

A special mention of appreciation must go to Michele Metcalf, Staff Assistant in the University of Connecticut's Center for International Business Education and Research (CIBER); and to Kelly Aceto, Associate Director in the CIBER office, for preparing the final manuscript. Thanks are due to our graduate students for their research help. We are indebted to many writers and publishers for granting permission to include excerpts from their works or their cases.

Throughout the development of this eighth edition, a number of reviewers made important contributions, and at the same time, many colleagues provided insightful suggestions. All these individuals had and important influence on our thinking:

John K. Rayan, Jr., Kent State University
P. Rajan Varadarajan, Texas A&M University
C.P. Rao, Kuwait University
Albert Stahli, GSBA Zurich
Sushil Vachanni, Boston University
Usha C. V. Haley, University of New Haven & Economic Policy Institute
Jerry Allen (Interim Dean), School of Business, University of New Haven

We owe a special word of thanks to our dean, Chris Earley, who encouraged us to undertake this project.

We are indebted to the talented staff at Cengage Learning for their role in shaping the eighth edition. Our editor, Greg Albert, furnished excellent advice on the structure of this edition. Our production editor K.A Espy and project coordinator Robin Richie did a superb job of seeing the book to completion.

Subhash C. Jain
University of Connecticut
Storrs, Connecticut

George T. Haley
University of New Haven
New Haven, CT

PART I

Introduction

Chapter 1
**Marketing and the Concept
of Planning and Strategy**

Chapter 2
Strategic Marketing

Chapter Outline

1.1 **Concept of Planning**
1.2 **Concept of Strategy**
1.3 **Concept of Strategic Planning**
    1.3.1 Managing for Competitive Advantage
    1.3.2 Viewing Change as an Opportunity
    1.3.3 Managing through People
    1.3.4 Shaping the Strategically Managed Organization
    1.3.5 Managing for Focus and Flexibility
    1.3.6 Managing Fit across All Functions
    1.3.7 Harnessing Information
1.4 **Strategic Business Units (SBUs)**
    1.4.1 Advertising
    1.4.2 Budgeting
    1.4.3 Packaging
    1.4.4 Manufacturing

Chapter **1**

Marketing and the Concept of Planning and Strategy

We must plan for the future, because people who stay in the present will remain in the past.
ABRAHAM LINCOLN

Over the years marketers have been presented with a series of philosophical approaches to marketing decision making. One widely used approach is the *marketing concept approach*, which directs the marketer to develop the product offering, and indeed the entire marketing program, to meet the needs of the customer base. A key element in this approach is the need for information flow from the market to the decision maker. Another approach is the *systems approach*, which instructs the marketer to view the product not as an individual entity but as just one aspect of the customer's total need-satisfaction system. A third approach, the *environmental approach*, portrays the marketing decision maker as the focal point of numerous environments within which the firm operates and that affect the success of the firm's marketing program. These environments frequently bear such labels as legal-political, economic, competitive, consumer, market structure, social, technological, and international.

Indeed, these and other philosophical approaches to marketing decision making are merely descriptive frameworks that stress certain aspects of the firm's role vis-a-vis the strategic planning process. No matter what approach a firm follows, it needs a reference point for its decisions that is provided by the strategy and the planning process involved in designing the strategy. Thus, the strategic planning process is the guiding force behind decision making, regardless of the approach one adopts. This relationship between the strategic planning process and approaches to marketing decision making is depicted in Exhibit 1.1.

Planning perspectives develop in response to needs that arise internally or that impinge on the organization from outside. During the 1950s and 1960s, growth was the dominant fact of the economic environment, and the planning processes developed during that time were typically geared to the discovery and exploitation of entrepreneurial opportunities. Decentralized planning was the order of the day. Top management focused on reviewing major investment proposals and approving annual operating budgets. Long-range corporate plans were occasionally put together, but they were primarily extrapolations and were rarely used for strategic decision making.

Planning perspectives changed in the 1970s. With the quadrupling of energy costs and the emergence of competition from new quarters, followed by a recession and reports of an impending capital crisis, companies found themselves surrounded by new needs. Reflecting these new management needs and concerns, a process aimed at more centralized control over resources soon pervaded planning efforts. Sorting out winners and losers, setting priorities, and conserving capital became the name of the game. A new era of strategic planning dawned over corporate America.

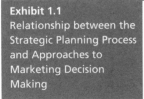

Exhibit 1.1
Relationship between the
Strategic Planning Process
and Approaches to
Marketing Decision
Making

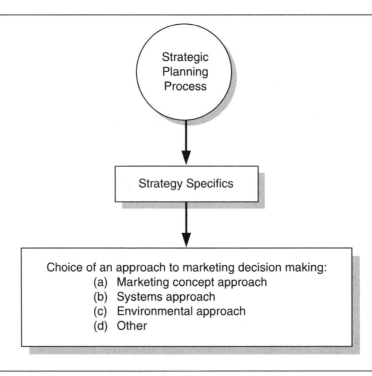

Today's enviornment has changed once again. The second largest and fastest growing source of multinational corporations (MNCs) is now the emerging markets. This change in the enviornment affects both our largest MNCs as well as small- and medium-sized enterprises (SMEs) with operations that are entirely domestic in nature. Emerging market multinationals (EMMs) originated in and operate in different business and socio-cultural environments than traditional MNCs. These differences permit EMMs significant advantages in speed and agility of managments if they are to remain effective in the new competitive environment. The effects of this change are compounded by the fact that many of these new EMMs, especially among those originating from the People's Republic of China, are state-owned enterprises (SOEs) and possess a government's deep pockets, and little of the slow, sclerotic decision processes many Westerners associate with SOEs.

The value of effective strategic planning is virtually unchallenged in today's business world. A majority of the *Fortune* 1000 firms in the United States, for instance, now have senior executives responsible for spearheading strategic planning efforts.[1]

In a recent *McKinsey Quarterly* survey of about 800 executives, 79 percent respondents claimed that strategic planning process played an important role in formulating strategies.[2]

Strategic planning requires that company assets (i.e., resources) be managed to maximize financial return through the selection of a viable business in accordance with the changing environment. One very important component of strategic planning is the establishment of the product/market scope of a business.[3] It is within this scope that strategic planning becomes relevant for marketers. Thus, as companies adopted and made progress in their strategic planning capabilities, a new strategic role for marketing emerged. In this strategic role, marketing concentrates on the markets to serve, the competition to be tackled, and the timing of market entry/exit.

1.1 CONCEPT OF PLANNING

Throughout human history, people have tried to achieve specific purposes, and in this effort some sort of planning has always found a place. In modern times, the former Soviet Union was the first nation to devise an economic plan for growth and development. After World War II, national economic planning became a popular activity, particularly among developing countries, with the goal of systematic and organized action designed to achieve stated objectives within a given period. Among market economies, France has gone the furthest in planning its economic affairs. In the business world, Henri Fayol, the French industrialist, is credited with the first successful attempts at formal planning.

Accomplishments attributed to planning can be summarized as follows:

1. Planning leads to a better position, or standing, for the organization.
2. Planning helps the organization progress in ways that its management considers most suitable.
3. Planning helps every manager think, decide, and act more effectively and progress in the desired direction.
4. Planning helps keep the organization flexible.
5. Planning stimulates a cooperative, integrated, enthusiastic approach to organizational problems.
6. Planning indicates to management how to evaluate and check up on progress toward planned objectives.
7. Planning leads to socially and economically useful results.

Planning in corporations emerged as an important activity in the 1960s. Several studies undertaken during that time showed that companies attached significant importance to planning. A Conference Board survey of 420 firms, for example, revealed that 85 percent had formalized corporate planning activity.[4] A 1983 survey by Coopers & Lybrand and Yankelovich, Skelly, and White confirmed the central role played by the planning function and the planner in running most large businesses.[5] A 1991 study by McDonalds noted that marketing planning is commonly practiced by companies of all sizes, and there is wide agreement on the benefits to be gained from such planning.[6] A 1996 survey by the Association of Management Consulting Firms found that business persons, academics, and consultants expect business planning to be their most pressing management issue[7] as they prepare to enter the next century.[6] The executives interviewed in a 2002 study indicated that planning was becoming more important and was receiving greater attention. Slywotzky and Wise emphasize the importance of planning for seeking growth in the midst of worldwide slowdown in the early years of the twenty-first century.[8]

Some companies that use formal planning believe that it improves profits and growth, finding it particularly useful in explicit objective setting and in monitoring results.[9] Certainly, the current business climate is generating a new posture among executives, with the planning process being identified by eight out of ten respondents as a key to implementing the chief executive officer's (CEO) chosen strategy.[10] Today most companies insist on some sort of planning exercise to meet the rapidly changing environment. For many, however, the exercise is cathartic rather than creative.[11]

Growth is an accepted expectation of a firm; however, growth does not happen by itself. Growth must be carefully planned: questions such as how much, when, in which areas, where to grow, and who will be responsible for different tasks must be answered. Unplanned growth will be haphazard and may fail to provide desired levels of profit. Therefore, for a company to realize orderly growth, to maintain a high level of operating efficiency, and to achieve its goals fully, it must plan for the future systematically. Products, markets, facilities, personnel, and financial resources must be evaluated wisely.

Today's business environment is more complex than ever. In addition to the keen competition that firms face from both domestic and overseas companies, a variety of other concerns, including environmental protection, employee welfare, consumerism, and antitrust action, impinge on business moves. Thus, it is desirable for a firm to be cautious in undertaking risks, which again calls for a planned effort.

Many firms pursue growth internally through research and development. This route to growth is not only time-consuming but also requires a heavy commitment of resources with a high degree of risk. In such a context, planning is needed to choose the right type of risk.

Since World War II, technology has had a major impact on markets and marketers. Presumably, the trend of accelerating technological change will continue in the future. The impact of technological innovations may be felt in any industry or in any firm. Therefore, such changes need to be anticipated as far in advance as possible in order for a firm to take advantage of new opportunities and to avoid the harmful consequences of not anticipating major new developments. Here again, planning is significant.

Finally, planning is required in making a choice among the many equally attractive alternative investment opportunities a firm may have. No firm can afford to invest in each and every ''good'' opportunity. Planning, thus, is essential in making the right selection.

Planning for future action has been called by many different names: long-range planning, corporate planning, comprehensive planning, and formal planning. Whatever its name, the reference is obviously to the future.

Planning is essentially a process directed toward making today's decisions with tomorrow in mind and a means of preparing for future decisions so that they may be made rapidly, economically, and with as little disruption to the business as possible.[7]

Though there are as many definitions of planning as there are writers on the subject, the emphasis on the future is the common thread underlying all planning theory. In practice, however, different meanings are attached to planning. A distinction is often made between a *budget* (a yearly program of operations) and a *long-range plan*. Some people consider planning as something done by staff specialists, whereas budgeting is seen to fall within the purview of line managers. Important aspects of planning frequently ignored in planning theory and discussions of planning are related to implementation, the importance of incorporating line managers into the planning process and the effects of line managment's adaptation of corporate plans to meet the exigenices of changing business and competitive environments.

It is necessary for a company to be clear about the nature and scope of the planning that it intends to adopt. A definition of planning should then be based on what planning is supposed to be in an organization. It is not necessary for every company to engage in the same style of comprehensive planning. The basis of all planning should be to design courses of action to be pursued for achieving stated objectives such that opportunities are seized and threats are guarded against, but the exact planning posture must be custom-made (i.e., based on the decision-making needs of the organization).

Operations management, which emphasizes the current programs of an organization, and planning, which essentially deals with the future, are two intimately related activities. Operations management or budgeted programs should emerge as the result of planning. In the outline of a five-year plan, for example, years two through five may be described in general terms, but the activities of the first year should be budgeted and accompanied by detailed operational programs.

A distinction should also be made between planning and forecasting. Forecasting considers future changes in areas of importance to a company and tries to assess the impact of these changes on company operations. Planning takes over from there to set objectives and goals and develop strategy.

Briefly, no business, however small or poorly managed, can do without planning. Although planning per se may be nothing new for an organization, the current emphasis on it is indeed different. No longer just one of several important functions of the organization, planning's new role demands linkage of various parts of an organization into an integrated system. The emphasis has shifted from planning as an aspect of the organization to planning as the basis of all efforts and decisions, the building of an entire organization toward the achievement of designated objectives.

There is little doubt about the importance of planning. Planning departments are key in critiquing strategies, crystallizing goals, setting priorities, and maintaining control;[12] but to be useful, planning should be done properly. Planning just for the sake of it can be injurious; half-hearted planning can cause more problems than it solves. In practice, however, many business executives simply pay lip service to planning, partly because they find it difficult to incorporate planning into the decision-making process and partly because they are uncertain how to adopt it.

If planning is to succeed, proper arrangements must be made to put it into operation. The Boston Consulting Group suggests the following concerns for effective planning:

- There is the matter of outlook, which can affect the degree to which functional and professional viewpoints, versus corporate needs, dominate the work of planning.
- There is the question of the extent of involvement for members of the management. Who should participate, and to what extent?
- There is the problem of determining what part of the work of planning should be accomplished through joint effort and how to achieve effective collaboration among participants in the planning process.
- There is the matter of incentive, of making planning an appropriately emphasized and rewarded kind of managerial work.
- There is the question of how to provide staff coordination for planning, which raises the issue of how a planning unit should be used in the organization.
- And there is the role of the chief executive in the planning process. What should it be?[13]

Though planning is conceptually rather simple, implementing it is far from easy. Successful planning requires a blend of many forces in different areas, not the least of which are behavioral, intellectual, structural, philosophical, and managerial. Achieving the proper blend of these forces requires making difficult decisions, as the Boston Consulting Group has suggested. Although planning is indeed complex, successful planning systems do have common fundamental characteristics despite differing operational details. First, it is essential that the CEO be completely supportive. Second, planning must be kept simple, in agreement with the managerial style, and unencumbered by detailed numbers and fancy equations. Third, planning is a shared responsibility, and it would be wrong to assume that the president or vice president of planning, staff specialists, or line managers can do it single-handedly. Fourth, the managerial incentive system should give due recognition to the fact that decisions made with long-term implications may not appear good in the short run. Fifth, the goals of planning should be achievable without excessive frustration and work load and with widespread understanding and acceptance of the process. Sixth, overall flexibility should be encouraged to accommodate changing conditions.[14]

There is no one best time for initiating planning activities in an organization; however, before developing a formal planning system, the organization should be prepared to establish a strong planning foundation. The CEO should be a central participant, spearheading the planning job. A planning framework should be developed to match the company's perspective and should be generally accepted by its executives. A manual outlining the work flow, information links, format of various documents, and schedules for completing various activities should be prepared by the planner. Once these foundations are completed, the company can initiate the planning process anytime.

Planning should not be put off until bad times prevail; it is not just a cure for poor performance. Although planning is probably the best way to avoid bad times, planning efforts that are begun when operational performance is at an ebb (i.e., at low or no profitability) will only make things worse, since planning efforts tend initially to create an upheaval by challenging the traditional patterns of decision making. The company facing the question of survival should concentrate on alleviating the current crisis.

Planning should evolve gradually. It is wishful thinking to expect full-scale planning to be instituted in a few weeks or months. Initial planning may be formalized in one or more functional areas; then, as experience is gained, a company-wide planning system may be designed. IBM, a pioneer in formalized planning, followed this pattern. First, financial planning and product planning were attempted in the post-World War II period. Gradual changes toward increased formality were made over the years. In the later half of 1960s, increased attention was given to planning contents, and a compatible network of planning data systems was initiated. Corporate-wide planning, which was introduced in the 1970s, forms the backbone of IBM's current global planning endeavors. Beginning in 1986, the company made several changes in its planning perspectives in response to the contingencies created by deteriorating performance. In the 1990s, planning at IBM became more centralized to fully seek resource control and coordination. In the new century, planning has a new purpose and a new destination for IBM. It is necessary to look at both the forest and the trees when developing and executing a dynamic business plan. Planning exercises should give decision-makers both an external, overarching perspective, and internal mechanisms to steer the organization toward the goal of sustained growth.

In an analysis of three different philosophies of planning, Ackoff established the labels satisfying, optimizing, and adaptivizing.[15] Planning on the basis of the **satisfying** philosophy aims at easily achievable goals and molds planning efforts accordingly. This type of planning requires setting objectives and goals that are ''high enough'' but not as ''high as possible.'' The satisfying planner, therefore, devises only one feasible and acceptable way of achieving goals, which may not necessarily be the best possible way. Under a satisfying philosophy, confrontations that might be caused by conflicts in programs are diffused through politicking, underplaying change, and accepting a fall in performance as unavoidable.

The philosophy of **optimizing** planning has its foundation in operations research. The optimizing planner seeks to model various aspects of the organization and define them as objective functions. Efforts are then directed so that an objective function is maximized (or minimized), subject to the constraints imposed by management or forced by the environment. For example, an objective may be to obtain the highest feasible market share; planning then amounts to searching for different variables that affect market share: price elasticity, plant capacity, competitive behavior, the product's stage in the life cycle, and so on. The effect of each variable is reduced to constraints on the market share. Then an analysis is undertaken to find out the optimum market share to target.

Unlike the satisfying planner, the optimizer endeavors, with the use of mathematical models, to find the best available course to realize objectives and goals. The success of an optimizing planner depends on how completely and accurately the model depicts the underlying situation and how well the planner can figure out solutions from the model once it has been built.

The philosophy of **adaptivizing** planning is an innovative approach not yet popular in practice. To understand the nature of this type of planning, let us compare it to optimizing planning. In optimization, the significant variables and their effects are taken for granted. Given these, an effort is made to achieve the optimal result. With an adaptivizing approach, on the other hand, planning may be undertaken to produce changes in the underlying relationships themselves and thereby create a desired future. Underlying relationships refer to an organization's internal and external environment and the dynamics of the values of the actors in these environments (i.e., how values relate to needs and to the satisfaction of needs, how changes in needs produce changes in values, and how changes in needs are produced).

1.2 CONCEPT OF STRATEGY

Strategy in a firm is

> the pattern of major objectives, purposes, or goals and essential policies and plans for achieving those goals, stated in such a way as to define what business the company is in or is to be in and the kind of company it is or is to be.

Any organization needs strategy (a) when resources are finite, (b) when there is uncertainty about competitive strengths and behavior, (c) when commitment of resources is irreversible, (d) when decisions must be coordinated between far-flung places and over time, and (e) when there is uncertainty about control of the initiative.

An explicit statement of strategy is the key to success in a changing business environment. Strategy provides a unified sense of direction to which all members of the organization can relate. Where there is no clear concept of strategy, decisions rest on either subjective or intuitive assessment and are made without regard to other decisions. Such decisions become increasingly unreliable as the pace of change accelerates or decelerates rapidly. Without a strategy, an organization is like a ship without a rudder going around in circles.

Strategy is concerned with the deployment of potential for results and the development of a reaction capability to adapt to environmental changes. Quite naturally, we find that there are hierarchies of strategies: corporate strategy and business strategy. At the corporate level, strategy is mainly concerned with defining the set of businesses that should form the company's overall profile. **Corporate strategy** seeks to unify all the business lines of a company and point them toward an overall goal. At the business level, strategy focuses on defining the manner of competition in a given industry or product/market segment. A **business strategy** usually covers a plan for a single product or a group of related products. Today, most strategic action takes place at the business unit level, where sophisticated tools and techniques permit the analysis of a business; the forecasting of such variables as market growth, pricing, and the impact of government regulation; and the establishment of a plan that can sidestep threats in an erratic environment from competitors, economic cycles, and social, political, and consumer changes.

Each functional area of a business (e.g., marketing) makes its own unique contribution to strategy formulation at different levels. In many firms, the marketing function represents the greatest degree of contact with the external environment, the environment least controllable by the firm. In such firms, marketing plays a pivotal role in strategy development.

In its strategic role, marketing consists of establishing a match between the firm and its environment. It seeks solutions to problems of deciding (a) what business the firm is in and what kinds of business it may enter in the future and (b) how the chosen field(s) of endeavor may be successfully run in a competitive environment by pursuing product, price, promotion, and distribution perspectives to serve target markets.[16] In the context of strategy formulation, marketing has two dimensions: present and future. The present dimension deals with the existing relationships of the firm to its environments. The future dimension encompasses intended future relationships (in the form of a set of objectives) and the action programs necessary to reach those objectives. The following example illustrates the point.

McDonald's, the hamburger chain, has among its corporate objectives the goal of increasing the productivity of its operating units. Given the high proportion of costs in fixed facilities, McDonald's decided to increase facility utilization during off-peak hours, particularly during the morning hours. The program developed to accomplish these goals, the Egg McMuffin, was followed by a breakfast menu consistent with the limited product line strategy of McDonald's regular fare. In this example, the corporate goal of increased productivity led to the marketing perspective of breakfast fare (intended relationship), which was built over favorable customer attitudes toward the chain (existing relationship). Similarly, a new marketing strategy in the form of McDonald's McGriddle (intended relationship) was pursued over the company's ability to serve food fast (existing relationship) to meet the corporate goal of growth. (The McGriddle is a pork-patty between two pancakes. It has been acclaimed to be McDonalds' biggest hit in a generations.[17])

Generally, organizations have identifiable existing strategic perspectives; however, not many organizations have an explicit strategy for the intended future. The absence of an explicit strategy is frequently the result of a lack of top management involvement and commitment required for the development of proper perspectives of the future within the scope of current corporate activities. Former GE CEO Jack Welch suggests a three-step approach in designing an explicit strategy[18]:

a. Come up with a big aha for your business, a smart, realisitic, relativley fast way to gain sustainable competitive advantage.
b. Put the right people in the right jobs to drive the big aha forward.
c. Relentlessly seek out the best practices to achieve your big aha, whether inside or out, adapt them, and contunally improve them.

Marketing provides the core element for future relationships between the firm and its environment. It specifies inputs for defining objectives and helps formulate plans to achieve them.

1.3 CONCEPT OF STRATEGIC PLANNING

Strategy specifies direction. Its intent is to influence the behavior of competitors and the evolution of the market to the advantage of the strategist. It seeks to change the competitive environment. Thus, a strategy statement includes a description of the new competitive equilibrium to be created, the cause-and-effect relationships that will bring it about, and the logic to support the course of action. Planning articulates the means of implementing strategy. A strategic plan specifies the sequence and the timing of steps that will alter competitive relationships.

The strategy and the strategic plan are quite different things. The strategy may be brilliant in content and logic; but the sequence and timing of the plan, inadequate. The plan may be the laudable implementation of a worthless strategy. Put together, strategic planning concerns the relationship of an organization to its environment. Conceptually, the organization monitors its environment, incorporates the effects of environmental changes into corporate decision making, and formulates new strategies. Exhibit 1.2 provides a scorecard to evaluate the viability of a company's strategic planning effort.

Exhibit 1.2 A Strategic Planning Scorecard	• Is our planning really strategic? Do we try to anticipate change or only project from the past? • Do our plans leave room to explore strategic alternatives? Or do they confine us to conventional thinking? • Do we have time and incentive to investigate truly important things? Or do we spend excessive planning time on trivia? • Have we ever seriously evaluated a new approach to an old market? Or are we locked into the status quo? • Do our plans critically document and examine strategic assumptions? Or do we not really understand the implications of the plans we review? • Do we consistently make an attempt to examine consumer, competitor, and distributor responses to our programs? Or do we assume the changes will not affect the relationships we have seen in the past?

Source: Thomas P. Justad and Ted J. Mitchell, "Creative Market Planning in a Partisan Environment," *Business Horizons* (March–April 1982): 64, copyright 1982 by the Foundation for the School of Business at Indiana University. Reprinted by permission.

Companies that do well in strategic planning define their goals clearly and develop rational plans to implement them. In addition, they take the following steps to make their strategic planning effective:

- They shape the company into logical business units that can identify markets, customers, competitors, and the external threats to their business. These business units are managed semi-autonomously by executives who operate under corporate financial guidelines and with an understanding of the unit's assigned role in the corporate plan.
- They demonstrate a willingness at the corporate level to compensate line managers on long-term achievements, not just the yearly bottom line; to fund research programs that could give the unit a long-term competitive edge; and to offer the unit the type of planning support that provides data on key issues and encourages and teaches sophisticated planning techniques.
- They develop at the corporate level the capacity to evaluate and balance competing requests from business units for corporate funds, based on the degree of risk and reward.
- They match shorter-term business unit goals to a long-term concept of the company's evolution over the next 15 to 20 years. Exclusively the CEO's function, effectiveness in matching business unit goals to the firm's evolution may be tested by the board of directors.

The importance of strategic planning for a company may be illustrated by the example of the Mead Corporation. The Mead Corporation is basically in the forest products business. More than 75 percent of its earnings are derived from trees, from the manufacture of pulp and paper, to the conversion of paperboard to beverage carriers, to the distribution of paper supplies to schools. Mead also has an array of businesses outside the forest products industry and is developing new technologies and businesses for its future, primarily in storing, retrieving, and reproducing data electronically. In short, Mead is a company growing in the industries in which it started as well as expanding into areas that fit the capabilities and style of its management.

Although Mead was founded in 1846, it did not begin to grow rapidly until around 1955, reaching the $1 billion mark in sales in the late 1960s. Unfortunately, its competitive position did not keep pace with this expansion. In 1982 the company ranked 12th among 15 forest products companies. Clearly, if Mead was to become a leading company, its philosophy, its management style and focus, and its sense of urgency—its whole corporate culture—had to change. The vehicle for that change was the company's strategic planning process.

When top managers began to discuss ways to improve Mead, they quickly arrived at the key question: What kind of performing company should Mead be? They decided that Mead should be in the top quartile of those companies with which it was normally compared. Articulation of such a clear and simple objective provided all levels of management with a sense of direction and with a frame of reference within which to make and test their own decisions. This objective was translated into specific long-term financial goals.

In 1982 a rigorous assessment of Mead's businesses was made. The results of this assessment were not comforting—several small units were in very weak competitive positions. They were substantial users of cash that was needed elsewhere in businesses where Mead had opportunities for significant growth. Mead's board decided that by 1987 the company should get out of certain businesses, even though some of those high cash users were profitable.

Setting goals and assessing Mead's mix of businesses were only the first steps. Strategic planning had to become a way of life if the corporate culture was going to be changed. Five major changes were instituted. First, the corporate goals were articulated throughout the company—over and over and over again.

Second, the management system was restructured. This restructuring was much easier said than done. In Mead's pulp and paper businesses, the culture expected top management to be heavily involved in the day-to-day operation of major facilities and intimately involved in major construction projects, a style that had served the company well when it was simply a producer of paper. By the early 1980s, however, Mead was simply too large and too diverse for such a hands-on approach. The nonpulp and paper businesses, which were managed with a variety of styles, needed to be integrated into a more balanced management system. Therefore, it was essential for top management to stay out of day-to-day operations. This decision allowed division managers to become stronger and to develop a greater sense of personal responsibility for their operations. By staying away from major construction projects, top managers allowed on-site managers to complete under budget and ahead of schedule the largest and most complex programs in the company's history.

Third, simultaneously with the restructuring of its management system, seminars were used to teach strategic planning concepts and techniques. These seminars, sometimes week-long sessions, were held off the premises with groups of 5 to 20 people at a time. Eventually, the top 300 managers in the company became graduates of Mead's approach to strategic planning.

Fourth, specific and distinctly different goals were developed and agreed upon for each of Mead's two dozen or so business units. Whereas the earlier Mead culture had charged each operation to grow in any way it could, each business unit now had to achieve a leadership position in its markets or, if a leadership position was not practical, to generate cash.

Finally, the board began to fund agreed-upon strategies instead of approving capital projects piecemeal or yielding to emotional pleas from favorite managers.

The first phase of change was the easiest to accomplish. Between 1983 and 1986, Mead disposed of 11 units that offered neither growth nor significant cash flow. Over $100 million was obtained from these divestitures, and that money was promptly reinvested in Mead's stronger businesses. As a result, Mead's mix of businesses showed substantial improvement by 1987. In fact, Mead achieved its portfolio goals one year ahead of schedule.

For the remaining businesses, developing better strategies and obtaining better operating performance were much harder to achieve. After all, on a relative basis, the company was performing well. With the exception of 1984, 1989, 1994, and 2003, the years from 1983 to 2006 set all-time records for performance. The evolution of Mead's strategic planning system and the role it played in helping the good businesses of the company improve their relative performance are public knowledge. The financial results speak for themselves. In spite of the divestitures of businesses with sales of over $500 million, Mead's sales grew at a compound rate of 9 percent from 1983 to reach $4.9 billion in 2006. In addition, by the end of 2006, Mead's return on total capital (ROTC) reached 11.1 percent. More important, among 15 forest products companies with which Mead is normally compared, it had moved from twelfth place in 1982 to second place in 1993, a position it continued to maintain in 2006. These were the results of using a strategic planning system as the vehicle for improving financial performance.

During the period from 2006 to 2007, Mead took additional measures to increase its focus in two areas: (a) its coated paper and board business and (b) its value-added, less capital-intensive businesses (the distribution and conversion of paper and related supplies and electronic publishing). Today Mead is a well-managed, highly focused, aggressive company. It is well positioned to be exceptionally successful in the current decade and beyond.

Many forces affected the way strategic planning developed in the 1980s and early 1990s. These forces included slower growth worldwide, intense global competition, burgeoning automation, obsolescence due to technological change, deregulation, an explosion in information availability, more rapid shifts in raw material prices, chaotic money markets, and major changes in macroeconomic and sociopolitical systems. As a result, destabilization and fluidity have become the norm in world business.

Today there are many, many strategic alternatives for all types of industries. Firms are constantly coming up with new ways of making products and getting them to market. Comfortable positions in industry after industry (e.g., in banking, telecommunications, airlines, automobiles) are disappearing, and barriers to entry are much more difficult to maintain. Markets are open, and new competitors are coming from unexpected directions.

To steadily prosper in such an environment, companies need new strategic planning perspectives. First, top management must assume a more explicit role in strategic planning, dedicating a large amount of time to deciding how things ought to be instead of listening to analyses of how they are. Second, strategic planning must become an exercise in creativity instead of an exercise in forecasting. Third, strategic planning processes and tools that assume that the future will be similar to the past must be replaced by a mindset obsessed with being first to recognize change and turn it into competitive advantage. Fourth, the role of the planner must change from being a purveyor of incrementalism to that of a crusader for action. Finally, strategic planning must be restored to the core of line management responsibilities.

These perspectives can be described along six action-oriented dimensions: managing a business for competitive advantage, viewing change as an opportunity, managing through people, shaping the strategically managed organization, managing for focus and flexibility, and managing fit across all functions. Considering these dimensions can make strategic planning more relevant and effective.

1.3.1 Managing for Competitive Advantage

Organizations in a market economy are concerned with delivering a service or product in the most profitable way. The key to profitability is to achieve a sustainable competitive advantage based on superior performance relative to the competition. Superior performance requires doing three things better than the competition. First, the firm must clearly designate the product/market, based on marketplace realities and a true understanding of its strengths and weaknesses. Second, it must design a winning business system or structure that enables the company to outperform competitors in producing and delivering the product or service. Third, management must do a better job of managing the overall business system, by managing not only relationships within the corporation but also critical external relationships with suppliers, customers, and competitors.[19]

In turn, the notion of white-space opportunities is proving especially compelling for highly decentralized companies such as Hewlett-Packard Co. Former HP CEO Carly Fiorina believed her most important role in strategy formulation was to build bridges among the compnay's various operations. "I don't create business strategies," argued Fiorina. "My role is to encourage discussion of the white spaces, the overlap and gap amoung business strategies, the important areas that are not addressed by the strategies of individual HP businesses."[20]

As an example, Hewlett-Packard Co. brings its customers and suppliers together with the general managers of its many business units in strategy sessions aimed at creating new market opportunities. In each case, HP defines a "business ecosystem," the framework for its managers to explore and analyze. In an ecosystem, companies sometimes compete and often cooperate to come up with innovations, create new products, and serve customers. Most of the business managers are so busy minding their current businesses that is is hard to step out and see threats or opportunities. But by looking at the entire ecosystem, it provides a broad perspective to them. It gets people out of their boxes.

A session on the ecosystem for the automotive industry saw HP assembling managers from divisions that make service-bay diagnostic systems for Ford Motor Co., workstations in auto manufacturing plants, and electronic components for cars. The company also invited customers and suppliers. What could all these divisions do together to create new value for the industry? "Many of the opportunities came right out of the mouth of customers."[21] Possibilities included creating "smart" highway systems or building integrated systems that would collect service problems and immediately feed them back to Detroit. It changes the vision of the business future, and managers start thinking about how they can get increased value from all the pieces of the company.

By inviting such a broad range of people to the strategy table, HP gained viewpoints that would normally not be heard. Yet those opinions are critical to creating future products and markets.[22]

1.3.2 Viewing Change as an Opportunity

A new culture should be created within the organization such that managers look to change as an opportunity and adapt their business system to continuously emerging conditions. In other words, change should not be viewed as a problem but as a source of opportunity, providing the potential for creativity and innovation.

1.3.3 Managing through People

Management's first task is to create a vision of the organization that includes (a) where the organization should be going, again based on a clear examination of the company's strengths and weaknesses; (b) what markets it should compete in; (c) how it will compete; and (d) major action programs required. The next task is to convert vision to reality—to develop the capabilities of the organization, to expedite change and remove obstacles, and to shape the environment. Central to both the establishment and execution of a corporate vision is the effective recruitment, development, and deployment of human resources. In the end, management is measured by the skill and sensitivity with which it manages and develops people, for it is only through the quality of their people that organizations can change effectively.

Electronic Data Systems Corp., which manages large-scale data centers, has opened its strategic-planning process to a broad range of players. In 1992, EDS launched a major strategy initiative that involved 2,500 of its 55,000 employees. The company picked a core group of 150 staffers from around the world for the yearlong assignment. The group ranged from a 26-year-old systems engineer who had been with EDS for two years to a sixty-something corporate vice-president with a quarter of a century of EDS experience. The staffers identified potential "discontinuities" that could threaten or pose opportunities for EDS. They isolated the company's core competencies—what it does best and how that differentiates it from the competition. And they crafted a "strategic intent"—a point of view about its future. The company discovered that in order for it to make information technology valuable to people, its people had to be able to go into a company and offer consulting to provide more complete solutions, and it couldn't do that without building a business strategy. So EDS began to create a management-consulting practice, acquiring A.T. Kearney Inc. for $600 million. Similar approaches have been used by a wide range of companies, including Marriott Hotel and Helene Curtis Industries.[23]

1.3.4 Shaping the Strategically Managed Organization[16]

Management should work toward developing an innovative, self-renewing organization that the future will demand. Organizational change depends on such factors as structure, strategy, systems, style, skills, staff, and shared values. Organizations that take an externally focused, forward-looking approach to the design of these factors have a much better chance of self-renewal than those whose perspective is predominantly internal and historical.

1.3.5 Managing for Focus and Flexibility

Today, strategic planning should be viewed differently than it was viewed in the past. A five-year plan, updated annually, should be replaced by an ongoing concern for the direction the organization is taking. Many scholars describe an ongoing concern for the direction of the firm; that is, concern with what a company must do to become smart, targeted, and nimble enough to prosper in an era of constant change, as strategic thinking. The key words in this pursuit are focus and flexibility.

Focus means figuring out and building on what the company does best. It involves identifying the evolving needs of customers, then developing the key skills—often called the *core competencies*—making sure that everyone in the company understands them. Flexibility means sketching rough scenarios of the future (i.e., bands of possibilities) and being ready to pounce on opportunities as they arise. The point may be illustrated with reference to Sears. From 1985 to 1994, about $163 billion of stock market value was created in the retail industry. Some 25 companies were responsible for creating 85% of that wealth, and many of them did it with "business designs" that featured stores outside shopping malls, with low prices, quality merchandise, and broad selection. While Wal-Mart Stores Inc. generated $42 billion and Home Depot Inc. added $20 billion in value, Sears' retail operations captured less that $1 billion in that 10-year period. How did it happen? Like so many American business icons, Sears lost sight of its customers. They did not know whom they wanted to serve. That was a huge hole in the company's strategy. It was also not clear on what basis they thought they could win against the competition.

A major strategy overhaul led to the disposal of non-retail assets and a renewed focus on Sears' core business. The company renovated dowdy stores, upgraded women's apparel, and launched a new ad campaign to engineer a major turnaround at the department-store giant. One of the things that got the company in trouble was its lack of focus on the customer. Extensive customer research discovered high levels of brand loyalty to Sears' hardware lines. The research also suggested that by segmenting the do-it-yourself market and focusing on home projects with a low degree of complexity, say, papering a bathroom or installing a dimmer switch, Sears could avoid a major competitive collision with Home Depot and other home-improvement giants. Customers, the Sears research showed, desired convenience more than breadth of category in such hardware stores.

After successfully testing the concept of hardware outlets, the company made a billion-dollar capital investment to gain growth in this new market. It now has 1,000 freestanding, 20,000-square-foot hardware stores in different parts of the country built at a cost of $1.25 – 2 million per outlet.

What is true of large companies applies to small businesses as well. Welch, in his book entitled *Winning*, describes the story of a pizza restaurant in a Boston neighborhood called Upper Crust Pizza. The place is a usual fast-food pizza noisey place with limited space, paper plates and soft drinks, with noncommittal staff. But its focus is on product with the unique sauce which has made it a successful operation. As has been said "But the pizza is to die for; you could just faint describing the flavor of the sauce, and the crust puts you over the edge." Investment bankers, activits, and cops start lining up at 11 A.M. to see the Slice of the Day posted on the door, and around lunch and dinner, the line can run 20 deep.[24]

1.3.6 Managing Fit across All Functions

Different functions or activities must reinforce each other for a successful strategy. A productive sales force, for example, confers a greater advantage when the company's product embodies premium technology and its marketing approach emphasizes customer assistance and support. A production line with high levels of model variety is more valuable when combined with an inventory and order-processing system that minimizes the need for stocking finished goods, a sales process equipped to explain and encourage customization, and an advertising theme that stresses the benefits of product variations that meet a customer's special needs. Such complementaries are pervasive in strategy.

1.3.7 Harnessing Information

Strategic planning future lies in harnessing all those day-to-day details for disparate divisions, and communicating and incorporating them regularly across the organization. It is no longer a paper-and-pencil activity. Rigorously tested vision teamed with enabling enterprise software pave the way, while staff, united in their purpose and able to execute their contributions to the plan, drive the organization to its unique destination.

1.4 STRATEGIC BUSINESS UNITS (SBUs)

Frequent reference has been made in this chapter to the business unit, a unit comprising one or more products having a common market base whose manager has complete responsibility for integrating all functions into a strategy against an identifiable competitor. Usually referred to as a **strategic business unit (SBU)**, business units have also been called strategy centers, strategic planning units, or independent business units. The philosophy behind the SBU concept has been described this way: The diversified firm should be managed as a "portfolio" of businesses, with each business unit serving a clearly defined product-market segment with a clearly defined strategy. Each business unit in the portfolio should develop a strategy tailored to its capabilities and competitive needs, but consistent with the overall corporate capabilities and needs. The total portfolio of businesses should be managed by allocating capital and managerial resources to serve the interests of the firm as a whole—to achieve balanced growth in sales, earnings, and assets mix at an acceptable and controlled level of risk. In essence, the portfolio should be designed and managed to achieve an overall corporate strategy.

Since formal strategic planning began to make inroads in corporations in the 1970s, a variety of new concepts have been developed for identifying a corporation's opportunities and for speeding up the process of strategy development. These newer concepts create problems of internal organization. In a dynamic economy, all functions of a corporation (e.g., research and development, finance, and marketing) are related. Optimizing certain functions instead of the company as a whole is far from adequate for achieving superior corporate performance. Such an organizational perspective leaves only the CEO in a position to think in terms of the corporation as a whole. Large corporations have tried many different structural designs to broaden the scope of the CEO in dealing with complexities. One such design is the profit center concept. Unfortunately, the profit center concept emphasizes short-term consequences; also, its emphasis is on optimizing the profit center instead of the corporation as a whole.

The SBU concept was developed to overcome the difficulties posed by the profit center type of organization. Thus, the first step in integrating product/market strategies is to identify the firm's SBUs. This amounts to identifying natural businesses in which the corporation is involved. SBUs are not necessarily synonymous with existing divisions or profit centers. An SBU is composed of a product or product lines having identifiable independence from other products or product lines in terms of competition, prices, substitutability of product, style/quality, and impact of product withdrawal. It is around this configuration of products that a business strategy should be designed. In today's organizations, this strategy may encompass products found in more than one division. By the same token, some managers may find themselves managing two or more natural businesses. This does not necessarily mean that divisional boundaries need to be redefined; an SBU can often overlap divisions, and a division can include more than one SBU.[25]

SBUs may be created by applying a set of criteria consisting of price, competitors, customer groups, and shared experience. To the extent that changes in a product's price entail a review of the pricing policy of other products may imply that these products have a natural alliance. If various products/markets of a company share the same group of competitors, they may be amalgamated into an SBU for the purpose of strategic planning. Likewise, products/markets sharing a common set of customers belong together. Finally, products/markets in different parts of the company having common research and development, manufacturing, and marketing components may be included in the same SBU. For purposes of illustration, consider the case of a large, diversified company, one division of which manufactures car radios. The following possibilities exist: the car radio division, as it stands, may represent a viable SBU; alternatively, luxury car radios with automatic tuning may constitute an SBU different from the SBU for standard models; or other areas of the company, such as the television division, may be combined with all or part of the car radio division to create an SBU.[26]

Overall, an SBU should be established at a level where it can rather freely address (a) all key segments of the customer group having similar objectives; (b) all key functions of the corporation so that it can deploy whatever functional expertise is needed to establish positive differentiation from the competition in the eyes of the customer; and (c) all key aspects of the competition so that the corporation can seize the advantage when opportunity presents itself and, conversely, so that competitors will not be able to catch the corporation off-balance by exploiting unsuspected sources of strength.

A conceptual question becomes relevant in identifying SBUs: How much aggregation is desirable? Higher levels of aggregation produce a relatively smaller and more manageable number of SBUs. Besides, the existing management information system may not need to be modified since a higher level of aggregation yields SBUs of the size and scope of present divisions or product groups. However, higher levels of aggregation at the SBU level permit only general notions of strategy that may lack relevance for promoting action at the operating level. For example, an SBU for medical care is probably too broad. It could embrace equipment, service, hospitals, education, self-discipline, and even social welfare.

On the other hand, lower levels of aggregation make SBUs identical to product/market segments that may lack "strategic autonomy." An SBU for farm tractor engines would be ineffective because it is at too low a level in the organization to (a) consider product applications and customer groups other than farmers or (b) cope with new competitors who might enter the farm tractor market at almost any time with a totally different product set of "boundary conditions." Further, at such a low organizational level, one SBU may compete with another, thereby shifting to higher levels of management the strategic issue of which SBU should formulate what strategy.

The optimum level of aggregation, one that is neither too broad nor too narrow, can be determined by applying the criteria discussed above, then further refining it by using managerial judgment. Briefly stated, an SBU must look and act like a freestanding business, satisfying the following conditions:

1. Have a unique business mission, independent of other SBUs.
2. Have a clearly definable set of competitors.
3. Be able to carry out integrative planning relatively independently of other SBUs.
4. Be able to manage resources in other areas.
5. Be large enough to justify senior management attention but small enough to serve as a useful focus for resource allocation.

The definition of an SBU always contains gray areas that may lead to dispute. It is helpful, therefore, to review the creation of an SBU, halfway into the strategy development process, by raising the following questions:

• Are customers' wants well defined and understood by the industry, and is the market segmented so that differences in these wants are treated differently?
• Is the business unit equipped to respond functionally to the basic wants and needs of customers in the defined segments?
• Do competitors have different sets of operating conditions that could give them an unfair advantage over the business unit in question?

If the answers give reason to doubt the SBU's ability to compete in the market, it is better to redefine the SBU with a view to increasing its strategic freedom in meeting customer needs and competitive threats.

The SBU concept may be illustrated with an example from Procter & Gamble. For more than 60 years the company's various brands were pitted against each other. The Camay soap manager competed against the Ivory soap manager as fiercely as if each were in different companies. The brand management system that grew out of this notion has been used by almost every consumer-products company.

In 1990s, however, Procter & Gamble reorganized according to the SBU concept (what the company called ''along the category lines''). The reorganization did not abolish brand managers, but it did make them accountable to a new corps of mini-general managers who were responsible for an entire product line—all laundry detergents, for example. By fostering internal competition among brand managers, the classic brand management system established strong incentives to excel. It also created conflicts and inefficiencies as brand managers squabbled over corporate resources, from ad spending to plant capacity. The system often meant that not enough thought was given to how brands could work together. Despite these shortcomings, brand management worked fine when markets were growing and money was available. But now, most packaged-goods businesses are growing slowly (if at all), brands are proliferating, the retail trade is accumulating more clout, and the consumer market is fragmenting. Procter & Gamble reorganized along SBU lines to cope with this bewildering array of pressures.

Under Procter & Gamble's SBU scheme, each of its 39 categories of U.S. businesses, from diapers to cake mixes, is run by a category manager with direct responsibility. Advertising, sales, manufacturing, research, engineering, and other disciplines all report to the category manager. The idea is to devise marketing strategies by looking at categories and by fitting brands together rather than by coming up with competing brand strategies and then dividing up resources among them. The paragraphs that follow discuss how Procter & Gamble's reorganization impacted select functions.

1.4.1 Advertising

Procter & Gamble advertises Tide as the best detergent for tough dirt. But when the brand manager for Cheer started making the same claim, Cheer's ads were pulled after the Tide group protested. Now the category manager decides how to position Tide and Cheer to avoid such conflicts.

1.4.2 Budgeting

Brand managers for Puritan and Crisco oils competed for a share of the same ad budget. Now a category manager decides when Puritan can benefit from stepped-up ad spending and when Crisco can coast on its strong market position.

1.4.3 Packaging

Brand managers for various detergents often demanded packages at the same time. Because of these conflicting demands, managers complained that projects were delayed and nobody got a first-rate job. Now the category manager decides which brand gets a new package first.

1.4.4 Manufacturing

Under the old system, a minor detergent, such as Dreft, had the same claim on plant resources as Tide— even if Tide was in the midst of a big promotion and needed more supplies. Now a manufacturing staff person who helps to coordinate production reports to the category manager.

The notion behind the SBU concept is that a company's activities in a marketplace ought to be understood and segmented strategically so that resources can be allocated for competitive advantage. That is, a company ought to be able to answer three questions: What business am I in? Who is my competition? What is my position relative to that competition? Getting an adequate answer to the first question is often difficult. (Answers to the other two questions can be relatively easy.) In addition, identifying SBUs is enormously difficult in organizations that share resources (e.g., research and development or sales).

There is no simple, definitive methodology for isolating SBUs. Although the criteria for designating SBUs are clear-cut, their application is judgmental and problematic. For example, in certain situations, real advantages can accrue to businesses sharing resources at the research and development, manufacturing, or distribution level. If autonomy and accountability are pursued as ends in themselves, these advantages may be overlooked or unnecessarily sacrificed.

SUMMARY

This chapter focused on the concepts of planning and strategy. Planning is the ongoing management process of choosing the objectives to be achieved during a certain period, setting up a plan of action, and maintaining continuous surveillance of results so as to make regular evaluations and, if necessary, to modify the objectives and plan of action. Also described were the requisites for successful planning, the time frame for initiating planning activities, and various philosophies of planning (i.e., satisfying, optimizing, and adaptivizing). Strategy, the course of action selected from possible alternatives as the optimum way to attain objectives, should be consistent with current policies and viewed in light of anticipated competitive actions.

The concept of strategic planning was also examined. Most large companies have made significant progress in the last 10 or 15 years in improving their strategic planning capabilities. Two levels of strategic planning were discussed: corporate and business unit level. Corporate strategic planning is concerned with the management of a firm's portfolio of businesses and with issues of firm-wide impact, such as resource allocation, cash flow management, government regulation, and capital market access. Business strategy focuses more narrowly on the SBU level and involves the design of plans of action and objectives based on analysis of both internal and external factors that affect each business unit's performance. An SBU is defined as a standalone business within a corporation that faces (an) identifiable competitor(s) in a given market.

For strategic planning to be effective and relevant, the CEO must play a central role, not simply as the apex of a multilayered planning effort, but as a strategic thinker and corporate culture leader.

DISCUSSION QUESTIONS

1. Why is planning significant?
2. Is the concept of strategic planning relevant only to profit-making organizations? Can nonprofit organizations also embrace planning?
3. Planning has always been considered an important function of management. How is strategic planning different from traditional planning?
4. What is an SBU? What criteria may be used to divide businesses into SBUs?
5. What are the requisites for successful strategic planning?
6. Differentiate between the planning philosophies of satisfying, optimizing, and adaptivizing.

NOTES

1. Andrew Campbell, ''Tailored, Not Benchmarked,'' *Harvard Business Review*, March/April, 1999, pp. 41–51.
2. Renee Dye and Oliver Sibony, ''How to Improve Strategic Planning,'' *The McKinsey Quarterly*, No. 3, 2007, pp. 40–49.
3. Gordon E. Greenley, ''Perceptions of Marketing Strategy and Strategic Marketing in UK Companies,'' *Journal of Strategic Marketing*, September 1993, pp. 189–210.
4. James Brown, Saul S. Sands, and G. Clark Thompson, ''The Status of Long Range Planning,'' *Conference Board Record*, September 1966, p. 11.
5. *Business Planning in the Eighties: The New Competitiveness of American Corporations*, New York: Coopers & Lybrand, 1984.
6. Malcolm McDonald, *The Marketing Audit: Translating Marketing Theory Into Practice*, Oxford, U.K.: Butterworth-Heinemann, 1991.
7. *The Economist*, March 1997, p. 65.
   Also see: Myung-su Chae and John S. Hill, ''High Versus Low Formality Marketing Planning in Global Industries: Determinants and Consequences,'' *Journal of Strategic Marketing*, Vol. 5, No. 1, March 1997, pp. 3–22.

8. Adrian Slywotzky and Richard Wise, *How to Grow When Markets Don't*, New York: Warner Business Books, 2003.

9. "Strategic Planning," *BusinessWeek*, August 26, 2003, p. 46.

10. Bryson, J.M. and P. Bromiley, "Critical Factors Affecting the Planning and Implementation of Major Products," *Strategic Management Journal*, July, 1993, pp. 319–338.

11. Andrew Campbell, *op. cit.*

12. See: Lawrence C. Rhyne, "The Relationship of Strategic Planning to Financial Performance," *Strategic Management Journal*, 1986, pp. 423–36.

13. *Perspectives on Corporate Planning* (Boston: Boston Consulting Group, 1968): 48.

14. See: W. Chan Kim and Renee Mauborgne, "Charting Your Company's Future," *Harvard Business Review*, June 2002, pp. 76–85.

15. Russell L. Ackoff, *A Concept of Corporate Planning* (New York: John Wiley & Sons, 1970): 13.

16. Shantanu Dutta and Om Narasimhan, "Success in High Technology Markets: Is Marketing Capability Critical?" Marketing Science Institute, 2000.

17. Michael Arndt, "McDonald's," *BusinessWeek*, February, 2007, pp. 65–72.

18. Jack Welch (with Suzy Welch), *Winning* (New York: Harper Collins, 2005).

19. Henry Mintzberg, "The Fall and Rise of Strategic Planning," *Harvard Business Review*, January–February 1994, p. 107.

20. Laurie Flynn, "Hewlett Posts Higher Earnings But Does Not See a Near Term Turnaround of the Technology Sector," *New York Times*, May 21, 2003, p. C-3.

21. Ibid.

22. Michael E. Portez, "The Five Competitive Forces," *Harvard Business Review*, January, 2008, pp. 78–93.

23. Michael E. Porter, "What is Strategy?" *Harvard Business Review*, November–December, 1996, pp. 61–80.

24. Clayton M. Christensen, "Strategy: Learning By Doing," *Harvard Business School*, November–December, 1997, pp. 141–160.

25. Jack Welch, *op. cit.* (from the abstract of the book in *Fortune*, April 18, 2005, p. 140).

26. Coskun A. Samli and Eric Shaw, "Strategic Business Units and Profit Centers Dichotomy: A Critical Distinction," Proceedings of Winter Educators' Conference, Chicago: American Marketing Association, 1997.

Chapter Outline

2.1 **Concept of Strategic Marketing**
2.2 **Aspects of Strategic Marketing**
    2.2.1 Emphasis on Long-Term
            Implications
    2.2.2 Corporate Inputs
    2.2.3 Varying Roles for Different
            Products/Markets
    2.2.4 Organizational Level
    2.2.5 Relationship to Finance
2.3 **Strategic Marketing and
    Marketing Management**
2.4 **The Process of Strategic
    Marketing: An Example**
    2.4.1 Portfolio Analysis
    2.4.2 Implementation of the
            Strategic Plan
2.5 **Strategic Marketing
    Implementation**
2.6 **Plan of the Book**

Chapter 2

Strategic Marketing

In its strategic role, marketing focuses on a business's intentions in a market and the means and timing of realizing those intentions. The strategic role of marketing is quite different from marketing management, which deals with developing, implementing, and directing programs to achieve designated intentions. To clearly differentiate between marketing management and marketing in its new role, a new term—*strategic marketing*—has been coined to represent the latter. This chapter discusses different aspects of strategic marketing and examines how it differs from marketing management. Also noted are the trends pointing to the continued importance of strategic marketing. The chapter ends with a plan for the rest of the book.

2.1 CONCEPT OF STRATEGIC MARKETING

Exhibit 2.1 shows the role that the marketing function plays at different levels in the organization. At the corporate level, marketing inputs (e.g., competitive analysis, market dynamics, environmental shifts) are essential for formulating a corporate strategic plan. Marketing represents the boundary between the marketplace and the company, and knowledge of current and emerging happenings in the marketplace is extremely important in any strategic planning exercise. At the other end of the scale, marketing management deals with the formulation and implementation of marketing programs to support the perspectives of strategic marketing, referring to marketing strategy of a product/market. Marketing strategy is developed at the business unit level.

Within a given environment, marketing strategy deals essentially with the interplay of three forces known as the **strategic three Cs:** the customer, the competition, and the corporation. Marketing strategies focus on ways in which the corporation can differentiate itself effectively from its competitors, capitalizing on its distinctive strengths to deliver better value to its customers[1] A good marketing strategy should be characterized by (a) a clear market definition; (b) a good match between corporate strengths and the needs of the market; and (c) superior performance, relative to the competition, in the key success factors of the business.

Together, the strategic three Cs form the marketing strategy triangle (see Exhibit 2.2). All three Cs— customer, corporation, and competition—are dynamic, living creatures with their own objectives to pursue. If what the customer wants does not match the needs of the corporation, the latter's long-term viability may be at stake. Positive matching of the needs and objectives of customer and corporation is required for a lasting good relationship. But such matching is relative, and if the competition is able to offer a better

Exhibit 2.1 Marketing's Role in the Organization	Organizational Level	Role of Marketing*	Formal Name
	Corporate	Provide customer and competitive perspective for corporate strategic planning.	Corporate marketing
	Business unit	Assist in the development of strategic perspective of the business unit to direct its future course.	Strategic marketing
	Product/market	Formulate and implement marketing programs.	Marketing management

* Like marketing, other functions (finance, research and development, production, accounting, and personnel) plan their own unique roles at each organizational level. The business unit strategy emerges from the interaction of marketing with other disciplines.

match, the corporation will be at a disadvantage over time. In other words, the matching of needs between customer and corporation must not only be positive, it must be better or stronger than the match between the customer and the competitor. When the corporation's approach to the customer is identical to that of the competition, the customer cannot differentiate between them. The result could be a price war that may satisfy the customer's but not the corporation's needs. **Marketing strategy**, in terms of these three key constituents, must be defined as an endeavor by a corporation to differentiate itself positively from its competitors, using its relative corporate strengths to better satisfy customer needs in a given environmental setting.

Exhibit 2.2
Key Elements of Marketing Strategy Formulation

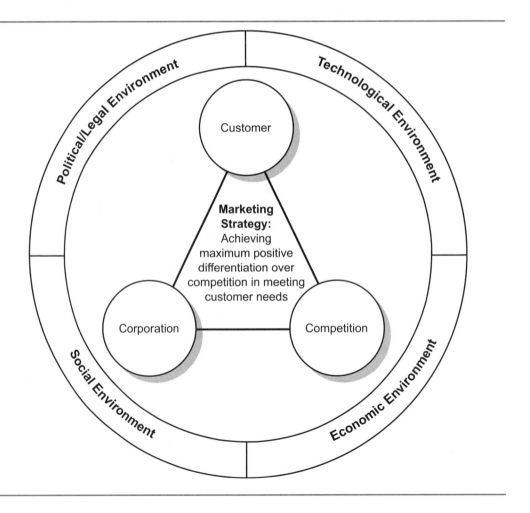

Based on the interplay of the strategic three Cs, formation of marketing strategy requires the following three decisions:

1. *Where to compete;* that is, it requires a definition of the market (for example, competing across an entire market or in one or more segments).
2. *How to compete;* that is, it requires a means for competing (for example, introducing a new product to meet a customer need or establishing a new position for an existing product).
3. *When to compete;* that is, it requires timing of market entry (for example, being first in the market or waiting until primary demand is established).

Thus, marketing strategy is the creation of a unique and valuable position, involving a set of activities and it requires choosing activities that are different from rivals.

The concept of strategic marketing may be illustrated with reference to Nokia corporation's decision in 2006 to regain lead in America.[2] Traditionally, Motorola has been the lead company in cell phones in the U.S. In the 1990s, Nokia overtook Motorola, which they did not expect. It took the top spot, in large part because Motorola lagged behind Nokia in shifting from analog to digital cell phones. But by 2004, Nokia lost the lead to Motorola since it failed to develop the right kind of products and introduce them at the right time.

Nokia has been broadening its product line and has developed clamshell-style phones with slimmer handsets to compete head on with Motorola's hit RAZR phones. The time was on Nokia's side. It needed something revolutionary to strengthen its market position in the U.S., and from all indication it had a portfolio of products which were highly suitable for the U.S. market.

Nokia delineated the following marketing strategy:

- *Market (where to compete)-* Nokia decided to focus on the entire U.S. market, not a particular region. While other countries were important for the company, it opted for more focus on the U.S.
- *Means (how to compete)-* Nokia decided to storm the U.S. market with new additions such as clamshell-style phones, like the 6101 and 6102 models. Later on, it planned to launch slimmer handsets, which supposedly were more sophisticated in technology and design than Motorola's phones.
- *Timing (when to compete)-* Nokia timed the product introductions so that the new phone models were launched in the U.S. at the same time they were launched elsewhere in the world.

In the past, there often had been a lag of several months before the new products reached the U.S. Now when the new products were ready to be launched, it was important for Nokia that they were introduced in the U.S. at the same time as in the other important markets (Nokia operated in over 130 different countries). Afterall, the U.S. represented about 8.3 percent of the company's sales, which in 2005 amounted to $25 billion.

Nokia's U.S. strategy emerged from a thorough consideration of the strategic 3Cs. First, the company had expanded its range of phone offerings to include models that were popular with U.S. consumers. At the same time, the company had been working more closely with U.S. service providers such as Cingular Wireless and T-Mobile to provide tailored products. For example, the company had been working with T-Mobile to develop a handset that connected both the regular cell phone networks and wireless broadband connections in the home via a technology known as unlicensed mobile access (UMA). The handset would allow users to make cheaper calls via Internet calling.

Second, the decision to regain the lead market position in the U.S. was based on full knowledge of the competition and Motorola, especially. As a part of its strategy, Nokia designated a team in its San Diego research facility dedicated to developing phones specifically for the U.S. market, that it had not done in the past. Further, as a part of its global distribution strategy, the company planned to open Nokia stores around the world. Its first U.S. location opened in June 2006 in Chicago, very close to Motorola's operations.

Third, Nokia's past leadership in the U.S., together with its advances in technology and adequate financial resources, properly equipped it to take over the U.S. market lead from Motorola. Finally, the environment (in this csae, a trend toward acceptance of technolocially advanced cell phones) substantiated the opportunity.

This strategy seems to have worked well for Nokia. In 2007, Nokia's market share in the U.S. increased by 5 percentage points. And yet, the company has to introduce its new line of slimmer phones.

2.2 ASPECTS OF STRATEGIC MARKETING

Strategic thinking represents a new perspective in the area of marketing. In this section we will examine the importance, characteristics, origin, and future of strategic marketing.

Marketing plays a vital role in the strategic management process of a firm. The experience of companies well versed in strategic planning indicates that failure in marketing can block the way to goals established by the strategic plan. ''Misguided marketing strategies have destroyed more shareholder value—and probably more careers—than shoddy accounting or shady fiscal practices have. In almost every industry—telecommunications, airlines, consumer products, finance—it is easy to point to poor marketing as a major cause of low growth and declining margins''.[3] A classic example is provided by Texas Instruments, a pioneer in developing a system of strategic planning called the OST system. Marketing negligence forced Texas Instruments to withdraw from the digital watch business. When the external environment is stable, a company can successfully ride on its technological lead, manufacturing efficiency, and financial acumen. As the environment shifts, however, lack of marketing perspective makes the best-planned strategies treacherous. With the intensification of competition in the watch business and the loss of uniqueness of the digital watch, Texas Instruments began to lose ground. Its experience can be summarized as follows:

> The lack of marketing skills certainly was a major factor in the ... demise of its watch business. T.I. did not try to understand the consumer, nor would it listen to the marketplace. They had the engineer's attitude.[4]

Philip Morris's success with Miller Beer illustrates how marketing's elevated strategic status can help in outperforming competitors. If Philip Morris had accepted the conventional marketing wisdom of the beer industry by basing its strategy on cost efficiencies of large breweries and competitive pricing, its Miller Beer subsidiary might still be in seventh place or lower. Instead, Miller Beer leapfrogged all competitors but Anheuser-Busch by emphasizing market and customer segmentation supported with large advertising and promotion budgets. A case of true strategic marketing, with the marketing function playing a crucial role in overall corporate strategy, Philip Morris relied on its corporate strengths and exploited its competitors' weaknesses to gain a leadership position in the brewing industry (In 2002, Philip Morris sold Miller to South African Breweries PLC for $5 billion.)

Indeed, marketing strategy is the most significant challenge that companies of all types and sizes face. Worldwide corporations are beginning to answer a ''new call to strategic marketing,'' as many of them shift their business planning priorities more toward strategic marketing and the market planning function.[5] As has been noted: ...what, then explains Xerox PARC's inability to exploit such innovative ideas as the graphical user interface, or AMD's failure to challenge Intel—despite the fact that AMD had designed the fastest chip in the industry? The missing link is marketing.[6]

Strategic marketing holds different perspectives from those of marketing management. Its salient features are described in the paragraphs that follow.

2.2.1 Emphasis on Long-Term Implications

Strategic marketing decisions usually have far-reaching implications. In the words of one marketing strategist, strategic marketing is a commitment, not an act. For example, a strategic marketing decision would not be a matter of simply providing an immediate delivery to a favorite customer but of offering 24-hour delivery service to all customers.

In 1980 the Goodyear Tire Company made a strategic decision to continue its focus on the tire business. At a time when other members of the industry were deemphasizing tires, Goodyear opted for the opposite route. This decision had wide-ranging implications for the company over the years. Looking back, Goodyear's strategy worked. Presently, it continues to be a globally dominant force in the tire industry.

The long-term orientation of strategic marketing requires greater concern for the environment. Environmental changes are more probable in the long run than in the short run. In other words, in the short run, one may assume that the environment will remain stable, but this assumption is not at all likely in the long run.

Proper monitoring of the environment requires strategic intelligence inputs. Strategic intelligence differs from traditional marketing research in requiring much deeper probing. For example, simply knowing that a competitor has a cost advantage is not enough. Strategically, one ought to find out how much flexibility the competitor has in further reducing price.

2.2.2 Corporate Inputs

Strategic marketing decisions require inputs from three corporate aspects: corporate culture, corporate publics, and corporate resources. **Corporate culture** refers to the style, whims, fancies, traits, taboos, customs, and rituals of top management that over time come to be accepted as intrinsic to the corporation. **Corporate publics** are the various stakeholders with an interest in the organization. Customers, employees, vendors, governments, and society typically constitute an organization's stakeholders. **Corporate resources** include the human, financial, physical, and technological assets/experience of the company. Corporate inputs set the degree of freedom a marketing strategist has in deciding which market to enter, which business to divest, which business to invest in, etc. The use of corporate-wide inputs in formulating marketing strategy also helps to maximize overall benefits for the organization.

2.2.3 Varying Roles for Different Products/Markets

Traditionally it has been held that all products exert effort to maximize profitability. Strategic marketing starts from the premise that different products have varying roles in the company. For example, some products may be in the growth stage of the product life cycle, some in the maturity stage, others in the introduction stage. Each position in the life cycle requires a different strategy and affords different expectations. Products in the growth stage need extra investment; those in the maturity stage should generate a cash surplus. Although conceptually this concept—different products serving different purposes—has been understood for many years, it has been articulated for real-world application only in recent years. The lead in this regard was provided by the Boston Consulting Group, which developed a portfolio matrix in which products are positioned on a two-dimensional matrix of market share and growth rate, both measured on a continuous scale from high to low.

The portfolio matrix essentially has two properties: (a) it ranks diverse businesses according to uniform criteria, and (b) it provides a tool to balance a company's resources by showing which businesses are likely to be resource providers and which are resource users.[7]

The practice of strategic marketing seeks first to examine each product/market before determining its appropriate role. Further, different products/markets are synergistically related to maximize total marketing effort. Finally, each product/market is paired with a manager who has the proper background and experience to direct it.

2.2.4 Organizational Level

Strategic marketing is conducted primarily at the business unit level in the organization. At General Electric, for example, major appliances are organized into separate business units for which strategy is separately formulated. At Gillette Company, strategy for the Duracell batteries is developed at the batteries business unit level.

2.2.5 Relationship to Finance

Strategic marketing decision making is closely related to the finance function.[8] The importance of maintaining a close relationship between marketing and finance and, for that matter, with other functional areas of a business is nothing new. But in recent years, frameworks have been developed that make it convenient to simultaneously relate marketing to finance in making strategic decisions.[9]

Strategic marketing did not originate systematically. The difficult environment of the early 1970s forced managers to develop strategic plans for more centralized control of resources. It happened that these pioneering efforts at strategic planning had a financial focus. Certainly, it was recognized that marketing inputs were required, but they were gathered as needed or were simply assumed. For example, most strategic planning approaches emphasized cash flow and return on investment, which of course must be examined in relation to market share. Perspectives on such marketing matters as market share, however, were either obtained on an ad hoc basis or assumed as constant. Consequently, marketing inputs, such as market share, became the result instead of the cause: a typical conclusion that was drawn was that market share must be increased to meet cash flow targets. The financial bias of strategic planning systems demoted marketing to a necessary but not important role in the long-term perspective of the corporation.

In a few years' time, as strategic planning became more firmly established, corporations began to realize that there was a missing link in the planning process. Without properly relating the strategic planning effort to marketing, the whole process tended to be static.[10] Business exists in a dynamic setting, and by and large, it is only through marketing inputs that perspectives of changing social, economic, political, and technological environments can be brought into the strategic planning process.

In brief, while marketing initially got lost in the emphasis on strategic planning, currently the role of marketing is better understood and has emerged in the form of strategic marketing.

A variety of factors point to an increasingly important role for strategic marketing in future years.[11] First, the battle for market share is intensifying in many industries as a result of declining growth rates. Faced with insignificant growth, companies have no choice but to grasp for new weapons to increase their share, and strategic marketing can provide extra leverage in share battles.

Second, deregulation in many industries is mandating a move to strategic marketing. For example, take the case of the airline, trucking, banking, and telecommunications industries. In the past, with territories protected and prices regulated, the need for strategic marketing was limited. With deregulation, it is an entirely different story. The prospect of Sears, Roebuck and Merrill Lynch as direct competitors would have been laughable as recently as twenty years ago. Thus, emphasis on strategic marketing is no longer a matter of choice if these companies are to perform well.

Third, many packaged-goods companies are acquiring companies in hitherto nonmarketing-oriented industries and are attempting to gain market share through strategic marketing. For example, apparel makers, with few exceptions, have traditionally depended on production excellence to gain competitive advantage. But when marketing-oriented consumer-products companies purchased apparel companies, the picture changed. General Mills, through marketing strategy, turned Izod (the alligator shirt) into a highly successful business. Chesebrough-Pond's has done much the same with Health-Tex, making it the leading marketer of children's apparel. On acquiring Columbia Pictures in 1982, the Coca-Cola Company successfully tested the proposition that it could sell movies like soft drinks. By using Coke's marketing prowess and a host of innovative financing packages, Columbia emerged as a dominant force in the motion picture business. It almost doubled its market share between 1982 and 1987 and increased profits by 20 percent annually.[12] Although in the last few years Izod, Health-Tex, and Columbia Pictures have been sold, they fetched these marketing powerhouses huge prices for their efforts in turning them around.[13] Borders group, Inc., the country's second largest book retailer has been emphasizing marketing strategy to choose books it would carry. It has planned to use category management to co-manage books in different areas divided into 250 categories. The co-managers determine which titles, the number of titles, and how those books are displayed. Similarly, Coach has been successfully able to revamp its product line through innovative marketing stategies.

Fourth, shifts in the channel structure of many industries have posed new problems. Traditional channels of distribution have become scrambled, and manufacturers find themselves using a mixture of wholesalers, retailers, chains, buying groups, and even captive outlets. In some cases, distributors and manufacturers' representatives are playing more important roles. In others, buying groups, chains, and cooperatives are becoming more significant. Because these groups bring greatly increased sophistication to the buying process, especially as the computer gives them access to more and better information, buying clout is being concentrated in fewer hands.

Fifth, competition from overseas companies operating both in the United States and abroad is intensifying. More and more countries around the world are developing the capacity to compete aggressively in world markets. Business-people in both developed and developing countries are aware of world market trends and are confident that they can reach new markets. Eager to improve their economic conditions and their living standards, they are willing to learn, adapt, and innovate. Thirty years ago, most American companies were confident that they could beat foreign competitors with relative ease. After all, they reasoned, we have the best technology, the best management skills, and the famous American ''can do'' attitude. Today competition from Europe, Japan, and elsewhere is seemingly insurmountable. To cope with worldwide competition, renewed emphasis on marketing strategy achieves significance.[14]

Sixth, the fragmentation of markets—the result of higher per capita incomes and more sophisticated consumers—is another factor driving the increased importance of strategic marketing. In the United States, for example, the number of segments in the automobile market increased by one-third, from 18 to 24, during the period from 1988 to 1995 (i.e., two subcompact, two compact, two intermediate, four full size, two luxury, three truck, two van, and one station wagon in 1978 to two minicompact, two subcompact, two compact, two midsized, two intermediate, two luxury, six truck, five van, and one station wagon in 1985).[15] Many of these segments remain unserved until a company introduces a product offering that is tailored to that niche. The competitive realities of fragmented markets require strategic marketing capability to identify untapped market segments and to develop and introduce products to meet their requirements.[16]

Seventh, in the wake of easy availability of base technologies and shortening product life cycles, getting to market quickly is a prerequisite for success in the marketplace. Early entrants not only can command premium prices, but they also achieve volume break points in purchasing, manufacturing, and marketing earlier than followers and, thus, gain market share. For example, in the European market, the first company to market car radios can typically charge 20 percent more for the product than a competitor who enters the market a year later.[17] In planning an early entry in the marketplace, strategic marketing achieves significance.

Eighth, the days are gone when companies could win market share by achieving cost and quality advantages in existing, well-defined markets. Today, companies need to conceive and create new and largely uncontested competitive market space. Corporate imagination and expeditionary policies are the keys that unlock new markets.[18] Corporate imagination involves going beyond served markets; that is, thinking about needs and functionalities instead of conventional customer-product grids; overturning traditional price/performance assumptions; and leading customers rather than following them.[19] Creating new markets is a risky business; however, through expeditionary policies, companies can minimize the risk not by being fast followers but by the process of low-cost, fast-paced market incursions designed to reach the target market. To successfully develop corporate imagination and expeditionary policies, companies need strategic marketing.[20] Consider this lesson in auto industry economics. Today it takes about 20 worker-hours to assemble a Ford Taurus with a retail price of, say, $18,000. Since labor costs about $42 an hour, the direct-assembly expense is $840, about 5% of the sticker price. By comparison, the cost of marketing and distributing the car can reach 30%.[21] The costs include advertising, promotions (such as cash rebates and lease incentives), and dealer rent and mortgage payments plus inventory financing. Controlling marketing costs begin, even before the vehicle leaves the drawing board or computer screen. By ensuring that a design meets the needs and desires of its customers—size, features, performance, and so on—a manufacturer can sell a new automobile for a higher price and avoid expensive rebates and other promotional gimmicks.

Finally, demographic shifts in American society have created a new customer environment that makes strategic marketing an imperative. In years past, the typical American family consisted of a working dad, a homemaker mom, and two kids. But the 2000 census revealed that only 24 percent of the 93.3 million households then surveyed fit that description. Of those families reporting children under the age of 18, 71 percent of the mothers worked full or part-time outside the home, up from 63 percent in 1990, 51 percent in 1985 and 42 percent in 1980. Smaller households now predominate: more than 60 percent of all households comprise only one or two persons. Even more startling, and frequently overlooked, is the fact that 10.3 million households are now headed by singles. This fastest-growing segment of all—up some 62 percent over the previous decade—expanded mainly because of an increase in the number of men living alone. Further, about 1 in 8 Americans is 65 years or older today. This group is expected to grow rapidly such that by 2030, 1 in 5 Americans will be elderly. And senior citizens are around for a lot longer as life expectancy has risen. The older population of the country is the fastest growing segment and they have turned out to be the wealthiest. Further, Hispanics, in the U.S. at 35. 3 million in 2000, have surpassed the black (34.7 million) as the largest minority group in the nation. These statistics have strategic significance. The mass market has splintered, and companies can't sell their products the way they used to. The largest number of households may fall into the two-wage-earner grouping, but that group includes everyone from manicurists to Wall Street brokers, a group whose lifestyles and incomes are too diverse to qualify as a mass market. Besides, age is less of a definer of who you are in maturity than it is when you are young. You may have five 55-year old men—one is retired, he is a grandfather; another one is new dad and he is starting a new business; the next one has had an open-heart surgery; the fourth one is training for a marathon; and the last one could be all these. We may see every market breaking into smaller and smaller units, with unique products being aimed at defined segments.

2.3 STRATEGIC MARKETING AND MARKETING MANAGEMENT

Strategic marketing focuses on choosing the right products for the right growth markets at the right time. It may be argued that these decisions are no different from those emphasized in marketing management. However, the two disciplines approach these decisions from different angles. For example, in marketing management, market segments are defined by grouping customers according to marketing mix variables. In the strategic marketing approach, market segments are formed to identify the group(s) that can provide the company with a sustainable economic advantage over the competition. To clarify the matter, Henderson labels the latter grouping a **strategic sector**. Henderson notes:

> A strategic sector is one in which you can obtain a competitive advantage and exploit it.... Strategic sectors are the key to strategy because each sector's frame of reference is competition. The largest competitor in an industry can be unprofitable in that the individual strategic sectors are dominated by smaller competitors.[22]

A further difference between strategic marketing and marketing management is that in marketing management the resources and objectives of the firm, however defined, are viewed as uncontrollable variables in developing a marketing mix. In strategic marketing, objectives are systematically defined at different levels after a thorough examination of necessary inputs. Resources are allocated to maximize overall corporate performance, and the resulting strategies are formulated with a more inclusive view. As Abell and Hammond have stated:

> A strategic market plan is not the same ... as a marketing plan; it is a plan of all aspects of an organization's strategy in the market place. A marketing plan, in contrast, deals primarily with the delineation of target segments and the product, communication, channel, and pricing policies for reaching and servicing those segments—the so-called marketing mix.[23]

Marketing management deals with developing a marketing mix to serve designated markets. The development of a marketing mix should be preceded by a definition of the market. Traditionally, however, market has been loosely defined. In an environment of expansion, even marginal operations could be profitable; therefore, there was no reason to be precise, especially when considering that the task of defining a market is at best difficult. Besides, corporate culture emphasized short-term orientation, which by implication stressed a winning marketing mix rather than an accurate definition of the market.

To illustrate how problematic it can be to define a market, consider the laundry product Wisk. The market for Wisk can be defined in many different ways: the laundry detergent market, the liquid laundry detergent market, or the prewash-treatment detergent market. In each market, the product would have a different market share and would be challenged by a different set of competitors. Which definition of the market is most viable for long-term healthy performance is a question that strategic marketing addresses. A market can be viewed in many different ways, and a product can be used in many different ways. Each time the product-market pairing is varied, the relative competitive strength is varied, too. Many businesspeople do not recognize that a key element in strategy is choosing the competitor whom you wish to challenge, as well as choosing the marketing segment and product characteristics with which you will compete.

Exhibit 2.3 summarizes the differences between strategic marketing and marketing management. Strategic marketing differs from marketing management in many respects: orientation, philosophy, approach, relationship with the environment and other parts of the organization, and the management style required. For example, strategic marketing requires a manager to forgo short-term performance in the interest of long-term results. Strategic marketing deals with the business to be in; marketing management stresses running a delineated business.

For a marketing manager, the question is: Given the array of environmental forces affecting my business, the past and the projected performance of the industry or market, and my current position in it, which kind of investments am I justified in making in this business? In strategic marketing, on the other hand, the question is rather: What are my options for upsetting the equilibrium of the marketplace and reestablishing it in my favor? Marketing management takes market projections and competitive position as a given and seeks to optimize within those constraints. Strategic marketing, by contrast, seeks to throw off those constraints wherever possible. Marketing management is deterministic; strategic marketing is opportunistic. Marketing management is deductive and analytical; strategic marketing is inductive and intuitive.

	Point of Difference	Strategic Marketing	Marketing Management
Exhibit 2.3 Major Differences between Strategic Marketing and Marketing Management*	Time frame	Long range; i.e., decisions have long-term implications	Day-to-day; i.e., decisions have relevance in a given financial year
	Orientation	Inductive and intuitive	Deductive and analytical
	Decision process	Primarily bottom-up	Mainly top-down
	Relationship with environment	Environment considered ever-changing and dynamic	Environment considered constant with occasional disturbances
	Opportunity sensitivity	Ongoing to seek new opportunities	Ad hoc search for a new opportunity
	Organizational behavior	Achieve synergy between different components of the organization, both horizontally and vertically	Pursue interests of the decentralized unit
	Nature of job	Requires high degree of creativity and originality	Requires maturity, experience, and control orientation
	Leadership style	Requires proactive perspective	Requires reactive perspective
	Mission	Deals with what business to emphasize	Deals with running a delineated business

*These differences are relative, not opposite ends of a continuum.

2.4 THE PROCESS OF STRATEGIC MARKETING: AN EXAMPLE

The process of strategic marketing planning, charted in Exhibit 2.4, may be illustrated with an SBU (Health and Well-Being) of Proctor & Gamble Company.[24] Headquartered in Cincinnati, Ohio, P&G is a worldwide manufacturer and marketer of a variety of food and nonfood products, including coffee, cake mixes, toothpaste, diapers, detergents, and health-related remedies. The company conducts its business in more than 100 countries, employs approximately 120,000 people, operates more than 149 manufacturing facilities, and maintains three major research centers. In (year ending June 30), the company's worldwide sales amounted to $76.5 billion.

The company has 23 brands in its portfolio that generate over one billion dollars in sales annually. In addition, it has 18 brands that generate at least $500 million in sales which were poised to be its next billion-dollar brands. In 12 countries, the company generated at least one billion dollars in sales annually. It did more than a billion dollars in sales each year with seven retail customers. The company's operating margins had increased from 15.5 percent in 2001 to 20.2 percent in 2007.

In 2000, the company's strategic plan established the following goals:

- To strengthen significantly the company's core businesses (i.e., toothpaste, diapers, and detergents).
- To view health-care products as a critical engine of growth.
- To boost the share of profits from health-related products from 20 percent to 30 percent over the next decade.
- To divest those businesses not meeting the company's criteria for profitability and growth, thus providing additional resources to achieve other objectives.
- To make an 18 percent return on total capital invested.
- To a great extent, to depend on retained earnings for financing growth.

This above strategy rested on the five factors, shown in Exhibit 2.4, that feed into corporate strategy:

- *Value system*—always to be strong and influential in marketing, achieving growth through developing and acquiring new products for specific niches.

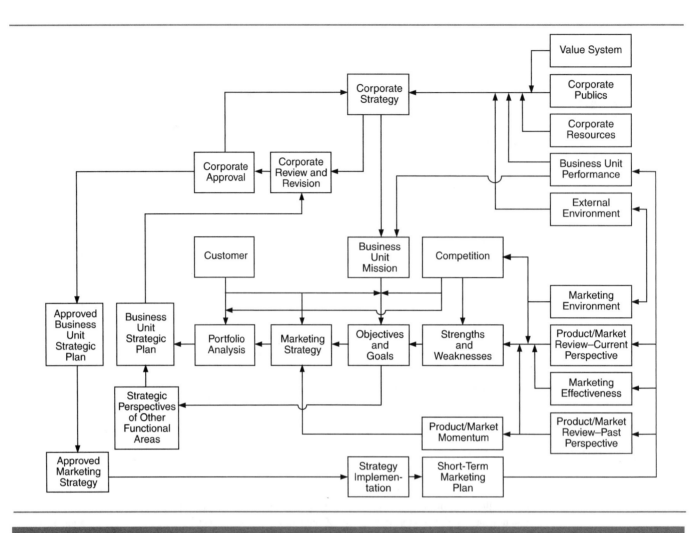

Exhibit 2.4 Process of Strategic Marketing

- *Corporate publics*—the willingness of P&G stockholders to forgo short-term profits and dividends in the interest of long-term growth and profitability.
- *Corporate resources*—strong financial position, high brand recognition, marketing powerhouse.
- *Business unit performance*—health-related remedies sales, for example, were higher worldwide despite recessionary conditions.
- *External environment*—increased health consciousness among consumers.

The mission for one of P&G's 42 business units, health and well-being, emerged from a simultaneous review of corporate strategy, competitive conditions, customers' perspectives, past performance of the business unit, and marketing environment, as charted in Exhibit 2.4. The business unit mission for health-related remedies was delineated as follows:

- To consolidate operations by combining recent acquisitions and newly developed products and by revamping old products.
- To accelerate business by proper positioning of products.
- To expand the product line to cover the entire human anatomy.

The mission for the business unit was translated into the following objectives and goals:

- To invest heavily to achieve $9.4 billion in sales by 2010, an increase of 50 percent over $6.2 billion in 2005.
- To achieve a leadership position in the United States.
- To introduce new products overseas as early as possible to preempt competition.

Marketing objectives for different products/markets emerged from these overall business unit objectives. For example, the marketing objectives for a product to combat indigestion were identified as follows:

- To accelerate research to seek new uses for the product.
- To develop new improvements in the product.

Marketing objectives, customer and competitive perspectives, and product/market momentum (i.e., extrapolation of past performance to the future) form the basis of marketing strategy. The major emphasis of marketing strategy for health-related remedies was on positioning through advertising and on new product development. Thus, the company decided to increase advertising support throughout the planning period and to broaden research and development efforts.

P&G's strategy was based on the following rationale. Consumers are extremely loyal to health products that deliver, as shown by their willingness to resume buying Johnson & Johnson's Tylenol after two poisoning episodes. But while brand loyalty makes consumers harder to lure away, it also makes them easier to keep, and good marketing can go a long way in this endeavor. The company was able to enlarge the market for its indigestion remedy, which experts thought had hit maturity, through savvy marketing. P&G used television advertising to sell it as a cure for overindulgence, which led to a 30 percent increase in business during 2002–2007.

As P&G pushes further into health products, its vast research and technological resources will be a major asset. P&G spends nearly $2 billion a year on research, and product improvements have always been an important key to the company's marketing prowess.

The overall strategy of the health and well-being business unit was determined by industry maturity and the unit's competitive position. The industry was found to be growing, while the competitive position was deemed strong.

With insurers and the government trying to drive health-care costs down, consumers are buying more and more over-the-counter nostrums. Advertisers are making health claims for products from cereal to chewing gum. As the fitness craze exemplifies, interest in health is higher than ever, and the aging of the population accentuates these trends: people are going to be older, but they are not going to want to feel older. Thus the health-related remedies industry has a significant potential for growth. P&G has been the largest over-the-counter remedies marketer. As shown in the list below, it has products for different ailments. The company's combined strength in marketing and research puts it in an enviable position in the market.

- *Skin*—P&G produces the leading facial moisturizer. P&G also leads the teenage acne treatment market. Work is now underway on a possible breakthrough antiaging product.
- *Mouth*—After being on the market for 34 years, P&G's mouthwash is the market leader. Another P&G product, a prescription plaque-fighting mouthwash, may go over the counter, or it may become an important ingredient in other P&G oral hygiene products.
- *Head*—A P&G weak spot, its aspirin holds an insignificant share of the analgesic market. P&G may decide to compete with an ibuprofen-caffeine combination painkiller.
- *Chest*—P&G's medicated chest rub is an original brand in a stable that now includes cough syrup, cough drops, a nighttime cold remedy, and nasal spray. Other line extensions and new products are coming, but at a fairly slow pace.
- *Abdomen*—The market share for P&G's indigestion remedy is up 22 percent in the last three years. Already being sold to prevent traveler's diarrhea, it may be marketed as an ulcer treatment. P&G also dominates the over-the-counter bulk laxative market. New clinical research shows that its laxative may reduce serum cholesterol.

Briefly, these inputs, along with the business unit's goals, led to the following business unit strategy: to attempt to improve position, to push for share.

2.4.1 Portfolio Analysis

The marketing strategy for each product/market was reviewed using the portfolio technique (see Chapter 10). By positioning different products/markets on a multifactor portfolio matrix (high/medium/low business strength and high/medium/low industry attractiveness), strategy for each product/market was examined and approved from the viewpoint of meeting business unit missions and goals. Following the portfolio analysis, the approved marketing strategy became a part of the business unit's strategic plan, which, when approved by top management, was ready to be implemented. As a part of implementation, an annual marketing plan was formulated and became the basis for operations managers to pursue their objectives.

2.4.2 Implementation of the Strategic Plan

A few highlights of the activities of the health-related remedies business unit during 2002-2007 show how the strategic plan was implemented.

- Steps were taken to sell its laxative as an anticholesterol agent.
- The company won FDA permission to promote its indigestion remedy to doctors as a preventive for traveler's diarrhea.
- Company research has shown that its indigestion remedy helps treat ulcers. Although some researchers have disputed this claim, the prospect of cracking the multibillion dollar ulcer treatment market is tantalizing.

2.5 STRATEGIC MARKETING IMPLEMENTATION

Strategic marketing has evolved by trial and error. In the 1980s, companies developed unique strategic marketing procedures, processes, systems, and models. Experience shows, however, that most companies' marketing strategies are burdened with undue complexity. They are bogged down in principles that produce similar responses to competition. Changes are needed to put speed and freshness into marketing strategy.

The following are the common problems associated with marketing strategy formulation and implementation.

1. **Too much emphasis on ''where'' to compete and not enough on ''how'' to compete.** Experience shows that companies have devoted much more attention to identifying markets in which to compete than to the means to compete in these markets. Information on where to compete is easy to obtain but seldom brings about sustainable competitive advantage. Further, ''where'' information is usually easy for competitors to copy. ''How'' information, on the other hand, is tough to get and tough to copy. It concerns the fundamental workings of the business and the company. For example, McDonald's motto, QSC & V, is a how-to-compete strategy—it translates into *quality* food products; fast, friendly *service*; restaurant *cleanliness*; and a menu that provides *value*. It is much more difficult to copy the ''how'' of McDonald's strategy than the ''where.''[25]

   In the next era of marketing strategy, companies will need to focus on how to compete in entirely new ways. In this endeavor, creativity will play a crucial role. For example, a large insurance company substantially improved its business by making improvements in underwriting, claim processing, and customer service, a ''how'' strategy that could not be replicated by competitors forthwith.

2. **Too little focus on uniqueness and adaptability in strategy.** Most marketing strategies lack uniqueness. For example, specialty stores increasingly look alike because they use the same layout and stock the same merchandise. In the past, when market information was scarce, companies pursued new and different approaches. But today's easy access to information often leads companies to follow identical strategies to the detriment of all.

   Ideas for uniqueness and adaptability may flow from unknown sources. Companies should, therefore, be sensitive and explore all possibilities. The point may be illustrated with reference to Arm and Hammer's advertising campaign that encouraged people to place baking soda in their refrigerators to reduce odors. The idea was suggested in a letter from a consumer. The introduction of that *unique* application for the product in the early 1970s caused sales of Arm and Hammer baking soda to double within two years.

3. **Inadequate emphasis on ''when'' to compete.** Because of the heavy emphasis on where and how to compete, many marketing strategies give inadequate attention to ''when'' to compete. Any move in the marketplace should be adequately timed. The optimum time is one that minimizes or eliminates competition and creates the desired impact on the market; in other words, the optimum time makes it easier for the firm to achieve its objectives. Timing also has strategy implementation significance. It serves as a guide for different managers in the firm to schedule their activities to meet the timing requirement.

Decisions on timing should be guided by the following:

a. *Market knowledge.* If you have adequate information, it is desirable to market readily; otherwise you must wait until additional information has been gathered.
b. *Competition.* A firm may decide on an early entry to beat minor competition. If you face major competition, you may delay entry if necessary; for example, to seek additional information.
c. *Company readiness.* For a variety of reasons, the company may not be ready to compete. These reasons could be lack of financial resources, labor problems, inability to meet existing commitments, and others.

Having the ability to do all the right things, however, is no guarantee that planned objectives will be realized. Any number of pitfalls may render the best strategies inappropriate. To counter the pitfalls, the following concerns should be addressed:

1. Develop attainable goals and objectives.
2. Involve key operating personnel.
3. Avoid becoming so engrossed in current problems that strategic marketing is neglected and thus becomes discredited in the eyes of others.
4. Don't keep marketing strategy separate from the rest of the management process.
5. Avoid formality in marketing strategy formulation that restrains flexibility and inhibits creativity.
6. Avoid creating a climate that is resistant to strategic marketing.
7. Don't assume that marketing strategy development can be delegated to a planner.
8. Don't overturn the strategy formulation mechanism with intuitive, conflicting decisions.

2.6 PLAN OF THE BOOK

Today's business and marketing managers are faced with a continuous stream of decisions, each with its own degree of risk, uncertainty, and payoff. These decisions may be categorized into two broad classes: operating and strategic. With reference to marketing, operating decisions are the domain of marketing management. Strategic decisions constitute the field of strategic marketing.

Operating decisions are those dealing with current operations of the business. The typical objective of these decisions in a business firm is profit maximization. During times of business stagnation or recession, as experienced in the early 1990s, efforts at profit maximization have typically encompassed a cost minimization perspective. Under these conditions, managers are pressured into shorter and shorter time horizons. All too frequently, decisions are made regarding pricing, discounts, promotional expenditures, collection of marketing research information, inventory levels, delivery schedules, and a host of other areas with far too little regard for the long-term impact of the decision. As might be expected, a decision that may be optimal for one time period may not be optimal in the long run.

The second category of decision making, **strategic decisions**, deals with the determination of strategy: the selection of the proper markets and the products that best suit the needs of those markets. Although strategic decisions may represent a very small fraction of the multitude of management decisions, they are truly the most important as they provide the definition of the business and the general relationship between the firm and its environment. Despite their importance, however, the need to make strategic decisions is not always as apparent as the need (sometimes urgency) for successfully completing operating decisions.

Strategic decisions are characterized by the following distinctions:

1. They are likely to effect a significant departure from the established product market mix. (This departure might involve branching out technologically or innovating in other ways.)
2. They are likely to hold provisions for undertaking programs with an unusually high degree of risk relative to previous experience (e.g., using untried resources or entering uncertain markets and competitive situations where predictability of success is noticeably limited).
3. They are likely to include a wide range of available alternatives to cope with a major competitive problem, the scope of these alternatives providing for significant differences in both the results and resources required.
4. They are likely to involve important timing options, both for starting development work and for deciding when to make the actual market commitment.

5. They are likely to call for major changes in the competitive "equilibrium," creating a new operating and customer acceptance pattern.

6. They are likely to resolve the choice of either leading or following certain market or competitive advances, based on a trade-off between the costs and risks of innovating and the timing vulnerability of letting others pioneer (in the expectation of catching up and moving ahead at a later date on the strength of a superior marketing force).

This book deals with strategic decisions in the area of marketing. Chapter 1 dealt with planning and strategy concepts, and this chapter examined various aspects of strategic marketing. Chapters 3 through 6 deal with analysis of strategic information relative to company (e.g., corporate appraisal), competition, customer, and external environment. Chapter 7 focuses on the measurement of strategic capabilities, and Chapter 8 concentrates on strategic direction via goals and objectives.

Chapters 9 and 10 are devoted to strategy formulation. Organization for strategy implementation and control are examined in Chapter 11. Chapter 12 discusses strategic techniques and models. The next five chapters, Chapters 13 through 17, review major market, product, price, distribution, and promotion strategies. The final chapter, Chapter 18, focuses on global market strategy.

SUMMARY

This chapter introduced the concept of strategic marketing and differentiated it from marketing management. Strategic marketing focuses on marketing strategy, which is achieved by identifying markets to serve, competition to be tackled, and the timing of market entry/exit. Marketing management deals with developing a marketing mix to serve a designated market.

The complex process of marketing strategy formulation was described. Marketing strategy, which is developed at the SBU level, essentially emerges from the interplay of three forces—customer, competition, and corporation—in a given environment.

A variety of internal and external information is needed to formulate marketing strategy. Internal information flows both down from top management (e.g., corporate strategy) and up from operations management (e.g., past performance of products/markets). External information pertains to social, economic, political, and technological trends and product/market environment. The effectiveness of marketing perspectives of the company is another input in strategy formulation. This information is analyzed to identify the SBU's strengths and weaknesses, which together with competition and customer, define SBU objectives. SBU objectives lead to marketing objectives and strategy formulation. The process of marketing strategy development was illustrated with an example of a health-related product.

Finally, this chapter articulated the plan of this book. Of the two types of business decisions, operating and strategic, this book will concentrate on strategic decision making with reference to marketing.

DISCUSSION QUESTIONS

1. Define strategic marketing. Differentiate it from marketing management.
2. What are the distinguishing characteristics of strategic marketing?
3. What emerging trends support the continuation of strategic marketing as an important area of business endeavor?
4. Differentiate between operating and strategic decisions. Suggest three examples of each type of decision from the viewpoint of a food processor.
5. How might the finance function have an impact on marketing strategy? Explain.
6. Adapt to a small business the process of marketing strategy formulation as presented in Exhibit 2.4.
7. Specify the corporate inputs needed to formulate marketing strategy.

NOTES

1. Brian Grow, "Renovating Home Depot," *BusinessWeek*, March 6, 2006, p. 50.
2. Adapted from: Cassell Bryan-Low, "New Nokia CEO Plans to Make U.S. House Calls," *The Wall Street Journal*, August 10, 2006, p. B1.
3. Gail J. McGovern, David Court, John A. Quelch and Blair Crawford, "Bringing Customers into the Board Room," *Harvard Business Review*, November 2004, pp. 70–80.
4. "When Marketing Failed at Texas Instruments," *BusinessWeek*, June 22, 1981, p. 91.
   See also Bro Uttal, "Texas Instruments Regroups," *Fortune*, August 9, 1982, p. 40.
5. Nirmalya Kumar, "Marketing's Drive to Recapture the Imagination," *Financial Times*, August 9, 1982, p. 7.
6. *Business Planning in the Eighties: The New Competitiveness of American Corporations* (New York: Coopers & Lybrand, 1984).
7. For further discussion of the portfolio matrix, see Chapter 10.
8. See Robert W. Ruekert and Orville C. Walker, Jr., "Marketing's Interaction with Other Functional Units: A Conceptual Framework and Empirical Evidence," *Journal of Marketing*, January 1987, pp. 1–19.
9. See Chapter 12.
10. David W. Cravens, "Examining the Impact of Market-Based Strategy Paradigms on Marketing Strategy," *Journal of Strategic Marketing*, September 1998, pp. 197–208.
11. "Strategic Planning," *BusinessWeek*, August 26, 1996, p. 46.
12. Laura Landro, "Parent and Partners Help Columbia Have Fun at the Movies," *Wall Street Journal*, December 7, 1984, p. 1.
13. "Come See My Movie – Please," *BusinessWeek*, May 8, 2000, p. 153.
14. R. Preston McAffee, *Competitive Solutions, The Strategiests' Tool Kit* (Princeton, NJ: Princeton University Press, 2002).
15. Alex Taylor III, "Rouge Road Ahead," *Fortune*, March 17, 1997, p. 115.
16. George Stalk and Rob Lachenauer (with John Butman), *Hardball—Are You Playing to Play or Playing to Win?* (Boston, MA: The Boston Consulting Group, 2007).
17. Don G. Reinertsen, "Whodunit? The Search for New Product Killers," *Electronic Business*, July 1983, pp. 62–66.
18. Gary Hamel and C. K. Prahalad, "Corporate Imagination and Expeditionary Marketing," *Harvard Business Review*, July–August 1991, pp. 81–92.
19. John Brady and Ian Davis, "Marketing's Mid-Life Crisis," *The McKinsey Quarterly* 2, 1993, pp. 17–28.
   Also see Adrian J. Slywotzky and Benson P. Shapiro, "Leveraging to Beat the Odds: The New Marketing Mind-Set," *Harvard Business Review*, September–October 1993, pp. 97–107.
20. See: Deborah L. Vance, "Bases Covered: Military Duty Transfers Well to Marketing," *Marketing News*, May 1, 2005. p. 16.
21. *Fortune*, April 4, 1994, p. 61.
22. Bruce D. Henderson, *Henderson on Corporate Strategy* (Cambridge, MA: Abt Books, 1981): 38.
23. Henderson, *op. cit.* p. 4.
24. The P&G example has been developed based on the company's annual reports and published material. The interpretations have been made by the authors as they understood P&G's perspectives.
25. Joel A. Bleeke, "Peak Strategies," *Across the Board*, February 1988, pp. 45–80.

PART II

Strategic Analysis

Chapter 3
Corporate Appraisal

Chapter 4
Understanding Competition

Chapter 5
Focusing on the Customer

Chapter 6
Scanning the Environment

Chapter Outline

3.1 Meaning of Corporate Appraisal
3.2 Factors in Appraisal: Corporate Publics
3.3 Factors in Appraisal: Value Orientation of Top Management
3.4 Factors in Appraisal: Corporate Resources
   3.4.1 Top Management
   3.4.2 Marketing
   3.4.3 Production
   3.4.4 Finance
   3.4.5 Research and Development
   3.4.6 Miscellaneous
3.5 Past Performance of Business Units

Chapter 3

Corporate Appraisal

One important reason for formulating marketing strategy is to prepare the company to interact with the changing environment in which it operates. Implicit here is the significance of predicting the shape the environment is likely to take in the future. Then, with a perspective of the company's present position, the task ahead can be determined. Study of the environment is reserved for a later chapter. This chapter is devoted to corporate appraisal.

An analogy to corporate appraisal is provided by a career counselor's job. Just as it is relatively easy to make a list of the jobs available to a young person, it is simple to produce a superficial list of investment opportunities open to a company. With the career counselor, the real skill comes in taking stock of each applicant; examining the applicant's qualifications, personality, and temperament; defining the areas in which some sort of further development or training may be required; and matching these characteristics and the applicant's aspirations against various options. Well-established techniques can be used to find out most of the necessary information about an individual. Digging deep into the psyche of a company is more complex but no less important. Failure by the company in the area of appraisal can be as stunting to future development in the corporate sense as the misplacement of a young graduate in the personal sense.

How should the strategist approach the task of appraising corporate perspectives? What needs to be discovered? These and other similar questions are explored in this chapter.

3.1 MEANING OF CORPORATE APPRAISAL

Broadly, **corporate appraisal** refers to an examination of the entire organization from different angles. It is a measurement of the readiness of the internal culture of the corporation to interact with the external environment. Marketing strategists are concerned with those aspects of the corporation that have a direct bearing on corporate-wide strategy because that must be referred in defining the business unit mission, the level at which marketing strategy is formulated. As shown in Exhibit 3.1, corporate strategy is affected by such factors as value orientation of top management, corporate publics, corporate resources, past performance of the business units, and the external environment. Of these, the first four factors are examined in this chapter.

Two important characteristics of strategic marketing are its concern with issues having far-reaching effects on the entire organization and change as an essential ingredient in its conduct. These characteristics make the process of marketing strategy formulation a difficult job and demand creativity and adaptability on the part of the organization. Creativity, however, is not common among all organizations. By the same token, adaptation to changing conditions is not easy. As has been said:

Success in the past always becomes enshrined in the present by the over-valuation of the policies and attitudes which accompanied that success.... With time these attitudes become embedded in a system

Exhibit 3.1
Scope of Corporate
Appraisal

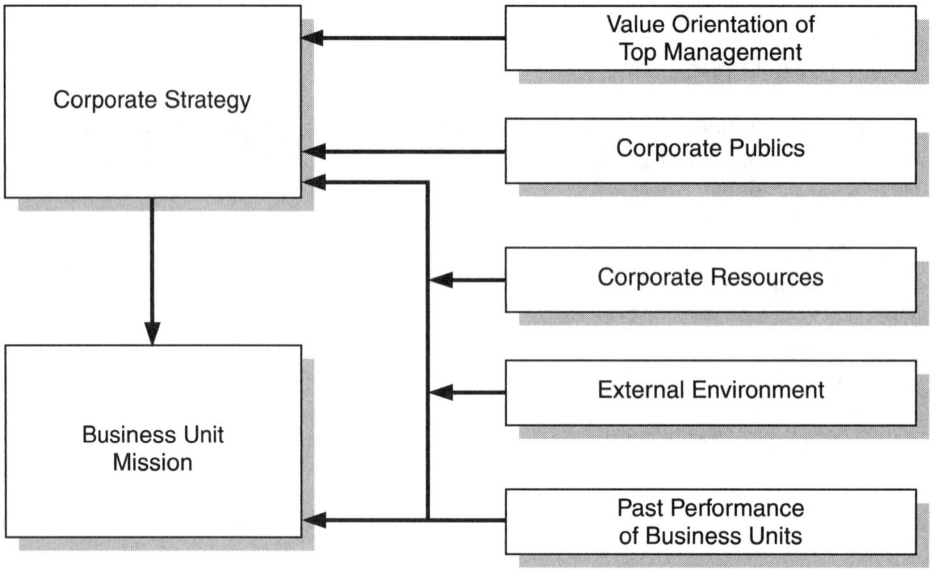

```
┌──────────────────┐          ┌──────────────────────┐
│                  │◄─────────│  Value Orientation of │
│                  │          │    Top Management     │
│  Corporate       │          └──────────────────────┘
│  Strategy        │          ┌──────────────────────┐
│                  │◄─────────│   Corporate Publics   │
│                  │          └──────────────────────┘
└────────┬─────────┘          ┌──────────────────────┐
         │         ◄──────────│   Corporate Resources │
         │                    └──────────────────────┘
         ▼                    ┌──────────────────────┐
┌──────────────────┐◄─────────│  External Environment │
│                  │          └──────────────────────┘
│  Business Unit   │          ┌──────────────────────┐
│  Mission         │◄─────────│   Past Performance    │
│                  │          │   of Business Units   │
└──────────────────┘          └──────────────────────┘
```

of beliefs, traditions, taboos, habits, customs, and inhibitions which constitute the distinctive culture of that firm. Such cultures are as distinctive as the cultural differences between nationalities or the personality differences between individuals. They do not adapt to change very easily.[1]

Human history is full of instances of communities and cultures being wiped out over time for the apparent reason of failing to change with the times. In the context of business, why is it that organizations such as Intel, Wal-Mart, Hewlett-Packard, and Microsoft, comparative newcomers among large organizations, are considered blue-chip companies? Why should United States Rubber, American Tobacco, and General Motors lag behind? Why are General Electric, Walt Disney, Citygroup, Du Pont, and 3M continually ranked as "successful" companies? The outstanding common denominator in the success of companies is the element of change. When time demands that the perspective of an organization change, and the company makes an appropriate response, success is the outcome.

Obviously, marketing strategists must take a close look at the perspectives of the organization before formulating future strategy. Strategies must bear a close relationship to the internal culture of the corporation if they are to be successfully implemented.

3.2 FACTORS IN APPRAISAL: CORPORATE PUBLICS

Business exists for people. Thus, the first consideration in the strategic process is to recognize the individuals and groups who have an interest in the fate of the corporation and the extent and nature of their expectations.

The following groups generally constitute the interest-holders in business organizations:

1. Owners
2. Employees
3. Customers
4. Suppliers
5. Banking community and other lenders
6. Government
7. Community in which the company does business
8. Society at large

For the healthy growth of the organization, all eight groups must be served adequately. Companies must balance the interests of multiple constituencies.[2] Of all the stakeholders, in the past corporations paid little attention to the communities in which they operated; today, however, the importance of service to community and to society is widely acknowledged. The community may force a company to refrain from activities that are detrimental to the environment. For example, the Boise Cascade Company was once denounced as harsh, stingy, socially insensitive, and considerably short of the highest ethical standards because of its unplanned land development. Community interests ultimately prevailed, forcing the company to either give up its land development activities or make proper arrangements for the disposal of waste and to introduce other environmental safeguards. Similarly, social concern may prevent a company from becoming involved in certain types of business. A publishing company responsive to community standards may refuse to publish pornographic material.

Johnson & Johnson exemplified responsible corporate behavior when it resolved the contingency created by the deaths of seven individuals who had consumed contaminated Tylenol capsules.[3] Within a few days, the company instituted a total product recall at a cost of $50 million after taxes, despite the fact that the problem did not occur because of negligence on the part of the company. Subsequently, the company took the initiative to develop more effective packaging to prevent tampering in the future. The company's commitment to socially responsible behavior was reaffirmed when it quit producing capsules entirely after the tampering occurred again. Johnson & Johnson put the well-being of the customer ahead of profitability in resolving this tampering problem. In brief, the requirements and expectations of today's society must serve as basic ingredients in the development of strategy:

> Large companies need to build social issues into strategy in a way which reflects their actual business importance. They need to articulate business's social contribution and define its ultimate purpose in a way that has more subtley than ''the business of business is business'' world view and is less defensive than most current corporate social responsibility (CSR) approaches. It can help to view the relationship between big business and society in this respect as an implicit ''Social Contract.'' This contract has obligations, opportunities and mutual advantage for both sides. To explain the basis for such an approach, however, it may help first to pinpoint the limitations with the two current ideological poles. Start with the ''business of business is buisness.'' The issue here is not primarily legal. In many countries, such as Germany, the legal obligation anyway is to stockholders, and even in America the legal primacy of shareholders is open to very broad interpretation. The problem with ''the busness of buisness'' mindset is rather that it can blind management to two important realities. The first is that social issues are not so much tangential to the business of buisness as fundamental to it. From a defensive point of view, companies that ignore public sentiment make themselves vulnerable to attack. But social pressures can also operate as early indicators of factors core to corporate profitability; for example, the regulations and public-policy environment in which companies must operate; the appetite for consumers for certain goods above others; and the motivation (and willingness to be hired in the first place) of employees. Companies that treat social issues as either irritating distractions or simply unjustified vehicles for attack on busines are turning a blind eye to impending forces that have the potential fundamentally to alter their strategic future. Although the effect of social pressure on these forces may not be immediate, this is not a reason for companies to delay preparing for or tackling them. Even from a strict shareholder-value perspective, most stockmarket value—typically over 80% in American and western European public markets—depends on expectations of companies' cashflow beyond the next three years.[4]

Historically, a business organization considered its sole purpose to be economic gain, concerning itself with other spheres of society only when required by law or self-interest or when motivated by philanthropy or charity. Charity was merely a celebration of a corporation's good fortune that it desired to share with ''outsiders'' or a display of pity for the unfortunate. Indirectly, of course, even this rather uninspired notion of charity gave the company a good name and thus served a public relations function. In slack times, a company reduced its activities in all areas, instituting both inside cost-cutting measures and the lowering of commitments to all publics other than stockholders. Such a perspective worked well until the mid-1960s; however, with economic prosperity almost assured, different stakeholders have begun to demand a more equitable deal from corporations.

Concern over global warming by corporations, for example, has become a major issue in both the public and the private sector. Similarly, customers expect products to be wholesome; employees want opportunities for advancement and self-improvement; and the community hopes that a corporation would assume some of its concerns, such as unemployment among minorities. Society now expects business corporations to help in resolving social problems. In brief, the role of the corporation has shifted from that of an economic institution solely responsible to its stockholders to that of a multifaceted force owing its existence to different stakeholders to whom it must be accountable.[5] As one of the most progressive institutions in the society, the corporation is expected to provide balanced prosperity in all fields. Two generations ago, the idea of a business being a party to a contract with society would have provoked an indignant snort from most businesspeople. Even 15 years ago, a business's contract with society was more likely material for a corporate president's speech to the stockholders than a basis for policy. It is a measure of how much the attitudes of middle-of-the-road businesspeople have changed that the notion of a social contract is now the basic assumption for their statements on the social responsibilities of a business. This new outlook extends the mission of the business beyond its primary obligation to owners.[6]

In today's environment, corporate strategy must be developed not simply to enhance financial performance, but also to maximize performance across the board, delivering the highest gains to all stakeholders, or corporate publics. And companies are responding to changing times. As former chairman Waldron of Avon Products noted, "We have 40,000 employees and 1.3 million representatives.... They have much deeper and more important stakes in our company than shareholders."[7]

In sum, capitalism is based on the principle that shareholders want their companies to be profitable over the long haul. And sustained and desired profitability is only feasible with satisfied customers, engaged employees, thriving communities, and healthy societies.

The "concept of stakeholders" is really an extension of the marketing concept, the central doctrine in marketing.[8]

> Marketing concept and the stakeholder concept are strongly related with a common root or core. Clearly, one commonality is that the stakeholder concept recognizes the consumer as a public with concerns central to the organization's purpose. Perhaps a further element of this common core is a realization of the importance of cooperative exchange with the consumer. In fact, all publics of an organization can be viewed in a cooperative vs. adversarial perspective. Cooperative strategies with labor, marketing channel members, etc., may result in eventual but not mutual symbiosis. For example, if a manufacturer cooperates with wholesalers, then these wholesalers may be more likely to cooperate with retailers. Similarly, retailers may then be more likely to treat the customer well. Consequently, the customer will be more loyal to certain brands, and this catalyzes the manufacturer to continue to be cooperative with channel members. This eventual, but not necessarily mutual, symbiosis may result in more long-run stability and evolutionary potential within the business system.[9]

One company that systematically and continuously examines and serves the interests of its stakeholders is Corning. It cooperates with labor, promotes diversity, and goes out of its way to improve the community. For example, the company's partnership with the glass workers' union promotes joint decision making. Worker teams determine job schedules and even factory design. All U.S. workers share a bonus based on point performance. All managers and salaried workers attend seminars to build sensitivity and support for women and African-American coworkers. A network of mentors helps minorities (i.e., African-Americans, Asians, Hispanics, and women) with career planning. Corning acquires and rehabilitates commercial properties, then finds tenants (some minority-owned) at market rates to locate their business there. It works to attract new business to the region and has invested in the local infrastructure by building a Hilton hotel, a museum, and a city library.

> More than the biggest employer in town, Corning plays benefactor, landlord, and social engineer. The company is half-owner of a racetrack and sponsors a professional golf tournament. Affordable housing, day care, new business development—it's doing all that, too. Corning is more directly involved in its community than most big U.S. corporations.... When a flood in 1972 put the town under 10 feet of water, the company paid area teenagers to rehabilitate damaged homes and appliances, then spent millions to build a new library and skating rink. But Corning's recent efforts have been more focused: They aim to turn a remote, insular town into a place that will appeal to the smart professionals Corning wants to attract—a place that offers social options for young singles, support for new families, and cultural diversity for minorities.

It's a strategy that often borders on corporate socialism. Corning bought the rundown bars—which "didn't fit with our objective," says one executive—as part of a block-long redevelopment of Market Street, the town's main commercial strip.

More important, Corning is working to create a region less dependent on its headquarters and 15 factories.... To help support the flagging local economy, Corning bought the Watkins Glen auto-racing track, which had slipped into bankruptcy. It rebuilt the facility, took in a managing partner, and last summer, saw the track host 200,000 visitors. Similarly, the company lobbied a supermarket chain to build an enormous new store. It persuaded United Parcel Service to locate a regional hub nearby.

In all, Corning expects its Corning Enterprises subsidiary, which spearheads community investments, to bring 200 new jobs to the Chemung River valley each year. It also wants to boost the number of tourists by 2% annually and attract four new businesses to town. Corning Enterprises funds its activities largely with rental income from real estate that it has purchased and rehabilitated.[10]

Another example of coporate social responsibility is provided by British Petroleum (BP). In 1997, Lord John Browne, the head of BP, publicly declared what many in the energy industry considered a blasphemous declaration. He said that global warming was indeed a problem and it was incumbent upon companies to take precautionary measures to address the long-term risks of climate change. By 2010, he pledged, BP would reduce its emissions of greenhouse gases to a level 10 percent below what it produced in 1990. He really meant what he said. In 2002, in another speech he announced that BP had reached the goal of reducing its emissions of greenhouse gases to below 1990 levels a full eight years ahead of schedule. According to him those reductions were made possible by, among other measures, increased efficiency throughout its global production facilities, and they came at no cost to the compnay.[11]

Although the expectations of different groups vary, in our society growth and improvement are the common expectations of any institution. But this broad view does not take into account the stakes of different groups within a business. For planning purposes, a clearer definition of each group's hopes is needed.

Exhibit 3.2 summarizes the factors against which the expectations of different groups can be measured. The broad categories shown here should be broken down into subcategories as far as possible. For example, in a community where juvenile delinquency is rampant, youth programs become an important area of corporate concern. One must be careful, however, not to make unrealistic or false assumptions about the expectations of different groups. Take owners, for example. Typically, 50 percent of earnings after taxes must be reinvested in the business to sustain normal growth, but the payout desired by the owners may render it difficult to finance growth. Thus, a balance must be struck between the payment of dividends and the plowing back of earnings. A vice president of finance for a chemical company with yearly sales over $500 million said in a conversation with the author:

> While we do recognize the significance of retaining more money, we must consider the desires of our stockholders. They happen to be people who actually live on dividend payments. Thus, a part of long-term growth must be given up in order to maintain their short-term needs for regular dividend payments.

Apparently this company would not be correct in assuming that growth alone is the objective of its stockholders. Thus, it behooves the marketing strategist to gain clear insight into the demands of different corporate publics.

Who in the company should study stakeholders' expectations? This task constitutes a project in itself and should be assigned either to someone inside the company (such as a strategic planner, an assistant to the president, a director of public affairs, or a marketing researcher) or to a consultant hired for this purpose. When this analysis is first undertaken, it will be fairly difficult to specify stakeholders, designate their areas of concern, and make their expectations explicit. After the initial study is made, updating it from year to year should be fairly routine.

The groups that constitute the stakeholders of a business organization are usually the same from one business to another. Mainly they are the owners, employees, customers, suppliers, the banking community and other lenders, government, the immediate community, and society at large. The areas of concern of each group and their expectations, however, require surveying. As with any other survey, this amounts to seeking information from an appropriate sample within each group. A structured questionnaire is preferable for obtaining objective answers. Before surveying the sample, however, it is desirable to conduct in-depth interviews with a few members of each group. The information provided by these interviews is helpful in developing the questionnaire. While overall areas of concern may not vary from one period to another,

Exhibit 3.2 Corporate Publics and their Concerns	

Publics	Areas of Concern
Owners	Payout
	Equity
	Stock price
	Nonmonetary desires
Customers	Business reliability
	Product reliability
	Product improvement
	Product price
	Product service
	Continuity
	Marketing efficiency
Employees of all ranks	Monetary reward
	Reward of recognition
	Reward of pride
	Environment
	Challenge
	Continuity
	Advancement
Suppliers	Price
	Stability
	Continuity
	Growth
Banking community and other lenders	Sound risk
	Interest payment
	Repayment of principal
Government (federal, state, and local)	Taxes
	Security and law enforcement
	Management expertise
	Democratic government
	Capitalistic system
	Implementation of programs
Immediate community	Economic growth and efficiency
	Education
	Employment and training
Society at large	Civil rights
	Urban renewal and development
	Pollution abatement
	Conservation and recreation
	Culture and arts
	Medical care

expectations certainly do. For example, during a recession stockholders may desire a higher payout in dividends than at other times. Besides, in a given period, the public may not articulate expectations in all of its areas of concern. During inflationary periods, for example, customers may emphasize stable prices only, while product improvement and marketing efficiency may figure prominently in times of prosperity.

The expectations of different publics provide the corporation with a focus for working out its objectives and goals. However, a company may not be able to satisfy the expectations of all stakeholders for two reasons: limited resources and conflicting expectations among stakeholders. For example, customers may want low prices and simultaneously ask for product improvements. Likewise, to meet exactly the expectations of the community, the company may be obliged to reduce dividends. Thus, a balance must be struck between the expectations of different stakeholders and the company's ability to honor them.

The corporate response to stakeholders' expectations emerges in the form of its objectives and goals, which in turn determine corporate strategy. While objectives and goals are discussed in detail in Chapter 8, a sample of corporate objectives with reference to customers is given here.

Assume the following customer expectations for a food-processing company:

1. The company should provide wholesome products.
2. The company should clearly state the ingredients of different products in words that are easily comprehensible to an ordinary consumer.
3. The company should make all efforts to keep prices down.

The company, based on these expectations, may set the following goals:

Wholesome Products

1. Create a new position—vice president, product quality. No new products will be introduced into the market until they are approved for wholesomeness by this vice president. The vice president's decision will be upheld no matter how bright a picture of consumer acceptance of a product is painted by marketing research and marketing planning.
2. Create a panel of nutrient testers to analyze and judge different products for their wholesomeness.
3. Communicate with consumers about the wholesomeness of the company's products, suggesting that they deal directly with the vice president of product quality should there be any questions. (Incidentally, a position similar to vice president of product quality was created at Gillette a few years ago. This executive's decisions overruled the market introduction of products despite numerous other reasons for early introduction.)

Information on Ingredients

1. Create a new position—director, consumer information. The person in this position will decide what information about product ingredients, nutritive value, etc., should be included on each package.
2. Seek feedback every other year from a sample of consumers concerning the effectiveness and clarity of the information provided.
3. Encourage customers, through various forms of promotions, to communicate with the director of consumer information on a toll-free phone line to clarify information that may be unclear.
4. Revise information contents based on numbers 2 and 3.

Keeping Prices Low

1. Communicate with customers on what leads the company to raise different prices (e.g., cost of labor is up, cost of ingredients is up, etc.).
2. Design various ways to reduce price pressure on consumers. For example, develop family packs.
3. Let customers know how much they can save by buying family packs. Assure them that the quality of the product will remain intact for a specified period.
4. Work on new ways to reduce costs. For example, a substitute may be found for a product ingredient whose cost has gone up tremendously.

By using this illustration, the expectations of each group of stakeholders can be translated into specific goals. Some firms, Adolph Coors Company, for example, define their commitment to stakeholders more broadly (see Exhibit 3.3). However, this company is not alone in articulating its concern for stakeholders. A whole corporate culture has sprung up that argues for the essential commonality of labor-management community-shareholder interests.

Overall, evaluation of corporate social responsibility can be undertaken using the following indicators[12]:

Marketplace Related:
Number of customer complaints.
Advertising complaints upheld.
Upheld cases of anti-competitive behaviour.
Customer satisfaction levels.
Provision for customers with special needs.

Exhibit 3.3
Coors' Commitment to its Stakeholders

Our corporate philosophy can be summed up by the statement, "Quality in all we are and all we do." This statement reflects our total commitment to quality relationships with customers, suppliers, community, stockholders and each other. Quality relationships are honorable, just, truthful, genuine, unselfish, and reputable.

We are committed first to our customers for whom we must provide products and services of recognizably superior quality. Our customers are essential to our existence. Every effort must be made to provide them with the highest quality products and services at fair and competitive prices.

We are committed to build quality relationships with suppliers because we require the highest quality goods and services. Contracts and prices should be mutually beneficial for the Company and the supplier and be honorably adhered to by both.

We are committed to improve the quality of life within our community. Our policy is to comply strictly with all local, state and federal laws, with our Corporate Code of Conduct and to promote the responsible use of our products. We strive to conserve our natural resources and minimize our impact on the environment. We pay our fair tax share and contribute resources to enhance community life. We boldly and visibly support the free enterprise system and individual freedom within a framework which also promotes personal responsibility and caring for others.

We are committed to the long-term financial success of our stockholders through consistent dividends and appreciation in the value of the capital they have put at risk. Reinvestment in facilities, research and development, marketing and new business opportunities which provide long-term earnings growth take precedence over short-term financial optimization.

These values can only be fulfilled by quality people dedicated to quality relationships within our Company. We are committed to provide fair compensation and a quality work environment that is safe and friendly. We value personal dignity. We recognize individual accomplishment and the success of the team. Quality relationships are built upon mutual respect, compassion and open communication among all employees. We foster personal and professional growth and development without bias or prejudice and encourage wellness in body, mind and spirit for all employees.

Source: Adolph Coors Company.

Environment Related:
Energy consumption.
Water usage.
Solid waste produced.
Successful enviornmental prosecutions.
CO_2/greenhouse gas emissions.
Other emissions such as ozone, radiation, SOX, NOX.
Net CO_2/greenhouse gas measures and offsetting effect.

Workplace Related:
Workforce profiles by gender, race, disability, age.
Staff absenteeism levels.
Number of legal non-compliances on health/safety, equal opportunities legislation.
Number of staff grievances.
Upheld cases of corrupt or unprofessional behavior.
Number of recordable safety incidents, (fatal and non-fatal).
Staff turnover.
Value of training and development provided to staff.
Perception measures of the company by its employees.
Existence of confidential grievance procedures for workers.

Community Related:
Cash value of company support as a percentage of pre-tax profit.
Individual value of staff time, gifts in kind, and management costs.

3.3 FACTORS IN APPRAISAL: VALUE ORIENTATION OF TOP MANAGEMENT

The ideologies and philosophies of top management as a team and of the CEO as the leader of the team have a profound effect on managerial policy and the strategic development process. According to Steiner:

> The CEO's aspirations about his personal life, the life of his company as an institution, and the lives of those involved in his business are major determinants of choice of strategy. His mores, habits, and ways of doing things determine how he behaves and decides. His sense of obligation to his company will decide his devotion and choice of subject matter to think about.[13]

Rene McPherson, former CEO of Dana Corporation, incessantly emphasized cost reduction and productivity improvement: the company doubled its productivity in seven years. IBM chairmen have always preached the importance of calling on customers—to the point of stressing the proper dress for a call. Over time, a certain way of dressing became an accepted norm of behavior for the entire corporation. Texas Instruments' ex-chairman Patrick Haggerty made it a point to drop in at a development laboratory on his way home each night when he was in Dallas to emphasize his view of the importance of new products for the company. Such single-minded focus on a value becomes an integral part of a company's culture. As employees steeped in the corporate culture move up the ladder, they become role models for newcomers, and the process continues.[14]

How companies in essentially the same business move in different strategic directions because of different top management values can be illustrated with an example from American Can Company and Continental Group. Throughout the 1970s, both Robert S. Hatfield, then Continental's chairman, and William F. May, his counterpart at American Can, made deep changes in their companies' product portfolios. Both closed numerous aged can-making plants. Both divested tangential businesses they deemed to have lackluster growth prospects. And both sought either to hire or promote executives who would steer their companies in profitable directions.

But similar as their overall strategies might seem, their concepts of their companies diverged markedly. May envisioned American Can as a corporate think tank, serving as both a trend spotter and a trend-setter. He put his trust in the advice of financial experts who, although lean on operating experience, were knowledgeable about business theory. They took American Can into such diverse fields as aluminum recycling, record distribution, and mail-order consumer products. By contrast, Hatfield sought executives with proven records in spotting new potential in old areas. The company acquired Richmond Corporation, an insurance holding company, and Florida Gas Company.[15]

It would be wrong to assume that every firm wants to grow. There are companies that probably could grow faster than their current rates indicate. But when top management is averse to expansion, sluggishness prevails throughout the organization, inhibiting growth. A large number of companies start small, perhaps with a family managing the organization. Some entrepreneurs at the helm of such companies are quite satisfied with what they are able to achieve. They would rather not grow than give up complete control of the organization. Obviously, if managerial values promote stability rather than growth, strategy will form accordingly. For Ben & Jerry's Homemade Ice Cream, social agenda is more important than business expansion. When a top supplier from Tokyo called to offer distribution in Japan, a lucrative ice-cream market, the company said no. It is because the Japanese company had no reputation for backing social causes.[16] Of course, if the owners find that their expectations are in conflict with the value system of top management, they may seek to replace the company's management with a more philosophically compatible team. As an example, a flamboyant CEO who emphasizes growth and introduces changes in the organization to the extent of creating suspicion among owners, board members, and colleagues may lead to the CEO's exit from the organization. An unconventionally high debt-to-equity ratio can be sufficient cause for a CEO to be dismissed. Conflict over the company's social agenda cost Ben & Jerry's the services of a CEO, Robert Holland Jr. He resigned after less than two years on the job because he ran into opposition from the co-founders into no-fat sorbet because that meant buying less hormone-free milk from those virtuous dairy farmers. And when Holland tried to distribute products in France, a dispute arose when Ben and Jerry issued a statement condemning France's nuclear-testing program.[17]

In brief, the value systems of the individual members of top management serve as important inputs in strategy development. If people at the top hold conflicting values, the chosen strategy will lack the willing cooperation and commitment of all executives. Generally, differing values are reflected in conflicts over policies, objectives, strategies, and structure.

This point may be illustrated with reference to Johnson & Johnson, a solidly profitable company. Its core businesses are entering market maturity and offer limited long-term growth potential. In the mid-1980s, therefore, the company embarked on a program to manufacture sophisticated technology products. But the development and marketing of high-tech products require a markedly different culture than that needed for Johnson & Johnson's traditional products. High-tech products require greater cooperation among corporate units, which is sometimes hard to obtain. Traditionally, Johnson & Johnson's various businesses have been run as completely decentralized units with total autonomy. To successfully achieve the shift to technology products, the CEO of the company, James E. Burke, had to tinker in subtle but important ways with a management style and corporate culture that had long been central to the company's success.[18] Similar efforts worked at Procter & Gamble: "Pressed by competitors and aided by new technology, P&G is, in fact, remodeling its corporate culture—a process bringing pain to some, relief to others and wonderment to most."[19]

Over time, top management values come to characterize the culture of the entire organization. Corporate culture in turn affects the entire perspective of the organization. It influences its product and service quality, advertising content, pricing policies, treatment of employees, and relationships with customers, suppliers, and the community.

Corporate culture gives employees a sense of direction, a sense of how to behave and what they ought to be doing. Employees who fail to live up to the cultural norms of the organization find the going tough. This point may be illustrated with reference to PepsiCo and J.C. Penney Company. At PepsiCo, beating the competition is the surest path to success. In its soft drink operation, Pepsi takes on Coke directly, asking consumers to compare the taste of the two colas. This kind of direct confrontation is reflected inside the company as well. Managers are pitted against each other to grab more market share, to work harder, and to wring more profits out of their businesses. Because winning is the key value at PepsiCo, losing has its penalties. Consistent runners-up find their jobs gone. Employees know they must win merely to stay in place and must devastate the competition to get ahead.[20]

But the aggressive manager who succeeds at Pepsi would be sorely out of place at J.C. Penney Company, where a quick victory is far less important than building long-term loyalty.

Indeed, a Penney store manager once was severely rebuked by the company's president for making too much profit. That was considered unfair to customers, whose trust Penney seeks to win. The business style set by the company's founder—which one competitor describes as avoiding "taking unfair advantage of anyone the company did business with"—still prevails today. Customers know they can return merchandise with no questions asked; suppliers know that Penney will not haggle over terms; and employees are comfortable in their jobs, knowing that Penney will avoid layoffs at all costs and will find easier jobs for those who cannot handle more demanding ones. Not surprisingly, Penney's average executive tenure is 33 years while Pepsi's is 10.[21]

These vastly different methods of doing business are just two examples of corporate culture. People who work at PepsiCo and at Penney sense that corporate values constitute the yardstick by which they will be measured. Just as tribal cultures have totems and taboos that dictate how each member should act toward fellow members and outsiders, a corporation's culture influences employees' actions toward customers, competitors, suppliers, and one another. Sometimes the rules are written, but more often they are tacit. Most often they are laid down by a strong founder and hardened by success into custom.

One authority describes four categories of corporate culture—academies, clubs, baseball teams, and fortresses.[22] Each category attracts certain personalities. The following are some of the traits among managers who gravitate to a particular corporate culture.

Academies
— Have parents who value self-reliance but put less emphasis on honesty and consideration.
— Tend to be less religious.
— Graduate from business school with high grades.
— Have more problems with subordinates in their first ten years of work.

Clubs
— Have parents who emphasize honesty and consideration.
— Have a lower regard for hard work and self-reliance.

— Tend to be more religious.
— Care more about health, family, and security and less about future income and autonomy.
— Are less likely to have substantial equity in their companies.

Baseball Teams
— Describe their fathers as unpredictable.
— Generally have more problems planning their careers in the first ten years after business school and work for more companies during that period than classmates do.
— Include personal growth and future income among their priorities.
— Value security less than others.

Fortresses
— Have parents who value curiosity.
— Were helped strongly by mentors in the first year out of school.
— Are less concerned than others with feelings of belonging, professional growth, and future income.
— Experience problems in career planning, on-the-job decisions, and job implementation.

An example of an academy is IBM, where managers spend at least 40 hours each year in training being carefully groomed to become experts in a particular function. United Parcel Service represents a club culture, which emphasizes grooming managers as generalists, with initiation beginning at the entry level. Generally speaking, accounting firms, law firms, and consulting, advertising, and software development companies exhibit baseball team cultures. Entrepreneurial in style, they seek out talent of all ages and experience and value inventiveness. Fortress companies are concerned with survival and are usually best represented by companies in a perpetual boom-and-bust cycle (e.g., retailers and natural resource companies).

Many companies cannot be neatly categorized in any one way. Many exhibit a blend of corporate cultures. For example, within General Electric, the NBC unit has baseball team qualities, whereas the aerospace division operates like a club, the electronics division like an academy, and the home appliance unit like a fortress. Companies may move from one category to another as they mature or as forced by the environment. For example, Apple started out as a baseball team but now appears to be emerging as an academy. Banks have traditionally exhibited a club culture, but with deregulation, they are evolving into baseball teams.

In the current environment, the changes that businesses are being forced to make merely to stay competitive—improving quality, increasing speed, becoming customer oriented—are so fundamental that they must take root in a company's very essence; that is, its culture. Cultural change, while difficult and time-consuming to achieve, is nevertheless feasible if approached properly. The CEO must direct change to make sure that it happens coherently. He or she must live the new culture, become the walking embodiment of it, and spot and celebrate subordinates who exemplify the values that are to be inculcated. The following are keys to cultural change:

— **Understand your old culture first.** You can't chart a course until you know where you are.
— **Encourage those employees** who are bucking the old culture and have ideas for a better one.
— **Find the best subculture** in your organization, and hold it up as an example from which others can learn.
— **Don't attack culture head on.** Help employees find their own new ways to accomplish their tasks, and a better culture will follow.
— **Don't count on a vision** to work miracles. At best, a vision acts as a guiding principle for change.
— **Figure on five to ten years** for significant, organization-wide improvement.
— **Live the culture you want.** As always, actions speak louder than words.[23]

Trying to change an institution's culture is certain to be frustrating. Most people resist change, and when the change goes to the basic character of the place where they earn a living, many people become upset. A company trying to improve its culture is like a person trying to improve his or her character. The process is long, difficult, often agonizing. The only reason that people put themselves through such difficulty is that it is correspondingly satisfying and valuable. As AT&T's CEO Robert Allen commented:

It's not easy to change a culture that was very control oriented and top down. We're trying to create an atmosphere of turning the organization chart upside down, putting the customers on top. The people close to the customer should be doing the key decision-making.[24]

In emphasizing the significance of the value system in strategic planning, several questions become pertinent. Should the corporation attempt to formally establish values for important members of management? If so, who should do it? What measures or techniques should be used? If the values of senior executives are in conflict, what should be done? Can values be changed?

It is desirable that the values of top management should be measured. If nothing else, such measurement will familiarize the CEO with the orientation of top executives and will help the CEO to better appreciate their viewpoints. Opinions differ, however, on who should do the measuring. Although a good case can be made for giving the assignment to a staff person, a strategic planner or a human resources planner, for example, hiring an outside consultant is probably the most effective way to gain an objective perspective on management values. If a consultant's findings appear to create conflict in the organization, they can be scrapped. With help from the consultant, the human resources planner in the company, working closely with the strategic planner, can design a system for the measurement of values once the initial effort is made.

Values can be measured in various ways. A popular technique is the self-evaluating scale developed by Allport, Vernon, and Lindzey.[25] This scale divides values into six classes: religious, political, theoretical, economic, aesthetic, and social. A manual is available that lists the average scores of different groups. Executives can complete the test in about 30 minutes and determine the structure of their values individually. Difficulties with using this scale lie in relating the executives' values to their jobs and in determining the impact of these values on corporate strategy.

A more specific way is to pinpoint those aspects of human values likely to affect strategy development and to measure one's score in relation to these values on a simple five- or seven-point scale. For example, we can measure an executive's orientation toward leadership image, performance standards and evaluation, decision-making techniques, use of authority, attitude about change, and nature of involvement. Exhibit 3.4 shows a sample scale for measuring these values.

As a matter of fact, a formal value orientation profile of each executive may not be entirely necessary. By raising questions such as the following about each top executive, one can gather insight into value orientations. Does the executive:

- Seem efficiency-minded?
- Like repetition?
- Like to be first in a new field instead of second?
- Revel in detail work?
- Seem willing to pay the price of keeping in personal touch with the customer, etc.?

Can the value system of an individual be changed? Traditionally, it has been held that a person's behavior is determined mainly by the inner self reacting within a given environment. In line with this thinking, major shifts in values should be difficult to achieve. In recent years, however, a new school of behaviorists has emerged that assigns a more significant role to the environment. These new behaviorists challenge the concept of "self" as the underlying force in determining behavior. If their "environmental" thesis is accepted, it should be possible to bring about a change in individual values so that senior executives can become more unified. However, the science of human behavior has yet to discover the tools that can be used to change values. Thus, it would be appropriate to say that minor changes in personal values can be produced through manipulation of the environment; but where the values of an individual executive differ significantly from those of a colleague, an attempt to alter an individual's values would be difficult.

A few years ago, differing values caused the Procter & Gamble's CEO Durk I. Jager leave the company after 17 months on the job. Other members of the company's management team found him too aggressive, too eager to experiment and change practices, and too quick to challenge established ways. He undertoook too much change too fast.[26]

The influence of the value orientation of top management on the perspectives of the business has already been emphasized. This section examines how a particular type of value orientation may lead to certain objectives and strategy perspectives. Two examples of this influence are presented below. In the first example, the president is rated high on social and aesthetic values, which seems to indicate a greater emphasis on the quality of a single product than on growth per se. In the second example, again, the theoretical and social orientation of top management appears to stress truth and honesty rather than strictly growth. If the strategic plans of these two companies were to emphasize growth as a major goal, they would undoubtedly fail. Planned perspectives may not be implemented if they are constrained by top management's value system.

Exhibit 3.4
Measuring Value
Orientation

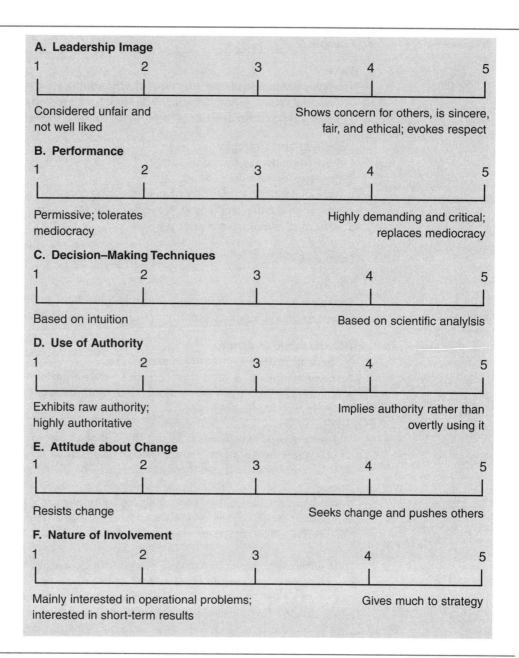

A. Leadership Image

1   2   3   4   5

Considered unfair and   Shows concern for others, is sincere,
not well liked   fair, and ethical; evokes respect

B. Performance

1   2   3   4   5

Permissive; tolerates   Highly demanding and critical;
mediocracy   replaces mediocracy

C. Decision–Making Techniques

1   2   3   4   5

Based on intuition   Based on scientific analylsis

D. Use of Authority

1   2   3   4   5

Exhibits raw authority;   Implies authority rather than
highly authoritative   overtly using it

E. Attitude about Change

1   2   3   4   5

Resists change   Seeks change and pushes others

F. Nature of Involvement

1   2   3   4   5

Mainly interested in operational problems;   Gives much to strategy
interested in short-term results

A corporation's culture can be its major strength when it is consistent with its strategies, as demonstrated by the following examples:

- At IBM, marketing drives a service philosophy that is almost unparalleled. The company keeps a hot line open 24 hours a day, seven days a week, to service IBM products.
- At International Telephone and Telegraph Corporation, financial discipline demands total dedication. To beat out the competition in a merger, an executive once called former chairman Harold S. Geneen at 3 a.m. to get his approval.
- At Microsoft, an emphasis on innovation creates freedom with responsibility. Employees can set their own hours and working style, but they are expected to articulate and support their activities with evidence of progress.
- At Delta Air Lines Inc., a focus on customer service produces a high degree of teamwork. Employees switch jobs to keep planes flying and baggage moving.

Example A

Values

The president of a small manufacturer of office duplicating equipment ranked relatively high on social values, giving particular attention to the security, welfare, and happiness of the employees. Second in order of importance to the president were aesthetic values.

Objectives and Strategies

1. Slow-to-moderate company growth.
2. Emphasis on a single product.
3. An independent-agent form of sales organization.
4. Very high-quality products with aesthetic appeal.
5. Refusal to compete on a price basis.

Example B

Values

The top-management team members of a high-fidelity loudspeaker systems manufacturer placed greater emphasis on theoretical and social values than on other values.

Objectives and Strategies

1. Scientific truth and integrity in advertising.
2. Lower margins to dealers than competitors were paying.
3. Maintenance of "truth and honesty" in relationships with suppliers, dealers, and employees

---

- At Toyota standards in efficiency, productivity, and quality are the most important pursuits. No wonder the company is the benchmark in manufacturing and product development.
- At GE every business unit should conduct continuous campaigns to become the lowest-cost producer in its area. One approach to reducing costs and improving productivity is work-outs, which are multi-day retreats. After the boss and outside consultants lay out the unit's achievements, problems and business environment, the participants brainstorm to come up with recommendations for improving operations. They receive on-the-spot responses and pledges that what is agreed upon will be implemented quickly.

In summary, an organization in the process of strategy formulation must study the values of its executives. While exact measurement of values may not be possible, some awareness of the values held by top management is helpful to planners. Care should be taken not to threaten or alienate executives by challenging their beliefs, traits, or outlooks. In the strategy formulation, the value package of the management team should be duly considered even if it means compromising on growth and profitability. Where no such compromise is feasible, it is better to transfer or change the assignment of a dissenting executive.

The experience of Interpace Corporation's CEO is relevant here. After moving from International Telephone and Telegraph Corporation (ITT) in the early 1980s, he drew on his ITT background to manage Interpace, a miniconglomerate with interests in such diverse products as teacups and concrete pipes. He used a formula that had worked well at ITT, which consisted of viewing assets primarily as financial pawns to be shifted around at the CEO's will, of compelling managers to abide by financial dicta, and of focusing on financial results. The approach seemed reasonable, but its implementation at Interpace was fraught with problems. ITT's management style did not fit the Interpace culture, despite the fact that the CEO replaced 35 members of a 51-person team.[27] Culture that prevents a company from meeting competitive threats or from adapting to changing economic or social environments can lead to stagnation and the company's ultimate demise unless the company makes a conscious effort to change.

3.4 FACTORS IN APPRAISAL: CORPORATE RESOURCES

The resources of a firm are its distinctive capabilities and strengths. Resources are relative in nature and must always be measured with reference to the competition. Resources can be categorized as financial strength, human resources, raw material reserve, engineering and production, overall management, and marketing strength. The marketing strategist needs to consider not only marketing resources but also resources of the company across the board. For example, price setting is a part of marketing strategy, yet it must be considered in the context of the financial strength of the company if the firm is to grow as rapidly as it should. It is obvious that profit margins on sales, combined with dividend policy, determine the amount of funds that a firm can generate internally. It is less well understood, but equally true, that if a firm uses more debt than its competitors or pays lower dividends, it can generate more funds for growth by decreasing profit margins. Thus, it is important in strategy development that all of the firm's resources are fully utilized in a truly integrated way. The firm that does not use its resources fully is a target for the firm that will—even if the latter has fewer resources. Full and skillful utilization of resources can give a firm a distinct competitive edge.

Consider the following resources of a company:

1. Has ample cash on hand (financial strength).
2. Average age of key management personnel is 42 years (human resources).
3. Has a superior raw material ingredient in reserve (raw material reserve).
4. Manufactures parts and components that go into the final product using the company's own facilities (plant and equipment).
5. The products of the company, if properly installed and serviced regularly, never stop while being used (technical competence).
6. Has knowledge of, a close relationship with, and expertise in doing business with grocery chains (marketing strength).

How do these resources affect marketing strategy? The cash-rich company, unlike the cash-tight company, is in a position to provide liberal credit accommodation to customers. General Electric, for example, established the General Electric Credit Corporation (now called GE Money) to help its dealers and ultimate customers to obtain credit. In the case of a manufacturer of durable goods whose products are usually bought on credit, the availability of easy credit can itself be the difference between success and failure in the marketplace.

If a company has a raw material reserve, it does not need to depend on outside suppliers when there are shortages. In the mid-1990s, there was a shortage of high-grade paper. A magazine publisher with its own forests and paper manufacturing facilities did not need to depend on paper companies to acquire paper. Thus, even when a shortage forced its competitors to reduce the sizes of their magazines, the company not dependent on outsiders was able to provide the same pre-shortage product to its customers.

In the initial stages of the development of color television, RCA was the only company that manufactured color picture tubes. In addition to using these tubes in its own television sets, RCA also sold them to other manufacturers/competitors such as GE. When the market for color television began to grow, RCA was in a strong position to obtain a larger share of the growth partly because of its easy access to picture tubes. GE, on the other hand, was weaker in this respect.

IBM's technical capabilities, among other things, helped it to be an innovator in developing data processing equipment and in introducing it to the market. IBM's excellent after-sale service facilities in themselves promoted the company's products. After-sale servicing put a promotional tool in the hands of salespeople to push the company's products.

Procter & Gamble is noted for its superior strength in dealing with grocery channels. The fact that this strength has served Procter & Gamble well hardly needs to be mentioned. More than anything else, marketing strength has helped Procter & Gamble to compete successfully with established companies in the introduction of new products. In brief, the resources of a company help it to establish and maintain itself in the marketplace. It is, of course, necessary for resources to be appraised objectively. It is the marketing power of big retailers like Wal-Mart that forces magazine publishers to share advance copies of forthcoming issues with them. They, then, decide if a particular issue would be sold in their stores. For example, Wal-Mart stores banned the April 1997 issue of *Vibe*, a magazine that focuses on rap music and urban culture, after viewing an early print of its cover and deeming it too risqué. Similarly, Winn-Dixie supermarkets (a 1,186 store chain) refused to carry the March 1997 issue of *Cosmopolitan* (the nation's best selling monthly magazine in terms of newsstand sales) because they judged it contained material that would be objectionable to many of their customers.''[28]

A firm is a conglomerate of different entities, each having a number of variables that affects performance. How far should a strategist probe into these variables to designate the resources of the firm? Exhibit 3.5

Exhibit 3.5
Strategic Factors
in Business

A. General Managerial

1. Ability to attract and maintain high-quality top management
2. Ability to develop future managers for overseas operations
3. Ability to develop future managers for domestic operations
4. Ability to develop a better organizational structure
5. Ability to develop a better strategic planning program
6. Ability to achieve better overall control of company operations
7. Ability to use more new quantitative tools and techniques in decision making at
   a. Top management levels
   b. Lower management levels
8. Ability to assure better judgment, creativity, and imagination in decision making at
   a. Top management levels
   b. Lower management levels
9. Ability to use computers for problem solving and planning
10. Ability to use computers for information handling and financial control
11. Ability to divest nonprofitable enterprises
12. Ability to perceive new needs and opportunities for products
13. Ability to motivate sufficient managerial drive for profits

B. Financial

1. Ability to raise long-term capital at low cost
   a. Debt
   b. Equity
2. Ability to raise short-term capital
3. Ability to maximize value of stockholder investment
4. Ability to provide a competitive return to stockholders
5. Willingness to take risks with commensurate returns in what appear to be excellent new business opportunities in order to achieve growth objectives
6. Ability to apply return on investment criteria to research and development investments
7. Ability to finance diversification by means of
   a. Acquisitions
   b. In-house research and development

C. Marketing

1. Ability to accumulate better knowledge about markets
2. Ability to establish a wide customer base
3. Ability to establish a selective consumer base
4. Ability to establish an efficient product distribution system
5. Ability to get good business contracts (government and others)
6. Ability to assure imaginative advertising and sales promotion campaigns
7. Ability to use pricing more effectively (including discounts, customer credit, product service, guarantees, delivery, etc.)
8. Ability to develop better relationships between marketing and new product engineering and production
9. Ability to produce vigor in sales organization

D. Engineering and Production

1. Ability to develop effective machinery and equipment replacement policies
2. Ability to provide more efficient plant layout
3. Ability to develop sufficient capacity for expansion
4. Ability to develop better materials and inventory control
5. Ability to improve product quality control
6. Ability to improve in-house product engineering

Exhibit 3.5 Strategic Factors in Business (*continued*)	7. Ability to improve in-house basic product research capabilities 8. Ability to develop more effective profit improvement (cost reduction) programs 9. Ability to develop better ability to mass produce at low per-unit cost 10. Ability to relocate present production facilities 11. Ability to automate production facilities 12. Ability to inspire better management of and better results from research and development expenditures 13. Ability to establish foreign production facilities 14. Ability to develop more flexibility in using facilities for different products 15. Ability to be in the forefront of technology and be extremely scientifically creative

E. Products

1. Ability to improve present products
2. Ability to develop more efficient and effective product line selection
3. Ability to develop new products to replace old ones
4. Ability to develop new products in new markets
5. Ability to develop sales for present products in new markets
6. Ability to diversify products by acquisition
7. Ability to attract more subcontracting
8. Ability to get bigger share of product market

F. Personnel

1. Ability to attract scientists and highly qualified technical employees
2. Ability to establish better relationships with employees
3. Ability to get along with labor unions
4. Ability to better utilize the skills of employees
5. Ability to motivate more employees to remain abreast of developments in their fields
6. Ability to level peaks and valleys of employment requirements
7. Ability to stimulate creativity in employees
8. Ability to optimize employee turnover (not too much and not too little)

G. Materials

1. Ability to get geographically closer to raw material sources
2. Ability to assure continuity of raw material supplies
3. Ability to find new sources of raw materials
4. Ability to own and control sources of raw materials
5. Ability to bring in house presently purchased materials and components
6. Ability to reduce raw material costs

is a list of possible strategic factors. Not all of these factors are important for every business; attention should be focused on those that could play a critical role in the success or failure of the particular firm. Therefore, the first step in designating resources is to have executives in different areas of the business go through the list and identify those variables that they deem strategic for success. Then each strategic factor may be evaluated either qualitatively or quantitatively. One way of conducting the evaluation is to frame relevant questions around each strategic factor, which may be rated on either a dichotomous or a continuous scale. As an example, the paragraphs that follow discuss questions relevant to a men's sportswear manufacturer.

3.4.1 Top Management

Which executives form the top management? Which manager can be held responsible for the firm's performance during the past few years? Is each manager capable of undertaking future challenges as successfully as past challenges were undertaken? Is something needed to boost the morale of top management?

What are the distinguishing characteristics of each top executive? Are there any conflicts, such as personality conflicts, among them? If so, between whom and for what reasons? What has been done and is being done for organizational development? What are the reasons for the company's performance during the past few years? Are the old ways of managing obsolete? What more can be done to enhance the company's capabilities?

3.4.2 Marketing

What are the company's major products/services? What are the basic facts about each product (e.g., market share, profitability, position in the life cycle, major competitors and their strengths and weaknesses, etc.)? In which field can the firm be considered a leader? Why? What can be said about the firm's pricing policies (i.e., compared with value and with the prices of competitors)? What is the nature of new product development efforts, the coordination between research and development and manufacturing? How does the market look in the future for the planning period? What steps are being taken or proposed to meet future challenges? What can be said about the company's channel arrangements, physical distribution, and promotional efforts? What is the behavior of marketing costs? What new products are expected to be launched, when, and with what expectations? What has been done about consumer satisfaction?

3.4.3 Production

Are people capable of working on new machines, new processes, new designs, etc., which may be developed in the future? What new plant, equipment, and facilities are needed? What are the basic facts about each product (e.g., cost structure, quality control, work stoppages)? What is the nature of labor relations? Are any problems anticipated? What steps have been proposed or taken to avert strikes, work stoppages, and so forth? Does production perform its part effectively in the manufacturing of new products? How flexible are operations? Can they be made suitable for future competition and new products well on the way to being produced and marketed commercially? What steps have been proposed or taken to control pollution? What are the important raw materials being used or likely to be used? What are the important sources for each raw material? How reliable are these sources?

3.4.4 Finance

What is the financial standing of the company as a whole and of its different products/divisions in terms of earnings, sales, tangible net worth, working capital, earnings per share, liquidity, inventory, cash flow position, and capital structure? What is the cost of capital? Can money be used more productively? What is the reputation of the company in the financial community? How does the company's performance compare with that of competitors and other similarly sized corporations? What steps have been proposed or taken to line up new sources of capital, to increase return on investment through more productive use of resources, and to lower break-even points? Has the company managed tax matters aggressively? What contingency steps are proposed to avert threats of capital shortage or a takeover?

3.4.5 Research and Development

What is the research and development reputation of the company? What percentage of sales and profits in the past can be directly attributed to research and development efforts? Are there any conflicts or personality clashes in the department? If so, what has been proposed and what is being done? What is the status of current major projects? When are they expected to be completed? In what way will they help the company's performance? What kind of relationships does research and development have with marketing and manufacturing? What steps have been proposed and are being taken to cut overhead and improve quality? Are all scientists/researchers adequately used? If not, why not? Can we expect any breakthroughs from research and development? Are there any resentments? If so, what are they and for what reason do they exist?

Exhibit 3.6 Success Factors for Different Industries		Specimen Industries	
Key Factor or Function	**To Increase Profit**	**To Gain Share**
Raw materials sourcing	Uranium	Petroleum
Product facilities (economies of scale)	Shipbuilding, steelmaking	Shipbuilding, steelmaking
Design	Aircraft	Aircraft, hi-fi
Production technology	Soda, semiconductors	Semiconductors
Product range/variety	Department stores	Components
Application engineering/ engineers	Minicomputers	Large-scale integration (LSI), microprocessors
Sales force (quality × quantity)	Electronic code recorders (ECR)	Automobiles
Distribution network	Beer	Films, home appliances
Servicing	Elevators	Commercial vehicles (e.g., taxis)

Source: Kenichi Ohmae, *The Mind of the Strategist* (New York: McGraw-Hill Book Co.,1982), 47.

3.4.6 Miscellaneous

What has been proposed or done to serve minorities, the community, the cause of education, and other such concerns? What is the nature of productivity gains for the company as a whole and for each part of the company? How does the company stand in comparison to industry trends and national goals? How well does the company compete in the world market? Which countries/companies constitute tough competitors? What are their strengths and weaknesses? What is the nature and scope of the company's public relations function? Is it adequate? How does it compare with that of competitors and other companies of similar size and character? Which government agencies—federal, state, or local—does the company deal with most often? Are the company's relationships with various levels of government satisfactory? Who are the company's stockholders? Do a few individuals/institutions hold majority stock? What are their corporate expectations? Do they prefer capital gains or dividend income?

Ratings on these questions may be added up to compute the total resource score in each area. It must be understood that not all questions can be evaluated using the same scale. In many cases, quantitative measurement may be difficult and subjective evaluation must be accepted. Further, measurement of resources should be done for current effectiveness and for future perspectives.

Strategic factors for success lie in different functional areas, the distribution network, for example, and they vary by industry. As shown in Exhibit 3.6, the success factors for different industries fall at different points along a continuum of functional activities that begins with raw materials sourcing and ends with servicing. In the uranium industry, raw materials sourcing is the key to success because low-quality ore requires much more complicated and costly processing. Inasmuch as the price of uranium does not vary among producers, the choice of the source of uranium supply is the crucial determinant of profitability. In contrast, the critical factor in the soda industry is production technology. Because the mercury process is more than twice as efficient as the semipermeable membrane method of obtaining soda of similar quality, a company using the latter process is at a disadvantage no matter what else it might do to reduce extra cost. In other words, the use of mercury technology is a strategic resource for a soda company if its competitors have chosen not to go to the expense and difficulty of changing over from the semipermeable membrane method.

3.5 PAST PERFORMANCE OF BUSINESS UNITS

The past performance of business units serves as an important input in formulating corporate-wide strategy. It helps in the assessment of the current situation and possible developments in the future. For example, if the profitability of an SBU has been declining over the past five years, an appraisal of current performance as satisfactory cannot be justified, assuming the trend continues. In addition, any projected rise in profitability must be thoroughly justified in the light of this trend. The perspectives of different SBUs over time, vis-à-vis other factors (top management values, concerns of stakeholders, corporate resources, and the socioeconomic-political-technological environment), show which have the potential for profitable growth.

SBU performance is based on such measures as financial strength (sales—dollar or volume—operating profit before taxes, cash flow, depreciation, sales per employee, profits per employee, investment per employee, return on investment/sales/assets, and asset turnover); human resources (use of employee skills, productivity, turnover, and ethnic and racial composition); facilities (rated capacity, capacity utilization, and modernization); inventories (raw materials, finished products, and obsolete inventory); marketing (research and development expenditures, new product introductions, number of salespersons, sales per salesperson, independent distributors, exclusive distributors, and promotion expenditures); international business (growth rate and geographic coverage); and managerial performance (leadership capabilities, planning, development of personnel, and delegation).

Usually the volume of data that the above information would generate is much greater than required. It is desirable, therefore, for management to specify what measures it considers important in appraising the performance of SBUs. From the viewpoint of corporate management, the following three measures are frequently the principal measures of performance:

1. **Effectiveness** measures the success of a business's products and programs in relation to those of its competitors in the market. Effectiveness commonly is measured by such items as sales growth in comparison with that of competitors or by changes in market share.
2. **Efficiency** is the outcome of a business's programs in relation to the resources employed in implementing them. Common measures of efficiency are profitability as a percentage of sales and return on investment.
3. **Adaptability** is the business's success in responding over time to changing conditions and opportunities in the environment. Adaptability can be measured in a variety of ways, but common measures are the number of successful new product introductions in relation to those of competitors and the percentage of sales accounted for by products introduced within some recent time period.

To ensure consistency in information received from different SBUs, it is worthwhile to develop a pro forma sheet listing the categories of information that corporate management desires. The general profile produced from the evaluation of information obtained through pro forma sheets provides a quick picture of how well things are going.

SUMMARY

Corporate appraisal constitutes an important ingredient in the strategy development process because it lays the foundation for the company to interact with the future environment. Corporate publics, value orientation of top management, and corporate resources are the three principal factors in appraisal discussed in this chapter. Appraisal of the past performance of business units, which also affects formulation of corporate strategy for the future, is covered briefly.

Corporate publics are all those groups having a stake in the organization; that is, owners, employees, customers, suppliers, the banking community and other lenders, government, the community in which the company does business, and society at large. Expectations of all stakeholders should be considered in formulating corporate strategy. Corporate strategy is also deeply influenced by the value orientation of the corporation's top management. Thus, the values of top management should be studied and duly assessed in setting objectives. Finally, the company's resources in different areas should be carefully evaluated. They serve as major criteria for the formulation of future perspectives.

DISCUSSION QUESTIONS

1. How often should a company undertake corporate appraisal? What are the arguments for and against yearly corporate appraisal?

2. Discuss the pros and cons of having a consultant conduct the appraisal.
3. Identify five companies that in your opinion have failed to change with time and have either pulled out of the marketplace or continue in it as laggards.
4. Identify five companies that in your opinion have kept pace with time as evidenced by their performance.
5. What expectations does a community have of (a) a bank, (b) a medical group, and (c) a manufacturer of cyclical goods?
6. What top management values are most likely to lead to a growth orientation?
7. Is growth orientation necessarily good? Discuss.
8. In your opinion, what marketing resources are the most critical for success in the cosmetics industry?

NOTES

1. *Perspectives on Corporate Strategy* (Boston: Boston Consulting Group, 1968): 93.
2. See: Richard R. Ellsworth, *Leading with Purpose: The New Corporate Realities* (Stanford, CA: Stanford University Press, 2003).
3. Donald P. Robin and R. Eric Reidenback, "Social Responsibility Ethics and Marketing Strategy: Closing the Gap between Concept and Application," *Journal of Marketing*, January 1987, p. 55.
4. Ian Davis "The Biggesst Contract," *The Economist*, May 28, 2005, p. 69.
5. "*The Good Company*, A Survey of Corporate Social Responsibility," *The Economist*, January 22, 2005.
6. Elizabeth Wine, "Socially Responsible Investment to Gain a Clearer Definition," *Financial Times*, May 14, 2001, p. 22.
7. "The Battle for Corporate Control," *BusinessWeek*, May 18, 1987, p. 102.
8. See: Richard R. Ellsworth, *Leading with Purpose: The New Corporate Realities, op. cit.*
9. Robert F. Lusch and Gene R. Laczniak, "The Evolving Marketing Concept, Competitive Intensity and Organizational Performance," *Journal of the Academy of Marketing Science*, Fall 1987, p. 10.
10. "Corning's Class Act," *BusinessWeek*, May 13, 1991, p. 76.
11. Chris Warren, "A Green Giant," *Continental Airlines Magazine*, May 2003, p. 35.
12. Roger Cowe, "Verifying the Facts is a Difficult Task," *Financial Times*, September 29, 2003, p. 4.
13. George A. Steiner, *Top Management Planning* (New York: Macmillan Co., 1969), p. 241.
14. Thomas J. Peters, "Putting Excellence into Management," *McKinsey Quarterly*, Autumn 1990, p. 37.
15. "Where Different Styles Have Led Two Canmakers," *BusinessWeek*, July 27, 1981, pp. 81–82. See also Bernard Wysocki, Jr., "The Chief's Personality Can Have a Big Impact For Better or Worse," *Wall Street Journal*, September 11, 1984, p. 1.
16. Alex Taylor III, "Yo Ben! Yo Jerry! It's Just Ice Cream!" *Fortune*, April 28, 1997, p. 374.
17. "Is It Rainforest Crunch Time?" *BusinessWeek*, July 15, 1996, p. 70.
18. "Changing a Corporate Culture," *BusinessWeek*, May 14, 1984, p. 130.
19. Brian Dumaine, "P&G Rewrites the Marketing Rules," *Fortune*, November 6, 1989, p. 34.
20. Mayron Magnet, "Let's Go for Growth," *Fortune*, March 7, 1994, p. 70.
21. "Corporate Culture," p. 34. See also Bro Uttal, "The Corporate Culture Vultures," *Fortune*, October 17, 1983, pp. 66–73; Trish Hall, "Demanding Pepsi Company Is Attempting to Make Work Nicer for Managers," *Wall Street Journal*, October 23, 1984, p. 31.
22. Carol Hymowitz, "Which Corporate Culture Fits You?" *Wall Street Journal*, July 17, 1989, p. B1.
23. Brian Dumaine, "Creating a New Company Culture," *Fortune*, January 15, 1990, p. 128.
24. David Kirpatrick, "Could AT&T Rule the World," *Fortune*, May 17, 1993, p. 57.
25. Gordon W. Allport, Philip E. Vernon, and Gardner Lindzey, *Study of Values and the Manual of Study of Values* (Boston: Houghton Mifflin Co., 1960).
26. Emily Nelson and Nikhil Deogun, "Reformer Jager was Too Much for P&G," *The Wall Street Journal*, June 9, 2000, p. 1.
27. "CEO Evolution," *Fortune*, November 18, 2002, p. 84.
28. G. Bruce Knecht, "Big Retail Chains Get Special Advance Looks at Magazine Contents," *The Wall Street Journal*, October 12, 1997, p. A1.

Chapter Outline

4.1 Meaning of Competition

4.2 Theory of Competition

4.3 Classifying Competitors

4.4 Intensity, or Degree, of Competition

4.5 Competitive Intelligence

4.6 Seeking Competitive Advantage

4.7 Sustaining Competitive Advantage

Chapter 4

Understanding Competition

The most complete and happy victory is this: to compel one's enemy to give up his purpose, while suffering no harm oneself.

BELISARIUS

In a free market economy, each company tries to outperform its competitors. A competitor is a rival. A company must know, therefore, how it stands up against each competitor with regard to "arms and ammunition"—skill in maneuvering opportunities, preparedness in reacting to threats, and so on. To obtain adequate knowledge about the competition, a company needs an excellent intelligence network.

Typically, whenever one talks about competition, emphasis is placed on price, quality of product, delivery time, and other marketing variables. For the purposes of strategy development, however, one needs to go far beyond these marketing tactics. Simply knowing that a competitor has been lowering prices, for example, is not sufficient. Over and above that, one must know how much flexibility the competitor has in further reducing the price. Implicit here is the need for information about the competitor's cost structure.

This chapter begins by examining the meaning of competition. The theory of competition is reviewed, and a scheme for classifying competitors is advanced. Various sources of competitive intelligence are mentioned, and models for understanding competitive behavior are discussed. Finally, the impact of competition in formulating marketing strategy is analyzed.

4.1 MEANING OF COMPETITION

The term *competition* defies definition because the view of competition held by different groups (e.g., lawyers, economists, government officials, and businesspeople) varies. Most firms define competition in crude, simplistic, and unrealistic terms. Some firms fail to identify the true sources of competition; others underestimate the capabilities and reactions of their competitors. When the business climate is stable, a shallow outlook toward the competition might work, but in the current environment, business strategies must be competitively oriented.

A useful way to define competition is to differentiate between natural and strategic competition. **Natural competition** refers to the survival of the fittest in a given environment. It is an evolutionary process that weeds out the weaker of two rivals. Applied to the business world, it means that no two firms doing business across the board the same way in the same market can coexist forever. To survive, each firm must have something uniquely superior to the other.

Natural competition is an extension of the biological phenomenon of Darwinian natural selection. Characteristically, this type of competition—evolution by adaptation—occurs by trial and error; is wildly opportunistic day to day; pursues growth for its own sake; and is very conservative, because growth from successful trials must prevail over death (i.e., bankruptcy) by random mistake.

Strategic competition is the studied deployment of resources based on a high degree of insight into the systematic cause and effect in the business ecological system.[1] It tries to leave nothing to chance. Strategic competition is a new phenomenon in the business world that may well have the same impact upon business productivity that the industrial revolution had upon individual productivity. Strategic competition requires (a) an adequate amount of information about the situation, (b) development of a framework to understand the dynamic interactive system, (c) postponement of current consumption to provide investment capital, (d) commitment to invest major resources to an irreversible outcome, and (e) an ability to predict the output consequences even with incomplete knowledge of inputs. The following are the basic elements of strategic competition:

• The ability to understand competitive interaction as a complete dynamic system that includes the interaction of competitors, customers, money, people, and resources.

- The ability to use this understanding to predict the consequences of a given intervention in the system and how that intervention will result in new patterns of equilibrium.
- The availability of uncommitted resources that can be dedicated to different uses and purposes in the present even though the dedication is permanent and the benefits will be deferred.
- The ability to predict risk and return with sufficient accuracy and confidence to justify the commitment of such resources.
- The willingness to deliberately act to make the commitment.

Japan's emergence as a major industrial power over a short span of time illustrates the practical application of strategic competition.

The differences between Japan and the U.S. deserve some comparative analysis. There are lessons to be learned. These two leading industrial powers came from different directions, developed different methods, and followed different strategies.

Japan is a small group of islands whose total land area is smaller than a number of our 50 states. The U.S., by comparison, is a vast land.

Japan is mountainous with very little arable land. The U.S. is the world's largest and most fertile agricultural area in a single country.

Japan has virtually no energy or natural resources. The U.S. is richly endowed with energy, minerals, and other vital resources.

Japan has one of the oldest, most homogenous, most stable cultures. For 2,000 years or more, there was virtually no immigration, no dilution of culture, or any foreign invasion. The U.S. has been a melting pot of immigrants from many cultures and many languages over one-tenth the time span. For most of its history, the U.S. has been an agrarian society and a frontier society.

The Japanese developed a high order of skill in living together in cooperation over many centuries. Americans developed a frontier mentality of self-reliance and individuality.

The evolution of the U.S. into a vast industrial society was a classic example of natural competition in a rich environment with no constraints or artificial barriers.

This option was not open to Japan. It had been in self-imposed isolation from the rest of the world for several hundred years until Commodore Perry sailed into Tokyo harbor and forced the signing of a navigation and trade treaty. Japan had been unaware of the industrial revolution already well underway in the West. It decided to compete in that world. But it had no resources.

To rise above a medieval economy, Japan had to obtain foreign materials. To obtain foreign materials, it had to buy them. To buy abroad required foreign exchange. To obtain foreign exchange, exports were required. Exports became Japan's lifeline. But effective exports meant the maximum value added, first with minimum material and then with minimum direct labor. Eventually this led Japan from labor intensive to capital intensive and then to technology intensive businesses. Japan was forced to develop strategic business competition as part of national policy.[2]

4.2 THEORY OF COMPETITION

Competition is basic to the free enterprise system. It is involved in all observable phenomena of the market—the prices at which products are exchanged, the kinds and qualities of products produced, the quantities exchanged, the methods of distribution employed, and the emphasis placed on promotion. Over many decades, economists have contributed to the theory of competition. A well-recognized body of theoretical knowledge about competition has emerged and can be grouped broadly into two categories: (a) economic theory and (b) industrial organization perspective. These and certain other hypotheses on competition from the viewpoint of businesspeople are discussed below.

Economists have worked with many different models of competition. Still central to much of their work is the model of *perfect competition*, which is based on the premise that, when a large number of buyers and sellers in the market are dealing in homogeneous products, there is complete freedom to enter or exit the market and everyone has complete and accurate knowledge about everyone else.

The essence of the industrial organization (IO) perspective is that a firm's position in the marketplace depends critically on the characteristics of the industry environment in which it competes. The industry environment comprises structure, conduct, and performance. The structure refers to the economic and technical perspectives of the industry in the context in which firms compete. It includes (a) concentration in the industry (i.e., the number and size distribution of firms), (b) barriers to entry in the industry, and (c) product differentiation among the offerings of different firms that make up the industry. Conduct, which is essentially strategy, refers to firms' behavior in such matters as pricing, advertising, and distribution. Performance includes social performance, measured in terms of allocative efficiency (profitability), technical efficiency (cost minimization), and innovativeness.

Following the IO thesis, the structure of each industry vis-à-vis concentration, product differentiation, and entry barriers varies. Structure plays an important role in the competitive behavior of different firms in the market.

Businesses must be continually aware of the structure of the markets they are presently in or of those they seek to enter. Their appraisal of their present and future competitive posture will be influenced substantially by the size and concentration of existing firms as well as by the extent of product differentiation and the presence or absence of significant barriers to entry.

If a manager has already introduced the firm's products into a market, the existence of certain structural features may provide the manager with a degree of insulation from the intrusion of firms not presently in that market. The absence, or relative unimportance, of one or more entry barriers, for example, supplies the manager with insights into the direction from which potential competition might come. Conversely, the presence or absence of entry barriers indicates the relative degree of effort required and the success that might be enjoyed if the manager attempted to enter a specific market. In short, a fundamental purpose of marketing strategy involves the building of entry barriers to protect present markets and the overcoming of existing entry barriers around markets that have an attractive potential.[3]

From the business perspective, **competition** refers to rivalry among firms operating in a market to fill the same customer need. The businessperson's major interest is to keep the market to himself or herself by adopting appropriate strategies. How and why competition occurs, its intensity, and what escape routes are feasible have not been conceptualized.[4] In other words, there does not exist a theory of competition from the business viewpoint.

In recent years, however, Henderson has developed the theory of strategic competition discussed above. Some of the hypotheses on which his theory rests derive from military warfare:

- Competitors who persist and survive have a unique advantage over all others. If they did not have this advantage, then others would crowd them out of the market.
- If competitors are different and coexist, then each must have a distinct advantage over the other. Such an advantage can only exist if differences in a competitor's characteristics match differences in the environment that give those characteristics their relative value.
- Any change in the environment changes the factor weighting of environmental characteristics and, therefore, shifts the boundaries of competitive equilibrium and "competitive segments." Competitors who adapt best or fastest gain an advantage from change in the environment.[5]

Henderson presents an interesting new way of looking at the marketplace: as a battleground where opposing forces (competitors) devise ways (strategies) to outperform each other. Some of his hypotheses can be readily observed, tested, and validated and could lead to a general theory of business competition. However, many of his interlocking hypotheses must still be revised and tested.

4.3 CLASSIFYING COMPETITORS

A business may face competition from various sources either within or outside its industry. Competition may come from essentially similar products or from substitutes. The competitor may be a small firm or a large multinational corporation. To gain an adequate perspective on the competition, a firm needs to identify all current and potential sources of competition.[6]

Competition is triggered when different industries try to serve the same customer needs and demands. For example, a customer's entertainment needs may be filled by television, sports, publishing, or travel.

New industries may also enter the arena to satisfy entertainment needs. In the early 1980s, for example, the computer industry entered the entertainment field with video games.

Different industries position themselves to serve different customer demands—existing, latent, and incipient. **Existing demand** occurs when a product is bought to satisfy a recognized need. An example is Swatch Watch to determine time. **Latent demand** refers to a situation where a particular need has been recognized, but no products have yet been offered to satisfy the need. Sony tapped the latent demand through Walkman for the attraction of ''music on the move.'' **Incipient demand** occurs when certain trends lead to the emergence of a need of which the customer is not yet aware. A product that makes it feasible to read books while sleeping would illustrate the incipient demand.

A competitor may be an existing firm or a new entrant. The new entrant may enter the market with a product developed through research and development or through acquisition.[7] For example, Apple entered the music business through research and development that led to the manufacture of their iPod product. Proctor and Gamble entered the razor blade market by acquiring the Gillette Company.

Often an industry competes by producing different product lines. General Foods Corporation, for example, offers ground, regular instant, freeze-dried, decaffeinated, and ''international'' coffee to the coffee market. Product lines can be grouped into three categories: a me-too product, an improved product, or a breakthrough product. A **me-too product** is similar to current offerings. One of many brands currently available in the market, it offers no special advantage over competing products. An **improved product** is one that, while not unique, is generally superior to many existing brands. A **breakthrough product** is an innovation and is usually technical in nature. The DVD player and iphone are breakthrough products.

In the watch business, companies have traditionally competed by offering me-too products. Occasionally, a competitor comes out with an improved product, as Seiko did in the 1970s by introducing quartz watches. Quartz watches were a little fancier and supposedly more accurate than other watches. Texas Instruments, however, entered the watch business via a breakthrough product, the digital watch.

Finally, the scope of a competing firm's activities may be limited or extensive. For example, General Mills may not worry if a regional chain of Italian eateries is established to compete against its Olive Garden chain of Italian restaurants subsidiary. However, if McDonalds were to start offering Italian food, General Mills would be concerned at the entry of such a strong and seasoned competitor.

Exhibit 4.1 illustrates various sources of competition available to fulfill the liquid requirements of the human body. Let us analyze the competition here for a company that maintains an interest in this field. Currently, the thrust of the market is to satisfy existing demand. An example of a product to satisfy latent demand would be a liquid that promises weight loss; a liquid to prevent aging would be an example of a product to satisfy incipient demand.

The industries that currently offer products to quench customer thirst are the liquor, beer, wine, soft drink, milk, coffee, tea, drinking water, and fruit juice industries. A relatively new entrant is health drinks. Looking just at the soft drink industry, assuming that this is the field that most interests our company, we see that the majority of competitors offer me-too products (e.g., regular cola, diet cola, lemonade, and other fruit-based drinks). However, caffeine-free cola has been introduced by two major competitors, Coca-Cola Company and PepsiCo. There has been a breakthrough in the form of low-calorie, caffeine-free drinks. A beverage containing a day's nutritional requirements is feasible in the future.

The companies that currently compete in the regular cola market are Coca-Cola, PepsiCo, Seven-Up, Dr. Pepper, Qibla Cola, Mecca-Cola, and a few others.[8] Among these, however, the first two have a major share of the cola market. Among new industry entrants, General Foods Corporation and Nestle Company are likely candidates (an assumption). The two principal competitors, Coca-Cola Company and PepsiCo, are large multinational, multibusiness firms. This is the competitive arena where our company will have to fight if it enters the soft drink business.

4.4 INTENSITY, OR DEGREE, OF COMPETITION

The degree of competition in a market depends on the moves and countermoves of various firms active in the market. It usually starts with one firm trying to achieve a favorable position by pursuing appropriate strategies. Because what is good for one firm may be harmful to rival firms, rival firms respond with counter strategies to protect their interests.

Exhibit 4.1 Source of Competition	

Customer Need: Liquid for the Body

Existing need	Thirst
Latent need	Liquid to reduce weight
Incipient need	Liquid to prevent aging

Industry Competition (How Can I Quench My Thirst?)

Existing industries	Hard liquor
	Beer
	Wine
	Soft drink
	Milk
	Coffee
	Tea
	Water
New industry	Mineral water

Product Line Competition (What Form of Product Do I Want?)

Me-too products	Regular cola
	Diet cola
	Lemonade
	Fruit-based drink
Improved product	Caffeine-free cola
Breakthrough product	Diet and caffeine-free cola providing full nutrition

Organizational Competition (What Brand Do I Want?)

Type of Firm	
Existing firms	Coca-Cola
	PepsiCo
	Seven-Up
	Dr. Pepper
New entrants	General Foods
	Nestle
Scope of Business	
Geographic	Regional, national, multinational
Product/market	Single versus multiproduct industry

Intense competitive activity may or may not be injurious to the industry as a whole. For example, while a price war may result in lower profits for all members of an industry, an advertising battle may increase demand and actually be mutually beneficial. Exhibit 4.2 lists the factors that affect the intensity of competition in the marketplace. In a given situation, a combination of factors determines the degree of competition.

A promising market is likely to attract firms seeking to capitalize on an available opportunity. As the number of firms interested in sharing the pie increases, the degree of rivalry increases. Take, for example, the home computer market. In the early 1980s, everyone from mighty IBM to such unknowns in the field as Timex Watch Company wanted a piece of the personal computer pie. As firms started jockeying for position, the intensity of competition increased manifold. A number of firms, for example, Texas Instruments and Atari, were forced to quit the market. At the same time, new competitors such as Dell and Compaq entered the market undermining even IBM.

When entry into an industry is relatively easy, many firms, including some marginal ones, are attracted to it. The long-standing, committed members of the industry, however, do not want "outsiders" to break

Exhibit 4.2 Factors Contributing to Competitive Rivalry	Opportunity potential Ease of entry Nature of product Exit barriers Homogeneity of market Industry structure or competitive position of firms Commitment to the industry Feasibility of technological innovations Scale economies Economic climate Diversity of firms

into their territory. Therefore, existing firms discourage potential entrants by adopting strategies that enhance competition.

For example, in 2008, McDonald's decided to directly compete with Starbucks by adding coffee bars with "baristas" in almost 14,000 of its U.S. restaurants, serving cappuccinos, lattes, mochas and the Frappe. Right away Starbucks planned offensive meaures to prevent McDonald's enroachment on what it considered its territory.[9]

When the products offered by different competitors are perceived by customers to be more or less similar, firms are forced into price and, to a lesser degree, service competition. In such situations, competition can be really severe.

For a variety of reasons, it may be difficult for a firm to get out of a particular business. Possible reasons include the relationship of the business to other businesses of the firm, high investment in assets for which there may not be an advantageous alternative use, high cost of discharging commitments (e.g., fixed labor contracts and future purchasing agreements), top management's emotional attachment to the business, and government regulations prohibiting exit (e.g., the legal requirement that a utility must serve all customers).

When the entire market represents one large homogeneous unit, the intensity of competition is much greater than when the market is segmented.[10] Even if the product sold is a commodity, segmentation of the market is possible. It is possible, for example, to identify frequent buyers of the commodity as one segment; and occasional buyers as another. But if a market is not suited to segmentation, firms must compete to serve it homogeneously, thus intensifying competition.

When the number of firms active in a market is large, there is a good chance that one of the firms may aggressively seek an advantageous position. Such aggression leads to intense competitive activity as firms retaliate. On the other hand, if only a few firms constitute an industry, there is usually little doubt about industry leadership. In situations where there is a clear industry leader, care is often taken not to irritate the leader since a resulting fight could be very costly.

When a firm has wholeheartedly committed itself to a business, it will do everything to hang on, even becoming a maverick that fearlessly makes moves without worrying about the impact on either the industry or its own resources. Polaroid Corporation, for example, with its strong commitment to instant photography, must maintain its position in the field at any cost. Another example is Budweiser's commitment to the beer business. Such an attachment to an industry enhances competitive activity.

In industries where technological innovations are frequent, each firm likes to do its best to cash in while the technology lasts, thus triggering greater competitive activity.

Where economies realizable through large-scale operations are substantial, a firm will do all it can to achieve scale economies. Attempts to capture scale economies may lead a firm to aggressively compete for market share, escalating pressures on other firms. A similar situation occurs when a business's fixed costs are high and the firm must spread them over a large volume. If capacity can only be added in large increments, the resulting excess capacity will also intensify competition.

Consider the airlines industry. Northwest Airlines commands 73% of the traffic at Detroit Metropolitan Wayne County Airport, and it wants to keep it that way by discouraging competitors. For example, a few years back, an upstart Spirit Airlines entered the Detroit-Philadelphia market with one-way fare of $49, while Northwest's average one-way fare was more than $170. Northwest soon slashed its fares to Philadelphia to $49 on virtually all seats at all times, and added 30% more seats. A few months later, Spirit abandoned the route and Northwest raised its fare to more than $220.[11]

During depressed economic conditions and otherwise slow growth, competition is much more volatile as each firm tries to make the best of a bad situation.

Firms active in a field over a long period come to acquire a kind of industry standard of behavior. But new participants invading an industry do not necessarily like to play the old game. Forsaking industry patterns, newcomers may have different strategic perspectives and may be willing to go to any lengths to achieve their goals. The Miller Brewing Company's unconventional marketing practices are a case in point. Miller, nurtured and guided by its parent, Philip Morris, segmented the market by introducing a light beer to an industry that had hitherto considered beer a commodity-type product. When different cultures meet in the marketplace, competition can be fierce.

4.5 COMPETITIVE INTELLIGENCE

Competitive intelligence is the publicly available information on competitors, current and potential, that serves as an important input in formulating marketing strategy. No general would order an army to march without first fully knowing the enemy's position and intentions. Likewise, before deciding which competitive moves to make, a firm must be aware of the perspectives of its competitors. Competitive intelligence includes information beyond industry statistics and trade gossip. It involves close observation of competitors to learn what they do best and why and where they are weak. No self-respecting business admits to not doing an adequate job of scanning the competitive environment, but what sets the outstanding companies apart from the merely self-respecting ones is that they watch their competition in such depth and with such dedication that, as a marketing executive once remarked to the author, ''The information on competitive moves reaches them before even the management of the competing company learns about it.''

Three types of competitive intelligence may be distinguished: defensive, passive, and offensive intelligence. **Defensive intelligence**, as the name suggests, is gathered to avoid being caught off-balance. A deliberate attempt is made to gather information on the competition in a structured fashion and to keep track of moves that are relevant to the firm's business. **Passive intelligence** is ad hoc information gathered for a specific decision. A company may, for example, seek information on a competitor's sales compensation plan when devising its own compensation plan. Finally, **offensive intelligence** is undertaken to identify new opportunities. From a strategic perspective, offensive intelligence is the most relevant.

Such information as how competitors make, test, distribute, price, and promote their products can go a long way in developing a viable marketing strategy. The Ford Motor Company, for example, has an ongoing program for tearing down competitors' products to learn about their cost structure. Exhibit 4.3 summarizes the process followed at Ford. This competitive knowledge has helped Ford in its strategic

Exhibit 4.3 Ford Motor Company's Competitive Product Tear-Down Process	1. **Purchase the product.** The high cost of product teardown, particularly for a carmaker, gives some indication of the value successful competitors place on the knowledge they gain.

1. **Purchase the product.** The high cost of product teardown, particularly for a carmaker, gives some indication of the value successful competitors place on the knowledge they gain.
2. **Tear the product down—literally.** First, every removable component is unscrewed or unbolted; the rivets are undone; finally, individual spot welds are broken.
3. **Reverse-engineer the product.** While the competitor's car is being dismantled, detailed drawings of parts are made and parts lists are assembled, together with analyses of the production processes that were evidently involved.
4. **Build up costs.** Parts are costed out in terms of make-or-buy, the variety of parts used in a single product, and the extent of common assemblies across model ranges. Among the important facts to be established in a product teardown, obviously, are the number and variety of components and the number of assembly operations. The costs of the processes are then built up from both direct labor requirements and overheads (often vital to an understanding of competitor cost structures).
5. **Establish economies of scale.** Once individual cost elements are known, they can be put together with the volume of cars produced by the competitor and the total number of people employed to develop some fairly reliable guides to the competitor's economies of scale. Having done this, Ford can calculate model-run lengths and volumes needed to achieve, first, break even and then profit.

Source: Robin Leaf, ''How to Pick Up Tips from Your Competitors,'' *Director* (February 1978): 60.

moves in Europe. For example, from regularly tearing down the Leyland Mini (a small truck), the company concluded that (a) Leyland was not making money on the Mini at its current price and (b) Ford should not enter the small truck market at current price levels. Based on these conclusions, Ford was able to arrive at a firm strategic decision not to assemble a "Mini."

The following example compares two companies that decided to enter the automatic dishwasher market at about the same time. One of the companies ignored the competition, floundered, and eventually abandoned the field; the other did a superior job of learning from the competition and came out on top. When the CEO of the first company, a British company, learned from his marketing department about the market growth potential for dishwashers and about current competitors' shares, he lost no time setting out to develop a suitable machine.

Finding little useful information available on dishwasher design, the director of research and development decided to begin by investigating the basic mechanics of the dishwashing process. Accordingly, she set up a series of pilot projects to evaluate the cleaning performance of different jet configurations, the merits of alternative washing-arm designs, and the varying results obtained with different types and quantities of detergent on different washing loads. At the end of a year she had amassed a great deal of useful knowledge. She also had a pilot machine running that cleaned dishes well and a design concept for a production version. But considerable development work was still needed before the prototype could be declared a satisfactory basis for manufacture.

To complicate matters, management had neglected to establish effective linkages among the company's three main functions—marketing, technology, and production. So it was not until the technologists had produced the prototype and design concepts that marketing and production began asking for revisions and suggesting new ideas, further delaying the development of a marketable product.

So much for the first company, with its fairly typical traditional response to market opportunities. The second company, which happened to be Japanese, started with the same marketing intelligence but responded in a very different fashion.

First, it bought three units of every available competitive dishwasher. Next, management formed four special teams: (a) a product test group of marketing and technical staff, (b) a design team of technologists and production people, (c) a distribution team of marketing and production staff, and (d) a field team of production staff.

The product test group was given one of each competitive model and asked to evaluate performance: dishwashing effectiveness, ease of use, and reliability (frequency and cause of breakdown). The remaining two units of each competitive model were given to the design team, who stripped down one of each pair to determine the number and variety of parts, the cost of each part, and the ease of assembly. The remaining units were stripped down to "life-test" each component, to identify design improvements and potential sources of supply, and to develop a comprehensive picture of each competitor's technology. Meanwhile, the distribution team was evaluating each competitor's sales and distribution system (numbers of outlets, product availability, and service offered), and the field team was investigating competitors' factories and evaluating their production facilities in terms of cost of labor, cost of supplies, and plant productivity.

All this investigating took a little less than a year. At the end of that time, the Japanese still knew a lot less about the physics and chemistry of dishwashing than their British rivals, but the knowledge developed by their business teams had put them far ahead. In two more months they had designed a product that outperformed the best of the competition, yet would cost 30 percent less to build, based on a preproduction prototype and production process design. They also had a marketing plan for introducing the new dishwasher to the Japanese domestic market before taking it overseas. This plan positioned the product relative to the competition and defined distribution system requirements in terms of stocking and service levels needed to meet the expected production rate. Finally, the Japanese had prepared detailed plans for building a new factory, establishing supply contracts, and training the labor force.

The denouement of this story is what one might expect: The competitive Japanese manufacturer brought its new product to market two years ahead of the more traditionally minded British manufacturer and achieved its planned market share 10 weeks later. The traditional company steadily lost money and eventually dropped out of the market.

As the above anecdote shows, competitive analysis has three major objectives:

1. It allows you to understand your position of comparative advantage and your competitors' positions of comparative advantage.
2. It allows you to understand your competitors' strategies—past, present, and as they are likely to be in the future.

3. It is a key criterion of strategy selection, the element that makes your strategies come alive in the real world.

Knowledge about the competition may be gained by raising the following questions. To answer each question requires systematic probing and data gathering on different aspects of competition.

- Who is the competition? now? five years from now?
- What are the strategies, objectives, and goals of each major competitor?
- How important is a specific market to each competitor and what is the level of its commitment?
- What are the relative strengths and limitations of each competitor?
- What weaknesses make competitors vulnerable?
- What changes are competitors likely to make in their future strategies?
- So what? What will be the effects of all competitors' strategies, on the industry, the market, and our strategy?

Essentially, knowledge about competitors comprise their size, growth, and profitability, the image and positioning of their brands, objectives and commitments, strengths and weaknesses, current and past strategies, cost structure, exit barriers limiting their ability to withdraw, and organization style and culture.

Consider the case of Motorola. In August 2007, it introuduced its next generation Razr2 cellular telephone, and the company was concerned how it would be received vis-à-vis Apple's iPhone, which was launched eight weeks earlier. Motorola executives were worried if iPhone has changed the dynamics of the industry establishing a new niche for itself, or would it directly compete with Razr2? Could Motorola charge a premium price for Razr2 considering its new features? What is the worth of Razr2's noise-filtering technology? And so on.[12]

As companies seek to build competitive advantage with new inventions, they need to determine the proper competitive position for the new product that would provide a long-term advantage over competitive products. This requires deep insights into their competitors, perspectives.

The following procedure may be adopted to gather competitive intelligence:

1. **Recognize key competitors in market segments in which the company is active.** Presumably a product will be positioned to serve one or more market segments. In each segment there may be different competitors to reckon with; an attempt should be made to recognize all important competitors in each segment. If the number of competitors is excessive, it is sufficient to limit consideration to the first three competitors. Each competitor should be briefly profiled to indicate total corporate proportion.
2. **Analyze the performance record of each competitor.** The performance of a competitor can be measured with reference to a number of criteria. As far as marketing is concerned, sales growth, market share, and profitability are the important measures of success. Thus, a review of each competitor's sales growth, market share, and profitability for the past several years is desirable. In addition, any ad hoc reasons that bear upon a competitor's performance should be noted. For example, a competitor may have lined up some business, in the nature of a windfall from Dubai, without making any strategic moves to secure the business. Similar missteps that may limit performance should be duly pointed out. Occasionally a competitor may intentionally pad results to reflect good performance at year end. Such tactics should be noted, too. Rothschild advises the following:

   > To make it really useful, you must probe how each participant keeps its books and records its profits. Some companies stress earnings; others report their condition in such a way as to delay the payment of taxes; still other bookkeep to increase cash availability.
   >
   > These measurements are important because they may affect the company's ability to procure financing and attract people as well as influence stockholders' and investors' satisfaction with current management.[13]

3. **Study how satisfied each competitor appears to be with its performance.** Refer to each competitor's objective(s) for the product. If results are in concert with the expectations of the firm's management and stakeholders, the competitor will be satisfied. A satisfied competitor is most likely to follow its current successful strategy. On the other hand, if results are at odds with management expectations, the competitor is most likely to come out with a new strategy.
4. **Probe each competitor's marketing strategy.** The strategy of each competitor can be inferred from game plans (i.e., different moves in the area of product, price, promotion, and distribution) that are pursued to achieve objectives. Information on game plans is available partly from published stories on the competitor and partly from the salespeople in contact with the competitor's customers and salespeople.

To clarify the point, consider a competitor in the small appliances business who spends heavily for consumer advertising and sells products mainly through discount stores. From this brief description, it is safe to conclude that, as a matter of strategy, the competitor wants to establish the brand in the mass market through discounters. In other words, the competitor is trying to reach customers who want to buy a reputable brand at discount prices and hopes to make money by creating a large sales base.

5. **Analyze current and future resources and competencies of each competitor.** In order to study a competitor's resources and competencies, first designate broad areas of concern: facilities and equipment, personnel skills, organizational capabilities, and management capabilities, for example. Refer to the checklist in Exhibit 4.4. Each area may then be examined with reference to different functional areas (general management, finance, research and development, operations, and especially marketing). In the area of finance, the availability of a large credit line would be listed as a strength under management capabilities. Owning a warehouse and refrigerated trucks is a marketing strength listed under facilities and equipment. A checklist should be developed to specifically pinpoint those strengths that a competitor can use to pursue goals against your firm as well as other firms in the market. Simultaneously, areas in which competitors look particularly vulnerable should also be noted. The purpose here is not to get involved in a ritualistic, detailed account of each competitor but to demarcate those aspects of a competitor's resources and competencies that may account for a substantial difference in performance.

6. **Predict the future marketing strategy of each competitor.** The above competitive analysis provides enough information to make predictions about future strategic directions that each competitor may pursue. Predictions, however, must be made qualitatively, using management consensus. The use of management consensus as the basic means for developing forecasts is based on the presumption that, by virtue of their experience in gauging market trends, executives should be able to make some credible predictions about each competitor's behavior in the future. A senior member of the marketing research staff may be assigned the task of soliciting executive opinions and consolidating the information into specific predictions on the moves competitors are likely to make.

7. **Assess the impact of competitive strategy on the company's product/market.** The *delphi technique*, examined in Chapter 12, can be used to specify the impact of competitive strategy. The impact should be analyzed by a senior marketing personnel, using competitive information and personal experiences on the job as a basis. Thereafter, the consensus of a larger group of executives can be obtained on the impact analysis performed previously.

Essentially, three sources of competitive intelligence can be distinguished: (a) what competitors say about themselves, (b) what others say about them, and (c) what employees of the firm engaged in competitive analysis have observed and learned about competitors. Information from the first two sources, as shown in Exhibit 4.5, is available through public documents, trade associations, government, and investors. Take, for example, information from government sources. Under the Freedom of Information Act, a great amount of information can be obtained at low cost.

As far as information from its own sources is concerned, the company should develop a structured program to gather competitive information. First, a tear-down program like Ford's (Exhibit 4.3) may be undertaken. Second, salespeople may be trained to carefully gather and provide information on the competition, using such sources as customers, distributors, dealers, and former salespeople. Third, senior marketing people should be encouraged to call on customers and speak to them in-depth. These contacts should provide valuable information on competitors' products and services. Fourth, other people in the company who happen to have some knowledge of competitors should be encouraged to channel this information to an appropriate office.

Information gathering on the competition has grown dramatically in recent years. Almost all large companies designate someone specially to seek competitive intelligence. A *Fortune* article has identified more than 20 techniques to keep tabs on the competition. These techniques, summarized below, fall into seven groups. Virtually all of them can be legally used to gain competitive insights, although some may involve questionable ethics. A responsible company should carefully review each technique before using it to avoid practices that might be considered illegal or unethical.

1. **Gathering information from recruits and employees of competing companies.** Firms can collect data about their competitors through interviews with new recruits or by speaking with employees of competing companies. According to the *Fortune* article:

When they interview students for jobs, some companies pay special attention to those who have worked for competitors, even temporarily. Job seekers are eager to impress and often have not been

	Facilities and Equipment	Personnel Skills	Organizational Capabilities	Management Capabilities
1. General Mgmt.				Large credit line
2. Finance				
3. R&D				
4. Operations				
5. Marketing	Warehousing	Door-to-door selling	Direct sales	Industrial marketing
	Retail outlets	Retail selling	Distributor chain	Customer purchasing
	Sales offices	Wholesale selling	Retail chain	Department of Defense marketing
	Service offices	Direct industry selling	Consumer service organization	State and municipality marketing
	Transportation equipment	Department of Defense selling	Industrial service organization	Well-informed and receptive management
	Training facilities for sales staff	Cross-industry selling	Department of Defense product support	Large customer base
	Data processing equipment	Applications engineering	Inventory distribution and control	Decentralized control
		Advertising	Ability to make quick response to customer requirements	Favorable public image
		Sales promotion	Ability to adapt to sociopolitical upheavals in the marketplace	Future orientation
		Servicing	Loyal set of customers	Ethical standards
		Contract administration	Cordial relations with media and channels	
		Sales analysis	Flexibility in all phases of corporate life	
		Data analysis	Consumer financing	
		Forecasting	Discount policy	
		Computer modeling	Teamwork	
		Product planning	Product quality	
		Background of people		
		Corporate culture		

Exhibit 4.4 Sources of Economic Leverage in the Business System

	Public	Trade Professionals	Government	Investors
What competitors say about themselves	• Advertising • Promotional materials • Press releases • Speeches • Books • Articles • Personnel changes • Want ads	• Manuals • Technical papers • Licenses • Patents • Courses • Seminars	• SEC reports • FIC • Testimony • Lawsuits • Antitrust	• Annual meetings • Annual reports • Prospectors • Stock/bond issues
What others say about them	• Books • Articles • Case studies • Consultants • Newspaper reporters • Environmental groups • Consumer groups • "Who's Who" • Recruiting firms	• Suppliers/ vendors • Trade press • Industry study • Customers • Subcontractors	• Lawsuits • Antitrust • State/federal agencies • National plans • Government programs	• Security analyst reports • Industry studies • Credit reports

Exhibit 4.5 Sources of Competitive Intelligence

warned about divulging what is proprietary. They sometimes volunteer valuable information.... Several companies now send teams of highly trained technicians instead of personnel executives to recruit on campus.

Companies send engineers to conferences and trade shows to question competitors' technical people. Often conversations start innocently—just a few fellow technicians discussing processes and problems ... [yet competitors'] engineers and scientists often brag about surmounting technical challenges, in the process divulging sensitive information.

Companies sometimes advertise and hold interviews for jobs that don't exist in order to entice competitors' employees to spill the beans.... Often applicants have toiled in obscurity or feel that their careers have stalled. They're dying to impress somebody.

In probably the hoariest tactic in corporate intelligence gathering, companies hire key executives from competitors to find out what they know.

2. **Gathering information from competitors' customers.** Some customers may give out information on competitors' products. For example, a while back Gillette told a large Canadian account the date on which it planned to begin selling its new Good News disposable razor in the United States. The Canadian distributor promptly called Bic about Gillette's impending product launch. Bic put on a crash program and was able to start selling its razor shortly after Gillette introduced its own.

3. **Gathering information by infiltrating customers' business operations.** Companies may provide their engineers free of charge to customers. The close, cooperative relationship that engineers on loan cultivate with the customer's staff often enables them to learn what new products competitors are pitching.

4. **Gathering information from published materials and public documents.** What may seem insignificant, a help wanted ad, for example, may provide information about a competitor's intentions or planned strategies. The types of people sought in help wanted ads can indicate something about a competitor's technological thrusts and new product development. Government agencies are another good source of information.

5. **Gathering information from government agencies under the Freedom of Information Act.** Some companies hire others to get this information more discreetly.

6. **Gathering information by observing competitors or by analyzing physical evidence.** Companies can get to know competitors better by buying their products or by examining other physical evidence. Companies increasingly buy competitors' products and take them apart to determine costs of production and even manufacturing methods.

In the absence of better information on market share and the volume of product being shipped, companies have measured the rust on the rails of railroad sidings to their competitors' plants and have counted tractor-trailers leaving loading bays.

7. **Gathering information from competitors' garbage.** Some firms actually purchase such garbage. Once it has left a competitor's premises, refuse is legally considered abandoned property. Although some companies shred paper generated by their design labs, they often neglect to shred almost-as-revealing refuse from marketing and public relations departments.[14]

Competitive, or business, intelligence is a powerful new management tool that enhances a corporation's ability to succeed in today's highly competitive global markets. It provides early warning intelligence and a framework for better understanding and countering competitors' initiatives. Competitive activities can be monitored in-house or assigned to an outside firm. A recent study indicates that over 500 U.S. firms are involved or interested in running their own competitive intelligence activities.[15] Usually, companies depend partly on their own people and partly on external help to scan the competitive environment.

Within the organization, competitive information should be acquired both at the corporate level and at the SBU level. At the corporate level, competitive intelligence is concerned with competitors' investment strengths and priorities. At the SBU level, the major interest is in marketing strategy; that is, product, pricing, distribution, and promotion strategies that a competitor is likely to pursue. The true payoff of competitive intelligence comes from the SBU review.

Organizationally, the competitive intelligence task can be assigned to an SBU strategic planner, to a marketing person within the SBU who may be a marketing research or a product/market manager, or to a staff person. Whoever is given the task of gathering competitive intelligence should be allowed adequate time and money to do a thorough job.

As far as outside help is concerned, three main types of organizations may be hired to gather competitive information. First, many marketing research firms (e.g., A.C. Nielsen, Frost and Sullivan, SRI International, Predicasts) provide different types of competitive information, some on a regular basis and others on an ad hoc arrangement. Second, clipping services scan newspapers, financial journals, trade journals, and business publications for articles concerning designated competitors and make copies of relevant clippings for their clients. Third, different brokerage firms specialize in gathering information on various industries. Arrangements may be made with brokerage firms to have regular access to their information on a particular industry.

4.6 SEEKING COMPETITIVE ADVANTAGE

To outperform competitors and to grow despite them, a company must understand why competition prevails, why firms attack, and how firms respond.[16] Insights into competitors' perspectives can be gained by undertaking two types of analysis: industry and comparative analysis. **Industry analysis** assesses the attractiveness of a market based on its economic structure. **Comparative analysis** indicates how every firm in a particular market is likely to perform, given the structure of the industry.[17]

Every industry has a few peculiar characteristics. These characteristics are bound by time and thus are subject to change. We may call them the dynamics of the industry. No matter how hard a company tries, if it fails to fit into the dynamics of the industry, ultimate success may be difficult to achieve.

An example of how the perspectives of an entire industry may change over time is provided by the cosmetics industry. The cosmetics business was traditionally run according to personal experience and judgment, by the seat-of-the-pants, so to speak, with ultimate dependence on the marketing genius of inventors. In the new century, a variety of pressures began to engulf the industry. The regulatory climate became tougher. Consumers have become more demanding and are fewer in number. Although the number of working women continues to rise, this increase has not offset another more significant demographic change: The population of teenagers—traditionally the heaviest and most experimental makeup users—has been declining. According to the 2000 census, there were 18 percent fewer 18- to 24-year-olds than in 1990. As a result, sales of cosmetics are projected to increase only about 2.5 percent per year to the year 2010. These shifts, along with unstable economic conditions and rising costs, have made profits smaller. In the 1980s, several pharmaceutical and packaged-goods companies, including Colgate-Palmolive Co., Eli Lilly and Co., Pfizer, and Schering Plough, acquired cosmetics companies. Among these, only Schering Plough, which makes the mass market Maybelline, has maintained a meaningful business. Colgate, which acquired Helena Rubenstein, sold the brand seven years later after it languished. At the start of the 1990s, the industry began to change again. New mass marketers Procter & Gamble and Unilever entered the arena, bringing with them their great experience producing mundane products such as soap and toilet paper, sparking disdain in the glamorous cosmetics trade. However, the mammoth marketing clout of these giant packaged-goods companies also sparked fear. Procter & Gamble bought Noxell Corporation, producer of Cover Girl and Clarion makeup, making it the top marketer of cosmetics in mass market outlets. Unilever acquired Faberge and Elizabeth Arden.

These changes made competition in the industry fierce. Although capital investment in the industry is small, inventory and distribution costs are extremely high, partly because of the number of shades and textures required in each product line. For example, nail polish and lipstick must be available in more than 50 different shades.

The cosmetics industry has gone through a tremendous change since the 1990s. In the past, success in the industry depended on having a glamorous product. As has been observed, Revlon was manufacturing lipstick in its factories, but it was selling beautiful lips. Today, however, success rests on such nuts-and-bolts matters as sharp positioning to serve a neatly defined segment and securing distribution to achieve specific objectives in sales, profit, and market share. Basic inventory and financial controls, budgeting, and planning are now utilized to the fullest extent to cut costs and waste: "In contrast to the glitzy, intuitive world of cosmetics, Unilever and P&G are the habitats of organization men in grey-flannel suits. Both companies rely on extensive market research."[18] This type of shift in direction and style in an industry has important ramifications for marketing strategy.

The dynamics of an industry may be understood by considering the following factors:

1. Scope of competitors' businesses (i.e., location and number of industries).
2. New entrants in the industry.
3. Other current and potential offerings that appear to serve similar functions or satisfy the same need.
4. Industry's ability to raise capital, attract people, avoid government probing, and compete effectively for consumer dollars.
5. Industry's current practices (price setting, warranties, distribution structure, after-sales service, etc.).
6. Trends in volume, costs, prices, and return on investment, compared with other industries.
7. Industry profit economics (the key factors determining profits: volume, materials, labor, capital investment, market penetration, and dealer strength).
8. Ease of entry into the industry, including capital investment.
9. Relationship between current and future demand and manufacturing capacity and its probable effects on prices and profits.
10. Effect of integration, both forward and backward.
11. Effect of cyclical swings in the relationship between supply and demand.

To formulate marketing strategy, a company should determine the relevance of each of these factors in its industry and the position it occupies with respect to competitors. An attempt should be made to highlight the dynamics of the company in the industry environment.

Conceptual framework for industry analysis has been provided by Porter.[19] He developed a five-factor model for industry analysis, as shown in Exhibit 4.6. The model identifies five key structural features that determine the strength of the competitive forces within an industry and hence industry profitability.

As shown in this model, the degree of rivalry among different firms is a function of the number of competitors, industry growth, asset intensity, product differentiation, and exit barriers. Among these variables, the number of competitors and industry growth are the most influential. Further, industries with high fixed costs tend to be more competitive because competing firms are forced to cut price to enable them to operate at capacity. Differentiation, both real and perceived, among competing offerings, however, lessens rivalry. Finally, difficulty of exit from an industry intensifies competition.

Threat of entry into the industry by new firms is likely to enhance competition. Several barriers, however, make it difficult to enter an industry. Two cost-related entry barriers are economies of scale and absolute cost advantage. Economies of scale require potential entrants either to establish high levels of production or to accept a cost disadvantage. Absolute cost advantage is enjoyed by firms with proprietary technology or favorable access to raw materials and by firms with production experience. In addition, high capital requirements, high switching costs (i.e., the cost to a buyer of changing suppliers), product differentiation, limited access to distribution channels, and government policy can act as entry barriers.

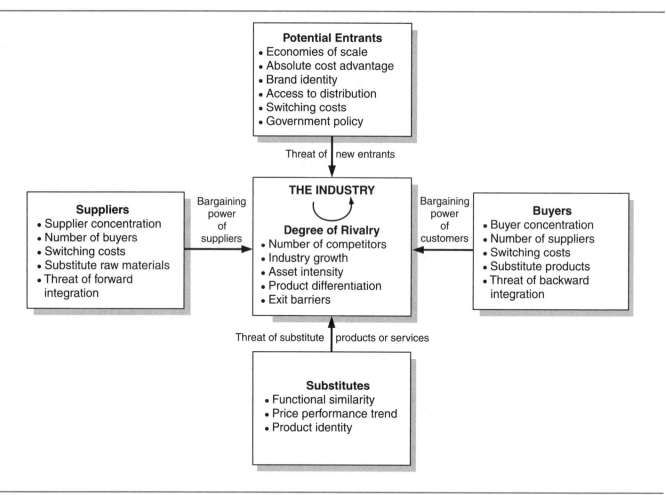

Source: Michael E. Porter, "Industry Structure and Competitive Strategy: Keys to Profitability," *Financial Analysis Journal* (July–August 1980): 33.

Exhibit 4.6 Porter's Model of Industry Competition

A substitute product that serves essentially the same function as an industry product is another source of competition. Since a substitute places a ceiling on the price that firms can charge, it affects industry potential. The threat posed by a substitute also depends on its long-term price/performance trend relative to the industry's product.

Bargaining power of buyers refers to the ability of the industry's customers to force the industry to reduce prices or increase features, thus bidding away profits. Buyers gain power when they have choices—when their needs can be met by a substitute product or by the same product offered by another supplier. In addition, high buyer concentration, the threat of backward integration, and low switching costs add to buyer power.

Bargaining power of suppliers is the degree to which suppliers of the industry's raw materials have the ability to force the industry to accept higher prices or reduced service, thus affecting profits. The factors influencing supplier power are the same as those influencing buyer power. In this case, however, industry members act as buyers.

These five forces of competition interact to determine the attractiveness of an industry. The strongest forces become the dominant factors in determining industry profitability and the focal points of strategy formulation, as the following example of the network television industry illustrates. Government regulations, which limited the number of networks to three, have had a great influence on the profile of the industry. This impenetrable entry barrier created weak buyers (advertisers), weak suppliers (writers, actors, etc.), and a very profitable industry. However, several exogenous events are now influencing the power of buyers and suppliers. Suppliers have gained power with the advent of cable television because the number of customers to whom artists can offer their services has increased rapidly. In addition, as cable television firms reduce the size of the network market, advertisers may find substitute advertising media more cost-effective. In conclusion, while the industry is still very attractive and profitable, the changes in its structure imply that future profitability may be reduced.

A firm should first diagnose the forces affecting competition in its industry and their underlying causes and then identify its own strengths and weaknesses relative to the industry. Only then should a firm formulate its strategy, which amounts to taking offensive or defensive action in order to achieve a secure position against each of the five competitive forces.[20] This involves:

- Positioning the firm so that its capabilities provide the best defense against the existing array of competitive forces.
- Influencing the balance of forces through strategic moves, thereby improving the firm's relative position.
- Anticipating shifts in the factors underlying the forces and responding to them, hopefully exploiting change by choosing a strategy appropriate to the new competitive balance before rivals recognize it.

Take, for example, the U.S. blue jeans industry. In the 1980s most firms except for Levi Strauss and Blue Bell, maker of Wrangler Jeans, took low profits. The situation can be explained with reference to industry structure (see Exhibit 4.7). The extremely low entry barriers allowed almost 100 small jeans manufacturers to join the competitive ranks; all that was needed to enter the industry was some equipment, an empty warehouse, and some relatively low-skilled labor. All such firms competed on price.

Further, these small firms had little control over raw materials pricing. The production of denim was in the hands of about four major textile companies. No one small blue jeans manufacturer was important enough to affect supplier prices or output; consequently, jeans makers had to take the price of denim or leave it. Suppliers of denim had strong bargaining power. Store buyers also were in a strong bargaining position. Most of the jeans sold in the United States were handled by relatively few buyers in major store chains. As a result, a small manufacturer basically had to sell at the price the buyers wanted to pay, or the buyers could easily find someone else who would sell at their price.

But then along came Jordache. Creating designer jeans with heavy up-front advertising, Jordache designed a new way to compete that changed industry forces. First, it significantly lowered the bargaining power of its customers (i.e., store buyers) by creating strong consumer preference. The buyer had to meet Jordache's price rather than the other way around. Second, emphasis on the designer's name created

Exhibit 4.7
Structure of Blue Jeans Industry

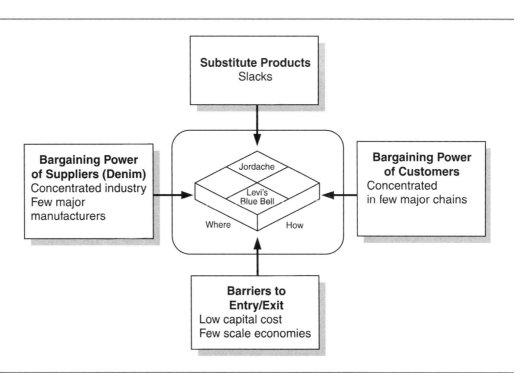

significant entry barriers. In summary, Jordache formulated a strategy that neutralized many of the structural forces surrounding the industry and gave itself a competitive advantage.

Comparative analysis examines the specific advantages of competitors within a given market. Two types of comparative advantage may be distinguished: structural and response. **Structural advantages** are those advantages built into the business. For example, a manufacturing plant in Indonesia may, because of low labor costs, have a built-in advantage over another firm. **Responsive advantages** refer to positions of comparative advantage that have accrued to a business over time as a result of certain decisions. This type of advantage is based on leveraging the strategic phenomena at work in the business.

Every business is a unique mixture of strategic phenomena. For example, in the soft drink industry a unit of investment in advertising may lead to a unit of market share. In contrast, the highest-volume producer in the electronics industry is usually the lowest-cost producer. In industrial product businesses, up to a point, sales and distribution costs tend to decline as the density of sales coverage (the number of salespeople in the field) increases. Beyond this optimum point, costs tend to rise dramatically. However, cost is only one way of achieving a competitive advantage. A firm may explore issues beyond cost to score over competition. For example, a company may find that distribution through authorized dealers gives it competitive leverage. Another company may find product differentiation strategically more desirable.

In order to survive, any company, regardless of size, must be different in one of two dimensions. It must have lower costs than its direct head-to-head competitors, or it must have unique values for which its customers will pay more. Competitive distinctiveness is essential to survival. Competitive distinctiveness can be achieved in different ways: (a) by concentrating on particular market segments, (b) by offering products that differ from rather than mirror competing products, (c) by using alternative distribution channels and manufacturing processes, and (d) by employing selective pricing and fundamentally different cost structures. An analytical tool that may be used by a company seeking a position of competitive advantage/ distinction is the business-system framework.

Examination of the business system operating in an industry is useful in analyzing competitors and in searching out innovative options for gaining a sustainable competitive advantage. The business-system framework enables a firm to discover the sources of greatest economic leverage, that is, stages in the system where it may build cost or investment barriers against competitors.[21] The framework may also be used to analyze a competitor's costs and to gain insights into the sources of a competitor's current advantage in either cost or economic value to the customer.

Exhibit 4.8 depicts the business system of a manufacturing company. At each stage of the system—technology, product design, manufacturing, and so on—a company may have several options. These options are often interdependent. For example, product design will partially constrain the choice of raw materials.

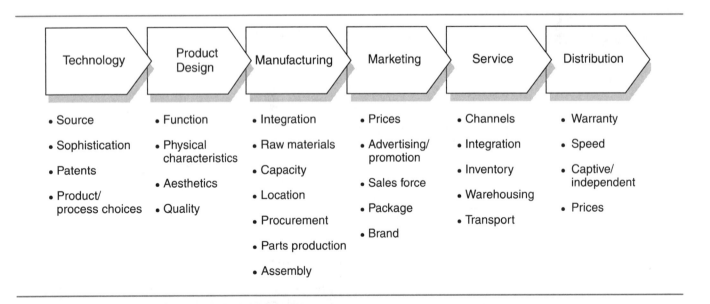

Exhibit 4.8 Business System of a Manufacturing Company

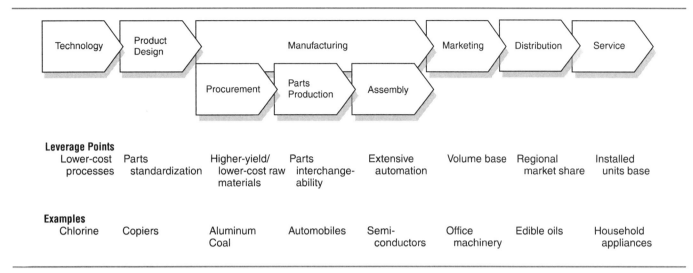

Leverage Points

| Lower-cost processes | Parts standardization | Higher-yield/ lower-cost raw materials | Parts interchange- ability | Extensive automation | Volume base | Regional market share | Installed units base |

Examples

| Chlorine | Copiers | Aluminum Coal | Automobiles | Semi- conductors | Office machinery | Edible oils | Household appliances |

Exhibit 4.9 Sources of Economic Leverage in the Business System

Likewise, the perspectives of physical distribution will affect manufacturing capacity and location and vice versa. At each stage, a variety of questions may be raised, the answers to which provide insights into the strategic alternatives a company may consider: How are we doing this now? How are our competitors doing it? What is better about their way? About ours? How else might it be done? How would these options affect our competitive position? If we change what we are doing at this stage, how would other stages be affected? Answers to these questions reveal the sources of leverage a business may employ to gain competitive advantage (see Exhibit 4.9).

The use of the business-system framework can be illustrated with reference to an old example. In 1975, the Savin Business Machines Corporation, with revenues of $63 million, was a minor factor in the U.S. office copier market. The market, at that time, was dominated by Xerox, whose domestic copier revenues were approaching $2 billion. Xerox accounted for almost 80 percent of plain-paper copiers in the United States. In November 1975, Savin introduced a plain-paper copier to serve customers who wanted low- and medium-speed machines (i.e., those producing fewer than 40 copies per minute). Two years later, Savin's annual revenues passed $200 million; the company had captured 40 percent of all new units installed in the low-end plain-paper copier market in the United States. Savin managed to earn a 64 percent return on equity while maintaining a conservative 27 percent debt ratio. In early 1980s, its sales surpassed $470 million, selling more copiers in the U.S. than any other company.[22] Meanwhile Xerox, which in 1974 had accounted for more than half of the low-end market, saw its share shrink to 10 percent in 1978. What reasons may be ascribed to Savin's success against mighty Xerox? Through careful analysis of the plain-paper copier business system, Savin combined various options at different stages of the system to develop a competitive advantage to successfully confront Xerox. As shown in Exhibit 4.10, by combining a different technology with different manufacturing, distribution, and service approaches, Savin was able to offer business customers, at some sacrifice in copy quality, a much cheaper machine. The option of installing several cheaper machines in key office locations in lieu of a single large, costly, centrally located unit proved attractive to many large customers.

At virtually every stage of the business system, Savin took a radically different approach. First, it used a low-cost technology that had been avoided by the industry because it produced a lower quality copy. Next, its product design was based on low-cost standardized parts available in volume from Japanese suppliers. Further, the company opted for low-cost assembly in Japan. These business-system innovations permitted Savin to offer a copier of comparable reliability and acceptable quality for half the price of Xerox's equivalent model. (Note: Starting from the mid-1980s, the Savin Corp. ran into all sorts of managerial problems. In 1993, it went into bankruptcy.)

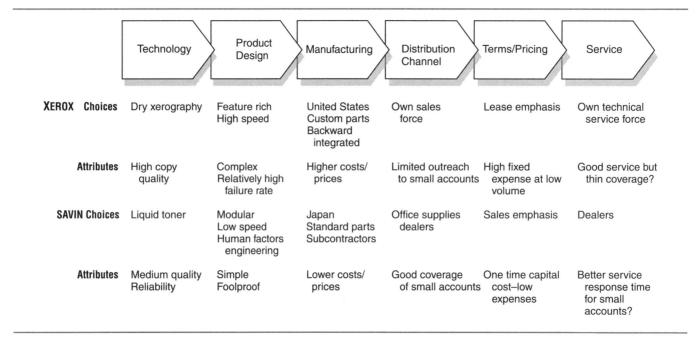

	Technology	Product Design	Manufacturing	Distribution Channel	Terms/Pricing	Service
XEROX Choices	Dry xerography	Feature rich High speed	United States Custom parts Backward integrated	Own sales force	Lease emphasis	Own technical service force
Attributes	High copy quality	Complex Relatively high failure rate	Higher costs/ prices	Limited outreach to small accounts	High fixed expense at low volume	Good service but thin coverage?
SAVIN Choices	Liquid toner	Modular Low speed Human factors engineering	Japan Standard parts Subcontractors	Office supplies dealers	Sales emphasis	Dealers
Attributes	Medium quality Reliability	Simple Foolproof	Lower costs/ prices	Good coverage of small accounts	One time capital cost–low expenses	Better service response time for small accounts?

Exhibit 4.10 Plain-Paper Copier Strategy: Xerox versus Savin

4.7 SUSTAINING COMPETITIVE ADVANTAGE

A good strategist seeks not only to "win the hill, but hold on to it." In other words, a business should not only seek competitive advantage but also sustain it over the long haul. Sustaining competitive advantage requires erecting barriers against the competition.

A barrier may be erected based on size in the targeted market, superior access to resources or customers, and restrictions on competitors' options. Scale economies, for example, may equip a firm with an unbeatable cost advantage that competitors cannot match. Preferred access to resources or to customers enables a company to secure a sustainable advantage if (a) the access is secured under better terms than competitors have and (b) the access can be maintained over the long run. Finally, a sustainable advantage can be gained if, for various reasons, competitors are restricted in their moves (e.g., pending antitrust action or given past investments or existing commitments).

In financial terms, barriers are based on competitive cost differentials or on price or service differentials. In all cases, a successful barrier returns higher margins than the competition earns. Further, a successful barrier must be sustainable and, in a practical sense, unbreachable by the competition; that is, it must cost the competition more to surmount than it costs the protected competitor to defend.

The nature of the feasible barrier depends on the competitive economics of the business. A heavily advertised consumer product with a leading market share enjoys a significant cost barrier and perhaps a price-realization barrier against its competition. If a consumer product has, for example, twice the market share of its competition, it need spend only one-half the advertising dollar per unit to produce the same impact in the marketplace. It will always cost the competition more, per unit, to attack than it costs the leader to defend.

On the other hand, barriers cost money to erect and defend. The expense of the barrier may become an umbrella under which new forms of competition can grow. For example, while advertising is a barrier that protects a leading consumer brand from other branded competitors, the cost of maintaining the barrier is an umbrella under which a private-label product may hide and grow.

A wide product line, large sales and service forces, and systems capabilities are all examples of major barriers. Each of these has a cost to erect and maintain. Each is effective against smaller competitors who are attempting to copy the leader but have less volume over which to amortize barrier costs.

Each barrier, however, holds a protective umbrella over focused competitors. The competitor with a narrow product line faces fewer costs than the wide-line leader. The mail-order house may live under the

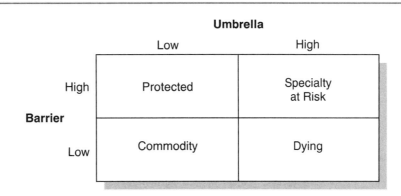

Exhibit 4.11
Strategies for Sustaining
Competitive Advantage

umbrella of costs associated with the large sales and service force of the leader. The "cherry picker" may produce components compatible with the systems of the leader without bearing the systems engineering costs.

Exhibit 4.11 shows the relationship between barrier and umbrella strategies in sustaining competitive advantage. The best position in the system is high barrier and low umbrella. A product or business with a position strong enough that the costs of maintaining the barrier are, on a per unit basis, insignificant is in a high-barrier, low-umbrella position. The low-barrier, low-umbrella quadrant is, by definition, a commodity without high profitability.

Most interesting is the high-barrier, high-umbrella quadrant. The business is protected by the existence of the barrier. At the same time, it is at risk because the cost of supporting the barrier is high. Profitability may be high, but the risk of competitive erosion, too, may be substantial. The marketplace issue is the trade-off between consumer preferences for more service, quality, choice, or "image" and lower prices from more narrowly focused competitors.

These businesses face profound decisions. Making no change in direction means continual threats from focused competition. Yet any change in spending to lower the umbrella means changing the nature of the competitive protection; that is, eroding the barrier.

Successful marketing strategy requires being aware of the size of the umbrella and continually testing whether to maintain investment to preserve or heighten the barrier or to withdraw investment to "cash out" as the barrier erodes.

A sustainable advantage is meaningful in marketing strategy only when the following conditions are met: (a) customers perceive a consistent difference in important attributes between the firm's product or service and those of its competitors, (b) the difference is the direct result of a capability gap between the firm and its competitors, and (c) both the difference in important attributes and the capability gap can be expected to endure over time.

To illustrate the point, consider competition between the Kellogg Co. and Quaker Oats Co. in the cereal market. Beginning in 1995, Kellogg could not maintain the barrier and the umbrella became too big. Quaker Oats (a relatively small fourth player in the industry) took advantage of this opportunity and introduced a line of bagged cereals that were cheaper versions of Kellogg's (the industry leader) national brands. By skimping on packaging and marketing costs, Quaker could sell bagged products for about $1 less than boxed counterparts. Since 1995, bagged cereals have skyrocketed from virtually nothing to account for 8% of all cereal packages sold in 1998.[23] The difference that Kellogg counted on could not be endured. The consumer did not care whether they are in a bag or box.

SUMMARY

Competition is a strategic factor that affects marketing strategy formulation. Traditionally, marketers have considered competition as one of the uncontrollable variables to be reckoned with in developing the marketing mix. It is only in the last few years that the focus of business strategy has shifted to the competition. It is becoming more and more evident that a chosen marketing strategy should be based on competitive advantage to achieve sustained business success. To implement such a perspective, resources should be concentrated in those areas of competitive activity that offer the best opportunity for continuing profitability and sound investment returns.

There are two very different forms of competition: natural and strategic. Natural competition implies survival of the fittest in a given environment. In business terms, it means firms compete from very similar strategic positions, relying on operating differences to separate the successful from the unsuccessful. With strategic competition, on the other hand, underlying strategy differences vis-à-vis market segments, product offerings, distribution channels, and manufacturing processes become paramount considerations.

Conceptually, competition may be examined from the viewpoint of economists, industrial organization theorists, and businesspeople. The major thrust of economic theories has centered on the model of perfect competition. Industrial organization emphasizes the industry environment (i.e., industry structure, conduct, and performance) as the key determinant of a firm's performance. A theoretical framework of competition from the viewpoint of the businessperson, other than the pioneering efforts of Bruce Henderson, hardly exists.

Firms compete to satisfy customer needs, which may be classified as existing, latent, or incipient. A firm may face competition from different sources, which may be categorized as industry competition, product line competition, or organizational competition. The intensity of competition is determined by a combination of factors.

A firm needs a competitive intelligence system to keep track of various facets of its rivals' businesses. The system should include proper data gathering and analysis of each major competitor's current and future perspectives. This chapter identified various sources of competitive information, including what competitors say about themselves, what others say about them, and what a firm's own people have observed. To gain competitive advantage, that is, to choose those product/market positions where victories are clearly attainable, two forms of analysis may be undertaken: industry analysis and comparative analysis. Porter's five-factor model is useful in industry analysis. Business-system framework can be gainfully employed for comparative analysis.

DISCUSSION QUESTIONS

1. Differentiate between natural and strategic competition. Give examples.
2. What are the basic elements of strategic competition? Are there any prerequisites to pursuing strategic competition?
3. How do economists approach competition? Does this approach suffice for businesspeople?
4. What is the industrial organization viewpoint of competition?
5. Identify, with examples, different sources of competition.
6. How does industry structure affect intensity of competition?
7. What are the major sources of competitive intelligence?
8. Briefly explain Porter's five-factor model of industry structure analysis.

NOTES

1. Joel E. Urbany, David B. Montegomery, and Marian Moore, "Competitive Reactions and Modes of Competitive Reasoning: Downplaying and Unpredictable?," Cambridge, MA: Marketing Science Institute, Working Paper, 2001.
2. Bruce D. Henderson, "New Strategies for the Global Competition," *A Special Commentary* (Boston: Boston Consulting Group, 1981): 5–6.
3. Louis W. Stern and John R. Grabner, Jr., *Competition in the Marketplace* (Glenview, IL: Scott, Foresman and Company, 1970): 29.
4. See Michael E. Porter, *Competitive Strategy* (New York: The Free Press, 1980): Chapter 1. See also E. T. Grether, *Marketing and Public Policy* (Englewood Cliffs, NJ: Prentice-Hall, 1960): 25; and George Fisk, *Marketing Systems: An Introductory Analysis* (New York: Harper & Row, 1967): 622.
5. Bruce D. Henderson, "The Anatomy of Competition," *Journal of Marketing*, Spring 1983, pp. 8–9.

6. See: Farshad Rafii and Raul J. Kampas, "How to Identify Your Enemies Before They Destroy You," *Harvard Business Review*, November, 2002, pp. 115–123.

7. Bruce H. Clark and David B. Montgomery, "Managerial Identification of Competitors," *Journal of Marketing*, July 1999, pp. 67–83.

8. Meg Carter, "New Colas Wage Battle for Hearts and Minds." *Financial Times*, January 8, 2004, p. 9.

9. Janet Adamy, "McDonald's Take on A Weakend Starbucks," *The Wall Street Journal*, January 7, 2008, p. A1.

10. Lauren Etter, "Is Wall Street Losing Its Competitive Edge," *The Wall Street Journal*, December 2–3, 2006, p. A6.

11. Wendy Zellner, "How Northwest Gives Competition a Bad Name," *BusinessWeek*, March 16, 1998, p. 34.

12. Richard A. D'Aveni, "Mapping Your Competitive Position," *Harvard Business Review*, November, 2007, pp. 110–120.

13. William E. Rothschild, *Putting It All Together* (New York: AMACOM, 1976): 85.

14. Steven Flax, "How to Snoop on Your Competitors," *Fortune*, May 14, 1984, pp. 29–33. Also see Richard Teitelbaum, "The New Race for Intelligence," *Fortune*, November 2, 1992, p. 104.

15. Patrick Marren, "Business Intelligence: Inside Out?" Outlook, The Futures Group, June 1996, p. 1.

16. Kim T. Gordon, "Dare to be Different," *Entrepreneur*, April, 2005, pp. 81–82.

17. See: "The Global Care Industry." *The Economist*, September 10, 2005, p. 63.

18. See George S. Day and Prakash Nedungadi, "Managerial Representations of Competetive Strategy," *Journal of Marketing*, April, 1994, pp. 31–44.

19. Michael E. Porter, "The Five Competitive Forces That Shape Strategy," *Harvard Business Review*, January, 2008, pp. 78–93.

20. George Stalk and Rob LaChenaver (with John Butman) *Hardball—Are You Playing to Play or Playing to Win?* (Boston, MA: The Boston Consulting Group, 2007).

21. Richard Normann and Rafael Ramirez, "From Value Chain to Value Constellation: Designing Interactive Strategy," *Harvard Business Review*, July–August 1993, pp. 65–77.

22. Tom Giordano, "From Riches to Rags," *The Hartford Courant*, December 12, 1993, p. 61.

23. "Cereal-Box Killers are on the Loose." *BusinessWeek*, October 5, 1998, p. 48.

Chapter Outline

5.1 **Identifying Markets**
5.2 **Customer Need**
5.3 **Market Emergence**
5.4 **Defining Market Boundaries**
    5.4.1 Technology
    5.4.2 Customer Function
    5.4.3 Customer Group
5.5 **Served Market**
5.6 **Customer Segmentation**

Chapter 5

Focusing on the Customer

Consumption is the sole end and purpose of production; and the interest of the producer ought to be attended to only so far as it may be necessary for promoting that of the consumer.

ADAM SMITH

Businesses compete to serve customer needs. Not only are there different types of customers, but their needs vary, too. Thus, most markets are not homogeneous. Further, the markets that are homogeneous today may not remain so in the future. In brief, a market represents a dynamic phenomenon that, influenced by customer needs, evolves over time.

In a free economy, each customer group tends to want a slightly different service or product. But a business unit cannot reach out to all customers with equal effectiveness; it must distinguish easily accessible customer groups from hard-to-reach customer groups. Moreover, a business unit faces competitors whose ability to respond to customer needs and cover customer groups differs from its own. To establish a strategic edge over its competition with a viable marketing strategy, it is important for the business unit to clearly define the market it intends to serve. It must segment the market, identifying one or more subsets of customers within the total market, and concentrate its efforts on meeting their needs. Fine targeting of the customer group to serve offers the opportunity to establish competitive leverage.

This chapter introduces a framework for identifying markets to serve. Various underlying concepts of market definition are examined. The chapter ends with a discussion of alternative ways of segmenting a market.

5.1 IDENTIFYING MARKETS

Contemporary approaches to strategic planning require proper definition of the market; however, questions about how to properly characterize a market make it difficult to arrive at an acceptable definition. Depending on how the market is defined, the relative market positions of two companies and their two products can be reversed.

	Percentage Market Share	
Brands	**Unsegmented (Mass)**	**Segmented**
S	32	40
T	24	30
U	16	20
V	8	10
X	12	60
Y	6	30
Z	2	10

Though brand X has a low share in the unsegmented, or mass, market (12 percent), it has a much higher share within its own segment of the mass market (60 percent) than does brand S (40 percent). Which of the two shares shown is better for the business: the total mass market for the product category or some segmented portion of that market? The arguments go both ways, some pointing out the merits of having a larger share of industry volume and others noting the favorable profit consequences of holding a larger share within a smaller market niche.[1] Does Sanka compete in the total mass market for coffee with

Exhibit 5.1
Identifying Markets
to Serve

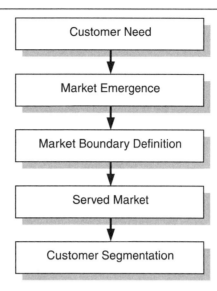

Maxwell House and Folgers or in a decaffeinated market segment against Brim and Nescafe? Does the market for personal computers include intelligent and dumb terminals as well as word processors, desktop and laptop computers, and intelligent telephones? Grape Nuts has 100 percent of the Grape Nuts market, a smaller percentage of the breakfast cereal market, an even smaller percentage of the packaged-foods market, a still smaller percentage of the packaged-goods market, a tiny percentage of the U.S. food market, a minuscule percentage of the world food market, and a microscopic percentage of total consumer expenditures. All descriptions of market share are meaningless, however, unless a company defines the market in terms of the boundaries separating it from its rivals.

Considering the importance of adequately defining the market, it is desirable to systematically develop a conceptual framework for that purpose. Exhibit 5.1 presents such a framework.

The first logical step in defining the market is to determine customer need. Based on need, the market emerges. Because customer need provides a broad perspective of the market, it is desirable to establish market boundaries. Traditionally, market boundaries have been defined in terms of product/market scope, but recent work suggests that markets should be defined multidimensionally.

The market boundary delineates the total limits of the market. An individual business must select and serve those parts, or segments, of the total market in which it is best equipped to compete over the long run. Consider Polaroid. It started as an instant photography firm. As such, it had only a 7 percent stake in the $15 billion photography industry. Over the years, it carried out a multi-billion dollar market for itself. But in the 1990s, the company realized it had little chance of any further growth. The developed world was already saturated with cameras, and photography itself was beginning to lose out to home videomaking. By aiming instead at the entire imaging industry—from photocopying to printing and video as well as photography—Polaroid saw a chance to compete in a rapidly growing, $150 billion global business.[2]

5.2 CUSTOMER NEED

Satisfaction of customer need is the ultimate test of a business unit's success. Thus, an effective marketing strategy should aim at serving customer needs and wants better than competitors do. Focus on customers is the essence of marketing strategy.[3] As Robertson and Wind have said:

> Marketing performs a boundary role function between the company and its markets. It guides the allocation of resources to product and service offerings designed to satisfy market needs while achieving corporate objectives. This boundary role function of marketing is critical to strategy development. Before marshaling a company's resources to acquire a new business, or to introduce a new product, or to reposition an existing product, management must use marketing research to cross the company-consumer boundary and to assess the likely market response.[4]

Toyota, for example, has established a "think tank" in the Toyota Motor Sales in Torrance, Califronia to study emerging consumer trends and develop cars and trucks in keeping with these trends. The "think tank" is staffed by 116 professionals Each one of them spends time meeting customers to learn first hand about their likings and dislikings. Such a perspective in Japan is called Genchi Genbutsu, i.e., "go to the scene and confirm the actual happenings."[5]

Unlike other big companies who also keep track of customers preferences, Toyota takes concrete actions to translate the preferences into products that hopefully would be accepted by the market. To illustrate the point, in the 1990s Toyota found it had been losing customers to brands like VW. The company, therefore, developed the Scion car which has been a success story. Similarly, although GM has been toying with the idea of an electric car for over 25 years, it was Toyota that in fact introduced the hybrid car Prius.

The logic and value of consumer needs assessment is generally beyond dispute, yet frequently ignored. It is estimated, for example, that a majority of new products fail. Yet, there is most often nothing wrong with the product itself; that is, it works. The problem is simply that consumers do not want the product.

AT&T's Picture Phone is a classic example of a technology-driven product that works; but people do not want to see each other on a telephone. It transforms a comfortable, low-involvement communication transaction into a demanding, high-involvement one. The benefit is not obvious to consumers. Of course, the benefit could become obvious if transportation costs continue to outpace communication costs, and if consumers could be "taught" the benefits of using a Picture Phone.

Marketing's boundary role function is similarly important in maintaining a viable competitive positioning in the marketplace. The passing of Korvette (a discount department store chain that went out of business in the late 1970s) from the American retail scene, for example, can be attributed to consumer confusion as to what Korvette represented—how it was positioned relative to competition. Korvette's strength was as a discount chain—high turnover and low margin. This basic mission of the business was violated, however, as Korvette traded-up in soft goods and fashion items and even opened a store on Manhattan's Fifth Avenue. The result was that Korvette became neither a discount store nor a department store and lost its previous customer base. Sears has encountered a similar phenomenon as it opted for higher margins in the 1970s and lost its reputation for "value" in the marketplace. The penalty has been declining sales and profitability for its retail store operation, which it is now trying valiantly to arrest by reestablishing its "middle America" value orientation. Nevertheless, consumer research could have indicated the beginning of the problem long before the crisis in sales and profits occurred.[6]

Customer need has always formed the basis of sound marketing. Yet, as Ohmae points out, it is often neglected or ignored:

Think for a moment about aching heads. Is my headache the same as yours? My cold? My shoulder pain? My stomach discomfort? Of course not. Yet when a pharmaceutical company asked for help . . . [it] asked 50 employees in the company to fill out a questionnaire—throughout a full year—about how they felt physically at all times of the day every day of the year. Then [it] pulled together a list of the symptoms described, sat down with the company's scientists, and asked them, item by item: Do you know why people feel this way? Do you have a drug for this kind of symptom? It turned out that there were no drugs for about 80 percent of the symptoms, these physical awarenesses of discomfort. For many of them, some combination of existing drugs worked just fine. For others, no one had ever thought to seek a particular remedy. The scientists were ignoring tons of profit.

Without understanding customers' needs—the specific types of discomfort they were feeling—the company found it all too easy to say, "Headache? Fine, here's a medicine, an aspirin, for headache. Case closed." It was easy not to take the next step and ask, "What does the headache feel like? Where does it come from? What is the underlying cause? How can we treat the cause, not just the symptom?" Many of these symptoms, for example, are psychological and culture-specific. Just look at television commercials. In the United States, the most common complaint is headache; in the United Kingdom, backache; in Japan, stomach ache. In the United States, people say that they have a splitting headache; in Japan it is an ulcer. How can we truly understand what these people are feeling and why?[7]

Looking closely at needs is the first step in delivering value to customers. Traditionally, needs have been classified according to Maslow's hierarchy of human needs. From lowest to highest, Maslow's hierarchy identifies five levels of needs: physiological, safety, belongingness, self-esteem, and self-actualization. Needs at each level of the hierarchy can be satisfied only after needs at the levels below it have been satisfied. A need unsatisfied becomes a source of frustration. When the frustration is sufficiently intense, it motivates a relief action—the purchase of a product, for example. Once a need is satisfied, it is forgotten, creating space for the awareness of other needs. In a marketing context, this suggests that customers need periodic reminders of their association with a product, particularly when satisfied.

Business strategy can be based on the certainty that needs exist. As we move up Maslow's hierarchy, needs become less and less obvious. The challenge in marketing is to expose non-obvious needs, to fill needs at all levels of the hierarchy.

Maslow's first two levels can be called survival levels. Most businesses operate at Level 2 (safety), with occasional spikes into higher levels. A business must satisfy a safety need to have a viable operation. The customer must feel both physically and economically safe in buying the product. The next higher levels—belongingness and self-esteem—are customer reward levels, where benefits of consuming a product accrue to the customer personally, enhancing his or her sense of worth. At the highest level, self-actualization, the customer feels a close identification with the product. Of course, not all needs can be filled, nor would it be economically feasible to attempt to do so. But a business can move further toward satisfaction of customer needs by utilizing the insights of the Maslow hierarchy.

5.3 MARKET EMERGENCE

Customer need gives rise to a market opportunity, and a market emerges. To judge the worth of this market, an estimate of market potential is important. If the market appears attractive, the strategist takes the next step of delineating the market boundary. This section examines the potential of the market.

Simply stated, **market potential** is the total demand for a product in a given environment. Market potential is measured to gain insights into five elements: market size, market growth, profitability, type of buying decision, and customer market structure. Exhibit 5.2 summarizes these elements and shows a pro forma scheme for measuring market potential.

The first element, *market size*, is best expressed in both units and dollars. Dollar expression in isolation is inadequate because of distortion by inflation and international currency fluctuations. Also, because of inflationary distortion, the screening criteria for new product concepts and product line extensions should separately specify both units and dollars. Market size can be expressed as total market sales potential or company market share, although most companies through custom utilize market share figures.

The second element, *market growth*, is meant to reflect the secular trend of the industry. Again, the screening criteria should be specified for new product concepts and product line extensions. The criteria and projections should be based on percentage growth in units. Projections in industrial settings often are heavily dependent on retrofit possibilities and plans for equipment replacement.

The third element in this evaluation of strategic potential is *profitability*. It usually is expressed in terms of contribution margin or in one of the family of return calculations. Most U.S. companies view profitability in terms of return on investment (ROI), return on sales (ROS), or return on net assets (RONA). Return on capital employed (ROCE) is often calculated in multinational companies. For measuring market potential, no one of these calculations appears to function better than another.

The fourth element is the *type of buying decision*. The basis for a buying decision must be predicated on whether the decision is a straight rebuy, a modified rebuy, or a new task.

The fifth and final element is the *customer market structure*. Based on the same criteria as competitive structure, the market can be classified as monopsony, oligopsony, differentiated competition (monopsonistic competition), or pure competition.

5.4 DEFINING MARKET BOUNDARIES

The crux of any strategy formulation effort is market definition:

The problem of identifying competitive product-market boundaries pervades all levels of marketing decisions. Such strategic issues as the basic definition of a business, the assessment of opportunities

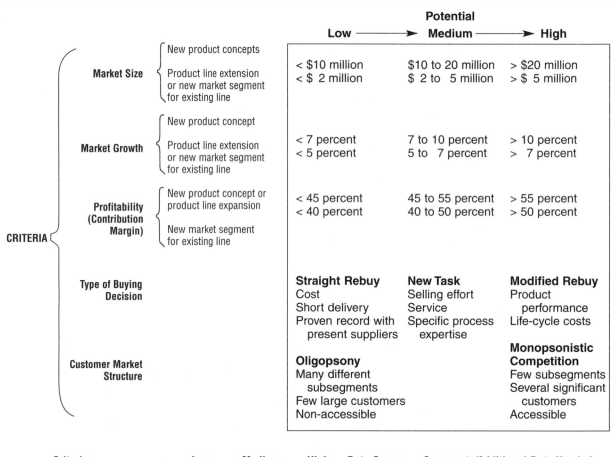

| | Potential | | |
| | Low ⟶ | Medium ⟶ | High |

CRITERIA

Market Size
- New product concepts
- Product line extension or new market segment for existing line

| | < $10 million | $10 to 20 million | > $20 million |
| | < $ 2 million | $ 2 to 5 million | > $ 5 million |

Market Growth
- New product concept
- Product line extension or new market segment for existing line

| | < 7 percent | 7 to 10 percent | > 10 percent |
| | < 5 percent | 5 to 7 percent | > 7 percent |

Profitability (Contribution Margin)
- New product concept or product line expansion
- New market segment for existing line

| | < 45 percent | 45 to 55 percent | > 55 percent |
| | < 40 percent | 40 to 50 percent | > 50 percent |

Type of Buying Decision

Straight Rebuy
Cost
Short delivery
Proven record with present suppliers

New Task
Selling effort
Service
Specific process expertise

Modified Rebuy
Product performance
Life-cycle costs

Customer Market Structure

Oligopsony
Many different subsegments
Few large customers
Non-accessible

Monopsonistic Competition
Few subsegments
Several significant customers
Accessible

Criteria	Low		Medium		High		Data Source	Comments/Additional Data Needed
Market								
Market Growth								
Profitability								
Type of Buying Decision								
Customer Market Structure								
Overall Rating								

Exhibit 5.2 Measurement of Market Potential

presented by gaps in the market, the reaction to threats posed by competitive actions, and the decisions on major resource allocations are strongly influenced by the breadth or narrowness of the definition of competitive boundaries. The importance of share of market for evaluating performance and for guiding territorial advertising, sales force, and other budget allocations and the growing number of antitrust prosecutions also call for defensible definitions of product-market boundaries.[8]

Defining the market is difficult, however, since market can be defined in many ways. Consider the cooking appliance business. Overall in 2007 about 24 million gas and electric ranges and microwave ovens were sold in the U.S. for household use. All these appliances serve the basic function of cooking, but their similarity ends there. They differ in many ways: (a) with reference to fuels—primarily gas versus electricity; (b) in cooking method—heat versus radiation; (c) with reference to type of cooking function—surface heating, baking, roasting, broiling, etc.; (d) in design—freestanding ranges, built-in countertop ranges, wall ovens, counter top microwave ovens, combinations of microwave units, and conventional ranges, etc.; and (e) in price and product features.

These differences raise an important question: Should all household cooking appliances be considered a single market or do they represent several distinct markets? If they represent several distinct markets, how should these markets be defined? There are different possibilities for defining the market: (a) with reference to product characteristics; (b) in terms of private brand sales versus manufacturers' brand sales; (c) with reference to sales in specific regions; and (d) in terms of sales target, for example, sales to building contractors for installation in new houses versus replacement sales for existing homes.

Depending on the criteria adopted to define the market, the size of a market varies considerably. The strategic question of how the marketer of home cooking appliances should define the market is explored below.

Traditionally, market boundaries have been defined in terms of product/market space. Consider the following:

A market is sometimes defined as a group of firms producing identical or closely related products.... A preferable approach is to define the markets in terms of products.... [What is meant by] a close relationship among products? Goods and services may be closely related in the sense that they are regarded as substitutes by consumers, or they may be close in that the factors of production used in each are similar.[9]

Some identify a market with a generic class of products. One hears of the beer market, the cake mix market, or the cigarette market. According to others, product markets refer to individuals who have purchased a given class of products.

These two definitions of the market—the market as a class of closely related products versus the market as a class of people who purchase a certain kind of product—view it from one of two perspectives: who are the buyers and what are the products. In the first definition, buyers are implicitly assumed to be homogeneous in their behavior. The second definition suggests that the products and brands within a category are easily identified and interchangeable and that the problem is to search for market segments.

In recent years, it has been considered inadequate to perceive market definition as simply a choice of products for chosen markets. Instead, the product may be considered a physical manifestation of a particular technology to a particular customer function for a particular customer group. Market boundaries should then be determined by choices along these three dimensions.

5.4.1 Technology

A particular customer function can be performed by different technologies. In other words, alternative technologies can be applied to satisfy a particular customer need. To illustrate, consider home cooking appliances again. In terms of fuel, the traditional alternative technologies have been gas and electricity. In recent years, a new form of technology, microwave radiation, has also been used. In another industry, alternative technologies may be based on the use of different materials. For example, containers may be made from metal, glass, or plastic. In defining market boundaries, a decision must be made whether the products of all relevant technologies or only those of a particular technology are to be included.

5.4.2 Customer Function

Products can be considered in terms of the functions they serve or in terms of the ways in which they are used. Some cooking appliances bake and roast, others fry and boil; some perform all these functions and perhaps more. Different functions provide varying customer benefits. In establishing market boundaries, customer benefits to be served should be spelled out.

5.4.3 Customer Group

A group refers to a homogeneous set of customers with similar needs and characteristics. The market for cooking appliances, for example, can be split into different groups: building contractors, individual households buying through retail stores, and so on. The retail stores segment can be further broken down into traditional appliance specialty stores, mass merchandisers, and so on. Decisions about market boundaries should indicate which types of customers are to be served.

In addition to these three dimensions for determining market boundaries, a fourth—level of production/ distribution can be added. A business has the option of operating at one or more levels of the production/distribution process. For example, producers of raw materials (e.g., aluminum) or component products (e.g., semiconductors, motors, compressors) may limit their business to selling only to other producers, they may produce finished products themselves, or they may do both. Decisions about production/distribution levels have a direct impact on the market boundary definition. Texas Instruments provides a classical example on the subject. The impact that a business unit's vertical integration strategy can have on competition in a market is dramatically illustrated by Texas Instruments' decision, in 1972, to enter the calculator business. At the time, it was a principal supplier of calculator components (integrated circuits) to the earlier entrants into the market, including the initial market leader, Bowmar Instruments. As most readers undoubtedly know, TI quickly took over a leadership position in calculators through a combination of "pricing down the experience curve" and aggressive promotion. For purposes of this discussion, the important point is one of a finished product. Some other component suppliers also entered the calculator business, while others continued to supply OEMs. In light of these varying strategies, is there a "calculator component market" and "calculator market," or do these constitute a single market?

Exhibit 5.3 depicts the three dimensions of the market boundary definition from the viewpoint of the personal financial transactions industry. Market boundaries are defined in terms of customer groups, customer functions, and technologies. The fourth dimension, level of production/distribution, is not included in the diagram because it is not possible to show four dimensions in a single chart. The exhibit shows a matrix developed around customer groups on the vertical axis, customer functions on the right axis, and technologies on the left axis. Any three-dimensional cell in the matrix constitutes an elementary "building block" of market definition. An automatic teller machine (ATM) for cash withdrawals at a commercial bank is an example of such a cell.

Exhibit 5.3
Dimensions of Market Boundary Definition for Personal Financial Transactions

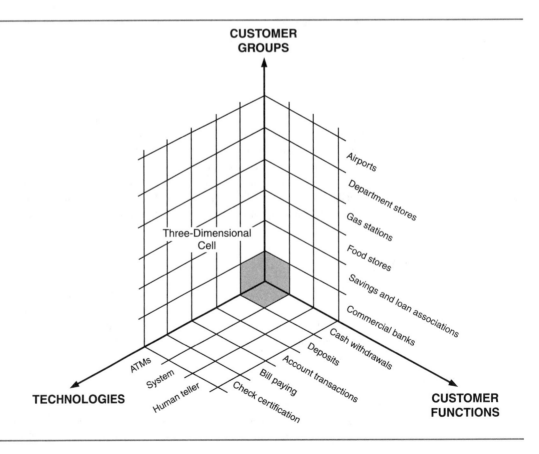

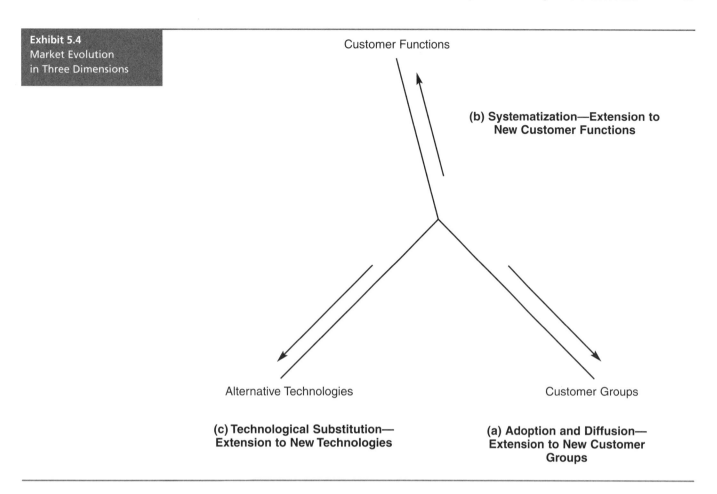

Exhibit 5.4
Market Evolution
in Three Dimensions

Customer Functions

(b) Systematization—Extension to New Customer Functions

Alternative Technologies

(c) Technological Substitution— Extension to New Technologies

Customer Groups

(a) Adoption and Diffusion— Extension to New Customer Groups

As markets evolve, boundaries may need to be restated. Five sets of "environmental influences" affect product/market boundaries. These influences are technological change (displacement by a new technology); market-oriented product development (e.g., combining the features of several products into one multipurpose offering); price changes and supply constraints (which influence the perceived set of substitutes); social, legal, or government trends (which influence patterns of competition); and international trade competition (which changes geographic boundaries). For example, when management introduces a new product, markets an existing product to new customers, diversifies the business through acquisition, or liquidates a part of the business, the market undergoes a process of evolution. Redefinition of market boundaries may be based on any one or a combination of the three basic dimensions. The market may be extended through the penetration of new customer groups, the addition of products serving related customer functions, or the development of products based on new technologies. As shown in Exhibit 5.4, these changes are caused by three fundamentally different phenomena: The adoption and diffusion process underlies the penetration of new customer groups, a process of systemization results in the operation of products to serve combinations of functions, and the technology substitution process underlies change on a technology dimension.

5.5 SERVED MARKET

Earlier in this chapter, it was concluded that the task of market boundary definition amounts to grouping together a set of market cells (see Exhibit 5.3), each defined in terms of three dimensions: customer groups, customer functions, and technologies. In other words, a market may comprise any combination of these cells. An additional question must now be answered. Should a business unit serve the entire market or limit itself to serving just a part of it? While it is conceivable that a business unit may decide to serve the total market, usually the served market is considerably narrower in scope and smaller in size than the total market. The decision about what market to serve is based on such factors as the following:

1. Perceptions of which product function and technology groupings can best be protected and dominated.
2. Internal resource limitations that force a narrow focus.
3. Cumulative trial-and-error experience in reacting to threats and opportunities.
4. Unusual competencies stemming from access to scarce resources or protected markets.

In practice, the choice of served market is not based on conscious, deliberate effort. Rather, circumstances and perceptions surrounding the business unit dictate the decision. For some businesses, lack of adequate resources limits the range of possibilities. A regional grocery chain, for example, would find it difficult to compete against Wal-Mart across the board. Further, as a business unit gains experience through trial and error, it may extend the scope of its served market. For example, the U.S. Post Office entered the overnight package delivery market to participate in an opportunity established by the Federal Express Company. The task of delineating the served market, however, is full of complications. As Day has noted:

> The task of grouping market cells to define a market is complicated. First, there is usually no one defensible criterion for grouping cells. There may be many ways to achieve the same function. Thus, boxed chocolates compete to some degree with flowers, records, and books as semicasual gifts. Do all of these products belong in the total market? To confound this problem, the available statistical and accounting data are often aggregated to a level where important distinctions between cells are completely obscured. Second, there are many products which evolve by adding new combinations of functions and technologies. Thus, radios are multifunctional products which include clocks, alarms, appearance options. To what extent do these variants dictate new market cells? Third, different competitors may choose different combinations of market cells to serve or to include in their total market definitions. In these situations there will be few direct competitors; instead, businesses will encounter each other in different but overlapping markets, and, as a result, may employ different strategies.[10]

Strategically, the choice of a business unit's served market may be based on the following approaches:

I. Breadth of Product Line

    A. Specialized in terms of technology, broad range of product uses
    B. Specialized in terms of product uses, multiple technologies
    C. Specialized in a single technology, narrow range of product uses
    D. Broad range of (related) technologies and uses
    E. Broad versus narrow range of quality/price levels

II. Types of Customers

    A. Single customer segment
    B. Multiple customer segments
        1. Undifferentiated treatment
        2. Differentiated treatment

III. Geographic Scope

    A. Local or regional
    B. National
    C. Multinational

IV. Level of Production/Distribution

    A. Raw or semifinished materials or components
    B. Finished products
    C. Wholesale or retail distribution

The choice of served market may be illustrated with reference to one company's entry into the snowmobile business. The management of this company considered snowmobiles an attractive market in terms of sales potential. The boundaries of this market are extensive. For example, in terms of technology, a snowmobile may be powered by gas, diesel fuel, or electricity. A snowmobile may fulfill such customer functions as delivery, recreation, and emergency transportation. Customer groups include household consumers, industrial buyers, and the military.

Since the company could not cover the total market, it had to define the market it would serve. To accomplish this task, the company developed a product/market matrix (see Exhibit 5.5a). The company could use any technology—gasoline, diesel, or electric—and it could design a snowmobile for any one of three customer groups: consumer, industrial, or military. The matrix in Exhibit 5.5a furnished nine possibilities for the company. Considering market potential and its competencies to compete, the part of the market that looked best was the diesel-powered snowmobile for the industrial market segment, the shaded area in Exhibit 5.5a.

But further narrowing of the market to be served was necessary. A second matrix (see Exhibit 5.5b) laid out the dimensions of customer use (function) and customer size. Thus, as shown in Exhibit 5.5b, snowmobiles could be designed for use as delivery vehicles (e.g., used by business firms and the post

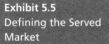

Exhibit 5.5
Defining the Served Market

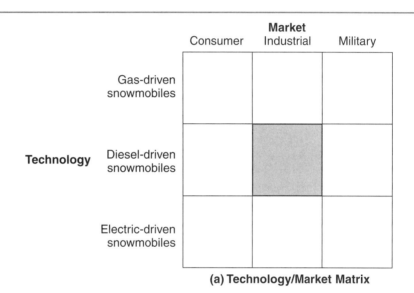

(a) Technology/Market Matrix

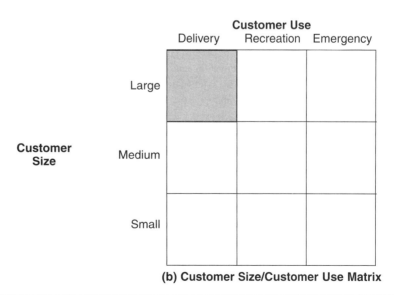

(b) Customer Size/Customer Use Matrix

Source: Philip Kotler, "Strategic Planning and the Marketing Process," *Business* (May-June 1980): 6–7. Reprinted by permission of the author.

office), as recreation vehicles (e.g., rented at resort hotel sites), or as emergency vehicles (e.g., used by hospitals and police forces). Further, the design of the snowmobile would be affected by whether the company would sell to large, medium, or small customers. After evaluating the nine alternatives in Exhibit 5.5b, the company found the large customer, delivery use market attractive, defining its served market as diesel-driven snowmobiles for use as delivery vehicles by large industrial customers.

In the preceding example, the company settled on a rather narrow definition of the served market. It could, however, expand the scope of the served market as it gains experience and as opportunities elsewhere in the market appear attractive. The following is a summary of the served market alternatives available to a business similar to this one.

1. Product/market concentration consists of the company's niching itself in only one part of the market. In the above example, the company's niche was making only diesel-driven snowmobiles for industrial buyers.
2. Product specialization consists of the company's deciding to produce only diesel-driven snowmobiles for all customer groups.
3. Market specialization consists of the company's deciding to make a variety of snowmobiles that serve the varied needs of a particular customer group, such as industrial buyers.
4. Selective specialization consists of the company's entering several product markets that have no relation to each other except that each provides an individually attractive opportunity.
5. Full coverage consists of the company's making a full range of snowmobiles to serve all market segments.

5.6 CUSTOMER SEGMENTATION

In the snowmobile example, the served market consisted of one segment. But conceivably, the served market could be much broader in scope. For example, the company could decide to serve all industrial customers (large, medium, small) by offering diesel-driven snowmobiles for delivery use. The ''broader'' served market, however, must be segmented because the market is not homogeneous; that is, it cannot be served by one type of product/service offering.

Currently, the United States represents the largest market in the world for most products; it is not a homogeneous market, however. Not all customers want the same thing. Particularly in well-supplied markets, customers generally prefer products or services that are tailored to their needs. Differences can be expressed in terms of product or service features, service levels, quality levels, or something else. In other words, the large market has a variety of submarkets, or segments, that vary substantially. One of the crucial elements of marketing strategy is to choose the segment or segments that are to be served. This, however, is not always easy because different methods for dissecting a market may be employed, and deciding which method to use may pose a problem.

Virtually all strategists segment their markets. Typically, they use SIC codes, annual purchase volume, age, and income as differentiating variables. Categories based on these variables, however, may not suffice as far as the development of strategy is concerned.

Sony, for example, initially classified potential customers for flat-panel television sets according to age, income, and social class. The company soon realized that these segments were not crucial for continued growth because potential buyers were not confined to those groups. Later analysis discovered that there were ''innovators'' and ''followers'' in each of the above groups. This finding led the company to tailor its marketing strategy to various segments according to their ''innovativeness.'' Mass acceptance of flat-panel television might have been delayed substantially if Sony had followed a more traditional approach.

An American food processor achieved rapid success in the French market after discovering that ''modern'' Frenchwomen liked processed foods while ''traditional'' French housewives looked upon them as a threat. A leading industrial manufacturer discovered that its critical variable was the amount of annual usage per item, not per order or per any other conventional variable. This proved to be critical since heavy users can be expected to be more sensitive to price and may be more aware of and responsive to promotional perspectives.

Segmentation aims at increasing the scope of business by closely aligning a product or brand with an identifiable customer group. Take, for example, beer. Thirty years ago, most beer drinkers chose from among three brands: Budweiser, Miller High Life, and Coors. Today more than 160 brands adorn retail shelves. In order to sell more beer, brewing companies have been dividing the drinking public into relatively tiny sociological groups and then aiming one or more brands at each group. Miller Lite, for example, is aimed at young women; Budweieser is aimed mostly at the working class. Beer marketing success hinges on how effectively a company can design a brand to appeal to a particular type of drinker and then on how well it can reach that drinker with sharply focused packaging, product design, and advertising.[11]

What is true of beer applies to many, many products; it applies even to services. Banks, for example, have been vying with one another for important customers by offering innovative services that set each bank apart from its competition.[12]

These illustrations underscore not only the significance of segmenting the market but also the importance of carefully choosing segmentation criteria.

Segmentation criteria vary depending on the nature of the market. In consumer-goods marketing, one may use simple demographic and socioeconomic variables, personality and lifestyle variables, or situation-specific events (such as use intensity, brand loyalty, and attitudes) as the bases of segmentation. In industrial ma_____ ____mentation is achieved by forming end use segments, product segments, geographic segments, _____ ___ and customer size segments. Exhibit 5.6 provides an inventory of differe_____ _____ _f these bases are self-explanatory. For a detailed account, however, refere_____ _____ _ marketing management.

I_____ _____ _ive analysts may well identify others. For example, a shipbuilding comp____ _____ _o large, medium, and small markets; similarly, its cargo ship market is cl____ _____ _low-grade markets. A forklift manufacturer divides its market on the basi_____ _____ _ments. Many consumer-goods companies, Nestle, Procter & Gamble, and _____ _eir segments on lifestyle analysis. Thomson Corporation, a B2B giant, div__ _____ _segments.[13]

Data for for_____ _____ _gments may be analyzed with the use of simple statistical techniques (e.g., averages) or multivariate methods. Conceptually, the following procedure may be adopted to choose a criterion for segmentation:

1. Identify potential customers and the nature of their needs.
2. Segment all customers into groups having
   a. Common requirements.
   b. The same value system with respect to the importance of these requirements.
3. Determine the theoretically most efficient means of serving each market segment, making sure that the distribution system selected differentiates each segment with respect to cost and price.
4. Adjust this ideal system to the constraints of the real world: existing commitments, legal restrictions, practicality, and so forth.

Exhibit 5.6
Bases for Customer Segmentation

A. Consumer Markets

1. Demographic factors (age, income, sex, etc.)
2. Socioeconomic factors (social class, stage in the family life cycle)
3. Geographic factors
4. Psychological factors (lifestyle, personality traits)
5. Consumption patterns (heavy, moderate, and light users)
6. Perceptual factors (benefit segmentation, perceptual mapping)
7. Brand loyalty patterns

B. Industrial Markets

1. End use segments (identified by SIC code)
2. Product segments (based on technological differences or production economics)
3. Geographic segments (defined by boundaries between countries or by regional differences within them)
4. Common buying factor segments (cut across product/market and geographic segments)
5. Customer size segments

A market can also be segmented by level of customer service, stage of production, price/performance characteristics, credit arrangements with customers, location of plants, characteristics of manufacturing equipment, channels of distribution, and financial policies. The key is to choose a variable or variables that so divide the market that customers in a segment respond similarly to some aspect of the marketer's strategy. The variable should be measurable; that is, it should represent an objective value, such as income, rate of consumption, or frequency of buying, not simply a qualitative viewpoint, such as the degree of customer happiness. Also, the variable should create segments that may be accessible through promotion. Even if it is feasible to measure happiness, segments based on the happiness variable cannot be reached by a specific promotional medium. Finally, segments should be substantial in size; that is, they should be sufficiently large to warrant a separate marketing effort.[14]

Once segments have been formed, the next strategic issue is deciding which segment should be selected. The selected segment should comply with the following conditions:

1. It should be one in which the maximum differential in competitive strategy can be developed.
2. It must be capable of being isolated so that competitive advantage can be preserved.
3. It must be valid even though imitated.

Initally, the success of Toyota in the United States can be attributed to its fit into a market segment that had two unique characteristics. First, the segment served by Toyota could not be adequately served by a modification to conventional U.S. cars. Second, U.S. manufacturers' economies of scale could not be brought to bear to the disadvantage of Toyota. In contrast, VW was equally successful in identifying a special segment to serve with its small car, the Beetle. The critical difference was that VW could not protect that segment from the superior scale of manufacturing volume of the other three U.S. automobile producers, especially after the DM (deutsche mark) was revalued.

The choice of strategically critical segments is not straightforward. It requires careful evaluation of business strengths as compared with the competition. It also requires analytical marketing research to uncover market segments in which these competitive strengths can be significant.

Rarely do market segments conveniently coincide with such obvious categories as religion, age, profession, or family income; in the industrial sector, with the size of company. For this reason, market segmentation is emphatically not a job for statisticians. Rather, it is a task that can be mastered only by the creative strategist. For example, an industrial company found that the key to segmenting customers is by the phase of the purchase decision process that they experienced. Accordingly, three segments were identified: (a) first-time prospects, (b) novices, and (c) sophisticates. These three segments valued different benefits, bought from different channels, and carried varying impressions of providers.

A technology-consulting firm, Forrester Research Inc., separates people into ten categories such as "fast forwards, techno-strivers, hand shakers, new age nurturers, digital hopefuls, traditionalists, mouse potatoes, gadget grabbers, media junkies, and sidelined citizens." For example, "Fast forwards" own on an average 20 technology products per household. Several of their clients have found this kind of classification useful in identifying segments to serve.[15]

Market segmentation has recently undergone several changes. These include:[16]

• Increased emphasis on segmentation criteria that represent "softer" data such as attitudes and needs. This is the case in both consumer and business-to-business marketing.[17]
• Increased awareness that the bases of segmentation depend on its purpose. For example, the same bank customers could be segmented by account ownership profiles, attitudes toward risk-taking and socioeconomic variables. Each segmentation could be useful for a different purpose, such as product cross-selling, preparation of advertising messages and media selection.[18]
• A move toward "letting the data speak for themselves," that is finding segments through the detection of patterns in survey or in house data. So-called "data mining" methods have become much more versatile over the past decade.
• Greater usage of "hybrid" segmentation methods. For example, a beer producer might first segment consumers according to favorite brand. Then, within each brand group, consumers could be further segmented according to similarities in attitudes toward beer drinking, occasions where beer is consumed, and so on.
• A closer connection between segmentation methods and new product development. Computer choice models (using information about the attribute trade-offs that consumers make) can now find the best segments for a given product profile of the best product profile for a given market segment.

- The growing availability of computer models (based on conjoint data) to find optimal additions to product lines—products that best balance the possibility of cannibalization of current products with competitive draw.
- Research on dynamic product/segment models that consider the possibility of competitive retaliation. Such models examine a company's vulnerability to competitive reactions over the short term and choose product/segment combinations that are most resistant to competitive encroachment.
- The development of pattern-recognition and consumer-clustering methods that seek segments on the basis of data but also respect managerial constraints on minimal segment size and managerial weightings of selected clustering variables.
- The development of flexible segmentations that permit the manager to loosen a clustering based only on buyer needs (by shifting a small number of people between clusters); the aim might be to increase the predictability of some external criterion measure such as household profitability to a company, say, selling mutual funds.

An interesting development in the past few years has been the emergence of a new segmentation concept called micromarketing, or segment-of-one marketing. Forced by competitive pressures, mass marketers have discovered that a segment can be trimmed down to smaller subsegments, even to an individual.[19] Micromarketing combines two independent concepts: information retrieval and service delivery. On one side is a proprietary database of customers' preferences and purchase behaviors; on the other is a disciplined, tightly engineered approach to service delivery that uses the database to tailor a service package for individual customers or a group of customers. Of course, such custom-designed service is nothing new, but until recently, only the very wealthy could afford it. Information technology has brought the level of service associated with the old carriage trade within reach of the middle class.[20]

Micromarketing requires:

1. **Knowing the customers**—Using high-tech techniques, find out who the customers are and aren't. By linking that knowledge with data about ads and coupons, fine-tune marketing strategy.
2. **Making what customers want**—Tailor products to individual tastes. Where once there were just Oreos, now there are Fudge Covered Oreos, Oreo Double Stufs, and Oreo Big Stufs.
3. **Using targeted and new media**—Advertising on cable television and in magazines can be used to reach special audiences. In addition, develop new ways to reach customers. For example, messages on walls in high-school lunchrooms, on videocassettes, and even on blood pressure monitors may be considered.
4. **Using nonmedia**—Sponsor sports, festivals, and other events to reach local or ethnic markets.
5. **Reaching customers in the store**—Consumers make most buying decisions while they are shopping, so put ads on supermarket loudspeakers, shopping carts, and in-store monitors.
6. **Sharpening promotions**—Couponing and price promotions are expensive and often harmful to a brand's image. Thanks to better data, some companies are using fewer, more effective promotions. One promising approach: aiming coupons at a competitor's customers.
7. **Working with retailers**—Consumer-goods manufacturers must learn to "micro market" to the retail trade, too. Some are linking their computers to retailers' computers, and some are tailoring their marketing and promotions to an individual retailer's needs.

An example of micromarketing is provided by a North Carolina bank, Wachovia Bank.[21] The bank's staff serves all customers the way it used to serve its best customer. The staff greets each customer by name and provides personalized information about her or his finances and how they relate to long-term objectives. Based on this knowledge, the staff suggests new products. In this way, the commodity retail banking has been turned into a customized, personalized service. This marketing strategy has resulted in more sales at lower marketing costs and powerful switching barriers relative to the competition. Three major investments are behind this seemingly effortless new level of service: a comprehensive customer database, accessible wherever the customer makes contact with the bank; an extensive training program that teaches a personalized service approach; and an ongoing personal communications program with each customer. Similarly, Noxell's Clarion line illustrates how micromarketing can be implemented. When the company introduced its line of mass market cosmetics in drugstores, it looked for a way to differentiate it in a crowded market. The answer was the Clarion computer. Customers type in the characteristics of their skin and receive a regimen selected from the Clarion line, thus providing department store-type personal advice without sales pressure in the much more convenient drug channel. Masterfoods, USA, the division of Mars, Inc. that makes M&M's, launched an online site called colorworks. It offered a palette of 21 colors to coat specially ordered

M&M's. Customers could pick any combo—maroon and gold, say, for their school colors, or silver for an anniversary. The company is using technology to give consumers the products they prefer. Briefly, from colored bits of candy to hockey sticks and complex plastics, lots of products and services are how being tailored to individual desires.[22] That is a part of a continuing industrial evolution—from mass production to mass customization. The result is mass market of one. And the Web is helping to bring it about.

SUMMARY

This chapter examined the role of the third strategic C—the customer—in formulating marketing strategy. One strategic consideration in determining marketing strategy is the definition of the market. A conceptual framework for defining the market was outlined.

The underlying factor in the formation of a market is customer need. The concept of need was discussed with reference to Maslow's hierarchy of needs. Once a market emerges, its worth must be determined through examining its potential. Different methods may be employed to study market potential.

Based on its potential, if a market appears worth tapping, its boundaries must be identified. Traditionally, market boundaries have been defined on the basis of product/market scope. Recent work on the subject recommends that market boundaries be established around the following dimensions: technology, customer function, and customer group. Level of production/distribution was suggested as a fourth dimension. The task of market boundary definition amounts to grouping together a set of market cells, each defined in terms of these dimensions.

Market boundaries set the limits of the market. Should a business unit serve a total market or just a part of it? Although it is conceivable to serve an entire market, usually the served market is considerably narrower in scope and smaller in size than the total market. Factors that influence the choice of served market were examined.

The served market may be too broad to be served by a single marketing program. If so, then the served market must be segmented. The rationale for segmentation was given, and a procedure for segmenting the market was outlined.

DISCUSSION QUESTIONS

1. Elaborate on marketing's boundary role function. How is it related to customer needs?
2. What dimensions may be used to define market boundaries?
3. Illustrate the use of these dimensions with a practical example.
4. What is meant by served market? What factors determine the served market?
5. How may a business unit choose the criteria for segmenting the market?
6. Describe the concept of micromarketing. How may a durable goods company adopt it to its business?

NOTES

1. David J. Bryce and Jeffrey H. Dyer, "Strategies to Crack Well-Guarded Markets," *Harvard Business Review*, May 2007, pp. 84–92.
2. Alec Klein, "The Techies Grumbled, But Polaroids Pocket Turned Into a Huge Hit," *The Wall Street Journal*, May 2, 2000, p. A1.
3. Kim Thomas, "Anthropoligists Get to the Bottom of Customers' Needs," *Financial Times*, August 24, 2005, p. 7.
4. Thomas S. Robertson and Yoram Wind, "Marketing Strategy," in *Handbook of Business Strategy* (New York: McGraw-Hill Book Co., 1982).
5. Alex Taylor III, "America's Best Car Company," *Fortune*, March 19, 2007, p. 98.

6. Thomas S. Robertson and Yoram Wind, "Marketing Strategy," in *Handbook of Business Strategy* (New York: McGraw-Hill Book Co., 1982). *See also* Yoram Wind and Thomas S. Robertson, "Marketing Strategy: New Directions for Theory and Research," *Journal of Marketing*, Spring 1983, pp. 12–25.

7. Kenichi Ohmae, "Getting Back to Strategy," *Harvard Business Review*, November–December 1988, pp. 155–56.

8. George S. Day and Allan D. Shocker, *Identifying Competitive Product-Market Boundaries: Strategic and Analytical Issues* (Cambridge, MA: Marketing Science Institute, 1976). 1.

9. Robert D. Buzzell, "Note on Market Definition and Segmentation," A Harvard Business School Note, 1978, distributed by HBS Case Services.

10. George S. Day, "Strategic Market Analysis and Definition: An Integrated Approach," *Strategic Management Journal* 2, 1981, p. 284.

11. Sarah Ellison, "After Making Beer Ever Lighter, Anhesier Faces a New Palate," *The Wall Street Journal*, April 26, 2006, p. A1.

12. See: Ronald Grover, "It's Your Call," *BusinessWeek*, May 15, 2005, p. 93.

13. Richard J. Harrington and Anthony K. Tjan, "Transforming Strategy: One Customer at at Time," *Harvard Business Review*, March 2008, pp. 62–73.

14. Sally Dibb and Lyndon Simkin, "Marketing Segmentation: Diagnosing and Treating the Barriers," *Industrial Marketing Management*, 30. November 2001, pp. 609–628.

15. "Are Tech Buyers Different," *BusinessWeek*, January 26, 1998, p. 64.

16. Paul Green and Abba Krieger, "Slicing and Dicing the Market," *Financial Times*, September 21, 1998.

17. Pamela Paul, "It's Mind Vending," *Time*, October, 2003 (Inside Business: the Bonus Section).

18. "How Europe's Banks Can Profit From Loyal Customers," *The McKinsey Quarterly*, February 6, 2006, pp. 18–27.

19. Anthony Bianco, "The Vanishing Mass Market," *BusinessWeek*, July 12, 2004, p. 6.

20. Edward Feitzinger and Hau L. Lee, "Mass Customization at Hewlett-Packard: The Power of Postponement," *Harvard Business Review*, January-February 1997, pp. 116–123.

21. Kathleen Deveny, "Segments of One," *Wall Street Journal*, March 22, 1991, p. B4. See also "Segment-of-One Marketing," *Perspectives* (Boston: Boston Consulting Group, 1989). Also see: Howard Schlossberg, "Packaged-goods Experts: Micromarketing the only way to Go," *Marketing News*, July 6, 1992, p. 8. Also see: Gregory A. Patterson, "Target 'Micromarkets' Its Way to Success; No 2 Stores Are Alike," *The Wall Street Journal*, May 31, 1995, p. 1.

22. "A Mass Market of One," *BusinessWeek*, December 2, 2002, p. 68. Also see: "Keeping the Customer Satisfied," *The Economist*, July 14, 2001, p. 9.; and "Mass Customization," *The McKinsey Quarterly*, #3, 2001, pp. 62–71.

Chapter Outline

6.1 **Importance of Environmental Scanning**

6.2 **What Scanning Can Accomplish**

6.3 **The Concept of Environment**

6.4 **State of the Art**

6.5 **Types of Environment**

    6.5.1   Orientation Toward Time

    6.5.2   Quality

    6.5.3   Health

    6.5.4   Environment

    6.5.5   Home

    6.5.6   Personal Finance

    6.5.7   Diversity of Lifestyles

6.6 **Environmental Scanning and Marketing Strategy**

6.7 **Environmental Scanning Procedure**

6.8 **Conducting Environmental Scanning: An Example**

6.9 **Organizational Arrangements and Problems**

Chapter 6

Scanning the Environment

I hold that man is in the right who is most in league with the future.

HENRIK IBSEN

An organization is a creature of its environment. Its very survival and all of its perspectives, resources, problems, and opportunities are generated and conditioned by the environment. Thus, it is important for an organization to monitor the relevant changes taking place in its environment and formulate strategies to adapt to these changes. In other words, for an organization to survive and prosper, the strategist must master the challenges of the profoundly changing political, economic, technological, social, and regulatory environment. To achieve this broad perspective, the strategist needs to develop and implement a systematic approach to environmental scanning. As the rate and magnitude of change increase, this scanning activity must be intensified and directed by explicit definitions of purpose, scope, and focus. The efforts of businesses to cope with these problems are contributing to the development of systems for exploring alternatives with greater sensitivity to long-run implications. This emerging science has the promise of providing a better framework for maximizing opportunities and allocating resources in anticipation of environmental changes.

This chapter reviews the state of the art of environmental scanning and suggests a general approach that may be used by a marketing strategist. Specifically, the chapter discusses the criteria for determining the scope and focus of scanning, the procedure for examining the relevance of environmental trends, the techniques for evaluating the impact of an environmental trend on a particular product/market, and the linking of environmental trends and other "early warning signals" to strategic planning processes.

6.1 IMPORTANCE OF ENVIRONMENTAL SCANNING

Without taking into account relevant environmental influences, a company cannot expect to develop its strategy. It was the environmental influences emerging out of the energy crisis that were responsible for the popularity of smaller, more fuel-efficient automobiles and that brought about the demise of less efficient rotary engines. It was the environmental influence of a coffee bean shortage and geometric price increases that spawned the "coffee-saver" modification in Mr. Coffee automatic drip coffee makers. Shopper and merchant complaints from an earlier era contributed to the virtual elimination of deposit bottles; recent pressures from environmental groups, however, have forced their return and have prompted companies to develop low-cost recyclable plastic bottles.

Another environmental trend, Americans' insatiable appetite for eating out (in 2003, restaurant sales accounted for $0.60 of every $1 spent on food; this number is expected to reach $0.67 by the year 2010), worries food companies such as Kraft. In response, Kraft is trying to make cooking as convenient as eating out (e.g., by providing high-quality convenience foods) to win back food dollars.[1]

The sad tales of companies that seemingly did everything right and yet lost competitive leadership as a result of technological change abound. Du Pont was beaten by Celanese when bias-ply tire cords changed from nylon to polyester. B.F. Goodrich was beaten by Michelin when the radial overtook the bias-ply tire. NCR wrote off $139 million in electro-mechanical inventory and the equipment to make it when solid-state point-of-sale terminals entered the market. Xerox let Canon create the small-copier market. Bucyrus-Erie allowed Caterpillar and Deere to take over the mechanical excavator market. These companies lost even though they were low-cost producers. They lost even though they were close to their customers. They lost even though they were market leaders. They lost because they failed to make an effective transition from old to new technology.

In brief, business derives its existence from the environment. The business should stop hankering after a mythical golen age when companies grew gradually into solid companies in which widows and orphans could safely park their money. This rosy view of the corporate past is an illusion. Comparison of *Forbes* magazine's 1917 list of the top 100 American companies with a similar list in 2002 showed that 77 of the original group had ceased to exist. Of the remainder, only 12 had managed to stay in top 100. They included such respected firms as Kodak, DuPont, General Electric, Ford, General Motors, and Procter & Gamble. But survival did not mean they were more profitable than their peers. Of the 12, only General Electric and Procter & Gamble out-performed the stock market.[2] Companies that stick with the past and make no attempt to change their business perspectives with time may fail. Business should scan the environment and incorporate the impact of environmental trends on the organization by continually reviewing the corporate strategy.[3]

The underlying importance of environmental scanning is captured in Darwinian laws: (a) the environment is ever-changing, (b) organisms have the ability to adapt to a changing environment, and (c) organisms that do not adapt do not survive. We are indeed living in a rapidly changing world. Many things that we take for granted today were not even imagined in the 1970s or even 1980s. In the future years, many more ''wonders'' will come to exist.

To survive and prosper in the midst of a changing environment, companies must stay at the forefront of changes affecting their industries.[4] First, it must be recognized that all products and processes have performance limits and that the closer one comes to these limits the more expensive it becomes to squeeze out the next generation of performance improvements. Second, one must take all competition seriously. Normally, competitor analyses seem to implicitly assume that the most serious competitors are the ones with the largest resources. But in the context of taking advantage of environmental shifts, this assumption is frequently not adequate. Texas Instruments was a $5- to $10-million company in 1955 when it took on the mighty vacuum tube manufacturers—RCA, GE, Sylvania, and Westinghouse—and beat them with its semiconductor technology. Boeing was nearly bankrupt when it successfully introduced the commercial jet plane, vanquishing larger and more financially secure Lockheed, McDonnell, and Douglas corporations.

Third, if the environmental change promises potential advantage, one must attack to win and attack even to play the game. Attack means gaining access to new technology, training people in its use, investing in capacity to use it, devising strategies to protect the position, and holding off on investments in mature lines. For example, IBM capitalized on the emerging personal computer market created by its competitor, Apple Computer. By becoming the low-cost producer, distributor, seller, and servicer of personal computers for business use, IBM took command of the marketplace in less than two years.

Fourth, the attack must begin early. The substitution of one product or process for another proceeds slowly and then predictably explodes. One cannot wait for the explosion to occur to react. There is simply not enough time. B.F. Goodrich lost 25 percentage points of market share to Michelin in four years. Texas Instruments passed RCA in sales of active electronic devices in five to six years.

Fifth, a close tie is needed between the CEO and the operating managers. Facing change means incorporating the environmental shifts in all aspects of the company's strategy.

6.2 WHAT SCANNING CAN ACCOMPLISH

Scanning improves an organization's abilities to deal with a rapidly changing environment in a number of ways:

1. It helps an organization capitalize on early opportunities rather than lose these to competitors.
2. It provides an early signal of impending problems, which can be defused if recognized well in advance.

3. It sensitizes an organization to the changing needs and wishes of its customers.

4. It provides a base of objective qualitative information about the environment that strategists can utilize.

5. It provides intellectual stimulation to strategists in their decision making.

6. It improves the image of the organization with its publics by showing that it is sensitive to its environment and responsive to it.

7. It is a means of continuing broad-based education for executives, especially for strategy developers.

6.3 THE CONCEPT OF ENVIRONMENT

Operationally, five different types of environments may be identified—technological, political, economic, regulatory, and social—and the environment may be scanned at three different levels in the organization—corporate, SBU, and product/market level (see Exhibit 6.1). Perspectives of environmental scanning vary from level to level. Corporate scanning broadly examines happenings in different environments and focuses on trends with corporate-wide implications. For example, at the corporate level Dell may review the impact of competition above and below in the telephone industry on the availability and rates of long-distance telephone lines to its customers. Emphasis at the SBU level focuses on those changes in the environment that may influence the future direction of the business. At Dell, the SBU concerned with personal computers may study such environmental perspectives as diffusion rate of personal computers, new developments in integrated circuit technology, and the political debates in progress on the registration (similar to automobile registration) of personal computers. At the product/market level, scanning is limited to day-to-day aspects. For example, a Dell personal computer marketing manager may review the significance of rebates, a popular practice among Dell's competitors.

The emphasis in this chapter is on environmental scanning from the viewpoint of the SBU. The primary purpose is to gain a comprehensive view of the future business world as a foundation on which to base major strategic decisions.

6.4 STATE OF THE ART

Scanning serves as an early warning system for the environmental forces that may impact a company's products and markets in the future. Environmental scanning is a comparatively new development. Traditionally, corporations evaluated themselves mainly on the basis of financial performance. In general, the environment was studied only for the purpose of making economic forecasts. Other environmental factors

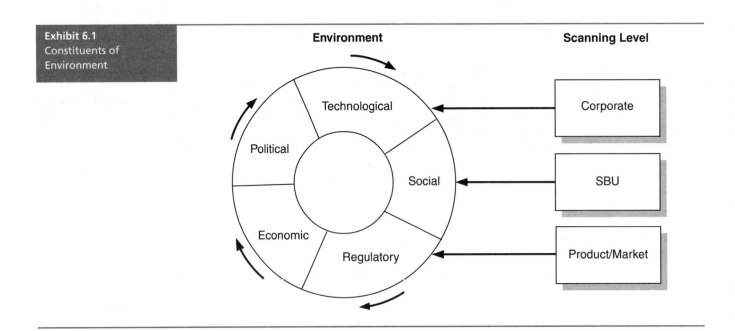

Exhibit 6.1
Constituents of Environment

were brought in haphazardly, if at all, and intuitively. In recent years, however, most large corporations have started doing systematic work in this area.

A pioneering study on environmental scanning was done by Francis Aguilar. In his investigation of selected chemical companies in the United States and Europe, he found no systematic approach to environmental scanning. Aguilar's different types of information about the environment that the companies found interesting have been consolidated into five groups: *market tidings* (market potential, structural change, competitors and industry, pricing, sales negotiations, customers); *acquisition leads* (leads for mergers, joint ventures); *technical tidings* (new products, processes, and technology; product problems; costs; licensing and patents); *broad issues* (general conditions relative to political, demographic, national issues; government actions and policies); *other tidings* (suppliers and raw materials, resources available, other). Among these groups, market tidings was found to be the dominant category and was of most interest to managers across the board.

Aguilar also identified four patterns for viewing information: *undirected viewing* (exposure without a specific purpose), *conditioned viewing* (directed exposure but without undertaking an active search), *informal search* (collection of purpose-oriented information in an informal manner), and *formal search* (a structured process for collection of specific information for a designated purpose). Both internal and external sources were used in seeking this information. The external comprised both personal sources (customers, suppliers, bankers, consultants, and other knowledgeable individuals) and impersonal sources (various publications, conferences, trade shows, exhibitions, and so on). The internal personal sources included peers, superiors, and subordinates. The internal impersonal sources included regular and general reports and scheduled meetings. Aguilar's study concluded that while the process is not simple, a company can systematize its environmental scanning activities for strategy development.[5]

Aguilar's framework may be illustrated with reference to the Coca-Cola Company. The company looks at its environment through a series of analyses. At the corporate level, considerable information is gathered on economic, social, and political factors affecting the business and on competition both in the United States and overseas. The corporate office also becomes involved in special studies when it feels that some aspect of the environment requires special attention. For example, in the 1990s, to address itself to a top management concern about healthy living, the company undertook a study to understand what was going on in the minds of their consumers and what they were looking for. How was the consumption of Coca-Cola related to their consumers' lifestyle, to their set of values, to their needs? This study spearheaded the work toward the introduction of Zero Coke. In the mid-1990s, the corporate office also made a study of the impact of antipollution trends on government regulations concerning packaging.

At the corporate level, environment was scanned rather broadly. Mostly market tidings, technical tidings, and broad issues were dealt with. Whenever necessary, in-depth studies were done on a particular area of concern, and corporate information was made available to different divisions of the company.

At the division level (e.g., Coca-Cola, USA), considerable attention is given to the market situation, acquisition leads, and new business ventures. The division also studies general economic conditions (trends in GNP, consumption, income), government regulation (especially antitrust actions), social factors, and even the political situation. Part of this division-level scanning duplicates the efforts of the corporate office, but the divisional planning staff felt that it was in a position to do a better job for its own purpose than could the corporate office, which had to serve the needs of other divisions as well. The division also undertakes special studies. For example, after the introduction of Zero Coke, it wondered whether a caffeine-free Zero Coke should be introduced and, if so, when.

The information received from the corporate office and that which the division had collected itself was analyzed for events and happenings that could affect the company's current and potential business. Analysis was done mostly through meetings and discussions rather than through the use of any statistical model. At the Coca-Cola Company, environmental analysis is a sort of forum. There is relatively little cohesion among managers; the meetings, therefore, respond to a need for exchange of information between people.

A recent study of environmental scanning identifies four evolutionary phases of activity, from primitive to proactive (see Exhibit 6.2). The scanning activities in most corporations can be characterized by one of these four phases.[6]

In Phase 1, the primitive phase, the environment is taken as something inevitable and random about which nothing can be done other than to accept each impact as it occurs. Management is exposed to information, both strategic and nonstrategic, without making any effort to distinguish the difference. No discrimination is used to discern strategic information, and the information is rarely related to strategic decision making. As a matter of fact, scanning takes place without management devoting any effort to it.

PHASE 1	PHASE 2	PHASE 3	PHASE 4
Primitive	**Ad Hoc**	**Reactive**	**Proactive**
Face the environment as it appears	*Watch out for a likely impact on the environment*	*Deal with the environment to protect the future*	*Predict the environment for a desired future*
• *Exposure to information without purpose and effort.*	• *No active search* • *Be sensitive to information on specific issues*	• *Unstructured and random effort* • *Less specific information collection*	• *Structured and deliberate effort* • *Specific information collection* • *Preestablished methodology*
Scanning without an Impetus	Scanning to Enhance Understanding of a Specific Event	Scanning to Make an Appropriate Response to Markets and Competition	Strategic Scanning to Be on the Lookout for Competitive Advantage

Exhibit 6.2 Four Phases in the Evolution of Environmental Scanning

Phase 2, the ad hoc phase, is an improvement over Phase 1 in that management identifies a few areas that need to be watched carefully; however, there is no formal system for scanning and no initiative is taken to scan the environment. In addition, that management is sensitive to information about specific areas does not imply that this information is subsequently related to strategy formulation. This phase is characterized by such statements as this: ''All reports seem to indicate that rates of interest will not increase substantially to the year 2010, but our management will never sit down to seriously consider what we might do or not do as a company to capitalize on this trend in the pursuit of our goals.'' Typically, the ad hoc phase characterizes companies that have traditionally done well and whose management, which is intimately tied to day-to-day operations, recently happened to hire a young M.B.A. to do strategic planning.

In Phase 3, the reactive phase, environmental scanning begins to be viewed as important, and efforts are made to monitor the environment to seek information in different areas. In other words, management fully recognizes the significance of the environment and dabbles in scanning but in an unplanned, unstructured fashion. Everything in the environment appears to be important, and the company is swamped with information. Some of the scanned information may never be looked into; some is analyzed, understood, and stored. As soon as the leading firm in the industry makes a strategic move in a particular matter, presumably in response to an environmental shift, the company in Phase 3 is quick to react, following the footsteps of the leader. For example, if the use of cardboard bottles for soft drinks appears uncertain, the Phase 3 company will understand the problem on the horizon but hesitate to take a strategic lead. If the leading firm decides to experiment with cardboard bottles, the Phase 3 firm will quickly respond in kind. In other words, the Phase 3 firm understands the problems and opportunities that the future holds, but its management is unwilling to be the first to take steps to avoid problems or to capitalize on opportunities. A Phase 3 company waits for a leading competitor to pave the way.

The firm in Phase 4, the proactive phase, practices environmental scanning with vigor and zeal, employing a structured effort. Careful screening focuses the scanning effort on specified areas considered crucial. Time is taken to establish proper methodology, disseminate scanned information, and incorporate it into strategy. A hallmark of scanning in Phase 4 is the distinction between macro and micro scanning. **Macro scanning** refers to scanning of interest to the entire corporation and is undertaken at the corporate level. **Micro scanning** is often practiced at the product/market or SBU level. A corporate-wide scanning system is created to ensure that macro and micro scanning complement each other. The system is designed to provide open communication between different micro scanners to avoid duplication of effort and information.

A multinational study on the subject concluded that environmental scanning is on its way to becoming a full-fledged formalized step in the strategic planning process. This commitment to environmental scanning has been triggered in part by the recognition of environmental turbulence and a willingness to confront relevant changes within the planning process. Commitment aside, there is yet no accepted, effective methodology for environmental scanning.[7]

6.5 TYPES OF ENVIRONMENT

Corporations today, more than ever before, are profoundly sensitive to technological, political, economic, social, and regulatory changes. Although environmental changes may be felt throughout an organization, the impact most affects strategic perspectives. To cope with a changing and shifting environment, the marketing strategist must find new ways to forecast the shape of things to come and to analyze strategic alternatives and, at the same time, develop greater sensitivity to long-term implications. Various techniques that are especially relevant for projecting long-range trends are discussed in the appendix at the end of this chapter. Suffice it to say here that environmental scanning necessarily implies a forecasting perspective.

Technological developments come out of the research effort. Two types of research can be distinguished: basic and applied. A company may engage in applied research only or may undertake both basic and applied research. In either case, a start must be made at the basic level, and from there the specific effect on a company's product or process must be derived. A company may choose not to undertake any research on its own, accepting a secondary role as an imitator. The research efforts of imitators will be limited mainly to the adaptation of a particular technological change to its business.

There are three different aspects of technology: type of technology, its process, and the impetus for its development. Technology itself can be grouped into five categories: energy, materials, transportation, communications and information, and genetic (includes agronomic and biomedical). The original impetus for technological breakthroughs can come from any or all of three sources: meeting defense needs, seeking the welfare of the masses, and making a mark commercially. The three stages in the process of technological development are invention, the creation of a new product or process; innovation, the introduction of that product or process into use; and diffusion, the spread of the product or process beyond first use.

The type of technology a company prefers is dictated, of course, by the company's interests. Impetus points to the market for technological development, and the process of development shows the state of technological development and whether the company is in a position to interface with the technology in any stage. For example, the invention and innovation stages may call for basic research beyond the resources of a company. Diffusion, however, may require adaptation, which may not be as difficult as the other two stages.

The point may be illustrated with reference to aluminum cans.[8] Gone are the days when almost every soda and beer product on store shelves came in identical aluminum cans. Sure, Coke was red and Pepsi was blue, but underneath the paint was the same sturdy, flip-top container. Just as technical advances allowed the aluminum industry to seize the can business from steel in the 1960s, today innovations from plastic, glass, and even steel, are undermining aluminum's hegemony. That is a problem for Aluminum Co. of America and its competitors in the aluminum industry. Over the past 20 years, they have come to dominate the $11 billion beverage container market. Cans account for one-fifth of the aluminum sold in North America, which makes it the industry's biggest business—bigger than airplane parts or siding for houses. Moreover, the can business has been the key to growth for aluminum companies, which scurried to build mills in the 1980s. Now they find themselves swamped with capacity. Although the industry produces a staggering 100 billion cans a year, the number has been flat since 1994. From 1985-1996, glass increased it's share of beer packaging from 31% to 37%, while aluminum's portion shrank from 56% to 51%. Meanwhile, in soda, innovations such as Coke's plastic contour bottle are muscling aluminum aside. Plastic bottles are even finding their way into vending machines, where aluminum was once invincible. Now plastic industry researchers are working to come up with a nonporous compound that could be used to hold beer. This materials war has forced aluminum to rethink the plain aluminum can and spend more on eye-catching shapes and textures. It will be interesting to see how far they succeed in dominating the beverage market.

Consider another example: Startling things have been happening to the television set in the last few years. For example, companies now offer color-projection systems with large screens. Some have developed large, flat-screen television sets that are so slim that they can hang on the wall like paintings. Even traditional 19-inch sets aren't just for looking at anymore; they are basic equipment on which to play video games, to learn how to spell, or to practice math. Videodisc players produce television images from discs; videocassette recorders tape television shows and play prerecorded videotapes. With two-way television, the viewer can respond to questions flashed on the screen. Teleprint enables the conversion of television sets into video-display tubes so that viewers can scan the contents of newspapers, magazines, catalogs, and the like and call up any sections of interest. Finally, cable television permits the viewer to call on the system's library for a game, movie, or even a French lesson.[9]

| | TECHNOLOGY POSITION | | |
| | | Different Technology | |
Product Position	Same Technology	Older Technology	Newer Technology
Behind competitors	Take traditional strategic actions — Assess marketing strategy and target markets — Enhance product features — Improve operational efficiency	Evaluate viability of your technology — Implement newer technology — Divest products based on older technology	Evaluate availability of resources to sustain technology development and full market acceptance — Continue to define new applications and product enhancements — Scale back operations
Ahead of competitors	Define new applications for the technology and enhance products accordingly	Take advantage of all possible profit	Define new applications for the technology and enhance products accordingly

Source: Susan J. Levine, "Marketers Need to Adopt a Technological Focus to Safeguard Against Obsolescence," *Marketing News* (28 October 1988): 16. Reprinted by permission of the American Marketing Association.

Exhibit 6.3 Technology Management Matrix

The 1990s were a period of technological change and true innovation. One of the areas of greatest impact is communications.[10] Until now, electronic communication has largely been confined to the traditional definition of voice (telephone), pictures (television), and graphics (computer): three distinct kinds of communication devices. From now on, electronics will increasingly produce total communications. Today it is possible to make simultaneous and instantaneous electronic transmission of voice, pictures, and graphics. People scattered over the face of the globe can now talk to each other directly, see each other, and, if need be, share the same reports, documents, and graphs without leaving their own offices or homes. Consider the impact of this innovation on the airline industry. Business travel should diminish in importance, though its place may well be taken by travel for vacations and learning.

To analyze technological changes and capitalize on them, marketing strategists may utilize the technology management matrix shown in Exhibit 6.3. The matrix should aid in choosing appropriate strategic options based on a business's technological position. The matrix has two dimensions: technology and product. The technology dimension describes technologies in terms of their relationships to one another; the product dimension establishes competitive position. The interaction of these two dimensions suggests desirable strategic action. For example, if a business's technology is superior to anything else on the market, the company should enhance its leadership by identifying and introducing new applications for the technology. On the other hand, if a business's technology lags behind the competition, it should either make a technological leap to the competitive process, abandon the market, or identify and pursue those elements that are laggards in terms of adopting new technologies.

Briefly, the rapid development and exploitation of new technologies are causing serious strategic headaches for companies in almost every type of industry. It has become vital for strategists to be able to recognize the limits of their core technologies, know which new technologies are emerging, and decide when to incorporate new technology in their products.

In stable governments, political trends may not be as important as in countries where governments are weak. Yet even in stable countries, political trends may have a significant impact on business. For example, in the United States one can typically expect greater emphasis on social programs and an increase in government spending when Democrats are in power in the White House. Therefore, companies in the business of providing social services may expect greater opportunities during Democratic administrations.

More important, however, are political trends overseas because the U.S. economy is intimately connected with the global economy. Therefore, what goes on in the political spheres of other countries may be significant for U.S. corporations, particularly multinational corporations.[11]

The following are examples of political trends and events that could affect business planning and strategy:

1. An increase in geopolitical federations.

   a. Economic interests: resource countries versus consumer countries.
   b. Political interests: Developed nations versus developing countries.

2. Rising nationalism versus world federalism.

   a. Failure of the United Nations.
   b. Trend toward world government or world law system.

3. Limited wars: Middle East, South Asia, Iraq War.
4. Increase in political terrorism; revolutions.
5. Third-party gains in the United States; rise of socialism.
6. Decline of the major powers; rise of emerging nations (e.g., China, India, Brazil).
7. Minority (female) president.
8. Rise in senior citizen power in developed nations.
9. Political turmoil in Saudi Arabia that threatens world oil supplies and peace in the Middle East.
10. Revolutionary change in Indonesia, jeopardizing Japanese oil supplies.
11. Revolutionary change in South Africa, limiting Western access to important minerals and threatening huge capital losses to the economies of Great Britain, the United States, and Germany.
12. Instability in other places where the economic consequences could be important, including Mexico, Turkey, Zaire, Nigeria, South Korea, Brazil, Chile, and the People's Republic of China.

Already in 2008 we have seen the overwhelming impact that political shocks can have on the world economy. The decline in the value of the dollar is the perfect illustration: it was not just the product of an arbitrary monetary policy that was temporarily out of control but a rational response to problems that were fundamentally political. The U.S. government continued to incur huge budget deficits and kept on borrowing, making itself dangerously dependent on the inflows of foreign capital. At the same time, this was disturbing for major U.S. trading partners since their goods became more expensive in the U.S.

Marketing strategy is deeply affected by political perspectives. For example, government decisions have significantly affected the U.S. automotive industry. Stringent requirements, such as fuel efficiency standards, have burdened the industry in several ways. The marketing strategist needs to study both domestic and foreign political happenings, reviewing selected published information to keep in touch with political trends and interpret the information as it relates to the particular company.

Governments around the world help their domestic industries strengthen their competitiveness through various fiscal and monetary measures. Political support can play a key role in an industry's search for markets abroad. Without it, an industry may face a difficult situation. For instance, the U.S. auto industry would benefit from a U.S. government concession favoring U.S. automotive exports. European countries rely on value-added taxes to help their industries. Value-added taxes are applied to all levels of manufacturing transactions up to and including the final sale to the end user. However, if the final sale is for export, the value-added tax is rebated, thus effectively reducing the price of European goods in international commerce. Japan imposes a commodity tax on selected lines of products, including automobiles. In the event of export, the commodity tax is waived. The United States has no corresponding arrangement. Thus, when a new automobile is shipped from the United States to Japan, its U.S. taxes upon export are not rebated, and the auto also must bear the cost of the Japanese commodity tax (15 or 20 percent, depending on the size of the vehicle) when it is sold in Japan. This illustrates how political decisions affect marketing strategy.

Economic trends and events affecting businesses include the following possibilities:

- Depression; worldwide economic collapse.
- Increasing foreign ownership of the U.S. economy.
- Increasing regulation and management of national economies.
- Several developing nations become superpowers (e.g., Brazil, India, China).
- World food production: famine relief versus holistic management.
- Decline in real world growth or stable growth.
- Collapse of world monetary system.
- High inflation.

- Significant employee-union ownership of U.S. businesses.
- Worldwide free trade.

It is not unrealistic to say that all companies, small or large, that are engaged in strategic planning examine the economic environment. Relevant published information is usually gathered, analyzed, and interpreted for use in planning. In some corporations, the entire process of dealing with economic information may be manual and intuitive. The large corporations, however, not only buy specific and detailed economic information from private sources, over and above what may be available from government sources, but they analyze the information for meaningful conclusions by constructing econometric models. For example, one large corporation with nine divisions has developed 26 econometric models of its different businesses. The data used for these models are stored in a database and are regularly updated. The information is available on-line to all divisions for further analysis at any time. Other companies may occasionally buy information from outside and selectively undertake modeling.

Usually the economic environment is analyzed with reference to the following key economic indicators: employment, consumer price index, housing starts, auto sales, weekly unemployment claims, real GNP, industrial production, personal income, savings rate, capacity utilization, productivity, money supply (weekly M1: currency and checking accounts), retail sales, inventories, and durable goods orders. Information on these indicators is available from government sources. These indicators are adequate for short-run analysis and decision making because, by and large, they track developments over the business cycle reasonably well. However, companies that try to base strategic plans on these indicators alone can run into serious trouble. Deficiencies in the data prove most dangerous when the government moves to take a more interventionist role in the economy. Further, when the ability of statistical agencies to respond has been hampered by unprecedented budget stringency, rapid changes in the structure of the economy cause a gradual deterioration in the quality of many of the economic statistics that the government publishes.

The problem of government-supplied data begins with a recondite document called the *Standard Industrial Classification (SIC) Manual*, which divides all economic activity into 12 divisions and 84 major groups of industries. The SIC Manual dictates the organization of and the amount of data available about production, income, employment, and other vital economic indicators. Each major group has a two-digit numerical code. The economy is then subdivided into hundreds of secondary groups, each with a three-digit code, and is further subdivided into thousands of industries, each with four-digit codes. But detail in most government statistical series is available only at the major group level; data at the three-digit level are scarce; at the four-digit level, almost nonexistent. Thus, information available from public sources may not suffice.

To illustrate the effect of economic climate on strategy, consider the following trends. In the more elderly capitalist countries, it is expected that old markets will become saturated much faster than new markets will take their place. Staple consumer goods, such as cars, radios, and television sets, already outnumber households in North America and in much of Western Europe; other products are fast approaching the same fate. The slow growth of populations in most of these countries means that the number of households is likely to grow at only about 2 percent annually to the year 2015 and that demand for consumer goods is unlikely to grow any faster. Furthermore, while demand in these markets decreases, supply will increase, leading to intensified price competition and pressure on profit margins.

For example, the auto industry is likely to suffer from overcapacity. It is expected that there will be three buyers for every four cars.[12] Already the market concentration in many consumer sectors has fallen significantly, mainly because of increased foreign competition. And the expansion of production capacity in such primary industries as metals and chemicals, especially in developing countries, may bring some kind of increased competition to producer goods.

These trends indicate the kind of economic issues that marketing strategists must take into account to determine their strategies.

The ultimate test of a business is its social relevance. This is particularly true in a society where survival needs are already being met. It therefore behooves the strategic planner to be familiar with emerging social trends and concerns. The relevance of the social environment to a particular business will, of course, vary depending on the nature of the business. For a technology-oriented business, scanning the social environment may be limited to aspects of pollution control and environmental safety. For a consumer-products company, however, the impact of the social environment may go much further.

An important aspect of the social environment concerns the values consumers hold. Observers have noted many value shifts that directly or indirectly influence business. Values mainly revolve around a number of fundamental concerns regarding time, quality, health, environment, home, personal finance, and diversity.

6.5.1 Orientation Toward Time

Given the scarcity of time and/or money to have products repaired or to buy new ones, consumers look for offerings that endure. Time has become the scarce resource as the result of the prevalence of dual income-earning households. Convenience is a critical source of differential advantage, particularly in foods and services. In addition, youth are making or influencing more household purchasing decisions than ever before. Moreover, as the population ages, time pressures become more widespread and acute. Consumers are going to need innovative and, in some cases, almost customized solutions. With time generally scarcer than money, offerings that ease time pressures will garner higher margins. For example, today's average consumer takes just 21 minutes to do her shopping - from the moment she slams her car door in a supermarket parking lot to the moment she climbs back in with her purchases. In that time, she buys an average of 18 items, out of 30,000 to 40,000 choices. She has less time to browse; it is down 25% from five years ago. She isn't even bothering to check prices. She wants the same product, at the same prices, in the same row, week after week. Under such a scenario, it does not make sense for P&G to make 55 price changes a day across 110 brands, offering 440 promotions a year, tinkering with package size, color and contents. To keep up with time, after 159 years P&G changed the name of its sales department to Customer Business Development, and let consumers drive supply than to force-feed retailers by making them buy more products than they can sell. To implement this concept involved everything from truck schedules to helping clean retailers' shelves of accumulated grime. It has prompted P & G to share its consumer research with retailers.[13]

6.5.2 Quality

Given the standards set by the influx of imported products, American consumers have developed a new set of expectations regarding quality; hence, they assign high priorities to those offerings that provide optimal price/quality. We are witnessing a move toward the adoption of a greater price/quality orientation in mass markets. There will continue to be a strong general desire for authenticity and lasting quality. Consumers will require fewer and more durable products rather than more ephemeral, novelty products. Heightened consumer expectations will translate into trying a manufacturer once. If the value, the quality, or the intrinsic characteristics that the consumer demands are not found, the consumer will not return to that manufacturer.

6.5.3 Health

A large and growing segment of the American population has become increasingly preoccupied with health. Health concerns are a function of both an aging population and changing predispositions. America is hungry for health and is impatient for its achievement. Industry experts are predicting that nutritional tags, such as "low in fat," will probably be the newest food fad to sweep the United States. No wonder, PepsiCo is pushing to make at least 50% of its food-and-beverage offerings "nutritious"—cutting fat and adding ingredients such as broccoli.[14] There is some consensus that a diet rich in soluble fiber and low in fat and a lifestyle that includes plenty of regular exercise reduces cholesterol. As an aging population strives to maintain its youth and vitality, alcohol and tobacco consumption and other unhealthy dietary habits will continue to decline. In short, American consumers have become highly health conscious.[15] The impact of this trend will not only be felt in the grocery store but in the travel and hospitality sectors of the economy, as well as in an array of services that contribute to lifelong wellness.

6.5.4 Environment

Perhaps the 1990s became the "earth decade." A growing number of Americans consider themselves "environmentalists." Outdoor activities, such as rock-climbing expeditions and whitewater rafting, are superseding more vicarious, passive ways of spending time. This heightened appreciation of the outdoors is being translated in choice criteria in the marketplace. Hence, more and more marketers are pressured into adopting "green" strategies; that is, offering products and services that are beneficial to the environment.

6.5.5 Home

In a more domesticated society, the many technological innovations of recent years are making staying at home more fun. Some of the most beneficial advances of this home-centered lifestyle are in the design and construction of houses that resemble self-contained entertainment/educational activity centers. Opportunities for marketers to provide creative, more personalized, high-value offerings in home furnishings evolved after the 2007-2008 housing slump rebounded.

6.5.6 Personal Finance

Most experts on consumer behavior expect that in the new century, people will be more frugal than they were in the past. The slow-and-steady consumer approach spawned by an attitude for upscale products that may outstrip finances makes every purchase especially important. We are witnessing several important consumer finance trends. First, consumers continue to seek out the best price/value before buying and accordingly place downward pressure on seller profit margins. Second, American consumers may have the income to spend freely, but recent economic difficulties nonetheless have caused them to remain cautious. Finally, quality is insisted upon, and a competitive premium price is willingly paid for performance and durability.

6.5.7 Diversity of Lifestyles

The predominance of diverse lifestyles is reflected by the significant increase in the number and the stature of women in the labor market. The increased presence of women in the labor force has dramatically influenced how men and women relate to one another and the personal and professional roles assumed by each. With 70 percent of women holding jobs outside the home, millions of men are doing chores their fathers would never have dreamed of. For example, men bought 41 percent of the groceries in the U.S. in 2002, up from 25 percent ten years earlier.[16] There has also been a dramatic change in racial integration and improved race relations. The United States has also witnessed the development of openly gay and lesbian lifestyles as well as an increase in the number of unmarried, cohabiting relationships. Significant changes in attitudes toward work and careers have also resulted in a new sense of independence and individuality. Accordingly, there has been an upsurge in the number of people who are self-employed. Experts hold that this pattern of social diversity will likely continue into the future.[17] Social diversity creates opportunities for marketers to develop personalized offerings that allow individuals to derive satisfaction in the pursuit of different living alternatives.

In conclusion, American consumers will continue to search for basic values and will experience heightened ethical awareness.[18] Consumers will still care about what things cost, but they will value only things that will endure—family, community, earth, faith.

Information on social trends may be derived from published sources. The impact of social trends on a particular business can be studied in-house or with the help of outside consultants. A number of consulting firms specialize in studying social trends.

Let us examine the strategic impact of two of the value shifts mentioned above: orientation toward time and concern for health. Consider the retail industry. Little is being done to support consumers in their quest to reduce shopping stress, although stress is a major consumer concern. Fast service has been the basis for growth for a number of well-known firms, among them American Express, McDonald's, and Federal Express; however, only a small but significant number of businesses have recognized and responded to the consumer's lack of free time for shopping and service transactions:

- Dayton-Hudson has moved away from a maze-like floor design to a center aisle design, making it easier for customers to find their way through the store. At Childworld, toys are coordinated in learning centers so that buyers can examine and play with products. Management feels that this arrangement enables buyers to shop more quickly.
- A new firm, Shopper's Express, is assisting large chains such as A&P and Safeway by taking telephone orders and delivering merchandise.
- Rather than forcing the consumer to sit at home for an entire day awaiting a service call, GE, for years, has been making specific service appointments.

- Sears now offers six-day-a-week and evening repair service. In addition, in specifying when a repair person will arrive, Sears assigns a two-hour window.
- Montgomery Ward authorizes 7,700 sales clerks to approve sales checks and handle merchandise returns on their own, eliminating the time needed to get a floor manager's approval.
- Burger King uses television monitors that enable drive-up customers to see the waiter and the order.
- Many retailers, including A&P, Shop Rite, Publix, and Home Depot use checkout systems that reduce waiting time in checkout lines.
- Wegman's, a supermarket chain in Rochester, New York, has a computer available for entering deli orders so that the customer does not have to wait to be served. The customer simply enters the order and picks it up on the way out of the store. Now, self-service technology in revolutionizing retailing. Tesco, a British Company, has opened Fresh & Easy grocery stores in the U.S. which are entirely run as self-service outlets.

More and more companies need to focus on developing shopping support systems and environments that help customers move through the buying process quickly. For firms that pride themselves for providing customers with a leisurely shopping environment, this will be a radical departure. Firms accepting this challenge will be able to support and stay closer to their customers through such changes. In addition, firms that help customers reduce shopping time will be able to differentiate themselves from competitors more easily.

For health reasons, salads and fish are replacing the traditional American dinner of meat and potatoes. Vegetarianism is on the rise. According to *Time*, about 12 million Americans call themselves vegetarians.[19,20] Increasing varieties of decaffeinated coffee and tea and substitutes for sugar and salt are crowding supermarket shelves. Shoppers are reading the small print to check for artificial ingredients in foods and beverages that they once bought without a thought. Smoking is finally declining. Manufacturers and retailers of natural foods are building a healthy ''health industry.'' Even products that do not easily accommodate healthier choices are being redeveloped in response to consumer concerns. For example, Dunkin' Donuts has yanked the egg yolks from all but four of its 52 varieties to make its donuts cholesterol-free.[21] Fast food firms—McDonald's Corporation and Hardee's Food Systems, for example—have introduced low-fat foods into their menus.[22]

The nation's dramatic new awareness of health is prompting these changes. The desire to feel better, look younger, and live longer exerts a powerful influence on what people put into their bodies. This strong force is now moving against a well-entrenched habit that affects millions and dates back to biblical times—the consumption of too much alcohol.[23]

Health substitutes for alcoholic beverages, labeled ''dealcoholized'' beverages, are now being offered to American consumers. For some time, gourmet food shops have stocked champagne-like bottles of carbonated grape juice and cans containing a not-fully-brewed mixture of water, malt, corn, yeast, and hops. Except for their packaging, these alcohol-free imitations failed to resemble wine and beer, especially in the crucial area of taste. New dealcoholized beverages, however, are fully fermented, or brewed, before their alcohol is separated out—either by pressure or heat—to below an unnoticeable 0.5 percent, the federal maximum before classifying a drink as alcoholic. The taste and body of the new beverages match that of their former alcoholized selves.

This 0.5 percent level is so low that a drinker would need to consume 24 glasses of dealcoholized wine or 8 cans of dealcoholized beer to obtain the amount of alcohol in one 4-ounce glass of regular wine or one 12-ounce can of regular beer. Thus, the drinker avoids not only intoxication but also worthless calories. A regular glass of wine or beer has about 150 calories, while their dealcoholized copies contain about 40 to 60 calories, respectively. And their prices are the same.[24] Introduced in Europe about five years ago, dealcoholized wines are slowly making headway in the United States.

Government influence on business appears to be increasing. It is estimated that businesses spend, on the average, twice as much time fulfilling government requirements today as they did 10 years ago. Consider the case of Frito-Lay, which has long been America's leading salty snack company.[25] In recent years, the PepsiCo subsidiary, whose offerings include Lay's Potato Chips to Rold Gold Pretzels, has boosted its industry market share from 38% to 55%. Because of this stellar performance, the Justice Department suspects that something must be rancid at Frito-Lay. The Justice Department is said to be looking hard at Frito-Lay's use of shelf allowances, a common retailing practice in which manufacturers pay stores up to $100,000 a foot for desirable shelf space. Among other things, investigators want to know if Frito-Lay has been purchasing more space than it needs in order to muscle out competitors. Since 1990, Frito-Lay has beaten a number of competitors. Anheuser-Busch sold its Eagle Snack division to Frito-Lay in 1996 after persistently losing money since they entered the field in 1979. Another well-known casualty was Borden, whose market share declined from 12% to 5%. Dozens of independent regional snack companies have folded in recent years. Frito-Lay makes no bones about it and asks, is it really a crime to be better than everyone else?

Interestingly, government in recent years has changed its emphasis from regulating specific industries to focusing on problem areas of national interest, including environmental cleanup, elimination of job discrimination, establishment of safe working conditions, and reduction of product hazards. A number of steps have been taken toward deregulation of various industries.

This shift in focus in the regulatory environment deeply affects the internal operations of business. To win or even survive in the competitive free-for-all environment that follows deregulation, companies in once-regulated industries must make some hard choices. Astute management can avoid some of the trauma by developing an explicit strategy to operate in a deregulated environment well in advance of the event, rethinking relationships with customers, considering new roles to play in the market, and realigning their organizations accordingly.

To study the impact of the regulatory environment, that is, of laws already on the books and of pending legislation, legal assistance is required. Small firms may seek legal assistance on an ad hoc basis. Large firms may maintain offices in Washington staffed by people with legal backgrounds who are well versed in the company's business, who know important government agencies from the point of view of their companies, who maintain a close liaison with them, and who pass on relevant information to planners in different departments of their companies.

6.6 ENVIRONMENTAL SCANNING AND MARKETING STRATEGY

The impact of environmental scanning on marketing strategy can be illustrated with reference to videotex technology.[26] Videotex technology—the merging of computer and communications technologies—delivers information directly to the consumer. The consumer may instantly view desired textual and visual information from on-line databases on television screens or other video receivers by pushing the appropriate buttons or typing the proper commands.

Possibilities for business and personal use of videotex are as endless as the imagination. Consumers are already utilizing videotex for shopping, travel, personal protection, financial transactions, and entertainment, in greater privacy and autonomy than ever before.

With the mechanism for getting things done most efficiently and cost effectively, marketing strategists have begun to explore the implications of videotex on marketing decisions. Videotex will alter the demand for certain kinds of goods and services and the ways in which consumers interact with marketing activities. For the first time, the average consumer, not just the affluent consumer, can interact directly with the production process, dictating final product specifications as the product is being manufactured. As small-batch production becomes more cost-effective, this type of consumer-producer interaction will become more common.

Product selection might also be enhanced by videotex, as sellers stock a more complete inventory at fewer, more central locations rather than dealing with many retail outlets. Because packages will no longer serve as the communications vehicle for selling the product, less money will be spent on packaging. Product changes can also be kept up-to-date. Information on videotex will be current, synthesized, and comprehensive. The user will have the power to access only desired information at the time it is desired. Advertising messages and articles will be available in index form.

Direct consumer interaction with manufacturers will eliminate distribution channels. Reduced or zero-based inventory will cut down obsolescence and turnover costs. Centrally located warehouses and new delivery routes will become increasingly cost-effective. The remaining retail stores will be transformed into showrooms with direct-order possibilities via viewdatalike terminals.

Promotional material will become more educational and information-based, including the provision of product specifications and independent product evaluations. Interactive video channels will provide advertisers and interested shoppers with prepackaged commercials and live shopping programs.

With more accurate price and product information, more perfect competition will result. Price discrepancies will be reduced. Consumers will engage in more preshopping planning, price-comparison shopping, and in-home shopping.

The market segment concept will be more important than ever before. The individualizing possibilities of videotex will enable the seller to measure and reach segments with unparalleled accuracy and will also enable consumers to effectively self-segment. Advertisers and consumers will benefit from 24-hour, 7-day-a-week salespeople. Everyone will be better prepared through videotex to satisfy customers.

6.7 ENVIRONMENTAL SCANNING PROCEDURE

Like any other new program, the scanning activity in a corporation evolves over time. There is no way to introduce a foolproof system from the beginning. If conditions are favorable—if there is an established system of strategic planning in place and the CEO is interested in a structured effort at scanning—the evolutionary period shortens, of course, but the state of the art may not permit the introduction of a fully developed system at the outset. Besides, behavioral and organizational constraints require that things be done over a period of time.[27] The level and type of scanning that a corporation undertakes should be custom designed, and a customized system takes time to emerge into a viable system.

Exhibit 6.4 shows the process by which environmental scanning is linked to marketing strategy. Listed below are the procedural steps that explain this relationship.

1. **Keep a tab on broad trends appearing in the environment**—Once the scope of environmental scanning is determined, broad trends in chosen areas may be reviewed from time to time. For example, in the area of technology, trends in energy utilization, material science, transportation capability, mechanization and automation, communications and information processing, and control over natural life may be studied.
2. **Determine the relevance of an environmental trend**—Not everything happening in the environment may be relevant for a company. Therefore, attempts must be made to select those trends that have significance for the company. There cannot be any hard-and-fast rules for making a distinction between

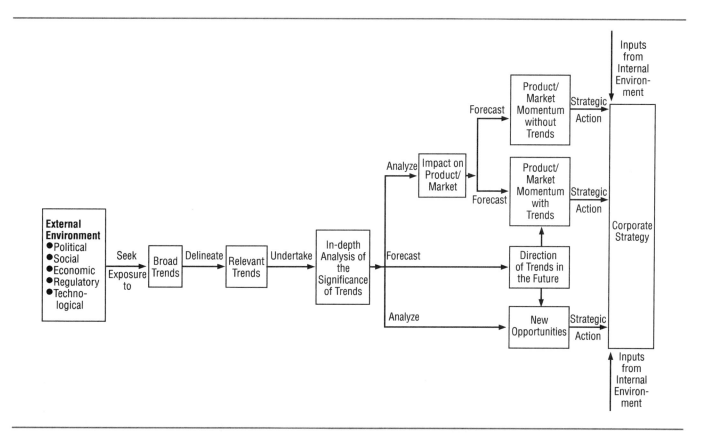

Exhibit 6.4 Linking Environmental Scanning to Corporate Strategy

relevant and irrelevant. Consider, for example, the demise of the steam locomotive industry. Management's creativity and farsightedness would play an important role in a company's ability to pinpoint relevant areas of concern. Described below is one way (for a large corporation) of identifying relevant trends in the environment:

- Place a senior person in charge of scanning.
- Identify a core list of about 100 relevant publications worldwide.
- Assign these publications to volunteers within the company, one per person. Selected publications considered extremely important should be scanned by the scanning manager.
- Each scanner reviews stories/articles/news items in the assigned publication that meet predetermined criteria based on the company's aims. Scanners might also review books, conference proceedings, lectures, and presentations.
- The scanned information is given a predetermined code. For example, a worldwide consumer-goods company used the following codes: subject (e.g., politics); geography (e.g., Middle East); function (e.g., marketing); application (e.g., promotion, distribution); and "uniterm," or keyword, for organizing the information. An abstract is then prepared on the story.
- The abstract, along with the codes, is submitted to a scanning committee, consisting of several managers, to determine its relevance in terms of effect on corporate, SBU, and product/market strategy. An additional relevance code is added at this time.
- The codes and the abstract are computerized.
- A newsletter is prepared to disseminate the information companywide. Managers whose areas are directly affected by the information are encouraged to contact the scanning department for further analysis.

3. **Study the impact of an environmental trend on a product/market**—An environmental trend can pose either a threat or an opportunity for a company's product/market; which one it turns out to be must be studied. The task of determining the impact of a change is the responsibility of the SBU manager. Alternatively, the determination may be assigned to another executive who is familiar with the product/market. If the whole subject appears controversial, it may be safer to have an ad hoc committee look into it; or consultants, either internal or external, may be approached. There is a good chance that a manager who has been involved with a product or service for many years will look at any change as a threat. That manager may, therefore, avoid the issue by declaring the impact to be irrelevant at the outset. If such nearsightedness is feared, perhaps it would be better to rely on a committee or a consultant.

4. **Forecast the direction of an environmental trend into the future**—If an environmental trend does appear to have significance for a product/market, it is desirable to determine the course that the trend is likely to adopt. In other words, attempts must be made at environmental forecasting.

5. **Analyze the momentum of the product/market business in the face of the environmental trend**—Assuming that the company takes no action, what will be the shape of the product/market performance in the midst of the environmental trend and its future direction? The impact of an environmental trend is usually gradual. While it is helpful to be the "first" to recognize a trend and take action, all is not lost if a company waits to see which way the trend proceeds. But how long one waits depends on the diffusion process, the rate at which the change necessitated by the trend is adopted. People are not jumping to replace their existing television sets with high-definition ones overnight. Similar examples abound. A variety of reasons may prohibit an overnight shift in markets due to an environmental trend that may deliver a new product or process. High prices, religious taboos, legal restrictions, and unfamiliarity with the product or service would restrict changeover. In brief, the diffusion process should be predicted before arriving at a conclusion.

6. **Study the new opportunities that an environmental trend appears to provide**—An environmental trend may not be relevant for a company's current product/market, but it may indicate promising new business opportunities. For example, the energy crisis provided an easy entry point for fuel-efficient Hondas into the United States. Such opportunities should be duly pinpointed and analyzed for action.

7. **Relate the outcome of an environmental trend to corporate strategy**—Based on environmental trends and their impacts, a company needs to review its strategy on two counts: changes that may be introduced in current products/markets and feasible opportunities that the company may embrace for action. Even if an environmental trend poses a threat to a company's product/market, it is not necessary for the company to come out with a new product to replace an existing one. Neither is it necessary for every competitor to embrace the "change." Even without developing a new product, a company may find a niche in the

market to which it could cater despite the introduction of a new product by a competitor. The electric razor did not make safety razor blades obsolete. Automatic transmissions did not throw the standard shift out of vogue. New markets and new uses can be found to give an existing product an advantage despite the overall popularity of a new product.

Although procedural steps for scanning the environment exist, scanning is nevertheless an art in which creativity plays an important role. Thus, to adequately study the changing environment and relate it to corporate strategy, companies should inculcate a habit of creative thinking on the part of its managers. The experience of one insurance company illustrates the point: in order to ''open up'' line managers to new ideas and to encourage innovation in their plans, they are, for a while, withdrawn from the line organization to serve as staff people. In staff positions, they are granted considerable freedom of action, which enhances their ability to manage creatively when they return to their management positions.

6.8 CONDUCTING ENVIRONMENTAL SCANNING: AN EXAMPLE

Following the steps in Exhibit 6.5, an attempt is made here to illustrate how specific trends in the environment may be systematically scanned.

A search of the literature in the area of politics shows that the following federal laws were considered in 2008:

1. Requiring that all ad claims be substantiated.
2. Publishing corporate actions that endanger the environment.
3. Disclosing lobbying efforts in detail.
4. Reducing a company's right to fire workers at will.
5. Eliminating inside directors.

The marketing strategist of a consumer-goods company may want to determine if any of these trends has any relevance for the company. To do so, the strategist may undertake trend-impact analysis. Trend-impact analysis requires the formation of a delphi panel (see Chapter 12) to determine the desirability (0-1), technical feasibility (0-1), probability of occurrence (0-1), and probable time of occurrence (2010, 2015, and beyond 2015) of each event listed. The panel may also be asked to suggest the area(s) that may be affected by each event (i.e., production, labor, markets [household, business, government, export], finance, or research and development).

Information about an event may be studied by managers in areas that, according to the delphi panel, are likely to be affected by the event. If their consensus is that the event is indeed important, scanning may continue (see Exhibit 6.6).

Exhibit 6.5
Systematic Approach to
Environmental Scanning
	1. Pick up events in different environments (via literature search).
	2. Delineate events of interest to the SBU in one or more of the following areas: production, labor, markets (household, business, government, foreign), finance, or research and development. This could be achieved via trend-impact analysis of the events.
	3. Undertake cross-impact analysis of the events of interest.
	4. Relate the trends of the noted events to current SBU strategies in different areas.
	5. Select the trends that appear either to provide new opportunities or to pose threats.
	6. Undertake forecasts of each trend
	   — wild card prediction
	   — most probable occurrence
	   — conservative estimate
	7. Develop three scenarios for each trend based on three types of forecasts.
	8. Pass on the information to strategists.
	9. Repeat Steps 4 to 7 and develop more specific scenarios vis-à-vis different products/markets. Incorporate these scenarios in the SBU strategy.

Exhibit 6.6 Trend-Impact Analysis: An Example		

Event	Requiring That All Ad Claims Be Substantiated	Reducing a Company's Right to Fire Workers at Will
Desirability	0.8	0.5
Feasibility	0.6	0.3
Probability of occurrence	0.5	0.1
Probable time of occurrence	2010	Beyond 2015
Area(s) impacted	Household markets Business markets Government markets Finance Research and development Production	Labor Finance
Decision	Carry on scanning	Drop from further consideration

Note: Two to three rounds of delphi would be needed to arrive at the above probabilities.

Next, cross-impact analysis may be undertaken. This type of analysis studies the impact of an event on other events. Where events are mutually exclusive, such analysis may not be necessary. But where an event seems to reinforce or inhibit other events, cross-impact analysis is highly desirable for uncovering the true strength of an event.

Cross-impact analysis amounts to studying the impact of an event (given its probability of occurrence) upon other events. The impact may be delineated either in qualitative terms (such as critical, major, significant, slight, or none) or in quantitative terms in the form of probabilities.

Exhibit 6.7 shows how cross-impact analysis may be undertaken. Cross-impact ratings, or probabilities, can best be determined with the help of another delphi panel. To further sharpen the analysis, whether the impact of an event on other events will be felt immediately or after a certain number of years may also be determined.

Cross-impact analysis provides the "time" probability of the occurrence of an event and indicates other key events that may be monitored to keep track of the first event. Cross-impact analysis is more useful for project-level scanning than for general scanning.

To relate environmental trends to strategy, consider the following environmental trends and strategies of a cigarette manufacturer:

Trends
T1: Requiring that all ad claims be substantiated.
T2: Publishing corporate actions that endanger workers or the environment.

Exhibit 6.7 Cross-Impact Analysis: An Example		

Event	Probability of Occurrence	Impact a	b	c	d	e
a. Requiring that all ad claims be substantiated	0.5				0.1*	
b. Publishing corporate actions that endanger workers or environment	0.4	0.7**				
c. Disclosing lobbying efforts in detail	0.4					
d. Reducing a company's right to fire workers at will	0.1					
e. Eliminating inside directors	0.6					

* This means that requiring that all claims be substantiated has no effect on the probability of Event d.
**This means that if publishing corporate actions that endanger workers or the environment occurs (probability 0.4), the probability of requiring that all ad claims be substantiated increases from 0.5 to 0.7.

Exhibit 6.8
Matrix to Determine the Impact of Selected Trends on Different Corporate Strategies

Trends	Strategies				Impact	
	S_1	S_2	S_3	S_4	+	−
T_1	−8	0	+2	−2	+	8
T_2	−4	−2	−6	0		12
T_3	0	+4	−4	+2	2	
T_4	0	−4	0	+6	2	
T_5	−2	+6	+4	+2	10	
+		−	4	−	8	
−		14	−	4	−	

Scale

+8	*Enhance the*	Critical
+6	*implementation*	Major
+2	*of strategy*	Significant
+2		Slight
0		**No effect**
−2	*Inhibit the*	Slight
−4	*implementation*	Significant
−6	*of strategy*	Major
−8		Critical

T3: Disclosing lobbying efforts in detail.
T4: Reducing a company's right to fire workers at will.
T5: Eliminating inside directors.

Strategies
S1: Heavy emphasis on advertising, using emotional appeals.
S2: Seasonal adjustments in labor force for agricultural operations of the company.
S3: Regular lobbying effort in Washington against further legislation imposing restrictions on the cigarette industry.
S4: Minimum number of outside directors on the board.

The analysis in Exhibit 6.8 shows that Strategy S_1, heavy emphasis on advertising, is most susceptible and requires immediate management action. Among the trends, Trend T_5, eliminating inside directors, will have the most positive overall impact. Trends T_1 and T_2, requiring that all ad claims be substantiated and publishing corporate actions that endanger the environment, will have a devastating impact. This type of analysis indicates where management concern and action should be directed. Thus, it will be desirable to undertake forecasts of Trends T_1 and T_2. The forecasts may predict when the legislation will be passed, what will be the major provisions of the legislation, and so on. Three different forecasts may be obtained:

1. Extremely unfavorable legislation.
2. Most probable legislation.
3. Most favorable legislation.

Three different scenarios (using three types of forecasts) may be developed to indicate the impact of each trend. This information may then be passed on to product/market managers for action. Product/market managers may repeat Steps 4 through 7 (see Exhibit 6.5), studying selected trend(s) in depth.

6.9 ORGANIZATIONAL ARRANGEMENTS AND PROBLEMS

Corporations organize scanning activity in three different ways: (a) line managers undertake environmental scanning in addition to their other work, (b) scanning is made a part of the strategic planner's job, (c) scanning responsibility is instituted in a new office of environmental scanning.

Most companies use a combination of the first two types of arrangements. The strategic planner may scan the corporate-wide environment while line managers concentrate on the product/market environment. In some companies, a new office of environmental scanning has been established with a responsibility for all types of scanning. The scanning office undertakes scanning both regularly and on an ad hoc basis (at the request of one of the groups in the company). Information scanned on a regular basis is passed on to all in the organization for whom it may have relevance. For example, General Electric is organized into sectors, groups, and SBUs. The SBU is the level at which product/market planning takes place. Thus, scanned information is channeled to those SBUs, groups, and sectors for which it has relevance. Ad hoc scanning may be undertaken at the request of one or more SBUs. These SBUs then share the cost of scanning and are the principal recipients of the information.

The environmental scanner serves to split the work of the planner. If the planner already has many responsibilities and if the environment of a corporation is complex, it is desirable to have a person specifically responsible for scanning. Further, it is desirable that both planners (and/or scanners) and line managers undertake scanning because managers usually limit their scanning perceptions to their own industry; that is, they may limit their scanning to the environment with which they are most familiar. At the corporate level, scanning should go beyond the industry.

Whoever is assigned to scan the environment should undertake the following six tasks:

1. **Trend monitoring**—Systematically and continuously monitoring trends in the external environments of the company and studying their impact upon the firm and its various constituencies.
2. **Forecast preparation**—Periodically developing alternative scenarios, forecasts, and other analyses that serve as inputs to various types of planning and issue management functions in the organization.
3. **Internal consulting**—Providing a consulting resource on long-term environmental matters and conducting special future research studies as needed to support decision-making and planning activities.
4. **Information center**—Providing a center to which intelligence and forecasts about the external environment from all over the organization can be sent for interpretation, analysis, and storage in a basic library on long-range environmental matters.
5. **Communications**—Communicating information on the external environment to interested decision makers through a variety of media, including newsletters, special reports, internal lectures, and periodic analyses of the environment.
6. **Process improvement**—Continually improving the process of environmental analysis by developing new tools and techniques, designing forecasting systems, applying methodologies developed elsewhere, and engaging in a continuing process of self-evaluation and self-correction.

Successful implementation of these tasks should provide increased awareness and understanding of long-term environments and improve the strategic planning capabilities of the firm. More specifically, environmental inputs are helpful in product design, formulation of marketing strategies, determination of marketing mix, and research and development strategies.

In addition, the scanner should train and motivate line managers to become sensitive to environmental trends, encouraging them to identify strategic versus tactical information and to understand the strategic problems of the firm as opposed to short-term sales policy and tactics.

Scanning may be for a short term or a long term. Short-term scanning is useful for programming various operations, and the term may last up to two years. Long-term scanning is needed for strategic planning, and the term may vary from three to twenty-five years. Rarely does the term of scanning go beyond twenty-five years. The actual time horizon is determined by the nature of the product. Forest products, for example, require a longer time horizon because the company must make decisions about tree planting almost twenty-five years ahead of harvesting those trees for lumber. Fashion designers, however, may not extend scanning beyond four years. As a rule of thumb, the appropriate time horizon for environmental scanning is twice as long as the duration of the company's strategic plan. For example, if a company's strategic plan extends eight years into the future, the environmental scanning time horizon should be sixteen years. Likewise, a company with a five-year planning horizon should scan the environment for ten years. Presumably, then, a multiproduct, multimarket company should have different time horizons for environmental scanning. Using this rule of thumb, a company can be sure not only of discovering relevant trends and their impact on its products/markets but also of implementing necessary changes in its strategy to marshal opportunities provided by the environment and to avert environmental threats.

Discussed below are the major problems companies face in the context of environmental scanning.[28] Many of these problems are, in fact, dilemmas that may be attributed to a lack of theoretical frameworks on the subject.

1. The environment per se is too broad to be tracked by an organization; thus, it is necessary to separate the relevant from the irrelevant environment. Separating the relevant from the irrelevant may not be easy since, in terms of perceptible realities, the environment of all large corporations is as broad as the world itself. Therefore, a company needs to determine what criteria to develop to select information on a practical basis.
2. Another problem is concerned with determining the impact of an environmental trend, that is, with determining its meaning for business. For example, what does the feminist movement mean for a company's sales and new business opportunities?
3. Even if the relevance of a trend and its impact are determined, making forecasts of the trend poses another problem. For example, how many women will be in managerial positions ten years from now?
4. A variety of organizational problems hinder environmental scanning. Presumably, managers are the company's ears and eyes and therefore should be good sources for perceiving, studying, and channeling pertinent information within the organization. But managers are usually so tied up mentally and physically within their specific roles that they simply ignore happenings in the environment. The structuring of organizations by specialized functions can be blamed for this problem to a certain extent. In addition, organizations often lack a formal system for receiving, analyzing, and finally disseminating environmental information to decision points.
5. Environmental scanning requires "blue sky" thinking and "ivory tower" working patterns to encourage creativity, but such work perspectives are often not justifiable in the midst of corporate culture.
6. Frequently top managers, because of their own values, consider dabbling in the future a waste of resources; therefore, they adopt unkind attitudes toward such projects.
7. Many companies, as a matter of corporate strategy, like to wait and see; therefore, they let industry leaders, the ones who want to be first in the field, act on their behalf.
8. Lack of normative approaches on environmental scanning is another problem.
9. Often, a change is too out of the way. It may be perceived, but its relationship to the company is not conceivable.
10. It is also problematic to decide what department of the organization should be responsible for environmental scanning. Should marketing research undertake environmental scanning? How about the strategic planning office? Who else should participate? Is it possible to divide the work? For example, the SBUs may concentrate on their products, product lines, markets, and industry. The corporate level may deal with the rest of the information.
11. Often, information is gathered that is overlapping, leading to a waste of resources. There are frequently informational gaps that require duplication of effort.

SUMMARY

The environment is ever-changing and complex; thus firms must constantly scan and monitor it. Environmental scanning may be undertaken at three levels in the organization: corporate level, SBU level, and product/market level. This chapter approaches scanning primarily from the SBU viewpoint. The environments discussed are technological, political, economic, social, and regulatory.

Environmental scanning evolves over a long haul. It is sufficient, therefore, to make a humble beginning rather than designing a fully structured system.

The impact of different environments on marketing strategy was illustrated by numerous examples. A step-by-step procedure for scanning the environment was outlined. A systematic approach to environmental scanning, using such techniques as trend-impact analysis, cross-impact analysis, and the delphi method, was illustrated. Feasible organizational arrangements for environmental scanning were examined, and problems that companies face in their scanning endeavors were discussed.

DISCUSSION QUESTIONS

1. Explain the meaning of environmental scanning. Which constituents of the environment, from the viewpoint of a corporation, require scanning?
2. Illustrate with examples the relevance of technological, political, economic, social, and regulatory environments in the context of marketing strategy.
3. Who in the organization should be responsible for scanning the environment? What role may consultants play in helping corporations in their environmental scanning activity?
4. Explain the use of trend-impact analysis and cross-impact analysis with reference to environmental scanning.
5. How may the delphi technique be useful in the context of environmental scanning? Give an example.
6. What types of responsibilities should be assigned to the person in charge of environmental scanning?
7. How may managers be involved in environmental scanning?

NOTES

1. Katy McLaughlin, "Sorry, We're Booked: The Restaurant Slump Ends," *The Wall Street Journal*, March 30, 2004, p. D1.
2. "Who Gets Eaten and Who Gets to Eat," *The Economist*, July 12, 2003, p. 61.
3. Anne Fisher, "America's Most Admired Companies," *Fortune*, March 19, 2007, p. 88.
4. Stan Davis and Christopher Meyer, *Blur* (Reading MA: Addison-Wesley, 1998).
5. Francis Joseph Aguilar, *Scanning the Business Environment* (New York: Macmillion Co., 1967): 40.
6. Subhash C. Jain, "Environmental Scanning: How the Best Companies Do It," *Long Range Planning*, April 1984, pp. 117–28. Also see: "Flying Solo," *Time*, October 24, 2000, p. 32.
7. "Mastering Uncertainty," *The Economist*, March 17, 2006.
8. "What's Foiling the Aluminum Can," *BusinessWeek*, October 6, 1997, p. 106. Also see: "Bar Codes Better Watch Their Backs," *BusinessWeek*, July 14, 2003, p. 42.
9. "A World of Connections," *The Economist*, April 28, 2007.
10. Brooks Barnes and Peter Grant, "CBS, NBC Deals Accelerate Shift in TV Landscape," *The Wall Street Journal*, November 8, 2005, p. A1. Also see: "The Cameraphone Revolution," *BusinessWeek*, April 12, 2004.
11. Moises Naim, "Megaplayers vs. Micropowers," *Foreign Policy*, July/August, 2006, p. 96.
12. Alex Taylor III, "Rough Road Ahead," *Fortune*, March 17, 1997, p. 115.
13. Raju Narisetti, "P&G, Seeing Shoppers Were Being Confused, Overhauls Marketing," *The Wall Street Journal*, January 15, 1997, p. A1.
14. Melanie Wells, "Pepsi's New Challenge," *Fortune*, January 20, 2003, p. 69.
15. Neil Buckley, "Finding a Taste for Profit: Obesity Forces Food Companies to Rethink Their Recipies," *Financial Times*, August 31, 2004, p. 13. Also see: "Coke Considers Mid-Calorie Drink," *Financial Times*, January 26, 2004, p. 18.
16. Michelle Conlin, "UnMarried America," *BusinessWeek*, October 20, 2003, p. 106, and Brad Dorfman "Help! Grocery Store Still Overwhelming to Men," reuters.com.
17. Deborah Orr, "Changing Appetites," *Forbes*, October 2, 2000, p. 76. Also see: "The Next Society," *The Economist*, November 3, 2001.
18. See Stan Rapp and Thomas L. Collins, *Beyond Maxi-Marketing: The New Power of Caring And Daring* (New York: McGraw-Hill, Inc., 1994): 10–11.
19. Barbara Kiviat, "The End of Customer Service," *Time*, March 24, 2008, p. 42.
20. *Time*, July 7, 2003, p. 68.
21. "Yolkless Dunkin' Donuts," *BusinessWeek*, April 6, 1991, p. 70.
22. Richard Gibson, "Lean and Mean: Hardee's Joins Low-Fat Fray," *Wall Street Journal*, July 15, 1991, 2003, p. B1. Also see: Eleena De Lisser, "Taco Bell, Low-Price King, Will Offer Low-Fat Line," *Wall Street Journal*, February 6, 1995, p. B1.

23. See: Clark Gilbert and Joseph L. Bower, "Disruptive Change: When Trying Harder Is Part of the Problem," *Harvard Business Review*, May 2002, pp. 94–101.
24. "This Merlot Is For You," *BusinessWeek*, September 30, 2002, p. 66.
25. John Greenwald, "Frito-Lay Under Snack Attack," *Time*, June 10, 1996, pp. 62–63.
26. Ravi S. Achrol and Philip Kotler, "Marketing in the Network Economy," *Journal of Marketing*, Special Issue, 1999, pp. 146–163.
27. Andy Serwer, "P&G's Covert Operation," *Fortune*, September 17, 2001, pp. 42–45.
28. See: Hugh Courtney, Jane Kirkland and Patrick Viguerie, "Strategy Under Uncertainty," *Havard Business Review*, November–December, 1997.

APPENDIX: SCANNING TECHNIQUES

Traditionally, environmental scanning has been implemented mainly with the use of conventional methods, including marketing research, economic indicators, demand forecasting, and industry studies. But the use of such conventional techniques for environmental scanning is not without pitfalls. These techniques have failed to provide reliable insights into the future. Discussed below are a variety of new techniques that have been adapted for use in environmental scanning.

Extrapolation Procedures

These procedures require the use of information from the past to explore the future. Obviously, their use assumes that the future is some function of the past. There are a variety of extrapolation procedures that range from a simple estimate of the future (based on past information) to regression analysis.

Historical Analogy

Where past data cannot be used to scan an environmental phenomenon, the phenomenon may be studied by establishing historical parallels with other phenomena. Assumed here is the availability of sufficient information on other phenomena. Turning points in the progression of these phenomena become guideposts for predicting the behavior of the phenomenon under study.

Intuitive Reasoning

This technique bases the future on the "rational feel" of the scanner. Intuitive reasoning requires free thinking unconstrained by past experience and personal biases. This technique, therefore, may provide better results when used by freelance think tanks than when used by managers on the job.

Scenario Building

This technique calls for developing a time-ordered sequence of events bearing a logical cause-and-effect relationship to one another. The ultimate forecast is based on multiple contingencies, each with its respective probability of occurrence.

Cross-Impact Matrices

When two different trends in the environment point toward conflicting futures, this technique may be used to study these trends simultaneously for their effect. As the name implies, this technique uses a two-dimensional matrix, arraying one trend along the rows and the other along the columns.

Some of the features of cross-impact analyses that make them attractive for strategic planning are (a) they can accommodate all types of eventualities (social or technological, quantitative or qualitative, and binary events or continuous functions), (b) they rapidly discriminate important from unimportant sequences of developments, and (c) their underlying rationale is fully retraceable from the analysis.

Morphological Analysis

This technique requires identification of all possible ways to achieve an objective. For example, the technique can be employed to anticipate innovations and to develop optimum configurations for a particular mission or task.

Network Models

There are two types of network methods: contingency trees and relevance trees. A contingency tree is simply a graphical display of logical relationships among environmental trends that focuses on branch-points where several alternative outcomes are possible. A relevance tree is a logical network similar to a contingency tree but is drawn in a way that assigns degrees of importance to various environmental trends with reference to an outcome.

Missing-Link Approach

The missing-link approach combines morphological analysis and the network method. Many developments and innovations that appear promising and marketable may be held back because something is missing. Under these circumstances, this technique may be used to scan new trends to see if they provide answers to any missing links.

Model Building

This technique emphasizes the construction of models following deductive or inductive procedures. Two types of models may be constructed: phenomenological models and analytic models. Phenomenological models identify trends as a basis for prediction but make no attempt to explain underlying causes. Analytic models seek to identify underlying causes of change so that future developments may be forecast on the basis of a knowledge of their causes.

Delphi Technique

The delphi technique is the systematic solicitation of expert opinion. Based on reiteration and feedback, this technique gathers opinions of a panel of experts on happenings in the environment.

PART III

Strategic Capabilities and Direction

Chapter 7
Measuring Strengths and Weaknesses

Chapter 8
Developing Marketing Objectives and Goals

Chapter Outline

7.1 Meaning of Strengths
    and Weaknesses
7.2 Studying Strengths and
    Weaknesses: State of the Art
7.3 Systematic Measurement of
    Strengths and Weaknesses
    7.3.1 What Markets Do We Have?
    7.3.2 How Is Each Market Served?
7.4 Analyzing Strengths
    and Weaknesses
7.5 Concept of Synergy

Chapter **7**

Measuring Strengths and Weaknesses

To measure is the first step to improve.

SIR WILLIAM PETTY

A business does not perform well by accident. Good performances occur because the people directing the affairs of the business interact well with the environment, capitalizing on its strengths and eliminating underlying weaknesses. In other words, to operate successfully in a changing environment, the business should plan its future objectives and strategies around its strengths and downplay moves that bear on its weaknesses. Thus, assessment of strengths and weaknesses becomes an essential task in the strategic process.

In this chapter, a framework will be presented for identifying and describing a business's strengths and weaknesses. The framework also provides a systematic scheme for an objective appraisal of the performance and strategic moves of the marketing side of business.

The appraisal of the marketing function has traditionally been pursued in the form of a marketing audit that stresses the review of current problems. From the strategic point of view, the review should go further to include the future as well.

Strengths and weaknesses in the context of marketing are relative phenomena. Strengths today may become weaknesses tomorrow and vice versa. This is why a penetrating look at the different aspects of a business's marketing program is essential. This chapter is directed toward these ends—searching for opportunities and the means for exploiting them and identifying weaknesses and the ways in which they may be eliminated.

7.1 MEANING OF STRENGTHS AND WEAKNESSES

Strengths refer to the competitive advantages and other distinctive competencies that a company can exert in the marketplace. Andrews notes that "the distinctive competence of an organization is more than what it can do; it is what it can do particularly well."[1] **Weaknesses** are constraints that hinder movements in certain directions. For example, a business short of cash cannot afford to undertake a large-scale promotional offensive. In developing marketing strategy, the business should, among other things, dig deeply into its skills and competencies and chart its future in accordance with these competencies.

As an example, in many businesses, service—speed, efficiency, personal attention—makes a crucial difference in gaining leverage in the marketplace.

Companies that score higher than their rivals in the category of service have a real competitive strength. McDonald's may not be everyone's idea of the best place in town to dine, but at its level, McDonald's provides a quality of service that is the envy of the industry. Whether at a McDonald's in a rural community or in the downtown area of a large city, the customer gets exactly the same service. Every McDonald's employee is supposed to strictly follow the rules. Cooks must turn, never flip, hamburgers one, never two, at a time. If they haven't been purchased, Big Macs must be discarded ten minutes after being cooked; french fries after seven minutes. Cashiers must make eye contact with and smile at every customer.

Similarly, visitors to Disney World come home impressed with its cleanliness and with the courtesy and competence of the staff. The Disney World management works hard to make sure that the 14,200 employees are, as described in a *Fortune* article, "people who fulfill an expectation of wholesomeness, always smiling, always warm, forever positive in their approach."[2]

7.2 STUDYING STRENGTHS AND WEAKNESSES: STATE OF THE ART

A systematic scheme for analyzing strengths and weaknesses is still in embryonic form.[3] One finds few scholarly works on the subject of strengths and weaknesses. An interesting study on the subject was done by Stevenson, who examined six companies.[4] He was interested in the process of defining strengths and weaknesses in the context of strategic planning. He was concerned with the company attributes examined, the organizational scope of the strengths and weaknesses identified, the measurement employed in the process of definition, the criteria used for distinguishing a strength from a weakness, and the sources of information used. Exhibit 7.1 illustrates the process in detail.

Companies should make targeted efforts to identify their competitive strengths and weaknesses. This is a far from easy process, however. Many companies, especially the large ones, have only the vaguest notion of the nature and degree of the competencies that they may possess. The sheer multiplicity of production stages and the overlapping among product lines hinder clear-cut assessment of the competitive strength of a single product line. Despite such problems, development of competitive strategy depends on having a complete perspective on strengths and weaknesses. Success requires putting the best foot forward.

Unique strengths may lie in different areas of the business and may impact the entire company. Stevenson found a general lack of agreement on suitable definitions, criteria, and information used to measure strengths and weaknesses. In addition to the procedural difficulties faced by managers in their attempts to measure strengths and weaknesses, the need for situational analysis, the need for self-protection, the desire to preserve the status quo, and the problems of definition and computational capacity complicated the process. Stevenson makes the following suggestions for improvement of the process of defining strengths and weaknesses. The manager should:

- Recognize that the process of defining strengths and weaknesses is primarily an aid to the individual manager in the accomplishment of his or her task.
- Develop lists of critical areas for examination that are tailored to the responsibility and authority of each individual manager.
- Make the measures and the criteria to be used in evaluation of strengths and weaknesses explicit so that managers can make their evaluations against a common framework.
- Recognize the important strategic role of defining attributes as opposed to efficiency or effectiveness.
- Understand the difference in the use of identified strengths and identified weaknesses.[5]

Despite the primitive state of the art, today many more companies review their strengths and weaknesses in the process of developing strategic plans than did 15 years ago. Strengths and weaknesses may be found in the functional areas of the business, or they may result from some unusual interaction of functions. The following example illustrates how a study of strengths and weaknesses may uncover opportunities that might otherwise have not been conceived. A national distiller and marketer of whiskeys may possess such strengths as sophistication in natural commodity trading associated with its grain purchasing procedures; knowledge of complex warehousing procedures and inventory control; ability and connections associated with dealing in state political structures (i.e., state liquor stores, licensing agencies, and so on); marketing experience associated with diverse wholesale and retail outlets; and advertising experience in creating brand images. If these strengths are properly analyzed with a view to seeking diversification opportunities, it appears that the distiller has unique abilities for successfully entering the business of selling building products, such as wood flooring or siding and composition board. The distiller's experience in commodity trading can be transferred to trading in lumber; its experience in dealing with political groups can be used to gain building code acceptances; and its experience in marketing can apply to wholesalers (e.g., hardware stores and do-it-yourself centers) of building products.

The case of XYZ Corporation, on the other hand, illustrates how a company can get into trouble if it does not carefully consider its strengths and weaknesses. XYZ was a Northfield, Illinois, company with a penchant for diversifying into businesses that were in vogue in the stock market. Until it was reorganized as the Lori Corporation in 1985, it had been in the following businesses: office copying machines, mobile homes, jewelry, speedboats and cabin cruisers, computers, video recording systems, and small buses. Despite entry into some glamorous fields, XYZ did not share the growth and profits that other companies in some of these fields achieved. This is because XYZ entered new and diverse businesses without relating its moves to its basic skills and competencies. For example, despite the fact that it was the first company to develop a photocopy process, developing its process even before Xerox, its total market share for all types

Which Attributes Can Be Examined?	With What Organizational Entity Is the Manager Concerned?	What Types of Measurements Can the Manager Make?	What Criteria Are Applicable to Judge a Strength or a Weakness?	How Can the Manager Get the Information to Make These Assessments?
Organizational structure	The corporation	Measure the existence of an attribute	Historical experience of the company	Personal observation
Major policies	Groups	Measure an attribute's efficiency	Intracompany competition	Customer contacts
Top manager's skills	Division	Measure an attribute's effectiveness	Direct competitors	Experience
Information system	Departments		Other companies	Control system documents
Operation procedures	Individual employees		Consultant's opinions	Meetings
Planning system			Normative judgments based on management's understanding of literature	Planning system documents
Employee attitudes			Personal opinions	Employees
Manager's attitudes			Specific targets of accomplishment, such as budgets, etc.	Subordinate managers
Union agreements				Superordinate managers
Technical skills				Peers
Research skills				Published documents
New product ideas				Competitive intelligence
Production facilities				Board members
Demographic characteristics of personnel				Consultants
Distribution network				Journals
Sales force's skill				Books
Breadth of product line				Magazines
Quality control procedures				Professional meetings
Stock market reputation				Government economic indicators
Knowledge of consumer's needs				
Market domination				

Source: Reprinted from "Defining Corporate Strengths and Weaknesses," by Howard H. Stevenson, *Sloan Management Review*, Vol. 17, No. 3 (Spring, 1976), p. 54, by permission of the publisher. Copyright © 1976 by Sloan Management Review Association. All rights reserved.

Exhibit 7.1 Steps in the Process of Assessing Strengths and Weaknesses

of copier machines and supplies in 1984 was well under 3 percent. XYZ Corporation could not keep pace with technological improvements nor with service on installed machines, an essential competency in the copier business. In addition, it overextended itself so much so that managerial controls were rendered inadequate. The company finally got out of all its *trendy* businesses and was reorganized in 1985 to design, manufacture, and distribute costume jewelry, fashion jewelry, and fashion accessories. Beginning in 1990, the company started making some money for its owners.[6]

7.3 SYSTEMATIC MEASUREMENT OF STRENGTHS AND WEAKNESSES

The strengths and weaknesses of a business can be measured at different levels in the organization: corporate, SBU, and product/market level. The thrust of this chapter is on the measurement of strengths and weaknesses at the SBU level. However, as the strengths and weaknesses of the SBU are a composite of the strengths and weaknesses of different products/markets, the major portion of the discussion will be devoted to the measurement of the marketing strengths and weaknesses of a product/market.

Exhibit 7.2 illustrates the factors that require examination in order to delineate the strengths and weaknesses of a product/market. These factors, along with competitive perspectives, describe the strengths and weaknesses of the product.

Current strategic posture constitutes a very important variable in developing future strategy. Although it is difficult and painful to try to understand current strategy if formal planning has not been done in the past, it is worth the effort to probe current strategy to achieve a good beginning in strategic planning.

The emphasis here is on the study of the current strategy of a product/market. Before undertaking such a study, however, it is desirable to assess company-wide perspectives by raising such questions as:

1. What underlies our company's success, given competitor's patterns of doing business?
2. Are there any characteristics and traits that have been followed regularly?
3. To what strategic posture do these characteristics and traits lead?
4. What are the critical factors that could make a difference in the success of the strategy?
5. To what extent are critical factors likely to undergo a change? What may be the direction of change?

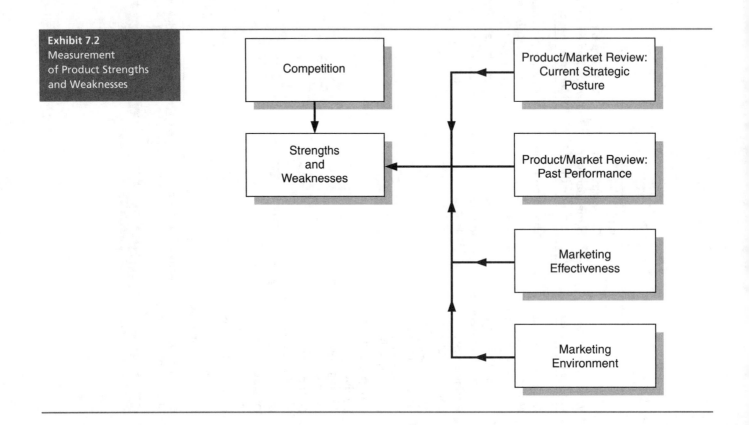

Exhibit 7.2
Measurement
of Product Strengths
and Weaknesses

Competition

Strengths and Weaknesses

Product/Market Review: Current Strategic Posture

Product/Market Review: Past Performance

Marketing Effectiveness

Marketing Environment

These questions cannot be answered entirely objectively; they call for creative responses. Managers often disagree on various issues. For example, the vice president of marketing of a company that had recently made a heavy investment in sales training considered this investment to be a critical success factor. He thought a well-trained sales staff was crucial for developing new business. On the other hand, the vice president of finance saw only that the investment in training had increased overhead. Though disagreements of this sort are inevitable, a review of current strategy is very important. The operational scheme for studying current strategy from the point of view of the entire corporation outlined below has been found useful.

1. Begin with an identification of the actual current scope of the company's activities. The delineation of customer/product/market emphasis and concentration will give an indication of what kind of a company the company is currently.
2. An analysis of current scope should be followed by identification of the pattern of actual past and existing resource deployments. This description will show which functions and activities receive the greatest management emphasis and where the greatest sources of strength currently lie.
3. Given the identification of scope and deployment patterns, an attempt should be made to deduce the actual basis on which the company has been competing. Such competitive advantages or distinctive competencies represent the central core of present performance and future opportunities.
4. Next, on the basis of observation of key management personnel, the actual performance criteria (specifications), emphasis, and priorities that have governed strategic choices in the past should be determined.

As far as marketing is concerned, the strategy for a product is formulated around one or more marketing mix variables. In examining present strategy, the purpose is to pinpoint those perspectives of the marketing mix that currently dominate strategy. The current strategy of a product may be examined by seeking answers to the following two questions:

1. What markets do we have?
2. How is each market served?

7.3.1 What Markets Do We Have?

Answering this question involves consideration of several aspects of the market:

1. Recognize different market segments in which the product is sold.
2. Build a demographic profile of each segment.
3. Identify important customers in each segment.
4. Identify those customers who, while important, also do business with competitors.
5. Identify reasons each important customer may have for buying the product from us. These reasons may be economic (e.g., lower prices), functional (e.g., product features not available in competing products), and psychological (e.g., "this perfume matches my individual chemistry").
6. Analyze the strategic perspective of each important customer as it concerns the purchase of our product. This analysis is relevant primarily for business customers. For example, an aluminum company should attempt to study the strategy of a can manufacturer as far as its aluminum can business is concerned. Suppose that the price of aluminum is consistently rising, and more and more can manufacturers are replacing all-aluminum cans with cans of a new alloy of plastic and paper. Such strategic perspectives of an important customer should be examined.
7. Consider changes in each customer's perspectives that may occur in the next few years. These changes may become necessary because of shifts in the customer's environment (both internal and external), abilities, and resources.

If properly analyzed, information concerning what markets a company has should provide insight into why customers buy the company's products and how likely it is that they will do business with the company in the future. For example, a paper manufacturer discovered that most of his customers did business with him because, in their opinion, his delivery schedules were more flexible than those of other suppliers. The quality of his paper might have been superior, too, but this was not strategically important to his customers.

7.3.2 How Is Each Market Served?

The means the company employs to serve different customers may be studied by analyzing the information contained in Exhibit 7.3. A careful examination of this information will reveal the current strategy the company utilizes to serve its main markets. For example, analysis of the information in Exhibit 7.3 may reveal the following facts pertaining to a breakfast cereal: Of the seven different segments in the market, the product is extremely popular in two segments. Customers buy the product mainly for health reasons or because of a desire to consume "natural" foods. This desire is strong enough for customers to pay a premium price for the product. Further, customers are willing to make a trip to another store (other than their regular grocery

Exhibit 7.3
Information for Recognizing Present Market Strategy

1. Basis for segmenting the market.
2. Definition of the markets for the product.
3. Profile of customers in each segment: age, income level, occupation, geographical location, etc.
4. Scope and dimensions of each market: size, profitability, etc.
5. Expected rate of growth of each segment.
6. Requirements for success in each market.
7. Market standing with established customers in each segment: market share, pattern of repeat business, expansion of customer's product use.
8. Benefits that customers in different segments derive from the product: economics, better performance, displaceable costs, etc.
9. Reasons for buying the product in different segments: product features, awareness, price, advertising, promotion, packaging, display, sales assistance, etc.
10. Customer attitudes in different segments: brand awareness, brand image (mapping), etc.
11. Overall reputation of the product in each segment.
12. Purchase or use habits that contribute to these attitudes.
13. Reasons that reinforce customer's faith in the company and product.
14. Reasons that force customers to turn elsewhere for help in using the product.
15. Life-cycle status of the product.
16. Story of the product line: quality development, delivery, service.
17. Product research and improvements planned.
18. Market share: overall and in different segments.
19. Deficiencies in serving or assisting customers in using the product.
20. Possibility of reducing services in areas where customers are becoming more self-sufficient.
21. Resource base: nature of emerging and developing resources—technical, marketing, financial—that could expand or open new markets for the product.
22. Geographic coverage of the product market.
23. Identification of principal channels: dealer or class of trade.
24. Buying habits and attitudes of these channels.
25. Sales history through each type of channel.
26. Industry sales by type of outlet: retail, wholesale, institutional; and by major types of outlets within each area: department store, chain store, specialty store, etc.
27. Overall price structure for the product.
28. Trade discount policy.
29. Variations in price in different segments.
30. Frequency of price changes.
31. Promotional deals offered for the product.
32. Emphasis on different advertising media.
33. Major thrust of advertising copy.
34. Sales tips or promotional devices used by salespeople.

store) to buy this product. Different promotional devices keep customers conscious of the "natural" ingredients in the product. This analysis may point toward the following strategy for the product:

1. Concentrate on limited segments.
2. Emphasize the naturalness of the product as its unique attribute.
3. Keep the price high.
4. Pull the product through with heavy doses of consumer advertising.

Where strategy in the past has not been systematically formulated, recognition of current strategy will be more difficult. In this case, strategy must be inferred from the perspectives of different marketing decisions.

Evaluation of past performance is invaluable in measuring strengths and weaknesses because it provides historical insights into a company's marketing strategy and its success. Historical examination should not be limited to simply noting the directions that the company adopted and the results it achieved but should also include a search for reasons for these results. Exhibit 7.4 shows the type of information that is helpful in measuring past performance.

Strategically, the following three types of analysis should be undertaken to measure past performance: product performance profile, market performance profile, and financial performance profile. Information used for developing a product performance profile is shown in Exhibit 7.5. A product may contribute to company performance in six different ways: through profitability, image of product leadership, furnishing a base for further technological growth, support of total product line, utilization of company resources (e.g., utilization of excess plant capacity), and provision of customer benefits (vis-à-vis the price paid). An example of this last type of contribution is a product that is a small but indispensable part of another product or process with low cost relative to the value of the finished product. Take the case of a manufacturer of oscilloscopes. An oscilloscope is sold along with a computer. It is used to help install the computer, to test it, and to monitor its performance. The cost of the oscilloscope is small when one considers the essential role it plays in the use of the much more expensive computer.

A market performance profile is illustrated in Exhibit 7.6. In analyzing how well a company is doing in the segments it serves, a good place to begin is with the marginal profit contribution of each customer or customer group. Other measures used are market share, growth of end user markets, size of customer base, distribution strength, and degree of customer loyalty. Of all these, only distribution strength requires some explanation. Distribution and dealer networks can greatly influence a company's performance because it takes an enormous effort to cultivate dealers' loyalty and get repeat business from them. Distribution strength, therefore, can make a significant difference in overall performance.

The real value of a strategy must be reflected in financial gains and market achievements. To measure financial performance, four standards may be employed for comparison: (a) the company's performance, (b) competitor's performance, (c) management expectations, and (d) performance in terms of resources committed. With these standards, for the purposes of marketing strategy, financial performance can be measured with respect to the following variables:

1. Growth rate (percentage).
2. Profitability (percentage), that is, rate of return on investment.
3. Market share (percentage as compared with that of principal competitors).
4. Cash flow.

It is desirable to analyze financial performance for a number of years to determine the historical trend of performance. To show how financial performance analysis may figure in formulating marketing strategy, consider the example:

A maker of confectioneries that offers more than one hundred brands, flavors, and packagings prunes its lines—regularly and routinely—of those items having the lowest profit contribution, sales volume, and vitality for future growth.

Each individual product has been ranked on these three factors, and an "index of gross profitability" has been prepared for each in conjunction with annual marketing plans. These plans take into account longer-term objectives for the business, trends in consumer wants and expectations, competitive factors in the marketplace and, lastly, a deliberately ordered "prioritization" of the company's resources. Sales and profit performance are then checked against projected targets at regular intervals through the year, and the indexes of gross profitability are adjusted when necessary.

Exhibit 7.4
Information for
Measuring Past
Performance

The Consumer

Identify if possible the current "light," "moderate," and "heavy" users of the product in terms of

1. Recent trends in percentage of brand's volume accounted for by each group.
2. The characteristics of each group as to sex, age, income, occupation, income group, and geographical location.
3. Attitudes toward the product and category and copy appeals most persuasive to each group.

The Product

Identify the current consumer preference of the brand versus primary competition (and secondary competition, if available), according to

1. Light, moderate, and heavy usage (if available).
2. The characteristics of each group as to sex, age, income, occupation, income group, geographical location, size of family, etc.

Shipment History

Identify the recent shipment trends of the brand by total units and units/M population (brand development), according to districts, regions, and nation.

Spending History

Identify the recent spending trends on the brand by total dollars, dollar/M population, and per unit sold for advertising, for promotion, and for total advertising and promotion by districts, regions, and nation.

Profitability History

Identify the recent trends of list price, average retail price (by sales areas), gross profit margins, and profit before taxes (PBT), *in addition* to trends in

1. Gross profit as a percentage of net sales.
2. Total marketing as percentage of gross profit and per unit sold.
3. PBT as a percentage of net sales and per unit sold.
4. ROFE (Return of Funds Employed) for each recent fiscal year.

Share of Market History

Identify recent trends of

1. The brand's share of market nationally, regionally, and district-wide.
2. Consumption by total units and percentage gain/loss versus year ago nationally, regionally, and district-wide.
3. Distribution by pack size nationally, regionally, and district-wide.

Where applicable, trends in all of the above data should also be identified by store classification: chain versus independent (large, medium, and small).

Total Market History

Identify recent trends of the total market in terms of units and percentage gain/loss versus year ago nationally, regionally, and district-wide per M population, store type, county size, type of user (exclusive versus partial user), retail price trends, and by user characteristics (age, income, etc.).

Competitive History (Major Brands), Where Available

Identify significant competitive trends in share; consumption levels by sales areas and store types; media and promotion expenditures; types of media and promotion; retail price differentials; etc.

Exhibit 7.5						
Product Performance Profile Contribution to Company Performance						
Product Line	Profitability	Product Leadership	Technological Growth	Support of Total Product Line	Utilization of Company Resources	Provision of Customer Benefits
⎯⎯						
⎯⎯						
⎯⎯						
⎯⎯						

The firm's chief executive emphasizes that even individual items whose indexes of profitability are ranked at the very bottom are nonetheless profitable and paying their way by any customary standard of return on sales and investment. But the very lowest-ranking items are regularly reviewed; and, on a judgmental basis, some are marked for pruning at the next convenient opportunity. This opportunity is most likely to arrive when stocks of special ingredients and packaging labels for the items have been exhausted.

In a recent year, the company dropped 16 items that were judged to be too low on its index of gross profitability. Calculated and selective pruning is regarded within the company as a healthy means of working toward the best possible mix of products at all times. It has the reported advantages of increasing efficiencies in manufacturing as a result of cutting the "down time" between small runs, reducing inventories, and freeing resources for the expansion of the most promising items—or the development of new ones—without having to expand productive capacity. Another important benefit is that the sales force concentrates on a smaller line containing only the most profitable products with the largest volumes. On the negative side, however, it is acknowledged that pruning, as the company practices it, may result in near-term loss of sales for a line until growth of the rest of the items can compensate.

Marketing is concerned with the activities required to facilitate the exchange process toward managing demand. The perspectives of these activities are founded on marketing strategy. To develop a strategy, a company needs a philosophical orientation. Four different types of orientation may be considered: manufacturing, sales, technology, and marketing. Manufacturing orientation emphasizes a physical product or a service and assumes that the customer will be pleased with it if it has been well conceived and developed. Sales orientation focuses on promoting the product to make the customer want it. The thrust of technology orientation is on reaching the customer through new and varied products made feasible through technological innovations. Under marketing orientation, first the customer group that the firm wishes to serve is designated. Then the requirements of the target group are carefully examined. These requirements become the basis of product or service conception and development, pricing, promotion, and distribution. Exhibit 7.7 contrasts marketing-oriented companies with manufacturing-, sales-, and technology-oriented firms.

An examination of Exhibit 7.7 shows that good marketers should think like general managers. Their approach should be unconstrained by functional boundaries. Without neglecting either near- or medium-term profitability, they should concentrate on building a position for tomorrow.[7]

Despite the lip service that has been paid to marketing for more than 30 years, it remains one of the most misunderstood functions of a business. According to Canning, only a few corporations, Procter & Gamble, McDonald's, General Electric, and Merck, for example, really understand and practice true

Exhibit 7.6						
Market Performance Profile Contribution to Company Performance						
Market Segments	Profitability	Market Share	Growth of End User Markets	Size of Customer Base	Distribution Strength	Degree of Customer Loyalty
⎯⎯						
⎯⎯						
⎯⎯						
⎯⎯						

Exhibit 7.7
Comparison of Four Kinds of Companies

	Orientation			
	Manufacturing	**Sales**	**Technology**	**Marketing**
Typical strategy	Lower cost	Increase	Push research	Build share profitability
Normal structure	Functional	Functional or profit centers	Profit centers	Market or product or brand; decentralized profit responsibility
Key systems	Plant P&L's Budgets	Sales forecasts Results vs. plan	Performance tests R&D plans	Marketing plans
Traditional skills	Engineering	Sales	Science and engineering	Analysis
Normal focus	Internal efficiencies	Distribution channels; short-term sales results	Product performance	Consumers Market share
Typical response to competitive pressure	Cut costs	Cut price Sell harder	Improve product	Consumer research, planning, resting, refining
Overall mental set	"What we need to do in this company is get our costs down and our quality up."	"Where can I sell what we make?"	"The best product wins the day."	"What will the consumer buy that we profitably make?"

Source: Edward G. Michaels, "Marketing Muscle: Who Needs It?" *Business Horizons*, May–June, 1982, p. 72. © 1982 by the foundation for the School of Business at Indiana University. Reprinted by permission.

marketing.[8] Inasmuch as marketing orientation is a prerequisite for developing a successful marketing strategy, it behooves a company to thoroughly examine its marketing orientation. The following checklist of ten questions provides a quick self-test for a company that wants a rough measure of its marketing capabilities.

- Has your company carefully segmented the various groups of the consumer market that it serves?
- Do you routinely measure the profitability of your key products or services in each of these consumer market segments?
- Do you use market research to keep abreast of the needs, preferences, and buying habits of consumers in each segment?
- Have you identified the key buying factors in each segment, and do you know how your company compares with its competitors on these factors?
- Is the impact of environmental trends (demographic, competitive, lifestyle, governmental) on your business carefully gauged?
- Does your company prepare and use an annual marketing plan?
- Is the concept of "marketing investment" understood—and practiced—in your company?
- Is profit responsibility for a product line pushed below the senior management level?
- Does your organization "talk" marketing?
- Did one of the top five executives in your company come up through marketing?

The number of "yes" answers to these questions determines the marketing orientation of a company. For example, a score of nine or ten "yes" answers would mean that the company has a strong marketing capability; six to eight would indicate that the firm is on the way; and fewer than six "yes" answers would stress that the firm is vulnerable to marketing-minded competitors. Essentially, truly marketing-oriented firms are consumer oriented, take an integrated approach to planning, look further ahead, and have highly developed marketing systems. In such firms, marketing dominates the corporate culture. A marketing-oriented culture is beneficial in creating sustainable competitive advantage. It becomes one of the internal strengths an organization possesses that is hard to imitate, is more durable, not transparent nor transferable.

This analysis reveals the overall marketing effectiveness of the company and highlights the areas that are weak and require management action. Management may take appropriate action—management training, reorganization, or installation of measures designed to yield improvements with or without the help of consultants. If weaknesses cannot be addressed, the company must live with them, and the marketing strategist should take note of them in the process of outlining the business's future direction. A marketing orientation perspective of a firm largely reflects its marketing excellence.

Chapter 6 was devoted to scanning the environment at the macro level. This section looks at the environment from the product/market perspective. Environmental scanning at the macro level is the job of a staff person positioned at the corporate, division, group, or business unit level. The person concerned may go by any of these titles: corporate planner, environmental analyst, environmental scanner, strategic planner, or marketing researcher.

Monitoring the environment from the viewpoint of products/markets is a line function that should be carried out by those involved in making marketing decisions because product/market managers, being in close touch with various marketing aspects of the product/market, are in a better position to read between the lines and make meaningful interpretations of the environment. The constituents of the product/market environment are social and cultural effects, political influences, ethical considerations, legal requirements, competition, economic climate, technological changes, institutional evolution, consumerism, population, location of consumers, income, expenditure patterns, and education. Not all aspects of the environment are relevant for every product/market. The scanner, therefore, should first choose which parts of the environment influence the product/market before attempting to monitor them.

The strategic significance of the product/market environment is well illustrated by the experience of Fanny Farmer Candy Shops, a familiar name in the candy industry. Review of the environment in the mid-1980s showed that Americans were watching their waistlines but that they were also indulging in chocolate. In 1983, the average American ate nearly 18 pounds of confections—up from a low of 16 pounds in 1975. Since the mid-1980s, the market for upscale chocolates has been growing rapidly. Chocolates are again popular gifts for dinner parties, providing a new opportunity for candy makers, who traditionally relied on Valentine's Day, Easter, and Christmas for over half of their annual sales.

Equipped with this analysis of the environment, Fanny Farmer decided to become a dominant competitor in the upscale segment. It introduced rich new specialty chocolates at $14 to $20 per pound, just below $25-per-pound designer chocolates (a market dominated by Godiva, a subsidiary of Campbell Soup Co., and imports such as Perugina of Italy) and above Russell Stover and Fannie May candies, whose chocolates averaged $10 per pound. The company thinks that its new strategic thrust will advance its position in the candy market, though implementing this strategy will require overcoming a variety of problems.[9]

7.4 ANALYZING STRENGTHS AND WEAKNESSES

The study of competition, current strategic perspectives, past performance, marketing effectiveness, and marketing environment provides insights into information necessary for designating strengths and weaknesses. Exhibit 7.8 provides a rundown of areas of strength as far as marketing is concerned. Where feasible, strengths should be stated in objective terms. Exhibit 7.8 is not an all-inclusive list, but it indicates the kind of strength a company may have over its competitors. It should be noted that most areas of strength relate to the excellence of personnel or are resource based. Not all factors have the same significance for every product/market; therefore, it is desirable to first recognize the critical factors that could directly or indirectly bear on a product's performance. For example, the development of an improved product may be strategic for drug companies. On the other hand, in the case of cosmetics, where image building is usually important, advertising may be a critical factor. After-sale service may have significance for products such as copying machines, computers, and elevators. Critical factors may be chosen with reference to Exhibit 3.6.

Exhibit 7.8 Areas of Strength	1. Excellence in product design and/or performance (engineering ingenuity). 2. Low-cost, high-efficiency operating skill in manufacturing and/or in distribution. 3. Leadership in product innovation. 4. Efficiency in customer service. 5. Personal relationships with customers. 6. Efficiency in transportation and logistics. 7. Effectiveness in sales promotion. 8. Merchandising efficiency—high turnover of inventories and/or of capital. 9. Skillful trading in volatile price movement commodities. 10. Ability to influence legislation. 11. Highly efficient, low-cost facilities. 12. Ownership or control of low-cost or scarce raw materials. 13. Control of intermediate distribution or processing units. 14. Massive availability of capital. 15. Widespread customer acceptance of company brand name (reputation). 16. Product availability, convenience. 17. Customer loyalty. 18. Dominant market share position, deal from a position of strength. 19. Effectiveness of advertising. 20. Quality sales force. 21. Make and sell products of highest quality. 22. High integrity as a company

From among the critical factors, an attempt should be made to sort out strengths. It is also desirable to rate different strengths for a more objective analysis.

An example from the personal computer business illustrates the measurement of strengths and weaknesses. In 1987, Apple, IBM, Tandy, and imports from Taiwan and South Korea were the major competitors. In 1990, the major firms in the industry included Apple, IBM, Tandy, Compaq Computers, Zenith Electronics, and imports from Taiwan and South Korea. In 1998, the front-runners in the business were IBM, Compaq, Apple, Dell, and Packard-Bell. Among these, Compaq Computer Corp. was the leader in worldwide PC shipments, followed by IBM. As a matter of fact, in the important U.S. market IBM ranked fourth, trailing even the late-entrant Packard Bell Electronics Inc. Five years later, in 2003, Hewlett-Packard (after the merger with Compaq) was the largest company in the business. It had a 20 percent market share in worldwide PC shipments followed by Dell with 12 percent, and IBM with 7.5 percent share.[10] By 2007, Dell had overtaken Hewlett-Packard as the largest PC company. Meanwhile, IBM sold its PC business to a Chinese company, Lenovo Group, and it continued to lose market share in the U.S. market. At the same time, Apple gained ground. Exhibit 7.9 lists the relative strengths of these firms in 2007.

Success in the personal computer business depends on mastery of the following three critical areas:

- **Low-cost production**—As personal computer hardware becomes increasingly standardized, the ability to provide the most value for the dollar greatly influences sales. The most vertically integrated companies have the edge.
- **Distribution**—Retailers have shelf space for just two or three brands; only those makers that are able to keep their products in the customer's line of sight are likely to survive. Dell developed a new distribution channel to its advantage, i.e., directly reaching the customers online and by phone.
- **IT Services**—Basic maintenance and support including choice of software.

Without these three strengths in place, a company cannot make it in the personal computer business. Thus, Texas Instruments withdrew from the field in 1983 because it did not have enough enterprise software. Fortune Systems dropped out in 1984. Zenith Electronics left the field in the early 1990s; Tandy became an insignificant contestant. Even imports from Taiwan and South Korea could not cope with changes in the fast-moving PC business, in which prices fall more than 20 percent a year, and product life cycles have shortened to as little as six months. Introducing a new generation of PCs just three months

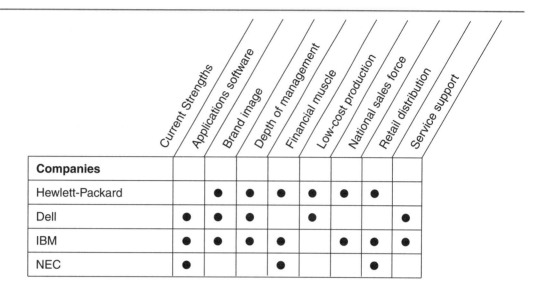

Exhibit 7.9
Relative Strengths of Personal Computer Firms in 2007

Companies	Current Strengths	Applications software	Brand image	Depth of management	Financial muscle	Low-cost production	National sales force	Retail distribution	Service support
Hewlett-Packard		●	●	●	●	●	●		
Dell	●	●	●		●				●
IBM	●	●	●	●			●	●	●
NEC	●				●		●		

behind schedule can cost a company 40 percent to 50 percent of the gross profit it had planned to make on the new line.[11]

Both IBM and Apple appeared to be in trouble in 1995. By 1998 however, both of them had been able to overcome their weaknesses in logistics, manufacturing, and research and development. IBM reorganized the PC division and hired seasoned executives to fix the problems. In addition, the company shifted the focus to push for market share instead of profit to realize production efficiencies and lower parts costs. IBM hopes that with these measures, and the company's unrivaled assets—the IBM name and the brand equity built over many years—in its favor, it can create a solid position in the coming years.[12] Apple made remarkable changes in its operations and it did overcome some of the weaknesses. Despite that in 2003 it lingered on as an insignificant player in the industry.[13] As mentioned above, toward the end of 2004, Lenovo Group Ltd., China's largest personal computer maker, bought IBM's PC-making business for $1.25 billion. Since then, two companies have played a leading role in the industry, i.e., Dell and Hewlett-Packard. At the end of 2007, Dell had a market share of 29% followed by Hewlett-Packard's (both HP and Compaq brands) 26%. Other companies active in the PC business were Apple, Toshiba and Gateway with market shares of 8%, 6% and 5% respectively.[14] The above discussion illustrates the importance of analyzing strengths and weaknesses to define objectives and strategies for the future.

As another example, consider the Walt Disney Company strengths. Its theme parks offer a *genuinely distinctive experience* built around universally recognized animated characters or *brand name*. The brand is supported by near-flawless delivery in every element of the business, coupled with a full range of marketing communications, all reinforcing the "childhood at any age" theme that Disney represents worldwide. Customers have powerful associations with the brands that often go back generations.[15] These strengths offer the following benefits in developing future strategy:

- **Substantial, often dominant, and sustained market share.** Disney occupies the dominant market position in animated features and theme parks, and is a leading producer of feature films.
- **Premium prices**. Disney theme parks, hotels, and merchandise command significantly higher prices than competitors' offerings.
- **A track record of extending the brand to new products**. The Disney brand was launched in 1923 with the first Mickey Mouse cartoon, and has since been extended to films, network and cable television programs and studios, theme parks, hotels, merchandise, and a National Hockey League team, the Mighty Ducks.
- **New markets.** From its original focus on children, the brand has been extended to the full range of demographic groups ("ages 8 to 80").
- **New geographic areas**. Disney's films and products are distributed worldwide. Theme parks are open or planned in the United States, Europe, and Asia.

Strengths should be further examined to undertake what may be called opportunity analysis (matching strengths, or competencies, to opportunity). Opportunity analysis serves as an input in establishing a company's economic mission. Opportunity analysis is also useful in developing an individual product's objectives. In Exhibit 7.10 the objectives for a food product are shown as they emerged from a study of its strengths. The objectives were to produce a premium product for an unscored segment and to develop a new channel outlet. In other words, at the product level, the opportunity analysis seeks to answer such questions as: What opportunity does the company have to capitalize on a competitor's weaknesses? Modify or improve the product line or add new products? Serve the needs of more customers in existing markets or develop new markets? Improve the efficiency of current marketing operations?

Opportunities emerge from the changing environment. Thus, environmental analysis is an important factor in identifying opportunities. Exhibit 7.11 suggests a simple format for analyzing the impact of the environment.

The concept of opportunity analysis may be illustrated with Procter & Gamble's moves in the over-the-counter (OTC) drug business. There is an increasing sense in the drug industry that the OTC side of the drug business will grow faster than prescription sales will grow. Consumers and insurers are becoming more interested in OTC medications, partly because of the steep cost of prescription drugs. Further, with the patents of many major medicines expiring, generic drugs will pose an even greater threat to prescription products. Consequently, drugmakers are taking another look at the OTC business, where a well-marketed brand can keep a franchise alive long after exclusive rights have expired. A case in point is the success of Advil, an ibuprofen-based painkiller.

To participate in the growing OTC market, Procter & Gamble has been making inroads into the industry. As a matter of fact, Procter & Gamble is already one of the largest marketers of OTC drugs. But to expand its position in the field, Procter & Gamble decided to speed things up by entering into partnerships

Exhibit 7.10 Matching Strengths with Opportunities			
Strength	**Likely Impact**	**Opportunity Furnished by the Environment**	**Objectives and Goals**
Customer loyalty	Incremental product volume increases	A trend of changing taste	Develop a premium product
	Price increases for premium quality/ service	An identified geographic shift of part of the market	Introduce the existing product in a segment hitherto not served
	New product introductions	A market segment neglected by the industry	Develop a new channel for the product, etc.
Cordial relationships with channels	New product introductions	A product-related subconscious need not solicited by the competition	
	Point-of-purchase advertising	A product weakness of the competition	
	Reduction of delivered costs through distribution innovations	A distribution weakness of the competition	
	Tied-in products	Technical feasibility for improving existing package design	
	Merchandising differentiation	A discovered new use for the product or container	

	Trends	Impact	Timing of Impact	Response Time	Urgency	Threats	Opportunities

Exhibit 7.11 Impact of Environmental Trends

with drugmakers and technology companies. By linking its formidable marketing strength with emerging technological advances in medicine, Procter & Gamble hopes to propel itself to the forefront of the health market.

Thus, the company is working on new formulations for minoxidil, a baldness remedy, and other new products promoting hair growth with UpJohn. It joined with Syntex to market Aleve, a nonprescription version of Anaprox, an anti-inflammatory drug that is popular with arthritis sufferers. It hopes to sell De-Nol, a gastrointestinal medicine made by Dutch drugmaker Gist-Brocades, as an ulcer treatment. It may use technology from Alcide, a Connecticut maker of disinfectants, in its toothpaste or mouthwash business. Finally, Procter & Gamble has an agreement with Triton Biosciences and Cetus to use Betaseron, a synthetic interferon, that it hopes will fight the common cold.[16]

In this case, it was Procter & Gamble's marketing strength that led it to enter the OTC drug industry. The opportunity was furnished by the environment—a concern for increasing health care costs—and many drug companies were glad to form alliances with this established OTC marketer.

In recent years flavored coffees have become popular and companies like Starbucks have established a new style of coffee drinking. Considering this as an opportunity to expand, Dunkin' Donuts expanded into coffee trendiness offering four or more blends of fresh-brewed coffee, even hot and cold specialty drinks—all at a fraction of the Starbucks price. Value, together with no-nonsense service, has made Dunkin' Donuts a favorable place for coffee lovers.

To continue to ride on this opportunity, the chain has decided to be the latest in fast-food business, offering in addition to specialty coffee, oven-baked bagels and fat-free muffins. In its redone stores, the tacky old pink décor is giving way to a more upscale "ripe raisin" hue. And not content to stop at morning munchies, the company has set its sights on the lunch crowd.[17] Similarly, McDonald's has decided to add coffee bars in practically all of its U.S. outlets, serving cappucinos, lattes, mochas and the Frappe.[18]

An interesting observation with regard to opportunity analysis, made by Andrews, is relevant here:

The match is designed to minimize organizational weakness and to maximize strength. In any case, risk attends it. And when opportunity seems to outrun present distinctive competence, the willingness to gamble that the latter can be built up to the required level is almost indispensable to a strategy that challenges the organization and the people in it. It appears to be true, in any case, that the potential capability of a company tends to be underestimated. Organizations, like individuals, rise to occasions, particularly when the latter provide attractive reward for the effort required.[19]

In the process of analyzing strengths, underlying weaknesses should also be noted. Exhibit 7.12 is a list of typical marketing weaknesses. Appropriate action must be taken to correct weaknesses. Some weaknesses have SBU-wide bearing; others may be weaknesses of a specific product. SBU weaknesses must be examined, and necessary corrective action must be incorporated into the overall marketing strategy. For example, weaknesses 3, 5, and 6 in Exhibit 7.12 could have SBU-wide ramifications. These must be addressed by the chief marketing strategist. The remaining three weaknesses can be corrected by the person in charge of the product/market with which these weaknesses are associated.

Exhibit 7.12 Typical Marketing Weaknesses	1. Inadequate definition of customer for product/market development. 2. Ambiguous service policies. 3. Too many levels of reporting in the organizational setup. 4. Overlapping channels. 5. Lack of top management involvement in new product development. 6. Lack of quantitative goals.

7.5 CONCEPT OF SYNERGY

Before concluding the discussion of strengths and weaknesses, it will be desirable to briefly introduce the concept of synergy. **Synergy**, simply stated, is the concept that the combined effect of certain parts is greater than the sum of their individual effects. Let us say, for example, that product 1 contributes X and product 2 contributes Y. If they are produced together, they may contribute X+Y+Z. We can say that Z is the synergistic effect of X and Y being brought together and that Z represents positive synergy. There can be negative synergy as well. The study of synergy helps in analyzing new growth opportunities. A new product, for instance, may have such a high synergistic effect on a company's existing product(s) that it may be an extremely desirable addition.

Conceptually, business synergies take one of six forms:[20]

(a) **Shared Know-How**. Units often benefit from sharing knowledge or skills. They may, for example, improve their results by pooling their insights into a particular process, function, or geographic area.

(b) **Coordinated Strategies**. It sometimes works to a company's advantage to align the strategies of two or more of its businesses. Divvying up markets among units may, for instance, reduce inter-unit competition. And coordinating responses to shared competitors may be a powerful and effective way to counter competitive threats.

(c) **Shared Tangible Resources.** Units can sometimes save a lot of money by sharing physical assets or resources. By using a common manufacturing facility or research laboratory, for example, they may gain economies of scale and avoid duplicated effort.

(d) **Vertical Integration.** Coordinating the flow of products or services from one unit to another can reduce inventory costs, speed product development, increase capacity utilization, and improve market access.

(e) **Pooled Negotiating Power.** By combining their purchases, different units can gain greater leverage over suppliers, reducing the cost or even improving the quality of the goods they buy. Companies can also gain similar benefits by negotiating jointly with other stakeholders, such as customers, governments, or universities.

(f) **Combined Business Creation.** The creation of new businesses can be facilitated by combining know-how from different units, by extracting discrete activities from various units and combining them in a new unit, or by establishing internal joint ventures or alliances.

	SYNERGY MEASURES						
	Startup Economies			**Operating Economies**			
Synergistic Contribution to:	**Investment**	**Operating**	**Timing**	**Investment**	**Operating**	**Expansion of Present Sales**	**New Product and Market Areas**	**Overall Synergy**
Parent								
New entry								
Joint opportunities								

Exhibit 7.13 Measurement of the Synergy of a New Product/Market Entry

Quantitative analysis of synergy is far from easy. However, synergy may be evaluated following the framework illustrated in Exhibit 7.13. This framework refers to a new product/market entry synergy measurement.

A new product/market entry contribution could take place at three levels: contribution to the parent company (from the entry), contribution to the new entry (from the parent), and joint opportunities (benefits that accrue to both as a result of consolidation). As far as it is feasible, entries in Exhibit 7.13 should be assigned a numerical value, such as increase in unit sales by 20 percent, time saving by two months, reduction in investment requirements by 10 percent, and so on. Finally, various numerical values may be given a common value in the form of return on investment or cash flow.

SUMMARY

This chapter outlined a scheme for the objective measurement of strengths and weaknesses of a product/market, which then become the basis of identifying SBU strengths and weaknesses. Strengths and weaknesses are tangible and intangible resources that may be utilized for seeking growth of the product. Factors that need to be studied in order to designate strengths and weaknesses are competition, current strategic perspectives, past performance, marketing effectiveness, and marketing environment. Present strategy may be examined with reference to the markets being served and the means used to serve these markets.

Past performance was considered in the form of financial analysis, ranging from simple measurements, such as market share and profitability, to developing product and market performance profiles. Marketing effectiveness was related to marketing orientation, which may be determined with reference to questions raised in the chapter. Finally, various aspects of the product/market marketing environment were analyzed.

These five factors were brought together to delineate strengths and weaknesses. An operational framework was introduced to conduct opportunity analysis. Also discussed was the concept of synergy. The analysis of strengths and weaknesses sets the stage for developing marketing objectives and goals, which will be discussed in the next chapter.

DISCUSSION QUESTIONS

1. Why is it necessary to measure strengths and weaknesses?
2. Because it is natural for managers and other employees to want to justify their actions and decisions, is it possible for a company to make a truly objective appraisal of its strengths and weaknesses?
3. Evaluate the current strategy of Hewlett-Packard related to personal computers and compare it with the strategy being pursued by Dell.
4. Develop a conceptual scheme to evaluate the current strategy of a bank.
5. Is it necessary for a firm to be marketing oriented to succeed? What may a firm do to overcome its lack of marketing orientation?
6. Making necessary assumptions, perform an opportunity analysis for a packaged-goods manufacturer.
7. Explain the meaning of synergy. Examine what sort of synergy Procter & Gamble achieved by going into the frozen orange juice business.

NOTES

1. Kenneth R. Andrews, *The Concept of Corporate Strategy* (Homewood, IL: Dow Jones-Irwin, 1971): 97.
2. Jeremy Main, ''Toward Service without a Snare,'' *Fortune*, March 23, 1981, pp. 64–66.
3. Philip Kotler, William T. Gregor, and William H. Rodgers III, ''The Marketing Audit Comes of Age,'' *Sloan Management Review*, Winter 1989, pp. 49–62.

4. Howard H. Stevenson, "Defining Corporate Strengths and Weaknesses: An Exploratory Study" (Ph.D. diss., Harvard Business School, 1969).

5. Howard H. Stevenson, "Defining Corporate Strengths and Weaknesses," *Sloan Management Review*, Spring 1976, p. 66.

6. *Moody's Industrial Manual*, 2006, pp. 5480–83.

7. Larry Selden and Ian C. MacMillan, "Manage Customer-Centric Innovation—Systematically," *Harvard Business Review*, April 2006, pp. 108–116.

8. Gordon Canning, Jr., "Is Your Company Marketing Oriented?" *Journal of Business Strategy*, May–June 1988, pp. 34–36. Also see: Charles Fomburn, "The Value to be Found in Corporate Reputation," *Financial Times*, November 27, 2002, p. 7.

9. David Tuller, "Repackaging Chocolates," *Working Women*, January 1997, pp. 45–46; updated based on interview with a company executive.

10. "Sheltering From The Storm," *The Economist*, September 8, 2001, p. 63.

11. Jeffrey A. Schmidt, "The Strategic Review," *Planning Review*, July/August 1998, pp. 14–19.

12. Eric Nee, "The Hard Truth Behind a Shotgun Wedding," *Fortune*, October 1, 2001, p. 190.

13. David Kirkpatrick, "The Second Coming of Apple," *Fortune*, November 9, 1998, p. 87.

14. Katie Massal, "Apple's U.S. Mac Market Share Rises to 8.1 Percent," Appleinsider.com, 2008.

15. Frank Rose, "Mickey Online," *Fortune*, September 28, 1995, p. 273.

16. "Where P&G's Brawn Doesn't Help Much," *BusinessWeek*, November 10, 1997, p. 112.

17. "Dunkin' Donuts is on a Coffee Rush," *BusinessWeek*, March 16, 1998, p. 7.

18. Janet Adamy, "McDonald's Takes on A Weakened Starbucks," *The Wall Street Journal,* January 7, 2008, p. A1.

19. Andrews, *op. cit.*, p. 100.

20. Michael Goold and Andrew Campbell, "Desperately Seeking Synergy," *Harvard Business Review*, September–October 1998, pp. 130–139.

Chapter Outline

8.1 **Framework for Defining Objectives**
8.2 **Corporate Strategic Direction**
  8.2.1 Strategic Direction and Organizational Perspectives
  8.2.2 Changing the Strategic Direction
  8.2.3 Corporate Strategic Direction and Strategy Development
8.3 **SBU Objectives**
8.4 **Business Mission**
8.5 **SBU Objectives and Goals**
8.6 **Product/Market Objectives**
  8.6.1 Technological Leadership
  8.6.2 Social Contribution
  8.6.3 Strengthening of National Security
  8.6.4 International Economic Development
8.7 **Process of Setting Objectives**

Chapter 8

Developing Marketing Objectives and Goals

"Would you tell me please, which way I ought to go from here?" said Alice. "That depends a good deal on where you want to get to," said the Cheshire Cat

LEWIS CARROLL (ALICE IN WONDERLAND)

An organization must have an objective to guide its destiny. Although the objective in itself cannot guarantee the success of a business, its presence will certainly mean more efficient and financially less wasteful management of operations.

Objectives form a specific expression of purpose, thus helping to remove any uncertainty about the company's policy or about the intended purpose of any effort. To be effective, objectives must present startling challenges to managers, jolting them away from traditional in-a-rut thinking. If properly designed, objectives permit the measurement of progress. Without some form of progress measurement, it may not be possible to know whether adequate resources are being applied or whether these resources are being managed effectively. Finally, objectives facilitate relationships between units, especially in a diversified corporation, where the separate goals of different units may not be consistent with some higher corporate purpose.

Despite its overriding importance, defining objectives is far from easy: there is no mechanical or expert instant-answer method. Rather, defining goals as the future becomes the present is a long, time-consuming, and continuous process. In practice, many businesses run either without any commonly accepted objectives and goals or with conflicting objectives and goals. In some cases, objectives may be understood in different ways by different executives. At times, objectives may be defined in such general terms that their significance for the job is not understood. For example, a product manager of a large company once observed that "our objective is to satisfy the customer and increase sales." After cross-checking with the vice president of sales, however, she found that the company's goal was making a minimum 10 percent after-tax profit even when it meant losing market share. "Our objective, or whatever you choose to call it, is to grow," the vice president of finance of another company said. "This is a profit-oriented company, and thus we must earn a minimum profit of 15 percent on everything we do. You may call this our objective." Different companies define their objectives differently. It is the task of the CEO to set the company's objectives and goals and to obtain for them the support of his or her senior colleagues, thus paving the way for other parts of the organization to do the same.

The purpose of this chapter is to provide a framework for goal setting in a large, complex organization. A first step in planning is usually to state objectives so that, knowing where you are trying to go, you can figure out how to get there. However, objectives cannot be stated in isolation; that is, objectives cannot be formed without the perspectives of the company's current business, its past performance, resources, and environment. Thus, the subject matter discussed in previous chapters becomes the background material for defining objectives and goals.

8.1 FRAMEWORK FOR DEFINING OBJECTIVES

This chapter deals with defining objectives and goals at the SBU level. Because SBU objectives should bear a close relationship to corporate strategic direction, we will start with a discussion of corporate direction and will then examine SBU objectives and goals. Product/market objectives will also be discussed, as they are usually defined at the SBU level and derived from SBU objectives.

The framework discussed here assumes the perspectives of a large corporation. In a small company that deals with a limited line of related products or services, corporate and SBU objectives may be identical. Likewise, in a company with a few unrelated products, an SBU's objectives may be no different from those of the product/market.

It is desirable to define a few terms one often confronts in the context of objective setting: mission, policy, objective, goal, and strategic direction. A **mission** (also referred to as corporate concept, vision, or aim) is the CEO's conception of the organization's raison d'être, or what it should work toward, in the light of long-range opportunity. A **policy** is a written definition of general intent or company position designed to guide and regulate certain actions and decisions, especially those of major significance or of a recurring nature. An **objective** is a long-range purpose that is not quantified or limited to a time period (e.g., increasing the return on stockholders' equity). A **goal** is a measurable objective of the business, judged by management to be attainable at some specific future date through planned actions. An example of a goal is to achieve 10 percent growth in sales within the next two years. **Strategic direction** is an all-inclusive term that refers to the network of mission, objectives, and goals. Although we recognize the distinction between an objective and a goal, we will consider these terms simultaneously in order to give the discussion more depth.

The following are frequently cited types of frustrations, disappointments, or troubling uncertainties that should be avoided when dealing with objectives:

1. Lack of credibility, motivation, or practicality.
2. Poor information inputs.
3. Defining objectives without considering different options.
4. Lack of consensus regarding corporate values.
5. Disappointing committee effort to define objectives.
6. Sterility (lack of uniqueness and competitive advantage).

Briefly, if objectives and goals are to serve their purpose well, they should represent a careful weighing of the balance between the performance desired and the probability of its being realized:

Strategic objectives which are too ambitious result in the dissipation of assets and the destruction of morale, and create the risk of losing past gains as well as future opportunities. Strategic objectives which are not ambitious enough represent lost opportunity and open the door to complacency.[1]

8.2 CORPORATE STRATEGIC DIRECTION

Corporate strategic direction is defined in different ways. In some corporations, it takes the form of a corporate creed, or code of conduct, that defines perspectives from the viewpoint of different stakeholders. At other corporations, strategic direction is stated in the form of policy statements that provide guidelines for implementing strategy. In still others, corporate direction is outlined in terms of objective statements. However expressed, corporate direction consists of broad statements that represent a company's position on various matters and serve as an input in defining objectives and in formulating strategy at lower echelons in the organization.

A company can reasonably expect to achieve a leadership position or superior financial results only when it has purposefully laid out its strategic direction. Every outstanding corporate success is based on a direction that differentiates the firm's approach from that of others. Specifically, strategic direction helps in

1. Identifying what "fits" and what needs the company is well suited to meet.
2. Analyzing potential synergies.
3. Undertaking risks that simply cannot be justified on a project basis (e.g., willingness to pay for what might appear, on a purely financial basis, to be a premium for acquisition).

4. Providing the ability to act fast (presence of strategic direction not only helps in adequately and quickly scanning opportunities in the environment but capitalizing on them without waiting).
5. Focusing the search for opportunities and options more clearly.

To illustrate the point, consider the corporate direction of Dow Chemical Company, which has persisted for more than 70 years.[2] Herbert Dow founded and built Dow Chemical on one fundamental and energizing idea: start with a cheap and basic raw material; then develop the soundest, lowest-cost process possible. This idea, or direction, defined certain imperatives Dow has pursued consistently over time:

1. First, don't copy or license anyone else's process. In other words, as Dow himself put it, "Don't make a product unless you can find a better way to do it."
2. Second, build large, vertically integrated complexes to achieve maximum economies of scale; that is, maintain cost leadership by building the most technologically advanced facilities in the industry.
3. Third, locate near and tie up abundant sources of cheap raw materials.
4. Fourth, build in bad times as well as good. In other words, become the large-volume supplier for the long pull and preempt competitors from coming in. Be there, in place, when the demand develops. The experience of Merck, the pharmaceutical company, is relevant here. In the early part of the new century the company had a number of major medicines going off patent. The stock price was falling, and revenues were flat—and this was before the Vioxx mess, which hurt the company badly. The whole industry was in a rut, and Merck's was deeper than most. So Merck increased investment in R&D from 12% of revenue in 1999 to 20% in 2004. Looking back, the company's CEO remarked that when you are "being hammered from all sides, it's important to reinforce your core values—and research excellence was one of ours." In this case, hindsight was rewarded: Merck now has the plumpest pipeline in the business, and investors have seen handsome returns.[3]
5. Fifth, maintain a strong cash flow so that the corporation can pursue its vision.

Over the years, Dow has consistently acted in concert with this direction, or vision. It has built enormous, vertically integrated complexes at Midland, Michigan; Freeport, Texas; Rotterdam, Holland; and the Louisiana Gulf Coast. And it has pursued with almost fanatical consistency the obtaining of secure, low-cost sources of raw materials.

8.2.1 Strategic Direction and Organizational Perspectives

Pursuing this direction has, in turn, mandated certain human and organizational characteristics of the company and its leadership. For example, Dow has been characterized as a company whose management shows exceptional willingness to take sweeping but carefully thought out gambles.[4] The company has had to make leaps of faith about the pace and direction of future market and technological developments. Sometimes, as in the case of shale oil, these have taken a very long time to materialize. Other times, these leaps of faith have resulted in failure. But as Ben Branch, a top Dow executive for many years, was fond of saying, "Dow encourages well-intentioned failure."

To balance this willingness to take large risks, the company has had to maintain an extraordinary degree of organizational flexibility to give it the ability to respond quickly to unexpected changes. For example, "Dow places little emphasis on, and does not publish, organization charts, preferring to define areas of broad responsibility without rigid compartments. Its informal style has given the company the flexibility to react quickly to change."[5]

8.2.2 Changing the Strategic Direction

Over the years, Dow's direction has had to expand to accommodate a changing world, its own growth, and expanding horizons of opportunity. The expansion of its direction, or vision, has included, for example:

1. Recognition of the opportunities and the need to diversify downstream into higher-value-added, technologically more sophisticated intermediate and end-use products, with the concomitant requirement for greater technical selling capability after World War II.

2. The opportunity and the imperative to expand abroad. In fact, Herbert Dow's core vision may have initially been retarded expansion abroad, since raw material availability was not as good in Europe or in Japan as it was in the United States and since it was harder to achieve comparable economies of scale.

3. The need to reorganize and decentralize foreign operations, setting them up on a semiautonomous basis to give them room for growth and flexibility.

But throughout its history, Dow's leadership has consistently held to a guiding concept that perhaps has been best articulated as this: "In this business, it's who's there with the vision, the money, and the guts to seize an opportunity."[6]

In the 1980s, Xerox Corporation faced the task of redefining its strategic direction in response to a new technological era. There were three different schools of thought within the company. One school believed it should stick to its core competency—copying—and that paper would be there for a long time. Another view, held by a smaller group, felt Xerox ought to quickly transform itself into a systems company. Based on its leading-edge technology at Palo Alto Research Center, this view suggested getting out of the paper world as quickly as possible. A third school of thought said that the company should finesse the differences and focus on being "the" office company. After all, it was reasoned, the company had a worldwide direct sales force that reached into almost every office around the world; it could sell anything through that direct sales force.

Looking carefully at the future, the company concluded that paper would not go away, but that its use would change. The creation, storage, and communication of documents will increasingly be in electronic form; however, for many years, people will prefer the paper document display to the electronic document display. They will print out their electronic documents closer to their end use and then throw them away, thereby making paper a transient display medium. Xerox chose to bridge the gap between the paper and electronic world. The strategic direction was defined to not remain the *copier* company, but to become the *document* company.[7]

Similarly, back in 2003, Kodak shifted its strategic direction from its traditional film and camera business to digital technology, challenging established rivals such as Fuji Film, Canon, Hewlett-Packard and Epson. It made new investments in digital color and inkjet printers, cameras and medical imagining. Kodak has been a leader in photographic equipment for more than a century but the threat posed by digital technology forced it to change its strategic direction.[8]

8.2.3 Corporate Strategic Direction and Strategy Development

What can be concluded from this brief history of Dow Chemical's corporate direction? First, it seems clear that, for more than 50 years, all of Dow's major strategic and operating decisions have been amazingly consistent. They have been consistent because they have been firmly grounded in some basic beliefs about where and how to compete. The direction has evidently made it easier to make the always difficult and risky long-term/short-term decisions, such as investing in research for the long haul or aggressively tying up sources of raw materials.[9]

This direction, or vision, has also driven Dow to be aggressive in generating the cash required to make risky investments possible. Most important, top management seems never to have eschewed its leadership role in favor of becoming merely stewards of a highly successful enterprise. They have been constantly aware of the need to question and reshape Dow's direction, while maintaining those elements that have been instrumental in achieving the company's long-term competitive success. Dow illustrates that corporate direction gives coherence to a wide range of apparently unrelated decisions, serving as the crucial link among them.

Without exception, the corporate direction of all successful companies is based not only on a clear notion of the markets in which they compete but also on specific concepts of how they can sustain an economically attractive position in those markets. Their direction is grounded in deep understanding of industry and competitive dynamics and company capabilities and potential. Corporate direction should focus in general on continually strengthening the company's economic or market position, or both, in some substantial way. For example, Dow was not immobilized by existing industry relationships, current market shares, or its past shortcomings. It sought and found new ways to influence industry dynamics in its favor. Corporate direction should foster creative thinking about realistic and achievable options, driving product, service and new business decisions. Its impact can actually be measured in the marketplace. In other words, in addition to having thought through the questions of where and how to compete, top management should also make realistic judgments about (a) the capital and human resources that are required to compete and where they should come from, (b) the changes in the corporation's functional and cultural biases that must be accomplished, (c) the unique contributions that are required of the corporation (top management and staff) to support pursuit of the new direction by the SBUs, and (d) a guiding notion of the timing or pace of change within which the corporation should realistically move toward the new vision.

Mentioned below is the strategic direction of a number of companies:[10]

Merck	Sony
• Corporate social responsibility • Unequivocal excellence in all aspects of the company • Science-based innovation • Honesty and integrity • Profit, but profit from work that benefits humanity	• Elevation of the Japanese culture and national status • Being a pioneer—not following others; doing the impossible • Encouraging individual ability and creativity

Nordstrom	Walt Disney
• Service to the customer above all else • Hard work and individual productivity • Never being satisfied • Excellence in reputation; being part of something special	• No cynicism • Nurturing and promulgation of "wholesome American values" • Creativity, dreams, and imagination • Fanatical attention to consistency and detail • Preservation and control of the Disney magic

Philip Morris	
• The right to freedom of choice • Winning—beating others in a good fight • Encouraging individual initiative • Opportunity based on merit; no one is entitled to anything • Hard work and continuous self-improvement	

As can be noted, strategic direction is not an abstruse construct based on the inspiration of a solitary genius. It is a hard-nosed, practical concept based on the thorough understanding of the dynamics of industries, markets, and competition and of the potential of the corporation for influencing and exploiting these dynamics. It is only rarely the result of a flash of insight; much more often it is the product of deep and disciplined analysis.

Strategic direction frequently starts out fuzzy and is refined through a messy process of trial and error. It generally emerges in its full clarity only when it is well on its way to being realized. Likewise, changes in corporate direction occur by a long process and in stages.

Changing an established direction is much more difficult than starting from scratch because one must overcome inherited biases and set norms of behavior. Change is effected through a sequence of steps. First, a need for change is recognized. Second, awareness of the need for change is built throughout the organization by commissioning study groups, staff, or consultants to examine problems, options, contingencies, or opportunities posed by the sensed need. Third, broad support for the change is sought through unstructured discussions, probing of positions, definition of differences of opinion, and so on, among executives. Fourth, pockets of commitment are created by building necessary skills or technologies within the organization, testing options, and taking opportunities to make decisions to build support. Fifth, a clear focus is established, either by creating an ad hoc committee to formulate a position or by expressing in written form the specific direction that the CEO desires. Sixth, a definite commitment to change is obtained by designating someone to champion the goal and be accountable for its accomplishment. Finally, after the organization arrives at the new direction, efforts are made to be sensitive to the need for further change in direction, if necessary.

Exhibit 8.1 Hewlett-Packard's Corporate Direction	
	Profit To achieve sufficient profit to finance our company growth and to provide the resources we need to achieve our other corporate objectives *Customers* To provide products and services of the greatest possible value to our customers, thereby gaining and holding their respect and loyalty *Field of Interest* To enter new fields only when the ideas we have, together with our technical, manufacturing and marketing skills, assure that we can make a needed and profitable contribution in the field *Growth* To let our growth be limited only by our profits and our ability to develop and produce technical products that satisfy real customer needs *People* To help our own people share in the company's success, which they make possible: to provide job security based on their performance, to recognize their individual achievements, and to help them gain a sense of satisfaction and accomplishment from their work *Management* To foster initiative and creativity by allowing the individual great freedom of action in attaining well-defined objectives *Citizenship* To honor our obligations to society by being an economic, intellectual and social asset to each nation and each community in which we operate

Source: Company records.

Many companies make specific statements to designate their direction. Usually these statements are made around such aspects as target customers and markets, principal products or services, geographic domain, core technologies, concern for survival, growth and profitability, company philosophy, company self-concept, and desired public image. Some companies make only brief statements of strategic direction (sometimes labeled corporate objectives); others elaborate on each aspect in detail. Avon products expressed its strategic direction rather briefly: "to be the company that best understands and satisfies the product, service and self-fulfillment needs of women globally."[11] IBM defines its direction, which it calls principles, separately for each functional area. For example, in the area of marketing, the IBM principle is: "The marketplace is the driving force behind everything we do." In technology, it is "at our core, we are a technology company with an overriding commitment to quality."[12] Apple Computer states its direction five years into the future with detailed statements under the following headings: corporate concept, internal growth, external growth, sales goal, financial, planning for growth and performance, management and personnel, corporate citizenship, and stockholders and financial community. Exhibit 8.1 shows the strategic direction of the Hewlett-Packard Corporation. As can be noted, this company defines its strategic perspective through brief statements.

No matter how corporate strategic direction is defined, it should meet the following criteria. First, it should present the firm's perspectives in a way that enables progress to be measured. Second, the strategic direction should differentiate the company from others. Third, strategic direction should define the business that the company wants to be in, not necessarily the business that it is in. Fourth, it should be relevant to all the firm's stakeholders. Finally, strategic direction should be exciting and inspiring, motivating people at the helm.

8.3 SBU OBJECTIVES

An SBU was defined in Chapter 1 as a unit comprising one or more products having a common market base whose manager has complete responsibility for integrating all functions into a strategy against an identifiable external competitor. The following is the rationale for defining objectives at the SBU level.

The development of marketing planning has paralleled the growing complexity of business organizations themselves. The first change to take place was the shift from functionally organized companies with relatively narrow product lines and served-market focus to large diversified firms serving multiple markets with multiple product lines. Such firms are usually divided into product or market divisions, divisions may be divided into departments, and these in turn are often further divided into product lines or market segments. As this change gradually took place over the last twenty five years, "sales planning" was gradually replaced by "marketing planning" in most of these organizations. Each product manager or market manager drew up a marketing plan for his product line or market segment. These were aggregated together into an overall divisional "marketing plan." Divisional plans in turn were aggregated into the overall corporate plan.

Then, a further change took place. There emerged a growing acceptance of the fact that individual units or subunits within a corporation, e.g., divisions, product departments, or even product lines or market segments, might play different roles in achieving overall corporate objectives. Not all units and subunits needed to produce the same level of profitability; not all units and subunits had to contribute equally to cash flow objectives.

This concept of the organization as a "portfolio" of units and subunits having different objectives is at the very root of contemporary approaches to strategic marketing. It is commonplace today to hear businesses defined as "cash cows," "stars," "question marks," "dogs," etc.* It is in sharp contrast to practice in the 1970s and earlier which emphasized primarily sales and earnings (or return on investment) as a major measure of performance. Although different divisions or departments were intuitively believed to have different capabilities to meet sales and earning goals, these differences were seldom made explicit. Instead, each unit was expected to "pull its weight" in the overall quest for growth and profits.

With the recognition that organizational entities may differ in their objectives and roles, a new organizational concept has also emerged. This is the concept of a "business unit." A business unit may be a division, a product department, or even a product line or major market, depending on the circumstances. It is, however, usually regarded by corporate management as a reasonably autonomous profit center. Usually it has its own "general manager" (even though he may not have that title, he has general managerial responsibilities). Often it has its own manufacturing, sales, research and development, and procurement functions although in some cases some of these may be shared with other businesses (e.g., pooled sales). A business unit usually has a clear market focus. In particular it usually has an identifiable strategy and an identifiable set of competitors. In some organizations (the General Electric Company, for example), business units were clearly identified and defined. In other organizations, divisions or product departments were treated as relatively autonomous business units although they were not explicitly defined as such.

A business unit usually comprises several "program" units. These may be product lines, geographic market segments, end-user industries to which the company sells, or units defined on the basis of any other relevant segmentation dimension. Program units may also sometimes differ in their objectives. In such cases, the concept of a portfolio exists both in terms of business units within a corporate structure (or substructure, such as a group) or in terms of programs within a business unit. Usually, however, the business unit is a major focus of strategic attention, and strategic market plans are of prime importance at this level.

Thus, a large, complex organization may have a number of SBUs, each playing its unique role in the organization. Obviously, then, at the corporate level, objectives can be defined only in generalities. It is only at each SBU level that more specific statements of objectives can be made. Actually, it is the SBU mission and its objectives and goals that product/market managers need to consider in their strategic plans.

8.4 BUSINESS MISSION

Mission is a broad term that refers to the total perspectives or purpose of a business. The mission of a corporation was traditionally framed around its product line and expressed in mottoes: "Our business is textiles," "We manufacture cameras," and so on. With the advent of marketing orientation and technological innovations, this method of defining the business mission has been decried. It has been held that building

*These terms are defined in Chapter 10.

the perspectives of a business around its product limits the scope of management to enter new fields and thus to make use of growth opportunities. In a key article published in 1960, Levitt observed:

> The railroads did not stop growing because the need for passengers and freight transportation declined. That grew. The railroads are in trouble today not because the need was filled by others (cars, trucks, airplanes, even telephones), but because it was not filled by the railroads themselves. They let others take customers away from them because they assumed themselves to be in the railroad business rather than in the transportation business. The reason they defined their industry wrong was because they were railroad-oriented instead of transportation-oriented; they were product-oriented instead of customer-oriented.[13]

According to Levitt's thesis, the mission of a business should be defined broadly: an airline might consider itself in the vacation business, a publisher in the education industry, an appliance manufacturer in the business of preparing nourishment. In recent times, Levitt's proposition has been criticized, and the question has been raised as to whether simply extending the scope of a business leads far enough. The Boston Consulting Group, for example, has pointed out that the railroads could not have protected themselves by defining their business as transportation:

> Unfortunately, there is a prevalent notion that if one merely defines one's business in increasingly general terms such as transportation rather than railroading the road to successful competitive strategy will be clear. Actually, that is hardly ever the case. More often, the opposite is true. For example, in the case of the railroads, passengers and freight represent very different problems, and short haul vs. longer haul are completely different strategic issues. Indeed, as the unit train demonstrates, just coal handling is a meaningful strategic issue.[14]

In the early 1980s, Coca-Cola extended its business mission from being a soft drink marketer to a beverage company. Subsequently, the company bought three wine companies. A few years later, the company decided to leave the wine business. What happened is simply this: Although soft drinks and wine both are parts of the beverage industry, the management skills required to run a soft drink business are quite different from those required for the wine business. Coca-Cola overlooked some basics. For example, because wine must be aged, inventory costs run much higher than for soft drinks. Further, grapes must be bought ahead of time. Coke added to its work by vastly overestimating the amount of grapes it needed. Another key characteristic of the wine business is a requirement for heavy capital investment; Coke did not want to make that investment.[15]

As the Coca-Cola example illustrates, the problem with Levitt's thesis is that it is too broad and does not provide a common thread: a relationship between a firm's past and future that indicates where the firm is headed and that helps management to institute directional perspectives. The common thread may be found in marketing, production technology, finance, or management. ITT took advantage of its managerial abilities when it ventured into such diverse businesses as hotels and bakeries. Merrill Lynch found a common thread via finance in entering the real estate business. Bic Pen Company used its marketing strength to involve itself in the razor blade business. Thus, the mission cannot be defined by making abstract statements that one hopes will pave the way for entry into new fields.

It would appear that the mission of a business is neither a statement of current business nor a random extension of current involvements. It signifies the scope and nature of business, not as it is today, but as it could be in the future. The mission plays an important role in designating opportunities for diversification, either through research and development or through acquisitions. To be meaningful, the mission should be based on a comprehensive analysis of the business's technology and customer mission. Examples of technology-based definitions are computer companies and aerospace companies. Customer mission refers to the fulfillment of a particular type of customer need, such as the need for basic nutrition, household maintenance, or entertainment.

Whether the company has a written business mission statement or not is immaterial. What is important, however, is that due consideration is given to technological and marketing factors (as related to particular segments and their needs) in defining the mission. Ideally, business definitions should be based on a combination of technology and market mission variables, but some companies venture into new fields on the basis of one variable only. For example, Texas Instruments entered the digital watch market on the basis of its lead in integrated circuits technology. Procter & Gamble added over-the-counter remedies to its business out of its experience in fulfilling the ordinary daily needs of customers.

To sum up, the mission deals with these questions: What type of business do we want to be in at some future time? What do we want to become? At any given point, most of the resources of a business are frozen or locked into current uses, and the outputs in services or products are for the most part defined by current operations. Over an interval of a few years, however, environmental changes place demands on the business for new types of resources. Further, because of personnel attrition and depreciation of capital resources, management has the option of choosing the environment in which the company will operate and acquiring commensurate new resources rather than replacing the old ones in kind. This explains the importance of defining the business's mission. The mission should be so defined that it has a bearing on the business's strengths and weaknesses.

In his pioneering work on the subject, Abell has argued against defining a business as simply a choice of products or markets.[16] He proposes that a business be defined in terms of three measures: (a) scope; (b) differentiation of the company's offerings, one from another, across segments; and (c) differentiation of the company's offerings from those of competitors. The scope pertains to the breadth of a business. For example, do life insurance companies consider themselves to be in the business of underwriting insurance only or do they provide complete family financial planning services? Likewise, should a manufacturer of toothpaste define the scope of its business as preventing tooth decay or as providing complete oral hygiene? There are two separate contexts in which differentiation can occur: differentiation across segments and across competitors. Differentiation across segments measures the degree to which business segments are treated differently. An example is personal computers marketed to young children as educational aids and to older people as financial planning aids. Differentiation across competitors measures the degree to which competitors' offerings differ.

These three measures should be viewed in three dimensions: (a) customer groups served, (b) customer functions served, and (c) technologies used. These three dimensions (and a fourth one, level of production/distribution) were examined at length in Chapter 5 in the context of defining market boundaries and will not be elaborated further here. An example will illustrate how a business may be defined using the above dimensions.

Customer groups describe who is being satisfied; customer functions describe what needs are being satisfied; technologies describe how needs are being satisfied. Consider a thermometer manufacturer. Depending on which measure is used, the business can be defined as follows:

Customer Groups	Customer Functions	Technologies Used
Households	Body temperature	Mercury-base
Restaurants	Cooking temperature	Alcohol-base
Health care facilities	Atmospheric temperature	Electronic-digital

The manufacturer can confine the business to just health care facilities or broaden the scope to include restaurants and households. Thermometers can be provided only for measurement of body temperature or the line can be extended to offer cooking or atmospheric thermometers. The manufacturer could decide to produce only mercury-base thermometers or could also produce alcohol-base or electronic-digital thermometers. The decisions that the manufacturer makes about customer groups, customer functions, and technologies ultimately affect the definition of the business in terms of both scope and differentiation.

Exhibit 8.2 and 8.3 graphically show how business can be defined narrowly or broadly around these three dimensions. In Exhibit 8.2, the manufacturer limits the business to service health care facilities only, offering just mercury-base thermometers for measuring body temperatures. In Exhibit 8.3, however, the definition has been broadened to serve three customer groups: households, restaurants, and health care facilities; two types of thermometers: mercury-base and alcohol-base; and three customer functions. The manufacturer could further expand the definition of the business in all three directions. Physicians could be added as a customer group. A line of electronic-digital thermometers could be offered. Finally, thermometers could be produced to measure temperatures of industrial processes.

An adequate business definition requires proper consideration of the strategic three Cs: customer (e.g., buying behavior), competition (e.g., competitive definitions of the business), and company (e.g., cost behavior, such as efficiencies via economies of scale; resources/skills, such as financial strength, managerial talent, engineering/manufacturing capability, physical distribution system, etc.; and differences in marketing, manufacturing, and research and development requirements and so on, resulting from market segmentation).

Earlier it was proposed that business be defined in terms of three measures: scope, differentiation across segments, and differentiation across competitors. Scope and both kinds of differentiation are related to one another in complex ways. One way to conceptualize these interrelationships is in terms of a typology

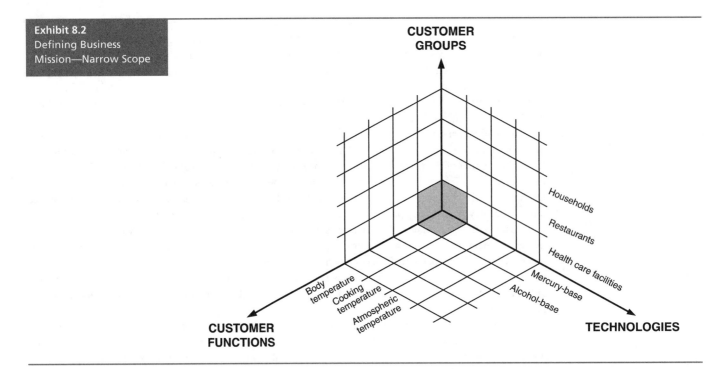

Exhibit 8.2
Defining Business
Mission—Narrow Scope

of business definitions. Three alternative strategies for defining a business are recommended: (a) a focused strategy, (b) a differentiated strategy, and (c) an undifferentiated strategy.

- *Focused strategy*—A business may choose to focus on a particular customer group, customer function, or technology segment. Focus implies a certain basis for segmentation along one or more of these dimensions, narrow scope involving only one or a few chosen segments, and differentiation from competitors through careful tailoring of the offering to the specific need of the segment(s) targeted.

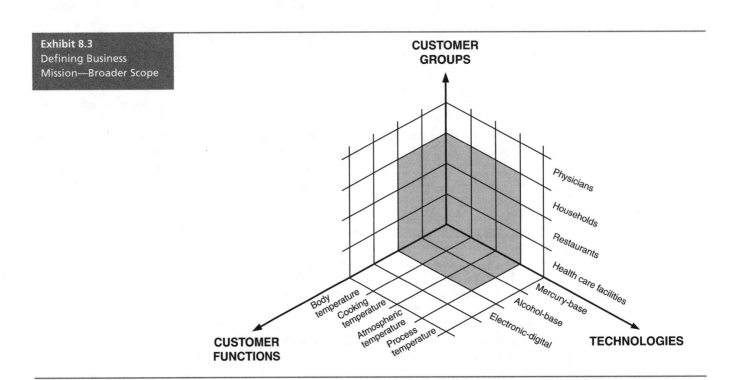

Exhibit 8.3
Defining Business
Mission—Broader Scope

- *Differentiated strategy*—When a business combines broad scope with differentiation across any or all of the three dimensions, it may be said to follow a differentiated strategy. Differentiation across segments may also be related to competitive differentiation. By tailoring the offering to the specific needs of each segment, a company automatically increases the chance for competitive superiority. Whether or not competitive differentiation also results is purely a function of the extent to which competitors have also tailored their offerings to the same specific segments. If they have, segment differentiation may be substantial, yet competitive differentiation may be small.
- *Undifferentiated strategy*—When a company combines broad scope across any or all of the three dimensions with an undifferentiated approach to customer group, customer function, or technology segments, it is said to follow an undifferentiated strategy.

Each of these strategies can be applied to the three dimensions (customer groups, customer functions, and technologies) separately. In other words, 27 different combinations are possible: (a) focused, differentiated, or undifferentiated across customer groups; (b) focused, differentiated, or undifferentiated across customer functions; (c) focused, differentiated, or undifferentiated across technologies, and so on.

A focused strategy serves a specific customer group, customer function, or technology segment. It has a narrow scope. Docutel Corporation's strategy exemplified a focused strategy relative to customer function. When Docutel first pioneered the development of the automated teller machine (ATM), it defined customer function very narrowly, concentrating on one function only—cash dispensing.

A differentiated strategy combines broad scope with differentiation across one or more of the three dimensions. A differentiated strategy serves several customer groups, functions, or technologies while tailoring the product offered to each segment's specific needs. An example of a differentiated strategy applied to customer groups is athletic footwear. Athletic footwear serves a broad range of customer groups and is differentiated across those groups. Tennis shoes are tailored to meet the needs of one specific customer group; basketball shoes, another.

An undifferentiated strategy combines a broad scope across one or more of the three dimensions. This strategy is applied to customer groups in a business that serves a wide range of customer groups but does not differentiate its offerings among those groups. Docutel's strategy was focused with respect to customer function but not with respect to customer groups: they offered exactly the same product to commercial banks, savings and loans, mutual savings banks, and credit unions. To sum up, the strategy that a business chooses to follow, based on the amount of scope and differentiation applied to the three dimensions, determines the definition of the business.

8.5 SBU OBJECTIVES AND GOALS

The objectives and goals of the SBU may be stated in terms of activities (manufacturing a specific product, selling in a particular market); financial indicators (achieving targeted return on investment); desired positions (market share, quality leadership); and combinations of these factors. Generally, an SBU has a series of objectives to cater to the interests of different stakeholders. One way of organizing objectives is to split them into the following classes: measurement objectives, growth/survival objectives, and constraint objectives. It must be emphasized that objectives and goals should not be based just on facts but on values and feelings as well. What facts should one look at? How should they be weighed and related to one another? It is in seeking answers to such questions that value judgments become crucial.

The perspectives of an SBU determine how far an objective can be broken down into minute details. If the objective applies to a number of products, only broad statements of objectives that specify the role of each product/market from the vantage point of the SBU are feasible. On the other hand, when an SBU is created around one or two products, objectives may be stated in detail.

Exhibit 8.4 illustrates how SBU objectives and goals can be identified and split into three groups: measurement, growth/survival, and constraint. Measurement objectives and goals define an SBU's aims from the point of view of the stockholders. The word profit has been traditionally used instead of measurement. But, as is widely recognized today, a corporation has several corporate publics besides stockholders; therefore, it is erroneous to use the word *profit*. On the other hand, the company's very existence and its ability to serve different stakeholders depend on financial viability. Thus, profit constitutes an important measurement objective.[17] To emphasize the real significance of profit, it is more appropriate to label it as a measurement tool.

Exhibit 8.4
Illustration of an SBU's
Objectives

I. SBU
Cooking Appliances

II. Mission
To market to individual homes cooking appliances that perform such functions as
baking, boiling, and roasting, using electric fuel technology

III. Objectives (general statements in the following areas):

A. Measurement
 1. Profitability
 2. Cash flow

B. Growth/Survival
 1. Market standing
 2. Productivity
 3. Innovation

C. Constraint
 1. Capitalize on our research in certain technologies
 2. Avoid style businesses with seasonal obsolescence
 3. Avoid antitrust problems
 4. Assume responsibility to public

IV. Goals
Specific targets and time frame for achievement of each objective listed above

It will be useful here to draw a distinction between corporate objectives and measurement objectives and goals at the level of an SBU. Corporate objectives define the company's outlook for various stakeholders as a general concept, but the SBU's objectives and goals are specific statements. For example, reducing the emissions generation may be a corporate objective. Using this corporate objective as a basis, in a particular time frame an SBU may define developing green products as one of its objectives. In other words, it is not necessary to repeat the company's obligation to various stakeholders in defining an SBU's objectives as this is already covered in the corporate objectives. Objectives and goals should underline the areas that need to be covered during the time horizon of planning.

Growth objectives and goals, with their implicit references to getting ahead, are accepted as normal goals in a capitalistic system. Thus, companies often aim at growth. Although measurements are usually stated in financial terms, growth is described with reference to the market. Constraint objectives and goals depend on the internal environment of the company and how it wishes to interact with the outside world.

An orderly description of objectives may not always work out, and the three types of objectives and goals may overlap. It is important, however, that the final draft of objectives be based on investigation, analysis, and contemplation.

8.6 PRODUCT/MARKET OBJECTIVES

Product/market objectives may be defined in terms of profitability, market share, or growth. Most businesses state their product/market purpose through a combination of these terms. Some companies, especially very small ones, may use just one of these terms to communicate product/market objectives. Usually, product/market objectives are stated at the SBU level.

Profits in one form or another constitute a desirable goal for a product/market venture. As objectives, they may be expressed either in absolute monetary terms or as a percentage of capital employed or of total assets.

At the corporate level, emphasis on profit in a statement of objectives is sometimes avoided because it seems to convey a limited perspective of the corporate purpose. But at the product/market level, an objective stated in terms of profitability provides a measurable criterion with which management can evaluate performance. Because product/market objectives are an internal matter, the corporation is not constrained by any ethical questions in its emphasis on profits.

An ardent user of the profitability objective is Georgia-Pacific Company. The company aims at achieving a return of 20 percent on stockholders' equity. The orthodox view has been that, in an industry where product differentiation is not feasible, the goal of profitability is irrelevant. But Georgia-Pacific insists on the profit goal, and the outcome had been very satisfactory. Georgia-Pacific's overall performance has been twice as good as any other competitor in the industry.[18]

How can the profitability goal be realized in practice? First, the corporate management determines the desired profitability, that is, the desired rate of return on investment. There may be a single goal set for the entire corporation, or goals may vary for different businesses. Using the given rate of return, the SBU may compute the percentage of markup on cost for its product(s). To do so, the normal rate of production, averaged over the business cycle, is computed. The total cost of normal production then becomes the standard cost. Next, the ratio of invested capital (in the SBU) to a year's standard cost (i.e., capital turnover) is computed. The capital turnover multiplied by the rate of return gives the markup percentage to be applied to standard cost. This markup is an average figure that may be adjusted both among products and over time.

In many industries, the beer industry, for example, gaining a few percentage points in market share has a positive effect on profits. Thus, market share has traditionally been considered a desirable goal to pursue. In recent years, extensive research on the subject has uncovered new evidence on the positive impact of market share on profitability.[19]

The importance of market share is explainable by the fact that it is related to cost. Cost is a function of scale or experience. Thus, the market leader may have a lower cost than other competitors because superior market share permits the accumulation of more experience. Prices, however, are determined by the cost structure of the least effective competitor. The high-cost competitor must generate enough cash to hold market share and meet expenses. If this is not accomplished, the high-cost competitor drops out and is replaced by a more effective, lower-cost competitor. The profitability of the market leader is ascertained by the same price level that determines the profit of even the least effective competitor. Thus, higher market share may give a competitive edge to a firm.

One strong proponent of market share goal is the Gillette Company. The company takes a long-term view and commits itself to obtaining a big share of growth markets. It keeps building new plants even though its first plant for a product has yet to run at full capacity. It does so hoping large-scale operations will provide a cost advantage that it can utilize in the form of lower prices to customers. Lower prices in turn lead to a higher market share.

Honda's experience in the motorcycle industry illustrates the point. In the 1950s, the two main motorcycle manufacturers in Japan were Tohatsu and Honda, with market shares of 22 percent and 20 percent respectively. Demand was growing over 40 percent a year and Honda opted to pursue market share. Toward the beginning of the 1950's its share grew to 45 percent simultaneously increasing the profitability. Tohatsu went bankrupt. At a time when market growth is high, increasing share is a desirable strategy in most businesses.[20]

While market share is a viable goal, tremendous foresight and effort are needed to achieve and maintain market share positions. A company aspiring toward a large share of the market should carefully consider two aspects: (1) its ability to finance the market share and (2) its ability to effectively defend itself against antitrust action that may be instigated by large increases in market share. For example, when General Electric considered entering the computer business, it found that to meet its corporate profitability objective it had to achieve a specific market share position. To realize its targeted market share position required huge investment. The question, then, was whether General Electric should gamble in an industry dominated by one large competitor (IBM) or invest its monies in fields where there was the probability of earning a return equal to or higher than returns in the computer field. General Electric decided to get out of the computer field.

Fear of antitrust suits also prohibits the seeking of higher market shares. A number of corporations—Kodak, Gillette, Xerox, and IBM, for example—have been the target of such action.

These reasons suggest that, although market share should be pursued as a desirable goal, companies should opt not for share maximization but for an optimal market share. Optimal market share can be determined in the following manner:

1. Estimate the relationship between market share and profitability.
2. Estimate the amount of risk associated with each share level.

3. Determine the point at which an increase in market share can no longer be expected to earn enough profit to compensate the company for the added risks to which it would expose itself.

The advantages of higher market share do not mean that a company with a lower share may not have a chance in the industry. There are companies that earn a respectable return on equity despite low market shares. Examples of such corporations are Crown Cork and Seal, American Eagle, Papa John's, and WellPoint. The following characteristics explain the success of low-share companies: (a) they compete only in those market segments where their strengths have the greatest impact, (b) they make efficient use of their modest research and development budgets, (c) they shun growth for growth's sake, and (d) they have innovative leaders.

Briefly, market share goals should not be taken lightly. Rather, a firm should aim at a market share after careful examination.

The following example illustrates the importance of market share. Exhibit 8.5 shows the experience of the industry leader in an industrial product. With an initially high share of a growing and competitive market, management shifted its emphasis from market share to high earnings. A manager with proven skills was put in charge of the business. Earnings increased for six years at the expense of some slow erosion in market share. In the seventh year, however, market share fell so rapidly that, though efforts to hold profits were redoubled, they dropped sharply. Share was never regained. The manager had been highly praised and richly rewarded for his profit results up to 2000. These results, however, were achieved in exchange for a certain unreported damage to the firm's long-term competitiveness. Only by knowing both and by weighing the gain in current income against the degree of market share liquidation that entailed could the true value of performance be judged. In other words, reported earnings do not tell the true story unless market share is constant. Loss of market share is liquidation of an unbooked asset upon which the value of all other assets depends. Gain in market share is like an addition to cost potential, just as real an asset as credit rating, brand image, organization resources, or technology. In brief, market share guarantees the long-term survival of the business. Liquidation of market share to realize short-term earnings should be avoided. High earnings make sense only when market share is stable.

Growth is an accepted phenomenon of a modern corporation. All institutions should progress and grow. Those that do not grow invite extinction. Static corporations are often subject to proxy fights.

There are a variety of reasons that make growth a viable objective: (a) growth expectations of the stockholders, (b) growth orientation of top management, (c) employees' enthusiasm, (d) growth opportunities furnished by the environment, (e) corporate need to compete effectively in the marketplace, and (f) corporate strengths and competencies that make it easy to grow. Exhibit 8.6 amplifies these reasons under the following categories: customer reasons; competitive reasons; company reasons; and distributor, dealer, and agent reasons.

Exhibit 8.5
Relationship between Market Share and After-Tax Profit

Exhibit 8.6 Reasons for Growth	

Customer Reasons

The product line or sizes too limited for customer convenience

Related products needed to serve a specific market

Purchasing economies: one source, one order, one bill

Service economies: one receiving and processing; one source of parts, service, and other assistance

Ability to give more and better services

Production capacity not enough to fill needs of important customers who may themselves be growing

Competitive Reasons

To maintain or better industry position; growth is necessary in any but a declining industry

To counter or better chief competitors on new offerings

To maintain or better position in specific product or market areas where competition is making strong moves

To permit more competitive pricing ability through greater volume

To possess greater survival strength in price wars, product competition, and economic slumps by greater size

Company Reasons

To fulfill the growth expectations of stockholders, directors, executives, and employees

To utilize available management, selling, distribution, research, or production capacity

To supplement existing products and services that are not growth markets or are on downgrade of the profit cycle

To stabilize seasonal or cyclical fluctuations

To add flexibility by broadening the market and product base of opportunities

To attain greater borrowing and financial influence with size

To be able to attract and pay for better management personnel

To attain the stability of size and move to management by planning

Distributor, Dealer, and Agent Reasons

To add products, sizes, and ranges necessary to attract interest of better distributors, dealers, and agents

To make additions necessary to obtain needed attention and selling effort from existing distributors, dealers, and agents

---

An example of growth encouraged by corporate strength is provided by R.J. Reynolds Industries. In the early 1980s, the company was in an extremely strong cash position, which helped it to acquire Heublein, Del Monte Corp., and Nabisco. H. S. Geneen's passion for growth led ITT into different industries (bakeries, car rental agencies, hotels, insurance firms, parking lots) in addition to its traditional communications business. Any field that promised growth was acceptable to him. Thus, the CEO's growth orientation is the most valuable prerequisite for growth. Similarly, growth ambitions led Procter & Gamble to venture into cosmetics and over-the-counter health remedies, and aquired the Gillette Company.

For most managers today, growth is the Holy Grail. When charting strategy, they focus on ways to expand revenues, believing that higher sales will bring higher profits. The assumption is that a company able to capture a large proportion of revenues in an industry—a large market share—will reap scale efficiencies, brand awareness, or other advantages that will translate directly into greater profits. If you can grow faster than your competitors, the thinking goes, profits will surely follow.

Unfortunately, profits do not necessarily follow revenues. Consider the recent experience of Gucci, one of the world's top names in luxury goods. In the 1980s, Gucci sought to capitalize on its prestigious brand by launching an aggressive strategy of revenue growth. It added a set of lower-priced canvas goods to its product line. It pushed its goods heavily into department stores and duty-free channels. In addition, it allowed its name to appear on a host of licensed items such as watches, eyeglasses, and perfumes. The strategy worked—sales soared—but it carried a high price: Gucci's indiscriminate approach to expanding its products and channels tarnished its sterling brand. Sales of its high-end goods fell, leading to erosion of profitability. Although the company was eventually able to retrench and recover, it lost a whole generation of image-conscious shoppers in some countries.

Gucci's misstep highlights the problem with growth: the strategies businesses use to expand their top line often have the unintended consequence of eroding their bottom line. Gucci attempted to extend its brand to gain sales—a common growth strategy—but ended up alienating its most profitable customer segments and attracting new segments that were less profitable. It was left with a larger set of customers but a much less attractive customer mix.[21]

In addition to the commonly held objectives of profitability, market share, and growth (discussed above), a company may sometimes pursue a unique objective. Such an objective might be technological leadership, social contribution, the strengthening of national security, or international economic development.

8.6.1 Technological Leadership

A company may consider technological leadership a worthwhile goal. In order to accomplish this, it may develop new products or processes or adopt innovations ahead of the competition, even when economics may not justify doing so. The underlying purpose in seeking this objective is to keep the name of the company in the forefront as a technological leader among security analysts, customers, distributors, and other stakeholders. To continue to be in the forefront of computer technology, in 2005 Apple introdouced the iPod and it continued its technological lead with the introduction of the iPhone in 2007.

8.6.2 Social Contribution

A company may pursue as an objective something that will make a social contribution. Ultimately, that something may lead to higher profitability, but initially it is intended to provide a solution to a social problem. A beverage company, for example, may attack the problem of litter by not offering its product in throwaway bottles. As another example, a pharmaceutical company may set its objective to develop and market an AIDS-preventive medicine.

8.6.3 Strengthening of National Security

In the interest of strengthening homeland defense, a company may undertake activities not otherwise justifiable. For example, concern for homeland security may lead a company to deploy resources to develop a new imaging machine for use at the airports. The company may do so despite little encouragement from the government, if only because the company sincerely feels that the country might need the machine in the coming years.

8.6.4 International Economic Development

Improvement in human welfare, the economic progress of less-developed countries, or the promotion of a worldwide free enterprise system may also serve as objectives. For example, a company may undertake the development of a foolproof method of birth control that can be easily afforded and conveniently used.

8.7 PROCESS OF SETTING OBJECTIVES

At the very beginning of the process of setting objectives, an SBU should attempt to take an inventory of objectives as they are currently understood. For example, the SBU head and senior executives may state the current objectives of the SBU and the type of SBU they want it to be in the future. Various executives perceive current objectives differently; and, of course, they will have varying ambitions for the SBU's future. It will take several top-level meetings and a good deal of effort on the part of the SBU head to settle on final objectives.

Each executive may be asked to make a presentation on the objectives and goals he or she would like the SBU to adopt for the future. Executives should be asked to justify the significance of each objective in terms of measuring performance, satisfying environmental conditions, and achieving growth. It is foreseeable that executives will have different objectives; they may express the same objectives in terms that make them appear different, but there should emerge, on analysis, a desire for a common destiny for the SBU. Disharmony of objectives may sometimes be based on diverse perceptions of a business's resource potential and corporate strategy. Thus, before embarking on setting SBU objectives, it is helpful if information on resource potential and corporate strategy is circulated.

Before finalizing the objectives, it is necessary that the executive team shows a consensus; that is, each member believes in the viability of the set objectives and willingly agrees to work toward their achievement. A way must be found to persuade a dissenting executive to cooperate. For example, if a very ambitious executive works with stability-oriented people, in the absence of an opportunity to be creative, the executive may fail to perform routine matters adequately, thus becoming a liability to the organization. In such a situation, it may be better to encourage the executive to look for another job. This option is useful for the organization as well as for the dissenting executive. This type of situation occurs when most of the executives have risen through the ranks and an ''outsider'' joins them. The dynamism of the latter is perceived as a threat, which may result in conflict. The authors are familiar with a $500 million company where the vice president of finance, an ''outsider,'' in his insistence on strategic planning came to be perceived as such a danger by the old-timers that they made it necessary for him to quit.

To sum up, objectives should be set through a series of executive meetings. The organizational head plays the role of mediator in the process of screening varying viewpoints and perceptions and developing consensus from them.

Once broad objectives have been worked out, they should be translated into specific goals, an equally challenging task. Should goals be set so high that only an outstanding manager can achieve them, or should they be set so that they are attainable by the average manager? At what level does frustration inhibit a manager's best efforts? Does an attainable budget lead to complacency? Presumably a company should start with three levels of goals: (a) easily attainable, (b) most desirable, and (c) optimistic. Thereafter, the company may choose a position somewhere between the most desirable goals and the optimistic goals, depending on the organization's resources and the value orientation of management. In no case, however, should performance fall below easily attainable levels, even if everything goes wrong. Attempts should be made to make the goals realistic and achievable. Overly elusive goals can discourage and affect motivation. As a matter of fact, realistic goals may provide higher rewards. A few years ago, Eastman Kodak lowered its 6 percent annual revenue growth from the core film and photographic paper business to 3 percent. Subsequently, its stock price went up from $40 to $50.[22]

There are no universally accepted standards, procedures, or measures for defining objectives. Each organization must work out its own definitions of objectives and goals—what constitutes growth, what measures to adopt for their evaluation, and so on. For example, consider the concept of return on investment, which for decades has been considered a good measure of corporate performance. A large number of corporations consider a specified return on investment as the most sacrosanct of goals. But ponder its limitations. In a large, complex organization, ROI tends to optimize divisional performance at the cost of total corporate performance. Further, its orientation is short-term. Investment refers to assets. Different projects require a varying amount of assets before beginning to yield results, and the return may be slow or fast, depending on the nature of the project. Thus, the value of assets may lose significance as an element in performance measurement. As the president of a large company remarked, ''Profits are often the result of expenses incurred several years previously.'' The president suggested that the current amount of net cash flow serves as a better measure of performance than the potential amount of net cash flow: ''The net cash contribution budget is a precise measure of expectations with given resources.''

The following six sources may be used to generate objectives and goals:

1. Focus on material resources (e.g., oil, minerals, forest).
2. Concern with fabricated objects (e.g., paper, nylon).
3. Major interest in events and activities requiring certain products or services, such as handling deliveries (Federal Express).
4. Emphasis on the kind of person whose needs are to be met: ''Babies Are Our Business'' (Gerber).
5. Catering to specific parts of the body: eyes (Maybelline), teeth (Dr. West), feet (Florsheim), skin (Noxzema), hair (Clairol), beard (Gillette), and legs (Hanes).

6. Examination of wants and needs and seeking to adapt to them: generic use to be satisfied (nutrition, comfort, energy, self-expression, development, conformity, etc.) and consumption systems (e.g., for satisfying nutritional needs).

Whichever procedure is utilized for finally coming out with a set of objectives and goals, the following serve as basic inputs in the process. At the corporate level, objectives are influenced by corporate publics, the value system of top management, corporate resources, the performance of business units, and the external environment. SBU objectives are based on the strategic three Cs of customer, competition, and corporation. Product/market objectives are dictated by product/market strengths and weaknesses and by momentum. Strengths and weaknesses are determined on the basis of current strategy, past performance, marketing excellence, and marketing environment. Momentum refers to future trends—extrapolation of past performance with the assumption that no major changes will occur either in the product/market environment or in its marketing mix.

Identified above are the conceptual framework and underlying information useful in defining objectives at different levels. Unfortunately, there is no computer model to neatly relate all available information to produce a set of acceptable objectives. Thus, whichever conceptual scheme is followed and no matter how much information is available, in the final analysis objective-setting remains a creative exercise.

Once an objective has been set, it may be tested for validity using the following criteria:

1. Is it, generally speaking, a guide to action? Does it facilitate decision making by helping management select the most desirable alternative courses of action?
2. Is it explicit enough to suggest certain types of action? In this sense, "to make profits" does not represent a particularly meaningful guide to action, but "to carry on a profitable business in electrical goods" does.
3. Is it suggestive of tools to measure and control effectiveness? "To be a leader in the insurance business" and "to be an innovator in child care services" are suggestive of measuring tools in a helpful way; but statements of desires merely to participate in the insurance field or child care field are not.
4. Is it ambitious enough to be challenging? The action called for should in most cases be something in addition to resting on one's laurels. Unless the enterprise sets objectives that involve reaching, there is the threat that the end of the road may be at hand.

Canon illustrates this point clearly. In 1975, Canon was a mediocre Japanese camera company. It was scarcely growing and had recently turned unprofitable for the first time since 1949. It set a few enormously aggressive goals, most of them quantitative. Its key goals were to increase sales *fivefold* over the next decade, to achieve 3 percent productivity improvement per *month*, to cut in half the time required to develop new products, and to build the premier manufacturing organization.

To achieve these goals, Canon established policies that focused on continuous improvement through the elimination of waste, broadly defined. Among other new policies, Canon put in place a number of organizational measures to promote active employee cooperation. A prime objective was to increase the number of suggestions per employee to 30 per year by 2002, up from one in 1995. This goal was achieved and then surpassed: by 2007, each employee was contributing, on average, 50 suggestions annually.

Planning within the company was refocused on methods to reach targets and, more importantly, on identifying internal capabilities required to achieve targets. Another policy was to make every performance measure visual, so employees could see at a glance where they were in relation to goals. In each factory, for example, there are visual representations of ongoing improvement activity in relation to goals.

By 2002, Canon had achieved each of its goals. It is now a significant and vigorous competitor in cameras, copiers, and computers.[23]

5. Does it suggest cognizance of external and internal constraints? Most enterprises operate within a framework of external constraints (e.g., legal and competitive restrictions) and internal constraints (e.g., limitations in financial resources).

In the late 1970s, Toyota set as its goal to defeat General Motors. It realized that to do so, it needed scale. To achieve scale, it needed first to defeat Nissan. Toyota initiated a battle against Nissan in which it rapidly introduced a vast array of new autos, capturing market share from Nissan. That battle won, Toyota could turn its attention to its long-term goal—besting General Motors. Targeting the leader is a great way to build momentum and create an organizational challenge.

6. Can it be related to both the broader and the more specific objectives at higher and lower levels in the organization? For example, can SBU objectives be related to corporate objectives, and in turn, do they also relate to the objectives of one of its products/markets?

SUMMARY

The thrust of this chapter was on defining objectives and goals at the SBU level. Objectives may be defined as general statements of the long-term purpose the business wants to pursue. Goals are specific targets the corporation would like to achieve within a given time frame. Because SBU objectives should bear a close relationship to overall corporate direction, the chapter first examined the networks of mission, objectives, and goals that make up a company's corporate direction. The example of the Dow Chemical Company was given.

The discussion of SBU objectives began with the business mission, which defines the total perspectives or purpose of a business. In addition to presenting the traditional viewpoint on business mission, a new framework for defining the business was introduced. SBU objectives and goals were defined in terms of either financial indicators or desired positions or combinations of these factors. Also considered were product/market objectives. Usually set at the SBU level, product/market objectives were defined in terms of profitability, market share, growth, and several other aspects. Finally, the process of setting objectives was outlined.

DISCUSSION QUESTIONS

1. Define the terms *policy*, *objective*, and *goal*.
2. What is meant by corporate direction? Why is it necessary to set corporate direction?
3. Does corporate direction undergo change? Discuss.
4. How does the traditional view of the business mission differ from the new approach?
5. Examine the perspectives of the new approach to defining the business mission.
6. Using the new approach, how may an airline define its business mission?
7. In what way is the market share objective viable?
8. Give examples of product/market objectives in terms of technological leadership, social contribution, and strengthening of national security.

NOTES

1. *Perspectives on Corporate Strategy* (Boston: Boston Consulting Group, 1970): 44.
2. The discussion on Dow Chemical Company draws heavily on the information available on the company's website.
3. Ram Charan, ''Ram's Rules,'' *Fortune*, February 18, 2008, p. 54.
4. Tony Jaques, ''Systematic Objective Setting for Effective Issues Management,'' *Journal of Public Affairs*, vol. 5, No. 1, 2005, pp. 33–42.
5. Michael McCoy, ''Dow Chemical,'' *Chemical & Engineering News*, June 18, 2001, pp. 21–25.
6. ''Dow Chemical's Drive to Change Its Market and Its Image,'' *BusinessWeek*, June 9, 1996, p. 92.
7. Roger E. Levien, ''Technological Transformation at Xerox,'' in *Strategic Management: Bridging Strategy and Performance* (New York: The Conference Board, Inc., 1992): 21–22.
8. James Bandler, ''Kodak Shifts Focus from Film, Betting Future on Digital Lines,'' *The Wall Street Journal*, September 25, 2003, p. A1.

9. Susan Avery, "Strategic Sourcing: Dow Chemical Turns Inward," *Purchasing*, January 17, 2008, pp. 14–19.

10. James C. Collins and Jerry F. Porras, "Behind your Company's Vision," *Harvard Business Review*, September–October 1996, pp. 65–78.

11. Robert F. McCracken, "Bringing Vision to Avon," in *Strategic Management: Bridging Strategy and Performance* (New York: The Conference Board, Inc., 1993): 25.

12. "Blue is the Colour," *The Economist*, June 6, 1998, p. 65.

13. Theodore Levitt, "Marketing Myopia," *Harvard Business Review*, July–August 1960, p. 46.

14. *Perspectives on Corporate Strategy*: 42.

15. "Coca-Cola: A Sobering Lesson from Its Journey into Wine," *BusinessWeek*, June 3, 1985, p. 96.

16. Derek F. Abell, *Defining the Business: The Starting Point of Strategic Planning* (Englewood Cliffs, NJ, Prentice Hall, 1980).

17. Michael Skapinker, "Measures of Success Must Go Beyond Financial Results," *Financial Times*, March 2, 2005, p. 9.

18. "Georgia Pacific Building Products Showcases Industry Leading Building Materials and Innovative Solutions at the 2008 International Builders Show," *BusinessWeek*, February 11, 2008, p. 22.

19. Catherine C. Langlois, "For Profit or for Market Share? The Pricing Strategy of Japanese Automakers on the U.S. Market," *Journal of the Japanese and International Economies* (March 1997): pp. 55–81.

20. Alex Taylor III, "Inside Hondas Brain," *Fortune*, March 17, 2008, p. 100. Also see: http://www.janhoo.com/skole/university/kaisha.html

21. Orit Gadiesh and James I. Gilbert, "Profit Pools: A Fresh Look at Strategy," *Harvard Business Review* (May–June 1998): 139–148. Also see: "Luxury Gods: When Profits Are Out of Fashion," *The Economist*, July 5, 2003, p. 55.

22. James Bandler, *Op. Cit.*

23. Clay Chandler, "Canon's Big Gun," *Fortune*, January 26, 2006, p. 56.

PART IV

Strategy Formulation

Chapter 9
Strategy Selection

Chapter 10
Portfolio Analysis

Chapter Outline

9.1 **Conceptual Scheme**
9.2 **Product/Market Strategy**
    9.2.1   Issue Assessment
    9.2.2   Identification of Key Variables
9.3 **Determining SBU Strategy**
9.4 **Strategy Evaluation**

Chapter 9

Strategy Selection

All men can see the tactics whereby I conquer, but what none can see is the strategy out of which victory is achieved.

SUN–TZU

Two things were achieved in the previous chapters. First, the internal and external information required for formulating marketing strategy was identified, and the methods for analyzing information were examined. Second, using the available information, the formulation of objectives was covered. This chapter takes us to the next step toward strategy formulation by establishing a framework for it.

Our principal concern in this chapter is with business unit strategy. Among several inputs required to formulate business unit strategy, one basic input is the strategic perspective of different products/markets that constitute the business unit. Therefore, as a first step toward formulating business unit strategy, a scheme for developing product/market strategies is introduced.

Bringing product/market strategies within a framework of business unit strategy formulation emphasizes the importance of inputs from both the top down and the bottom up. As a matter of fact, it can be said that strategic decisions in a diversified company are best made at three different levels: jointly by product/market managers and the SBU manager when questions of implementation are involved, jointly by the CEO and the SBU manager when formulation of strategy is the concern, and by the CEO when the mission of the business is at issue.

9.1 CONCEPTUAL SCHEME

Exhibit 9.1 depicts the framework for developing marketing strategy. As delineated earlier, marketing strategy is based on three key factors: corporation, customer, and competition. The interaction among these three factors is rather complex. For example, the corporation factor impacts marketing strategy formulation through (a) business unit mission and its goals and objectives, (b) perspectives of strengths and weaknesses in different functional areas of the business at different levels, and (c) perspectives of different products/markets that constitute the business unit. Competition affects the business unit mission as well as the measurement of strengths and weaknesses. The customer factor is omnipresent, affecting the formation of goals and objectives to support the business unit mission and directly affecting marketing strategy.

9.2 PRODUCT/MARKET STRATEGY

The following step-by-step procedure is used for formulating product/market strategy:

1. Start with the present business. Predict what the momentum of the business will be over the planning period if no significant changes are made in the policies or methods of operation. The prediction should be based on historical performance.
2. Forecast what will happen to the environment over the planning period. This forecast will include overall marketing environment and product/market environment.
3. Modify the prediction in Step 1 in light of forecasted shifts in the environment in Step 2.
4. Stop if predicted performance is fully satisfactory vis-à-vis objectives. Continue if the prediction is not fully satisfying.
5. Appraise the significant strengths and weaknesses of the business in comparison with those of important competitors. This appraisal should include any factors that may become important both in marketing

Exhibit 9.1
Framework for
Formulating Marketing
Strategy

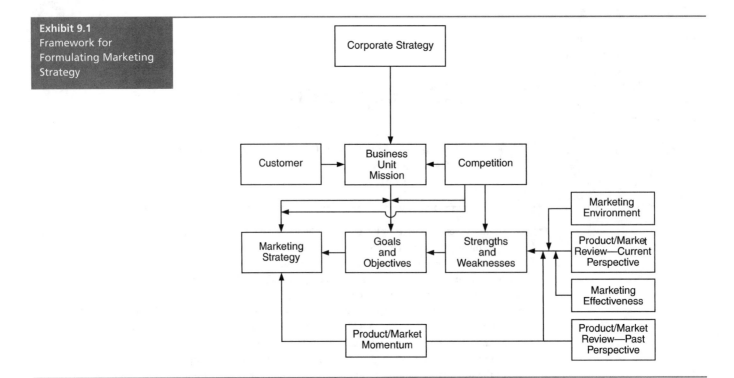

(market, product, price, promotion, and distribution) and in other functional areas (finance, research and development, costs, organization, morale, reputation, management depth, etc.).

6. Evaluate the differences between your marketing strategies and those of your major competitors.

7. Undertake an analysis to discover some variation in marketing strategy that would produce a more favorable relationship in your competitive posture in the future.

8. Evaluate the proposed alternate strategy in terms of possible risks, competitive response, and potential payout.

9. Stop if the alternate strategy appears satisfactory in terms of objectives.

10. Broaden the definition of the present business and repeat Steps 7, 8, and 9 if there is still a gap between the objective and the alternative strategy. Here, redefining the business means looking at other products that can be supplied to a market that is known and understood. Sometimes this means supplying existing products to a different market. It may also mean applying technical or financial abilities to new products and new markets simultaneously.

11. The process of broadening the definition of the business to provide a wider horizon can be continued until one of the following occurs:

 a. The knowledge of the new area becomes so thin that a choice of the sector to be studied is determined by intuition or by obviously inadequate judgment.

 b. The cost of studying the new area becomes prohibitively expensive because of lack of related experience.

 c. It becomes clear that the prospects of finding a competitive opportunity are remote.

12. Lower the objectives if the existing business is not satisfactory and if broadening the definition of the business offers unsatisfactory prospects.

There are three tasks involved in this strategy procedure: information analysis, strategy formulation, and implementation. At the product/market level, these tasks are performed by either the product/market manager or an SBU executive. In practice, analysis and implementation are usually handled entirely by the product/ market manager; strategy formulation is done jointly by the product/ market manager and the SBU executive.

Essentially, all firms have some kind of strategy and plans to carry on their operations. In the past, both plans and strategy were made intuitively. However, the increasing pace of change is forcing businesses to make their strategies explicit and often to change them. Strategy per se is getting more and more attention.

Any approach to strategy formulation leads to a conflict between objectives and capabilities. Attempting the impossible is not a good strategy; it is just a waste of resources. On the other hand, setting inadequate objectives is obviously self-defeating. Setting the proper objectives depends upon prejudgment of the potential success of the strategy; however, you cannot determine the strategy until you know the objectives. Strategy development is a reiterative process requiring art as well as science. This dilemma may explain why many strategies are intuitively made rather than logically and tightly reasoned. But there are concepts that can be usefully applied in approximating opportunities and in speeding up the process of strategy development. The above procedure is designed not only to analyze information systematically but also to formulate or change strategy in an explicit fashion and implement it.

The first phase in developing product/market plans is to predict the future state of affairs, assuming that the environment and the strategy remain the same. This future state of affairs may be called *momentum*. If the momentum projects a desirable future, no change in strategy is needed. More often, however, the future implied by the momentum may not be the desired future.

The momentum may be predicted using modeling, forecasting, and simulation techniques. Let us describe how these techniques were applied at a bank. This bank grew by opening two to three new branches per year in its trading area. The measurement of momentum consisted of projecting income statement and balance sheet figures for new branches and merging them with the projected income statement and balance sheet of the original bank. A model was constructed to project the bank's future performance. The first step in construction of the model was the prediction of B_{ijt}, that is, balances for an account of type i in area j and in time period t. Account types included checking, savings, and certificates of deposit; areas were chosen to coincide with counties in the state. County areas were desirable because most data at the state level were available by county and because current branching areas were defined by counties. Balances were projected using multiple linear regression. County per capita income and rate of population growth were found to be important variables for predicting total checking account balances, and these variables, along with the last period's savings balance, were shown to be important in describing savings account balances.

The next step was to predict M_{jt} (i.e., the market share of the bank being considered in area j and time period t). This was done using a combination of data of past performances and managerial judgment. The total expected deposit level for the branch being considered, D_{it}, was then calculated as:

$$D_{it} = \sum_{jb}(B_{ijt}M_{jt})$$

For the existing operations of the bank, past data were utilized to produce a 10-year set of deposit balances. These deposit projections were added to those of new branches. Turning to other figures, certain line items on the income statement could be attributed directly to checking accounts, others to savings accounts. The remaining figures were related to the total of account balances.

For this model, ratios of income and expense items to appropriate deposit balances were predicted by a least-squares regression on historical data. This was not considered the most satisfactory method because some changing patterns of incurring income and expenses were not taken into account. However, more sophisticated forecasting techniques, such as exponential smoothing and Box-Jenkins, were rejected because of the potential management misunderstanding they could generate.

Once the ratio matrix was developed, income statements could be generated by simply multiplying the ratios by the proper account balance projection to arrive at the 10-year projection for income statement line items. These income statements, in conjunction with the bank's policy on dividends and capitalization, were then used to generate a 10-year balance sheet projection. The net results were presented to the bank's senior executive committee to be reviewed and modified. After incorporating executive judgment, final 10-year income statements and balance sheets were obtained, indicating the bank's momentum into the future.

In the banking example, momentum was extrapolated from historical data. Little attention was given to either internal or external environmental considerations in developing the momentum. However, for a realistic projection of future outcomes, careful analysis of the overall marketing environment as well as the product/market environment is necessary.

As a part of gap analysis, therefore, the momentum should be examined and adjusted with reference to environmental assumptions. The industry, the market, and the competitive environment should be analyzed to identify important threats and opportunities. This analysis should be combined with a careful evaluation of product/market competitive strengths and weaknesses. On the basis of this information, the momentum should be evaluated and refined.

For example, in the midst of continued concern about the weakness of the economy in 2007–2008, the Federal Reserve Bank decided to increase the money supply. To do so, the prime and short-term interest rates were decreased many times. For instance, the rate of interest on many 30-month certificates of deposit went down from 5 percent in 2006 to 1.5 percent in 2008. This decrease led many depositors to choose other forms of investment over certificates of deposit. In the illustration discussed in the last section, the impact of such a decline in interest rates was not considered in arriving at the momentum (i.e., in making forecasts of deposit balances). As a part of gap analysis, this shift in the environment would be duly taken into account and the momentum would be adequately adjusted.

The "new" momentum should then be measured against objectives to see if there is a gap between expectation and potential realization. More often than not, there will be a gap between desired objectives and what the projected momentum, as revised with reference to environmental assumptions, can deliver. How this gap may be filled is discussed next.

The gap must be filled to bring planned results as close to objectives as possible. Essentially, gap filling amounts to reformulating product/market strategy.[1] A three-step procedure may be used for examining current strategy and coming up with a new one to fill the gap. These steps are issue assessment, identification of key variables, and strategy selection. The experience of some companies suggests that gap filling should be assigned to a multifunctional team. Nonmarketing people often provide fresh inputs; their objectivity and healthy skepticism are generally of great help in sharpening focus and in maintaining business-wide perspectives. The process the team follows should be carefully structured and the analytical work punctuated with regular review meetings to synthesize findings, check progress, and refocus work when desirable. The SBU staff should be deeply involved in the evaluation and approval of the strategies.

9.2.1 Issue Assessment

The primary purpose of this step is to raise issues about the status quo to evaluate the business's competitive standing in view of present and expected market conditions. To begin, a team would typically work through a series of general questions about the industry to identify those few issues that will most crucially affect the future of the business. The following questions might be included: How mature is the product/market segment under review? What new avenues of market growth are conceivable? Is the industry becoming more cyclical? Are competitive factors changing (e.g., Is product line elaboration declining and cost control gaining in importance?)? Is our industry as a whole likely to be hurt by continuing inflation? Are new regulatory restrictions pending?

Next, the company should evaluate its own competitive position, for which the following questions may be raised: How mature is our product line? How do our products perform compared with those of leading competitors? How does our marketing capability compare? What about our cost position? What are our customers' most common criticisms? Where are we most vulnerable to competitors? How strong are we in our distribution channels? How productive is our technology? How good is our record in new product introduction?[2]

Some critical issues are immediately apparent in many companies. For example, a company in a highly concentrated industry might find it difficult to hold on to its market share if a stronger, larger competitor were to launch a new low-priced product with intensive promotional support. Also, in a capital-intensive industry, the cyclical pattern and possible pressures on pricing are usually critical. If a product's transport costs are high, preemptive investments in regional manufacturing facilities may be desirable. Other important issues may be concerned with threats of backward integration by customers or forward integration by suppliers, technological upset, new regulatory action, or the entry of foreign competition into the home market. Most strategy teams supplement this brainstorming exercise with certain basic analyses that often lead to fresh insights and a more focused list of critical business issues. Three such issues that may be mentioned here are profit economics analysis, market segmentation analysis, and competitor profiling.

Profit Economics Analysis. Profit economics analysis indicates how product costs are physically generated and where economic leverage lies. The contribution of the product to fixed costs and profits may be calculated by classifying the elements of cost as fixed, variable, or semivariable and by subtracting variable cost from product price to yield contribution per item sold. It is then possible to test the sensitivity of profits to possible variations in volume, price, and cost elements. Similar computations may be made for manufacturing facilities, distribution channels, and customers.

Market Segmentation Analysis. Market segmentation analysis shows alternate methods of segmentation and whether there are any segments not being properly cultivated. Once the appropriate segment is determined, efforts should be made to project the determinants of demand (including cyclical factors and any constraints on market size or growth rate) and to explain pricing patterns, relative market shares, and other determinants of profitability.

Competitor Profiling. Profiling competitors may involve examining their sales literature, talking with experts or representatives of industry associations, and interviewing shared customers and any known former employees of competitors. If more information is needed, the team may acquire and analyze competing products and perhaps even arrange to have competitors interviewed by a third party. With these data, competitors may be compared in terms of product features and performance, pricing, likely product costs and profitability, marketing and service efforts, manufacturing facilities and efficiency, and technology and product development capabilities. Finally, each competitor's basic strategy may be inferred from these comparisons. Consider Toyota, Dell, and Wal-Mart:

> Toyota has steadily attacked the Big Three where their will to defend was weakest, moving up the line from compact cars to mid- and full-size vehicles and on to Detroit's last remaining profit centers, light trucks and SUVs. All the while, Toyota has dared its rivals to duplicate a production system that gives the company unmatchable productivity and quality. Dell is similarly relentless, and ruthless, in dealing with competitiors. In 2003, the day after Hewlett-Packard announced weak results because of price competition in PCs, Dell announced a further across-the-board-cut, delivering a swift kick to a tough rival when it was down. Wal-Mart is well known for its uncompromosing stance toward suppliers. In 1996, Rubbermaid, a $2 billion business that a few years earlier had been Fortune's most admired company, ventured to contest Wal-Mart's pressure on suppliers to lower their prices—and Wal-Mart simply cut Rubbermaid off. Wal-Mart doesn't pull punches with competitors, either. In recent years, as Kmart floundered in bankruptcy proceedings, Wal-Mart rolled out a knockoff of Kmart's Martha Stewart product line, putting pressue on one of their tottering retailer's few areas of success.[3]

All three are hardball players. They pursue with a single-minded focus competitve advantage and the benefits it offers-leading market share, great margins, rapid growth, and all the intangibles of being in command. They pick their shots, seek out competitive encounters, set the pace of innovation, test the edges of the possible. They play to win.

9.2.2 Identification of Key Variables

The information on issues described above should be analyzed to isolate the critical factors on which success in the industry depends. In any business, there are usually about five to ten factors with a decisive effect on performance. As a matter of fact, in some industries one single factor may be the key to success. For example, in the airline industry, with its high fixed costs, a high load factor is critical to success. In the automobile industry, a strong dealer network is a key success factor because the manufacturer's sales crucially depend on the dealer's ability to finance a wide range of model choices and offer competitive prices to the customer. In a commodity component market, such as switches, timers, and relays, both market share and profitability are heavily influenced by product range. An engineer who is designing circuitry normally reaches for the thickest catalog with the richest product selection. In this industry, therefore, the manufacturer with a wide selection can collect more share points with only a meager sales force.

Key factors may vary from industry to industry. Even within a single company, factors may vary according to shifts in industry position, product superiority, distribution methods, economic conditions, availability of raw materials, and the like. Therefore, suggested here is a set of questions that may be raised to identify the key success factors in any given situation:

1. What things must be done exceptionally well to win in this industry? In particular, what must we do well today to lead the industry in profit results and competitive vitality in the years ahead?
2. What factors have caused or could cause companies in this industry to fail?
3. What are the unique strengths of our principal competitors?
4. What are the risks of product or process obsolescence? How likely are they to occur and how critical could they be?
5. What things must be done to increase sales volume? How does a company in this industry go about increasing its share of the market? How could each of these ways of growing affect profits?

6. What are our major elements of cost? In what ways might each of them be reduced?
7. What are the big profit leverage points in this industry (i.e., What would be the comparative impact on profits of equal management efforts expended on each of a whole series of possible improvement opportunities?)?
8. What key recurring decisions must be made in each major functional segment of the business? What impact on profits could a good or bad decision in each of these categories have?
9. How, if at all, could the performance of this function give the company a competitive advantage?

Once these key factors have been identified, they should be examined with reference to the current status of the product/market to define alternative strategies that may be pursued to gain competitive advantage over the long term. Each alternative strategy should be evaluated for profit payoff, investment costs, feasibility, and risk.

It is important that strategy alternatives be described as specifically as possible. Simply stating "maintain product quality," "provide high-quality service," or "expand market overseas" is not enough. Precise and concrete descriptions, such as "extend the warranty period from one year to two years," "enter U.K., French, and German markets by appointing agents in these countries," and "provide a $100 cash rebate to every buyer to be handed over by the company directly," are essential before alternatives can be adequately evaluated.

Initially, the strategy group may generate a long list of alternatives, but informal discussion with management can soon pare these down to a handful. Each surviving alternative should be weighted in terms of projected financial consequences (sales, fixed and variable costs, profitability, investment, and cash flow) and relevant nonfinancial measures (market shares, product quality and reliability indices, channel efficiency, and so on) over the planning period.[4]

At this time, due attention should be paid to examining any contingencies and to making appropriate responses to them. For example, if market share increases by only half of what was planned, what pricing and promotional actions might be undertaken? If customer demand instantly shoots up, how can orders be filled? What ought to be done if the Consumer Product Safety Commission should promulgate new product usage controls? In addition, if the business is in a cyclical industry, each alternative should also be tested against several market-size scenarios, simultaneously incorporating varying assumptions about competitive pricing pressures. In industries dominated by a few competitors, an evaluation should be made of the ability of the business to adapt each strategy to competitive actions—pricing moves, shifts in advertising strategy, or attempts to dominate a distribution channel, for example.

Strategy Selection. After information on trade-offs between alternative strategies has been gathered as discussed above, a preferred strategy should be chosen for recommendation to management. Usually, there are three core marketing strategies that a company may use: (a) operational excellence, (b) product leadership, and (c) customer intimacy. Operational excellence strategy amounts to offering middle-of-the-market products at the best price with the least inconvenience. Under this strategy, the proposition to the customer is simple: low price or hassle-free service or both. Wal-Mart, Price/Costco, Best Buy, and Dell Computer epitomize this kind of strategy.[5] The product leadership strategy concentrates on offering products that push performance boundaries. In other words, the basic premise of this strategy is that customers receive the best product. Moreover, product leaders don't build their propositions with just one innovation: they continue to innovate year after year. Johnson & Johnson, for instance, is a product leader in the medical equipment field. With Nike, the superior value does not reside just in its athletic footwear, but also in the comfort customers can take from knowing that whatever product they buy from Nike will represent the hottest style and technology on the market.[6] For product leaders, competition is not about price or customer service, it is about product performance. The customer intimacy strategy focuses not on what the market wants but on what specific customers want. Businesses following this strategy do not pursue one-time transactions; they cultivate relationships. They specialize in satisfying unique needs, which often only they recognize, through a close relationship with and intimate knowledge of the customer. The underlying proposition of this strategy is: we have the best solution for you, and provide all the support you need to achieve optimum results.[7] Long-distance telephone carrier Cable and Wireless, for example, follows this strategy with a vengeance, achieving success in a highly competitive market by consistently going the extra mile for its selectively chosen, small business customers. Exhibit 9.2 summarizes the differentiating aspects of the three core strategies examined above.

| | | Core Strategy | |
| | | | |
Managerial Attributes	**Operational Excellence**	**Product Leadership**	**Customer Intimacy**
Strategic Direction	Sharpen distribution systems and provide no-hassle service	Nurture ideas, translate them into products, and market them skillfully	Provide solutions and help customers run their businesses
Organizational Arrangement	Has strong, central authority and a finite level of empowerment	Acts in an ad hoc organic, loosely knit, and ever-changing way	Pushes empower-ment close to cus-tomer contact
Systems Support	Maintain standard operating procedures	Reward individuals' innovative capacity and new product success	Measure the cost of providing service and of maintaining customer loyalty
Corporate Culture	Acts predictably and believes "one size fits all"	Experiments and thinks "out-of-the-box"	Is flexible and thinks "have it your way"

Exhibit 9.2
Distinguishing Aspects of Different Core Marketing Strategies

The core strategy combines one or more areas of the marketing mix. For example, the preferred strategy may be product leadership. Here the emphasis of the strategy is on product, the area of primary concern. Thus product represents the *core strategy*. However, in order to make an integrated marketing decision, appropriate changes may have to be made in price, promotion, and distribution areas. The strategic perspectives in these areas may be called *supporting strategies*. Thus, once core strategy has been selected, supporting strategies should be delineated. Core and supporting strategies should fit the needs of the marketplace, the skills of the company, and the vagaries of the competition.

The concept of core and supporting strategies may be examined with reference to the Ikea furniture chain.[8] Ikea, the giant Swedish home-furnishings business, has done well in the U.S. market by pursuing operational excellence as its core strategy. Where other Scandinavian furniture stores have faltered in the United States, Ikea keeps growing. Despite its poor service, customers keep coming to buy trendy furniture at bargain basement prices. The company has well aligned its supporting strategies of product, promotion, and distribution with its core strategy. For example, it selects highly visible sites easily accessible from major highways to generate traffic. Few competitors can match the selection offered by its cavernous 200,000-square-foot branches, which on average are five times larger than full-line competitors. The products are stylish and durable as well as functional; the quality is good. Advertising attempts to mold Ikea's image as hip and appealing. Ikea's enticing in-store models, easy-to-find price tags, and attractive displays create instant interest in the merchandise. But all these supporting strategies are fully price relevant. The company is so price conscious that it has used components from as many as four different manufacturers to make a single chair. Briefly, Ikea follows a strategy to satisfy the desire for contemporary furniture at moderate prices.

It is rather common for firms competing in the same industry to choose different core and supporting strategies through which to compete.[9] The chosen strategy reflects the particular strength of the firm, the specific demands of the market, and the competitive thrust. As has been noted:

Coca-Cola was born a winner, but Pepsi had to fight to survive by distinguishing itself from the leader. For most of its history, Pepsi differentiated itself purely on price: ''Twice as much for a nickel, too.'' Only in the early 1970s did Pepsi start to believe that its product actually may be as good as if not better than Coke's. The resulting strategy was: ''The Pepsi challenge.''

The first belief of Coca-Cola was that its product was sacred. The resulting strategy was simple: ''Don't touch the recipe'' and ''don't put lesser products under the same brand name'' (call them ''Tab''). Coca-Cola's second belief was that anyone should be able to buy Coke within a few steps of anywhere on earth. This belief drove the company to make its product available in every conceivable outlet and required a distribution strategy that allowed all outlets a reasonable profit at competitive prices.

While Coca-Cola was driven by a product focus, Pepsi developed a more market-oriented perspective. Pepsi was the first to offer new sizes and packages. When consumer trends toward health, fitness and sweeter taste emerged, Pepsi again was the innovator: It was the first to market diet and light varieties and it quickly sweetened its formula. Unencumbered by reverence for its base brand, it introduced the new varieties as extensions of the Pepsi signature. Where Coca-Cola feared a dilution of its brand name, Pepsi saw an opportunity to exploit the cost advantages and advertising of an umbrella brand.[10]

It is important to remember that the core strategy is formulated around the critical variable(s) that may differ from one segment to another for the same product. This is well supported by the following quotation taken from a case study of the petroloids business. Petroloids, a family of such unique materials as oils, petro-rubbers, foams, adhesives, and sealants, are manufactured substances based on the synthesis of organic hydrocarbons:

> Major producers competed with one another on a variety of dimensions. Among the most important were price, technical assistance, advertising and promotion, and product availability. Price was used as a competitive weapon primarily in those segments of the market where products and applications had become standardized. However, where products had been developed for highly specialized purposes and represented only a small fraction of a customer's total material cost, the market was often less price sensitive. Here customers were chiefly concerned with the physical properties of the product and operating performance.
>
> Technical assistance was an important means of obtaining business. A sizable percentage of total petroloid sales were accounted for by products developed to meet the unique needs of particular customers. Products for the aerospace industry were a primary example. Research engineers of petroloid producers were expected to work closely with customers to define performance requirements and to insure the development of acceptable products.
>
> Advertising and promotional activities were important marketing tools in those segments which utilized distribution channels and/or which reached end users as opposed to OEMs. This was particularly true of foams, adhesives, and sealants which were sold both to industrial and consumer markets. A variety of packaged consumer products were sold to hardware, supermarkets, and "do-it-yourself" outlets by our company as well as other competitors. Advertising increased awareness and stimulated interest among the general public while promotional activities improved the effectiveness of distribution networks. Since speciality petroloid products accounted for only a small percentage of a distributor's total sales, product promotion insured that specific products received adequate attention.
>
> Product availability was a fourth dimension on which producers competed. With manufacturing cycles from 2–16 weeks in length and thousands of different products, no supplier could afford to keep all his items in stock. In periods of heavy demand, many products were often in short supply. Those competitors with adequate supplies and quick deliveries could readily attract new business.[11]

Apparently, strategy development is difficult because different emphases may be needed in different product/market situations. Emphasis is built around critical variables that may themselves be difficult to identify.[12] Luck plays a part in making the right move; occasionally, sheer intuition suffices. Despite all this, a careful review of past performance, current perspectives, and environmental changes go a long way in choosing the right areas on which to concentrate.

Reformulation of current strategy may range from making slight modifications in existing perspectives to coming out with an entirely different strategy. For example, in the area of pricing, one alternative for an automobile manufacturer may be to keep prices stable from year to year (i.e., no yearly price increases). A different alternative is to lease cars directly to consumers instead of selling them. The decision on the first alternative may be made by the SBU executive. But the second alternative, being far-reaching in nature, may require the review and approval of top management. In other words, how much examination and review a product/market strategy requires depends on the nature of the strategy (in terms of the change it seeks from existing perspectives) and the resource commitment required.

Another point to remember in developing core strategy is that the emphasis should always be placed on searching for new ways to compete. The marketing strategist should develop strategy around those key factors in which the business has more freedom than its competitors have. The point may be illustrated with reference to Body Shop International, a cosmetic company that spends nothing on advertising, even though it is in one of the most image-conscious industries in the business world. Based in England, this company operates in 56 nations. Unlike typical cosmetic manufacturers, which sell through drugstores and department stores, Body Shop sells its own franchise stores. Further, in a business in which packaging costs often outstrip product costs, the Body Shop offers its products in plain, identical rows of bottles and gives discounts to customers who bring Body Shop bottles in for refills. The company has succeeded because it is so different from its rivals. Instead of assailing its customers with promotions and ads, it educates them. A great deal of Body Shop's budget is spent on training store personnel on the detailed nature of how its products are made and how they ought to be used. Training, which is accomplished through newsletters, videotapes, and classroom study, enables salesclerks to educate consumers on hair care, problem skin treatments, and the ecological benefits of such exotic products as rhassoul and mud shampoo, white grape skin tonic, and peppermint foot lotion. Consumers have also responded to Body Shop's environmental policies: the company uses only natural ingredients in its products, doesn't use animals for lab testing, and publicly supports saving whales and preserving Brazilian rain forests.

Another example is provided by Enterprise Rent-a-Car Company. While Hertz, Avis, and other members of the car rental industry were aggressively competing to win a point or two of the business and vacation travelers market at airports, Enterprise invaded the hinterlands with a completely different strategy— "one that relies heavily on doughnuts, ex-college frat house jocks, and your problems with your family car."[13] The company's approach is simple: It aims to provide a spare family car. Say a person's car has been hit or has broken down, or is in for routine maintenance. Once upon a time, the person could have asked his spouse for a ride or he could have borrowed her car, but now she is commuting to her own job. "Lo and behold, even before you have time to kick the repair shop's Coke machine, a well-dressed, intelligent young Enterprise agent materializes with some paperwork and a car for you."[14] Typically, an Enterprise car rents for one-third less than one from an airport.

Instead of massing 10,000 cars at a few dozen airports, Enterprise sets up inexpensive rental offices just about everywhere. As soon as one branch grows to about 150 cars, the company opens another a few miles away. The company claims that 90% of the American population lives within 15 minutes of an Enterprise office. Once a new office opens, employees fan out to develop relationships with the service managers of every good-size auto dealership and body shop in the area. When a person's car is being towed, he/she is in no mood to figure out which local rent-a-car company to use. Enterprise knows that the recommendations of the garage service managers will carry enormous weight, so it has turned courting them into an art form.

The end result is Enterprise has bypassed everybody in the industry. It owns over 500,000 cars and operates in more locations than Hertz. The company accounts for more than 22% of the $20 billion-a-year car rental business, versus 18% for Hertz and about 11% for Avis.

In the final analysis, companies with the following characteristics are most likely to develop successful strategies:

1. **Informed opportunism**—Information is the main strategic advantage, and flexibility is the main strategic weapon. Management assumes that opportunity will keep knocking but that it will knock softly and in unpredictable ways.
2. **Direction and empowerment**—Managers define the boundaries, and their subordinates figure out the best way to do the job within them. Managers give up some control to gain results.
3. **Friendly facts, congenial controls**—Share information that provides context and removes decision making from the realm of mere opinion. Managers regard financial controls as the benign checks and balances that allow them to be creative and free.
4. **A different mirror**—Leaders are open and inquisitive. They get ideas from almost anyone in and out of the hierarchy: customers, competitors, even next-door neighbors.
5. **Teamwork, trust, politics, and power**—Stress the value of teamwork and trust the employees to do the job. Be relentless at fighting office politics, since politics are inevitable in the workplace.
6. **Stability in motion**—Keep changing but have a base of underlying stability. Understand the need for consistency and norms, but also realize that the only way to respond to change is to deliberately break the rules.
7. **Attitudes and attention**—Visible management attention, rather than exhortation, gets things done. Action may start with words, but it must be backed by symbolic behavior that makes those words come alive.
8. **Causes and commitment**—Commitment results from management's ability to turn grand causes into small actions so that everyone can contribute to the central purpose.

9.3 DETERMINING SBU STRATEGY

SBU strategy concerns how to create competitive advantage in each of the products/markets it competes with. The business-unit-level strategy is determined by the three Cs (customer, competition, and company). The experience of different companies shows that, for the purposes of strategy formulation, the strategic three Cs can be articulated by placing SBUs on a two-by-two matrix with industry maturity or attractiveness as one dimension and strategic competitive position as the other.

Industry attractiveness may be studied with reference to the life-cycle stage of the industry (i.e., embryonic, growth, mature, or aging). Such factors as growth rate, industry potential, breadth of product line, number of competitors, market share perspectives, purchasing patterns of customers, ease of entry, and technology development determine the maturity of the industry. As illustrated in Exhibit 9.3, these factors behave in different ways according to the stage of industry maturity. For example, in the embryonic stage, the product line is generally narrow, and frequent changes to tailor the line to customer needs are common. In the growth stage, product lines undergo rapid proliferation. In the mature stage, attempts are made to orient products to specific segments. During the aging stage, the product line begins to shrink.

Going through the four stages of the industry life cycle can take decades or a few years. The different stages are generally of unequal duration. To cite a few examples, iPhone and solar energy devices are in the embryonic category. Home smoke alarms and sporting goods in general fall into the growth category. Golf equipment and steel represent mature industries. Men's hats and rail cars are in the aging category. It is important to remember that industries can experience reversals in the aging processes. For example, roller skates have experienced a tremendous resurgence (i.e., moving from the aging stage back to the growth stage) because of the introduction of polyurethane wheels. It should also be emphasized that there is no "good" or "bad" life-cycle position. A particular stage of maturity becomes "bad" only if the expectations or strategies adopted by an industry participant are inappropriate for its stage of maturity. The particular characteristics of the four different stages in the life cycle are discussed in the following paragraphs.

Embryonic industries usually experience rapid sales growth, frequent changes in technology, and fragmented, shifting market shares. The cash deployment to these businesses is often high relative to sales as investment is made in market development, facilities, and technology. Embryonic businesses are generally not profitable, but investment is usually warranted in anticipation of gaining position in a developing market.

The growth stage is generally characterized by a rapid expansion of sales as the market develops. Customers, shares, and technology are better known than in the embryonic stage, and entry into the industry can be more difficult. Growth businesses are usually capital borrowers from the corporation, producing low-to-good earnings.

In mature industries, competitors, technology, and customers are all known and there is little volatility in market shares. The growth rate of these industries is usually about equal to GNP. Businesses in mature industries tend to provide cash for the corporation through high earnings.

The aging stage of maturity is characterized by

1. Falling demand for the product and limited growth potential.
2. A shrinking number of competitors (survivors gain market share through attrition).
3. Little product line variety.
4. Little, if any, investment in research and development or plant and equipment.

The competitive position of an SBU should depend not only on market share but also on such factors as capacity utilization, current profitability, degree of integration (forward or backward), distinctive product advantages (e.g., patent protection), and management strength (e.g., willingness to take risks). These factors may be studied for classifying a given SBU in one of the following competitive positions: dominant, strong, favorable, tenable, or weak.

Exhibit 9.4 summarizes the typical characteristics of firms in different competitive positions. An example of a dominant firm is Wal-Mart in the retailing field; its competitors pattern their behavior and strategies on what Wal-Mart does. In the beer industry, Anheuser-Busch exemplifies a strong firm, a firm able to make an independent move without being punished by the major competitor.

Determining strategic competitive position is one of the most complex elements of business analysis and one of the least researched. With little state-of-the-art guidance available, the temptation is to fall back

Stages of Industry Maturity

Descriptors	Embryonic	Growth	Mature	Aging
Growth rate	Accelerating; meaningful rate cannot be calculated because base is too small	Substantially faster than GNP; industry sales expanding significantly	Growth at rate equal to or slower than GNP; more subject to cyclicality	Industry volume declining
Industry potential	Usually difficult to determine	Demand exceeds current industry volume but is subject to unforeseen developments	Well known; primary markets approach saturation	Saturation is reached; supply capability exceeds demand
Product line	Line generally narrow; frequent changes tailored to customer needs	Product lines undergo rapid proliferation; some evidence of products oriented toward multiple industry segments	Product line turnover but little or no change in breadth; products frequently oriented toward narrow industry segments	Product line shrinking but tailored to major customer needs
Number of competitors	Few competing at first but number increasing rapidly	Number and types are unstable; increase to peak followed by shakeout and consolidation	Generally stable or declining slightly	Declines or industry may break up into many small regional suppliers
Market share stability	Volatile; share difficult to measure; share frequently concentrated	Rankings can change; a few firms have major shares	Little share volatility; firms with major shares are entrenched; significant niche competition; firms with minor shares are unlikely to gain major shares	Some change as marginal firms drop out; as market declines, market share generally becomes more concentrated
Purchasing patterns	Varies; some customers have strong loyalties; others have none	Some customer loyalty; buyers are aggressive but show evidence of repeat or add-on purchases; some price sensitivity	Suppliers are well known; buying patterns are established; customers generally loyal to limited number of acceptable suppliers; increasing price sensitivity	Strong customer loyalty as number of alternatives decreases; customers and suppliers may be tied to each other
Ease of entry (exclusive of capital considerations)	Usually easy; opportunity may not be apparent	Usually easy; presence of competitors is offset by growth	Difficult; competitors are entrenched; growth slowing	Little incentive
Technology	Important to match performance to market needs; industries started on technological breakthrough or application; multiple technologies	Fewer competing technologies; significant product line refinements or extensions likely; performance enhancement is important	Process and materials refinement; technologies developed outside this industry are used in seeking efficiencies	Minimal role in ongoing products; new technology sought to renew growth

Exhibit 9.3 Industry Maturity Guide

Exhibit 9.4 Classification of Competitive Strategic Positions	Dominant	• Controls behavior and/or strategies of other competitors • Can choose from widest range of strategic options, independent of competitor's actions
	Strong	• Can take independent stance or action without endangering long-term position • Can generally maintain long-term position in the face of competitor's actions
	Favorable	• Has strengths that are exploitable with certain strategies if industry conditions are favorable • Has more than average ability to improve position • If in a niche, holds a commanding position relatively secure from attack
	Tenable	• Has sufficient potential and/or strengths to warrant continuation in business • May maintain position with tacit consent of dominant company or of the industry in general but is unlikely to significantly improve position • Tends to be only marginally profitable • If in a niche, is profitable but clearly vulnerable to competitors' actions
	Weak	• Has currently unsatisfactory performance but has strengths that may lead to improvement • Has many characteristics of a better position but suffers from past mistakes or current weaknesses • Inherently short-term position; must change (up or out)
	Nonviable	• Has currently unsatisfactory performance and few, if any, strengths that may lead to improvement (may take years to die)

on the single criterion of market share, but the experiences of successful companies make it clear that determining competitive position is a multifaceted problem embracing, for example, technology, breadth of product line, market share, share movement, and special market relationships. Such factors change in relative importance as industry maturity changes.

Once the position of an SBU is located on the industry maturity/competitive position matrix, the guide shown in Exhibit 9.5 may be used to determine what strategy the SBU should pursue. Actually, the strategies shown in the exhibit are guides to strategic thrust rather than strategies per se. They show the normal strategic path a business unit may adopt, given its industry maturity and competitive position. The Appendix at the end of this chapter further examines the strategic thrusts identified in Exhibit 9.5. Each strategic thrust is defined, and its objective, requirements, and expected results are noted.

To bridge the gap between broad guidelines and specific strategies for implementation, further analysis is required. A three-stage process is suggested here. First, using broad guidelines, the SBU management may be asked to state strategies pursued during previous years. Second, these strategies may be reviewed by using selected performance ratios to analyze the extent to which strategies were successfully implemented. Similarly, current strategies may be identified and their link to past strategies established. Third, having identified and analyzed past and current strategy with the help of strategic guidelines, the management, using the same guidelines, selects the strategy it proposes to pursue in the future. The future perspective may call for the continuation of current strategies or the development of new ones. Before accepting the future strategic course, however, it is desirable to measure its cash consequences or internal deployment (i.e., percentage of funds generated that are reinvested). Exhibit 9.6 illustrates an SBU earning 22 percent on assets with an internal deployment of 80 percent. Such an SBU would normally be considered in the mature stage. However, if the previous analysis showed that the SBU was in fact operating in a growth

Competitive Position	Stages of Industry Maturity			
	Embryonic	**Growth**	**Mature**	**Aging**
Dominant	Grow fast Start up	Grow fast Attain cost leadership Renew Defend position	Defend position Focus Renew Grow fast	Defend position Renew Grow into maturity
Strong	Start up Differentiate Grow fast	Grow fast Catch up Attain cost leadership Differentiate	Attain cost leadership Renew, focus Differentiate Grow with industry	Find niche Hold niche Hang in Grow with industry Harvest
Favorable	Start up Differentiate Catch up Focus Grow fast	Differentiate, focus Find niche, hold niche Grow with industry	Harvest, hang in Turn around Renew, turn around Differentiate, focus Grow with industry	Retrench
Tenable	Start up Grow with industry Focus	Harvest, catch up Hold niche, hang in Find niche Turn around Focus Grow with industry	Harvest Turn around Find niche Retrench	Divest Retrench
Weak	Find niche Catch up Grow with industry	Turn around Retrench	Withdraw Divest	Withdraw

Exhibit 9.5 Guide to Strategic Thrust Options

industry, the corporation would need to rethink its investment policy. All quantitative information pertaining to an SBU may be summarized on one form, as shown in Exhibit 9.7.

Different product/market plans are reviewed at the SBU level. The purpose of this review is twofold: (a) to consider product/market strategies in finalizing SBU strategies and (b) to approve product/market strategies. The underlying criterion for evaluation is a balanced achievement of SBU goals, which may be specified in terms of profitability and cash consequences. If there is a conflict of interest between two product/market groups in the way the strategy is either articulated or implemented, the conflict should be resolved so that SBU goals are maximized.

Assume that both product/market groups seek additional investments during the next two years. Of these, the first product/market will start delivering positive cash flow in the third year. The second one is not likely to generate positive cash flow until the fourth year, but it will provide a higher overall return on capital. If the SBU's need for cash is urgent and if it desires additional cash for its goals during the third year, the first product/market group will appear more attractive. Thus, despite higher profit expectations from the second product/market group, the SBU may approve investment in the first product/market group with a view to maximizing the realization of its own goals.

At times, the SBU may require a product/market group to make additional changes in its strategic perspective before giving its final approval. On the other hand, a product/market plan may be totally rejected and the group instructed to pursue its current perspective.

Industry maturity and competitive position analysis may also be used in further refining the SBU itself. In other words, after an SBU has been created and is analyzed for industry maturity and competitive position, it may be found that it has not been properly constituted. This would require redefining the SBU and undertaking the analysis again. Drawing an example from the car radio industry, considerable differences in industry maturity may become apparent between car radios with built-in CD players and traditional car radios. Differences in industry maturity or competitive position may also exist with regard to regional

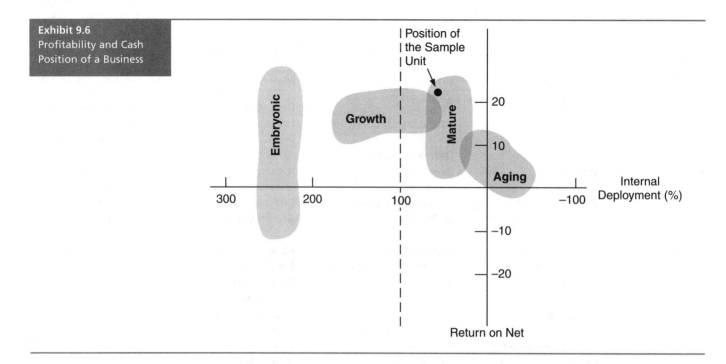

Exhibit 9.6
Profitability and Cash Position of a Business

markets, consumer groups, and distribution channels. For example, the market for cheap car radios sold by discount stores to end users doing their own installations may be growing faster than the market served by specialty retail stores providing installation services. Such revelations may require further refinement in formulating SBUs. This may continue until the SBUs represent the highest possible level of aggregation consistent with the need for clear-cut analyses of industry maturity and competitive position.

9.4 STRATEGY EVALUATION

The time required to develop resources is so extended, and the timescale of opportunities is so brief and fleeting, that a company which has not carefully delineated and appraised its strategy is adrift in white water. This underlines the importance of strategy evaluation. The adequacy of a strategy may be evaluated using the following criteria:[15]

1. **Suitability**—Is there a sustainable advantage?
2. **Validity**—Are the assumptions realistic?
3. **Feasibility**—Do we have the skills, resources, and commitments?
4. **Internal consistency**—Does the strategy hang together?
5. **Vulnerability**—What are the risks and contingencies?
6. **Workability**—Can we retain our flexibility?
7. **Appropriate time horizon**.

Strategy should offer some sort of competitive advantage. In other words, strategy should lead to a future advantage or an adaptation to forces eroding current competitive advantage. The following steps may be followed to judge the competitive advantage a strategy may provide: (a) review the potential threats and opportunities to the business, (b) assess each option in light of the capabilities of the business, (c) anticipate the likely competitive response to each option, and (d) modify or eliminate unsuitable options.

Strategy should be consistent with the assumptions about the external product/market environment. At a time when more and more women are seeking jobs, a strategy assuming traditional roles for women (i.e., raising children and staying home) would be inconsistent with the environment.

Money, competence, and physical facilities are the critical resources a manager should be aware of in finalizing strategy. A resource may be examined in two different ways: as a constraint limiting the achievement of goals and as an opportunity to be exploited as the basis for strategy. It is desirable for a strategist to make correct estimates of resources available without being excessively optimistic about them. Further, even if resources are available in the corporation, a particular product/market group may not be able to lay

PERFORMANCE

| Year | Indices of: | | | | Return | | | | | | |
	Industry Capacity (A)	Business Unit's Product Capacity (B)	Business Unit's Sales (C)	Profits after Taxes (D)	New Assets (E)	Receivables (F)	Inventories (G)	Investment (per $ sales) New Current Liabilities (H)	Working Capital (I)	Other Assets (J)	Total Net Assets (K)

INVESTMENT

| Yr. | Return (continued) | | | | | | | | Funds Generation and Deployment | | | |
| | Cost and Earnings (per $ sales) | | | | | | | | (per $ sales) | | | (%) |
	Cost of Goods Sold (L)	Research and Development (M)	Sales and Marketing (N)	General and Administrative (O)	Other Income and Expenses (P)	Profit before Taxes (Q)	Profit after Taxes (R)	Return on Net Assets (S)	Operating Funds Flow (T)	Changes in Assets (U)	Net Cash Flow to Corporation (V)	Internal Development (U ÷ T) (W)

Source: Arthur D. Little, Inc. Reprinted by permission.

Exhibit 9.7 Sources of Competitive Information

claim to them. Alternatively, resources currently available to a product/market group may be transferred to another group if the SBU strategy deems it necessary.

Strategy should be in tune with the different policies of the corporation, the SBU, and the product/market arena. For example, if the corporation decided to limit the government business of any unit to 40 percent of total sales, a product/market strategy emphasizing greater than 40 percent reliance on the government market would be internally inconsistent.

The degree of risk may be determined on the basis of the perspectives of the strategy and available resources. A pertinent question here is: Will the resources be available as planned in appropriate quantities and for as long as it is necessary to implement the strategy? The overall proportion of resources committed to a venture becomes a factor to be reckoned with: the greater these quantities, the greater the degree of risk.[16]

The workability of a strategy should be realistically evaluated with quantitative data. Sometimes, however, it may be difficult to undertake such objective analysis.[17] In that case, other indications may be used to assess the contributions of a strategy. One such indication could be the degree of consensus among key executives about the viability of the strategy. Identifying ahead of time alternate strategies for achieving the goal is another indication of the workability of a strategy. Finally, establishing resource requirements in advance, which eliminates the need to institute crash programs of cost reduction or to seek reduction in planned programs, also substantiates the workability of the strategy.

A viable strategy has a time frame for its realization. The time horizon of a strategy should allow implementation without creating havoc in the organization or missing market availability. For example, in introducing a new product to the market, enough time should be allotted for market testing, training of salespeople, and so on. But the time frame should not be so long that a competitor can enter the market first and skim the cream off the top.

SUMMARY

This chapter was devoted to strategy formulation for the SBU. A conceptual framework for developing SBU strategy was outlined. Strategy formulation at the SBU level requires, among different inputs, the perspectives of product/market strategies. For this reason, a procedure for developing product/market strategy was discussed first.

Product/market strategy development requires predicting the momentum of current operations into the future (assuming constant conditions), modifying the momentum in the light of environmental changes, and reviewing the adjusted momentum against goals. If there is no gap between the set goal and the prediction, the present strategy may well be continued. Usually, however, there is a gap between the goal and expectations from current operations. Thus, the gap must be filled.

The following three-step process was suggested for filling the gap: (a) issue assessment (i.e., raising issues with the status quo vis-à-vis the future), (b) identification of key variables (i.e., isolating the key variables on which success in the industry depends) and development of alternative strategies, and (c) strategy selection (i.e., choosing the preferred strategy). The thrust of the preferred strategy is on one or more of the four variables in the marketing mix—product, price, promotion, or distribution. The major emphasis of marketing strategy, the core strategy, is on this chosen variable. Strategies for the remaining variables are supporting strategies. Usually, the three core marketing strategies are operational excellence, product leadership, and customer intimacy.

The SBU strategy is based on the three Cs (customer, competition, and company). SBUs were placed on a two-by-two matrix with industry maturity or attractiveness as one dimension and strategic competitive position as the other. Stages of industry maturity—embryonic, growth, mature, and aging—were identified. Competitive position can be classified as dominant, strong, favorable, tenable, or weak. Classification by industry maturity and competitive position generates 20 different quadrants in the matrix. In each quadrant, an SBU requires a different strategic perspective. A compendium of strategies was provided to figure out the appropriate strategy in a particular case.

The chapter concluded with a procedure for evaluating the selected strategy. This procedure consists of examining the following aspects of the strategy: suitability, validity, feasibility, internal consistency, vulnerability, workability, and appropriateness of time horizon.

DISCUSSION QUESTIONS

1. Describe how a manufacturer of washing machines may measure the momentum of the business for the next five years.

2. List five issues Sears may raise to review its strategy for large appliances.
3. List five key variables on which success in the home construction industry depends.
4. In what industry state would you position (a) light beer and (b) color television?
5. Based on your knowledge of the company, what would you consider to be Miller's competitive position in the light beer business and GE's position in the appliance business?
6. Discuss how strategy evaluation criteria may be employed to review the strategy of an industrial goods manufacturer.

NOTES

1. Gary Hamel, "Strategy as Revolution," *Harvard Business Review*, July–August 1996, pp. 48–56. Also see Jim Collins, *Good to Great* (New York: HarperCollins, 2001).
2. David J. Collis and Michael G. Rukstad, "Can You Say What Your Strategy Is?" *Harvard Business Review,* April 2008, pp. 82–93.
3. George Stalk, Jr. and Rob Lachenauer, "Five Killer Strategies for Trouncing the Competition," *Harvard Business Review*, April 2004, pp. 62–71.
4. Robert S. Kaplan and David P. Norton, "Having Trouble with Your Strategy," *Harvard Business Review*, September–October 2000, pp. 167–176.
5. Michael E. Porter, "The Five Competitive Forces That Shape Strategy," *Harvard Business Review*, January 2008, pp. 78–93.
6. Gary Hamel, "Killer Strategies," *Fortune*, June 23, 1997, p. 70.
7. Ian C. MacMillan and Rita Gunther McGrath, "Discovering New Points of Differentiation," *Harvard Business Review*, July–August 1997, pp. 133–145.
8. "Ikea," in Subhash C. Jain, *Essentials of Global Marketing* (Lombard, IL, Marsh Publications, 2008): 448–450.
9. Alex Taylor III, "Inside Honda's Brain," *Fortune*, March 17, 2008, p. 100.
10. Michael Norkus, "Soft Drink Wars: A Lot More Than Just Good Taste," *The Wall Street Journal*, July 8, 1985, p. 12.
11. "Tex-Fiber Industries Petroloid Products Division (A)," a case developed by John Craig under the supervision of Derek F. Abell, copyrighted by the President and Fellows of Harvard College, 1970, 7.
12. "Who Gets Eaten and Who Gets to Eat," *The Economist*, July 12, 2003, p. 61.
13. Brian O'Reilly, "The Rent-a-Car Jocks Who Make Enterprise #1," *Fortune*, October 1996, p. 125.
14. Ibid.
15. See George S. Day, "Tough Questions for Developing Strategies," *Journal of Business*, Winter 1986, pp. 60–68.
16. Natalie Mizik and Robert Jacobson, "Trading Off Between Value Creation and Value Appropriation: The Financial Implications of Shifts in Strategic Emphasis," *Journal of Marketing*, January 2003, pp. 63–76.
17. Eric D. Beinhocker and Sarah Kaplan, "Tired of Strategic Planning," *McKinsey Quarterly*, 2002 Special Edition: Risk and Resilience, pp. 49–57.

APPENDIX: PERSPECTIVES ON STRATEGIC THRUSTS

A. Start Up

Definition: Introduction of new product or service with clear, significant technology breakthrough.

Objective: To develop a totally new industry to create and satisfy new demand where none existed before.

Requirements: Risk-taking attitude of management; capital expenditures; expense.

Expected Results: Negative cash flow; low-to-negative returns; a leadership position in new industry.

B. Grow with Industry

Definition: To limit efforts to those necessary to maintain market share.

Objective: To free resources to correct market, product, management, or production weaknesses.

Requirements: Management restraint; market intelligence; some capital and expense investments; time-limited strategy.

Expected Results: Stable market share; profit, cash flow, and RONA not significantly worse than recent history, fluctuating only as do industry averages.

C. Grow Fast

Definition: To pursue aggressively larger share and/or stronger position relative to competition.

Objective: To grow volume and share faster than competition and faster than general industry growth rate.

Requirements: Available resources for investment and follow-up; risk-taking management attitude; and appropriate investment strategy.

Expected Results: Higher market share; in the short term, perhaps lower returns; above average returns in the longer term; competitive retaliation.

D. Attain Cost Leadership

Definition: To achieve lowest delivered costs relative to competition with acceptable quality levels.

Objective: To increase freedom to defend against powerful entries, strong customer blocks, vigorous competitors, or potential substitute products.

Requirements: Relatively high market share; disciplined, persistent management efforts; favorable access to raw materials; substantial capital expenditures; aggressive pricing.

Expected Results: In early stages, may result in start-up losses to build share; ultimately, high margins; relatively low capital turnover rates.

E. Differentiate

Definition: To achieve the highest degree of product/quality/service difference (as perceived by customers) in the industry with acceptable costs.

Objective: To insulate the company from switching, substitution, price competition, and strong blocks of customers or suppliers.

Requirements: Willingness to sacrifice high market share; careful target marketing; focused technological and market research; strong brand loyalty.

Expected Results: Possibly lowered market share; high margins; above-average earnings; highly defensible position.

F. Focus

Definition: To select a particular segment of the market/product line more narrow in scope than competing firms.

Objective: To serve the strategic target area (geographic, product, or market) more efficiently, fully, and profitably than it can be served by broad-line competitors.

Requirements: Disciplined management; persistent pursuit of well-defined scope and mission; premium pricing; careful target selection.

Expected Results: Above-average earnings; may be low-cost producer in its area; may attain high differentiation.

G. Review

Definition: To restore the competitiveness of a product line in anticipation of future industry sales.

Objective: To overcome weakness in product/market mix in order to improve share or to prepare for a new generation of demand, competition, or substitute products.

Requirements: Strong-enough competitive position to generate necessary resources for renewal efforts; capital and expense investments; management capable of taking risk; recognition of potential threats to existing line.

Expected Results: Short-term decline in sales, then sudden or gradual breakout of old volume/profit patterns.

H. Defend Position

Definition: To ensure that relative competitive position is stable or improved.

Objective: To create barriers that make it difficult, costly, and risky for competitors, suppliers, customer blocks, or new entries to erode your firm's market share, profitability, and growth.

Requirements: Establishment of one or more of the following: proprietary technology, strong brand, protected sourcing, favorable locations, economies of scale, government protection, exclusive distribution, or customer loyalty.

Expected Results: Stable or increasing market share.

I. Harvest

Definition: To convert market share or competitive position into higher returns.

Objective: To bring returns up to industry averages by trading, leasing, or selling technology, distribution rights, patents, brands, production capacity, locations, or exclusive sources to competitors.

Requirements: A better-than-average market share; rights to entry or mobility barriers that the industry values; alternative investment opportunities.

Expected Results: Sudden surge in profitability and return; a gradual decline of position, perhaps leading to withdrawal strategy.

J. Find Niche

Definition: To opt for retaining a small, defensible portion of the available market rather than withdraw.

Objective: To define the opportunity so narrowly that large competitors with broad lines do not find it attractive enough to dislodge you.

Requirements: "Think small" management style; alternative uses for excess production capacity; reliable sources for supplies and materials; superior quality and/or service with selected sector.

Expected Results: Pronounced decline in volume and share; improved return in medium to longer term.

K. Hold Niche

Definition: To protect a narrow position in the larger product/market arena from larger competitors.

Objective: To create barriers (real or imagined) that make it unattractive for competitors, suppliers, or customer blocks to enter your segment or switch to alternative products.

Requirements: Designing, building, and promoting "switching costs" into your product.

Expected Results: Lower-than-industry average but steady and acceptable returns.

L. Catch Up

Definition: To make up for poor or late entry into an industry by aggressive product/market activities.

Objective: To overcome early gains made by first entrants into the market by careful choice of optimum product, production, distribution, promotion, and marketing tactics.

Requirements: Management capable of taking risk in flexible environment; resources to make high investments of capital and expense; corporate understanding of short-term low returns; probably necessary to dislodge weak competitors.

Expected Results: Low-to-negative returns in near term; should result in favorable to strong position by late growth stage of industry.

M. Hang In

Definition: To prolong existence of the unit in anticipation of some specific favorable change in the environment.

Objective: To continue funding a tenable (or better) unit only long enough to take advantage of unusual opportunity known to be at hand; this might take the form of patent expiration, management change, government action, technology breakthrough, or socioeconomic shift.

Requirements: Clear view of expected environmental shift; a management willing and able to sustain poor performance; opportunity and resources to capitalize on new environment; a time limit.

Expected Results: Poorer-than-average performance, perhaps losses; later, substantial growth and high returns.

N. Turn Around

Definition: To overcome inherent, severe weaknesses in performance in a limited time.

Objective: To halt further declines in share and/or volume; to bring about at least stability or, preferably, a small improvement in position; to protect the line from competitive and substitute products.

Requirements: Fast action to prevent disaster; reductions or redirection to reduce losses; change in morale.

Expected Results: Stable condition and average performance.

O. Retrench

Definition: To cut back investment in the business and reduce level of risk and exposure to losses.

Objective: To stop unacceptable losses or risks; to prepare the business for divestment or withdrawal; to strip away loss operations in hopes of exposing a "little jewel."

Requirements: Highly disciplined management system; good communication with employees to prevent wholesale departures; clear strategic objective and timetable.

Expected Results: Reduced losses or modestly improved performance.

P. Divest

Definition: To strip the business of some or all of its assets through sale of the product line, brands, distribution facilities, or production capacity.

Objective: To recover losses sustained through earlier strategic errors; to free up funds for alternative corporate investments; to abandon part or all of a business to competition.

Requirements: Assets desirable to others competing or desiring to compete in the industry; a recognition of the futility of further investments.

Expected Results: Increase in cash flow; reduction of asset base; probable reduction in performance levels and/or losses.

Q. Withdraw

Definition: To remove the business from competition.

Objective: To take back from the business whatever corporate assets or expenses can be recovered through shutdown, sale, auction, or scrapping of operations.

Requirements: A decision to abandon; a caretaker management; a phased timetable; a public relations plan.

Expected Results: Losses and write-offs.

Chapter Outline

10.1 Product Life Cycle (PLC)
10.2 Portfolio Matrix
    10.2.1 Stars
    10.2.2 Cash Cows
    10.2.3 Question Marks
    10.2.4 Dogs
10.3 Multifactor Portfolio Matrix
10.4 Portfolio Matrix: Critical Analysis
10.5 A New Product Portfolio
    Approach: Porter's Generic
    Strategies Framework
10.6 Portfolio Analysis Conclusion

Chapter 10

Portfolio Analysis

Induce your competitors not to invest in those products, markets, and services where you expect to invest the most. That is the most fundamental rule of strategy.

BRUCE D. HENDERSON

The previous chapters dealt with strategy development for individual SBUs. Different SBU strategies must ultimately be judged from the viewpoint of the total organization before being implemented. In today's environment, most companies operate with a variety of businesses. Even if a company is primarily involved in a single broad business area, it may actually be operating in multiple product/market segments. From a strategy angle, different products/markets may constitute different businesses of a company because they have different roles to play. This chapter is devoted to the analysis of the different businesses of an organization so that each may be assigned the unique role for which it is suited, thus maximizing long-term growth and earnings of the company.

Years ago, Peter Drucker suggested classifying products into six categories that reveal the potential for future sales growth: tomorrow's breadwinners, today's breadwinners, products capable of becoming net contributors if something drastic is done, yesterday's breadwinners, the ''also rans,'' and the failures. Drucker's classification provides an interesting scheme for determining whether a company is developing enough new products to ensure future growth and profits.

In the past few years, the emphasis has shifted from product to business. Usually a company discovers that some of its business units are competitively well placed, whereas others are not. Because resources, particularly cash resources, are limited, not all SBUs can be treated alike. In this chapter, three different frameworks are presented to enable management to select the optimum combination of individual SBU strategies from a spectrum of possible alternatives and opportunities open to the company, still satisfying the resource limitations within which the company must operate. The frameworks may also be used at the SBU level to review the strategic perspective of its different product/market segments.

The first framework to be discussed, the **product life cycle**, is a tool many marketers have traditionally used to formulate marketing strategies for different products. The second framework was developed by the Boston Consulting Group and is commonly called the product portfolio approach. The third, the multifactor portfolio approach, owes its development to the General Electric Company. The chapter concludes with the Porter's generic strategies framework. One important caveat to keep in mind with all the frameworks that will be discussed is that, while certain strategies are implicit in their categorizations, these implied strategies are not set in stone—diametrically divergent strategies implemented well may be equally successful.

10.1 PRODUCT LIFE CYCLE (PLC)

Products tend to go through different stages, each stage being affected by different competitive conditions. These stages require different marketing and product management strategies at different times if sales and profits are to be efficiently realized. The length of a product's life cycle is in no way a fixed period of time. It can last from weeks to years, depending on the type of product. In most texts, the discussion of the PLC portrays the sales history of a typical product as following an S-shaped curve. The curve is has traditionally been divided into four stages: introduction, growth, maturity, and decline. (Some authors include a fifth stage, saturation.)

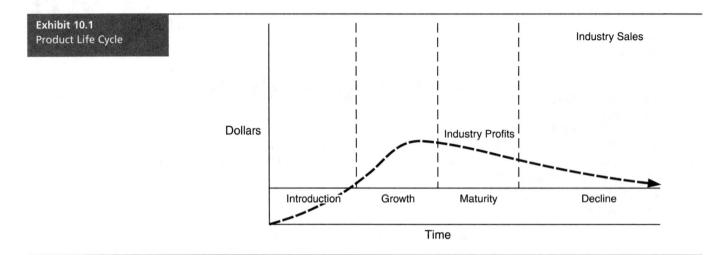

Exhibit 10.1
Product Life Cycle

However, not all products follow an S-shaped curve. Marketing scholars have identified varying product life-cycle patterns. For example, Tellis and Crawford[1] identify 17 product life-cycle patterns, while Swan and Rink name 10.[2] Exhibit 10.1 conceptualizes a typical product life-cycle curve, which shows the relationship between profits and corresponding sales throughout a product's life.

Introduction is the period during which initial market acceptance is in doubt; thus, it is a period of slow growth. Profits are almost nonexistent because of high marketing and other expenses. Setbacks in the product's development, manufacturing, and market introduction exact a heavy toll. Marketing strategy during this stage is based on different combinations of product, price, promotion, and distribution. For example, price and promotion variables may be combined to generate the following strategy alternatives: (a) high price/high promotion, (b) high price/low promotion, (c) low price/heavy promotion, and (d) low price/low promotion.

Strategy during the Introduction Stage is dominated by two factors: First, the fact that the product is new and unknown to the market, and second, the fact that the product initially has no direct competitors, and at the end of the stage, generally still has only a few competitors. Hence, promotion and advertising should focus on creating **primary demand**—that is demand for the product category. In the latter part of the Introduction Stage and in subsequest stages, when competition has entered the market, promotion and advertising should focus on creating **secondary demand**—that is demand for the specific company brand—and brand equity. During subsequent stages w Certain environmental influences that influence product strategy are associated with each stage of the PLC.

Survivors of the introduction stage enjoy a period of rapid growth. During this **growth** period, there is substantial profit improvement. Strategy in this stage takes the following shape: (a) product improvement, addition of new features and models; (b) development of new market segments; (c) addition of new channels; (d) secondary demand stimulation (building demand for a company's specific product); and (e) price reductions to vie for new, targeted customers.

During the next stage, **maturity**, there is intense rivalry for a mature market. Efforts may be limited to attracting a new population, leading to a proliferation of sizes, colors, attachments, perfomance characteristics and other product variants. Battling to retain the company's share, each marketer steps up persuasive advertising, opens new channels of distribution, and grants price concessions where appropriate. Unless new competitors are obstructed by patents or other barriers, entry is easy. Thus, maturity is a period when sales growth slows down, margins tighten and profits peak and then start to decline.

Strategy in the maturity stage comprises the following steps: (a) search for new markets and new and varied uses for the product, (b) improvement of product quality through changes in features and style, (c) new marketing mix perspectives, and (d) production and/or delivery efficiencies begin to be implemented. For the leader firm, Step c may mean introducing an innovative product, fortifying the market through multibrand strategy, or engaging in a price-promotion war against the weaker members of the industry; the nonleader may seek a differential advantage, finding a niche in the market through either product or promotional variables.

Finally, there is the **decline** period. Though sales and profits continue their downward trend, the declining product is not necessarily unprofitable. Some of the competition may have left the market by this stage and assets are generally fully depreciated. Promotion and other costs are cut wherever possible. Customers who remain committed to the product may be willing to use standard models, pay higher prices, and buy at selected outlets.

An important consideration in strategy determination in the decline stage is exit barrier. Even when it appears appropriate to leave the industry, there may be one or more barriers to prevent easy exit. For example, there may be durable and specialized assets peculiar to the business that have little value outside the business; the cost of exit may be prohibitive because of labor settlement costs or contingent liabilities for land use; there may be managerial resistance; the business may be important in gaining access to financial markets; quitting the business may have a negative impact on other businesses and products in the company; or there may be government pressure to continue in the business, a situation that a multinational corporation may face, particularly in developing countries.

Overall, in the decline stage, the choice of a specific alternative strategy is based on the business's strengths and weaknesses and the attractiveness of the industry to the company. The following alternative strategies appear appropriate:

1. Increasing the firm's investment (to dominate or get a good competitive position).
2. Holding the firm's investment level until the uncertainties about the industry are resolved.
3. Decreasing the firm's investment posture selectively by sloughing off unpromising customer groups, while simultaneously strengthening the firm's investment posture within the lucrative niches of enduring customer demand.
4. Harvesting (or milking) the firm's investment to recover cash quickly, regardless of the resulting investment posture.
5. Divesting the business quickly by disposing of its assets as advantageously as possible.[3]

In summary, in the introduction stage, the choices are primarily with what force to enter the market and whether to target a relatively narrow segment of customers or a broader customer group. In the growth stage, the choices appear to be to fortify and consolidate previously established market positions or to develop new primary demand and establishing secondary demand. Developing new primary demand may be accomplished by a variety of means, including developing new applications, extending geographic coverage, trading down to previously untapped consumer groups, or adding related products. Developing secondary demand involves building brand awareness and demand. In the late growth and early maturity stages, the choices lie among various alternatives for achieving a larger share of the existing market. This may involve product improvement, product line extension, finer positioning of the product line, a shift from breadth of offering to in-depth focus, invading the market of a competitor that has invaded one's own market, or cutting out some of the "frills" associated with the product to appeal better to certain classes of customers. In the maturity stage, market positions have become established and the primary emphasis is on nose-to-nose competition in various segments of the market. This type of close competition may take the form of price competition, minor feature competition, or promotional competition. In the decline stage, the choices are to continue current product/market perspectives as is, to continue selectively, or to divest. If one continues in the product/market, improving costs efficiencies in all the controllable variables becomes paramount.

Exhibit 10.2 identifies the characteristics, marketing objectives, and marketing strategies of each stage of the S-shaped product life cycle. The characteristics help locate products on the curve. The objectives and strategies indicate what marketing perspective is relevant in each stage. Actual choice of strategies rests on the objective set for the product, the nature of the product, and environmental influences operating at the time. For example, in the introductory stage, if a new product is launched without any competition and the firm has spent huge amounts of money on research and development, the firm may pursue a high price/low promotion strategy (i.e., skim the cream off the top of the market). As the product becomes established and enters the growth stage, the price may be cut to bring new segments into the fold—the strategic perspective Panasonic used this for its VCRs.

On the other hand, if a product is introduced into a market where there is already a well-established brand, the firm may follow a high price/high promotion strategy. Seiko, for example, introduced its digital watch among well-to-do buyers with a high price and heavy promotion without any intention of competing against Texas Instruments head on.

Of the four stages, the maturity stage of the life cycle offers the greatest opportunity to shape the duration of a product's life cycle. These critical questions must be answered: Why have sales tapered off? Has the product approached obsolescence because of a superior substitute or because of a fundamental change in

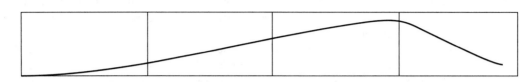

	Introduction	**Growth**	**Maturity**	**Decline**
Characteristics				
Sales	Low sales	Rapidly rising sales	Peak sales	Declining sales
Costs	High cost per customer	Average cost per customer	Low cost per customer	Low cost per customer
Profits	Negative	Rising profits	High profits	Declining profits
Customers	Innovators	Early adopters	Middle majority	Laggards
Competitors	Few	Growing number	Stable number beginning to decline	Declining number
Marketing Objectives				
	Create a product awareness and trial	**Maximize market share**	**Maximize profit while defending market share**	**Reduce expenditure and milk the brand**
Strategies				
Product	Offer a basic product	Offer product extensions, service warranty	Diversify brands and models	Phase out weak items
Price	Use cost-plus	Price to penetrate market	Price to match or beat competitors	Cut price
Distribution	Build selective distribution	Build intensive distribution	Build more intensive distribution	Go selective; phase out unprofitable outlets
Advertising	Build product awareness among early adopters and dealers	Build awareness and interest in the mass market	Stress brand differences and benefits	Reduce to level needed to retain hardcore loyals
Sales Promotion	Use heavy sales promotion to entice trial	Reduce to take advantage of heavy consumer demand	Increase to encourage brand switching	Reduce to minimal level

Source: Philip Kotler, *Marketing Management: Analysis, Planning and Control,* 8th Ed., © 1994, p. 373. Reprinted by permission of Prentice-Hall, Inc., Englewood Cliffs, N.J.

Exhibit 10.2 Perspectives of the Product Life Cycle

consumer needs? Can obsolescence be attributed to management's failure to identify and reach the right consumer needs or has a competitor done a better marketing job? Answers to these questions are crucial if an appropriate strategy is to be employed to strengthen the product's position. For example, the product may be redirected on a growth path through repackaging, physical modification, repricing, appeals to new users, the addition of new distribution channels, or the use of some combination of marketing strategy changes. The choice of a right strategy at the maturity stage can be extremely beneficial, since a successfully revitalized product offers a higher return on management time and funds invested than does a new product.

This point may be illustrated with reference to a Du Pont product, Lycra, a superstretching polymer invented in its labs in 1959. Fifty years after its humble start as an ingredient for girdles, demand for Lycra continues to explode so fast that the company cannot keep up with demand. The product's success may be directly attributed to a shrewd marketing strategy, initiated during the maturity stage, that allowed Lycra's use to expand steadily, from bathing suits in the 1970s to cycling pants and aerobic outfits in the 1980s and Indian saris, kites and parasails in the first decade of the 21st century. Teenagers were lured to it and use it in their everyday fashion wardrobes. Avant-garde designers picked up on the trend, using Lycra in new, body-hugging designs. Now, this distinctly unnatural fiber is part of the fashion mainstream. Du Pont's marketing strategy has paid off well. A recent study showed that consumers would pay 20 percent more for a wool-Lycra skirt than for an all-wool version.[4]

The product life cycle is a useful concept that may be an important aid in marketing planning and strategy. A concept familiar to most marketers, it is given a prominent place in every marketing textbook. Its use in practice remains limited, however, partly because of the lack of normative models available for its application and partly because of the vast amount of data needed for and the level of subjectivity involved in its use.

One caution that is in order when using the product life cycle is to keep in mind that not all products follow the typical life-cycle pattern. The same product may be viewed in different ways: as a brand (Pepsi Light), as a product form (diet cola), and as a product category (cola drink), for example. Among these, the product life-cycle concept is most relevant for product forms.

The easiest way to locate a product in its life cycle is to study its past performance, competitive history, and current position and to match this information with the characteristics of a particular stage of the life cycle. Analysis of past performance of the product includes examination of the following:

1. Sales growth progression since introduction.
2. Any design problems and technical bugs that need to be sorted out.
3. Sales and profit history of allied products (those similar in general character or function as well as products directly competitive).
4. Number of years the product has been on the market.
5. Casualty history of similar products in the past.
6. Product variations on the market.
7. The market's familiarity with the product, its uses, benefits and technologies.

The review of competition focuses on:

1. Profit history.
2. Ease with which other firms can get into the business.
3. Extent of initial investment needed to enter the business.
4. Number of competitors and their strength.
5. Number of competitors that have left the industry.
6. Life cycle of the industry.
7. Critical factors for success in the business.

In addition, current perspectives may be reviewed to gauge whether sales are on the upswing, have leveled out for the last couple of years, or are heading down; whether any competitive products are moving up to replace the product under consideration; whether customers are becoming more demanding vis-à-vis price, service, or special features; whether additional sales efforts are necessary to keep the sales going up; and whether it is becoming harder to sign up dealers and distributors.

This information on the product may be related to the characteristics of different stages of the product life cycle as discussed above; the product perspectives that match the product life cycle indicate the position of the product in its life cycle. Needless to say, the whole process is highly qualitative in nature, and managerial intuition and judgment bear heavily on the final placement of the product in its life cycle. As a matter of fact, making the appropriate assumptions about the types of information described here can be used to construct a model to predict the industry volume of a newly introduced product through each stage of the product life cycle.[5]

A slightly different approach for locating a product in its life cycle is to use past accounting information for the purpose. Listed below are the steps that may be followed to position a product in its life cycle:

1. Develop historical trend information for a period of three to five years (longer for some products). Data included should be unit and dollar sales, profit margins, total profit contribution, return on invested capital, market share, and prices.

2. Check recent trends in the number and nature of competitors, number and market share rankings of competing products and their quality and performance advantages, shifts in distribution channels, and relative advantages enjoyed by products in each channel.

3. Analyze developments in short-term competitive tactics, such as competitors' recent announcements of new products or plans for expanding production capacity.

4. Obtain (or update) historical information on the life cycle of similar or related products.

5. Project sales for the product over the next three to five years, based on all information gathered, and estimate an incremental profit ratio for the product during each of these years (the ratio of total direct costs—manufacturing, advertising, product development, sales, distribution, etc.—to pretax profits). Expressed as a ratio (e.g., 4.8 to 1 or 6.3 to 1), this measure indicates the number of dollars required to generate each additional dollar of profit. The ratio typically improves (becomes lower) as the product enters its growth period, begins to deteriorate (rise) as the product approaches maturity, and climbs more sharply as it reaches decline.

6. Estimate the length of profitable time remaining in the product's life cycle and, based on all information at hand, fix the product's position on its life-cycle curve: (a) introduction, (b) early or late growth, (c) early or late maturity, or (d) early or late decline. Keep in mind that a product's life cycle may be measured in decades (e.g., Coca Cola and Lycra), one or two years (e.g., high tech products with relatively rapid onset of obsolesence), or a matter of months (e.g., high fashion clothing), and that a product's life cycle may be restarted in the late growth or early maturity stage.

The current positions of different products in the product life cycle may be determined by following the procedure described above, and the net results (i.e., the cash flow and profitability) of these positions may be computed. Similar analyses may be performed for a future period. The difference between current and future positions indicates what results management may expect if no strategic changes are made. These results may be compared with corporate expectations to determine the gap. The gap can be filled either by making strategic changes to extend the life cycle of a product or by bringing in new products through research and development or acquisition. This procedure may be put into operation by following these steps:

1. Determine what percentage of the company's sales and profits fall within each phase of the product life cycle. These percentages indicate the present life-cycle (sales) profile and the present profit profile of the company's current line.

2. Calculate changes in life-cycle and profit profiles over the past five years and project these profiles over the next five years.

3. Develop a target life-cycle profile for the company and measure the company's present life-cycle profile against it. The target profile, established by marketing management, specifies the desirable share of company sales that should fall within each phase of the product life cycle. It can be determined by industry obsolescence trends, the pace of new product introductions in the field, the average length of product life cycles in the company's line, and top management's objectives for growth and profitability. As a rule, the target profile for growth-minded companies whose life cycles tend to be short calls for a high proportion of sales in introductory and growth phases.

With these steps completed, management can assign priorities to such functions as new product development, acquisition, and product line pruning, based on the discrepancies between the company's target profile and its present life-cycle profile. Once corporate effort has been broadly allocated in this way among products at various stages of their life cycles, marketing plans can be detailed for individual product lines.

10.2 PORTFOLIO MATRIX

A good planning system must guide the development of strategic alternatives for each of the company's current businesses and new business possibilities. It must also provide for management's review of these strategic alternatives and for corresponding resource allocation decisions. The result is a set of approved business plans that, taken as a whole, represent the direction of the firm. This process starts with, and its success is largely determined by, the creation of sound strategic alternatives.

The top management of a multibusiness firm cannot generate these strategic alternatives. It must rely on the managers of its business ventures and on its corporate development personnel. However, top management can and should establish a conceptual framework within which these alternatives can be developed. One such framework is the portfolio matrix associated with the Boston Consulting Group (BCG). Briefly, the **portfolio matrix** is used to establish the best mix of businesses in order to maximize the long-term earnings growth of the firm. The portfolio matrix represents a real advance in strategic planning in several ways:

• It encourages top management to evaluate the prospects of each of the company's businesses individually and to set tailored objectives for each business based on the contribution it can realistically make to corporate goals.
• It stimulates the use of externally focused empirical data to supplement managerial judgment in evaluating the potential of a particular business.
• It explicitly raises the issue of cash flow balancing as management plans for expansion and growth.
• It gives managers a potent new tool for analyzing competitors and for predicting competitive responses to strategic moves.
• It provides not just a financial but a strategic context for evaluating acquisitions and divestitures.[6]

As a consequence of these benefits, the widespread application of the portfolio matrix approach to corporate planning has sounded the death knell for planning by exhortation, the kind of strategic planning that sets uniform financial performance goals across an entire company—15 percent growth in earnings or 15 percent return on equity—and then expects each business to meet those goals year in and year out. The portfolio matrix approach has given top management the tools to evaluate each business in the context of both its environment and its unique contribution to the goals of the company as a whole and to weigh the entire array of business opportunities available to the company against the financial resources required to support them.

The portfolio matrix concept addresses the issue of the potential value of a particular business for the firm. This value has two variables: first, the potential for generating attractive earnings levels now; second, the potential for growth or, in other words, for significantly increased earnings levels in the future. The portfolio matrix concept holds that these two variables can be quantified. Current earnings potential is measured by comparing the market position of the business to that of its competitors.

Growth potential is measured by the growth rate of the market segment in which the business competes. Clearly, if the segment is in the decline stage of its life cycle, the only way the business can increase its market share is by taking volume away from competitors. Although this is sometimes possible and economically desirable, it is usually expensive, leads to destructive pricing and erosion of profitability for all competitors, and ultimately results in a market that is ill served. On the other hand, if a market is in its rapid growth stage, the business can gain share by preempting the incremental growth in the market. So if these two dimensions of value are arrayed in matrix form, we have the basis for a business classification scheme. This is essentially what the Boston Consulting Group portfolio matrix is. Each of the four business categories tends to have specific characteristics associated with it. The two quadrants corresponding to high market leadership have current earnings potential, and the two corresponding to high market growth have growth potential.

The basic assumptions of the BCG Matrix are that:

1. Increased market share will result in increased cash generation.
2. Growing markets require additional investment.
3. The additional investment needed for growing, high market share businesses can be taken by more mature, slower growth businesses.
4. Each business unit is independent from the others.

Use of the BCG Matrix should keep these assumptions in mind and application of the matrix is questionable when these assumptions are seriously breached.

Exhibit 10.3 shows a matrix with its two sides labeled *product sales growth rate* and *relative market share*. The area of each circle represents dollar sales. The market share position of each circle is determined by its horizontal position. Each circle's product sales growth rate (corrected for inflation) in the market in which it competes is shown by its vertical position.

With regard to the two axes of the matrix, relative market share is plotted on a logarithmic scale in order to be consistent with the experience curve effect, which implies that profit margin or rate of cash

Exhibit 10.3
Product Portfolio Matrix

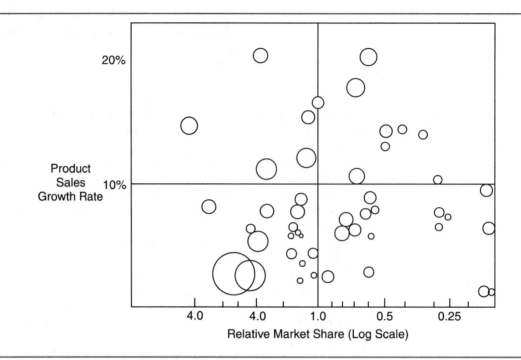

generation differences between two competitors tends to be proportionate to the ratio of their competitive positions. A linear axis is used for growth, for which the most generally useful measure is volume growth of the business concerned; in general, rates of cash use should be directly proportional to growth.

The lines dividing the matrix into four quadrants are arbitrary. Usually, high growth is taken to include all businesses growing in excess of 10 percent annually in volume. The line separating areas of high and low relative competitive position is set at 1.0.

The importance of growth variables for strategy development is based on two factors. First, growth is a major influence in reducing cost because it is easier to gain experience or build market share in a growth market than in a low-growth situation. Second, growth provides opportunity for investment. The relative market share affects the rate at which a business will generate cash. The stronger the relative market share position of a product, the higher the margins it will have because of the scale effect.

Using the two dimensions discussed here in Exhibit 10.4, one can classify businesses and products into four categories. Businesses in each category exhibit different financial characteristics and offer different strategic choices.

Exhibit 10.4
Matrix Quadrants

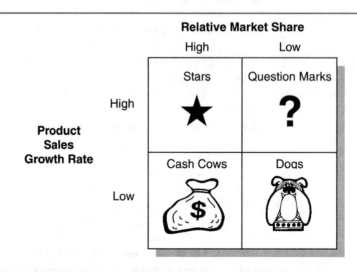

10.2.1 Stars

High-growth market leaders are called stars. They generate large amounts of cash, but the cash they generate from earnings and depreciation is more than offset by the cash that must be put back in the form of capital expenditures and increased working capital. Such heavy reinvestment is necessary to fund the capacity increases and inventory and receivable investment that go along with market share gains. Thus, star products represent probably the best profit opportunity available to a company, and their competitive position must be maintained. If a star's share is allowed to slip because the star has been used to provide large amounts of cash in the short run or because of cutbacks in investment and rising prices (creating an umbrella for competitors), the star will ultimately become a dog.

The ultimate value of any product or service is reflected in the stream of cash it generates net of its own reinvestment. For a star, this stream of cash lies in the future—sometimes in the distant future. To obtain real value, the stream of cash must be discounted back to the present at a rate equal to the return on alternative opportunities. It is the future payoff of the star that counts, not the present reported profit. For GE, the plastics business is a star in which it keeps investing. As a matter of fact, the company even acquired Thomson's plastics operations (a French company) to further strengthen its position in the business.

10.2.2 Cash Cows

Cash cows are characterized by low growth and high market share. They are net providers of cash. Their high earnings, coupled with their depreciation, represent high cash inflows, and they need very little in the way of reinvestment. Thus, these businesses generate large cash surpluses that help to pay dividends and interest, provide debt capacity, supply funds for research and development, meet overheads, and also make cash available for investment in other products. Thus, cash cows are the foundation on which everything else depends. These products must be protected. Technically speaking, a cash cow has a return on assets that exceeds its growth rate. Only if this is true will the cash cow generate more cash than it uses. For NCR Company, the mechanical cash register business is a cash cow. The company still maintains a dominant share of this business even though growth has slowed down since the introduction of electronic cash registers. The company uses the surplus cash from its mechanical cash registers to develop electronic machines with a view to creating a new star. Likewise, the tire business can be categorized as a cash cow for Goodyear Tire and Rubber Company. The tire industry is characterized by slow market growth, and Goodyear has a major share of the market.

10.2.3 Question Marks

Products in a growth market with a low share are categorized as question marks. Because of growth, these products require more cash than they are able to generate on their own. If nothing is done to increase market share, a question mark will simply absorb large amounts of cash in the short run and later, as the growth slows down, become a dog. Thus, unless something is done to change its perspective, a question mark remains a cash loser throughout its existence and ultimately becomes a cash trap.

What can be done to make a question mark more viable? One alternative is to gain share increases for it. Because the business is growing, it can be funded to dominance. It may then become a star and later, when growth slows down, a cash cow. This strategy is a costly one in the short run. An abundance of cash must be poured into a question mark in order for it to win a major share of the market, but in the long run, this strategy is the only way to develop a sound business from the question mark stage. Another strategy is to divest the business. Outright sale is the most desirable alternative. But if this does not work out, a firm decision must be made not to invest further in the business. The business must simply be allowed to generate whatever cash it can while none is reinvested.

When Joseph E. Seagram and Sons bought Tropicana from Beatrice Co. in 1988, it was a question mark. The product had been trailing behind Coke's Minute Maid and was losing ground to Procter & Gamble's new entry in the field, Citrus Hill. Since then, Seagram has invested heavily in Tropicana to develop it into a star product. After just two years, Tropicana has emerged as a leader in the not-from-concentrate orange juice market, far ahead of Minute Maid, and has been trying to make inroads into other segments.[7] Meanwhile, P&G withdraw its citrus Hill brand.

10.2.4 Dogs

Products with low market share positioned in low-growth situations are called dogs. Their poor competitive position condemns them to poor profits. Because growth is low, dogs have little potential for gaining sufficient share to achieve viable cost positions. Usually they are net users of cash. Their earnings are low, and the reinvestment required just to keep the business together eats cash inflow. The business, therefore, becomes a cash trap that is likely to regularly absorb cash unless further investment is rigorously avoided. An alternative is to convert dogs into cash, if there is an opportunity to do so. GE's consumer electronics business had been in the dog category, maintaining only a small percentage of the available market in a period of slow growth, when the company decided to unload the business (including the RCA brand acquired in late 1985) to Thomson, France's state-owned, leading electronics manufacturer. (Recently, Thomson sold its consumer electronics business to a Korean firm.)

Exhibit 10.5 summarizes the investment, earning, and cash flow characteristics of stars, cash cows, question marks, and dogs. Also shown are viable strategy alternatives for products in each category.

In a typical company, products could be scattered in all four quadrants of the portfolio matrix. The appropriate strategy for products in each cell is given briefly in Exhibit 10.5. The first goal of a company should be to secure a position with cash cows but to guard against the frequent temptation to reinvest in them excessively. The cash generated from cash cows should first be used to support those stars that are not self-sustaining. Surplus cash may then be used to finance selected question marks to dominance. Any question mark that cannot be funded should be divested. A dog may be restored to a position of viability by shrewdly segmenting the market; that is, by rationalizing and specializing the business into a small niche that the product may dominate. If this is not practical, a firm should manage the dog for cash; it should cut off all investment in the business and liquidate it when an opportunity develops.

Exhibit 10.6 shows the consequences of a correct/incorrect strategic move. If a question mark is given adequate support, it may become a star and ultimately a cash cow (success sequence). On the other hand, if a star is not appropriately funded, it may become a question mark and finally a dog (disaster sequence).

Top management needs to answer two strategic questions: (a) How promising is the current set of businesses with respect to long-term return and growth? (b) Which businesses should be developed? maintained as is? liquidated? Following the portfolio matrix approach, a company needs a cash-balanced portfolio of businesses; that is, it needs cash cows and dogs to throw off sufficient cash to fund stars and question marks. It needs an ample supply of question marks to ensure long-term growth and businesses with return levels appropriate to their matrix position. In response to the second question, capital budgeting theory requires the lining up of capital project proposals, assessment of incremental cash flows attributable to each project, computation of discounted rate of return on each, and approval of the project with the

Quadrant	Investment Characteristics	Earning Characteristics	Cash Flow Characteristics	Strategy Implication
Stars	— Continual expenditures for capacity expansion — Pipeline filling with cash	Low to high	Negative cash flow (net cash user)	Continue to increase market share, if necessary at the expense of short-term earnings
Cash cows	— Capacity maintenance expenditures	High	Positive cash flow (net cash contributor)	Maintain share and leadership until further investment becomes marginal
Question marks	— Heavy initial capacity expenditures — High research and development costs	Negative to low	Negative cash flow (net cash user)	Assess chances of dominating segment: if good, go after share; if bad, redefine business or withdraw
Dogs	— Gradually deplete capacity	High to low	Positive cash flow (net cash contributor)	Plan an orderly withdrawal so as to maximize cash flow

Exhibit 10.5 Characteristics and Strategy Implications of Products in the Strategy Quadrants

Exhibit 10.6
Product Portfolio Matrix:
Strategic Consequences

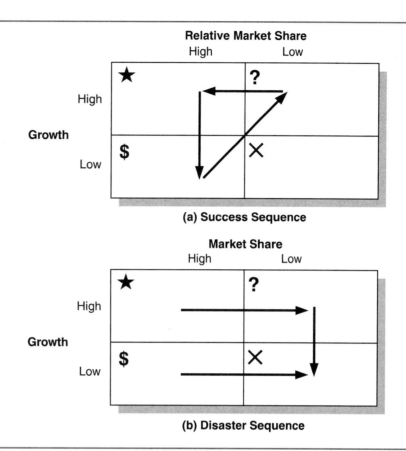

highest rate of return until available funds are exhausted. But the capital budgeting approach misses the strategic content; that is, it ignores questions of how to validate assumptions about volume, price, cost, and investment and how to eliminate natural biases. This problem is solved by the portfolio matrix approach.

The product portfolio matrix approach propounded by the Boston Consulting Group may be related to the product life cycle by letting the introduction stage begin in the question mark quadrant; growth starts toward the end of this quadrant and continues well into the star quadrant. Going down from the star to the cash cow quadrant, the maturity stage begins. Decline is positioned between the cash cow and the dog quadrants (see Exhibit 10.7). Ideally, a company should enter the product/market segment in its introduction stage, gain market share in the growth stage, attain a position of dominance when the product/market segment enters its maturity stage, maintain this dominant position until the product/market segment enters its decline stage, and then determine the optimum point for liquidation.

Exhibit 10.8 is an example of a balanced portfolio. With three cash cows, this company is well positioned with stars to provide growth and to yield high cash returns in the future when they mature. The company has four question marks, two of which present good opportunities to emerge as stars at an investment level that the cash cows should be able to support (based on the area of the circles). The company does have dogs, but they can be managed to avoid drain on cash resources.

Unbalanced portfolios may be classified into four types:

1. Too many losers (due to inadequate cash flow, inadequate profits, and inadequate growth).
2. Too many question marks (due to inadequate cash flow and inadequate profits).
3. Too many profit producers (due to inadequate growth and excessive cash flow).
4. Too many developing winners (due to excessive cash demands, excessive demands on management, and unstable growth and profits).

Exhibit 10.9 illustrates an unbalanced portfolio. The company has just one cash cow, three question marks, and no stars. Thus, the cash base of the company is inadequate and cannot support the question marks. The company may allocate available cash among all question marks in equal proportion. Dogs may

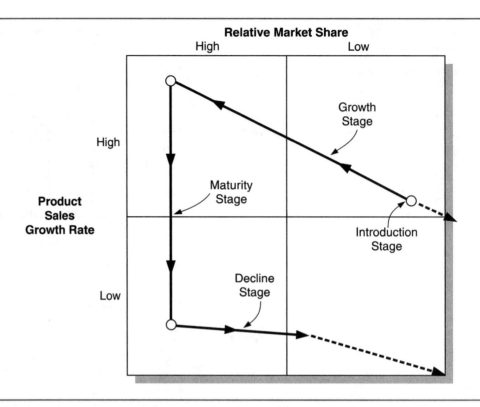

also be given occasional cash nourishment. If the company continues its current strategy, it may find itself in a dangerous position in five years, particularly when the cash cow moves closer to becoming a dog. To take corrective action, the company must face the fact that it cannot support all its question marks. It must choose one or maybe two of its three question marks and fund them adequately to make them stars. In addition, disbursement of cash in dogs should be totally prohibited. In brief, the strategic choice for the company, considered in portfolio terms, is obvious. It cannot fund all question marks and dogs equally.

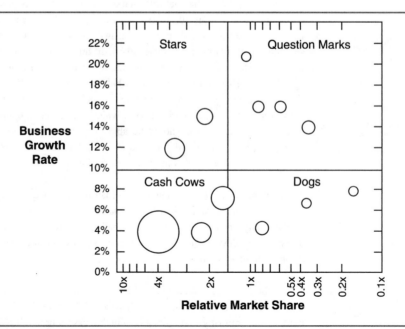

Exhibit 10.9
Illustration of an
Unbalanced Portfolio

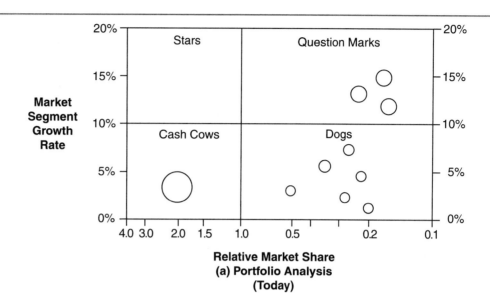

Relative Market Share
(a) Portfolio Analysis
(Today)

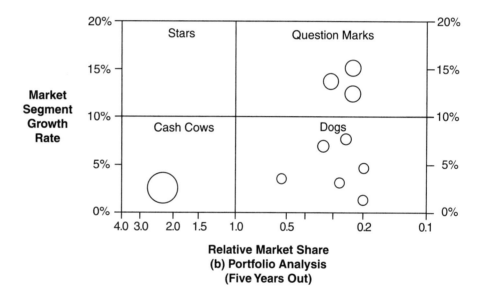

Relative Market Share
(b) Portfolio Analysis
(Five Years Out)

The portfolio matrix focuses on the real fundamentals of businesses and their relationships to each other within the portfolio. It is not possible to develop effective strategy in a multiproduct, multimarket company without considering the mutual relationships of different businesses.

The portfolio matrix approach provides for the simultaneous comparison of different products. It also underlines the importance of cash flow as a strategic variable. Thus, when continuous long-term growth in earnings is the objective, it is necessary to identify high-growth product/market segments early, develop businesses, and preempt the growth in these segments. If necessary, short-term profitability in these segments may be forgone to ensure achievement of the dominant share. Costs must be managed to meet scale-effect standards. The appropriate point at which to shift from an earnings focus to a cash flow focus must be determined and a liquidation plan for cash flow maximization established. A cash-balanced mix of businesses should be maintained.

Many companies worldwide have used the portfolio matrix approach in their strategic planning. The first companies to use this approach were the Norton Company, Mead, Borg-Warner, Eaton, and Monsanto. Since then, virtually all large corporations have reported following it.

The portfolio matrix approach, however, is not a panacea for strategy development. In reality, many difficulties limit the workability of this approach. Some potential mistakes associated with the portfolio matrix concept are

1. Overinvesting in low-growth segments (lack of objectivity and "hard" analysis).
2. Underinvesting in high-growth segments (lack of guts).
3. Misjudging the segment growth rate (poor market research).
4. Not achieving market share (because of improper market strategy, sales capabilities, or promotion).
5. Losing cost effectiveness (lack of operating talent and control system).
6. Not uncovering emerging high-growth segments (lack of corporate development effort).
7. Unbalanced business mix (lack of planning and financial resources).

Thus, the portfolio matrix approach should be used with great care.

10.3 MULTIFACTOR PORTFOLIO MATRIX

The two-factor portfolio matrix discussed above provides a useful approach for reviewing the roles of different products in a company. However, the growth rate-relative market share matrix approach leads to many difficulties. At times, factors other than market share and growth rate bear heavily on cash flow, the mainstay of this approach. Some managers may consider return on investment a more suitable criterion than cash flow for making investment decisions. Further, the two-factor portfolio matrix approach does not address major investment decisions between dissimilar businesses. These difficulties can lead a company into too many traps and errors. For this reason, many companies (such as GE and the Shell Group) have developed the multifactor portfolio approach.

Exhibit 10.10 illustrates the GE matrix. Its two dimensions, industry attractiveness and business strengths, are based on a variety of factors. It is this multifactor characteristic that differentiates this approach from the one discussed in the previous section. In its early attempts with the portfolio matrix, GE used the criteria and measures shown in Exhibit 10.11 to determine industry attractiveness and business strengths. These criteria and measures are only suggestions; another company may adopt a different list. For example, GE later added cyclicality as a criterion under industry attractiveness. The measure of relative profitability, as shown in the exhibit, was used for the first time in 1985.

Exhibit 10.10
Relationship between the Strategic Planning Process and Approaches to Marketing

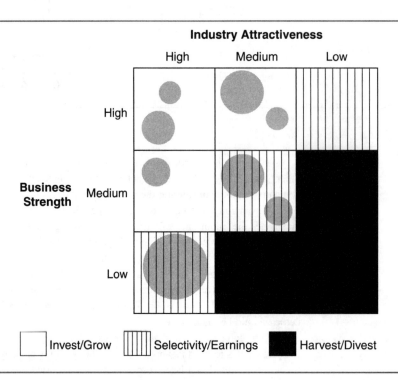

☐ Invest/Grow   ▥ Selectivity/Earnings   ■ Harvest/Divest

Industry Attractiveness		Business Strengths	
Criterion	**Measure**	**Criterion**	**Measure**
1. Market size	• Three-year average served industry market dollars	1. Market position	• Three-year average market share (total dollars)
2. Market growth	• Ten-year constant dollar average market growth rate		• Three-year average international market share
			• Two-year average relative market share (SBU/Big Three competitors)
3. Industry profitability	• Three-year average ROS, SBU and Big Three competitors: • Nominal • Inflation adjusted	2. Competitive position	Superior, equal, or inferior to competition in 1980: • Product quality • Technological leadership • Manufacturing/cost leadership • Distribution/marketing leadership
4. Cyclicality	• Average annual percent variation of sales from trend		
5. Inflation recovery	• Five-year average ratio of combined selling price and productivity change to change in cost due to inflation	3. Relative profitability	Three-year average SBU ROS less average ROS, Big Three competitors: • Nominal • Inflation adjusted
6. Importance of non-U.S. markets	• Ten-year average ratio of international to total market		

☐ Indicates measure used for first time in 1980

Source: General Electric Co. Reprinted by permission. The measurements do not reflect current GE practice.

Exhibit 10.11 Portfolio Considerations and Measures Used by GE in 1980

Exhibits 10.12 and 10.13 illustrate how the factors may be weighed and how a final industry attractiveness and business strengths score may be computed. Management may establish cutoff points for high, medium, and low industry attractiveness and competitive position scores.

It is worthwhile to mention that the development of a multifactor matrix may not be as easy as it appears. The actual analysis required may take a considerable amount of foresight and experience and many, many days of work. The major difficulties lie in identifying relevant factors, relating factors to industry attractiveness and business strengths, and weighing the factors.

The overall strategy for a business in a particular position is illustrated in Exhibit 10.10. The area of the circle refers to the business's sales. Investment priority is given to products in the high area (upper left), where a stronger position is supported by the attractiveness of an industry. Along the diagonal, selectivity is desired to achieve a balanced earnings performance. The businesses in the low area (lower right) are the candidates for harvesting and divestment.

A company may position its products or businesses on the matrix to study its present standing. Forecasts may be made to examine the directions different businesses may go in the future, assuming no changes are made in strategy. Future perspectives may be compared to the corporate mission to identify gaps between what is desired and what may be expected if no measures are taken now. Filling the gap requires making strategic moves for different businesses. Once strategic alternatives for an individual business have been identified, the final choice of a strategy should be based on the scope of the overall corporation vis-à-vis the matrix. For example, the prospects for a business along the diagonal may appear good, but this business cannot be funded in preference to a business in the high-high cell. In devising future

Criteria	Weights*	× Ratings** =	Values
Market size	.15	4	.60
Growth rate	.12	3	.36
Profit margin	.05	3	.15
Market diversity	.05	2	.10
Demand cyclicality	.05	2	.10
Expert opportunities	.05	5	.25
Competitive structure	.05	3	.15
Industry profitability	.20	3	.60
Inflation vulnerability	.05	2	.10
Value added	.10	5	.50
Capital intensity	GO	4	—
Raw material availability	GO	4	—
Technological role	.05	4	.20
Energy impact	.08	4	.32
Social	GO	4	—
Environmental impact	GO	4	—
Legal	GO	4	—
Human	GO	4	—
	1.00	1 to 5	3.43

* Some criteria may be of a GO/NO GO type. For example, many
Fortune 500 firms would probably not invest in industries viewed
negatively by society even if it were legal and profitable to do so.
**"1" denotes very unattractive; "5" denotes very attractive.

strategy, a company generally likes to have a few businesses on the left to provide growth and to furnish potential for investment and a few on the right to generate cash for investment in the former. The businesses along the diagonal may be selectively supported (based on resources) for relocation on the left. If this is not feasible, they may be slowly harvested or divested. Exhibit 10.14 summarizes desired strategic perspective in different cell positions.

For an individual business, there can be four strategy options: investing to maintain, investing to grow, investing to regain, and investing to exit. The choice of a strategy depends on the current position of the business in the matrix (i.e., toward the high side, along the diagonal, or toward the low side) and its future direction, assuming the current strategic perspective continues to be followed. If the future appears unpromising, a new strategy for the business is called for.

Analysis of present position on the matrix may not pose any problem. At GE, for example, there was little disagreement on the position of the business.[8] The mapping of future direction, however, may not be easy. A rigorous analysis must be performed, taking into account environmental shifts, competitors' perspectives, and internal strengths and weaknesses.

The four strategy options are shown in Exhibit 10.15. Strategy to maintain the current position (Strategy 1 in the exhibit) may be adopted if, in the absence of a new strategy, erosion is expected in the future. Investment will be sought to hold the position; hence, the name invest-to-maintain strategy. The second option is the invest-to-grow strategy. Here, the product's current position is perceived as less than optimum vis-à-vis industry attractiveness and business strengths. In other words, considering the opportunities furnished by the industry and the strengths exhibited by the business, the current position is considered inadequate. A growth strategy is adopted with the aim of shifting the product position upward or toward the left. Movement in both directions is an expensive option with high risk.

The invest-to-regain strategy (Strategy 3 in Exhibit 10.15) is an attempt to rebuild the product or business to its previous position. Usually, when the environment (i.e., industry) continues to be relatively attractive but the business position has slipped because of some strategic past mistake (e.g., premature harvesting), the company may decide to revitalize the business through new investments. The fourth and

Exhibit 10.13
Assessing Business
Strengths

Criteria	Weights*	× Ratings**	= Values
Market share	.10	5	.50
SBU growth rate	X	3	—
Breadth of product line	.05	4	.20
Sales/distribution effectiveness	.20	4	.80
Proprietary and key account effectiveness	X	3	—
Price competitiveness	X	4	—
Advertising and promotion effectiveness	.05	4	.20
Facilities location and newness	.05	5	—
Capacity and productivity	X	3	.10
Experience curve effects	.15	4	.60
Value added	X	4	—
Investment utilization	.05	5	.25
Raw materials cost	.05	4	.20
Relative product quality	.15	4	.60
R&D advantage/position	.05	4	.20
Cash throwoff	.10	5	.50
Organizational synergies	X	5	—
General image	X	5	—
	1.00	1 to 5	4.30

* For any particular industry, there will be some factors that, while important in general, will have little or no effect on the relative competitive position of firms within that industry.

**"1" denotes very weak competitive position; "5" denotes a very strong competitive position.

final option, the invest-to-exit strategy, is directed toward leaving the market through harvesting or divesting. Harvesting amounts to making very low investments in the business so that in the short run the business will secure positive cash flow and in a few years die out. (With no new investments, the position will continue to deteriorate.) Alternatively, the whole business may be divested, that is, sold to another party in a one-time deal. Sometimes small investments may be made to maintain the viability of business if divestment is desired but there is no immediate suitor. In this way the business can eventually be sold at a higher price than would have been possible right away.

The framework discussed here may be applied to either a product/market or an SBU. As a matter of fact, it may be equally applicable to a much higher level of aggregation in the organization, such as a division or a group. Of course, at the group or division level, it may be very difficult to measure industry attractiveness and business strengths unless the group or division happens to be in one business.

In the scheme followed in this book, the analysis may be performed first at the SBU level to determine the strategic perspective of different products/markets. Finally, all SBUs may be simultaneously positioned on the matrix to determine a corporate-wide portfolio.

A slightly different technique, the directional policy matrix, is popularly used in Europe. It was initially worked out at the Shell Group but later caught the fancy of many businesses across the Atlantic. Exhibit 10.16 illustrates a directional policy matrix. The two sides of the matrix are labeled business sector prospects (industry attractiveness) and company's competitive capabilities (business strengths). *Business sector prospects* are categorized as unattractive, average, and attractive; and the *company's competitive capabilities* are categorized as weak, average, and strong. Within each cell is the overall strategy direction for a business depicted by the cell. The consideration of factors used to measure business sector prospects and a company's competitive capabilities follows the same logic and analyses discussed above.

Exhibit 10.14
Prescriptive Strategies for
Businesses in Different
Cells

Competitive Position

		Strong	Medium	Weak
Market Attractive-ness	High	**Protect Position** • Invest to grow at maximum digestible rate • Concentrate effort on maintaining strength	**Invest to Build** • Challenge for leadership • Build selectively on strengths • Reinforce vulnerable areas	**Build Selectively** • Specialize around limited strengths • Seek ways to overcome weaknesses • Withdraw if indications of sustainable growth are lacking
	Medium	**Build Selectively** • Invest heavily in most attractive segments • Build up ability to counter competition • Emphasize profitability by raising productivity	**Selectivity/Manage for Earnings** • Protect existing program • Concentrate investments in segments where profitability is good and risk is relatively low	**Limited Expansion or Harvest** • Look for ways to expand without high risk; otherwise, minimize investment and rationalize investment
	Low	**Protect and Refocus** • Manage for current earnings • Concentrate on attractive strengths • Defend strengths	**Manage for Earnings** • Protect position in most profitable segments • Upgrade product line • Minimize investment	**Divest** • Sell at time that will maximize cash value • Cut fixed costs and avoid investment meanwhile

10.4 PORTFOLIO MATRIX: CRITICAL ANALYSIS

In recent years, a variety of criticisms have been leveled at the portfolio framework. Most of the criticism has centered on the Boston Consulting Group matrix.

1. A question has been raised about the use of market share as the most important influence on marketing strategy. The BCG matrix is derived from an application of the learning curve to manufacturing and other costs. It was observed that, as a firm's product output (and thus market share) increases, total cost declines by a fixed percentage. This may be true for commodities; however, in most product/market situations, products are differentiated, new products and brands are continually introduced, and the pace of technological changes keeps increasing. As a result, one may move from learning curve to learning curve or encounter a discontinuity. More concrete evidence is needed before the validity of market share as a dimension in strategy formulation is established or rejected.

2. Another criticism, closely related to the first, is how product/market boundaries are defined. Market share varies depending on the definition of the corresponding product/market. Hence, a product may be classified in different cells, depending on the market boundaries used.

3. The stability of product life cycles is implicitly assumed in some portfolio models. However, as in the case of the learning curve, it is possible for the product life cycle to change during the life of the

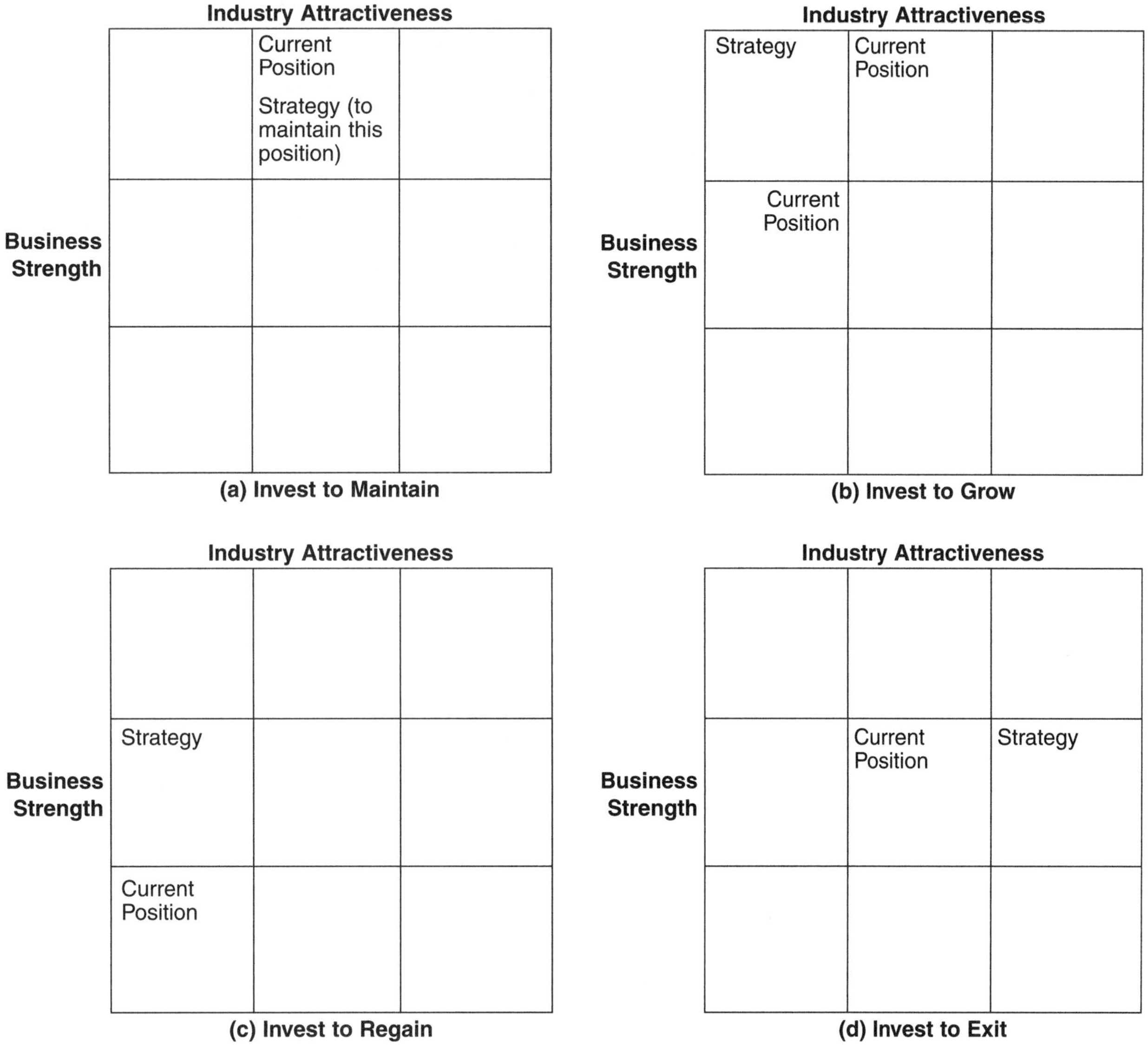

Industry Attractiveness

	Current Position Strategy (to maintain this position)	

Business Strength

(a) Invest to Maintain

Industry Attractiveness

Strategy	Current Position	
	Current Position	

Business Strength

(b) Invest to Grow

Industry Attractiveness

Strategy		
Current Position		

Business Strength

(c) Invest to Regain

Industry Attractiveness

	Current Position	Strategy

Business Strength

(d) Invest to Exit

Exhibit 10.15 Strategy Options

product. For example, recycling can extend the life cycle of a product, sparking a second growth stage after maturity. A related subissue concerns the assumption that investment is more desirable in high-growth markets than in low-growth ones. There is insufficient evidence to support this proposition.[9] This overall issue becomes more problematic for international firms because a given product may be in different stages of its life cycle in different countries.

4. The portfolio framework assumes that investments in all products/markets are equally risky, but this is not the case. In fact, financial portfolio management theory does take risk into account. The more risky an investment, the higher the return expected of it. The portfolio matrix does not consider the risk factor.

5. The BCG portfolio model assumes that there is no interdependency between products/markets. This assumption can be questioned on various grounds. For instance, different products/markets might share technology or costs.[10] These interdependencies should be accounted for in a portfolio framework.

Exhibit 10.16
Directional Policy Matrix

Business Sector Prospects

		Unattractive	Average	Attractive
Company's Competitive Capabilities	Weak	Disinvest	Phased withdrawal Proceed with care	Double or quit
	Average	Phased withdrawal	Proceed with care	Try
	Strong	Cash generator	Growth Leader	Leader

6. Most portfolio approaches are retrospective and overly dependent on conventional wisdom in the way in which they treat both market attractiveness and business strengths.[11] For example, despite evidence to the contrary, conventional wisdom suggests the following:

a. Dominant market share endows companies with sufficient power to maintain price above a competitive level or to obtain massive cost advantages through economies of scale and the experience curve. However, the returns for such companies as Goodyear and Maytag show that this is not always the case.

Market Situation	Conventional Wisdom	Examples	Return on Total Capital Employed 1975–85
Dominant market	Market leader gains — Premium prices — Cost advantages due to scale and experience curve	Goodyear: 40% of U.S. tire market; market leader	7.0%
		Maytag: 5% of U.S. appliance industry; niche competitor	26.7%

b. High market growth means that rivals can expand output and show profits without having to take demand out of each other's plants and provoking price warfare. But the experience of industries as different as the European tungsten carbide industry and the U.S. airline industry suggests that it is not always true.

Market Situation	Conventional Wisdom	Examples	Return on Total Capital Employed 1975–85
High market growth	High market growth allows companies to expand output without provoking price competition and leads to higher profits	European tungsten carbide industry: 1% annual growth	15.0%
		U.S. airline industry: 13.6% annual growth	5.7%

c. High barriers to entry allow existing competitors to keep prices high and earn high profits. But the experience of the U.S. brewing industry seems to refute conventional wisdom.

Market Situation	Conventional Wisdom	Examples	Return on Total Capital Employed 1975–85
High barriers to entry	High barriers prevent new entrants from competing away previously excess profits	U.S. brewing industry is highly concentrated with very high barriers to entry	8.6%

7. There are also issues of measurement and weighting. Different measures have been proposed and used for the dimensions of portfolio models; however, a product's position on a matrix may vary depending on the measures used.[12] In addition, the weights used for models having composite dimensions may impact the results, and the position of a business on the matrix may change with the weighting scheme used.

8. Portfolio models, when applied, must take into account both the external and internal environments of a company. Because a firm's strategic decisions are made within its environments, their potential impact must be taken into account. Day highlights a few situational factors that might affect a firm's strategic plan. As examples of internal factors, he cites rate of capacity utilization, union pressures, barriers to entry, and extent of captive business. GNP, interest rates, and social, legal, and regulatory environment are cited as examples of external factors.[13] No systematic treatment has been accorded to such environmental influences in the portfolio models. These influences are always unique to a company, so the importance of customizing a portfolio approach becomes clear.

9. The relevance of a particular strategy for a business depends on its correct categorization on the matrix. If a mistake is made in locating a business in a particular cell of the matrix, the failure of the implied strategy cannot be blamed on the framework. In other words, superficial and uncritical application of the portfolio framework can misdirect a business's strategy. As Gluck has observed:

> Portfolio approaches have their limitations, of course. First, it's just not all that easy to define the businesses or product/market units appropriately before you begin to analyze them. Second, some attractive strategic opportunities can be overlooked if management treats its businesses as independent entities when there may be real advantages in their sharing resources at the research or manufacturing or distribution level. And third, like more sophisticated models, when it's used uncritically the portfolio can give its users the illusion that they're being rigorous and scientific when in fact they've fallen prey to the old garbage-in, garbage-out syndrome.[14]

10. Most portfolio approaches suggest standard or generic strategies based on the portfolio position of individual SBUs. But these kinds of responses can often result in lost opportunities, turn out to be impractical or unrealistic, and stifle creativity. For example, the standard strategy for managing dogs (SBUs that have a low share of a mature market) is to treat them as candidates for divestment or liquidation. New evidence demonstrates, however, that, with proper management, dogs can be assets to a diversified corporation. One recent study of the performance of more than a thousand industrial-product businesses slotted into the four cells of the BCG matrix found that the average dog had a positive cash flow even greater than the cash needs of the average question mark. Moreover, in a slow-growth economy, more than half of a company's businesses might qualify as dogs. Disposing of them all would be neither feasible nor desirable. Yet the portfolio approach provides no help in suggesting how to improve the performance of such businesses.[15]

11. Portfolio models fail to answer such questions as (a) how a company may determine whether its strategic goals are consistent with its financial objectives, (b) how a company may relate strategic goals to its affordable growth, and (c) how relevant the designated strategies are vis-à-vis competition from overseas companies. In addition, many marketers have raised other questions about the viability of portfolio approaches as a strategy development tool. For example, it has been claimed that the BCG matrix approach is relevant only for positioning existing businesses and fails to prescribe how a question mark may be reared to emerge as a star, how new stars can be located, and so on. Empirical support for limitations of portfolio planning methods come from the work of Armstrong and Brodie. According to them, the limitations are so serious that portfolio matrices are detrimental since they produce poorer decisions.[16]

In response to these criticisms, it should be pointed out that the the portfolio frameworks were developed as an aids in formulating business strategies in complex environments. Their aim was not to prescribe strategy, though many executives and academicians have misused it in this way. As one writer has noted:

> No simple, monolithic set of rules or strategy imperatives will point automatically to the right course. No planning system guarantees the development of successful strategies. Nor does any technique. The Business Portfolio (the growth/share matrix) made a major contribution to strategic thought. Today it is misused and overexposed. It can be a helpful tool, but it can also be misleading or, worse, a straitjacket.[17]

Thus, many of the above criticisms are not actually criticisms of the techniques, but of their misapplication.

10.5 A NEW PRODUCT PORTFOLIO APPROACH: PORTER'S GENERIC STRATEGIES FRAMEWORK

Porter has identified three generic strategies: (a) overall cost leadership (i.e., making units of a fairly standardized product and underpricing everybody else); (b) differentiation (i.e., turning out something customers perceive as unique—an item whose quality, design, brand name, or reputation for service commands higher-than-average prices); and (c) focus (i.e., concentrating on a particular group of customers, geographic market, channel of distribution, or distinct segment of the product line).[18]

Porter's choice of strategy is based on two factors: the **strategic target** at which the business aims and the **strategic advantage** that the business has in aiming at that target. According to Porter, forging successful strategy begins with understanding of what is happening in one's industry and deciding which of the available competitive niches one should attempt to dominate. For example, a firm may discover that the largest competitor in an industry is aggressively pursuing cost leadership, that others are trying the differentiation route, and that no one is attempting to focus on some small specialty market.[19] On the basis of this information, the firm might sharpen its efforts to distinguish its product from others or switch to a focus game plan. As Porter says, the idea is to position the firm ''so it won't be slugging it out with everybody else in the industry; if it does it right, it won't be directly toe-to-toe with anyone.'' The objective is to mark out a defensible competitive position—defensible not just against rival companies but also against the forces driving industry competition (discussed in Chapter 4).

What it means is that the give-and-take between firms already in the business represents only one such force. Others are the bargaining power of suppliers, the bargaining power of buyers, the threat of substitute products or services, and the threat of new entrants. In conclusion, Porter's framework emphasizes not only that certain characteristics of the industry must be considered in choosing a generic strategy, but that they in fact dictate the proper choice.

10.6 PORTFOLIO ANALYSIS CONCLUSION

Portfolio approaches provide a useful tool for strategists. Granted, these approaches have limitations, but all these limitations can be overcome with a little imagination and foresight. The real concern about the portfolio approach is that its elegant simplicity often tempts managers to believe that it can solve all problems of corporate choices and resource allocation. The truth is that it addresses only half of the problem: the back half. The portfolio approach is a powerful tool for helping the strategist select from a menu of available opportunities, but it does not put the menu into his or her hands. That is the front half of the problem. The other critical dimension in making strategic choices is the need to generate a rich array of business options from which to choose. No simple tool is available that can provide this option-generating capability. Here only creative thinking about one's environment, one's business, one's customers, and one's competitors can help.

For a successful introduction of the portfolio framework, the strategist should heed the following advice:[20]

1. Once introduced, move quickly to establish the legitimacy of portfolio analysis.
2. Educate line managers in its relevance and use.
3. Redefine SBUs explicitly because their definition is the "genesis and nemesis" of adequately using the portfolio framework.
4. Use the portfolio framework to seek the strategic direction for different businesses without haggling over the fancy labels by which to call them.
5. Make top management acknowledge SBUs as portfolios to be managed.
6. Seek top management time for reviewing different businesses using the portfolio framework.
7. Rely on a flexible, informal management process to differentiate influence patterns at the SBU level.
8. Tie resource allocation to the business plan.
9. Consider strategic expenses and human resources as explicitly as capital investment.
10. Plan explicitly for new business development.
11. Make a clear strategic commitment to a few selected technologies or markets early.

SUMMARY

A diversified organization needs to examine its widely different businesses at the corporate level to see how each business fits within the overall corporate purpose and to come to grips with the resource allocation problem. The portfolio approaches described in this chapter help management determine the role that each business plays in the corporation and allocate resources accordingly.

Three portfolio approaches were introduced: product life cycle, growth rate-relative market share matrix, and multifactor portfolio matrix. The product life-cycle approach determines the life status of different products and whether the company has enough viable products to provide desired growth in the future. If the company lacks new products with which to generate growth in coming years, investments may be made in new products. If growth is hurt by the early maturity of promising products, the strategic effort may be directed toward extension of their life cycles.

The second approach, the growth rate-relative market share matrix, suggests locating products or businesses on a matrix with relative market share and growth rate as its dimensions. The four cells in the matrix, whose positions are based on whether growth is high or low and whether relative market share is high or low, are labeled stars, cash cows, question marks, and dogs. The strategy for a product or business in each cell, which is primarily based on the business's cash flow implications, was outlined.

The third approach, the multifactor portfolio matrix, again uses two variables (industry attractiveness and business strengths), but these two variables are based on a variety of factors. Here, again, a desired strategy for a product/business in each cell was recommended. The focus of the multifactor matrix approach is on the return-on-investment implications of strategy alternatives rather than on cash flow, as in the growth rate-relative market share matrix approach.

Various portfolio approaches were critically examined. The criticisms relate mainly to operational definitions of dimensions used, weighting of variables, and product/market boundary determination. The chapter concluded with a discussion of Porter's generic strategies framework.

DISCUSSION QUESTIONS

1. What purpose may a product portfolio serve in the context of marketing strategy?
2. How can the position of a product in its life cycle be located?
3. What is the strategic significance of products in the maturity stage of the product life cycle?
4. What is the meaning of relative market share?
5. What sequence should products follow for success? What may management do to ensure this sequence?
6. What factors may a company consider when measuring industry attractiveness and business strengths? Should these factors vary from one business to another in a company?
7. What is the basic difference between the growth rate-relative market share matrix approach and the multifactor portfolio matrix approach?
8. What major problems with portfolio approaches have critics identified?
9. What generic strategies does Porter recommend? Discuss.

NOTES

1. Gerald J. Tellis and C. Merle Crawford, "An Evolutionary Approach to Product Growth Theory," *Journal of Marketing*, Fall 1981, pp. 125–34.

2. John E. Swan and David R. Rink, "Fitting Market Strategy to Varying Product Life Cycles," *Business Horizons*, January–February 1982, pp. 72–76; and Yoram J. Wind, *Product Policy: Concepts, Methods, and Strategy* (Reading, MA, Addison-Wesley Publishing Co., 1982).

3. Kathryn Rudie Harrigan, "Strategies for Declining Industries," *Journal of Business Strategy*, Fall 1980, p. 27.

4. "How Du Pont Keeps Them Coming Back for More," *BusinessWeek*, August 20, 1990, p. 80; and "India: Modern Spin on Traditional Clothing with Lycra," off the web site, www.fibre2fibre.com, January 29, 2008.

5. Stephen G. Harrell and Elmer D. Taylor, "Modeling the Product Life Cycle for Consumer Durables," *Journal of Marketing*, Fall 1981, pp. 68–75.

6. See Philippe Haspeslagh, "Portfolio Planning: Uses and Limits," *Harvard Business Review*, January–February 1982, pp. 60, 73.

7. "They're All Juiced Up at Tropicana," *BusinessWeek*, May 13, 1991. Information updated through company sources.

8. *Organizing and Managing the Planning Function* (Fairfield, CT, GE Company, n.d.).

9. Robin Wensley, "Strategic Marketing: Betas, Boxes, or Basics," *Journal of Marketing*, Summer 1981, pp. 173–182.

10. Michael E. Porter, *Competitive Strategy* (New York, The Free Press, 1981).

11. Fred Gluck, "A Fresh Look at Strategic Management," *Journal of Business Strategy*, Fall 1987, p. 23.

12. Yoram Wind, Vijay Mahajan, and Donald J. Swire, "An Empirical Comparison of Standardized Portfolio Models," *Journal of Marketing*, Spring 1983, pp. 89–99.

13. George Day, "Diagnosing the Product Portfolio," *Journal of Marketing*, April 1977, pp. 29–38.

14. Frederick W. Gluck, "Strategic Choice and Resource Allocation," *McKinsey Quarterly*, Winter 1980, p. 24.

15. Donald Hambrick and Ian MacMillan, "The Product Portfolio and Man's Best Friend," *California Management Review*, Fall 1982, pp. 16–23.

16. J. Scott Armstrong and Roderick J. Brodie, "Effects of Portfolio Planning Methods on Decision Making: Experimental Results," *International Journal of Research in Marketing*, Vol. 11, 1994, pp. 73–84.

17. *The Boston Consulting Group Annual Perspective* (Boston, Boston Consulting Group, 1981).

18. Porter, *Competitive Strategy*.

19. Christian Homburg, Horby Kohmer and John P. Workman, Jr., "Strategic Consensus and Performance: The Role of Strategy Type and Market-Related Dynamism," *Strategic Management Journal*, April 1999, pp. 339–357.

20. See: Gary Hamel, "Reinvent Your Company," *Fortune*, June 12, 2000.

PART **V**

Strategy Implementation and Control

Chapter 11
Organizational Structure

Chapter 12
Strategic Tools

Chapter Outline

11.1 The Traditional Organization
11.2 Creating Market-Responsive
     Organizations
     11.2.1 Determine Corporate
            Strategic Boundaries
     11.2.2 Balance the Demands
            of Scale and Market
            Responsiveness
     11.2.3 Organize for Strategic
            Effectiveness
11.3 Role of Systems in Implementing
     Strategy
11.4 Executive Reward Systems
11.5 Leadership Style
11.6 Measuring Strategic Performance
11.7 Achieving Strategic Planning
     Effectiveness
11.8 Strategic Planning
     and Marketing Organization

Chapter 11

Organizational Structure

Whatever action is performed by a great man, common men follow in his footsteps, and whatever standards he sets by exemplary acts, all the world pursues.

BHAGAVAD GITA

A strategic planning system should provide answers to two basic questions: what to do and how to do it. The first question refers to selection of a strategy; the second, to organizational arrangements. An organization must have not only a winning strategy to pursue but also a matching structure to facilitate its implementation. The emphasis in the preceding chapters has been on strategy formulation. This chapter is devoted to building a viable organizational structure to administer the strategy.

In the last twenty-five years, principles of strategic analysis and planning have been fully integrated into corporate decision making at all levels. Yet, although these precepts now enjoy global acceptance, the need to translate strategic guidelines into long-term results and adapt them to rapidly changing market conditions continues to rank among the major challenges confronting today's companies. Essentially, there are three aspects of implementation that, if properly organized, can lead to superior corporate performance and competitive advantage: organization planning, management systems, and executive reward programs.

Fitting these aspects to the underlying strategy requires strategic reorganization. There is no magic formula to ensure successful reorganization and, generally, no ''perfect'' prototype to follow. Reorganization is a delicate process that above all requires a finely tuned management sense.

The discussion in this chapter focuses on five dimensions: (a) the creation of market-responsive organizations, (b) the role of systems in implementing strategy, (c) executive reward systems, (d) leadership style (i.e., the establishment of an internal environment conducive to strategy implementation), and (e) the measurement of strategic performance (i.e., the development of a network of control and communication to monitor and evaluate progress in achieving strategic goals). In addition, the impact of strategic planning on marketing organization is studied.

11.1 THE TRADITIONAL ORGANIZATION

Corporations have traditionally been organized with a strong emphasis on pursuing and achieving established objectives. Such organizations adapt well to growing internal complexities and provide adequate incentive mechanisms and systems of accountability to support objectives. However, they fail to provide a congenial environment for strategic planning. For example, one of the organizational capabilities needed for strategic planning is that of modifying, or redefining, the objectives themselves so that the corporation

Exhibit 11.1 Organizational Characteristics	**Command and Control Structure**	**Strategic Planning**
	1. Concerned with goals derived from established objectives	1. Concerned with the identification and evaluation of new objectives and strategies.
	2. Goals usually have been validated through extensive experience.	2. New objectives and strategies can be highly debatable; experience within the organization or in other companies may be minimal.
	3. Goals are reduced to specific subgoals for functional units.	3. Objectives usually are evaluated primarily for corporate significance.
	4. Managers tend to identify with functions or professions and to be preoccupied with means.	4. Managers need a corporate point of view oriented to the environment.
	5. Managers obtain relatively prompt evidence of their performance against goals.	5. Evidence of the merit of new objectives or strategies is often available only after several years.
	6. Incentives, formal and social, are tied to operating goals.	6. Incentives are at best only loosely associated with planning.
	7. The "rules of the game" become well understood. Experienced individuals feel competent and secure.	7. New fields of endeavor may be considered. Past experience may not provide competence in a "new game."
	8. The issues are immediate, concrete, and familiar.	8. Issues are abstract, deferrable (to some extent), and may be unfamiliar.

is prepared to meet future competition. The traditional organizational structure, based on "command and control" principles, resists change, which is why a new type of structure is needed for strategic planning:

> The forces shaping organization today are dramatically different from those facing Frederick Taylor and Alfred Sloan. End-use markets are fragmenting, requiring faster and more targeted responses. Advances in the ability to capture, manipulate, and transmit information electronically make it possible to distribute decision making ("command") without losing "control." Gone is the abundant, primarily male, blue-collar workforce. Workers today are better educated, in short supply, and demanding greater participation and variety in their jobs.
>
> Individually all these changes are dramatic; collectively they shape a new era in organization and strategy. Strategies are increasingly shifting from cost- and volume-based sources of competitive advantage to those focusing on increased value to the customer. Competitive strength is derived from the skills, speed, specificity, and service levels provided to customers. The Command and Control organization is under strain. Indeed, many businesses are finding that C&C principles now result in competitive disadvantage.[1]

Exhibit 11.1 differentiates the characteristics of command and control structure (i.e., traditional organization with emphasis on the achievement of established objectives) and strategic planning. By and large, command and control structure works in known territory and is concerned with immediate issues. Strategic planning stresses unfamiliar perspectives and is oriented toward the future.

11.2 CREATING MARKET-RESPONSIVE ORGANIZATIONS

As markets and technologies change more and more rapidly, organizations must respond quickly and frequently to strategic moves if they are to sustain competitive advantage. Although corporations have learned to make changes in strategy quickly, their organizations may lack parallel market responsiveness. One major reason for this failure is the conflict between scale economics, which is geared to the expansion and aggregation of resources, and the economics of vertical integration, which links differentiated functions and resources for maximum efficiency in responding to market changes.

The opposing pressures fueling this conflict are both subtle and complex. On one side of the equation are all the forces contributing to the need to reap maximum scale advantage. On the other side of the equation, the accelerated pace of change—environmental, competitive, and technological—drives corporations toward increased flexibility, high levels of internal integration, and smaller operating units.

Although scale advantage has traditionally held high ground, evidence is mounting that highly integrated organizations can increase productive capacity through the efficient coordination of functions and resources while remaining highly adaptive and market sensitive.[2] Such organizations respond to the strategic need for change more quickly, smoothly, and successfully than centralized, large-unit organizations oriented toward scale aggregation. Their advantages lie in their greater knowledge of their product/markets, their greater knowledge of the various environments in which the organization operates and the greater speed and responsiveness made possible by the smaller and genereally also flatter organization.[3]

Management has basically three options for resolving the conflict between scale and integration. First, a company can choose to centralize its functions in order to achieve scale at the expense of market responsiveness. Second, it can opt for market responsiveness over scale; that is, it can emphasize small, independent units. Third, it can adopt another, more difficult approach, exploiting the strengths associated with both large and small organizational units to achieve benefits of scale and market responsiveness simultaneously. The key to sustainable competitive advantage lies in successful pursuit of the third alternative.

Exploiting the benefits of both large and small organizational structures involves creating market-responsive units within a framework of shared resources. Such units can combine the strengths of a small company (lean, entrepreneurial management; sharp focus on the business; immediacy of the relationship with the customer; dedication to growth; and action-oriented viewpoint) with those of the large company (extensive financial information and resources; availability of multiple technologies; recognition as an established business; people with diverse skills to draw on; and an intimate knowledge of markets and functions).[4]

The creation of such units demands that planners determine, as precisely as possible, in what form and to what degree resources must be integrated to ensure the level of market responsiveness dictated by their business strategy. This process can be successful only when it is undertaken in the context of a rigorous analytical framework that links strategy to organization.

To create a market-responsive organization, management can use a three-phase process: (a) determine corporate strategic boundaries, (b) balance the demands of scale and market responsiveness, and (c) organize for strategic effectiveness.

11.2.1 Determine Corporate Strategic Boundaries

How successfully a corporation aligns its structure with its strategic objectives depends on its success in making a number of key decisions: determining the stage of the value-added process at which it will compete, identifying those activities in which it has a competitive edge, selecting the functions it should execute internally, and developing a plan of action for integrating those functions most productively. These decisions determine how resources should be allocated and how external and internal boundaries should be drawn. They define the company's business—its products, services, customers, and markets—and determine both long- and short-term strategic potential. How well the company exploits its assets and the degree to which each division's performance supports strategic objectives determine how close it will come to achieving that potential.

How strategic boundary setting reflects the trade-offs between scale and integration becomes clearer when one considers the case of an assembler facing a typical make-or-buy decision for components. As long as the components manufacturer is able to produce common components for several customers, the assembler among them, the components manufacturer enjoys scale advantage. As the products ordered by the assembler become more specialized in response to market demands or increased competitive pressures, however, the benefits the components manufacturer gains from scale begin to decline. At the same time, the cost of integrating operations with those of the assembler increases as technical specifications become more complex and as manufacturing operations become more interdependent. To continue their relationship and sustain their respective advantages, the components manufacturer and the assembler are required to make additional investments: the components manufacturer in capital equipment outlays and product design; the assembler in negotiating terms, research and development planning, quality control, and related areas. As a result, a substantial "disruption cost" is incurred if the components manufacturer and the assembler decide to end their business relationship. Both parties attempt to guard against this potential loss through longer-term contracts, whether explicit or implicit. As interdependence increases, prices and contract negotiations become cumbersome and unresponsive. At some point, the economies of scale may decline enough and the integration costs climb high enough that the assembler finds it more cost effective to produce components internally—to bring that particular function inside the assembler's corporate boundaries.

In this classic make-or-buy example, economic trade-offs between scale and integration costs are direct and relatively clear-cut. As we move from simple make-or-buy decisions to issues of full-scale vertical integration, the economic impact can be far more subtle and far-reaching. Scale advantage is not expressed solely in terms of lower unit manufacturing costs but may also flow from the critical mass of skills gained or from the transferability of new product or process technologies. Valuable integration benefits, on the other hand, may be gained from the willingness to undertake more profitable research and development investments because vertical integration ensures a ''market'' in downstream operations.

11.2.2 Balance the Demands of Scale and Market Responsiveness

The balancing of scale and market responsiveness demands may be illustrated with reference to a large insurance company. The company faced a complex set of internal and market-based organizational trade-offs in its core business—property and casualty insurance. Lagging market growth, increased price sensitivity, new forms of product distribution, new information technology, and escalating competition were all placing enormous pressures on the company's traditional mode of operation. Top management realized that fundamental changes in organization were needed in both its home office and in its field network if the company was to remain competitive and meet aggressive new growth and profit goals.

In responding to these pressures, the company found itself facing a familiar dilemma. On the one hand, it was vital that its organizational structure become more responsive to local market demand, particularly in terms of regional product pricing and agent deployment. This need pointed to decentralization as the logical method for restructuring operations, with the field divided into smaller sales and marketing regions and more responsibility assigned to local management. On the other hand, however, management was determined to reduce the costs of transaction processing. Meeting this need for administrative streamlining appeared to require that field offices around the country be reorganized into larger regional centers to exploit fully the scale economies offered by improvements in automated processing capacity.

Initially, these strategic requirements seemed to set large centers against locally responsive marketing and sales units. Yet, by carefully analyzing and ''rewiring'' its structure, the company was able to resolve the apparent conflict cost-effectively and efficiently. Here is the approach it pursued. The company's field operations consisted of essentially self-sufficient regional centers; each center included all functional departments under its umbrella, ranging from sales, claims, and underwriting to operations and personnel. Two of these functions dominated field operations: customer interaction through sales and marketing and transaction processing. Originally, the field organization was designed around exploiting administrative scale in the processing function and balancing the need to locate sales and marketing functions to serve the customer base effectively. The underlying basis for the organizational design was the need to coordinate sales and processing functions because of the high volume of transactions and interactions between them. A layer of management between the home office and the regional centers coordinated programs and enforced company policies.

In line with its new strategic objectives (greater market responsiveness and increased productivity), the company instituted major organizational changes. First, the layer of management between the home office and regional centers was eliminated to improve communications and to facilitate more market-responsive decision making. Second, to achieve scale economies and contain costs, the reporting relationships of the processing centers were shifted from the regional level directly to the home office. New information technology allowed the company to ''unhook'' processing centers from sales functions and still remain adequately integrated. As a result, the number of regions of independent sale organizations was no longer tied to the number of processing centers. The number of processing centers was reduced as information-technology innovations allowed additional processing capacity, whereas the number of marketing and sales regions was increased as market requirements demanded, allowing the entire sales organization to move closer to its local client base. The needs for both market responsiveness and scale economies in processing was fully satisfied.

11.2.3 Organize for Strategic Effectiveness

To organize for strategic effectiveness, it is important to recognize that the ultimate goal of a business organization is competitive advantage, and the drive for competitive advantage must be expressed in economic terms and pursued through the use of economic tools. Only by placing organizational decisions in an economic context can the value of alternative forms of structure, incentive, and management process be determined.[5] It is only in the light of these assessments that the steps needed to strike the proper balance between scale and market responsiveness can be taken. Needless complexity, excessive layers of management, and nonessential integration of channels must all be eliminated. The design phase is easy when compared to the difficulties of execution (i.e., implementing organizational change). It requires strong leadership, consistent signals and actions, and strategically driven incentive programs.

Designing and managing a market-responsive organization requires overturning old assumptions. First, the linearity from strategy to structure and on to systems, staff, etc., cannot be reasoned. The process is instead iterative: a team is formed to meet a strategic need; it sizes up the situation, develops a specific strategy, and reorganizes itself as necessary. What's more, the structure is temporary. The organization needs to be ready to change its configuration quickly to respond to new needs and circumstances. Second, the organization's purpose is not to control from the top; it is to empower a group of people to get a job done. Management occurs through training, incentives, and strongly articulated goals, strategies, and standards.[6]

Market-responsive organizations are found most often in businesses that are driven by product development and customer service—electronics and software companies, for example—and are often smaller, younger organizations where traditional boundaries are weaker. Some large-scale models include parts of Honda and Panasonic, 3M, GE, and also, in some ways, Hewlett-Packard, which has developed extraordinary flexibility in recent years in reshaping its organization and pushing authority down to frontline managers.

Market-responsive organizations have obvious drawbacks: they lack tight controls, they are ill-suited to exploit scale or to accomplish massive tasks, and they depend on capable and motivated people at the working level. However, companies that cannot use the full market-responsive model can appropriate aspects of it—new product development teams, for instance.

Some large companies, such as IBM, Microsoft, and Dow Chemical, with the need for both innovation and coordination of resources among markets, product lines, and technologies, often use the concept in modified form. They frequently change the focus of resources and control by reshuffling product groups—shifting power among parts of the organization or by using ad hoc teams.

Experience suggests that people are quite willing and able to change as long as they have a clear understanding of what's expected of them, know why it is important to change, and have latitude in designing the new organization. Five key elements that companies should carefully consider in seeking strategic effectiveness are discussed below:[7]

1. **Forge a clear link between strategy and skills**—A company's strategy, which should embody the value it proposes to deliver to its customers, determines the skills it needs. Many companies, however, are not sufficiently clear or rigorous about this linkage. Because Frank Perdue promises to deliver more tender chickens, his organization must excel at the breeding and logistics skills necessary to deliver them. Because Volvo promises to deliver more reliable, tougher, and safer cars, it must be skilled in designing and manufacturing them. Because Domino's Pizza says it will deliver fresh pizza hot to your door within 30 minutes, each of its 5,000 outlets needs to be skilled at making a good pizza quickly and at customer order processing and delivery. Strategy drives skills, but if this linkage is missed, a company may end up doing some things right but not the right things right.

2. **Be specific and selective about core skills**—Managers often describe the core skills their companies need in terms that are too general. Saying that you need to be first rate at customer service or marketing is not good enough. For example, the employees of a department store committed to being better at customer service will not know what to do differently because the term *customer service* doesn't paint a specific enough picture of the behavior desired of them. In fact, a department store needs to be good in at least three different types of customer services: with hard goods such as refrigerators or furniture, customer service must have a high component of product and technical knowledge; with fine apparel, what counts is expertise in fashion counseling; with basics and sundries, the need is for friendly, efficient self-service. Each of these service goals translates into a different set of day-to-day behaviors expected of employees. Unless these behaviors are precisely defined, even willing employees won't change their behavior very much because they won't know how.

3. **Clarify the implications for pivotal jobs**—Consider the department store again. The definition of different types of customer services drives through to the identification of several specific jobs whose performance determines whether customers think the store is good at customer service: the product salesperson for refrigerators, the fashion counselor for fine apparel, and the cashier for sundries. Pushing the skill definition to these specific jobs, which may be called pivotal jobs, allows the company to describe in specific

terms what the holders of these jobs should do or not do, which kind of people to hire, which kind of training and coaching to give them, which rewards motivate them, and which kind of information they need. For example, at Nordstrom, the excellent Seattle-based fashion specialty retailer, the pivotal job is the frontline sales associate. Because Nordstrom is clear about the type of person it wants for this job—someone interested in a career, not just a summer position—it looks more for a service orientation than prior experience. It pays better than the industry average and offers incentives that allow top sales associates to make over $80,000 a year. Nordstrom stresses customer service above all else. The company philosophy is to offer the customer, in this order, "the best service, selection, quality, and value."

This clarity about priorities helps sales associates determine appropriate service behavior. So does the excellent product and service training they receive. And so does the customer information system that provides sales associates with up-to-date sales and service records on their customers. Nordstrom recognizes that its business success depends on the success of pivotal jobholders in delivering value to customers, and the company has geared its entire organization to support these frontline associates.

4. **Provide leadership from the top**—The key ingredients that have been found workable in this task include

- Appealing to the pride of the organization. Most people want to do a superior job, especially for a company that expresses its mission with an idea bigger than just making money. Providing them with a single noble purpose—be it "quality, service, cleanliness, value" or "innovation"—will unleash energy but keep it focused.
- Clarifying the importance and value of building core skills. Provide the organization with a good economic understanding of the value as well as a clear picture of the consequences of not paying attention to core skills.
- Being willing to do the tough things that break bottlenecks and establish credibility for the belief that "this change is for real." Usually, the toughest things involve replacing people who are change blockers, committing key managers to the skill-building effort, and spending money on it.

Li & Fung's John Wayne Structure*

Li & Fung has grown into the world's largest trading organization based on the organizational principal that building uniformity and centralized control where necessary grants independence of action where it is most effective. Victor Fung calls it the John Wayne structure and says that he wants his line managers to be a bunch of John Waynes. In his most memorable roles, the Li & Fung CEO argues, John Wayne played people who were fiercely independent, highly determined and driven to achieve their goals through any honorable actions possible. That is the type of manager he wants. They are people that, "if they did not work for Li & Fung, would rather start their own business than work for a more traditionally structured company. They must be able to operate on their own, without strict supervision; they must be entrepreneurial." Li & Fung's trading operations are structured around their customers and their product markets. Each John Wayne manages thirty to forty people who focus on specific customers' needs within the product markets focused on by Li & Fung, primarily textiles, toys, health and beauty, and the importation of packaged foods into their home markets. Their goal is to become their customers' extended supply chains, and that is the job of the John Waynes. This structure evolved at Li & Fung due to the sheer number of transactions to be managed—there was no way a centralized structure could manage the transactions efficiently and, at the same time, interface effectively with their customers and provide the kind of rapid and thorough service management that has driven them to their present level of success. Each John Wayne structure is a corporate profit center and has complete authority in the areas of marketing, customer service, product selection and development, purchasing, logistics, distribution and sales. The only thing that is entirely centralized is corporate finance and IT. The John Waynes must live within the funding constraints management sets for them or justify any additional funding required. What makes this possible? Extensive investment in IT and an enforced uniformity of all IT documents and corporate communications—all corporate communications are in English and all IT forms are uniform throughout Li & Fung.

New Asian Emperors: The Overseas Chinese After the Crises (2008), George T. Haley, Chin Tiong Tan and Usha C. V. Haley.

- Treat the program to build skills as something special, not as business as usual. Reflect this in the leader's own time allocation, in the questions he or she asks subordinates, in the special assignments he or she gives people, in the choice of the special measurements he or she looks at, and so on.
- Over-communicate to superiors, subordinates, customers, and especially to pivotal jobholders. Talk and write incessantly about the skill-building program—about the skills the company is trying to build and about why they are critical; about early wins, heroes, and lessons learned from failures; about milestones achieved.

5. **Empower the organization to learn**—Organizations, like individuals, learn best by doing. Building new core skills is preeminently a learning process. Sketch out for employees the boundaries of their playing field by defining the strategy, the skills the company is trying to build, the pivotal job behaviors required, and the convictions they must hold about what is right. But within these boundaries, give them a lot of room to run—to try things, succeed, fail and to learn for themselves exactly what works and what doesn't. They will figure out for themselves details that could never be prescribed from above.[8]

To illustrate the point, take, for example, the 10,000 route salespeople of Frito-Lay. Michael Jordan, the company's president, says that these people with their "store to door service" control the destiny of Frito-Lay. Wayne Calloway, PepsiCo's former president and past CEO of Frito-Lay, describes this pivotal job as follows: "Our sales people are entrepreneurs of the first order. Over 100,000 times a day they encounter customers who are making buying decisions on the spot. How in the world could an old-fashioned sort of management deal with those kinds of conditions? Our approach is to find good people and to give them as much responsibility as possible because they're closest to the customer, they know what's going on."[9]

11.3 ROLE OF SYSTEMS IN IMPLEMENTING STRATEGY

The term *systems* refers to management systems, which include any of the formally organized procedures that pervade a business. Three types of systems may be distinguished: execution systems, monitoring systems, and control systems.

1. **Execution systems** focus directly on the basic processes for conducting the firm's business. They include systems that enable products to be designed, supplies to be ordered, production to be scheduled, goods to be shipped, cash to be applied, and employees to be paid.
2. **Monitoring systems** are any procedures that measure and assess basic processes. They can be designed to gather information in different ways to serve a number of internal or external reporting purposes: to meet SEC or other regulatory requirements, to control budgets, to pay taxes, and to serve the strategic and organizational intent of the company.
3. **Control systems** are the means through which processes are made to conform or are kept within tolerable limits. At the broadest level, they include separation of duties, authority limits, product inspection, and plan submittals.

As can be seen from this brief description, systems pervade the conduct of business. For that very reason, systems provide ample opportunity for strategies to fail. In most companies, the major emphasis is on execution systems. But creating systems that support strategies and organizational intent requires top management to include monitoring and control systems in addition to executing systems in strategic thinking and to focus on systems in strategy implementation. It means, as part of the strategic planning, answering such key questions as: What are the critical success factors? How do they translate into operational performance? How should that operational performance be measured and motivated? How should information about financial performance be derived? What business cycles are important? How should systems support them? What is the role of financial controls and measures? Where should control of information reside? How should strategic objectives and organizational performance be monitored and modified? How should internal and external information be linked?

In short, integrating all systems with strategy requires great vision—the ability to see the firm as an organic whole. Unfortunately, too many systems managers lack vision or clout and too many executives lack the understanding or the inclination to make this integration happen.

To create systems that support strategic and organizational intent, top management must include systems in strategic thinking and focus on systems in strategy implementation. Once critical success factors have been identified and translated into operational measurements, good systems design techniques are needed to ensure that those factors and measurements are appropriately accommodated by all systems. Following are some guidelines for good systems design:

1. **Design an effective information-capturing procedure**—Data should be captured close to the source, and source documents should be linked. For example, at one company, data processing personnel collected information on raw materials from receiving reports two days after delivery and entered that information into purchasing control and inventory management systems. Two days later, accounting gathered information on the same delivery from invoices, this time entering it into accounting systems. The failure to link source documents led to apparent inventory discrepancies. Purchasing and inventory processes focused on inventory codes and quantities; accounting processes dealt with accounting codes and monetary amounts, which were available only at the end of the month.

   These problems required a three-part solution: placing terminals at the receiving dock, where receiving clerks could enter operating information; using internal links to accounting codes; and creating a reconciliation proof on which quantities and amounts were entered as invoices were received.

2. **Manage commonly used data elements for firm-wide accessibility and control**—If a multidivisional firm allows each unit to code inventory discretely, stock that is commonly used cannot be traded and rebalanced. Traditionally, auto dealers maintained independent inventory controls. By contrast, Ford Motor Company has worked to keep its inventory records consistent and thus accessible to dealers so that imbalances at one lead to opportunities for another.

3. **Decide which applications are common and which tolerate distributed processing**—Typical considerations here include pinpointing the need to share data, determining the availability of hardware and software offerings that make a distributed approach feasible, and investigating the effect of geographical distance. Once a particular application or function is judged appropriate for a distributed approach, it must be integrated into an information network.

4. **Manage information, not reports**—Systems are often developed with end reports in mind, focusing on output, not content. If needs change or if developers and users misunderstand each other, the results can lead to frustration at best or the inability to modify output at worst. When the development focus is on content, on information that has been strategically identified as critical to success, users can tailor the presentation of output to their purposes. For example, in one company with a well-constructed receivables database, one manager chose to compare cash collections to target amounts, another used days outstanding, and a third used turnover ratios.

5. **Examine cost-effectiveness**—Questioning the value of a system and of the work required to support it is healthy. But such questioning must be handled properly. As an example, to escape merely chipping away at existing processes through cost reduction, Procter & Gamble developed its elimination approach, which is based on the key ''if'' question: If it were not for this [reason], this [cost] would be eliminated.[10]

Designing and maintaining systems that focus on strategic intent and that assess performance in terms of that intent is crucial to the success of a strategy. In fact, a lack of integration between systems and strategy is an important reason why sound strategic and organizational concepts get bogged down in implementation and do not achieve the results their creators intended. Soundly designed and managed systems do not happen casually: they emerge only with top management involvement and with a clear vision of the importance of systems to strategic outcomes.

11.4 EXECUTIVE REWARD SYSTEMS

Executive compensation and strategy are mutually dependent and reinforcing. A good reward system should have three characteristics:[11] (a) it should optimize value to all key stakeholders, including both shareholders and management alike (the so-called agency problem); (b) it should properly measure and recapture value; and (c) it should integrate compensation signals with those implicit in strategy and structure. Although these issues are generally addressed from the perspective of plan implementation, they also have an important but rarely noted strategic dimension. And that strategic dimension actually has a make-or-break impact on plan effectiveness.

The agency problem refers to the potential conflict of interest between shareholders and their agents, the executives charged with implementing corporate strategy. The executives of a corporation serve as agents of the corporation's shareholders. Yet, though both executives and shareholders are stakeholders in a corporation, their interests do not coincide. In fact, they naturally diverge on three counts: risk position (e.g., shareholders stand last in line among claimants to the resources of the corporation, whereas executives have the right to payment of salaries and benefits before the claims of shareholders are met); ability to redeploy (e.g., shareholders can freely redeploy their investments; the executives' human capital invested in the course of a career may not be easily redeployable at full value); time horizon (e.g., shareholders embrace long time horizons to earn competitive returns; time horizons of executives are usually shorter). These differences lead to differences in the ways each group measures the risks and rewards of any corporate action. In general, the differences in risk evaluation make a company's executives more averse to risk than are its shareholders.

Resolving the agency problem requires bridging the gap between the inherently divergent interests of shareholders and the executives entrusted with the responsibility of safeguarding and increasing shareholder investments. Though executive compensation plans can and should help resolve this problem, they often compound it. Most incentive plans, for example, are based on improvements in short-term earnings; therefore, they actually inhibit the very risk decisions required to provide highly competitive returns to shareholders.

New and creative ways of compensating executives must be developed to synchronize their interests with those of shareholders.

From the company's viewpoint, the value issue is twofold. One aspect revolves around the need to reward executive performance in a way that is systematically related to the market value of the corporation. The other is the need to create incentive plans for managers of individual business units.

In this book, our major concern is with creating incentive plans for managers of individual business units. Compensation planning for individual business units is illustrated with reference to a hypothetical company, Hellenic Corporation.

Hellenic Corporation consists of four businesses: Alpha, Beta, Gamma, and Delta. Alpha operates in a promising market but needs to increase market share rapidly. Beta is an efficient, well-run business that already has the largest share of a mature market. Gamma, once a top performer, has suffered recently from serious management mistakes; nevertheless, it has the potential to be a winner again. Delta is a mediocre performer in a mediocre market; moreover, its business is largely unrelated to the other businesses of the corporation.

Hellenic's strategic plan calls for Alpha to grow rapidly, for Beta to capitalize on its well-established position, for Gamma to turn itself around, and for Delta to be divested. This plan maximizes the value of the corporation as a whole. Each division is vital to the corporation's success; however, the management objectives of the chiefs at Alpha, Beta, Gamma, and Delta differ from one another and influence the market value of the firm in distinct ways. This conflict, however, does not mean that shareholder value is an impractical standard for determining executive reward. Even when a manager's performance is related only indirectly to shareholder value, increasing shareholder value need not be abandoned as the aim of executive compensation planning. The challenge is to craft a plan that links performance to value in a way that is consistent with the corporation's long-term strategy. To do this requires tailoring a specific compensation package for the manager of each business unit. The determinants of compensation at Alpha must be different from those at Beta, which again must be different from those at Gamma and at Delta.

This overall plan can be created by analyzing how risk and time horizons in executive pay plans suit the strategic objectives of each business unit. For example, the top manager at Alpha is engaged in a very long-term project. Exceptional growth and profitability are planned, and the risks incurred in executing the plan are considerable. These circumstances call for a pay package geared to the entrepreneurial challenges facing Alpha. Accordingly, the time horizon is very long and the risk posture is high. At Beta, where the prime objective is to maximize returns from a well-established market position, the time horizon and risk posture are moderate. At Gamma, the turnaround candidate, the time horizon is short and the risk posture is very high. At Delta, being managed for window dressing, the time horizon is short and the risk posture is low. In addition, other special sell-off compensation arrangements (e.g., a percentage of the sale price) may be needed.

A *signal* is simply an inducement to action. Because pay is clearly a powerful inducement to action, compensation systems are powerful signaling devices. Other signaling devices include financial controls, the planning process, and the top management succession plan. All these factors convey messages about what a corporation expects and what it values. Collectively, these signals shape the corporation's culture and determine the actions it takes in given situations.

When management sends consistent signals through all channels, it adheres to a clear strategic track. Unfortunately, conflicting internal signals are common, and compensation is frequently the area of greatest dissonance. Companies must tackle the signaling problem directly. Winners should be paid like winners, and poor performers must not be rewarded. Briefly, executive compensation plans require more risk taking based on real value.

Incentive plans should be designed to induce risk taking. They should make executives think like owners. That is, the plan must bring the interests of executives in line with the interests of shareholders.[12] By resolving the problems of agency and value, by ensuring that high levels of risk taking reap commensurate rewards, and by eliminating conflicting signals, companies can put in place the kinds of incentives required to create exceptional value for owners and agents alike.

11.5 LEADERSHIP STYLE

However strategic plans are arrived at, only one person, the CEO, can ensure that energies and efforts throughout the organization are orchestrated to attain desired objectives. What the Chinese general and philosopher Sun-tzu said in 514 B.C. is still true today: ''Weak leadership can wreck the soundest strategy; forceful execution of even a poor plan can often bring victory.'' This section examines the key role of the CEO in shaping the organization for strategy implementation. Also discussed is the role of the strategic planner, whose activities also have a major impact on the organization and its attitude toward strategic change.

The CEO of a company is the chief strategist. He or she communicates the importance of strategic planning to the organization. Personal commitment on the part of the CEO to the significance of planning must not only be highly visible—it must also be consistent with all other decisions that the CEO makes to influence the work of the organization.[13] To be accepted within the organization, the strategic planning process needs the CEO's support. People accustomed to a short-term orientation may resist the strategic planning process, which requires different methods. But the CEO can set an example for them by adhering to the planning process. Essentially, the CEO is responsible for creating a corporate climate conducive to strategic planning. The CEO can also set a future perspective for the organization. One CEO remarked:

> My people cannot plan or work beyond the distance of my own vision. If I focus on next year, I'll force them to become preoccupied with next year. If I can try to look five to ten years ahead, at least I'll make it possible for the rest of the organization to raise their eyes off the ground immediately in front of them.[14]

The CEO should focus attention on the corporate purpose and approve strategic decisions accordingly. To perform these tasks well, the CEO should support the staff work and analysis upon which his or her decisions are based. Along the same lines, the CEO should ensure the establishment of a noise-free communications network in the organization. Communications should flow downward from the CEO with respect to organizational goals and aspirations and the values of top management. Similarly, information about risks, results, plans, concepts, capabilities, competition, and the environment should flow upward. The CEO should avoid seeking false uniformity, trying to eliminate risk, trusting tradition, dominating discussion, and delegating strategy development.[15] A CEO who does these things could inadvertently discourage strategy implementation.

Concern for the future may require a change in organizational perspectives, as discussed above. The CEO should not only perceive the need for a change but should also be instrumental in making it happen. Change is not easy, however, because past success provides a strong motive for preserving the status quo. As long as the environment and competitive behavior do not change, past perspectives are fine. However, as the environment shifts, changes in policies and attitudes become essential. The CEO must rise to the occasion and not only initiate change but encourage others to accept it and adapt to it.[16] The timing of a change may be more important than the change itself. The need for change must be realized before the optimum time for it has passed so that competitive advantage and flexibility are not lost. Exhibit 11.2 summarizes the qualities and attributes of a chief strategist.

Zaleznik makes a distinction between the CEO who is a manager and the CEO who is a leader. Managers keep things running smoothly; leaders provide longer-term direction and thrust.[17] Successful strategic planning requires that the CEO be a good leader. In this capacity, the CEO should

Exhibit 11.2 Qualities and Attributes of a Chief Strategist

1. **Trustworthiness.** Trustworthiness is one of the most important qualities required by any leader. In other words, anyone seeking to be a leader should always tell the truth, if for no other reason than it is simpler.

2. **Fairness.** Americans will forgive much, but seldom unfairness. Unfairness in a chief executive (or for that matter in any executive) is particularly serious, because he or she sets the example for everyone else. In fact, to be called an unfair leader is damning, and even implies a flawed character.

3. **Unassuming behavior.** Arrogance, haughtiness, and egotism are poisonous to leadership. Having a "servant" leadership viewpoint helps any CEO focus on company performance and on the needs of constituents rather than on his or her own performance or image. Successful leaders are as unassuming in the surroundings they create—or tolerate—as they are in their behavior.

4. **Leaders listen.** Active listening helps assure the other person that he or she is being heard and understood. Unfortunately, of all the skills of leadership, listening is one of the most valuable; yet one of the least understood.

5. **Open-mindedness.** Any leader with an open mind makes better judgements, learns more of what he or she needs to know, and establishes more positive relations with subordinates and constituents. In such an environment, people in the organization can be more productive.

6. **Sensitivity to people.** A leader cannot motivate or persuade constituents or others effectively without having some sense of what is on their minds. Sensitivity to people also means that leaders are sensitive to their feelings. Leaders are polite, considerate, understanding, and careful that what they say to someone is not dispiriting unless criticism is intended.

7. **Sensitivity to situations.** Situations are created by people and must be dealt with by people. Any company leader who is called on to resolve a dispute or disagreement must combine a careful analysis of the facts with an acute sensitivity to the feelings and attitudes of the people involved.

8. **Leaders take initiative.** Initiative is one of the most important attributes of any leader. Just think a bit, use judgment, and act. Nothing happens except at the initiative of a single person.

9. **Good judgment.** Judgment is the ability to combine hard data, questionable data, and intuitive guesses to arrive at a conclusion that events prove to be correct.

10. **Broad-mindedness.** Broad-mindedness refers to tolerance of varied views and willingness to condone minor departures from conventional behavior. This attribute is closely related to being open-minded, adaptable, and flexible. Other aspects of broad-mindedness are being undisturbed by little things, willing to overlook small errors, and easy to talk with.

11. **Flexibility and adaptability.** The leader should be ready to consider change and be willing to make changes when most agree they are needed.

12. **Capacity to make sound and timely decisions.** All decisions will be of higher quality where subordinates are free to speak up and disagree. The leader should recognize that the speed as well as the quality of his or her decisions will set an example for others to follow in the organization.

13. **Capacity to motivate.** A leader should have the capacity to move people to action, to communicate persuasively, and to strengthen the confidence of followers.

14. **Sense of urgency.** A sense of urgency should underlie everything that the leader does—for example, bring new products out on time, deliver orders promptly, or get things done faster than competitors. When a sense of urgency has spread through a company, it can make a substantial difference in both effectiveness and efficiency, making it easier to speed up activities further when necessary.

Source: See Marvin Bower, *The Will To Lead* (Boston, MA, Harvard Business School Press, 1997).

1. Gain complete and willing acceptance of his or her leadership.
2. Determine those business goals, objectives, and standards of behavior that are as ambitious as the potential abilities of the organization will permit.

3. Introduce these objectives and motivate the organization to accept them as their own. The rate of introduction should be the maximum that is consistent with continued acceptance of the CEO's leadership. Because of this need for acceptance, the new manager must always go slowly, except in emergencies. In emergencies, the boss must not go slowly if he or she is to maintain leadership.
4. Change the organizational relationships internally as necessary to facilitate both the acceptance and attainment of the new objectives.

A coordinated program of change in pursuit of a sound and relevant strategy under the active direction of the chief executive and the chief planner can lead to significant progress. Although this may only begin a long-term program, it should yield benefits far beyond the time and effort invested. Although pace and effectiveness of strategic change cannot be judged in quantitative terms, there are useful criteria by which they may be assessed. Some of the more important hallmarks of progress are listed here:

- Strategies are principally developed by line managers, with direct, constructive support by the staff.
- Real strategic alternatives are openly discussed at all levels within the corporation.
- Corporate priorities are relatively clear to senior management, but they permit flexible response to new opportunities and threats.
- Corporate resources are allocated based on these priorities and in view of future potential as well as historical performance.
- The strategic roles of business units are clearly differentiated as are the performance measures applied to their managers.
- Realistic responses to likely future events are worked out well in advance.
- The corporate staff adds real value to the consideration of strategic issues and receives cooperation from most divisions.

A strategic planner is a staff person who helps line executives in their planning efforts. Thus, there may be a corporate strategic planner working closely with the CEO. A strategic planner may also be attached to an SBU. This section examines the role of a strategic planner at the SBU level.

The planner conceptualizes the planning process and helps translate it for line executives who actually do the planning. As part of this function, the planner works out a planning schedule and may develop a planning manual. He or she may also design a variety of forms, charts, and tables that may be used to collect, analyze, and communicate planning-oriented information. The planner may also serve as a trainer in orienting line managers to strategic planning.

The planner generates innovative ways of performing difficult tasks and educates line managers in new techniques and tools needed for an efficient job of strategic planning. The planner also coordinates the efforts of other specialists (i.e., marketing researchers, systems persons, econometricians, environmental monitors, and management scientists) with those of line management. In this role, the planner exposes managers to the newest and most sophisticated concepts and techniques in planning.

The planner serves as an adviser to the head of the SBU. In matters of concern, the SBU head may ask the planner to undertake a study. For example, the SBU head may seek the advice of the SBU strategic planner in deciding whether private branding should be accepted so as to increase market share or whether it should be rejected for eroding the quality image of the brand.

Another key role the planner plays is that of evaluator of strategic plans. For example, strategic plans relative to various products/markets are submitted to the SBU head. The latter may ask the planner to develop an evaluation system for products/markets. In addition, the planner may also be asked to express an opinion on strategic issues.

The planner may be involved in integrating different plans. For example, the planner may integrate different product/market plans into an SBU strategic plan. Similarly, an SBU's plans may be integrated by the corporate strategic planner from the perspectives of the entire corporation. For example, if a company uses the growth rate-relative market share matrix (see Exhibit 10.4) to judge plans submitted by different businesses, the planner may be asked not only to establish the position of these businesses on the matrix but also to furnish a recommendation on such matters as which of two question marks (businesses in the high-growth-rate, low-market-share quadrant of the matrix) should be selected for additional funding. The planner's recommendation on such strategic issues helps crystallize executive thinking.

Matters of a nonroutine nature may be assigned to the planner for study and recommendation. For example, the planner may head a committee to recommend structural changes in the organization.

Obviously, the job of strategic planner is not an easy one. The strategic planner must

1. Be well versed in theoretical frameworks relevant to planning and, at the same time, realize their limitations as far as practical applications are concerned.
2. Be capable of making a point with conviction and firmness and, at the same time, be a practical politician who can avoid creating conflict in the organization.
3. Maintain a working alliance with other units in the organization.
4. Command the respect of other executives and managers.
5. Be a salesperson who can help managers accept new and difficult tools and techniques.

In short, a planner needs to be a jack-of-all-trades.

11.6 MEASURING STRATEGIC PERFORMANCE

Tracking strategy, or evaluating progress toward established objectives, is an important task in strategy implementation. There are three basic considerations in putting together a performance measurement system: (a) selecting performance measures, (b) setting performance standards, and (c) designing reports. A strategic performance measurement system requires reporting not by profit center or cost center but by SBU. It may require allocation or restatement of financial results based on the new type of reporting center. Most management reporting is geared to SEC (Security and Exchange Commission) and FASB (Financial Accounting Standards Board) requirements and focuses on the bottom line. For many business units, however, profit is not the pertinent measure of a unit's strategic performance.

In selecting performance measures, only those measures that are relevant to the strategies adopted by each SBU should be chosen. For example, brand building, advertising, and many public relations activities are commonly designed to build long-term value for the brand and the organization. In reality, most marketing expenses are investments. They are investments in customers. A marketing investment that makes certain customers more loyal can deliver a return by persuading these customers to buy and pay more, by costing less in sales and service, and by referring new customers through existing customers' visible use of the product or service and their advocacy. Ford estimates that each percentage point gained in car-owner loyalty is worth $100 million in profit every year.[18]

Further, when setting performance standards, the targets, or expected values, should be established so that they are consistent with both the strategic position of business units and the strategies selected. Finally, reports should focus management attention on key performance measures. Exhibit 11.3 summarizes significant issues in measuring strategic performance.

11.7 ACHIEVING STRATEGIC PLANNING EFFECTIVENESS

As mentioned above, most companies have made significant progress in the last twenty years in improving their strategic planning capabilities. Clear, concise methods have been developed for analyzing and evaluating market segments, business performance, and pricing and cost structures. Creative, even elegant, methods have been devised for displaying the results of these strategic analyses to top management.

Few today would argue the value—in theory at least—of the strategic approach to business planning. RJR Nabisco's former CEO, Lou Gerstner (now CEO at IBM), describes that value in the following words: ''It is my absolute conviction that you can out-manage your competition by having brilliant strategies.''[19] Unfortunately, RJR Nabisco's successful experience appears to be more the exception than the rule. Much more typical are reports of dissatisfaction with the results of strategic planning.

Why the achievement gap between strategic planning and strategic performance? Reasons undoubtedly will vary from corporation to corporation, but certain ones appear to be critical. First, many companies have found that top-down strategic planning produces resistance on the part of operating managers. Second, strategic planning efforts have failed to encourage innovative ideas and techniques to implement the strategy. Third, even in companies known for excellence in strategic planning, lack of adequate emphasis on marketing has led to poor implementation of strategic plans. Fourth, many senior managers and strategic planners have failed to comprehend that middle and lower level managers and employees are a market that has to brought on board in favor of the strategy if implementation of a strategic plan is to be successful.

Exhibit 11.3
Strategic Performance
Measurements

1. To be effective, strategic performance measures must be tailored to the particular strategy of each individual business unit. While there is a basket of generic strategic measurement tools, selection and application is highly dependent on detailed understanding of the particular business strategy and situation.
2. Strategic performance measurements have two dimensions:

   • **Monitoring key program implementation** to ensure that the necessary elements of strategy are being provided.
   • **Monitoring results** to ensure that the programs are having the desired effects.

3. Strategy performance necessarily involves trade-offs—costs and benefits. Both must be recognized in any useful strategic performance measurement system:

   • **Objectives**—assessing progress toward primary goals.
   • **Constraints**—monitoring other dimensions of performance that may be sacrificed, to some degree and for some period, in order to achieve strategic objectives.

4. Strategic performance measurements do not replace, but rather supplement, short-term financial measurements. They do provide management with a view of long-term progress in contrast to short-term performance. They may indicate that fundamental objectives are being met in spite of short-term problems, and that strategic programs should be sustained despite adversity. They may also show that fundamentals are not being met although short-term performance is satisfactory, and, therefore, strategy needs to be changed.
5. Strategic performance measurement is linked to competitive analysis. Performance measurements should be stated in competitive terms (share, relative profitability, relative growth). While quantitative goals must be established, evaluating performance against them should include an assessment of what competition has been able to attain.
6. Strategic performance measurement is linked to environmental monitoring. Reasonable goals cannot always be met by dint of effort if the external world turns against us. Strategic performance measurement systems must attempt to filter uncontrollable from controllable performance, and provide signals when the measures themselves may be the problem, rather than performance against them.

Source: Rochelle O'Connor, *Tracking the Strategic Plan* (New York, The Conference Board, Inc., no date): 11. Reprinted by permission of the publisher.

Finally, too many strategic planners and analysts, and even many CEOs, have no line management experience, and thus do not have adequate grounding in the day-to-day issues faced by the line managers in sales, production and operations that will have to implement their plans.

Strategic planning as currently practiced has produced resistance on the part of operating managers. One observer has identified three types of resistance: measurement myopia (i.e., managers behave in ways that show good short-term performance), measurement invalidation (i.e., managers supply top management with distorted or selected biased data), and measurement justification (i.e., managers justify their behavior excessively and become excessively cautious about specific factors identified as critical cash flow or ROI determinants).[20]

To solve this resistance problem, it is important to remember that, although sophisticated management tools and the up-to-the-minute techniques of business schools may help identify a desirable strategic course, implementation of a strategy requires time-honored simple and straightforward approaches. As a matter of fact, the latter are still vital prerequisites for success. Experience shows the following specific steps are helpful in effective implementation.[21]

• **Benchmark using world standards.** Find the world champions in every process you measure, from inventory turns to customer service, and try to exceed them.
• **Use process mapping.** Break down your organization's activities to their component parts. Identify the inefficiencies, then redesign each process as if from scratch. For each step, ask whether customers would pay for it if they knew about it.
• **Communicate with employees to encourage them to focus on external reality—customers and competitors.** Define a clear vision that creates a sense of urgency. Help them understand the impact of their own behavior.

- **Distinguish what needs to be done from how hard it is to do it.** The difficulty of doing is irrelevant; real emphasis should be on what is to be done.
- **Set stretch targets.** There is nothing wrong with asking employees to perform as well as the best in the world. But don't tell them how to do it. They will come out with ideas to accomplish what has to be done.
- **Never stop.** When you get ahead of the pack, don't relax. That is just when your competitors are getting energized by benchmarking against you.

Effective strategic planning should eliminate organizational restraints, not multiply them; it should contribute to innovation, not inhibit it. In the coming years, strategic planners face a unique challenge because innovation and new product development must be stimulated within the structure of large, multinational corporate enterprises. A number of companies have proved that innovation and entrepreneurial drive can be institutionalized and fostered by a responsive organizational structure. 3M and IBM, for example, have established technology review boards to ensure that promising product ideas and new technologies receive adequate start-up support. Adopting another approach, Dow Chemical has instituted an "innovation department" to streamline technology commercialization.

To encourage perpetuation of new ideas and innovation, management should:[22]

1. Focus attention on the goals of strategic planning rather than on process; that is, concentrate on substance, not form.
2. Integrate into its business strategy the analysis of emerging technologies and technology management, consumer trends and demographic shifts, regulatory impact, and global economics.
3. Design totally new planning processes and review standards and acceptance criteria for technological advances and new business "thrusts" that may not conform completely to the current corporate base.
4. Adopt a longer planning horizon to ensure that a promising business or technological development will not be cut off prematurely.
5. Ensure that overly stringent financial requirements aren't imposed during the start-up phase of a promising project.
6. Create special organizational "satellites," such as new venture groups, whose mission is to pursue new ideas free from the pressures of day-to-day operations.
7. Institute financial and career reward systems that encourage bold, innovative development programs.

11.8 STRATEGIC PLANNING AND MARKETING ORGANIZATION

Strategic planning deals with the relationship of the organization to its environment and thus relates to all areas of a business. Among all these areas, however, marketing is the most susceptible to outside influences. Thus, marketing concerns are pivotal to strategic planning. Initially, however, the role of marketing in the organization declined with the advent of strategic planning. As Kotler noted in 1978:

> Strategic planning threatens to demote marketing from a strategic to an operational function. Instead of marketing being in the driver's seat, strategic planning has moved into the driver's seat. Marketing has moved into the passenger seat and in some companies into the back seat.[23]

It has generally been believed that the only marketing decision that has strategic content is the one concerned with product/market perspectives. As far as other marketing decisions are concerned, they are mainly operational in nature; that is, they deal with short-term performance, although they may occasionally have strategic marketing significance. Product/market decisions, however, being the most far-reaching in nature as far as strategy is concerned, are frequently made by top management; the marketing organization is relegated to making operating decisions. In brief, the inroads of strategic planning have tended to lower marketing's status in the organization.

Many marketers have opined that marketing would continue to be important, but mainly for day-to-day operations. For example, Kotler predicted that

1. The marketer's job would be harder than ever in the 1980s because of the tough environment.
2. The strategic planner would provide the directive force to the company's growth, not the marketer.

3. The marketer would be relied on to contribute a great deal of data and appraisal of corporate purposes, objectives and goals, growth decisions, and portfolio decisions.

4. The marketer would assume more of an operational and less of a strategic role in the company.

5. The marketer would still need to champion the customer concept because companies tend to forget it.[24]

Experience has shown, however, that marketing definitely has an important strategic role to play. How neglect of marketing can affect strategy implementation and performance can be illustrated by Atari's problems. This company had been a pioneer in developing video games. Because of negligence in marketing, however, Atari failed to realize how quickly the market for video games would mature. Atari based earnings projections on the assumption that demand would grow at the same rate as in the past and that the company would hold its share of the market. But its assumption proved to be wrong. The market for video games grew at a much lower rate than anticipated.

Continuous close contact with the marketplace is an important prerequisite to excellent performance that no firm can ignore:

> Stay close to the customer. No company, high tech or low, can afford to ignore it. Successful companies always ask what the customer needs. Even if they have strong technology, they do their marketing homework.[25]

More businesses today than during the establishment years of strategic planning are making organizational arrangements to bring in marketing perspectives—an understandable development because, with the emergence of strategic planning (particularly in organizations that have adopted the SBU concept), marketing has become a more pervasive function. Thus, although marketing positions at the corporate level may have vanished, the marketing function still plays a key strategic role at the SBU level.

Businesses, by and large, have recognized that an important link is missing in their strategic planning processes: inadequate attention to marketing. Without properly relating the strategic planning effort to marketing, the whole process tends to become static. Business exists in a dynamic setting. It is only through marketing inputs that perspectives of changing social, economic, political, and technological environments can be brought into the strategic planning process.

Overall, marketing is once again assuming prominence. Businesses are finding that marketing is not just an operations function relevant to day-to-day decision making. It has strategic content as well.

As has been mentioned before, strategic planning emerged largely as an outgrowth of the budgeting and financial planning process, which demoted marketing to a secondary role. However, things are different now. In some companies, of course, concern with broad strategy considerations has long forced routine, high-level attention to issues closely related to markets and marketing. There is abundant evidence, however, of renewed emphasis on such issues on the part of senior management and hence of staff planners in a growing number of other companies as well. Moreover, both marketers and planners are drawing increasingly from the same growing body of analytical techniques for futurist studies, market forecasts, competitive appraisals, and the like. Such overlapping in orientation, resources, and methods no doubt helps to reinstate the crucial importance of marketing in the strategic planning effort.

Accumulating forces have caused most firms to reassess their marketing perspectives at both the corporate and the SBU level. Although initially marketing got lost in the midst of the emphasis on strategic planning, now the role of marketing is better understood and is reemerging in the form of strategic marketing.[26] The decade of the 1990s was considered as a period of marketing renaissance. The present decade has seen an increasing emphasis on developing much more precise and informative metrics on which to build analyses and input into strategic planning processes.

SUMMARY

The chapter examined five dimensions of strategy implementation and control: creation of a market-responsive organization, the role of systems in implementing strategy, executive reward systems, leadership style, and measurement of strategic performance. It is not enough for an organization to develop a sound strategy. It must, at the same time, structure the organization in a manner that ensures the implementation of the strategy. This chapter examined how to accomplish this task, that is, to match organizational structure to strategy.

Inasmuch as strategic planning is a recent activity in most corporations, no basic principles have been developed on the subject. As a matter of fact, limited academic research has been reported in this area. However, it is clear that one fundamental aspect that deeply impacts strategy implementation is the proper linking of organization, systems, and compensation. This chapter examined how to ensure maximum market responsiveness, how to fully exploit management systems as a strategic tool, and how to tie the reward system to the strategic mission.

Strategy implementation requires establishing an appropriate climate in the organization. The CEO plays a key role in adapting the organization for strategic planning. Also examined was the role of the strategic planner in the context of strategic planning and its implementation.

Many companies have not been satisfied with their strategic planning experiences. Three reasons were given for the gap between strategic planning and strategic performance: (a) resistance on the part of operating managers, (b) lack of emphasis on innovations, and (c) neglect of marketing. Suggestions were made for eliminating dysfunctional behavior among managers and for improving innovation planning.

As far as the strategic role of marketing is concerned, with the advent of strategic planning, marketing appears to have lost ground. Lately, however, marketing is reemerging as an important force in strategy formulation and implementation.

DISCUSSION QUESTIONS

1. What is the meaning of scale integration in the context of creating a market-responsive organization?
2. Discuss the three broad principles of establishing a market-responsive organization.
3. Define the term *systems*. Discuss the three categories of systems examined in this chapter.
4. Discuss the three problems that affect the establishment of a sound executive reward system.
5. What is the significance of the office of the CEO in strategic planning?
6. How does the role of a strategic planner at the corporate level differ from the role of a planner within the SBU?

NOTES

1. Steven F. Dichter, ''The Organization of the '90s,'' *McKinsey Quarterly*, Fall 1991, pp. 146–147.
2. Nora A. Aufreiter, Teri L. Lawver, and Candace D. Lun, ''A New Way to Market,'' *The McKinsey Quarterly*, No. 2, 2000, pp. 52–61.
3. Michael Treacy and Fred Wiersema, ''How Market Leaders Keep Their Edge,'' *Fortune*, February 6, 1995, p. 88.
4. Geoffrey Colvin, ''The Ultimate Manager,'' *Financial Times*, November 22, 1999, pp. 185–187; Alan Webber, ''Business Race Isn't Always to the Swift, But Bet That Way,'' *USA Today*, February 3, 1998, p. 15A.
5. Rahul Jacob, ''The Struggle to Create an Organization,'' *Fortune*, April 3, 1995, p. 90.
6. Pui-Wing Tam, ''The Chief Does Double Duty,'' *The Wall Street Journal*, February 7, 2002, p. B1.
7. See Diniel Goleman, Richard Boyatzis, and Annie McKee, ''Primal Leadership: The Hidden Drive of Great Performance,'' *Harvard Business Review*, December 2001, pp. 42–53. Also see Ram Charan and Geoffrey Colvin, ''Managing for the Slowdown,'' *Fortune*, February 5, 2001, pp. 78–88.
8. Nigel Freedman, ''Operation Centurion: Managing Transformation at Philips,'' *Long Range Planning*, Vol. 29, No. 5, 1997, pp. 607–615.
9. Ron Zemke and Dick Schaaf, *The Service Edge* (New York, New American Library, 1989): 342.
10. For a complete discussion of systems design see Jamshid Gharajedaghi, Systems Thinking: Managing Chaos and Complexity 2d Ed. (Amsterdam: Butterworth-Heinemann, 2006).
11. See Alfred Rappaport, ''New Thinking on How to Link Executive Pay with Performance,'' *Harvard Business Review*, March–April 1999, pp. 91–105.
12. Charles Elson, ''What's Wrong with Executive Compensation?'' *Harvard Business Review*, January 2003, pp. 68–77.

13. See Frank J. Sulloway, *Born to Rebel: Birth Order, Family Dynamics, and Creative Lives* (New York, Pantheon, 1998).

14. Frederick G. Hilmer, "Real Jobs for Real Managers," *McKinsey Quarterly*, Summer 1989, p. 24.

15. Sumantra Ghoshal and Christopher A. Bartlett, "Changing the Role of Top Management: Beyond Structure to Process," *Harvard Business Review*, January–February 1995, pp. 86–96.

16. Charles M. Farkas and Suzy Wetlaufer, "The Ways Chief Executive Officers Lead," *Harvard Business Review*, May–June 1996, pp. 110–122. Also see Gary Hamel, *Leading the Revolution* (Boston, MA, Harvard Business School Publishing, 2000).

17. See Abraham Zaleznink, "Managers and Leaders: Are They Different?" *Harvard Business Review*, May–June 1977, pp. 67–68.

18. Don E. Schultz and Anders Cronstedt, "Making Marcom an Investment," *Marketing Management*, Fall 1997, pp. 41–49.

19. Treacy and Wiersema, "How Market Leaders . . . ," 92.

20. Thomas V. Bonoma and Victoria L. Crittenden, "Managing Marketing Implementation," *Sloan Management Review*, Winter 1988, pp. 7–14.

21. Stratford Sherman, "Are You As Good As the Best in the World," *Fortune*, December 13, 1993, p. 95. Also see "What Is So Effective About Stephen Covey," *Fortune*, December 12, 1994, p. 116.

22. See Ray Stata, "Organizational Learning: The Key to Management Innovation," *Sloan Management Review*, Spring 1989, pp. 63–74.

23. Philip Kotler, "The Future Marketing Manager," in *Marketing Expansion in a Shrinking World: 1978 Business Proceedings*, ed. Betsy D. Gelb (Chicago, American Marketing Association, 1978): 3.

24. Kotler, "The Future Marketing Manager," 5.

25. Susan Fraker, "High-Speed Management for the High-Tech Age," *Fortune*, March 5, 1984, p. 62.

26. Ravi S. Achrol, "Evolution of the Marketing Organization: New Forms for Turbulent Environments," *Journal of Marketing*, October 1991, pp. 77–93.

Chapter Outline

12.1 Experience Curve Concept
12.2 Profit Impact of Marketing
      Strategy (PIMS)
12.3 Measuring the Value
      of Marketing Strategies
12.4 Game Theory
12.5 Delphi Technique
12.6 Trend-impact Analysis
12.7 Cross-impact Analysis
12.8 Scenario Building
12.9 Other Tools
      12.9.1 Benchmarking
      12.9.2 Core Competencies
      12.9.3 Customer Satisfaction
             Measurement
      12.9.4 Pay for Performance
      12.9.5 Reengineering
      12.9.6 Strategic Alliances
      12.9.7 Total Quality Management

Chapter 12

Strategic Tools

The Red Queen said: "Now, here, it takes all the running you can do to keep in the same place. If you want to get somewhere else, you must run twice as fast as that."

LEWIS CARROLL (ALICE IN WONDERLAND)

Strategy development is by no means an easy job. Not only must decision makers review a variety of inside factors, they must also incorporate the impact of environmental changes in order to design viable strategies. Strategists have become increasingly aware that the old way of "muddling through" is not adequate when confronted by the complexities involved in designing a future for a corporation.

Economic uncertainty, leveling off of productivity, international competition, and environmental problems pose new challenges with which corporations must cope when planning their strategies. There is, therefore, a need for systematic procedures for formulating strategy. This chapter discusses selected tools and models that serve as aids in strategy development.

A **model** may be defined as an instrument that serves as an aid in searching, screening, analyzing, selecting, and implementing a course of action. Because marketing strategy interfaces with and affects the perspectives of an entire corporation, the tools and models of the entire science of management can be considered relevant here. In this chapter, however, we deal with eight models that exhibit direct application to marketing strategies: the experience curve concept, PIMS model, value-based planning, game theory, the delphi technique, trend-impact analysis, cross-impact analysis, and scenario building. In addition, a variety of new tools that are commonly used by strategic planners are summarily listed.

12.1 EXPERIENCE CURVE CONCEPT

Experience shows that practice makes perfect. It is common knowledge that beginners are slow and clumsy and that with practice they generally improve to the point where they reach their own permanent level of skill. Anyone with business experience knows that the initial period of a new venture or expansion into a new area is frequently not immediately profitable. Many factors, such as making a product name known to potential customers, are often cited as reasons for this nonprofitability. In brief, even the most unsophisticated businessperson acknowledges that experience and learning lead to improvement. Unfortunately, the significance of experience is realized only in abstract terms. For example, managers in a new and unprofitable situation tend to think of experience in vague terms without ever analyzing it in terms of cost. This statement applies to all functions of a business where cost improvements are commonly sought—except for production management.

As growth continues, we anticipate greater efficiency and more productive output. But how much improvement can one reasonably expect? Generally, management makes an arbitrary decision to ascertain what level of output reflects the optimum level. Obviously, in the great majority of situations, this decision is primarily based on pure conjecture. Ideally, however, one should be able to use historical data to predict cost/volume relationships and learning patterns. Many companies have, in fact, developed their own learning curves—but only in the areas of production or manufacturing where tangible data are readily available and most variables can be quantified.

Several years ago the Boston Consulting Group observed that the concept of experience is not limited to production alone. The experience curve concept embraces almost all cost areas of business.

> Unlike the well-known "learning curve" and "progress function," the experience curve effect is observed to encompass all costs—capital, administrative, research and marketing—and to have transferred impact from technological displacements and product evolution.[1]

The experience effect was first observed in the aircraft industry. Because the expense incurred in building the first unit is exceptionally high in this industry, any reduction in the cost of manufacturing succeeding units is readily apparent and becomes extremely pertinent in any management decision regarding future production. For example, it has been observed that an "80 percent air frame curve" could be developed for the manufacture of airplanes. This curve depicts a 20 percent improvement every time production doubles (i.e., to produce the fourth unit requires 80 percent of the time needed to produce the second unit, and so on).[2] Studies of the aircraft industry suggest that this rate of improvement seems to prevail consistently over the range of production under study; hence, the label *experience* is applied to the curve.

Although the significance of the experience curve concept is corporate-wide, it bears most heavily on the setting of marketing objectives and the pricing decision. As already mentioned, according to the experience curve concept, all costs go down as experience increases. Thus, if a company acquired a higher market share, its costs would decline, enabling it to reduce prices. The lowering of prices would enable the company to acquire a still higher market share. This process is unending as long as the market continues to grow. But as a matter of strategy, while aiming at a dominant position in the industry, the company may be wise to stop short of raising the eyebrows of the Antitrust Division of the U.S. Department of Justice.

During the growth phase, a company keeps making the desired level of profit, but in order to provide for its growth, a company needs to reinvest profits. In fact, further resources might need to be diverted from elsewhere to support such growth. Once the growth comes to an end, the product makes available huge cash throw-offs that can be invested in a new product.

The Boston Consulting Group claims that, in the case of a second product, the accumulated experience of the first product should provide an extra advantage to the firm in reducing costs. However, experience is transferable only imperfectly. There is a transfer effect between identical products in different locations, but the transfer effect between different products occurs only if the products are somewhat the same (i.e., in the same family). This is true, for instance, in the case of the marketing cost component of two products distributed through the same trade channel. Even in this case, however, the loss of buyer "franchise" can result in some lack of experience transferability. Exhibit 12.1 is a diagram of the implications of the experience curve concept.

Some of the Boston Consulting Group's claims about the experience effect are hard to substantiate. In fact, until enough empirical studies have been done on the subject, many claims may even be disputed.[3] For example, conventional wisdom holds that market share drives profitability. Certainly, in some industries, such as chemicals, paper, and steel, market share and profitability are inextricably linked. But profitability of premium brands—brands that sell for 25% to 30% more than private-label brands—in 40 categories of consumer goods was not driven by market share alone.

Instead, both market share and the nature of the category, or product market, in which the brand competes, drive a brand's profitability. A brand's relative market share has a different impact on profitability depending on whether the overall category is dominated by premium brands or by value brands. If a category is composed largely of premium brands, then most of the brands in the category are—or should be—quite profitable. If the category is composed mostly of value and private-label brands, then returns will be lower across the board.[4]

To summarize, the experience curve concept leads to the conclusion that all producers must achieve and maintain the full cost-reduction potential of their experience gains if they hope to survive. Furthermore, the experience framework has implications for strategy development, as shown in Exhibit 12.2. The appendix at the end of this chapter describes construction of experience curves, showing how the relationship between costs and accumulated experience can be empirically developed.

The application of the experience curve concept to marketing requires sorting out various marketing costs and projecting their behavior for different sales volumes. It is hoped that the analyses will show a close relationship between increases in cumulative sales volume and declines in costs. The widening gap

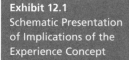

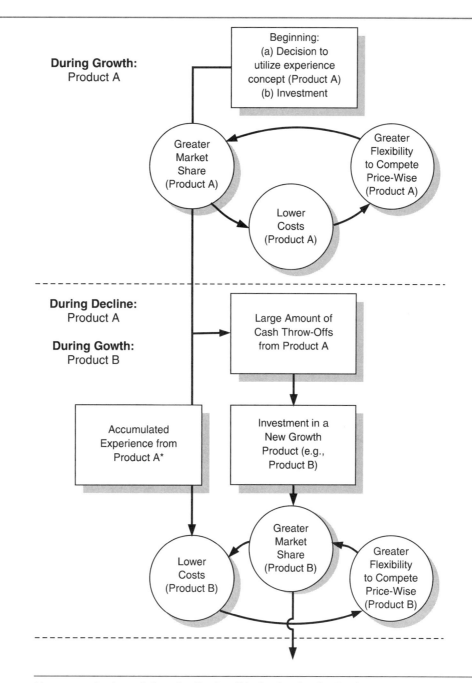

*An assumption is made here that Product B is closely related to Product A.

between volume and costs establishes the company's flexibility in cutting prices in order to gain higher market share.

Declines in costs are logical and occur for reasons such as the following:

1. Economies of scale (e.g., lower advertising media costs per unit).
2. Increase in efficiency across the board (e.g., ability of salespersons to reduce time per call).
3. Technological advances.

Conceivably, four different techniques could be used to project costs at different levels of volume: regression, simulation, analogy, and intuition. Because historical information on growing products may be

Exhibit 12.2
Experience Curves Strategy Implications

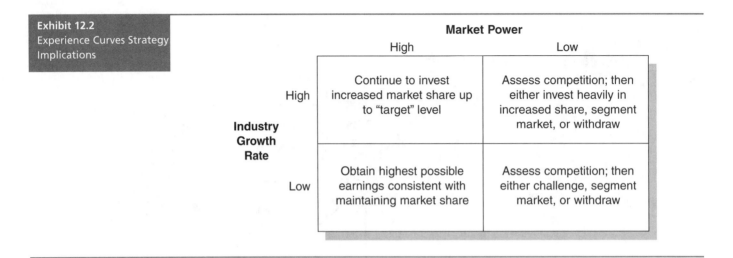

lacking, the regression technique may not work. In addition, though in many instances projecting a regression line beyond the most extreme data points is often possible due to the robustness of the technique, doing so with limited data points to work with should be done with great caution as it breaks a fundamental assumption of regression analysis—that the regression line does not extend beyond its data points. Simulation is a possibility, but it continues to be rarely practiced because it is strenuous. Drawing an analogy between the subject product and the one that has matured perhaps provides the most feasible means of projecting various marketing costs as a function of cumulative sales. But analogy alone may not suffice. As with any other managerial decision, analogy may need to be combined with intuition.

The cost characteristics of experience curves can be observed in all types of costs: labor costs, advertising costs, overhead costs, distribution costs, development costs, or manufacturing costs. Thus, marketing costs as well as those for production, research and development, accounting, service, etc., should be combined to see how total cost varies with volume. Further, total costs over different ranges of volume should be projected while considering the company's ability to finance an increased volume of business, to undertake an increased level of risk, and to maintain cordial relations with the Antitrust Division.

Each element of cost included in total cost may have a different slope on a graph. The aggregation of these elements does not necessarily produce a straight line on logarithmic coordinates. Thus, the relationship between cost and volume is necessarily an approximation of a trend line. Also, the cost derivatives of the curve are not based on accounting costs but on accumulated cash input divided by accumulated end-product unit output. The cost decline of the experience curve is the rate of change in that ratio.

Management should establish a market share objective that projects well into the future. Estimates should be made of the timing of price cuts in order to achieve designated market share. If at any time a competitor happens to challenge a firm's market share position, the firm should go all out to protect its market share and never surrender it without an awareness of its value. Needless to say, the perspective of the entire corporation must change if the gains expected from a particular market share strategy are to become reality. Thus, proper coordination among different functions becomes essential for the timely implementation of related tasks.

Although the experience effect is independent of the life cycle, of growth rate, and of initial market share, as a matter of strategy it is safer to base one's actions on experience when the following conditions are operating: (a) the product is in the early stages of growth in its life cycle, (b) no one competitor holds a dominant position in the market, (c) the product is not amenable to nonprice competition (e.g., emotional appeals, packaging), and (d) the different competitors have relative equality in their cost structures. Because the concept demands undertaking a big offensive in a battle that might last many years, a well-drawn long-range plan should be in existence. Top management should be capable of undertaking risks and going through the initial period of fast activity involved in sudden moves to enlarge the company's operations; the company should also have enough resources to support the enlargement of operations.

The experience effect has been widely accepted as a basis for strategy in a number of industries, the aircraft, petroleum, consumer electronics, and a variety of durable and maintenance-related industries among them. The application of this concept to marketing has been minimal for the following reasons:

1. Skepticism that improvement can continue.
2. Difficulty with the exact quantification of different relationships in marketing.
3. Inability to recognize experience patterns even though they are already occurring.
4. Lack of awareness that the improvement pattern can be subjectively approximated and that the concept can apply to groups of employees as well as to individual performance across the board in different functions of the business.
5. Inability to predict the effect of future technological advances, which can badly distort any historical data.
6. Accounting practices that may make it difficult to segregate costs adequately.

Despite these obstacles, the concept adds new importance to the market share strategy.

12.2 PROFIT IMPACT OF MARKETING STRATEGY (PIMS)

In 1960, the vice president of marketing services at GE authorized a large-scale project (called PROM, for profitability optimization model) to examine the profit impact of marketing strategies. Several years of effort produced a computer-based model that identified the major factors responsible for a great deal of the variation in return on investment. Because the data used to support the model came from diverse markets and industries, the PROM model is often referred to as a cross-sectional model. Even today, cross-sectional models are popularly used at GE.

In 1972, the PROM program, henceforth called PIMS, was moved to the Marketing Science Institute, a nonprofit organization associated with the Harvard Business School. The scope of the PIMS program has increased so much and its popularity has gained such momentum that its administration was moved to the Strategic Planning Institute, a new organization established for PIMS.

The PIMS program is based on the experience of more than 500 companies in nearly 3,800 "businesses" for periods that range from two to twelve years. "Business" is synonymous with "SBU" and is defined as an operative unit that sells a distinct set of products to an identifiable group of customers in competition with a well-defined set of competitors. Essentially, PIMS is a cross-sectional study of the strategic experience of profit organizations. The information gathered from participating businesses is supplied to the PIMS program in a standardized format in the form of about 200 pieces of data. The PIMS database covers large and small companies; markets in North America, Europe, and elsewhere; and a wide variety of products and services, ranging from candy to heavy capital goods to financial services. The information deals with such items as

- A description of the market conditions in which the business operates, including such things as the distribution channels used by the SBU, the number and size of its customers, and rates of market growth and inflation.
- The business unit's competitive position in its marketplace, including market share, relative quality, prices and costs relative to the competition, and degree of vertical integration relative to the competition.
- Annual measures of the SBU's financial and operating performance over periods ranging from two to twelve years.

The PIMS project indicated that the profitability of a business is affected by 37 basic factors, explaining more than 80 percent of profitability variation among businesses studied. Of the 37 basic factors, seven proved to be of primary importance (see Exhibit 12.3).

Based on analysis of information available in the PIMS database, Buzzell and Gale hypothesized the following strategy principles, or links between strategy and performance:

1. In the long run, the most important single factor affecting a business unit's performance is the quality of its products and services relative to those of competitors. A quality edge boosts performance in two ways. In the short run, superior quality yields increased profits via premium prices. In the longer term, superior or improving relative quality is the more effective way for a business to grow, leading to both market expansion and gains in market share.

Return on Investment (ROI):

The ratio of net pretax operating income to average investment. Operating income is what is available after deduction of allocated corporate overhead expenses but before deduction of any financial charges on assets employed. "Investment" equals equity plus long-term debt, or, equivalently, total assets employed minus current liabilities attributed to the business.

Market Share:

The ratio of dollar sales by a business, in a given time period, to total sales by all competitors in the same market. The "market" includes all of the products or services, customer types, and geographic areas that are directly related to the activities of the business. For example, it includes all products and services that are competitive with those sold by the business.

Product (Service) Quality:

The quality of each participating company's offerings, appraised in the following terms: What was the percentage of sales of products or services from each business in each year that were superior to those of competitors? What was the percentage of equivalent products? Inferior products?

Marketing Expenditures:

Total costs for sales force, advertising, sales promotion, marketing research, and marketing administration. The figures do not include costs of physical distribution.

R&D Expenditures:

Total costs of product development and process improvement, including those costs incurred by corporate-level units that can be directly attributed to the individual business.

Investment Intensity:

Ratio of total investment to sales.

Corporate Diversity:

An index that reflects (1) the number of different 4-digit Standard Industrial Classification industries in which a corporation operates, (2) the percentage of total corporate employment in each industry, and (3) the degree of similarity or difference among the industries in which it participates.

Source: Reprinted by permission of the *Harvard Business Review.* Exhibit from "Impact of Strategic Planning on Profit Performance" by Sidney Schoeffler, Robert D. Buzzell, and Donald F. Heany (March–April 1974): 140. Copyright © 1974 by the President and Fellows of Harvard College, all rights reserved.

2. Market share and profitability are strongly related. Business units with very large shares—over 50 percent of their served markets—enjoy rates of return more than three times greater than small-share SBUs (those that serve under 10 percent of their markets). The primary reason for the market share-profitability link, apart from the connection with relative quality, is that large-share businesses benefit from scale economies. They simply have lower per-unit costs than their smaller competitors.

3. High-investment intensity acts as a powerful drag on profitability. Investment-intensive businesses are those that employ a great deal of capital per dollar of sales, per dollar of value added, or per employee.

4. Many so-called ''dog'' and ''question mark'' businesses generate cash, while many ''cash cows'' are dry. The guiding principle of the growth-share matrix approach to planning (see Chapter 10) is that cash flows largely depend on market growth and competitive position (your share relative to that of your largest competitor). However, the PIMS-based research shows that, while market growth and relative share are linked to cash flows, many other factors also influence this dimension of performance. As a result, forecasts of cash flow based solely on the growth-share matrix are often misleading.

5. Vertical integration is a profitable strategy for some kinds of businesses, but not for others. Whether increased vertical integration helps or hurts depends on the situation, quite apart from the question of the cost of achieving it.

6. Most of the strategic factors that boost ROI also contribute to long-term value.[5]

These principles are derived from the premise that business performance depends on three major kinds of factors: the characteristics of the market (i.e., market differentiation, market growth rate, entry conditions, unionization, capital intensity, and purchase amount), the business's competitive position in that market (i.e., relative perceived quality, relative market share, relative capital intensity, and relative cost), and the strategy it follows (i.e., pricing, research and development spending, new product introductions, change in relative quality, variety of products/services, marketing expenses, distribution channels, and relative vertical integration). Performance refers to such measures as profitability (ROS, ROI, etc.), growth, cash flow, value enhancement, and stock prices.

The PIMS approach is to gather data on as many actual business experiences as possible and to search for relationships that appear to have the most significant effect on performance. A model of these relationships is then developed so that an estimate of a business's return on investment can be made from the structural competitive/strategy factors associated with the business. Obviously, the PIMS conceptual framework must be modified on occasion. For example, repositioning structural factors may be impossible and the costs of doing so prohibitive. Besides, actual performance may reflect some element of luck or some unusual event.[6] In addition, results may be influenced by the transitional effect of a conscious change in strategic direction.[7] Despite these reservations, the PIMS framework can be beneficial in the following ways:

1. It provides a realistic and consistent method for establishing potential return levels for individual businesses.
2. It stimulates managerial thinking on the reasons for deviations from par performance.
3. It provides insight into strategic moves that will improve the par return on investment.
4. It encourages a more discerning appraisal of business unit performance.

The PIMS database has been used by managers and planning specialists in many ways. Applications include developing business plans, evaluating forecasts submitted by divisional managers, and appraising possible strategies. The data suggests that[8]

- For followers, current profitability is adversely affected by a high level of product innovation, measured either by the ratio of new product sales to total sales or by research and development spending. The penalty paid for innovation is especially heavy for businesses ranked fourth or lower in their served markets. The market leader's profitability, on the other hand, is not hurt by new product activity or research and development spending.
- High rates of marketing expenditure depress return on investment for followers, not for leaders.
- Low-ranking market followers benefit from high inflation. For businesses ranked first, second, and third, inflation has no relation to return on investment.

12.3 MEASURING THE VALUE OF MARKETING STRATEGIES

In the last few years, a new yardstick for measuring the worth of marketing strategies has been suggested. This new approach, called **value-based planning**, judges marketing strategies by their ability to enhance shareholders' value. It emphasizes the impact a strategic move has on the *value* investors place on the equity portion of a firm's assets.[9] The principal feature of value-based planning is that managers should be evaluated on their ability to make strategic investments that produce returns greater than their cost of capital.

Value-based planning draws ideas from contemporary financial theory. For example, a company's primary obligation is to maximize returns from capital appreciation. Similarly, the market value of a stock depends on investors' expectations of the ability of each business unit in the firm to generate cash.[10]

Value is created when the financial benefits of a strategic activity exceed costs. To account for differences in the timing and riskiness of the costs and benefits, value-based planning estimates overall value by discounting all relevant cash flows.

A company that has used the value-based approach for a long time is the Connecticut-based Dexter Corporation. Its value-based planning uses four subsystems:[11]

- The Dexter financial decision support system (DSS), which provides strategic business segments (SBS) with financial data. The DSS provides a monthly profit and loss and balance sheet statement of each strategic business segment. All divisional expenses, assets, and current liabilities are allocated to the SBSs.
- A microcomputer-based system, which transforms this data for use in the two following subsystems: corporate financial reports system and value planner system. The financial data generated by DSS must be transformed to fit the input specifications of these two subsystems.

- The corporate financial reports system estimates the cost of capital of an SBS. For estimating cost of capital, Dexter uses two models. The first is the bond-rating simulation model. This model is used to estimate the capital structure appropriate to each of its SBSs, given its six-year financial history. Each SBS is assigned the highest debt-to-total capital ratio that would allow it to receive an A bond rating. The second model, which is used to compute cost of capital, is the business risk index estimation model. This model allows cost of equity to be estimated for business segments that are not publicly traded.
- The value planner system estimates a business's future cash flows. The basic premise of the value planner system is that business decisions should be based on a rigorous consideration of expected future cash flows. Dexter uses the 12 most recent quarters of SBS data to produce a first-cut projection of future cash flows. As information on a new quarter becomes available, the oldest quarter in the model is deleted. These historical trends are used for projecting financial ratios into the future. The following assumptions are made to compute future cash flows:

> **Sales growth**—Based on the expectation that each SBS will maintain market share.
>
> **Net plant investment**—Based on the growth rate in unit volume deemed necessary to maintain Dexter's market share.
>
> **Unallocated divisional expenses**—Projected for each SBS using the same percentage of sales used for the division as a whole.
>
> **The appropriate time horizon for cash flow projections**—Based on the expected number of years that a business can reinvest at an expected rate of return.

These assumptions are controversial because they do not allow cash flow projections to be tailored to each SBS. Dexter management terms its historical forecast a *naive* projection and uses it to challenge its managers to explain why the future will be different from the recent past.

The next step in the value-based planning process is to compute the value of projected future cash flows and to discount them by the cost of capital for an SBS. If the estimated value of an SBS is in excess of its book value, the SBS contributes positively to the wealth of Dexter's stockholders, which means it makes sense to reinvest in it.

The major strengths of Dexter's SBS value planner system have been articulated as follows:

- **Its emphasis on being intelligible to line managers**—A value-based planning model can indicate which SBSs are not creating value for the firm's stockholders. However, it is the SBS manager who must initiate action to rectify problems that the analysis uncovers.
- **Its degree of accuracy**—The real dilemma in designing models for value-based planning is to make them easy to use while improving the accuracy with which they reflect or predict the firm's market value.
- **Its integration with existing systems and databases**—By developing a system that works with existing systems, costs are reduced and upgrades are easier to implement. Also, it is easier to gain the acceptance of line managers if the value-based planning system is presented as an extension of the decision support system they are currently using.

The value-based approach has made important contributions to the decision-making process at Dexter. Using this approach, Dexter managers made the following decisions:

- Not to invest further in an SBS with high-growth prospects until its valuation, based on actual performance, increases significantly.
- To harvest and downsize an SBS with a negative value.
- To sell an SBS with negative value to its employees for book value.
- To sell an SBS with a value higher than book value but for which an offer was received that was significantly greater than any valuation that could be reasonably modeled in Dexter's hands.

The interesting characteristic of these decisions is that they can run somewhat counter to the prescriptions that flow out of a typical portfolio-planning approach. The first decision, for example, refers to a star business, presumably worthy of further investment. Unlike portfolio planning, in which growth is desirable in and of itself, under value-based planning, growth is healthy only if the business is creating value.

Dexter used value-based planning as a guideline for decision making, not as an absolute rule. The approach is, in general, understood and accepted, but many managers question its relevance. They now know whether their divisions create value for the company, but they do not understand how they can use that information to make or change important business decisions. Top management understands that value-added planning needs more time before it is completely accepted. However, its value in formulating strategy is limited in that its focus is on returns of historically implemented and assumes they will continue into the future. It does not provide for the potential for a new strategy to increase market share, nor does it do anything to offset the difficulties involved in projecting cash flows into the future.

12.4 GAME THEORY

Game theory is a useful technique for companies to rapidly respond to changes in products, technologies, and prices. It helps companies pay attention to interactions with competitors, customers, and suppliers, and induces companies to focus on the end-game so that their near-term actions promote their long-term interest by influencing what these players do.

The theory is reasonably straightforward to use. There are two competitors, Ace and Smith. Ace expects Smith to enter the market and is trying to understand Smith's likely pricing strategy. To do so, Ace uses something called a *payoff matrix* (see Exhibit 12.4). Each quadrant in the matrix contains the payoffs—or financial impact—to each player for each possible strategy. If both players maintain prices at current levels, they will both be better off: Ace will earn $100 million and Smith will earn $60 million (Quadrant A). Unfortunately for both Ace and Smith, however, they have perverse incentives to cut prices.

Ace calculates that if he maintains prices, Smith will cut prices to increase earnings to $70 million from $60 million. (See the arrow moving from Quadrant A to Quadrant B.) Smith makes a similar calculation that if it maintains prices, Ace will cut. The logic eventually drives them both to Quadrant D, with both cutting prices and both earning lower returns than they would with current prices in place. This equilibrium is unattractive for both parties. If each party perceives this, then there is some prospect that each will separately determine to try to compete largely on other factors, such as product features, service levels, sales force deployment, or advertising.

But it is necessary to have in-depth knowledge of the industry before game theory is truly valuable. Whether the goal is to implement by fully quantifying the outcomes of a payoff matrix or by more qualitatively assessing the outcome of the matrix, it is necessary to understand entry costs, exit costs, demand functions, revenue structures, cost curves, etc. Without that understanding, the game theory may not provide correct answers.

The following are the rules to observe to make the best use of the theory:

- **Examine the number, concentration, and size distribution of the players.** Industries with four or fewer significant competitors have the greatest potential for using game theory to gain an edge because (a) the competitors will usually be large enough to benefit more from an improvement in general industry conditions than they would from improving their position at the expense of others, and (b) with smaller numbers of

Exhibit 12.4
Game Theory: An Illustration of the Pricing Game

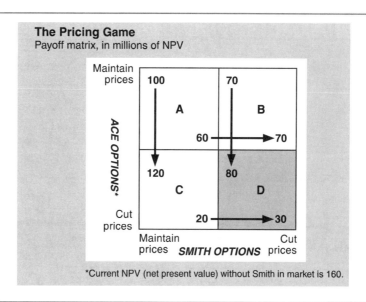

The Pricing Game
Payoff matrix, in millions of NPV

*Current NPV (net present value) without Smith in market is 160.

competitors it is possible for managers to think through the different combinations of moves and counter-moves. Similarly, the number of customers, suppliers, etc., affects the usefulness of game theory.

- **Keep an eye out for strategies inherent in one's market share.** Small players can use ''judo economics'' to take advantage of larger companies that may be more concerned with maintaining the status quo than with retaliating against a small entrant. In 1992, for instance, Kiwi Airlines got away with undercutting Delta's and Continental's prices between Atlanta and Newark by as much as 75 percent. The reason: When Kiwi first entered the market it represented less then 7 percent of that route's capacity, and the cost of a significant pricing response by the incumbents would have likely exceeded the benefits.[12] Conversely, large players can create economies of scale or scope. Companies such as United and American have used frequent-flier programs to create switching barriers, whereas most small airlines would not have the route structure required to make their frequent-flier programs very attractive.
- **Understand the nature of the buying decision.** If there are only a few deals signed in an industry each year, it will be hard to avoid aggressive competition. In the jet engine industry, for example, three manufacturers (GE, Pratt & Whitney, and Rolls Royce) compete ruthlessly for scarce orders. If a producer loses several large bids in a row, layoffs will be likely, and it might even go out of business. In this kind of situation, the challenge for game theory is to improve the bidding process to shift the power balance between the industry and its customers.
- **Scrutinize the competitors' cost and revenue structures.** Industries where competitors have a high proportion of fixed-to-variable cost will probably behave more aggressively than those where production costs are more variable. In the paper, steel, and refining industries, for example, high profit contributions on extra volume give most producers strong incentives to cut prices to get volume.
- **Examine the similarity of firms.** Industries where competitors have similar cost and revenue structures often exhibit independently determined but similar behavior. Consider the U.S. cellular telephone industry: Competitors share similar technologies, and have similar cost structures. Given their similar economic incentives, the challenge is to find prices that create the largest markets and then to compete largely on factors such as distribution and service quality.
- **Analyze the nature of demand.** The best chances to create value with less aggressive strategies are in markets where demand is stable or growing at a moderate rate. For example, even in oil-field services in the early 1980s after drilling activity had plummeted, declining demand did not lead to lower prices in all sectors. In those more-technology-demanding parts of the industry where there were only a limited number of competitors (e.g., open-hole logging and well-pressure control), prices were more stable than in other sectors. It should be kept in mind that demand in business-to-business markets is generally inelastic.

Done right, game theory can turn conventional strategies on their heads and dramatically improve a company's ability to create economic value. Sometimes it can increase the size of the pie; on other occasions it can make a company's slice of the pie bigger, and it may even help do both.

12.5 DELPHI TECHNIQUE

The **delphi technique**, named after Apollo's oracle at Delphi, is a method of making forecasts based on expert opinion. Its history is an interesting one. It was developed by the Rand Corporation under contract to the U.S. Air Force for the express purpose of forecasting future technological trends and their impact on future strategic environments and needs. Its critics were responsible for naming the technique when they claimed that its forecasts were as ''nebulous as those of the Oracle at Delphi.'' Traditionally, expert opinions were pooled in committee. The delphi technique was developed to overcome the weaknesses of the committee method. Some of the problems that occur when issues are discussed in committee include:

1. The influence of a dominant individual.
2. The introduction of a lot of redundant or irrelevant material into committee workings.
3. Group pressure that places a premium on compromise.
4. Reaching decisions is slow, expensive, and sometimes painful.
5. Holding members accountable for the actions of a group.

All of these factors provide certain psychological drawbacks to people in face-to-face communication. Because people often feel pressure to conform, the most popular solution, instead of the best one, prevails.

With the delphi technique, a staff coordinator questions selected individuals on various issues. The following is a sample of questions asked:

1. What is the probability of a future event occurring? For example, by what year do you think there will be widespread use of robot services for refuse collection, as household slaves, as sewer inspectors, etc.?

   a. 2010
   b. 2020
   c. 2030
   d. 2040

2. How desirable is the event in Question 1?

   a. needed desperately
   b. desirable
   c. undesirable but possible

3. What is the feasibility of the event in Question 1?

   a. highly feasible
   b. likely
   c. unlikely but possible

4. What is your familiarity with the material in Question 1?

   a. fair
   b. good
   c. excellent

The coordinator compiles the responses, splitting them into three groups: lower, upper, and inner. The division into groups may vary from one investigation to another. Frequently, however, the lower and upper groups each represent 10 percent, whereas the inner group takes the remaining 80 percent. When a person makes a response in either the upper or lower group, it is customary to ask about the reasons for his or her extreme opinion.

In the next round, the respondents are given the same questionnaire, along with a summary of the results from the first round. The data feedback includes the consensus and the minority opinion. During the second round, the respondents are asked to specify by what year the particular product or service will come to exist with 50 percent probability and with 90 percent probability. Results are once again compiled and fed back. This process of repeating rounds can be continued indefinitely; however, rarely has any research been conducted past the sixth round, and generally no significant change in projections occurs after three iterations. In recent years, the delphi technique has been refined by the use of interactive computer programs to obtain inputs from experts, to present summary estimates, and to store revised judgments in data files that are retrievable at user terminals.

The delphi technique is gradually becoming important for predicting future events objectively. Most large corporations use this technique for long-range forecasting. Some of the advantages of the delphi technique are listed below:

1. It is a rapid and efficient way to gain objective information from a group of experts.
2. It involves less effort for a respondent to answer a well-designed questionnaire than to participate in a conference or write a paper.
3. It can be highly motivating for a group of experts to see the responses of knowledgeable persons.
4. The use of systematic procedures applies an air of objectivity to the outcomes.
5. The results of delphi exercises are subject to greater acceptance on the part of the group than are the consequences arrived at by more direct forms of interaction.
6. The delphi is more capable of making accurate forecasts during periods of developmental change (defined below) than traditional statistical techniques.

Change is an accepted phenomenon in the modern world. Change coupled with competition forces a corporation to pick up the trends in the environment and to determine their significance for company operations. In light of the changing environment, the corporation must evaluate and define strategic posture to be able to face the future boldly. Two types of changes can be distinguished: cyclical and developmental. A **cyclical change** is repetitive in nature; managers usually develop routine procedures to meet cyclical changes. A **developmental change** is innovative and irregular; having no use for the "good" old ways, managers abandon them. Developmental change appears on the horizon so slowly that it may go unrecognized or be ignored until it becomes an accomplished fact with drastic consequences. It is this latter category of change that assumes importance in the context of strategy development. The delphi technique can be fruitfully used to analyze developmental changes. Functionally, a change may fall into one of the following categories: social, economic, political, regulatory, or technological. The delphi technique has been used by organizations to study emerging perspectives in all these areas.

One drawback of the delphi technique is that each trend is given unilateral consideration on its own merits. Thus, one may end up with conflicting forecasts; that is, one trend may suggest that something will happen, whereas another may lead in the opposite direction. To resolve this problem, another forecasting technique, the cross-impact matrix (discussed later) has been used by some researchers. With this technique, the effect of potential interactions among items in a forecasted set of occurrences can be investigated. If the behavior of an individual item is predictable (i.e., if it varies positively or negatively with the occurrence or nonoccurrence of other items), the cross-impact effect is present. It is thus possible to determine whether a predicted event will have an enhancing or inhibiting influence upon each of the other events under study by using a cross-impact matrix.

Recent research shows that the use of the delphi technique has undergone quite a change. The salient features of the revised delphi technique are (a) identifying recognized experts in the field of interest; (b) seeking their cooperation and sending them a summary paper on the topic being examined (based on a literature search); and (c) conducting personal interviews with each expert based on a structured questionnaire, usually by two interviewers. Feedback and repeated rounds of responding to written questionnaires are no longer considered necessary. Though the first two features listed were commonly used from the beginning, not all practioners of the technique accept the third modification.

12.6 TREND-IMPACT ANALYSIS

Trend-impact analysis is a technique for projecting future trends from information gathered on past behavior. The uniqueness of this method lies in its combination of statistical method and human judgment. If predictions are based on quantitative data alone, they will fail to reflect the impact of unprecedented future events. On the other hand, human judgment provides only subjective insights into the future. Therefore, because both human judgment and statistical extrapolation have their shortcomings, both should be taken into consideration when predicting future trends.

In trend-impact analysis (TIA), past history is first extrapolated with the help of a computer. Then the judgment of experts is sought (usually by means of the delphi technique) to specify a set of unique future events that may have a bearing on the phenomenon under study and to indicate how the trend extrapolation may be affected by the occurrence of each of these events. The computer then uses these judgments to modify its trend extrapolation. Finally, the experts review the adjusted extrapolation and modify the inputs in those cases in which an input appears unreasonable.

To illustrate TIA methods, let us consider the case of the average price of a new prescription drug to the year 2010. As shown in Exhibit 12.5, statistical extrapolation of historical data shows that price will rise to $23 by the year 2005 and to $24.23 by the year 2010. The events considered relevant include (a) generic dispensing, which increases 20 percent of all prescriptions filled; (b) Medicaid and Medicare prescription reimbursement, which is based on a fixed monthly fee per covered patient ("capitation plan"); and (c) a 50 percent decrease in the average rate of growth in prescription size. Consider the first event, i.e., 20 percent increase in generic dispensing. Expert judgment may show that this event has a 75 percent chance of occurring by 2000. If this event does occur, it is expected that its first impact on the average price of a new prescription will begin right away. The maximum impact, a 3 percent reduction in the average price, will occur after five years.

The combination of these events, probabilities, and impacts with the baseline extrapolation leads to a forecast markedly different from the baseline extrapolation (see Exhibit 12.5). The curve even begins to taper off in the year 2010. The level of uncertainty is indicated by quartiles above and below the mean forecast. (The quartiles indicate the middle 50 percent of future values of the curve, with 25 percent lying on each side of the forecast curve.) The uncertainty shown by these quartiles results from the fact that many of the events that have large impacts also have relatively low probabilities.

At this juncture, it is desirable to determine the sensitivity of these results to the individual estimates upon which they are based. For example, one might raise valid questions about the estimates of event

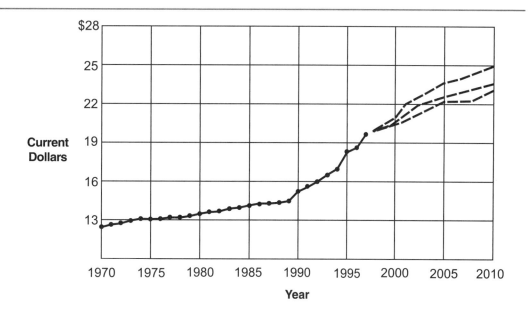

Exhibit 12.5
Average Retail Price of a New Prescription

	Historical Data				Forecast		
					Lower Quartile	Mean	Upper Quartile
1969	12.17	1984	13.86	1998	20.65	20.70	20.75
1970	12.41	1985	14.02	1999	20.92	21.03	21.14
1971	12.78	1986	14.19	2000	21.21	21.40	21.61
1972	12.92	1987	14.32	2001	21.54	21.79	22.10
1973	12.99	1988	14.45	2002	21.83	22.15	22.54
1974	13.15	1989	14.70	2003	22.08	22.45	22.92
1975	13.22	1990	15.20	2004	22.30	22.74	23.25
1976	13.27	1991	15.60	2005	22.52	23.00	23.55
1977	13.26	1992	15.98	2006	22.74	23.25	23.83
1978	13.35	1993	16.44	2007	22.95	23.50	24.10
1979	13.42	1994	17.03	2008	23.17	23.75	24.38
1980	13.48	1995	17.66	2009	23.39	23.99	24.64
1981	13.56	1996	18.63	2010	23.60	24.23	24.90
1982	13.63	1997	20.37				
1983	13.70						

probability, the magnitude of the impacts used, and the lag time associated with these impacts. Having prepared these data in a disaggregated fashion, one can very easily vary such estimates and view the change in results. It may also be observed that intervention policies, whether they are institutional (such as lobbying, advertising, or new marketing approaches) or technological (such as increased research and development expenditures), can be viewed as a means of influencing event probabilities or impacts.

TIA can be used not only to improve forecasts of time series variables but also to study the sensitivity of these forecasts to policy. Of course, any policy under consideration should attempt to influence as many events as possible rather than one, as in this example. Corporate actions often have both beneficial and detrimental effects because they may increase both desirable and undesirable possibilities. The use of TIA can make such uncertainties more clearly visible than can traditional methods.

12.7 CROSS-IMPACT ANALYSIS

Cross-impact analysis, as mentioned earlier, is a technique used for examining the impacts of potential future events upon each other. It indicates the relative importance of specific events, identifies groups of reinforcing or inhibiting events, and reveals relationships between events that appear unrelated. In brief, cross-impact analysis provides a future forecast, making due allowance for the effect of interacting forces on the shape of things to come.

Essentially, this technique consists of selecting a group of five to ten project participants who are asked to specify critical events having any relationship with the subject of the analysis. For example, in an analysis of a marketing project, events may fall into any of the following categories:

1. Corporate objectives and goals.
2. Corporate strategy.
3. Markets or customers (potential volume, market share, possible strategies of key customers, etc.).
4. Competitors (product, price, promotion, and distribution strategies).
5. Overall competitive strategic posture, whether aggressive or defensive.
6. Internally or externally developed strategies that might affect the project.
7. Legal or regulatory activities having favorable or unfavorable effects.
8. Other social, demographic, or economic events.

The initial attempt at specifying critical events presumably will generate a long list of alternatives that should be consolidated into a manageable size (e.g., 25 to 30 events) by means of group discussion, concentrated thinking, elimination of duplications, and refinement of the problem. It is desirable for each event to contain one and only one variable, thus avoiding double counting. Selected events are represented in an $n \times n$ matrix for developing the estimated impact of each event on every other event. This is done by assuming that each specific event has already occurred and that it will have an enhancing, an inhibiting, or no effect on other events. If desired, impacts may be weighted. The project coordinator seeks impact estimates from each project participant individually and consolidates the estimates in the matrix form. Individual results, in summary form, are presented to the group. Project participants vote on the impact of each event. If the spread of votes is too wide, the coordinator asks those persons voting at the extremes to justify their positions. The participants are encouraged to discuss differences in the hope of clarifying problems. Another round of voting takes place. During this second round, opinions usually converge, and the median value of the votes is entered in the appropriate cell in the matrix. This procedure is repeated until the entire matrix is complete.

In the process of completing the matrix, a review of occurrences and interactions identifies events that are strong actors and significant reactors and provides a subjective opinion of their relative strengths. This information then serves as an important input in formulating strategy.

The use of cross-impact analysis may be illustrated with reference to a study concerning the future of U.S. automobile component suppliers. The following events were set forth in the study:

1. Motor vehicle safety standards that come into effect between 2000 and 2004 will result in an additional 150 pounds of weight for the average-sized U.S. car.
2. The 2001 NOX emissions regulations will be relaxed by the EPA.
3. The retail price of gasoline (regular grade) will be $2 per gallon.
4. U.S. automakers will introduce passenger cars that will achieve at least 40 mpg under average summer driving conditions.

These events are arranged in matrix form in Exhibit 12.6. The arrows show the direction of the analysis. For example, the occurrence of Event A would be likely to bring more pressure to bear upon regulatory officials; consequently, Event B would be more likely to occur. An enhancing arrow is therefore placed in the cell where Row A and Column B intersect. Moving to Column C, it is not expected that the occurrence of Event A will have any effect on Event C, so a horizontal line is placed in this cell. It is judged that the occurrence of Event A would make Event D less likely to occur, and an inhibiting arrow is placed in this cell. If Event B were to occur, the consensus is that Event A would be more likely; hence the enhancing arrow. Event B is not expected to affect Event C but would make Event D more likely. Cells are completed in accordance with these judgments. Similar analyses for Events C and D complete the matrix.

The completed matrix shows the direction of the impact of rows (actors) upon columns (reactors). An analysis of the matrix at this point reveals that Reactor C has only one actor (Event D) because there is only one reaction in Column C. If interest is primarily focused on Event D, Column D should be studied for actor events. Then each actor should be examined to determine what degree of influence, if any, it is likely to have on other actors in order to bring about Event D.

If This Event Were to Occur

Then the Impact upon This Event Would Be

A   MVSS (2000 through 2004) requires 150 pounds additional weight for average-sized U.S. autos

B   2001 NO_x emissions requirements are relaxed by EPA

C   Retail price of gasoline is $2/gallon

D   U.S. automakers introduce cars capable of 40 mpg in average summer driving

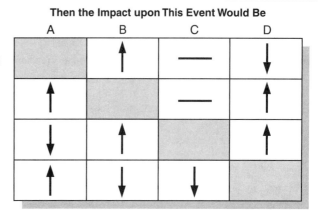

= enhancing

— = no effect

= inhibiting

Exhibit 12.6 Basic Format for Cross-Impact Matrix

Next, impacts should be quantified to show linkage strengths (i.e., to determine how strongly the occurrence or nonoccurrence of one event would influence the occurrence of every other event). To assist in quantifying interactions, a subjective rating scale, such as the one shown on page 307, may be used.

Voting Scale	Subjective Scale	
+8	Critical: essential for success	**Enhancing**
+6	Major: major item for success	
+4	Significant: positive and helpful but not essential	
+2	Slight: noticeable enhancing effect	
0	**No effect**	
−2	Slight: noticeable inhibiting effect	**Inhibiting**
−4	Significant: retarding effect	
−6	Major: major obstacle to success	
−8	Critical: almost insurmountable hurdle	

Consider the impact of Event A upon Event B. It is felt that the occurrence of Event A would significantly improve the likelihood of the occurrence of Event B. Both the direction and the degree of enhancing impact are shown in Exhibit 12.7 by the +4 rating in the appropriate cell. Event A's occurrence would make Event D less likely; therefore, the consensus rating is –4. This process continues until all interactions have been evaluated and the matrix is complete.

There are a number of variations for quantifying interactions. For example, the subjective scale could be 0 to 10 rather than –8 to +8, as shown in the example above.

Another technique for quantifying interactions involves the use of probabilities. If the probability of the occurrence of each event is assessed before the construction of the matrix, then the change in that probability can be assessed for each interaction. As shown in Exhibit 12.8, the probabilities of occurrence can be entered in a column preceding the matrix, and the matrix is constructed in the conventional manner. Consider the impact of Event A on the probable occurrence of Event B. It is judged to be an enhancing effect, and the consensus is that the probability of Event B occurring will change from 0.8 to 0.9. The new probability is therefore entered in the appropriate cell. Event A is judged to have no effect upon Event C; therefore, the original probability, 0.5, is unchanged. Event D is inhibited by the occurrence of Event A, and the resulting probability of occurrence is lowered from 0.5 to 0.4. The occurrence of Event B increases the probability of Event A occurring from 0.7 to 0.8. Event B has no impact upon Event C (0.5, unchanged) and increases the probability of Event D to 0.7. This procedure is followed until all cells are completed.

If This Event Were to Occur	Then the Impact upon This Event Would Be			
	A	B	C	D
A MVSS (2000 through 2004) requires 150 pounds additional weight for average-sized U.S. autos		+4	0	−4
B 2001 NOx emissions requirements are relaxed by EPA	+2		0	+4
C Retail price of gasoline is $2/gallon	−4	+4		+2
D U.S. automakers introduce cars capable of 40 mpg in average summer driving	+2	−2	−2	

Exhibit 12.7 Cross-Impact Matrix Showing Degrees of Impact

An examination of the matrix at this stage reveals several important relationships. For example, if we wanted Event D to occur, then the most likely actors are Events B and C. We would then examine Columns B and C to determine what actors might be influenced. Influences that bring about desired results at a critical moment are often secondary, tertiary, or beyond. In many instances, the degree of impact is not the only important information to be gathered from a consideration of interactions. Time relationships are often very important and can be shown in a number of ways. For example, in Exhibit 12.8 information about time has been added in parentheses. It shows that if Event A were to occur, it would have an enhancing effect upon Event B, raising B's probability of occurrence from 0.8 to 0.9, and that this enhancement would occur immediately. If Event B were to occur, it would raise the probability of the occurrence of Event D from 0.5 to 0.7. It would also take two years to reach the probable time of occurrence of Event D.

12.8 SCENARIO BUILDING

Plans for the future were traditionally developed on a single set of assumptions. Restricting one's assumptions may have been acceptable during times of relative stability, but as we enter the new century experience has shown that it may not be desirable to commit an organization to the most probable future alone. It is equally important to make allowances for unexpected or less probable future trends that may seriously

If This Event Were to Occur	Probability of Occurrence	Then the Impact upon This Event Would Be			
		A	B	C	D
A MVSS (2000 through 2004) requires 150 pounds additional weight for average-sized U.S. autos	0.7		0.9 (immed.)	0.5	0.4 (immed.)
B 2001 NOx emissions requirements are relaxed by EPA	0.8	0.8 (immed.)		0.5	0.7 (+2 yrs.)
C Retail price of gasoline is $2/gallon	0.5	0.6 (+1 yr.)	0.9 (+1 yr.)		0.7 (+2 yrs.)
D U.S. automakers introduce cars capable of 40 mpg in average summer driving	0.5	0.8 (immed.)	0.6 (immed.)	0.4 (+1 yr.)	

Exhibit 12.8 Cross-Impact Matrix Showing Interactive Probabilities of Occurrence

jeopardize strategy. One way to focus on different future outcomes within the planning process is to develop scenarios and to design strategy so that it has enough flexibility to accommodate whatever outcome occurs. In other words, by developing multiple scenarios of the shape of things to come, a company can make a better strategic response to the future environment. Scenario building in this sense is a synopsis that depicts potential actions and events in a likely order of development, beginning with a set of conditions that describe a current situation or set of circumstances.[13] In addition, scenarios depict a possible course of evolution in a given field. Identification of changes and evolution of programs are two stages in scenario building.

Changes in the environment can be grouped into two classes: (a) scientific and technological changes and (b) socioeconomic-political changes. Chapter 6 dealt with environmental scanning and the identification of these changes. Identification should take into consideration the total environment and its possibilities: What changes are taking place? What shape will change take in the future? How are other areas related to environmental change? What effect will change have on other related fields? What opportunities and threats are likely?

A scenario should be developed without any intention of predicting the future. It should be a time-ordered sequence of events that reflects logical cause-and-effect relationships among events. The objective of a scenario building should be to clarify certain phenomena or to study the key points in a series of developments in order to evolve new programs. One can follow an inductive or a deductive approach in building a scenario. The deductive approach, which is predictive in nature, studies broad changes, analyzes the impact of each change on a company's existing lines, and at the same time generates ideas about new areas of potential exploitation. Under the inductive approach, the future of each product line is simulated by exposing its current environment to various foreseen changes. Through a process of elimination, those changes that have relevance for one's business can be studied more deeply for possible action. Both approaches have their merits and limitations. The deductive approach is much more demanding, however, because it calls for proceeding from the unknown to the specific.

Exhibit 12.9 summarizes how scenarios may be constructed. Scenarios are not a set of random thoughts: They are logical conclusions based on past behaviors, future expectations, and the likely interactions of the two. As a matter of fact, a variety of analytical techniques (e.g., the delphi technique, trend impact analysis, and cross-impact analysis) may be used to formulate scenarios.

The following procedure may be utilized to analyze the scenarios:

- Identify and make explicit your company's mission, basic objective, and policies.
- Determine how far into the future you wish to plan.
- Develop a good understanding of your company's points of leverage and vulnerability.
- Determine factors that you think will definitely occur within your planning time frame.
- Make a list of key variables that will have make-or-break consequences for your company.
- Assign reasonable values to each key variable.
- Build scenarios in which your company may operate.
- Develop a strategy for each scenario that will most likely achieve your company's objectives.
- Check the flexibility of each strategy in each scenario by testing its effectiveness in the other scenarios.
- Select or develop an "optimum response" strategy.

12.9 OTHER TOOLS

Traditionally, tool usage was in favor of cost-reduction techniques. In recent years, the tool preferences are shifting toward models for retaining customers, outsmarting competitors, motivating employees, and accelerating innovation. Here is a listing of select new tools that are commonly used by strategists.

12.9.1 Benchmarking

This process measures a company against the standards and practices of other companies. The use of benchmarking is growing quickly among small companies, as it becomes easier to do due to the vast amount of information accessible through the web and availability of special software for benchmarking. Benchmarking falls into two main categories: (a) comparison of financial measures, (b) qualitative and systematic search to identify the best practices of a relevant industry.

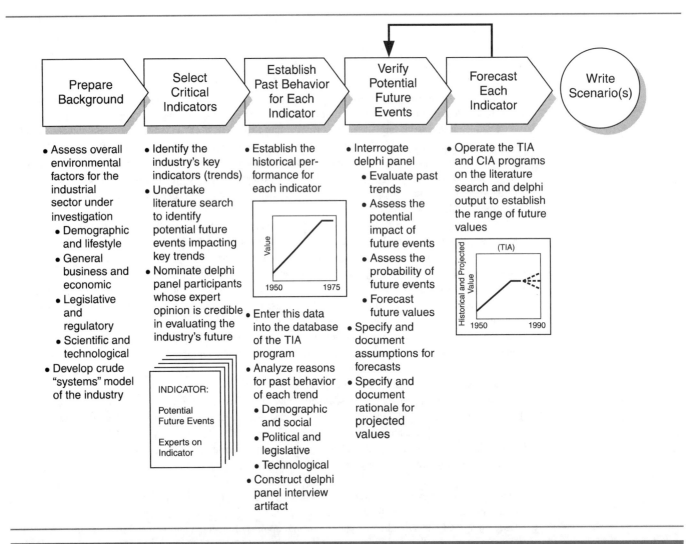

Exhibit 12.9 Scenario-Building Method at GE

12.9.2 Core Competencies

Core competencies are the capabilities of a firm or its product that are important in the eyes of customers and at the same time difficult to replicate by competition. In other words, a core competence has three traits:

1. It makes a contribution to perceived customer benefits.
2. It is difficult for competitors to imitate.
3. It can be leveraged to a wide variety of markets.

It is important to know that core competencies do change over time; thus companies must be proactive in developing new ones in response to market needs. Another trend that can be observed is that external relationship competencies are becoming more important than internal technological and process competencies.

12.9.3 Customer Satisfaction Measurement

Customer satisfaction measurement follows the perspectives of the marketing concept, i.e., first, firms need to be able to identify and understand customer needs; second, they need to be able to satisfy those needs. The customer satisfaction measurement is critical in evaluating how well the needs have been satisfied. A well-designed customer satisfaction measurement system has a direct and indirect impact in meeting many common business requirements: (a) design and development of a market-driven business plan; (b) design, analysis, and use of essential performance indicators; (c) product design and development; (d) assessment of the effectiveness of servicing; (e) continuous improvement; and (f) benchmarking.

There are 15 steps in the creation of an effective customer satisfaction measurement system. They include

1. Define the scope and purpose of the survey.
2. Determine the data collection method.
3. Determine how the data should be segmented by market, titles, etc.
4. Determine the appropriate sample sizes.
5. Determine the drivers of satisfaction.
6. Design the instrument to assess the relative importance of the drivers of customer satisfaction.
7. Develop a method to verify the buying criteria.
8. Develop open-ended questions.
9. Structure the competitive analysis section.
10. Develop the scale.
11. Test the instrument.
12. Pre-notify customers.
13. Administer the survey.
14. Develop the report.
15. Use the results and do it again.

12.9.4 Pay for Performance

This system of compensation is tied to performance, as the name indicates. Although it may sound like a very straightforward system, the main challenge for compensation managers here is to tie the right rewards to the right outcomes. Issues that need to be taken under consideration in designing pay-for-performance plans are

1. Specific outcomes that should be measured
2. Competency-based pay programs for senior management compensation
3. Accounting and tax issues for stock and executive compensation programs
4. Retirement planning

12.9.5 Reengineering

Reengineering is a strategy of radically redesigning business processes to increase productivity. Specifically, reengineering often deals with reassigning job tasks and downsizing. Some authors suggest that empowerment should be an important aspect of reengineering, while others argue that empowerment does not really increase performance because people have difficulty with defining their own jobs.

12.9.6 Strategic Alliances

Many businesses today realize that they "can't go it alone." Thus, they form business partnerships with their customers, suppliers, or even competitors. Such alliances are not only present in the domestic market but also in the international arena (joint ventures). The main issue here is: Are alliances a successful method of conducting business? Many of them fail—this brings up a challenge of identifying the success and failure factors in such ventures.

12.9.7 Total Quality Management

Total Quality Management (TMQ) is a management technique that focuses on continuous improvement of business operations and practices to eliminate errors (thus improve quality and cut costs) and improve quality of customer satisfaction. Several success factors have been identified for TQM, among others:

1. Process focus (improving how things should be done to make them better)
2. Systematic and continuous improvement

3. Company-wide emphasis
4. Customer focus (e.g., quality defined from the customer perspective)
5. Employee involvement and development
6. Cross-functional management
7. Supplier relationships
8. Recognition of TQM as a critical competitive strategy

SUMMARY

This chapter presented a variety of tools and techniques that are helpful in different aspects of strategy formulation and implementation. These tools and techniques include experience curves, the PIMS model, a model for measuring the value of marketing strategies, game theory, the delphi technique, trend-impact analysis, cross-impact analysis, and scenario building. Most of these techniques require data inputs both from within the organization and from outside. Each tool or technique was examined for its application and usefulness. In some cases, procedural details for using a technique were illustrated with examples from the field.

DISCUSSION QUESTIONS

1. Explain the relevance of experience curves in formulating pricing strategy.
2. Discuss how the delphi technique may be used to generate innovative ideas for new types of distribution channels for automobiles.
3. Explain how PIMS judgments can be useful in developing marketing strategy.
4. Experience curves and the PIMS model both seem to imply that market share is an essential ingredient of a winning strategy. Does that mean that a company with a low market share has no way of running a profitable business?
5. One of the PIMS principles states that quality is the most important single factor affecting an SBU's performance. Comment on the link between quality and business performance.

NOTES

1. *Perspective on Experience* (Boston, Boston Consulting Group, 1970): 1. Also see James Aley, ''The Theory That Made Microsoft,'' *Fortune*, April 29, 1996, p. 65.
2. See John Dutton and Annie Thomas, ''Treating Progress Functions as a Managerial Opportunity,'' *Academy of Management Review*, April 1984.
3. See Richard Minter, ''The Myth of Market Share,'' *The Wall Street Journal*, June 15, 1998, p. A17. Also see William W. Alberts, ''The Experience Curve Doctrine Reconsidered,'' *Journal of Marketing*, July 1989, pp. 36–49 and Robert Jacobson, ''Distinguishing among Competing Theories of the Market Share Effect,'' *Journal of Marketing*, October 1988, pp. 68–80.
4. Vijay Vishwahath and Jonathon Mark, ''Your Brand's Best Strategy,'' *Harvard Business Review*, May–June 1997, pp. 123–131.
5. Robert D. Buzzell and Robert T. Gale, *The PIMS Principles: Linking Strategy to Performance* (New York, The Free Press, 1987): 2.
6. Robert Jacobson and David A. Aaker, ''Is Market Share All It's Cracked Up to Be?'' *Journal of Marketing*, Fall 1985, pp. 11–22. Also see John E. Prescott, Ajay K. Kohli, and N. Venkatraman, ''The Market Share-Profitability Relationship: An Empirical Assessment of Major Assertions and Contradictions,'' *Strategic Management Journal*, Vol. 7, 1986, pp. 377–394.
7. See Cheri T. Marshall and Robert D. Buzzell, ''PIMS and the FTC Line-of-Business Data: A Comparison,'' *Strategic Management Journal*, Vol. 11, 1990, pp. 269–282.

8. Buzzell and Gale, *PIMS Principles*, 192–193. Also see V. Ramanujan and N. Venkatraman, "An Inventory and Critique of Strategy Research Using the PIMS Data Base," *Academy of Management Review*, January 1984, pp. 138–151.

9. George S. Day and Liam Fahey, "Valuing Market Strategies," *Journal of Marketing*, July 1988, pp. 45–57. Also see Eric Almquist and Gordon Wyner, "Boost your Marketing ROI with Experimental Design," *Harvard Business Review*, October 2001, pp. 135–151.

10. Sharon Tully, "The Real Key to Creating Wealth," *Fortune*, September 20, 1993, p. 38. Also see Laura Walbert, "America's Best Wealth Creators," *Fortune*, December 27, 1993, p. 64.

11. See Bala Chakravarthy and Worth Loomis, "Dexter Corporation's Value-Based Strategic Planning System," *Planning Review*, January–February 1988, pp. 34–41. Also see Rajendra K. Srirastara, Tasadduq A. Shervani, and Liam Fahey, "Marketing, Business Process, and Shareholder Value: An Organizationally Embedded View of Marketing Activities and the Discipline of Marketing," *Journal of Marketing*, Special Issue, 1999, pp. 168–179.

12. F. William Barnett, "Making Game Theory Work in Practice," *The Wall Street Journal*, February 13, 1995, p. B8.

13. "Scenario Planning: The Next Big Surprise," *The Economist*, October 13, 2001, p. 60; Pierre Wack, "Scenarios: Uncharted Waters Ahead," *Harvard Business Review*, September–October, 1985, Reprint # 85516; and Pierre Wack, "Scenarios: Shooting the Rapids," *Harvard Business Review*, November–December, 1985, Reprint # 85617.

APPENDIX: EXPERIENCE CURVE CONSTRUCTION

The experience curve concept can be used as an aid in developing marketing strategy. The procedure for constructing curves discussed below describes how the relationship between costs and accumulated experience can be empirically developed.

The first step in the process of constructing the experience curve is to compute experience and accumulated cost information. Experience for a particular year is the accumulation of all volume up to and including that year. It is computed by adding the year's volume to the experience of previous years. Accumulated cost (constant dollars) is the total of all constant costs incurred for the product up to and including that year. It is computed by adding the year's constant dollar cost to the accumulated costs of previous years. A year's constant dollar cost is the real dollar cost for that year, corrected by inflation. It is computed by dividing cost (actual dollars) by the appropriate deflator.

The second step is to plot the initial and annual experience/accumulated cost (constant dollars) data on log-log graph paper (see Exhibit 12.A). It is important that the experience axis of this graph be calibrated so that its point of intersection with the accumulated cost axis is at one unit of experience. The accumulated cost axis may be calibrated in any convenient manner.

The next step is to fit a straight line to the points on the graph, which may be accomplished by using the least-squares method (Exhibit 12.A).

It is useful at this point to stop and analyze the accumulated cost diagram. In general, the closer the data points are to the accumulated cost curve, the stronger the evidence that the experience effect is present. Deviations of the data points from the curve, however, do not necessarily disprove the presence of the experience effect. If the deviations can be attributed to heavy investment in plant, equipment, etc. (as is common in very capital-intensive industries), the experience effect still holds, but only in the long run because, in the long run, the fluctuations are averaged out. If, on the other hand, significant deviations from the line cannot be explained as necessary periodic changes in the rate of investment, then the presence of the experience effect, or at least its consistency, is open to question. In Exhibit 12.B there is one deviation (see Point X) that stands out as significant. If this can be ascribed to heavy investment (in plant, equipment, etc.), the experience effect is still viable here.

The next step in the process of constructing the experience curve is to calculate the intensity of the product's experience effect. Intensity is the percentage in unit cost reduction achieved each time the product's experience is doubled. As such, it determines the slope of the experience curve. To compute the intensity from the accumulated cost curve, arbitrarily select an experience level on the experience axis (e.g., Point $E1$ in Exhibit 12.C). Draw a line vertically up from $E1$ until it intersects the accumulated cost curve. From that point on the curve, draw a horizontal line left until it intersects the accumulated cost axis. Read

Exhibit 12.A
Accumulated
Cost Diagram

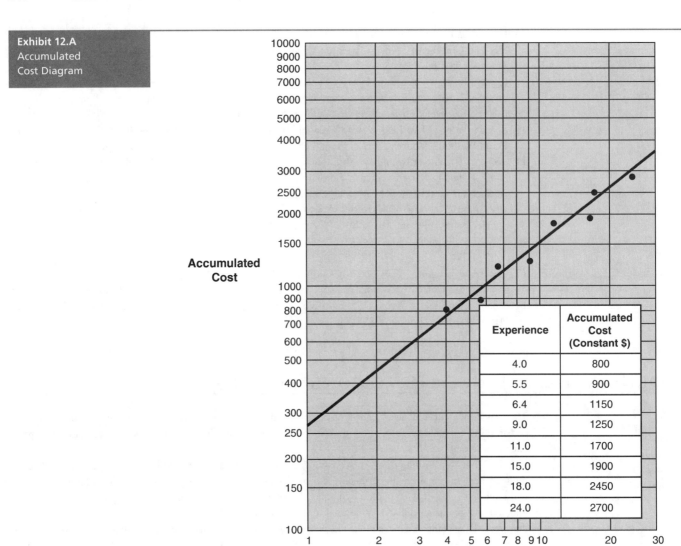

Experience	Accumulated Cost (Constant $)
4.0	800
5.5	900
6.4	1150
9.0	1250
11.0	1700
15.0	1900
18.0	2450
24.0	2700

Exhibit 12.B
Interpretation of
Deviations from
Accumulated Cost Curve

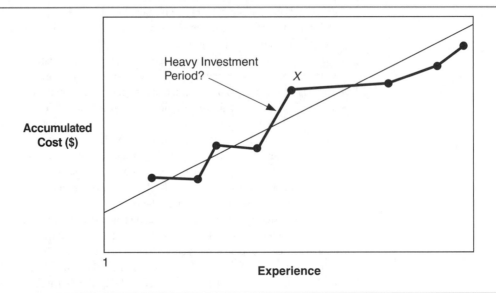

Heavy Investment
Period?

X

Accumulated
Cost ($)

Experience

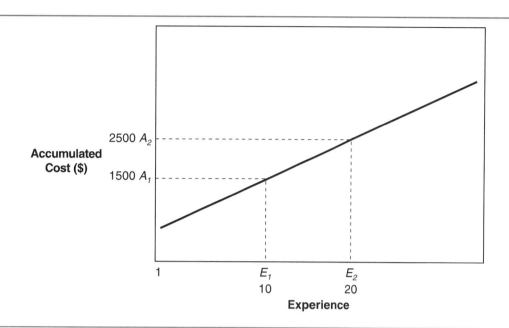

Exhibit 12.C
Product Intensity
Computation

the corresponding accumulated cost ($A1$) from the scale. Follow the same procedure for experience level $E2$, where $E2$ equals $E1 \times 2$, to obtain $A2$. Divide $A2$ by $A1$, divide the result by 2, and subtract the second result from the number 1. The final answer is the product's intensity. With the information given in Exhibit 12.C, the intensity equals 16.7 percent:

When the intensity has been computed, the slope of the experience curve is determined. However, as shown in Exhibit 12.D, this information in itself is not sufficient for constructing the curve. Because all of the lines in Exhibit 12.D are parallel, they have the same slope and represent the same intensity. To construct the experience curve, it is necessary to find a point ($C1$) on the unit cost axis. This can be achieved in the following manner: Find the *intensity multiplier* corresponding to the product's intensity from the table specially prepared for the purpose (Exhibit 12.E). If the intensity falls between two values in Exhibit 12.E, the appropriate intensity multiplier should be determined by implementation and control interpolation. Read the value on the accumulated cost axis where the curve intersects that axis. Multiply this value by the intensity multiplier. The result is $C1$.

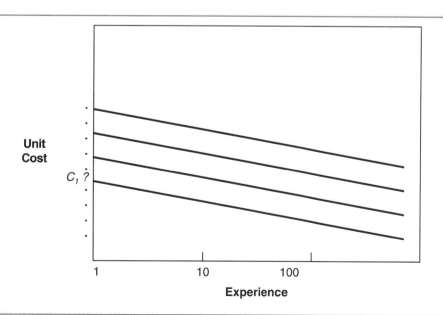

Exhibit 12.D
Slopes of Parallel Lines

Exhibit 12.E
Intensity Multipliers

Intensity	Intensity Multiplier	Intensity	Intensity Multiplier
5.0%	.926	20.5%	.669
5.5	.918	21.0	.660
6.0	.911	21.5	.651
6.5	.903	22.0	.642
7.0	.895	22.5	.632
7.5	.888	23.0	.623
8.0	.880	23.5	.614
8.5	.872	24.0	.604
9.0	.864	24.5	.595
9.5	.856	25.0	.585
10.0	.848	25.5	.575
10.5	.840	26.0	.566
11.0	.832	26.5	.556
11.5	.824	27.0	.546
12.0	.816	27.5	.536
12.5	.807	28.0	.526
13.0	.799	28.5	.516
13.5	.791	29.0	.506
14.0	.782	29.5	.496
14.5	.774	30.0	.485
15.0	.766	30.5	.475
15.5	.757	31.0	.465
16.0	.748	31.5	.454
16.5	.740	32.0	.444
17.0	.731	32.5	.433
17.5	.722	33.0	.422
18.0	.714	33.5	.411
18.5	.705	34.0	.401
19.0	.696	34.5	.390
19.5	.687	35.0	.379
20.0	.678	35.5	.367

The intensity was calculated above as 16.7 percent. By using Exhibit 12.E, the corresponding intensity multiplier can be interpolated as approximately 0.736. As shown in Exhibit 12.A, the accumulated cost at the point of intersection can be read as approximately $260. Multiplying $260 by 0.736 yields a $C1$ of $191. The experience curve can now be plotted on log-log graph paper. Position $C1$ on the unit cost axis. Multiply $C1$ by the quantity (1 – intensity) to obtain $C2$:

$$\$191 \times (1 - 0.167) = \$159$$

Locate $C2$ on the unit cost axis. Find the point of intersection (y) of a line drawn vertically up from 2 on the experience axis and a line drawn horizontally right from $C2$ on the unit cost axis. Draw a straight line through the points $C1$ and y. The result is the product's experience curve (Exhibit 12.F).

The application of the experience curve concept to marketing strategy requires the forecasting of costs. This can be achieved by using the curve. Determine the current cumulative experience of the product. Add to this value the planned cumulative volume from the present to the future time point. The result is the planned experience level at that point. Locate the planned experience level on the experience axis of the graph. Move vertically up from that point until the line extension of the experience curve is reached. Move horizontally left from the line to the unit cost axis. Read the estimated unit cost value from the scale. The unit cost obtained is expressed in constant dollars, but it can be converted to an actual dollar cost by multiplying it by the projected inflator for the future year.

Cost forecasts can also be used to determine the minimum rate of volume growth necessary to offset an assumed rate of inflation. For example, with an assumed inflation rate of 3.8 percent, a producer having

Exhibit 12.F
Experience Curve
Estimation

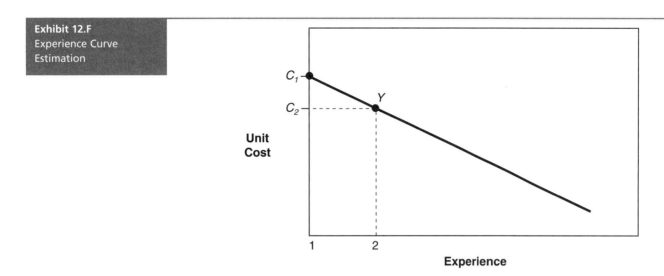

an intensity of 20 percent must realize a volume growth of approximately 13 percent per year just to maintain unit cost in real dollars. Should growth be slower or should full cost-reduction potential not be realized, the producer's unit cost would rise.

Competitor cost is one of the most fundamental yet elusive information needs of the producer attempting to develop marketing strategy. The experience curve concept provides a sound basis for estimating the cost positions of competitors as well. With certain assumptions, competitors' curves can be estimated.

PART **VI**

Marketing Strategies

Chapter 13
Market Strategies

Chapter 14
Product Strategies

Chapter 15
Pricing Strategies

Chapter 16
Distribution Strategies

Chapter 17
Promotion Strategies

Chapter 18
Global Market Strategies

Chapter Outline

13.1 Dimensions of Market Strategies
13.2 Market-Scope Strategy
13.3 Market-Geography Strategy
13.4 Market-Entry Strategy
13.5 Market-Commitment Strategy
13.6 Market-Dilution Strategy

Chapter 13

Market Strategies

Three women and a goose make a marketplace.

ITALIAN PROVERB

In the final analysis, all business strategies must be justified by the availability of a viable market. When there is no viable market, even the best strategy will flop. In addition, the development of marketing strategies for each business should be realistically tied to the target market. Because the market should be the focus of successful marketing, strategies aligned to the market point the way for each present business, serve as underpinnings for overall corporate-wide strategy, and provide direction for programming key activities and projects in all functional areas.

When corporate resources are scarce and corporate strengths are limited, it is fatal to spread them across too many markets. Rather, these critical resources should be concentrated on those key markets (key in terms of type of market, geographic location, time of entry, and commitment) that are decisive for the business's success. Merely allocating resources in the same way that other firms do yields no competitive differential. If, however, it can be discovered which markets really hold potential, the business will be able to lever itself into a position of relative competitive superiority.

This chapter will identify different aspects of market strategies that companies commonly pursue and will analyze their impact on performance vis-à-vis SBU objectives. The use of these strategies will be illustrated with examples from the marketing literature. The appendix at the end of this chapter will summarize each strategy in terms of definition, objectives, requirements, and expected results.

13.1 DIMENSIONS OF MARKET STRATEGIES

Market strategies deal with the perspectives of markets to be served. These perspectives can be determined in different ways. For example, a company may serve an entire market or dissect it into key segments on which to concentrate its major effort. Thus, market scope is one aspect of market strategy. The geographic dimensions of a market constitute another aspect: a company may focus on a local, regional, national, or international market. Another strategic variable is the time of entry into a market. A company may be the first, among the first few, or among the last to enter a market. Commitment to a market is still another aspect of market strategy. This commitment can be to achieve market dominance, to become a major factor in the market, or merely to play a minor role in it. Finally, a company may intentionally decide to dilute a part of its market as a matter of strategy. Briefly, then, the following constitute the major market strategies that a company may pursue:

- Market-scope strategy
- Market-geography strategy
- Market-entry strategy
- Market-commitment strategy
- Market-dilution strategy

13.2 MARKET-SCOPE STRATEGY

Market-scope strategy deals with the coverage of the market. A business unit may serve an entire market or concentrate on one or more of its parts. Three major alternatives in market-scope strategy are single-market strategy, multimarket strategy, and total-market strategy.

A variety of reasons may lead a company to concentrate its efforts on a single segment of a market, often called a market niche strategy. For example, in order to avoid confrontation with large competitors, a small company may find a unique niche in a market and devote its energies to serving this niche. Design and Manufacturing Corporation (D&M) is a classic example of a successful single-market strategy. In the late 1950s, Samuel Regenstrief studied the dishwasher market and found (a) high growth potential; (b) market domination by GE; and (c) absence of a manufacturer to supply large retailers, such as Sears, with their own private brand. These conclusions led him to enter the dishwasher market and to concentrate his efforts on a single segment: national retailers. The company emerged as the largest producer of dishwashers in the world with over 25 percent of the U.S. market. A D&M executive describes the company's strategy in the following words: "Sam knew precisely what segment of the market he was going after; he hit it at exactly the right time; and he has set up a tightly run organization to take full advantage of these opportunities."[1]

The story of Tampax also illustrates the success of the single-market strategy. Tampax had a minimal share of a market dominated by Kimberly-Clark's Kotex and Personal Product's Modess. Tampax (in 1997 Procter & Gamble purchased this business) could not afford to compete head-on with these major brands. To sell its different concept of sanitary protection—internal protection—the company found that newer, younger users were more open-minded and very brand loyal. Starting from a premise that had great appeal for the young user, that internal protection offers greater freedom of action, Tampax concentrated on reaching young women. Its single-market strategy has proved to be highly beneficial.[2] Even today the company's advertising is scarcely distinguishable from the firm's first efforts.

In the competitive field of cosmetics, Noxell Corporation (a division of Procter & Gamble), marketer of the popular Noxzema and Cover Girl brands of makeup and skin cream, found success in a single segment of the $15-billion cosmetics industry that its rivals disdain: the mass market. Noxell's products are aimed primarily at teenagers and evoke the image of fresh-faced natural beauty. Widely distributed and heavily advertised, Noxell's brands are easily recognizable by their low price. Content to sell its products in chains such as Kmart and Wal-Mart, the company avoids more prestigious, but cutthroat, department and specialty store businesses. The determination to sell exclusively through mass merchandisers is based on Noxell's belief that distribution through department stores is unattractive: it requires leasing counter space, keeping large inventories on hand, and paying commissions to salespeople. Noxell's continued sales growth and healthy profit performance attest to the viability of concentrating on a single segment of the market.[3]

There is no magic formula for choosing a segment. A business should analyze the market carefully to find a segment that is currently being ignored or served inadequately. Then it should concentrate on the chosen segment wholeheartedly, despite initial difficulties, and avoid competition from the established firms.

New market segments often emerge as a result of changes in the environment. For example, the women's movement motivated Smith and Wesson Corp. to launch Lady Smith in 1989, a line of guns specifically designed for women. The result: sales to women jumped from 5 percent of the company's total to nearly 20 percent.[4] Despite the cutthroat competition from mass merchandisers such as Toys "R" Us, FAO Schwartz continues to successfully operate by targeting upscale children. P&G's latest growth strategy is to launch a gender-specific toothpaste with crest "Rejuvenating Effects" for women. Although teeth are not different among men and women, P&G thinks a shimmery box and a hint of vanilla and cinnamon flavoring will make the product feminine. In addition, the notion of "rejuvenating" is intended to resonate with women concerned about aging.[5] Candy makers find their traditional markets slowing down since birth rates in developed countries have been declining. In Spain, for example, only 1.3 children are born per family. On the other hand ex-smokers appear to emerging into a new viable segment. Therefore, market leader Tootsie Roll Industries, Inc., has started offering Yogurt-flavored fruit-smoothies and hot-chocolate lollipops. Spangler Candy Co. has introduced three new kinds of Dum Dums-buttered popcorn, fruit punch and orange cream. Mars, Inc., has added Starburst Fruit chew lollipops to its offerings, while Hershey Foods Corp. introduced Jolly Rancher lollipops.[6]

The single-market strategy generally consists of seeking out a market segment that larger competitors consider too small, too risky, or just plain unappealing. The strategy will not work in areas where the market power of big companies is important in realizing economies of scale, as in the extractive and process industries, for example. Companies concentrating on a single market have the advantage of being able to make quick responses to market opportunities and threats through appropriate changes in policies. The single-market, or niche, strategy is often born of necessity. Lacking the resources to fight head-to-head battles across the board with larger entrenched competitors, winners typically seek out niches that are too small to interest the giants or that can be captured and protected by sheer perseverance and by serving customers surpassingly well.

As far as the impact of the single-market strategy is concerned, it affects profitability in a positive direction. When effort is concentrated on a single market, particularly when competition is minimal, it is feasible to keep costs down while prices are kept high, thus earning substantially higher profits. Although its growth objective may not be achieved when this strategy is followed, a company may be able to increase its market share if the chosen segment is large enough vis-à-vis the overall market, or if, as in the case of tampons, is a markets that takes off and begins to grow significantly.

Instead of limiting business to one segment and thus putting all its eggs in one basket, a company may opt to serve several distinct segments. To implement a multimarket strategy successfully, it is necessary to choose those segments with which the company feels most comfortable and in which the company is able to avoid confronting companies that serve the entire market.[7] This point may be illustrated with reference to Crown Cork and Seal Company. The company is a major producer of metal cans, crowns (bottle caps), closures (screw caps and bottle lids), and filling machinery for beer and soft drink cans. The industry is characterized by a really dynamic environment: technological breakthroughs, new concepts of packaging, new materials, and threats of self-manufacture by large users are common. Crown Cork and Seal, as a matter of strategy, decided to concentrate on two segments: (a) cans for such "hard-to-hold" products as beer and soft drinks and (b) aerosol containers. Its new strategy paid off. The company outperformed its competitors both in sales growth and in return on sales in the 1980s and 1990s. As it should be with any strategic choice, the company fully committed itself to its strategy despite the lure of serving other segments. For example, in spite of its 50 percent share in the motor oil can business, Crown Cork decided not to continue to compete aggressively in that market.[8]

The multimarket strategy can be executed in one of two ways: either by selling different products in different segments or by distributing the same product in a number of segments. Toyota Motor Corporation, for example, introduced its Lexus line of cars in 1989. The car was directed toward luxury car buyers who traditionally had looked to BMW and Mercedes-Benz. Toyota entered a different segment with a different product. In recent years, outdoor sports (e.g., biking, backpacking, and hiking) have experienced terrific growth. Counting on the continued strength of this outdoor trend, Timex Corporation decided to introduce a line of rugged watches. The company decided to license Timberland Co., a well-established name in outdoor products, to sell its watches under the brand name Timberland. The company has introduced as many as 82 styles to keep the competitors at bay.[9]

In contrast, North Face, Inc., the leader in high-performance outdoor clothing, decided to broaden its market base by extending the business to the casual sportswear market. The company increased the number of stores selling North Face after 2001 from 1,500 specialty stores up to 4,000 retailers, including such stores as Nordstrom and Footlocker.[10]

A company using the total-market strategy serves an entire spectrum of a market. There are two approaches to the total market strategy. The first is by selling different products directed toward different segments of the market. The strategy evolves over a great number of years of operation. A company may start with a single product. As the market grows and as different segments emerge, leading competitors may attempt to compete in all segments by employing different combinations of product, price, promotion, and distribution strategies. These dominant companies may also attempt to enter new segments as they emerge. As a matter of fact, the leading companies may themselves create new segments and try to control them from the outset. The second alternative strategy is to focus on the mass market, the largest single segment in the market, and try and serve the entire market with their mass market offering. The classic example of this strategy is Ford Motors under its founder, Henry Ford, where it was said, "You can buy a car any color you want so long as it is black."

The two strategies have their own respective advantages and weaknesses. The mass market strategy is much more cost efficient. Due to economies of scale, all aspects of unit cost, e.g., production costs, advertising and promotion costs, research cost, acquisition costs, quality control costs inventory costs, and etc., can be driven down to their minimum. However brand equity will tend to be weaker as the producer is trying to serve all markets with one, or a very few products. In addition, if the company encounters a competitor with a cost structure that is lower across all levels of production, it is difficult to remain competitive since the primary competitive premise is low prices. The multisegment strategy generally creates greater brand loyalty and higher levels of customer satisfaction, but all costs tend to be higher also so prices must also be higher to maintain margins.

A number of companies in different industries have followed this strategy. General Motors, for one, has traditionally directed its effort to securing an entire market: "A car for every pocket and taste." With its five auto lines (Chevrolet, Pontiac, Oldsmobile, Buick, and Cadillac), along with a variety of small trucks, the company attempts to compete in all conceivable segments. The clearest indication of the strength of this strategy is the fact that General Motors overtook Ford, a devotee of the mass market strategy at the time with its classic Model A, as the World's largest industrial company in 1932, the worst year of the Great Depression and a year in which it could have been expected that the low cost Model A should have had a significant advantage.

IBM now also follows an across-the-board strategy. It has a system for meeting the requirements of all types of customers. In the mid-1980s, as the personal computer segment emerged, IBM was somewhat slow to respond but finally developed a personal computer of its own, came to dominate the market, and as the economics of the market changed towards being more cost and price oriented, sold its PC division when margins were sqeezed and profits evaporated. Similarly, in the consumer products area, the Coca-Cola Company has Coca-Cola, Diet Coke, Tab, Sprite, Fresca, and Fanta to satisfy different drinking tastes and needs. The company even has a brand of orange juice, Minute Maid, for the segment of consumers who drink juice rather than carbonated beverages.

The total-market strategy is highly risky. For this reason, only a very small number of companies in an industry may follow it. Embracing an entire market requires top management commitment. In addition, a company needs ample resources to implement it. Finally, only companies in a strong financial position may find this strategy attractive. As a matter of fact, a deteriorating financial position may force a company to move backward from an across-the-board market strategy. Chrysler Corporation's financial woes in the 1990s led it to reduce the scope of its markets overseas at a time when experts were anticipating the emergence of a single global market. The total-market strategy can be highly rewarding in terms of achieving growth and market share, but it may or may not lead to increased profitability.

There are only limited periods during which the fit between the key requirements of a market and the particular competencies of a firm competing in that market is at an optimum. Companies should not, therefore, tie themselves to a particular market strategy permanently. Environmental shifts may necessitate a change in perspective from one period to another. Consider the American Express credit card. At one time, it had potent snob appeal meant for upscale customers. But as competition in the credit card business intensified, many American Express card holders exchanged their cards for others that required no annual fee and provided revolving credit at modest interest rates. This forced American Express to redefine its market. In 1994, it began offering a number of new cards, each one targeted at a different segment of the consumer market. Some cards bore the exclusive imprimatur of AmEx with annual fee waived, others shared billing with other companies that offered a range of enticements, such as frequent-flier miles and car discounts. All offered revolving credit at competitive rates. Where business travelers were once AmEx's preferred clientele, every creditworthy American was now being wooed. Similarly, Gerber Products long dominated the U.S. baby food market, but declining birth rates forced it to seek growth elsewhere. The company has been planning to introduce foods for older people. In the mid-1990s as microbrewers became popular, the industry leaders, Anheuser and Miller, decided to introduce their own specialty beers with the mystique of the micros. For example Anheuser-Busch added Redhook Ale, Red Wolf, Elk Mountain, and Crossroads; Miller offered Red Dog, Icehouse, and Celis; and Coors came out with Sandlot and George Killian. They did so since future industry growth is dependent on specialty beers. While the U.S. beer industry continues to stagnate, the specialty beers have been growing over 40% annually.[11]

The J.C. Penney Company, after 75 years of being identified as a retailer of private-label soft goods to price-conscious customers, decided in the 1980s to change the scope of its market. The company transformed itself so that it occupied a position between a traditional department store and a discount store (something along the lines of a moderately priced department store with emphasis on higher-priced fashion) in hard goods, housewares, and especially apparel. The company continues to upgrade and has successfully been able to attract more upscale customers.

Disney's emphasis on the 5- to 13-year-old age market has been a phenomenon in itself. During the 1960s, this segment continued to grow, providing the company with opportunities for expansion. In the 1970s, however, this segment shrank; it declined further in the 1980s, leading the company to change its strategic perspectives. It began serving the over-25 age group by making changes in its current offerings and by undertaking new projects: Epcot Center, Disney MGM Studios theme park, and a water park are all attached to Disney World in Florida.[12]

Briefly, then, markets are moving targets, and a company's strategic perspectives must change accordingly.

13.3 MARKET-GEOGRAPHY STRATEGY

Geography has long been used as a strategic variable in shaping market strategy. History provides many examples of how businesses started locally and gradually expanded nationally, even internationally. Trains, automobiles, telephones, televisions, and jet aircraft have brought all parts of the country together so that distance ceases to be important, thus making geographic expansion an attractive choice when seeking growth.

Consider the case of Ponderosa System, a fast-food chain of steak houses (a division of Metromedia Steak Houses, Inc.). The company started in 1969 with four restaurants in Indiana. By 1970 it had added 10 more restaurants in Indiana and southern Ohio. At the end of 1994, there were almost 800 Ponderosa Steak Houses all over the country.

There are a variety of reasons for seeking geographic expansion: to achieve growth, reduce dependence on a small geographic base, use national advertising media, realize experience (i.e., economies of scale), utilize excess capacity, and guard against competitive inroads by moving into more distant regional markets. This section examines various alternatives of market-geography strategy. The purpose here is to highlight strategic issues that may dictate the choice of a geographic dimension in the context of market strategy.

In modern days, the relevance of local-market strategy may be limited to (a) retailers and (b) service organizations, such as airlines, banks, and medical centers. In many cases, the geographic dimensions of doing business are decided by law. For example, until recently, an airline needed permission from the Civil Aeronautics Board (which was dissolved in 1983 after the airline industry deregulation) to choose the areas it could cover. By the same token, banks traditionally could only operate locally.

Of the 2 million retailers in the United States, about half have annual sales of less than $100,000. Presumably, these are all local operations. Even manufacturers may initially limit the distribution of new products to a local market. Local-market strategy enables a firm to prosper by serving customers in a narrow geographic area well. The strategy emphasizes personal service, which bigger rivals may shun.

The regional scope of a business may vary from operations in two or three states to those spread over larger sections of the country: New England, the Southwest, the Midwest, or the West, for example. Regional expansion provides a good compromise between doing business locally and going national.

Regional expansion ensures that, if business in one city is depressed, favorable conditions prevailing in other regions allow the overall business to remain satisfactory. In the 1980s, Marshall Field, the Chicago-based department store (now a division of Dayton-Hudson Company), found itself pummeled by recent demographic and competitive trends in that city. Therefore, it decided to expand into new regions in the South and West. This way it could lessen its concentration in the Midwest and expand into areas where growth was expected.

Further, it is culturally easier to handle a region than an entire country. The logistics of conducting business regionally are also much simpler. As a matter of fact, many companies prefer to limit themselves to a region in order to avoid competition and to keep control centralized. Regional-market strategy allows companies to address America's diversity by dividing the country into well-defined geographic areas, choosing one or more areas to serve, and formulating a unique marketing mix to serve each region. The point may be illustrated with reference to D.A. Davidson & Company, a regional brokerage firm based in Great Falls, Montana. While large brokerage houses, such as Merrill Lynch and Smith Barney, invest the bulk of their research dollars following large, well-established corporations, regional firms mainly concentrate on local companies.[13] This helps in establishing a long-term relation such that when these companies need financial guidance, they turn to the firm that understands them.

Many businesses continue to operate successfully on a regional scale. The following large grocery chains, for example, are regional in character: Safeway in the West, Kroger in the Midwest, HEB in the Southwest, and Stop & Shop in the East. Regional expansion of a business helps achieve growth and, to an extent, gains market share. Simply expanding a business regionally, however, may or may not affect profitability.

Geographic expansion of a business to a region may become necessary either to achieve growth or to keep up with a competitor. For example, a small pizza chain with about 30 restaurants in an Ohio metropolitan area had to expand its territory when Pizza Hut started to compete aggressively with it.

At times, a regional strategy is much more desirable than going national. A company operating nationally may do a major portion of its business in one region, with the remainder spread over the rest of the country, or it may find it much more profitable to concentrate its effort in a region where it is most successful and divest itself of its business elsewhere.

Going from a regional to a national market presumably opens up opportunities for growth. This may be illustrated with reference to Borden, Inc. A dairy business by tradition, in the 1980s Borden decided to become a major player in the snack food arena. It acquired seven regional companies, among them Snacktime, Jays, and Laura Scudder's, to compete nationally, to grow, and to provide stiffer competition for PepsiCo's Frito-Lay division.

It was the prospect of growth that influenced the Radisson Hotel Corporation of Minneapolis to go national and to become a major competitor in the hotel business. Radisson decided to move into prime "gateway" markets—New York, Los Angeles, Boston, Chicago, and San Francisco—where it could compete against such giants as Marriott and Hyatt. Growth opportunity led CVS Corp., a drugstore chain, based in Woonsocket, R.I., to go national by acquiring Revco D.S., Inc., and Arbor Drugs, Inc. In 2001, it had 4,133 stores in 34 states while its close rival Walgreen Co. had 3,165 stores in 43 states.[14]

In some cases, the profit economics of an industry requires going national. For example, success in the beer industry today demands huge advertising outlays, new product introductions (e.g., light beer), production efficiencies, and wide distribution. These characteristics forced Adolph Coors to go national.

Going national, however, is far from easy. Each year a number of products enter the market, hoping eventually to become national brands. Ultimately, however, only a small percentage of them hit the national market; a still smaller percentage succeed.

A national-market strategy requires top management commitment because a large initial investment is needed for promotion and distribution. This requirement makes it easier for large companies to introduce new brands nationally, partly because they have the resources and are in the position to take the risk and partly because a new brand can be sheltered under the umbrella of a successful brand. For example, a new product introduced under GE's name has a better chance of succeeding than one introduced by an unknown company.

To implement a national-market strategy successfully, a company needs to institute proper controls to make sure that things are satisfactory in different regions. Where controls are lacking, competitors, especially regional ones, may find it easy to break in. If that situation comes about, the company may find itself losing business in region after region. Still, a properly implemented national-market strategy can go a long way in providing growth, market share, and profitability.

A number of corporations have adopted international-market postures. The Singer Company, for example, has been operating overseas for a long time. The international-market strategy became a popular method for achieving growth objectives among large corporations in the post–World War II period.

In its attempts to reconstruct war-torn economies, the U.S. government provided financial assistance to European countries through the Marshall Plan. Because the postwar American economy emerged as the strongest in the world, its economic assistance programs, in the absence of competition, stimulated extensive corporate development of international strategies.

At the end of 2002, according to a U.S. Department of Commerce report, U.S. direct investment abroad was estimated at $986 billion, up from $716 billion in 1996. About 70 percent of U.S. investment overseas has traditionally been in developed countries. However, as many developing countries gained political freedom after World War II, their governments also sought U.S. help to modernize their economies and to improve their living standards. Thus, developing countries have provided additional investment opportunities for U.S. corporations, especially in more politically stable countries. It is interesting, however, that although for cultural, political, and economic reasons more viable opportunities were found in Western Europe, Canada, and, to a lesser extent, Japan, developing countries provided a better return on direct U.S. investment. For example, in 2000 developing countries accounted for about 40 percent of income but less than 30 percent of investment.[15]

In recent years, overseas business has become a matter of necessity from the viewpoint of both U.S. corporations and the U.S. government. The increased competition facing many industries, resulting from the saturation of markets and competitive threats from overseas corporations doing business domestically, has forced U.S. corporations to look to overseas markets. At the same time, the unfavorable balance of trade, partly due to increasing energy imports, has made the need to expand exports a matter of vital national interest. Thus, although in the 1950s and 1960s international business was considered a means of capitalizing on a new opportunity, in today's changing economic environment it has become a matter of survival.

Generally speaking, international markets provide additional opportunities over and above domestic markets. In some cases, however, a company may find the international market an alternative to the domestic market. Massey-Ferguson decided long ago to concentrate on sales outside of North America rather than compete with powerful U.S. farm equipment producers. Massey's entire organization, including engineering, research, and production, is geared to market changes overseas. It has learned to live with the instability of foreign markets and to put millions of dollars into building its worldwide manufacturing and marketing networks. The payoff for the company from its emphasis on the international market has been encouraging. The company continues to outperform both Deere and International Harvester. Similarly, the Colgate-Palmolive Company has flourished through concentration in markets abroad despite tough competitors, i.e., Procter & Gamble and Unilever, at home.

With the world's biggest private inventory of commercial softwood, Weyerhaeuser has been able to build an enviable export business—a market its competitors have virtually ignored until recently. This focus has given Weyerhaeuser a unique advantage in a rapidly changing world market. Consumption of forest products overseas in the 1990s has been increasing at double the domestic rate of 2 to 3 percent annually. Future prospects overseas continue to be attractive. Particularly dramatic growth is expected in the Pacific Basin, which Weyerhaeuser is ideally located to serve. Moreover, dwindling timber supplies and high oil costs are putting European and Japanese producers at an increasing disadvantage even in their own markets, creating a vacuum that North American producers have rushed to fill. With a product mix already heavily weighted toward export commodities and with unmatched access to deep-water ports, Weyerhaeuser is far ahead of its competitors in what became an export boom in U.S. forest products. Exports, which in 1998 accounted for 40 percent of Weyerhaeuser's sales and an even higher percentage of its profits, could account for fully half of the company's total revenues in future years.[16]

A company may be regional or national in character, yet it may not cover its entire trading area. These gaps in the market provide another opportunity for growth. For example, the Southland Corporation has traditionally avoided putting its 7-Eleven stores (now a division of the Yokado Group of Japan) in downtown areas. About 6,500 of these stores in suburban areas provide it with more than $2 billion in sales. A few years ago, the company opened a store at 34th and Lexington in New York City, signaling the beginning of a major drive into the last of the U.S. markets that 7-Eleven had not yet tapped. Similarly, Hyatt Corp. has hotels in all major cities but not in all resort and suburban areas. To continue to grow, this is the gap the company plans to fill in the years to come.

Gaps in the market are left unfilled either because certain markets do not initially promise sufficient potential or because local competition appears too strong to confront. However, a corporation may later find that these markets are easy to tap if it consolidates its position in other markets or if changes in the environment create favorable conditions.

13.4 MARKET-ENTRY STRATEGY

Market-entry strategy refers to the timing of market entry. Basically, there are three market-entry options from which a company can choose: (a) be first in the market, (b) be among the early entrants, or (c) be a laggard. The importance of the time of entry can be illustrated with reference to computers. Experience has shown that if new product lines are acceptable to users and if their impact is properly controlled through pricing and contractual arrangements, sales of an older line can be stimulated. Customers are more content to upgrade within the current product line if they know that a more advanced machine is available whenever they need it. A successful introduction, therefore, requires that the right product is announced at the right time. If it is announced too early, the manufacturer will suffer a drop in revenues and will lose customers to the competition.

To be the first in the market with a product provides definite advantages. The company can create a lead for itself that others will find difficult to match. Following the experience curve concept, if the first entrant gains a respectable share of the market, across-the-board costs should go down by a fixed percentage every time experience doubles. This cost advantage can be passed on to customers in the form of lower prices. Thus, competitors will find it difficult to challenge the first entrant in a market because, in the absence of experience, their costs and hence their prices for a similar product will be higher. If the new introduction is protected by a patent, the first entrant has an additional advantage because it will have a virtual monopoly for the life of the patent.

The success story of Kinder-Care Learning Centers illustrates the significance of being first in the market. In 1968 a real estate developer, Perry Mendel, had an idea that many people thought was outrageous, impractical, and probably immoral. He wanted to create a chain of child care centers, and he wanted to use the same techniques of standardization that he had seen work for motels and fast-food chains. Convinced that the number of women working outside the home would continue to increase, Mendel started Kinder-Care Learning Centers. Since its founding the company has become a dominant force in the commercial child care industry. The strategic perspective of the first in strategy are most easily stated by the FIDO Principle:

First
In
Defeats
Others

The strategy to be the first, however, is not without risks. The first entrant must stay ahead of technology or risk being dethroned by competitors. It is also succeptible to be bested by competitors that possess a significant competitive advantage in a factor, such as customer service or superior product performance, that is of great importance to the market. Docutel Corporation provides an interesting case. This Dallas-based company was the first to introduce automated teller machines (ATMs) in the late 1960s. These machines made it possible for customers to withdraw cash from and make deposits to their savings and checking accounts at any time by pushing a few buttons. Docutel had virtually no competition until 1975, and in 1976 the company had a 60 percent share of the market for ATMs. Then the downfall began. Market share fell to 20 percent in 1977 and to 8 percent in 1978. Docutel's fortunes changed because the company failed to maintain its technological lead. Its second-generation ATM failed miserably and thus made room for competitors. Diebold was the major beneficiary of Docutel's troubles: its share of the market jumped to 70 percent in 1978 from barely 15 percent in 1976. Although Docutel's comeback efforts have been encouraging, the company may never again occupy a dominant position in the ATM industry.

Similarly, Micro Instrumentation and Telemetry Systems invented the PC in the mid-1970s, but ceded market leadership to latecomers (such as Apple computers and IBM) that invested heavily to turn the PC into a mass-market product. Royal Crown was a pioneer in the consumer market for diet colas, a product that had previously been sold only to diabetics. However, PepsiCo and Coca-Cola were able to use their vast financial muscle in other parts of the cola market to crush Royal Crown, despite their late arrival. Indeed, it took Diet Coke only a year to establish market leadership after Coca-Cola launched it in 1983.[17]

A company whose strategy is to be the first in the market must stay ahead no matter what happens because the cost of yielding the first position to someone else later can be very high. Through heavy investment in promotion, the first entrant must create a primary demand for a product where none exists. Competitors will find it convenient to piggyback because by the time they enter the market, primary demand is already established. Thus, even if a company has been able to develop a new product for an entirely new need, it should carefully evaluate whether it has sufficient technological and marketing strength to command the market for a long time. Competitors will make every effort to break in, and if the first company is unsure of itself, it should wait. Apple Computer, for example, was the leading company in the personal computer field. Despite its best efforts, it could not compete against IBM. The upstart company that always talked confrontation with IBM finally decided to play second fiddle. If properly implemented, however, the strategy to be first can be highly rewarding in terms of growth, market share, and profitability.

Several firms may be working on the same track to develop a new product. When one introduces the product first, the remaining firms are forced into an early-entry strategy, whether they had planned to be first or had purposely waited for someone else to take the lead. If the early entry takes place on the heels of the first entry, there is usually a dogfight between the firms involved. By and large, the fight is between two firms, the leader and a strong follower (even though there may be several other followers). The reason for the fight is that both firms have worked hard on the new product, both aspire to be the first in the market, both have made a strong commitment to the product in terms of resources. In the final phases of their new-product development, if one of the firms introduces the product first, the other one must rush to the market right away to prevent the first company from creating a stronghold. Ultimately, the competitor with a superior marketing strategy in terms of positioning, product, price, promotion, and distribution comes out ahead.

After the first two firms find their natural positions in the market and the market launches itself on a growth course, other entrants may follow. These firms exist on the growth wave of the market and exit as the market matures.

When Sara Lee Corp. introduced its new Wonderbra in the United States in 1994, the rival VF Corp. watched closely. Only after American shoppers began buying it in large numbers did VF offer up its own It

Must Be Magic version. But once VF decided to enter the market, it moved swiftly using state-of-the-art distribution, surging with nationwide distribution ahead of Sara Lee. VF's "second-to-the-market" approach, bringing high technology to the nitty-gritty details of distribution, have helped it avoid the financial risk that beset clothing makers.[18]

Early entry on the heels of a leader is desirable if a company has an across-the-board superior marketing strategy and the resources to fight the leader. As a matter of fact, the later entrant may get an additional boost from the groundwork laid by the leader (in the form of the creation of primary demand). A weak early entrant, however, will be conveniently swallowed by the leader. The Docutel case discussed above illustrates the point. Docutel was the leader in the ATM market. However, being a weak leader, it paved the way for a later entrant, Diebold, to take over the market it had developed. The disposable diaper was introduced in the mid-1930s by a small company under the brand name Chux. Although it was probably the best product in the early 1960s, it was relatively expensive, limiting the market to wealthy households, or for use while traveling. However, P&G's experience in grocery marketing and its early research with Pampers prompted it to aim at the mass market. Through making huge investments, P&G expanded the market from $10 million to $370 million in seven years.[19]

As the market reaches the growth phase, a number of other firms may enter it. Depending on the length of the growth phase and the point at which firms enter the market, some could be labeled as early entrants. Most of these early entrants prefer to operate in specific market niches rather than compete against major firms. For example, a firm may concentrate on doing private branding for a major retailer. Many of these firms, particularly marginal operations, may be forced out of the market as growth slows down. In summary, an early-entry strategy is justifiable in the following circumstances:

1. When the firm can develop strong customer loyalty based on perceived product quality and retain this loyalty as the market evolves.
2. When the firm can develop a broad product line to help discourage entries and combat competitors who choose a single-market niche.
3. When either current investment is not substantial or when technological change is not anticipated to be so rapid and abrupt as to create obsolescence problems.
4. When an early entrant can initiate the experience curve and when the amount of learning is closely associated with accumulated experience that cannot readily be acquired by later entrants.
5. When absolute cost advantages can be achieved by early commitment to raw materials, component manufacture, distribution channels, and so forth.
6. When the initial price structure is likely to be high because the product offers superior value to products being displaced.
7. When prospective competitors can be discouraged as the market is not strategically crucial to them and existing competitors are willing to see their market shares erode.

Early entry, therefore, can be a rewarding experience if the entry is made with a really strong thrust directed against the leader's market or if it is carefully planned to serve an untapped market. Early entry can contribute significantly to profitability and growth. For the firm that takes on the leader, the early entry may also help in gaining market share.

The laggard-entry strategy refers to entering the market toward the tail end of the growth phase or in the maturity phase of the market. There are two principal alternatives to choose from in making an entry in the market as a laggard: to enter as imitator or as initiator. An **imitator** enters the market as a me-too competitor; that is, imitators develop a product that, for all intents and purposes, is similar to one already on the market. An **initiator**, on the other hand, questions the status quo and, after doing some innovative thinking, enters the market with a new product. Between these two extremes are companies that enter stagnant markets with modified products.

Entry into a market as an imitator is short-lived. A company may be able to tap a portion of a market initially by capitalizing on the customer base of the major competitor(s). In the long run, however, as the leader discards the product in favor of a new or improved one, the imitator is left with nowhere to go. When Enterprise Rent-a-Car, Inc., entered the business, it had to decide whether to follow the strategy that the early starters, Hertz and Avis, had pursued or consider an alternative strategy. It decided to go against all the conventional wisdom. Not only has it ceded the bread-and-butter airport business to Hertz, Avis, and others, but it has also done without celebrity-driven advertisements and catchy slogans. Sticking close to the niche it developed—providing rentals for customers whose cars are being repaired or who need an extra car—Enterprise is the leader in fleet size and locations. Its sales in 1996 were $3.1 billion versus $3.8 billion for Hertz, but it probably was number one in profits, estimated to be $500 million (Hertz was a division of the Ford Motor Company at the time and did not disclose earnings).[20]

Imitators have many inherent advantages that make it possible to run a profitable business. These advantages include availability of the latest technological improvements; feasibility of achieving greater economies of scale; ability to obtain better terms from suppliers, employees, or customers; and ability to offer lower prices. Thus, even without superior skills and resources, an imitator may perform well.

The initiator starts by seeking ways to dislodge the established competitor(s) in some way. Consider the following examples:

> The blankets produced by an electrical appliance manufacturer carried the warning: "Do not fold or lie on this blanket." One of the company's engineers wondered why no one had designed a blanket that was safe to sleep on while in operation. His questioning resulted in the production of an electric underblanket that was not only safe to sleep on while in operation, but was much more efficient: being insulated by the other bed clothes, it wasted far less energy than conventional electric blankets, which dissipate most of their heat directly into the air.
>
> A camera manufacturer wondered why a camera couldn't have a built-in flash that would spare users the trouble of finding and fixing an attachment. To ask the question was to answer it. The company proceeded to design a 35 mm camera with built-in flash, which has met with enormous success and swept the Japanese medium-priced single-lens market.[21]

These two examples illustrate how a latecomer may be able to make a mark in the market through creativity and initiative. In other words, by exploiting technological change, avoiding direct competition, or changing the accepted business structure (e.g., a new form of distribution), the initiator has an opportunity to establish itself in the market successfully.[22]

The Wilmington Corporation adopted the middle course when entering the pressed glass-ceramic cookware market in 1977. Until that time, Corning Glass Works was the sole producer of this product. Corning held a patent that expired in January 1977. The Wilmington Corporation opted not to enter the market with a me-too product. It sought entry into the market with a modified product line: round containers in solid colors. Corning's product was square-shaped and white, with a cornflower design. The company felt that its product would enlarge the market by appealing to a broader range of consumer tastes.[23]

Whatever course a company may pursue to enter the market, as a laggard, it cannot expect much in terms of profitability, growth, or market share. When laggards enter the market, it is already saturated; only established firms can operate profitably. As a matter of fact, their built-in experience affords the established competitors an even greater advantage. An initiator, however, may be able to make a profitable entry, at least until an established firm adds innovation to its own line.

13.5 MARKET-COMMITMENT STRATEGY

The **market-commitment strategy** refers to the degree of involvement a company seeks in a particular market. It is widely held that not all customers are equally important to a company. Often, such statements as "17 percent of our customers account for 60 percent of our sales" and "56 percent of our customers provide 11 percent of our sales" are made, which indicate that a company should make varying commitments to different customer groups. The commitment can be in the form of financial or managerial resources or both. Presumably, the results from any venture are commensurate with the commitment made, which explains the importance of the commitment strategy.

Commitment to a market may be categorized as strong, average, or light. Whatever the nature of the commitment, it must be honored: a company that fails to regard its commitment can get into trouble. In 1946, the Liggett and Myers Tobacco Company had a 22 percent share of the U.S. cigarette market. In 1978, its share of the market was less than 3.5 percent; in 1989, slightly less than 3 percent.[24] A variety of reasons has been given for the company's declining fortunes, all amounting to a lack of commitment to a market that at one time it had commanded with an imposing market share. These reasons included responding too slowly to changing market conditions, using poor judgment in positioning brands, and failing to attract new and younger customers. The company lagged behind when filters were introduced and missed industry moves to both king-size and extra-long cigarettes. It also missed the market move toward low-tar cigarettes. Its major entry in that category, Decade, was not introduced until 1977, well after competitors had established similar brands. Liggett and Myers illustrates that a company can lose a comfortable position in any market if it fails to commit itself adequately to it.

The strong-commitment strategy requires a company to operate in a market optimally by realizing economies of scale in promotion, distribution, manufacturing, and so on. If a competitor challenges a company's position in the market, the latter must fight back aggressively by employing different forms of product, price, promotion, and distribution strategies. In other words, because the company has a high stake in the market, it should do all it can do to defend its position.

A company with a strong commitment to a market should refuse to be content with the status quo. It should foresee its own obsolescence by developing new products, improving product quality, and increasing expenditures for sales force, advertising, and sales promotion relative to the market's growth rate. To do this a company must develop and maintain a significant base of knowledge about its markets and continuously use its market knowledge to either accurately forecast changing market needs and tastes, or react rapidly to those changing needs and tastes.

This point may be illustrated with reference to the Polaroid Corporation. The company continues to do research and development to stay ahead of the field. The original Land camera, introduced in 1948, produced brown-and-white pictures. Thereafter, the company developed film that took truly black-and-white pictures with different ASA speeds. Also, the time involved in the development of film was reduced from the original 60 seconds to 10 seconds. In 1963 the company introduced color-print film with a development time of 60 seconds; in the early 1970s, the company introduced the SX-70 camera, which made earlier Polaroid cameras obsolete. Since its introduction, a variety of changes and improvements have been made both in the SX-70 camera and in the film that goes into it. A few years later, the company introduced yet another much-improved camera, Spectra. In 1976 Kodak introduced its own version of the instant camera. Polaroid charged Kodak with violating seven Polaroid patents and legally forced Kodak out of the instant photography business.[25] The result: Polaroid retained its supremacy in the instant photography field, as long as it has been solely committed. Porsche continues to excel in the crowded auto industry by making a firm commitment to a well-defined market niche (a 40-something male college graduate earning over $200,000 per year). The company sells only about 6000 cars a year (each costing between $46,000 and $130,000), but does well in terms of profits.[26] RCA pioneered color television in 1954, yet their product did not sell well since the vast majority of programs were broadcast in black and white. But RCA did not give up and made a long-term commitment to the business. It started broadcasting color TV programs through its NBC subsidiary at a time when the majority of consumers owned black-and-white TVs. RCA's persistence over ten years was rewarded with long-term market leadership of color TVs.

The nature of a company's commitment to a market may, of course, change with time. Consider Levi Strauss & Co. Its brand name is synonymous with rebellious youth. But while it retains its hold over the baby boomers who built the brand into mythic proportions, it has neglected the whims of the new generation of youth, and these are the future customers. This lack of commitment has cost the company dearly. Its sales have been declining since 1990, forcing it to close many factories. As a company executive put: "It was, in part, the classic corporate goof: taking your eyes off the ball. Projects during the last decade, such as expanding the casual clothing line Dockers and launching its upscale cousin Slates, distracted executives from the threat to Levi's core jeans brand."[27]

Strong commitment to a market can be highly rewarding in terms of achieving growth, market share, and profitability. A warning is in order, however. The commitment made to a market should be based on a company's resources, its strengths, and its willingness to take risks to live up to its commitment. For example, Procter & Gamble could afford to implement its commitment to the Pittsburgh coffee market because it had a good rapport with distributors and dealers and the resources to launch an effective promotional campaign. A small company could not have afforded to do all of that.

When a company has a stable interest in a market, it must stress the maintenance of the status quo, leading to an only average commitment to the market. Adoption of the average-commitment strategy may be triggered by the fact that a strong-commitment strategy is not feasible. The company may lack the resources to make a strong commitment; a strong commitment may be in conflict with top management's value orientation; or the market in question may not constitute a major thrust of the business in, for example, a diversified company.

In April 1976, when the Eastman Kodak Company announced its entry into the instant photography field, the company most worried about this move was Polaroid. Because Polaroid had a strong commitment to the instant photography market, it did not like Kodak being there just for the sake of competition. As Polaroid's president commented, "This is our very soul that we are involved with. This is our whole life. For them it's just another field."[28] Similarly, when Frito-Lay (a division of PepsiCo) entered the cookie business in 1982, the industry leader, Nabisco, had to adopt a new strategy to defend its title in the business. As an executive of the company noted, "We aren't going to sit on our haunches and let 82 years of business go down the drain."[29]

A company with an average commitment to a market can afford to make occasional mistakes because it has other businesses to compensate for them. Essentially, the average-commitment strategy requires keeping customers happy by providing them with what they are accustomed to. This can be accomplished by making appropriate changes in a marketing program as required by environmental shifts, thus making it difficult for competitors to lure customers away. Where commitment is average, however, the company becomes vulnerable to the lead company as well as the underdog. The leader may wipe out the average-commitment company by price cutting, a feasible strategy because of the experience effect. The underdog may challenge the average-commitment company by introducing new products, focusing on new segments within the market, trying out new forms of distribution, or launching new types of promotional thrusts. The best defense for a company with an average commitment to a market is to keep customers satisfied by being vigilant about developments in its market.

An average commitment may be adequate, as far as profitability is concerned, if the market is growing. In a slow-growth market, an average commitment is not conducive to achieving either growth or profitability.

A company may have only a passing interest in a market; consequently, it may make only a light commitment to it. The passing interest may be explained by the fact that the market is stagnant, its potential is limited, it is overcrowded with many large companies, and so on. In addition, a company may opt for light commitment to a market to avoid antitrust difficulties. GE maintained a light commitment in the color television market because the field was overcrowded, particularly by Japanese companies. (In 1988, GE sold its television business to Thomson, a French company, which, in turn, a few years later sold to a Korean company.) In the early 1970s, Procter & Gamble adopted the light-commitment strategy in the shampoo market, presumably to avoid antitrust difficulties such as those it had encountered with Clorox several years previously; Procter & Gamble let its share of the shampoo market slip from around 50 percent to a little over 20 percent, delayed reformulating its established brands (Prell and Head & Shoulders), introduced only one new brand in many years, and substantially cut its promotional efforts.[30]

A company with a light commitment to a market operates passively and does not make any new moves. It is satisfied as long as the business continues to be in the black and thus seeks very few changes in its marketing perspectives. Overall, this strategy is not of much significance for a company pursuing increasing profitability, greater market share, or growth.

13.6 MARKET-DILUTION STRATEGY

In many situations, a company may find reducing a part of its business strategically more useful than expanding it. The **market-dilution strategy** works out well when the overall benefit that a company derives from a market, either currently or potentially, is less than it could achieve elsewhere. Unsatisfactory profit performance, desire for concentration in fewer markets, lack of top management knowledge of the market, negative synergy vis-à-vis other markets that the company serves, and lack of resources to develop the market fully are other reasons for diluting market position.

There was a time when dilution of a market was considered an admission of failure. In the 1970s, however, dilution came to be accepted purely as a matter of strategy. Different ways of diluting a market include demarketing, pruning marginal markets, key account strategy, and harvesting strategy.

Demarketing, in a nutshell, is the reverse of marketing. This term became popular in the early 1970s when, as a result of the Arab oil embargo, the supply of a variety of products became short. **Demarketing** is the attempt to discourage customers in general or a certain class of customers in particular on either a temporary or permanent basis.

The demarketing strategy may be implemented in different ways. One way involves keeping close track of time requirements of different customers. Thus, if one customer needs the product in July and another in September, the former's order is filled first even though the latter confirmed the order first. A second way of demarketing is rationing supplies to different customers on an equitable basis. Shell Oil followed this route toward the end of 1978 when a gasoline shortage occurred. Each customer was sold a maximum of 10 gallons of gasoline at each filling. Third, recommending that customers use a substitute product temporarily is a form of demarketing. The fourth demarketing method is to divert a customer with an immediate need for a product to another customer to whom the product was recently supplied and who is unlikely to use it immediately. The company becomes an intermediary between two customers, providing supplies of the product to one customer whenever they are needed if present supplies are transferred to the customer in need.

The demarketing strategy is directed toward maintaining customer goodwill during times when customer demands cannot be adequately met. By helping customers in the different ways discussed above, the company hopes that the situation requiring demarketing is temporary and that, when conditions are normal again, customers will be inclined favorably toward the company. In the long run, the demarketing strategy should lead to increased profitability.

A company must undertake a conscious search for those markets that do not provide rates of return comparable to those rates that could be attained if it were to shift its resources to other markets. These markets potentially become candidates for pruning. The pruning of marginal markets may result in a much higher growth rate for the company as a whole. Consider two markets, one providing 10 percent and the other 20 percent on original investments of $1 million. After 15 years, the first market will show an equity value of $4 million, as opposed to $16 million for the second one. Pruning can improve return on investment and growth rate by ridding the company of markets that are growing more slowly than the rest of its markets and by providing cash for investment in faster-growing, higher-return markets. Several years ago, A&P closed more than 100 stores in markets where its competitive position was weak. This pruning effort helped the company to fortify its position and to concentrate on markets where it felt strong.

Pruning also helps to restore balance. A company may be out of balance when it has too many diverse and difficult markets to serve. By pruning, the company may limit its operations to growth markets only. Because growth markets require heavy doses of investment (in the form of price reductions, promotion, and market development) and because the company may have limited resources, the pruning strategy can be very beneficial. Gateway in 2001, for example, closed its operations in non-US markets so that it could use its limited resources to restore its position in the U.S. PC market.[31]

In most industries, a few customers account for a major portion of volume. This characteristic may be extended to markets. If the breakdown of markets is properly done, a company may find that a few markets account for a very large share of its revenues. Strategically, these key markets may call for extra emphasis in terms of selling effort, after-sales service, product availability, and so on. As a matter of fact, the company may decide to limit its business to these key markets alone.

The key-markets strategy requires:

1. A strong focus tailored to environmental differences (i.e., don't try to do everything; rather, compete in carefully selected ways with the competitive emphasis differing according to the market environment).
2. A reputation for high quality (i.e., turn out high-quality products with superior performance potential and reliability).
3. Medium to low relative prices complementing high quality.
4. Low total cost to permit offering high-quality products at low prices and still show high profits.

The harvesting strategy refers to a situation where a company may decide to let its market share slide deliberately. The harvesting strategy may be pursued for a variety of reasons: to increase badly needed cash flow, to increase short-term earnings, or to avoid antitrust action. Usually, only companies with high market share can expect to harvest successfully.

If a product reaches the stage where continued support can no longer be justified, it may be desirable to realize a short-term gain by raising the price or by lowering quality and cutting advertising to turn an active brand into a passive one. In any event, the momentum of the product may continue for years with sales declining but with useful revenues still coming in.

Because they reduce a firm's strategic flexibility, exit barriers may prevent a company from implementing a harvesting strategy. Exit barriers refer to circumstances within an industry that discourage the exit of competitors whose performance in that particular business may be marginal. Three types of exit barriers are (a) a thin resale market for the business's assets, (b) intangible strategic barriers as deterrents to timely exit (e.g., value of distribution networks, customer goodwill for the other products of the company, or strong corporate identification with the product), and (c) management's reluctance to terminate a sick line. When exit barriers disappear or when their effect ceases to be of concern, a harvesting strategy may be pursued.

SUMMARY

This chapter illustrated various types of market strategies that a company may pursue. Market strategies rest on a company's perspective of the customer. Customer focus is a very important factor in market strategy. By diligently delineating the markets to be served, a company can effectively compete in an industry even with established firms.

The five different types of market strategies and the various alternatives under each strategy that were examined in this chapter are outlined below:

1. Market-scope strategy.

   a. Single-market strategy
   b. Multimarket strategy
   c. Total-market strategy

2. Market-geography strategy.

   a. Local-market strategy
   b. Regional-market strategy
   c. National-market strategy
   d. International-market strategy

3. Market-entry strategy.

   a. First-in strategy
   b. Early-entry strategy
   c. Laggard-entry strategy

4. Market-commitment strategy.

   a. Strong-commitment strategy
   b. Average-commitment strategy
   c. Light-commitment strategy

5. Market-dilution strategy.

   a. Demarketing strategy
   b. Pruning-of-marginal-markets strategy
   c. Key-markets strategy
   d. Harvesting strategy

Application of each strategy was illustrated with examples from marketing literature. The impact of each strategy was considered in terms of its effect on marketing objectives (i.e., profitability, growth, and market share).

DISCUSSION QUESTIONS

1. What circumstances may lead a business unit to change the scope of its market?
2. Under what conditions may a company adopt across-the-board market strategy?

3. Can a company operating only locally go international? Discuss and give examples.

4. Examine the pros and cons of being the first in a market.

5. What underlying conditions must be present before a company can make a strong commitment to a market?

6. Define the term *demarketing*. What circumstances dictate the choice of demarketing strategy?

7. List exit barriers that may prevent a company from implementing a harvesting strategy.

NOTES

1. "Design and Manufacturing Corporation," a case copyrighted in 1972 by the President and Fellows of Harvard College, 4.

2. "P&G May Spark Agency Battle for Tambrands," *Advertising Age*, April 14, 1997, p. 10.

3. Raju Narisetti, "P&G, Seeing Shoppers Were Being Confused, Overhauls Marketing," *The Wall Street Journal*, January 15, 1997, p. A1.

4. "Crowning Achievement," *Forbes*, October 29, 1990, p. 178.

5. Sarah Ellison, "P&G Latest Growth Strategy: His and Hers Toothpaste," *The Wall Street Journal*, September 5, 2002, p. B1.

6. Sydney B. Leavens, "Seeking Broader Market, Candy Makers Aim New Lollipops at Adults," *The Wall Street Journal*, August 24, 2001, p. B1. Also see Richard Morais, "Listen Up, Sucker," *Forbes*, January 8, 2001, p. 212.

7. See Satish Jayachandran, Javier Gimeno, and P. Rajan Varadarajan, "The Theory of Multimarket Competition: A Synthesis and Implications for Marketing Strategy," *Journal of Marketing*, July 1999, pp. 49–66.

8. By Any Other Means," *Beverage-World*, June 15, 1997, p. 50.

9. Patricia Seremet, "Timex Get Watches for Outdoors Market," *Hartford Courant*, March 15, 1996, p. F2.

10. "A Slippery Slope for North Face," *BusinessWeek*, December 7, 1998, p. 66.

11. "From the Microbrewers Who Brought You Bud, Coors...," *BusinessWeek*, April 24, 1995, p. 66.

12. John Huey, "Eisner Explains Everything," *Fortune*, April 17, 1995, p. 44.

13. Dom Del Prete, "How Regional Firms Find Their Niches," *Marketing News*, October 13, 1997, p. 8.

14. CVS: Will Its Growth Elixir Work," *BusinessWeek*, July 9, 2001, p. 50.

15. *Statistical Abstract of the United States* (2002): 788.

16. Marc Beauchamp, "Lost in the Woods," *Forbes*, October 16, 1999, p. 22; Also see *Weyerhaeuser Company's Annual Report* for 2001.

17. "Why First May Not Last," *The Economist*, March 16, 1996, p. 65.

18. "Sara Lee: Playing with the Recipe," *BusinessWeek*, April 27, 1998, p. 114.

19. Gerald J. Tellis and Peter N. Golder, "First to Market, First to Fail? Real Causes of Enduring Market Leadership," *Slogan Management Review*, Winter 1996, pp. 65–75.

20. Gianna Jacobson, "Comfortable in the Driver's Seat," *New York Times*, January 23, 1997, p. D1.

21. Kenichi Ohmae, "Effective Strategies for Competitive Success," *McKinsey Quarterly*, Winter 1978, p. 55.

22. C.K. Prahalad and Venkatram Ramaswamy, "Co-opting Customer Competence," *Harvard Business Review*, January–February 2000, pp. 79–90.

23. "Wilmington Corporation," a case copyrighted in 1976 by the President and Fellows of Harvard College.

24. "How Badly Is Liggett Getting Burned?" *BusinessWeek*, July 7, 1997, p. 36.

25. Alex Taylor III, "Kodak Scrambles to Refocus," *Fortune*, March 3, 1986, p. 34. Also see James Champy, "Ending Your Company's Slump," *Sales and Marketing Management*, May 1998, p. 26.

26. Alex Taylor, "Porsche Slices Up Its Buyers," *Fortune*, January 16, 1995, p. 24.

27. "Levi's Is Hiking Up Its Pants," *BusinessWeek*, December 1, 1997, p. 70.

28. *New York Times*, April 28, 1976, p. 23.

29. Ann M. Morrison, "Cookies Are Frito-Lay's New Bag," *Fortune*, August 9, 1982, p. 64.

30. Nancy Giges, "Shampoo Rivals Wonder When P&G Will Seek Old Dominance," *Advertising Age*, September 23, 1974, p. 3.

31. Scott Morrison, "Gateway May Quit Markets Outside U.S." *Financial Times*, August 9, 2001, p. 13.

APPENDIX: PERSPECTIVES OF MARKET STRATEGIES

A. Single-Market Strategy

Definition: Concentration of efforts in a single segment.
Objective: To find a segment currently being ignored or served inadequately and meet its needs.
Requirements: (a) Serve the market wholeheartedly despite initial difficulties. (b) Avoid competition with established firms.
Expected Results: (a) Low costs. (b) Higher profits.

B. Multimarket Strategy

Definition: Serving several distinct markets.
Objective: To diversify the risk of serving only one market.
Requirements: (a) Carefully select segments to serve. (b) Avoid confrontation with companies serving the entire market.
Expected Results: (a) Higher sales. (b) Higher market share.

C. Total-Market Strategy

Definition: Serving the entire spectrum of the market by selling differentiated products to different segments in the market.
Objective: To compete across the board in the entire market.
Requirements: (a) Employ different combinations of price, product, promotion, and distribution strategies in different segments. (b) Top management commitment to embrace entire market. (c) Strong financial position.
Expected Results: (a) Increased growth. (b) Higher market share.

A. Local-Market Strategy

Definition: Concentration of efforts in the immediate vicinity.
Objective: To maintain control of the business.
Requirements: (a) Good reputation in the geographic area. (b) Good hold on requirements of the market.
Expected Results: Short-term success; ultimately must expand to other areas.

B. Regional-Market Strategy

Definition: Operating in two or three states or over a region of the country (e.g., New England).
Objectives: (a) To diversify risk of dependence on one part of a region. (b) To keep control centralized.
Requirements: (a) Management commitment to expansion. (b) Adequate resources. (c) Logistical ability to serve a regional area.
Expected Results: (a) Increased growth. (b) Increased market share. (c) Keep up with competitors.

C. National-Market Strategy

Definition: Operating nationally.
Objective: To seek growth.
Requirements: (a) Top management commitment. (b) Capital resources. (c) Willingness to take risks.
Expected Results: (a) Increased growth. (b) Increased market share. (c) Increased profitability.

D. International-Market Strategy

Definition: Operating outside national boundaries.
Objective: To seek opportunities beyond domestic business.

Requirements: (a) Top management commitment. (b) Capital resources. (c) Understanding of international markets.

Expected Results: (a) Increased growth. (b) Increased market share. (c) Increased profits.

A. First-In Strategy

Definition: Entering the market before all others.

Objective: To create a lead over competition that will be difficult for them to match.

Requirements: (a) Be willing and able to take risks. (b) Be technologically competent. (c) Strive to stay ahead. (d) Promote heavily. (e) Create primary demand. (f) Carefully evaluate strengths.

Expected Results: (a) Reduced costs via experience. (b) Increased growth. (c) Increased market share. (d) Increased profits.

B. Early-Entry Strategy

Definition: Entering the market in quick succession after the leader.

Objective: To prevent the first entrant from creating a stronghold in the market.

Requirements: (a) Superior marketing strategy. (b) Ample resources. (c) Strong commitment to challenge the market leader.

Expected Results: (a) Increased profits. (b) Increased growth. (c) Increased market share.

C. Laggard-Entry Strategy

Definition: Entering the market toward the tail end of growth phase or during maturity phase. Two modes of entry are feasible: (a) Imitator—Entering market with me-too product; (b) Initiator— Entering market with unconventional marketing strategies.

Objectives: Imitator—To capture that part of the market that is not brand loyal. Initiator—To serve the needs of the market better than present firms.

Requirements: Imitator—(a) Market research ability. (b) Production capability. Initiator—(a) Market research ability. (b) Ability to generate creative marketing strategies.

Expected Results: Imitator—Increased short-term profits. Initiator—(a) Putting market on a new growth path. (b) Increased profits. (c) Some growth opportunities.

A. Strong-Commitment Strategy

Definition: Fighting off challenges aggressively by employing different forms of product, price, promotion, and distribution strategies.

Objective: To defend position at all costs.

Requirements: (a) Operate optimally by realizing economies of scale in promotion, distribution, manufacturing, etc. (b) Refuse to be content with present situation or position. (c) Have ample resources. (d) Be willing and able to take risks.

Expected Results: (a) Increased growth. (b) Increased profits. (c) Increased market share.

B. Average-Commitment Strategy

Definition: Maintaining stable interest in the market.

Objective: To maintain the status quo.

Requirements: Keep customers satisfied and happy.

Expected Results: Acceptable profitability.

C. Light-Commitment Strategy

Definition: Having only a passing interest in the market.

Objective: To operate in the black.

Requirements: Avoid investing for any long-run benefit.

Expected Results: Maintenance of status quo (no increase in growth, profits, or market share).

A. Demarketing Strategy

Definition: Discouraging customers in general or a certain class of customers in particular, either temporarily or permanently, from seeking the product.

Objective: To maintain customer goodwill during periods of shortages.

Requirements: (a) Monitor customer time requirements. (b) Ration product supplies. (c) Divert customers with immediate needs to customers who have a supply of the product but no immediate need for it. (d) Find out and suggest alternative products for meeting customer needs.

Expected Results: (a) Increased profits. (b) Strong customer goodwill and loyalty.

B. Pruning-of-Marginal-Markets Strategy

Definition: Weeding out markets that do not provide acceptable rates of return.

Objective: To divert investments in growth markets.

Requirements: (a) Gain good knowledge of the chosen markets. (b) Concentrate all energies on these markets. (c) Develop unique strategies to serve the chosen markets.

Expected Results: (a) Long-term growth. (b) Improved return on investment. (c) Decrease in market share.

C. Key-Markets Strategy

Definition: Focusing efforts on selected markets.

Objective: To serve the selected markets extremely well.

Requirements: (a) Gain good knowledge of the chosen markets. (b) Concentrate all energies on these markets. (c) Develop unique strategies to serve the chosen markets.

Expected Results: (a) Increased profits. (b) Increased market share in the selected markets.

D. Harvesting Strategy

Definition: Deliberate effort to let market share slide.

Objectives: (a) To generate additional cash flow. (b) To increase short-term earnings. (c) To avoid antitrust action.

Requirements: High-market share.

Expected Results: Sales decline but useful revenues still come in.

Chapter Outline

14.1 Dimensions of Product
     Strategies
14.2 Product-Positioning Strategy
14.3 Product-Repositioning Strategy
14.4 Product-Overlap Strategy
14.5 Product-Scope Strategy
14.6 Product-Design Strategy
14.7 Product-Elimination Strategy
14.8 New-Product Strategy
14.9 Diversification Strategy
14.10 Value-Marketing Strategy

Chapter 14

Product Strategies

Product strategies specify market needs that may be served by different product offerings. It is a company's product strategies, duly related to market strategies, that eventually come to dominate both overall strategy and the spirit of the company. Product strategies deal with such matters as number and diversity of products, product innovations, product scope, and product design. In this chapter, different dimensions of product strategies are examined for their essence, their significance, their limitations, if any, and their contributions to objectives and goals. Each strategy will be exemplified with illustrations from marketing literature.

14.1 DIMENSIONS OF PRODUCT STRATEGIES

The implementation of product strategies requires cooperation among different groups: finance, research and development, the corporate staff, and marketing. This level of integration makes product strategies difficult to develop and implement. In many companies, to achieve proper coordination among diverse business units, product strategy decisions are made by top management. At Gould, for example, the top management decides what kind of business Gould is and what type it wants to be. The company pursues products in the areas of electromechanics, electrochemistry, metallurgy, and electronics. The company works to dispose of products that do not fall strictly into its areas of interest.[1]

In some companies, the overall scope of product strategy is laid out at the corporate level, whereas actual design is left to business units. These companies contend that this alternative is more desirable than other arrangements because it is difficult for top management to deal with the details of product strategy in a diverse company. In this chapter, the following product strategies are recognized:

- Product-positioning strategy
- Product-repositioning strategy
- Product-overlap strategy
- Product-scope strategy
- Product-design strategy
- Product-elimination strategy
- New-product strategy
- Diversification strategy
- Value-marketing strategy

Each strategy is examined from the point of view of an SBU. The appendix at the end of this chapter summarizes each strategy, giving its definition, objectives, requirements, and expected results.

14.2 PRODUCT-POSITIONING STRATEGY

The term *positioning* refers to placing a brand in that part of the market where it will receive a favorable reception compared to competing products. Because the market is heterogeneous, one brand cannot make an impact on the entire market. As a matter of strategy, therefore, a product should be matched with that segment of the market in which it is most likely to succeed. The product should be positioned so that it stands apart from competing brands. Positioning tells what the product stands for, what it is, and how customers should evaluate it.

Positioning is achieved by using marketing mix variables, especially design and communication. Although differentiation through positioning is more visible in consumer goods, it is equally true of industrial goods. With some products, positioning can be achieved on the basis of tangible differences (e.g., product features); with many others, intangibles are used to differentiate and position products. As Levitt has observed:

> Fabricators of consumer and industrial goods seek competitive distinction via product features—some visually or measurably identifiable, some cosmetically implied, and some rhetorically claimed by reference to real or suggested hidden attributes that promise results or values different from those of competitors' products.
>
> So too with consumer and industrial services—what I call, to be accurate, 'intangibles.' On the commodities exchanges, for example, dealers in metals, grains, and pork bellies trade in totally undifferentiated generic products. But what they "sell" is the claimed distinction of their execution—the efficiency of their transactions in their client's behalf, their responsiveness to inquiries, the clarity and speed of their confirmations, and the like. In short, the offered product is differentiated, though the generic product is identical.[2]

The desired position for a product may be determined using the following procedure:

1. Analyze product attributes that are salient to customers.
2. Examine the distribution of these attributes among different market segments.
3. Determine the optimal position for the product in regard to each attribute, taking into consideration the positions occupied by existing brands.
4. Choose an overall position for the product (based on the overall match between product attributes and their distribution in the population and the positions of existing brands).

For example, cosmetics for the career woman may be positioned as "natural," cosmetics that supposedly make the user appear as if she were wearing no makeup at all. An alternate position could be "fast" cosmetics, cosmetics to give the user a mysterious aura in the evenings. A third position might be "light" cosmetics, cosmetics to be worn for tennis and other leisure activities.

Consider the positioning of beer. Two positioning decisions for beer are light versus heavy and bitter versus mild. The desired position for a new brand of beer can be determined by discovering its rating on these attributes and by considering the size of the beer market. The beer market is divided into segments according to these attributes and the positions of other brands. It may be found that the heavy and mild beer market is large and that Coors and Budweiser compete in it. In the light and mild beer market, another big segment, Miller and Anheuser-Busch are the dominant competitors. Management may decide to position a new brand in competition with Miller Lite and Bud Light.

Disney stores demonstrate how adequate positioning can lead to instant success.[3] Disney stores earn more than three times what other specialty stores earn per every square foot of floor space. Disney has created retail environments with entertainment as their chief motif. As a customer enters the store, he/she sees the Magic Kingdom, a land of bright lights and merry sounds packed full of Mickey Mouse merchandise. From a phone at the front of each store, a customer can get the Disney channel or book a room in a Disney World hotel. Disney designers got down on their hands and knees when they laid out the stores to be sure that their sight lines would work for a three-year-old. The back wall, normally a prime display area, is given over to a large video screen that continuously plays clips from Disney's animated movies and cartoons. Below the screen, at kid level, sit tiers of stuffed animals that toddlers are encouraged to play with. Adult apparel hangs at the front of the stores to announce that they are for shoppers of all ages. Floor fixtures that hold the merchandise angle inward to steer shoppers deeper into this flashy money trap. Managers spend six weeks in intensive preparatory classes and training before being assigned to a store. Garnished with theatrical lighting and elaborate ceiling displays, the stores have relatively high start-up and fixed costs, but once up and running, they earn high margins.

Six different approaches to positioning may be distinguished:

1. Positioning by attribute (i.e., associating a product with an attribute, feature, or customer benefit).
2. Positioning by price/quality (i.e., the price/quality attribute is so pervasive that it can be considered a separate approach to promotion).

3. Positioning with respect to use or application (i.e., associating the product with a use or application).

4. Positioning by the product user (i.e., associating a product with a user or a class of users).

5. Positioning with respect to a product class (e.g., positioning Caress soap as a bath oil product rather than as soap).

6. Positioning with respect to a competitor (i.e., making a reference to competition, as in Avis's now-famous campaign: "We're number two, so we try harder.").

Two types of positioning strategy are discussed here: single-brand strategy and multiple-brand strategy. A company may have just one brand that it may place in one or more chosen market segments, or, alternatively, it may have several brands positioned in different segments.

To maximize its benefits with a single brand, a company must try to associate itself with a core segment in a market where it can play a dominant role. In addition, it may attract customers from other segments outside its core as a fringe benefit. BMW does very well, for example, positioning its cars mainly in a limited segment to high-income young professionals.

An alternative single-brand strategy is to consider the market undifferentiated and to cover it with a single brand. Several years ago, for example, the Coca-Cola Company followed a strategy that proclaimed that Coke quenched the thirst of the total market. Such a policy, however, can work only in the short run. To seek entry into a market, competitors segment and challenge the dominance of the single brand by positioning themselves in small, viable niches. Even the Coca-Cola Company now has a number of brands to serve different segments: Classic Coke and Diet Coke, both with multiple flavorings, Coke Zero, Fanta, Sprite, Tab, Fresca, and even Minute Maid juice.

Consider the case of beer. Traditionally, brewers operated as if there were one homogeneous market for beer that could be served by one product in one package. Miller, in order to seek growth, took the initiative to segment the market and positioned its High Life brand to younger customers. Thereafter, it introduced a seven-ounce pony bottle that turned out to be a favorite among women and older people who thought that the standard 12-ounce size was simply too much beer to drink. But Miller's big success came in 1975 with the introduction of another brand, low-calorie Lite. Lite, probably, is the most successful new beer introduced in the United States in in the 20th century. Gatorade's positioning as a sports-drink is a success story as well. Its dominance appears to be unassailable. Many brands lose ground when rivals come along. But Gatorade lost only a few points of market share even after competitors PepsiCo Inc. and Coca-Cola Co. entered the sports-drink business in the 1990s. Years after facing the two dominant soft drink companies in its market, Gatorade's share remained at 80% plus. In 2001, PepsiCo finally decided that if it couldn't beat Gatorade, it should buy it. Today, it retains an 80% market share in the hottest-selling segment of the beverage industry.[4]

To protect the position of a single brand, sometimes a company may be forced to introduce other brands. Kotler reported that Heublein's Smirnoff brand had a 23 percent share of the vodka market when its position was challenged by Wolfschmidt, priced at $1 less a bottle. Instead of cutting the price of its Smirnoff brand to meet the competition, Heublein raised the price by one dollar and used the increased revenues for advertising. At the same time, it introduced a new brand, Relska, positioning it against Wolfschmidt, and also marketed Popov, a low-price vodka. This strategy effectively met Wolfschmidt's challenge and gave Smirnoff an even higher status. Heublein resorted to multiple brands to protect a single brand that had been challenged by a competitor.[5]

Anheuser-Busch has been dependent on Bud and Bud Light for more than two-thirds of its brewery volume and for over half of its sales revenues. It was this dependence on a single brand that led the company to introduce Michelob. This brand, however, is not doing as well as expected, and at the same time, rivals are showing signs of fresh energy and determination, making it urgent for the company to diversify.[6] It built its collection of brand and product offerings tremendously, with eight product offerings under the Budweiser label, ten product offerings under the Michelob label, 21 imported brands, ten specialty beers, and 22 regional and other beers, malt liquors and special malt beverages.

Whether a single brand should be positioned in direct competition with a dominant brand already on the market or be placed in a secondary position is another strategic issue. The head-on route is usually risky, but some variation of this type of strategy is quite common. Avis seemingly accepted a number two position in the market next to Hertz. Gillette, on the other hand, positioned Silkience shampoo directly against Johnson's Baby Shampoo and Procter & Gamble's Prell. Generally, a single-brand strategy is a desirable choice in the short run, particularly when the task of managing multiple brands is beyond the managerial and financial capability of a company. Supposedly, this strategy is more conducive to achieving higher profitability because a single brand permits better control of operations than do multiple brands.

There are two requisites to managing a single brand successfully: a single brand must be so positioned that it can stand competition from the toughest rival, and its unique position should be maintained by creating an aura of a distinctive product. Consider the case of Cover Girl. The cosmetics field is a crowded and highly competitive industry. The segment Cover Girl picked out—sales in supermarkets and discount stores—is one that large companies, such as Revlon, Avon, and Estee Lauder, have not tapped. Cover Girl products are sold at a freestanding display without sales help or demonstration. As far as the second requisite is concerned, creating an aura of a distinctive product, an example is Perrier. It continues to protect its position through the mystique attached to its name. In other words, a single brand must have some advantage to protect it from competitive inroads.

Business units introduce multiple brands to a market for two major reasons: (a) to seek growth by offering varied products in different segments of the market and (b) to avoid competitive threats to a single brand. General Motors has a car to sell in all conceivable segments of the market. Coca-Cola has a soft drink for each different taste. Dell sells computers for different customer needs. Procter & Gamble offers a laundry detergent for each laundering need. Offering multiple brands to different segments of the same market is an accepted route to growth.

To realize desired growth, multiple brands should be diligently positioned in the market so that they minimize cannibalism. For example, 20 to 25 percent of sales of Anheuser-Busch's Michelob Light are to customers who previously bought regular Michelob but switched because of the Light brand's low-calorie appeal.[7] The introduction of Maxim by General Foods took sales away from its established Maxwell House brand. About 20 percent of sales of Miller's Genuine Draft beer come from Miller High Life.[8] Thus, it is necessary to be careful in segmenting the market and to position the product, through design and promotion, as uniquely suited to a particular segment.

Of course, some cannibalism is unavoidable. But the question is how much cannibalism is acceptable when introducing another brand. It has been said that 70 percent of Mustang sales in its introductory year were to buyers who would have purchased another Ford had the Mustang not been introduced; the remaining 30 percent of its sales came from new customers. Cadbury's experience with the introduction of a chocolate bar in England indicates that more than 50 percent of its volume came from market expansion, with the remaining volume coming from the company's existing products. Both the Mustang and the chocolate bar were rated as successful introductions by their companies. The apparent difference in cannibalism rates shows that cost structure, degree of market maturity, and the competitive appeal of alternative offerings affect cannibalism sales and their importance to the sales and profitability of a product line and to individual items.[9]

An additional factor to consider in determining actual cannibalism is the vulnerability of an existing brand to a competitor's entry into a presumably open spot in the market. For example, suppose that a company's new brand derives 50 percent of its sales from customers who would have bought its existing brand. However, if 20 percent of the sales of this existing brand were susceptible to a competitor's entry (assuming a fairly high probability that the competitor would have indeed positioned its new brand in that open spot), the actual level of cannibalism should be set at 30 percent. This is because 20 percent of the revenue from sales of the existing brand would have been lost to a competitive brand had there been no new brand.

Multiple brands can be positioned in the market either in head-on, direct competition with the leading brand or with an idea. The relative strengths of the new entry and the established brand dictate which of the two positioning routes is more desirable. Although head-on positioning usually appears risky, some companies have successfully carried it out. IBM's personal computer was positioned in head-on competition with Apple's. Datril, a Bristol-Myers painkiller, was introduced to compete directly with Tylenol.

Positioning with an idea, however, can prove to be a better alternative, especially when the leading brand is well established. Positioning with an idea was attempted by Kraft when it positioned three brands (Breyers and Sealtest ice cream and Light 'n' Lively ice milk) as complements rather than as competitors. Vick Chemical positioned Nyquil, a cold remedy, with the idea that Nyquil assured a good night's sleep. Seagram successfully introduced its line of cocktail mixes, Party Tyme, against heavy odds in favor of Holland House, a National Distillers brand, by promoting it with the Snowbird winter drink. Lexus was positioned to directly challenge the European luxury cars.

Positioning of multiple brands and their management in a dynamic environment call for ample managerial and financial resources. When these resources are lacking, a company is better off with a single brand. In addition, if a company already has a dominant position, its attempt to increase its share of the market by introducing an additional brand may invite antitrust action. Such an eventuality should be guarded against. On the other hand, there is also a defensive, or share-maintenance, issue to be considered here even if one has the dominant entry. A product with high market share may not remain in this position forever if competitors are permitted to chip away at its lead with unchallenged positions.

As a strategy, the positioning of multiple brands, if properly implemented, can lead to increases in growth, market share, and profitability.

14.3 PRODUCT-REPOSITIONING STRATEGY

Often, a product may require repositioning. This can happen if (a) a competitive entry is positioned next to the brand, creating an adverse effect on its share of the market; (b) consumer preferences change; (c) new customer preference clusters with promising opportunities are discovered; or (d) a mistake is made in the original positioning.

Citations from the marketing literature serve to illustrate how repositioning becomes desirable under different circumstances. When A & W went national in 1989 with its cream soda, it failed to clearly articulate the position. As a result, research showed that consumers perceived cream soda as an extension of the root beer family. To correct this, the company repositioned the brand as a separate soda category by emphasizing the vanilla flavor through advertising and packaging. Following the repositioning, cream soda's sales increased rapidly.[10]

Over the years, Coca-Cola's position has shifted to keep up with the changing mood of the market. In recent years, the theme of Coca-Cola's advertising has evolved from ''Things go better with Coke'' to ''It's the real thing'' to ''Coke is it'' to ''Can't beat the feeling'' to ''Catch the Wave'' to ''Always new, always real, always you, always Coke.'' The current perspective of Coca-Cola's positioning is to reach a generation of young people and those young at heart.

The risks involved in positioning or repositioning a product or service are high. The technique of perceptual mapping may be used gainfully to substantially reduce those risks. Perceptual mapping helps in examining the position of a product relative to competing products. It helps marketing strategists to

• Understand how competing products or services are perceived by various consumer groups in terms of strengths and weaknesses.
• Understand the similarities and dissimilarities between competing products and services.
• Understand how to reposition a current product in the perceptual space of consumer segments.
• Position a new product or service in an established marketplace.
• Track the progress of a promotional or marketing campaign on the perceptions of targeted consumer segments.

The use of perceptual mapping may be illustrated with reference to the automobile industry. Exhibit 14.1 shows how different cars are positioned on a perceptual map. The map helps the marketing strategist in calculating whether a company's cars are on target. The concentration of dots, which represent competing models, shows how much opposition there is likely to be in a specific territory on the map. Presumably, cars higher up on the graph fetch a higher price than models ranked toward the bottom, where the stress is on economy and practicality. After looking at the map, General Motors might find that its Chevrolet division, traditionally geared to entry-level buyers, should move down in practicality and more to the right in youthfulness. Another problem for General Motors, which the map so clearly demonstrated, was the close proximity of its Buick and Oldsmobile divisions. This close proximity suggested that the two divisions were, in effect, waging a marketing war more against each other than against the competition (In 2000, General Motors discontinued the Oldsmobile line of cars.)

Basically, there are three ways to reposition a product: among existing users, among new users, and for new uses. The discussion that follows will elaborate on these repositioning alternatives.

Repositioning a product among existing customers can be accomplished by promoting alternative uses for it. To revitalize its stocking business, Du Pont adopted a repositioning strategy by promoting the ''fashion smartness'' of tinted hose. Efforts were directed toward expanding women's collections of hosiery by creating a new fashion image for hosiery: hosiery was not simply a neutral accessory; rather, a suitable tint and pattern could complement each garment in a woman's wardrobe.

General Foods Corporation repositioned Jell-O to boost its sales by promoting it as a base for salads. To encourage this usage, the company introduced a variety of vegetable-flavored Jell-Os. A similar strategy

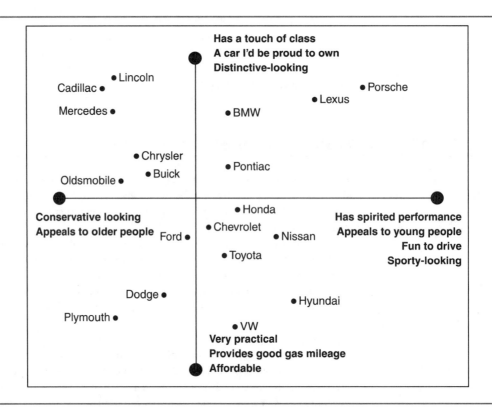

Exhibit 14.1
Perceptual Map of Brand Images

was adopted by 3M Company, which introduced a line of colored, patterned, waterproof, invisible, and write-on Scotch tapes for different types of gift wrapping.

The purpose of repositioning among current users is to revitalize a product's life by giving it a new character as something needed not merely as a staple product but as a product able to keep up with new trends and new ideas. Repositioning among users should help the brand in its sales growth as well as increasing its profitability.

Repositioning among new users requires that the product be presented with a different twist to people who have not hitherto been favorably inclined toward it. In so doing, care must be taken to see that, in the process of enticing new customers, current customers are not alienated. Miller's attempts to win over new customers for Miller High Life beer are noteworthy. Approximately 15 percent of the population consumes 85 percent of all the beer sold in the United States. Miller's slogan "the champagne of bottled beer" had more appeal for light users than for heavy users. Also, the image projected too much elegance for a product like beer. Miller decided to reposition the product slightly to appeal to a wider range of beer drinkers without weakening its current franchise: "Put another way, the need was to take Miller High Life out of the champagne bucket, but not to put it in the bathtub."[11] After conducting a variety of studies, Miller came up with a new promotional campaign built around this slogan: "If you've got the time, we've got the beer." The campaign proved to be highly successful. Through its new slogan, the brand communicated three things: that it was a quality product worth taking time out for; that it was friendly, low-key, and informal; and that it offered relaxation and reward after the pressures of the workday.

At Du Pont, new users of stockings were created by legitimizing the wearing of hosiery among early teenagers and subteenagers. This was achieved by working out a new ad campaign with an emphasis on the merchandising of youthful products and styles to tempt young consumers. Similarly, Jell-O attempted to develop new users among consumers who did not perceive Jell-O as a dessert or salad product. Jell-O was advertised with a new concept—a fashion-oriented, weight-control appeal.

The addition of new users to a product's customer base helps enlarge the overall market and thus puts the product on a growth route. Repositioning among new users also helps increase profitability because very few new investments, except for promotional costs, need to be made.

Repositioning for new uses requires searching for latent uses of the product. The case of Arm and Hammer's baking soda is a classic example of an unexplored use of a product. Today this product is popular as a deodorizer, yet deodorizing was not the use originally conceived for the product. Although new uses for a product can be discovered in a variety of ways, the best way to discover them is to gain insights into the customer's way of using a product. If it is found that a large number of customers are using the product for a purpose other than the one originally intended, this other use could be developed with whatever modifications are necessary.

Repositioning for new uses may be illustrated with reference to Disney World's efforts to expand its business. In 1991, it opened a Disney Fairy Tale Weddings Department, which puts on more than 200 full-service weddings a year, each costing about $10,000.[12]

At Du Pont, new uses for nylon sprang up in varied types of hosiery (stretch stockings and stretch socks), tires, bearings, etc. Its new uses have kept nylon on the growth path: wrap knits in 1945, tire cord in 1948, textured yarns in 1955, carpet yarns in 1959, and so on. Without these new uses, nylon would have hit the saturation level as far back as 1962.

General Foods found that women used powdered gelatin dissolved in liquid to strengthen their finger-nails. Working on this clue, General Foods introduced a flavorless Jell-O as a nail-building agent.

The new-use strategy is directed toward revamping the sales of a product whose growth, based on its original conceived use, has slowed down. This strategy has the potential to increase sales growth, market share, and profitability.

14.4 PRODUCT-OVERLAP STRATEGY

The product-overlap strategy refers to a situation where a company decides to compete against its own brand. Many factors lead companies to adopt such a strategic posture. For example, A&P stores alone cannot keep the company's 42 manufacturing operations working at full capacity. Therefore, A&P decided to distribute many of its products through independent food retailers. A&P's Eight O'Clock coffee, for example, is sold through 7-Eleven stores. Procter & Gamble has different brands of detergents virtually competing in the same market. Each brand has its own organization for marketing research, product development, merchandising, and promotion. Although sharing the same sales force, each brand behaves aggressively to outdo others in the marketplace. Sears' large appliance brands are actually manufactured by the Whirlpool Corporation. Thus, Whirlpool's branded appliances compete against those that it sells to Sears.

There are alternative ways in which the product-overlap strategy may be operationalized. Principal among them are having competing lines, doing private labeling, and dealing with original-equipment manufacturers.

In order to gain a larger share of the total market, many companies introduce competing products to the market. When a market is not neatly delineated, a single brand of a product may not be able to make an adequate impact. If a second brand is placed to compete with the first one, overall sales of the two brands should increase substantially, although there will be some cannibalism. In other words, two competing brands provide a more aggressive front against competitors.

Often the competing-brands strategy works out to be a short-term phenomenon. When a new version of a product is introduced, the previous version is allowed to continue until the new one has fully established itself. In this way, the competition is prevented from stealing sales during the time that the new product is coming into its own. In 1989, Gillette introduced the Sensor razor, a revolutionary new product that featured flexible blades that adjusted to follow the unique contours of the face. At the same time, its previous razor, Atra, continued to be promoted as before. It is claimed that together the two brands were very effective in the market. It is estimated that 36 percent of Sensor users converted from Atra. If Atra had not been promoted, this figure would have been much more, and Sensor would have been more vulnerable to the Schick Tracer and other rigid Atra look-alikes.[13] Interestingly, however, when Gillette introduced the Mach 3 razor in 1998, it decided to run down stocks of its Sensor and Atra shavers ahead of the new product's launch.[14]

To expand its overall coffee market, Procter & Gamble introduced a more economical form of ground coffee under the Folgers label. A more efficient milling process that refines coffee into flakes allows hot water to come into contact with more of each coffee particle when brewing, resulting in savings of up to 15 percent per cup. The new product, packaged in 13-, 26-, and 32-ounce cans, yielded the same number of cups of coffee as standard 16-, 32-, and 48-ounce cans, respectively. Both the new and the old formulations were promoted aggressively, competing with each other and, at the same time, providing a strong front against brands belonging to other manufacturers.

Reebok International products under the Reebok brand name directly compete with its subsidiary's brand, Avia. As noted earlier, the competing-brands strategy is useful in the short run only. Ultimately, each brand, Avia and Reebok, should find its special niche in the market. If that does not happen, they will create confusion among customers and sales will be hurt. Alternatively, in the long run, one of the brands may be withdrawn, thereby yielding its position to the other brand. This strategy is a useful device for achieving growth and for increasing market share.

Private labeling refers to manufacturing a product under another company's brand name. In the case of goods whose intermediaries have significant control of the distribution sector, private labeling, or branding, has become quite common. For large food chains, items produced with their label by an outside manufacturer contribute significantly to sales. Wal-Mart, Target, Sears, J.C. Penney, and other such companies merchandise many different types of goods—textile goods, electronic goods, large appliances, sporting goods, etc.—each carrying the company's brand name.

The private-label strategy from the viewpoint of the manufacturer is viable for the following reasons:

- Private labeling represents a large (and usually growing) market segment.
- Economies of scale at each step in the business system (manufacturing capacity, distribution, merchandising, and so on) justify the search for additional volume.
- Supplying private labeling will improve relationships with a powerful organized trade.
- Control over technology and raw materials reduces the risk.
- There is a clear consumer segmentation between branded and unbranded goods that supports providing private labels.
- Private labeling helps eliminate small, local competitors.
- Private labeling offers an opportunity to compete on price against other branded products.
- Private labeling increases share of shelf space—a critical factor in motivating impulse purchases.

But here are also strong arguments against the private-label strategy:

- Market share growth through private-label supply always happens at the expense of profitability, as price sensitivity rises and margins fall.
- Disclosing cost information to the trade—usually essential for a private-label supplier—can threaten a firm's branded products.
- In order to displace existing private-label suppliers, new entrants must undercut current prices, and thus risk starting a price war—in an environment where trade loyalty offers little protection.
- In young, growing markets, it is the brand leaders, not the private-label suppliers, that influence whether the market will develop toward branded or commodity goods.
- Private labeling is inconsistent with a leader's global brand and product strategy—it raises questions about quality and standards, dilutes management attention, and affects consumers' perception of the main branded business.

Many large manufacturers deal in private brands while simultaneously offering their own brands. In this situation, they are competing against themselves. They do so, however, hoping that overall revenues will be higher with the offering of the private brand than without it. Coca-Cola, for example, supplies to A&P stores both its own brand of orange juice, Minute Maid, and the brand it produces with the A&P label. At one time, many companies equated supplying private brands with lowering their brands' images. But the business swings of the 1980s changed attitudes on this issue. Frigidaire appliances at one time were not offered under a private label. However, in the 1980s Frigidaire began offering them under Montgomery Ward's name (For readers' information, Montgomery Ward's went out of business in 1999.) An interesting question that can be raised about private branding is whether cars can be sold under a distributor's own label. The idea has surfaced at AutoNation, the country's biggest car retailer, who might one day buy a car manufactured in, say, South Korea, and sell it under its own label.[15]

A retailer's interest in selling goods under its own brand name is also motivated by economic considerations. The retailer buys goods with its brand name at low cost, then offers the goods to customers at a slightly lower price than the price of a manufacturer's brand (also referred to as a national brand). The assumption is that the customer, motivated by the lower price, will buy a private brand, assuming that its quality is on a par with that of the national brand. This assumption is, of course, based on the premise that a reputable retailer will not offer something under its name if it is not high quality. Consider the

Save-A-Lot chain, a unit of Minneapolis food distribution Super Valu Inc., whose 85% of sales come from private-label items. With a total of 706 stores in 31 states, with sales amounting to $3 billion, it is one of the nation's fastest growing grocery chains.[16]

Following the strategy of dealing with an OEM, a company may sell to competitors the components used in its own product. This enables competitors to compete with the company in the market. For example, in the initial stages of color television, RCA was the only company that manufactured picture tubes. It sold these picture tubes to GE and to other competitors, enabling them to compete with RCA color television sets in the market.

The relevance of this strategy may be discussed from the viewpoint of both the seller and the OEM. The motivation for the seller comes from two sources: the desire to work at near-capacity level and the desire to have help in promoting primary demand. Working at full capacity is essential for capitalizing on the experience effect (see Chapter 12). Thus, by selling a component to competitors, a company may reduce the across-the-board costs of the component for itself, and it will have the price leverage to compete with those manufacturers to whom it sold the component. Besides, the company will always have the option of refusing to do business with a competitor who becomes a problem.

The second source of motivation is the support competitors can provide in stimulating primary demand for a new product. Many companies may be working on a new-product idea. When one of them successfully introduces the product, the others may be unable to do so because they lack an essential component or the technology that the former has. Since the product is new, the innovator may find the task of developing primary demand by itself tedious. It may make a strategic decision to share the essential-component technology with other competitors, thus encouraging them to enter the market and share the burden of stimulating primary demand.

A number of companies follow the OEM strategy. Auto manufacturers sell parts to each other. Texas Instruments sold electronic chips to its competitors during the initial stages of the calculator's development. In the 1950s, Polaroid bought certain essential ingredients from Kodak to manufacture film. IBM has shared a variety of technological components with other computer producers. In many situations, however, the OEM strategy may be forced upon companies by the Justice Department in its efforts to promote competition in an industry. Both Kodak and Xerox shared the products of their technology with competitors at the behest of the government. Thus, as a matter of strategy, when government interference may be expected, a company will gain more by sharing its components with others and assuming industry leadership. From the standpoint of results, this strategy is useful in seeking increased profitability, though it may not have much effect on market share or growth.

As far as the OEMs are concerned, the strategy of depending upon a competitor for an essential component only works in the short run because the supplier may at some point refuse entirely to sell the component or may make it difficult for the buyer to purchase it by delaying deliveries or by increasing prices enormously.

14.5 PRODUCT-SCOPE STRATEGY

The product-scope strategy deals with the perspective of the product mix of a company (i.e., the number of product lines and items in each line that the company may offer). The product-scope strategy is determined by making reference to the business unit mission. Presumably, the mission defines what sort of business it is going to be, which helps in selecting the products and services that are to become a part of the product mix.

The product-scope strategy must be finalized after a careful review of all facets of the business because it involves long-term commitment. In addition, the strategy must be reviewed from time to time to make any changes called for because of shifts in the environment. The point may be elaborated with reference to Eastman Kodak Company's decision to enter the instant photography market in the early 1970s. Traditionally, Polaroid bought negatives for its films, worth $50 million, from Kodak. In 1969, Polaroid built its own negative plant. This meant that Kodak would lose some $50 million of Polaroid's business and be left with idle machinery that had been dedicated to filling Polaroid's needs. Further, by producing its own film, Polaroid could lower its costs; if it then cut prices, instant photography might become more competitive with Kodak's business. Alternatively, if Polaroid held prices high, it would realize high margins and would soon be very rich indeed. Encouraged by such achievements, Polaroid could even develop a marketing organization rivaling Kodak's and threaten it in every sphere. In brief, Kodak was convinced that it would be shut out of the instant photography market forever if it delayed its entry any longer. Subsequently, however, a variety of reasons led Kodak to change its decision to go ahead with instant photography. Its pocket instamatic cameras turned out to be highly successful, and some of the machinery and equipment allocated to instant photography had to be switched over to pocket instamatics. A capital shortage also occurred, and Kodak, as a matter of financial policy, did not want to borrow to support the instant photography project. In 1976, Kodak again revised its position and did enter the field of instant photography but withdrew quickly.[17]

In brief, commitment to the product-scope strategy requires a thorough review of a large number of factors both inside and outside the organization. The three variants of product-scope strategy that will be discussed in this section are single-product strategy, multiple-products strategy, and system-of-products strategy. It will be recalled that in the previous chapter three alternatives were discussed under market-scope strategy: single-market strategy, multimarket strategy, and total-market strategy. These market strategies may be related to the three variants of product-scope strategy, providing nine different product/market-scope alternatives.

A business unit may have just one product in its line and must try to live on the success of this one product. There are several advantages to this strategy. First, concentration on a single product leads to specialization, which helps achieve scale and productivity gains. Second, management of operations is much more efficient when a single product is the focus. Third, in today's environment, where growth leads most companies to offer multiple products, a single-product company may become so specialized in its field that it can stand any competition.

A narrow product focus, for example, cancer insurance, has given American Family Life Assurance Company of Columbus, Georgia, a fast track record. Cancer is probably more feared than any other disease in the United States today. Although it kills fewer people than heart ailments, suffering is often lingering and severe. Cashing in on this fear, American Family Life became the nation's first marketer of insurance policies that cover the expenses of treating cancer.

Despite its obvious advantages, the single-product company has two drawbacks: First, if changes in the environment make the product obsolete, the single-product company can be in deep trouble. American history is full of instances where entire industries were wiped out. The disposable diaper, initially introduced by Procter & Gamble via its brand Pampers, pushed the cloth diaper business out of the market. The Baldwin Locomotive Company's steam locomotives were made obsolete by General Motors' diesel locomotives.

Second, the single-product strategy is not conducive to growth or market share. Its main advantage is profitability. If a company with a single-product focus is not able to earn high margins, it is better to seek a new posture. Companies interested in growth or market share will find the single-product strategy of limited value.

The multiple-products strategy amounts to offering two or more products. A variety of factors lead companies to choose this strategic posture. A company with a single product has nowhere to go if that product gets into trouble; with multiple products, however, poor performance by one product can be balanced out. In addition, it is essential for a company seeking growth to have multiple product offerings.

In 1970, when Philip Morris bought the Miller Brewing Company, it was a one-product business ranking seventh in beer sales. Growth prospects led the company to offer a number of other products. By 1978, Miller had acquired the number two position in the industry with 15 percent of the market. Miller continues to maintain its position (market share in 1998 was 18.2 percent), although Anheuser-Busch, the industry leader, has taken many steps to dislodge it. (In 2002, Philip Morris sold the Miller Brewing Company to South African Breweries, which now ranks as the second largest beer company in the world.)[18] As another example, consider Chicago-based Dean Foods Company, which traditionally has been a dairy concern. Over the years, diet-conscious and aging consumers have increasingly shunned high-fat dairy products in favor of low-calorie foods, and competition for the business that remains is increasingly fierce. To successfully operate in such an environment, the company decided to add other faster-growing, higher-margin refrigerated foods, such as party dips and cranberry drink, to the company's traditional dairy business. Dean's moves have been so successful that, although many milk processors were looking to sell out, Dean was concerned that it might be bought out. Similarly, Nike began with a shoe solely for serious athletes. Over the years, the company has added a number of new products to its line. It now makes shoes, for both males and females, for running, jogging, tennis, aerobics, soccer, basketball, and walking. Lately, it has expanded its offerings to include children.

Multiple products can be either related or unrelated. Unrelated products will be discussed later in the section on diversification. Related products consist of different product lines and items. A food company may have a frozen vegetable line, a yogurt line, a cheese line, and a pizza line. In each line, the company may produce different items (e.g., strawberry, pineapple, apricot, peach, plain, and blueberry yogurt). Note, in this example, the consistency among the different food lines: (a) they are sold through grocery stores, (b) they must be refrigerated, and (c) they are meant for the same target market. These underpinnings make them related products.

Although not all products may be fast moving, they must complement each other in a portfolio of products. The subject of product portfolios was examined in Chapter 10. Suffice it to say, the multiple-products strategy is directed toward achieving growth, market share, and profitability. Not all companies get rich simply by having multiple products: growth, market share, and profitability are functions of a large number of variables, only one of which is having multiple products.

The word *system*, as applied to products, is a post-World War II phenomenon. Two related forces were responsible for the emergence of this phenomenon: (a) the popularity of the marketing concept that businesses sell satisfaction, not products; and (b) the complexities of products themselves often call for the use of complementary products and after-sale services. A cosmetics company does not sell lipstick, it sells the hope of looking pretty; an airline should not sell plane tickets, it should sell pleasurable vacations. However, vacationers need more than an airline ticket. Vacationers also need hotel accommodations, ground transportation, and sightseeing arrangements. Following the systems concept, an airline may define itself as a vacation packager that sells air transportation, hotel reservations, meals, sightseeing, and so on. IBM is a single source for hardware, operating systems, packaged software, maintenance, emergency repairs, and consulting services. Thus, IBM offers its customers a system of different products and services to solve data management problems. Likewise, ADT Ltd. is a company whose product is security systems. Beginning with consulting on the type of security systems needed, ADT also provides the sales, installation, service, updating on new technologies to existing systems, and the actual monitoring of these alarm systems either by computer or with patrol services and security watchmen.

Offering a system of products rather than a single product is a viable strategy for a number of reasons. It makes the customer fully dependent, thus allowing the company to gain monopolistic control over the market. The system-of-products strategy also blocks the way for the competition to move in. With such benefits, this strategy is extremely useful in meeting growth, profitability, and market share objectives. If this strategy is stretched beyond its limits, however, a company can get into legal problems. Several years ago, IBM was charged by the Justice Department with monopolizing the computer market. In the aftermath of this charge, IBM has had to make changes in its strategy. Lately, Microsoft has been under fire for its dominant hold on the Internet technology.

The successful implementation of the system-of-products strategy requires a thorough understanding of customer requirements, including the processes and functions the consumer must perform when using the product. Effective implementation of this strategy broadens both the company's concept of its product and market opportunities for it, which in turn support product/market objectives of growth, profitability, and market share.

14.6 PRODUCT-DESIGN STRATEGY

A business unit may offer a standard or a custom-designed product to each individual customer. The decision about whether to offer a standard or a customized product can be simplified by asking these questions, among others: What are our capabilities? What business are we in? With respect to the first question, there is a danger of overidentification of capabilities for a specific product. If capabilities are overidentified, the business unit may be in trouble. When the need for the product declines, the business unit will have difficulty in relating its product's capabilities to other products. It is, therefore, desirable for a business unit to have a clear perspective about its capabilities. The answer to the second question determines the limits within which customizing may be pursued.

Between the two extremes of standard and custom products, a business unit may also offer standard products with modifications. These three strategic alternatives, which come under the product-design strategy, are discussed below.

Offering standard products leads to two benefits. First, standard products are more amenable to the experience effect than are customized products; consequently, they yield cost benefits. Second, standard products can be merchandised nationally much more efficiently. Ford's Model T is a classic example of a successful standard product. The standard product has one major problem, however. It orients management thinking toward the realization of per-unit cost savings to such an extent that even the need for small changes in product design may be ignored.

There is considerable evidence to suggest that larger firms derive greater profits from standardization by taking advantage of economies of scale and long production runs to produce at a low price. Small companies, on the other hand, must use the major advantage they have over the giants, that is, flexibility. Hence, the standard-product strategy is generally more suitable for large companies. Small companies are better off as job shops, doing customized work at a higher margin.

A standard product is usually offered in different grades and styles with varying prices. In this manner, even though a product is standard, customers have broader choices. Likewise, distribution channels get the product in different price ranges. The result: standard-product strategy helps achieve the product/market objectives for growth, market share, and profitability.

Customized products are sold on the basis of the quality of the finished product, that is, on the extent to which the product meets the customer's specifications. The producer usually works closely with the customer, reviewing the progress of the product until completion. Unlike standard products, price is not a factor for customized products. A customer expects to pay a premium for a customized product. As mentioned above, a customized product is more suitable for small companies to offer. This broad statement should not be interpreted to mean that large companies cannot successfully offer customized products. The ability to sell customized products successfully actually depends on the nature of the product. A small men's clothing outlet is in a better position to offer custom suits than a large men's suit manufacturer. On the other hand, GE is better suited to manufacture a custom-designed engine for military aircraft than a smaller business.

An innovative aspect of this product strategy is mass customization, making goods to each customer's requirements. One company that practices mass customization is Customer Foot. It makes shoes that meet individual tastes and size requirements, yet does so on a mass-production basis, at slightly lower prices than many premium brands sold off the shelf.[19] This requires a flexible manufacturing system that anticipates a wide range of options. Many companies can find an important competitive edge in mass customization. If Company X offers a one-size-fits-all product and Company Y can tailor the same product to individual tastes without charging much more, the latter will be more successful. It is a powerful tool for building relationships with customers, since it requires a company to gather information, often of a very personal nature, about customers' tastes and needs. In 1999 Toyota Motor Corp. began offering Camry Solara to customer order in just five days. It was a surprise move since a typical car requires 30 to 60 days to produce a custom order. Currently, Toyota offers a number of other car models that are custom-designed and delivered in 5 to 10 days. This gives Toyota a significant competitive advantage. By making and delivering personal computers to order, Dell computer catapulted from a crowded field to become an industry leader. Toyota's customization strategy may force other members of the industry to adopt build-to-order strategy.[20]

Over and above price flexibility, dealing in customized products provides a company with useful experience in developing new standard products. A number of companies have been able to develop mass market products out of their custom work for NASA projects. The microwave oven, for example, is an offshoot of the experience gained from government contracts. Customized products also provide opportunities for inventing new products to meet other specific needs. In terms of results, this strategy is directed more toward realizing higher profitability than are other product-design strategies.

The strategy of modifying standard products represents a compromise between the two strategies already discussed. With this strategy, a customer may be given the option to specify a limited number of desired modifications to a standard product. A familiar example of this strategy derives from the auto industry. The buyer of a new car can choose type of shift (standard or automatic), air conditioning, power brakes, power steering, size of engine, type of tires, and color. Although some modifications may be free, for the most part the customer is expected to pay extra for modifications.

This strategy is directed toward realizing the benefits of both a standard and a customized product. By manufacturing a standard product, the business unit seeks economies of scale; at the same time, by offering modifications, the product is individualized to meet the specific requirements of the customer. The experience of a small water pump manufacturer that sold its products nationally through distributors provides some insights into this phenomenon. The company manufactured the basic pump in its facilities in Ohio and then shipped it to its four branches in different parts of the country. At each branch, the pumps were finished according to specifications requested by distributors. Following this strategy, the company lowered its transportation costs (because the standard pump could be shipped in quantity) even while it provided customized pumps to its distributors.

Among other benefits, this strategy permits the business unit to keep in close contact with market needs that may be satisfied through product improvements and modifications. It also enhances the organization's reputation for flexibility in meeting customer requirements. It may also encourage new uses of existing products. Other things being equal, this strategy can be useful in achieving growth, market share, and profitability.

14.7 PRODUCT-ELIMINATION STRATEGY

Marketers have believed for a long time that sick products should be eliminated. It is only in recent years that this belief has become a matter of strategy. A business unit's various products represent a portfolio, with each product playing a unique role in making the business viable. If a product's role diminishes or if it does not fit into the portfolio, it ceases to be important.

When a product reaches the stage where continued support is no longer justified because performance is falling short of expectations, it is desirable to pull the product out of the marketplace. Poor performance is easy to spot. It may be characterized by any of the following:

1. Low profitability.
2. Stagnant or declining sales volume or market share that is too costly to rebuild.
3. Risk of technological obsolescence.
4. Entry into a mature or declining phase of the product life cycle.
5. Poor fit with the business unit's strengths or declared mission.

Products that are not able to limp along must be eliminated. They drain a business unit's financial and managerial resources, resources that could be used more profitably elsewhere. Hise, Parasuraman, and Viswanathan cite examples of a number of companies, among them Hunt Foods, Standard Brands, and Crown Zellerbach, that have reported substantial positive results from eliminating products.[21] The three alternatives in the product-elimination strategy are harvesting, line simplification, and total-line divestment.

Harvesting refers to getting the most from a product while it lasts. It is a controlled divestment whereby the business unit seeks to get the most cash flow it can from the product. The harvesting strategy is usually applied to a product or business whose sales volume or market share is slowly declining. An effort is made to cut the costs associated with the business to improve cash flow. Alternatively, price is increased without simultaneous increase in costs. Harvesting leads to a slow decline in sales. When the business ceases to provide a positive cash flow, it is divested.

Du Pont followed the harvesting strategy in the case of its rayon business. Similarly, BASF Wyandotte applied harvesting to soda ash. As another example, GE harvested its artillery business a few years ago. Even without making any investments or raising prices, the business continued to provide GE with positive cash flow and substantial profits. Lever Brothers applied this strategy to its Lifebuoy soap. The company continued to distribute this product for a long time because, despite higher price and virtually no promotional support, it continued to be in popular demand.

Implementation of the harvesting strategy requires severely curtailing new investment, reducing maintenance of facilities, slicing advertising and research budgets, reducing the number of models produced, curtailing the number of distribution channels, eliminating small customers, and cutting service in terms of delivery time, speed of repair, and sales assistance. Though a harvesting strategy may be implemented successfully in various situations, ideally, a harvesting strategy should be pursued when the following conditions are present:

1. The business entity is in a stable or declining market.
2. The business entity has a small market share, but building it up would be too costly; or it has a respectable market share that is becoming increasingly costly to defend or maintain.
3. The business entity is not producing especially good profits or may even be producing losses.
4. Sales would not decline too rapidly as a result of reduced investment.
5. The company has better uses for the freed-up resources.
6. The business entity is not a major component of the company's business portfolio.
7. The business entity does not contribute other desired features to the business portfolio, such as sales stability or prestige.

Line-simplification strategy refers to a situation where a product line is trimmed to a manageable size by pruning the number and variety of products or services offered. This is a defensive strategy that is adopted to keep a falling line stable. It is hoped that the simplification effort will restore the health of the line. This strategy becomes especially relevant during times of rising costs and resource shortages.

The application of this strategy in practice may be illustrated with an example from GE's housewares business. In the early 1970s, the housewares industry faced soaring costs and stiff competition from Japan. GE took a hard look at its housewares business and raised such questions as: Is this product segment mature? Is it one we should be harvesting? Is it one we should be investing money in and expanding? Analysis showed that there was a demand for housewares, but demand was just not attractive enough for GE at that time. The company ended production of blenders, fans, heaters, and vacuum cleaners because they were found to be on the downside of the growth curve and did not fit in with GE's strategy for growth.

Similarly, Sears, Roebuck & Co. overhauled its retail business in 1993, dropping its famous catalog business, which contributed over $3 billion in annual sales. Sears's huge catalog operations had been losing money for nearly a decade (about $175 million in 1992), as specialty catalogs and specialty stores grabbed market share from the country's once-supreme mail-order house.[22] Kodak discovered that more than 80% of all its sales are achieved by less than 20% of the product line. Therefore, the company eliminated 27% of all sales items.[23] Procter & Gamble got rid of marginal brands such as Bain de Soleil sun-care products. In addition, the company cut product items by axing extraneous sizes, flavors, and other variants.

The implementation of a line-simplification strategy can lead to a variety of benefits: potential cost savings from longer production runs; reduced inventories; and a more forceful concentration of marketing, research and development, and other efforts behind a shorter list of products.

However, despite obvious merits, simplification efforts may sometimes be sabotaged. Those who have been closely involved with a product may sincerely feel either that the line as it is will revive when appropriate changes are made in the marketing mix, or that sales and profits will turn up once temporary conditions in the marketplace turn around. Thus, careful maneuvering is needed on the part of management to simplify a line unhindered by corporate rivalries and intergroup pressures.

The decision to drop a product is more difficult if it is a core product that has served as a foundation for the company. Such a product achieves the status of motherhood, and a company may like to keep it for nostalgic reasons. For example, the decision by General Motors to drop the Cadillac convertible was probably a difficult one to make in light of the prestige attached to the vehicle. Despite the emotional aspects of a product-deletion decision, the need to be objective in this matter cannot be overemphasized. Companies establish their own criteria to screen different products for elimination.

In finalizing the decision, attention should be given to honoring prior commitments. For example, replacement parts must be provided even though an item is dropped. A well-implemented program of product simplification can lead to both growth and profitability. It may, however, be done at the cost of market share.

Divestment is a situation of reverse acquisition. It may also be a dimension of market strategy. But to the extent that the decision is approached from the product's perspective (i.e., to get rid of a product that is not doing well even in a growing market), it is an aspect of product strategy. Traditionally, companies resisted divestment for the following reasons, which are principally either economic or psychological in nature:

1. Divestment means negative growth in sales and assets, which runs counter to the business ethic of expansion.
2. Divestment suggests defeat.
3. Divestment requires changes in personnel, which can be painful and can result in perceived or real changes in status or have an adverse effect on the entire organization.
4. Divestment may need to be effected at a price below book and thus may have an adverse effect on the year's earnings.
5. The candidate for divestment may be carrying overhead, buying from other business units of the company, or contributing to earnings.

With the advent of strategic planning in the 1970s, divestment became an accepted option for seeking faster growth. More and more companies are now willing to sell a business if the company will be better off strategically. These companies feel that divestment should not be regarded solely as a means of ridding the company of an unprofitable division or plan; rather, there are some persuasive reasons supporting the divestment of even a profitable and growing business. Businesses that no longer fit the corporate strategic plan can be divested for a number of reasons:

- There is no longer a strategic connection between the base business and the part to be divested.
- The business experiences a permanent downturn, resulting in excess capacity for which no profitable alternative use can be identified.
- There may be inadequate capital to support the natural growth and development of the business.
- It may be dictated in the estate planning of the owner that a business is not to remain in the family.
- Selling a part of the business may release assets for use in other parts of the business where opportunities are growing.
- Divestment can improve the return on investment and growth rate both by ridding the company of units growing more slowly than the basic business and by providing cash for investment in faster-growing, higher-return operations.

Whatever the reason, a business that may have once fit well into the overall corporate plan can suddenly find itself in an environment that causes it to become a drain on the corporation, either financially, managerially, or opportunistically. Such circumstances suggest divestment.

Divestment helps restore balance to a business portfolio. If the company has too many high-growth businesses, particularly those at an early stage of development, its resources may be inadequate to fund growth. On the other hand, if a company has too many low-growth businesses, it will often generate more cash than is required for investment and will build up redundant equity. For a business to grow evenly over time while showing regular increments in earnings, a portfolio of fast- and slow-growth businesses is necessary. Divestment can help achieve this kind of balance. Finally, divestment helps restore a business to a size that will not lead to an antitrust action.

The use of this strategy is reflected in GE's decision to divest its consumer electronics business in the early 1980s. In order to realize a return that GE considered adequate, the company would have had to make additional heavy investments in this business. GE figured that it could use the money to greater advantage in an area other than consumer electronics. Hence, it divested the business by selling it to Thomson, a French company.

Essentially following the same reasoning, Olin Corporation divested its aluminum business on the grounds that maintaining its small four percent share required big capital expenditures that could be employed more usefully elsewhere in the company. Westinghouse sold its major appliance line because it needed at least an additional three percent beyond the five percent share it held before it could compete effectively against industry leaders GE and Whirlpool. GE and Whirlpool divided about half the total market between them. Between 1986 and 1988, Beatrice sold two-thirds of its business, including such well-known names as Playtex, Avis, Tropicana, and Meadow Gold. The company considered these divestments necessary to transform itself into a manageable organization.[24]

It is difficult to prescribe generalized criteria to determine whether to divest a business. However, the following questions may be raised, the answers to which should provide a starting point for considering divestment:

1. **What is the earnings pattern of the unit?** A key question is whether the unit is acting as a drag on corporate growth. If so, then management must determine whether there are any offsetting values. For example, are earnings stable compared to the fluctuation in other parts of the company? If so, is the low-growth unit a substantial contributor to the overall debt capacity of the business? Management should also ask a whole series of ''what-if'' questions relating to earnings: What if we borrowed additional funds? What if we brought in new management? What if we made a change in location? etc.
2. **Does the business generate any cash?** In many situations, a part of a company may be showing a profit but may not be generating any discretionary cash. That is, every dime of cash flow must be pumped right back into the operation just to keep it going at existing levels. Does this operation make any real contribution to the company? Will it eventually? What could the unit be sold for? What would be done with the cash from this sale?
3. **Is there any tie-in value—financial or operating—with existing business?** Are there any synergies in marketing, production, or research and development? Is the business countercyclical? Does it represent a platform for growth internally based or through acquisitions?
4. **Will selling the unit help or hurt the acquisitions effort?** What will be the immediate impact on earnings (write-offs, operating expenses)? What effect, if any, will the sale have on the company's image in

the stock market? Will the sale have any effect on potential acquisitions? (Will I, too, be sold down the river?) Will the divestment be functional in terms of the new size achieved? Will a smaller size facilitate acquisitions by broadening the "market" of acceptable candidates, or, by contrast, will the company become less credible because of the smaller size?

5. **Is the business unit central to accomplishing the core mission of the company?** There are times when a business unit is not truly profitable but remains central to accomplishing the company's strategic goals. This may occur through the business unit serving to block a competition from entering a market, through being so thoroughly identified with the company that closing the business unit would damage the company's perceived viability in the view of the market, through drawing attention to the company that is needed for growth or for changing the company's image into one that is more desirable, or any number of other reasons.

In conclusion, a company should undertake continual in-depth analysis of the market share, growth prospects, profitability, and cash-generating power of each business. As a result of such reviews, a business may need to be divested to maintain balance in the company's total business. This, however, is feasible only when the company develops enough self-discipline to avoid increasing sales volume beyond a desirable size and instead buys and sells businesses with the sole objective of enhancing overall corporate performance.

14.8 NEW-PRODUCT STRATEGY

New-product development is an essential activity for companies seeking growth. By adopting the new-product strategy as their posture, companies are better able to sustain competitive pressures on their existing products and make headway. The implementation of this strategy has become easier because of technological innovations and the willingness of customers to accept new ways of doing things.[25]

Despite their importance in strategy determination, however, implementation of new-product programs is far from easy. Too many products never make it in the marketplace. Bic is remembered for its ballpoint pens, disposable lighters, and razors. But many other products of the company never succeeded. Bic hosiery, including a brand called "fannyhose," failed in two product launches in the 1970s. Then the company blundered into sports with Bic sailboards, also short lived. But the biggest failure was probably Parfum Bic.[26] The drugstore fragrance was introduced in 1989 with $20 million in marketing support. It was such a colossal flop that the company called it quits within a few months. The risks and penalties of product failure require that companies move judiciously in adopting new-product strategies.

Interestingly, however, the mortality rate of new product ideas has declined considerably since the 1960s. In 1968, on average, 58 new-product ideas were considered for every successful new product. In 1981, only seven ideas were required to generate one successful new product. However, these statistics vary by industry. Consumer nondurable companies consider more than twice as many new-product ideas in order to generate one successful new product, compared to industrial or consumer durable manufacturers.[27]

Top management can affect the implementation of new-product strategy; first, by establishing policies and broad strategic directions for the kinds of new products the company should seek; second, by providing the kind of leadership that creates the environmental climate needed to stimulate innovation in the organization; and third, by instituting review and monitoring procedures so that managers are involved at the right decision points and can know whether or not work schedules are being met in ways that are consistent with broad policy directions.

The term *new product* is used in different senses. For our purposes, the new-product strategy will be split into three alternatives: (a) product improvement/modification, (b) product imitation, and (c) product innovation.

Product improvement/modification is the introduction of a new version or an improved model of an existing product, such as "new, improved Crest." Improvements and modifications are usually achieved by adding new features or styles, changing processing requirements, or altering product ingredients. When a company introduces a product that is already on the market but new to the company, it is following a product-imitation strategy. For example, Schick was imitating when it introduced its Tracer razor to compete with Gillette's Sensor. For our purposes, a product innovation will be defined as a strategy with a completely new approach in fulfilling customer desires (e.g., Polaroid camera, television, typewriter) or one that replaces existing ways of satisfying customer desires (e.g., the replacement of slide rules by pocket calculators). About 90% of new products are simply line extensions, such as Frito-Lay's Doritos Flamin, Hot Tortilla Chips in snack-size bags. This is despite the fact that truly original products—the remaining 10%—possess the real profit potential.[28]

New-product development follows the experience curve concept; that is, the more you do something, the more efficient you become at doing it (for additional details, see Chapter 12). Experience in introducing products enables companies to improve new-product performance. Specifically, with increased new-product experience, companies improve new-product profitability by reducing the cost per introduction. More precisely, with each doubling of the number of new-product introductions, the cost of each introduction declines at a predictable and constant rate. For example, among the 13,000 new products introduced by 700 companies surveyed by Booz, Allen, and Hamilton between 1976 and 1981, the experience effect yielded a 71 percent cost curve. At each doubling of the number of new products introduced, the cost of each introduction declined by 29 percent.[29]

An existing product may reach a stage that requires that something be done to keep it viable. The product may have reached the maturity stage of the product life cycle because of shifts in the environment and thus has ceased to provide an adequate return. Or product, pricing, distribution, and promotion strategies employed by competitors may have reduced the product to the me-too category. At this stage, management has two options: either eliminate the product or revitalize it by making improvements or modifications. Improvements or modifications are achieved by redesigning, remodeling, or reformulating the product so that it satisfies customer needs more fully. This strategy seeks not only to restore the health of the product but sometimes seeks to help distinguish it from competitors' products as well. For example, it has become fashionable these days to target an upscale, or premium, version of a product at the upper end of the price performance pyramid. *Fortune's* description of Kodak's traditional product strategy is relevant here:

On the one hand, the longer a particular generation of cameras can be sold, the more profitable it will become. On the other hand, amateur photographers tend to use less film as their cameras age and lose their novelty; hence, it is critical that Kodak keep the camera population eternally young by bringing on new generations from time to time. In each successive generation, Kodak tries to increase convenience and reliability in order to encourage even greater film consumption per camera—a high ''burn rate,'' as the company calls it. In general, the idea is to introduce as few major new models as possible while ringing in frequent minor changes powerful enough to stimulate new purchases.

Kodak has become a master of this marketing strategy. Amateur film sales took off with a rush after 1963. That year the company brought out the first cartridge-loading, easy-to-use instamatic, which converted many people to photography and doubled film usage per camera. A succession of new features and variously priced models followed to help stimulate film consumption for a decade. Then Kodak introduced the pocket instamatic, which once again boosted film use both because of its novelty and because of its convenience. Seven models of that generation have since appeared.[30]

Kodak's strategy points out that it is never enough just to introduce a new product. The real payoff comes if the product is managed in such a way that it continues to flourish year after year in a changing and competitive marketplace. It also points out a significant problem that can exist in even the best market oriented companies. Due to its focus on film, rather than the true end product—the captue of memories—Kodak missed staying on top of the market's move toward digital cameras and has been hard pressed to catch up to the newer technology.

In the 1990s, the company continued to pursue the strategy with yet another new product, the throwaway camera. Fun, cheap, and easy to use are the features that have turned the disposable camera (basically a roll of film with a cheap plastic case and lens) into a substantial business. In 1992, the sales at retail reached over $200 million with Kodak holding over 65% of the market.[31]

There is no magic formula for restoring the health of a product. Occasionally, it is the ingenuity of the manager that may bring to light a desired cure. Generally, however, a complete review of the product from marketing perspectives is needed to analyze underlying causes and to come up with the modifications and improvements necessary to restore the product to health. For example, General Mills continues to realize greater profits by rejuvenating its old products—cake mixes, Cheerios, and Hamburger Helper. The company successfully builds excitement for old products better than anyone else in the food business by periodically improving them. Compared with Kellogg, which tends not to fiddle with its core products, General

Mills takes much greater risks with established brands. For instance, the company introduced two varieties of Cheerios—Honey Nut in 1979 and Apple Cinnamon in 1988—and successfully created a megabrand.[32]

To identify options for restoring a damaged product to health, it may be necessary to tear down competing products and make detailed comparative analyses of quality and price.

By comparing its product with that of its competitors, a company can identify unique product strengths on which to pursue modifications and improvements. The use of this analysis may be illustrated with reference to a Japanese manufacturer. In 1978, Japan's amateur color film market was dominated by Kodak, Fuji, and Sakura, the last two being Japanese companies. For the previous 15 years, Fuji had been gaining market share, whereas Sakura, the market leader in the early 1950s with over half the market, was losing ground to both its competitors. By 1976, Sakura had only about a 16 percent market share. Marketing research showed that, more than anything else, Sakura was the victim of an unfortunate word association. Its name in Japanese means "cherry blossom," suggesting a soft, blurry, pinkish image. The name Fuji, however, was associated with the blue skies and white snow of Japan's sacred mountain. Being in no position to change perceptions, the company decided to analyze the market from structural, economic, and customer points of view. Sakura found a growing cost consciousness among film customers: to wit, amateur photographers commonly left one or two frames unexposed in a 36-exposure roll, but they almost invariably tried to squeeze extra exposures onto 20-exposure rolls. Here Sakura saw an opportunity. It decided to introduce a 24-exposure film. Its marginal costs would be trivial, but its big competitors would face significant penalties in following suit. Sakura was prepared to cut its price if the competition lowered the price of their 20-frame rolls. Its aim was twofold. First, it would exploit the growing number of cost-minded users. Second, and more important, it would be drawing attention to the issue of economics, where it had a relative advantage, and away from the image issue, where it could not win. Sakura's strategy paid off. Its market share increased from 16 percent to more than 30 percent.[33] PepsiCo has developed a new product, Pepsi One, to fulfill the unmet needs of young men. The company launched the product with about $100 million promotion and hoped to generate $1 billion in annual retail sales.[34] Overall, the product-improvement strategy is conducive to achieving growth, market share, and profitability alike.

Not all companies like to be first in the market with a new product. Some let others take the initiative. If the innovation is successful, they ride the bandwagon of the successful innovation by imitating it. In the case of innovations protected by patents, imitators must wait until patents expire. In the absence of a patent, however, the imitators work diligently to design and produce products not very different from the innovator's product to compete vigorously with the innovator.

The imitation strategy can be justified in that it transfers the risk of introducing an unproven idea/product to someone else. It also saves investment in research and development. This strategy particularly suits companies with limited resources. Many companies, as a matter of fact, develop such talent that they can imitate any product, no matter how complicated. With a limited investment in research and development, the imitator may sometimes have a lower cost, giving it a price advantage in the market over the leader.

Another important reason for pursuing an imitation strategy may be to gainfully transfer the special talent a company may have for one product to other similar products. For example, the Bic Pen Corporation decided to enter the razor business because it thought it could successfully use its aggressive marketing posture in that market. In the early 1970s, Hanes Corporation gained resounding success with L'eggs, an inexpensive pantyhose that it sold from freestanding racks in food and drugstore outlets.

The imitation strategy may also be adopted on defensive grounds. Being sure of its existing product(s), a company may initially ignore new developments in the field. If new developments become overbearing, however, they may cut into the share held by an existing product. In this situation, a company may be forced to imitate the new development as a matter of survival. Colorado's Adolph Coors Company conveniently ignored the introduction of light beer and dismissed Miller Lite as a fad. Many years later, however, the company was getting bludgeoned by Miller Lite. Also, Anheuser-Busch began to challenge the supremacy of Coors in the California market with its light beer. The matter became so serious that Coors decided to abandon its one-product tradition and introduced a low-calorie light beer.

Another example of product imitation is the introduction of specialty beers by major brewers. While the U.S. beer industry has been stagnating throughout the 1990s, the specialty brews have been growing at better than a 40 percent annual rate. This has led the four major beer companies that control 80 percent of the market to offer their own brands of specialty beers: Anheuser (Ray Hill's American Pilsner, Zeigen-Bock, Shock Top Belgian White, Bare Knuckle Stout); Miller (Henry Weinhard's, Icehouse, Southpaw Light); and Coors (Blue Moon, George Killian).

Imitation also works well for companies that want to enter new markets without resorting to expensive acquisitions or special new-product development programs. For example, Owens-Illinois adapted heavy-duty laboratory glassware into novelty drinking glasses for home use. Victoria's Secret extended its brand to offer such common products as laundry detergent (Lavish Laundry), soap for delicates (Gentle Affection), and fabric softener (Soften It Up.) The company's objectives is to expand into lifestyle products.[35,36]

Although imitation does avoid the risks involved in innovation, it is wrong to assume that every imitation of a successful product will succeed. The marketing program of an imitation should be as carefully chalked out and implemented as that of an innovation. Imitation strategy is most useful for achieving increases in market share and growth.

Product-innovation strategy includes introducing a new product to replace an existing product in order to satisfy a need in an entirely different way or to provide a new approach to satisfy an existing or latent need. This strategy suggests that the entrant is the first firm to develop and introduce the product. The ballpoint pen is an example of a new product; it replaced the fountain pen. The VCR was a new product introduced to answer home entertainment needs.

Product innovation is an important characteristic of U.S. industry. Year after year companies spend billions of dollars on research and development to innovate. In 2001, for example, American industry spent almost $110 billion on research and development. Research and development expenditures are expected to continue rising at an average of 10 percent annually as we enter the next century. This shows that industry takes a purposeful attitude toward new-product and new-process development.

Product innovation, however, does not come easy. Besides involving major financial commitments, it requires heavy doses of managerial time to cut across organizational lines. And still the innovation may fail to make a mark in the market. A number of companies have discovered the risks of this game. Among them is Texas Instruments, which lost $660 million before withdrawing from the home computer market. RCA lost $500 million on ill-fated videodisc players. RCA, GE, and Sylvania, leaders in vacuum-tube technology, lost out when transistor technology revolutionized the radio business. RJR Nabisco abandoned the "smokeless" cigarette, Premier, after a 10-year struggle and after spending over $500 million.[37]

Most recognized, innovative products are produced by large organizations. Initially, an individual or a group of individuals may be behind it, but a stage is eventually reached where individual efforts require corporate support to finally develop and launch the product. To encourage innovation and creativity, many large companies are spinning off companies. For example, Colgate-Palmolive Co. launched Colgate Venture Co. to support entrepreneurship and risk taking. In this way, a congenial environment within the large corporation is maintained for generating and following creative pursuits.[38]

In essence, innovation flourishes where divisions are kept small (permitting better interaction among managers and staffers), where there is willingness to tolerate failure (encouraging plenty of experimentation and risk taking), where champions are motivated (through encouragement, salaries, and promotions), where close liaison is maintained with the customer (visiting customers routinely; inviting them to brainstorm product ideas), where technology is shared corporate wide (technology, wherever it is developed, belongs to everyone), and where projects are sustained, even if initial results are discouraging.

The development of a product innovation typically passes through various stages: idea generation, screening, business analysis, development of a prototype, test market, and commercialization. The idea may emerge from different sources: customers, private researchers, university researchers, employees, or research labs. An idea may be generated by recognizing a consumer need or just by pursuing a scientific endeavor, hoping that it may lead to a viable product. Companies follow different procedures to screen ideas and to choose a few for further study. If an idea appears promising, it may be carried to the stage of business analysis, which may consist of investment requirements, revenue and expenditure projections, and financial analysis of return on investment, pay-back period, and cash flow. Thereafter, a few prototype products may be produced to examine engineering and manufacturing aspects of the product. A few sample products based on the prototype may be produced for market testing. After changes suggested in market testing have been incorporated, the innovation may be commercially launched.

Procter & Gamble's development of Pringles is a classic case of recognizing a need in a consumer market and then painstakingly hammering away to meet it.[39] Americans consume about one billion dollars' worth of potato chips annually, but manufacturers of potato chips face a variety of problems. Chips made in the traditional way are so fragile that they can rarely be shipped for more than 200 miles; even then, a quarter of the chips get broken. They also spoil quickly; their shelf life is barely two months. These characteristics have kept potato chip manufacturers split into many small regional operations. Nobody, before Procter & Gamble, had applied much technology to the product since it was invented in 1853.

Procter & Gamble knew these problems because it sold edible oils to the potato chip industry, and it set out to solve them. Instead of slicing potatoes and frying them in the traditional way, Procter & Gamble's engineers developed a process somewhat akin to paper making. They dehydrated and mashed potatoes and pressed them for frying into a precise shape, which permitted the chips to be stacked neatly on top of one another in hermetically sealed containers that resemble tennis ball cans. Pringles potato chips stay whole and have a shelf life of at least a year.

After a new product is screened through the lab, the division that will manufacture it takes over and finances all further development and testing. In some companies, division managers show little interest in taking on new products because the costs of introduction are heavy and hold down short-term profits. At Procter & Gamble, executives ensure that a manager's short-term record is not marred by the cost of a new introduction.

Before a new Procter & Gamble product is actually introduced to the market, it must prove that it has a demonstrable margin of superiority over its prospective competitors. A development team begins refining the product by trying variations of the basic formula, testing its performance under almost any conceivable condition, and altering its appearance. Eventually, a few alternative versions of the product are produced and tested among a large number of Procter & Gamble employees. If the product gets the approval of employees, the company presents it to panels of consumers for further testing. Procter & Gamble feels satisfied if a proposed product is chosen by fifty-five out of one hundred consumers tested. Though Pringles potato chips passed all these tests, they only recently started showing any profits for Procter & Gamble.

There is hardly any doubt that, if an innovation is successful, it pays off lavishly. For example, nylon still makes so much money for Du Pont that the company would qualify for the Fortune 500 list even if it made nothing else.[40] However, developing a new product is a high-risk strategy requiring heavy commitment and having a low probability of achieving a breakthrough. Thus, the choice of this strategy should be dictated by a company's financial and managerial strengths and by its willingness to take risks. Consider the case of Kevlar, a super-tough fiber (lightweight but five times stronger than steel) invented by Du Pont. It took the company 25 years and $900 million to come out with this product, more time and money than the company had ever spent on a single product. Starting in 1985, however, the payoff began: annual sales reached $300 million. Du Pont forecasts Kevlar's annual sales growth at 10 percent during the 1990s and 8 percent in the next ten years to 2010. Meanwhile, the company continues its quest for new applications that it hopes will make Kevlar a blockbuster.[41]

Exhibit 14.2 suggests an approach that may be used to manage innovations successfully. As a company grows more complex and decentralized, its new-product development efforts may fail to keep pace with change, weakening vital lines between marketing and technical people and leaving key decisions to be made by default. The possible result is the ultimate loss of competitive edge. To solve the problem, as shown in Exhibit 14.2a, both technical and market opportunity may be plotted on a grid. From this grid, innovations may be grouped into three classes: heavy emphasis (deserving full support, including basic research and development); selective opportunistic development (i.e., may be good or may be bad; may require a careful approach and top management attention); and limited defense support (i.e., merits only minimum support). Exhibit 14.2b lists the relevant kinds of programs for each area. This approach helps gear research efforts to priority strategic projects.

14.9 DIVERSIFICATION STRATEGY

Diversification refers to seeking unfamiliar products or markets or both in the pursuit of growth. Every company is best at certain products; diversification requires substantially different knowledge, thinking, skills, and processes. Thus, diversification is at best a risky strategy, and a company should choose this path only when current product/market orientation does not seem to provide further opportunities for growth. A few examples will illustrate the point that diversification does not automatically bring success. CNA Financial Corporation faced catastrophe when it expanded the scope of its business from insurance to real estate and mutual funds: it ended up being acquired by Loews Corporation. Schrafft's restaurants did little for Pet Incorporated. Pacific Southwest Airlines acquired rental cars and hotels, only to see its stock decline quickly. Diversification into the wine business (by acquiring Taylor Wines) did not work for the Coca-Cola Company.[42]

Exhibit 14.2
Managing Innovations

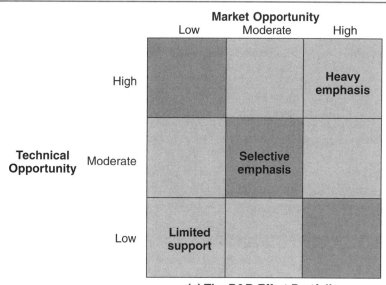

(a) The R&D Effort Portfolio

R&D Program Elements						
R&D Emphasis	Primary Level of Funding	Focus of Work	Level of Basic Research	Technical Risk	Acceptable Time for Payoff	Projects to Exceed or Maintain Competitive Parity
Heavy	High	Balance between new and existing products	High	High	Long	Many
Selective	Medium	Mainly existing products	Low	Medium	Medium	Few
Limited	Low	Existing processes	Very low	Low	Short	Very few

(b) Implied Nature of R&D Effort

Source: Richard N. Foster, "Linkage comes to United International, A fable for strategists," *Business Horizons,* December 1980, pages 66–67. Copyright © 1980, by the Foundation for the School of Business at Indiana University. Reprinted by permission.

The diversification decision is a major step that must be taken carefully. On the basis of a sample from 200 Fortune 500 firms and the PIMS database (see Chapter 12), Biggadike notes that it takes an average of 10 to 12 years before the return on investment from diversification equals that of mature businesses.[43]

The term *diversification* must be distinguished from integration and merger. *Integration* refers to the accumulation of additional business in a field through participation in more of the stages between raw materials and the ultimate market or through more intensive coverage of a single stage. *Merger* implies a combination of corporate entities that may or may not result in integration. Diversification is a strategic alternative that implies deriving revenues and profits from different products and markets. The following factors usually lead companies to seek diversification:

1. Firms diversify when their objectives can no longer be met within the product/market scope defined by expansion.
2. A firm may diversify because retained cash exceeds total expansion needs.
3. A firm may diversify when diversification opportunities promise greater profitability than expansion opportunities.
4. Firms may continue to explore diversification when the available information is not reliable enough to permit a conclusive comparison between expansion and diversification.

Diversification can take place at either the corporate or the business unit level. At the corporate level, it typically entails entering a promising business outside the scope of existing business units. At the business unit level, it is most likely to involve expanding into a new segment of the industry in which the business presently participates. The problems encountered at both levels are similar and may differ only in magnitude.

Diversification strategies include internal development of new products or markets (including development of international markets for current products), acquisition of an appropriate firm or firms, a strategic alliance with a complementary organization, licensing of new product technologies, and importing or distributing a line of products manufactured by another company. The final choice of an entry strategy involves a combination of these alternatives in most cases. This combination is determined on the basis of available opportunities and of consistency with the company's objectives and available resources.

Caterpillar Tractor Company's entry into the field of diesel engines is a case of internal diversification. Since 1972, the company has poured more than $1 billion into developing new diesel engines "in what must rank as one of the largest internal diversifications by a U.S. corporation."[44] Hershey Foods ventured into the restaurant business by buying the Friendly Ice Cream Corporation, illustrating diversification by acquisition. Hershey adopted the diversification strategy for growth because its traditional business, chocolate and candy, was stagnant because of a decline in candy consumption, sharp increases in cocoa prices, and changes in customer habits. Hershey subsequently sold Friendly in 1988 to a private company, Tennessee Restaurant Co.[45]

An empirical study of entry strategy shows that higher barriers are more likely to be associated with acquisition than with entry through internal development. Thus, in choosing between these two entry modes, business unit managers should take into account, among other factors, the entry barriers surrounding the market and the cost of breaching them. Despite high apparent barriers, the entrant's relatedness to the new entry may make entry financially more desirable.

Essentially, there are three different forms of diversification a company may pursue: concentric diversification, horizontal diversification, and conglomerate diversification. No matter what kind of diversification a company seeks, the three essential tests of success are

1. **The attractiveness test**—The industries chosen for diversification must be structurally attractive or capable of being made attractive.
2. **The cost-of-entry test**—The cost of entry must not capitalize all future profits.
3. **The better-off test**—The new unit must either gain competitive advantage from its link with the corporation or vice versa.[46]

Concentric diversification bears a close synergistic relationship to either the company's marketing or its technology, or both. Thus, new products that are introduced share a common thread with the firm's existing products, either through marketing or production. Usually, the new products are directed to a new group of customers. Texas Instrument's venture into pocket calculators illustrates this type of diversification. Using its expertise in integrated circuits, the company developed a new product that appealed to a new set of customers. On the other hand, PepsiCo's venture into the fast-food business through the acquisition of Pizza Hut is a case of concentric diversification in which the new product bears a synergistic relationship to the company's existing marketing experience. (Recently, PepsiCo spun off Pizza Hut along with Taco Bell and Kentucky Fried Chicken into a new $8.5 billion-a-year company called Tricon and now named Yum Brands.) Another example of concentric diversification is the joint venture between Coca-Cola Co. and Procter & Gamble Co. that develops and markets juices, juice-based drinks, and snacks.[47] The joint venture is a marriage between Coke's global distribution system and P&G's research expertise.

Toys "R" Us branched into children's clothing on the ground that its marketing as well as technological skills (purchasing power, brand name, storage facilities, retail outlets, and sophisticated information systems) would give it an edge in the new business. Similar logic persuaded Honda to diversify from motorcycles to lawn mowers and cars; and Black & Decker from power tools to home appliances.[48]

Although a diversification move per se is risky, concentric diversification does not lead a company into an entirely new world because in one of two major fields (technology or marketing), the company will operate in familiar territory. The relationship of the new product to the firm's existing product(s), however, may or may not mean much. All that the realization of synergy does is make the task easier; it does not necessarily make it successful. For example, Gillette entered the market for pocket calculators in 1974 and for digital watches in 1976. Later it abandoned both businesses. Both pocket calculators and digital watches were sold to mass markets where Gillette had expertise and experience. Despite this marketing synergy, it failed to sell either calculators or digital watches successfully. Gillette found that these lines of business called for strategies totally different from those it followed in selling its existing products. Two lessons can be drawn from Gillette's experience. One, there may be other strategic reasons for successfully launching a new product in the market besides commonality of markets or technology. Two, the commonality should be analyzed in breadth and depth before drawing conclusions about the transferability of current strengths to the new product.

Philip Morris's acquisition of Miller Brewing Company illustrates how a company may achieve marketing synergies through concentric diversification. Cigarettes and beer are distributed through many of the same retail outlets, and Philip Morris had been dealing with them for years. In addition, both products serve hedonistic consumer markets. Small wonder, therefore, that the marketing research techniques and emotional promotion appeals of cigarette merchandising worked equally well for beer. Miller moved from seventh to second place in the beer industry in the short span of six years.

Horizontal diversification refers to new products that technologically are unrelated to a company's existing products but that can be sold to the same group of customers to whom existing products are sold. A classic case of this form of diversification is Procter & Gamble's entry into potato chips (Pringles), toothpaste (Crest), coffee (Folgers), and orange juice (Citrus Hill). Traditionally a soap company, Procter & Gamble diversified into these products, which were aimed at the same customers who bought soap. Similarly, Maytag's entry into the medium-priced mass market to sell refrigerators and ranges, in addition to selling its traditional line of premium-priced dishwashers, washers, and dryers, is a form of horizontal diversification. Mattel's introduction of clothing items (skirts, shoes, jeans, shirts, and pajamas) for little girls, sizes 4 to 6x, under the Barbie brand name is another example of horizontal diversification. Using the Barbie phenomenon, the company has successfully launched the new business. As a company executive puts it, "Barbie is a designer brand for the little customers, their Calvin Klein."[49] Staples, plan to enter office supplies delivery business which is currently controlled by 6,000 small dealers is another example of horizontal diversification.[50]

Note that in the case of concentric diversification, the new product may have certain common ties with the marketing of a company's existing product except that it is sold to a new set of customers. In horizontal diversification, by contrast, the customers for the new product are drawn from the same ranks as those for an existing product.

Other things being equal, in a competitive environment horizontal diversification is more desirable if present customers are favorably disposed toward the company and if one can expect this loyalty to carry over to the new product; in the long run, however, a new product must stand on its own. For example, if product quality is lacking, if promotion is not effective, or if the price is not right, a new product will flop despite customer loyalty to the company's other products. Thus, while Crest and Folgers made it for Procter & Gamble, Citrus Hill struggled, and Pringles has been disappointing, even though all these products are sold to the same "loyal" customers (P&G dropped Citrus Hill from its line in 1998.) In other words, horizontal diversification should not be regarded as a route to success in all cases. An important limitation of horizontal diversification is that the new product is introduced and marketed in the same economic environment as the existing products, which can lead to rigidity and instability. Stated differently, horizontal diversification tends to increase the company's dependence on a few market segments.

In conglomerate diversification, the new product bears no relationship to either the marketing or the technology of the existing product(s). In other words, through conglomerate diversification, a company launches itself into an entirely new product/market arena. ITT's ventures into bakery products (Continental Baking Company), insurance (Hartford Insurance Group), car rentals (Avis Rent-A-Car System, Inc.), and the hotel business (Sheraton Corporation) illustrate the implementation of conglomerate diversification. (ITT divested its car rental business a few years ago.)

Dover Corp. provides another example of conglomerate diversification. The company, with annual sales of over $3 billion, is a manufacturer with 54 operating companies engaged in more than 70 diverse businesses, from elevators and garbage trucks to valves and welding torches.[51]

It is necessary to remember here that companies do not flirt with unknown products in unknown markets without having some hidden strengths to handle conglomerate diversification. For example, the managerial style required for a new product to prosper may be just the same as the style the company already has. Thus, managerial style becomes the basis of synergy between the new product and an existing product. By the same token, another single element may serve as a dominant factor in making a business attractive for diversification.

Inasmuch as conglomerate diversification does not bear an obvious relationship to a company's existing business, there is some question as to why companies adopt it. There are two major advantages of conglomerate diversification. One, it can improve the profitability and flexibility of a firm by venturing into businesses that have better economic prospects than those of the firm's existing businesses. Two, a conglomerate firm, because of its size, gets a better reception in capital markets.

Conglomerate is often criticized by Western management theorists. For the most part traditional management theory calls for companies to remain focused on their core industries and products. In emerging markets, however, conglomerate diversification is the norm for most emerging market multinationals (Haley and Tan, 1996, 1999; Haley, Tan and Haley, 1998; Haley and Haley, 1998 and 1999; Haley, Haley & Tan, 2004).[52]

Overall, this type of diversification, if successful, has the potential of providing increased growth and profitability.

14.10 VALUE-MARKETING STRATEGY

In the 1990s, *value* has become the marketer's watchword. Today, customers are demanding something different than they did in the past. They want the right combination of product quality, price, good service, and timely delivery. These are the keys to performing well in the next century. It is for this reason that we examine this new strategic focus.

Value marketing strategy stresses real product performance and delivering on promises. Value marketing doesn't mean high quality if it is only available at ever-higher prices. It doesn't necessarily mean cheap, if cheap means bare bones or low-grade. It doesn't mean high prestige, if the prestige is viewed as snobbish or self-indulgent. At the same time, value is not about positioning and image mongering. It simply means providing a product that works as claimed, is accompanied by decent service, and is delivered on time and at a price that is considered fair value for the combination of benefits offered by the vendor. More recently, some buyers are factoring social benefits, such as how relatively green a product is, into the evaluation of a product's fair value.

The emphasis on value is part atmospherics, part economics, and part demographics. Consumers are repudiating the wretched excesses of the 1980s and are searching for more traditional rewards of home and family. They are concerned about the seemingly nonending economic ups and down. The growing focus on value also stems from profound changes in the American consumer marketplace.

For example, real income growth for families got a boost when women entered the work force. But now, with many women already working and many baby boomers assuming new family responsibilities, the growth in disposable income is scarily slow. Aging baby boomers whose debt burden is already high realize that they must worry about their children's college tuitions and their own retirement. At the same time, the new generation of consumers is both more savvy and more cynical than were its predecessors. Briefly, consumers want products that perform, sold by advertising that informs. They are concerned about intrinsic value, not simply buying to impress others.

Traditionally, quality has been viewed as a manufacturing concern. Strategically, however, the idea of total quality is perceived in the market; that is, quality must exude from the offering itself and from all the services that come with it. The important point is that quality perspectives should be based on customer preferences, not on internal evaluations. The ultimate objective of quality should be to delight the customer in every way possible, providing levels of service, product quality, product performance, and support that are beyond his/her expectations. Ultimately, quality may mean striving for excellence throughout the entire organization. For assessing perceived quality, the step-by-step procedure used by the Strategic Planning Institute may be followed:

1. A meeting is held, in which a multifunctional team of managers and staff specialists identify the non-price product and service attributes that affect customer buying decisions. For an office equipment product, these might include durability, maintenance costs, flexibility, credit terms, and appearance.
2. The team is then asked to assign "importance weights" for each attribute representing their relative decisions. These relative importance weights sum to 100. (For markets in which there are important segments with different importance weights, separate weights are assigned to each segment.)
3. The management team creates its business unit's product line, and those of leading competitors, on each of the performance dimensions identified in Step 1. From these attribute-by-attribute ratings, each weighted by its respective importance weight, an overall relative quality score is constructed.

4. The overall relative quality score and other measures of competitive position (relative price and market share) and financial performance (ROI, ROS, and ROE) are validated against benchmarks based on the experience of "look-alike" businesses in similar strategic positions in order to check the internal consistency of strategic and financial data and confirm the business and market definition.

5. Finally, the management team tests its plans and budgets for reality, develops a blueprint for improving market perceived quality, relative to competitors', and calibrates the financial payoff.

In many cases, the judgmental ratings assigned by the management team are tested (and, when appropriate, modified) by collecting ratings from customers via field interviews.[53]

This approach to assessing relative quality is similar to the multiattribute methods used in marketing research. These research methods are, however, employed primarily for evaluating or comparing individual products (actual or prospective), whereas the scores here apply to a business unit's entire product line.

Attaining adequate levels of excellence and customer satisfaction often requires significant cultural change; that is, change in decision-making processes, interfunctional relationships, and the attitudes of each member of the company. In other words, achieving total quality objectives requires teamwork and cooperation. People are encouraged and rewarded for doing their jobs right the first time rather than for their success in resolving crises. People are empowered to make decisions and instilled with the feeling that quality is everyone's responsibility.

The following are the keys to success in achieving world-class total quality. First, the program requires unequivocal support of top management. The second key to success is understanding customer need. The third key is to fix the business process, if there are gaps in meeting customer needs. The fourth key is to compress cycle time to avoid bureaucratic hassles and delays. The next is empowering people so that they are able to exert their best talents. Further, measurement and reward systems must be reassessed and revamped to recognize people. Finally, the total quality program should be a continuous concern, a constant focus on identifying and eliminating waste and inefficiency throughout the organization.

Organizationally, the single most important aspect of implementing a quality strategy is to maintain a close liaison with the customer. Honda's experience in this matter in designing the new Accord is noteworthy:

When Honda's engineers began to design the third-generation (or 1986) Accord in the early 1980s, they did not start with a sketch of a car. The engineers started with a concept—"man maximum, machine minimum" that captured in a short, evocative phrase the way they wanted customers to feel about the car. The concept and the car have been remarkably successful: since 1982, the Accord has been one of the best-selling cars in the United States; in 1989, it was the top-selling car. Yet when it was time to design the 1990 Accord, Honda listened to the market, not to its own success. Market trends were indicating a shift away from sporty sedans toward family models. To satisfy future customers' expectations and to reposition the Accord, moving it up-market just a bit, the 1990 model would have to send a new set of product messages—"an adult sense of reliability." The ideal family car would allow the driver to transport family and friends with confidence, whatever the weather or road conditions; passengers would always feel safe and secure.

This message was still too abstract to guide the engineers who would later be making concrete choices about the new Accord's specifications, parts, and manufacturing processes. So the next step was finding an image that would personify the car's message to consumers. The image that managers emerged with was "a rugby player in a business suit." It evoked rugged, physical contact, sportsmanship, and gentlemanly behavior—disparate qualities the new car would have to convey. The image was also concrete enough to translate clearly into design details. The decision to replace the old Accord's retractable head lamps with headlights made with a pioneering technology developed by Honda's supplier, Stanley, is a good example. To the designers and engineers, the new lights' totally transparent cover glass symbolized the will of a rugby player looking into the future calmly, with clear eyes.

The next and last step in creating the Accord's product concept was to break down the rugby player image into specific attributes the new car would have to possess. Five sets of key words captured what the product leader envisioned: "open minded," "friendly communication," "tough spirit," "stress-free," and "love forever." Individually and as a whole, these key words reinforced the car's message to consumers. "Tough spirit" in the car, for example, meant maneuverability, power, and sure handling in extreme driving conditions, while "love forever" translated into long-term reliability and customer satisfaction. Throughout the course of the project, these phrases provided a kind of shorthand to help people make coherent design and hardware choices in the face of competing demands.[54]

There are three generic approaches to improving quality performance: catching up, pulling ahead, and leapfrogging. Catching up involves restoring those aspects about which the firm has been behind to standard. Catching up is a defensive strategy where the emphasis is either to be as good as the competition or to barely meet market requirements. Pulling ahead, going further than the customer asks or achieving superiority over the competition, provides a firm competitive advantage that may lead to greater profitability. Thus, it makes sense to resist the temptation to focus on just catching up and to find a way to make a sustainable move to pull ahead. Finally, leapfrogging involves negating competitive disadvantage, that is, creating a sustainable competitive advantage through differentiation. In other words, leapfrogging comprises coming from behind and getting ahead of the competition through providing a quality product in keeping with customer demands. For example, by leapfrogging Detroit on several key attributes, Japanese companies rolled further up the "quality-for-price curve"; that is, they shifted into better value positions.

Several benefits accrue to businesses that offer superior perceived quality, including stronger customer loyalty, more repeat purchases, less vulnerability to price wars, ability to command higher relative price without affecting share, lower marketing costs, and share improvements.

Customer service has come to occupy an important place in today's competitive market. Invariably, customers want personal service, the kind of service delivered by live bodies behind a sales counter, a human voice at the other end of a telephone, or people in the teller's cage at the bank. Paying attention to the customer is not a new concept. In the 1950s, General Motors went all the way toward consumer satisfaction by designing cars for every lifestyle and pocketbook, a breakthrough for an industry that had been largely driven by production needs ever since Henry Ford promised to deliver any color car as long as it was black. General Motors rode its insights into customers' needs to a 52 percent share of the U.S. car market in 1962.[55] But with a booming economy, a rising population, and virtually no foreign competition, many U.S. companies had it too easy. Through the 1960s and into the 1970s, many U.S. car makers could sell just about anything they could produce. With customers seemingly satisfied, management concentrated on cutting production costs and making splashy acquisitions. To manage these growing behemoths, CEOs turned to strategic planning, which focused on winning market share, not on getting in touch with remote customers. Markets came to be defined as aggregations of competitors, not as customers.

In recent times, Japanese companies were the first to recognize a problem. They started to rescue customers from the limbo of so-so merchandise and take-it-or-leave-it service. They built loyalty among U.S. car buyers by assiduously uncovering and accommodating customer needs. The growing influence of Japanese firms as well as demographics and hard economic times have forced American companies to realize the need to listen to customers.

Creative changes in service can make the difference. For example, companies offering better service can charge 10 percent more for their products than competitors.[56] B2B marketers have long known that personal relationships between senior executives and sales representative with customers can help in various ways. Many companies attach so much importance to service that they require their senior managers to put in time at the front lines. For example, Xerox requires that its executives spend one day a month taking complaints from customers about machines, bills, and service. Similarly, at Hyatt Hotels, senior executives put in time as bellhops.[57]

Briefly, a company must decide who it wants to serve, discover what those customers want, and set a strategy that single-mindedly provides that service to those customers. With such clearly articulated goals, top management can give frontline employees responsibility for responding instantly to customer needs in those crucial moments that determine the company's success or failure. The following episode, which underlines Scandinavian Airlines' emphasis on service, shows how far a company can go to stand by the customer.

Rudy Peterson was an American businessman staying at the Grand Hotel in Stockholm. Arriving at Stockholm's Arlanda airport for an important day trip with a colleague to Copenhagen on a Scandinavian Airlines (SAS) flight, he realized he'd left his ticket in his hotel room.

Everyone knows you can't board an airplane without a ticket, so Rudy Peterson resigned himself to missing the flight and his business meeting in Copenhagen. But when he explained his dilemma to the ticket agent, he got a pleasant surprise. "Don't worry, Mr. Peterson," she said with a smile. "Here's your boarding card. I'll insert a temporary ticket in here. If you just tell me your room number at the Grand Hotel and your destination in Copenhagen, I'll take care of the rest."

While Rudy and his colleague waited in the passenger lounge, the ticket agent dialed the hotel. A bellhop checked the room and found the ticket. The ticket agent then sent an SAS limo to retrieve it from the hotel and bring it directly to her. They moved so quickly that the ticket arrived before the

Copenhagen flight departed. No one was more surprised than Rudy Peterson when the flight attendant approached him and said calmly, "Mr. Peterson? Here's your ticket."

What would have happened at a more traditional airline? Most airline manuals are clear: "No ticket, no flight." At best, the ticket agent would have informed her supervisor of the problem, but Rudy Peterson almost certainly would have missed his flight. Instead, because of the way SAS handled his situation, he was both impressed and on time for his meeting.[58]

The SAS experience shows how far a business must be willing to go to become a truly customer-driven company, a company that recognizes that its only true assets are satisfied customers, all of whom expect to be treated as individuals.

Many firms argue that service by definition is difficult to guarantee. Services are generally delivered by human beings, who are less predictable than machines. Services are also usually produced at the same time that they are consumed. Although there can be exceptions to the rule, service can be guaranteed in any field. Consider the guarantee offered by "Bugs" Burger Bug Killers (BBBK), a Miami-based pest extermination company, a division of S.C. Johnson and Sons:

Most of BBBK's competitors claim that they will reduce pests to "acceptable levels"; BBBK promises to eliminate them entirely. Its service guarantee to hotel and restaurant clients promises:

- You don't owe one penny until all pests on your premises have been eradicated.
- If you are ever dissatisfied with BBBK's service, you will receive a refund for up to 12 months of the company's services plus fees for another exterminator of your choice for the next year.
- If a guest spots a pest on your premises, BBBK will pay for the guest's meal or room, send a letter of apology, and pay for a future meal or stay.
- If your facility is closed down due to the presence of roaches or rodents, BBBK will pay any fines, as well as all lost profits, plus $5,000. In short, BBBK says, "If we don't satisfy you 100%, we don't take your money."[59]

The company's service program has been extremely successful. It charges up to 10 times more than its competitors and yet has a disproportionately high market share in its operating areas.

In designing a good service program, a company should be conversant with a number of important trends. First, most customers don't read (e.g., customers don't read assembly and operation instructions). Second, customers don't understand ownership responsibilities (e.g., some hotels require customers to program their own wake-up calls into a confusing computerized system). Third, high technology and product complexity make product differentiation difficult (i.e., with like products, better service can become an important differentiating factor). Fourth, consumers have lower confidence and expectations for products and services (i.e., customer service can have an enormous impact on consumer confidence). Fifth, high-quality service has become a product attribute (i.e., consumers rate qualitative service factors as more important than product cost and features). Sixth, consumer attention is drawn to negative publicity (i.e., negative word of mouth is extremely detrimental). Seventh, consumers believe they are not getting their money's worth.

Improved customer service can play a major role in changing customer perceptions about a product and its value and can directly affect a company's success and profitability. The quality of service a company provides depends largely on people, not only those with direct customer responsibility but also with managers, supervisors, and support staff. Thus, success in providing adequate service largely depends on preparing employees for it.

When a product market changes quickly, companies must respond quickly if they want to preserve their positions. In today's changing markets, time-based strategy that aims to beat the competition has assumed new dimensions.

GE has cut the time to deliver a custom-made industrial circuit breaker box from three weeks to three days. In the past, AT&T needed two years to design a new phone; now it needs only one year. Motorola used to take three weeks to turn out electronic pagers after the factory received the order; now it takes two hours.[60]

Time-based strategy brings about important competitive benefits. Market share grows because customers love getting their orders now. Inventories of finished goods shrink because they are not necessary to ensure quick delivery; the fastest manufacturers can make and ship an order the day it is received. For this and other reasons, costs fall. Many employees become satisfied because they are working for a more responsive, more successful company and because speeding operations requires giving them more flexibility and responsibility. Quality also improves. Briefly, doing it fast forces a firm to do it right the first time.

Speed can also pay off in product development even if it means going over budget by as much as fifty percent. For example, a model developed by McKinsey and Co. shows that high-tech products that come to market on budget but six months late earn 33 percent less profit over five years. In contrast, coming out fifty percent over budget but on time cuts profits only by four percent.[61]

To implement a time-based strategy, the entire production process must be redesigned for speed. GE's experience is relevant here. Its circuit breaker business was old and stagnant. Market growth was slow and Siemens and Westinghouse were strong competitors. GE assembled a team of manufacturing, design, and marketing experts to focus on overhauling the entire process. The goal was to cut the time between order and delivery from three weeks to three days. Six plants around the United States were producing circuit breaker boxes. The team consolidated production into one plant and automated its facilities. But the team did not automate operations as they were. In the old system, engineers custom-designed each box, a task that took about a week. Engineers chose from 28,000 unique parts to create a box. To set up an automated system to handle that many parts would have been a nightmare. The design team reduced the number of parts to 1,275, making most parts interchangeable. Even with this drastic reduction in parts, customers were still given 40,000 different sizes, shapes, and configurations from which to choose.

The team also devised a way to phase out the engineers, by replacing them with computers. Now a salesperson enters the specifications for a circuit breaker into a computer at GE's main office and the order flows to a computer at the plant, which automatically programs factory machines to custom-make the order with minimum waste.

Although these advances are indeed impressive, the team still had to conquer another source of delay—solving problems and making decisions on the factory floor. The solution was to eliminate all line supervisors and quality inspectors, reducing the organizational layers between worker and plant manager from three to one. Everything middle managers used to handle—vacation scheduling, quality, work rules—became the responsibility of the 129 workers on the floor, who were divided into teams of fifteen to twenty. It worked. The more responsibility GE gave the workers, the faster problems were solved and decisions were made.

The results: The plant that used to have a two-month backlog of orders now works with a two-day backlog. Productivity has increased twenty percent over the past year. Manufacturing costs have dropped thirty percent, or $5.5 million a year, and return on investment is running at over twenty percent. The speed of delivery for a higher-quality product with more features has shrunk from three weeks to three days. And GE is gaining share in a flat market.[62]

Another area ripe for time-based strategy is the administrative/approval area. According to the Thomas Group, a Dallas-based consulting firm specializing in speed, manufacturing typically takes only five to twenty percent of the total time that is needed to get an order for a given product to market; the rest is administrative.[63] For example, at Adca Bank, a subsidiary of West Germany's Reebobank (with assets of $90 billion), an application for a loan used to go through numerous layers of bureaucracy. A branch would send a loan application to a loan officer at headquarters, who would look at it and change it. Then the loan officer's manager would look at the application and change it, and so on. The bank eventually got rid of five layers of management and gave officers in all branches more authority to make loans. It used to take 24 managers to approve a loan. Now it takes twelve.

Teamwork seems to be the key ingredient among the fastest companies. Nearly all of them form multi-department teams. AT&T formed teams of six to twelve members, including engineers, manufacturers, and marketers, with complete authority to make every decision about how a product would look, work, be made, and cost. At AT&T the key was setting rigid speed requirements, such as six weeks, and leaving the rest to the team. Teams could meet these strict deadlines because they did not need to send each decision up the line for approval. With this new approach, AT&T cut development time for its new 4200 phone from two years to just a year while lowering costs and increasing quality.

Application of time-based strategy to distribution is equally important. Even the world's fastest factory cannot provide much of a competitive advantage if everything it produces gets snagged in the distribution chain. For example, Benetton takes its distribution very seriously and has created an electronic loop that links sales agent, factory, and warehouse. If a saleswoman in one of Benetton's Los Angeles shops finds that she is starting to run out of a best-selling sweater, she calls one of Benetton's 80 sales agents, who enters the order in a personal computer, which sends it to a mainframe in Italy. The mainframe computer, which has all of the measurements for the sweater, sets the knitting machines in motion. Once the sweaters are finished, workers box them up and label the box with a bar code containing the Los Angeles address. The box then goes into the warehouse. The computer next sends a robot flying. The robot finds the box and any others going to Los Angeles, picks them up, and loads them onto a truck. Including manufacturing time, Benetton can get an order to Los Angeles in four weeks.

Implementation of time-based strategy requires a number of steps. First, start from scratch (i.e., set a time goal and revamp entire operations to meet this goal rather than simply improving efficiency in current operations). Second, wipe out approvals (i.e., cut down bureaucratic layers of control and let people make decisions on the spot). Third, emphasize teamwork (i.e., establish multidepartment teams to handle the work). Fourth, worship the schedule (i.e., nothing short of disaster should be a valid excuse for delay). Fifth, develop time-effective distribution (i.e., snags in distribution must be simultaneously worked out). Sixth, put speed in the culture (i.e., train people in the company at all levels to understand and appreciate the significance of speed).

The advantages of speed are undeniably impressive. Although it is a common precept that time is money, in practice, companies have paid only lip service to it. The time it took to do a job, whatever the amount, was considered a necessity to meet organizational requirements, systems, procedures, and hierarchical relationships. Now, however, there is a new realization that time saved is a strategic factor for gaining competitive advantage. Companies that grasp and appreciate the unprecedented advantages of getting new products to market sooner and orders to customers faster hold the key for achieving competitive preeminence today and beyond.

SUMMARY

Product strategies reflect the mission of the business unit and the business it is in. Following the marketing concept, the choice of product strategy should bear a close relationship to the market strategy of the company. The various product strategies and the alternatives under each strategy that were discussed in this chapter are outlined below:

1. Product-positioning strategy

   a. Positioning a single brand
   b. Positioning multiple brands

2. Product-repositioning strategy

   a. Repositioning among existing customers
   b. Repositioning among new users
   c. Repositioning for new uses

3. Product-overlap strategy

   a. Competing brands
   b. Private labeling
   c. Dealing with original-equipment manufacturers (OEMs)

4. Product-scope strategy

   a. Single product
   b. Multiple products
   c. System of products

5. Product-design strategy

   a. Standard products
   b. Customized products
   c. Standard product with modifications

6. Product-elimination strategy

   a. Harvesting
   b. Line simplification
   c. Total-line divestment

7. New-product strategy

   a. Product improvement/modification
   b. Product imitation
   c. Product innovation

8. Diversification strategy

   a. Concentric diversification
   b. Horizontal diversification
   c. Conglomerate diversification

9. Value-marketing strategy

   a. Quality strategy
   b. Customer-service strategy
   c. Time-based strategy

The nature of different strategies was discussed, and their relevance for different types of companies was examined. Adaptations of different strategies in practice were illustrated with citations from published sources.

DISCUSSION QUESTIONS

1. Discuss how a business unit may avoid problems of cannibalism among competing brands.
2. Conceptualize how a lagging brand (assume a grocery product) may be repositioned for new uses.
3. What criteria may be employed to determine the viable position for a brand in the market?
4. What conditions justify a company's dealing in multiple products?
5. Are there reasons other than profitability for eliminating a product? Discuss.
6. What factors must be weighed to determine the viability of divesting an entire product line?
7. Under what circumstances is it desirable to adopt a product-imitation strategy?

NOTES

1. Edward H. Kolcum, "Gould Will Use Same Market Strategy under Encore Ownership," *Aviation Week and Space Technology,* April 17, 1989, p. 53.
2. Theodore Levitt, "Marketing Success through Differentiation of Anything," *Harvard Business Review,* January–February 1980, p. 82.
3. See Frank Rose, "Mickey Online," *Fortune,* September 28, 1995, p. 273.
4. Daren Rovell, *First in Thirst* (Saranac Lake, NY: Amacom Books, 2007).
5. Philip Kotler, *Marketing Management,* 11th ed. (Englewood Cliffs, NJ: Prentice-Hall, 2002): 314.
6. Subhash C. Jain, "Global Competitiveness in the Beer Industry: A Case Study," Food Marketing Policy Center, University of Connecticut, Research Report No. 28, November 1994.
7. Prudential Securities Incorporated, *Anheuser-Busch Company Update,* June 1993.
8. Ira Teinowitz, "Beer Battle Heats Up: New Brands Score," *Advertising Age,* August 13, 1990, p. 21.
9. Roger A. Kerin, Michael G. Harvey, and James T. Rothe, "Cannibalism and New Product Development," *Business Horizons,* October 1978, p. 31.

10. Alison Fahey, "A&W Aims Younger," *Advertising Age,* January 27, 1992, p. 12.

11. Ira Teinowitz, "Beer Battle Heats Up: New Brands Score," *Advertising Age,* August 13, 1990, p. 21.

12. Eric Morgenthaler, "People Are So Goofy About Disney World, They Marry There," *The Wall Street Journal,* October 28, 1992, p. A1.

13. Based on an interview with a Gillette executive. See also Lawrence Ingrassia, "Schick Razor to Try for Edge against Gillette," *The Wall Street Journal,* October 9, 1990, p. B1.

14. See "The Gillette Company," in Subhash C. Jain, *International Marketing Management*, 6th edition, (Storrs, CT: Digital Publishing Company, 1999): 852–856.

15. "Sticky Label?" *The Economist,* July 25, 1998, p. 63.

16. Colmetta Y. Coleman, "Dr. Pop and Frisk Help a Grocery Chain Grow," *The Wall Street Journal,* April 13, 1998, p. B1.

17. Alex Taylor III, "Kodak Scrambles to Reform," *Fortune,* March 3, 1986, p. 34.

18. "From the Microbrewers Who Brought You Bud, Coors . . . ," *BusinessWeek,* April 24, 1995, p. 66.

19. Justin Martin, "Give 'em Exactly What They Want," *Fortune,* November 1997, p. 283.

20. Jeffrey Bodenstab, "An Automaker Tries the Dell Way," *The Wall Street Journal,* August 30, 1999, p. A26.

21. Richard T. Hise, A. Parasuraman, and Ramaswamy Viswanathan, "Product Elimination: The Neglected Management Responsibility," *Journal of Business Strategy*, Spring 1984, pp. 56–63.

22. Gregory A. Patterson and Christina Duff, "Sears Trims Operations, Ending an Era," *The Wall Street Journal,* January 26, 1993, p. B1.

23. Linda Grant, "Why Kodak Still Isn't Fixed," *Fortune,* May 11, 1998, p. 179.

24. "How Sweet It Is to Be out from under Beatrice's Thumb," *BusinessWeek,* May 9, 1988, p. 98.

25. Christine Moorman and Anne S. Miner, "The Convergence of Planning and Execution: Improvisation in New Product Development," *Journal of Marketing*, July 1998, pp. 1–20.

26. "Ballpoint Perfume," *Forbes*, July 3, 2000, p. 154.

27. *New Products Management for the 1980s* (New York: Booz, Allen, & Hamilton Inc., 1982): 14.

28. Justin Martin, "Ignore Your Customer," *Fortune,* May 1, 1995, p. 121.

29. *New Products Management for the 1980s, op. cit.*, p. 18.

30. Bro Uttal, "Eastman Kodak's Orderly Two-Front War," *Fortune,* September 1976, p. 123.

31. Linda Grant, *Fortune,* "Why Kodak Still Isn't Fixed." *Also see Eastman Kodak Company's Annual Report* for 1998.

32. Patricia Sellers, "A Boring Brand Can Be Beautiful," *Fortune,* November 18, 1991, p. 48.

33. Kenichi Ohmae, "Effective Strategies for Competitive Success," *McKinsey Quarterly,* Winter 1978, pp. 56–57.

34. Nikhil Deogun, "Pepsi Takes Aim at Coke With New One-Calorie Drink," *The Wall Street Journal,* October 6, 1998, p. B4.

35. "From the Microbrewers Who Brought You Bud, Coors. . . . ," *BusinessWeek*, May 15, 1995, p. 66.

36. "The Joy of Laundry," *BusinessWeek*, July 17, 2000, p. 8.

37. "Flops," *BusinessWeek,* August 16, 1993, p. 76.

38. Ronald Alsop, "Consumer-Product Giants Relying on "Intrapreneurs' in New Ventures," *The Wall Street Journal,* April 22, 1988, p. 35.

39. Peter Vanderwicken, "P&G's Secret Ingredient," *Fortune,* July 1974, p. 75. *See also* "The Miracle Company," *BusinessWeek,* October 19, 1987 p. 84.

40. *The Economist,* January 23, 1988, p. 75.

41. Laurie Hays, "Du Pont's Difficulties in Selling Kevlar Show Hurdles of Innovation," *The Wall Street Journal,* September 29, 1987, p. 1. See also: E. I. du Pont de Nemours and Company, *Annual Report for 2001.*

42. "Coke's Man on the Spot," *BusinessWeek,* July 25, 1985, p. 56.

43. E. Ralph Biggadike, "The Risky Business of Diversification," *Harvard Business Review,* May–June 1979, pp. 103–111. See also: E. Ralph Biggadike, *Corporate Diversification: Entry Strategy and Performance* (Boston: Division of Research, Harvard Business School, 1979).

44. "A Revved-up Market for Diesel Engine Makers," *BusinessWeek,* February 5, 1979, p. 76.

45. Richard Gibson, "Restaurant Rescuer Don Smith Hopes for More Than Potluck at Friendly's," *The Wall Street Journal,* August 11, 1988, p. 34.

46. Michael E. Porter, "From Competitive Advantage to Corporate Strategy," *McKinsey Quarterly*, Spring 1988, p. 43.

47. Nikhil Deogun and Betsy McKay, "Coke and P&G Plan to Create $4.2 Billion Juice and Snack Company," *The Wall Street Journal*, February 21, 2001, p. B1.

48. "Hopelessly Seeking Synergy," *The Economist,* August 20, 1994, p. 53.

49. "Barbie's Secret Plan for World Domination," *Fortune,* November 23, 1998, p. 38.

50. "Thinking Outside the Big Box," *BusinessWeek*, August 11, 2003, p. 63.

51. "Who Says the Conglomerate Is Dead?" *BusinessWeek,* January 23, 1995, p. 92.

52. George T. Haley and Chin Tiong Tan (1996), "The Black Hole of South-East Asia: Strategic Decision-Making in an Informational Void," *Management Decision*, Vol. 34, No. 9, pp. 37–48; George T. Haley and Chin Tiong Tan (1999), "East versus West: Strategic Marketing Management Meets the Asian Networks," *Journal of Business & Industrial Marketing*, Vol. 14, No. 2, pp. 91–101; George T. Haley, Chin Tiong Tan and Usha C. V. Haley (1998), *New Asian Emperors: The Overseas Chinese, their Strategies and Competitive Advantages* (Oxford, Butterworth-Heinemann); George T. Haley and Usha C. V. Haley (1999), "Managing Effectively in Southeast and East Asia," *General Management Review*, "A Special Compilation by the Indian Institute of Management, Calcutta," Vol. 1, No. 1, pp. 37–46; George T. Haley and Usha C. V. Haley (1998), "Boxing with Shadows: Competing Effectively with the Overseas Chinese and Overseas Indian Business Networks in the Asian Arena," *Journal of Organizational Change Management*, Vol. 11, No. 4, pp. 301–320; George T. Haley, Usha C. V. Haley and Chin Tiong Tan (2004), *The Chinese Tao of Business: The Logic of Successful Business Strategy* (Singapore & New York: John Wiley & Sons).

53. Bradley T. Grale and Robert D. Buzzell, "Market Perceived Quality: Key Strategic Concept," *Planning Review*, March–April 1989, p. 11.

54. Kim B. Clark and Takahiro Fujimoto, "The Power of Product Integrity," *Harvard Business Review*, November–December 1990, p. 110.

55. Frank Rose, "Now Quality Means Service Too," *Fortune,* April 22, 1991, p. 98.

56. "King Customer," *BusinessWeek,* March 12, 1990, p. 90.

57. Frank Rose, "Now Quality Means Service Too," *Fortune,* April 22, 1991, p. 100.

58. Jan Carlzon, "Putting the Customer First: The Key to Service Strategy," *McKinsey Quarterly*, Summer 1987, pp. 38–39.

59. Christopher W. L. Hart, "The Power of Unconditional Service Guarantees," *Harvard Business Review*, July–August 1988, p. 54.

60. Brian Dumaine, "How Managers Can Succeed through Speed," *Fortune,* February 13, 1989, p. 54. *See also:* Warren B. Brown and Necmi Karagozoglu, "Leading the Product Development," *Academy of Management Executive*, 1993, pp. 36–47.

61. Edward G. Krubasik, "Customize Your Product Development," *Harvard Business Review,* November–December 1989, pp. 46–52.

62. Dumaine, "How Managers Can Succeed through Speed," *op. cit.*, pp. 57–58. *See also:* "Mattel's Wild Race to Market," *BusinessWeek,* February 12, 1994, p. 62.

63. This example and the ones that follow are based on Dumaine, "How Managers Can Succeed through Speed," *op. cit.*

APPENDIX: PERSPECTIVES OF PRODUCT STRATEGIES

Definition: Placing a brand in that part of the market where it will have a favorable reception compared with competing brands.

Objectives: (a) To position the product in the market so that it stands apart from competing brands. (b) To position the product so that it tells customers what you stand for, what you are, and how you would like customers to evaluate you. In the case of positioning multiple brands: (a) To seek growth by offering varied products in differing segments of the market. (b) To avoid competitive threats to a single brand.

Requirements: Use of marketing mix variables, especially design and communication efforts. (a) Successful management of a single brand requires positioning the brand in the market so that it can stand competition from the toughest rival and maintaining its unique position by creating the aura of a distinctive product. (b) Successful management of multiple brands requires careful positioning in the market so that multiple brands do not compete with nor cannibalize each other. Thus it is important to be careful in segmenting the market and to position an individual product as uniquely suited to a particular segment through design and promotion.

Expected Results: (a) Meet as much as possible the needs of specific segments of the market. (b) Limit sudden changes in sales. (c) Make customers faithful to the brands.

Definition: Reviewing the current positioning of the product and its marketing mix and seeking a new position for it that seems more appropriate.

Objectives: (a) To increase the life of the product. (b) To correct an original positioning mistake.

Requirements: (a) If this strategy is directed toward existing customers, repositioning is sought through promotion of more varied uses of the product. (b) If the business unit wants to reach new users, this strategy requires that the product be presented with a different twist to the people who have not been favorably inclined toward it. In doing so, care should be taken to see that, in the process of enticing new customers, current ones are not alienated. (c) If this strategy aims at presenting new uses of the product, it requires searching for latent uses of the product, if any. Although all products may not have latent uses, there are products that may be used for purposes not originally intended.

Expected Results: (a) Among existing customers: increase in sales growth and profitability. (b) Among new users: enlargement of the overall market, thus putting the product on a growth route, and increased profitability. (c) New product uses: increased sales, market share, and profitability.

Definition: Competing against one's own brand through introduction of competing products, use of private labeling, and selling to original-equipment manufacturers.

Objectives: (a) To attract more customers to the product and thereby increase the overall market. (b) To work at full capacity and spread overhead. (c) To sell to competitors; to realize economies of scale and cost reduction.

Requirements: (a) Each competing product must have its own marketing organization to compete in the market. (b) Private brands should not become profit drains. (c) Each brand should find its special niche in the market. If that doesn't happen, it will create confusion among customers and sales will be hurt. (d) In the long run, one of the brands may be withdrawn, yielding its position to the other brand.

Expected Results: (a) Increased market share. (b) Increased growth.

Definition: The product-scope strategy deals with the perspectives of the product mix of a company. The product-scope strategy is determined by taking into account the overall mission of the business unit. The company may adopt a single-product strategy, a multiple-product strategy, or a system-of-products strategy.

Objectives: (a) Single product: to increase economies of scale by developing specialization. (b) Multiple products: to cover the risk of potential obsolescence of the single product by adding additional products. (c) System of products: to increase the dependence of the customer on the company's products as well as to prevent competitors from moving into the market.

Requirements: (a) Single product: company must stay up-to-date on the product and even become the technology leader to avoid obsolescence. (b) Multiple products: products must complement one another in a portfolio of products. (c) System of products: company must have a close understanding of customer needs and uses of the products.

Expected Results: Increased growth, market share, and profits with all three strategies. With system-of-products strategy, the company achieves monopolistic control over the market, which may lead to some problems with the Justice Department, and enlarges the concept of its product/market opportunities.

Definition: The product-design strategy deals with the degree of standardization of a product. The company has a choice among the following strategic options: standard product, customized product, and standard product with modifications.

Objectives: (a) Standard product: to increase economies of scale of the company. (b) Customized product: to compete against mass producers of standardized products through product-design flexibility. (c) Standard product with modifications: to combine the benefits of the two previous strategies.

Requirements: Close analysis of product/market perspectives and environmental changes, especially technological changes.

Expected Results: Increase in growth, market share, and profits. In addition, the third strategy allows the company to keep close contacts with the market and gain experience in developing new standard products.

Definition: Cuts in the composition of a company's business unit product portfolio by pruning the number of products within a line or by totally divesting a division or business.

Objectives: To eliminate undesirable products because their contribution to fixed cost and profit is too low, because their future performance looks grim, or because they do not fit in the business's overall strategy. The product-elimination strategy aims at shaping the best possible mix of products and balancing the total business.

Requirements: No special resources are required to eliminate a product or a division. However, because it is impossible to reverse the decision once the elimination has been achieved, an in-depth analysis must be done to determine (a) the causes of current problems; (b) the possible alternatives, other than elimination, that may solve problems (e.g., Are any improvements in the marketing mix possible?); and (c) the repercussions that elimination may have on remaining products or units (e.g., Is the product being considered for elimination complementary to another product in the portfolio? What are the side effects on the company's image? What are the social costs of an elimination?).

Expected Results: In the short run, cost savings from production runs, reduced inventories, and in some cases an improved return on investment can be expected. In the long run, the sales of the remaining products may increase because more efforts are now concentrated on them.

Definition: A set of operations that introduces (a) within the business, a product new to its previous line of products; (b) on the market, a product that provides a new type of satisfaction. Three alternatives emerge from the above: product improvement/modification, product imitation, and product innovation.

Objectives: To meet new needs and to sustain competitive pressures on existing products. In the first case, the new-product strategy is an offensive one; in the second case, it is a defensive one.

Requirements: A new-product strategy is difficult to implement if a "new product development system" does not exist within a company. Five components of this system should be assessed: (a) corporate aspirations toward new products, (b) organizational openness to creativity, (c) environmental favor toward creativity, (d) screening method for new ideas, and (e) evaluation process.

Expected Results: Increased market share and profitability.

Definition: Developing unfamiliar products and markets through (a) concentric diversification (products introduced are related to existing ones in terms of marketing or technology), (b) horizontal diversification (new products are unrelated to existing ones but are sold to the same customers), and (c) conglomerate diversification (products are entirely new).

Objectives: Diversification strategies respond to the desire for (a) growth when current products/markets have reached maturity, (b) stability by spreading the risks of fluctuations in earnings, (c) security when the company may fear backward integration from one of its major customers, and (d) credibility to have more weight in capital markets.

Requirements: In order to reduce the risks inherent in a diversification strategy, a business unit should (a) diversify its activities only if current product/market opportunities are limited, (b) have good knowledge of the area in which it diversifies, (c) provide the products introduced with adequate support, and (d) forecast the effects of diversification on existing lines of products.

Expected Results: (a) Increase in sales. (b) Greater profitability and flexibility.

Definition: The value-marketing strategy concerns delivering on promises made for the product or service. These promises involve product quality, customer service, and meeting time commitments.

Objectives: Value-marketing strategies are directed toward seeking total customer satisfaction. It means striving for excellence to meet customer expectations.

Requirements: (a) Examine customer value perspectives. (b) Design programs to meet customer quality, service, and time requirements. (c) Train employees and distributors to deliver on promises.

Expected Results: This strategy enhances customer satisfaction, which leads to customer loyalty and, hence, to higher market share. This strategy makes the firm less vulnerable to price wars, permitting the firm to charge higher prices and, thus, earn higher profits.

Good is not good where better is expected.

Chapter Outline

15.1 Review of Pricing Factors
  15.1.1 Industry Demand Elasticity
    Business-to-Business Markets
  15.1.2 Demand for an Individual
    Firm's Products
15.2 Pricing Strategy for New Products
**15.3 Pricing Strategies for Established
  Products**
15.4 Price-Flexibility Strategy
15.5 Product Line-Pricing Strategy
15.6 Leasing Strategy
15.7 Bundling-Pricing Strategy
15.8 Price-Leadership Strategy
**15.9 Pricing Strategy to Build Market
  Share**

Chapter 15

Pricing Strategies

Pricing has traditionally been considered a me-too variable in marketing strategy. The stable economic conditions that prevailed during the 1960s may be particularly responsible for the low status ascribed to the pricing variable. Strategically, the function of pricing has been to provide adequate return on investment. Thus, the timeworn cost-plus method of pricing and its sophisticated version, return-on-investment pricing, have historically been the basis for arriving at price. In the 1970s, however, a variety of events gave a new twist to the task of making pricing decisions. Double-digit inflation, material shortages, the high cost of money, consumerism, and post-price controls behavior all made pricing important. Since then pricing continues to play a key role in formulating marketing strategy.

Despite the importance attached to it, effective pricing is not an easy task, even under the most favorable conditions. A large number of internal and external variables must be studied systematically before price can be set. For example, the reactions of a competitor often stand out as an important consideration in developing pricing strategy. Simply knowing that a competitor has a lower price is insufficient; a price strategist must know how much flexibility a competitor has in further lowering price. This presupposes a knowledge of the competitor's cost structure. In the dynamics of today's environment, however, where unexpected economic changes can render cost and revenue projections obsolete as soon as they are developed, pricing strategy is much more difficult to formulate.

This chapter provides a composite of pricing strategies. Each strategy is examined for its underlying assumptions and relevance in specific situations. The application of different strategies is illustrated with examples from pricing literature. The appendix at the end of this chapter summarizes each strategy by giving its definition, objectives, requirements, and expected results.

15.1 REVIEW OF PRICING FACTORS

Basically, a pricer needs to review four factors to arrive at a price: pricing objectives, cost, competition, and demand. This section briefly reviews these factors, which underlie every pricing strategy alternative. Many business people cite a common rule of thumb when considering pricing strategy: "One's costs set the minimum price one can charge, one's competitors the maximum."

Broadly speaking, pricing objectives can be either profit oriented or volume oriented. The profit-oriented objective may be defined either in terms of desired net profit percentage or as a target return on investment. The latter objective has been more popular among large corporations. The volume-oriented objective may be stated as the percentage of market share that the firm would like to achieve. Alternatively, it may simply be stated as the desired sales growth rate. Many firms also consider the maintenance of a stable price as a pricing goal. Particularly in cyclical industries, price stability helps to sustain the confidence of customers and thus keeps operations running smoothly through peaks and valleys.

For many firms, there can be pricing objectives other than those of profitability and volume, as shown in Exhibit 15.1. Each firm should evaluate different objectives and choose its own priorities in the context

Exhibit 15.1 Potential Pricing Objectives	1. Maximum long-run profits 2. Maximum short-run profits 3. Growth 4. Stabilize market 5. Desensitize customers to price 6. Maintain price-leadership arrangement 7. Discourage entrants 8. Speed exit of marginal firms 9. Avoid government investigation and control 10. Maintain loyalty of middlemen and get their sales support 11. Avoid demands for "more" from suppliers 12. Enhance image of firm and its offerings 13. Be regarded as "fair" by customers (ultimate) 14. Create interest and excitement about the item 15. Be considered trustworthy and reliable by rivals 16. Help in the sale of weak items in the line 17. Discourage others from cutting prices 18. Make a product "visible" 19. "Spoil market" to obtain high price for sale of business 20. Build traffic

Source: Alfred R. Oxenfeldt, "A Decision-Making Structure for Price Decisions," *Journal of Marketing* (January 1973): 50. Reprinted by permission of the American Marketing Association.

of the pricing problems that it may be facing. The following list contains illustrations of typical pricing problems:

1. Decline in sales.
2. Higher or lower prices than competitors.
3. Excessive pressure on middlemen to generate sales.
4. Imbalance in product line prices.
5. Distortion vis-à-vis the offering in the customer's perceptions of the firm's price.
6. Frequent changes in price without any relationship to environmental realities.

These problems suggest that a firm may have more than one pricing objective, even though these objectives may not be articulated as such. Essentially, pricing objectives deal directly or indirectly with three areas: profit (setting a high enough price to enable the company to earn an adequate margin for profit and reinvestment), competition (setting a low enough price to discourage competitors from adding capacity), and market share (setting a price below competition to gain market share).

As an example of pricing objectives, consider the goals that Apple Computer set for Macintosh:[1]

1. To make the product affordable and a good value for most college students.
2. To get certain target market segments to see the Macintosh as a better value than the IBM PC.
3. To encourage at least 90 percent of all Apple retailers to carry the Macintosh while providing a strong selling effort.
4. To accomplish all this within 18 months.

Fixed and variable costs are the major concerns of a pricer. In addition, the pricer may sometimes need to consider other types of costs, such as out-of-pocket costs, incremental costs, opportunity costs, controllable costs, and replacement costs.

To study the impact of costs on pricing strategy, the following three relationships may be considered: (a) the ratio of fixed costs to variable costs, (b) the economies of scale available to a firm, and (c) the cost structure of a firm vis-à-vis competitors. If the fixed costs of a company in comparison to its variable costs form a high proportion of its total costs, adding sales volume will be a great help in increasing earnings. Consider, for example, the case of the airlines, whose fixed costs are as high as 60 to 70 percent of total

Exhibit 15.2 Effect of Costs on Pricing	**Cost Pricing**

Cost Pricing

Costs	Product A	Product B
Labor (L)	$ 80	$120
Material (M)	160	80
Overhead (O)	40	80
Full cost (L + M + O)	280	280
Incremental cost (L + M)	240	200
Conversion cost (L + O)	120	200

Product Line Pricing

	Markup (M′)	Product A	Product B
Full-Cost Pricing			
P = FC + (M′)FC	20%	$336	$336
Incremental-Cost Pricing			
P = (L + M) + M′(L + M)	40%	336	280
Conversion-Cost Pricing			
P = (L + O) + M′(L + O)	180%	336	560

costs. Once fixed costs are recovered, any additional tickets sold add greatly to earnings. Such an industry is called volume sensitive. There are some industries, such as the consumer electronics industry, where variable costs constitute a higher proportion of total costs than do fixed costs. Such industries are price sensitive because even a small increase in price adds much to earnings.

If the economies of scale obtainable from a company's operations are substantial, the firm should plan to expand market share and, with respect to long-term prices, take expected declines in costs into account. Alternatively, if operations are expected to produce a decline in costs, then prices may be lowered in the long run to gain higher market share.

If a manufacturer is a low-cost producer relative to its competitors, it will earn additional profits by maintaining prices at competitive levels. The additional profits can be used to promote the product aggressively and increase the overall market share of the business. If, however, the costs of a manufacturer are high compared to those of its competitors, the manufacturer is in no position to reduce prices because that tactic may lead to a price war that it would most likely lose.

Different elements of cost must be differently related in setting price. Exhibit 15.2 shows, for example, how computations of full cost, incremental cost, and conversion cost may vary and how these costs affect product line prices. Exhibit 15.3 shows the procedure followed for setting target-return pricing.

Exhibit 15.4 shows the competitive information needed to formulate a pricing strategy. The information may be analyzed with reference to these competitive characteristics: number of firms in the industry, relative size of different members of the industry, product differentiation, and ease of entry.

In an industry where there is only one firm, there is no competitive activity. The firm is free to set any price, subject to constraints imposed by law. As an Illinois Bell executive said about pricing (before the

Exhibit 15.3 Computation of Target-Return Pricing		
Manufacturing capacity		200,000
Standard volume (80%)		160,000
Standard full cost before profit		$100/unit
Target profit		
Investment		$20,000,000
ROI target		20%
ROI target		$4,000,000
Profit per unit at standard ($4,000,000 ÷ 160,000)		$25/unit
Price		$125/unit

Exhibit 15.4 Competitive Information Needed for Pricing Strategy	1. Published competitive price lists and advertising 2. Competitive reaction to price moves in the past 3. Timing of competitors' price changes and initiating factors 4. Information on competitors' special campaigns 5. Competitive product line comparison 6. Assumptions about competitors' pricing/marketing objectives 7. Competitors' reported financial performance 8. Estimates of competitors' costs—fixed and variable 9. Expected pricing retaliation 10. Analysis of competitors' capacity to retaliate 11. Financial viability of engaging in price war 12. Strategic posture of competitors 13. Overall competitive aggressiveness

AT&T split): "All we had to do was determine our costs, and then we would go to the commission—the Illinois Commerce Commission, and they would give us the allowable rate of return."[2] Conversely, in an industry comprising a large number of active firms, competition is fierce. Fierce competition limits the discretion of a firm in setting price. Where there are a few firms manufacturing an undifferentiated product (such as in the steel industry), only the industry leader may have the discretion to change prices. Other industry members will tend to follow the leader in setting price.

The firm with a large market share is in a position to initiate price changes without worrying about competitors' reactions. Presumably, a competitor with a large market share has the lowest costs. The firm can, therefore, keep its prices low, thus discouraging other members of the industry from adding capacity, and further its cost advantage in a growing market.

If a firm operates in an industry that has opportunities for product differentiation, it can exert some control over pricing even if the firm is small and competitors are many. This latitude concerning price may occur if customers perceive one brand to be different from competing brands: whether the difference is real or imaginary, customers do not object to paying a higher price for preferred brands. To establish product differentiation of a brand in the minds of consumers, companies spend heavily for promotion. Product differentiation, however, offers an opportunity to control prices only within a certain range.

In an industry that is easy to enter, the price setter has less discretion in establishing prices; if there are barriers to market entry, however, a firm already in the industry has greater control over prices. Barriers to entry may take any of the following forms:

1. Capital investment.
2. Technological requirements.
3. Nonavailability of essential materials.
4. Economies of scale that existing firms enjoy and that would be difficult for a newcomer to achieve.
5. Control over natural resources by existing firms.
6. Marketing expertise.
7. Marketing expense.

In an industry where barriers to entry are relatively easy to surmount, a new entrant will follow what can be called *keep-away pricing*. This pricing strategy is necessarily on the lower side of the pricing spectrum.

Exhibit 15.5 contains the information required for analyzing demand. Demand is based on a variety of considerations, of which price is just one. Some of these considerations are

1. Ability of customers to buy.
2. Willingness of customers to buy.
3. Place of the product in the customer's lifestyle (whether a status symbol or a product used daily).
4. Benefits that the product provides to customers.
5. Prices of substitute products.

Exhibit 15.5
Customer Information
Needed for Pricing
Strategy

1. The customer's value analysis of the product: performance, utility, profit-rendering potential, quality, etc.
2. Market acceptance level: the price level of acceptance in each major market, including the influence of substitutes.
3. The price the market expects and the differences in different markets.
4. Price stability.
5. The product's S curve and its present position on it.
6. Seasonal and cyclical characteristics of the industry.
7. The economic conditions now and during the next few periods.
8. The anticipated effect of recessions; the effect of price change on demand in a declining market (e.g., very little with luxury items).
9. Customer relations.
10. Channel relations and channel costs to figure in calculations.
11. The markup at each channel level (company versus intermediary costs).
12. Advertising and promotion requirements and costs.
13. Trade-in, replacement parts, service, delivery, installation, maintenance, preorder and postorder engineering, inventory, obsolescence, and spoilage problems and costs.
14. The product differentiation that is necessary.
15. Existing industry customs and reaction of the industry.
16. Stockholder, government, labor, employee, and community relations.

6. Potential market for the product (is demand unfulfilled or is the market saturated?).
7. Nature of nonprice competition.
8. Customer behavior in general.
9. Segments in the market.

All these factors are interdependent, and it may not be easy to estimate their relationship to each other precisely.

Demand analysis involves predicting the relationship between price level and demand while considering the effects of other variables on demand. The relationship between price and demand is called elasticity of demand or sensitivity of price. **Elasticity of demand** refers to the number of units of a product that would be demanded at different prices. Price sensitivity should be considered at two different levels: total industry price sensitivity and price sensitivity for a particular firm.

Industry demand for a product is considered to be elastic if, by lowering prices, demand can be substantially increased. If lowering price has little effect on demand, demand is considered inelastic. The environmental factors previously mentioned have a definite influence on demand elasticity. Let us illustrate with a few examples. During the energy crisis, the price of gasoline went up, leading consumers to reduce gasoline usage. By the same token, when gasoline prices go down, people again start using gas more freely. Thus, demand for gasoline can be considered somewhat elastic.

A case of inelastic demand is provided by salt. No matter how much the price fluctuates, people are not going to change the amount of salt that they consume. Similarly, the demand for luxury goods—yachts—for example, is inelastic because only a small proportion of the total population can afford to buy yachts.

Sometimes the market for a product is segmented so that demand elasticity in each segment must be studied. The demand for certain types of beverages by senior citizens might be inelastic, though demand for the same products among a younger audience may be especially elastic. If the price of a product goes up, customers have the option of switching to another product. Thus, availability of substitute products is another factor that should be considered.

When the total demand of an industry is highly elastic, the industry leader may take the initiative to lower prices. The loss in revenue due to decreased prices will be more than compensated for by the additional demand expected to be generated; therefore, the total dollar market expands. Such a strategy is highly attractive in an industry where economies of scale are achievable. Where demand is inelastic and there are no conceivable substitutes, price may be increased, at least in the short run. In the long run, however, the government may impose controls, or substitutes may be developed.

15.1.1 Industry Demand Elasticity Business-to-Business Markets

B2B markets tend to be inelastic. B2B demand is inelastic because it tends to be both **derived demand** and **joint demand**. Derived demand is demand which is derived from the demand for the purchaser's own product. This is true whether the vendor is selling goods or services. If the purchaser has no need for additional product from a vendor, it will not purchase additional product regardless of what price reductions are being offered. To do so would only require the purchaser to hold additional inventory for extended periods, thereby increasing inventory holding costs, spoilage costs and quality control costs. Joint demand refers to the fact that if a purchaser cannot obtain additional components, raw materials or supplies that are necessary for the prodcution of its product, it has no need for the other components, raw materials or supplies that would be used in producing the purchaser's product. Thus, when there are shortages among any one item or material needed for producing a product, demand for the other items and materials needed for the production of the customer company's product will also fall regardless of prices cuts. A third factor of importance where demand elasticity for an individual company's product is concerned is **market transparency**. Market transparency is the degree of ease with which members of the market, both vendors and purchasers, can determine what the latest transaction price for a product has been. Where a market is opaque, an individual company can offer price reductions to an invidual customer to obtain a sale without other vendors and purchasers learning of the price reduction. In a relatively transparent market this is not possible. If a company offers a single customer a price reduction, its other customers will learn of it relatively quickly and demand price reductions also, and competing vendors will learn of the price reduction, and in order to retain market share, offer price reductions of their own. Hence, unless a company's market is opaque, it is generally counterproductive to reduce prices—demand will not rise and the only effect will be to reduce all vendors' margins. Hence, to try and increase market share through reducing one's prices is generally an act of desperation in B2B markets, especially for those companies that are not the lowest-cost producer.

15.1.2 Demand for an Individual Firm's Products

The demand for the products of an individual firm derives from total industry demand. An individual firm is interested in finding out how much market share it can command by changing its own prices. In the case of undifferentiated standardized products, lower prices should help a firm increase its market share as long as competitors do not retaliate by matching the firm's prices. Similarly, when business is sought through bidding prices, lower prices should help achieve the firm's objectives. In the case of differentiated products, however, market share can be improved even when higher prices are maintained (within a certain range). Products may be differentiated in various real and imaginary ways. For example, by providing adequate guarantees and after-sale service, an appliance manufacturer may maintain higher prices and still increase market share. A favorably considered brand name, an image of prestige, and the perception of high quality are other factors that may help to differentiate a product in the marketplace and thus create an opportunity for the firm to increase prices and not lose market share. Of course, other elements of the marketing mix should reinforce the product's image suggested by its price. In brief, a firm's best opportunity lies in differentiating the product and then communicating this fact to the customer. A differentiated product offers more opportunity for increasing earnings through price increases.

The sensitivity of price can be measured by taking into account historical data, consumer surveys, and experimentation. Historical data can either be studied intuitively or analyzed through quantitative tools, such as regression, to see how demand goes up or down based on price. A consumer survey to study the sensitivity of prices is no different from any other market research study. Experiments to judge what level of price generates what level of demand can be conducted either in a laboratory situation or in the real world. For example, a company interested in studying the sensitivity of prices may introduce a newly developed grocery product in a few selected markets for a short period at different prices. Information obtained from this experiment should provide insights into the elasticity of demand for the product. In one study, the prices of seventeen food products were varied in thirty food stores. It was found that the product sales generally followed the law of demand: when prices were raised ten percent, sales decreased about 25 percent; a price increase of five percent led to a decrease in sales of about thirteen percent; a lowering of prices by five percent increased sales by twelve percent; and a ten percent decrease in price improved sales by 26 percent. In another study, a new deodorant that was priced at 63 cents and at 85 cents in different markets resulted in the same volume of sales. Thus, price elasticity was found to be absent, and the manufacturer set the product price at 85 cents.[3]

A recent study of the top 500 brands in the United Kingdom showed that a ten percent price cut produced an 18.5 percent increase in sales. This excludes a small group of mainly luxury brands with a positive price elasticity whose sales increase when their price goes up. The study found wide variation across brands and categories. The household cleaning products were much less price-sensitive than, say dairy and bakery products.[4]

To conclude this discussion on pricing factors, it would not be out of place to say that, while everybody thinks businesses go about setting prices scientifically, very often the process is incredibly arbitrary. Packaged goods companies for example, have long recognized that pricing is a key lever in managing brands for profitability. Yet it is so neglected at present that improving price management can raise margins substantially. Companies seeking to capture this potential must make efforts to understand the behavior of consumers and find ways to apply this understanding to the thousands of frontline pricing decisions they make every year. Although businesses of all types devote a great deal of time and study to determine the prices to put on their products, pricing practices are often more art than science, and many feel that pricing is one field that is sorely in need of becoming more science and less art (Lester, 2005).[5] In some cases, setting prices does involve the use of a straightforward equation:

$$\text{material \& labor costs} + \text{overhead \& other expenses} + \text{profit} = \text{price}.$$

But in many other cases, the equation includes psychological and other such subtle subjective factors that the pricing decision may essentially rest on gut feeling. Exhibit 15.6 suggests one way of combining information on different pricing factors to make an objective pricing decision in industrial marketing. For example, price sensitivity, visibility to competition, and strength of supplier relationships are used to rank various customers, allowing a different pricing strategy to be adopted for each customer to effectively achieve profit, share, and communication objectives.

The following eight steps deal with the essentials of setting the right price and then monitoring that decision so that the benefits are sustainable.[6]

1. Assess what value your customers place on a product or service.
2. Look for variations in the way customers value the product.
3. Assess customers' price sensitivity.
4. Identify an optimal pricing structure.
5. Consider competitors' reactions.
6. Monitor prices realized at the transaction level.
7. Assess customers' emotional response.
8. Analyze whether the returns are worth the cost to serve.

The above eight steps assess the factors affecting price. Companies need to assess their customers to discover how a product or service is valued. Variations in the way customers value the same product may be turned to a company's benefit through clever pricing.

Exhibit 15.6
Pricing Guide

Company Relationship with Customer (Leverage)	Visibility of Price to Competition (Knowledge)	Customer's Price Sensitivity	
		Low	High
Strong	High	To gain profit and communicate high price	To maintain share and communicate willingness to fight
	Low	To gain profit	
Weak	High	To communicate high price	
	Low	To gain share	

Source: Robert A. Garda, "Industrial Pricing: Strategy vs. Tactics." Reprinted by permission of publisher, from *Management Review,* November 1983, © 1983. American Management Association, New York. All rights reserved.

15.2 PRICING STRATEGY FOR NEW PRODUCTS

The pricing strategy for a new product should be developed so that the desired impact on the market is achieved while the emergence of competition is discouraged. Two basic strategies that may be used in pricing a new product are skimming pricing and penetration pricing.

Skimming pricing is the strategy of establishing a high initial price for a product with a view to "skimming the cream off the market" at the upper end of the demand curve. It is accompanied by heavy expenditure on promotion. A skimming strategy may be recommended when the nature of demand is uncertain, when a company has expended large sums of money on research and development for a new product, when a company's patents are expected to hold the competition at bay, when the competition is expected to develop and market a similar, but different product in the near future (e.g., the three early standards for the VCR could not play films recorded in a competing standard), or when the product is so innovative that the market is expected to mature very slowly. Under these circumstances, a skimming strategy has several advantages. At the top of the demand curve, price elasticity is low. Besides, in the absence of any close substitute, cross-elasticity is also low. These factors, along with heavy emphasis on promotion, tend to help the product make significant inroads into the market. The high price also helps segment the market. Only nonprice-conscious customers will buy a new product during its initial stage. Later on, the mass market can be tapped by lowering the price.

If there are doubts about the shape of the demand curve for a given product and the initial price is found to be too high, price may be cut. However, it is very difficult to start low and then raise the price. Raising a low price may annoy potential customers, and anticipated drops in price may retard demand at a particular price. For a financially weak company, a skimming strategy may provide immediate relief. This model depends on selling enough units at the higher price to cover promotion and development costs. If price elasticity is higher than anticipated, a lower price will be more profitable and "relief giving."

Modern patented drugs provide a good example of skimming pricing. At the time of its introduction in 1978, Smithkline Beecham's anti-ulcer drug, Tagamet, was priced as high as $10 per unit. By 1990, the price came down to less than $2; it was sold for about 60 cents in 1994. (Tagamet was to lose patent protection in the United States in 1995, unleashing a flood of cheaper generics onto the American market.)[7] Many new products are priced following this policy. VCRs, frozen foods, and instant coffee were all priced very high at the time of their initial appearance in the market. But different versions of these products are now available at prices ranging from very high to very low. No conclusive research has yet been done to indicate how high an initial price should be in relation to cost. As a rule of thumb, the final price to the consumer should be at least three or four times the factory door cost.

The decision about how high a skimming price should be depends on two factors: (a) the probability of competitors entering the market and (b) price elasticity at the upper end of the demand curve. If competitors are expected to introduce their own brands quickly, it may be safe to price rather high. On the other hand, if competitors are years behind in product development and a low rate of return to the firm would slow the pace of research at competing firms, a low skimming price can be useful. However, price skimming in the face of impending competition may not be wise if a larger market share makes entry more difficult. If limiting the sale of a new product to a few selected individuals produces sufficient sales, a very high price may be desirable.

Determining the duration of time for keeping prices high depends on the both the competition's activities and the rate of technical development of product enhancements. In the absence of patent protection, skimming prices may be forced down as soon as competitors join the race. However, in the case of products that are protected through patents (e.g., drugs), the manufacturer slowly brings down the price as the patent period draws near an end; then, a year or so before the expiration of the patent period, the manufacturer saturates the market with a very low price. This strategy establishes a foothold for the manufacturer in the mass market before competitors enter it, thereby frustrating their expectations.

So far, skimming prices have been discussed as high prices in the initial stage of a product's life. Premium and umbrella prices are two other forms of price skimming. Some products carry premium prices (high prices) permanently and build an image of superiority for themselves. When a mass market cannot be developed and upper-end demand seems adequate, manufacturers will not risk tarnishing the prestigious image of their products by lowering prices, thereby offering the product to everybody. Estee Lauder cosmetics, Olga intimate apparel, Rolex watches, Waterford Crystal, Armani suits, and Hermes accessories are products that fall into this category.

Sometimes, higher prices are maintained in order to provide an umbrella for small high-cost competitors. Umbrella prices have been aided by limitation laws that specify minimum prices for a variety of products, such as milk.

Du Pont provides an interesting example of skimming pricing. The company tends to focus on high-margin specialty products. Initially, it prices its products high; it then gradually lowers price as the market builds and as competition grows. Polaroid also pursues a skimming pricing strategy. The company introduces an expensive model of a new camera and follows up the introduction with simpler lower-priced versions to attract new segments.

Penetration pricing is the strategy of entering the market with a low initial price so that a greater share of the market can be captured. The penetration strategy is used when an elite market does not exist and demand seems to be elastic over the entire demand curve, when a company has decided to focus on the mass market or when patent protection does not seem likely to hold competitors at bay. High price elasticity of demand and significant learning curve effects are probably the most important reasons for adopting a penetration strategy. The penetration strategy is also used to discourage competitors from entering the market. When competitors seem to be encroaching on a market, an attempt is made to discourage them by means of penetration pricing, which yields lower margins. A weakness in the strategy occurs when a competitor hold a cost advantage over the existing manufacturer across all levels of production. When this happens and a lower cost new entrant can convince the market its product possesses accceptable quality, it will prevail in the market due to the price sensitivity of most mass markets.

One may also turn to a penetration strategy with a view to achieving economies of scale. Savings in production costs alone may not be an important factor in setting low prices because, in the absence of price elasticity, it is difficult to generate sufficient sales. Finally, before adopting penetration pricing, one must make sure that the product fits the lifestyles of the mass market. For example, although it might not be difficult for people to accept imitation milk, cereals made from petroleum products would probably have difficulty in becoming popular.

How low the penetration price should be differs from case to case. There are several different types of prices used in penetration strategies: restrained prices, elimination prices, promotional prices, and keep-out prices. Restraint is applied so that prices can be maintained at a certain point during inflationary periods. In this case, environmental circumstances serve as a guide to what the price level should be. Elimination prices are fixed at a point that threatens the survival of a competitor. A large, multiproduct company can lower prices to a level where a smaller competitor might be wiped out of the market, although the larger company must take care not to cross the line into predatory pricing, a practice that is illegal in the U.S. and most industrialized economies. The pricing of suits at factory outlets illustrates promotional prices. Factory outlets constantly stress low prices for comparable department-store-quality suits. Keep-out prices are fixed at a level that prevents competitors from entering the market. Here the objective is to keep the market to oneself at the highest chargeable price.

A low price acts as the sole selling point under penetration strategy, but the market should be broad enough to justify low prices. Thus, price elasticity of demand is probably the most important factor in determining how low prices can go. This point can be easily illustrated.[8] Convinced that shoppers would willingly sacrifice convenience for price savings, an entrepreneur in 1991 introduced a concentrated cleaner called 4 + 1. Unlike such higher-priced cleaners as Windex, Fantastik, and Formula 409, this product did not come in a spray bottle. It also needed to be diluted with water before use. The entrepreneur hoped for ten percent of the $270 million market. But the product did not sell well. The product was not as price elastic as the entrepreneur had assumed. Though the consumer tends to talk a lot about economy, the lure of convenience is apparently stronger than the desire to save a few cents. Ultimately, 4 + 1 had to be withdrawn from most markets.

Unlike Du Pont, Dow Chemical Company stresses penetration pricing. It concentrates on lower-margin commodity products and low prices, builds a dominant market share, and holds on for the long haul. Texas Instruments also practices penetration pricing. Texas Instruments starts by building a large plant capacity. By setting the price as low as possible, it hopes to penetrate the market fast and gain a large market share.

Penetration pricing reflects a long-term perspective in which short-term profits are sacrificed in order to establish sustainable competitive advantage. Penetration policy usually leads to above-average long-run returns that fall in a relatively narrow range. Price skimming, on the other hand, yields a wider range of lower average returns.

15.3 PRICING STRATEGIES FOR ESTABLISHED PRODUCTS

Changes in the marketing environment may require a review of the prices of products already on the market. For example, an announcement by a large firm that it is going to lower its prices makes it necessary for other firms in the industry to examine their prices. In 1976, Texas Instruments announced that it would soon sell a digital watch for about $20. The announcement jolted the entire industry because only fifteen months earlier the lowest-priced digital was selling for $125. It forced a change in everyone's strategy and gave some producers real problems. Fairchild Camera and Instrument Corporation reacted with its own version of a $20 plastic-cased digital watch. So did National Semiconductor Corporation. American Microsystems, however, decided to get completely out of the finished watch business.[9]

A review of pricing strategy may also become necessary because of shifts in demand. In the late 1960s, for example, it seemed that, with the popularity of miniskirts, the pantyhose market would continue to boom. But its growth slowed when the fashion emphasis shifted from skirts to pants. Pants hid runs, or tears, making it unnecessary to buy as many pairs of pantyhose. The popularity of pants also led to a preference for knee-high hose over pantyhose. Knee-high hose, which cost less, meant lower profits for manufacturers. Although the pantyhose market was dwindling, two new entrants, Bic Pen Corporation and Playtex Corporation, were readying their brands for introduction. Their participation made it necessary for the big three hosiery manufacturers—Hanes, Burlington, and Kayser-Roth—to review their prices and protect their market shares. An examination of existing prices may lead to one of three strategic alternatives: maintaining the price, reducing the price, or increasing the price.

If the market segment from which the company derives a big portion of its sales is not affected by changes in the environment, the company may decide not to initiate any change in its pricing strategy. The gasoline shortage in the aftermath of the fall of the Shah of Iran did not affect the luxury car market because buyers of Cadillac, Mercedes-Benz, and Rolls-Royce were not concerned about higher gas prices. Thus, General Motors did not need to redesign the Cadillac to reduce its gas consumption or lower its price to make it attractive to the average customer.

The strategy of maintaining price is appropriate in circumstances where a price change may be desirable, but the magnitude of change is indeterminable. If the reaction of customers and competitors to a price change cannot be predicted, maintaining the present price level may be appropriate. Alternatively, a price change may have an impact on product image or sales of other products in a company's line that it is not practical to assess. Several years ago, when Magnavox and Sylvania cut the prices of their color television sets, Zenith maintained prices at current levels. Because the industry appeared to be in good shape, Zenith could not determine why its competitors adopted such a strategic posture. Zenith continued to maintain prices and earned higher profits.

Politics may be another reason for maintaining prices. During the year from 1978 to 1979, President Carter urged voluntary control of wages and prices. Many companies restrained themselves from seeking price changes in order to align themselves behind the government's efforts to control inflation.

Concern for the welfare of society may be another reason for maintaining prices at current levels. Even when supply is temporarily short of demand, some businesses may adopt a socially responsible posture and continue to charge current prices. For example, taxi drivers may choose not to hike fares when subway and bus service operators are on strike.

There are three main reasons for lowering prices. First, as a defensive strategy, prices may be cut in response to competition. For example, in October 1978, Congress authorized the deregulation of the airline industry. Deregulation gave airlines almost total freedom to set ticket prices. Thus, in spring of 2003, in response to Continental Airline's $298 round-trip fare on its New York–Los Angeles route, United Airlines acted to meet this competitive fare. United's regular round-trip coach fare at the time was about $750. Similarly, other carriers were forced to reduce their fares on different routes to match these prices. In addition, to successfully compete in mature industries, many companies reduce prices, following a strategy that is often called value pricing. For example, in light of slipping profit margins and lower customer counts, McDonald's cut prices under pressure from major rivals Burger King, Wendy's, and Taco Bell.[10]

A second reason for lowering prices is offensive in nature. Following the experience curve concept (see Chapter 12), costs across the board go down by a fixed percentage every time experience doubles. Consequently, a company with greater experience has lower costs than one whose experience is limited. Lower costs have a favorable impact on profits. Thus, as a matter of strategy, it behooves a company to shoot for higher market share and to secure as much experience as possible in order to gain a cost and, hence, a profit advantage. A company that has successfully followed this strategy is Home Depot, the largest home repair chain in the country. The policy of everyday low prices has enabled the company to grow into a $77.0 billion chain of over 1500 stores in the U.S. and over 2500 stores in the U.S., Canada, Mexico, Puerto Rico, the U.S. Virgin Islands and China.[11] Costco Waterhouse clubs follow a low price, artfully affixed to high-quality, high-end merchandise, strategy that has become a powerful middle-class elixir.[12]

Technological advances have made possible the low-cost production of high-quality electronics gear. Many companies have translated these advances into low retail prices to gain competitive leverage. For example, in 1978 a Sony clock radio, with no power backup and a face that showed nothing more than the current time, sold for $80. In 1988, a Sony clock radio priced at about $40 had auxiliary power and showed the time at which the alarm was set as well as the current time. In 2002, the same radio was available for less than $18.

Texas Instruments has followed the experience curve concept in achieving cost reductions in the manufacture of integrated circuits. This achievement is duly reflected in its strategy to slowly lower prices of such products as electronic calculators. Compaq Computer Corp. followed a similar strategy to make a dramatic comeback in the PC market. Even in other businesses where technological advances have a less critical role to play in the success of the business, a price reduction strategy may work out. Consider the case of Metpath, a clinical laboratory. In the late 1960s, at about the time Metpath was formed, the industry leader, Damon Corporation, was acquiring local labs all around the country; by the early 1980s, other large corporations in the business—Revlon, Bristol-Myers, Diamond Shamrock, and W.R. Grace—began doing the same. Metpath, however, adopted a price-cutting strategy. In order to implement this strategy, it took a variety of measures to achieve economies of scale. Figuring that there were not many economies of scale involved in simply putting together a chain of local labs that operated mostly as separate entities, to reduce costs, Metpath focused on centralizing its testing. A super lab that did have those economies of scale was created, along with a nationwide network to collect specimens and distribute test results. Metpath's strategy paid off well. It emerged as the industry leader in the clinical lab-testing field. Heavy price competition, much of it attributed to Metpath, led some of the big diversified companies, including W.R. Grace and Diamond Shamrock, to pull out of the business.[13]

The recession in the early 1990s caused consumers to tighten belts and to be more sensitive to prices. Sears, therefore, adopted a new pricing policy whereby prices on practically all products were permanently lowered. The company closed its 824 stores for two days to remark price tags and to implement its "everyday low pricing" strategy. A number of other companies, such as Wal-Mart, Toys "R" Us, and Circuit City, also pursue this strategy by keeping prices low year-round, avoiding the practice of marking them up and down. Consumers like year-round low prices because constantly changing sale prices makes it hard to recognize a fair deal.[14] Similarly, fast-food chains have started offering "value" menus of higher-priced items.

The third and final reason for price cutting may be a response to customer need. If low prices are a prerequisite for inducing the market to grow, customer need may then become the pivot of a marketing strategy, all other aspects of the marketing mix being developed accordingly.[15]

As an example, in 1993 Philip Morris used price as an aggressive marketing tactic to seek growth for its Marlboro brand of cigarette. Its 40-cents-per-pack cut grabbed consumers' attention, narrowed the gap with discount brands, and squeezed competitors. In less than a year, Marlboro's share of the U.S. cigarette market increased from twenty percent to 25 percent, higher than it has been before.[16]

However, Philip Morris's move depressed the profits of the entire industry, since other cigarette manufacturers responded by reducing their own brands' prices. Philip Morris repeated the same strategy by cutting down prices about twenty percent on its Post and Nabisco ready-to-eat cereals. However, other cereal companies, such as Kellogg and General Mills, did not go along with Philip Morris's lead.[17]

In adopting a low-price strategy for an existing product, a variety of considerations must be taken into account. The long-term impact of a price cut against a major competitor is a factor to be reckoned with. For example, a regional pizza chain can cut prices to prevent Pizza Hut from gaining a foothold in its market only in the short run. Eventually, Pizza Hut will prevail over the local chain through price competition. Pizza Hut may lower prices to such an extent that the local chain may find it difficult even to recover its costs. Thus, competitive strength should be duly evaluated in opting for low-price strategy.

In a highly competitive situation, a product may command a higher price than other brands if it is marketed as a "different" product—for example, as one of deluxe quality. If the price of a deluxe product is reduced, the likely impact on its position should be looked into. Sony television sets have traditionally sold at premium prices because they have been promoted as quality products. Sony's higher-price strategy paid off: the Sony television rose to prominence as a quality product and captured a respectable share of the market. A few years later, however, consumer pressures led Sony dealers to reduce prices. This action not only hurt Sony's overall prestige, it made some retailers stop selling Sony because it had now become just one of the many brands they carried. In other words, the price cut, though partly initiated by its dealers, cost Sony its distinction. Even if its sales increased in the short run, the price cut did not prove to be a viable strategy in the long run because it went against the perception consumers had of Sony's being a distinctive brand. Ultimately, consumers may perceive Sony as just another brand, which will affect both sales and profits.

It is also necessary to examine thoroughly the impact of a price cut of one product on other products in the line.

Finally, the impact of a price cut on a product's financial performance must be reviewed before the strategy is implemented. If a company is so positioned financially that a price cut will weaken its profitability, it may decide not to lower the price even if lowering price may be in all other ways the best course to follow. For instance, a mere one percent price decrease for an average company might destroy over eleven percent of the company's operating profit dollars.[18]

An increase in price may be implemented for various reasons. First, in an inflationary economy, prices may need to be adjusted upward in order to maintain profitability. During periods of inflation, all types of costs go up, and to maintain adequate profits, an increase in price becomes necessary. How much the price should be increased is a matter of strategy that varies from case to case. Conceptually, however, price should be increased to such a level that the profits before and after inflation are approximately equal. An increase in price should also take into account any decline in revenue caused by shifts in demand due to price increases. Strategically, the decision to minimize the effects of inflationary pressures on the company through price increases should be based on the long-term implications of achieving a short-run vantage.

It must also be mentioned that it is not always necessary for a company to increase prices to offset inflationary pressures. A company can take nonprice measures as well to reduce the effects of inflation. For example, many fast-food chains expanded menus and seating capacity to partially offset rising costs. Similarly, a firm may substantially increase prices, much more than justified by inflation alone, by improving product quality or by raising the level of accompanying services. High quality should help keep prices and profits up because inflation-weary customers search for value in the marketplace. Improved product quality and additional services should provide such value.

Price may also be increased by downsizing (i.e., decreasing) package size while maintaining price. In a recession, downsizing helps hold the line on prices despite rising costs. Under inflationary conditions, downsizing provides a way of keeping prices from rising beyond psychological barriers. Downsizing is commonly practiced by packaged-goods companies. For example, recently Procter & Gamble cut the number of diapers in a package from 88 to 80 while leaving the price the same. In this example, downsizing effectively resulted in a price increase of 9.1 percent. Similarly, H. J. Heinz reduced the contents of its 6.5-ounce StarKist Seafood (tuna) can by three-eighths of an ounce. By keeping exactly the same price as before, the company gained an invisible 5.8 percent price increase.[19]

Prices may also be increased when a brand has a monopolistic control over the market segments it serves. In other words, when a brand has a differential advantage over competing brands in the market, it may take advantage of its unique position, increasing its price to maximize its benefits. Such a differential advantage may be real or may exist just in the mind of the consumer. In seeking a price increase in a monopolistic situation, the increase should be such that customers will absorb it and still remain loyal to the brand. If the price increase is abnormal, differential advantage may be lost, and the customer will choose a brand based on price.

The downside of increasing price may be illustrated with reference to coffee. Let us say that there is a segment of customers who ardently drink Maxwell House coffee. In their minds, Maxwell House has something special. If the price of Maxwell House goes up (assuming that the prices of other brands remain unchanged), these coffee drinkers may continue to purchase it because the brand has a virtual monopoly over their coffee-drinking behavior. There is a limit, however, to what these Maxwell House loyalists will pay for their favorite brand of coffee. Thus, if the price of Maxwell House is increased too much, these customers may shift their preference.

From the perspective of strategy, this example indicates that, in monopolistic situations, the price of a brand may be set high to increase revenues and profits. The extent of the increase, however, depends on many factors. Each competitor has a different optimum price level for a given end product for a given customer group. It is rare that such optimum prices are the same for any two competitors. Each competitor has different options based on different cost components, capacity constraints, financial structure, product mix, customer mix, logistics, culture, and growth rate. The competitor with the lowest optimum price has the option of setting the common price; all others must follow or retreat. However, the continued existence of competitors depends on each firm retreating from competition when it is at a disadvantage until each competes primarily in a "competitive segment," a monopolistic situation where it has an advantage compared to all others. This unique combination of characteristics, matched with differentials in the competitive environment, enables each firm to coexist and prosper in its chosen area (i.e., where it has monopolistic control).

Sometimes prices must be increased to adhere to an industry situation. Of the few firms in an industry, one (usually the largest) emerges as a leader. If the leader raises its price, other members of the industry must follow suit, if only to maintain the balance of strength in the industry. If they refuse to do so, they are liable to be challenged by the leader. Usually, no firm likes to fight the industry leader because it has more at stake than the leader.

In the U.S. auto industry, there are three domestic firms: General Motors, Ford, and Chrysler. General Motors has historically been the industry leader in terms of market share. When General Motors increased its prices, all other members of the industry increased prices. This characteristic of the industry has faded as General Motors and the other U.S. brands lost market share to Toyota, Nissan, Volkswagon and the other foreign brands. Thus, a firm may be compelled to increase price in response to a similar increase by the industry leader. The leader also sets a limit on price increases, with followers frequently setting their prices very close to those of the leader. Although an increase is forced on a firm in this situation, it is a good strategic move to set a price that, without being obviously different, is higher than the leader's price.

Prices may also be increased to segment the market. For example, a soft-drink company may come out with a new brand and direct it toward busy executives/professionals. This brand may be differentiated as one that provides stamina and invigoration without adding calories. To substantiate the brand's worth and make it appear different, the price may be set at double the price of existing soft drinks. Similarly, the market may be segmented by geography, with varying prices serving different segments. For example, in New York City, a 6.4-ounce tube of Crest toothpaste may sell for $3.89 on Park Avenue, for $3.29 on the Upper East Side, and for $2.39 on the Lower East Side. Furthermore, companies with products that customers want and that are not easily matched by competitors may increase the price without any negative repercussions. For example, in 1998 when inflation was merely 2.1 percent, some industries, such as airlines, mutual-fund houses, sellers of mainframe software, and entertainment companies, boosted their prices far faster.[20]

Hewlett-Packard Company operates in the highly competitive pocket calculator industry, where the practice of price cutting is quite common. Nonetheless, Hewlett-Packard thrives by offering high-priced products to a select segment of the market. It seems to appeal to a market segment that is highly inelastic with respect to price but highly elastic with respect to quality. The company equips its calculators with special features and then offers them at a price that is much higher than the industry average. In other words, rather than running the business on the basis of overall volume, Hewlett-Packard realizes high prices by being a specialist that serves a narrow segment. In cosmetics or automobiles, for example, there may be a tenfold cost difference between mass market products and those designed, produced, packaged, distributed, and promoted for small, high-quality niches. Up-market products are often produced by specialists, companies such as Daimler-Benz or BMW, that can compete successfully around much larger producers of standard products.

Many airlines have successfully used price structure to differentiate market segments and objectives based on customer price sensitivity. Business travelers are relatively price insensitive, whereas tourists are very sensitive to the price of tickets. In order to increase the volume of tourist traffic without forgoing bread-and-butter revenues from business customers, airlines have developed price structures based on characteristics that differentiate these two customer segments.

For example, tourists generally spend a weekend at their destination; business travelers do not. By changing the structure from pricing flights to pricing itineraries, the airlines can discount itineraries that include a Saturday night stay. Most business customers cannot take advantage of such discounts without incurring substantial inconvenience. This enables the airline to increase tourist volume while maintaining high prices among the business customer segment. Such pricing policies have led to as much as 10 times the difference in fares paid for the same seat. Thus, a flexible pricing strategy permits a company to realize high prices from customers who are willing to pay them without sacrificing volume from customers who are not.

Increase in price is seductive in nature. After all, improvements in price typically have three to four times the effect on profitability as proportionate increases in volume. But the increase should be considered for its effect on long-term profitability, demand elasticity, and competitive moves. Although a higher price may mean higher profits in the short run, the long-run effect of a price increase may be disastrous. The increase may encourage new entrants to flock to the industry and competition from substitutes. Thus, before a price increase strategy is implemented, its long-term effect should be thoroughly examined. Further, an increase in price may lead to shifts in demand that could be detrimental. Likewise, the increase may negatively affect market share if the competition decides not to seek similar increases in price. Thus, competitive posture must be studied and predicted. In addition, a company should review its own ability to live with higher prices. A price increase may mean a decline in revenues but an increase in profits. Whether such a situation will create any problem needs to be looked into. Will laying off people or reassigning sales territories be problematic? Is a limit to price increases called for as a matter of social responsibility? In the last few years, there has been a backlash against pharmaceutical firms about rising drug prices. In such a situation, should a company that otherwise finds a ten percent increase in price strategically sound go ahead with it? Finally, the price increase should be duly reinforced by other factors in the marketing mix. A Chevy cannot be sold at a Cadillac price. A man's suit bearing a Kmart label cannot be sold on a par with one manufactured by Brooks Brothers. Chanel No. 5 cannot be promoted by placing an ad in *TV Guide*. The increased price must be evaluated before being finalized to see whether the posture of other market mix variables will substantiate it.

Finally, the timing of a price increase can be nearly as important as the increase itself. For example, a simple tactic of lagging competitors in announcing price increases can produce the perception among customers that you are the most customer-responsive supplier. The extent of the lag can also be important.

15.4 PRICE-FLEXIBILITY STRATEGY

A price-flexibility strategy usually consists of two alternatives: a one-price policy and a flexible-pricing policy. Influenced by a variety of changes in the environment, such as saturation of markets, slow growth, global competition, and the consumer movement, more and more companies have been adhering in recent years to flexibility in pricing of different forms. Pricing flexibility may consist of setting different prices in different markets based on geographic location, varying prices depending on the time of delivery, or customizing prices based on the complexity of the product desired.

A one-price strategy means that the same price is set for all customers who purchase goods under essentially the same conditions and in the same quantities. The one-price strategy is fairly typical in situations where mass distribution and mass selling are employed. There are several advantages and disadvantages that may be attributed to a one-price strategy. One advantage of this pricing strategy is administrative convenience. It also makes the pricing process easier and contributes to the maintenance of goodwill among customers because no single customer receives special pricing favors over another.

A general disadvantage of a one-price strategy is that the firm usually ends up broadcasting its prices to competitors who may be capable of undercutting the price. Total inflexibility in pricing may undermine the product in the marketplace. Total inflexibility in pricing may also have highly adverse effects on corporate growth and profits in certain situations. It is very important that a company remain responsive to general trends in economic, social, technological, political/legal, and competitive environments. Realistically, then, a pricing strategy should be periodically reviewed to incorporate environmental changes as they become pronounced. Any review of this type would need to include a close look at a company's position relative to the actions of other firms operating within its industry. As an example, it is generally believed that one reason for the success of discount houses is that conventional retailers have rigidly held to traditional prices and margins.

A flexible-pricing strategy refers to situations where the same products or quantities are offered to different customers at different prices. A flexible-pricing strategy is more common in industrial markets than in consumer markets. An advantage of a flexible-pricing strategy is the freedom allowed to sales representatives to make adjustments for competitive conditions rather than refuse an order. Also, a firm is able to charge a higher price to customers who are willing to pay it and a lower price to those who are unwilling, although legal difficulties may be encountered if price discrimination becomes an issue. Besides, other customers may become upset upon learning that they have been charged more than their competitors. In addition, bargaining tends to increase the cost of selling, and some sales representatives may let price cutting become a habit.

Recently, many large U.S. companies have added new dimensions of flexibility to their pricing strategies. Although companies have always shown some willingness to adjust prices or profit margins on specific products when market conditions have varied, this kind of flexibility is now being carried to the state of high art. As a matter of fact, electronic commerce is further likely to accelerate the flexible-pricing trend. The Internet, corporate networks, and wireless setups are linking people, machines, and companies around the globe and connecting sellers and buyers as never before. This is enabling buyers to quickly and easily compare products and prices, putting them in a better bargaining position. At the same time, the technology allows sellers to know customers' buying habits, preferences, and spending limits, enabling them to tailor products and prices.[21] The concept of price flexibility can be implemented in four different ways: by market, by product, by timing, and by technology.

Price flexibility with reference to the market can be achieved either from one geographic area to another or from one segment to another. Both Ford and General Motors charge less for their compact cars marketed on the West Coast than for those marketed anywhere else in the country. Different segments make different uses of a product: many companies, therefore, consider customer usage in setting price. For example, a plastic sold to industry might command only thirty cents a pound; sold to a dentist, it might bring $25 a pound. Here again, the flexible-pricing strategy calls for different prices in the two segments.

Price flexibility with reference to the product is implemented by considering the value that a product provides to the customer. Careful analysis may show that some products are underpriced and can stand an upgrading in the marketplace. Others, competitively priced to begin with, may not support any additional margin because the matchup between value and cost would be lost.

Costs of all transactions from raw material to delivery may be analyzed, and if some costs are unnecessary in a particular case, adjustments may be made in pricing a product to sell to a particular customer. Such cost optimization is very effective from the customer's point of view because he or she does not pay for those costs for which no value is received.

Price flexibility can also be practiced by adding to the price an escalation clause based on cost fluctuations. Escalation clauses are especially relevant in situations where there is a substantial time gap between confirmation of an order and delivery of the finished product. In the case of products susceptible to technological obsolescence, price is set to recover all sunken costs within a reasonable period.

The flexible-pricing strategy has two main characteristics: an emphasis on profit or margins rather than simply on volume and a willingness to change price with reference to the existing climate. Caution is in order here. In many instances, building market share may be essential to cutting costs and, hence, to increasing profits. Thus, where the experience curve concept makes sense, companies may find it advantageous to reduce prices to hold or increase market share. However, a reduction in price simply as a reactionary measure to win a contract is discounted. Implementation of this strategy requires that the pricing decision be instituted by someone high up in the organization away from salespeople in the field. In some companies, the pricing executive may report directly to the CEO.

In addition, a systematic procedure for reviewing price at quarterly or semiannual intervals must be established. Finally, an adequate information system is required to help the pricing executive examine different pricing factors.

15.5 PRODUCT LINE-PRICING STRATEGY

A modern business enterprise manufactures and markets a number of product items in a line with differences in quality, design, size, and style. Products in a line may be complementary to or competitive with each other. The relationships among products in a given product line influence the cross-elasticities of demand between competing products and the package-deal buying of products complementary to each other. For example, instant coffee prices must bear some relationship to the prices of a company's regular coffee because these items are substitutes for one another; therefore, this represents a case of cross-elasticity. Similarly, the price of a pesticide must be related to that of a fertilizer if customers are to use both. In other words, a multiproduct company cannot afford to price one product without giving due consideration to the effect its price produces on other products in its line.

The pricing strategy of a multiproduct firm should be developed to maximize the profits of the entire organization rather than the profitability of a single product. For products already in the line, pricing strategy may be formulated by classifying them according to their contribution as follows:

1. Products that contribute more than their pro rata share toward overhead after direct costs are covered.
2. Products that just cover their pro rata share.

3. Products that contribute more than incremental costs but do not cover their pro rata share.
4. Products that fail to cover the costs savable by their elimination.

With such a classification in mind, management is in a better position to study ways of strengthening the performance of its total product line. Pricing decisions on individual products in the four categories listed here are made in the light of demand and competitive conditions facing each product in the line. Consequently, some products (new products) may be priced to yield a very high margin of profit; others (highly competitive standard products) may need to show an actual loss. By retaining these marginal products to "keep the machines running" and to help absorb fixed overhead costs, management may be able to maximize total profit from all of its lines combined. A few items that make no contribution may need to be kept to round out the line offered.

General Motors' pricing structure provides a good illustration of this procedure. To offset lower profit margins on lower-priced small cars, the company raises the prices of its large cars. The prices of its luxury cars are raised much more than those of its standard cars. For example, in 2008 a Cadillac XLR Roadster sold for more than $85,000, eight times the price of the company's lowest-priced car. Fifteen years ago, the top of the line was three times as costly as the lowest-priced car. The gap is widening, however, because the growing market for small cars with low markups makes it necessary for the company to generate high profits on luxury cars to meet its profit goals. Thus, in 2010, General Motors might sell a Cadillac for $100,000.

For a new product being considered for addition to the line, strategy development proceeds with an evaluation of the role assigned to it. The following questions could be asked:

1. What would the effect be on the company's competing products at different prices?
2. What would be the best new-product price (or range), considering its impact on the total company offerings as a whole? Should other prices be adjusted? What, therefore, would be the incremental gain or loss (volumes and profits of existing lines plus volumes and profits of the new line at different prices)?
3. Is the new product necessary for staying ahead of or catching up with the competition?
4. Can it enhance the corporate image, and if so, how much is the enhancement worth?

If product/market strategy has been adequately worked out, it will be obvious whether the new product can profitably cater to a particular segment. If so, the pricing decision will be considerably easier to make; costs, profit goals, marketing goals, experience, and external competition will be the factors around which price will be determined.

Where there is no specific product/market match, pricing strategy for a new product considered for the line will vary depending on whether the product is complementary or competitive vis-à-vis other products in the line. For the complementary product, examination of the industry price schedule, which is the primary guide for the bottom price, top price, and conventional spread between product prices in a given industry, may be necessary. There are three particularly significant factors in product line-pricing strategy. The lowest price in the market is always the most remembered and unquestionably generates the most interest, if not the most traffic; the top market price implies the ability to manufacture quality products; and a well-planned schedule structure (one that optimizes profit and, at the same time, is logical to customers) is usually carefully studied and eventually followed by the competition regardless of who initiated it. In addition, however, there can be a product in the line with the objective of pricing to obtain the principal profit from a product's supplies or supplementary components.

If the anticipated product is competitive, a start will need to be made with the following market analysis:

1. Knowledge of the industry's pricing history and characteristics regarding the line.
2. Comparison of company and competitor products and volumes, showing gaps and areas of popularity.
3. Volume and profit potentials of the company line as is.
4. Volume and profit potentials with the new internally competitive product.
5. Effect on company volume and profit if competition introduced the proposed product and the company did not.
6. Impact of a possible introduction delay or speedup.

With this information on hand, computations for cost-plus markup should be undertaken. Thereafter, the pricer has three alternatives to set price: (a) add a uniform or individual markup rate to the total cost of the product, (b) add a markup rate that covers all the constant costs of the line, and (c) add the rate necessary for achieving the profit goal. These three alternatives have different characteristics. The first one hides the contribution margin opportunities. The second alternative, although revealing the minimum feasible price, tends to spread constant-cost coverage in such a manner that the product absorbing the most overhead is made the most price attractive. The third alternative assigns the burden to the product with the highest material cost, an action that may be competitively necessary. No matter which alternative is pursued, however, the final price should be arrived at only after it has been duly examined with reference to the market and the competition.

15.6 LEASING STRATEGY

The major emphasis of a pricing strategy is on buying a product outright rather than leasing it. Except in housing, leasing is more common in the marketing of industrial goods than among consumer goods, though in recent years there has been a growing trend toward the leasing of consumer goods. For example, some people lease cars. Usually, by paying a specified sum of money every month, similar to a rental on an apartment, one can lease a new car. Again, as in the case of housing, a lease is binding for a minimum period, such as two years. Thus, the consumer can lease a new car every other year. Because repairs in the first two years of a car's life may not amount to much, one is saved the bother of such problems.

At the same time, overall the lease may cost slightly more than what a customer would pay by buying the car on loan. The net price of a fully equipped 2003 Ford Escort with a sticker price of $23,650, after negotiations and a $1,000 manufacturer's rebate, was $20,494. Payments on a two-year lease from Ford Motor Credit Co. were $457.43 a month, or total payout of $10,520, assuming that the rebate is used for the first payment and a security deposit. At the end of the lease, the car would have a residual value—the value after depreciation—of $14,663. That is what the customer would have to pay if he/she decides to buy it, bringing the total cost to $25,183. On the other hand, monthly payments on a four-year loan at 9.9 percent would be $518.79. The total paid over the term of the loan would be $24,901, and the customer would have a vehicle valued at more than $7,000 at the end.[22]

Although there may be different alternatives for setting the lease price, the lessor usually likes to recover the investment within a few years. Thereafter, a very large portion of the lease price (or rent) is profit. A lessor may set the monthly rental on a car so that within a few months, say 30, the entire cost of the car can be recovered. For example, the monthly rental on a Toyota Corolla, based on its 2003 price (assuming no extras), was about $239 a month (the sticker price was $15,985). With the term set at 36 months, the dealer captured all his or her money back in about 32 months. (It should be noted that a dealer gets a car at the wholesale price, not the sticker price, which is the suggested retail price.) The important thing is to set the monthly lease rate and the minimum period for which the lease is binding in such proportions that the total amount that the lessee pays for the duration of the lease is less than what he or she would pay in monthly installments on a new car. As a matter of fact, the lease rate must be substantially less than that in order for the buyer to opt to lease.

Automobile leasing represents a major share of the auto market. In 1998, one-fourth of all cars and trucks sold went out under lease. Though it was predicted that by the year 2005, half of all cars and trucks would be leased, the share of market has remained fairly constant. In 2007, 27 percent of all auto sales were actually leases.[23] The reason for the importance of leasing is easy to understand. About 75 percent of car buyers need some sort of financing, and with interest on car loans no longer deductible, leasing's relatively low monthly payments are enticing. For the auto companies, leasing camouflages price increases, and restores brand loyalty. It offers companies an opportunity to strike up a relationship with the customers. Further, it attracts younger buyers to luxury brands and smoothes industry sales throughout the year.

Leasing works out to be a viable strategy for other products as well. For example, furniture renting may be attractive to young adults, people of high mobility (e.g., executives, airline stewards), and senior citizens who may need appropriate furnishings only temporarily when their children's families come to visit. In addition, apartment owners may rent furniture to provide furnished units to tenants.

In industrial markets, the leasing strategy is employed by essentially all capital goods and equipment manufacturers. Traditionally, shoe machinery, postage meters, packaging machinery, textile machinery, and other heavy equipment have been leased. Recent applications of the strategy include the leasing of computers, copiers, cars, and trucks. As a matter of fact, just about any item of capital machinery and equipment can be leased. From the customer's point of view, the leasing strategy makes sense for a variety of reasons. First, it reduces the capital required to enter a business. Second, it protects the customer against technological obsolescence. Third, the entire lease price, or rental, may be written off as an expense for income tax purposes. This advantage, of course, may or may not be relevant depending on the source of funds the customer would have used for the outright purchase (i.e., his or her own money or borrowed funds). Finally, leasing gives the customer the freedom not to get stuck with a product that may later prove not to be useful.

From the viewpoint of the manufacturer, the leasing strategy is advantageous in many ways. First, income is smoothed out over a period of years, which is very helpful in the case of equipment of high unit value in a cyclical business. Second, market growth can be boosted because more customers can afford to lease a product than can afford to buy. Third, revenues are usually higher when a product is leased than when it is sold.

15.7 BUNDLING-PRICING STRATEGY

Bundling, also called **iceberg pricing**, refers to the inclusion of an extra margin (for support services) in the price over and above the price of the product as such. This type of pricing strategy has been popular with companies that lease rather than sell their products. Thus, the rental price, when using a bundling strategy, includes an extra charge to cover a variety of support functions and services needed to maintain the product throughout its useful life. Because unit profit increases sharply after a product completes its planned amortization, it is desirable for firms that lease their products to keep the product in good condition, thus enhancing its working life for high resale or re-leasing value. The bundling strategy permits a company to do so because a charge for upkeep, or iceberg, services is included in the price.

IBM once followed a bundling strategy, whereby it charged one fee for hardware, service, software, and consultancy. In 1969, however, the Justice Department charged IBM with monopolizing the computer market. Subsequently, the company unbundled its price and started selling computers, software, service, and technical input separately.

Under the bundling strategy, not only are costs of hardware and profits covered, anticipated expenses for extra technical sales assistance, design and engineering of the system concept, software and applications to be used on the system, training of personnel, and maintenance are also included. Although the bundling strategy can be criticized for tending to discourage competition, one must consider the complexities involved in delivering and maintaining a fault-free sophisticated system. Without the manufacturer taking the lead in adequately keeping the system in working condition, customers would have to deal with a variety of people to make use of such products as computers. At least in the initial stages of a technologically oriented product, a bundling strategy is highly useful from the customer's point of view.

For the company, this strategy (a) covers the anticipated expenses of providing services and maintaining the product, (b) provides revenues for supporting after-sales service personnel, (c) provides contingency funds to meet unanticipated happenings, and (d) ensures the proper care and maintenance of the leased products. The bundling strategy also permits an ongoing relationship with the customer. In this way the company gains firsthand knowledge of the customer's needs that may help to shift the customer to a new generation of the product. Needless to say, the very nature of the bundling strategy makes it most relevant to technologically sophisticated products, particularly those marked by rapid technological obsolescence.

On the negative side, the bundling strategy tends to inflate costs and distort prices and profitability. For this reason, during unfavorable economic conditions, it may not be an appropriate strategy to pursue. Grocery wholesalers, for instance, may pass through a straight invoice cost and then charge separately for delivery, packaging, and so on. A growing number of department stores now charge extra for home delivery, gift wrapping, and shopping bags. Thus, people who don't want a service need not pay for it.

15.8 PRICE-LEADERSHIP STRATEGY

The price-leadership strategy prevails in oligopolistic situations. One member of an industry, because of its size or command over the market, emerges as the leader of an entire industry. The leading firm then makes pricing moves that are duly acknowledged by other members of the industry. Thus, this strategy places the burden of making critical pricing decisions on the leading firm; others simply follow the leader. The leader is expected to be careful in making pricing decisions. A faulty decision could cost the firm its leadership because other members of the industry would then stop following in its footsteps. For example, if, in increasing prices, the leader is motivated only by self-interest, its price leadership will not be emulated. Ultimately the leader will be forced to withdraw the increase in price.

The price-leadership strategy is a static concept. In an environment where growth opportunities are adequate, companies would rather maintain stability than fight each other by means of price wars. Thus, the leadership concept works out well in this case. In the auto industry, General Motors was the leader, based on market share. The other two domestic members of the industry adjusted their prices to come very close to any price increase by General Motors.

Usually, the leader is the company with the largest market share. The leadership strategy is designed to stave off price wars and "predatory" competition that tend to force down prices and hurt all parties. Companies that deviate from this form are chastised through discounting or shaving by the leaders. Price deviation is quickly disciplined.

Successful price leaders are characterized by the following:

1. Large share of the industry's production capacity.
2. Large market share.
3. Commitment to a particular product class or grade.
4. New cost-efficient plants.
5. Strong distribution system, perhaps including captive wholesale outlets.
6. Good customer relations, such as technical assistance for industrial buyers, programs directed at end users, and special attention to important customers during shortages.
7. An effective market information system that provides analysis of the realities of supply and demand.
8. Sensitivity to the price and profit needs of the rest of the industry.
9. A sense of timing to know when price changes should be made.
10. Sound management organization for pricing.
11. Effective product line financial controls, which are needed to make sound price-leadership decisions.
12. Attention to legal issues.

In an unfavorable business environment, it may not be feasible to implement a leadership strategy because firms may be placed differently to interact with the environment. Thus, the leader hesitates to make decisions on behalf of an entire industry because other firms may not always find its decisions to their advantage. For this reason, the price leader/follower pattern may be violated.

In order to survive during unfavorable conditions, even smaller firms may take the initiative to undercut the price leader. For example, during 1998 when the list prices of steel were similar, companies freely discounted their prices. In the chemical industry, with increasing competition from overseas, the price-leadership strategy does not work. Companies thus plan a variety of temporary allowances to generate business.

An automatic response to a leader's price adjustment assumes that all firms are more or less similarly positioned vis-à-vis different price variables (i.e., cost, competition, and demand) and that different firms have common pricing objectives. Such an assumption, however, is far from being justified. The leadership strategy is an artificial way to enforce similar pricing responses throughout an industry. Strategically, it is a mistake for a company to price in a manner identical to that of its competitors. It should price either above or below the competition to set itself apart.

15.9 PRICING STRATEGY TO BUILD MARKET SHARE

Recent work in the area of marketing strategy has delineated the importance of market share as a key variable in strategy formulation. Although market share has been discussed earlier with reference to other matters, this section examines the impact of market share on pricing strategy.

Time and again it has been noted that higher market share and experience lead to lower costs. Thus, unless it is targeted towards a luxury or premium market, a new product should be priced to improve experience and market share. The combination of enhanced market share and experience gives a company such a cost advantage that it cannot ever profitably be overcome by any competitor of normal performance. Competitors are prevented from entering the market and must learn to live in a subordinate position.

Assuming the market is price sensitive, it is desirable to develop the market as early as possible. One way of achieving this is to reduce price. Unit costs are necessarily very high in the early stages of any product; if price is set to recover all costs, there may be no market for the product at its initial price in competition with existing alternatives. Following the impact of market share and experience on prices, it may be worthwhile to set price at a level that will move the product. During the early stages of a product introduction, operations may need to be conducted even at a loss. As volume is gained, costs go down, and even at an initial low price the company makes money, implying that future competitive cost differentials should be of greater concern than current profitability. Of course, such a strategic posture makes sense only in a competitive situation. In the absence of competition there is every reason to set prices as high as possible, to be lowered only when total revenue will not be affected by such an action.

The lower the initial price set by the first producer, the more rapidly that producer builds up volume and a differential cost advantage over succeeding competitors and the faster the market develops. In a sense, employing a pricing strategy that builds market share is a purchase of time advantage. However, the lower the initial price, the greater the investment required before the progressive reduction of cost results in a profit. This in turn means that the comparative investment resources of competitors can become a significant or even the critical determinant of competitive survival.

Two limitations, however, make the implementation of this type of strategy difficult. First, the resources required to institute this strategy are more than those normally available to a firm. Second, the price, once set, must not be raised and should be maintained until costs fall below price; therefore, the lower the price, the longer the time needed to realize any returns and the larger the investment required. When a future return is discounted to present value, there is obviously a limit.

It is these difficulties that lead many firms to set initial price to cover all costs. This policy is particularly likely to be adopted when there is no clear competitive threat. As volume builds and costs decline, visible profitability results, which in turn induces new competitors to enter the field. As competitors make their moves, the innovating firm has the problem of choosing between current profitability and market share. Strategically, however, the pricing of a new product, following the relationship between market share and cost, should be dictated by a product's projected future growth.

SUMMARY

Pricing strategy is of interest to the very highest management levels of a company. Yet few management decisions are more subject to intuition than pricing. There is a reason for this. Pricing decisions are primarily affected by factors, such as pricing objectives, cost, competition, and demand, that are difficult to articulate and analyze. For example, assumptions must be made about what a competitor will do under certain hypothetical circumstances. There is no way to know that for certain; hence the characteristic reliance on intuition.

This chapter reviewed the pricing factors mentioned above and examined important strategies that a pricer may pursue. The following strategies were discussed:

1. Pricing strategies for new products.
2. Pricing strategies for established products.
3. Price-flexibility strategy.
4. Product line-pricing strategy.
5. Leasing strategy.
6. Bundling-pricing strategy.
7. Price-leadership strategy.
8. Pricing strategy to build market share.

There are two principal pricing strategies for new products, skimming and penetration. Skimming is a high-price strategy; penetration strategy sets a low initial price to generate volume. Three strategies for established products were discussed: maintaining the price, reducing the price, and increasing the price. A flexible-pricing strategy provides leverage to the pricer in terms of duration of commitment both from market to market and from product to product. Product line-pricing strategy is directed toward maintaining a balance among different products offered by a company. The leasing strategy constitutes an alternative to outright sale of the product. The bundling strategy is concerned with packaging products and associated services together for the purposes of pricing. Price-leadership strategy is a characteristic of an oligopoly, where one firm in an industry emerges as a leader and sets the pricing strategy to build market share. Setting price to build market share emphasizes the strategic significance of setting an initially low price to gain volume and market share, thereby enabling the firm to achieve additional cost reductions in the future.

DISCUSSION QUESTIONS

1. Is the maintenance of a stable price a viable objective? Why?
2. Is there a conflict between profit and volume objectives? Doesn't one lead to the other? Discuss.
3. What are the advantages of using incremental costs instead of full costs for pricing? Are there any negative implications of using incremental costs that a pricing strategist needs to be aware of?
4. What assumptions need to be made about competitive behavior for formulating pricing strategy?
5. ''Short-term price increases tend to depress industry profits in the long run by accelerating the introduction of new capacity and depressing market demand.'' Discuss.
6. Following the experience curve concept, the initial price of a new product should be set rather low; as a matter of fact, it may be set below cost. Taking into account the popularity of this thesis, discuss the relevance of the skimming strategy.
7. What factors are ascribed to the decline in popularity of the price-leadership strategy?

NOTES

1. Thomas T. Nagle, *The Strategy and Tactics of Pricing* (Englewood Cliffs, NJ: Prentice-Hall, 1987): 8.
2. Heywood Klein, ''Illinois Bell Faces New Environment as Era of Competitive Pricing Nears,'' *The Wall Street Journal,* December 31, 1891, p. 9.
3. Mark I. Alpert, *Pricing Decisions* (Glenview, IL: Scott, Foresman, 1971): 96.
4. ''Marketing in Britain: Elastic Brands,'' *The Economist,* November 19, 1994, p. 75.
5. Tom Lester, Find the Right Pricing Strategy—at Any Cost,'' *Financial Times,* December 5, 2005, p. 8.
6. Robert J. Dolan, ''How Do You Know When the Price is Right?'' *Harvard Business Review* (September–October 1995): 174–183.
7. ''Having an Ulcer is Getting a Lot Cheaper,'' *BusinessWeek* (May 9, 1994): 30.
8. *The Wall Street Journal,* December 31, 1981, p. 9.
9. ''How T.I. Beat the Clock on Its $20 Digital Watch,'' *BusinessWeek,* May 31, 1976, pp. 62–63. (For different reasons, T.I. quit the digital watch business itself a few years later. But the point made here with reference to pricing is still relevant.)
10. Richard Gibson, ''How Burger King Finally Became a Contender.'' *The Wall Street Journal,* February 27, 1997, p. B1. *Also see:* ''The Heat in Kraft's Kitchen,'' *BusinessWeek,* August 4, 2003, p. 82.
11. From May 6, 2008, Home Depot press release taken off www.Homedepot.com.
12. Selly Branch, ''Inside Costco,'' *Fortune,* September 6, 1999, p. 184.
13. Ignatics Chitbebhen, ''Clinical Case,'' *Forbes,* May 20, 1989, p. 178.
14. ''Looking Downscale Without Looking Down,'' *BusinessWeek,* October 8, 1990, p. 62.
15. John Gourville and Dilip Soman, ''Pricing and the Psychology of Consumption,'' *Harvard Business Review*, September 2002, pp. 90–96.
16. ''The Smoke Clears at Marlboro,'' *BusinessWeek,* January 31, 1994, p. 76.
17. ''Cereal Wars: A Tale of Bran, Oats, and Air,'' *Fortune,* May 13, 1996, p. 30.
18. Michael V. Marn and Robert L. Rosiello, ''Managing Price, Gaining Profit,'' *Harvard Business Review* (September–October 1992): 48.

19. John B. Hinge, "Critics Call Cuts in Package Size Deceptive Move," *The Wall Street Journal,* February 15, 1991, p. B1.

20. "The Power To Raise Prices," *BusinessWeek,* May 4, 1998, p. 37.

21. Akshay R. Rao, Mark E. Bergen and Scott Davis, "How to Fight a Price War?" *Harvard Business Review*, March–April 2000, pp. 107–120.

22. "Good-bye to Fixed Pricing," *BusinessWeek,* May 4, 1998, p. 71. *See also*: Hermann Simon and Robert J. Dolan, "Price Customization," *Marketing Management* (Fall 1998): 11–17.

23. Consumer Reports, April 2008, off web site: http://www.consumerreports.org/cro/money/credit-loan/auto-lease-or-buy-4-08/overview/auto-lease-or-buy-ov.htm

APPENDIX: PERSPECTIVES OF PRICING STRATEGIES

A. Skimming Pricing

Defintion: Setting a relatively high price during the initial stage of a product's life.

Objectives: (a) To serve customers who are not price conscious while the market is at the upper end of the demand curve and competition has not yet entered the market. (b) To recover a significant portion of promotional and research and development costs through a high margin.

Requirements: (a) Heavy promotional expenditure to introduce product, educate consumers, and induce early buying. (b) Relatively inelastic demand at the upper end of the demand curve. (c) Lack of direct competition and substitutes.

Expected Results: (a) Market segmented by price-conscious and not so price-conscious customers. (b) High margin on sales that will cover promotion and research and development costs. (c) Opportunity for the firm to lower its price and sell to the mass market before competition enters.

B. Penetration Pricing

Defintion: Setting a relatively low price during the initial stages of a product's life.

Objective: To discourage competition from entering the market by quickly taking a large market share and by gaining a cost advantage through realizing economies of scale.

Requirements: (a) Product must appeal to a market large enough to support the cost advantage. (b) Demand must be highly elastic in order for the firm to guard its cost advantage.

Expected Results: (a) High sales volume and large market share. (b) Low margin on sales. (c) Lower unit costs relative to competition due to economies of scale.

A. Maintaining the Price

Objectives: (a) To maintain position in the marketplace (i.e., market share, profitability, etc.). (b) To enhance public image.

Requirements: (a) Firm's served market is not significantly affected by changes in the environment. (b) Uncertainty exists concerning the need for or result of a price change. (c) Firm's public image could be enhanced by responding to government requests or public opinion to maintain price.

Expected Results: (a) Status quo for the firm's market position. (b) Enhancement of the firm's public image.

B. Reducing the Price

Objectives: (a) To act defensively and cut price to meet the competition. (b) To act offensively and attempt to beat the competition. (c) To respond to a customer need created by a change in the environment.

Requirements: (a) Firm must be financially and competitively strong to fight in a price war if that becomes necessary. (b) Must have a good understanding of the demand function of its product.

Expected Results: Lower profit margins (assuming costs are held constant). Higher market share might be expected, but this will depend upon the price change relative to competitive prices and upon price elasticity.

C. Increasing the Price

Objectives: (a) To maintain profitability during an inflationary period. (b) To take advantage of product differences, real or perceived. (c) To segment the current served market.

Requirements: (a) Relatively low price elasticity but relatively high elasticity with respect to some other factor such as quality or distribution. (b) Reinforcement from other ingredients of the marketing mix; for example, if a firm decides to increase price and differentiate its product by quality, then promotion and distribution must address product quality.

Expected Results: (a) Higher sales margin. (b) Segmented market (price conscious, quality conscious, etc.). (c) Possibly higher unit sales, if differentiation is effective.

A. One-Price Strategy

Defintion: Charging the same price to all customers under similar conditions and for the same quantities.

Objectives: (a) To simplify pricing decisions. (b) To maintain goodwill among customers.

Requirements: (a) Detailed analysis of the firm's position and cost structure as compared with the rest of the industry. (b) Information concerning the cost variability of offering the same price to everyone. (c) Knowledge of the economies of scale available to the firm. (d) Information on competitive prices; information on the price that customers are ready to pay.

Expected Results: (a) Decreased administrative and selling costs. (b) Constant profit margins. (c) Favorable and fair image among customers. (d) Stable market.

B. Flexible-Pricing Strategy

Defintion: Charging different prices to different customers for the same product and quantity.

Objective: To maximize short-term profits and build traffic by allowing upward and downward adjustments in price depending on competitive conditions and how much the customer is willing to pay for the product.

Requirements: Have the information needed to implement the strategy. Usually this strategy is implemented in one of four ways: (a) by market, (b) by product, (c) by timing, (d) by technology. Other requirements include (a) a customer-value analysis of the product, (b) an emphasis on profit margin rather than just volume, and (c) a record of competitive reactions to price moves in the past.

Expected Results: (a) Increased sales, leading to greater market share. (b) Increased short-term profits. (c) Increased selling and administrative costs. (d) Legal difficulties stemming from price discrimination.

Defintion: Pricing a product line according to each product's effect on and relationship with other products in that line, whether competitive or complementary.

Objective: To maximize profits from the whole line, not just certain members of it.

Requirements: (a) For a product already in the line, strategy is developed according to the product's contributions to its pro rata share of overhead and direct costs. (b) For a new product, a product/market analysis determines whether the product will be profitable. Pricing is then a function of costs, profit goals, experience, and external competition.

Expected Results: (a) Well-balanced and consistent pricing schedule across the product line. (b) Greater profits in the long term. (c) Better performance of the line as a whole.

Defintion: An agreement by which an owner (lessor) of an asset rents that asset to a second party (lessee). The lessee pays a specified sum of money, which includes principal and interest, each month as a rental payment.

Objectives: (a) To enhance market growth by attracting customers who cannot buy outright. (b) To realize greater long-term profits; once the production costs are fully amortized, the rental fee is mainly profit. (c) To increase cash flow. (d) To have a stable flow of earnings. (e) To have protection against losing revenue because of technological obsolescence.

Requirements: (a) Necessary financial resources to continue production of subsequent products for future sales or leases. (b) Adequate computation of lease rate and minimum period for which lease is binding such that the total amount the lessee pays for the duration of the lease is less than would be paid in monthly installments on an outright purchase. (c) Customers who are restrained by large capital requirements necessary for outright purchase or need write-offs for income tax purposes. (d) The capability to match competitors' product improvements that may make the lessor's product obsolete.

Expected Results: (a) Increased market share because customers include those who would have forgone purchase of product. (b) Consistent earnings over a period of years. (c) Greater cash flow due to lower income tax expense from depreciation write-offs. (d) Increased sales as customers exercise their purchase options.

Defintion: Inclusion of an extra margin in the price to cover a variety of support functions and services needed to sell and maintain the product throughout its useful life.

Objectives: (a) In a leasing arrangement, to have assurance that the asset will be properly maintained and kept in good working condition so that it can be resold or re-leased. (b) To generate extra revenues to cover the anticipated expenses of providing services and maintaining the product. (c) To generate revenues for supporting after-sales service personnel. (d) To establish a contingency fund for unanticipated happenings. (e) To develop an ongoing relationship with the customer. (f) To discourage competition with "free" after-sales support and service.

Requirements: This strategy is ideally suited for technologically sophisticated products that are susceptible to rapid technological obsolescence because these products are generally sold in systems and usually require the following: (a) extra technical sales assistance, (b) custom design and engineering concept for the customer, (c) peripheral equipment and applications, (d) training of the customer's personnel, and (e) a strong service/maintenance department offering prompt responses and solutions to customer problems.

Expected Results: (a) Asset is kept in an acceptable condition for resale or re-lease. (b) Positive cash flow. (c) Instant information on changing customer needs. (d) Increased sales due to "total package" concept of selling because customers feel they are getting their money's worth.

Defintion: This strategy is used by the leading firm in an industry in making major pricing moves, which are followed by other firms in the industry.

Objective: To gain control of pricing decisions within an industry in order to support the leading firm's own marketing strategy (i.e., create barriers to entry, increase profit margin, etc.).

Requirements: (a) An oligopolistic situation. (b) An industry in which all firms are affected by the same price variables (i.e., cost, competition, demand). (c) An industry in which all firms have common pricing objectives. (d) Perfect knowledge of industry conditions; an error in pricing means losing control.

Expected Results: (a) Prevention of price wars, which are liable to hurt all parties involved. (b) Stable pricing moves. (c) Stable market share.

Defintion: Setting the lowest price possible for a new product.

Objective: To seek such a cost advantage that it cannot ever be profitably overcome by any competitor.

Requirements: (a) Enough resources to withstand initial operating losses that will be recovered later through economies of scale. (b) Price-sensitive market. (c) Large market. (d) High elasticity of demand.

Expected Results: (a) Start-up losses to build market share. (b) Creation of a barrier to entry to the industry. (c) Ultimately, cost leadership within the industry.

Chapter Outline

16.1 Channel-Structure Strategy
16.2 Distribution-Scope Strategy
16.3 Multiple-Channel Strategy
16.4 Channel-Modification Strategy
    16.4.1 Cost of Distribution
    16.4.2 Coverage of the Market
    16.4.3 Customer Service
    16.4.4 Communication and Control
16.5 Channel-Control Strategy
16.6 Conflict-Management Strategy

Chapter 16

Distribution Strategies

D istribution strategies are concerned with the channels a firm may employ to make its goods and services available to customers. **Channels** are organized structures of buyers and sellers that bridge the gap of time and space between the manufacturer and the end user.

Marketing is defined as an exchange process. In relation to distribution, exchange poses two problems. First, goods must be moved to a central location from the warehouses of producers who make heterogeneous goods and who are geographically widespread. Second, the goods that are accumulated from diversified sources should represent a desired assortment from the viewpoint of customers. These two problems can be solved by the process of sorting, which combines concentration (i.e., bringing the goods from different sources to a central location) and dispersion (i.e., picking an assortment of goods from different points of concentration). Two basic questions need to be answered here. Who should perform the concentration and dispersion tasks—the manufacturer or the intermediaries? Which intermediaries should the manufacturer select to bring goods close to the customer? These questions are central to distribution strategies.

Other strategy-related matters discussed in this chapter include scope of distribution (i.e., how widespread distribution may be), use of multiple channels to serve different segments, modification of channels to accommodate environmental shifts, resolution of conflict among channels, importance of maintaining control over the product presentation to the customer, and use of vertical systems to institute control over channels. Each strategic issue is examined for its relevance in different circumstances. The application of each strategy is illustrated with examples from marketing literature.

16.1 CHANNEL-STRUCTURE STRATEGY

The **channel-structure strategy** refers to the number of intermediaries that may be employed in moving goods from manufacturers to customers. A company may undertake to distribute its goods to customers or retailers without involving any intermediary. This strategy constitutes the shortest channel and may be labeled a *direct distribution strategy*. Alternatively, goods may pass through one or more intermediaries, such as wholesalers or agents. This is an *indirect distribution strategy*. Exhibit 16.1 shows alternative channel structures for consumer and industrial products.

Decisions about channel structure are based on a variety of factors. To a significant extent, channel structure is determined by where inventories should be maintained to offer adequate customer service, fulfill required sorting processes, and still deliver a satisfactory return to channel members.

An underlying factor in determining channel-structure strategy is the use of intermediaries. The importance of using intermediaries is illustrated with reference to an example of a primitive economy used by Alderson.[1] In a primitive economy, five producers produce one type of item each: hats, hoes, knives, baskets, or pots. Because each producer needs all the other producers' products, a total of 10 exchanges are required to accomplish trade. However, with a market (or middlemen), once the economy reaches equilibrium (i.e., each producer-consumer has visited the market once), only five exchanges need to take place to meet everyone's needs. Let n denote the number of producer-consumers. Then the total number of transactions (T) without a market is given by:

$$T_{without} = \frac{n(n-1)}{2}$$

Exhibit 16.1
Typical Channel
Structures

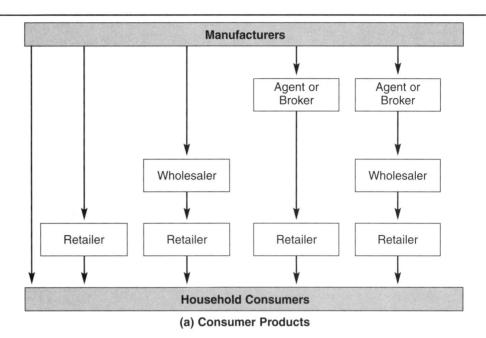

(a) Consumer Products

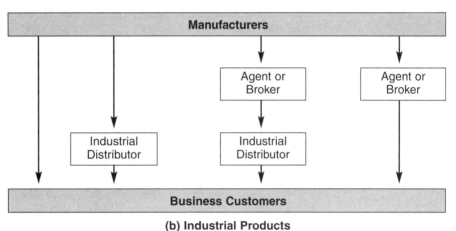

(b) Industrial Products

and the total number of transactions with a market is given by:

$$T_{with} = n$$

The efficiency created in distribution by using an intermediary may be viewed using this equation:

$$\text{Efficiency} = \frac{T_{without}}{T_{with}} = \frac{n(n-1)}{2} \times \frac{1}{n} = \frac{n-1}{2}$$

In the example of five producer-consumers, the efficiency of having a middleman is two. The efficiency increases as n increases. Thus, usually, intermediaries perform the task of distribution more efficiently than manufacturers alone.

Conceptually, the selection of channel structure may be explained with reference to Bucklin's postponement-speculation framework.[2] The framework is based on risk, uncertainty, and costs involved in facilitating exchanges. Postponement seeks to eliminate risk by matching production/distribution with actual customer demand. Presumably, postponement should produce efficiency in marketing channels. For example, the manufacturer may produce and ship goods only on confirmed orders. Speculation, on the other hand, requires undertaking risk through changes in form and movement of goods within channels. Speculation leads to economies of scale in manufacturing, reduces costs of frequent ordering, and eliminates opportunity cost.

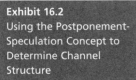

Exhibit 16.2
Using the Postponement-Speculation Concept to Determine Channel Structure

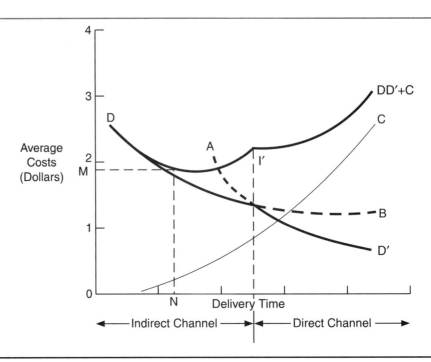

Source: Louis P. Bucklin and Leslie Halpert, "Exploring Channels of Distribution for Cement with the Principle of Postponement-Speculation," in *Marketing and Economic Development*, ed. Peter D. Bennett (Chicago: American Marketing Association, 1965): 698. Reprinted by permission of the American Marketing Association.

Exhibit 16.2 shows the behavior of variables involved in the postponement-speculation framework. The vertical axis shows the average cost of undertaking a function for one unit of any given commodity; the horizontal axis shows the time involved in delivering a confirmed order. Together, the average cost and the delivery time measure the cost of marketing tasks performed in a channel with reference to delivery time. The nature of the three curves depicted in Exhibit 16.2 should be understood: C represents costs to the buyer for holding an inventory; AD′, costs involved in supplying goods directly from a manufacturer to a buyer; and DB, costs involved in shipping and maintaining speculative inventories (i.e., in anticipation of demand).

Following Bucklin's framework, one determines the channel structure by examining the behavior of the C, AD′, and DB curves:

1. The minimal cost of supplying the buyer for every possible delivery time is derived from curves AD′ and DB. As may be seen in Exhibit 16.2, especially fast delivery service can be provided only by the indirect channel (i.e., by using a stocking intermediary). However, at some delivery time, I′, the cost of serving the consumer directly from the producer will intersect and fall below the cost of indirect shipment. The minimal costs derived from both curves are designated DD′. From the perspective of channel cost, it will be cheaper to service the buyer from a speculative inventory if delivery times shorter than I′ are demanded. If the consumer is willing to accept delivery times longer than I′, then direct shipment will be the least expensive.

2. The minimal total cost curve for the channel with respect to delivery time is derived by summing the cost of moving goods to the buyer, DD′, and the buyer's costs of holding inventory, C. The curve is represented in Exhibit 16.2 by DD′ + C. Total channel costs initially fall as delivery time lengthens because increased buyer expenses are more than made up for by savings in other parts of the channel. Gradually, however, the savings from these sources diminish and buyer costs begin to rise more rapidly. A minimal cost point is reached, and expenses for the channel rise thereafter. Channel structure is controlled by the location of this minimum point. If, as in the present case, it falls to the left of I′, then goods would be expected to flow through the speculative inventory (i.e., an intermediary). If, on the other hand, the savings of the buyer from postponement had not been as great as those depicted, the minimum point would have fallen to the right of I′ and shipments would have been made directly from the producer to the consumer.[3]

Benetton, an Italian apparel maker, offers an excellent example of a distribution strategy that combines speculation with postponement in an effort to optimize both service and cost. Speculation involves commitment by retailers to specific inventory items months before the start of the selling season. It leads to such advantages for Benetton as low-cost production (via use of subcontractors) and good quality control (via centralized warehousing and assembly of orders). Postponement of orders requires last-minute dyeing of woolen items at an added cost. The advantages of speculation are flexibility in meeting market needs and reduced inventory levels.[4]

The postponement-speculation theory provides an economic explanation of the way the channels are structured. Examined in this section are a variety of environmental influences on channel-structure strategy formulation. These influences may be technological, social and ethical, governmental, geographical, or cultural.

Many aspects of channel structure are affected by technological advances. For example, mass retailing in food has become feasible because of the development of automobiles, highways, refrigerated cars, cash registers, packaging improvements, and mass communications (television). In the coming years, television shopping with household computer terminals should have a far-reaching impact on distribution structures. Technological advances permitted Sony to become dominant in the U.S. market for low-priced CD players. Sony developed prepackaged players that could be sold through mass retailers so that even sales clerks without technical know-how could handle customers.

How technology may be used to revamp the operations of a wholesaler, making it worthwhile to adopt indirect channels, is illustrated by the case of Foremost-McKesson, the nation's largest wholesale distributor. A few years ago, the company found itself in a precarious position. Distribution, though one of the company's most pervasive business functions, did not pay. Foremost-McKesson merely took manufacturers' goods and resold them to small retailers through a routine process of warehousing, transportation, and simple marketing that offered thin profits. As a matter of fact, at one time the company came close to selling off drug wholesaling, its biggest business. Instead, however, its new chief executive decided to add sophisticated technology to its operations in order to make the company so efficient at distribution that manufacturers could not possibly do as well on their own. It virtually redefined the function of the intermediary. Having used the computer to make its own operations efficient, it devised ways to make its data processing useful to suppliers and customers, in essence making Foremost part of their marketing teams. Since the company computerized its operations, Foremost has turned around dramatically. Here are the highlights of Foremost's steps in reshaping its role:

- Acting as middleman between drugstores and insurance offices by processing medical insurance claims.
- Creating a massive "rack jobbing" service by providing crews to set up racks of goods inside retail stores, offering what amounts to a temporary labor force that brings both marketing know-how and Foremost merchandise along with it.
- Taking waste products as well as finished goods from chemical manufacturers, and recycling the wastes through its own plants—its first entry into chemical waste management.
- Designing, as well as supplying, drugstores.
- Researching new uses for products it receives from manufacturers. Foremost found new customers, for example, for a Monsanto Co. food preservative from among its contacts in the cosmetics industry.[5]

Another example of the use of technology to overhaul distribution is provided by Britain's supermarket chain Tesco. The firm's nine composite (variable temperature) distribution centers use a just-in-time system (known as pick-by-line or cross-docking). That means goods amounting to around 40 percent of total sales go straight out to the stores within hours of arrival.[6] Retailing has always been an inefficient business. Retailers, particularly those that operate large chains have to predict the desires of fickle consumers, buy and allocate complex sets of merchandise, set the right promotions for each individual item. Inevitably, there are gaps between supply and demand, leaving stores holding too much of what customers don't want and too little of what they do. In recent years, however, a new set of software tools have revolutionized the entire merchandising chain. These tools help in determining the right quantity, allocation, and price of items to maximize retailers' returns.[7]

Social taboos and ethical standards may also affect the channel-structure decision. For example, *Viva*, a woman's magazine, had achieved a high circulation in supermarkets and drugstores in Canada. When *Viva* responded to readers' insistence and to competition from *Playgirl* by introducing nude male photos, most supermarkets banned the magazine. Because supermarkets accounted for more than half of *Viva's* circulation, *Viva* dropped the photos so that it could continue to be sold through this channel.

The channel-structure strategy can also be influenced by local, state, and federal laws in a variety of ways. For example, door-to-door selling of certain goods may be prohibited by local laws. In many states (e.g., California and Ohio) wine can be sold through supermarkets, but other states (e.g., Connecticut) do not permit this.

Geographic size, population patterns, and typology also influence the channel-structure strategy. In urban areas, direct distribution to large retailers may make sense. Rural areas, however, may be covered only by wholesalers.

With the inception of large grocery chains, it may often appear that independent grocery stores are dying. The truth is, however, that independent grocery stores as recently as 1999 accounted for 46 percent of all grocery sales in the country—over $175 billion. Thus, a manufacturer can ill afford not to deal with independents and to reach them it must go through wholesalers. Wetterau, for example, is a grocery wholesale firm in Hazelwood, Missouri, which did over $6 billion worth of business serving almost 3,000 retail grocery stores. It does not do any business with chain stores. But because of Wetterau's determination to offer its customers relatively low prices, a wide selection of brands, service programs carefully designed to make brands more profitable, and a personal interest in their success, its customers are almost fanatically loyal. The company offers its customers—small independent retail stores—a variety of services, including lease arrangements, store design, financing packages, training, and computerized inventory systems. These services tend to enhance customers' competitiveness by reducing their operating costs and by simplifying their bookkeeping, which in turn helps Wetterau to earn profits.[8] The Wetterau example shows that to reach smaller retailers, particularly in areas far removed from large metropolises, the indirect distribution strategy is appropriate. The wholesaler provides services to small retailers that a large manufacturer can never match on its own.

Finally, cultural traits may require the adoption of a certain channel structure in a setting that otherwise might seem an odd place for it. For example, in many parts of Switzerland, fruits and vegetables are sold in a central marketplace in the morning by small vendors, even though there are modern supermarkets all over. This practice continues because it gives customers a chance to socialize while shopping. Similarly, changing lifestyles among average American consumers and their desire to have more discretionary income for life-fulfillment activities appear to be making warehouse retailing (e.g., Sam's Club) more popular. This is so because prices at warehouse outlets—grocery warehouses, for example—are substantially lower than at traditional stores.

Presented below is a channel design model that can be used to make the direct/indirect distribution decision. The model involves six basic steps.

1. List the factors that could potentially influence the direct/indirect decision. Each factor must be evaluated carefully in terms of the firm's industry position and competitive strategy.
2. Pick out the factors that will have the most impact on the channel design decision. No factor with a dominant impact should be left out. For example, assume that the following four factors have been identified as having particular significance: market concentration, customer service level, asset specificity, and availability of working capital.
3. Decide how each factor identified is related to the attractiveness of a direct or an indirect channel. For example, market concentration reflects the size distribution of the firm's customers as well as their geographical dispersion. Therefore, the more concentrated the market, the more desirable the direct channel because of the lower costs of serving that market (high concentration = direct; low concentration = indirect). Customer service level is made up of at least three factors: delivery time, lot size, and product availability. The more customer service required by customers, the less desirable is the direct channel (high customer service = indirect; low customer service = direct). The direct channel is more desirable, at least under conditions of high uncertainty in the environment, with a high level of asset specificity (high asset specificity = direct; low asset specificity = indirect). Finally, the greater the availability of working capital, the more likely it is that a manufacturer can afford and consider a direct channel (high working capital = direct; low working capital = indirect). Note that a high level on a factor does not always correspond to a direct channel.
4. Create a matrix based on the key factors to consider the interactions among key factors. If only two factors are being considered, a two-by-two matrix of four cells would result. For three factors, a three-by-three matrix of nine cells would result. For four factors, a four-by-four matrix of sixteen cells would result, and so on. If more than five or six factors are involved, a series of smaller models could be constructed to make this fourth step more manageable. Exhibit 16.3 presents a four-by-four matrix developed for this example.

			Asset Specificity: Low		Asset Specificity: High	
			Capital Availability		Capital Availability	
Market Concentration	Customer Service Level		Low	High	Low	High
Low	Customer Service Level	High	*cell 1* indirect	*cell 3* indirect	*cell 2* indirect	*cell 4* combination
Low	Customer Service Level	Low	*cell 5* indirect	*cell 7* combination	*cell 6* combination	*cell 8* direct
High	Customer Service Level	High	*cell 9* indirect	*cell 11* combination	*cell 10* direct	*cell 12* direct
High	Customer Service Level	Low	*cell 13* combination	*cell 15* combination	*cell 14* direct	*cell 16* direct

Source: Gary L. Frazier, "Designing Channels of Distribution," *The Channel for Communication* (Seattle, Wash.: Center for Retail Distribution Management, University of Washington, 1987): 3–7.

Exhibit 16.3 Designing a Distribution Channel Matrix

5. Decide (for each cell in the matrix) whether a direct channel, an indirect channel, or a combination of both a direct and an indirect channel is most appropriate, considering the factors involved. Combination channels are becoming more common in business practice, especially in industrial markets.

   For some cells in the matrix, deciding which channel design is best is rather easy to do. For example, Cell 1 in Exhibit 16.3 has all four factors in agreement that an indirect channel is best. This is also true for Cell 16: a direct channel is the obvious choice. For other cells, choosing between a direct channel and an indirect channel is not as easy because factors conflict with each other to some extent. For example, in Cell 14, asset specificity is low, suggesting that an indirect channel is best. The other three factors suggest otherwise, however; the market is concentrated, customer service requirements are low, and the availability of capital to the manufacturer is high. Taken together, the factors in Cell 14 reveal that a direct channel would be most attractive. In the cells that have factors that conflict with one another, the strategist must make trade-offs among them to decide whether a direct channel, indirect channel, or combination of channels is best.
6. For each product or service in question, locate the corresponding cell in the box model. The prediction in this cell is the one that should be followed or at least the one that should be most seriously considered by the firm.

The accuracy of the model generated by this method depends totally on the expertise and skills of the person who builds and uses it. If carefully constructed, such a model can be invaluable in designing more efficient and effective channels of distribution.

16.2 DISTRIBUTION-SCOPE STRATEGY

For an efficient channel network, the manufacturer should clearly define the target customers it intends to reach. Implicit in the definition of target customers is a decision about the scope of distribution the manufacturer wants to pursue. The strategic alternatives here are exclusive distribution, selective distribution, and intensive distribution.

Exclusive distribution means that one particular retailer serving a given area is granted sole rights to carry a product. For example, Coach leather goods are distributed exclusively through select stores in an area. Several advantages may be gained by the use of exclusive distribution. It promotes tremendous dealer loyalty, greater sales support, a higher degree of control over the retail market, better forecasting, and better inventory and merchandising control. The impact of dealer loyalty can be helpful when a manufacturer has seasonal or other kinds of fluctuating sales. An exclusive dealership is more willing to finance inventories and thus bear a higher degree of risk than a more extensive dealership. Having a smaller number of dealers gives a manufacturer or wholesaler greater opportunity to provide each dealer with promotional support and training for the dealer's sales personnel. It also provides a degree of exclusivity to a product, hence it is generally used for luxury products that people are willing to search for the location of a product's dealership in order to make a purchase. For instance Houston, fourth largest city in the U.S., has one authorized local McIntosh Stereo dealer (with three locations), and San Antonio, the seventh largest, has one authorized dealer with only a single location. With fewer outlets, it is easier to control such aspects as margin, price, and inventory. Dealers are also more willing to provide data that may be used for marketing research and forecasts. Other examples of products distributed through exclusive distribution channels include Rolex watches, Gucci bags, Regal shoes, Celine neckties, and Mark Cross wallets.

On the other hand, there are several obvious disadvantages to exclusive distribution. First, sales volume may be lost. Second, the manufacturer places all its fortunes in a geographic area in the hands of one dealer. Exclusive distribution brings with it the characteristics of high price, high margin, and low volume. If the product is highly price elastic in nature, this combination of characteristics can mean significantly less than optimal performance. Relying on one retailer can mean that if sales are depressed for any reason, the retailer is then likely to be in a position to dictate terms to other channel members (i.e., the retailer becomes the channel captain). To avoid this, it is crucial for the maker of products distributed exclusively to maintain the aura of high quality and desirability of its products.

As an example of losing such an aura, assume that a company manufacturing traditional toys deals exclusively with Toys "R" Us. For a variety of reasons, its line of toys may not do well. These reasons may be a continuing decline in the birthrate, an economic recession, the emerging popularity of electronic toys, higher prices of the company's toys compared to competitive brands, a poor promotional effort by Toys "R" Us, and so on. Because it is the exclusive distributor, however, Toys "R" Us may put the blame on the manufacturer's prices, and it may demand a reduction in prices from the manufacturer. Inasmuch as the manufacturer has no other reasons to give that could explain its poor performance, it must depend on Toys "R" Us's analysis.

The last disadvantage of exclusive distribution is one that is easy to overlook. In certain circumstances, exclusive distribution has been found to be in violation of antitrust laws because of its restraint on trade. The legality of an exclusive contract varies from case to case. As long as an exclusive contract does not undermine competition and create a monopoly, it is acceptable. The courts appear to use the following criteria to determine if indeed an exclusive distribution lessens competition:

1. Whether the volume of the product in question is a substantial part of the total volume for that product type.
2. Whether the exclusive dealership excludes competitive products from a substantial share of the market.

Thus, a company considering an exclusive distribution strategy should review its decision in the light of these two ground rules.

The inverse of exclusive distribution is intensive distribution. **Intensive distribution** makes a product available at all possible retail outlets. This may mean that the product is carried at a wide variety of different and also competing retail institutions in a given area. The distribution of convenience goods is most consistent with this strategy. If the nature of a product is such that a consumer generally does not bother to seek out the product but will buy it on sight if available, then it is to the seller's advantage to have the product visible in as many places as possible. The Bic Pen Corporation is an example of a firm that uses this type of strategy. Bic makes its products available in a wide variety of retail establishments, ranging from drugstores, to "the corner grocery store," to large supermarkets. In all, Bic sells through 250,000 retail outlets, which represent competing as well as noncompeting stores. The advantages to be gained from this strategy are increased sales, wider customer recognition, and impulse buying. All of these qualities are desirable for convenience goods. It also requires that manufacturers using an intensive distribution strategy must generally use a greater number of channels of distribution and much longer channels of distribution that manufacturers using less intensive distribution strategies.

There are two main disadvantages associated with intensive distribution. First, intensively distributed goods are characteristically low-priced and low-margin products that require a fast turnover. Second, it is difficult to provide any degree of control over a large number of retailers. In the short run, uncontrolled distribution may not pose any problem if the intensive distribution leads to increased sales. In the long run, however, it may have a variety of devastating effects. For example, if durable products such as Sony television sets were to be intensively distributed (i.e., through drugstores, discount stores, variety stores, etc.), Sony's sales would probably increase. But such intensive distribution could lead to the problems of price discounting, inadequate customer service, and noncooperation among traditional channels (e.g., department stores), and loss of brand equity. Not only might these problems affect sales revenues in the long run, but the manufacturer might also lose some of its established channels. For example, a department store might decide to drop the Sony line for another brand of television sets. In addition, Sony's distinctive brand image could suffer. In other words, the advantages furnished by intensive distribution should be related carefully to product type to decide if this form of distribution is suitable. It is because of the problems outlined above that one finds intensive distribution limited to such products as candy, newspapers, cigarettes, aspirin, and soft drinks. For these types of products, turnover is usually high and channel control is usually not as strategic as it would be, say, for television sets. Classic products for intensive distribution are soft drinks, low priced candies/snacks and newspapers.

Between exclusive and intensive distribution, there is selective distribution. **Selective distribution** is the strategy in which several but not all retail outlets in a given area distribute a product. **Shopping goods**—goods that consumers seek on the basis of the most attractive price or quality characteristics—are frequently distributed through selective distribution. Because of this, competition among retailers is far greater for shopping goods than for convenience goods. Naturally, retailers wish to reduce competition as much as possible. This causes them to pressure manufacturers to reduce the number of retail outlets in their area distributing a given product in order to reduce competition.

The number of retailers under a selective distribution strategy should be limited by criteria that allow the manufacturer to choose only those retailers who will make a contribution to the firm's overall distribution objectives. For example, some firms may choose retail outlets that can provide acceptable repair and maintenance service to consumers who purchase their products. In the automotive industry, selective criteria are used by manufacturers in granting dealerships. These criteria consist of such considerations as showroom space, service facilities, and inventory levels.

The point may be illustrated with reference to Pennsylvania House, a furniture company. The company used to have 800 retail accounts, but it cut this number to 500. This planned cut obviously limited the number of stores in which the company's product line was exposed. More limited distribution provided the company with much stronger support among surviving dealers. Among these 500 dealers, there was a higher average amount of floor space devoted to Pennsylvania House merchandise, better customer service, better supplier relations, and most important for the company, substantially increased sales per account.

Selective distribution is best applied under circumstances in which high sales volume can be generated by a relatively small number of retailers or, in other words, in which the manufacturer would not appreciably increase its coverage by adding additional dealers. Selective distribution can also be used effectively in situations in which a manufacturer requires a high-caliber firm to carry a full product line and provide necessary services. A dealer in this position is likely to require promotional and technical assistance. The technical assistance is needed not only in conjunction with the sale but also after the sale in the form of repair and maintenance service. Again, by limiting the number of retail outlets to a select few capable of covering the market, the manufacturer can avoid unnecessary costs associated with signing on additional dealers.

Obviously, the greatest danger associated with a strategy of selective distribution is the risk of not adequately covering the market. The consequences of this error are greater than the consequences of initially having one or two extra dealers. Therefore, when in doubt, it is better to have too much coverage than not enough.

In selective distribution, it is extremely important for a manufacturer to choose dealers (retailers) who most closely match the marketing goals and image intended for the product. There can be segments within retail markets; therefore, identifying the right retailers can be the key to penetrating a chosen market. Every department store cannot be considered the same. Among them there can be price, age, and image segmentation. One does not need to be very accurate in distinguishing among stores of the same type in the case of products that have no special image (i.e., those that lend themselves to unsegmented market strategies and mass distribution). But for products with any degree of fashion or style content or with highly segmented customer groups, a selective distribution strategy requires a careful choice of outlets.

Exhibit 16.4 Selection of Suitable Distribution Policies Based on the Relationship between Type of Product and Type of Store		

Classification	Consumer Behavior	Most Likely Form of Distribution
Convenience store/ convenience good	The consumer prefers to buy the most readily available brand of a product at the most accessible store.	Intensive
Convenience store/ shopping good	The consumer selects his or her purchase from among the assortment carried by the most accessible store.	Intensive
Convenience store/ specialty good	The consumer purchases his or her favorite brand from the most accessible store carrying the item in stock.	Selective/exclusive
Shopping store/ convenience good	The consumer is indifferent to the brand of product he or she buys but shops different stores to secure better retail service and/or retail price.	Intensive
Shopping store/ shopping good	The consumer makes comparisons among both retail-controlled factors and factors associated with the product (brand).	Intensive
Shopping store/ specialty good	The consumer has a strong preference as to product brand but shops a number of stores to secure the best retail service and/or price for this brand.	Selective/exclusive
Specialty store/ convenience good	The consumer prefers to trade at a specific store but is indifferent to the brand of product purchased.	Selective/exclusive
Specialty store/ shopping good	The consumer prefers to trade at a certain store but is uncertain as to which product he or she wishes to buy and examines the store's assortment for the best purchase.	Selective/exclusive
Specialty store/ specialty good	The consumer has both a preference for a particular store and for a specific brand.	Selective/exclusive

Source: Louis P. Bucklin, "Retail Strategy and the Classification of Consumer Goods," *Journal of Marketing* (January 1963): 50–55; published by the American Marketing Association.

To appraise what type of product is suitable for what form of distribution, refer to Exhibit 16.4. This exhibit combines the traditional threefold classification of consumer goods (convenience, shopping, and specialty goods) with a threefold classification of retail stores (convenience, shopping, and specialty stores) to determine the appropriate form of distribution. This initial selection may then be examined in the light of other considerations to make a final decision on the scope of distribution.

16.3 MULTIPLE-CHANNEL STRATEGY

The multiple-channel strategy refers to a situation in which two or more different channels are employed to distribute goods and services. The market must be segmented so that each segment gets the services it needs and pays only for them, not for services it does not need. This type of segmentation usually cannot be done effectively by direct selling alone or by exclusive reliance upon distributors. The Robinson-Patman Act makes the use of price for segmentation almost impossible when selling to the same kind of customer through the same distribution channel. Market segmentation, however, may be possible when selling directly to one class of customer and to another only through distributors, which usually requires different services, prices, and support. Thus, a multiple-channel strategy permits optimal access to each individual segment.

Basically, there are two types of multiple channels of distribution, complementary and competitive.

Exhibit 16.5	Brand Name	Price	Retailers	Retails
Mass Levi's, Class Levi's	Levi's Vintage	$145–$220	Neiman Marcus, Sharon Segal	Replica of vintage styles with special treatments
	Levi's Red Tab	$27–$35	Macy's Sears, Kohl's	Trendy embellishment designed to appeal to a broad audience
	Levi's Strauss Signature	Under $30	Wal-Mart	Newly designed label without the famous two-horse design

Complementary channels exist when each channel handles a different noncompeting product or non-competing market segment. An important reason to promote complementary channels is to reach market segments that cannot otherwise be served. For example, Avon Products, which had sold directly to consumers for 100 years, broke the tradition in 1986 and began selling some perfumes (e.g., Deneuve fragrance, which sells for as much as $165 an ounce) through department stores. The rationale behind this move was to serve customer segments that the company could not reach through direct selling.[9] Samsonite Corporation sells the same type of luggage to discount stores that it distributes through department stores, with some cosmetic changes in design. In this way the company is able to reach middle- and low-income segments that may never shop for luggage in department stores. Similarly, magazines use newsstand distribution as a complementary channel to subscriptions. Catalogs serve as complementary channels for large retailers such as J.C. Penney. Levi Strauss & Co. markets a large number of different styles at different prices sold through a range of retailers as shown in Exhibit 16.5.[10]

The simplest way to create complementary channels is through private branding. This permits entry into markets that would otherwise be lost. The Coca-Cola Company sells its Minute Maid frozen orange juice to A&P to be sold under the A&P name. At the same time, the Minute Maid brand is available in A&P stores. Presumably, there are customers who perceive the private brand to be no different in quality from the manufacturer's brand. Inasmuch as the private brand is always a little less expensive than a manufacturer's brand, such customers prefer the lower-priced private brand. Thus, private branding helps broaden the market base.

There is another reason that may lead a manufacturer to choose this strategy. In instances where other firms in an industry have saturated traditional distribution channels for a product, a new entry may be distributed through a different channel. This new channel may then in turn be different from the traditional channel used for the rest of the manufacturer's product line. Hanes, for example, decided to develop a new channel for L'eggs (supermarkets and drugstores) because traditional channels were already crowded with competing brands. Likewise, R. Dakin developed nontraditional complementary channels to distribute its toys. Although most toy manufacturers sell their wares through toy shops and department stores, Dakin distributes more than 60 percent of its products through a variety of previously ignored outlets such as airports, hospital gift shops, restaurants, amusement parks, stationery stores, and drugstores. This strategy lets Dakin avoid direct competition. In recent years, many companies have developed new channels in the form of direct mail and internet based sales for such diverse products as men's suits, shoes, insurance, records, newly published books, computers, CDs and individual songs, and jewelry.

The Internet is changing where and how consumers shop and retailers sell. It has become the location to buy almost anything a person wants—fast, easy, and whenever he/she wants it. But that does not mean that traditional retail stores will become relics. The physical limits of buying on the Web mean that not every product is suited to online purchasing.[11] To date, with some notable exceptions such as Amazon and Ebay, the most successful retailers have combined Internet-based selling with brick-and-mortar outlets.

U.S. consumers spent $136.4 billion on purchases on the Web in 2007. In 2000, when Web-based sales were $90 billion, it was estimated that there would be $150 billion in Web-based sales in the year 2005, and that they would soar to $250 billion in 2010. Though Web-based sales have not lived up to projections, their growth has obviously been quite substantial. As personal computers and online services penetrate more and more households, the number of cybershoppers will grow. In their 2007 Internet activities survey (at www.pewinternet.org/trends.asp), Pew Internet and American Life found that 75 percent of U.S. adults used the Internet, and of those adults 92 percent sent or read email. Eighty-one percent used Internet services to get information on a product or dervice they were considering buying, and 66 percent bought products over the Internet.[12]

A company may also develop complementary channels to broaden the market when its traditional channel happens to be a large account. For example, Easco Corporation, the nation's second-largest maker of hand tools, had for years tied itself to Sears, Roebuck and Company, supplying wrenches, sockets, and other tools for the retailer's Craftsman line. Sears accounted for about 47 percent of Easco's sales and about 62 percent of its pretax earnings in the mid-1980s. But as Sears's growth slowed, Easco had a critical strategic dilemma: What do you do when one dominant customer stops growing and starts to slip? The company decided to lessen its dependence on Sears by adding some 500 new hardware and home-center stores for its hand tools.[13]

To broaden their markets in recent years, many clothing manufacturers, including Ralph Lauren, Liz Claiborne, Calvin Klein, Anne Klein, and Adrienne Vittadini, have opened their own stores to sell a full array of their clothes and accessories. Again, to broaden the market, brand-name fast-food companies, Pizza Hut, Subway Sandwiches, Salads Kiosk, and others, have started selling their products in public school cafeterias.[14] After years of deriding personal-computer dealers as costly middlemen, in 2001 Dell computer Corp. began selling its PCs through the dealers. This move came as the company looked beyond its traditional business model to spur sales growth.[15]

Complementary channels may also be necessitated by geography. Many industrial companies undertake direct distribution of their products in such large metropolitan areas as New York, Chicago, Detroit, and Cleveland. Because the market is dense and because of the proximity of customers to each other, a salesperson can make more than 10 calls a day. The same company that sells directly to its customers in urban environments, however, may use manufacturer's representatives or some other type of intermediary in the hinterlands because the market there is too thin to support full-time salespeople.

Another reason to promote complementary channels is to enhance the distribution of noncompeting items. For example, many food processors package fruits and vegetables for institutional customers in giant cans that have little market among household customers. These products, therefore, are distributed through different channels. Procter & Gamble manufactures toiletries for hotels, motels, hospitals, airlines, and so on, which are distributed through different channel arrangements. The volume of business may also require the use of different channels. Many appliance manufacturers sell directly to builders but use distributors and dealers for selling to household consumers.

The basis for employing complementary channels is to enlist customers and segments that cannot be served when distribution is limited to a single channel. Thus, the addition of a complementary channel may be the result of simple cost-benefit analysis. If by employing an additional channel the overall business can be increased without jeopardizing quality or service and without any negative impact on long-term profitability, it may be worthwhile to do so. However, care is needed to ensure that the enhancement of the market through multiple channels does not lead the Justice Department to charge the company with monopolizing the market.

The second type of multiple-channel strategy is the competitive channel. **Competitive channels** exist when the same product is sold through two different and competing channels. This distribution posture may be illustrated with reference to a boat manufacturer, the Luhrs Company. Luhrs sells and ships boats directly to dealers, using one franchise to sell Ulrichsen wood boats and Alura fiberglass boats and another franchise to sell Luhrs wood and fiberglass/wood boats. The two franchises could be issued to the same dealer, but they are normally issued to separate dealers. Competition between dealers holding separate franchises is both possible and encouraged. The two dealers compete against each other to the extent that their products satisfy similar consumer needs in the same segment.

The reason for choosing this competitive strategy is the hope that it will increase sales. It is thought that if dealers must compete against themselves as well as against other manufacturers' dealers, the extra effort will benefit overall sales. The effectiveness of this strategy is debatable. It could be argued that a program using different incentives, such as special discounts for attaining certain levels of sales, could be just as effective as this type of competition. It could be even more effective because the company would eliminate costs associated with developing additional channels.

Sometimes a company may be forced into developing competing channels in response to changing environments. For example, nonprescription drugs were traditionally sold through drugstores. But as the merchandising perspectives of supermarkets underwent a change during the post-World War II period, grocery stores became a viable channel for such products because shoppers expected to find convenience drug products there. This made it necessary for drug companies to deal with grocery wholesalers and retail grocery stores along with drug wholesalers and drugstores. In the 1980s, Capital Holding Corp. (a life insurance company located in Louisville, Kentucky) adopted a variety of marketing innovations. For example, in 1985 it began selling life insurance in novel ways, notably through supermarkets. Impressed by Capital Holding's steady growth and strong financial performance, many other insurance companies were forced to develop new channels to sell their insurance products.[16]

The argument behind the competitive channel strategy is that, although two brands of the same manufacturer may be essentially the same, they may appeal to different sets of customers. Thus, General Motors engages different dealers for its Buick, Cadillac, Chevrolet, and Pontiac cars. These dealers vigorously compete with one another. A more interesting example of competing multiple channels adopted by automobile manufacturers is provided by their dealings with car rental companies. Carmakers sell cars directly to car rental agencies. Hertz, for example, buys from an assembly plant and regularly resells some of its slightly used cars in competition with new cars through its more than 100 offices across the United States. Many of these offices are located in close proximity to dealers of new cars. Despite such competition, a manufacturer undertakes distribution through multiple channels to come off, on the whole, with increased business.

In adopting multiple competing channels, a company needs to make sure that it does not overextend itself; otherwise it may spread itself too thin and face competition to such an extent that ultimate results are disastrous. McCammon cites the case of a wholesaler who adopted multiple channels and thus exposed itself to a grave situation:

Consider, for example, the competitive milieu of Stratton & Terstegge, a large hardware wholesaler in Louisville. At the present time, the company sells to independent retailers, sponsors a voluntary group program, and operates its own stores. In these multiple capacities, it competes against conventional wholesalers (Belknap), cash and carry wholesalers (Atlas), specialty wholesalers (Garcia), corporate chains (Wiches), voluntary groups (Western Auto), cooperative groups (Colter), free-form corporations (Interco), and others. Given the complexity of its competitive environment, it is not surprising to observe that Stratton & Terstegge generates a relatively modest rate of return on net worth.[17]

One of the dangers involved in setting up multiple channels is dealer resentment. This is particularly true when competitive channels are established. When this happens, it obviously means that an otherwise exclusive retailer will now suffer a loss in sales. Such a policy can result in the retailer electing to carry a different manufacturer's product line, if a comparable product line is available. For example, if a major department store such as Lord & Taylor is upset with a manufacturer such as the Hathaway Shirt Company for doing business with discounters (i.e., for adopting competing channels), it can very easily give its business to another shirt manufacturer.

Consider the following examples.[18] Hill's Science Diet pet food lost a great deal of support in pet shops and feed stores as a result of the company's experiments with a "store within a store" pet shop concept in the competing grocery channel. In the auto market, ATK, the dominant seller of replacement engines for Japanese cars, lost its virtual monopoly when it attempted to undercut distributors and sell direct to individual mechanics and installers.

Quaker Oats's recent $1.4 billion write-off from the divestiture of its Snapple business was caused in part by channel conflict. Quaker had planned to consolidate its highly efficient grocery channel supporting the Gatorade brand with Snapple's channels for reaching convenience stores. Snapple distributors were supposed to focus on delivering small quantities of both brands to convenience store accounts while Gatorade's warehouse delivery channel handled larger orders to grocery chains and major accounts, leveraging Quaker's established strength in this area.

However, the strategy backfired. As Quaker suggested moving larger Snapple accounts to Gatorade's delivery system, Snapple's distributors revolted. They saw the value of their Snapple business as an exclusive geographic franchise that the split channel strategy would undermine. Several Snapple distributors took legal action against Quaker. The company ultimately backed down, but the dispute had created a considerable distraction at a time when competition from Arizona and Nantucket Nectars was intensifying.

Multiple channels also create control problems. National Distillers and Chemical Corporation had a wholly owned New York distributor, Peel Richards, that strictly enforced manufacturer-stipulated retail prices and refused to do business with price cutters. Since R.H. Macy discounted National Distiller's products, Peel Richards stopped selling to them. R.H. Macy retaliated by placing an order with an upstate New York distributor of National Distillers.[19] National Distillers had no legal recourse against either R.H. Macy or the upstate New York distributor, who was an independent businessperson.

These problems do not diminish the importance of multiple distribution: they only suggest the difficulties that may arise with multiple channels and the difficulties with which management must contend. A manufacturer's failure to use multiple channels gives competitors an opportunity to segment the market by

Exhibit 16.6 Ten Ways to Manage Channel Conflict	Two or more channels target the same customer segment	Channel economics deteriorate	Threatened channel stops performing or retaliates against the supplier
	1. Differentiate channel offer 2. Define exclusive territories 3. Enhance or change the channel's value proposition (e.g., by building skills in value chain)	4. Change the channel's economic formula: • Grant rebates if an intermediary fulfills certain program requirements • Adjust margins between products to support different channel economics • Treat channels fairly to create level playing field 5. Create segment-specific programs (e.g., certain services not available via direct channels) 6. Complement value proposition of the existing channel by introducing a new channel 7. Foster consolidation among intermediaries in a declining channel	8. Leverage power (e.g., a strong brand) against the channel to prevent retaliation 9. Migrate volume to winning channel (e.g., to warehouse clubs for packaged goods) 10. Back off

Source: Christine B. Bucklin, Pamela A. Thomas-Graham, and Elizabeth A. Webster, "Channel conflict: When is it dangerous?", August 1997, *The McKinsey Quarterly*, www.mckinseyquarterly.com. Copyright © 2008 McKinsey & Company. All rights reserved. Reprinted by permission.

concentrating on one or the other end of the market spectrum. This is particularly disastrous for a leading manufacturer because it must automatically forgo access to a large portion of market potential for not being able to use the economies of multiple distribution. If a manufacturer determines that multiple channels could cause problems, solutions must be found to resolve those problems. Exhibit 16.6 outlines a variety of ways to tackle multiple channel conflicts at different stages in its development. For example, if conflict has recently arisen between channels focused on the same segments, suppliers might respond by introducing separate products or brands tailored to each channel.

16.4 CHANNEL-MODIFICATION STRATEGY

The **channel-modification strategy** is the introduction of a change in existing distribution arrangements based on evaluation and critical review. Channels should be evaluated on an ongoing basis so that appropriate modification may be made as necessary. A shift in existing channels may become desirable for any of the following reasons:

1. Changes in consumer markets and buying habits.
2. Development of new needs in relation to service, parts, or technical help.
3. Changes in competitors' perspectives.
4. Changes in relative importance of outlet types.
5. Changes in a manufacturer's financial strength.
6. Changes in a major intermediary's financial strength.
7. Changes in the sales volume level of existing products.
8. Changes in product (addition of new products), price (substantial reduction in price to gain dominant position), or promotion (greater emphasis on advertising) strategies.

To illustrate the importance of modifying channel arrangements to keep up with changing climate, consider GM's efforts to remake its distribution system. GM's objective is to catch up with population shifts by moving stores out of small towns and declining cities and into bustling retail zones along suburban highways. At the same time, it is pushing dealers to reconfigure their holdings to match the way GM has realigned its divisions, and either to spiff up stores or build new ones. The company's ultimate goal: fewer but better dealers. Although the auto maker has made progress in revamping the distribution, the going has been tough as expected. GM launched a $1 billion project in 1990 to relocate some dealers, merge others, and shrink its dealer count from 9,500 in 1990 to 7,000 by the end of 2000.[20]

Channels of distribution may be evaluated on such primary criteria as cost of distribution, coverage of market (penetration), customer service, communication with the market, and control of distribution networks. Occasionally, such secondary factors as support of channels in the successful introduction of a new product and cooperation with the company's promotional effort also become evaluative criteria. To arrive at a distribution channel that satisfies all these criteria requires simultaneous optimization of every facet of distribution, something that is usually not operationally possible. Consequently, a piecemeal approach may be followed.

16.4.1 Cost of Distribution

A detailed cost analysis of distribution is the first step in evaluating various channel alternatives on a sales-cost basis. This requires classification of total distribution costs under various heads and subheads. Exhibit 16.7 illustrates such a cost classification based on general accounting practices; information about each item should be conveniently available from the controller's office.

The question of evaluation comes up only when the company has been following a particular channel strategy for a number of years. Presumably, the company has pertinent information to undertake distribution cost analysis by customer segment and product line. This sort of data allows the analyzer to find out how cost under each head varies with sales volume; for example, how warehousing expenses vary with sales volume, how packaging and delivery expenses are related to sales, and so on. In other words, the purpose here is to establish a relationship between annual sales and different types of cost. These relationships are useful in predicting the future cost behavior for established dollar-sales objectives, assuming present channel arrangements are continued.

To find out the cost of distribution for alternative channels, estimates should be made of all relevant costs under various sales estimates. Cost information can be obtained from published sources and interviews with selected informants. For example, assume that a company has been selling through wholesalers for a number of years and is now considering distribution through its own branches. To follow the latter course, the company needs to rent a number of offices in important markets. Estimates of the cost of renting or purchasing an office can be furnished by real estate agents. Similarly, the cost of recruiting and hiring additional help to staff the offices should be available through the personnel office. With the relevant information gathered, simple break-even analysis can be used to compute the attractiveness of the alternative channel.

Assume that a company has 20,000 potential customers and, on an average, that each of them must be contacted every two weeks. A salesperson who makes 10 calls a day and who works five days a week can contact 100 customers every two weeks. Thus, the company needs $20,000 \div 100 = 200$ salespeople. If each salesperson receives $30,000 in salary and $20,000 in expenses, the annual cost of its salespeople is $10,000,000. Further, assume that 10 sales managers are required for control and supervision and that each one is paid, say, $50,000 a year. The cost of supervision would then be $500,000. Let $9,500,000 be the cost of other overhead, such as office and warehouse expenses. The total cost of direct distribution will then be $10,000,000 + $500,000 + $9,500,000, or $20 million. Assume that distribution through wholesalers (the arrangement currently being pursued) costs the company 25 percent of sales. Assuming sales to be x, we can set up an equation, $0.25x + $20 million, and solve for x ($x + $80 million). If the company decides to go to direct distribution, it must generate a sales volume of $80 million before it can break even on costs. Thus, if sales potential is well above the $80 million mark, direct distribution is worth considering.

One problem with break-even analysis is that distribution alternatives that are considered equally effective may not always be so. It is a pervasive belief that the choice of a distribution channel affects total sales revenue just as the selection of an advertising strategy does. For example, a retailer may receive the same number of calls under either of two channel alternatives: from the company's salesperson or from a wholesaler's salesperson. The question, however, is whether the effect of these calls is the same. The best

1. Direct Selling

Salaries: administrative and supervisory
Clerical
Salespeople
Commission
Travel and entertainment
Training
Insurance: real and property; liability; workmen's comp
Taxes: personal property; social security; unemployment insurance
Returned-goods expense chargeable to salespeople
Pension
Rent
Utilities
Repair and maintenance
Depreciation
Postage and office supplies

2. Advertising and Sales Promotion

Salaries: administrative and supervisory; clerical; advertising production
Publication space: trade journals; newspapers
Product promotion: advertising supplier; advertising agency fees; direct-mail expenses; contests; catalogs and price list
Cooperative advertising: dealers; retail stores; billboards

3. Product and Package Design

Salaries: administrative and supervisory
Wages
Materials
Depreciation

4. Sales Discounts and Allowances

Cash discounts on sales
Quantity discounts
Sales allowances

5. Credit Extension

Salaries: administrative and supervisory; credit representatives; clerical
Bad debt losses
Forms and postage
Credit rating services
Legal fees: collection efforts
Travel
Financial cost of accounts receivable

6. Market Research

Salaries: administrative; clerical
Surveys: distributors; consumers
Industry trade data
Travel

7. Warehousing and Handling

Salaries: administrative
Wages: warehouse services
Depreciation: furniture; fixtures
Insurance
Taxes
Repair and maintenance
Unsalable merchandise
Warehouse responsibility
Supplies
Utilities

8. Inventory Levels

Obsolescence markdown
Financial cost of carrying inventories

9. Packing, Shipping, and Delivery

Salaries: administrative; clerical
Wages: truck drivers; truck maintenance persons; packers
Shipping clerks
Truck operators
Truck repairs
Depreciation: furniture; fixtures; trucks
Insurance
Taxes
Utilities
Packing supplies
Postage and forms
Freight: factory to warehouse; warehouse to customer; factory to customer
Outside trucking service

10. Order Processing

Order forms
Salaries: administrative
Wages: order review clerks; order processing clerks; equipment operators
Depreciation: Order processing equipment

11. Customer Service

Salaries: administrative; customer service representatives; clerical
Stationery and supplies

12. Printing and Recording of Accounts Receivable

Sales invoice forms
Salaries: clerical; administrative; accounts receivable clerks; sales invoicing equipment operators
Depreciation: sales invoicing equipment

13. Returned Merchandise

Freight
Salaries: administrative; clerical; returned-goods clerical
Returned-goods processing: material labor
Forms and supplies

Exhibit 16.7 Representative List of Distribution Costs by Function

way to handle this problem is to calculate the changes that would be necessary in order to make channel alternatives equally effective. To an extent, this can be achieved either intuitively or by using one of the mathematical models reported in the marketing literature.

16.4.2 Coverage of the Market

An important aspect of predicting future sales response is the penetration that will eventually be achieved in the market. For example, in the case of a drug company, customers can be divided into three groups: (a) drugstores, (b) doctors, and (c) hospitals.

One measure of the coverage of the market (or penetration of the market) is the number of customers in a group contacted or sold, divided by the total number of customers in that group. Another measure may be penetration in terms of geographical coverage of territory. But these measures are too general. Using just the ratio of customers contacted to the total number of customers does not give a proper indication of coverage because not all types of customers are equally important. Therefore, customers may be further classified, as shown in the accompanying display:

Customer Group	Classification	Basis of Classification
Drugstores	Large, medium, and small	Annual turnover
Hospitals	Large, medium, and small	Number of beds
Doctors	Large, medium, and small	Number of patients attended

Then the desired level of penetration for each subgroup should be specified (e.g., penetrate 90 percent of the large, 75 percent of the medium, and 50 percent of the small drugstores). These percentages can be used for examining the effectiveness of an alternative channel.

An advanced analysis is possible, however, by building a penetration model. The basis of the model is that increments in penetration for equal periods are proportional to the remaining distance to the aimed penetration. The increments in penetration in a period t will be: $t = rp(1 - r)t - 1$, where p = targeted or aimed penetration and r = penetration ratio. This ratio signifies how rapidly the cumulative penetration approaches aimed penetration. For example, if aimed penetration is 80 percent and if $r = 0.3$, then first-year penetration is $80 \times 0.3 = 24$ percent. Next year, the increment in penetration will be $80 \times 0.3 \times 0.7 = 16.8$ percent. Hence, cumulative penetration at the end of the second year will be $24 + 16.8 = 40.8$. The value of p for each subgroup is a matter of policy decision on the part of the company. The value of r depends on the period during which aimed penetration is to be achieved and on sales efforts in terms of the number of medical representatives/salespeople and their call pattern for each subgroup. For the existing channel (selling through the wholesalers), the value of r can be determined from past records. For the alternate channel (direct distribution), the approximate value of r can be computed in one of two ways:

1. Company executives should know how many salespeople would be kept on the rolls if the alternate channel were used. The executives can also estimate the average number of calls a day a salesperson can make and hence the average number of customers in a subgroup he or she can contact. With this information, the value of r can be determined as follows:

$$\frac{\text{Number of customers in a subgroup contacted under existing channel}}{\text{Number of customers in a subgroup that would be contacted in alternate channel}} = \frac{\text{Value of } r \text{ for existing channel}}{\text{Value of } r \text{ for alternate channel}}$$

2. A second approach may be to find out (or estimate) the penetration that would be possible after one year if the alternate channel is used, then to substitute this in the penetration equation to find r when p and t are known.

The penetration model makes it easier to predict the exact coverage in each subgroup of customers over a planning period (say, five years hence). The marketing strategist should determine the ultimate desired penetration p and the time period in which it is to be achieved. Then the model would be able to predict which channel would take the penetration closer to the objective.

16.4.3 Customer Service

The level of customer service differs from customer to customer for each business. Generally speaking, the sales department, with feedback from the field force, should be able to designate the various services that the company should offer to different consumer segments. If this is not feasible, a sample survey may be planned to find out which services customers expect and which services are currently being offered by competitors. This information can be used to develop a viable service package. Then the capability and willingness of each channel alternative to provide these services may be matched to single out the most desirable channel. This can be done intuitively. A more scientific approach would be to list and assign weights to each type of service, then rate different channels according to their ability to handle these services. Cumulative scores can be used for the service ranking of channel alternatives. Conjoint measurement can be used to determine which services are most important to a particular segment of customers.

16.4.4 Communication and Control

Control may be defined as the process of taking steps to bring actual results and desired results closer together. **Communication** refers to the information flow between the company and its customers. To evaluate alternate channels on these two criteria, communication and control objectives should be defined. With reference to communication, for example, information may be desired on the activities of competitors, new products from competitors, the special promotional efforts of competitors, the attitudes of customers toward the company's and toward competitors' services, and the reasons for success of a particular product line of the company. Each channel alternative may then be evaluated in terms of its willingness, capabilities, and interest in providing the required information. In the case of wholesalers, the communication perspective may also depend on the terms of the contract. But the mere fact that they are legally bound by a contract may not motivate wholesalers to cooperate willingly. Finally, the information should be judged for accuracy, timeliness, and relevance.

Environmental shifts, internal or external, may require a company to modify existing channel arrangements. A shift in trade practice, for instance, may render distribution through a manufacturer's representative obsolete. Similarly, technological changes in product design may require frequent service calls on customers that wholesalers may not be able to make, thus leading the company to opt for direct distribution.

To illustrate the point, consider jewelry distribution. For centuries, jewelry was distributed through jewelry shops that relied on uniqueness, craftsmanship, and mystique to reap fat margins on very small volumes. Traditionally, big retailers shunned jewelry as a highly specialized, slow-moving business that tied up too much money in inventory. But this attitude has changed in the last few years. For example, between 1978 and 1982, jewelry stores' share of the jewelry market declined from 65 percent to less than 50 percent. On the other hand, relying on hefty advertising and deep discounting, mass merchandisers (e.g., J.C. Penney, Sears, Wal-Mart, Target, and others) have been making fast inroads into the jewelry business. For example, in 1995 J.C. Penney became the fourth-largest retail jewelry merchant in the United States behind Zale, Gordon Jewelry, and Best Products, the catalog showroom chain. Such a shift in trade practice requires that jewelry manufacturers modify their distribution arrangements.[21]

Similarly, as computer makers try to reach ever-broadening audiences with lower-priced machines, they need new distribution channels. Many of them, IBM and Apple, for example, have turned to retail stores. In the 1970s, people would have laughed at the idea of selling computers over the counter; now it is a preferred way of doing business. The tantalizing opportunity to sell computers to consumers has also given birth to specialty chains specializing in computer and related items.

Ben & Jerry's Homemade, Inc., had to change their distribution arrangements for a different reason. Dreyer's Grand Ice Cream controlled 70 percent of its distribution, and the relationship was regarded as a cornerstone of Ben & Jerry's success. Then, Dreyer made an unwanted takeover offer which Ben & Jerry's resented. The company decided to end the relationship with Dreyer and forged a new alliance with Diage PLC's Haagen-Dazs, until now regarded as an arch competitor, to deliver its products.[22]

Generally speaking, a new company in the market starts distribution through intermediaries. This is necessary because, during the initial period, technical and manufacturing problems are big enough to keep management busy. Besides, at this stage, the company has neither the insight nor the capabilities needed to deal successfully with the vagaries of the market. Therefore, intermediaries are used. With their knowledge of the market, they play an important role in establishing a demand for a company's product. But once the company establishes a foothold in the market, it may discover that it does not have the control of distribution it needs to make further headway. At this time, channel modification becomes necessary.

Managerial astuteness requires that the company do a thorough study before deciding to change existing channel arrangements. Taking a few halfhearted measures could create insurmountable problems resulting in loose control and poor communication. Further, the intermediaries affected should be duly taken into confidence about a company's plans and compensated for any breach of terms. Any modification of channels should match the perspectives of the total marketing strategy. This means that the effect of a modified plan on other ingredients of the marketing mix (such as product, price, and promotion) should be considered. The managers of different departments (as well as the customers) should be informed so that the change does not come as a surprise. In other words, care needs to be taken to ensure that a modification in channel arrangements does not cause any distortion in the overall distribution system.

The point may be illustrated with reference to Caterpillar.[23] A decade ago, many observers predicted Caterpillar's demise. Yet today the company's overall share of the world market for construction and mining equipment is the highest in its history. And the biggest reason for the turnaround has been the company's system of distribution and product support and the close customer relationships it fosters. The backbone of that system is Caterpillar's 186 independent dealers around the world. They have played a central role in helping the company build close relationships with customers and gain insights into how it can improve products and services. The company's success may be attributed to several factors. For one thing, the company stands by its dealers in goods times and in bad. In addition, it gives them extraordinary support, helps ensure that the dealerships are well run, and emphasizes full and honest two-way communication. Finally, it stresses the emotional ties that have developed between the company and its dealers over time.

16.5 CHANNEL-CONTROL STRATEGY

Channel arrangements traditionally consisted of loosely aligned manufacturers, wholesalers, and retailers, all of whom were trying to serve their own ends regardless of what went on elsewhere in the channel structure. In such arrangements, channel control was generally missing. Each member of the channel negotiated aggressively with others and performed a conventionally defined set of marketing functions.

For a variety of reasons, control is a necessary ingredient in running a successful system. Having control is likely to have a positive impact on profits because inefficiencies are caught and corrected in time. This is evidenced by the success of voluntary and cooperative chains, corporate chains, franchise alignments, manufacturers' dealer organizations, and sales branches and offices. Control also helps to realize cost effectiveness vis-à-vis experience curves. For example, centralized organization of warehousing, data processing, and other facilities provides scale efficiencies. Through a planned perspective of the total system, effort is directed to achieving common goals in an integrated fashion.

The focus of channel control may be on any member of a channel system: the manufacturer, wholesaler, or retailer. Unfortunately, there is no established theory to indicate whether any one of them makes a better channel controller than the others. For example, one appliance retailer in Philadelphia with a ten percent market share, Silo Incorporated, served as the channel controller there. This firm had no special relationship with any manufacturer, but if a supplier's line did not do well, Silo immediately contacted the supplier to ask that something be done about it. Wal-Mart can be expected to be the channel controller for a variety of products. Among manufacturers, Kraft ought to be the channel controller for refrigerated goods in supermarkets. Likewise, Procter & Gamble is a channel controller for detergents and related items. Ethan Allen decided to control the distribution channels for its line of Early American furniture by establishing a network of 200 dealer outlets. Sherwin-Williams decided to take over channel control to guide its own destiny because traditional channels were not showing enough aggressiveness. The company established its own chain of 2,000 retail outlets.

These examples underscore the importance of someone taking over channel leadership in order to establish control. Conventionally, market leadership and the size of a firm determine its suitability for channel control. Strategically, a firm should attempt to control the channel for a product if it can make a commitment to fulfill its leadership obligations and if such a move is likely to be economically beneficial in the long run for the entire channel system. For example, the thought of winning a contract to supply a mass retailer may lead a company to modify existing channel arrangements. After all, Toys "R" Us accounted for a fifth of the U.S. toy market in 2001.[24] The Home Depot sold more home improvement products than all hardware stores combined, and one quarter of the underwear purchased by Americans came from Wal-Mart (an estimated 23 percent of the U.S. population shops in Wal-Mart on an average day).[25] Landing an account with one of these mass retailers can double or even triple a supplier's annual sales. However, rapid revenue growth is not always accompanied by a surge in profits. The strain of coping with high volumes and the service needs of powerful customers can put tremendous pressure on suppliers' profit margins if they attempt to conduct business as usual. Some manufacturers that supply mass retailers even find that although their sales rise faster than those of other manufacturers, their earnings growth is slower. As a matter of fact, in some cases dealing with a stronger partner may force a retailer out of buisness. The failure of Toy Mart.Com Inc., one of the first high-profile casualties of the Web-retailing shakeout, shows how things can go wrong when a small distributor turns to big companies for funding and support.[26]

Vertical marketing systems may be defined as professionally managed and centrally programmed networks that are pre-engineered to achieve operating economies and maximum market impact. Stated alternatively, vertical marketing systems are rationalized and capital-intensive networks designed to achieve technological, managerial, and promotional economies through the integration, coordination, and synchronization of marketing flows from points of production to points of ultimate use.[27]

The vertical marketing system is an emerging trend in the American economy. It seems to be replacing all conventional marketing channels as the mainstay of distribution. As a matter of fact, according to one estimate, vertical marketing systems in the consumer-goods sector account for about 70 to 80 percent of the available market.[28] In brief, vertical marketing systems (sometimes also referred to as centrally coordinated systems) have emerged as the dominant ingredient in the competitive process and thus play a strategic role in the formulation of distribution strategy.

Vertical marketing systems may be classified into three types: corporate, administered, and contractual. Under the corporate vertical marketing system, successive stages of production and distribution are owned by a single entity. This is achieved through forward and backward integration. Sherwin-Williams owns and operates its 2,000 retail outlets in a corporate vertical marketing system (a case of forward integration). Other examples of such systems are Hart, Schaffner, and Marx (operating more than 275 stores), International Harvester, Goodyear, and Sohio. Not only a manufacturer but also a corporate vertical system might be owned and operated by a retailer (a case of backward integration). Sears, like many other large retailers, has financial interests in many of its suppliers' businesses. For example, about one-third of DeSoto (a furniture and home furnishings manufacturer) stock is owned by Sears. Finally, W. W. Grainger provides an example of a wholesaler-run vertical marketing system. This firm, an electrical distributor with 2007 sales of $6.4 billion, has nine manufacturing facilities.

Another outstanding example of a vertical marketing system is provided by Gallo, the wine company.

The Gallo brothers own Fairbanks Trucking company, one of the largest intrastate truckers in California. Its 200 semis and 500 trailers are constantly hauling wine out of Modesto and raw materials back in including ... lime from Gallo's quarry east of Sacramento. Alone among wine producers, Gallo makes bottles—two million a day—and its Midcal Aluminum Co. spews out screw tops as fast as the bottles are filled. Most of the country's 1,300 or so wineries concentrate on production to the neglect of marketing. Gallo, by contrast, participates in every aspect of selling short of whispering in the ear of each imbiber. The company owns its distributors in about a dozen markets and probably would buy many ... more ... if the laws in most states did not prohibit doing so.[29]

In an **administered vertical marketing system**, a dominant firm within the channel system, such as the manufacturer, wholesaler, or retailer, coordinates the flow of goods by virtue of its market power. For example, the firm may exert influence to achieve economies in transportation, order processing, warehousing, advertising, or merchandising. As can be expected, it is large organizations like Wal-Mart, Safeway, J.C. Penney, General Motors, Kraft, GE, Procter & Gamble, Lever Brothers, Nabisco, and General Foods that emerge as channel captains to guide their channel networks, while not actually owning them, to achieve economies and efficiencies.

In a **contractual vertical marketing system**, independent firms within the channel structure integrate their programs on a contractual basis to realize economies and market impact. Primarily, there are three types of contractual vertical marketing systems: wholesaler-sponsored voluntary groups, retailer-sponsored cooperative groups, and franchise systems. Independent Grocers Alliance (IGA) is an example of a wholesaler-sponsored voluntary group. At the initiative of the wholesaler, small grocery stores agree to form a chain to achieve economies with which to compete against corporate chains. The joining members agree to adhere to a variety of contractual terms, such as the use of a common name, to help realize economies on large order. Except for these terms, each store continues to operate independently. A retailer-sponsored cooperative group is essentially the same. Retailers form their own association (cooperative) to compete against corporate chains by undertaking wholesaler functions (and possibly even a limited amount of production); that is, they operate their own wholesale companies to serve member retailers. This type of contractual vertical marketing system is operated primarily, though not exclusively, in the food line. Associated Grocers Co-op and Certified Grocers are examples of retailer-sponsored food cooperative groups. Value-Rite, a group of 2,298 stores, is a drugstore cooperative.[30]

A **franchise system** is an arrangement whereby a firm licenses others to market a product or service using its trade name in a defined geographic area under specified terms and conditions. In 2007, there were more than 3,000 franchisers in the United States, over twice as many as in 1984. Practically any business that can be taught to someone is being franchised. From 2001–2005, The franchising industry grew by eighteen percent, adding more than 140,000 new businesses and 1.2 million new jobs to the U.S. economy. The direct economic output grew by forty percent over the five year period to $880 billion.

In addition to traditional franchising businesses (e.g., fast-food), banks are doing it, as are accountants, dating services, skin care centers, tub and tile refinishers, tutors, funeral homes, bookkeepers, dentists, nurses, bird seed shops, gift wrappers, wedding consultants, cookie bakers, popcorn poppers, beauty shops, baby-sitters, and suppliers of maid service, lawn care, and solar greenhouses. Four different types of franchise systems can be distinguished:

1. The manufacturer-retailer franchise is exemplified by franchised automobile dealers and franchised service stations.
2. The manufacturer-wholesaler franchise is exemplified by Coca-Cola and PepsiCo, who sell the soft drink syrups they manufacture to franchised wholesalers who, in turn, bottle and distribute soft drinks to retailers.
3. The wholesaler-retailer franchise is exemplified by Rexall Drug Stores, Sentry Drug Centers, and CompUSA.
4. The service sponsor-retailer franchise is exemplified by Avis, Hertz, and National in the car rental business; McDonald's, Chicken Delight, Kentucky Fried Chicken, and Taco Bell in the prepared foods industry; Comfort Inn and Holiday Inn in the lodging and food industry; Midas and AAMCO in the auto repair business; and Kelly Girl and Manpower in the employment service business.

Vertical marketing systems help achieve economies that cannot be realized through the use of conventional marketing channels. In strategic terms, vertical marketing systems provide opportunities for building experience, thus allowing even small firms to derive the benefits of market power. Considering their growing importance, conventional channels will need to adopt new distribution strategies to compete against vertical marketing systems. For example, they may

1. Develop programs to strengthen customers' competitive capabilities. This alternative involves manufacturers and wholesalers in such activities as sponsoring centralized accounting and management reporting services, formulating cooperative promotional programs, and cosigning shopping center leases.
2. Enter new markets. For example, building supply distributors have initiated cash-and-carry outlets. Steel warehouses have added glass and plastic product lines to their traditional product lines. Industrial distributors have initiated stockless buying plans and blanket order contracts so that they may compete effectively for customers who buy on a direct basis.
3. Effect economies of operation by developing management information systems. For example, some middlemen in conventional channels have installed the IBM IMPACT program to improve their control over inventory.
4. Determine through research the focus of power in the channel and urge the channel member designated to undertake a reorganization of marketing flows.[31]

Despite the growing trend toward vertical integration, it would be naive to consider it an unmixed blessing. Vertical integration has both pluses and minuses—more of the latter, according to one empirical study on the subject.[32] For example, vertical integration requires a huge commitment of resources: in mid-1981, Du Pont acquired Conoco in a $7.3 billion transaction. The strategy may not be worthwhile unless the company gains needed insurance as well as cost savings. As a matter of fact, some observers have blamed the U.S. automobile industry's woes, in part, on excessive vertical integration: "In deciding to integrate backward because of apparent short-term rewards, managers often restrict their ability to strike out in innovative directions in the future."[33]

16.6 CONFLICT-MANAGEMENT STRATEGY

It is quite conceivable that the independent firms that constitute a channel of distribution (i.e., manufacturer, wholesaler, retailer) may sometimes find themselves in conflict with each other. The underlying causes of conflict are the divergent goals that different firms may pursue. If the goals of one firm are being challenged because of the strategies followed by another channel member, conflict is the natural outcome. Thus, channel conflict may be defined as a situation in which one channel member perceives another channel member or members to be engaged in behavior that is preventing or impeding it from achieving its goals.

Disagreement between channel members may arise from incompatible desires and needs. Weigand and Wasson give four examples of the kinds of conflict that may arise:

A manufacturer promises an exclusive territory to a retailer in return for the retailer's "majority effort" to generate business in the area. Sales increase nicely, but the manufacturer believes it is due more to population growth in the area than to the effort of the store owner, who is spending too much time on the golf course.

A fast-food franchiser promises "expert promotional assistance" to his retailers as partial explanation for the franchise fee. One of the retailers believes that the help he is getting is anything but expert and that the benefits do not correspond with what he was promised.

Another franchiser agrees to furnish accounting services and financial analysis as a regular part of his service. The franchisee believes that the accountant is nothing more than a "glorified bookkeeper" and that the financial analysis consists of several pages of ratios that are incomprehensible.

A third franchiser insists that his franchisees should maintain a minimum stock of certain items that are regularly promoted throughout the area. Arguments arise as to whether the franchiser's recommendations constitute a threat, while the franchisee is particularly concerned about protecting his trade name.[34]

The four strategic alternatives available for resolving conflicts between channel members are bargaining, boundary, interpenetration, and superorganizational strategies. Under the **bargaining strategy**, one member of the channel takes the lead in activating the bargaining process by being willing to concede something, with the expectation that the other party will reciprocate. For example, a manufacturer may agree to provide interest-free loans for up to ninety days to a distributor if the distributor will carry twice the level of inventory that it previously did and will furnish warehousing for the purpose. Or a retailer may propose to continue to carry the television line of a manufacturer if the manufacturer will supply television sets under the retailer's own name (i.e., the retailer's private brand). The bargaining strategy works out only if both parties are willing to adopt the attitude of give-and-take and if bottom-line results for both are favorable enough to induce them to accept the terms of the bargain.

The **boundary strategy** handles the conflict through diplomacy; that is, by nominating the employee most familiar with the perspectives of the other party to take up the matter with his or her counterpart. For example, a manufacturer may nominate a veteran salesperson to communicate with the purchasing agent of the customer to see if some basis can be established to resolve the conflict. For example, North Face, the manufacturer of high-performance outdoor clothes, decided to expand beyond the $5 billion specialty outdoor market to the broader $30-billion casual sportswear market. To implement the strategy, it plans to increase the number of stores selling North Face after 2001, from 1,500 specialty stores up to 4,000 retailers.[35]

This has upset the specialty stores since they fear that the expansion will undercut the brand, putting pressure on their margins. To resolve the conflict, the North Face salesperson may meet the specialty store buyers to talk over business in general. In between the talks, he or she may indicate in a subtle way that the company's decision to broaden the distribution would be mutually beneficial. In the end, the specialty stores will reap the benefits of the brand name popularity triggered by the mass distribution. Besides, the salesperson may be authorized to propose that his or her company will agree not to sell the top of the line to "new retailers," thus ensuring that it will continue to be available only through the specialty stores. In order for this strategy to succeed, it is necessary that the diplomat (the salesperson in the example) be fully briefed on the situation and provided leverage with which to negotiate.

The **interpenetration strategy** is directed toward resolving conflict through frequent informal interactions with the other party to gain a proper appreciation of each other's perspectives. One of the easiest ways to develop interaction is for one party to invite the other to join its trade association. For example, several years ago television dealers were concerned because they felt that the manufacturers of television sets did not understand their problems. To help correct the situation, the dealers invited the manufacturers to become members of the National Appliance and Radio-TV Dealers Association (NARDA). Currently, manufacturers take an active interest in NARDA conventions and seminars.

Finally, the focus of **superorganizational strategy** is to employ conciliation, mediation, and arbitration to resolve conflict. Essentially, a neutral third party is brought into the conflict to resolve the matter. **Conciliation** is an informal attempt by a third party to bring two conflicting organizations together and help them come to an agreement amicably. For example, an independent wholesaler may serve as a conciliator between a manufacturer and its customers. Under **mediation**, the third party plays a more active role. If the parties in conflict fail to come to an agreement, they may be willing to consider the procedural or substantive recommendations of the mediator.

Arbitration may also be applied to resolve channel conflict. Arbitration may be compulsory or voluntary. Under compulsory arbitration, the dispute must by law be submitted to a third party, the decision being final and binding on both conflicting parties. For example, the courts may arbitrate between two parties in dispute. Years ago, when automobile manufacturers and their dealers had problems relative to distribution policies, the court arbitrated. Voluntary arbitration is a process whereby the parties in conflict submit their disputes for resolution to a third party on their own. For example, in 1955 the Federal Trade Commission arbitrated between television set manufacturers, distributors, and dealers by setting up 32 industry rules to protect the consumer and to reduce conflicts over distribution. The conflict areas involved were tie-in sales; price fixing; mass shipments used to clog outlets and foreclose competitors; discriminatory billing; and special rebates, bribes, refunds, and discounts.[36]

Of all the methods of resolving conflict, arbitration is the fastest. In addition, under arbitration, secrecy is preserved and less expense is incurred. Inasmuch as industry experts serve as arbitrators, one can expect a fairer decision. Thus, as a matter of strategy, arbitration may be more desirable than other methods for managing conflict. Exhibit 16.6 lists different ways of managing channel conflict.

SUMMARY

Distribution strategies are concerned with the flow of goods and services from manufacturers to customers. The discussion in this chapter was conducted from the manufacturer's viewpoint. Six major distribution strategies were distinguished: channel-structure strategy, distribution-scope strategy, multiple-channel strategy, channel-modification strategy, channel-control strategy, and conflict-management strategy.

Channel-structure strategy determines whether the goods should be distributed directly from manufacturer to customer or indirectly through one or more intermediaries. Formulation of this strategy was discussed with reference to Bucklin's postponement-speculation theory. Distribution-scope strategy specifies whether exclusive, selective, or intensive distribution should be pursued. The question of simultaneously employing more than one channel was discussed under multiple-channel strategy. Channel-modification strategy involves evaluating current channels and making necessary changes in distribution perspectives to accommodate environmental shifts. Channel-control strategy focuses on vertical marketing systems to institute control. Finally, resolution of conflict among channel members was examined under conflict-management strategy.

The merits and drawbacks of each strategy were discussed. Examples from marketing literature were given to illustrate the practical applications of different strategies.

DISCUSSION QUESTIONS

1. What factors may a manufacturer consider to determine whether to distribute products directly to customers? Can automobiles be distributed directly to customers?
2. Is intensive distribution a prerequisite for gaining experience? Discuss.
3. What precautions are necessary to ensure that exclusive distribution is not liable to challenge as a restraint of trade?
4. What strategic factor makes the multiple-channel strategy a necessity for a multiproduct company?

5. What criteria may a food processor adopt to evaluate its channels of distribution?

6. What kinds of environmental shifts require a change in channel arrangements?

7. What reasons may be ascribed to the emergence of vertical marketing systems?

8. What strategies may conventional channels adopt to meet the threat of vertical marketing systems?

9. What are the underlying sources of conflict in distribution channel relations? Give examples.

10. What is the most appropriate strategy for resolving a channel conflict?

NOTES

1. Wroe Alderson, "Factors Governing the Development of Marketing Channels," in *Marketing Channels for Manufactured Products*, ed. Richard M. Clewett (Homewood, IL, Richard D. Irwin, 1964): 7.

2. Louis P. Bucklin, *A Theory of Distribution Channel Structure* (Berkeley, IBER Special Publications, University of California, 1966); and "Postponement, Speculation and Structure of Distribution Channels," in *The Marketing Channel: A Conceptual Viewpoint*, ed. Bruce E. Mallen (New York, John Wiley & Sons, 1967): 67–74.

3. Louis P. Bucklin and Leslie Halpert, "Exploring Channel of Distribution for Cement with the Principle of Postponement-Speculation," in *Marketing and Economic Development*, ed. Peter D. Bennett (Chicago, American Marketing Association, 1965): 699.

4. See "Benetton," in Robert D. Buzzell and John A. Quelch, *Multinational Marketing Management* (Reading, MA, Addison-Wesley Publishing Co., 1988): 47–76.

5. Leslie Easton, "Distributing Value: A Revamped McKesson Corporation Is Producing Surprises," *Barron's*, August 3, 1977, pp. 13, 41, 42.

6. "Tesco's New Tricks," *The Economist*, April 15, 1995, p. 61.

7. Scott C. Friend and Patricia H. Walker, "Welcome to the New World of Merchandising," *Harvard Business Review*, November 2001, pp. 133–141. Also see Leonard L. Berry, "The Old Pillars of New Retailing," *Harvard Business Review*, pp. 131–140; and Bertrand Benoit, "Checkout the Supermarket of the Future," *Financial Times*, May 14, 2003, p. 8.

8. *Wetterau, Inc., Annual Report for 1998.*

9. Katarzyna Moreno, "Unbecoming," *Forbes*, June 10, 2002, p. 151.

10. "Why Levi's Still Looks Faded," *BusinessWeek*, July 22, 2002, p. 54.

11. "Home Alone?" *The Economist*, October 12, 1996, p. 67.

12. "A Survey of E-Management," *The Economist*, November 11, 2000. Also see Penelope Ody, "Consumers Again Turn the Tables on Retail Values," *Financial Times*, March 7, 2001, p. 14; US Census Bureau News: Quarterly. Retail E-Commerce Sales, 4th Quarter, 2007, released February 15, 2008; Pew Internet and American Life Project (www.pewinternet.org/trends.asp).

13. "Easco: Turning to New Customers While Helping Sears Promote Tools," *BusinessWeek*, October 6, 1990, p. 62.

14. Louise Lee, "School's Back, and So Are the Marketers," *The Wall Street Journal*, September 1, 1997, p. B1.

15. Gary McWilliams, "In About Face, Dell Will Sell PCs to Dealers," *The Wall Street Journal*, August 20, 2002, p. B1.

16. "Even Star Insurers Are Feeling the Heat," *BusinessWeek*, January 14, 1985, p. 119.

17. Bert C. McCammon, Jr., "Future Shock and the Practice of Management" (Paper presented at the Fifth Annual Research Conference of the American Marketing Association, Madrid, Spain, 1973): 9.

18. Christine B. Bucklin, Pamela A. Thomas-Graham, and Elizabeth A. Webster, "Channel Conflict: When Is It Dangerous?" *The McKinsey Quarterly*, Vol. 3, 1997, pp. 36–43.

19. Robert E. Weigand, "Fit Products and Channels to Your Market," *Harvard Business Review*, January–February 1977, pp. 95–105.

20. "GM Brings Its Dealers Up to Speed," *BusinessWeek*, February 23, 1998, p. 82.

21. "Chain Stores Strike Gold in Jewelry Sales," *BusinessWeek*, February 6, 1984, p. 56.

22. Laura Johannes, "Ben & Jerry's Plans to End Ties with Dreyer's," *The Wall Street Journal*, September 1, 1998, p. A4.

23. Donald V. Fifties, "Make Your Dealers Your Partners," *Harvard Business Review*, March–April 1996, pp. 84–96.

24. "A Showstopper on Bradway," *BusinessWeek,* December 24, 2001, p. 54.

25. Bruce Upbia, "Profit in a Big Orange," *Forbes*, January 24, 2000; and Constance L. Hays, "The Wal-Mart Way Becomes Topic A in Business Schools," *New York Times*, July 27, 2003, p. 18.

26. William M. Bulkeley, Joseph Pereira, and Bruce Orwall, "Toysmart and Disney Found a Tangled Web of Conflicting Goals," *The Wall Street Journal*, June 7, 2000, p. A1.

27. Bert C. McCammon, Jr., "Perspectives for Distribution Programming," in *Vertical Marketing Systems*, ed. Louis P. Bucklin (Glenview, IL, Scott, Foresman, 1970): 43.

28. Philip Kotler, *Marketing Management*, 11th ed. (Englewood Cliffs, NJ, Prentice-Hall, 2001): 508.

29. Jaclyn Fireman, "How Gallo Crushes the Competition," *Fortune*, September 1, 1986, p. 27.

30. *The Wall Street Journal*, October 2, 1986, p. 1.

31. Louis W. Stern, Adel I. El-Ansary, and James R. Brown, *Management in Marketing Channels* (Englewood Cliffs, NJ, Prentice-Hall, 2000): 190.

32. Robert D. Buzzell, "Is Vertical Integration Profitable?" *Harvard Business Review*, January–February 1983, pp. 92–102.

33. Robert H. Hayes and William J. Abernathy, "Managing Our Way to Economic Decline," *Harvard Business Review*, July–August 1980, p. 72.

34. Robert Weigand and Hilda C. Wasson, "Arbitration in the Marketing Channel," *Business Horizons*, October 1974, p. 40.

35. "A Slippery Slope for North Face," *BusinessWeek,* December 7, 1998, p. 66.

36. Stern and El-Ansary, *Marketing Channels*.

APPENDIX: PERSPECTIVES ON DISTRIBUTION STRATEGIES

Definition: Using perspectives of intermediaries in the flow of goods from manufacturers to customers. Distribution may be either direct (from manufacturer to retailer or from manufacturer to customer) or indirect (involving the use of one or more intermediaries, such as wholesalers or agents, to reach the customer).

Objective: To reach the optimal number of customers in a timely manner at the lowest possible cost while maintaining the desired degree of control.

Requirements: Comparison of direct versus indirect distribution on the basis of (a) cost, (b) product characteristics, (c) degree of control, and (d) other factors.

Costs: (a) Distribution costs. (b) Opportunity costs incurred because product not available. (c) Inventory holding and shipping costs.

Product Characteristics: (a) Replacement rate. (b) Gross margin. (c) Service requirements. (d) Search time.

Degree of Control: Greater when direct distribution used.

Other Factors: (a) Adaptability. (b) Technological changes (e.g., computer technology). (c) Social/cultural values.

Expected Results: (a) Direct distribution: (i) high marketing costs, (ii) large degree of control, (iii) informed customers, and (iv) strong image. (b) Indirect distribution: (i) lower marketing costs, (ii) less control, and (iii) reduced channel management responsibilities.

Definition: Establishing the scope of distribution, that is, the target customers. Choices are exclusive distribution (one retailer is granted sole rights in serving a given area), intensive distribution (a product is made available at all possible retail outlets), and selective distribution (many but not all retail outlets in a given area distribute a product).

Objective: To serve chosen markets at a minimal cost while maintaining desired product image.

Requirements: Assessment of (a) customer buying habits, (b) gross margin/turnover rate, (c) capability of dealer to provide service, (d) capability of dealer to carry full product line, and (e) product styling.

Expected Results: (a) Exclusive distribution: (i) strong dealer loyalty, (ii) high degree of control, (iii) good forecasting capability, (iv) sales promotion assistance from manufacturer, (v) possible loss in sales volume, and (vi) possible antitrust violation. (b) Selective distribution: (i) extreme competition in marketplace, (ii) price discounting, and (iii) pressure from channel members to reduce number of outlets. (c) Intensive distribution: (i) low degree of control, (ii) higher sales volume, (iii) wide customer recognition, (iv) high turnover, and (v) price discounting.

Definition: Employing two or more different channels for distribution of goods and services. Multiple-channel distribution is of two basic types: complementary (each channel handles a different noncompeting product or market segment) and competitive (two different and competing channels sell the same product).

Objective: To achieve optimal access to each individual market segment to increase business. Complementary channels are used to reach market segments otherwise left unserved; competitive channels are used with the hope of increasing sales.

Requirements: (a) Market segmentation. (b) Cost/benefit analysis. Use of complementary channels prompted by (i) geographic considerations, (ii) volume of business, (iii) need to distribute noncompeting items, and (iv) saturation of traditional distribution channels. Use of competitive channels can be a response to environmental changes.

Expected Results: (a) Different services, prices, and support provided to different segments. (b) Broader market base. (c) Increased sales. (d) Possible dealer resentment. (e) Control problems. (f) Possible over-extension. Over-extension can result in (i) decrease in quality/service and (ii) negative effects on long-run profitability.

Definition: Introducing a change in the existing distribution arrangements on the basis of evaluation and critical review.

Objective: To maintain an optimal distribution system given a changing environment.

Requirements: (a) Evaluation of internal/external environmental shifts: (i) changes in consumer markets and buying habits, (ii) changes in the retail life cycle, (iii) changes in the manufacturer's financial strength, and (iv) changes in the product life cycle. (b) Continuous evaluation of existing channels. (c) Cost/benefit analysis. (d) Consideration of the effect of the modified channels on other aspects of the marketing mix. (e) Ability of management to adapt to modified plan.

Expected Results: (a) Maintenance of an optimal distribution system given environmental changes. (b) Disgruntled dealers and customers (in the short run).

Definition: Takeover by a member of the channel structure in order to establish control of the channel and provide a centrally organized effort to achieve common goals.

Objectives: (a) To increase control. (b) To correct inefficiencies. (c) To realize cost-effectiveness through experience curves. (d) To gain efficiencies of scale.

Requirements: Commitment and resources to fulfill leadership obligations. Typically, though not always, the channel controller is a large firm with market leadership/influence.

Expected Results (Vertical Marketing System): (a) Increased control. (b) Professional management. (c) Central programming. (d) Achievement of operating economies. (e) Maximum market impact. (f) Increased profitability. (g) Elimination of inefficiencies.

Definition: Resolving conflict among channel members.

Objective: To devise a solution acceptable to the conflicting members so that they will cooperate to make it work.

Requirements: Choice of a strategy for solving the conflict. (a) Bargaining: (i) both parties adopt give-and-take attitude and (ii) bottom line is favorable enough to both parties to induce them to accept the terms of the bargain. (b) Boundary: (i) nomination of an employee to act as diplomat, (ii) diplomat is fully briefed on the situation and provided with leverages with which to negotiate, and (iii) both parties are willing to negotiate. (c) Interpenetration: (i) frequent formal interactions with the other party to develop an appreciation of each other's perspectives and (ii) willingness to interact to solve problems. (d) Superorganizational: A neutral third party is brought into the conflict to resolve the matter by means of (i) conciliation, (ii) mediation, or (iii) arbitration (compulsory or voluntary).

Expected Results: (a) Elimination of snags in the channel. (b) Results that are mutually beneficial to the parties involved. (c) Need for management time and effort. (d) Increased costs. (e) Costs incurred by both parties in the form of concessions.

Chapter Outline

17.1 **Strategies for Developing Promotional Perspectives**
    17.1.1 Breakdown Methods
    17.1.2 Buildup Method
    17.1.3 Product Factors
    17.1.4 Market Factors
    17.1.5 Customer Factors
    17.1.6 Budget Factors
    17.1.7 Marketing Mix Factors
17.2 **Advertising Strategies**
    17.2.1 Advertising Objectives
    17.2.2 Inventory Approach
    17.2.3 Hierarchy Approach
    17.2.4 Attitudinal Approach
    17.2.5 Media-Selection Procedure
    17.2.6 Cost-per-Thousand-Contacts Comparison
    17.2.7 Matching of Audience and Media Characteristics
    17.2.8 Evaluation Criteria
    17.2.9 Balance of Argument
    17.2.10 Message Repetition
    17.2.11 Rational versus Emotional Appeals
    17.2.12 Comparison Advertising
17.3 **Personal Selling Strategies**
    17.3.1 Objectives
    17.3.2 Strategic Matters
    17.3.3 Motivation
    17.3.4 Compensation
    17.3.5 Evaluation
    17.3.6 Supervision

Chapter **17**

Promotion Strategies

Advertisements contain the only truths to be relied on in a newspaper.

THOMAS JEFFERSON

Promotion strategies are concerned with the planning, implementation, and control of persuasive communication with customers. These strategies may be designed around advertising, personal selling, sales promotion, or any combination of these. The first strategic issue involved here is how much money may be spent on the promotion of a specific product/market. The distribution of the total promotional budget among advertising, personal selling, and sales promotion is another strategic matter. The formulation of strategies dealing with these two issues determines the role that each type of promotion plays in a particular situation.

Clear-cut objectives and a sharp focus on target customers are necessary for an effective promotional program. In other words, merely undertaking an advertising campaign or hiring a few salespeople to call on customers may not suffice. Rather, an integrated communication plan consisting of various promotion methods should be designed to ensure that customers in a product/market cluster get the right message and maintain a long-term cordial relationship with the company. Promotional perspectives must also be properly matched with product, price, and distribution perspectives.

In addition to the strategic issues mentioned above, this chapter discusses strategies in advertising and personal selling. The advertising strategies examined are media strategy and copy strategy. Strategic matters explored in the area of personal selling are those concerned with designing a selling program and supervising salespeople. The formulation of each strategy is illustrated with reference to examples from the literature.

17.1 STRATEGIES FOR DEVELOPING PROMOTIONAL PERSPECTIVES

The amount that a company may spend on its total promotional effort, which consists of advertising, personal selling, and sales promotion, is not easy to determine. There are no unvarying standards to indicate how much should be spent on promotion in a given product/market situation. This is so because decisions about promotion expenditure are influenced by a complex set of circumstances.

Promotion expenditure makes up one part of the total marketing budget. Thus, the allocation of funds to one department, such as advertising, affects the level of expenditure elsewhere within the marketing function. For example, a company may need to choose between additional expenditures on advertising or a new package design. In addition, the perspectives of promotion expenditure must be examined in the context of pricing strategy. A higher price obviously provides more funds for promotion than does a lower price. The amount set aside for promotion is also affected by the sales response to the product, which is very difficult to estimate accurately. A related matter is the question of the cumulative effect of promotion. The major emphasis of research in this area, even where the issue is far from being resolved, has been on the duration of advertising effects. Although it is generally accepted that the effects of advertising and maybe the effects of other forms of promotion as well may last over a long period, there is no certainty about the duration of these benefits. The cumulative effect depends on the loyalty of customers, frequency of purchase, and competitive efforts, each of which may be influenced in turn by a different set of variables.

Promotion expenditures vary from one product/market situation to another. Consider the case of McDonald's. It spent $520.5 million on television advertising in 2002, over twice as much as its rival Burger King. Yet the research showed that viewers remembered and liked Burger King's ads better than McDonald's. There is no way to be sure if McDonald's advertising budget was more than optimum. Similarly, the best-known and best-liked television ad in 2002 was for Miller Lite, a commercial showing people arguing whether Miller tasted great or was less filling. This campaign performed better than all other beer commercials even though several companies spent more money on their campaigns than Miller did.[1] Again, despite the ad's success, it is difficult to say if Miller's budget was optimum.

Promotion, however, is the key to success in many businesses. To illustrate this point, take the case of Isordil, a brand of nitrate prescribed to heart patients to prevent severe chest pains. Made by the Ives Laboratories division of the American Home Products Corporation, it was introduced in 1959 and has since grown to claim almost fifty percent of a $200-million-a-year market. Ives claims that Isordil is longer acting and in certain ways more effective than other nitrate drugs on the market. No matter that the Food and Drug Administration has not yet approved all of the manufacturer's claims, nor that some doctors think that Isordil differs little from competing drugs—Ives has promoted its nitrate so aggressively for so long that many doctors think only of Isordil when they think of nitrates. The success of Isordil illustrates the key importance of promotion: Indeed, the very survival of a drug in today's highly competitive marketplace often depends as much on a company's promotion talents as it does on the quality of its medicine.

Promotion induces competitors to react, but there is no way to anticipate competitive response accurately, thus making it difficult to decide on a budget. For example, during the decade from 1990 to 2000, the promotional costs of Anheuser-Busch rose by $7 a barrel of beer (from $9 in 1990 to $16 in 2000).[2] Although the company has been able to prevent Miller's inroads into its markets, the question remains if continuing to increase ad budgets is the best strategy.

Despite the difficulties involved, practitioners have developed rules of thumb for determining promotion expenditures that are strategically sound. These rules of thumb are of two types: they either take the form of a breakdown method or they employ the buildup method.

17.1.1 Breakdown Methods

There are a number of breakdown methods that can be helpful in determining promotion expenditures. Under the percentage-of-sales approach, promotion expenditure is a specified percentage of the previous year's or predicted future sales. Initially, this percentage is arrived at by hunch. Later, historical information is used to decide what percentage of sales should be allocated for promotion expenditure. The rationale behind the use of this approach is that expenditure on promotion must be justified by sales. This approach is followed by many companies because it is simple, it is easy to understand, and it gives managers the flexibility to cut corners during periods of economic slowdown. Among its flaws is the fact that basing promotion appropriation on sales puts the cart before the horse. Further, the logic of this approach fails to consider the cumulative effect of promotion and to cut promotion expenditures when sales are falling would tend to add to the downward sales trend. In brief, this approach considers promotion a necessary expenditure that must be apportioned from sales revenue without considering the relationship of promotion to competitor's activities or its influence on sales revenues.

Another approach for allocating promotion expenditure is to spend as much as can be afforded. In this approach, the availability of funds or liquid resources is the main consideration in making a decision about promotion expenditure. In other words, even if a company's sales expectations are high, the level of promotion is kept low if its cash position is tight. This approach can be questioned on several grounds. It makes promotion expenditures dependent on a company's liquid resources when the best move for a cash-short company may be to spend more on promotion with the hope of improving sales. Further, this approach involves an element of risk. At a time when the market is tight and sales are slow, a company may spend more on promotion if it happens to have resources available. This approach does, however, consider the fact that promotion outlays have long-term value; that is, advertising has a cumulative effect. Also, under conditions of complete uncertainty, this approach is a cautious one.

Under the *return-on-investment approach*, promotion expenditures are considered as an investment, the benefits of which are derived over the years. Thus, as in the case of any other investment, the appropriate level of promotion expenditure is determined by comparing the expected return with the desired return. The expected return on promotion may be computed by using present values of future returns. Inasmuch as some promotion is likely to produce immediate results, the total promotion expenditure may be partitioned between current expense and investment. Alternatively, the entire promotion expenditure can be considered an investment, in which case the immediate effect of promotion can be conceived as a return in period zero. The basic validity and soundness of the return-on-investment approach cannot be disputed. But there are several problems in its application. First, it may be difficult to determine the outcomes of different forms of promotion over time. Second, what is the appropriate return to be expected from an advertising investment? Third, as the effectiveness of promotions can change when the promotion is changed, for example when the advertising theme changes, an estimated return on investment based on previous years promotions may be invalid. These limitations put severe constraints on the practical use of this approach.

The *competitive-parity approach* assumes that promotion expenditure is directly related to market share. The promotion expenditure of a firm should, therefore, be in proportion to that of competitors in order to maintain its position in the market. Thus, if the leader in the industry allocates two percent of its sales revenue for advertising, other members of the industry should spend about the same percentage of their sales on advertising. Considering the competitive nature of our economy, this seems a reasonable approach. It has, however, a number of limitations. First, the approach requires a knowledge of competitors' perspectives on promotion, and this information may not always be available. For example, the market leader may have decided to put its emphasis not on promotion per se but on reducing prices. Following this firm's lead in advertising expenditures without reference to its prices would be an unreliable guide. Second, one firm may get more for its promotion dollar through judicious selection of media, timing of advertising, skillful preparation of ads, a good sales supervision program, and so on. Thus, it could realize the same results as another firm that has twice as much to spend. Because promotion is just one of the variables affecting market performance, simply maintaining promotional parity with competitors may not be enough for a firm to preserve its market share.

17.1.2 Buildup Method

Many companies have advertising, sales, and sales promotion (merchandising) managers who report to the marketing manager. The marketing manager specifies the objectives of promotion separately for the advertising, personal selling, and sales promotion of each product line. Ideally, the spadework of defining objectives should be done by a committee consisting of executives concerned with product development, pricing, distribution, and promotion. Committee work helps incorporate inputs from different areas; thus, a decision about promotion expenditure is made in the context of the total marketing mix. For example, the committee may decide that promotion should be undertaken to expose at least 100,000 households to the product; institutional customers may be sought through reductions in price.

In practice, it may not always be easy to pinpoint the separate roles of advertising, personal selling, and sales promotion because these three methods of promotion usually overlap to some degree. Each company must work out its own rules for a promotion mix. Once the tasks to be performed by each method of promotion have been designated, they may be defined formally as objectives and communicated to the respective managers. On the basis of these objectives, each promotion manager probably redefines his or her own goals in more operational terms. These redefined objectives then become the modus operandi of each department.

Once departmental objectives have been defined, each area works out a detailed budget, costing each item required to accomplish the objectives of the program. As each department prepares its own budget, the marketing manager may also prepare a summary budget for each of them, simply listing the major expenditures in light of the overall marketing strategy. A marketing manager's budget is primarily a control device.

When individual departments have arrived at their estimates of necessary allocation, the marketing manager meets with each of them to approve budgets. At that time, the marketing manager's own estimates help assess department budgets. Finally, an appropriation is made to each department. Needless to say, the emphasis on different tasks is revised and the total budget refigured several times before an acceptable program emerges. A committee instead of just the marketing manager may approve the final appropriation for each department.

The buildup method forces managers to analyze scientifically the role they expect promotion to play and the contribution it can make toward achieving marketing objectives. It also helps maintain control over promotion expenditure and avoid the frustrations often faced by promotion managers as a result of cuts in promotion appropriations due to economic slowdown. On the other hand, this approach can become overly scientific. Sometimes profit opportunities that require additional promotion expenditure may appear unannounced. Involvement with the objective and task exercise to decide how much more should be spent on promotion takes time, perhaps leading to the loss of an unexpected opportunity.

Another strategic decision in the area of promotion concerns the allocation of effort among the three different methods of promotion. Advertising refers to nonpersonal communication transmitted through the mass media (radio, television, print, outdoors, and mail). The communication is identified with a sponsor who compensates the media for the transmission. Personal selling refers to face-to-face interaction with the customer. Unlike advertising, personal selling involves communication in both directions, from the source to the destination and back. All other forms of communication with the customer other than those included in advertising and personal selling constitute sales promotion. Thus, coupons, samples, demonstrations, exhibits, premiums, sweepstakes, trade allowances, sales and dealer incentives, cents-off packs, rebates, and point-of-purchase material are all sales promotion devices.

A variety of new ways have been developed to communicate with customers. These include telemarketing (i.e., telephone selling), demonstration centers (i.e., specially designed showrooms to allow customers to observe and try out complex industrial equipment), and Internet word-of-mouth advertising. The discussion in this chapter will be limited to the three traditional methods of promotion. In some cases, the three types of promotion may be largely interchangeable; however, they should be blended judiciously to complement each other for a balanced promotional perspective. Illustrated below is the manner in which a chemical company mixed advertising with personal selling and sales promotion to achieve optimum promotional performance:

> An advertising campaign aimed at customer industries, employees, and plant communities carried the theme, "The little chemical giant." It appeared in *Adhesive Age*, *American Paint & Coating Journal*, *Chemical & Engineering News*, *Chemical Marketing Reporter*, *Chemical Purchasing*, *Chemical Week*, *Modern Plastics*, and *Plastics World*.
>
> Sales promotion and personal selling were supported by publicity. Editorial tours of the company's new plants, programs to develop employee understanding and involvement in the expansion, and briefings for local people in towns and cities where USIC [the company] had facilities provided a catalyst for publicity.
>
> Personal selling was aggressive and provided direct communication about the firm's continued service. USIC reassured producers of ethyl alcohol, vinyl acetate monomer, and polyethylene that "we will not lose personal touch with our customers."[3]

Development of an optimum promotion mix is by no means easy. Companies often use haphazard, seat-of-the-pants procedures to determine the respective roles of advertising, personal selling, and sales promotion in a product/market situation.

Exhibit 17.1
Criteria for Determining
Promotion Mix

Product Factors
1. Nature of product
2. Perceived risk
3. Durable versus nondurable
4. Typical purchase amount

Market Factors
1. Position in its life cycle
2. Market share
3. Industry concentration
4. Intensity of competition
5. Demand perspectives

Customer Factors
1. Household versus business customers
2. Number of customers
3. Concentration of customers

Budget Factors
1. Financial resources of the organization
2. Traditional promotional perspectives

Marketing Mix Factors
1. Relative price/relative quality
2. Distribution strategy
3. Brand life cycle
4. Geographic scope of market

Decisions about the promotional mix are often diffused among many decision makers, impeding the formation of a unified promotion strategy. Personal selling plans are sometimes divorced from the planning of advertising and sales promotion. Frequently, decision makers are not adequately aware of the objectives and broad strategies of the overall product program that the promotion plan is designed to implement. Sales and market share goals tend to be constant, regardless of decreases or increases in promotional expenditures. Thus they are unrealistic as guides and directives for planning, as criteria for promotional effectiveness, or even as a fair basis for application of the judgment of decision makers. Briefly, the present state of the art in the administration of the promotion function is such that cause-and-effect relationships as well as other basic insights are not sufficiently understood to permit knowledgeable forecasts of what to expect from alternate courses of action. Even identifying feasible alternatives can prove difficult.[4]

A variety of factors should be considered to determine the appropriate promotion mix in a particular product/market situation. These factors may be categorized as product factors, market factors, customer factors, budget factors, and marketing mix factors, as outlined in Exhibit 17.1.

17.1.3 Product Factors

Factors in this category relate principally to the way in which a product is bought, consumed, and perceived by the customer. For industrial goods, especially technical products, personal selling is more significant than advertising because these goods usually need to be inspected and compared before being bought. Salespeople can explain the workings of a product and provide on-the-spot answers to customer queries. For customer goods such as cosmetics and processed foods, advertising is of primary importance. In addition, advertising plays a dominant role for products that provide an opportunity for differentiation and for those being purchased with emotional motives.

The perceived risk of a purchase decision is another variable here. Generally speaking, the more risk a buyer perceives to be associated with buying a particular product, the higher the importance of personal selling over advertising. A buyer generally desires specific information on a product when the perceived risk is high. This necessitates an emphasis on personal selling. Durable goods are bought less frequently than nondurables and usually require a heavy commitment of resources. These characteristics make personal selling of greater significance for durable goods than advertising. However, because many durable goods are sold through franchised dealerships, the influence of each type of promotion should be determined in light of the additional push it would provide in moving the product. Finally, products purchased in small quantities are presumably purchased frequently and require routine decision making. For these products, advertising should be preferable to personal selling. Such products are often of low value; therefore, a profitable business in these products can only be conducted on volume. This underlines the importance of advertising in this case.

17.1.4 Market Factors

The first market factor is the position of a product in its life cycle. The creation of primary demand, hitherto nonexistent, is the primary task during the introductory stage; therefore, a great promotion effort is needed to explain a new product to potential customers. For consumer goods in the introductory stage, the major thrust is on heavy advertising supported by missionary selling to help distributors move the product. In addition, different devices of sales promotion (e.g., sampling, couponing, free demonstrations) are employed to entice the customer to try the product. In the case of industrial products, personal selling alone is useful during this period. During the growth phase, there is increasing demand, which means enough business for all competitors. In the case of consumer goods, however, the promotional effort shifts to reliance on advertising. Industrial goods, on the other hand, begin to be advertised as the market broadens. However, they continue to require a personal selling effort. In the maturity phase, competition becomes intense, and advertising, along with sales promotion, is required to differentiate the product (a consumer good) from competitive brands and to provide an incentive to the customer to buy a particular product. Industrial goods during maturity call for intensive personal selling. During the decline phase, the promotional effort does not vary much initially from that during the maturity phase except that the intensity of promotion declines. Later, as price competition becomes keen and demand continues to decline, overall promotional perspectives are reduced.

For a given product class, if market share is high, both advertising and personal selling are used. If the market share is low, the emphasis is placed on either personal selling or advertising. This is because high market share seems to indicate that the company does business in more than one segment and uses multiple channels of distribution. Thus, both personal selling and advertising are used to promote the product. Where market share is low, the perspectives of the business are limited, and either advertising or personal selling will suffice, depending on the nature of the product.

If the industry is concentrated among a few firms, advertising has additional significance for two reasons: (a) heavy advertising may help discourage other firms from entering the field, and (b) heavy advertising sustains a desired position for the product in the market. Heavy advertising constitutes an implied warranty of product performance and perhaps decreases the uncertainty consumers associate with new products. In this way, new competition is discouraged and existing positions are reinforced.

Intensity of competition tends to affect promotional blending in the same way that market share does. When competition is keen, all three types of promotion are needed to sustain a product's position in the market. This is because promotion is needed to inform, remind, and persuade customers to buy the product. On the other hand, if competitive activity is limited, the major function of promotion is to inform and perhaps remind customers about the product. Thus, either advertising or personal selling is emphasized.

Hypothetically, advertising is more suited for products that have relatively latent demand. This is because advertising investment should open up new opportunities in the long run, and if the carryover effect is counted, expenditure per sales dollar would be more beneficial. If demand is limited and new demand is not expected to be created, advertising outlay would be uneconomical. Thus, future potential becomes a significant factor in determining the role of advertising.

17.1.5 Customer Factors

One of the major dimensions used to differentiate businesses is whether products are marketed for household consumption or for organizational use. There are several significant differences in the way products are marketed to these two customer groups, and these differences exert considerable influence on the type of promotion that should be used. In the case of household customers, it is relatively easy to identify the decision maker for a particular product; therefore, advertising is more desirable. Also, the self-service nature of many consumer-product sales makes personal selling relatively unimportant. Finally, household customers do not ordinarily go through a formal buying process using objective criteria as organizational customers do. This again makes advertising more useful for reaching household customers. Essentially the same reasons make personal selling more relevant in promoting a product among organizational customers.

The number of customers and their geographic concentration also influence promotional blending. For a small customer base, especially if it is geographically concentrated, advertising does not make as much sense as it does in cases where customers are widely scattered and represent a significant mass. Caution is needed here because some advertising may always be necessary for consumer goods, no matter what the market perspectives are. Thus, these statements provide only a conceptual framework and should not be interpreted as exact yes/no criteria.

17.1.6 Budget Factors

Ideally, the budget should be based on the promotional tasks to be performed. However, intuitively and traditionally, companies place an upper limit on the amount that they spend on promotion. Such limits may influence the type of promotion that may be undertaken in two ways. First, a financially weak company is constrained in undertaking certain types of promotion. For example, television advertising necessitates a heavy commitment of resources. Second, in many companies the advertising budget is, by tradition, linked to revenues as a percentage. This method of allocation continues to be used so that expected revenues indicate how much may be spent on advertising in the future. The allocated funds, then, automatically determine the role of advertising.

17.1.7 Marketing Mix Factors

The promotion decision should be made in the context of other aspects of the marketing mix. The price and quality of a product relative to competition affect the nature of its promotional perspectives. Higher prices must be justified to the consumer by actual or presumed product superiority. Thus, in the case of a product that is priced substantially higher than competing goods, advertising achieves significance in communicating and establishing the product's superior quality in the minds of customers.

The promotion mix is also influenced by the distribution structure employed for the product. If the product is distributed directly, the sales force can largely be counted on to promote the product. Indirect distribution, on the other hand, requires greater emphasis on advertising because the push of a sales force is limited. As a matter of fact, the further the manufacturer is from the ultimate user, the greater the need for the advertising effort to stimulate and maintain demand. The influence of the distribution strategy may be illustrated with reference to two cosmetics companies that deal in similar products, Revlon and Avon. Revlon distributes its products through different types of intermediaries and advertises them heavily. Avon, on the other hand, distributes primarily directly to end users in their homes and spends less on advertising relative to Revlon.

Earlier we examined the effect on the promotion mix of a product's position in its life cycle. The position of a brand in its life cycle also influences promotional perspectives. Positioning a new brand in the desired slot in the market during its introduction phase requires a higher degree of advertising. As a product enters the growth phase, advertising should be blended with personal selling. In the growth phase, the overall level of promotion declines in scope. When an existing brand reaches the maturity phase in its life cycle, the marketer has three options: to employ life-extension strategies, to harvest the brand for profits, and/or to introduce a new brand that may be targeted at a more specific segment of the market. The first two options were discussed in Chapter 13. As far as the third option is concerned, for promotional purposes, the new brand will need to be treated like a new product.

Finally, the geographic scope of the market to be served is another consideration. Advertising, relatively speaking, is more significant for products marketed nationally than for those marketed locally or regionally. When the market is geographically limited, one study showed that even spot television advertising proved to be more expensive vis-à-vis the target group exposures gained.[5] Thus, because advertising is an expensive proposition, regional marketers should rely less on advertising and more on other forms of promotion, or they should substitute another element of the marketing mix for it. For example, a regional marketer may manufacture private label brands.

Although these factors are helpful in establishing roles for different methods of promotion, actual appropriation among them should take into consideration the effect of any changes in the environment. For example, in the 1980s soft drink companies frequently used sales promotion (mainly cents off) to vie for customers. In the 1990s, however, the makers of soft drinks changed their promotion mix strategy to concentrate more on advertising. This is evidenced by the fact that the five largest soft drink makers spent about $500 million on advertising in 1999, forty percent more than they spent in 1989. One reason for this change in promotional perspective was the realization that price discounting hurt brand loyalties; because Coke and Pepsi had turned their colas into commodities by means of cents-off promotion, the consumer now shopped for price.

An empirical study on this topic has shown that consumers prefer incentives other than price. Price cuts also appear to have little lasting effect on sales volumes. For example, consumers exposed to repeated price cuts learn to ignore the "usual" price. Instead, they wait for the next discount and then stockpile the product. They also tend to become discount junkies, stimulated into buying only by ever-steeper discounts.[6] In brief, price promotions not only cut margins, but also leave manufacturers to cope with costly fluctuations in stocks.

In addition, the promotion mix may also be affected by a desire to be innovative. For example, Puritan Fashions Corporation, an apparel company, traditionally spent little on advertising. In the late 1970s, the company was continually losing money. Then, in the 1980s, the company introduced a new product, body-hugging jeans, and employed an unconventional promotion strategy. It placed Calvin Klein's label on its jeans, sold them as a prestige trouser priced at $55 (double the price of nonlabeled styles), and advertised them heavily. This promotion mix provided the company with instant success. Another example of promotion innovation is provided by Kellogg, which, instead of plastic toys and other gimmicks, now featured Microsoft Corp. software for children and adults. Although promotional innovation may not last long because competitors may soon copy it, it does provide the innovator with a head start.

Promotional blending requires consideration of a large number of variables, as outlined above. Unfortunately, it is difficult to assign quantitative values to the effect that these variables have on promotion. Thus, decisions about promotional blending must necessarily be made subjectively. These factors, however, provide a checklist for reviewing the soundness and viability of subjective decisions.

Research conducted by the Strategic Planning Institute for Cahners Publishing Co. identified the following decision rules that can be used in formulating ad budgets. These rules may be helpful in finalizing promotion mix decisions.[7]

1. Market share—A company that has a higher market share must generally spend more on advertising to maintain its share.
2. Sales from new products—If a company has a high percentage of its sales resulting from new products, it must spend more on advertising compared to companies that have well-established products.
3. Market growth—Companies competing in fast-growing markets should spend comparatively more on advertising.
4. Plant capacity—If a company has a lot of unused plant capacity, it should spend more on advertising to stimulate sales and production.
5. Unit price (per sales transaction)—The lower the unit price of a company's products, the more it should spend on advertising because of the greater likelihood of brand switching.
6. Importance of product to customers (in relation to their total purchases)—Products that constitute a lower proportion of customers' purchases generally require higher advertising expenditures.
7. Product price—Both very high-priced (or premium) products and very low-priced (or discount) products require higher ad expenditures because, in both cases, price is an important factor in the buying decision and the buyer must be convinced (through advertising) that the product is a good value.
8. Product quality—Higher-quality products require a greater advertising effort because of the need to convince the consumer that the product is unique.

9. Breadth of product line—Companies with a broad line of products must spend more on advertising compared to companies with specialized product lines.

10. Degree of standardization—Standardized products produced in large quantities should be backed by higher advertising outlays because they are likely to have more competition in the market.

17.2 ADVERTISING STRATEGIES

Companies typically plan and execute their advertising through five stages: developing the budget, planning the advertising, copy development and approval, execution, and monitoring response. Exhibit 17.2 summarizes who participates in each stage and the end product.

Media may be defined as those channels through which messages concerning a product or service are transmitted to targets. The following media are available to advertisers: newspapers, magazines, television, radio, outdoor advertising, transit advertising, direct mail, telemarketing, theater advertising, fliers, spectaculars (found in some emerging markets and including such activities as sculpting the plant life on a hillside next to a major thoroughfare into a commercial message) and the Internet.

Selection of an advertising medium is influenced by such factors as the product or service itself, the target market, the extent and type of distribution, the type of message to be communicated, the budget, and competitors' advertising strategies. Except for the advertising perspectives employed by the competition, information on most of these factors is presumably available inside the company. It may be necessary to undertake a marketing research project to find out what sorts of advertising strategies competitors have used in the past and what might be expected of them in the future. In addition, selection of a medium also depends on the advertising objectives for the product/market concerned. With this information in place, different methods may be used to select a medium.

Mention must be made here of an emerging medium, i.e., Internet advertising. In 2007, ad agencies had total revenues of $31.1 billion dollars, of which 10.2 percent, or about $3.2 billion, was digital advertising.[8] Internet advertising offers a variety of advantages. It offers an exceptional ability to target specific customers. Besides, it blurs the division between content and advertising, which the traditional media regard as sacred. If the money is right, many online publishers are willing to strike whatever sort of partnerships an advertiser might want.

Exhibit 17.2 The Advertising Planning Process	Stage	Preliminary Players	End Product
	Developing the marketing plan and budget	Product manager	Budget Spending guidelines Profit projections
	Planning the Market	Product manager Advertising manager Ad agency	Identification of the target advertising Allocating of spending Statement of advertising strategy and message
	Copy development and approval	Ad agency Copy research company Product manager Advertising manager Senior management	Finished copy Media plan (with reach and frequency projections)
	Execution	Ad agency or media buying company	Actual placement
	Monitoring	Market research manager Product manager Ad agency (research)	Awareness, recognition, and perception tracking Perceptual maps Sales/share tracking

However, ad rates on the Net are steep enough to justify the cost. Most advertisers pay at least as much to reach an Internet audience, typically $10 to $40 per 1000 viewers, as they would for TV or magazine ads.[9] Further, the emotion-laden vignettes that work so well on TV simply don't woo viewers in cyberspace. In addition, the new media has spawned new forms of abuse such as click fraud (where agencies pay people to click through ads to increase fees to advertisers). Presently, most marketers see Internet advertising as little more than a complement to traditional media.

Despite the above problems, Internet advertising will account for a growing proportion of overall advertising expenditure. As the technology improves, the impact of Internet advertising will increase and become easier to measure, and the gap between this new precise, interactive marketing capability and conventional ''fuzzy'' passive media will widen. The following reasons are advanced for the growing popularity of Internet advertising:[10]

(a) The Web presents great advertising opportunities for marketers because of its continuing growth, its user demographics, its effectiveness, and its cost-competitiveness.

(b) The overall Web population is reaching critical mass. Recent surveys show there are 25 to 40 million adult Web users in the United States—between one-eighth and one-fifth of the population. Twenty-five million Americans use the Web at least once a week, according to one source, and 8.4 million are daily users. The average user spends 8.6 hours a month on line.

(c) The demographics of Internet users are broadening, but remain attractive. More women are now using the Internet: in 2007 the Pew Internet & American Life Project put the figure at 70 percent of adult women as compared with 71 percent of adult men. In financial terms, 55 percent of families with a household income of $30,000 or less, while 93 percent of families with household income of greater than $75,000 or more. Marketers pursuing certain segments of the population are finding the Internet increasingly useful. For those interested in, say, American men aged 35 to 44 with incomes over $75,000, the Web can provide access to about 2 million—over 40 percent of the target demographic segment, and a critical mass in itself.

(d) Studies have shown that the Internet is reasonably good at achieving standard advertising objectives, such as shaping attitudes. However, it also has capabilities that traditional media cannot match. Features that make the Internet a superior medium include its addressability, its interactivity, and its scope for customization. Advertisers can do things on the Internet that are impossible in traditional media: identify individual users, target and talk to them one at a time, and engage in a genuine two-way dialogue.

(e) In terms of advertising economics, the Internet can already compete with existing media, both in response as measured by click-throughs and in exposure as measured by cost per thousand. Moreover, the Internet's economics look better and better the more precisely a target consumer segment is defined. The cost to an Internet advertiser of reaching families that earn over $70,000 and own a foreign car, for instance, can be less than a quarter the cost of using a specialty magazine such as *Car and Driver*.

(f) Like traditional media, the Internet needs consistent metrics and auditing in order to gain broad acceptance from marketers. Both are emerging slowly, driven by old players such as Nielsen and new ones such as Web Track.

(g) Advertisers and agencies cannot afford to produce a different ad and negotiate a different price for every site. Standards for size, position, content, and pricing are badly needed and are now being developed; an example is CASIE, the Coalition for Advertising Supported Information and Entertainment, a joint project of the Association of National Advertisers and the American Association of Advertising Agencies.

(h) Unless they place their ads on one of the few highly trafficked sites, advertisers find it difficult to ensure that sufficient people see them. Responding to advertisers' need for scale, placement networks such as DoubleClick do the aggregating for them, making sure that a specified number of people will be exposed to their ads.

17.2.1 Advertising Objectives

To build a good advertising program, it is necessary first to pinpoint the objectives of the ad campaign. It would be wrong to assume that all advertising leads directly to sales. A sale is a multiphase phenomenon, and advertising can be used to transfer the customer from one phase to the next: from unawareness of a product or service, to awareness, to comprehension, to conviction, to action. Thus, the advertiser must specify at what stage or stages he or she wants advertising to work. The objectives of advertising may be defined by any one of the following approaches: inventory approach, hierarchy approach, or attitudinal approach.

17.2.2 Inventory Approach

A number of scholars have articulated inventories of functions performed by advertising. The objectives of an ad campaign may be defined from an inventory based on a firm's overall marketing perspective. For example, the following inventory may be used to develop a firm's advertising objectives:

A. *Increase sales by*
   1. Encouraging potential purchasers to visit the company or its dealers.
   2. Obtaining leads for salespeople or dealers.
   3. Inducing professional people (e.g., doctors, architects) to recommend the product.
   4. Securing new distributors.
   5. Prompting immediate purchases through announcements of special sales and contests.

B. *Create an awareness about a company's product or service by*
   1. Informing potential customers about product features.
   2. Announcing new models.
   3. Highlighting the unique features of the product.
   4. Informing customers as to where the product may be bought.
   5. Announcing price changes.
   6. Demonstrating the product in use.

The inventory approach is helpful in highlighting the fact that different objectives can be emphasized in advertising and that these objectives cannot be selected without reference to the overall marketing plan. Thus, this approach helps the advertiser avoid operating in a vacuum. However, inherent in this approach is the danger that the decision maker may choose nonfeasible and conflicting objectives if everything listed in an inventory seems worth pursuing.

17.2.3 Hierarchy Approach

Following this approach, the objectives of advertising should be stated in an action-oriented psychological form. Thus, the objectives of advertising may be defined as (a) gaining customers' initial attention, perception, continued favorable attention, and interest; or (b) affecting customers' comprehension, feeling, emotion, motivation, belief, intentions, decision, imagery, association, recall, and recognition. The thesis behind this approach is that customers move from one psychological state to another before actually buying a product. Thus, the purpose of advertising should be to move customers from state to state and ultimately toward purchasing the product. Although it makes sense to define the purpose of an individual ad in hierarchical terms, it may be difficult to relate the purpose so defined to marketing goals. Besides, measurement of psychological states that form the basis of this approach is difficult and subjective compared to the measurement of goals such as market share.

17.2.4 Attitudinal Approach

According to this approach, advertising is instrumental in producing changes in attitudes; therefore, advertising goals should be defined to influence attitudinal structures. Thus, advertising may be undertaken to accomplish any of the following goals:

1. Affect those forces that influence strongly the choice of criteria used for evaluating brands belonging to the product class.
2. Add characteristic(s) to those considered salient for the product class.
3. Increase/decrease the rating for a salient product class characteristic.

4. Change the perception of the company's brand with regard to some particular salient product characteristic.
5. Change the perception of competitive brands with regard to some particular salient product characteristic.

The attitudinal approach is an improvement over the hierarchical approach because it attempts to relate advertising objectives to product/market objectives. This approach indicates not only the functions advertising performs, it also targets the specific results it can achieve.

Advertising objectives should be defined by a person completely familiar with all product/market perspectives. A good definition of objectives aids in the writing of appropriate ad copy and in selecting the right media. It should be recognized that different ad campaigns for the same product can have varied objectives. But all ad campaigns should be complementary to each other to maximize total advertising impact.

Product/market advertising objectives may be used to derive media objectives. Media objectives should be defined so as to answer such questions as: Are we trying to reach everybody? Are we aiming to be selective? If housewives under 30 with children under 10 are really our target, what media objectives should we develop? Are we national or regional? Do we need to concentrate in selected counties? Do we need reach or frequency or both? Are there creative considerations to control our thinking? Do we need color or permanence (which might mean magazines and supplements), personalities and demonstration (which might mean television), the best reminder for the least money (which might mean radio or outdoor), superselectivity (which might mean direct mail), or going all the way up and down in the market (which could mean newspapers)? The following is a list of sample media objectives based on these questions:

1. We need a national audience of women.
2. We want them between 18 and 34.
3. Because the product is a considered purchase, we need room to explain it thoroughly.
4. We need color to show the product to best advantage.
5. We must keep after these women more than once, so we need frequency.
6. There's no way to demonstrate the product except in a store.

17.2.5 Media-Selection Procedure

Media selection calls for two decisions: (a) which particular medium to use and (b) which specific vehicles to choose within a given medium. For example, if magazines are to be used, in which particular magazines should ads be placed? The following two approaches can be used in media selection: cost-per-thousand-contacts comparison and matching of audience and medium characteristics.

17.2.6 Cost-per-Thousand-Contacts Comparison

The cost-per-thousand-contacts comparison has traditionally been the most popular method of media selection. Although simple to apply, the cost-per-thousand method leaves much to be desired. Basing media selection entirely on the number of contacts to be reached ignores the quality of contacts made. For example, an advertisement for a women's dress line appearing in *Vogue* would make a greater impact on those exposed to it than would the same ad appearing in *True Confessions*. Similarly, *Esquire* would perhaps be more appropriate than many less-specialized magazines for introducing men's fashions.

Further, the cost-per-thousand method can be highly misleading if one considers the way in which advertisers define the term *exposure*. According to the media definition, exposure occurs as soon as an ad is inserted in the magazine. Whether the exposure actually occurs is never considered. This method also fails to consider editorial images and the impact power of different channels of a medium.

17.2.7 Matching of Audience and Media Characteristics

An alternative approach to media selection is to specify the target audience and match its characteristics to a particular medium. A step-by-step procedure for using this method is described as follows:

1. Build a profile of customers, detailing who they are, where they are located, when they can be reached, and what their demographic characteristics are. Setting media objectives (discussed earlier) is helpful in building customer profiles.

2. Study media profiles in terms of audience coverage. Implicit in this step is the study of the audience's media habits (i.e., an examination of who constitutes a particular medium's audience).

3. Match customer profiles to media profiles. The customer characteristics for a product should be matched to the audience characteristics of different media. This comparison should lead to the preliminary selection of a medium, based primarily on the grounds of coverage.

4. The preliminary selection should be examined further in regard to product and cost considerations. For some products, other things being equal, one medium is superior to another. For example, in the case of beauty aids, a product demonstration is helpful; hence, television would be a better choice than radio. Cost is another concern in media selection; information on cost is available from the media themselves. Cost should be balanced against the benefit expected from the campaign under consideration.

5. Finally, the total budget should be allocated to different media and to various media vehicles. The final selection of a medium should maximize the achievement of media objectives. For example, if the objective is to make people aware of a product, then the medium selected should be the one that reaches a wide audience.

Basically, two types of information are required for media selection: customer profile and media characteristics. The advertiser should build a customer profile for his or her product/market. Information about various media is usually available from media owners. Practically all media owners have complete information available to them concerning their audiences (demographics and circulation figures). Each medium, however, presents the information in a way that makes it look best. It is desirable, therefore, to validate the audience information supplied by media owners with data from bureaus that audit various media. The Audit Bureau of Circulations, the Traffic Audit Bureau, and the Business Publications Audit of Circulation are examples of such audit bureaus.

17.2.8 Evaluation Criteria

Before money is committed to a selected medium, it is desirable to review the medium's viability against evaluation criteria. Is the decision maker being thorough, progressive (imaginative), measure-minded, practical, and optimistic? Thoroughness requires that all aspects of media selection be given full consideration. For maximum impact, the chosen medium should be progressive: it should have a unique way of doing the job. An example of progressiveness is putting a sample envelope of Maxwell House coffee in millions of copies of *TV Guide*. Because of postal regulations, this sampling could not be done in a magazine that is purchased primarily through subscriptions. But *TV Guide* is mainly a newsstand magazine. Measure-mindedness refers to more than just the number of exposures. It refers not only to frequency and timing in reaching the target audience but also to the quality of the audience; that is, to the proportion of heavy to light television viewers reached, proportion of men to women, working to nonworking women, and so on. Practicality requires choosing a medium on factual, not emotional, grounds. For example, it is not desirable to substitute a weak newspaper for a strong one just because the top management of the company does not agree with the editorial policy of the latter. Finally, the overall media plan should be optimistic in that it takes advantage of lessons learned from experience.

Three factors need to be considered in media selection and budgeting: *audience reach, frequency of exposure*, and *competitive matching*. The latter two factors are dominant. Audience reach is the total number of individuals within a target audience that will be exposed to an ad at least once through a particular medium. Frequency of exposure is crucial because an advertisement must be viewed a minimum number of times in order to have an effect on the target audience. Hence, when an advertiser must compromise between audience reach and frequency of exposure, it is frequency of exposure that will dominate. Competitive matching is important because, for an ad campaign in a specific medium to have an effect, a company must roughly match their primary competitors' in frequency of exposures. If a rough equivalency cannot be purchased, many advertisers prefer to abandon a medium and focus on alternative media.

Copy refers to the content of an advertisement. In the advertising industry, the term is sometimes used in a broad sense to include the words, pictures, symbols, colors, layout, and other ingredients of an ad. Copywriting is a creative job, and its quality depends to a large extent on the creative ability of writers in the advertising agency or in the company. However, creativity alone may not produce good ad copy. A marketing strategist needs to have his or her own perspectives incorporated in the copy (what to say, how to say it, and to whom to say it) and needs to furnish information on ad objectives, product, target customers, competitive activity, and ethical and legal considerations. The creative person carries on from there. In brief, although copywriting may be the outcome of a flash of inspiration on the part of an advertising genius, it must rest on a systematic, logical, step-by-step presentation of ideas.

This point may be illustrated with reference to Perrier, a brand of bottled water that comes from mineral springs located in southern France. In Europe, this product has been quite popular for some years; in the United States, however, it used to be available in gourmet shops only. In 1977, the company introduced the product to the U.S. market as a soft drink by tapping the adult user market with heavy advertising. Perrier's major product distinction is that its water is naturally carbonated spring water. The product was aimed at the affluent adult population, particularly those concerned with diet and health, as a status symbol and a sign of maturity. Perrier faced competition from two sources: regular soft drink makers and potential makers of mineral water. The company took care of its soft drink competition by segmenting the market on the basis of price (Perrier was priced 50 percent above the average soft drink) and thus avoided direct confrontation. In regard to competition from new brands of mineral water, Perrier's association with France and the fact that it is constituted of naturally carbonated spring water were expected to continue as viable strengths. This information was used to develop ad copy for placement in high-fashion women's magazines and in television commercials narrated by Orson Welles. The results were astonishing. In less than five years, Perrier became a major liquid drink in the U.S. market.[11]

Take another example. Back in 1998, packs of Thomas' English Muffins carried the following announcement: "Coming Soon . . . New Package, Same Great Taste!" An illustration of the forthcoming design appeared along with the burst.[12] This campaign set a new standard in postmodern promotion. Instead of simply crowing about itself, this package was actually heralding its own replacement. The new design showed up in stores about six weeks later. If there ever was a case study that demonstrates the value of a highly creative program, it is about Absolut Vodka. Absolut has taken a colorless, tasteless, orderless liquid and made it the object of our desire inspite of Smirnoff's solidly established position.[13]

Essentially, ad copy constitutes an advertiser's message to the customer. To ensure that the proper message gets across, it is important that there is no distortion of the message because of what in communication theory is called noise. Noise may emerge from three sources: (a) dearth of facts (e.g., the company is unaware of the unique distinctions of its product), (b) competitors (e.g., competitors make changes in their marketing mix to counter the company's claims or position), and (c) behavior traits of the customers or audience. Failure to take into account the last source of noise is often the missing link in developing ad copy. It is not safe to assume that one's own perspectives on what appeals to the audience are accurate. It is desirable, therefore, to gain, through some sort of marketing research, insights into behavior patterns of the audience and to make this information available to the copywriter.[14] For example, a 1993 Research International Organization (RIO) study of teenagers in 26 countries provides the following clues for making an effective appeal to young customers.

1. Never talk down to a teenager. While "hip" phraseology and the generally flippant tone observed in the teenager's conversation may be coin of the realm from one youngster to another, it comes across as phony, foolish, and condescending when directed at him or her by an advertiser. Sincerity is infinitely more effective than cuteness. Entertainment and attention-getting approaches by themselves do little to attract a teenager to the merits of a product. In fact, they often dissuade the youngster from making a purchase decision.

2. Be totally, absolutely, and unswervingly straightforward. Teenagers may act cocky and confident in front of adults, but most of them are still rather unsure of themselves and are wary of being misled. They are not sure they know enough to avoid being taken advantage of, and they do not like to risk looking foolish by falling for a commercial gimmick. Moreover, teenagers as a group are far more suspicious of things commercial than adults are. Advertising must not only be noticed; it must be believed.

3. Give the teenager credit for being motivated by rational values. When making a buying selection, adults like to think they are doing so on the basis of the benefits the product or service offers. Teenagers instinctively perceive what's "really there" in an offering. Advertising must clearly expose for their consideration the value a product or service claims to represent.

4. Be as personal as possible. Derived from the adult world of marketing, this rule has an exaggerated importance with teenagers. In this automated age, with so many complaining of being reduced en masse to anonymity, people are becoming progressively more aware of their own individuality. The desire to be personally known and recognized is particularly strong with young people, who are urgently searching for a clear sense of their own identity.[15]

Findings from communications research are helpful in further refining the attributes of ad copy that an advertising strategist needs to spell out for the copywriter.

Source Credibility. *An ad may show a celebrity recommending the use of a product. It is hoped that this endorsement will help give the ad additional credibility, credibility that will be reflected in higher sales.*

Research on the subject has shown that an initially credible source, such as Miss America claiming to use a certain brand of hair spray, is more effective in changing the opinion of an audience than if a similar claim is made by a lesser-known source, such as an unknown homemaker. However, as time passes, the audience tends to forget the source or to dissociate the source from the message.[16] Some consumers who might have been swayed in favor of a particular brand because it was recommended by Miss America may revert to their original choice, whereas those who did not initially accept the homemaker's word may later become favorably inclined toward the product she is recommending. The decreasing importance of the source behind a message over time has been called the sleeper effect.[17]

Several conclusions can be drawn from the sleeper effect. In some cases, it may be helpful if the advertiser is disassociated as much as possible from the ad, particularly when the audience may perceive that a manufacturer is trying to push something.[18] On the other hand, when source credibility is important, advertisements should be scheduled so that the source may reappear to reinforce the message.

An example of source credibility is provided by Nike. It attracted popular sports heroes as credible sources to build new product lines and marketing campaigns around them. Consumers seemed to respond best to athletes who combined a passion to win with a maverick disregard for convention: "outlaws with morals."[19]

17.2.9 Balance of Argument

When preparing copy, there is a question of whether only the good and distinctive features of a brand should be highlighted or whether its demerits should be mentioned as well. Traditionally, the argument has been, "Put your best foot forward." In other words, messages should be designed to emphasize only the favorable aspects of a product. Recent research in the field of communication has questioned the validity of indiscriminately detailing the favorable side. It has been found that

1. Presenting both sides of an issue is more effective than giving only one side among individuals who are initially opposed to the point of view being presented.
2. Better-educated people are more favorably affected by presentation of both sides; poorly educated persons are more favorably affected by communication that gives only supporting arguments.
3. For those already convinced of the point of view presented, the presentation of both sides is less effective than a presentation featuring only those items favoring the general position being advanced.
4. Presentation of both sides is least effective among the poorly educated who are already convinced of the position advocated.
5. Leaving out a relevant argument is more noticeable and detracts more from effectiveness when both sides are presented than when only the side favorable to the proposition is being advanced.[20]

These findings have important implications for developing copy. If one is trying to reach executive customers through an ad in the *Harvard Business Review*, it probably is better to present both favorable and unfavorable qualities of a product. On the other hand, for such status products and services as Rolex diamond watches and Chanel No. 5 perfume, emphasis on both pros and cons can distort the image. Thus, when status is already established, a simple message is more desirable.

17.2.10 Message Repetition

Should the same message be repeated time and again? According to learning theory, reinforcement over time from different directions increases learning. It has been said that a good slogan never dies and that repetition is the surest way of getting the message across. However, some feel that, although the central theme should be maintained, a message should be presented with variations.

Communication research questions the value of wholesale repetition. Repetition, it has been found, leads to increased learning up to a certain point. Thereafter, learning levels off and may, in fact, change to boredom and loss of attention. Continuous repetition may even counteract the good effect created earlier. Thus, advertisers must keep track of the shape of the learning curve and develop a new product theme when the curve appears to be flattening out. The Coca-Cola Company, for example, regularly changes its message to maintain audience interest.[21]

1886—Coca-Cola
1905—Coca-Cola revives and sustains
1906—The Great National Temperance Beverage
1922—Thirst knows no season
1925—Six million a day
1927—Around the corner from everywhere
1929—The pause that refreshes
1938—The best friend thirst ever had
1948—Where there's Coke there's hospitality
1949—Along the highway to anywhere
1952—What you want is a Coke
1956—Makes good things taste better
1957—Sign of good taste
1958—The cold, crisp taste of Coke
1963—Things go better with Coke
1970—It's the real thing
1971—I'd like to buy the world a Coke
1975—Look up, America
1976—Coke adds life
1979—Have a Coke and a smile
1982—Coke is it
1985—We've got a taste for you
1986—Catch the wave
1987—When Coca-Cola is a part of your life, you can't beat the feeling
1988—Can't beat the feeling
1990—Always new, always real
1992—Always you, always Coke
1995—Always spring, always Coke
1998—Something should stay the same, like Coke
2001—Life tastes good

17.2.11 Rational versus Emotional Appeals

Results of studies on the effect of rational and emotional appeals presented in advertisements are not conclusive. Some studies show that emotional appeals have definite positive results.[22] However, arousing emotions may not be sufficient unless the ad can rationally convince the subject that the product in question will fulfill a need. It appears that emphasis on one type of appeal—rational or emotional—is not enough. The advertiser must strike a balance between emotional and rational appeals. For example, Procter & Gamble's Crest toothpaste ad, "Crest has been recommended by the American Dental Association," has a rational content; but its reference to cavity prevention also excites emotions. Similarly, a Close-up toothpaste ad produced for Lever Brothers is primarily emotional in nature: "Put your money where your mouth is." However, it also has an economic aspect: "Use Close-up both as a toothpaste and mouthwash."

An example of how emotional appeal complemented by service created a market niche for an unknown company is provided by Singapore Airlines. Singapore is a Southeast Asian nation barely larger than Cleveland. Many airlines have tried to sell the notion that they have something unique to offer, but not many have succeeded. Singapore Airlines, however, thrives mainly on the charm of its cabin attendants, who serve passengers with warm smiles and copious attention. A gently persuasive advertising campaign glamorizes the attendants and tries to convey the idea of in-flight pleasure of a lyrical quality. Most of the airline's ads are essentially large, soft-focus color photographs of various attendants. A commercial announces: ''Singapore girl, you look so good I want to stay up here with you forever.'' Of course, its emotional appeals are duly supported by excellent service (rational appeals to complement emotional ones). The airline provides gifts, free cocktails, and free French wines and brandy even to economy-class passengers. Small wonder that it flies with an above-average load factor higher than that of any other major international carrier. In brief, emotional appeal can go a long way in the development of an effective ad campaign, but it must have rational underpinnings to support it.

17.2.12 Comparison Advertising

Comparison advertising refers to the comparison of one brand with one or more competitive brands by explicitly naming them on a variety of specific product or service attributes. Comparison advertising became popular in the early 1970s; today one finds comparison ads for all forms of goods and services. Although it is debatable whether comparative ads are more or less effective than individual ads, limited research on the subject indicates that in some cases comparative ads are more useful.

Many companies have successfully used comparison advertising. One that stands out is Helene Curtis Industries. The company used comparison ads on television for its Suave brand of shampoo. The ads said: ''We do what theirs does for less than half the price.'' Competitors were either named or their labels were clearly shown. The message that Suave is comparable to top-ranking shampoos was designed to allay public suspicion that low-priced merchandise is somehow shoddy. The campaign was so successful that within a few years Suave's sales surpassed those of both Procter & Gamble's Head & Shoulders and Johnson & Johnson's Baby Shampoo in volume. The company continues to use the same approach in its advertising today. Comparison advertising clearly provides an underdog with the chance to catch up with the leader.[23]

In using comparison advertising, a company should make sure that its claim of superiority will hold up in a court of law. More businesses today are counterattacking by suing when rivals mention their products in ads or promotions. For example, MCI has sought to stop an AT&T ad campaign (aimed at MCI) that claims that AT&T's long-distance and other services are better and cheaper.

It will be appropriate to mention here that in recent years, companies have come up with alternative promotional approaches that bypass the use of traditional media. For example, in the United Kingdom, Nestle's Buitoni brand grew through programs that taught the English how to cook Italian food. The Body Shop gathered loyalty with its support of environmental and social causes. Cadbury funded a theme park tied to its history in the chocolate business. Haagen-Dazs opened posh ice-cream parlors and got itself featured by a name on the menus of fine restaurants. Hugo Boss and Swatch backed athletic or cultural events that became associated with their brands. At a time when promotional costs are rising and markets have fragmented, novel approaches for promoting the product in the ever more competitive world could be rewarding.

17.3 PERSONAL SELLING STRATEGIES

There was a time when the problems of selling were simpler than they are today. Recent years have produced a variety of changes in the selling strategies of businesses. The complexities involved in selling as we approach the next century are different from those in the past. As an example, today a high-principled style of selling that favors a close, trusting, long-term relationship over a quick sell is recommended. The philosophy is to serve the customer as a consultant, not as a peddler. Discussed below are objectives and strategic matters pertaining to selling strategies.

17.3.1 Objectives

Selling objectives should be derived from overall marketing objectives and should be properly linked with promotional objectives. For example, if the marketing goal is to raise the current 35 percent market share in a product line to 40 percent, the sales manager may stipulate the objective to increase sales of specific products by different percentage points in various sales regions under his or her control.

Selling objectives are usually defined in terms of sales volume. Objectives, however, may also be defined for (a) gross margin targets, (b) maximum expenditure levels, and (c) fulfillment of specific activities, such as converting a stated number of competitors' customers into company customers.

The sales strategist should also specify the role of selling in terms of personal selling push (vis-à-vis advertising pull). Selling strategies depend on the buyer's decision process, the influence of different communication alternatives, and the cost of these alternatives. The flexibility associated with personal selling allows sales presentations to be tailored to individual customers. Further, personal selling offers an opportunity to develop a tangible personal rapport with customers that can go far toward building long-term relationships. Finally, personal selling is the only method that secures immediate feedback. Feedback helps in taking timely corrective action and in avoiding mistakes. The benefits of personal selling, however, must be considered in relation to its costs. For example, according to the research department of the McGraw-Hill Publications Company, per call personal selling expenditures for all types of personal selling in 1998 came to $241.80, up 19.2 percent from 1995.[24] Thus, the high impact of personal selling should be considered in light of its high cost.

17.3.2 Strategic Matters

As a part of selling strategy, several strategic matters should be resolved. A decision must be made on whether greater emphasis should be put on maintaining existing accounts or on converting customers. Retention and conversion of customers are related to the time salespeople spend with them. Thus, before salespeople can make the best use of their efforts, they must know how much importance is to be attached to each of these two functions. The decision is influenced by such factors as the growth status of the industry, the company's strengths and weaknesses, competitors' strengths, and marketing goals. For example, a manufacturer of laundry detergent will think twice before attempting to convert customers from Tide (Procter & Gamble's brand) to its own brand. On the other hand, some factors may make a company challenge the leader. For example, Bic Pen Corporation aggressively promotes its disposable razor to Gillette customers. The decision to maintain or convert customers cannot be made in isolation and must be considered in the context of total marketing strategy.[25]

An important strategic concern is how to make productive use of the sales force. In recent years, high expenses (i.e., cost of keeping a salesperson on the road), affordable technological advances (e.g., prices of technology used in telemarketing, teleconferencing, and computerized sales have gone down substantially), and innovative sales techniques (e.g., video presentations) have made it feasible for marketers to turn to electronic marketing to make the most productive use of sales force resources. For example, Gould's medical products division in Oxnard, California, uses video to support sales efforts for one of its new products, a disposable transducer that translates blood pressure into readable electronic impulses. Gould produced two videotapes—a six-minute sales presentation and a nine-minute training film—costing $200,000. Salespeople were equipped with videorecorders—an additional $75,000 investment—to take on calls. According to Gould executives, video gives a concise, clear version of the intended communication and adds professionalism to their sales effort. Gould targeted its competitors' customers and maintains that it captured 45 percent of the $75 million transducer market in less than a year. At the end of nine months, the company had achieved sales of more than 25,000 units per month, achieving significant penetration in markets that it had not been able to get into before.[26]

Another aspect of selling strategy deals with the question of who should be contacted in the customer organization. The buying process may be divided into four phases: consideration, acceptance, selection, and evaluation. Different executives in the customer organization may exert influence on any of the four phases. The sales strategist may work out a plan specifying which salesperson should call upon various individuals in the customer organization and when. On occasion, a person other than the salesperson may be asked to call on a customer. Sometimes, as a matter of selling strategy, a team of people may visit the customer. For example, Northrop Corporation, an aerospace contractor, assigns aircraft designers and technicians—not salespeople—to call on potential customers. When Singapore indicated interest in Northrop's F-5 fighter, Northrop dispatched a team to Singapore that included an engineer, a lawyer, a pricing expert, a test pilot, and a maintenance specialist.

A manufacturer of vinyl acetate latex (used as a base for latex paint) built its sales volume by having its people call on the "right people" in the customer organization. The manufacturer recognized that its product was used by the customer to produce paint sold through its marketing department, not the purchasing agent or the manager of research. So the manufacturer planned for its people to meet with the customer's sales and marketing personnel to find out what their problems were, what kept them from selling more latex paint, and what role the manufacturer could play in helping the customer. It was only after the marketing personnel had been sold on the product that the purchasing department was contacted. Thus, a good selling strategy requires a careful analysis of the situation to determine the key people to contact in the customer organization. A routine call on a purchasing agent may not suffice.

The selling strategy should also determine the size of the sales force needed to perform an effective job. This decision is usually made intuitively. A company starts with a few salespeople, adding more as it gains experience. Some companies may go a step beyond the intuitive approach to determine how many salespeople should be recruited. For instance, consideration may be given to factors such as the number of customers who must be visited, the amount of market potential in a territory, and so on. But all these factors are weighed subjectively. This work load approach requires the following steps:

1. Customers are grouped into size classes according to their annual sales volume.
2. Desirable call frequencies (number of sales calls on an account per year) are established for each class.
3. The number of accounts in each size class is multiplied by the corresponding call frequency to arrive at the total work load for the country in sales calls per year.
4. The average number of calls a sales representative can make per year is determined.
5. The number of sales representatives needed is determined by dividing the total annual calls required by the average annual calls made by a sales representative.

To ensure that salespersons perform to their utmost capacity, they must be motivated adequately and properly supervised. It has often been found that salespeople fail to do well because management fails to carry out its part of the job, especially in the areas of motivation and supervision. Although motivation and supervision may appear to be mundane day-to-day matters, they have far-reaching implications for marketing strategy. The purpose of this section is to provide insights into the strategic aspects of motivation and supervision.

17.3.3 Motivation

Salespeople may be motivated through financial and nonfinancial means. Financial motivation is provided by monetary compensation. Nonfinancial motivation is usually tied in with evaluation programs.[27]

17.3.4 Compensation

Most people work to earn a living; their motivation to work is deeply affected by the remuneration they receive. A well-designed compensation plan keeps turnover low and helps to increase an employee's productivity. A compensation plan should be simple, understandable, flexible (cognizant of the differences between individuals), and economically equitable. It should also provide incentive and build morale. It should not penalize salespeople for conditions beyond their control, and it should help develop new business, provide stable income, and meet the objectives of the corporation. Above all, compensation should be in line with the market price for salespeople. Because some of these requisites may conflict with each other, there can be no one perfect plan. All that can be done is to try to balance each variable properly and design a custom-made plan for each sales force.

Different methods of compensating salespeople are the salary plan, the commission plan, and the combination plan. Exhibit 17.3 shows the relative advantages and disadvantages of each plan.

The greatest virtue of the straight-salary method is the guaranteed income and security that it provides. However, it fails to provide any incentive for the ambitious salesperson and therefore may adversely affect productivity. Most companies work on a combination plan, which means that salespeople receive a percentage of sales as a commission for exceeding periodic quotas. Conceptually, the first step in designing a compensation plan is to define the objective. Objectives may focus on rewarding extraordinary performance, providing security, and so on. Every company probably prefers to grant some security to its people and, at the same time, distinguish top employees through incentive schemes. In designing such a plan, the company may first determine the going salary rate for the type of sales staff it is interested in hiring. The company

Exhibit 17.3
Advantages and
Disadvantages of Various
Sales Compensation
Alternatives

Salary Plan

Advantages

1. Assures a regular income.
2. Develops a high degree of loyalty.
3. Makes it simple to switch territories or quotas or to reassign salespeople.
4. Ensures that nonselling activities will be performed.
5. Facilitates administration.
6. Provides relatively fixed sales costs.

Disadvantages

1. Fails to give balanced sales mix because salespeople would concentrate on products with greatest customer appeal.
2. Provides little, if any, financial incentive for the salesperson.
3. Offers few reasons for putting forth extra effort.
4. Favors salespeople who are the least productive.
5. Tends to increase direct selling costs over other types of plans.
6. Creates the possibility of salary compression where new trainees may earn almost as much as experienced salespeople.

Commission Plan

Advantages

1. Pay relates directly to performance and results achieved.
2. System is easy to understand and compute.
3. Salespeople have the greatest possible incentive.
4. Unit sales costs are proportional to net sales.
5. Company's selling investment is reduced.

Disadvantages

1. Emphasis is more likely to be on volume than on profits.
2. Little or no loyalty to the company is generated.
3. Wide variances in income between salespeople may occur.
4. Salespeople are encouraged to neglect nonselling duties.
5. Some salespeople may be tempted to "skim" their territories.
6. Service aspect of selling may be slighted.
7. Problems arise in cutting territories or shifting people or accounts.
8. Pay is often excessive in boom times and very low in recession periods.
9. Salespeople may sell themselves rather than the company and stress short-term rather than long-term relationships.
10. Highly paid salespeople may be reluctant to move into supervisory or managerial positions.
11. Excessive turnover of sales personnel occurs when business turns bad.

Combination Plan

Advantages

1. Offers participants the advantage of both salary and commission.
2. Provides greater range of earnings possibilities.
3. Gives salespeople greater security because of steady base income.
4. Makes possible a favorable ratio of selling expense to sales.
5. Compensates salespeople for all activities.

Exhibit 17.3
Advantages and
Disadvantages of Various
Sales Compensation
Alternatives (*continued*)

6. Allows a greater latitude of motivation possibilities so that goals and objectives can be achieved on schedule

Disadvantages

1. Is often complex and difficult to understand.
2. Can, where low salary and high bonus or commission exist, develop a bonus that is too high a percentage of earnings; when sales fall, salary is too low to retain salespeople.
3. Is sometimes costly to administer.
4. Unless a decreasing commission rate for increasing sales volume exists, can result in a "windfall" of new accounts and a runaway of earnings.
5. Has a tendency to offer too many objectives at one time so that really important ones can be neglected, forgotten, or overlooked.

should match the market rate to retain people of caliber. The total wage should be fixed somewhere near the market rate after making adjustments for the company's overall wage policy, environment, and fringe benefits. A study of the spending habits of those in the salary range of salespeople should be made. Based on this study, the percentage of nondiscretionary spending may be linked to an incentive income scheme whereby extra income could be paid as a commission on sales, as a bonus, or both. Care must be taken in constructing a compensation plan. In addition to being equitable, the plan should be simple enough to be comprehensible to the salespeople.

A compensation plan must also reflect and support the activities which a company desires of its sales force. For example, if a company requires that it sales force provide significant levels of service to its customers, acompensation plan which is primarily salary based should be implemented. Providing service to a customer takes time away from selling, hence a sales force cannot be expected to provide significant service to customers if the primary form of compensation is commission based—the company would literally be demanding that its sales representatives reduce their own income. If service is not an important duty and sales are fairly consistent over the year, then a primarily commission-based compensation plan is desirable as the sales representative will be free to sell and move on, maximizing their own income as well as the company's sales.

Once compensation has been established for an individual, it is difficult to reduce it. It is desirable, therefore, for management to consider all the pros and cons of fixed compensation for a salesperson before finalizing a salary agreement.

17.3.5 Evaluation

Evaluation is the measurement of a salesperson's contribution to corporate goals. For any evaluation, one needs standards. Establishment of standards, however, is a difficult task, particularly when salespeople are asked to perform different types of jobs. In pure selling jobs, quotas can be set for minimal performance, and salespeople achieving these quotas can be considered as doing satisfactory work. Achievement of quotas can be classified as follows: salespeople exceeding quotas between 1 to 15 percent may be designated as average; those between 16 and 30 percent as well-performing; finally, those over 30 percent can be considered extraordinary salespeople. Sales contests and awards, both financial and nonfinancial, may be instituted to give recognition to salespeople in various categories. In evaluating sales performance it is important to use several measures other than straight sales volume. To use only straight sales volume will encourage a sales representative to make the easiest sales, i.e., to sell the company's loss leaders—this is not a formula for profit. Hence a sales representatives quotas should require minimum proportions of sales of the company's more profitable products and product lines.

17.3.6 Supervision

Despite the best efforts in selecting, training, and compensating salespeople, they may not perform as expected. Supervision is important to ensure that salespeople provide the services expected of them.

Supervision of salespeople is defined in a broader sense to include the assignment of a territory to a salesperson, control over his or her activities, and communication with the salesperson in the field.

Salespeople are assigned to different geographic territories. An assignment requires solving two problems: (a) forming territories so that they are as much alike as possible in business potential and (b) assigning territories so that each salesperson is able to realize his or her full potential. Territories may be formed by analyzing customers' locations and the potential business they represent. Customers can be categorized as having high, average, or low potential. Further, probabilities in terms of sales can be assigned to indicate how much potential is realizable. Thus, a territory with a large number of high-potential customers with a high probability of buying may be smaller in size (geographically) than a territory with a large number of low-potential customers with a low probability of buying.

Matching salespeople to territories should not be difficult once the territories have been laid out. Regional preferences and the individual affiliations of salespeople require that employees be placed where they will be happiest. It may be difficult to attract salespeople to some territories, whereas other places may be in great demand. Living in big metropolitan areas is expensive and not always comfortable. Similarly, people may avoid places with poor weather. It may become necessary to provide extra compensation to salespeople assigned to unpopular places.

Although salespeople are their own bosses in the field, the manager must keep informed of their activities. To achieve an adequate level of control, a system must be created for maintaining communication with employees in the field, for guiding their work, and for employing remedial methods if performance slackens. Firms use different types of control devices. Some companies require salespeople to fill in a call form that gives all particulars about each visit to each customer. Some require salespeople to submit weekly reports on work performed during the previous week. Salespeople may be asked to complete several forms about sales generated, special problems they face, market information collected, and so on. Using a good reporting system to control the sales force should have a positive influence on performance. In recent years, more and more companies have begun to use computer-assisted techniques to maintain control of the activities of their sales forces.

Management communicates with salespeople through periodic mailings, regional and national conferences, and telephone calls. Two areas of communication in which management needs to be extra careful to maintain the morale of good salespeople are (a) in representing the problems of the field force to people at headquarters and (b) in giving patient consideration to the salesperson's complaints. A sales manager serves as the link between the people in the field and the company and must try to bring their problems and difficulties to the attention of top management. Top management, not being fully aware of operations in the field, may fail to appreciate problems. It is, therefore, the duty of the sales manager to keep top management fully posted about field activities and to secure for salespeople its favor. For example, a salesperson in a mountainous area may not be able to maintain his or her work tempo during the winter because of weather conditions. Management must consider this factor in reviewing the salesperson's work. It is the manager's duty to stand by and help with occupational or personal problems bothering salespeople.

Close rapport with salespeople and patient listening can be very helpful in recognizing and solving sales force problems. More often than not, a salesperson's problem is something that the company can take care of with a little effort and expenditure if it is only willing to accept such responsibility. The primary thing, however, is to know the salesperson's mind. This is where the role of the supervisor comes in. It is said that the sales manager should be as much a therapist in solving the problems of his or her salespeople as the latter should be in handling customers' problems.

SUMMARY

Promotion strategies are directed toward establishing communication with customers. Three types of promotion strategies may be distinguished. Advertising strategies are concerned with communication transmitted through the mass media. Personal selling strategies refer to face-to-face interactions with the customer. All other forms of communication, such as sampling, demonstration, cents off, contests, etc., are known as sales promotion strategies. Two main promotion strategies were examined in this chapter: promotion-expenditure strategy, which deals with the question of how much may be spent on overall promotion, and promotion mix strategy, which specifies the roles that the three ingredients of promotion (i.e., advertising, personal selling, and sales promotion) play in promoting a product.

Discussed also were two advertising strategies. The first, media-selection strategy, focuses on the choice of different media to launch an ad campaign. The second, advertising-copy strategy, deals with the development of appropriate ad copy to convey intended messages. Two personal selling strategies were examined: selling strategy and sales motivation and supervision strategy. Selling strategy emphasizes the approach that is adopted to interact with the customer (i.e., who may call on the customer, whom to call on in the customer organization, when, and how frequently). Sales motivation and supervision strategy is concerned with the management of the sales force and refers to such issues as sales compensation, nonfinancial incentives, territory formation, territory assignments, control, and communication.

DISCUSSION QUESTIONS

1. Outline promotion objectives for a packaged food product in an assumed market segment.
2. Develop a promotion-expenditure strategy for a household computer to be marketed through a large retail chain.
3. Will promotion-expenditure strategy for a product in the growth stage of the product life cycle be different from that for a product in the maturity stage? Discuss.
4. How may a promotion budget be allocated among advertising, personal selling, and sales promotion? Can a simulation model be developed to figure out an optimum promotion mix?
5. Is comparison advertising socially desirable? Comment.
6. Should the media decision be made before or after the copy is first developed?
7. Which is more effective, an emotional appeal or a rational appeal? Are emotional appeals relevant for all consumer products?

NOTES

1. James B. Arndorfer, "Brewers Fight for Hispanic Market," *Advertising Age*, June 8, 2003, p. 40.
2. Richard Gibson, "Marketers' Mantra: Reap More with Less," *The Wall Street Journal*, April 14, 2001, p. B1.
3. "USIC Chem. Ads Start to Support Effort to Double Sales in 5 Years," *Industrial Marketing*, June 1986, pp. 1–4.
4. See Mark Ritson, "Integration As the Way Ahead for Marketing," *Financial Times*, October 18, 2001, p. 2 (Mastering Management).
5. Michael E. Porter, "Interbrand Choice: Media Mix and Market Performance," *American Economic Review*, May 6, 1976, pp. 190–203.
6. "Market Makers," *The Economist*, March 14, 1998, p. 67.
7. See *Workbook for Estimating Your Advertising Budget* (Boston, Cahners Publishing Co., 1994).
8. "Ad Agencies Thrive on Digital Revenue," EMarketer.com, May 6, 2008.
9. George Anders, "Internet Advertising, Just Like Its Medium, Is Pushing Boundaries," *The Wall Street Journal*, November 30, 1998, p. A1.
10. Caroling Cartellieri, Andrew J. Parsons, Varsha Rao, and Michael P. Zeisser, "The Real Impact of Internet Advertising," *The McKinsey Quarterly*, Vol. 3, 1997, pp. 44–63.
11. E. S. Browning, "Perrier's Vincent Plans Wave of Change as a Fresh Regime Displaces the Old?" *The Wall Street Journal*, February 14, 1991, p. B1.
12. "New Headline, Same Great Column," *Fortune*, February 16, 1998, p. 42.
13. Bob Lamons, "Absolut Fortune: One Liquor's Success Story," *Marketing News*, February 12, 2001, p. 8.
14. Kevin Lane Keller, Brian Sternthal, and Alice Tybout, "Three Questions You Need to Ask About Your Brand," *Harvard Business Review*, September 2002, pp. 80–89.
15. "The Generation Gap in Point Form: Some Recent Reflections on the Vital Signs and Values of the Youth Market," *Marketing* (U.K.), February 14, 1994, p. 21. Also see Jeanne Whalen, "Market Trends: Retailers Aim Straight at Teens," *Advertising Age*, September 5, 1994, p. 1.

16. See Stratford P. Sherman, ''When You Wish upon a Star,'' *Fortune*, August 19, 1985, p. 66.

17. See Carl I. Hoveland, Irving L. Janis, and Harold H. Kelley, *Communication and Persuasion* (New Haven, Yale University Press, 1953): 225.

18. Thomas R. King, ''Credibility Gap: More Consumers Find Celebrity Ads Unpersuasive,'' *The Wall Street Journal*, July 5, 1985, p. B5.

19. Kenneth Labich, ''Nike vs. Reebok,'' *Fortune*, September 18, 1995, p. 90.

20. Carl I. Hoveland, Arthur A. Lumsdaine, and Fred D. Sheffield, ''The Effect of Presenting 'One Side' versus 'Both Sides' in Changing Opinions on a Controversial Subject,'' in *The Process and Effect of Mass Communication*, ed. Wilbur Schramm (Urbana, University of Illinois Press, 1960): 274.

21. Based on information supplied by the Coca-Cola Company.

22. Hoveland, Janis, and Kelley, *Communication and Persuasion*, 57.

23. Joanne Lipman, ''Amex Card Takes on Visa Over Olympics,'' *The Wall Street Journal*, February 3, 1992, p. B1.

24. ''Average Cost Almost Hits $20 Mark for Industrial Sales Calls,'' *Marketing News*, February 21, 2001, p. 14. The study also showed that the larger the sales force, the lower the cost. For instance, companies with fewer than 10 salespeople spent more than $298.85 per call; companies with more than 100 spent $158.55. This underscores the significance of the experience effect (see Chapter 12).

25. Jaclyn Fireman, ''The Death and Rebirth of the Salesman,'' *Fortune*, July 25, 1994, p. 80.

26. ''Rebirth of a Salesman: Willy Loman Goes Electronic,'' *BusinessWeek*, February 27, 1984, p. 103.

27. Alan Farnham, ''Mary Kay's Lessons in Leadership,'' *Fortune*, September 20, 1993, p. 68.

APPENDIX: PERSPECTIVES ON PROMOTION STRATEGIES

Definition: Determination of the amount that a company may spend on its total promotional effort, which includes advertising, personal selling, and sales promotion.

Objective: To allocate enough funds to each promotional task so that each is utilized to its fullest potential.

Requirements: (a) Adequate resources to finance the promotion expenditure. (b) Understanding of the products/services sales response. (c) Estimate of the duration of the advertising effect. (d) Understanding of each product/market situation relative to different forms of promotion. (e) Understanding of competitive response to promotion.

Expected Results: Allocation of sufficient funds to the promotional tasks to accomplish overall marketing objectives.

Definition: Determination of a judicious mix of different types of promotion.

Objective: To adequately blend the three types of promotion to complement each other for a balanced promotional perspective.

Requirements: (a) Product factors: (i) nature of product, (ii) perceived risk, (iii) durable versus nondurable, and (iv) typical purchase amount. (b) Market factors: (i) position in the life cycle, (ii) market share, (iii) industry concentration, (iv) intensity of competition, and (v) demand perspectives. (c) Customers factors: (i) household versus business customers, (ii) number of customers, and (iii) concentration of customers. (d) Budget factors: (i) financial resources of the organization and (ii) traditional promotional perspectives. (e) Marketing mix factors: (i) relative price/relative quality, (ii) distribution strategy, (iii) brand life cycle, and (iv) geographic scope of the market. (f) Environmental factors.

Expected Results: The three types of promotion are assigned roles in a way that provides the best communication.

Definition: Choosing the channels (newspapers, magazines, television, radio, outdoor advertising, transit advertising, and direct mail) through which messages concerning a product/service are transmitted to the targets.

Objective: To move customers from unawareness of a product/service, to awareness, to comprehension, to conviction, to the buying action.

Requirements: (a) Relate media-selection objectives to product/market objectives. (b) Media chosen should have a unique way of promoting the business. (c) Media should be measure-minded not only in frequency, in timing, and in reaching the target audience but also in evaluating the quality of the audience. (d) Base media selection on factual not connotational grounds. (e) Media plan should be optimistic in that it takes advantage of the lessons learned from experience. (f) Seek information on customer profiles and audience characteristics.

Expected Results: Customers are moved along the desired path of the purchase process.

Definition: Designing the content of an advertisement.

Objective: To transmit a particular product/service message to a particular target.

Requirements: (a) Eliminate ''noise'' for a clear transmission of message. (b) Consider importance of (i) source credibility, (ii) balance of argument, (iii) message repetition, (iv) rational versus emotional appeals, (v) humor appeals, (vi) presentation of model's eyes in pictorial ads, and (vii) comparison advertising.

Expected Results: The intended message is adequately transmitted to the target audience.

Definition: Moving customers to the purchase phase of the decision-making process through the use of face-to-face contact.

Objective: Achievement of stated sales volume and gross margin targets and the fulfillment of specific activities.

Requirements: (a) The selling strategy should be derived from overall marketing objectives and properly linked with promotional objectives. (b) Decision on maintenance of existing accounts versus lining up new customers. (c) Decision on who should be contacted in customer's organization. (d) Determine optimal size of sales force.

Expected Results: (a) Sales and profit targets are met at minimum expense. (b) Overall marketing goals are achieved.

Definition: Achieving superior sales force performance.

Objective: To ensure optimal performance of the sales force.

Requirements: (a) Motivation financial and nonfinancial. (b) Adequate compensation package. (c) Evaluation standards. (d) Appropriate territory assignment, activity control, and communication.

Expected Results: Business objectives are met adequately at minimum expense.

Chapter Outline

18.1 **Identifying Target Markets**
18.2 **Entry Strategies**
  18.2.1 Advantages of Licensing
  18.2.2 Disadvantages of Licensing
18.3 **Global Market Environment**
18.4 **Strategy for Global Marketing Programs**
18.5 **Marketing in Global Business Strategy**
18.6 **Developing Global Market Strategy: An Example**

Chapter 18

Global Market Strategies

Competition in the U.S. marketplace is no longer national, but international. American businesses that adapt to changing circumstances and recognize opportunities will prosper; those that do not will at best survive temporarily.

PRESIDENT'S TASK FORCE ON INTERNATIONAL PRIVATE ENTERPRISE

One of the most significant developments in recent years has been the emergence of global markets. Today's market provides not only a multiplicity of goods but goods from many places. It would not be surprising to discover that your shirt comes from Taiwan, your jeans from Mexico, and your shoes from Italy. You may drive a Japanese car equipped with tires manufactured in France, with nuts and bolts produced in India, and with paint from a U.S. company. Gucci bags, Sony Walkmans, and McDonald's golden arches are seen on the streets of Tokyo, London, Paris, and New York. Thai goods wind up on U.S. grocery shelves as Dole canned pineapple and on French farms as livestock feed. Millions of consumers worldwide want all the things that they have heard about, seen, or experienced via new communication technologies. Firms today are enmeshed in world competition to serve these consumers, no matter where they live.

A number of broad forces have led to growing globalization of markets.[1] These include

1. **Growing similarity of countries**—Because of growing commonality of infrastructure, distribution channels, and marketing approaches, more and more products and brands are available everywhere. Similar buyer needs thus manifest themselves in different countries. Large retail chains, television advertising, and credit cards are just a few examples of once-isolated phenomena that are rapidly becoming universal.
2. **Falling tariff barriers**—Successive rounds of bilateral and multilateral agreements have lowered tariffs markedly since World War II. At the same time, regional economic agreements, such as the European Union (EU), have facilitated trade relations.
3. **Strategic role of technology**—Technology is not only reshaping industries but contributing toward market homogenization. For example, electronic innovations have permitted the development of more compact, lighter products that are less costly to ship. Transportation costs themselves have fallen with the use of containerization and larger-capacity ships. Increasing ease of communication and data transfer make it feasible to link operations in different countries. At the same time, technology leads to an easy flow of information among buyers, making them aware of new and quality products and thus creating demand for them.

The impact of these forces on the globalization of markets may be illustrated with reference to a few examples. Kids everywhereplay Nintendo and stroll along streets to the sound of Sony Walkmans. The videocassette recorder market took off simultaneously in Japan, Europe, and the United States, but the most extensive use of videocassette recorders today is probably in places like Riyadh and Caracas. Shopping centers from Dusseldorf to Rio to Singapore and Shanghai sell Gucci shoes, Yves St. Laurent suits, and Gloria Vanderbilt jeans. Siemens and ITT telephones can be found almost everywhere in the world. The Mercedes-Benz and the Toyota Corolla are as much objects of passion in Manila as in California.

Just about every gas turbine sold in the world has some GE technology or component in it, and what country doesn't need gas turbines? How many airlines around the world could survive without Boeing or Airbus? Third World markets for high-voltage transmission equipment and diesel-electric locomotives are bigger than those in developed countries. And today's new industries—robotics, videodisks, fiber optics, satellite networks, high-technology plastics, artificial diamonds—seem global from birth.

Briefly, these forces have homogenized worldwide markets, triggering opportunities for firms to seek business across national borders. For U.S. corporations, the real impetus to overseas expansion occurred after World War II. Attempting to reconstruct war-torn economies, the U.S. government, through the Marshall Plan, provided financial assistance to European countries. As the postwar American economy emerged as the strongest in the world, its economic assistance programs, in the absence of competition, stimulated extensive corporate development of international strategies. Since then, many new players, not only from Europe and Japan, but from emerging markets in Southeast Asia, Latin America and China as well, have entered the arena to serve global markets. Emerging market competitors have been quick to exploit new international competitive conditions as well as cross-cutting technologies to leapfrog well-established rivals. Emerging market multinationals (EMNCs) have overtaken their European counterparts and now form the second largest group of multinationals in the world after those from the United States.

Global markets offer unlimited opportunities. But competition in these markets is intense. To be globally successful, companies must learn to operate and compete as if the world were one large complex market. Corporations geared to this new reality can often benefit from enormous economies of scale in production, distribution, marketing, and management. By translating these benefits into reduced world prices, they can dislodge competitors who still operate under the perspectives of the 1980s. Companies willing to change their perspectives and become global can attain sustainable competitive advantage.

18.1 IDENTIFYING TARGET MARKETS

There are over 200 countries in the world. Different countries represent varying market potentials due to economic, cultural, and political contrasts. These contrasts mean that a global marketer cannot select target customers randomly but must employ workable criteria to choose countries where the company's product/service has the best opportunity for success.

The most basic information needed to identify markets concerns population because people, of course, constitute a market. The population of the world reached an estimated 6.8 billion on May 1, 2008. According to the latest estimates from the United Nations, this total is expected to increase to almost 8.5 billion by 2025. Current world population is growing at about 1.167 percent per year. This is a decline from the peak rate of 1.9 percent.

Population growth rates vary significantly by region. Europe has the lowest rate of population growth at only about 0.3 percent per year. Several European countries, including Austria, Denmark, West Germany, Luxembourg and Sweden, and Japan, are experiencing declining populations. Growth rates are also below 1 percent per year in North America.

The regions with the highest population growth rates are Africa (3 percent per year), Latin America (2 percent per year) and South Asia (1.9 percent per year). China, the world's most populous country, is growing at only about 1.2 percent per year. Even so, it means that China's population increases by over 12 million people each year. The world's second most populous country, India with curent population of 1 billion, is growing at over 1.5 percent per year.

One striking aspect of population growth in developing countries is the rapid rate of urbanization. The urban population is growing at less than 1 percent in Europe and in North America, but it is growing at almost 3.5 percent in the developing world. Today 20 of the 25 largest urban agglomerations are in the developing world. The only cities in the top 20 located in developed countries are Tokyo, New York, and Los Angeles. Tough different sources provide significantly different population estimates, in 2007 the world's largest cities were believed to be Tokyo (33.6 million) and Seoul (23.4 million).

The above information shows that the total market in Europe, Japan and North America will not be increasing substantially or rapidly; the population of the industrialized countries will not add much to total market size. Of course, these populations are growing older, so certain segments will increase in number. For example, the total population of Europe was expected to increase only 2.8 percent between 2000–2010, but the over-65 population in Europe was estimated to increase by 14 percent during the same period.

In the developing world, the increase in numbers does not necessarily mean increased markets for U.S. business. The fastest-growing region in the world, Africa, experienced low or negative rates of economic growth per capita for many years, although recent years have shown an economic turnaround in sub-Saharan Africa is taking place, especially in countries like Ghana, South Africa and Nigeria. Many

Exhibit 18.1
Consuming Capacities of
Selected Countries

Country	Population	Per Capita GNP	Index of Consuming Capacity
United States	270	29,340	7,921,800
Japan	126	32,380	4,079,880
Germany	82	25,850	2,119,700
France	59	24,940	1,471,460
United Kingdom	59	21,400	1,262,600
Italy	58	20,250	1,174,500
Brazil	166	4,570	758,620
Canada	31	20,020	620,620
India	980	430	421,400
Netherlands	16	24,760	396,160
Australia	19	20,300	385,700
Mexico	96	3,970	381,120
Argentina	36	8,970	322,920
Switzerland	7	40,080	280,560
Belgium	10	25,380	253,800
Turkey	63	3,160	199,080
Denmark	5	33,260	166,300
Thailand	61	2,200	134,200
South Africa	41	2,880	118,080
Israel	6	15,940	95,640
Philippines	75	1,050	78,750
Peru	25	2,460	61,500
New Zealand	4	14,700	58,800
Ecuador	12	1,530	18,360
Paraguay	5	1,760	8,800
Uganda	21	320	6,720

Source: World Bank Report 2000 (Washington, DC, The World Bank, 2000).

Latin American countries, Brazil in particular, have been hampered by huge external debts that force them to try to limit imports while using their resources to generate foreign exchange for debt service. However over the latter half of the 20th century Latin America was the second fastest growing region in the world behind Southeast Asia, and year to year, Mexico ranks as the U.S.'s second or third largest trading partner. Canada is the U.S.'s largest trading partner. With the rise of China, Latin America has dropped into the position of being the third fastest growing region.

Obviously, population figures alone provide little information about market potential because people must have the means in terms of income to become viable customers and competitive conditions in different countries can significantly impact profitability. For example, in 2004 affiliates of U.S. companies operating in China (with a popolation of 1.2 billion) had total earnings of $8.2 billion; total earnings for affilliates of U.S. companies operating in Australia (population 19 million), Taiwan and South Korea (combined population 70 million) and Mexico (population 95 million) were $7.1 billion, $8.9 billion and $14.3 billion, respectively.[2] In Exhibit 18.1, population combined with per capita GNP provides an estimate of consuming capacity. An index of consuming capacity depicts absolute, or aggregate, consumption, both in the entire world and in individual economies. Consumption rates can be satisfied either domestically or through imports.

The information in Exhibit 18.1 should be interpreted cautiously because it makes no allowances for difference in the purchasing power among different countries. Two conclusions are obvious, however: (a) aggregate consuming capacity depends upon total population as well as per capital income and (b) currently advanced countries dominate as potential customers.

Although population and income variables provide a snapshot of the market opportunity in a given country, a variety of other factors must be considered to identify viable markets. These factors are urbanization, consumption patterns, infrastructure, and overall industrialization. Taking these factors into account,

Exhibit 18.2
Top Fifteen Economies by GDP

International Monetary Fund Rankings			CIA World Fact Book Rankings		
Rank	Country	GDP (millions of USD)	Rank	Country	GDP (millions of USD)
—	World	54,311,608	—	World	53,640,000
—	European Union	16,830,100	—	European Union	16,370,000
1	United States	13,843,825	1	United States	13,790,000
2	Japan	4,383,762	2	Japan	4,346,000
3	Germany	3,322,147	3	Germany	3,259,000
4	China	3,250,827	4	China	3,249,000
5	United Kingdom	2,772,570	5	United Kingdom	2,756,000
6	France	2,560,255	6	France	2,515,000
7	Italy	2,104,666	7	Italy	2,068,000
8	Spain	1,438,959	8	Spain	1,415,000
9	Canada	1,432,140	9	Canada	1,406,000
10	Brazil	1,313,590	10	Russia	1,286,000
11	Russia	1,289,582	11	Brazil	1,269,000
12	India	1,098,945	12	India	1,090,000
13	South Korea	957,053	13	South Korea	981,900
14	Australia	908,826	14	Australia	889,700
15	Mexico	893,365	15	Mexico	886,400

the International Monetary Fund and the CIA World Fact Book both rank countries by the size of their economy. The fifteen largest countries are listed in Exhibit 18.2.[3] Interestingly, six of these fifteen countries—China, Brazil, Russia, India, Mexico and South Korea—are emerging economies.

Although these fifteen countries have been identified as the principal global markets by *Business International,* they may not all be viable markets from the viewpoint of U.S. firms. A variety of environmental factors (political, legal, cultural) affect market opportunity in a nation. For example, Brazil is burdened with debt, which limits the amount of export potential in that country; China's political control limits freedom of choice; India's regulations make it difficult for foreign corporations to conduct business there. Thus, many countries may not have large market potential, yet they may constitute important markets for U.S. business.

Exhibit 18.3 lists the top 25 U.S. export markets. Also shown is the dollar amount of exports to each country in 2007. It should be noted that, globally speaking, although Canada ranks as the ninth largest market in the world and Mexico as the fifteenth (see Exhibit 18.2), they represent the largest and second largest markets for the United States, accounting for over 33 percent of its trade.

Traditionally, a major proportion of international business activities of U.S. corporations has been limited to developed countries. For example, at the end of 2000, total U.S. direct investment was estimated to be $952 billion, of which almost 70 percent was in developed countries. Slowly, however, new markets are unfolding. Consider the newly industrializing countries. During the decade of the 1980s, South Korea, Singapore, Taiwan, and Hong Kong were the world's fastest-growing economies and consequently offered new opportunities for U.S. firms.

In recent years, emerging economies, at least the more politically stable ones, have begun to show viable market potential. A number of developing countries are achieving higher and higher growth rates every year. With GDPs adjusted for purchasing power parity, the emerging economies' share of world GDP overtook the industrialized economies in 2004.[4] Although an individual country may not provide adequate potential for U.S. corporations, developing countries as a group constitute a major market. In 2002, almost 30 percent of U.S. trade was with developing countries. In future years, the flow of U.S. trade with developing countries should increase. An Organization of Economic Cooperation and Development (OECD) study showed that, in 1970, OECD countries, with just 20 percent of the world's people, had 83 percent of the world's trade in manufactures; whereas developing countries, with 70 percent of the world's people, captured just 11 percent of the trade. In the year 2000, however, the OECD countries, with 15 percent of

1.	Canada	248.4
2.	Mexico	136.5
3.	China	65.2
4.	Japan	62.7
5.	United Kingdom	50.3
6.	Germany	49.7
7.	South Korea	34.7
8.	Netherlands	33.0
9.	France	27.4
10.	Taiwan	26.4
11.	Singapore	26.3
12.	Belgium	25.3
13.	Brazil	24.6
14.	Hong Kong	20.1
15.	Australia	19.2
16.	India	17.6
17.	Switzerland	17.0
18.	Italy	14.1
19.	Israel	13.0
20.	Malaysia	11.7
21.	United Arab Emirates	
	Thailand	11.6
22.	Saudi Arabia	10.4
23.	Venezuela	10.2
24.	Spain	9.9
25.	Ireland	9.0

Source: U.S. Department of Commerce

the population, account for 63 percent of the world's trade in manufactures; developing countries, with 78 percent of the population, generated 28 percent of world trade.[5] Today almost 50 percent of direct foreign investment and well over 10 percent of portfolio capital flows are directed toward emerging markets, even though they account for less than 25 percent of the world GDP.[6] Interestingly, although for cultural, political, and economic reasons, Western Europe, Canada, and to a lesser extent Japan have always been predominantly important for business, many developing countries provide a better return on U.S. investment.[7]

The relevance of emerging markets for the United States can be illustrated with reference to Pacific basin countries. Over the last quarter century, streams of food, fuels, textiles, cameras, cars, and videocassette recorders flowing from countries all across Asia exerted heavy pressure on Western economies. This outpouring of exports has increased the Asian/Pacific share of world trade from less than 10 percent in the 1970s to over 25 percent in 2000 and has pushed one Asian economy after another out of the Dark Ages and into the global marketplace.

For U.S. marketers, rising Pacific power holds both a threat and a promise. The threat is dramatically increased competition for sales and market share, both at home and abroad. Since 2000 alone, U.S. imports from Asia have increased $140 billion. As for the promise, there is the emergence of a market of more than two billion potential consumers. In the last 25 years, as the Pacific region began its time-bending leap into the twentieth century, millions of Asians began an equally rapid transition from rural to urban, from agrarian to industrial, and from feudal to contemporary society. With more of the Pacific region's rural population traveling to cities to shop every day, the demand for goods and services—from the most basic household commodities to sophisticated technical devices—is soaring. In the coming years, as rising incomes continue to bolster the spending power of Asia's new consumer population, the opportunities for shrewd marketers will be unparalleled.

Barriers to conducting business in the region are beginning to fall, too. Increasingly, throughout the region English is the language of commerce, and an allegiance to free market economics is widespread. And, as companies such as McDonald's, P&G, Unilever, and Coca-Cola have already discovered, from Penang to Taipei, this is a region where well-made and well-marketed products and services are witnessing increasing acceptance.

As modern influences exert greater pressure on traditional Asian cultures, two trends with important implications for marketers are starting to take shape:

- Although each Asian nation is culturally distinct, consumers throughout the Pacific region are gradually sharing more of the same wants and needs. As Asian homogenization progresses, sophisticated strategies and considerable economies of scale in regional and global marketing and advertising will become increasingly relevant.
- Many Western marketers misinterpret the nature of current changes in the Pacific region. Despite the Big Macs, the Levi's, the Nikes, and all the other familiar trappings, Asia is not Westernizing—it's modernizing. Asian consumers are buying Western goods and services, not Western values and cultures.

Elsewhere in the East, India and China are two large markets that should provide unprecedented opportunities for U.S. corporations year after year as their economies become fully market oriented. A growing number of U.S. consumer-goods companies have begun to make inroads in China. In November 1987, Kentucky Fried Chicken Corp. opened the first Western fast-food restaurant in China. Coca-Cola and PepsiCo are aggressively expanding distribution. Kodak and other foreign film suppliers have attained a 70 percent share of the color film market. Nescafé and Maxwell House are waging coffee combat in a land of tea. It should be remembered however that opportunity does not automatically equal profits. A 2004 survey by the U.S. Chamber of Commerce-Beijing have shown that 80 percent of U.S. companies operating in China have either never made a profit in China or failed to attain expected profit levels.[8]

A number of U.S. companies—Pepsi, Timex, General Foods, Kellogg—have entered India to serve its emerging middle class.[9] Thus, the developing countries provide new opportunities for U.S. corporations to expand business overseas: as their wealth grows, U.S. marketing possibilities expand.

It has been observed that in not too distant a future, Latin American countries, too, will emerge as modern, Northern-styled marketplaces with improved transportation systems, subsidized credit to native businesses, and marketing education programs. All of these changes should result in more efficient channels of distribution, more local marketing support services, and fewer bottlenecks that hamper exchanges. All of these indications point toward a variety of emerging opportunities for U.S. corporations in Latin America.[10]

For example, a few years ago, the Gillette Company discovered that only 8 percent of Mexican men who shave used shaving cream. Sensing an opportunity, Gillette introduced plastic tubes of shaving cream in Guadalajara, Mexico, that sold for half the price of its aerosol. In a year's time, 13 percent of Guadalajaran men began to use shaving cream. Gillette has been selling its new product, Prestobarba (Spanish for "quick shave"), in the rest of Mexico, in Colombia, and in Brazil.[11]

These emerging markets can help many U.S. corporations to counter the results of demographic changes in Western nations examined above. As mentioned above, in most advanced nations of the world, birthrates are declining while population in the developing countries is growing. Though population growth in the U.S. has slowed, its historically more liberal immigration policies have given the U.S. a much better market environment than those of Japan and Western Europe. This increasing population holds significant future growth potential for U.S. business, and is an absolute necessity for European and Japanese businesses.

With the fall of the Berlin Wall and the lifting of the Iron Curtain, new opportunities await Western managers in Eastern Europe, previously a forbidden region. In many ways, the opening of Eastern Europe could prove even more important than the drive for a single market in Western Europe. Take, for example, Poland, Hungary, and Czech Republic. Their combined GNP is larger than that of China. These three countries also have relatively well-trained and reliable workers who work for less than a quarter of what Western Europeans are paid.[12] Giving them access to their developed neighbors' markets and hefty injections of Western capital, they could become the tigers of Europe. As their economies grow, they should develop into viable markets for a variety of goods and services.

Developments in Eastern Europe will benefit American companies in two ways. First, as Eastern Europe's backward economies finally integrate into the global economy and take off, new market opportunities should emerge. Second, sales to Western Europe by U.S. firms, made even more dynamic by its expanding Eastern frontier, will increase. Just as markets in the 1980s were developed by Reaganomics and Thatcherism, markets in future years will be developed by the shifting of the ideological plates that have separated the world's geopolitical land masses. Companies that aim for global market and remain competitive will be the winners.

From a global perspective, the United States, Canada, Japan, and Western Europe, often referred to as *triad countries*, constitute the major market. Although elsewhere opportunities are emerging, in the foreseeable future these countries continue to be the leading markets. They account for approximately 14 percent of the world's population, but they represent a greatly disproportionate percentage world gross product. As such, these countries absorb a major proportion of capital and consumer products and, thus, are the most advanced consuming societies in the world. Not only do most product innovations take place in these countries, but they also serve as the opinion leaders and mold the purchasing and consumption behavior of the emerging markets' growing middle classes.

For example, over 90 percent of the world's computers are used by triad countries. In the case of numerically controlled machine tools, almost 100 percent are distributed in the triad markets. The same pattern follows in consumer products. The triad accounts for 90 percent of the demand for electronic consumer goods. What these statistics point to is that a company that ignores the market potential of the triad does so at its own peril.

An interesting characteristic of the triad markets is the universalization of needs. For example, not too long ago manufacturers of capital equipment produced machinery that reflected strong cultural distinctions. West German machines reflected that nation's penchant for craftsmanship; American equipment was often extravagant in its use of raw materials. But these distinctions have disappeared. The best-selling factory machines have lost the "art" element that once distinguished them and have become both in appearance and in the level of skill that they require much more similar. The current revolution in production engineering has brought about ever-increasing global standards of performance. In an era when productivity improvements can quickly determine life or death on a global scale, companies cannot afford to indulge in a metallic piece of art that will last 30 years.

At the same time, consumer markets have become fairly homogeneous. Ohmae notes that

> Triad consumption patterns, which is both a cause and an effect of cultural patterns, has its roots to a large extent in the educational system. As educational systems enable more people to use technology, they tend to become more similar to each other. It follows, therefore, that education leading to higher levels of technological achievement also tends to eradicate differences in lifestyles. Penetration of television, which enables everyone possessing a television set to share sophisticated behavioral information instantaneously throughout the world, has also accelerated this trend. There are, for example, 750 million consumers in all three parts of the Triad (Japan, the United States and Canada, the nations of Western Europe) with strikingly similar needs and preferences. A new generation worships the universal "now" gods—ABBA, Levi's and Arpege. Youngsters in Denmark, West Germany, Japan, and California are all growing up with ketchup, jeans, and guitars. Their lifestyles, aspirations, and desires are so similar that you might call them "OECDites" or Triadians, rather than by names denoting their national identity.[13]

There are many reasons for the similarities and commonalities in the triad's consumer demand and lifestyle patterns. First, the purchasing power of triad residents, as expressed in discretionary income per individual, is more than 10 times greater than that of residents of emerging economies. For example, television penetration in triad countries is greater than 94 percent, whereas in newly industrialized countries it is 25 percent; for other emerging economies, it is less than 10 percent. Second, their technological infrastructure is more advanced. For example, over 70 percent of triadian households have a telephone. This makes it feasible to use such products as facsimile, teletext, and digital data transmission/processing equipment. Third, the educational level is much higher in triad nations than in other parts of the world. Fourth, the number of physicians per 10,000 in triad countries, which creates demand for pharmaceuticals and medical electronics, exceeds 30. Fifth, better infrastructure in the triad leads to opportunities not feasible in less-developed markets. For example, paved roads have made rapid penetration of radial tires and sports cars possible.

18.2 ENTRY STRATEGIES

Four different modes of business offer a company entry into foreign markets: (a) exporting, (b) contractual agreement, (c) joint venture, and (d) manufacturing.

A company may minimize the risk of dealing internationally by exporting domestically manufactured products either by minimal response to inquiries or by systematic development of demand in foreign markets. Exporting requires minimal capital and is easy to initiate. Exporting is also a good way to gain international experience. A major part of overseas involvement among large U.S. firms is through export trade.

There are several types of contractual agreements:

- **Patent licensing agreements**—These agreements are based on either a fixed-fee or a royalty basis and include managerial training.
- **Turnkey operations**—These operations are based on a fixed-fee or cost-plus arrangement and include plant construction, personnel training, and initial production runs.
- **Coproduction agreements**—These agreements are most common in socialist countries, where plants are built and then paid for with part of the output.
- **Management contracts**—Currently widely used in the Middle East, these contracts require that a multinational corporation provide key personnel to operate a foreign enterprise for a fee until local people acquire the ability to manage the business independently. For example, Whittaker Corp. of Los Angeles operates government-owned hospitals in several cities in Saudi Arabia.
- **Licensing**—Licensing works as a viable alternative in some contractual agreement situations where risk of expropriation and resistance to foreign investments create uncertainty. *Licensing* encompasses a variety of contractual agreements whereby a multinational marketer makes available intangible assets—such as patents, trade secrets, know-how, trademarks, and company name—to foreign companies in return for royalties or other forms of payment. Transfer of these assets usually is accompanied by technical services to ensure proper use. Licensing, however, has some advantages and disadvantages as summarized below.

18.2.1 Advantages of Licensing

1. Licensing requires little capital and serves as a quick and easy entry to foreign markets.
2. In some countries, licensing is the only way to tap the market.
3. Licensing provides life extension for products in the maturity stage of their life cycles.
4. Licensing is a good alternative to foreign production and marketing in an environment where there is worldwide inflation, shortages of skilled labor, increasing domestic and foreign governmental regulation and restriction, and tough international competition.
5. Licensing royalties are guaranteed and periodic, whereas shared income from investment fluctuates and is risky.
6. Domestically based firms can benefit from product development abroad without incurring research expense through technical feedback arrangements.
7. When exports no longer are profitable because of intense competition, licensing provides an alternative.
8. Licensing can overcome high transportation costs, which make some exports noncompetitive in target markets.
9. Licensing is also immune to expropriation.
10. In some countries, manufacturers of military equipment or any product deemed critical to the national interest (including communications equipment) may be compelled to enter licensing agreements.

18.2.2 Disadvantages of Licensing

1. To attract licensees, a firm must possess distinctive technology, a trademark, and a company or brand name that is attractive to potential foreign users.
2. The licensor often has little control over production and marketing by the licensee even when certain standards are incorporated into the contract.
3. Licensing royalties are negligible compared with equity investment potential. Royalty rates seldom exceed 5 percent of gross sales because of government restrictions in the host country.
4. The licensee may lose interest in renewing the contract unless the licensor holds interest through innovation and new technology.
5. There is a danger of creating competition in third, or even home, markets if the licensee violates territorial agreements or the licensor fails to incorporate the necessary restrictions in the contract. Going to court in these situations is expensive and time-consuming, and no international adjudicatory body exists.

Joint venture represents a higher-risk alternative than exporting or contractual agreements because it requires various levels of direct investment. A joint venture between a U.S. firm and a native operation abroad involves sharing risks to accomplish mutual enterprise. Once a firm moves beyond the exporting stage, joint ventures, incidentally, are the next most common form of entry. One example of a joint venture is General Motors Corporation's partnership with Egypt's state-owned Nasar Car Company, a joint venture for the assembly of trucks and diesel engines. Another example is between Matsushita of Japan and IBM, a joint venture established to manufacture small computers. Joint ventures normally are designed to take advantage of the strong functions of the partners and to supplement their weak functions, be they management, research, or marketing.

Joint ventures provide a mutually beneficial arrangement for domestic and foreign businesses to join forces. For both parties, the venture is a means to share capital and risk and make use of each other's technical strength. Japanese companies, for example, prefer entering into joint ventures with U.S. firms because such arrangements help ensure against possible American trade barriers. American firms, on the other hand, like the opportunity to enter a previously forbidden market, to utilize established channels, to link American product innovation with Japanese manufacturing technology, and to curb a potentially tough competitor.

As a case in point, General Foods Corporation tried for more than a decade to succeed in Japan on its own but watched the market share of its instant coffee (Maxwell House) drop from 20 to 14 percent. Then, in 1975, the firm established a joint venture with Ajinomoto, a food manufacturer, to use the full power of Ajinomoto's product distribution system and personnel and managerial capabilities. Within two years, Maxwell House's share of the Japanese instant coffee market recovered.[14]

Joint ventures, however, are not an unmixed blessing. The major problem in managing joint ventures stems from one cause: there is more than one partner and one of the partners must play a key dominant role to steer the business to success.

Joint ventures should be designed to supplement each partner's shortcomings, not to exploit each other's strengths and weaknesses. It takes as much effort to make a joint venture a success as to start a grass roots operation and eventually bring it up to a successful level. In both cases, each partner must be fully prepared to expend the effort necessary to understand customers, competitors, and itself. A joint venture is a means of resource appropriation and of easing a foreign business's entry into a new terrain. It should not be viewed as a handy vehicle to reap money without effort, interest, and/or additional resources.

Joint ventures are a wave of the future. There is hardly a Fortune 500 company active overseas that does not have at least one joint venture. Widespread interest in joint ventures is related to the following:

1. **Seeing market opportunities**—Companies in mature industries in the United States find joint venture a desirable entry mode to enter attractive new markets overseas.
2. **Dealing with rising economic nationalism**—Host governments are often more receptive to or require joint ventures.
3. **Preempting raw materials**—Countries with raw materials, such as petroleum or extractable material, usually do not allow foreign firms to be active there other than through joint venture.
4. **Sharing risk**—Rather than taking the entire risk, a joint venture allows the risk to be shared with a partner, which can be especially important in politically sensitive areas.
5. **Developing an export base**—In areas where economic blocs play a significant role, joint venture with a local firm smooths the entry into the entire region, such as entry into the European Union through a joint venture with an English company.
6. **Selling technology**—Selling technology to developing countries becomes easier through a joint venture.
7. **Learning skills**—Many companies enter into joint ventures with a partner with an exceptional skill in some element of management, production, market knowledge, or distribution in order to enhance their own skills in the area.

Even a joint venture with a well-qualified majority foreign partner may provide significant advantages:

1. **Participation in income and growth**—The minority partner shares in the earnings and growth of the venture even if its own technology becomes obsolete.
2. **Low cash requirements**—Know-how and patents or both can be considered as partial capital contribution.
3. **Preferred treatment**—Because it is locally controlled, the venture is treated with preference by government.
4. **Easier access to a market and to market information**—A locally controlled firm can seek market access and information much more easily than can a firm controlled by foreigners.

5. **Less drain on managerial resources**—The local partner takes care of most managerial responsibilities.
6. **U.S. income tax deferral**—Income to the U.S. minority partner is not subject to U.S. taxation until distribution.

A multinational corporation may also establish itself in an overseas market by direct investment in a manufacturing and/or assembly subsidiary. Because of the volatility of worldwide economic, social, and political conditions, this form of involvement is most risky. An example of a direct investment situation is Chesebrough-Pond's operation of overseas manufacturing plants in Japan, England, and Monte Carlo.

Manufacturing around the world is riskier, as illustrated by Union Carbide's disaster in Bhopal, India: in the worst industrial accident that has ever occurred, a poisonous gas leak killed over 2,000 people and permanently disabled thousands. It is suggested that multinational corporations should not manufacture overseas where the risk of a mishap may jeopardize the survival of the whole company. As a matter of fact, in the wake of the Bhopal accident, many host countries tightened safety and environmental regulations. For example, Brazil, the world's fourth-largest user of agricultural chemicals, restricted the use of the deadly methyl isocyanate.[15]

A firm interested in entering the international market must evaluate the risk and commitment involved with each entry and choose the entry mode that best fits the company's objectives and resources. Entry risk and commitment can be examined by considering five factors:

1. Characteristics of the product.
2. The market's external macroenvironment, particularly economic and political factors, and the demand and buying patterns of potential customers.
3. The firm's competitive position, especially the product's life-cycle stage, as well as various corporate strengths and weaknesses.
4. Dynamic capital budgeting considerations, including resource costs and availabilities.
5. Internal corporate perceptions that affect corporate selection of information and the psychic distance between a firm's decision makers and its target customers as well as control and risk-taking preferences.

These five factors combined indicate that risk should be reviewed vis-à-vis a company's resources before determining a mode of entry.

Computerized simulation models can be employed to determine the desired entry route by simultaneously evaluating such factors as environmental opportunity, risk index, competitive risk index, corporate strength index, product channel direction index, comparative cost index, and corporate policy and perception index.

18.3 GLOBAL MARKET ENVIRONMENT

Not only are the risk factors underlying the mode of entry largely contingent on the nature of the foreign environment, but these environmental forces also influence the development of marketing strategies. Decision making for expansion into global markets is strategically similar to the decision-making process guiding domestic marketing endeavors. More specifically, four marketing strategy variables—product, price, distribution, and promotion—need to be as systematically addressed in the context of international marketing as they are in formulating domestic marketing strategies. What is different about international marketing, however, is the environment in which marketing decisions must be made and the influence that environment has in shaping marketing strategies. The principal components of the international marketing environment include cultural, political, legal, commercial, and economic forces. Each of these forces represents informational inputs that must enter into the strategy formulation process.

Culture refers to learned behavior over time, passed on from generation to generation. This behavior manifests itself in the form of social structure, habits, faith, customs, rituals, and religion, each of which tends to affect individual lifestyles, which in turn shape consumption patterns in the marketplace. Thus, what people of a particular country buy, why they buy, when they buy, where they buy, and how they buy are largely culturally determined. There are five elements of culture: material culture, social institutions, man and universe, aesthetics, and language. Each of these elements varies from country to country. The importance to marketers of understanding these often subtle variations has been illustrated by Dichter:

In puritanical cultures it is customary to think of cleanliness as being next to godliness. The body and its functions are covered up as much as possible.

But in Catholic and Latin countries, to fool too much with one's body, to overindulge in bathing or toiletries, has opposite meaning. Accordingly, an advertising approach based on puritanical principles, threatening Frenchmen that if they didn't brush their teeth regularly, they would develop cavities or would not find a lover, failed to impress. To fit the accepted concept of morality, the French advertising agency changed this approach to a permissive one.[16]

Similarly, language differences from one country to another could lead to problems because literal translations of words often connote different meanings. Two classic examples of marketing blunders include "Body by Fisher," which when literally translated into Flemish meant "Corpse by Fisher," and "Let Hertz Put You in the Driver's Seat," which when literally translated into Spanish meant "Let Hertz Make You a Chauffeur."[17] When dealing with many widely spoken languages, such as Spanish or Chinese it should also be remembered that the same word can have different meanings and/or pronunciations in different countries or even different regions of the same country. Even the choice of color for packaging and advertising may influence marketing decisions. For example, in the United States, white is equated with purity. In most Asian countries, however, white is associated with death in the same way that black is a symbol of mourning in American culture. In short, culture could have and has had far-reaching effects on the success of overseas marketing strategies.

The laissez-faire era when governments had little if anything to do with the conduct of business is past history. Today, even in democratic societies, governments exercise a pervasive influence on business decisions. In fact, it is not uncommon to find that the governments of many overseas countries actually own and operate certain businesses. One example of a government-owned and -operated business is Air France, the French airline company. In China, not only is virtually every major company is government owned, but companies are owned at all levels of government, central, provincial, municipal and village.

Although the degree of intervention varies across countries, developments in developing countries perhaps represent situations where government policies are most extreme. Therefore, to be successful overseas, a global marketer should determine the most favorable political climates and exploit those opportunities first. Robinson suggests that the degree of political vulnerability in a given overseas market can be ascertained by researching certain key issues. Positive answers to the following questions signal political troubles for a foreign marketer:

1. Is the supply of the product ever subject to important political debates? (sugar, salt, gasoline, public utilities, medicines, foodstuffs)
2. Do other industries depend upon the production of the product? (cement, power, machine tools, construction machinery, steel)
3. Is the product considered socially or economically essential? (key drugs, laboratory equipment, medicines)
4. Is the product essential to agricultural industries? (farm tools and machinery, crops, fertilizers, seed)
5. Does the product affect national defense capabilities? (transportation industry, communications)
6. Does the product require important components that would be available from local sources and that otherwise would not be used as effectively? (labor, skill, materials)
7. Is there competition or is it likely from local manufacturers in the near future? (small, low-investment manufacturing)
8. Does the product relate to channels of mass communication media? (newsprint, radio equipment)
9. Is the product primarily a service?
10. Does the use of the product, or its design, rest upon some legal requirements?
11. Is the product potentially dangerous to the user? (explosives, drugs)
12. Does the product induce a net drain on scarce foreign exchange?[18]

Despite the best intentions, differences may reasonably arise between parties doing business. What recourse exists for the resolution of differences and whose laws will apply are of vital concern to global marketers. Although there is no simple solution to such a complex problem, it is important that marketers anticipate areas where disputes are likely to arise and establish beforehand agreements on the means to use and which country will have jurisdiction in the resolution of differences. Legal difficulties in marketing are most prevalent regarding the following issues:

1. Rules of competition about
   a. collusion
   b. discrimination against certain buyers
   c. promotional methods

d. variable pricing

e. exclusive territory agreement.

2. Retail price maintenance laws.
3. Cancellation of distributor or wholesaler agreements.
4. Product quality laws and controls.
5. Packaging laws.
6. Warranty and after-sales exposure.
7. Price controls and limitations on markups or markdowns.
8. Patents, trademarks, and copyright laws and practices.

Needless to say, the marketer in conjunction with legal counsel should probe these areas and establish with the buyer various contingencies prior to the making of commitments. It should be noted that familiar legal terms may be defined very differently in overseas markets, and hence marketers should ensure that legal counsel is familiar with local laws, legal interpretations and definitions, and legal customs.

An international marketer must be thoroughly familiar with the business customs and practices in effect in overseas markets. Although some evidence suggests that business traditions in a country may undergo a change as a result of dealing with foreign corporations, such transformations are long-term processes. Thus, local customs and practices must be researched and adhered to in order to gain the confidence and support of local buyers, channel intermediaries, and other business operatives. The specific customs and practices of a country may be studied with reference to the following factors:

Business Structure
Size

Ownership

Various business publics

Sources and level of authority

    Top management decision making

    Decentralized decision making

    Committee decision making

Management Attitudes and Behavior
Personal background

Business status

Objectives and aspirations

    Security and mobility

    Personal life

    Social acceptance

    Advancement

    Power

Patterns of Competition
Mode of Doing Business
Level of contact

Communications emphasis

Formality and tempo

Business ethics

Negotiation emphasis

Only a small percentage of people in the world approach the standard of living experienced in the United States and in other advanced industrialized countries. The level of economic development in various countries can be explained and described through a number of measures. One common measure used to rank nations economically is per capita GNP.

According to Rostow, the countries of the world can be grouped into the following stages of economic development: (a) the traditional, (b) the precondition for take-off, (c) the takeoff, (d) the drive to maturity, and (e) mass consumption.[19] Most African, Asian, and Latin American countries would be categorized as underdeveloped, having lower living standards and limited discretionary income. The amount of work required to earn enough to purchase a product varies greatly among different countries. For example, to buy one kilogram of sugar, a person in the United States needs to work a little over five minutes; in Greece it takes 53 minutes of labor to earn an equivalent amount. In many African and Asian countries, the effort needed to buy a kilogram of sugar and, for that matter, other similar products is even higher.

18.4 STRATEGY FOR GLOBAL MARKETING PROGRAMS

Two opposite viewpoints for developing global marketing strategy are commonly expounded. According to one school of thought, marketing is an inherently local problem. Due to cultural and other differences among countries, marketing programs should be tailor-made for each country.[20] The opposing view treats marketing as know-how that can be transferred from country to country. It has been argued that the worldwide marketplace has become so homogenized that multinational corporations can market standardized products and services all over the world with identical strategies, thus lowering their costs and earning higher margins.

The proponents of localized marketing strategies support their viewpoint based on four differences across countries:[21] (a) buyer behavior characteristics, (b) socioeconomic condition, (c) marketing infrastructure, and (d) competitive environment. A review of the marketing literature shows how companies often experience difficulties in foreign markets because they did not fully understand differences in buyer behavior. For example, Campbell's canned soups—mostly vegetable and beef combinations packed in extra-large cans—did not catch on in soup-loving Brazil. A postmortem study showed that most Brazilian housewives felt they were not fulfilling their roles if they served soup that they could not call their own. Brazilian housewives had no problems using dehydrated competitive products, such as Knorr and Maggi, which they could use as soup starters and still add their own ingredients and flair.[22] Also, Johnson & Johnson's baby powder did not sell well in Japan until its original package was changed to a flat box with a powder puff. Japanese mothers feared that powder would fly around their small homes and enter their spotlessly clean kitchens when sprinkled from a plastic bottle. Powder puffs allowed them to apply powder sparingly.[23] Similarly, advertisers have encountered difficulty when using colors in certain foreign countries. For example, purple is a death color in Brazil, white is for funerals in Hong Kong, India and Turkey, and yellow signifies jealousy in Thailand. In Egypt the use of green, which is the national color, is frowned upon for packaging.[24]

Socioeconomic differences (i.e., per capita income, level of education, level of unemployment) among countries also call for a localized approach toward international marketing. For example, limited economic means may prevent masses in developing countries from buying the variety of products that U.S. consumers consider essential. To bring such products as automobiles and appliances within the reach of the middle class in developing countries, for example, the products must be appropriately modified to cut costs without reducing functional quality.

Differences in the character of local marketing infrastructure across countries may suggest pursuing country-specific marketing strategies. The marketing infrastructure consists of the institutions and functions necessary to create, develop, and service demand, including retailers, wholesalers, sales agents, warehousing, transportation, credit, media, and more. Consider the case of media. Commercial television is not available in many countries. Sweden, for example, lacks this element of the marketing infrastructure. In many countries, for example, Switzerland, commercials on television are allowed on a limited scale. Suntory (a Japanese liquor company) considers the ban on advertising liquor on U.S. television as a main deterrent for not entering the U.S. market in a big way.[25] Similarly, the physical conditions of a country (i.e., climate, topography, and resources) may require localized strategies. In hot climates, as in the Middle East, such products as cars and air conditioners must have additional features. Differences in telephone systems, road networks, postal practices, and the like may require modifications in marketing practices. For example, mail-order retailing is popular in the United States but is virtually nonexistent in Italy because of differences in its mail system.[26]

Finally, differences in the competitive environment among countries may require following localized marketing strategies. Nestlé, for example, achieved more than a 60 percent market share in the instant coffee market in Japan but less than 30 percent in the United States. Nestlé had to contend with two strong domestic competitors in the United States, namely General Foods, which markets the Maxwell House, and other brands, and more recently Procter & Gamble, which markets Folgers and High Point. Nestlé faced relatively weak domestic competitors in Japan. IBM, which is the leading computer company in the world, slipped to third place in the Japanese market behind Fujitsu Ltd. and NEC Corporation in terms of total revenue. Nestlé and IBM must reflect differences in their competitive environments in such marketing choices as pricing, sales force behavior, and advertising.

In contrast to the view that marketing strategies must be localized, many scholars and practitioners argue that significant benefits can be achieved through standardization of marketing strategies on a global basis. As a matter of fact, some people recommend an extreme strategy: offering identical products at identical prices through identical distribution channels and supporting these identical products by identical sales and promotional programs throughout the world. Levitt asserts that "commercially, nothing confirms this as much as the success of McDonald's from the Champs Elysees to the Ginza, of Coca-Cola in Bahrain and Pepsi-Cola in Moscow, and of rock music, Greek salad, Hollywood movies, Revlon cosmetics, Sony televisions, and Levi's jeans everywhere."[27] Although across-the-board standardization, as proposed by Levitt, may be difficult, it is commonly accepted that the marketplace is becoming increasingly global, and indeed standardized strategies have been successfully pursued in many cases. Among consumer durable goods, Mercedes-Benz sells its cars by following a universal marketing program. Among nondurable goods, Coca-Cola is ubiquitous. Among industrial goods, Boeing jets are sold worldwide based on common marketing perspectives.

Past research shows that, other things being equal, companies usually opt for standardization. A recent study on the subject lends support to the high propensity to standardize all or parts of marketing strategy in foreign markets. For example, an extremely high degree of standardization appears to exist in brand names, physical characteristics of products, and packaging. More than half of the products that multinational corporations sell in less-developed countries originate in the parent companies' home markets. Of the 2,200 products sold by the 61 subsidiaries in the sample, 1,200 had originated in the United States or the United Kingdom.[28]

The arguments in favor of standardization are realization of cost savings, development of worldwide products, and achievement of better marketing performance. Standardization of products across national borders eliminates duplication of such costs as research and development, product design, and packaging. Further, standardization permits realization of economies of scale. Also, standardization makes it feasible to achieve consistency in dealing with customers and in product design. Consistency in product style—features, design, brand name, packaging—should establish a common image of the product worldwide and help increase overall sales. For example, a person accustomed to a particular brand is likely to buy the same brand overseas if it is available. The global exposure that brands receive these days as a result of extensive world travel and mass media requires the consistency that is feasible through standardization. Finally, standardization may be urged on the grounds that a product that has proved to be successful in one country should do equally well in other countries that present more or less similar markets and similar competitive conditions.[29]

Although standardization offers benefits, too much attachment to standardization can be counterproductive. Marketing environments vary from country to country, and thus a standard product originally conceived and developed in the United States may not really match the conditions in each and every market. In other words, standardization can lead to substantial opportunity loss.

Pond's cold cream, Coca-Cola, and Colgate toothpaste have been cited as evidence that a universal product and marketing strategy for consumer goods can win worldwide success. However, the applicability of a universal approach for consumer goods appears to be limited to products that have certain characteristics, among them universal brand name recognition (generally earned by huge financial outlays), minimal product knowledge requirements for consumer use, and product advertisements that demand low information content. Clearly, Coca-Cola, Colgate toothpaste, McDonald's, Levi's jeans, and Pond's cold cream display these traits. Thus, whereas a universal strategy can be effective for some consumer products, it is clearly an exception rather than the general rule. Those who argue that consumer products no longer require market tailoring due to the globalization of markets brought about by today's advanced technology are not always correct.

A multinational corporation that intends to launch a new product into a foreign market should consider the nature of its products, its organizational capabilities, and the level of adaptation required to accommodate cultural differences between the home and the host country. A multinational corporation should also analyze such factors as market structures, competitors' strategic orientations, and host government demands.

The international marketplace is far more competitive today than in the 1980s and most likely will remain so as we enter the next century.[30] Thus, to enhance competitive advantage some sort of adaptation might provide a better match between a product and local marketing conditions. Ohmae's charges against American companies for not adapting their products to Japanese needs are revealing:

Yet, American merchandisers push such products as oversize cars with left-wheel drive, devices measuring in inches, appliances not adapted to lower voltage and frequencies, office equipment without kanji capabilities and clothes not cut to smaller dimensions. Most Japanese like sweet oranges and sour cherries, not visa versa. That is because they compare imported oranges with domestic mikans (very sweet tangerines) and cherries with plums (somewhat tangy and sour).[31]

There are several patterns and various degrees of differentiation that firms can adopt to do business on an international scale. The most common of these are obligatory and discretionary product adaptation. An **obligatory**, or **minimal**, **product adaptation** implies that a manufacturer is forced to introduce minor changes or modifications in product design for either of two reasons. First, adaptation is mandatory in order to seek entry into particular foreign markets. Second, adaptation is imposed on a firm by external environmental factors, including the special needs of a foreign market. In brief, obligatory adaptation is related to safety regulations, trademark registration, quality standards, and media standards. An obligatory adaptation requires mostly physical changes in a product. **Discretionary**, or **voluntary**, **product adaptation** reflects a sort of self-imposed discipline and a deliberate move on the part of an exporter to build stable foreign markets through a better alignment of product with market needs and/or cultural preferences.[32]

Swiss-based pharmaceutical maker Ciba-Geigy's efforts in adapting its products to local conditions are noteworthy. Basic to the company's adaptation program are quality circles. These circles include local executives with line responsibilities for packaging, labeling, advertising, and manufacturing. They are responsible for determining (a) if Ciba-Geigy's products are appropriate for the cultures in which they are sold and meet users' needs, (b) if products are promoted in such a way that they can be used correctly for purposes intended, and (c) if, when used properly, products present no unresponsible hazards to human health and safety.[33]

18.5 MARKETING IN GLOBAL BUSINESS STRATEGY

International marketing strategy is significant in formulating global business strategy in three different ways.[34] First, what should be the global *configuration* of marketing activities? That is, where should such activities as new product development advertising, sales promotion, channel selection, marketing research, etc., be performed? Second, how should global marketing activities performed in different countries be *coordinated*? Third, how should marketing activities be *linked* with other activities of the firm? Each of these aspects is examined below.

Marketing activities, unlike those in other functional areas of a business, must be dispersed in each host country to make an adequate response to local environments. Although this configuration is valuable in being customer oriented, not all marketing activities need to be performed on a dispersed basis. In many cases, competitive advantage is gained in the form of lower cost or enhanced differentiation if selected activities are performed centrally as a result of technological changes, buyer shifts, and evolution of marketing media. These activities comprise production of promotional materials, sales force, service support organization, training, and advertising.

The centralized production of advertisements, sales promotion materials, and user manuals can lead to a variety of benefits. Economies of scale can be reaped in both development and production. For example, experienced art directors and producers can be hired to create better ads at a greater speed or lower cost. The use of centralized printing permits the latest technology to be adopted. On the other hand, excessive transportation costs and cultural differences among nations may make the production of some materials (e.g., user manuals) impractical.

Sales force, at least for some businesses, can be centralized in one location. Alternatively, highly skilled sales specialists can be stationed at the headquarters or in a regional office to provide sales support in different countries. Centralization of the sales force is most effective when the complexity of the selling task is very high, and the products being sold are high-ticket items purchased infrequently.

As with the sales force, highly-skilled service specialists can be located at world or regional headquarters. They can visit different subsidiaries to provide nonroutine service. Along the same lines, service facilities (service center, repair shop) can be regionalized at a few locations, especially for complex jobs. Such centralization should permit the use of state-of-the-art facilities and qualified service people, resulting in better service at lower cost.

Training of marketing personnel can be effectively centralized and lead to economies of scale in production and delivery of training programs, faster accumulated learning (brought by people with varied experiences assembled in one place), and increased uniformity around the world in implementing marketing programs. Training centralization, however, must be weighed against travel time and cost.

Although cultural differences between nations require advertising to be tailored to each country, in many ways global advertising is gaining acceptance. First, a company may select one ad agency to handle its global campaign, economizing in campaign development, seeking better coordination between the parent and subsidiaries, and facilitating a consistent advertising approach worldwide. For example, British Airways uses one agency worldwide. Second, many companies advertise in the global media, for example, in *The Economist*, in certain trade magazines, or at international sports events seen by viewers around the world, such as at U.S. Open tennis matches. Finally, many media (e.g., airport billboards, airline and hotel magazines) have a decidedly international reach. For these reasons, centralization of advertising makes sense. Yet government rules and regulations relative to advertising, distinct national habits, language differences, and lack of media outlets may require dispersion of advertising to different countries.

International marketing activities dispersed in different countries should be properly coordinated to gain competitive advantage. Such coordination can be achieved in the following ways:

1. **Performing marketing activities using similar methods across countries**—This form of coordination implies standardizing activities across nations. Some strategies, including brand name, product positioning, service standards, warranties, and advertising theme, are easier to coordinate than are other marketing strategies. On the other hand, distribution, personal selling, sales training, pricing, and media selection are difficult to coordinate across nations.

2. **Transferring marketing know-how and skills from country to country**—For example, a market entry strategy successfully tried in one country can be transferred and applied in another country. Likewise, customer and market information can be transferred for use by other subsidiaries. Such information may relate to shifts in buyer purchasing patterns, recent trends in technology, lifestyle changes, successful new product or feature introductions, new promotion ideas, and early market signals by competitors.

3. **Sequencing of marketing programs across countries**—For example, new products or new marketing practices may be introduced in various countries in a planned sequence. In this way, programs developed by one subsidiary can be shared by others to their mutual advantage and, thus, should result in substantial cost savings. To reap the benefits of sequencing, a company must create organizational mechanisms to manage the product line from a worldwide perspective and to overcome manager resistance to change in all participating countries.

4. **Integrating the efforts of various marketing groups in different countries**—Perhaps the most common form of such integration is managing relationships with important multinational customers, often called *international account management.* International account management systems are commonly used in service firms. For example, Citibank handles some accounts on a worldwide basis. It has account officers responsible for coordinating services to its large corporate customers anywhere in the world.

Competitive advantage can result from international account management systems in a variety of ways. They can lead to economies in the utilization of the sales force if duplication of selling effort is avoided. They can allow a company to differentiate itself from its competitors by offering a single contact for international buyers. They can also leverage the skills of top salespersons by giving them more influence over the entire relationship with major customers. Some of the potential impediments to using international account management include increased travel time, language barriers, and cultural differences in how business is conducted. Dealing with a major customer through a single coordinator may also heighten the customer's awareness of its bargaining power.

Integration of effort across countries can lead to competitive advantage in other areas as well; for example, after-sale service. Some international companies have come to realize that the availability of after-sale service is often as important as the product itself, especially when a multinational customer has operations in remote areas of the world or when the customer moves from country to country.

A global view of international marketing permits linking marketing functions to upstream and support activities of the firm, which can lead to advantage in various ways. For example, marketing can unlock economies of scale and learning in production and/or research and development by (a) supporting the development of universal products by providing the information necessary to develop a physical product design that can be sold worldwide; (b) creating demand for more universal products even if historical demand has been for more varied products in different countries; (c) identifying and penetrating segments in many countries to allow the sale of universal products; and (d) providing services and/or local accessories that effectively tailor the standard physical product.

18.6 DEVELOPING GLOBAL MARKET STRATEGY: AN EXAMPLE

Decisions related to foreign market entry, expansion, and conversion as well as to phasing out of foreign markets call for systematic effort. Illustrated here is one method of developing a global market strategy. The method consists of three phases:

1. Appropriate national markets are selected by quickly screening the full range of options without regard to any preconceived notions.
2. Specific strategic approaches are devised for each country or group of countries based on the company's specific product technologies.
3. Marketing plans for each country or group of countries are developed, reviewed, revised, and incorporated into the overall corporate concept without regard to conventional wisdom or stereotypes.

There are over 132 countries in the world; of these, the majority may appear to present entry opportunities. Many countries go out of their way to attract foreign investment by offering lures ranging from tax exemptions to low-paid, amply skilled labor. These inducements, valid as they may be in individual cases, have repeatedly led to hasty foreign market entry.

A good basis for selecting national markets is arrived at through a comparative analysis of different countries, with long-term economic environment having the greatest weight. First, certain countries, because of their political situations (e.g., Libya under Qaddafi), may be considered unsuitable for market entry. It might help to consult a political index that rates different countries for business attractiveness. The final choice should be based on the company's own needs, assessment and risk preference. Further, markets that are either too small in terms of population and per capita income or that are economically too weak should be eliminated. For example, a number of countries with populations of less than 20 million and with annual per capita incomes below $2,000 are of little interest to many companies because of limited demand potential.

The markets surviving this screening should then be assessed for strategic attractiveness. A battery of criteria should be developed to fit the specific requirements of the corporation. Basically, the criteria should focus on the following six factors (industry/product characteristics may require slight modification):

1. Future demand and economic potential.
2. Distribution of purchasing power by population groups or market segments.
3. Country-specific technical product standards.
4. Spillover from the national market (e.g., the Andes Pact provides for low-duty exports from Colombia to Peru).
5. Access to vital resources (qualified labor force, raw materials sources, suppliers).
6. Are the company's infrastructural needs, both hard (ports, rail lines, roads, and etc.) and soft (legal, political and regulatory environments, trained work force, government policies and etc.), met in the market?

There is no reason to expand the list because additional criteria are rarely significant enough to result in useful new insights. Rather, management should concentrate on developing truly meaningful and practical parameters for each of the five criteria listed above so that the selection process does not become unnecessarily costly and the results are fully relevant to the company concerned. For example, a German flooring manufacturer, selling principally to the building industry, selected the following yardsticks:

1. **Economic potential**—New housing needs and GNP growth.
2. **Wealth**—Per capita income, per capita market size for institutional building or private dwellings (the higher the per captia income, market volume, and share of institutional buildings, the more attractive the market).
3. **Technical product standards**—Price level of similar products, for example, price per square meter for floor coverings (the higher the price level, the more attractive the market tends to be for a technically advanced producer).
4. **Spillover**—Area in which the same building standards (especially fire safety standards) apply (e.g., the U.S. National Electrical Manufacturers' Association standards are widely applicable in Latin America; British standards apply in most Commonwealth countries).
5. **Resource availability**—Annual production volume of PVC (an important raw material for the company).

Through these criteria, the analysis of economic potential was based on two factors: housing needs and economic base (see Exhibit 18.4). In specifying these criteria, the company deliberately confined itself to measures that (a) could readily be developed from existing sources of macroeconomic data, (b) would show trends as well as current positions, and (c) matched the company's particular characteristics as closely as possible.

Since German producers of floor covering employ a highly sophisticated technology, it would have been senseless to give a high ranking to a country with only rudimentary production technology in this particular facet. Companies in other industries, of course, would consider other factors—auto registrations per 1,000 population, percentage of households with telephones, density of household appliance installations, and the like.

The resulting values are rated for each criterion on a scale of one to five so that, by weighting the criteria on a percentage basis, each country can be assigned an index number indicating its overall attractiveness. In this particular case, the result was that, out of the 49 countries surviving the initial screening,

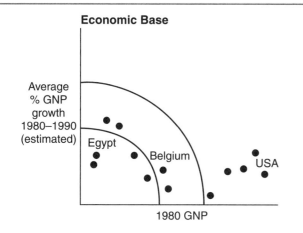

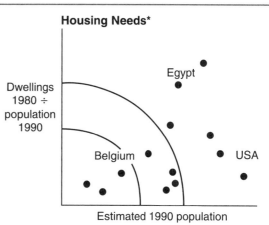

	Economic Base		
	Weak	Medium	Strong
High	Egypt Pakistan	Korea Nigeria	USA Japan
Housing Needs **Medium**	Yugoslavia	United Kingdom	Germany France
Low	Denmark	Belgium	Sweden

Examples: Sweden—needs only in replacement sector; Pakistan—economically too weak to meet needs.

Exhibit 18.4 Assessing Country Economic Potential: The Case of a Building Industry Flooring Supplier

16 were ultimately judged attractive enough on the basis of market potential, per capita market size, level of technical sophistication, prevailing regulations, and resource availability to warrant serious attention.

Interestingly, the traditionally German-favored markets of Austria and Belgium emerged with low rankings from this strategically based assessment because the level of potential demand was judged to be insufficient. Some new markets, Egypt and Pakistan, for example, were also downgraded because of inadequate economic base. Likewise, even such high-potential markets as Italy and Indonesia were eliminated for objective reasons (in the latter case, the low technical standard of most products).

After a short list of attractive foreign markets has been compiled, the next step is to group these countries according to their respective stages of economic development. Here the criterion of classification is not per capita income but the degree of market penetration by the generic product in question. For example, the floor covering manufacturer grouped countries into three categories—developing, takeoff, and mature—as defined by these factors (see Exhibit 18.5):

1. **Accessibility of markets**—Crucial for the choice between export and import production.
2. **Local competitive situation**—Crucial for the choice between independent construction, joint venture, and acquisition.
3. **Customer structure**—Crucial for sales and distribution strategy.
4. **Re-import potential**—Crucial for international product/market strategy.

The established development phases and their defining criteria must be very closely geared to the company situation because it is these factors, not the apparent attractiveness of markets, that will make or break the company's strategic thrust into a given country.

This being the case, for each country or group of countries on the short list, management should formulate a generic marketing strategy with respect to investment, risk, product, and pricing policies; that is,

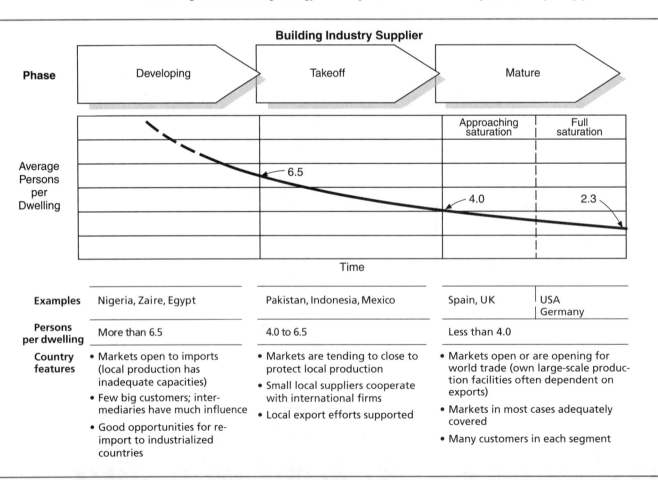

Exhibit 18.5 Grouping Countries by Phase of Development

Phase	Developing	Takeoff	Mature
Basic Strategy	**Test Market**	**Build Base**	**Expand/Round Off Operations**
	Pursue profitable individual projects and/or export activities	Allocate substantial resources to establish leading position in market	Allocate resources selectively to develop market niches
Elements of Strategy			
Investment	Minimize (distribution and services)	Invest to expand capacity (relatively long payback)	Expand selectively in R&D, production, and distribution (relatively short payback)
Risk	Avoid	Accept	Limit
Know-how transfer (R&D)	Document know-how on reference projects	Use local know-how in • Product technology • Production engineering	Transfer know-how in special product lines; acquire local know-how to round off own base
Market share objective	Concentrate on key projects; possibly build position in profitable businesses with local support	Extend base with • New products • New outlets • New applications	Expand/defend
Cost leadership objective	Minimum acceptable (especially reduction of guarantee risks)	Economies of scale; reduction of fixed costs	Rationalize; optimize resources
Product	Standard technology; simple products	Aim for wide range; "innovator" role	Full product line in selected areas; products of high technical quality
Price	Price high	Aim for price leadership (at both ends)	Back stable market price level
Distribution	Use select local distributors (exclusive distribution)	Use a large number of small distributors (intensive distribution)	Use company sales force (selective distribution)
Promotion	Selective advertising • With typical high prestige products • Aiming at decision makers	Active utilization of selective marketing resources	Selected product advertising

Exhibit 18.6 Developing Standard Strategies

a unified strategic framework applicable to all the countries in each stage of development should be prepared. This step should yield a clear understanding of what the respective stages of economic development of each country entail for the company's marketing strategies (see Exhibit 18.6).

Companies are too often inclined to regard "overseas" as a single market or at least to differentiate very little among individual overseas markets. Another common error is the assumption that product or service concepts suited to a highly developed consumer economy work as well in any foreign market. This is rarely true: different markets demand different approaches.

Across-the-board strategic approaches typically result in ill-advised and inappropriate allocation of resources. In less-developed markets that could be perfectly well served by a few distributors, companies have in some cases established production facilities that are doomed to permanent unprofitability. In markets already at the takeoff point, companies have failed to build the necessary local plants and instead have complained about declining exports only to finally abandon the field to competitors. In markets already approaching saturation, companies have often sought to impose domestic technical standards where adequate standards and knowledge already exist or have tried to operate like mini replicas of parent corporations, marketing too many product lines with too few salespeople. Again and again, product line offerings are weighted toward either cheaper- or higher-quality products than the local market will accept. Clearly, the best insurance against such errors is to select strategies appropriate to the country.

In developing detailed marketing plans, it is first necessary to determine which product lines fit which local markets as well as the appropriate allocation of resources. A rough analysis of potential international business, global sales, and profit targets based on the estimates worked out in Phase 1 help in assigning product lines. A framework for resource allocation can then be mapped according to rough comparative figures for investment quotas, management needs, and skilled labor requirements. This framework should be supplemented by company-specific examples of standard marketing strategies for each group of countries.

Exhibit 18.7 illustrates the resource allocation process. Different product lines are assigned to different country groups, and for each country category, different strategic approaches—for example, support on large-scale products, establishment of local production facilities, cooperation with local manufacturers—are specified.

The level of detail in this resource allocation decision framework depends on a number of factors: company history and philosophy, business policy objectives, scope and variety of product lines, and the number of countries to be served. Working within this decision framework, each product division should analyze its own market in terms of size, growth, and competitive situations; assess its profitability prospects, opportunities, and risks; and identify its own current strategic position on the basis of market share, profit situation, and vulnerability to local risks.[33] Each product division is then in a position to develop country-specific marketing alternatives for servicing each national market. Top management's role

		Resource Allocation by Product Division					
Phase	Specimen Countries	PVC Floor Coverings	Carpeting	Suspended Ceilings	Wall Paneling	PVC Tubes	Plastic-Coated Roof Insulation
Developing "Test market"	Nigeria	Intensive	No operations	Moderate	No operations	Intensive	Intensive
(Share of total resources: 20%)	Specific plans • Develop own plastics-processing facilities. • Acquire plastics processors.						
Takeoff "Build base"	Indonesia	Moderate	No operations	No operations	No operations	Moderate	Moderate
(Share of total resources: 50%)	Specific plans • Give support in key projects. • Cooperative with state-owned construction organization.						
Mature "Expand/round off operations"	Spain	Moderate	Moderate	Intensive	Intensive	No operations	No operations
(Share of total resources: 30%)	Specific plans • Develop local facilities for tufting and paneling. • Acquire/cooperate with suppliers using unique product and production technology. • Develop own distribution channel. • Extend range to provide complete interior equipment program (system concept).						

Legend: ■ No operations. ▨ Moderate. ▨ Intensive.

Exhibit 18.7 A Specimen Framework for Resource Allocation

throughout is to coordinate marketing strategy development efforts of various divisions and continually to monitor the strategic decision framework.

The three-phase approach illustrated above exhibits a number of advantages:

- It allows management to set up, with a minimum of planning effort, a strategic framework that gives clear priority to market selection decisions, thus making it much easier for divisions to work out effective product line strategies unhampered by the usual chicken-or-egg problem.
- Division managers can foresee at a fairly early stage what reallocations of management, labor, and capital resources are needed and what adjustments may need to be imposed from the top due to inadequate resources.
- The company's future risk profile can be worked out in terms of resource commitment by country group and type of investment.
- The usual plethora of "exceptional" (and mostly opportunistic) product/market situations is sharply reduced. Only the really unique opportunities pass through the filter; exceptions are no longer the rule.
- The dazzling-in-theory but unrealistic-in-practice concept of establishing production bases in low-wage countries, buying from the world's lowest-cost sources, and selling products wherever best prices can be had is replaced by a realistic country-by-country market evaluation.
- Issues of organization, personnel assignment, and integration of overseas operations into corporate planning and control systems reach management's attention only after the fundamental strategic aspects of the company's overseas involvement have been thoroughly prepared.

In brief, the three-phase approach enables management to profitably concentrate resources and attention on a handful of really attractive countries instead of dissipating its efforts in vain attempts to serve the entire world.

SUMMARY

Internationalization of business has become a fact of life. Company after company finds that decisions made elsewhere in the world have a deep impact on its business. Although many firms have long been engaged in foreign business ventures, the real impetus to overseas expansion came after World War II. The globalization of business is accounted by such forces as (a) growing similarity of countries (e.g., commonality of infrastructure and channels of distribution); (b) falling tariff barriers; and (c) technological developments that, for example, permit the development of compact, easy-to-ship products.

Traditionally, major U.S. business activities overseas have been concentrated in developed countries. In recent years, developing countries have provided additional opportunities for U.S. corporations, especially in more politically stable countries. Yet although an individual developing country may not provide adequate potential for U.S. companies, developing countries as a group constitute a major market. The emerging markets in developing countries can help many U.S. corporations counter the results of matured markets in Western nations.

A firm aspiring to enter the international market may choose among various entry modes—exporting, contractual agreement, joint venture, or manufacturing. Each entry mode provides different opportunities and risks. The differentiation of global and domestic marketing largely revolves around the nature of environmental forces impinging on the formulation of strategy. International marketers must be sensitive to the environmental influences operating in overseas markets. The principal components of the international marketing environment include cultural, political, legal, commercial, and economic forces. Each of these forces represents informational inputs that must be factored into the decision-making process.

An important question that global marketers need to answer is whether the same product, price, distribution and promotion approach is adequate in foreign markets. In other words, a decision must be made about which is the more appropriate of two marketing strategies: localization or standardization. On the one hand, environmental differences between nations suggest using localization. On the other hand, there are potential gains to consider in standardizing market strategy. International marketers must examine all criteria in order to decide the extent to which marketing perspectives should vary from country to country.

International marketing plays three important roles in global business strategy. These are *configuration* of marketing activities (i.e., where different marketing activities should be performed), *coordination* (i.e., how international marketing activities dispersed in different countries should be coordinated), and the *linkage* of international marketing with other functions of the business.

The chapter ended with a framework for designing global market strategy. The framework consists of three steps: (a) selecting national markets, (b) determining marketing strategy, and (c) developing marketing plans.

DISCUSSION QUESTIONS

1. What forces are responsible for the globalization of markets?
2. How does culture affect international marketing decisions? Explain with examples.
3. Given their low per capita income, why should companies be interested in developing countries?
4. What are the different modes of entry into the international market? What are the relative advantages and disadvantages of each mode?
5. What are the advantages of international marketing strategy standardization?
6. Under what circumstances should marketing be adapted to local conditions?
7. What role does marketing play in global business strategy?

NOTES

1. George S. Yip, ''Global Strategy in a World of Nations?'' *Sloan Management Review*, Fall 1991, pp. 29–39. Also see Thomas A. Stewart, ''Welcome to the Revolution,'' *Fortune*, December 13, 1993, p. 66.
2. Usha C. V. Haley, ''Chinese Economic Planning and the Role of Subsidies,'' Presentation before the U.S.-China Economic Security and Review Commission of the U.S. Congress, April 4, 2006.
3. *Crossborder Monitor*, August 18, 2003, p. 14.
4. Jane Fraser and Jeremy Oppenheim, ''What's New About Globalization?'' *The McKinsey Quarterly*, No. 2, 1997, pp. 168–179; George T. Haley and Usha C. V. Haley, ''Emerging Market Multinational Corporations' Business Environments and Strategies,'' Presentation before the National Intelligence Council, February 28, 2006.
5. ''Leap Forward or Sink Back,'' *Development Forum*, March 1982, p. 3.
6. ''Face Value: The Mixer,'' *The Economist*, February 9, 2002, p. 56.
7. *The Global Century: A Source Book on U.S. Business and the Third World* (Washington, D.C., National Cooperative Business Association, 1997).
8. ''Laying Foundation for the Great Mall of China,'' *BusinessWeek*, January 25, 1988, p. 68; George T. Haley, Usha C. V. Haley, and Chin Tiong Tan, *The Chinese Tao of Business: The Logic of Successful Business Strategy* (Singapore, John Wiley and Sons, 2004).
9. Subhash C. Jain, *Market Evolution in Developing Countries: Unfolding of the Indian Market* (Binghamton, N.Y., The Haworth Press, Inc., 1993).
10. Paula L. Andruss and Lisa Bertagnoli, ''Europe, Latin America Hold Most Marketing Promise,'' *Marketing News*, January 1, 2001, p. 11.
11. David Wessel, ''Gillette Keys Sales to Third World Tastes,'' *The Wall Street Journal*, January 23, 1986, p. 35.
12. Richard I. Kirkland, Jr., ''Who Gains from the New Europe,'' *Fortune*, December 18, 1989, p. 83.
13. Kenichi Ohmae, *Triad Power* (New York, The Free Press, 1985), Chapter 4.
14. Ohmae, *Triad Power*, 116.
15. ''For Multinationals It Will Never Be the Same,'' *BusinessWeek*, December 24, 1984, p. 57.
16. Ernest Dichter, ''The World Customer,'' *Harvard Business Review*, July–August 1962, p. 116.
17. David A. Ricks, *Big Business Blunders* (Homewood, IL, Dow Jones-Irwin, 1983): 83–85.
18. Richard D. Robinson, ''Background Concepts and Philosophy of International Business from World War II to the Present,'' *Journal of International Business Studies*, Spring–Summer 1981, pp. 13–21.
19. Walt W. Rostow, *The Stages of Economic Growth* (London, Cambridge University Press, 1960): 10.

20. Cecilie Rohwedder, "Viva La Differenza!" *The Wall Street Journal*, January 29, 2003, B1.

21. Subhash C. Jain, "Standardization of International Marketing Strategy," *Journal of Marketing*, January 1989, pp. 70–79.

22. "Brazil: Campbell Soup Fails to Make It to the Table," *BusinessWeek*, October 21, 1981, p. 66.

23. Louis Kraar, "Inside Japan's 'Open' Market," *Fortune*, October 5, 1981, p. 122.

24. C. L. Lapp, "Marketing Goofs in International Trade," *The Diary of Alpha Kappa Psi*, February 1983, p. 4.

25. Hirotaka Takeuchi and Michael E. Porter, "Three Roles of International Marketing in Global Strategy," in *Competition in Global Industries*, ed. Michael Porter (Boston, Harvard Business School Press, 1986): 113.

26. Takeuchi and Porter, "Three Roles of International Marketing," 114.

27. Ted Levitt, "The Globalization of Markets," *Harvard Business Review*, May–June 1983, pp. 92–102.

28. John S. Hill and Richard R. Still, "Adapting Products to LDC Tastes," *Harvard Business Review*, March–April 1984, pp. 93–94.

29. William W. Lewis and Marvin Harris, "Why Globalization Must Prevail," *The McKinsey Quarterly*, Vol. 2, 1992, pp. 114–31.

30. Lisa T. Cullen, "Foreign Invaders," *Time*, February 5, 2002, p. B18.

31. Ohmae, *Triad Power*, 101–02. Also see C.K. Prahalad and Kenneth Lieberthal, "The End of Corporate Imperialism," *Harvard Business Review*, July–August 1996, pp. 68–79.

32. W. Chan Kim and R. A. Manborgue, "Cross-cultural Strategies," *Journal of Business Strategy*, Spring 1987, pp. 30–31.

33. See Takeuchi and Porter, "Three Roles of International Marketing," 111–46.

34. Walter Kuemmerle, "Go Global or Not?" *Harvard Business Review*, June 2001, pp. 37–49.

CASE 1
Lipitor Market

In 2002, Lipitor was the largest-selling pharmaceutical in history. Within the next few years it could very well become the world's first $10 billion-a-year drug. Lipitor is a product of Pfizer. Not many people know about it since Pfizer is linked in the national consciousness with its blue impotence pill, Viagra. That drug received so much publicity after its release in 1998 that one would think it would be the main force behind Pfizer's estimated $35 billion in 2002 revenues. But compared with Lipitor, the vaunted "Pfizer riser," with an estimated $1.75 billion in sales in 2002 was a pretty penny. In 2002, Lipitor achieved estimated sales of $7.4 billion while commanding a 42% market share in its class of drugs known as statins (see Exhibit 1). Its closet rival, Merck's Zocor, held 32% of the market.

Even as Lipitor's sales continued to grow, Pfizer faced challenges. Concerns about statins' long-term effects did not disappear. In 2001, Bayer voluntarily withdrew its statin, Baycol, from the market after the FDA linked it to 31 deaths from muscle deterioration. And a study in 2001 by Dr. Peter Langsjoen, a cardiologist at East Texas Medical Center in Tyler, Texas, found that two-thirds of patients showed signs of heart muscle weakening after only six months of statin therapy. The study was far from conclusive, but the FDA was reviewing Langsjoen's request for a government-funded study of long-term statin use. He also petitioned the FDA in May 2002 to order a warning on all statin pill bottles. Above all, people need to exercise caution, Langsjoen argued: "Doctors are prescribing statins with reckless abandon. They are really, really tricky drugs."

Pfizer's marketing team could also soon be put to the test. By the end of 2003, AstraZeneca planned to release Crestor, a statin that purports not only to lower bad cholesterol but also to raise good cholesterol far more effectively than other statins. Crestor had encountered snags and still needed FDA approval, but its lead marketer, Adele Gulfo, knew the competition well. She was part of the Pfizer-Warner-Lambert prelaunch marketing team for Lipitor. Because Crestor does things that Lipitor did not, this was not likely to be a traditional Coke vs. Pepsi market war. This market was still in its infancy; 52 million Americans needed cholesterol therapy, and Crestor had a much more aggressive stance on how to treat it. For its part, Pfizer had no plans to change its marketing tack: Doctors know Lipitor. They had been shown the data. Why did they need anything else?

Even if Crestor turned out to be a hit, there was probably room for both drugs in this growing market. With baby-boomers aging, the global market was expected to expand from $18.8 billion in 2002 to $23.6 billion by 2007. That was not even counting the possibility that statins might prove effective against Alzheimer's disease and multiple sclerosis.

The outlook for statins couldn't be healthier. In the U.S. alone, some 52 million people needed medical attention for high cholesterol, but only a third were getting it. As new patients sought out statins, Lipitor could well continue to gain share; Pfizer was a powerhouse marketer, and the drug would stay under patent protection until at least 2009.

LIPITOR STORY

Pfizer's status as the sultan of statins was even more remarkable considering it was a latecomer to the cholesterol reduction game. Lipitor entered the market a full decade after the first statins became available. The story of how Pfizer acquired the rights to an improved statin and turned it into the all-time biggest blockbuster was a tale of hyperaggressive marketing, deft timing, financial power, and plain dumb luck. It was also a story of missteps and missed opportunities by Merck, the company that pioneered statins.

The statin saga began in an unlikely place—Japan. In 1971, Dr. Akira Endo, working for the small Tokyo drug company Sankyo, set out to create a cholesterol-lowering drug. Research a decade earlier had shown that most of the body's cholesterol is manufactured in the liver with the help of an enzyme know as HMG-CoA (the rest comes directly from food). Despite decades of research, no one had been able to locate a compound that inhibited the enzyme's production.

Endo was determined to do so. He and his team at Sankyo spent years sifting through more than 6,000 microbes, looking for one that naturally produced an HMG-CoA inhibitor as a defense against other microorganisms. Eventually he identified mevastatin, the world's first cholesterol-fighting compound.

Word of the breakthrough spread quickly in the global medical community—as did rumors that Endo's statin caused tumors, muscle deterioration, and sometimes death in laboratory dogs. The stories scared off researchers at several drug companies, but not P. Roy Vagelos, the chief scientist at Merck. His $1.5-billion-a-year company was betting heavily on applied research in molecular biology and biochemistry, and Endo's work intrigued him.

Starting in 1975, Vagelos made several trips to Japan; before long, Merck had successfully duplicated Endo's experiments. By 1978 its scientists had identified another cholesterol-lowering compound, lovastatin, and begun the long process of clinical trials needed for FDA approval. When lovastatin finally hit the market in 1987 under the brand name Mevacor, it was the first drug in its class. Vagelos had become CEO by then, and Merck had grown into one of the largest and most profitable drug companies.

Merck faced a dual challenge as the market pioneer. It needed to help educate the public about the dangers of high cholesterol in the blood. (Reducing heart attack risk in the mid-1980s was

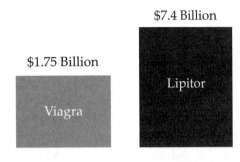

Exhibit 1 Lipitor vs. Viagra (2002 estimated sales)

mainly a matter of avoiding saturated fat and of eating high-fiber foods like oat bran.) Merck also had to convince doctors that statins would extend their patients' lives. Few doctors had experience with Mevacor, so they were reluctant to prescribe it. For doctors, the questions were: How safe are these drugs, and can they change overall mortality?

As Merck conducted research to prove that statins could stave off death, the public-awareness campaign took hold. Americans began drawing the connection between high cholesterol and heart attacks. Heart patients got to know their cholesterol numbers; people even learned the distinction between high-density lipoprotein (HDL), or "good" cholesterol, and low-density lipoprotein (LDL), or "bad" cholesterol. Food marketers responded with products like low-fat frozen pizzas and cholesterol-free potato chips. And rival drugmakers began to crowd into the statin market. Sankyo, for example, teamed with Bristol-Myers Squibb to market a drug called Pravachol.

More and more doctors were prescribing statins, yet questions lingered about the long-term benefits. Then, in April 1994, researchers announced the findings of the Merck-sponsored Scandinavian Simvastatin Survival Study, known as the Four-S. It had tested a new Merck statin on 4,444 patients with high cholesterol who had also experienced heart attacks. After five years of simvastatin use, the patients saw a 35% reduction in their cholesterol. Better yet, simvastatin had reduced the likelihood that a patient would die of a heart attack by 42%. That was a golden moment for Merck's publicity campaign for the Four-S. Merck quickly won FDA approval for simvastatin, which it branded Zocor. With market-leading products and groundbreaking research, Merck soon made its name synonymous with cholesterol control. Zocor quickly rose to No.1, and in 1995 both it and Mevacor were $1-billion-plus blockbusters. Though clearly a godsend for Merck, the Four-S would prove to be a curse. By lifting sales for the entire class of statins, it paved the way for Lipitor.

Back in 1982, when Mevacor was still five years from FDA approval, Bruce Roth was a 28-year-old postdoctoral fellow in the University of Rochester chemistry department. He had a fascination with statins and experimented with replicating their chemical structures. That spring he succeeded in synthesizing a statin that was very close to the one Sankyo's Dr. Endo had discovered a decade earlier. Roth's work wasn't groundbreaking, but his skill at piecing together and analyzing molecular structure attracted the attention of executives at Warner-Lambert's Ann Arbor labs. They

invited him for an interview. "I though it was intriguing," said Roth. "But honestly, I had never heard of the company." He'd probably used its products. Once primarily a consumer goods company, Warner-Lambert was the maker of Schick razors, Visine, and Listerine. In 1970 the company had joined the ranks of Big Pharma by acquiring Parke-Davis. During Roth's visit to its labs, he was impressed by how Warner-Lambert was using cutting-edge computerized molecular modeling to speed the search for new drugs. He decided to sign on and by 1984 was head of an 18-scientist atherosclerosis discovery group.

Warner-Lambert had high expectations: It wanted to become a serious player in statins, and Roth's job was to make that happen. In August 1985 he synthesized Lipitor. At first, though, he didn't know what he had: Animal testing showed that while Lipitor worked, it wasn't any better than Merck's Mevacor. Roth knew Warner-Lambert wouldn't tolerate a me-too drug after all the resources it had poured into his project.

There were other concerns. Mervacor was already well along in its final round of clinical trials, but Roth didn't even have a process for manufacturing Lipitor in commercial quantities. That took two years; meanwhile, Roth's bosses grew increasingly anxious. By 1987, Warner-Lambert was floundering; its pipeline of new drugs had virtually run dry, and it had fallen from the fourth-largest drug company to the ninth. "People in '87, '88, and '89 were telling me it was too late for a cholesterol reducer," Roth said.

Whispers began to circulate that Warner-Lambert was close to terminating the project. It seemed clear that at best Lipitor would be the third statin in a still-unproven market. Roth argued for one last chance to test Lipitor in a human clinical trial. Ronald Cresswell, head of the labs, took the pleas to Warner-Lambert's top managers. They agreed to fund one attempt to bring a cholesterol compound forward. If it failed, the company would end its statin effort. "We just rolled the dice," Roth said.

The dice came up sevens. A clinical trial of 24 Warner-Lambert employees showed that the earlier animal studies had greatly underestimated Lipitor. The drug's lowest dose for human subjects, ten milligrams, wound up reducing bad cholesterol by 38%, making it more effective than rival drugs at their highest FDA-recommended doses. Exhibit 2 summarizes the historical development of Lipitor.

KEY ROLE OF MARKETING

Suddenly Warner-Lambert knew it was on to something big. But to play catch-up in the market, it also knew it would need extra marketing muscle. Pfizer, then the No. 5 drugmaker, was known for its sales and marketing prowess and had no statin of its own. So when Warner-Lambert came knocking, Pfizer pounced at the chance. In 1996 the two companies entered an agreement to co-market Lipitor.

At first the partnership proved to be just what the doctor ordered. The marketers at Pfizer understood there might be advantages to Lipitor's late entry. By commissioning clinical trials, the companies could test their still-secret product against statins

I. Early to mid-1970s: In the Doghouse
Endo's statin is rumored to cause tumors, muscle deterioration, and even death in lab-tested dogs. Sankyo abandons the product. Other companies are hesitant to delve into statin research.

II. Late 1970s to early 1980s: Oat Bran Revolution
The medical community accepts the idea that cholesterol can be somewhat managed. Doctors begin recommending a diet high in fiber and low in saturated fat. Merck devotes 100 researchers and 25% of its research budget to creating a safe statin.

III. 1987 to 2001: Knights in White Statin
Merck's Mevacor, the first viable statin, wins FDA approval in August 1987. Five other statins hit the pharmacists' shelves in the '90s—including Lipitor. The cholesterol drug market flourishes, growing from $1.8 billion in 1991 to $17.8 billion in 2001.

IV. 2002 to 2004: Sick at Heart
Some 52 million Americans need cholesterol therapy, says the National Institutes of Health. Five million of the most severe cases have congestive heart failure—what the FDA calls "congestive heart failure epidemic." By 2004, Lipitor is expected to hit $10 billion in sales.

Exhibit 2 Historical Development of Lipitor

---

already on the market. The makers of those statins couldn't do the same because they couldn't get their hands on Lipitor.

In the spring of 1996 the results of a head-to-head trial landed on Pat Kelly, then senior marketing executive at Pfizer's New York City headquarters. The packet contained lots of paper, but one page stood out. It was a chart with color-coded curved lines, comparing Lipitor with each of the major cholesterol drugs—Merck's Zocor and Mevacor, Novartis's Lescol, and Bristol-Myers's Pravachol—in effectiveness at lowering cholesterol over time. "I will never forget seeing that chart," said Kelly. Lipitor's curve began at a higher point than those of all the other medicines and showed a steeper upswing. That meant not only that Lipitor had a more effective starting dose, but also that it reduced cholesterol by proportions that the others couldn't. Pfizer marketers nicknamed the study the curves trial. With that graphic, it was like, Aha! When the FDA approved Lipitor in January 1997, it allowed Pfizer and Warner-Lambert to include the curves data in the packet insert found in each prescription bottle of the drug. It was also part of the literature salespeople handed out to physicians.

In further preparation for Lipitor market blitz, Pfizer conducted focus groups with doctors. The sessions uncovered a selling point that other statin makers had missed: Though doctors were prescribing statins in record numbers, they were still spooked at the idea of recommending high doses. The insight led Pfizer to push the FDA to approve a low starting dose for Lipitor. The agency agreed. It approved Lipitor for use in the range of ten to 80 milligrams a day. Other statins had been approved in the 20-to 40-milligram range. When doctors heard that, they thought, if the FDA approved Lipitor up to 80 milligrams, ten milligrams must be really safe. It was a major psychological advantage.

Pfizer's marketers now focused on toppling Merck's Zocor. To do so, they decided they needed an additional tactic: They would undercut Merck's price. The pricing was based on feedback from doctors and managed care. They wanted to make sure Lipitor was within reach of all patients. (In 2002, a month's supply of Lipitor cost about $66, vs. about $120 for Zocor.)

When Lipitor hit the market in spring 1997, it piggybacked on the work other companies had done to raise consumer awareness

and doctors' confidence. By June 1998, Lipitor had garnered nearly 18% of the market, making it No. 2 behind Zocor, which held 37%. Wall Street analysts nicknamed Lipitor the turbostatin; between mid-1997 and mid-1998 the stocks of Pfizer and Warner-Lambert leaped 102% and 83%, respectively. The success of Pfizer's doctor-savvy marketing was especially frustrating for executives at Merck. "We were so busy patting ourselves on the back for doing the Four-S study that we didn't realize doctors were prescribing based on potency and price, not the outcomes that we showed in the study," recalled a Merck executive.

By linking up with Pfizer, however, Warner-Lambert had gotten more than it bargained for. In late 1999, Warner-Lambert agreed to be acquired by American Home Products. Its hard-charging Lipitor partner wasn't about to swallow that. Breaking with genteel drug industry tradition, Pfizer made an unsolicited bid for Warner-Lambert, touching off a bidding war. After seven months, Pfizer won, paying $90 billion in the biggest drug takeover in history.

With Lipitor fully under its control, Pfizer went into overdrive in 2001 with direct-to-consumer advertising. Its campaign aimed at conveying two simple messages. The first: You don't have to be visibly unhealthy to have dangerously high cholesterol. The second: "Know your number"—that is, the level of bad cholesterol in your blood. A reading above 160 milligrams per deciliter of blood is considered risky, while a reading below 100 is optimal.

Pfizer's sales campaign in doctors' offices had been no less aggressive. Selling drugs to physicians was not easy. To get their foot in the door, sales reps had to be almost as knowledgeable as doctors about health-care trends. So Pfizer continually trained and tested its 13,000 salespeople. A five-week boot camp for recruits included courses in anatomy and physiology. Nothing was left to chance. The trainees went through weeks of simulated sales calls in a mock physician's office, built like a movie set on one of Pfizer's upstate New York campuses. On the simulation stage, former sales reps played harried and irritable doctors. Trainees were timed and judged on their ability to deliver a pitch for a Pfizer drug.

All this reflected the company's guiding sales principle: It wanted doctors to think of Pfizer sales reps as vital suppliers not only of drugs but also of new, useful medical information. What was important was that [the reps] got access to doctors who were incredibly crunched for time. The approach seemed to work. In a national survey of doctors by industry consultant Verispan in 2002, Pfizer's sales force ranks as most esteemed. That reputation helped make Pfizer's sale reps the most productive in the industry, with an average of 552 calls per year, vs. 409 for GlaxoSmith Kline and 379 for Merck, according to Verispan.

The sales and marketing forces sometimes get carried away. In October 2001, Pfizer was forced to pay the U.S. government $49 million to settle charges that it overcharged Medicaid for Lipitor. Company officials say the incident occurred before the Warner-Lambert acquisition happened on the Warner-Lambert side of the co-marketing deal. Also last fall the FDA asked Pfizer to stop running magazine ads that claimed inaccurately that Lipitor might not have side effects of other statins. Pfizer changed the wording.

UPS vs. FedEx

In spring, 2000, FDX, the parent company of FedEx, was under attack from UPS and it must develop a viable strategy to counter the attack. Fed Ex was concerned about a huge, slow moving, decidedly unglamorous foe: United Parcel Service, also know as "Big Brown" and "the Brown Blizzard." UPS handled three times as many packages as the purple and orange company and it made four times as much money. Exhibit 1 shows the market breakdown for the two companies. Ignoring the relatively unsophisticated (not to mention relatively unreliable) U.S. Postal Service, UPS practically owned the business of moving packages economically by ground and delivering them to any address in the country. Several years ago it began going after FedEx's high-margin core business, next-day air express, with surprising success. And just in case it wasn't big enough already, once-private UPS raised $5.4 billion in November 1999 in the largest IPO ever, the better to kick butt here and in Europe. James Kelly, 56, the burly former truck driver who in 2000 served as the company's President, remarked: "We are going to involve ourselves in global commerce more deeply and more extensively than ever. The consumer will have access to goods anywhere in the world."

FDX PERSPECTIVIES

FDX, the parent company of FedEX was counterattacking. In 1999 it bought a trucking company to wage turf war against UPS; think of that strategy as racing for lower ground. In mid-January, 2000 FDX announced that is would change its name back to FedEx Corp. (the company was originally called Federal Express, than FedEx, than FDX) and apply the FedEx brand to its cheaper, slower delivery arms. RPS, the existing trucking company, would be named FedEx Ground; it would make only business-to-business deliveries. A new operation, FedEx Home Delivery, would specialize in deliveries to residences. FDX was gambling that its sterling reputation for service wouldn't be tarnished by using independent contractors, instead of employees, as carriers at FedEx Ground and FedEx Home.

At the high end of the shipping business, FedEx was investing $100 million in operations that would enable it to deliver packages more quickly and with greater control than it already did. Fred Smith, FDX's founder and CEO, saw the world's manufacturing process going to a build-to-order model, much as Dell Computer had already done. He said his company would be there with sophisticated shipping systems to choreograph the flow of goods anywhere. If FDX could not succeed at that, warned Smith, 55, an intense ex-Marine, "we won't succeed at anything."

Although it might seem that UPS and FedEx were locked in a struggle to the death, it's not as bad as that. Both companies were well run and likely to flourish. They were fighting over shares of a pie that kept getting bigger. Why? Very simply, fewer and fewer products today moved by cargo pallet—thousands of identical units at a time—to factories or warehouses. They went instead into cardboard boxes to be delivered to specific business or to individuals.

The Internet deserved much, but not all, of the credit for changes in the transportation business. The Net made e-tailing possible, of course. And it had made interconnected information system—essential to ordering and tracking—cheaper and more widespread than ever. Beyond the Internet, however, corporations looking for ways to cut the cost of shipping and inventories had discovered that moving goods by the boxful instead of the boatload was cheaper in the long run. With an 80% share between them, UPS (55%) and FDX (25%) practically owned the on-time package delivery business. Companies like Airborne and DHL were also-rans. UPS, a $27-million-a-year colossus, delivered more than 12.4 million packages a day. The Atlanta-based company claimed to move goods worth 6% of the nation's GDP every night. FDX, with headquarters in Memphis, was enormous too. It grossed an estimated $17.5 billion during 1999. FDX hauled far fewer packages than UPS—about 4.5 million a day—but since 3.2 million went by plane, not truck, FDX's yield, or revenue per package, was much higher.

Lately UPS had been gaining on FedEx in its core business. UPS noticed a long time ago that air express was a fast-growing and potentially lucrative part of the package delivery business. It began buying airplanes in the early 1980s and built a huge sorting hub at Louisville airport that nearly rivaled FedEx's in Memphis. But for years the growth of UPS's air-express business lagged far behind FedEx's. Big Brown couldn't match FedEx's reputation for reliability. FedEx was the first to install elaborate scanning equipment, which enabled it to tell customers exactly where their package was. In Fred Smith's memorable phrase, "The information about the package is almost as important as the package itself."

Because its airplanes and tracking equipment were expensive and required large capital investments, FedEx's return on equity for the past ten years had been a fairly pedestrian 8%—far below UPS's 20% return. UPS, it turned out, had a big advantage over FedEx. Because it already had an army of 150,000 trucks and drivers making ground-based shipments to virtually every address in the country, it was easy to simply take air-express packages off UPS planes and ferry them to one of the company's 1,700 truck depots. Then the packages could travel the last few miles at little additional cost.

UPS had gradually eroded FedEx's share of the air-express business, until it now carried two million overnight and next-day air packages, vs. FedEx's three million. Overall growth for the air-express business had slowed considerably in the recent years, from

20% or more annually a decade ago to roughly 7% in 1999. But while FedEx's air-express business grew just 3.6% in the first three quarters of last year, according to Bear Stearns, UPS's grew an astounding 9.3%.

For most of the past decade, UPS spent $1 billion a year on information systems that gradually improved its ability to track packages and its on-time performance. Although executives at UPS and FedEx each claimed that their company had the best overnight-air reliability, outsiders say it was a wash. According to James Tompkins, head of a logistics consulting firm in Raleigh, "There was no difference." It's hype and image. A company shipped 100 boxes with FedEx and 100 with UPS and repeated it ten times; it came out the same. UPS used to be bad. They have improved. The thing that made the most difference in any given night was the weather over the companies' airport hubs in Memphis and Louisville.

UPS hadn't just made inroads into FedEx's air express business. It had also engineered the shift of a lot of packages away from expensive airplanes and onto cheaper trucks. The company accomplished that by greatly boosting the tracking and on-time performance of its ground fleet, so that when UPS said a package would arrive somewhere by mid-afternoon three days from now, it did so better than 90% of the time. To publicize and back up its claim, UPS announced a money-back guarantee for its ground deliveries in April 1999. That was a very big deal for the customers. It really changed perceptions about the usefulness of ground.

FDX MOVES INTO TRUCKING BUSINESS

FDX, it seemed, didn't have much choice but to get into the trucking business too. In January 1999 it bought Caliber Systems, a Pittsburgh company whose trucking operations included a package delivery division called RPS. With $2 billion a year in revenues RPS was not even one-tenth the size of Big Brown. Nor did it deliver to homes. But because its drivers were independent contractors who severed a franchise area and supplied their own trucks, RPS's labor costs were low, and its operating income— 12% of revenues—was considerably better than the 6% at FedEx.

The on-time delivery performance of RPS—the outfits soon to be renamed FedEx Ground—was mixed. As a matter of fact it was horrible. If the driver had to make a delivery in some suburban part of his franchise area, he didn't go until he was good and ready. Things were days late. Customers were extremely frustrated. However, FedEx had remedied many of RPS's service problems and would continue to upgrade technology and improve training at the company.

The most intriguing of FDX's recent announcements was its plan to create a new operation solely dedicated to home deliveries. Like RPS, FedEx Home Delivery will hire independent contractors to serve defined areas. The drivers would use smaller, more economical vans (decorated with the image of a friendly dog), and would make deliveries in evenings and on Saturday, when residents were most likely to be home. According to a company

executive, "They will be like the milkman of the old days. They'll know the neighborhoods and know the people. But instead of delivering milk, they'll deliver just about anything else." FedEx planned to have its new drivers serving half the U.S. population by the end of 2005, but it declined to say how many trucks and drivers it would actually engage.

Shippers and customers using FedEx Home Delivery and FedEx Ground (business-to-business) would be able to call up the same Website that FedEx's air-express customers used to track the whereabouts of a package. But the truckers won't share the express group's hubs or sorting center, and none of the divisions would deliver packages for the other. According to FedEx this is their strength. Because UPS had combined its express and ground businesses, its flexibility was limited. For instance, the UPS pickup schedules were built around the needs of the ground operation, so its drop-off locations closed before FedEx's. With FedEx, one could still drop off an air express package at 7:30 in the evening.

But until FedEx got its trucking act on the road, it would continue to be vulnerable to UPS. Not only was UPS luring some air-express business back to the ground, but it offered on-stop shopping to companies that needed both air and ground transportation—and volume discounts to boot. UPS sales reps seemed more aggressive than ever in taking business away from FedEx. It used to be that when you'd go to UPS and tell them your client was pretty big, they'd give you a standard 10% discount. But now if you tell UPS that your client had been using FedEx for last three years, their pencils came out in a hurry.

In reality, the price difference between UPS and FedEx for the same services might be as little as 2%; careful cost analysis was difficult because volume discounts differed sharply from list and were kept secret. Some companies that shipped lots of packages had learned they could profit from widespread public misconceptions that FedEx was quicker and more reliable than UPS. Although both companies charged shippers similar prices for similar services, many consumers willingly paid a few dollars more to get something via FedEx.

CORPORATE CULTURE

FedEx deliberately pursed that tony image. It sponsored golf tournaments and even had the Orange Bowl renamed the FedEx Orange Bowl. UPS would not do that in a million years. There was far less pizzazz in UPS's marketing. The different histories of the two companies helped explain why. FedEx was founded by Smith, a Yale graduate with a background in economics. At UPS, on the other hand, virtually every executive—including CEO Kelly—began by driving the truck. The UPS guys get ahead by scrambling all the time. They get promoted and hustle like mad and yell at their drivers to make their section profitable and get their bonus. They did care about image. The are tough. Their attitude is, 'Whaddaya mean, I can't drive through that brick wall?'

Even as the two companies invaded each other's turf, they had different visions of where the package delivery business was going and where they wanted to be. United Parcel is eager to capture the traffic to homes that the Internet would generate. Federal

Express thought the Internet would drive demand for high-end shipping services for corporations; it is intent on capturing that so-called supply-chain management.

Although both companies claimed to be capable of matching any service the other provided, United Parcel clearly had a leg up on FedEx in delivering to homes. According to Forrester Research, a Cambridge, Mass., consulting firm, UPS delivered 55% of the items ordered over the Web and shipped to homes during Christmas in 1999. It estimated that UPS handled at least that proportion during Christmas of 1998. The U.S. Postal Service made about 30% of e-tail deliveries. FedEx, with its less-developed ground-based system, handled about 10%. United Parcel was much more focused on the movement of goods from business to consumer. That's not a big part of their overall business now (about 80% of UPS's deliveries were business to business.) But deliveries to consumers were expected to grow exponentially in the next few years.

IMPACT OF E-COMMERCE

The value of goods ordered over the Net and shipped to homes was a fairly modest $20 billion in 1999, about 1% of traditional retail sales. That was expected to rise to $180 billion by 2005. During the same time the volume of homeward-bound parcels should rise from three million to eight million a day.

Delivering to homes was less profitable than delivering to business because homes were more scattered. (UPS charged an extra dollar for residential delivery to help cover the additional costs.) But margins should rise as the Internet would boost the flow of boxes to apartments and suburbs. According to UPS, business-to-residential added to profit and it filled the network. The delivery person could do air express in the early morning, business deliveries in the late morning, and residential in the afternoon. Density and scale were a big part of this.

The looming rival to UPS in the home delivery business was more likely to be the U.S. Postal Service than Federal Express. The merry mailmen were not much of a threat now, because the post office lacked the sophisticated computer systems that would enable it and its customers to track packages. Customers of both UPS and FedEx could check the status of shipments themselves on the Internet to learn exactly when a package was received and who signed for it. The post office had hired Lockheed Martin to devise just such a tracking system, which should be ready in about five years. Expectedly, when completed it should be as good or better than UPS and FedEx had now.

Because the post office already delivered letters to virtually every address in the country, the added cost of packages would be low. FedEx and UPS executives railed at the intrusion of the post office, noting that it could subsidize its package delivery operations with money from its monopoly on mail and that the post office did not even pay taxes. Most galling, federal law required FedEx and UPS to set their package list prices twice as high as those of the post office. It was predicted that the post office's share of Internet-driven package deliveries to homes would rise from about 30% now to 50% in a few years. Exhibit 2 summarizes the expected evaluation of two companies in the context of Internet business.

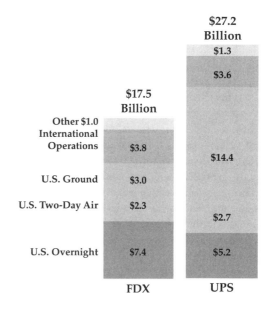

Exhibit 1 Big Bundles 1999 Revenue

DEPENDENCE ON NEW SYSTEMS

Over the long term, FedEx was placing its biggest bets on the build-to-order revolution underway in manufacturing, epitomized by Dell Computer. Dell did not build a zillion identical computers, flood them out to retailers, and hope customers would like what they saw. It waited until it had your customer order (any your money), then ordered components from suppliers and assembled the parts. Some components, like the monitor or speakers, might be sent directly from the supplier to your home (never passing through Dell) and arrive on your doorstep at the same time as everything else.

That might sound like old news. Just-in-time inventory and delivery systems that were popularized by the Japanese in the 1970s were adopted by Western corporations in the 1980s. But they required private data networks that were expensive and difficult to use. Even the automakers got only about 20% of their suppliers to connect to their systems. The Internet, vastly cheaper and easier to use, promised to make it possible for a small widget maker in Sri Lanka to receive an order and ship parts to an assembly plant in San Jose or even directly to a customer. Because transportation and warehousing account for about 10% of the price of all goods, cutting costs with sophisticated Internet-based logistics and supply-chain management tools had become a minor obsession for many corporations.

Both FedEx and UPS had seen the opportunities here. Both were working to tie their tracking systems to warehouse and inventory software from the likes of Oracle, SAP, and PeopleSoft. Both did sophisticated warehousing for hundreds of big and small companies; UPS boxed and shipped sneakers for Nike, while FedEx did the same with computer peripherals for Hewlett-Packard. FedEx, however, seemed hungrier. When Cisco Systems wanted a more precisely timed way of delivering routers to customers, it approached both FedEx and UPS. UPS's response was rather ho-hum: Give us a few million and we would scratch it for you. FedEx, by contrast, jumped: They pulled out their wallets and said they'd do whatever it took.

The problem for Cisco was that a big client might order 100 routers at a time. (Routers control the flow of information on computer networks.) Some might be shipped from San Jose, others from Mexico, the rest from Asia. Unfortunately for Cisco, customers wanted all the routers to arrive at the same time. FedEx could easily coordinate shipments when Cisco's factories were running smoothly. But suppose Cisco discovered that a bunch of routers at the San Jose plant had a problem and would be delayed for two days? Meanwhile, the routers made in Asia and Mexico were already their way to the customer. How did Cisco keep them from arriving ahead of the California routers?

It was not a trivial matter. Items arriving in dribs and drabs caused all sorts of frustration. If the routers from Mexico got to the customer before the ones from California, the guy who signed for them on the receiving dock might think the order was botched. He would not know whether to send along what had gotten to the tech center or hold everything in storage until the entire order arrived. Might be the customer had hired a group of technicians to install the routers, but now they were standing around doing nothing because the full shipment wasn't in.

In the old days, the way to guarantee coordinated shipments was to keep plenty of routers in a warehouse and put them all on one truck. But Cisco wanted to avoid the cost of keeping millions of dollars' worth of routers in inventory. FedEx agrees to install systems for Cisco that would enable the company to accelerate or retard parts of an order on short notice, thus ensuring coordinated deliveries.

One shipping expert familiar with the deal said Cisco was impressed with FedEx's enthusiasm for the proposal: FedEx told Cisco, the way you're looking at this was very much the way we saw the world going, and we'd like to develop this product for

---

Will FDX and UPS deliver the goods to your portfolio? Wall Street thought so and had been pushing both stocks as backdoor Internet plays. Buy one of the shipping giants and get a piece of the e-commerce boom without astronomical prices or the risks of an untested startup. As good as gold—or fool's gold? Shares of UPS, priced at $50 when the company went public in November, quickly soared to $74 and had held most of their first-day gain. FDX was a different story. After reaching a 52-week high of 61 and 7/8 in May 1999, the Federal Express parent plunged to 34 and 3/4 when investors decided UPS was better equipped to rule online shipping. More than $10 billion abandoned FDX—much of it heading to Big Brown.

But now things looked overdone. UPS was trading at 44 times earnings, unprecedented for a shipping stock. And FDX, at 22 times, looked like a remnant from Filene's Basement. "Anyone who says there can be only one winner is an idiot," says Jeffrey Kauffman, an analyst at Merrill Lynch. There's no question that both UPS and FDX would be busier because of online retail and business-to-business deliveries. UPS already handled 55% of the merchandise sold online, while FDX was repositioning itself to increase its 10% share. A year ago Barron's called FDX the "cheapest Internet stock; today it is not cheap, it's unwanted. Meanwhile, UPS was trading above the most bullish expectations. Should UPS, which did have a recorded for dealing with shareholders, really be priced like a dot-com? Should FDX, until recently the most innovative shipping company, be left on the loading dock?

Even without the dot-com bonus, UPS was a powerhouse. It earned about $2.3 billion last year on estimated sales of $27.2 billion. It had billions in cash to pay for acquisitions that could deepen its reach into Europe and Asia, where analysts saw potential gains that dwarf those of e-commerce back home. Profits were expected to grow 13% this year, to $2.6 billion. FDX was no cream puff either. It earned $631 million last year on $17.5 billion in sales. Despite a 6% decline in profits last quarter because of higher jet fuel prices, FDX had a strong outlook, particularly with trade barriers falling in Asia and a recent fuel surcharge providing a buffer from higher prices. Profits were expected to be $659 million this year, on sales of $18 billion. In 1999, the return on equity for UPS was 35% while it was 14% for FDX.

Based on market and financial leadership analysts felt UPS should trade at a 30% to 40% premium to FDX. The fact that the premium was 100% has spooked some. Rich Crable at Loomis Sayles bought UPS at the offering, then sold when it sprinted up like a no-name-dot-come. He had earlier sold FDX near its high because it, too, was overpriced. Says Crable of UPS: "At $50 a share, UPS would have a substantial premium over FDX."

Even in the wired world, transporters could escape the economy. Unlike dot-come stocks that soared in a universe disconnected from traditional valuation methods, the fortunes of FDX and UPS still turned on such old-economy events as rising fuel prices, interest rates, and business sentiment. E-commerce might give the shippers a broader base of customers, but those customers won't be placing as many orders if Federal Reserve rate hikes slowed the economy.

The bottom line: If you're an investor with a five-year horizon, UPS on a 10% pullback would look ripe. It was fast becoming a must-own blue chip. If trading was your thing, battered FDX oozed opportunity. One of two quarters that top estimates could help it win back fans who left for Big Brown. But this was not likely to happen in the short run.

Source: Fortune, February–March, 2000, p. 104.

Exhibit 2 Net Effects: UPS vs. FedEx

you. He estimated that FedEx would spend $100 million on the project. It meant system changes and ripping up the physical plant and changing how drivers did things.

All this was just beginning, but if it worked it would make a big difference for Cisco: It would blow away warehouses. The cost of doing this with warehouses looked like it would be twice the cost of doing it the new way. And it would give Cisco so much flexibility about where it put its factories around the world.

Whether FedEx would benefit from the improvements as much as Cisco remained to be seen. Certainly FedEx would have many admirers if it could become the brains and brawn of a global, Internet-based system that moved and tracked goods around the world with the precision of a master chess player—and that wiped out trillions of dollars in costly inventories. But would

this new system pay? Experts worry that the company was infatuated with technology at the expense of earnings. In the basic operations where FedEx did something that UPS did not, it was not clear that FedEx made money.

FedEx officials said they weren't concerned. United Parcel might have taken the early lead in capturing what the Internet had to offer, but that was like Russia bragging that it launched Sputnik. Russia didn't put a man on the moon.

One got the sense, though, that UPS was not chasing the moon right now. It seemed content with its wheels on the ground and 12 million boxes a day passing through its trucks. The battle between Big Brown on the ground and FedEx in the air seemed certain to get more heated. And it won't be over anytime soon. Exhibit 2 summarizes the financial outlook on the two companies.

CASE 3
Loblaws

"It's been a year since we introduced green products at Loblaws and the decisions still are not getting any easier." In early July 1990, Scott Lindsay was reflecting upon his decision as to which, if any, of three possible products he would recommend for the G·R·E·E·N line: an energy-efficient light bulb, toilet tissue made from recycled paper, or a high-fiber cereal.

As Director of International Trade for Intersave Buying & Merchandising Services (a buying division for Loblaws), it was Scott's job to source and manage about 400 corporate brands (No Name, President's Choice, G·R·E·E·N)[1] for Loblaws in Canada. In four days, Scott would have to make his recommendations to the buyers' meeting.

The "green line" for which Scott was sourcing products was a new concept for Loblaws and its customers. Launched in 1989 as part of the corporate President's Choice brands, green products had characteristics that were less hazardous to the environment and/or contributed to a more healthy life-style. At issue for Scott was deciding what was "green" and balancing the financial requirements of the company with the socially responsible initiative of the green line.

As well, his most pressing concern was his ability to convince the president, Dave Nichol, of the merits of his recommendations. Mr. Nichol was the driving force behind the corporate brands, and he maintained involvement and final authority on these important product decisions.

In preparation for the buyers' meeting, Scott had to have his written recommendations on Dave Nichol's desk that day. Dave Nichol required that recommendations include retail price and cost data, projected annual sales in units and dollars, as well as total gross margin expected. In addition to the expected results, best and worst case scenarios were also required. As well, primary reasons for and against the proposal needed to be given. Typically, the recommendations were made based on the Ontario market as it was the proving ground for new products.

The first product Scott was considering was a new energy-efficient light bulb, which had been successfully marketed in Germany. The bulb lasted at least ten times longer than a regular light bulb but was substantially more expensive. There was no question in Scott's mind that the energy-efficient bulb had strong "green" characteristics and would enhance Loblaws' green image.

However, a potential consumer price of $20 and low retail margins were a troubling combination. He knew that store managers, who were measured on sales volume and profits, would not be enthusiastic about a product that would not deliver sales or profits. These store managers controlled the individual products and brands that were carried in their stores.

The second new product was, in fact, not a new product at all. Loblaws had been selling a toilet tissue manufactured with 100% recycled material under its No Name corporate label. The existing product could be repackaged under the G·R·E·E·N label and sold beside the No Name line of products. The green packaging might alert consumers sensitive to the recycled feature, thereby generating greater volumes for the product. Further, Scott realized there was an opportunity to price the "green" toilet tissue at a higher price than the No Name, providing a higher profit margin.

The final product under consideration was a new corn flake product for the very "crowded" breakfast cereal category. The new cereal had an unusually high fiber content. The "body friendly" nature of the cereal was the basis for considering it for the green line. Its additional feature was that it could be sourced at a cost much lower than the national brands.

LOBLAWS COMPANIES LIMITED

Loblaw Companies Limited is part of George Weston Ltd., a conglomerate of companies that operate in three basic areas: food processing, food distribution, and natural resources. George Weston is the sixth largest company in Canada with sales of $10.5 billion and net income of $988 million in 1989. The Loblaw Companies, an integrated group of food wholesaling and retailing companies, had total sales and net earnings in 1989 of $7,934 million and $70 million respectively.

THE GREEN IDEA

The G·R·E·E·N line launch had its origins in one of Dave Nichol's buying trips to Germany in 1988, where he was struck by the number of grocery products that were promoted as "environmentally friendly." He discovered that *The Green Consumer Guide*, a "how-to" book for consumers to become environmentally responsible, had become a best-seller in England. In late 1988, Loblaws began collecting information on Canadian attitudes about the environment. The results suggested that an increasing number of Canadians were concerned about environmental issues, and some expressed a willingness to pay extra to purchase environmentally safe products. Further, many said they were willing to change supermarkets to acquire these products. (See Exhibit 1.)

---

[1]No Name, President's Choice, and G·R·E·E·N are all trademarks, owned by Loblaws Companies Limited.

This case was written by Professor Gordon H. G. McDougall and Professor Douglas Snetsinger of Wilfrid Laurier University as a basis of classroom discussion rather than to illustrate either effective or ineffective handling of an administrative situation. Reprinted by permission of the authors.

Copyright © 1991. Some data are disguised.

1. National survey on issues.
   What is the most important issue facing Canada today?

Issues	1985	1986	1987	1988	1989
Environment	*	*	2	10	18
Goods and services tax	*	*	*	*	15
Inflation/Economy	16	12	12	5	10
Deficit/Government	6	10	10	6	10
National unity	*	*	*	*	7
Free trade	2	5	26	42	7
Abortion	*	*	*	*	6
Employment	45	39	20	10	6

Source: Maclean's/Decima Research

*Not cited by a significant number of poll respondents.

Note: Survey conducted in early January of each year.

2. Loblaws customers surveys.

   How concerned are you about the environment? (%)
   Extremely (32), Quite (37), Somewhat (24), Not Very (5), Don't Care (2)

   How likely is it that you would purchase environmentally friendly products?
   Very (49), Somewhat (43), Not too (2), Not at all (4)

   How likely is it that you would switch supermarkets to purchase environmentally friendly products?
   Very (2), Somewhat (45), Not too (24), Not at all (10)

   Note: Survey conducted in early 1989.

Exhibit 1 Consumer Attitudes on Environment

THE G·R·E·E·N LAUNCH

Armed with this supportive data, in late January 1989, Loblaws management decided to launch, by July 1989, a line of 100 products that were either environmentally friendly or healthy for the body. These products would be added to the family of the corporate line and called G·R·E·E·N. Although the task was considered ambitious, the corporation believed it had the requisite size, strength, influence, network, imagination, and courage to be successful. Loblaws contacted a number of prominent environmental groups to assist in the choice of products. These groups were requested to make a "wish list" of environmentally safe products. Using this as a guide, Loblaws began to source the products for the G·R·E·E·N launch.

A few products, such as baking soda, simply required repackaging to advertise the already existing environmentally friendly qualities of the product. Intersave Buying and Merchandising Services was able to source some products through foreign suppliers, such as the Ecover line of household cleaning products, to be marketed under the G·R·E·E·N umbrella. All G·R·E·E·N products were rigorously tested as well as screened by environmental groups such as Pollution Probe and Friends of the Earth. This collaboration was developed to such an extent that a few of the products were endorsed by Pollution Probe.

The G·R·E·E·N product line, consisting of about 60 products, was launched on June 3, 1989. Initial G·R·E·E·N products included phosphate-free laundry detergent, low-acid coffee, pet foods, and biodegradable garbage bags. (See Exhibit 2.) A holistic approach was taken in selecting these initial products; for example, the pet food products were included because they provided a more healthful blend of ingredients for cats and dogs. The G·R·E·E·N products were offered in a distinctively designed package with vivid green coloring. When the package design decisions were being made, it was learned that 20 percent of the Canadian population is functionally illiterate. Management felt that the distinct design would give these consumers a chance to readily identify these brands.

The G·R·E·E·N launch was supported with a $3 million television and print campaign. Consumers were informed of the new product line using the June 1989 issue of the *Insider's Report.* In an open letter to consumers, Mr. Nichol addressed Loblaws' motivation for the G·R·E·E·N launch. Part of the motivation was also to offer consumers a choice that could, in the longer term, provide educational benefits for consumers on specific green issues. As well, by offering the choice, consumers could "vote at the cash register" and, in a sense, tell Loblaws what they were willing to buy and what green products they would accept. The G·R·E·E·N line was to be typically priced below national brand products.

The G·R·E·E·N introduction was not without its problems. Shortly after the launch, members of the Pollution Probe rejected their previous endorsement of the G·R·E·E·N disposable diaper. These members felt that the group should not support a less than perfect product. The G·R·E·E·N diaper was more environmentally

Food

- Just Peanuts Peanut Butter
- Smart Snack Popcorn
- "The Virtuous" Soda Cracker
- Cox's Orange Pippin Apple Juice
- White Hull-less Popcorn
- Reduced Acid Coffee
- Boneless and Skinless Sardines
- "Green" Natural Oat Bran
- Naturally Flavoured Raisins: Lemon, Cherry, Strawberry
- "Green" Turkey Frankfurters
- 100% Natural Rose Food
- Norwegian Crackers
- Whole Frozen Turkey
- Gourmet Frozen Foods (low-fat)
- "If the World Were PERFECT" Water

Cleaning/Detergent Products

- All-Purpose Liquid Cleaner with Bitrex
- "Green" Automatic Dishwasher Detergent
- Ecover 100% Biodegradable Laundry Powder*
- Ecover Dishwasher Detergent
- Laundry Soil and Stain Remover with Bitrex
- Drain Opener with Bitrex
- Ecover Fabric Softener
- Ecover 100% Biodegradable Toilet Cleaner
- Ecover 100% Biodegradable Wool Wash
- Ecover Floor Soap
- "Green" 100% Phosphate-Free Laundry Detergent

Pet Food

- Low Ash Cat Food
- Slim & Trim Cat Food
- All Natural Dog Biscuits

Cooking Products

- "The Virtuous" Canola Oil
- "The Virtuous" Cooking Spray
- Baking Soda

Paper-Based Products

- Bathroom Tissue
- "Green" Ultra Diapers
- "Green" Foam Plates
- Swedish 100% Chlorine-Free Coffee Filters
- "Green" Baby Wipes
- "Green" Maxi Pads

Oil-Based Products

- Biodegradable Garbage Bags
- Hi-Performance Motor Oil
- Natural Fertilizer
- Lawn and Garden Soil

Other Products

- Green T-Shirt/Sweatshirt
- Green Panda Stuffed Toy
- Green Polar Bear Stuffed Toy
- Cedar Balls

---

* The Ecover brands are a line of cleaning products made by Ecover of Belgium. These products are vegetable oil based and are rapidly biodegradable. Loblaws marketed these products under the G·R·E·E·N umbrella.

Exhibit 2 The Initial G·R·E·E·N Products

---

friendly than any other disposable brand. However, it was not, in Pollution Probe's opinion, environmentally pure. Further, it was felt that endorsing such products compromised the integrity and independence of the organization. This prompted the resignation of Colin Issac, the director of Pollution Probe. The group subsequently discontinued its endorsement of the diaper, but continued its support of six other G·R·E·E·N products.

Controversy also arose around the introduction of the G·R·E·E·N fertilizer. Greenpeace, a prominent environmental group, rejected Loblaws' claims that the fertilizer had no toxic elements and therefore was environmentally pure. The group did not know that Loblaws had spent substantial funds to determine that the product was free of toxic chemicals.

Both incidents, although unfortunate, focused the attention of Canadians on the G·R·E·E·N product line. The media highlighted Loblaws as the only North American retailer to offer a line of environmentally friendly products. The publicity also prompted letters of encouragement from the public who supported Loblaws' initiative. Surveys conducted four weeks after the line introduction revealed an

82 percent awareness of the G·R·E·E·N line with 27 percent of the consumers actually purchasing at least one of the G·R·E·E·N products. In Ontario alone, the G·R·E·E·N line doubled its projected sales and sold $5 million in June 1989.

THE FIRST YEAR OF G·R·E·E·N

The launch of G·R·E·E·N was soon followed by a virtual avalanche of "environmentally friendly" products. Major consumer goods companies such as Procter & Gamble, Lever Brothers, and Colgate-Palmolive introduced Enviro-Paks, phosphate-free detergents, and biodegradable cleaning products. Competing supermarket chains had varied responses from launching their own "green" line (Miracle Mart introduced three "Green Circle" products, Oshawa Foods introduced about 10 "Green-care" products) to highlighting environmentally sensitive products in their stores (Safeway) to improving its internal practices through recycling and other activities (Provigo).

During the year, Loblaws continued to develop and promote the G·R·E·E·N product line. In the first year of G·R·E·E·N, Loblaws sold approximately $60 million worth of G·R·E·E·N products and "broke even" on the line.

THE DECISIONS

As Scott began to make his decisions on the three products, he reflected on the past year. He thought that $60 million in sales for the G·R·E·E·N line was reasonable, but he had hoped the line would do better. He remembered some of the products that just didn't fit in the line, such as "green" sardines. "I don't think we sold 20 cans of that stuff." Scott and the other buyers at Intersave were very concerned when a product didn't sell. Individual store managers, who were held accountable for the sales and profits of their stores, did not have to list (that is, stock in the store that he or she managed) any product, including any in the G·R·E·E·N line. If a store manager thought the product was unsuitable for the store, it wasn't listed. As well, if a buyer got a product listed and it didn't sell, his or her reputation with the store managers would suffer.

LIGHT BULB

The proposal by Osram, a well-known German manufacturer, was a true green product. The Osram light bulb was a compact fluorescent bulb that could replace the traditional incandescent light bulb in specific applications. The unique aspect of this product was that while fluorescent light technology was commonplace (these long-tube lights were common in office buildings), only recently had the product been modified for use as a replacement for traditional light bulbs. The major benefits of fluorescent light bulbs were that they used considerably less energy than incandescent light bulbs (for example, a nine watt fluorescent bulb could replace a 40 watt incandescent bulb and still provide the same lighting level, while using only 22.5 percent of the energy) and it lasted at least 10 times longer (an estimated 2,000 hours versus 200 hours for the incandescent bulb). To date, the major application for compact fluorescents had been in apartment buildings in stairwells where lights remained on 24 hours a day. Apartment building owners purchased them because the bulbs lowered both energy costs and maintenance costs (less frequent replacement).

The compact fluorescent had limited applications in the home. Because of its unique shape, it could not be used with a typical lampshade. The main application was likely to be in hallways where it was difficult to replace a burned-out bulb. Even in these situations, a new fixture (that is, an enclosure) might be required so that the compact fluorescent would fit.

The bulb's energy efficiency and long-lasting features were well tested and had been sold for specialized industrial use for several years. The bulb was making satisfactory inroads in Germany even though it was priced at the equivalent of $40 Canadian.

Loblaws sold a variety of 60 and 100 watt No Name and Phillips light bulbs in packages of four. In total, the light bulb category generated over $1 million in gross margin for Loblaws in 1989. (See Exhibit 3.)

The initial Osram proposal was to sell the product to Loblaws at $19.00 per bulb. Even if the mark-up was set at 5 percent, Loblaw's retail price would be $19.99. Scott talked this over with a number of people at Loblaws and concluded that the price was too high to be accepted by Canadian consumers. At this time, Ontario Hydro entered the picture. Ontario Hydro was extremely concerned about its ability to meet the power demands of its

	Average Retail Price* ($)	Average Cost ($)	Annual Sales ($000)	Total Gross Margin ($000)	Market Share (%)
Loblaws					
60 Watt	2.25	1.25	470	209	18
60 Watt Soft	2.75	1.50	426	193	16
100 Watt	2.25	1.25	294	130	11
100 Watt Soft	2.75	1.50	279	127	11
Total Loblaws			1,468	659	56
Phillips					
60 Watt	2.40	1.50	367	138	14
60 Watt Soft	3.20	1.65	341	165	13
100 Watt	2.40	1.50	236	88	9
100 Watt Soft	3.20	1.65	102	102	8
Total Phillips			1,153	493	44
Total			2,621	1,152	100

* Based on four-packs (that is, four light bulbs in a package). Total unit sales were 1,019,000 (four-packs).

Exhibit 3 Light Bulbs (1989)

customers in the next decade and was engaged in aggressive energy conservation programs. Ontario Hydro was prepared to offer a $5 rebate for every light bulb that was sold in Ontario in the three months following the launch. Although it meant customers would need to request the rebate by mail, it reduced the effective price of the bulb to the consumer to $14.99.

Scott felt that the combination of the rebate, a retail price at only half that paid by German consumers, and a strong environmental message had strong merchandising appeal that could be exploited in the launch of the bulb. Nevertheless, the sales potential was still unclear. Loblaws' annual sales in Ontario were nearly four million bulbs, or $2.7 million. Because this product was unique and new, Scott had difficulty estimating its sales potential. His best guess was that Loblaws might sell anywhere from 10,000 to 50,000 Osram bulbs in one year. Scott thought that half the sales would come from regular customers and the other half from customers coming to Loblaws specifically to buy the bulb. Scott also felt that after three months, the price should be raised to $24.99 retail to generate a reasonable margin for Loblaws.

Scott thought that if half the volume were generated at the higher price, it would certainly be easier to maintain the support of the store managers. At the $24.99 price, the margin would be

$5.99 per bulb. Even considering the cannibalization issue, the margin on the higher priced Osram would be about four times higher than the margin for a four-pack of regular bulbs. However, it would be necessary to calculate the contribution for the year to see what the net effect would be for the line. The shelf space required for these bulbs would be minimal and could be handled by some minor changes to the layout of the existing bulbs.

BATHROOM TISSUE

The bathroom tissue category was a highly competitive, price-sensitive market. The category was one of the largest in the Loblaws lineup, generating over $31 million in retail sales in Ontario and $7 million in contribution. (See Exhibit 4.) Bathroom tissue was more important to Loblaws than just a volume generator. It was one of the few product categories that would draw price-conscious buyers into the store. Loblaws listed 40 different sizes and colors from various manufacturers. There were six Loblaws brands in the category. Loblaws was aggressive at delisting any competitive or corporate brand that did not meet turnover or profitability goals. Manufacturers were just as aggressive at providing

	Average Retail Price[1] ($)	Average Cost ($)	Annual Sales ($000)	Total Gross Margin ($000)	Market Share (%)
Loblaws[2]					
President's Choice	2.50	1.95	1,542	339	5
No Name White	1.75	1.15	3,084	1,052	10
No Name Coloured	1.80	1.35	386	96	1
Loblaws Total			5,012	1,487	16
Royale					
White	1.85	1.55	10,795	1,751	34
Coloured	2.00	1.60	3,855	771	12
Royale Total			14,650	2,522	46
Cottonelle					
White	1.85	1.45	4,627	1,000	15
Coloured	1.95	1.50	4,627	1,068	15
Cottonelle Total			9,254	2,068	30
Other Brands					
Capri	1.50	0.90	945	378	3
April Soft	1.40	0.95	721	232	2
Jubilee	1.35	0.70	386	186	1
Dunet	2.45	1.60	405	140	1
White Swan	1.55	1.00	463	164	1
Other Brands Total			2,920	1,100	8
Total			31,836	7,177	100

[1] Statistics for the prices, costs, and sales have been collapsed over the various sizes and reported in equivalent four-roll packs. Total unit sales were 17,125,000 (four-roll packs).

[2] With respect to colors and sizes, Loblaws offered six varieties, Royale (eight varieties), Cottonelle (eight varieties), Capri (four varieties), April Soft (three varieties), Jubilee (two varieties), Dunet (one variety), and White Swan (eight varieties).

Exhibit 4 Bathroom Tissue (1989)

allowance and merchandising incentives to ensure satisfactory margins for Loblaws and to facilitate retail price reductions that in turn would enhance turnover and maintain volume goals. Two national brands—Royale and Cottonelle—held shares of 46 percent and 30 percent, respectively.

For 1989, Loblaws' brands held 16 percent of the market with No Name White providing a total gross margin of over $1 million. Loblaws' No Name White was sourced for an average cost of $1.15 for a 4-roll package. These lower costs were largely based

on the fact that the tissue was manufactured with totally recycled material. This product feature made it a candidate for G·R·E·E·N line consideration. The existing product could simply be repackaged with the distinctive G·R·E·E·N labeling and an emphasis placed on the recycled character of the product. No development or testing costs would be required, and art work and new labeling costs would be minimal.

Several decisions needed to be considered with respect to the repackaging of the No Name product. Should the new product

	Average Retail Price* ($)	Average Cost ($)	Annual Sales ($000)	Total Gross Margin ($000)	Market Share (%)
President's Choice					
Bran with Raisins	2.35	1.50	1,051	380	7.4
Honey Nut Cereal	3.00	1.40	324	173	2.3
Toasted Oats	3.00	1.45	221	114	1.5
Corn Flakes	1.75	1.20	193	60	1.4
Crispy Rice	3.20	1.50	263	139	1.8
Loblaws Total			2,052	866	14.3
Kellogg's					
Corn Flakes	2.30	1.80	1,436	312	10.1
Raisin Bran	2.75	2.00	1,236	324	8.7
Honey Nut Corn Flakes	3.95	2.70	460	141	3.2
Rice Krispies	3.95	2.52	899	315	6.3
Common Sense	4.40	2.70	433	167	3.0
Mini-Wheat	3.30	2.00	326	129	2.3
Variety Pack	5.90	3.90	309	105	2.2
Other Kellogg's	3.41	2.26	258	87	1.8
Kellogg's Total			5,357	1,580	37.5
Nabisco					
Shreddies	2.35	1.70	2,725	754	19.1
Apple/Cinnamon	2.25	1.50	169	57	1.2
Raisin Wheat	3.30	2.10	139	50	1.0
Nabisco Total			3,033	861	21.2
General Mills					
Cheerios	3.80	2.60	1,171	370	8.2
Cheerios/Honey Nut	3.90	2.60	1,017	339	7.1
General Mills Total			2,188	709	15.3
Quaker					
Corn Bran	3.50	2.25	389	139	2.7
Life	3.15	2.10	358	119	2.5
Oat Bran	4.10	2.80	281	89	2.0
Muffets	2.65	1.60	92	36	0.6
Quaker Total			1,120	383	7.8
Others	2.40	1.45	573	227	4.0
Total			14,323	4,626	100.0

* Based on 500-gram size. Total unit sales were 4,950,000 (500-gram size).

Cereals are packaged in several different sizes. Some brands, such as Kellogg's Corn Flakes, could have four different sizes (e.g., 350g, 425g, 675g, 800g) on the shelf at one time. To facilitate comparisons, all figures have been converted to a standard 500g size; where brands had multiple sizes, the figures are reported as averages, weighted by the sales volume of the size.

Exhibit 5 Family Cereals (1989)

replace the old or simply be added to an already crowded category? Should the price of the new product be set higher than that set for the old? Should the product be launched at all?

READY-TO-EAT CEREAL

Loblaws sold more than $14 million worth of family cereals (that is, cereals targeted at the ''family'' market) in Ontario in 1989. (See Exhibit 5.) Loblaws corporate brand share of the family cereal segment, at 14 percent, was lower than corporate objectives for this category. One of Scott Lindsay's goals was to increase Loblaws' share for this category. The brand leaders, such as Kellogg's Corn Flakes, Nabisco Shreddies, and General Mills' Cheerios, were as familiar to shoppers as any other product or brand in a store. With decades of advertising and promotional support, these brands had become thoroughly entrenched in the minds and pantries of generations of Canadians.

The brand names of these market leaders provided the manufacturers with strong protection against competitors. However, the manufacturing process did not. The manufacturing processes were well known in the industry, and many firms could produce identical products at favorable costs. Loblaws had found several products from domestic sources that appeared to be as good if not better than the national brands. One such product was a corn flake product that had a very high fiber content. The new product would appeal to those customers who had been primed by the health claims of high-fiber diets. In sensory tests, it had proven to have an excellent taste and texture profile and was equal to or preferred in blind taste tests to some of the market leaders. Moreover, the product could be obtained for $1.40 per 500g package.

The President's Choice brands were beginning to make inroads in this market, and this new product could increase the share. However, it was not clear how to position the high-fiber corn flake product. Should it go in the regular President's Choice line as a line extension of the current corn flake product, or should it be packaged as a G·R·E·E·N product? As a regular President's Choice product, it would be positioned directly against Kellogg's as an all-around cereal with extra value. As a G·R·E·E·N product, it would be positioned less against Kellogg's and much more towards a health/''good-for-you'' claim. G·R·E·E·N positioning might also minimize any cannibalization of the President's Choice corn flakes. The lower sourcing costs provided some flexibility on pricing. It could be priced as low as $1.75, like the current President's Choice corn flakes, and still maintain good margins; or it could be priced as high as Kellogg's Corn Flakes at $2.30 and generate superior margins.

Having reviewed the three proposals, Scott began the process of preparing his recommendations. ''I'll start with the financial projections,'' thought Scott, ''then consider the pros and cons of each proposal. Then it's decision time.''

CASE 4
CIBC: Introduction

The morning meeting was on her mind as Pat Skene, vice president of the Consumer Credit Division of the CIBC Personal and Commercial Bank, entered her office on June 5, 1995. Pat was not sure if her department had the time, energy, or budget to continue promoting Bankware II. Bankware II was a software diskette that provided users with information on CIBC products and services and allowed users to do financial planning, including calculating mortgage and loan plans. While Bankware had been well received by customers, Pat wondered whether the software contributed to the new strategic direction in which the bank was moving. Hopefully, the meeting would decide once and for all what to do about Bankware.

THE COMPANY

Over the last 125 years, CIBC had grown to become North America's fifth largest bank and the second largest bank in Canada.[1] Consumers were most familiar with CIBC's Personal and Commercial Bank, which provided a full range of financial services to 6 million Canadian customers. Personal banking involved basic transaction services, deposits and investments, consumer loans, residential mortgages, VISA issuing and merchant services, and other related financial services. The CIBC Personal and Commercial Bank provided Canadians with these banking services through its network of 1,428 branches, 2,887 automated banking machines (ABMs), and 40,800 full-time personnel. Services such as CIBC LinkUp, CIBC Contact, and Commcash augmented the delivery network.[2] In fiscal year 1994, CIBC managed

$115,462 million in deposits and $99,938 million worth of loans for individuals, businesses, governments, and banks. In 1994, CIBC had its best year ever, with a net income of $890 million, a 22 percent increase from 1993.[3] (Exhibit 1 provides selected financial information for CIBC.)

In recent years, CIBC had increased its liquidity, improved the quality of its lending portfolio, and refined key business strategies as the bank moved toward its goal of becoming the preeminent Canadian financial services company. CIBC strove to accomplish this initiative by focusing on meeting the needs of its customers, and by building a corporate culture that encouraged employees to maintain this focus. The CIBC 1994 Annual Report contained the following statement by A. L. Flood, Chairman and Chief Executive Officer:

> In the Personal and Commercial Bank, we are working to better align our services and delivery systems with customer preferences. We want to ensure that we can meet our customers' basic banking needs in efficient and accessible ways. At the same time, we will enhance how we deliver, value-added service to customers with more complex financial requirements.

THE INDUSTRY

Collectively, Canada's banks had assets in excess of $777 billion. There were nine domestic chartered banks in Canada and 51 foreign bank subsidiaries in Canada. Canadian chartered banks managed liabilities of $642,126 million, demand deposits of $41,332 million, notice deposits of $141,420 million, and loans worth over $470,464 million. There were 7,971 domestic bank branches across Canada.

The Royal Bank of Canada was the largest financial institution in Canada, with assets of $173,079 million and a net income of $1,169 million for fiscal year 1994, up from $300 million in 1993. The Royal Bank served more than 9.5 million personal and business clients through its 1,600 Canadian branches, 3,900 ABMS, 442 account updaters, and 30,000 point-of-sale merchant terminals. The Royal managed $135,815 million in deposits and $115,386 million worth of loans for Canadian individuals, businesses, governments, and banks.

The second largest financial institution in Canada was CIBC; the Bank of Montreal—with assets of $138,175 million and a 1994 net income of $825 million, up from $709 million in 1993—was a close third. The Bank of Montreal had 34,769 employees, 1,248 branches, and 1,708 ABMs in Canada and managed $98,241 million in deposits and $88,634 million worth of loans.

---

[1] CIBC was the corporate identity for a number of related corporations and operating units. These included the Personal and Commercial Bank, the Investment and Corporate Bank, CIBC Development Corporation, CIBC Finance, CIBC Mortgage, CIBC Trust, CIBC Insurance, CIBC Wood Gundy Securities, and foreign subsidiaries throughout the world.

[2] CIBC Contact provided toll free telephone access to staff able to provide information on CIBC products and services. The telephone lines were open Mon.-Fri. 8a.m.-9p.m. and Sat. 8a.m.-6p.m. (Eastern times). CIBC LinkUp was a service available to customers wishing to use their telephones to transact banking activities. Commcash was a similar service offered to commercial customers.

This case was prepared by Ian McKillop, Gordon McDougall, and Natasha White, School of Business & Economics, Wilfrid Laurier University, Waterloo, Ontario, Canada. The case was written solely for the purpose of stimulating student discussion. The assistance provided by the Consumer Credit division of CIBC is gratefully acknowledged. Certain data have been disguised. All amounts are in Canadian dollars unless indicated otherwise. It is reprinted here by permission. Copyright © 1996 by the *Case Research Journal* and Ian McKillop, Gordon McDougall, and Natasha White.

---

[3] All corporations and operating units.

	1994	1993	1992	1991	1990
Net income	$890	$730	$12	$811	$802
Net income applicable to common shares	749	599	(108)	710	709
Total assets	151,033	141,299	132,212	121,025	114,196
Loans					
Residential mortgages	32,225	30,720	28,927	25,616	24,196
Personal and credit card loans	16,807	14,650	14,318	14,608	14,715
Business and government loans	50,906	51,811	51,682	46,137	44,420
Deposits					
Individuals	59,040	57,265	54,233	50,412	47,534
Businesses and governments	36,313	34,357	26,873	34,095	31,605
Banks	20,209	19,283	15,912	10,964	10,971
Return on Assets, %	0.60	0.53	0.01	9.68	0.74
Return on common equity, %	11.7	10.6	(2.0)	13.9	15.8
Ratio of noninterest expenses to revenue	61.2	61.5	64.6	N/A	N/A
Ratio of net nonperforming loans to loans and acceptances	1.4	2.3	3.0	2.0	0.9
Ratio of credit losses to loans and acceptances	0.8	0.9	1.8	N/A	N/A
Earnings per share	$3.52	$2.99	$(0.59)	$3.93	$4.03
Book value per common share	31.18	28.9	27.44	29.41	26.90

Exhibit 1 CIBC Selected Financial Results 1990–1994 (Dollar Figures, Canadian $, in Millions)

Collectively, Canada's six largest domestic banks, which controlled over 80 percent of all bank assets in Canada, had net income of $4,266 million in 1994, up from $2,903 million in 1993 and $1,844 million in 1992. The increase in net income reflected, in part, the improvement in the Canadian economy, which had experienced a deep recession up to 1992 but had begun a recovery in 1993 which had continued in 1994 and 1995.

CONSUMER BANKING IN THE NINETIES

The delivery of banking services had changed considerably in the past ten years. Automated banking machines and other on-line processing technologies had allowed banks to move work out of branches and into the "back room." This had freed branch staff to concentrate on providing improved customer service and marketing the bank's deposit and credit products.

For many consumers, "convenience" was the watchword of the '90s. Consumers increasingly counted on their banks to provide basic transaction services quickly, cheaply, and accurately. Drive-through banking machines, telephone banking systems (such as CIBC LinkUp), 800 numbers that provided 24-hour access to personal banking representatives, and self-serve passbook updating machines were examples of technologies introduced by banks to offer customers increased levels of convenience and service.

Banks had also recognized that, for some customers, additional levels of personalized service might be more appropriate. These customers often had more complex banking needs and might look to their bank for investment counseling and other

forms of asset management services. These customers were often highly profitable because they made use of a wider range of bank services and thus contributed to the bank's profits through fees and interest earnings to a greater degree than customers who relied on their banks only or primarily for automated services related to individual transactions. One study of bank customers indicated that "transaction-oriented" customers were marginally unprofitable while "personalized service" customers were very profitable. Another study of bank customers revealed that, on average, Canadians dealt with 2.2 banks; 26 percent used one bank, 37 percent used two banks, and 37 percent used three or more banks. Multiple bank users tended to have more complex banking needs. At many banks, customers with complex or extensive banking requirements were assigned a personal banking representative or "account manager." Incentives or premiums were sometimes offered to reward these customers for their loyalty to a specific bank. For example, at one bank, if a customer had at least three products in his or her portfolio that together added up to $50,000 the client automatically received a 1/4 percent discount on a credit product such as a car loan. If the client's bank portfolio exceeded $100,000, the client received an automatic 1/2 percent discount on a loan. Similar premiums were offered for deposit products such as Guaranteed Investment Certificates. There was intensive competition to attract and hold the more profitable customers.

HOW CIBC COMPETED

The CIBC's Personal and Commercial Bank competed on quality, service, and personal relationships with its customers. The bank's corporate philosophy was best illustrated by Holger Kluge, president, Personal and Commercial Bank:

> We're not in the business of selling financial products. We're in the business of helping our customers achieve their financial goals.

Over the past year, the CIBC had completely repositioned itself to respond to the needs of its customers. In the past, the bank had been very focused on products which were sold based on price and product attributes. Now, CIBC's corporate strategy was based on two fundamental concepts. The first was relationship banking: a focus on serving the 'whole client' instead of a focus on selling products. The second component of the strategy was customer segmentation: grouping customers according to similar needs and expectations and then tailoring the way in which services were delivered to meet these needs.

Relationship banking encouraged bankers to move away from a product-focused marketing strategy (e.g., selling car loans, term deposits, mutual funds, etc.) and to concentrate instead on providing an integrated, tailored package of banking services designed to meet the needs of individual clients and households. For example, a client with $20,000 in a checking account (which had low interest rates) might be encouraged to invest in a money market fund (which had higher interest rates). The customer profited from the increased interest earnings, and the bank profited because the funds were now co-mingled with other monies with which the bank could pursue various investment strategies of its own.

CIBC grouped its customers into two broad segments: customers who valued convenience and customers whose banking needs caused them to value personal service. The customers who valued the convenience of "anywhere" banking counted on the bank to provide quick, efficient, economical, and accurate handling of their transaction-oriented activities. The advanced features available through ABMs and CIBC's LinkUp service met many of the banking needs of these customers. Personal banking representatives were available in every branch to assist with transactions that could not be processed through an ABM.[4]

Customers who valued personalized service made up about 10 percent of a typical branch's clientele and about 20 percent of the bank's overall client base.[5] While many of these customers also valued convenience (in that they also wanted their banking activities handled quickly, efficiently, and cost effectively), customers in this category usually had more complex banking requirements. These customers typically purchased a wider range of bank products. In addition, many had Hearings with CIBC partner organizations such as CIBC Trust or CIBC Wood Gundy

Securities, or might be expected to have such needs in the future. To meet the needs of these clients, CICB had created the position of "relationship banker." Relationship bankers were specially trained personal banking representatives with good product knowledge, excellent money-management skills, and a strong people-oriented service focus. They worked closely with clients to provide a comprehensive and personalized package of banking services. A relationship banker in a typical branch might have 200 clients.

CIBC's emphasis on personal relationships was reflected in the bank's advertising. The bank no longer advertised individual products such as car loans. All advertising and promotional materials now reflected the changing needs of the customer and the customer's family. Instead of a car loan brochure that featured an illustration of a new car on the cover, a customer might find a brochure that offered comprehensive guidance to home ownership with a picture of a family on the cover. Inside would be descriptions of CIBC products applicable to home ownership such as mortgages, credit cards, and personal lines of credit.

In a service industry where it was becoming more and more difficult to differentiate through products, CIBC was differentiating itself based on its relationship with the client. CIBC believed that customers were more concerned with how well a financial institution helped them meet their needs and realize their financial aspirations than with what products the bank had for sale.

SYSTEMS SUPPORT

For relationship banking to succeed, bankers required access to a completely integrated, comprehensive customer database that consolidated all of a customer's interactions with the bank into a single client portfolio.

Relationship bankers at CIBC had access to a number of software products developed by the CIBC's Information Technology division to help with this task. These software products could: (1) track the various banking services used by a household, (2) help bankers process credit applications and monitor credit products currently "on the books," and (3) help bankers assess customer profitability. (A banker could see the current contribution to branch operations generated by a particular household, including information on the total value of deposits and loans held by the household.)

In the near future, a new software system currently under development would allow personal banking representatives not only to process deposits and withdrawals, but also to determine the profitability of each client and even identify clients who were good candidates to approach about investment or lending opportunities.

CONSUMER CREDIT

The Consumer Credit Division was one of a number of divisions within the Personal and Commercial Bank.[6] Consumer Credit,

---

[4]Applying for a term loan or arranging for a Guaranteed Investment Certificate were examples of services with which a Personal Banking Representative could offer assistance. Customers who valued convenience were also able to call CIBC Contact to access a Personal Banking Representative, freeing the customer from the need to actually come into a branch.

[5]The segmentation ratios are slightly different between a typical branch and the bank overall because there is a high concentration of customers with extensive banking requirements at main branches in major centres such as Toronto, Montreal and Vancouver.

---

[6]Some of the other divisions included VISA, Retail Deposits, Mortgages, Private Banking, Investments, Marketing, Commercial Banking, Collections, and Delivery Network.

Personal Loans

There are two types of personal loans: demand loans and term loans. Demand loans must be repaid immediately upon request by the bank. Term loans must be repaid in full by an agreed upon date, although the loan can be paid out at any time without penalty. Term loans typically run less than 72 months, but can go as long as 300 months in special circumstances.

Term loans require the borrower to make regular (usually monthly) payments during the period of the loan. The payments are designed to "pay out" the loan in full during the period of the loan. Payments consist of both an interest and a principal portion. The amount of the payment is determined using annuity formulas for daily compounding interest.

Demand loans are similar to term loans except that in return for the customer agreeing to repay the bank immediately upon its request, the customer is charged an interest rate less than that charged for a similar term loan. In order to ensure that the customer has the ability to honour a possible "demand" for payment, customers seeking demand loans must usually have liquid assets equal to the amount of the loan.

Typical uses for personal loans are to purchase a car, consolidate debt, or finance minor home renovations. Once a personal loan is paid off, the customer needs to initiate a new application should financing be required for another purpose.

Personal Lines of Credit (PLCs)

A line of credit allows customers to establish a set lending limit against which they can borrow by simply writing a cheque on a special "line of credit account." Writing a cheque has the effect of establishing a loan on the date the cheque is processed by the bank. Interest charges begin on that day, and interest rates are similar to those offered on term loans. Once the loan is paid off, however, the credit line continues to be available for use by the client without a subsequent application to the bank.

Many customers choose to "secure" their line of credit by offering their house or other forms of equity as collateral. In return for the reduced risk that this form of credit line presents to the bank, the bank usually offers a discount on the interest rate charged.

Overdraft Protection

Overdraft protection provides customers with the knowledge that should they inadvertently write cheques for which there are insufficient funds in their accounts, the bank will honour the cheques up to the amount of the pre-established overdraft protection limit. Overdraft limits could be anywhere from $100 to $5,000 depending on the customer's needs and credit worthiness.

The customer is not charged for overdraft protection until the overdraft position is required. Interest charges are then hefty, often 21 percent.

Exhibit 2 Main Credit Products Managed by the Consumer Credit Division

located in Toronto, had a staff of 120 employees and six regional consumer loan departments across Canada. Vice President Pat Skene managed a $10 billion portfolio of consumer credit products and was responsible for the marketing, operations, credit policy, and head office administration for all of Consumer Credit's products and services which were sold by CIBC branches across Canada.

Products Sold by the Consumer Credit Division

Overall, CIBC marketed 106 different products, which included various types of deposit accounts, investment instruments, RSPs, VISA cards, loans, and mortgages. The average client made use of three of the 106 products sold by the bank.

The Consumer Credit Division was currently responsible for managing all retail loans, which included three of the bank's main product lines: personal loans, personal lines of credit (PLCs), and overdraft protection. (Exhibit 2 provides an overview of these product lines.)

Deposit instruments (including money lying dormant in transaction accounts) were the bank's most profitable product line, followed closely by mortgages.[7] Credit products (such as those managed by Consumer Credit) came in third. In recent years, there had been an increase in personal lines of credit, while the number

---

[7]While deposit instruments in general were very profitable, customers who maintained chequing and savings accounts with balances of less than $100 were generally unprofitable. Customers with very small chequing or savings account balances could represent up to 20 percent of a typical branch's clientele.

and dollars of personal loans issued had been decreasing. Banks (and their customers) were turning more and more to PLCs alternative to the personal loan. PLCs required less paperwork than personal loans, and were generally less intimidating for the customer. (Consider that with a PLC, customers only had to apply for credit once. Thereafter, they were free to use the credit as they chose without having to explain their purchase wishes to a banker.) CIBC had more than 17 percent of the Canadian market in PLCs and 22.5 percent of the market in personal loans.

About one quarter of households in a typical branch purchased a PLC product, while 13 percent of households in a typical branch had overdraft protection. About 11 percent of PLC users chose to secure their PLC in order to take advantage of lower interest rates. A typical PLC customer had a credit line of $20,000 with an outstanding balance of $15,000.

Pricing and Costs Associated with Personal Loan Products

Credit products were priced in relation to the bank's cost of funds—the rate that the bank paid to purchase the money it wanted to lend. The difference between the bank's cost of funds and the interest rate charged to a customer determined the revenue stream the bank would receive from the sale of the credit product.

Branches had total price discretion on loans. Personal banking representatives examined the profit in relation to the customer's financial strength and the total relationship with the client when making pricing decisions on credit products. Personal banking representatives might even grant a customer a loan at a rate slightly over the bank's cost of funds if they felt that the overall relationship warranted such a step.

Years 1990–1994 in Consumer Credit

In 1991, the Consumer Credit division was suffering from the effects that the recession was having on CIBC's client base. A strong focus on marketing CIBC credit products, combined with a lack of sophisticated risk management and assessment tools accessible to branch staff, compounded the problem. Although Consumer Credit had a large number of loans under administration (which under normal circumstances would have been very profitable), arrears, delinquent loans, and loan writeoffs were having a significant impact on profitability (Exhibit 1).

Pat Skene and the Senior Vice President, Brian Cassidy, both joined the division in 1991 and assumed responsibility for turning things around. Credit policies needed to be revised and better risk management tools needed to be developed. In the short term, credit-granting procedures were tightened and branch staffs were encouraged to avoid extending loans of marginal quality.

Resources were dedicated within Consumer Credit to enhancing existing credit scoring systems and implementing new on-line credit administration systems. Significant enhancements to software were made during this period to assist in new application assessments and portfolio management. Organizational improvements were also made. For example, a ''line of business'' approach to management was introduced. Bottom-line responsibility was given to cross-functional teams responsible for specific product lines (like PLCS.) This was in contrast to the previous organizational structure built around three functional areas: marketing, operations, and credit management. A special risk management unit was added to oversee the new Consumer Credit teams who now had a bottom-line responsibility for their product line.

At the same time, however, loan products were assuming a less significant role in the activities of CIBC branches. With stringent controls placed on the granting of credit, many bankers had moved on to marketing other products (such as deposit instruments, RSPs, etc.). It was hard to find a banker who considered himself or herself to be a lender during this period. It had been said that even a creditworthy customer had to ''come out and ask, and then insist'' to get branch staff to sit down and consider selling a credit product.

THE NEW CAMPAIGN

By late 1992, Consumer Credit was ready to begin the process of attracting new, quality loans. A significant challenge lay ahead. Branch staff, who were once empowered to make credit decisions had that authority reduced during the restructuring process. Now the Consumer Credit wanted to convince branch staff that the appropriate systems, policies, and controls were in place to actively meet customers' credit needs. Three things were needed: to disseminate the new approach throughout the organization, to explain the new software, and to find ways to differentiate CIBC products from the competition.

The first step was to communicate to branch staff (Personal Banking Representatives, Managers, etc.) what had happened and to share with lending staff that CIBC wanted to write new personal loans. To accomplish this, two senior executives from the Consumer Credit group (Brian Cassidy and Pat Skene) set out in November 1992 to travel across Canada meeting with front-line bankers in every district. Their message was clear: ''We are changing the loan experience.'' A second step was to share with branch staff how the new enhancements to the software system would help them better serve their customers. Training and education seminars on the new credit scoring system were held across the country.

The last step was to find ways to differentiate CIBC loan products from competitors' products. This was important because loans were a commodity. Unless CIBC loan products had value-added features that somehow distinguished them from those of the competition, CIBC bankers would have difficulty attracting customers away from the other sources of credit that they had discovered during the previous year and a half.

The Consumer Credit team met in 1992 to brainstorm ideas that would add value to the personal credit products, and that would help differentiate CIBC loans from those offered by other banks. Many innovative ideas emerged from these sessions. Six of these ideas were implemented as a part of a campaign targeted at branch staff called "We're Changing the Loan Experience." The six main elements of this campaign were as follows.

1. *Roadside assistance.* Lenders were able to offer one year of roadside automobile assistance (at no cost) to customers taking out a new loan. This was a great selling feature for car loans, although Roadside Assistance could be offered as a premium with a loan taken out for any purpose.

2. *Discount coupon for loans.* Bankers were provided with a promotional tool designed to thank customers and reward them for their business. After making the last payment on a loan, customers would receive a thank-you note from a personal banking representative. A coupon for a $1/2$ percent discount on the customer's next loan with CIBC was included with the note. There was also a place for the banker to include two copies of his or her card. One card could be kept by the customer, and the customer was encouraged to pass the second card along to a friend.

   This promotional item was well received by both lenders and customers. Bankers liked how they could formally thank customers for their business with a small token of their appreciation (the discount coupon) and, in the process, possibly attract new business in the future. Customers liked the fact that the bank had rewarded them for their business with a coupon that could save them hundreds of dollars on their next loan.

3. *Bankware.* A software diskette was developed containing information about products and services offered by the bank. The diskette also included credit planning tools such as a mortgage payment calculator and a budgeting template. Customers could even use the diskette to learn how much credit their income and current lifestyle could support.

4. *An informational booklet.* A well-written, informative booklet, "Credit Smart," was developed that answered questions people commonly ask about credit and how credit is granted. Much of the contents of the booklet could also be found in the Bankware software. However, unlike the software, the booklet did not have automated scenario calculation capabilities.

5. *Free VISA Classic card for a year or Free CIBC LinkUp for a year.* For customers applying for a CIBC consumer credit product, bankers could provide vouchers waiving the normal fee for a CIBC Classic VISA card for a year, or they could provide one year's free CIBC LinkUp service.

6. *The "valued customer" portfolio.* A burgundy slipcase with a gold elastic binding was introduced that branch staff could provide to customers when a loan was approved. The slipcase contained slots to store loan documents, informational brochures, a copy of the Bankware disk, and the banker's business card. While this seemed like a value-added idea, branch staff never warmed to the concept. Thousands of the burgundy slipcases languished in the Toronto warehouse.

In March 1993, an additional promotion was introduced called Last Payment on Us. The Last Payment on Us program offered customers the opportunity to have the bank make the final payment on their personal loan (up to $500), provided that the loan was kept up to date with regular payments during its amortization period. This program was enthusiastically received by branch staff, and customers appeared to respond positively.

Bankware I and Bankware II

While the idea for Bankware came out of the brainstorming sessions at Consumer Credit, the seed for the idea had been planted in Brian Cassidy's mind when he saw a similar, but simpler, product from Wells Fargo, a large U.S. bank, at a U.S. trade show. The Wells Fargo diskette had been developed by Interactive Media from San Francisco. CIBC contacted Interactive Media to see if they could produce an enhanced diskette for the Canadian market. The resulting software, Bankware, allowed users to explore features of CIBC loan, mortgage, and other credit products. Consumer Credit paid for the software development and distribution costs from its own operating budget. Total cost for Bankware was U.S. $250,000.

Bankware was introduced to the Canadian public in early 1993. Using Bankware, customers could calculate a budget, determine their net worth, apply for a mortgage or loan, and learn how to save on interest costs. The software was distributed to branch managers who, in turn, gave copies to interested customers. A full-page advertisement was run in *Globe & Mail*, Canada's national newspaper, encouraging people to mail in a coupon in response to which the bank would send out a copy of Bankware. Over 144,000 copies of the software were produced and distributed. Customers (and potential customers) could now explore the various options open to them before entering a branch to apply for a loan, mortgage, or line of credit.

As Brian Cassidy observed:

> Bankware was a great idea. As an advertising and promotional tool, consider its staying power. You give away a brochure and it gets thrown out. You give away a diskette and it gets copied.

Bankware was well received, but many people, including customers, had ideas for additional features that should be incorporated into the software. The Consumer Credit division decided to commit resources to develop an improved version, Bankware II.

While Bankware concentrated on services and products offered primarily by the Consumer Credit group, Bankware II showcased the much wider range of products and services available from CIBC. Features of deposit accounts, investments, VISA, mutual funds, mortgages, and loans were all to be added to the software to present a comprehensive overview of products offered by CIBC. A section targeted at introducing children to the world of banking was planned. The new version was to have a strong customer focus.

Other divisions of the bank (such as VISA, CIBC Wood Gundy, etc.) were invited to participate in the development of Bankware II. Although coordinated by Consumer Credit, the division looked forward to being able to include promotional materials submitted by the other divisions. However, most divisions chose to have Consumer Credit staff prepare the marketing material to describe their products. As Consumer Credit prepared materials, they were sent to the other divisions for their review and approval. Despite the fact that Bankware II would promote products from many other divisions and entities within CIBC, the full cost of the software's development was sponsored by Consumer Credit.

Consumer Credit had initially planned to contract out Bankware II's development (as had been done with Bankware), but soon found it necessary to produce the script for the disk themselves, and then work with an outside programmer to complete the disk. Working as a team, Consumer Credit's product staff created the diskette's content, while Consumer Credit's marketing staff handled packaging and distribution. From start to finish, Bankware II cost $250,000 to produce. The direct production costs were as follows:

Software development	$100,000.00
Disk duplication (including virus scanning)	88,000.00
Jacket printing	19,000.00
Assembly (insert disk into jacket, collate, wrap)	23,000.00
French translation	20,000.00

The indirect costs were 462 person days of effort from Consumer Credit staff time committed to meetings, product brainstorming, developing scripts, testing, etc.

Bankware II was launched in September 1994. Among other features, the new version offered users the ability to print personalized mortgage amortization tables and to compare cash back car offers with discounted loan interest rate offers. There was even a section designed so that children could explore the services offered by a major bank. Bankware II allowed customers to learn, explore, compute, make decisions, and print out information on virtually any of CIBC's products and services. A total of 150,000 English and 25,000 French copies of Bankware II were produced.

Competition for Bankware II was minor. The Toronto Dominion Bank and the Bank of Montreal had information diskettes, and the Royal Bank had a small business diskette. As far as anyone knew, no other bank had a promotional product similar to Bankware II.

Two focus groups were held to gain insight into customer perceptions of the original Bankware. Results from the focus groups suggested that customers might be undervaluing the true value of Bankware because it was being given to them for free. The groups suggested that the bank charge a $15 fee for the disk in order to increase the perceived value of Bankware II to the customer. Bank officials disagreed. They thought that Bankware II was a promotional tool to help the customer and should not be seen as a way to generate revenue.

Branch managers had been given 100 free copies of the first version of Bankware, after which they were able to obtain additional copies from Head Office for $0.50 each. This charge was debited to the branch's marketing budget, just as the branch paid for posters and other promotional items such as certain brochures and CIBC crested pens. Branches were encouraged to load Bankware on their personal computers so that staff could familiarize themselves with the product and be able to demonstrate it to clients. No free copies

of Bankware II were given to branches. Given the penetration of the first version of Bankware, it was thought that branch staff would know the product well enough to order copies of Bankware II from Head Office with their regular promotional items order. Over 85,000 copies of Bankware II were ordered by branches, but it became clear by early 1995 that branches were shying away from ordering Bankware II. Head Office then removed the nominal fee ($0.50), and almost overnight the branches requested another 41,650 copies. Clearly, there was a pent-up demand for the diskette. It was estimated that 80 percent of the Bankware II diskettes distributed to branches were passed along to customers. As with the first version of Bankware, many of these diskettes were copied by customers and passed along to friends.

Bankware II was available free of charge to CIBC customers. Unfortunately, many of the bank's customers were unaware that the product existed. Branch managers often kept copies of Bankware II in their desk drawer and only distributed the diskette to customers upon request. This might have been a hold-over from the days of the We're Changing the Loan Experience campaign when the diskette was considered to be a premium to be offered to customers to thank them for their business. Other than at one Toronto branch, the diskettes had never been left out on a table for customers to pick up as they passed by. The reason for this given by one banker was, "If you were to leave huge piles of diskettes on a table some people might scoop up a whole bunch to take home and reformat as blank floppies!"

Many bank managers and personal banking representatives were enthusiastic about Bankware II. One Montreal bank manager raved:

> Bankware II is one of the best promotional tools the bank has developed.... It helps the customers help themselves. Customers can see what they qualify for and become a better educated consumer by exploring the various options available to them. This knowledge reduces the customer's feelings that the bank works in mysterious and unpredictable ways. Designing a loan to meet the needs of a customer is hard. Bankware II makes it easier for me to serve my customers because the customer is already aware of his or her options.

An Edmonton branch manager agreed:

> Bankware II is great! A good customer is an informed customer, and Bankware II helps to show customers what their best options are. For ourselves, Bankware II not only provides control, but has the potential to lower the cost of dealing with a transaction in the future. Right now all inquiries generated in response to fax-back screens in Bankware II[8] go through CIBC Contact, but in the future I could see the customer bringing me

---

[8]One of the features added to Bankware II was the ability for customers to automatically fax their completed loan applications to CIBC Contact. Customers whose computers did not have built-in fax capabilities could print a copy of their loan application and either mail it to CIBC Contact or take it into a local branch. Bankware II did not include the ability to directly connect via modem with CIBC's information system.

an electronic file all ready for processing. This would reduce paperwork and data capture time at my end, freeing me up to spend more time with the customer on other financial planning issues.

At other branches, few disks were distributed. One problem was that CIBC's Information System Division had changed the operating system at the branches from DOS to OS/2 just before the release of Bankware II. For integrity and security reasons, only software developed or supported by the Information System Division was loaded on the network servers. This meant that Bankware II could not be loaded at the branch level and customers could not be shown how to use it at the branches.

Within the Consumer Credit division, the staff felt that the need for Bankware was apparent. In the opinion of one Consumer Credit employee:

> Sometimes bankers don't realize that some customers feel incredibly intimidated when seeking a loan. Approval of a loan is an everyday occurrence from the bank's perspective while it is a rare occurrence for the customer. Furthermore, bankers often feel that customers are aware of the various financial options while customers themselves feel that they have no other options. The bank's offer is often seen as a "take it or leave it" situation. With Bankware II, the borrowing transaction is not such an ordeal for the typical customer.

Pat Skene had her own interest in promoting Bankware II. She knew first-hand the tremendous job that her staff had done in developing and putting Bankware II together. She was, moreover, a true believer in Bankware II's advantages:

> Customers really need Bankware II. If the bank wants to build strong, binding relationships with customers, it must look to customer needs. Bankware II helps the bank address these needs, allowing customers to make informed decisions about their finances.

To: All CC Staff Involved in the Development of
             Bankware or Bankware II
When: June 5, 1995, 10:00 a.m.
Location: 1st floor conference room—CC operations
             Centre. Coffee available.

Agenda:

- Welcome and Introduction
- Review of Bankware Project
- Future Plans

Bring your thinking cap and your coffee mug!

Telephone regrets to Michelle at ext. 8501.

Exhibit 3 Notice of June 5, 1995, Board Meeting

THE TEAM MEETING

The managers and staff from all of Pat Skene's Consumer Credit departments were chatting about Bankware II around the boardroom table as Pat arrived. The agenda for the team meeting had been set for weeks. (See Exhibit 3.) In attendance were:

Pat Skene	Vice President, Consumer Credit
Rita Ripenburg	General Manager, Retail Lending
Catherine Gardner	Senior Manager, Personal Loan Portfolio
Warren Wood	Product Manager
Rosemary Naltchadjian	Product Manager
Michelle Thomas	Secretary to Pat Skene
Denise Fawcitt	Manager, Marketing (Consumer Credit)
Ming Wong	Systems Manager (Consumer Credit)
Sherwin Lui	Manager, Office Systems

and seven representatives from the operations and the risk management groups.

Pat opened the meeting, "I would like to begin by thanking everyone for the countless hours that you have all put into the development of Bankware II. I am extremely proud of the Consumer Credit department and all of the innovative work that each of you has put into Bankware II."

Pat: When we started working on Bankware II we thought branch staff would love the product and could not help but get excited about all the capabilities Bankware II gives our customers. But since the launch of Bankware II, the product hasn't taken off as we had anticipated. Warren tells me that we still have 48,350 copies in inventory (Exhibit 4), and this is after we told the branches that they could have copies for free. We need to make some tough decisions.

Consumer Credit launched Bankware back in '93 as a part of our initiative to regain a dominant position in the personal credit marketplace. We have accomplished this. In fact, as you know, we have just finished our best year ever. Bankware was a part of that turnaround. Now we have to decide where we want to go in the future.

Depending on what happens next with Bankware II's development, some people have suggested that the software has the potential to change the way the bank operates and interacts with its customers. Maybe we could begin with some general discussion.

Denise: As Pat has said, our We're Changing the Loan Experience campaign combined with the Last Payment on Us campaign was extremely successful. We have increased our portfolio by over $2 billion since the start of these programs. Some of you have been asking about how much the premiums cost that we used during these campaigns. I've put together some numbers and you will find them attached to your agenda (Exhibit 5). Don't forget that for many branches, the budget out of which they pay for these promotional items might only be $2,500. If a manager has to choose between hosting an investment seminar at a local hotel for $500

Campaign Items Central Stores Inventory Report 3420-B-332
Inventory Status of Campaign Promotional Materials
Campaign 34F-CC: We're Changing the Loan Experience
Report Created: June 1, 1995
Run By: JSM
Forward To: Denise Fawcitt, Consumer Credit

Item Code	Description	Instock	Backordered
CC3453-1	THANKYOU BROCHURE—ENGLISH	12,000	
CC3453-2	THANKYOU BROCHURE—FRENCH	3,000	
CC3488-3	$1/2$ OFF COUPON—BILINGUAL	15,330	
CC3493-1	CREDIT WISE BOOKLET—ENGLISH	0	0
CC3493-2	CREDIT WISE BOOKLET—FRENCH	130	
CC3498-3	VISA CLASSIC FREE YEAR	217,320	
CC3499-3	LINKUP FREE YEAR	257,870	
CC3520-3	VALUED CUSTOMER PORTFOLIO	60,000	
CC3532-1	BANKWARE $3^1/2$ ENGLISH	560	
CC3532-2	BANKWARE $3^1/2$ FRENCH	430	
CC3576-1	BANKWARE II $3^1/2$ ENGLISH	33,650	
CC3576-2	BANKWARE II $3^1/2$ FRENCH	14,700	

Exhibit 4 Inventory Status of "We're Changing the Loan Experience"

Memo from the Desk of Denise Fawcitt, Manager, Marketing

Consumer Credit—Operations Centre, North York

May 31, 1995

Details on premiums used for the We're Changing the Loan Experience campaign.

Roadside Assistance
Cost is $25.00 per membership. Consumer Credit buys the memberships as needed. (Branch isn't charged.) No figures are available on how many Roadside Assistance memberships have been purchased for customers.

$1/2$% Off Coupons + Thank You Brochure
Coupon + Thank You brochure costs $0.35 per set to print. 210,000 units have been ordered by branches. No data is available on how many coupons have been used. (We can't spot this because Personal Banking Reps simply adjust the interest rate in CLASS to account for the coupon.) We provide these items to branches free of charge.

Credit Wise Booklet
The booklet costs about $0.95 to print. Branches are charged $0.75 each. We printed 250,000.

VISA Classic Card
Coupon has a value of $12.00 (1 year's VISA Classic fee). The coupon itself costs us hardly anything to print. Branches aren't charged for the coupons or for the cost of the foregone VISA fee revenue.

Free LinkUp Service
Situation is similar to that for the VISA Classic card coupons. CISC LinkUp is worth $2.25 per month, and the coupon is good for one year's service.

The Valued Customer Portfolio
Cost to us was $5.50 each. We charged branches $5.00 each. 100,000 were printed.

Bankware
Warren previously provided you with information on Bankware's development costs.

Exhibit 5 Cost Premiums for We're Changing the Loan Experience Campaign

and buying 100 Valued Customer Portfolios or 1,000 Bankware disks, she might be inclined to host the seminar. The "payback" is probably faster in that she'll make some RSP sales for sure after the seminar. The irony is that while it may take longer in coming, the return to the bank will be much larger from a customer who uses Bankware II to choose one of our mortgage or loan products.

(Papers rustled as team members flipped through the agenda looking for Denise's memo. Someone asked about how many loans were a part of the Last Payment on Us campaign.)

Warren: It is hard to know how many people will be taking us up on our Last Payment on Us campaign, as the loans involved in this campaign are just beginning to reach their term. First impressions, based on the amount of voice mail I'm receiving from branches asking how to process the final "free" payment, suggest that the campaign was very successful. I think the neat thing about this campaign is how it attracted the very customers we wanted ... people who keep their loans up to date, pay them out on time, and never get into arrears.

Rosemary: And I'm sure that astute Personal Banking Reps are making sure that every one of these customers gets a "1/2% off" coupon along with a thank you note at the end of their loan. These are just the customers that a branch will want to hang onto.

Rita: Wouldn't it be interesting to know how much loan business we attracted because of Bankware II? Remember how in Bankware II we have that great feature where customers could compare a CIBC loan with a loan offered by a car dealership at a seemingly unbelievable interest rate? By the time you factored in the "cash back" option, which you usually had to give up to get the "unbelievable" rate, our loan almost always came out as the cheaper one. Imagine the edge we'd have if we updated Bankware II to show the additional effect on the total loan cost of having the bank make the final payment!

Warren: Rita has a good point, but the Last Payment on Us promotion is no longer offered to customers. But what Rita has pointed out is that the static nature of Bankware II doesn't allow it to reflect the new innovations and campaigns we develop both here in Consumer Credit and elsewhere in the bank.

(Pat drew everyone's attention to the memo [Exhibit 6] she had received from the Strategy Planning Group in the Marketing Division regarding the promotion and distribution of Bankware II.)

Pat: I think this memo is along the lines of Warren's comment. It basically says that Bankware II is now "off strategy" because the diskette's strong product focus is not in keeping with the bank's current strategic thrust of enhancing relationships with our clients.

Denise: But Bankware II is much more than a product-focused advertisement. It's an educational tool that provides consumers with the very information they need so that we can form an informed and mutually beneficial relationship with each customer.

(A number of silent nods signaled unanimous agreement. She continued.)

Denise: In fact, I think Bankware's strength lies in its ability to better inform clients about our services. The software allows customers to interact with the bank in a manner that is convenient, quick and technologically advanced. Heck ... that is part of the bank's strategy! I think that our next version of Bankware, and I want to go on record as thinking there should be such a product, should be designed to do just that ... make banking even easier for the customer who values convenience.

Pat: What do the rest of you feel that it will take to make Bankware a success in the future?

Rita: I think we need to focus on four dimensions of competition in the '90s. Where does Bankware fit in terms of price, cost, quality and timeliness?

Warren: I think that we need to put more effort into the technological development of the product before we can look into promoting Bankware III effectively. Although released in 1994, Bankware II's interface is already becoming dated. We should also look into making the product available on CD-ROM. Bankware III should have a full featured graphical user interface, and we need to upgrade Bankware to work with the bank's PC system.

Did you know that while bankers were able to explore the features of the first version of Bankware, many bankers have never

---

To: Pat Skene, VP Consumer Credit
From: Marketing-Strategy Planning Group
Re: Bankware

Date: April 28, 1995

As you are aware, the bank recently launched a major repositioning of itself in the marketplace. The cornerstones of our new strategy are relationship banking and customer segmentation. We want to provide the right services at the right place at the right time, tailored to the needs of each customer.

While we think that Bankware is an innovative product, we are not sure that it fits well with the bank's current strategy. The diskette is completely product focused. While we think that CIBC products are very well presented in Bankware II, the diskette is not a good fit with our current relationship-focused strategy.

We would like to suggest that you hold off further development of Bankware until we have a chance to meet to discuss this issue.

Exhibit 6 Interoffice Memorandum to Pat Skene from Marketing Strategy Planning Group

seen how Bankware II works because they can't load a copy on the network. It is impossible for Personal Banking Representatives to show customers how to use Bankware II.

Ming: The Information Systems division is concerned about maintaining the integrity of our cross-Canada network. I've heard suggestions that we should allow customers to have direct access to the network. Wow. Then we'd really have to make sure that we have the right security in place.

Sherwin: I agree, and yet this seems to be the way of the future. Everyone talks about the information superhighway. Did you see the full-colour advertising supplement the Royal Bank ran in the *Globe & Mail* few months ago? RBC even has their own "home page" on the World Wide Web.

Rita: That's true, but they don't have a product like Bankware II to give to customers. Right now, we are at the leading edge of technology with respect to how banking will be done in the next century. We cannot afford to let go of this opportunity. I think we need to decide when to expand and where to expand. I think we should develop Bankware III and distribute it in an all-out nationwide campaign. What does everyone else think?

Rosemary: What's our goal here? Are we trying to attract new customers to the bank, or to sell additional products to the customers we already have. My friends in Delivery Network tell me that it is expensive to attract business from other banks, particularly profitable business. We end up giving so many interest rate concessions that it's hard to make a profit. Why not focus Bankware so that it helps cement relationships with existing clients?

Catherine: Look, Bankware is a great product, and along with the other initiatives that we put in place as a part of the We're Changing the Loan Experience program, it helped contribute to our success in attracting new loan business. But let's not forget that Bankware II was expensive to produce, and took a huge amount of personal commitment on the part of everyone around this table.

We've got lots of people who love Bankware. People also love our "1/2% off" coupons and the free Roadside Assistance program. How do we know where we're getting the best bang for the buck? I bet we've spent thousands buying Roadside Assistance memberships for customers.

Warren: I think what we really need to do is to get the other divisions as excited about Bankware as we are. Think of what Bankware could do to promote an understanding of CIBC Insurance products, or of brokerage services available through Wood Gundy. If Bankware III is going to succeed, it can't be as a Consumer Credit initiative, it's got to be as a CIBC initiative.

(A voice piped up from the back of the room.)

Voice: Great idea. But we're a huge corporation. That's like asking Prince Edward Island lobster boat owners on the East Coast to help plan salmon quotas on the West Coast. They might be interested. They might have lots of experience. But, bottom line—they've got too much to take care of in their own backyard to be able to spare the time.

(Warren tried to see who was talking, but couldn't.)

Rita: Let's get back to what Catherine was talking about. While some of the other premiums are expensive, the per unit cost of Bankware is peanuts in the big scheme of things. We are a multibillion dollar bank. What I think is important to recognize is that if the soft-

ware is not able to do everything a customer would like it to, then Bankware is useless in promoting CIBC's products and services.

For example, Bankware III should have the ability to do more financial planning. We could use the software to show people the value of contributing regularly to their retirement savings plan. The planner should show the impact of various interest rate scenarios. Instead of showing how much your money will grow to at, say 10 percent, show comparative columns with a low, medium, and high rate of return.

I disagree with Denise on who the target audience for Bankware III should be. If we develop Bankware III, it should be aimed at customers who are profitable to the bank and who have more comprehensive banking needs than those clients who look to us to help with their transaction-oriented requirements.

Rosemary: Remember that the focus groups told us that customers would perceive Bankware to be a more valuable tool if they had to pay for it. Some customers might be willing to pay $15.00 for a financial planning tool, but would everyone? What we really need to decide today is who should receive I Bankware. I think every customer should be given a copy of Bankware free of charge.

Ming: It would be very expensive for the branches to give every customer a copy. The average branch has about 2000 customers. Bankware III would cost much more than Bankware II if this is our strategy.

(Pat decided she should focus the discussion.)

Pat: We've had a lot of discussion about how we can improve Bankware, but we haven't really talked about whether we should improve Bankware.

Rita: Marketing has correctly identified that the diskette is product focused. How appropriate is this given that we are encouraging our branch staff to move away from a product focus toward a more integrated client service approach?

Catherine: Let's also not lose track of the fact that while the branches are adopting a more integrated, total customer focus, the organization back here at Head Office is still functionally oriented. We have done a great job reorganizing ourselves so that we have product teams with bottom-line responsibility, but in the end, we are still product focused. If a branch offers RSP loans at prime to encourage investing in CIBC Mutual Funds, the mutual fund division watches their profits soar, while we end up booking a bunch of loans with no profit, and therefore no contribution to our division.

Denise: What really matters is that the personal banking rep made a good decision from the bank's standpoint. That's because once the loan is paid off, profits will continue to be made from the RSP investments. This is why I think that it is so important that all the other players be invited to sit at this table and decide what to do with Bankware.

Pat: Let's think "big picture" for a moment. We had a real problem in 1992. Through the efforts of everyone here, together with our retail delivery network, we accomplished a remarkable turnaround. Maybe Bankware helped with the turnaround. Maybe it didn't. Bottom line ... we did change the loan experience.

The bank's profits are higher than they've ever been. The loan portfolio is growing every day. We are the number two bank in Canada. I guess my question is, where do we go now? What do we do next? I've heard the following points this morning.

1. We could either develop Bankware III or devote resources elsewhere.
2. If we think it's worthwhile to develop Bankware III, should Bankware III be ... aimed at providing financial planning tools for customers who count on CIBC to provide support and guidance in managing their financial affairs, or designed to make it even easier for convenience-oriented customers to interact with the bank? The features needed in Bankware III would be very different under each option.
3. If we choose to devote resources elsewhere, what are examples of value-added initiatives that we could undertake instead of Bankware III to help promote and support the sale of Consumer Credit products?
4. What role can we play in the development of a relationship-focused approach to banking given that we are product focused?

Warren, I wonder if you and three or four people could get together to examine and report back on these issues? There might be some other points that also deserve attention. If everyone is free on Friday morning, why don't we meet back here to review what Warren and the smaller group has come up with.

CASE 5
NACSW's Growth Endeavors

I n the spring of 2002, Rick Chamiec-Case, executive director of NACSW, was growing increasingly concerned about the prospects for the future growth of this professional social work membership association. In spite of the past five years, the past couple of years had seen NACSW's membership retention rate slip to just 55–60% per year. This meant that although NACSW was continuing to bring in a large number of new members, about 40–45% of its members were dropping their memberships each year. Rick realized that in order to sustain and continue to build on the growth it had achieved during the past five years, NACSW would have to significantly increase this membership retention rate.

History of NACSW

NACSW (the North American Association of Christians in Social Work) is an interdenominational and international professional social work association that grew out of a series of annual conferences beginning in 1950. In 1954, NACSW was incorporated in the state of Illinois. Its purpose was to supports its members' efforts to tap the resources of their faith and faith communities to become more effective social workers.

Leadership of LACSW was vested in a Board of Directors composed of at least twelve NACSW members elected by the membership for three-year terms. The Board employed an executive director, who carried out the operations of the organization.

NACSW was incorporated in the state of Illinois and registered as a foreign corporation in the state of Connecticut. It was exempt from federal income tax under the provisions of Section 501C(3) of the Internal Revenue Service Code.

NACSW's mission, adopted in 1998, was "to support the integration of Christian faith and professional social work practice in the lives of its members, the profession and the church, promoting love and justice in social service and social reform." Its goals include:

- Supporting and encouraging members in the integration of Christian faith and professional practice through fellowship, education, and service opportunities
- Articulating an informed Christian voice on social welfare practice and policies to the social work profession
- Providing professional understanding and help for the social ministry of the church
- Promoting social welfare services and policies in society which bring about greater justice and meet basic human needs

It strived to meet these goals by providing a range of member services such as providing:

- Networking Opportunities (chapter/small group meetings, listserves, chatroom sessions, member interest groups, mentoring program, etc.)
- Publications and Materials (books, videos, bimonthly newsletter, professional journal, book reviews, etc.)
- Conventions & Training Events (in person, via the Internet, via telephone, etc.)
- Job Information Services
- Professional Liability Insurance

During late 1980's and early 1990's, NACSW was in the midst of a major organizational crisis. Although it had existed since 1954, by the mid-1990s NACSW had spent down most of its fund balance, and its membership base had eroded significantly. There was a legitimate concern that unless these trends could be reserved, NACSW would have to "close its doors."

In 1997, NACSW closed its office in Pennsylvania, and moved to a new executive director's home in Connecticut. The new staff and Board worked together to rebuild the association. Drawing largely on the energy and expertise of its volunteer leadership, NACSW was able to greatly expand member services, and develop collaborative relationships with leaders in both the professional social work and faith communities. As a result of these efforts, NACSW experienced a remarkable turnaround. In just five years, NACSW's membership base almost doubled, member satisfaction risen significantly, and NACSW finished financially "in the black" for five consecutive years, enabling it to build back a significant fund balance. Yet although the NACSW Board and membership were pleased with the progress NACSW had made over the past five years, they were also clear that NACSW must continue to grow in order to make a more tangible contribution to and have a more vital impact on the professional social work and faith communities in the years ahead. The current low membership retention rate was a significant obstacle to achieving that goal.

Current NACSW Information

NACSW currently had about 1925 members (up over 80% from 1050 in 1997), mostly living in the U.S. and Canada. The majority of NACSW's members were either professional social workers or social work students. The first goal from NACSW's current strategic plan was specifically related to membership growth defined by the following goal for the association.

> Increase membership 15% each year from 2001–2003, from 1,650 (as of January, 2001), to 1,900 as of January 2002, to 2,175 by the end of 2002, and to 2,500 by the end of 2003.

All other things remaining equal, simply increasing its renewal rate from 55% to 75% would in and of itself increase NACSW's membership by an additional 380 members to 2,310 by the end of 2002 (given its total of 1920 members at the end of 2001), and then an additional 460 members to 2,765 by the end of 2003, enabling it to exceed its goal without a single additional growth intervention. The amount of increased revenue this would raise for the association would be approximately $17,000 the first year (based on an average membership rate of $45), and $20,000 the second year—even before factoring in any additional revenue generated by these retained members, such as revenue from their convention registrations, publication purchases, etc. This alone amounted to increases of over 7% and 8.5, respectively, in total budgeted revenue for the next two years. As was evident from these numbers, increasing the retention rate would be an extremely significant step in an overall strategy toward increasing NACSW's growth and financial viability.

This was not the first time that NACSW had made a concerted effort to increase its renewal rate as a strategy to stimulate membership growth. Back in 1997, the renewal rate was slightly below 60%. A number of strategies were put into place between 1997 and 1999 in an attempt to increase this rate, including: a. developing a more consistent practice of sending out renewal reminders (four altogether); b. upgrading the content of renewal letters to highlight significant organizational accomplishments and new member benefits; c. sending renewal kits as a sales promotion strategy (members would be offered a set of gifts to choose at the point that they renewed their memberships.) This combination of strategies, along with an overall increase in membership satisfaction, had a significant impact, increasing membership retention rates from about 60% in 1997, to a high of 71% in 1999.

However, beginning in about 1999, NACSW's overall membership numbers began to significantly increase, primarily because of the success of several strategies designed to bring new members into the association. As was anticipated, this increase of new members renewed their memberships as compared to longer standing members. Importantly, because of significant and steady membership growth, by the end of 2001, for the first time in its history, NACSW had more new members (members who belonged to NACSW for less than one year) than members who had belonged to the association for more than one year. While this had many positive benefits for the association, it also both contributed to and served to highlight NACSW's difficulty in building long-term member loyalty, as by the beginning of 2002, NACSW renewal rate had dropped to about 55%.

By contrast, one of NACSW's current competitors, CAPS (Christian Association for Psychological Studies), reported that their membership retention rate in 2001 was about 80%. This was significantly above NACSW's retention rate, although CAPS' overall growth in membership from 1997 to 2001 had only been about 10% (from 1,909 members in 1997, to 2,108 in 2001) compared to NACSW's 80+%, and so their percentage of new to long-standing members was probably much lower than NACSW's. A larger competitor, AACC (American Association of Christian Counseling), had increased its membership by about 400% during this same five-year period, from about 5,000 in 1997 to about 40,000 in 2002. Unfortunately, AACC's staff did not respond to my inquiry about their current membership renewal rate. Another large competitor of NACSW's, NASW (the National Association

of Social Workers), currently had an 88% member retention rate, although they had seen about a 17% decrease in their membership from 1997 to the present time (from 174,000 in 1997 to 147,000 in 2002.)

These 80% and 88% membership retention rates of two of NACSW's key competitors highlight the importance of NACSW significantly improving its current 55% retention rate.

Possible Contributors to Current Retention Rate

A key question that must be addressed before focusing on a set of strategies to increase NACSW's retention rate was this: what were the most important factors that contributed to NACSW's current low retention rate? Or asked another way, what obstacles currently prevented more NACSW members from renewing their memberships?

For the past couple of years, NACSW had asked all of its members who did not renew their memberships (and who had provided NACSW with an email address—about 70% their membership) to provide feedback related to their reasons for not renewing (see Exhibit 1 for a copy of the "Exit Interview Email" NACSW used for this purpose). Although the response rate was extremely low (less than 5%), responses to this exit interview email fell into the following categories, in order of frequency:

Hi, <First_Name>. I hope this email finds you well.

I was wondering if you could take a few minutes to help me out. Each month I contact former NACSW members who have not renewed their memberships during this last membership cycle. My goal is to find out some of the reasons individuals have decided not to renew, in the hopes that the information will help me shape and improve NACSW to be more responsive, and a better support for Christians in social work.

If you have a few minutes, would you be willing to drop me a line or give me a quick call (toll-free) to let me know some of the reasons why you decided not to renew your NACSW membership, as well as anything we could have done differently that would have made it more likely that you would have chosen to renew?

Any thoughts or ideas you have on this matter, even just a few brief sentences, would be most helpful and greatly appreciated. Thanks for considering my request!

Sincerely,

Rick Chamiec-Case, MSW, MAR
Executive Director, North American Association Of Christians in Social Work (NACSW)

Exhibit 1 NACSW Exit Interview Email

A. Former member could not afford the dues (basic dues rate: $71; student rate: $22)—57%

B. Benefits/services were not relevant to the former members' work—18%

C. Former member was no longer in the field—15%

D. Former member did not have adequate time to take advantage of the benefits—10%

Clearly there were several considerations that NACSW should explore to improve the quality of the information it gathered from its members who choose not to renew their memberships. For example, it could begin conducting sampling telephone interviews (especially for members who had not supplied NACSW with an email address) for more interactive exit interviews. Also, it could focus the questions in the exit interview emails more carefully—for example, ''what additional benefits/services (or price reduction) could NACSW had offered that would have made it likely you would have renewed your membership?'').

In addition, NACSW could explore more fully the typical decision-making process a member goes through when deciding whether or not to renew his/her membership (including the roles of other key persons involved in this decision-making process), as well as examining key environmental variables that potentially impacted membership retention (such as the current state of the economy, the impact of NACSW's main competitors on renewal decisions, etc.).

Based on the responses received to date from exit interviews with non-renewing members, the working hypothesis was that the majority of non-renewing NACSW members did not renew their memberships because the benefits and services currently offered by NACSW did not provide sufficient value for them to justify paying the current membership rates (which were already low for the industry), even though they generally held the work and mission of the association in positive regard, and even though the number of quality of services and benefits had risen significantly over the past several years.

Extending this hypothesis an additional step, it would be safe to assume that the majority of current services and benefits (including those added during the past few years) did not have a more significant impact on member retention because most could be described as a ''one size fits all'' benefits, not taking into account the specific and varied needs of NACSW's current membership.

MARKETING STRATEGY

A web of marketing strategies designed to promote a significant increase in NACSW's membership retention rate over the next two to three years were proposed.

A. Clarifying Marketing Segments and Selecting Target Markets

1. Market Segmentation: Given that NACSW's resource base would not allow NACSW to provide more customized, targeted benefits and services for the wide variety of diverse segments currently represented within NACSW's membership, it appeared clear that NACSW must consider segmenting its market and making some hard decisions about where to focus its energy and scarce resources in the services and benefits it provided for its membership. So one of the first questions NACSW must face is this: what would be the most effective way to segment the market currently broadly defined as ''Christians in social work?''

There were number of plausible segmentation schemes to consider. Several leading contenders include:

a. Segment the market by the type of social work methods or primary work responsibilities of its members (segments defined by using this criteria could include social work educators, administrators, researchers, policy/planners, consultants, and direct service practitioners, which could be further subdivided into social work case managers, counselors/therapists, community organizers, community developers, etc.)

b. Segment the market by the stages in members' career cycles (segments defined by using this criteria could include undergraduate students, graduate students, doctoral students, young professionals, mid-career professionals, end-of-career professionals, retirees, etc.)

c. Segment the market by the type of organizational auspices or settings in which its members worked (segments defined by using this criteria could include social workers who work in private practice, faith-based service organizations, congregations/churches, non-faith-based service organizations, public schools, governmental organizations, faith-based colleges, non-faith-based colleges, etc.)

d. Segment the market by the primary fields of specialization or populations served by its members (segments defined by using this criteria could include social workers who worked in homelessness/poverty, addictions, mental health, developmental disabilities, aging, education, criminal justice, medical social work, housing/income maintenance, industry/labor, legal services, and child welfare, which could be further subdivided into residential services, adoption/foster care services, family services, etc.)

e. Since NACSW had recently begun offering organizational memberships (in addition to its traditional individual memberships), the segments outlined in ''c'' or ''d'' above might be applied to organizations as well as individuals and, as such, be considered as additional organizational member segments.

2. More traditional segmentation schemes (markets segmented by variables such as gender, ethnicity, geography, etc.) appear to be somewhat less useful for segmenting the NACSW market at the current time, although they should be kept in mind in ongoing market research efforts.

Given this broad range of possible segmentation schemes, how should NACSW proceed to decide which criterion (or criteria) to use to segment its market? Over the next three to five months, the executive director would pitch several segmentation schemes/criteria outlined above to NACSW's leadership/key members, and use their feedback to make a final decision regarding the most effective segmentation scheme for NACSW's market by no later than 11/02.

Target Segment Selection: However, even after a segmentation scheme was selected, there would still be the critical question: how would NACSW know which segment(s) to serve? This decision should be guided by some of the following considerations:

a. Which segment(s) was NACSW most effective at serving (or potentially effective at serving), and most highly values the services and benefits that NACSW offers?

b. Which segment(s) exhibits the greatest need for services and benefits that were not being offered by any of NACSW's competitors?

c. Which segment(s) had the greatest need for services and benefits that NACSW could offer without over-extending its scarce resource base?

d. Which segment(s) already known and was well known by NACSW?

e. Which segment(s) was most accessible to NACSW and its services and benefits?

f. Which segment(s) had sufficient resources to be able to adequately reimburse NACSW at levels that would ensure NACSW's financial viability?

3. Immediately after a segmentation scheme was selected by 11/02, NACSW's executive director would present several proposed target segments to NACSW's leadership/key members for their consideration, help them to wrestle with the pros and cons associated with targeting each proposed segment, and use their feedback to make a decision by no later than 4/03 regarding the target segment(s) that NACSW would focus on for the next couple of years.

One additional point needed to be considered in this discussion of target market selection. Given NACSW's history of defining its market very broadly (all "Christians in Social Work"), NACSW must consider whether there would be a negative reaction from many of its long-standing, supportive members who were not in one of the targeted segments selected by NACSW. To address this concern, and to maintain at least some continuity with its long history, NACSW should consider identifying one additional market segment to serve (over and above the one or more specific segments suggested above)—the broad "Christian in Social Work" segment. However, if it did decide to target this broad segment, it must do so with a clear understanding that it could only provide very general ("one size fits all") services and benefits for this particular segment, and market itself within this segment accordingly.

B. Market Research to Support Improved Membership Renewal

Once NACSW selected market segment(s) it would serve, how should NACSW go about discovering what the customers in these segments value most? In other words, how would NACSW determine these segments' stated needs, wants, and demands? NACSW must develop a web of market research strategies that would enable it to gather data from any of the segments it targeted in the following areas:

1. For current members of NACSW in this targeted segment(s), what were the most valued services or benefits that NACSW provided? Which were the ones they actually used the most?

2. What were the most challenging problems individuals in this segment(s) currently faced in their work? What outcomes or solutions to these problems would they be delighted to see occur, and how did they feel NACSW might contribute to these solutions?

3. If there were any new (or greatly improved) services or benefits that persons in this segment(s) would like to see NACSW provide, what would these be?

4. For current members of NACSW in this targeted segment(s), how satisfied would they say that they were with their membership? What were the main reasons they would give for their level of satisfaction with NACSW?

5. When a person mentions "NACSW," what words or images quickly came to mind that described or identified NACSW for them?

6. How did individuals in this segment(s) feel about the current costs and levels of service of NACSW's benefits (membership; trainings; publications, etc.)?

7. How accessible did individuals in this segment(s) feel that NACSW's services and benefits were for them?

8. Were individuals in this segment(s) more interested in "broad" or deep" NACSW benefits and services (provide examples of each type)?

9. For those who were long-standing NACSW members, what were the primary reasons that they maintained their membership in NACSW?

Sample representatives would need to be chosen from each target segment, and research methods would include website surveys, telephone interviews, and face-to-face interviews/focus groups facilitated by NACSW leadership teams (staff and board members could meet with focus groups at NACSW conferences and chapter events, etc.)

Another helpful marketing research approach would be to develop "customer scenarios" for each of the targeted segments. A customer scenario would sketch out the major steps for some of the key tasks members in each of these segments were responsible for. (For example, for individuals in the social work faculty segment, developing new course curricula, or for individuals in the social work administrator segment, designing new faith-based service programs or program evaluation tools). The goal of conducting customer scenarios would be to identify the kinds of supports that would help individuals in these segments do their jobs more effectively, and therefore that NACSW could consider adding to its portfolio of benefits and services. Exhibit 2 illustrates a customer scenario and how it helps in product/service development.

Because of the challenges involved in identifying commonly shared needs, wants, and demands for broader market segments, particular attention would need to be paid to the broad "Christians in Social Work" segment, if it is selected as one of NACSW's target markets. The challenge here would be to identify sufficiently relevant needs, wants, and demands that were shared by a large number of social workers, but who had very different

The following steps represent the key tasks associated with developing new course curricula and syllabi:

1. Faculty receives course assignment or proposes new course based on needs of the college's social work program
2. Faculty does research and brainstorms with colleagues regarding possible course topics
3. Faculty develops tentative course learning goals and objectives for selected course topic
4. Faculty researches appropriate materials/readings to use both in the development of the course outline, as well as to add to the student reading list and/or course
5. Faculty develops broad outline for the course
6. Faculty designs course syllabus, including possible topics for each class, required and supplementary readings, bibliography, etc.
7. Faculty develops detailed notes in preparation for each topic addressed by the course
8. Faculty design mix of presentation modalities (lectures, distance learning resources, guest presenters, student presentations, etc.) for presenting course material
9. Faculty develops class requirements and grading criteria
10. Class curricula is completed

NACSW should next run this customer scenario analysis by several NACSW members who teach in college social work programs, refine it based on their feedback, and then use it as a tool to facilitate several focus groups consisting of a larger sample of NACSW members who teach in faith-based colleges or universities. Key questions and topics to discuss during these focus groups include:

1. Which aspects of developing course curricula and syllabi do social work faculty usually find most challenging?
2. For which steps in the customer scenario would members find support or additional resources to be most useful?
3. What other specific support or resources would members find most useful in helping them more effectively and efficiently develop course curricula and syllabi?
4. What tangible outcomes would members like to be able to meet related to the task of developing course curricula and syllabi?

Generating and Screening New Product Ideas: In generating possible new product/service ideas for this target market segment, NACSW would be interested in the following question: Is there something NACSW could do – uniquely, differently, and more effectively than it has been done before – that would support faculty members related to these steps outlined in the course curriculum and syllabi development scenario?

To continue exploring how this product development process could play out, let's proceed on the assumption that this case scenario analysis led to the generation of two innovative ideas for developing new NACSW products/services for this target group: 1. developing an on-line database of curricula development reference materials, sample faculty syllabi and bibliography for a wide range of courses that integrate faith and social work; 2. developing a "publication on demand" service that would allow faculty members to view on-line copies of NACSW's books and journals, and pick and choose from among the chapters and articles in those books and journals to order their own, customized on-line NACSW publications with just the specific content they want for one or more of their courses.

Currently, NACSW only has the resources available to develop one of these two new product/service ideas. Let proceed on the assumption that in weighing these two options, NACSW selects option "2":

1. NACSW is already an established publisher in the textbook market for faith-based social work colleges, and so has experience and brand recognition in this area.
2. NACSW has sufficient in-house technological expertise to produce customized, on-line publications at a very low cost
3. There has been increasing competition from other publishers who have begun to produce books on themes related to the integration of spirituality and social work practice, and NACSW recognizes that this increases the importance of developing products/services that remain differentiated from those of its competition. To the knowledge of the individuals involved in this new product/service screening process, there are currently no other academic publishers that offer a "publication on demand" service.

Concept Testing: Next would come the concept testing phase, in which additional specifics regarding this new service idea would be fleshed out in more detail. Some of these details related to on-demand publishing include:

1. Copies of all current/recent NACSW books and publications would be posted on-line, and all NACSW members who teach in college programs would be given instant access to these on-line copies, which would be available to them 24 hours a day, 7 days a week. (Previously, faculty members would have had to request a review copy of any materials they were interested in reviewing, and then wait for them to arrive via the mail 5-7 days later).

Exhibit 2 Customer Scenario Analysis: Developing or Upgrading Course Curricula and Syllabi

2. After reviewing NACSW's materials, faculty members would be able to select any chapters, specific page ranges, or articles they would be interested in making available to their students for a specific course or series of courses. Within 48 hours, NACSW would electronically merge the selected chapters, pages, or articles (in the specified order) into a customized on-line publication for use by this faculty member and her or his class(es).

3. Faculty members would be able to access and download this new on-line publication at no cost, and students from their classes could purchase/download this new on-line publication at a fraction of the cost of purchasing all the books from which the chapters/articles were extracted.

Market Test: As with the development of any new product or service, there would be a number of important concerns/ risks raised that would have to be carefully considered. Potential risk associated with this new product or service would include:

1. It could lead to an overall reduction in NACSW books sales. It is possible that students might end up ordering fewer books overall since faculty are able to combine just those chapters/articles they need into one book, rather than ordering the several publications from which the materials have been extracted.) This has the potential to adversely impact book sales revenue.

2. It would be relatively easy for one or more students in any given class to purchase/download a copy of a customized publication and distribute it directly to their peers, thereby significantly undercutting book sales revenue.

3. Making it possible for faculty members to extract individual chapters or sections from its publications could inadvertently dilute the distinctiveness of each of its individual books, which to a certain degree depend on the integration and inter-relatedness of its various chapters set out in a specified order.

4. It could reduce the motivation of faculty to use as many chapters from NACSW books as possible for their classes since it would be easy for them to place orders just for the specific chapters with which they were already familiar. This in turn could lead to a reduction in both overall volume of book sales as well as impact of NACSW material in the market.

To explore these important concerns more carefully, following a careful business analysis (which unfortunately is beyond the scope of this paper), the project would move to the market testing phase.

And in fact, that is what NACSW plans to this Fall. It will set up a small test market for its on-demand publishing service consisting of 10 potential customers who have ordered NACSW publications previously, and 10 potential customers who have never ordered an NACSW publication. Cost for products offered to this test market will be set at just cost plus a 20% margin. Customer response to this new service, as well as the potency of the concerns/risks listed above, will be carefully studied and evaluated during an initial six-month test period.

If the market test proves successful (and the concerns/risk are shown to be manageable), NACSW will develop a plan for full marketing mix for this new product/service, including pricing considerations, promotional strategies, and distribution channels for offering this product more widely based on the information it gathered from the testing period. Perhaps the developing of a plan for a full marketing mix for this new product/service will turn out to be an appropriate subject for another paper in the Fall.

Exhibit 2 Customer Scenario Analysis: Developing or Upgrading Course Curricula and Syllabi *(continued)*

responsibilities, practice in very different practice environments, work with very different client groups, and were at different points in their careers. Some broad needs areas that might be tested in the market research process included: a. Desire to "keep a finger on the pulse" of what's going on in various areas within the field of faith-based social work; b. Need for a range of networking/connecting opportunities with other social workers of faith; c. Need for range of publications that tackle broad questions related to the integration of faith and practice; d. Need for on-going training, particularly with the potential to earn continuing education contact hours needed for licensing requirements; e. Desire to have a faith-based presence/advocacy arm within the general social work profession.

C. Developing a Market Mix for NACSW Membership to Enhance Membership Renewal

1. **Product/Services:** Once it identified the customer wants, needs, and demands from its selected segment(s), how would NACSW determine and develop the portfolio of products/services that would best meet the needs of the these customers? Although developing a full-blown product development process was beyond the scope of this case, there were several key considerations that NACSW would need to keep in mind related to the upgrading and development of new products and services:

a. NACSW must keep a clear focus on its how its membership services and benefits were differentiated from those offered by its competitors. Briefly put, the focus of NACSW's services and benefits was to enable members to integrate faith on the one hand, with professional social work practice on the other. Some of NACSW's main competitors addressed the faith component, but not the professional social work component (AACC, CAPS, for example). Others addressed the professional social work components, but not the faith component (NASW, for example). NACSW's niche and potential competitive advantage rested with its ability to help members intentionally integrate the two.

b. Because NACSW's resource and customer bases were relatively small, its products and services must be highly individualized to retain member interest. If they were not, members could easily go to one of its competitors, who because of economies of scale could produce a wider range of products and services for a very competitive price. One of NACSW's competitive advantages had to be in its ability to tailor personalized services and solutions to its small customer base. In addition, highly individualized services and benefits were NACSW's best strategy to develop lifetime members, who renew because they came to depend on customized services and benefits that meet their individual needs.

c. NACSW products and services must be developed in response to increasingly specific information from marketing research that successfully teased out the most critical needs, wants, and demands of the individuals in NACSW's targeted segment(s), and specifically those areas that research indicates renewal decisions were most decisively based on.

d. Because NACSW did not have a large staffing infrastructure (less than 1.5 staff FTEs), NACSW must set up a process for new product/service development that was volunteer, rather than staff-intensive. NACSW must recruit volunteers from among its membership (its customers) to assist with generating and screening new services ideas, as well as supporting staff efforts in the area of market testing and promotion.

e. NACSW must develop a process to more systematically track the new product/service ideas of its main competitors, including: AACC (faith-based counseling services); NASW (professional social work membership association); CMA (faith-based management membership association); NAACFA (faith-based child and family membership association); CAPS (faith-based membership services for the discipline of psychology); Social Work Managers (membership association for social work managers); CSWE (professional social work educators membership association); ASAE (non-profit executive membership association); Haworth Press (publisher of social services materials, some written from a faith-based perspective). Brooks-Cole (publisher of social services materials, some written from a faith-based perspective). NACSW must also continue to expand this list to identify other potential competitors in related industries.

f. Based on decisions it made with regard to selecting targeted market segments, NACSW should evaluate all of its current services and benefits, and decide which need to be tweaked, which need to be significantly upgraded, and which need to be scrapped entirely, so that its services and benefits portfolio was maximally attractive and relevant to its target market segment(s). For example, some of NACSW's current services like convention trainings and publications should clearly be continued, but the content should be more focused on meeting the training needs and interests of the target market segment(s) it selects.

2. **Pricing of NACSW membership:** Once it determines the portfolio of products/services that would best meet the needs of its target market segment(s), NACSW should re-evaluate its membership rates, as well as the pricing structure of any additional benefits and services that it offers. Once again, there are several key considerations that NACSW would need to keep in mind related to re-evaluating its price for services:

a. Because NACSW's customer base was small, and because NACSW was committed to focusing on highly individualized services and benefits, NACSW must be cautious not to underprice its membership rates or its prices for any additional services and benefits. Rates must be set at a level to ensure long-term financial viability of the association, since it cannot count on high volume to generate the revenue it needs to sustain itself. This would be a challenge for NACSW, which had historically set its prices at below market rates (compared to other membership associations in the industry). With an upgrading of services and benefits, it was possible that prices would need to follow.

b. At the same time (and somewhat in tension with ''a'' above), NACSW should be cautious not to set price too high, as its goal of continued membership growth would be best supported by achieving high levels of market penetration. In turn, high levels of market penetration were often most successfully accomplished by employing a moderate pricing strategy.

c. One way of dealing creatively with the natural tension between ''a'' and ''b'' above would be for NACSW to consider setting different pricing levels for different services and/or target segments. One strategy might be to set higher prices for those target segments that would obtain more value from expanded services for their segment, particularly if those segments were better resourced and be less sensitive to higher price. Different rates could also be established based on customer use of benefits (for example, members who chose to access information materials on-line could pay a lower membership rate than members who access information materials both on-line as well as in hard copy format). NACSW could even create a ''preferred'' customer status that charged higher prices in exchange for an even higher level of service (such as receiving targeted emails with special information, personal invitations to events of particular interest to those customers, ''frequent user'' discounts for attendance at multiple conferences, etc.)

3. **Promotion as a Strategy to Increase Membership Renewal:** Given NACSW's limited resources, selecting an optimal promotional mix that supports the goal of increased membership retention would be no small challenge. What were some considerations NACSW should weight when deciding on the best

mix of advertising, sales promotion, and personal selling initiatives to increase its membership retention rate?

a. Because NACSW's resource and customer bases were small, it must seek ways to turn its size into strength by providing communication that is personal, direct, and responsive. Members must feel like they can readily speak to anyone in the association, including the executive director or a board member, and the association must take a personal interest in its members. NACSWs must parlay its size into a distinctive advantage so that members felt they were part of a "family," not just an impersonal association.

b. NACSW must begin to develop its brand management and positioning strategies. It should start by evaluating its current slogan, "A Vital Christian Presence in Social Work," to determine: 1. Was this the image/description that came to most members' minds when they thought of NACSW? 2. Was this the image/message that would most effectively motivate members to renew their memberships when they were at the point of making a renewal decision? 3. What other messages did NACSW's brand convey to members (and which messages does NACSW want its brand to convey to members)? 4. Were there some specific brand relationships that NACSW needs to work harder to cultivate, and/or others to avoid? In addition, it would be necessary to develop separate brand management and position strategies for each targeted market segment it decides to serve.

c. NACSW would need to develop the capacity to run multiple promotional strategies, with at least one different strategy customized to each targeted market segment (at the current time, NACSW used a "one size fits all" promotional approach). Particular care would need to be given to the broad "Christians in Social Work" segment, if NACSW selects this as a target segment. On the other hand, a promotional strategy for this broad segment would need to define clear, useful benefits (such as "helping members to keep their fingers on the pulse of what's going on in the field of faith-based social work") that would prove useful to as many as possible within this broad segment (but that are not in any of the other more specific targeted segments). On the other hand, it would need to guard against making promises that NACSW could deliver more specific services for this broad a group than NACSW would be able to produce given its limited resource base (a mistake NACSW had arguably made in the past).

d. Because NACSW had limited resources for advertising, most of its advertisements have currently targeted to recruit new members (who had not yet heard about NACSW). However, NACSW should take a look at upgrading ads and information that it provided in its own publications (for example, its newsletter and journal) with an eye toward encouraging members to renew their memberships.

e. NACSW should experiment with a variety of sales promotional ideas to encourage membership renewal. One approach would be to provide targeted members (those who were members for the first time, for example, whose renewal rates were especially low) with a coupon offering 25–35% off any NACSW product or service upon their renewing their memberships. In addition, NACSW should consider offering even more lucrative renewal benefits (for example, a complimentary copy of NACSW's newest publication) for those members who renewed for two years at a time, or renewed at least 60 days before their renewal date.

f. NACSW should consider adding membership renewal "sales calls" to the job descriptions of its current office staff so that all staff members make a minimum number of telephone calls each week to targeted members coming up on membership renewal. Scripts could be developed for these sales calls, with a focus on crafting messages customized for each targeted segment. In addition, NACSW could recruit students from colleges that were organizational members to make additional renewal sales calls. In exchange, participating colleges could be given conspicuous recognition for the contribution of their students' paid time for making these calls, and/or NACSW could offer virtual memberships or NACSW publications for non-paid student volunteers.

4. Place—Distribution/Channels: Even though NACSW dealt almost exclusively in direct marketing, there were still a couple of key considerations that NACSW could keep in mind as it strived to make the process of renewing memberships—as well as accessing all NACSW benefits and services—as quick, easy, and convenient as possible:

a. NACSW must continue to make it easy for members to keep track of when it was time to renew their memberships, provide them with compelling reasons to renew at exactly the point in time when they were making their renewal decision, and make the renewal or purchase decision as convenient as possible. Offering members a variety of ways to renew their memberships (toll-free number, snail mail, email, website forms, etc.) is also important. In other words, NACSW needs to offer a strong "process benefit" to its members.

b. NACSW should consider viewing and treating its growing number of organizational members as "distributors" of individual memberships. That way NACSW could offer to organizational members blocks of individual memberships (in increments of 5 or 10 at a time) for them to distribute among their employees (as professional development perks) each year as desired. In this way, NACSW would only have to deal with one contact (the representative of the organizational membership) for the annual renewal of multiple members. It would become the organization's responsibility to broker the individual memberships in the block of individual members they order, in exchange for reduced individual membership rates and additional organizational member benefits.

CASE 6
The Nottoway Plantation, Restaurant, and Inn: The White Castle of Louisiana

In early 1994, Faye Russell, marketing director, and Cindy Hidalgo, general manager, considered the future of Nottoway Plantation of White Castle, Louisiana. Nottoway, which was listed in the *National Registry of Historic Places*, was an enterprise in the hospitality industry, attracting visitors to tour the mansion that contained many original furnishings. In addition to tours, the plantation offered overnight accommodations, dining and banquet facilities, and a gift shop. Nottoway competed with several other plantations for tourist trade along the Mississippi River, seven of which provided similar tours and elegant bed-and-breakfast facilities.

Although Cindy and Faye felt that Nottoway was operating "in the black," they thought they were missing an opportunity; tour groups visited the plantation homes, but stayed overnight in the nearby cities of Port Allen or Baton Rouge in a Holiday Inn or similar facility. Couldn't Nottoway expand its facilities to provide enough overnight accommodations for bus tours and other groups?

BACKGROUND

Nottoway plantation home, constructed in 1859, was the largest existing Southern antebellum residence in 1994. John Hampden Randolph, the son of a prominent man from Nottoway County, Virginia, built Nottoway plantation to house his growing family. Randolph, who left Virginia in 1841, was an enterprising businessman. He first settled in Woodville, Mississippi. Six years later he moved to Iberville Parish, Louisiana, where he built a sugar empire on the Mississippi River. A series of expansions resulted in a plantation of over 7,000 acres. The crown jewel of the plantation was the magnificent home Randolph built for his wife, Emily, and their four sons and seven daughters, six of whom would later

marry there. The complete home consisted of a 53,000 square foot, 64-room mansion surrounded by graceful grounds, including formal gardens, a carriage house, and a caretaker's cottage (20 years older than the mansion itself). Nottoway was a gem of Italianate and Greek Revival style. The mansion reflected the splendor, luxury, and innovation of its time, featuring coal fireplaces, gas lighting, and indoor plumbing with hot and cold running water.

As Union troops approached during the Civil War, Randolph, who never officially declared allegiance to the Confederacy, left Nottoway for Texas, taking his slaves. During his exile, his wife remained at Nottoway. Despite a shelling from a gunboat on the Mississippi, the plantation home was spared from total destruction by a Union officer who had been a guest of the Randolphs. However, Mrs. Randolph did endure a three-week encampment by Union troops.

Randolph died in 1883 at age 70. Mrs. Randolph continued to run the plantation until she auctioned it for $100,000 in 1889.

Restoration

Nottoway remained in private use until 1980, when Arlin Dease purchased and restored it. As part of the purchase agreement, the prior owner negotiated the rights to continue to live in a suite in the mansion until her death; she was still living there in 1994. In 1981, Dease opened the plantation to the public for the first time in its 122-year history. In 1985, Paul Ramsay of Sydney, Australia, acquired the property and continued the restoration.

Ramsay grew up in Australia. After attending a university for a year, he left school to join his father in a series of real estate ventures. Over the years, he acquired many different types of real estate, and by 1985 he had become a wealthy man. He also owned a large health care company in New Orleans, which included a medical center. By 1995, he was highly respected in the health care community, and had received an honorary doctorate in mental health from Louisiana State University.

Ramsay bought Nottoway, a small investment by his standards, with plans to restore and expand it. As general manager of Nottoway, Ramsay brought in Cindy Hidalgo, who had been assistant administrator of the medical center owned by Ramsay for the prior three years. They both felt that the transition from managing the medical center to managing Nottoway would be easy. Hidalgo perceived the two operations to be "very similar" since

This case was prepared by Caroline M. Fisher, Loyola University New Orleans, and Claire Anderson, Old Dominion University. This case was originally presented at the annual conference of the North American Case Research Association. Management cooperated in the field research for this case, which was written solely for the purpose of class discussion. All events and individuals are real, but financial data has been disguised at the request of the organization. The authors thank Brandi Abraham, Tricia Bollinger, and Jason Murphy for their assistance in collecting information for this case. Copyright © 1996 by the *Case Research Journal* and Caroline M. Fisher and Claire Anderson. It is reprinted here by permission.

both were service organizations and offered gift shops, food service, and overnight accommodations. Together Ramsay and Hidalgo made significant changes in both the physical plant and the operations of the plantation.

First, they constructed a new building to house a gift shop and restrooms. Previously, the only gift shop was operated by the former owner in a small room on the first floor of the plantation home itself, where it was frequently missed by visitors. The new building, which was strategically placed between the parking area and the mansion, provided greater space for display of the gift inventory.

To further encourage its use, Cindy decided to sell tickets for the mansion tours in the gift shop. The new building also served as a gathering area for tour groups at both the beginning and the end of their visits.

Another significant change was the upgrading of the menu offered at the restaurant. Under the prior management, the restaurant offered three menu choices at both lunch and dinner: chicken, shrimp, or jambalaya. Cindy hired an executive chef John Percle, away from a competitive plantation, and brought in the chef's wife, Terry Percle, to manage the restaurant. Under their management, the restaurant flourished and developed an outstanding reputation for fine food and service.

TOURISM IN LOUISIANA

The state of Louisiana had suffered severely from the oil-patch depression of the 1980s; the economic downturn continued well into the 1990s. One industry that withstood the spillover effects from the oil industry was tourism. While New Orleans was a well-established international attraction, Louisiana conducted a nationwide media promotion in the 1980s and 1990s to lure additional leisure trade to the rest of the state with appeal to such attractions as Cajun cuisine and the ''Bayou lifestyle.''

The heart of tourism in Louisiana in the 1990s remained New Orleans. Over 7.6 million visitors flocked to New Orleans in 1992, attracted by its charm, its festivals, and its superior convention facilities. October through May was the peak time for conventions, but individual tourists, combined with a smaller number of conference attendees, kept the city busy throughout the year.

For the visitor satiated with the attractions of downtown New Orleans, an alternative side trip was to visit the nostalgic, historic plantations along the ''mighty Mississippi.'' A number of antebellum homes competed for the tourist trade through tours and overnight accommodations. (See Exhibit 1 for a listing and a map of the major plantation homes near New Orleans.)

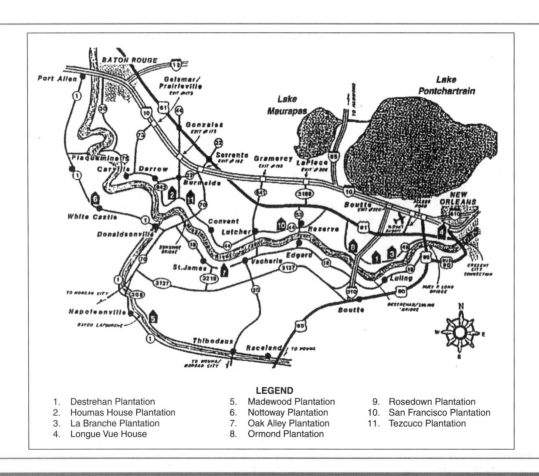

LEGEND

1. Destrehan Plantation
2. Houmas House Plantation
3. La Branche Plantation
4. Longue Vue House
5. Madewood Plantation
6. Nottoway Plantation
7. Oak Alley Plantation
8. Ormond Plantation
9. Rosedown Plantation
10. San Francisco Plantation
11. Tezcuco Plantation

Exhibit 1 Map of Plantations in Southeast Louisiana

Visits to these plantations required special efforts. Tourists who owned or rented a car had to plan their excursions carefully. The plantations were not located near expressways, and required considerable backroads driving. A map, like that shown in Exhibit 1, was a necessity. For tourists without their own transportation, organized tours were the only way they could get to the plantation homes.

A visitor could obtain specific information about the plantation tours in two basic ways. First, the tourist might contact a travel agent either specifically inquiring about a plantation visit or wanting general information on the attractions available in the New Orleans area. The travel agent would then provide information and make reservations for the tourist. Second, upon arriving in New Orleans, the visitor might pick up information on the plantation tours from a hotel concierge or a tourism office. They could then contact the tour agencies directly to make reservations.

The 1994 New Orleans Yellow Pages contained 40 listings under the "tour" category, and another four listings under limousines mentioned plantation tours. Most of those offering tours were small local organizations that contracted with groups which wanted to offer tours to their members. Convention organizers who wanted to include plantation tours among the activity choices for attendees were important customers. Two organizations offered regularly scheduled tours which individuals could join. New Orleans Tours offered two half-day plantation tours seven days a week. These $24 bus tours visited the Destrehan, Ormond, and San Francisco plantations. While capacity on the bus was 49, the tours averaged about 35 people, with the number varying depending on the convention activity in New Orleans.

Grayline Tours offered two different plantation tours. The first, an all-day tour, cost $35 and visited Nottoway Plantation and Houmas House. The second was a half-day tour for $27 to Oak Alley Plantation. The full-day tour ran three days a week; the half-day tour ran four days. Both operated all year. Bus capacity was 43 passengers.

NOTTOWAY PLANTATION, 1994

Nottoway was located 18 miles (about 30 minutes) south of Baton Rouge and 69 miles (approximately 1.5 hours) from New Orleans. Facilities were open daily all year, with the exception of Christmas Day.

Plantation tours provided Nottoway's prime source of profit. Other sources were its elegant dining, overnight accommodations, and gift purchases. (See Exhibits 2, 3, and 4 for financial data.) Exhibit 5 shows a diagram of the facilities.

TOURS

Nottoway was open for public viewing with guided tours available from 9 A.M. to 5 P.M. seven days a week. Evening candlelight tours required reservations. The guided tour lasted 45 minutes.

Visitors entered the mansion, just as in John Randolph's time, through immense 11-foot doors into a spacious entrance hall with

**Budget July 1, 1993–June 30, 1994
(Dollar Figures in Thousands)**

Revenues	
Rooms	$ 439
Tours	$ 742
Restaurant	$ 964
Gift Shop	$ 373
Total Revenues	$ 2,518

Expenses	
Rooms	
Salaries	$ 38
Housekeeping	$ 56
Other	$ 52
Total Rooms	$ 146
Tours	
Salaries	$ 64
Landscaping	$ 5
Total Tours	$ 69
Restaurant	
Salaries	$ 279
Food	$ 231
Liquor	$ 32
Linen	$ 29
Other	$ 26
Total Restaurant	$ 597
Gift Shop	$ 249
Overhead	
Administrative Salaries	$ 164
Maintenance Salaries	$ 74
Advertising	$ 62
Insurance	$ 120
Credit Card	$ 25
Property Tax	$ 25
Security	$ 29
Benefits	$ 86
Utilities	$ 69
Maintenance	$ 38
Other	$ 76
Total Overhead	$ 768
Total Expenses	$ 1,829

Source: Nottoway Plantation.

Exhibit 2 Nottoway Plantation

a 16-foot-high ceiling. Looking at Nottoway's original intricate lacy plaster friezework, hand-painted Dresden porcelain doorknobs, and hand-carved marble mantels, visitors could sense the splendor of a bygone era in the old South. The grand white ballroom and dining room, which contained a 17-foot-long American Empire table with Chippendale chairs, attested to Randolph's commitment to opulence. Most of the mansion's furnishings were authentic period pieces, many of them original pieces that Arlin Dease had retrieved from around the country.

Income Statement
Year Ending June 30
(Dollar Figures in Thousands)

	1994	1993
Income		
Restaurant	$ 852	$ 844
Guest Rooms	$ 410	$ 405
Tours	$ 648	$ 740
Gift Shop	$ 316	$ 351
Revenue from Operations	$ 2,226	$ 2,340
Other Income	$ 9	$ 45
Total Income	$ 2,235	$ 2,385
Expenses		
Cost of Sales	$ 455	$ 471
Operating Expenses	$ 1,994	$ 1,929
Total Expenses	$ 2,449	$ 2,400
Net Gain (Loss) before Taxes	($214)	($15)
Income Taxes		
Current	$ 31	$ 37
Deferred	$ 31	$ 38
Net	$ 0	($1)
Net Gain (Loss)	($214)	($14)

Source: Nottoway Plantation.

Exhibit 3 Nottoway Plantation

ACCOMMODATIONS

The Nottoway Plantation Restaurant and Inn offered accommodations in the mansion itself and in the overseer's cottage (circa 1839). The visitor could choose among six rooms and three suites in the mansion and four rooms in the overseer's cottage. Guest rooms were individually decorated with period furnishings, each unique. (Exhibit 6 describes these rooms and their rates.)

Room rates included sherry (champagne in the bridal suite), a tour of the mansion, an in-room wake-up breakfast, and a full plantation breakfast served on the veranda. The plantation breakfast consisted of "pain perdu" (French toast), eggs, ham or sausage, grits, toast, and fresh fruit.

Swimming and tennis facilities were available. Nightly room prices ranged from $95 to $175 for a single; $125 to $175, double; and $155 to $190, triple. Suites ranged from $200 to $250.

DINING AND BANQUET FACILITIES

Randolph Hall, a 300-seat dining facility, provided on-site dining services, and was also available for banquets and receptions. Other banquet facilities included the Magnolia and the Camellia Rooms on the ground floor of the mansion, which seated 50 and 20 respec-

Balance Sheet
Year Ending June 30
(Dollar Amounts in Thousands)

	1994	1993
Assets		
Cash	$ 399	$ 348
Accounts Receivable—Trade	$ 41	$ 71
Accounts Receivable—Insurance	$ 0	$ 79
Inventory	$ 130	$ 128
Prepaid Insurance	$ 33	$ 27
Total Current Assets	$ 603	$ 653
Buildings	$ 3,595	$ 3,559
Building Improvements	$ 424	$ 413
Furniture and Fixtures	$ 323	$ 302
Automobiles	$ 12	$ 27
Accumulated Depreciation	($1,013)	($ 893)
Net	$ 3,341	$ 3,408
Land	$ 323	$ 323
Restricted Cash	$ 7	$ 7
Deferred Income Tax	$ 69	$ 38
Other Assets	$ 3	$ 0
Total Noncurrent Assets	$ 3,743	$ 3,776
Total Assets	$ 4,346	$ 4,429
Liabilities and Stockholders' Equity		
Liabilities		
Accounts Payable—Trade	$ 52	$ 50
Accounts Payable—Affiliates	$ 150	$ 83
Room Deposits/Gift Certs.	$ 59	$ 52
Notes Payable—Affiliates	$ 3,660	$ 3,406
Income Tax Payable	$ 21	$ 35
Other Accrued Liabilities	$ 100	$ 114
Notes Payable with 1 Year*	$ 797	$ 172
Total Current Liabilities	$ 4,839	$ 3,912
Notes Payable Over 1 Year	$ 0	$ 797
Total Liabilities	$ 4,839	$ 4,709
Stockholders' Equity		
Common Stock (100 Shares @$1)	$ 0	$ 0
Additional Paid in Capital	$ 445	$ 445
Accumulated Deficit	($ 938)	($ 725)
Total Net Equity	($ 493)	($ 280)
Total Equity and Liabilities	$ 4,346	$ 4,429

* Represents money owned to Paul Ramsay which will be rolled over.

Source: Nottoway Plantation.

Exhibit 4 Nottoway Plantation

tively. Randolph Hall was open for lunch 11 A.M. to 3 P.M., and dinner, 6 P.M. to 9 P.M. Reservations were recommended for dinner.

The cuisine included Cajun and other traditional local dishes. Among the specialties were alligator sauce picante, medallions of veal, prime rib, homemade gumbo, and a "Cajun two-step: a levee of jambalaya surrounded by a river of shrimp creole."

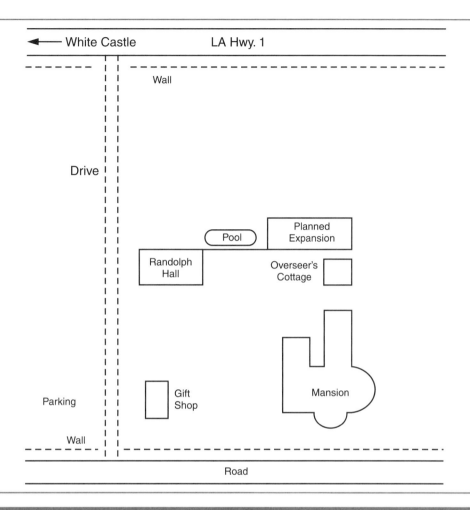

Exhibit 5 Nottoway Plantation Ground and Facilities

Dining was leisurely and elegant. Guests sat on hand-carved mahogany chairs, and light was provided by crystal and bronze chandeliers. A regular pianist performed on a hand-carved concert grand piano produced by Webber of London in 1896.

OTHER OFFERINGS

Hidalgo offered a variety of other activities at Nottoway to attract and satisfy visitors and supplement revenues. After the guided tour, besides enjoying a meal at the restaurant, visitors could stroll on the levee (the protective barrier between the Mississippi River and the plantation grounds), picnic on the grounds, or visit the gift shop. The gift shop offered antique accessories, Louisiana specialty foods, books, and other fine gifts.

To attract visitors other than tourists, the facilities were available for receptions, dinner parties, banquets, business meetings, or other special events. Weddings were performed in the Ballroom followed by a reception in the mansion or Randolph Hall.

ORGANIZATION

When Cindy Hidalgo was hired as general manager in 1985, she was 27 years old with an accounting degree, a start on an MBA, and three years of management experience. She did not become a CPA because she "felt that it would be a waste of time to study for the exam" while she could be concentrating on climbing the corporate ladder. Her goal for Nottoway was continual improvement. Ramsay essentially left the running of Nottoway to Hidalgo, visiting four to six times a year for reports.

Hidalgo directed a staff of five: an assistant manager/marketing director, Faye Russell; a restaurant manager, Terry Percle; an executive chef John Percle; a maintenance engineer, Randy LaPrairie; and a gift shop manager, Susan Rockforte, who also acted as bookkeeper. Three others reported to the marketing director: a house manager who was responsible for tours, a housekeeping supervisor, and a sales manager. Assistant restaurant managers (maître d's), reporting to the restaurant manager, supervised the bellmen and the wait, banquet, and service staff.

Faye Russell, the assistant manager and marketing director, had been with Nottoway since 1987. She came to Nottoway with a

All rooms include sherry, tour of the mansion, full plantation breakfast, and use of the pool. Rates are effective January 1, 1992 and do not include 7.66 percent tax.

Mansion and Wings

Room 1*	Cornelia's Bedroom: Third floor of mansion overlooking the river, mahogany four poster double bed and three-quarter day bed. $175 single or double; $190 triple.
Room 2*	Third floor of mansion, mahogany half-tester double bed and three-quarter day bed, view of the gardens from the veranda. $175 single or double; $190 triple.
Room 3*	Second floor of boy's wing, queen size bed with canopy, view of the gardens from the veranda. $95 single, $135 double.
Room 4*	Second floor of boy's wing, antique brass double bed, view of the gardens from the veranda. $95 single, $135 double.
Room 5*	Ground floor of girl's wing, antique double sleigh bed. $95 single, $135 double.
Room 6*	Ground floor of girl's wing, antique walnut double bed, twin day bed. $95 single, $135 double, $155 triple.

Overseer's Cottage (Circa 1839)

Room 7*	Ground floor of cottage, antique brass queen bed, twin day bed, view of duck pond. $95 single, $135 double, $155 triple.
Room 8*	Ground floor of cottage, antique brass queen bed, three-quarter day bed, view of patio with fountain. $95 single, $135 double, $155 triple.
Room 9*	Second floor of cottage, antique brass queen bed, three-quarter day bed, view of duck pond, private veranda. $95 single, $135 double, $155 triple.
Room 10*	Second floor of cottage, rosewood double bed, overlooks patio and pond, private veranda. $95 single, $135 double.

Suites

Master Bedroom[†]	Third floor of mansion, only bedroom furniture original to Nottoway, rosewood half-tester double bed, twin bed in sitting room. Room is on tour. $200 single or double, $215 triple.
Randolph Suite[†]	Third floor of mansion, wicker morning room, four poster double bed, overlooks the river. Room is on tour. $200 single or double.
Bridal Suite[†]	Ground floor of boy's wing, three-room suite with half-tester canopy queen bed, parlor, wet bar, sleeper sofa, jacuzzi, and private pool. $250 single, double, or triple.

* Check in: 2:30 P.M.; check out: 11:00 A.M.
† Check in: 5:00 P.M.; check out: 9:00 A.M.

Exhibit 6 Nottoway's Rooms and Rates

degree in communications and 7½ years of experience with the Louisiana Office of Tourism. Her experience in the destination marketing field included meeting and convention planning, managing special projects and trade shows, and developing brochures.

The administrative offices were housed in the attic of the overseer's cottage above the two floors of rooms rented to the public for overnight accommodations. The offices were cramped, with Cindy sharing one office with the reservationist, files, and a microwave oven. Faye shared the other office with the sales manager and another salesperson. In total, Nottoway employed 85 people in the restaurant, gift shop, and mansion.

OPERATIONS

Like much of the hospitality trade, Nottoway's business was seasonal, reflecting the locale's tropical climate. (Although the home was not air-conditioned, it did benefit from breezes which came in through large windows.) Room occupancy ranged from less than 45 percent in January up to 90 percent in the peak months. (See Exhibit 7.) Tours, accommodations, and the gift shop experienced peak months in March through May; January was the slowest month. Exhibit 7 shows projected visitors by month. In addition to the March through May peak, the dining facilities also enjoyed a second peak in October. The dining business, and the tours, died off in January.

The largest revenue producer was the restaurant. Lunch and special events (weddings, receptions, and business meetings) made up most of its income; dinner accounted for only a small portion, mostly generated by overnight guests. Tours were the second most important source of revenue. Budgets were determined from historical data and conventions scheduled for the coming year in New Orleans and Baton Rouge. (Exhibit 2 shows the budget for the fiscal year ending June 30, 1994, and Exhibits 3 and 4 provide financial statements.)

	July	Aug.	Sept.	Oct.	Nov.	Dec.	Jan.	Feb.	March	April	May	June	Total
Tours (Number of People)													
Group	2150	2330	3020	5550	4000	2600	1550	2950	4250	5400	6100	2700	42600
Individual	7850	7450	4825	6050	5350	4950	3725	5000	7800	7675	7550	6250	74475
Candlelight	75	250	50	450	300	600	50	200	200	500	600	350	3625
Weddings	50	200	0	200	200	0	150	0	0	100	350	100	1350
Total	10125	10230	7895	12250	9850	8150	5475	8150	12250	13675	14600	9400	122050
Weddings (Number of Guests)	50	200	0	200	200	0	150	0	0	100	350	100	1350
Rooms (Number Rented)	260	285	230	330	300	200	175	200	330	345	350	275	3280
Meals (Number Served)													
Lunches	3275	3050	3250	4350	3550	3600	1900	3200	4500	5100	5300	3475	44550
Dinners	750	620	550	700	700	850	450	600	750	700	800	700	8170
Functions	300	400	400	450	525	1000	175	600	400	900	800	500	6450
Weddings	50	200	0	200	200	0	150	0	0	50	400	100	1350
Total	4375	4270	4200	5700	4975	5450	2675	4400	5650	6750	7300	4775	60520

Source: Nottoway Plantation.

Exhibit 7 Nottoway Plantation—Projected Visitors by Month, 1994

COMPETITION

Several historic Louisiana plantations, inns, or cottages vied for the bed-and-breakfast trade. The famous Oak Alley Plantation of Vacherie (just outside New Orleans) featured overnight cottages on its grounds, which included a quarter-mile alley of 28 sheltering oaks that were over 250 years old. Rosedown Plantation in St. Francisville included magnificent formal gardens. Tezcuco in Burnside offered bed and breakfast in one two-bedroom suite in the main house or one of ten cottages on the plantation estate, which also included a chapel, blacksmith shop, museum, and gazebo. (Exhibit 8 lists the major competitors and their features.)

Cindy and Faye considered the competition to be a challenge. While the elegance of the mansion itself was a distinctive feature, the two women also tried to provide first-class service. For example, weddings were limited to no more than one a day, even on Saturday, to make the wedding party feel that they were special, that this was their "mansion" for the day.

Similarly, they wanted all of their guests to feel special, even those receiving a discount as part of a tour group. "I tell my people that there are no second-class citizens at Nottoway, even though they aren't paying full price," declared Cindy.

MARKETING

Cindy and Faye were concerned with Nottoway's ability to serve the tourism market, their main source of guests. "We're looking at where we want to go to fully serve our clients," stated Cindy.

"We want to provide a well-rounded, balanced product. Currently, we can't fully service motor coaches or business groups."

Faye had no data concerning the source of individual visitors (local, out of state, etc.) or how visitors learned of Nottoway, but she believed that most people learned about the plantation directly from prior visitors. They did know, however, that slightly over 96 percent of tour visitors were adults. The majority came by private automobile, although all the major tour lines offered trips to Nottoway. Grayline, the prime tour line that brought visitors to Nottoway, offered the only regularly scheduled tour which included the plantation. Grayline's tour was offered three times a week.

Walk-in guests, including both tourists and people who worked in the area, made up approximately 65 percent of the luncheon trade; tour groups accounted for the remainder. Special event promotions for holiday meals such as Easter Sunday and Thanksgiving dinners were directed at local residents, who were also thought to be a significant part of the lunch and dinner trade.

Promotion was primarily aimed directly at the end consumer, although Nottoway was also promoted to tour operators. Advertising budgets were $59,000, $61,000, $73,000, $55,000 and $62,000 for fiscal years ending June 1990 through June 1994, respectively (exclusive of salaries and travel). These costs included advertisements in local media such as *New Orleans Magazine*, the Baton Rouge *State-Times/Morning Advocate*, the *Acadiana Dining Guide, LeGuide—What's Happening in Acadiana*, and various American Automobile Association publications. The Nottoway plantation was listed in the promotional materials of the Greater New Orleans Tourist Commission; national publications such as *The Annual Directory of American Bed &*

Destrehan Plantation. Destrehan is the oldest plantation in the Mississippi valley, originally constructed in 1787. Tours daily 9:30–4:00. Nominal admission fee. Group tours welcome, gift shop. Closed holidays. 22 miles from New Orleans.

Houmas House. Houmas House is one of Louisiana's most imposing Greek Revival plantation homes; known for its distinctive three-story spiral staircase. Tours with costumed guides 10:00–5:00. Fee: $6.50 adults, $3.25 children, $4.50 13–17 years. Special arrangements for large groups. Gift shop. 60 miles from New Orleans.

La Branche Plantation Dependency House. La Branche Plantation is known for its exceptional display of Federal woodwork and its rarity as a plantation dependency. Grounds tour includes slave quarters, gazebo, restaurant, and more. Fee: $5 adults, $3 children, $4 seniors. Open all days except major holidays, 10:00–4:00. 20 miles from New Orleans.

Longue Vue House and Gardens. Greek Revival style mansion, original furnishings, 8-acre garden, changing exhibits. Self-guided tour of gardens. Guided tour of the house. Fee: $6 adults, $3 children, $5.40 seniors. Open Mon.–Sat. 10:00–4:30, Sun. 1:00–5:00. Closed major holidays. In New Orleans.

Madewood Plantation. Magnificent 1846 Greek Revival style home with period furnishings. Group lunches and dinners can be arranged. Overnight guests sleep in canopied beds and dine by candlelight in formal family dining room. Scheduled tours. Fee: $5 adults, $3 children, $3.50 seniors. Open 10:00–4:30 daily; closed Thanksgiving and Christmas. 72 miles from New Orleans.

Nottoway Plantation. Largest plantation home in the South. Daily tours, gift shop, weddings, award-winning restaurant serving lunch and dinner. Fee: $8 adults, $3 children, $8 seniors. Group rates available. Open 9:00–5:00 daily except Christmas day. 69 miles from New Orleans.

Oak Alley Plantation. Antebellum home and grounds famous for its alley of 28 evenly spaced live oaks. Overnight cottages. Scheduled tours. Fee: $6.50 adults, $3.50 13–18 years, $2 6–12 years. Group rates available. Open 9:00–5:30 daily. 60 miles from New Orleans.

Ormond Plantation. Colonial plantation furnished with various periods of antique furniture. Available for private parties. Scheduled tours. Fee: $5 adults, $2.50 children, $4 seniors. Group rates available. Dining on-site. Overnight accommodations. 23 miles from New Orleans.

Rosedown Plantation Home and Gardens. Antebellum home restored to museum quality with original furnishings and 28 acres of formal gardens. Scheduled tours 9:00–5:00. Fee: $9 adults, $4 children. 110 miles from New Orleans.

San Francisco Plantation. One of the most elaborate homes of the period. Guided tours daily 10:00–4:00. Fee: $6.50 adults, $2.50 6–11 years, $3.75 12–17 years. Group rates available, gift shop. Closed main holidays. 45 miles from New Orleans.

Tezcuco Plantation. One of the last plantations built before the Civil War in 1856, Tezcuco is a Greek Revival style raised cottage. Tours daily 9:00–5:00. Closed major holidays. Fee: $5.50 adults, $2.75 children, $4.50 seniors and teens. Group rates available; bed and breakfast cottages. Antique and gift shop. Restaurant open daily 8:30–3:00. 60 miles from New Orleans.

Exhibit 8 Major Competitors

Breakfasts and the *Christian Bed & Breakfast Directory*; and books such as *Plantation Homes of Louisiana and Natchez Area* (David King Gleason, Baton Rouge: Louisiana State University Press, 1982). Brochures were provided to all New Orleans hotels and tourism offices.

Advertising materials billed Nottoway as ''The largest plantation home in the South!'' The message in the print media was one of refinement and elegance. Print advertisements appealed to customers to ''step back in time and marvel at how the ravages of war and time could not mar the beauty of the White Castle of Louisiana–Nottoway.'' Another suggested ''19th Century charm and elegance for all bridal celebrations,'' offering bridal lun-

cheons, honeymoon accommodations, rehearsal dinners, weddings, and receptions.

FUTURE PLANS

Cindy and Faye realized that tour operators represented an essentially untapped market for Nottoway. While many groups stopped to tour the mansion, few actually dined at Nottoway or stayed overnight. Most group tours required significantly more rooms, usually 22 to 24 rooms to handle 44 to 46 passengers, than were available at Nottoway or any one plantation for overnight accommodations. ''We just can't service the motor coaches with our current facilities,'' stated Cindy in frustration.

Other groups required larger facilities as well. ''Why just last week I had to turn away three reservations from groups who needed rooms for 40 people,'' noted the reservationist.

Small business meetings were one other type of group needing more rooms. ''We're in the middle of the oil industry; they are our potential clients too. They look for facilities for housing visitors and conducting off-site meetings and retreats,'' Faye stated.

One option that they were considering was to add another building on the mansion grounds that would provide 22 to 28 additional units. Construction costs typically ranged from $30,000 to $50,000 per room, according to industry statistics. They felt that they needed to make some strategic decisions before they could present their idea to the owner, Paul Ramsay. Faye and Cindy investigated small hotels that serviced motor coaches and business meetings, and found that most of the rooms in these hotels had two queen-sized beds, and a few had king-sized beds.

A motel-quality building would be the lowest-cost alternative. The units could be rented slightly below the low end of their current rate schedule to the general public, and at even lower rates to the tour operators. Many tour operators were looking for discounts and lower room rates; Faye thought they might need to offer tour operators rates in the $50 to $70 range to attract any significant business away from similar facilities in nearby cities.

To stay with something closer to their current type of accommodations would require considerably more capital; based on some preliminary discussions with an architect, Cindy estimated a cost of $1.5 million. Just obtaining period furniture would be very expensive, and they didn't know if they could attract tour operators if they charged even the low end of the current rate structure.

The additional building could also house office space and ''meeting rooms designed to be meeting rooms.'' With the existing facilities, meetings had to be held in Randolph Hall or in rooms in the basement of the mansion. Neither option was fully satisfactory to Faye and Cindy.

While the grounds surrounding the mansion were spacious, the most likely place to build the additional rooms was on the far side of the pool from the mansion, running from Randolph Hall to the pond. Initial consultations with an architect suggested that three connected buildings could easily house the needed rooms.

Cindy and Faye wanted to develop a marketing strategy and plan for the additional rooms that they could present to Ramsay. They did not want to destroy the image of Nottoway in the process of trying to create additional business. Could they develop a reasonable plan to add rooms? What sort of rate structure would be needed to cover the costs? Were they missing some alternative way to increase revenues? The challenge of developing a workable plan excited them.

I t was early 1995 and Margarita Farga, Farggi's marketing director, was turning over in her mind the situation of her company's different businesses. The Farga/Farggi Corporation was a group of family companies, whose annual sales were expected to amount to between 2.8 and 3.0 billion pesetas in 1995 (1 U.S. dollar = 130 Spanish pesetas).

From its humble beginnings as a small traditional cake and pastry shop in 1957, its businesses had been expanded and diversified. By the end of 1994, it had three traditional cake shops operating under the name "Farga." It also manufactured and sold ice cream and frozen cakes for the catering market under the "Farggi" brand name.

However, its latest "great leap forward" had been in 1993, when it started to manufacture and market luxury ice cream for sale in "Farggi" stores—either owned by the company or franchised—and in supermarkets and other non-exclusive shops. As a result of the latter activity, their positioning was now very similar to that of the famous Häagen Dazs ice creams. In fact, it was rumored that someone had heard an unidentified Häagen Dazs manager say that, of all its competitors in the entire world, Farggi had been the one most able to adopt its concept, positioning, and way of selling premium ice cream with the greatest speed and precision.

In July 1993, the first exclusive "Farggi Tub's & Ice Cream" parlour was opened in Barcelona's upmarket Paseo de Gracia and, by the end of 1994, 13 such parlours had been opened, five owned by the company and eight franchises.

While she reviewed everything that had been achieved so far, Margarita tried to think what her company's action priorities should be, both in the short and in the medium term. Jesús Farga, her father and the company's president, insisted that all these questions needed to be clearly defined, as the future consolidation of the company depended on it.

HISTORY OF THE COMPANY

In 1957, Jesús Farga opened a traditional food retail store on Mayor de Gracia Street in Barcelona, near Plaza Lesseps. About five years later, after attending occupational training courses in cake making, he turned his food shop into a cake shop, keeping the same name "Farga." With the cake shop operating, he married Magdalena Bertrán and had four children: Elena, Margarita, Luís and Eduard.

This case was prepared by Professor Lluis Renart and Francisco Parés, lecturer at IESE, Barcelona, Spain. Copyright © 1995, IESE. Reprinted by permission.

About five years after that, Jesús Farga opened his second cake shop, on the Paseo de San Gervasio, in a neighborhood with a higher socioeconomic level, manufacturing and selling fresh cakes and pastry.

The First Diversification: "Tartas y Helados Farga"

With both cake shops operating at full capacity, in the late 1960s, Jesús Farga started to sell cakes outside of his shops, delivering them frozen to nearby cafeterias and restaurants, where they were thawed in a refrigerator or at room temperature before being served to customers.

Jesús Farga and his employees managed to perfect their formulas and processes to such a point that it was impossible for the end customers in the restaurants and cafeterias to tell that the cakes they were eating had been frozen and thawed beforehand.

The transportation and delivery service was carried out by José Manuel Garrido. In the course of time, he was to become one of Jesús Farga's right-hand men and, in 1994, he was still sales director. Also, at about that time, Farga started to make and sell ice cream.

Thus, slowly but surely, a second business activity, separate from that of the retail stores, came into being and consolidated itself under the name of "Tartas y helados Farga." Legally, both activities continued to be a single business activity owned by Jesús Farga.

The "Farggi" Brand

In spite of the excellent performance of both activities (sales in the cake and pastry stores, and the sale of frozen cakes and ice creams by delivery to cafeterias and restaurants), close monitoring of the second of these two lines of business convinced Jesús Farga of the need to use a different brand name.

Shortly before, during a trip to Italy, his friends and travelling companions had jokingly called him "Comendatore Farggi." Jesús decided to use his own italianized name to give a distinctive identity to his second business activity.

When, in 1974, he started to use the name "Farggi," the business's name was extended to "Farggi: tartas, helados y sorbetes de lujo" (Farggi: luxury cakes, ice creams and sorbets), to prevent any connotation of a second, lower quality brand name.

The First Factory in Badalona

In 1975, Jesús moved production to a factory measuring just under 1,000 meters in Badalona. One of the innovations at that time was the production and sale of individual portions of frozen cake and ice cream, with the same "luxury" quality.[1]

Jesús Farga observed with satisfaction that when he sold portions of ice cream or cake of between 100 and 150 millilitres, priced by the portion and in a market niche which he had practically all to himself, his sales revenues were substantially higher than when he sold by the litre. Although the production process had a somewhat higher skill and labour content, his margins improved considerably.

With the opening of the new factory in Badalona and due to the sudden economic downturn as a result of the oil crisis, Jesús Farga decided to legally reform his business as a limited company under the name Lacrem, S.A. At the same time, he brought his brother-in-law into the business as financial director and minority shareholder. For many years, the company's management team consisted of Jesús Farga, Miguel Bertrán, and José Manuel Garrido.

As a result of the increase in production capacity, the company was now able to sell its products virtually throughout Catalonia, although still basically focused on the catering sector.

Farggi's products and salesmen consistently used the image of the Farga cake retail stores as their reference point, quality guarantee, and visiting card. This enabled them to gain entry in restaurants and cafeterias with relative ease, smoothing their path in a market that was coveted by many other companies. Farga's guarantee also gave them a solid argument for defending higher sales prices.

Often, the "secret weapon" used by Farggi's salesmen and distributors was to get a foot in a new customer's door by first offering him the more typical frozen cake products, i.e., apple, chocolate, almond cakes, and the like. Once the restaurant or cafeteria had become a customer for the cakes and trusted the salesman, the service, the products and Farggi in general, the salesmen gradually introduced new articles, particularly ice creams.

This process was also facilitated by the fact that Farggi always differentiated itself from its possible competitors in the way it did things: it offered higher quality products, with a more craftlike appearance and a more attractive presentation, a more extensive and creative collection, etc. Therefore, it was usual for restaurants and cafeterias to always have some Farggi products in stock.

Regarding distribution and logistics, Farggi had its own distribution organization, delivering directly to the restaurants in Barcelona and its metropolitan area. In the rest of Catalonia, Farggi sold through independent distributors.

These distributors were almost always small local companies, enabling distribution to be fragmented into small units. The distributors were required to have their own warehouse, equipped with cold-storage chambers suitable for handling frozen products, a fleet of delivery vehicles and a minimum sales team. However, they were not required to work exclusively for Farggi, so it was common for Farggi's distributors to distribute other brands of ice cream such as Frigo, Camy, or Marisa, which targeted other market segments with less demanding quality requirements.

When it started to sell through distributors, Farggi offered them a 28 percent discount on ice creams and a 26 percent discount on cakes, applied on their own direct sales price, so that the distributor could sell to its restaurant customers at the same prices that Farggi would have charged if they had been direct customers. Following an "oil stain" strategy, distribution was gradually extended to other parts of Spain, using the same system of independent distributors.

The New Factory in Montgat and the Third Cake Shop in the Avenida Diagonal in Barcelona

In 1982–83, the new Montgat factory was opened.[2] With a floor area of 8,000 meters, it completely replaced the previous Badalona factory, which was closed. With the new factory operating, both capacity and service were improved.

Almost at the same time, Jesús Farga had the opportunity to rent premises on the prestigious Avenida Diagonal, in Barcelona, between the Paseo de Gracia and the Rambla de Cataluña, where it opened its third Farga cake shop, with restaurant service. A veritable flagship, it consisted of a ground floor, a mezzanine, and two basements where the kitchen and the workshop were installed. In total, it measured about 1,500 meters, in one the best locations in Barcelona.

After opening the new factory in Montgat, Farga's turnover amounted to about 400 million pesetas between the three cake shops, whose workforce now stood at 45 employees. For its part, the Farggi business was billing another 600 million pesetas, with 60 employees and 18 independent distributors. With its present distribution network, its ice creams and frozen cakes now reached cities as far afield as Madrid, Malaga, and Corunna.

The new shop, large and well-located, enhanced the reflected glory of the Farga cake shops that was projected on the Farggi brand, and increased general brand awareness.

The years until 1987–1988 were the company's period of greatest prosperity. It had excellent sales margins and was able to sell without any major marketing or advertising efforts, as it was virtually the sole player in the high quality ice cream and frozen cake segment in Spain.

Farggi was, and defined itself as, "luxury cakes, ice creams and desserts for restaurants." It utilized a single product concept, with about 250 products or stock keeping units, serving a single market: the catering trade.

COMPETITION GETS TOUGHER AND IT BECOMES NECESSARY TO INSTALL FREEZER CABINETS IN RESTAURANTS

Unfortunately for Farggi, in the late 1980s and early 1990s, the big Spanish ice cream companies, many of them owned by

---

[1]Individual portions of sorbet or ice cream were already common in Spain, but only in the impulse sale market segments and/or in the medium-10" quality segments.

[2]Small coastal town located to the north of Barcelona and adjoining Badalona.

multinationals, started to develop their own *ad hoc* product lines for the catering segment.

Companies such as La Menorquina (previously Marisa), Frigo, and Miko started to launch products with formats (sizes and appearance) similar to those of Farggi, although without seeking to position themselves on the same high quality level. They sold at lower prices, with advertising backing, and provided the restaurants with menu cards showing the desserts.

One of the consequences of the stiffening in competition was a fashion whereby a manufacturer had to install a freezer cabinet on deposit in the restaurant in order to be able to sell ice cream to it. Each freezer cost the ice cream manufacturer about 100,000 pesetas. The restaurants' order of priorities when buying ice cream now became freezer-price-quality-service.

Faced with this new market situation, Farggi had to invest considerable sums in installing freezers: 40 million pesetas in 1989, 70 million pesetas in 1990 and between 80 and 100 million pesetas in 1991.

An Offer to Buy Farggi

In 1989–90, Camy (Nestlé) started talks with a view to buying Farggi. At that time, Farggi was billing about 800 million pesetas and the entire group, including the cake shops, had a turnover of about 1.5 billion pesetas. It appears that the purchase offer was considerably above this figure and was therefore very tempting. Finally, it was decided to turn the offer down.

The Second Generation Joins the Company

In June 1989, Margarita Farga, the second daughter of Jesús Farga and Magdalena Bertrán, graduated in business studies from ESADE. Immediately afterwards, she went to Boston, in the United States, where she stayed until March 1990, following an extension management studies course at the renowned Harvard Business School. Margarita would be the first daughter to join the company.

In addition to her formal studies, Margarita recalled having accompanied her father on many business trips; he made her visit supermarkets and restaurants in various countries in order to find out about the prices, the products sold, who bought them and how, and other details.

First Awareness of the Existence of Häagen Dazs

When she was in Boston, Margarita first saw a Häagen Dazs ice cream parlour:

> I was struck by the fact that it sold a much more expensive ice cream and that it used the word ''luxury.'' The containers seemed very unsightly to me, but when I tried the ice cream, I realized that it tasted different, although I did not know why.

Another detail that caught her attention was that Häagen Dazs also sold ice creams on a stick. In Spain, this sort of ice folly or Popsicle had traditionally been little more than ''a chunk of ice with some sort of flavoring'' (usually orange or lemon), and occupied the lowest quality segments; one did not think of an ice folly as a ''luxury'' product.

The Häagen Dazs stores that Margarita saw seemed unappealing to her, and also fairly empty, in spite of the fact that they sold a good product which could be served with toppings. In her opinion, they lacked ''a touch of European design,'' which would give them more class.

Margarita's reaction could be summed up by saying that she noticed and appreciated the containers[3] and the presentation of the ice creams, their taste and the variety of flavors offered, the use of the word ''luxury'' and of the color gold in the materials and designs (although accompanied by other decorative details in black which she did not find so pleasing). At the same time, the stores, which she felt could be improved on in several respects, showed her ''what Farggi would like to be when it was grown up,'' as a commercial mechanism for reaching the end consumer more directly (selling ice cream for consumption in the store itself, strolling along the street, or to take home).

Although Margarita felt that ''it could be done even better,'' she was well aware that in Spain the few retailers who specialized in the sale of ice cream were almost without exception open only in summer, with inadequate fluorescent lighting, white tiles on the walls, and, as the only form of decoration, posters showing the various ice creams on sale and rows of glasses upside down on the shelves. With very few exceptions, the stores were independent, family-run businesses. Consequently, the staff usually wore no uniform or each person wore his own; and obviously, each store used its own name and had its own sign, with very poor quality lettering.

For Margarita, the concept of the Häagen Dazs-type ice cream parlour was ''love at first sight.'' However, if she was to introduce similar ice cream parlours in her own country, the first problem would be to find the way to make them viable throughout the year, since ice cream consumption in Spain had always been highly seasonal, falling to almost zero during the winter.[4] Also, unlike in the United States, there was very little ice cream consumption at home.

Margarita invited her parents to visit her, among other reasons so that they could see the Häagen Dazs ice cream parlours and share with her all these opinions and concerns. Jesús Farga decided that the matter had to be looked into in greater depth and that the first thing to do was to thoroughly analyze the product. So, when he went back to Barcelona, he took several samples of ice cream with him in his hand luggage.

---

[3]For example, she observed that, in the United States in general, round tubs were generally accepted as indicating that the ice cream they contained was higher quality and were labeled ''super premium,'' whereas the lower quality, lower price ice creams were sold in square-shaped packs.

[4]According to some estimates by industry sources, in 1989, 80 percent of ice cream consumption in Spain took place between May and October. The statistics indicated that ice cream consumption in Spain was about three litres per inhabitant per year, whereas in the United States it was about 15 litres.

By then, Farggi's ice cream was already being manufactured without stabilizers and with low air content. This was stated in the sales brochures as features indicative of its high quality.

The results of the analyses carried out in Barcelona showed that half a litre of Häagen Dazs weighed about 470 grammes, while the same volume of Farggi ice cream weighed between 300 and 350 grammes, and the ice creams of the major domestic brands weighed between 200 and 250 grammes. This was because Farggi had always sold ice cream with a low air content; in fact, every 100 litres of solid ingredients used to make Farggi ice cream yielded only about 150 litres of ice cream. From the same quantity of solid ingredients, the major Spanish brands might obtain about 200 litres of finished ice cream ready for consumption. Another significant difference was that the Häagen Dazs ice creams (and most of the North American ice creams) had a fat content of 16 percent, whereas the norm in Spain was 5 to 6 percent, including Farggi.

Margarita Returns to Barcelona

By the time Margarita returned to Barcelona in March 1990 and joined the company as "head" of marketing, Farggi's managers had realized that, if in previous years they had grown at annual rates of up to 30 percent, now they were growing more slowly and they had to invest more to obtain that growth. Also, because of the economic recession, restaurants were buying less, which made it even more difficult to recoup the investment in freezer cabinets, which the company bought on a lease.

The first thing Margarita did was to spend six months riding in the delivery trucks, crossing Barcelona from one end to the other, accompanying the company's salesmen and visiting distributors throughout Spain. This enabled her to acquire a certain degree of authority both inside and outside the company.

At about this time, it was also observed that the company's mousse cakes were very popular and had relatively little competition. Furthermore, in the course of his travels to other European countries, Jesús Farga had noticed that this was a widely accepted product in many of the more developed countries' markets. They were sold frozen in supermarkets in somewhat smaller sizes than those normally sold by Farggi to Spanish restaurants.

CONCERNS IN 1991, LEADING TO THE LAUNCH OF "PASTIMÚS" AND "CHEESECAKE," FROZEN CAKES TARGETING THE HOME CONSUMPTION MARKET AND SOLD IN FOOD RETAIL STORES[5]

By 1991, the entire management team in Farggi was reflecting on what seemed to them to be their chief strategic dilemma: whether to try to maintain growth in the catering market or to try to expand their market by entering another distribution channel with products for consumption in the home. All were aware that they had to find something that would enable them to achieve two objectives at the same time: to preserve and improve their image, and to sustain and improve the company's profitability.

One of the fruits of this search for new openings was the idea of launching frozen cakes targeted at the home consumption market, to be sold in supermarkets, select food shops, and the like, offering to install a Farggi freezer cabinet. They would be the first to launch this type of product in Spain.

It seemed to them that the traditional cake shop, although it continued to play a very important role, had probably entered a phase of gradual decline.

An extensive survey was carried out from the supply of frozen cakes in Europe and the United States.

While the frozen cakes made and sold by Farggi on the catering market measured 26 centimeters in diameter and 4.5 centimeters in height, the new cakes for home consumption would measure 19 centimeters in diameter and 3 centimeters in height, giving a net weight of 550 grammes. However, being mousse cakes, because they had light, airy bodies, it was considered that they were large enough to serve between six and eight portions.

A range of nine flavors was defined; five mousse flavors and four cheesecake flavors.[6] Following the serving recommendations for the products used by the catering market, on the packs of these cakes for home consumption it was clearly stated that they should not be eaten frozen but that they should be taken out of the freezer about two hours before serving to allow them to thaw. The names "Pastimús" and "Cheesecake de Farggi" were registered as trademarks, and all the other details regarding finish, formulas, processes, packaging, etc., were defined.

Farggi's sale price to the retailer was set at 920 pesetas, plus VAT, per unit, so that retailers, in turn, could sell them to the public at 1300 pesetas per unit; that is, with a gross margin of 380 pesetas. This retail sale price was higher than that of the ice cream bars and frozen cakes sold by the major national ice cream manufacturers but significantly lower than a fresh cake bought in a traditional cake shop.

Everyone was aware that, in some way which was still not clear at that time, the mousse cakes were laying the foundations for opening the distribution channel to ice cream for home consumption. Consequently, in 1991, it was decided to build a new cold storage chamber with a capacity of 10,000 m3 on a piece of land adjoining the Montgat factory. With this decision, Farggi took a step forward, anticipating future needs, whereas in the past its decisions to increase production and storage capacity had almost always been reactive. They had not expanded capacity until they had first created the market and the need.

---

[5]Throughout this case, we will call these shops non-exclusive retail stores because they sell Farggi products together with other food products, possibly including other ice cream brands.

[6]Mousse flavors were fresh pears with truffled chocolate; fresh lemon; vanilla and Irish coffee, dairy cream and fresh strawberries; and chocolate with walnuts. The cheesecake flavors were bitter orange, cranberries, pineapple, and raspberry. In total, there were nine Stock Keeping Units (SKUs).

LUIS FARGA ALSO GOES TO HARVARD. FIRST DIRECT CONTACT WITH HÄAGEN DAZS MANAGERS

In June 1991, Luis Farga, Jesús Farga's third child and Margarita's brother, graduated in economics. Then, like his sister, he went to Harvard University to follow an extension management course. Once there, he too was fascinated by the quality of North American premium ice cream and, like Margarita, insisted that Farggi should start to make and sell it in Spain.

During a visit made by his father, they decided to make an appointment with Häagen Dazs in order to explore the possibility of doing something together in Spain. The meeting took place at the end of 1991 and was rather cold. The Häagen Dazs executive they spoke to told them that any matter related to a European market should be discussed at Häagen Dazs' European headquarters in Paris.

In January 1992, they had another meeting with a senior Häagen Dazs manager in Paris, but there did not seem to be any possibility of collaboration between the two companies. In fact, the only clear impression they got from the meeting was that Häagen Dazs had not yet decided whether or not to try to penetrate the Spanish market.

He visited the Häagen Dazs parlour in the Av. Victor Hugo, where he saw that the company had managed to improve the appearance of their ice cream parlours, giving them more class. Jesús Farga traveled on to Brussels and London, where he observed and gathered information on the Häagen Dazs parlours open there.

In March 1992, Alimentaria (Food Industry Trade Fair) was held in Barcelona. Farggi was present with a stand of its own, where they were visited by the manager responsible for Häagen Dazs parlours in all Europe. He told them that Häagen Dazs was about to open their first ice cream parlour in Barcelona and that he wished to explore the possibilities of cooperation between the two companies.

In August 1992, while the Olympic Games were in fall swing in Barcelona, the first Häagen Dazs ice cream parlour was opened at number 85 in the centrally-located and classy Rambla de Cataluña. On their packaging, it was stated that the product was manufactured in France and imported by Helados Häagen Dazs, S.A.

MEANWHILE, THE "PASTIMÚS" PROJECT . . .

A few months earlier, in January 1992, Farggi had vigorously launched the frozen cakes "Pastimús" and "Cheesecake" on the Spanish market, targeting the home consumption market.

In a period of only three months, they installed about 300 freezer cabinets in supermarkets and other select food shops in Barcelona and the surrounding area, where Farggi continued to have direct physical distribution, and a further 500 freezers, through its distributors, in the rest of Spain.

The new range of frozen cakes for home consumption was readily accepted by this kind of retailer. However, the sales volume grew at a rate substantially lower than forecast. Farggi's managers considered that this was because fresh cakes were withstanding the incursion better than expected, and that the habit of buying their cakes fresh in the cake shops, rather than in supermarkets and food shops such as bakeries, delicatessens, or frozen food shops, was deeply ingrained in the public.

In any case, the market and customer surveys seemed to indicate that the low turnover was not due to the product itself, which people liked when they bought and tried it. They thought that perhaps it was because the Farggi trademark, traditionally centered on the catering market, was not sufficiently well known and did not have enough strength to persuade the final consumers to try the new cakes.

The lower turnover of frozen cakes for home consumption led Farggi to speed up the project to launch the ice creams—which were to be displayed in the same freezers—as soon as possible in order to recoup the heavy investment made in freezer cabinets. However, it should be pointed out that, at that time, Farggi's managers had not yet decided whether the launching of ice creams through the freezers already installed in retail outlets would be accompanied by the opening of exclusive Farggi ice cream parlours or not.

FURTHER CONTACT WITH HÄAGEN DAZS: POSSIBLE COOPERATION IN LOGISTICS

In September 1992, right after having opened their first Häagen Dazs parlour in the Rambla de Cataluña, in Barcelona, the multinational company's management took the initiative to contact Farggi again in order to explore the possibility of the Spanish company taking care of the physical distribution of its ice creams to the freezer cabinets it intended to install in supermarkets throughout Catalonia.

In the ensuing discussions, Häagen Dazs' managers provided the necessary detailed information on the number and foreseeable location of their freezers, the expected turnover, ice cream SKU numbers, restocking frequencies, etc., to enable Farggi's managers to study the foreseeable workload volumes, compatibility with their delivery schedules, etc.

For their part, Farggi's managers informed them of the areas and types of outlets that they could cover with their logistics distribution system, including the fact, which apparently seemed to be completely new to Häagen Dazs, that they were already distributing their frozen cakes in bakeries, delicatessens, and the like, in addition to selling in supermarkets.

Margarita Farga remarked:

I had my eyes and ears wide open because they were telling me the story I had dreamed of doing with our brand. The fact is that we were very unsure whether we should agree to carry out the physical distribution of Häagen Dazs. We knew that the company belonged to the extremely powerful Grand Metropolitan Group and its enormous economic potential inspired a certain amount of awe.

The talks went on, with both parties exploring the projects viability until, on a certain day in November 1992, something unexpected happened:

"We had already explored all the data and details of the proposed cooperation," said Margarita, "and we were relatively close to an agreement. But at that moment, the Häagen Dazs manager we mainly spoke with (a delightful person and very competent), possibly carried away by his enthusiasm at the way things were starting to come together, exclaimed, 'Fantastic, we'll install the first Häagen Dazs freezers in the three Farga cake shops!' That sentence, no doubt uttered with the best of intentions, made something snap inside us. It came as a thunderbolt! As if suddenly a veil had fallen from our eyes and it was crystal clear to us what we should not do!''

There were at least another three reasons against closing the physical distribution agreement. First, Häagen Dazs offered to pay Farggi only 13 percent on its list price to the retailer, while the latter, just for selling the product to the public, had a gross margin of more than 38 percent on the retail sale price.[7]

Furthermore, in the event that Farggi was to physically distribute Häagen Dazs ice creams outside of the metropolitan area of Barcelona, its direct distribution area, the money received would have to be shared in some way between Farggi and its 30 independent distributors.[8] In any case, taking into account the direct costs of storage, delivery, administration and control, Farggi estimated that 13 percent was not a very good rate for them.

---

[7]A food shop equipped with a freezer cabinet (belonging to Häagen Dazs) bought the ice creams at 440 pesetas + 6% VAT and resold them to the public at 675 pesetas, with a gross margin of 235 pesetas per 500 ml tub. From the supermarket's point of view, this was not only an excellent gross margin in absolute terms, but was even more so when the fast turnover and small area occupied by the freezer in the shop (approximately one meter) were worked into the calculation.

[8]The logistics process that had been designed would have been the following: Häagen Dazs would be responsible, on the one hand, for placing its ice creams (manufactured in France) in Farggi's central cold storage warehouse in Montgat, which would act as central warehouse. On the other hand, Häagen Dazs, through its own team of sales representatives, would carry out all the initial sales work with the supermarkets and would install the freezer cabinets. It would then notify Farggi of the new customer. Farggi would serve the initial order to load the freezer. From then on, Farggi's delivery/salesperson would visit the sales outlet at least twice a week. At each visit, he would verify stock status, replace the sold articles (placing the ice creams inside the freezer), and obtain the retailer's signature on the delivery note, which detailed what had been delivered. Farggi's delivery person would not collect payment, but would hand in the signed delivery notes at his operations base at the end of the day's work for verification, control, and subsequent dispatch to Häagen Dazs, who would issue the corresponding invoice and take care of collecting payment. (Apparently, it was Häagen Dazs' intention to issue only one monthly invoice, summarizing everything that had been delivered to a particular shop during each calendar month.) In return for its cooperation in this process, Farggi would receive 13 percent of Häagen Dazs' selling price to the retailer. It was estimated that the average order per visit and delivery would be at least about 12–14 "pints" (500 ml tubs). In autumn 1992, Häagen Dazs' selling price to the retailer was 440 pesetas (+ 6% VAT) per "pint." Consequently, Farggi's average revenue per visit would have been 13 percent of this amount, or about 744 pesetas per visit made by its own delivery personnel (13 pints sold per visit × 440 pesetas/pint × 13%). Obviously, the more successful and better accepted Häagen Dazs's ice creams became, the higher the average sale per visit. At that time, Häagen Dazs had installed only three freezers, but it intended to initiate an aggressive sales and freezer installation campaign as soon as it had solved the physical distribution issue.

The second, and perhaps most important and decisive reason against a logistics cooperation between Farggi and Häagen Dazs, was that José Manuel Garrido, Farggi's sales director, was never quite sure that the distribution of Häagen Dazs products was really compatible with the delivery of Farggi products, from the commercial and image viewpoints (signage on the vans, etc.).

Finally, Farggi's managers also thought that, if they acted merely as a logistics service for storage and delivery, any time that Häagen Dazs received a more attractive offer from another logistics company, they could decide to discontinue their relationship with Farggi, which could leave Farggi with excess storage and transport capacity, which it would not be easy to reoccupy.

In the end, the negotiations were broken off and, almost without giving it a second thought, Farggi's management team took the momentous decision: ''We must open our own Farggi parlours as soon as possible!'' Initially, the plan was to open five Farggi-owned ice cream parlours, the first of which had to be open by June 1993 to gain maximum benefit from the summer season. They knew that they would need bank financing for this. Consequently, right from the start, they planned and executed the entire project on the understanding that subsequent growth of the number of exclusive Farggi parlours would be by franchising.

Farggi's managers were well aware that both Farggi, through its Farga cake shops, and Häagen Dazs created and developed their image through establishments that bore their name. Thus, one of the key success factors would be to get customers to buy the luxury ice creams in the supermarket thanks to the memory and image they took away from their visit to the exclusive ice cream parlour.

A FEW MORE MONTHS OF FRENETIC ACTIVITY: THE DESIGN OF ''FARGGI TUB'S & ICE CREAM''

Once the decision to open their own parlours had been made, there began a frantic race against time. Numerous operational details concerning the new ice cream parlours and the range of ice creams had to be decided.

They designed a new logo with the ''Farggi'' brand name and considered different names for their new establishments (they did not want to call them ''ice cream parlours''). They did not know what name to give their ice cream containers either.

Finally, they decided that the formal name would be ''*Farggi Tub's & Ice Cream.*''[9] Generally, they referred to them as their ''shops.''

In addition, they had to resolve, decide, and define a large number of operational details, such as:

1. Find a container manufacturer who could supply food-quality printed cardboard tubs. Apparently, there was no such manufacturer in Spain. It was also difficult to find a suitable supplier of plastic lids for the tubs. Then, the tub had to be ''dressed.'' Its decoration had to be designed so that it

---

[9]''Tub's'' is a registered trademark of Farggi.

conveyed the idea of "luxury ice cream," using gold and navy blue, which became the "corporate livery."

However, there was another problem: the tub manufacturer (which was not a Spanish company), stipulated minimum runs of 100,000 units for each model or type of decoration. The solution was to print and manufacture a standard or universal tub model, a preprinted base to which two labels would be added: one on the tub front or side, with the name of the flavor (and stamped with the outline of the object defining the flavor, for example, a strawberry), and another with the barcode, which would be stuck on the tub base. Likewise, it was decided to buy lids made of white plastic, to which a round sticker was added. Initially, on a temporary basis, these labels would have to be stuck on by hand, which would slow down and increase the cost of the production process. The primary goal was to get the product on the market as soon as possible. These production details could be improved at a later date.

2. Define the range of ice cream flavors to sell. Then, develop the corresponding formulas and production processes. For this purpose, besides using the knowledge and experience of Farggi's production and management team, numerous trips were made to the United States to make contact with various manufacturers of machinery for making ice cream. Jesús Farga also contacted experts in formulas and production processes for North American-style ice cream.

During these months, Farggi's management team and technical and production staff, with outside help when necessary, developed the formulas and processes for the 25 flavors[10] that made up the new range of ice creams for sale both in Farggi's exclusive ice cream parlours and through the 800 freezer cabinets that were already installed in supermarkets and other non-exclusive food shops to sell the "Pastimús" and "Cheesecake" frozen cakes.

Establishing the formulas and production processes for the new range of ice creams involved serious technical difficulties because Farggi wanted to use only absolutely natural ingredients and because the new ice cream had to meet the following specifications: about 16 percent fat content (instead of the 5 to 6 percent that was usual in Spain, even in the ice cream previously manufactured by Farggi), a very low air content, and no stabilizers or artificial coloring.

In fact, so great were the technical difficulties that the formulas and processes were not considered to have been finalized until June 1993, when the opening of the first Farggi ice cream parlour was imminent.

These formulas produced ice creams that were very similar to those of Häagen Dazs. On the other hand, both companies' premium ice creams were clearly different from any other ice creams manufactured at that time in Spain.

3. It was necessary to purchase, install, and start up a number of new machines in the Montgat factory in order to manufacture and/or package the new types of ice cream.

---

[10]Of these 25 flavours, at least three were typically Spanish and therefore had no Häagen Dazs counterpart: milk meringue streaked with cinnamon, mandarin sorbet, and Spanish nougat.

4. It was also difficult to find a manufacturer who could supply the 9.5-litre cardboard cylinders that were required as bulk containers for use in the glass-fronted freezer cabinets in the Farggi parlours, for serving to the public in individual scoops. In Spain, the normal size was five litres, but Farggi's managers wanted them bigger, so that they would not have to be changed so often and so that they would fit better in the freezer cabinet.

5. Much to their surprise, they also found that there was no Spanish manufacturer capable of supplying freezer cabinets with the machines and thermostats needed to keep the ice cream precisely between $-18°C$ and $-20°C$. This was an essential detail, not only to keep the ice cream in perfect condition (manufactured with a high milk solids content), but also to ensure that the consumer would find it cold enough when he ate it. Finally, after a hard search, they managed to locate a manufacturer of freezer cabinets in the United States, to whom they sent their first orders.

However, a surprising incident occurred: when these freezer chests were ready, the North American manufacturer shipped them to Europe. When Farggi's managers asked for the address and telephone number of the collection point, they discovered to their horror that the North American manufacturer had assumed that they were Häagen Dazs licensees and had sent the freezer chests to the Häagen Dazs warehouse in Paris! So, in March 1993, Häagen Dazs found out that Farggi was planning to open its own ice cream parlours.

6. The interior of the freezer cabinets installed in the retail outlets where the frozen cakes were being sold had to be redesigned so that they could also be used to store the new tubs in such a way that customers could help themselves directly from the freezer.

7. A large number of decisions had to be made regarding the range of products to be sold in the Farggi ice cream parlours, the functional design of the parlours, and their decoration. For example, one of the key decisions was whether only ice creams would be served, as seemed to be the case in Häagen Dazs, or whether coffee, soft drinks, and pastries would also be served. If coffee was to be served, the establishment's decoration depended, among other things, on whether the coffee machine would be located in a place where it was visible to the public, as in most bars and cafeterias, or not. If they served coffee and pastries, would the typical bar counter be installed or would they only be served to be taken away or to be eaten sitting at the tables?

There was never any doubt that portions of Pastimús and Cheesecake would be served in Farggi's parlours, and this feature would clearly differentiate them from Häagen Dazs.

In the end, it was decided that coffee, soft drinks, and pastries would be served, in addition to ice creams and cakes. There were at least two reasons for this decision: on the one hand, Farggi's managers were continually concerned about ensuring their parlours' commercial and economic viability during the winter months, when ice cream consumption drops off considerably. In fact, the thought process followed by Farggi's management team had been the following: "Our growth will necessarily depend on granting franchises. Therefore, inevitably, the exclusive Farggi parlours must be profitable for our future franchisees. Consequently, the parlours and the range of products served in them must be designed so that they make good business sense in their own right, even if we stay with the idea that most of their sales should be ice creams.''

Secondly, by offering and serving combinations of scoops of ice cream with portions of cake (possibly with toppings, such as whipped cream, melted chocolate, caramel sauce, or other fruit sauces), the aim was to inspire consumers to imitate them and prepare similar dessert combinations in their own homes, after purchasing the ingredients in the Farggi parlours or from the freezers at the supermarkets. As Margarita Farga added ''. . . by this means, we wanted to get the final consumer to identify with the sweet world of Farggi.''

8. It was also decided that they would manufacture and sell three varieties[11] of premium ice cream on sticks, to be called ''batonets,'' a name that was unique in Spain.

9. Having established the products and services to be sold in their own parlours, menus were printed so that customers wishing to consume the products sitting at the establishment's tables could choose in complete comfort and ask the waiters to bring them what they wanted.

10. Regarding the decoration of the first Farggi parlour, it was necessary to contact a number of contractors and interior decorators. One of the prerequisites was that these companies should be organizations large enough to be able to fit out and decorate other exclusive Farggi parlours (either owned by Farggi or franchised) in any part of Spain. Also, right from the start, there was a serious and persistent effort to define designs that used standard measurements and specifications, so that they could easily be reproduced in other premises of a different size, in different locations and with different floor layouts.

The idea was that Farggi parlours would have two parts: the entrance had always to be ''very Farggi,'' with a more striking and direct style of decoration, lighting and signage. Further inside, on the other hand, in what Farggi's managers called the ''tea room,'' the style of decoration would be softer and more flexible, and could vary from one parlour to another, although they would always use fine materials such as marble and wood.

11. The last three important decisions were, first, to run a number of blind tests of the ice cream developed at the Montgat factory, comparing them with Häagen Dazs' ice cream. Farggi's managers reached the conclusion that, at least when the test was carried out blind, when the customer did not know which brand of ice cream he or she was tasting, the result was a draw between the two companies. In actual fact, what happened was that with certain flavors there was a preference for the ice creams of one manufacturer, while in other flavors there was a preference for the ice creams of the other manufacturer. There

was a third group of flavors where there was no significant preference in either direction.

Encouraged by this result, Farggi's managers then decided that their ice creams would be sold at exactly the same retail price as Häagen Dazs' products, both in their parlours and in the freezer cabinets installed in supermarkets and other sales outlets. First, this would give them the same (substantial!) unit margins that Häagen Dazs enjoyed. Second, selling at lower prices could have been interpreted by the consumers as an indication that Farggi's ice creams were lower quality. Finally, they did not have any wish or intention to start a hypothetical price war with Häagen Dazs.[12]

The final decision concerned the location of their first parlour. After considering various options as regards site, size and rent, it was decided that their first parlour would be at number 94 of the stately Paseo de Gracia, a few yards along the street from Saudis world famous building ''La Pedrera'' and a few blocks from Häagen Dazs first parlour on the Rambla de Cataluña.

THE FIRST ''FARGGI TUB'S & ICE CREAM'' PARLOUR IS OPENED

The first Farggi parlour opened its doors to the public in July 1993, almost one year after Häagen Dazs opened its first parlour. A few months later, in November of the same year, the second Farggi parlour was opened in the Rambla de Cataluña, barely three blocks away from the first Häagen Dazs parlour and on the same side of the street. A few weeks later, on 2 December, the third parlour was opened in the ''L'Illa Diagonal'' shopping centre, on the Avenida Diagonal.

These three parlours were owned and operated by Farggi.[13] The necessary investments had been made by the company itself and they were run by Farggi personnel. Responsibility for the day-to-day management and supervision of the parlours was assigned to Marcos Serra. Eduard Farga was made responsible for planning and initiating relationships with franchisees: identification of future franchisees, negotiation, implementation, start-up and monitoring.

On his return from the United States, Luís Farga had also joined the company as assistant sales director, with direct responsibility for the distribution of Farggi products in supermarkets and other types of non-exclusive food shops. His first task was to study the performance of each of the freezers where frozen mousse

---

[11]Swiss chocolate with black chocolate, vanilla with mild chocolate and almonds, and vanilla with milk chocolate.

---

[12]This price policy would be continued during the following months: Farggi accepted a role as price ''follower'' with respect to Häagen Dazs, so that when Häagen Dazs took the initiative to increase prices, Farggi followed suit, raising prices by the same amount.

[13]All Farggi parlours are exclusive, that is, they only sell products made by Farggi. In this text, we use the expression ''Farggi-owned parlours'' to refer to the parlours in which the investment and operation are Farggi's responsibility, using the expression ''franchised parlours'' when the investment and operation are the responsibility of an independent licensee, although always under Farggi's control and supervision.

cakes were sold. Any freezer that did not reach certain minimum sales levels was reinstalled in a different shop.

The opening of these first three Farggi-owned parlours—true flagships for "Farggi Tub's & Ice Cream"—attracted a lot of attention and the company started to receive unsolicited requests to open franchised Farggi parlours.

This fitted in perfectly with the company's intentions and plans, since they had all been aware, right from the start of the new project, that franchises would be indispensable if they were to continue growing at a high enough rate. Indeed, opening the first three parlours had required an investment of about 140 million pesetas, which the company had financed with bank loans.

Therefore, in early 1994, on the basis of the experience acquired during the first months of operation of the three Farggi-owned parlours and other sources of information, Margarita Farga drew up an operating manual running to more than 200 pages detailing, from A to Z, the operation of a Farggi parlour.

THE FIRST FRANCHISED FARGGI PARLOUR IS OPENED; THE OTHER PARLOURS OPENED IN 1994

With the manual now available, in February 1994 the owner of a restaurant that was a customer for Farggi products opened the first franchised Farggi parlour in Vilanova i La Geltrd.[14]

The agreement initially took the form of a pre-contract, while Elena Farga, who had a degree in law and worked in a law firm unrelated to the company, worked against the clock to draw up a highly detailed franchise contract that eventually ran to over 40 pages.

In May 1994, the fourth Farggi-owned parlour was opened in the Port Olimpic in Barcelona. A trial run had been carried out beforehand by opening a corner franchise, almost a window franchise, in "El Túnel del Port," one of the many restaurants in the area. In view of the enormous success of the window, it was decided to open the parlour while maintaining the corner franchise. This "double sale" in the same area was still operating at the time of writing this case.

In May 1994, the seventh exclusive sales outlet was opened (the third of the franchised outlets) in Conde de Penalver Street in Madrid, near the El Corte Inglés department store. In this case, the licensee was Farggi's own distributor in Madrid.

In June, the fifth Farggi-owned parlour was opened in the heart of Barcelona: the Plaza de Cataluña. Located between El Corte Inglés and the head of the Ramblas, Barcelona's most famous boulevard, this parlour would benefit from high visibility and high pedestrian traffic. With this parlour, Farggi's management team had a certain sensation of having achieved, in barely one year and a half, the objective that they had set themselves in November 1992 of opening five Farggi-owned parlours. They were

frankly pleased with the impact they had in Barcelona and on the ice cream market.

In the same month, the fourth franchised parlour was opened in Salou, a well-known coastal town located a few kilometers to the south of Tarragona. Finally, in the next few months, another three franchised parlours were opened: in the port of Mataró, in Malaga, and in Calella de Palafrugell, on the Costa Brava.

Thus, the first full year of activity of Farggi Tub's & Ice Cream (July 1993–July 1994) ended with 12 parlours open: five Farggi-owned in the city of Barcelona, and seven franchises (one corner franchise in Barcelona's Port Olimpic, four in towns on the Catalonian coast, one in Madrid and another in Malaga). After the summer, in September 1994, a second franchised parlour was opened in Madrid (Pintor Sorolla–Santa Engracia).

In order to make sure that the franchisees properly complied with the conditions contained in Farggi's manual, the services of an independent company that specialized in the control and monitoring of food franchises were hired. This company used the "mystery buyer" method, which basically consists of visiting the establishments without any prior announcement or identification to verify the level and quality of service to customers, the establishment's cleanness and appearance, and other details.

New Parlours that Would Be Opened in 1995 and After

In February 1995, the third Farggi franchised parlour would be opened in Madrid. A further nine new franchised Farggi parlours were scheduled: in the "Maremagnum" shopping and entertainment complex in the port of Barcelona; in the Calle del Pi, also in Barcelona; in Vic (province of Barcelona); in L'Escala (province of Gerona); in Benidorm (province of Alicante); in Puerto Banús (province of Malaga); in Marbella (province of Malaga); in Lloret de Mar (province of Barcelona); in Corunna; in Las Arenas, near Bilbao; and in Ciutadella, in Menorca.

In short, if these plans worked out, by the end of 1995, Farggi would have a chain of 25 exclusive ice cream parlours, five owned by the company itself and located in the city of Barcelona, and 20 franchises.

By the end of the fifth year of operations, Eduard Farga expected to have about 100 exclusive Farggi parlours open, of which 90 would be franchises and perhaps 10 Farggi-owned.

EVOLUTION OF THE SALE OF FARGGI PRODUCTS IN SUPERMARKETS AND OTHER TYPES OF NON-EXCLUSIVE SHOP FOR HOME CONSUMPTION

The first Farggi products for consumption at home had been the "Pastimús" and "Cheesecake" cakes, which were distributed and sold frozen, but were to be eaten after thawing. They had been

---

[14]A coastal town with about 40,000 inhabitants located about 40km south of Barcelona.

introduced in early 1992 by installing about 800 freezer cabinets in supermarkets and other types of retailers.

Even back then, Farggi's management team had guessed that this range of cakes would eventually be complemented with another range of ice creams to be eaten at home, possibly taken from or based on the range of Farggi ice creams sold to restaurants.

Unfortunately, sales of this range of frozen cakes were growing at a much slower rate than expected. Margarita Farga attributed this slowness to the need to induce and allow time for a double change in the end customers' purchasing and eating habits, since, in Spain, it was not the custom for people to buy frozen cakes in the supermarket. Normally, people either ate fresh cakes bought in a traditional cake shop, or ice cream bars and frozen cakes bought in supermarkets and eaten while still frozen.

In spite of this difficulty, Farggi had never advertised its frozen mousse cakes in the mass media.

As a result of all this, sales of the Pastimús and Cheesecake range in some of the freezers were just above 100,000 pesetas per freezer per year, at Farggi's selling prices to the retailer. Although this was a minimum figure, the company's managers admitted that the project would only have been profitable in the long term. There were even cases where some freezers had to be relocated, installing them in restaurants and cafeterias.

Throughout 1992, these freezers were installed in various kinds of sales outlets. From November 1992 onwards, the attention of Farggi's management team was concentrated on preparing the launch of ''Farggi Tub's & Ice Cream,'' so little attention was paid to the Pastimús and Cheesecake range during that period.

Of course, these cakes were included in the range of products to be sold in the Farggi ice cream parlours.

However, once the first Farggi parlour had been opened in Paseo de Gracia, modifications were made to the freezers' shelving to be able to display the ice cream ''Tub's'' in them, starting with the freezers installed in Barcelona. At the same time, Farggi's sales teams reopened negotiations with some supermarket chains with a view to relaunching the installation of new freezer cabinets which would sell the ice cream ''Tub's'' and the Farggi frozen mousse cakes right from the start.

Like Häagen Dazs, Farggi's policy was first to open an exclusive Farggi parlour in a city, to create the product's image, and then start distributing ice creams in supermarkets through the freezer cabinets. Of course, Farggi had the advantage of the fact that a large number of freezers had already been installed.

Consequently, all that was needed in order to expand the product range was to change the inside shelving and obtain the retailer's agreement, which was relatively easy as the sales turnover of a Farggi freezer cabinet increased very substantially, almost always to about 500,000 pesetas per year, at Farggi prices to the retailer.

Although both Farggi and Häagen Dazs maintained a discreet silence regarding their costs and margins, a number of experts in ice cream manufacture indicated that, even taking into account the fact that both brands used only top quality natural ingredients, the cost of the raw materials and packaging would probably not be more than 35 percent of their sale price for ''Tub's'' and ''pints'' to retailers.

Generally speaking, although both had started in Barcelona, there was relatively little confrontation between Farggi and Häagen Dazs. First, because both were still in an early phase of market entry.

Second, because Farggi already had a large installed base of freezer cabinets. Third, because both realized that they could coexist perfectly, sharing presence in many supermarkets and even in smaller shops.

In spite of this, there were a few clashes. For example, Farggi managed to be present in all the Caprabo supermarkets (55 points of sale), whereas Häagen Dazs would only be present in the 15 largest, sharing presence with Farggi. In those supermarkets where both brands' freezers were installed side by side, their sales volumes were very similar.

On the other hand, in the Pizza Hut chain, even though Farggi had managed to get its foot in first, in March 1994 Häagen Dazs became the sole supplier of ice creams. However, Farggi remained as a cake supplier for Pizza Hut, so the business relationship was not broken. Much the same thing happened in the Pans & Company sandwich chain, which bought ice creams from Häagen Dazs and cakes from Farggi.

In August 1993, Farggi signed a contract with the Barcelona Football Club for the exclusive sale of ice creams in its sports facilities. The purpose of this contract was to create brand impact and enable a large number of people to taste Farggi's products. ''Mini Tub's'' (100 ml) and ''Batonets'' were sold from 25 carts at 350 pesetas each. The contract would run for three years, with Farggi paying 15 million pesetas/year.

MEANWHILE, HÄAGEN DAZS . . .

Farggi's managers believed that, by the end of 1994, Häagen Dazs had about 25 parlours operating, of which two were actually owned by the company: one in the Rambla de Cataluña in Barcelona and the other in the centre of Madrid.

Regarding distribution, it was estimated that they had about 600 freezer cabinets installed in Barcelona and a further 400 in Madrid, mainly in relatively small outlets, but with presence in some supermarket and hypermarket chains. The physical distribution in the Barcelona area was carried out by La Menorquina, although this relationship seemed to have ended by the end of 1994. In other parts of Spain, they used the services of professional frozen product logistics companies.

In June 1994, Häagen Dazs had introduced a range of four varieties of ice cream under the name ''Exträas,'' which it sold in its parlours but not in supermarkets. This range had a distinctive presentation and seemed to have achieved a relative success.

By the end of 1994, one or two Häagen Dazs franchisees had raised the possibility with Farggi of changing flag and joining its chain.

MAIN STRATEGIC DILEMMAS FACING THE FARGA/FARGGI GROUP IN EARLY 1995

In early 1995, Margarita Farga, as Farggi's marketing director, was reflecting on what had been done so far and what had been achieved.

To help her organize her thoughts about the Farga/Farggi Group's business activities, she sometimes used the following "branch system:"

Farga/Farggi Group:
 1. Farga traditional cake shops
 2. Farggi businesses
 2.1 Farggi products sold to restaurants
 2.2. Farggi products sold to retail shops
 2.2.1. Sold to non-exclusive shops (supermarkets, etc.)
 2.2.2. Sold to the exclusive Farggi parlours
 2.2.2.1. Farggi-owned parlours
 2.2.2.2. Franchised parlours

Some of her thoughts and concerns about each of these "branches of the Farga/Farggi tree" were the following:

On the one hand, the three Farga cake shops (item 1) were carrying on as usual, with 37 years of professional and trade experience, as upmarket establishments making fresh cakes and high-quality pastries, sold directly to the public either for consumption on the premises or to take home. There did not seem to be any intention of modifying their activities or increasing the number of such establishments.

On the other hand, there were all the Farggi products (item 2).

First among these, both for historical reasons of "order of appearance" and because of its basic economic importance, was the sale of ice creams and frozen cakes to restaurants and cafeterias (item 2.1), which was still the group's largest business in terms of sales: excluding sales by the Farga cake shops, it had accounted for 60 percent of total ice cream and frozen cake sales under the Farggi brand name in 1994.

Margarita was aware that, since November 1992, this "business 2.1" had been somewhat neglected as a result of the strategic priority given by all the company's personnel to designing and starting up the "Farggi Tub's & Ice Cream" project. Consequently, it seemed to her that the time had come to redefine and refocus it strategically, both as a brand and as its product range or collection.

Restaurants and cafeterias were a mature market, but one in which some fast food chains were growing rapidly. However, during 1993 and 1994, Margarita had not had the impression that Farggi's customary competitors in this field (Frigo, Camy, Menorquina, Avidesa, etc.) were introducing any striking novelties.

In third place was "business 2.2," the sale of Farggi products in shops and parlours for consumption at home, on the premises, or on the street (impulse sale). It seemed clear to Margarita that Farggi's management team's chief achievement during the previous three years (1992–1994) had been the creation of a relatively complex strategic platform for the sale of Farggi ice creams and frozen cakes for consumption in Farggi ice cream parlours and at home. Over a period of three years, they had taken this business from zero to 40 percent of the total sales of Farggi products, "business 2" in 1994.

According to a market survey carried out in September 1994, their only competitor in this "business 2.2," in the opinion of a sample of final consumers in Barcelona, was Häagen Dazs. It seemed that Farggi and Häagen Dazs were the only two ice cream brands that had really succeeded in positioning and consolidating themselves in the high quality, premium price segment of the ice cream market in Spain. However, at the same time, it seemed obvious to her that both "luxury" ice cream brands competed with the major brands, such as Frigo, Camy, Avidesa, Miko, etc., given that the consumer, when buying ice cream, had to decide whether he wanted high quality ice cream at a high price or medium quality ice cream at a medium price.

Regarding sales in non-exclusive shops (item 2.2.1), by the end of 1994, Farggi was distributing its ice cream "Tub's" and frozen cakes (Pastimús and Cheesecake) in Catalonia, Madrid, and Malaga through 800 freezer cabinets installed in supermarkets and other retail sales outlets. Farggi's management team were of the opinion that, in these three areas, the market was still a long way from being saturated and that in Catalonia, Madrid, and Malaga-Costa del Sol, they could install up to a maximum of 6,000 freezers.

It was also their intention to expand the distribution of "Tub's" and frozen cakes as new exclusive Farggi parlours were opened in other locations; the parlours would create the brand image in each location, paving the way for sales in non-exclusive shops. The brand image was also needed to justify the price premium of Farggi ice creams, which were sold to the public in supermarkets at 675 pesetas for half a litre, whereas the usual price for Frigo, Camy and Miko ranged between 400 and 450 pesetas per litre, although they often ran promotions during which the price could be reduced to as little as 350 pesetas per litre.

By the end of 1994, Farggi had about 80 applications to open new franchised Farggi parlours, so Margarita was sure that there would be no obstacle to growth due to lack of parlours. However, depending on the rate at which new parlours were opened and the market size and potential of each town or city in which they were to be opened, a limiting factor might be their financial capacity to invest in the purchase of freezer cabinets. By the end of 1994, each freezer cost 150,000 pesetas. The upside of this was that, thanks to the sale of "Tub's" and cakes in the same freezer, sales figures exceeding 600,000 pesetas per freezer per year were being achieved, at Farggi's sales prices to the retailer. In a large supermarket, the figure could easily be double this amount. When Farggi sold to retailers through its local distributor, it granted the distributor a 20 percent discount, giving a net billing for Farggi per freezer of 480,000 pesetas/year. Even so, with such figures, it was possible to depreciate a freezer over a reasonable period of five years, financing them by credit lines or leasing operations.

Finally, regarding sales in exclusive Farggi parlours (item 2.2.2.), a distinction had to be made between Farggi-owned parlours and franchised parlours.

As stated earlier, by the end of 1994, Farggi had five parlours of its own (item 2.2.2.1), all of them located in the city of Barcelona. The parlours in Paseo de Gracia, Rambla de Cataluña and L'Illa had been operating for barely a year. Port Olimpic and Plaza de Cataluña, which were opened in mid-1994, had only been going for a few months and had yet to pass the acid test of the winter season.

In Margarita Farga's opinion, these five Farggi-owned parlours were "perfect as flagships," to create the necessary Farggi image: (a) to sell "Tub's" in the supermarkets; (b) to promote sales of new franchises; and (c) to generate a good image, in general, with a very broad range of groups and audiences, such as gastronomic journalists, retailers, financial institutions, etc. Their profitability was in some cases "very high," while in others she considered it to be "satisfactory."

The company's immediate plans were not to open any more Farggi-owned parlours, except in cities or streets which might be considered "strategic," necessary for the process of creating or strengthening the company's image.

There could perhaps be a middle road, consisting of having part-owned parlours, in which Farggi would share ownership of the parlour with a local partner.

Regarding the franchised parlours (item 2.2.2.2), one point that had to be remembered was that some of them were seasonal, open to the public for only about six months. Such was the case of the parlours in Salou, Calella, Mataró.... It appeared that the seasonal parlours, located in coastal resorts, were "extremely profitable." Other parlours were open all the year round: Madrid and Malaga. The key profitability factor for these parlours would be their performance during the difficult winter months.

At least until the end of 1994, these franchised parlours did not pay any royalties nor had they made any initial down payment to buy their franchising rights when they signed the contract. Farggi obtained its profits from the captive sale to its franchisees of five products or groups of products:

1. Ice cream, in 9.5 litre packs ("bulks"), which they resold "by the scoop."
2. Ice cream in "Tub's" for taking away.
3. "Pastimús" and "Cheesecake" frozen cakes for taking home whole.
4. Frozen cakes for selling in the parlour in portions.
5. Various complementary articles, such as paper napkins, cone wafers and paper cups for serving the balls of ice cream, toppings and sauces, uniforms, etc....

The margin, the difference between the purchase price from Farggi and the selling price to the public in the parlour, was very high, about 65 percent of the retail price. To put it the other way round, the cost of the products sold to the public was 35 percent of the selling price. Of course, the parlour owner had to pay the rent, wages and social security, financial expenses (if any), electricity, water, amortize the machinery and facilities, etc.

Farggi required that parlours which were to be open all year round should have a minimum surface area of 100 meters. A parlour of this size required investments of about 20–25 million pesetas in machinery, equipment, and decoration.

In the case of parlours that were open only during the summer season, Farggi allowed them to be smaller, with a minimum of about 50 meters. The investment to fit out an ice cream parlour of this size usually ran to between 12 and 15 million pesetas.

SOME FINANCIAL INFORMATION

Being a family-owned company, Lacrem, S.A. did not publish its balance sheets. Traditionally, it had always made a profit which had enabled it to finance its growth from self-generated funds. Exceptionally, in 1993, the company had recorded a negative cash flow. However, cash flow had been moderately positive again in 1994. The economic forecasts for 1995 and 1996 were for a strong increase in cash flow, which would enable the company to progressively decrease its level of indebtedness, open new Farggi-owned parlours, or buy more freezer cabinets.

As marketing director, Margarita had a relatively modest budget of about 25 or 30 million pesetas, which she used to carry out typical marketing activities, such as local promotional events when new parlours were opened, tasting events, preparing the new menus for the company's parlours, a number of public relations activities, etc.

The Group's turnover, which consists of Lacrem, S.A.'s turnover plus the final turnover (sales to the public) of the five Farggi-owned parlours, less Lacrem, S.A.'s billing to these five parlours (so as not to count twice), was expected to double between 1993 and 1995, as follows:

	1992	+5%
	1993	−15%
	1994	+40%
Forecast	1995	+30%
Forecast	1996	+30%

The investments in the factory had amounted to about 350 million pesetas. Total investments in Farggi-owned parlours and freezer cabinets had amounted to another 350 million pesetas.

By the end of 1994, for all its sales activities, including sales to restaurants and cafeterias, the company had an installed base of about 3,000 freezer cabinets and a further 2,000 top-opening freezer chests, used by restaurants and cafeterias to store their stocks of Farggi products.

SOME QUESTIONS ABOUT THE FUTURE

Faced with this situation, Margarita Farga was turning over a number of questions in her mind. For example:

- Who were they really competing against? Against Häagen Dazs? Against the traditional big ice cream companies: Frigo, Camy, etc.? Against the traditional cake shops? Were they perhaps expanding the market, expanding consumption among people who would not otherwise eat ice cream?
- How quickly should they grow? In which cities or geographical areas? Farggi was already receiving a large number of franchise applications from outside of Spain. Should it start to internationalize itself? If so, which countries should it go to first? Should they open directly in other countries or reach an agreement with a master franchiser who would be given exclusive rights for an entire country?

- Were five Farggi-owned parlours enough or should they try and open more? Should they maintain a certain percentage or proportion of Farggi-owned parlours out of the total number of exclusive Farggi parlours?
- Would it be enough to open exclusive parlours to create the necessary image or should they also run advertising campaigns in the mass media? In the case of the latter, what should be their positioning and message? It was clear that such advertising would have to promote high quality, premium price products, but should they aim for an ''adult'' positioning like Häagen Dazs? Would a more family-style positioning be better, with advertisements showing children with their parents and/or grandparents or perhaps a ''for gourmets of all ages'' positioning?
- What things should they, try and do like Häagen Dazs and what things should they do differently in order to achieve a distinct, differentiated image? For example, on the subject of ice cream flavors, should they make ''international flavors'' or should they differentiate themselves by creating flavors more in tune with the Spanish palate?

  In short, what were the key success factors of ''Farggi Tub's & Ice Cream?'' What things could Farggi do that Häagen Dazs could not or did not want to do? Looking at it the other way round, what things could Häagen Dazs do that Farggi could not do, or at least could not do so well? What things could both of them do with more or less equal cost-effectiveness, without any differential competitive advantages on either side?

- Finally, Farggi's management team was aware of a significant dilemma: (a) They could either go on alone, self-financing their growth, in which case they might not be able to keep up with Häagen Dazs and other competitors might appear in the same segment;[15] or (b) it might be better to allow a non-family investor to come in with a view to accelerating their market penetration at home and abroad.

  No doubt, this list of questions was not exhaustive and what most worried Margarita was the possibility that she might have left out some key decision in this maze of decisions and opportunities.

---

[15]On 5 February 1995, the newspaper *Expansión* published an article stating that the North American ice cream company Ben & Jerry had recruited Robert Holland as its new CEO. The article closed by quoting Holland, an ex-McKinsey consultant, as saying, ''We will be in Europe next year.'' According to the same article, Ben & Jerry's sales in 1993 totaled 140 million dollars, with a net income of 7.2 million U.S. dollars.

The Spanish ice cream market had a total volume of almost 182 million litres (some 48 million U.S. gallons) in 1994.

According to industry sources, this figure includes only "industrial" ice cream, manufactured by companies which were members of the Asociación Española de Fabricantes de Helados. Therefore, to obtain the real total market volume, one should add a further 20 to 25 million litres of ice cream homemade or made by small artisan-like manufacturers, plus some 20 to 25 million litres manufactured by small industrial companies which were not members of the Asociación.

Bearing in mind that Spain has a permanent population of some 40 million, the annual consumption of ice cream would be around five litres per person. It may be even less than that, bearing in mind that Spain received some 60 million tourists and visitors in 1994.

According to industry sources, the total market may be broken down in the following manner:

1. Some 42 percent of the total market would be made up of products classified as "impulse," sold in individual portions, individually packed or wrapped, frequently sold by street or beach stand vendors, or from ice cream freezers located at the door of bars, supermarkets or miscellaneous food retailers. The most common products in this category would be pre-packaged ice cream cones, small cups, and ice lollies or Popsicles. It may be necessary to clarify that this classification refers to product categories, and not to how or where it is consumed. In other words, whether an "impulse" product, is bought at a bar or in a restaurant, if it is a product in an individual portion, individually packaged, it continues to be classified as "impulse."

   In the last few years, formats of "impulse" products have appeared in the market, such as ice cream sandwiches, or small ice cream bars, such as Crunch by Nestlé, or frozen Mars bars.

2. A further 11 percent of the total market is made up of "home" consumption products. These are frequently packaged in one litre packs, such as the product ranges of "La Cremería" (Nestlé), "Carte d'Or" (Frigo), or "Etiqueta Negra" (Miko). We would also find in this group the large ice cream bars or blocks which have to be cut into smaller individual portions for consumption. as well as frozen cakes or confections, such as "Gala," "Comtessa," crocanti, or whisky frozen cakes. We also find here multipacks containing several portions usually sold as "impulse," but in a special multiple pack to be sold in supermarkets and food stores, to be consumed at home.

3. A further 11 percent of the total market is made up of products sold in "restaurants," cafeterias, and food service outlets. This product category is made up of larger ice cream bars or blocks for restaurants (intended to be cut into individual portions just before serving), and ice cream prepared by the manufacturer in individual portions to be sold in restaurants, mostly as desserts: individual portions with fruit or packaged in ceramic terrines, bonbons, tartuffi, small cartons or plastic cups for food service cafeterias, etc.

4. Finally, the remaining 25 percent of the total market is defined as "blocks and bulks." This product category would be made up of ice cream in large bars or blocks, sold directly to consumers using the same freezers out of which "impulse" products are sold to the public. We would also find here the large ice cream carton cylinders of 2, 4, and even 6 litres each, out of which ice cream parlours or restaurants serve cones or cups by the ball. These ice cream balls will be eaten at the restaurant or walking in the street. These portions are never individually packed and are meant to be consumed immediately. Maybe as much as 50 percent of the volume sold in this way is really an "impulse" purchase, bought and consumed without any previous planning on the part of the consumer.

Industry sources estimated that ice cream consumption by impulse and in restaurants and cafeterias amounted to some 75 percent of the total market, while ice cream consumed at home would account for only around 25 percent of the total volume. These same sources expected that consumption at home would increase in the immediate future, attaining maybe 40 percent total market volume by the year 2000.

Some observers said that the Spanish market had witnessed a significant improvement in the average quality of ice cream. The traditional water-based ice lollies or Popsicles had given way to richer and more nutritive products. It was estimated that maybe 50 percent of the total Spanish ice cream market was now manufactured with milk fats, while the other 50 percent was manufactured using modern and advanced vegetable fats.

Regarding the main competitors and their products, Frigo (Unilever) had been the traditional leader in the Spanish ice cream market for many years, with a market share of around 30 percent (*Source: El Pais-Negocios*, 2 July 1995, page 5). In 1993, Frigo had a total turnover of some 27,780 million pesetas (1 US$ = 130 Spanish pesetas), of which 87 percent had been by its ice cream division, while the other 13 percent had been in frozen foods (*Fomento* magazine, October l994, page 260). According to *IP mark* magazine (16–30 September 1995, page 45), Frigo was said to have spent around 1,100 million pesetas on media advertising in 1994.

However, Frigo's leadership had just been lost to Nestlé. After a premature announcement in August 1994, in March 1995 Nestlé-Camy had finally bought Avidesa and Miko. According to Carina Farreras (*La Vanguardia*, July 22, 1995, *Economia y Negocios*, page 7), Nestlé would now be the new leader of the Spanish ice cream market with a total market

(*continued*)

share of around 40 percent, with its three brands Camy, Avidesa, and Miko. According to the same issue of *IP mark* magazine, Nestlé spent some 900 million pesetas on media advertising to promote their ice cream in 1994 (presumably, just to promote their Camy brand). However, sources close to Nestlé indicated that their media spending in that year was close to 350 million pesetas.

In other words, some 70 percent of the total Spanish ice cream market would now be jointly held by Nestlé (Camy + Avidesa + Miko) and Unilever (Frigo). TLC Beatrice-La Menorquina would be the third contender, with a total turnover of some 12,800 million pesetas in 1993 (*Fomento*, October 1994, page 259). This turnover was slightly less than the 13,950 million pesetas sold in 1993 by Helados y Congelados, S.A. (Conelsa-Miko), recently acquired by Nestlé. However, Beatrice Foods and its partner Mr. Delfín Suárez also owned Interglás, S.A. (Kalise), which had a turnover of 7,800 million pesetas in 1993, including yoghurt.

Finally, the U.S. market was estimated to be worth between 3.2 and 3.3 billion U.S. dollars. Out of these, the "super premium" segment had a share of about 11 percent. In the last few years, the total U.S. market was said to have grown at an annual rate of about 3.5 percent, while the "super premium" segment would have grown faster.

The two major competitors in the "super premium" segment were Häagen Dazs and Ben & Jerry's with some 40 percent each. The remaining 20 percent was in the hands of other "super premium" brands such as *Frutsen Gladge*, *Steve's Homemade*, some "ethnic" brands such as *Goya*, or private brands such as *Dag's Select*, owned by D'Augostino supermarkets.

Exhibit 1 FARGGI The Spanish Ice Cream Market

CASE **8**
Revolution in the Jumbo Jet Market: Airbus – Boeing in 2001[1]

"Just as the 747 introduced a new way of flying compared to what was in existence before that, we are absolutely convinced the A380 will create that same quantum change in the way people fly ..."
(Airbus)[2]

Having proclaimed victory in one competitive arena, Airbus was now committed to the biggest pie in the industry: intercontinental jumbo jets. In June 2000, Airbus announced the launch of the super jumbo A380. The A380 would enable Airbus to enter the category of over 400-seat aircraft where Boeing's 747 had been the only plane in that arena.

This was Boeing's territory, the lucrative Boeing 747 market. When it first introduced these jets in 1966, Boeing sold 747s for about $18 million each. In 2000, the price of the very same airframe (albeit with some improvement and renovations) was about $150 million apiece. One industry analyst estimated that Boeing's 2000 profit on each 747 sold was about $45 million.

Boeing and Airbus had two different strategies for the over 400-seater aircraft market. Airbus was betting that what the world needed was a 555-passenger jumbo jet, and wanted to offer in this double-deck aircraft various amenities (a casino, hairdresser, showers). Boeing, on the other hand, speculated that there was not market for such planes and instead intended to launch a stretch version of the 747-400. Which strategy makes sense?

AIRBUS INDUSTRY

Airbus Industry was formed in 1970 as part of the GIE (Groupe d'Interet Economique), an entity of French origin under which separate companies pooled their interests and activities for mutual gain. All of the financial accounts associated with the Airbus programs were incorporated into the partners' own accounts, therefore the GIE did not report its financial results.

A major reason for Airbus' existence was the desire of several European governments to have a viable aerospace industry. The initial two members of the consortium were France's Aerospatiale and West Germany's Deutsche Airbus. Later British Aerospace and Spain's CASA joined as well.

EADS (European Aerospace and Defense Company) was created in 2000 with the fusion of French Aerospatiale Matra, German Dasa and Spanish Casa and Airbus became a subsidiary company of EADS. The EADS made Airbus as flexible as any multinational company, able to switch production to where it was most efficient, thereby enabling significant cost-savings. Before, without company status, Airbus had struggled to raise the money it needed to compete with Boeing and to rebut the attack from the American government that Airbus was heavily subsidized by European governments and thus it had an unfair advantage against Boeing. The EADS realized revenues of 24 billion euros in 2000, and 70% of its sales came from Airbus.

In 1970, discussions on cooperation stemmed from perceived opportunities in the short- to medium-range market. At that time, over 60% of the world's airline traffic flew routes less than 2,500 nautical miles and the short- to medium-range airliner market was virtually untapped. The A300, delivered in 1974, was the world's first twin-engine wide-bodied aircraft, seated 240 to 345 passengers, and had a range of 2,000 to 4,000 nautical miles. Later, the A300 was improved when the consortium launched the A310 in 1983, with its smaller and longer-range wide body. Recognizing the importance of having a range of aircraft "families" available to fill various niches for customers, Airbus followed with the A320 in 1988, a small-capacity, short-range craft. The A330 and A340, first delivered in 1993, were to compete with the MD-11 and 747 on medium- to long-range routes, and were a way to access the expected increase in intercontinental (especially trans-Pacific) travel. Only one category where Airbus was not present in the year 2000 was the over 400-seater. Exhibit 1 shows the whole family of Airbus aircrafts.

Airbus aircraft boasted technological advances over U.S. planes. Technological firsts for Airbus on the A320, A330 and A340 included, among other features, active controls, variable camber wing, fly-by-wire, digital auto-flight systems, side-stick controllers, and advanced composite materials in the aircraft's structure. Later on several of these technologies were incorporated into the new versions of Boeing and MD designs like the 777 and MD-11.

Over the past decade, Airbus had steadily eaten into the home market of Boeing. Today, about 10% of the big commercial airplanes flying around the U.S. were Airbus models. They expect to have 20% of the market share by 2005.

Had either of them developed a twin-engine wide body aircraft, it would have avoided head-to-head competition with the

---

[1]Student Claire A. Breviere prepared this case under the supervision of Professor Subhash C. Jain.

[2]Airbus' top salesman John Leahy, interviewed in 2000.

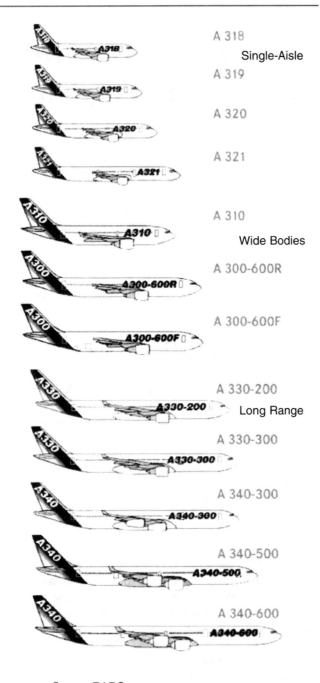

A 318

Single-Aisle

A 319

A 320

A 321

A 310

Wide Bodies

A 300-600R

A 300-600F

A 330-200

Long Range

A 330-300

A 340-300

A 340-500

A 340-600

Source: EADS

Exhibit 1 The Airbus Family of Aircraft

747, and might have prevented Airbus from getting off the ground. Instead, over the past 20 years the European consortium had encroached on Boeing's dominant market share. Boeing used to account for well over two-thirds of orders, but it was being challenged in most parts of the market by Airbus. Exhibit 2 presents in a matrix the aircraft offerings of both Airbus and Boeing, and

shows how Airbus offered an aircraft in every market segment, except the over 400-seater. Boeing now reigns supreme only with the largest 747s.

THE BOEING COMPANY

The Boeing Company was founded in 1916 in Seattle, Washington. In 1987 Boeing bought rival and leading military aircraft maker McDonnell Douglas Corporation for $16 billion. This merger made Boeing the world's largest aerospace company and second largest defense supplier, and combined the last two remaining commercial jet airplane manufacturers in the United States. In 1999, Boeing realized revenues of $58 billion, 60% of which came from its commercial airplane activity. Boeing was also America's largest exporter (40% of its sales were foreign sales.) The order level of aircraft was 640 aircrafts in 2000 (530 commercial aircraft), rising from 620 in 1999 (490 commercial aircraft.) Boeing also produced military aircraft and products for NASA and other aerospace organizations.

Boeing developed a family of basic models for a wide variety of flight ranges and passenger capacity (see Exhibit 3). From these, derivatives could be developed to expand markets and to extend product life cycles. In 2000, Boeing's airframe families included the 727 and 737, both short-range aircraft; the 757 and 767, both larger, medium-range craft; the 777, a medium- to long-range wide body aircraft that Boeing successfully launched in 1995; and the 747, a massive wide body airplane that could carry 400 passengers and could fly farther than any other commercial airliner.

With the increase of competition with Airbus, Boeing had to improve its efficiency in the 1990s. In March 1998, it introduced a new system to control the supply and stock of all of its parts in order to cut inventory costs. At the same time, Boeing made efforts to trim the number of special features it had to produce for different airlines. The several production changes Boeing initiated included halting the manufacture of its MD-11, -80, and -90 lines (from McDonnell Douglas), and cutting back its workforce.

Boeing announced in May 2001 that it would move its headquarters out of Seattle, where it had been founded 85 years earlier. It considered Chicago, Denver, or Houston and finally chose Chicago.

AIRBUS IN 2000

Within 20 years, Airbus managed to become the major competitor of Boeing with an airplane in each category except the 747 segment. The 747 had been in production for 30 years, could carry in its current version 416 passengers, and had earned the company $20 billion in profits since its first flight. Because there was no price competition, Boeing realized significant profits from this sector. Airbus suspected that Boeing was able to use its monopoly profits on the 747 to keep down its prices for smaller aircraft, thereby snatching away Airbus sales in the other categories. Airbus had been content to attack the 747 from below, with bigger

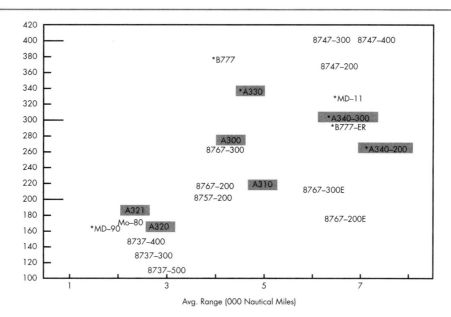

Exhibit 2 Matrix of Aircraft by Range (000 Nautical Miles) and Number of Seats

versions of its long-range A340, but now it was looking to challenge the Boeing 747's monopoly of over 400-seaters.

When it came to new products, few businesses were more perilous than making civilian aircraft. Aeroplanes cost billions to develop and were designed to last a generation. Boeing bet the company when it launched the 747, spending $2 billion on the project, or 2½ times the value of the firm. Airbus had been looking at the jumbo jet since 1993 when Boeing and the four Airbus Industry partners launched the Very Large Commercial Transport study to jointly produce a large airplane. The Boeing-Airbus collaboration lasted two years, after which the companies concluded they would not build anything together. People from Airbus felt that this joint study with Boeing was a ploy to prolong the 747's dominance.

Airbus decided to make its entry in the over 400-seater segment and announced the launch of the A380 in June 2000. The A380 had a proposed sticker price of between $213 million and $225 million. There would be dual rows of windows running the full length of the fuselage.

Airbus believed that a 1200 passenger megaliner and 300 freighters could be sold, while Boeing said that the market was only 500 planes deep. Fifty orders were needed to launch the project. Airbus got 66 firm orders from several airlines like Air France, Dubai-based Emirates, Singapore Airlines, Australia's Qantas Airlines, and International Lease Finance Corporation of the United States. But airlines that rushed to become launch customers got fantastic discounts from manufacturers. Therefore, Airbus would need to sell 229 aircraft before it could earn a profit, and sell at least 780 before it could recover the investment made not just by Airbus, but by its suppliers and governments. In effect, EADS was betting the company on this aircraft, because civilian aircraft accounted for about 70% of the company's turnover.

The first version of the A380 would be a 555-passenger jetliner. Its configuration would be finalized at the end of 2001, its first flight in mid-2004, and entry into service in October 2005, with delivery of the first freighter version two years later. Configured all in economy seats, a stretched A380 could carry 800 people.

Launch-aid subsidies by Airbus member governments would account for around $4 billion of the $12 billion that it would cost to develop the aircraft. Launch aid would be paid back to the governments, as a royalty on sales. Thus governments could end up making money if the aircraft sold well, but taxpayers did bear some of the risk.

THE AIRBUS A380

Airbus wanted to differentiate itself from Boeing by inventing a new way to fly. The A380 would allow airlines a really competitive advantage in passenger comfort. The main deck of the A380 would be the widest in the world. Its floor area would be 49% more floor space and 35% more seats than the 747-400. So airlines could make their seats wider and provide each seat with its own separate armrest, which was a frequent passenger demand. It would also be looking to add a grand staircase (as opposed to the spiral staircase in the 747) for passengers assigned to the upper deck.

The A380 would also have a lower deck on which lavatories, sleeper cabins, crew rest area, business center, a health spa or a casino could be located. Airbus had been considering various interior design proposals for the interior of the aircraft, such as a stylish lounge with a cocktail bar and very modern seating, eating, and sleeping pods. The intention has been to have as much space for passenger amenities as for seats, to make the aircraft more comfortable and attractive to passengers in economy, club or first class.

747-400

The Boeing 747–400
The 747–400 seats 416 to 568 passengers, depending on seating configuration and, with the recent launch of the Longer–Range 747–400, has a range of 8,850 miles. With its huge capacity, long range and fuel efficiency, the 747 offers the lowest operating cost per seat of any twin–aisle commercial jetliner. The 747–400 is available in all–cargo freighter version as well as combi model for passengers and cargo. Boeing continues to study 747 derivatives that will fly farther or carry more passengers to continue the 747 leadership in meeting the world's need for high–capacity, long–range airplanes.

orders: 1,338* Deliveries: 1,261

777-200

777-300

The Boeing 777–200 and 777–300
The 777–200, which seats 305 to 440 passengers depending on configuration, a range of up to 5,925 miles. The777–200ER (Extended range) can fly the same number of passengers up to 8,861 miles. the 777–300 is about 33 feet longer than the –200 and can carry from 368 to 550 passengers, depending on seating configuration, with a range of 6,854 miles. The company recently introduced two longer–range 777s.

orders: 563* Deliveries: 316

767-200

767-300

767-400

The Boeing 767–200, 767–300, and 767–400
The 767–200 will typically fly 181 to 224 passengers up to 7,618 miles in its extended–range version. The 767–300, also offered in an extended–range version, offers 20 percent more passenger seating. A freighter version of the 767–300 is also available. The first extended–range 767–400ERs were delivered to Delta Air Lines and Continental Airlines in August 2000. The airplane typically will carry between 245 and 304 passengers up to 6, 501 miles. In a high–density inclusive tour arrangement, the 767–400ER can carry up to 375 passengers. Boeing commintted to production in September 2000 a longer–range 767–400ER. This longer–range version is the same size as the 767–400ER, but has the equivalent range of the 767–300ER.

orders: 901* Deliveries: 817

757-200

757-300

The Boeing 757–200 and 757–300
Seating 194 passengers in two classes, the 757–200 is ideal for high–demand, short–to medium–range operations and can fly nonstop intercontinental routes up to 4,500 miles. It is also available in a freighter version. The 757–300 can carry 240 to 289 passengers on routes of up to 3,900 miles.

orders: 1,027* Deliveries: 948

737-600

737-700

737-800

737-900

The Boeing 737–600, 737–700, 737–800 and 737–900
The Boeing 737 is the best-selling commercial jetliner of all time. The Next–Generation 737–600/–700/–800/–900 have outsold all other airplanes in their market segment. These new 737s incorporate advanced technology and design features that translate into cost–efficient, high–reliability operations and outstanding passenger comfort. The 737 is the only airplane family to span the entire 100–to–189–seat market, with maximum ranges from 3,159 (the –900) to 3,752 (the –700) miles. The 737 family also includes two boeing business jets, derivatives of the 737–700 and –800.

orders: 4,873* Deliveries: 3,857

717-200

The Boeing 717–200
The Boeing 717–200 twinjet meets the grpwing need worldwide for a 100–seat, high frequency, short–range jet, flying a maximum range of 1,647 miles. The durable, simple, ultra–quiet and clean twinjet's effective use of technology results in the lowest operating costs.

Orders: 151* Deliveries: 44.

Source: The Boeing Company Annual Report, 2000.

Exhibit 3 Boeing Family Commercial Aircraft

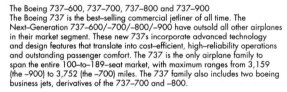

The competition was also an exercise in probing the limits of gigantism. The A380 would use advanced materials like carbon composite. It would fly at about Mach 0.85 cruise speed, and would have a 555-passenger capacity across two decks. The basic version would list for $216 million.

The A380 would allow savings in operating cost. Airbus claimed the A380 would have 17% lower operating costs than the 747-400 and, on certain Asian routes, Airbus even claimed that the modern A380 design would save airlines up to 45% on

operating costs compared with the 747. Exhibit 4 gives the technical characteristics of the A380, airliner and freighter version.

Demand for very large aircraft was a function of several factors- air travel growth, and also basic airport infrastructure. If the air travel market grew but airport capacity (particularly the availability of slots) did not, the extra passenger base would have to be accommodated by flying larger aircraft.

Air traffic was expected to grow by 5% per year. The inexorable growth in the global number of passengers over the next

Airbus A380 Airliner

WING SPAN	79.8 m / 261ft 10in
LENGTH	73 m / 239ft 6in
HEIGHT	24.1 m / 79ft 1in
Typical payload	555 pax plus 38 LD3s
RANGE	8,000 nm (= 14800 km)
MTOW*	580 t
MLW**	386 t
MZFW***	361 t
OWE	276.5 t
MAX PAYLOAD	83 t
FUEL CAPACITY	325 000 l
ENGINE THRUST (slst)	70,000 lb
Take-Off Field Length	<11,000 ft (3,350 m)
Max Range Cruise	MO.85, flexibility to MO.87 / MO.88
VMO /MMO	340 kts / MO.89
Initial Cruise Altitude	FL350
Time & Distance to ICA	30 min. & 200 NM
Max Altitude Capability	FL430
Approach Speed	<145 kts CAS

*MTOW: Maximum takeoff weight
**MLW: Maximum landing weight
***MZFW: Maximum zero-fuel weight

Source: EADS.

Exhibit 4 A380 Airliner Characteristics

20 years would require a larger plane on popular routes. Airbus was predicting a 127% increase in passenger numbers over the next 20 years.

Asia would be the place where growth would be the highest. The populations of most Asian countries were much more concentrated than those of European or North American nations. The Asian region is more congested than any other, making it more difficult to boost airport capacity than in other regions of the world. So there was a need for larger capacity airplanes. It was a good sign for the future of Airbus that Singapore Airlines ordered A380 planes, because it was one of the most respected airlines in Asia, which would encourage other Asian companies to buy the A380. According to Noel Forgeard, president of Airbus, only about 20 airlines, half of them in Asia, were seen as potential customers and only 10% of the total number of planes would be super-jumbos. But they would be worth 25% of the market, or $300 billion.

The Impact of curfews also favored larger airplanes. Airlines couldn't simply space out their flights through the day. Market demand and the early-morning and late-night curfews at many European and Asia/Pacific airports made this not very realistic.

Only 10 new airports were planned to open within the next 15 years while only 18 airports had approved plans for growth, according to Airbus. But there was still an uncertainty about airport developments. If the market growth was as rapid as Airbus forecast, even taking into account very ambitious expansion plans, slot constraints would be severe.

Airbus had to examine different technical challenges like to fulfill international certification requirements to insure safety. Airplanes must permit evacuation of all passengers within 90 seconds. Airbus was working on the appropriate slides for evacuation of the people of the upper deck.

Airbus had to face also the challenge of lack of airport capacity. Airbus met with 60 major international airport executives to make sure that the new jet would fit airport size specifications. Airbus said that the A380 would be compatible with existing airport infrastructure. The A380 would be only 72 to 73 meters in length. It was only when aircraft was beyond 80 meters in length that it became difficult for most airports to handle it. The runways, taxiways, and aprons that had been designed to be large enough for the 747 should then be alright for A380.

Airbus would also have to face the challenge of maintaining the same level of convenience for the passenger. A large airplane

---

Boeing sees the market for super jumbo jets more fragmented than Airbus. A fragmented market is a market that does not rely so heavily on major hubs to distribute regional or domestic traffic, but more on non-stop direct flights between cities large and small. This trend is encouraged by the ongoing liberalization of the Asian/U.S. market.

The Sonic Cruiser 20XX will fly at 95% of the speed of sound, or about 20% faster than today's jets. The plane, which will seat 175 to 250 passengers, will fly at higher altitudes than conventional jets and save about one hour for every 3,000 miles it travels. This will be equivalent to an hour off for transcontinental flights in the United States, three hours on flights from California to Europe.

Analysts have estimated that the cost of developing the 20XX will be between $9 billion to $10 billion (the cost of developing the stretched version of the 30-year-old 747 was $4 billion). It will have twin-engine jet and a double delta-shaped wing with a horizontal stabilizer near the nose. Many of its design features must still be worked out. The Sonic Cruiser should be built with conventional materials and be powered by the same engines now used on Boeing's wide body 777. The 20XX should not enter service until the end of the 2010.

But there are some limits to the 20XX. Boeing pretends that even though the 20XX will fly faster, it will still have about the same operating costs as today's jets. But most experts agree that a new supersonic jet built today would still be too expensive for most airlines to operate. It also could not fly at top speed over land because of the noisy sonic boom and would fly so high that it would damage the ozone layer.

Exhibit 5 The Sonic Cruiser 20XX

might lead to increased congestion in departure lounges and swarms of individuals collecting their luggage and longer boarding lineups. Airbus claimed that the A380 would operate to the same ground schedule as a 747-400, which was 90 minutes. To address for example the issue of boarding lineup, the A380 would allow simultaneously loading on both the upper and lower decks, by having doublewide doors and doublewide stairs.

BOEING'S RESPONSE

After the announcement of the launch of the A380, Boeing proposed the 747X stretch program. The airplane would be based on the design of the 747 (which was designed in the 1960s), and would seat 522 (compared with the 416 seats on the largest of today's 747s).

Boeing didn't want to launch a totally new model because it estimated that there was not enough demand for large airplanes.

Boeing estimated that only 330 aircraft larger than 500 seats would be in service by 2019. Indeed, Boeing estimated that the market for more than 400-seater aircraft (including all 747 passenger variants) would not be that much larger than Airbus' estimates for the above 500-seater market alone, amounting to only 1,905 aircraft in 2019.

Since Boeing didn't receive any order from the airlines for the 747X stretch, it decided in March 2001 to drop the project and launch the Supersonic 20XX instead (see Exhibit 5). But Boeing announced that it was still working on a larger version of the 747, even if it would not be as big as the 747X stretch. The new aircraft would only add eight more seats to the existing 747-400, which seats 416 people in a typical configuration, and would have a range of about 8,400 miles. But it would enable the plane to fly an additional 775 miles without affecting its speed or cargo capacity.

Which strategy will work on the over 400-seater segment? Airbus' strategy to launch the A380 or will Boeing prevail in the over 400-seater segment with their extension of the 747-400? Only time will tell who is right.

CASE 9
SR Corp: Decisions for an Emerging Technology: Introduction

I n January 1994, Darr Hastings, vice president of Marketing for SR Corp, was flying back to Boston from a conference in San Francisco. Hastings knew that he had to deliver a recommendation to the company's board the next day regarding a major strategic marketing direction.

SR Corp was about to announce its new product, the Colloquial Speech Platform 2000, a revolutionary speech recognition system that was at least three to four years ahead of the competition. Hastings's research had shown three primary markets for the new technology: Fortune 500 corporations, telephone companies, and telephone switch manufacturers. He felt that SR Corp's products and organization were not sufficiently mature to pursue all three market niches at once, particularly since each niche would use speech recognition for significantly different applications. Even within a particular niche, Hastings believed that SR Corp could only support the systems integration activity in three companies during the first 18 months of commercialization. He thought that SR Corp's best hope for success would be to successfully install the system in a first customer, and then leverage that experience as much as possible by targeting a similar type of company as the next customer.

Making the wrong decision with respect to which market niche to pursue first would waste precious time and could cost the company its lead in technology. By working directly with end-user companies, such as Fortune 500 corporations or telephone companies, SR Corp could capture more margin on its product sales and have greater control over specific accounts. On the other hand, working through strong intermediaries, such as telephone switch manufacturers, might provide SR Corp with more rapid market penetration and help it reach the goal of becoming the de facto industry, standard for speech recognition technology.

The wrong decision could easily put the firm out of business. Much larger firms, such as AT&T, were aggressively trying to achieve SR Corp's level of technical performance. The financial resources of SR Corp, like those of most small firms, were precarious. Having been capitalized to date with approximately $10 million in venture funding, the firm's investors now needed to see tangible sales before providing additional funding.

This case was prepared by Marc H. Meyer and G. Thomas Aley, Northeastern University. This case was written solely for the purpose of stimulating student discussions. All events and individuals are real but names have been disguised at the company's request. Copyright © 1995 by the *Case Research Journal* and Marc H. Meyer and G. Thomas Aley. It is reprinted here with permission.

As he leaned back in his seat, Hastings thought about all the marketing he had recently studied in an executive M.B.A. program. He felt insufficiently prepared to tackle the job ahead of him: market prioritization for an innovative, preemptive technology. He thought to himself:

I've read Porter and many of the leading books available on positioning and competitive strategy to help in this effort. They are great for providing strategic recommendations for stable markets that contain clear distribution patterns and no real threat of predatory invasion from new technologies. However, most of the concepts do not apply to our situation—an emerging industry where no markets are certain and the threat of obsolescence is around every corner.

COMPANY BACKGROUND

SR Corp was formed in 1986 to develop and commercialize speaker-independent speech recognition, the ability of a computer to recognize and take action on the spoken word. SR Corp's mission was to deploy a new generation of speech transaction technologies, products, and systems that could be easily integrated into telephone and computer networks. The company's goal was to become the leader in a new realm of human communication.

SR Corp had been financed over the last eight years through a private investor who had been a successful entrepreneur in the publishing industry in the early 1980s. By 1994, the firm had 20 employees. The management of the firm was comprised of Dr. Gary York (president and CEO), Hastings (vice president of Marketing), and Dr. Paul Schall (vice president of Engineering). The company also had a chief operating officer, Ms. Sheila Garris, who was responsible for systems manufacturing and finance. Most employees were software and hardware engineers, reporting to Dr. Schall. Dr. York was the inventor of several key parts of SR Corp's proprietary technology, and several of the firm's patents were in his name. Hastings had only one administrative assistant and knew that he would have to expand his sales force over the next several years in order for the firm to grow.

Between 1986 and 1994, the company focused on developing its core technology while working with major telephone companies and Fortune 500 corporations to find out what they wanted in large-scale speech recognition systems. On the basis of feedback from these organizations, SR Corp created a system that Hastings's competitive research had shown to be years ahead of the industry.

THE INDUSTRY

A leading market research firm's 1993 report on speech recognition summarized the common industry opinion: "Voice recognition is the least developed of voice technologies and is widely considered to be a technology still in its infancy. Industry experts agree it will be at least a decade before a mature voice recognition product is introduced in the market."[1] The power of SR Corp's systems, if successfully commercialized, could shatter this perception.

Speech recognition had a history of research long on promise but short on tangible results. Bell labs initiated work in this area nearly 30 years ago. The initial technology worked only in the most constrained situations—understanding a few single isolated words using a high-bandwidth microphone in a noise-free environment. Progress had moved slowly toward the goal: computer understanding of unconstrained conversation with any caller under difficult telephone network conditions.

TYPES OF SPEECH RECOGNITION

The most popular form of speech recognition deployed in 1993 was called speaker-dependent speech recognition (SDSR). The term *speaker-dependent* referred to the fact that the person using its first "trained" the system by loading it with his or her own voice patterns for a selected set of words necessary for the application. For example, Sprint Corporation developed a system, the Voice FonCard, which allowed users to record up to thirty names over the phone and store them in a central database at the telephone company. When someone wanted to place a call, he or she would simply speak the name of the person they wanted to call into the phone for automated dialing.

Speaker-independent speech recognition (SISR), on the other hand, would allow any person to use a system without first training it. AT&T had recently implemented a speaker-independent collect-call application in which an automated attendant instructed the person to say "yes" or "no" in order to accept a collect call.

Speaker-dependent systems were accurate 95 percent of the time, while speaker-independent systems had achieved only 80 percent accuracy. The most important factor in weighing the technical capabilities of different speech recognition vendors lay in their ability to improve accuracy levels on an annual basis. In the past decade, it had typically taken about one year to achieve a one to two percent improvement in accuracy.

In 1994, speaker-independent speech recognition could be subclassified into two different types of systems: discrete and continuous. Discrete speaker-independent speech recognition was used

for command and control of speech applications where users say one word at a time. Continuous speaker-independent speech recognition allowed users to speak naturally into the computer system.

Discrete speaker-independent systems were commonly referred to as "voice-buttons" because the technology replaced pressing buttons on the telephone. This technology was available in 1994, but was limited in its application because accuracy levels had reached only 90 percent. The pressing short-term challenge for vendors was to reach 99 percent accuracy. Following historical progress rates, industry experts predicted that this goal would be achieved around the year 2000.

The longer-term challenge for speech recognition was to reach 99 percent or better accuracy levels for continuous speaker-independent speech recognition. Once again, most industry experts did not expect highly accurate continuous speech systems to achieve this level of accuracy until after the turn of the century.

Speech recognition vendors such as AT&T and Texas Instruments (TI) used the Hidden Markov Method as the central process for algorithms in their products. Programmed into software, this method provided voice pattern-recognition based on complex statistical programming. These statistical patterns had been developed utilizing laboratory data and generic language models. The resulting systems had large processing power requirements and typically operated on workstations running in excess of 20 mips (millions of instructions per second) for the central processor. Each system needed at least one workstation per telephone line of speech recognition. In addition, an important part of any system was its ability to allow companies to build new applications. Existing systems came with very limited software development environments; users were dependent on vendors for sophisticated applications development.

SR CORP'S PRODUCT: THE CORE TECHNOLOGY

By 1994, SR Corp developed a speech recognition system that industry experts had not expected to be available until 2000: a discrete, speaker-independent speech recognition system that operated with 99 percent accuracy for numbers zero through 10, "yes" and "no," and an application-specific vocabulary of words spoken in sequence. That vocabulary could exceed thousands of words for complex applications, such as automating directory assistance in a large telephone company. Like existing discrete systems, the typical application built with SR Corp's system would have menus to guide a user's transactions. However, unlike these systems, SR Corp's technology would allow the user to speak a stream of words (with short breaks between them) to totally bypass the application menu. This was a direct step toward the highly accurate speaker-independent continuous speech recognition system that SR Corp expected to have operational within three years. The combination of accuracy and menu bypass made SR Corp's current system highly distinctive; the prospect of delivering continuous speech capability within a few years made the company even more attractive for prospective customers.

To achieve these results, SR Corp had proceeded along a different technological path than AT&T and other large vendors.

---

[1] Rettig, Hillary, "Not Quite the Last Word." VARBUSINESS Networking Annual, Oct. 15, 1993, p. 4.

It developed a pattern-recognition approach based on a neural network model, and its algorithms differed fundamentally from existing approaches. Further, the company had achieved constraint-free telephone recognition using Intel 486-based personal computers running in the 20- to 30-mips range. Seven U.S. and foreign patents for SR Corp's technology had been issued and others were pending. These patents were issued between 1990 and 1994 and would, therefore, be in force well into the next century unless successfully challenged in court. The company had also developed a Transaction Dialogue Authoring System that allowed new applications to be developed by the user in a higher level language. Exhibit 1 is a flowchart of an SR Corp conversational transaction.

SR Corp's product was designed to be integrated at reasonable cost into any network, whether it be a central office of a telephone company or a local area network of a major corporation. The system could be delivered in a variety of configurations, with two PC boards supporting one telephone line of speech recognition. The boards shipped in a chassis; each chassis contained ten boards, and thus supported five lines of recognition. The approximate cost of goods sold for the five-line system was $3,000.

SR CORP'S MARKET

SR Corp hoped to gain a cost advantage with its technology over Hidden-Markov based systems. Hasting's research had shown that the speaker-independent discrete voice recognition systems were currently selling at an effective price of about $6,000 per line of recognition, including the cost of the workstation itself. Hastings found that, in large-volume orders (10,000 units were not unusual for telephone companies), discounting drove competitors' pricing down to about $3,000 per line of recognition.

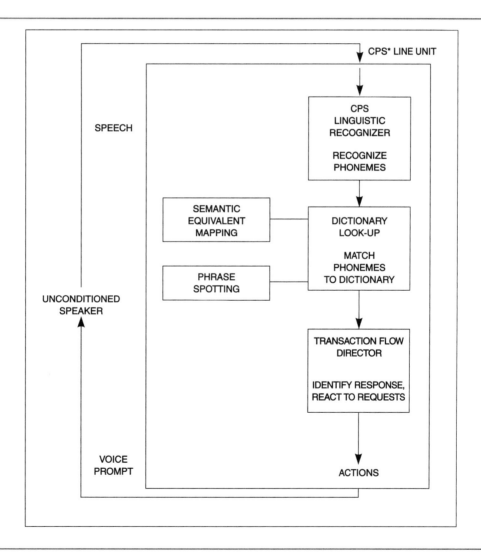

* CPS is the Colloquial Platform for Speech
Source: SR Corp Internal Document.

Exhibit 1 SR Corp's Conversational Transaction Flow

Since SR Corp's product could handle at least two and as many as five lines of recognition per workstation (compared to the single-line systems of competitors), Hastings believed that SR Corp's product could be priced between $5,000 and $10,000, depending on the size and type of customer. Even with large-volume orders, Hastings believed that the SR Corp's cost advantage over competitors for equivalent processing process configurations would remain 3 to 1.

The 99 percent accuracy of the system would also allow many customers to apply speech recognition to applications that they had previously avoided due to the error rates of competitors' systems. Further, while existing speech recognition systems were single-application products, SR Corp's system could be used as a single platform for developing many applications. For example, a telephone company using a competitor's system would have to develop software running on two completely separate sets of workstations to implement both voice dialing and voice mail. Using SR Corp's technology, a single set of workstations could be used to perform both applications. For large users, the resulting cost differential could be considerable. For example, if a telephone company was to purchase a single unit for each application, the two-application (two line) scenario would cost approximately $12,000 with a competitor's technology. SR Corp's solution would cost $10,000 for a maximum of five lines of speech recognition, for an effective cost per line of $2,000. Therefore, the two-line scenario would be priced at $4,000, providing SR Corp with an $8,000 cost advantage over competitors. For large-volume orders, both SR Corp and its competitors would discount their prices by about 50 percent. This would still yield a full system cost of $3,000 per line for competitors versus $1,000 per line for SR Corp. This was a substantial cost advantage because large customers might purchase thousands of units for any single application.

Most companies in SR Corp's target markets had many potential applications for speech recognition. Hastings's discussions with representative customers in various market segments revealed that the typical customer would wish to buy between 100 and 500 systems for an initial speech recognition application such as automating a customer service function. This would produce initial revenues in the range of $1 million to $.5 million per customer.

By 1994, the entire U.S. speech recognition market was a $350 million industry. Its market segments included telephony, data entry, dictation, consumer products, computer control, and voice verification. (Exhibit 2 shows the speech recognition market forecast through 1996, and 1992 revenue by market shares.) The VARBUSINESS Networking Annual, a leading industry forum, forecast that annual sales of speech recognition equipment would exceed $3 billion by the year 2000.[2]

SR Corp's product was targeted at the telephony market segment. Telephone-based speech recognition offered great potential due to the pervasiveness of voice communication and the lack of alternative methods for high-bandwidth input. It was also the largest market segment, representing 27 percent of the market. Teleph-

ony applications were expected to grow rapidly and expand to 60 percent of installed speech recognition systems by the turn of the century, according to *VARBUSINESS Networking Annual*.[3]

Hastings divided the telephony segment into three major niches:

1. Fortune 500 companies
2. Telephone companies
3. Telephone switch manufacturers, which sold equipment to telephone companies

Hastings also realized that telephony applications could be difficult due to the lack of control over the conditions of use. Problems included a large and unpredictable user population, differences in handset microphones, the presence of channel noise, and low signal bandwidth. In 1994, the most successful speech recognition systems used by large industrial, transportation, and financial firms, and by telephone companies, were limited to very small vocabularies (10 to 20 words spoken in a discrete, noncontinuous manner). Yet even these systems had provided substantial payback by reducing the need for telephone operators and/or customer support personnel.

SR CORP'S COMPETITORS

The major competitors in the telephony market segment included, AT&T, Texas Instruments (TI), Northern Telecom, Nynex, Bolt Beranek & Newman, Voice Control Systems, and Voice Processing Systems.

All of these companies were selling speaker dependent and limited discrete speaker-independent systems. Each competitor had approximately 10 percent market share of the telephony segment. None had achieved technical leadership with regard to accuracy levels, with all averaging 90 percent for speaker-dependent systems and 80 percent for speaker-independent systems.

AT&T, the largest and most threatening competitor, had stated that it would deliver discrete, speaker-independent speech recognition reaching 99 percent accuracy no earlier than 1998. AT&T made no claims with respect to more advanced continuous speech recognition. Although by mid-1994 SR Corp had not sold any discrete, speaker-independent systems, its internal tests proved that the system they developed was 98 to 99 percent accurate.

All the competitors had been extraordinarily secretive about their R&D. The speech recognition industry had been litigious: lawsuits had been initiated to challenge patents, intellectual property, and even the loss of scientists from one firm to another. In one case, TI had the federal government raid Voice Control Systems three weeks after two former TI scientists began working for Voice Control Systems. The case was settled out of court.

Therefore, while Hastings was ecstatic about the technological breakthroughs achieved by his firm, he thought that he had to be very careful about who he talked to in this early stage of commercialization. Hastings believed that SR Corp's technology had

---

[2]Rettig, op. cit.

[3]Rettig, op. cit.

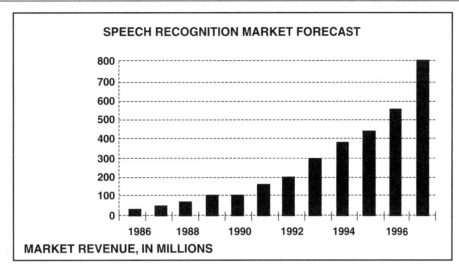

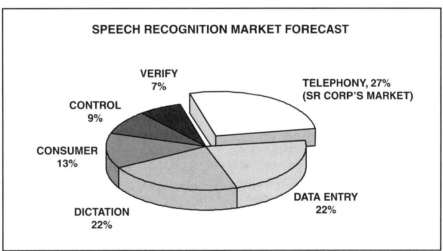

Source: Voice Information Associates, Lexington, Mass.

Exhibit 2 Market Forecast and Segments

to be kept secret until market share was secured. SR Corp had thoroughly researched existing speech recognition patents and was confident that its patents did not violate any of them. However, any large firm seeking to block SR Corp's entry into its market (be it a firm selling voice-button systems that SR Corp's technology would make obsolete, or a firm such as AT&T that was trying to develop its own advanced system) might be a problem. In Hastings's view, an intellectual property suit filed against SR Corp by AT&T or TI would consume scarce management and financial resources and could drive the company out of business.

STRATEGIC MARKETING ALTERNATIVES

The day after Hastings's return from San Francisco, an executive management committee meeting was convened comprised of him-

self, Dr. York (president), Dr. Schall (vice president of Engineering), and the lead investor. Together, they had to make a decision regarding which niche within the telephony segment to pursue during the coming year, e.g., Fortune 500 corporations, telephone companies, or telephone switch manufacturers.

Dr. Schall described the continued positive results of the most recent field tests of SR Corp's product. He was deeply concerned about selecting the company's first set of target customers:

This will be a critical step in our success because we need to utilize our initial customers as references for future sales. We also need knowledgeable customers, or else we will never get past the first installation. At the same time, we must try to avoid becoming entangled and delayed by the red tape of the bureaucratic organizations of some of these customers, such as a mutual fund company or a telephone company. Time is of the essence.

Hastings concurred, and then added:

We can't afford to pick a strategy that brings us to the wrong customers. Once we dive in with a customer, we'll be devoting most of our efforts toward integration and deployment. These ramp up issues are of strategic concern because if we are six months into a project and suddenly discover that a customer's lack of technical skill or bureaucratic politics will delay final implementation, we could be in serious trouble; we'll have hired 10, maybe 15 people, set up a satellite office, and the bills will have to be paid. Further, we could have been working with a better customer either in the same or some other niche in telephony.

Hastings gave examples of how the sales cycle could be lengthened by a prospective customer's bureaucratic decision making. For example, a telephone company might have more than a half dozen departments, ranging from operator services to consumer marketing, that would be users of the same integrated speech recognition system. Each department would have a separate budget for systems procurement, and therefore all would have to agree to "pitch in" resources for a major systems procurement.

He also spoke about complications that could occur after the sale was completed. For example, several telephone companies had agreed to contracts for existing speech recognition technology with SR Corp's competitors only to cancel the projects after a year of effort, even though they had already spent in the range of $1 to $2 million. The telecommunications industry was undergoing dramatic consolidation, and these project cancellations were dramatic evidence of how efforts involving exotic technologies could come to naught. Further, some of SR Corp's smaller competitors had been stalled in their attempts to market their own technologies by intellectual property lawsuits filed by larger, better established companies. The stakes were high and companies played "hardball."

Both Dr. York and the lead investor wanted to forge ahead with sales. Installing SR Corp's system at a large customer site would require allocation of a significant portion of the company's resources. While everyone believed that securing three large accounts was a reasonable objective in the next 18 months, SR Corp's limited resources would require that implementation to the three customer sites be performed sequentially. Dr. York said that the company would also have to create remote offices near each major customer to provide field support and technical training. Hastings also believed that SR Corp would have to ramp up investment in its marketing activities for direct sales and trade show exhibitions.

The lead investor indicated a willingness to supply additional funding. However, he wanted to see a clear marketing plan and customer contracts that garnered a significant portion of the total sale up front to help cover systems integration expenses.

Hastings then presented the data he had gathered from company visits and industry expert sources, addressing first the Fortune 500 niche, then the telephone company niche, and lastly, the telephone switch manufacturer niche. From these data, SR Corp's attack plan would be formed.

The Fortune 500 Market Niche

The Fortune 500 niche was comprised of large corporations in a variety of industrial, consumer products, and financial industries. More than half of these companies had already purchased interactive voice response and voice messaging customer premise equipment used for customer service and ordering applications. SR Corp's product would be marketed as the next generation of voice response and voice messaging technology, featuring greater accuracy, menu bypass capability, a multiapplication functionality, and at least a 3 to 1 cost advantage on an equivalent processing power basis.

In 1994, voice response systems only allowed companies to automate certain customer service functions. For example, callers might be greeted by menus such as "press 1 for sales, press 2 for service," etc. Callers navigated through menus by pressing the right buttons on their touch-tone phones. With speech recognition, the caller would reach a truly automated "operator," who would ask: "Would you like sales, service ...?" etc., and wait for the caller to say what he or she wanted.

Voice messaging enabled callers to leave messages for employees in companies. Users pushed buttons on their phones to manage their voice mail (e.g., they would press 1 to delete a message, press 2 to go to the next message, and so on). With a speech recognition system, users could simply say "Delete the first message," "Go to the next message," etc.

SR Corp's product was a substitute system for both voice response and voice messaging systems. Companies using voice response and voice messaging systems needed a gateway to voice services that was easy and quick to use. Users often expressed dissatisfaction with the limitations of voice response and voice messaging, and in particular, were annoyed by the long, cumbersome, and inflexible menus contained in these systems.

For example, a voice-button system in an airline might result in the following dialogue:

System: Thank you for calling American Airlines. In order to expedite your call, please press 1 if you're calling from a touch-tone phone. If you have a rotary phone, please hold the line and a customer service representative will be with you shortly.

User: Presses 1.

System: Please make your selection from the following menu:

- For flight arrival times, departure times or gate information, press 1.
- For domestic reservations and fare information in the 50 states, press 2.
- For international travel, including Canada and the Caribbean, press 3.
- For Fly Away Vacations, press 4.
- For Frequent Flier Mileage accounts and information, press 5.
- For all other inquiries, press 6.
- Press 7 to repeat the menu.

The user might then be able to press a button corresponding to what he or she actually wanted. However, if after listening to the entire menu, the user still did not know what button to press, he or she might press 6, calling up yet another automated menu, or 7, to hear the menu again.

With SR Corp's system, such a call could be greatly simplified—for either a touch-tone or rotary phone:

System: Thank you for calling American Airlines. Tell us how we can help you. Be sure to leave short breaks between your words.

User: I need to check my frequent flier miles.

System: The call transfers to the Frequent Flier Division.

Hasting's interviews with prospective customers in the Fortune 500 niche showed that they wanted a system that would allow this type of natural, conversational exchange with a high degree of accuracy. These large companies needed systems that their own customers would find easy to use for performing automated, non-human-assisted transactions. Replacing touch-tone keypad operation with speech would accelerate user acceptance, particularly if the user could skip ahead through menus once they became familiar with routine transactions. Any system would have to function accurately with "unconditioned" speakers, that is, speakers who were not trained beforehand to use an artificial protocol for interacting with the system. Companies would also require a flexible and productive software development environment so that their own computer staffs could build customized applications without overreliance on the vendor. SR Corp believed that it was well ahead of its competitors in providing this type of solution for the Fortune 500 market.

SR Corp could initially target industries that had the largest number of telephone transactions per day using voice response and voice messaging systems. These industries included the competitive access telephone services providers (CAPs), airlines, financial services companies, and catalog mail order companies. (See Exhibits 3 and 4.) Almost every major Fortune 500 company that completed transactions over the phone utilized some form of interactive voice processing and many used an alternative access provider rather than their local phone company to save money. In 1993, the typical CAP processed over 250,000 calls per day. The travel industry also had high volumes. By 1989, American Airlines was taking 100 million reservation calls per year.[4] This translated into about 274,000 calls per day (or about 3 calls per second). Similarly, large banks, on average, processed about 65,000 calls per day.

Companies in these industries had looked to voice response and messaging systems as a way to create efficiencies and automate portions of their operations. The total 1993 revenue for the domestic voice response and voice messaging systems in the Fortune 500 niche was $1.1 billion. Vendors of these systems were also highly profitable. Their average profit before tax was approximately 23 percent.

Systems enhanced with speech recognition capabilities were available, but accounted only for $33 million in revenues, or 3 percent of the total voice response and voice messaging markets. This small penetration rate was due primarily to the existing low accuracy levels. Experts agreed that companies would feel more comfortable replacing push-button commands with voice commands once accuracy rates exceeded 95 percent. Experts further predicted that sales of speech enhanced substitutes for existing voice response and messaging systems would increase dramatically and represent $600 million out of the total forecasted $1.5 billion for the voice response and messaging markets by the year 2000.[5]

Hastings's visits to prospective customers had indicated that the typical company in this market niche might purchase SR Corp's system to support 3,000 telephone lines. He anticipated that he could price the system at approximately $6,000 per line. SR Corp would also have to hire a team of three engineers per customer for approximately one year in order to help with the integration of its system with the customer's existing equipment For planning purposes, Hastings used a fully loaded cost of $100,000 per engineer per year, a figure that had been provided by Dr. Schall.

A customer would install SR Corp's system for a single, targeted speech recognition application. To develop follow-on business and generate more revenue from each customer, Hastings planned to hire one account manager per customer at an equivalent cost of $100,000 per person per year. Both field engineers and account representatives would work out of a single field office located near the customer's central office. Hastings did not expect that customers would necessarily agree to provide office space for SR Corp's field personnel. The figures he used for planning were 250 square feet of office space per person leased on an annual basis for $10 per square foot.

Hastings had to factor in another concern. He expected that Fortune 500 customers would have a steeper learning curve, and hence a longer sales and implementation cycle, than either telephone companies or telephone switch manufacturers. MIS departments in typical Fortune 500 customers were not familiar with the application of speech recognition technologies. Because of this, Hastings believed it would take approximately 10 to 12 months to achieve full implementation of SR Corp's system for an initial application with each new customer. Customers would not see that time scale as a drawback, they measured deployment of older technology systems in years.

At the same time, because of the compelling need of these companies to reduce operating costs, he believed that SR Corp could land five Fortune 500 customers during the first two years. The current voice-button systems in industry did not allow firms to completely replace their customer service representatives. For example, a major airline found that voice-buttons could only accommodate 25 percent of a standard flight reservation transaction, and in particular, only that part where the customer needed to be directed to a particular department for human-assisted reservation making. In fact, many Fortune 500 companies had decided not to implement voice-button systems because of the limitations of those systems in handling complex transactions. Their customers were found to be frustrated and annoyed with the inflexible, "hard-wired" menus of voice-button systems. SR Corp's technology was sufficiently dynamic to handle complex transactions. For example, internal tests by SR Corp found that 100 percent of a standard flight reservation could be done through its system. Fortune 500 companies could eliminate major portions of their total human telephone operator or service representative costs.

---

[4]"AMR Wields SABRE, Private Net," *ComputerWorld*, May 1, 1989.

[5]Rettig, op. cit.

Industry or Company	No. Transactions per Day	Forcing Function	Applications
Telcos (CAPs)* Metropolitan Fiber Services Corp. Teleport Inner Media	250,000	Extremely competitive with other CAPs, local exchange carriers.† Interexchange carriers.‡ Access provision 80% of business. Adoption high (50% NYC); increase new services.	Centrex services only Voice dial Operator services
Travel United American AmEx TRS	1,000,000	Airlines hate paying commissions to travel agents, but they represent 90% of overall business. Volatile pricing environment, monopolistic competition. Extremely competitive; razor thin margins.	Reservations, flight times, schedules, weather, personal flight information
Banks Bank of America Banc One Chemical	65,000	Rapid consolidation and acquisitions from drop in regulations. Savings from consolidations going into tech spending. Intense competition, and SR tech could give edge that would do more than just increasing CD rates by 1%. With regs dropping, new services are the rise.	Obtain checking, credit card, stock, mutual fund info. & services Loan/mortgage Acceptance ATM locator service
Catalogs Home Shopping Network J.C. Penney QVC	200,000	Heavy competition. Immense cost for customers to hold to place order, ties up potential sales revenue; if hold is too long, customer could leave and buy product elsewhere. Heavy automation within the industry.	Preview customer info Automate order process Obtain shipment status Obtain account and billing info

* Competitive access providers (CAPs) are competitors to local telephone companies in major metropolitan areas, and primarily serve Fortune 1000 customers.
† Local telephone companies such as Regional Bells and GTE.
‡ Long distance companies such as AT&T and MCI.
Source: SR Corp Internal Document.

Exhibit 3 Target Fortune 500 Industries

Industry or Company	Pros for Leading Company	Cons for Leading Company
CAPS Metropolitan Fiber Services Corp. Teleport Inner Media	MFS: Highest growth rate in switches and cities. Only CAP dedicated to operator services. Need SR Tech for Oper Service efficiencies. Fast, driven, innovative, $, national. Not as large as LEC, fast sales cycle. Only CAP going after providing LDist service.	Not adding oper service until next year; most money comes from providing access. Wouldn't be ready for us just yet.
Travel United American AmEx TRS	United: 4800 operators, have skipped IVR system because transactions are not static. Said they have been looking for effective speech recog, but AT&T can only do 95% on 0 through 9; if anyone could get higher, "we could keep them busy just doing hundreds of apps for our company."	Affordability a major concern. Testing would take approximately 10–16 months.
Banks Bank of America Banc One Chemical	Bank of America: The Security Pacific acquisition brought a high tech focus to the company operations and they are extremely committed to technology to drive business. Corporate clientele on rise with Continental acquisition.	Any bank will need solid, large references before they purchase technology-based solutions. Very cautious.
Catalogs Home Shopping Network J.C. Penney QVC	Home Shopping Network: Incredibly devoted to technology-driven processes. In fact, their Annual Report discusses their different methods for 6 pages. Phones so important, HSN built own IVR company and later spun it off.	Potential use as a reference may be difficult. Would Home Shopping Net work be as good as an airline or telco?

Source: SR Corp Internal Document.

Exhibit 4 Advantages and Disadvantages of Prospective Fortune 500 Targets

Given the complexity and newness of the technology, the best channel for reaching this market niche was to sell directly to customers. Fortune 500 companies were more likely to buy hardware from large vendors such as IBM or AT&T, but they had shown a willingness to buy specialized software and turnkey systems from small vendors. SR Corp could expect to establish long-term relationships with Fortune 500 accounts because they would want SR Corp's continued assistance in developing a "family" of speech recognition applications for their respective businesses.

By 1994, more than half of the Fortune 500 companies had implemented interactive voice-button systems to automate customer service. SR Corp would have to replace these systems, and therefore faced the prospect of counterarguments from the vendors. From the customer's perspective, buying into a new system would specifically mean replacing systems that might only be a few years old and therefore not fully amortized. SR Corp's system would have to be connected to a heterogeneous mix of PCs, mainframes, and networks. Development and maintenance software tools would also be critical.

Hastings summarized his thoughts on this niche:

The Fortune 500 niche holds excellent opportunities with regard to potential sales volume and a solid reference base. I've already spoken to two airlines who want to start right away evaluating our technology. These two airlines have the second highest number of daily transactions after the largest telephone companies. They really want our stuff.

My concern is the level of effort we'll need to provide in order to serve these airlines or large banks or mutual fund companies, during the first two years. We'll have to hire engineers and set up a field office at each customer site. These things may all put a resource drain on the company during its initial years of marketing, particularly when compared to either telephone companies or telephone switch manufacturers, who basically know what they are doing technically. The lack of knowledge in this market niche about speech recognition deployed in a local area network environment would also lengthen our sales cycle. Lastly, an airline reservation application is much more complicated than directory assistance or hands-free dialing.

The Telephone Companies

Telephone company prospects included all telephone companies in the United States that owned and maintained telephone lines. The majority of these lines were owned by local exchange carriers (LECS) and long distance providers. Telephone companies would put speech recognition systems in their central office locations where telephone lines were connected. For example, in 1994 Bell

Atlantic had approximately 19 million phone lines and as many as 500 central offices in its Mid-Atlantic region.

Voice processing technologies such as messaging, speech synthesis, and speech recognition offered substantial opportunities in the operator services arena. Hastings believed that implementation of these capabilities should be worth hundreds of millions of low-risk dollars in cost containment and new enhanced service revenues to each of the local exchange carriers (including Baby Bells & GTE) and interexchange carriers (including the long distance companies such as AT&T, Sprint, and MCI).

Many large telephone companies had already made substantial investments in new operator services platforms that integrated directory assistance, intercepts and toll assistance functions. Further, some had developed voice messaging and speech controlled services for calling cards and 800 and 900 service.

Directory assistance was a compelling example of how speech recognition could save a company money. Industry experts believed that operator services enhanced with speaker-independent voice recognition technology could save telephone companies $600 million annually in equipment and operational costs. One Baby Bell shared the results of a recent internal study with Hastings that showed impressive savings through automation. The company's average directory assistance work time was 18 seconds. Eliminating just a single second would translate into $8 million in annual savings.

SR Corp was shooting for a high level of automation of directory assistance services which would include names of cities and individuals. The system incorporated alphabet recognition, so that a user could spell the last name and city if he or she needed to. The system also understood the majority of foreign accents in English. Even a speech recognition system that automatically recognized only city and state words (not name and address) could save as much as 10 seconds on average.

Even with the best technology, however, telephone companies would still provide users with the option of speaking to a human operator. With its 99 percent accuracy, SR Corp's system would provide an effective automation rate of 98 percent (99 percent for the city words times 99 percent for the state words; in general, the effective accuracy rate would decrease by 0.99 times the number of words in the transaction). Human operators would be required to handle the remaining 2 percent of the city and state part of transactions.

The combined local and long distance carrier industry reached $150 billion in 1994. There were 130 million telephone access lines controlled by local exchange carriers in the United States. (See Exhibits 5 and 6.) Of the 130 million lines, only about 200,000 were trunks, where individual lines came together and provided logical targets for embedding speech recognition.

Sales of speech recognition enhanced products to telephone companies totaled $44 million in 1994. However, industry experts predicted sales would rise to $1 billion by the year 2000. Based on his own field research in several telephone companies, Hastings expected that most telephone companies would be interested in speech recognition for at least 25 percent of their trunks over the next several years and would gradually move toward 50 to 75 percent within 5 to 10 years.

SR Corp's product could be configured for any number of phone lines. Speech recognition offered a telephone company an opportunity to generate new incremental revenues from innovative applications. One Baby Bell, for example, concluded it could sell voice dialing services to seven million customers by mid-1996 at a $5 monthly charge, producing approximately $400 million in additional revenue per year. Speech recognition could also serve as a means to overhaul and automate many internal functions.

A growing subset of the telephone company niche was cellular companies. By 1994, most telephone companies had an equity interest in a major cellular company in the United States. (See Exhibit 7.) Revenues for the cellular industry totaled $11 billion in 1993, and the industry served a total of seven million subscribers. Cellular markets were growing at 45 percent per year versus the 3 percent annual growth of line-based telephony. New types of digital cellular technology, such as personal communications services and global mobile services, were emerging on the scene. Cellular telephony provided a strong market for speech recognition services. Hands-free command and control for voice dialing and

| | **Total Access Lines Serviced** | | | | |
| | | | | 1993 Revenue | Estimated Number |
Carrier	1992	1993	% Growth	(000,000)	of Calls per Day
GTE	16,819,000	17,000,000	1.08	$ 12,400	95,119,112
Bell Atlantic	18,180,700	18,612,700	2.38	$ 10,700	104,142,559
BellSouth	18,621,600	19,296,500	3.62	$ 13,000	107,968,585
Ameritech	17,001,000	17,471,581	2.77	$ 10,000	97,757,722
NYNEX	15,700,000	15,700,000		$ 11,000	87,845,298
US West	13,300,000	13,700,000	3.01	$ 8,000	76,654,814
SNET	1,936,577	1,959,555	1.19	$ 1,000	10,964,184
Pacific Bell	14,306,000	14,600,000	2.06	$ 9,000	81,690,532
Southwestern Bell	12,700,000	13,200,000	3.94	$ 7,000	73,857,193
Total	128,564,877	131,540,336		$ 82,100	736,000,000

Source: Annual Review & Forecast, TE&M, Jan. 15, 1994.

Exhibit 5 Local Exchange Carrier Access Line Information and Corporate Data

Interexchange Carriers Market Shares 1992 (percent)

	AT&T	MCI	Sprint	Other	Total
Toll revenues	65	14	10	11	$ 52B
Switched minutes	63				$324B
Premium minutes	64				$318B
Private line	62	11	8	19	$ 8B
Presubscribed	79	11	6	4	
Business customers	52	17	16	15	$132B

Total Market Share Long-Distance Market (percent)

Vendor	Total market share	Hospitality industry	Public payphone	Private payphone	Traditional
AT&T	71.00	74.00	76.00	51.00	68.00
MCI	9.00	7.00	6.00	4.00	13.00
Sprint	6.00	5.00	8.00		9.00
Int'l Telecharge	2.20	2.00	4.00	21.00	
Nat'l Tele Serv	1.60		3.00		
Others	10.20	12.00	3.00	24.00	10.00

Source: 1993 Geodesic Network, Geodesic Co., Washington D.C.

Exhibit 6 Long Distance Company Information

messaging were two examples. These factors made cellular companies good candidates for SR Corp's marketing efforts.

Judging from telephone company buying patterns and their need to reduce operational costs, Hastings believed that a large telephone company would want to introduce speaker-independent speech recognition capability into 5,000 lines in the first year and could pay up to $10,000 per line. SR Corp's system could handle up to five lines per workstation, which translated into 1,000 systems delivered to a customer's central offices.

Given the complexity of the technology, Hastings thought that the best channel for reaching this market niche was to sell directly to customers. When compared to Fortune 500 firms, telephone companies were even more likely to buy hardware from large vendors such as IBM or AT&T because a telephone company's fault-tolerant environment required proven hardware and strong technical support. However, telephone companies had looked to emerging telecommunications firms for specialized solutions, particularly in software. SR Corp could expect to establish

	Ameritech	Bell Atlantic	BellSouth	NYNEX
Cellular subscribers	860,000	1,039,000	1,559,132	575,000
POPS (millions)	21	31	39	20
Cellular penetration	4.00%	3.30%	4.00%	2.90%
1993 growth in subscribers	47%	48%	39%	47%
Avg. monthly revenue per subscriber	$68	$77	$63	$82
Cellular's share of total company value	13.50%	11.10%	25.30%	11.40%

	PACTEL	Southwestern Bell	US West	LEC Average
Cellular subscribers	1,046,000	2,049,000	601,000	1,104,162
POPS (millions)	33	36	18	28
Cellular penetration	3.10%	5.70%	3.30%	3.76%
1993 growth in subscribers	41%	45%	45%	45%
Avg. monthly revenue per subscriber	$83	$63	$72	$73
Cellular's share of total company value	35.30%	28.10%	11.00%	19.39%

Source: 1993 Geodesic Network, Geodesic Co., Washington D.C.

Exhibit 7 Cellular Market Information

long-term relationships with such companies because they would want its help building new applications.

By 1994, most telephone companies had implemented interactive voice response systems as well as voice mail systems. The switching costs facing a telephone company considering SR Corp would be large. These voice response and mail systems were typically large computers placed in central offices. Not only was amortization of installed equipment an issue, but substitution with a new speech recognition system would require simultaneous replacement of old systems in numerous geographical sites.

Dr. Schall figured that he would need to hire a team of about 20 engineers per telephone company in order to help with the complex integration of the speech recognition technology into the central offices. To develop follow-on business, Hastings also expected to hire one account manager per telephone company at a cost of $100,000 per person per year. Both field engineers and account representatives would work from a single field office located near the customer's central office. Once again, the figures used for planning were 250 square feet of office space per person leased on an annual basis for $10 per square foot.

Based on his discussions with several companies, Hastings believed that SR Corp could obtain 10 percent of the typical 5,000 line sale upon contract signing. Integration would take approximately a year. He felt confident that two telephone companies could be converted into customers during the first two years.

Hastings summarized the telephone company niche for his colleagues:

Telcos offer a high-growth market and can definitely deliver the volume for SR Corp to achieve strong profitability. Furthermore, Telcos would have the most knowledge about speech recognition and its implementation. Their learning curve would be quick. Also, because Telcos could use this technology, both inside their companies as well as outside by selling it to their own commercial customers, the technology would provide a quick payback.

There are a couple of catches, though. Telcos are multibillion-dollar customers who could slow us down and drag out the sales process. I've heard of some Telcos agreeing to a contract and then, after wasting 12 months of a vendor's time, canceling the program—we cannot afford that type of a problem at this early stage. In addition, AT&T and several Baby Bells are experimenting with their own homegrown versions of speaker-independent speech recognition. We would not want to alert them to what we have already done. This would invite legal battles over intellectual property. This particular threat is a very real—they might try to hire away our best engineers or tie us up in court.

The Telephone Switch Manufacturers (OEMS)

This last niche in telephony was comprised of original equipment manufacturers (OEMs) making switch equipment for telephone companies. Telephone switches were presently digital, computer-based systems. The largest switch OEMs included Northern Telecom, AT&T, Alcatel, GTE, British Telecom, and Ericsson. This market brought in revenues of $2.5 billion in 1993.

SR Corp's strategy in this market niche would be to license its speech recognition system to switch manufacturers who would bundle the technology into their switches. SR Corp would provide the integration of its technology under contract into an OEM's system and then receive a royalty on units sold. Switch manufacturers would most likely choose to manufacture the speech recognition boards themselves. They would also be wholly responsible for the selling of their switches, including that portion containing SR Corp's technology. They would neither demand nor expect exclusive rights to SR Corp's technology or that of any other vendor of speech recognition technology.

The average advanced switch was priced at approximately $100,000, and 45,000 units were sold in 1993 to telephone companies. Northern Telecom had 24 percent of the global market, AT&T had 24 percent, GTE had 18 percent, Alcatel had 11 percent, and other switch OEMs held the remaining 23 percent. The current "action" in this market was the development of a new generation of switches based on the asynchronous transfer mode (ATM) networking protocols—a method that allowed more reliable communications for data, voice, and video.

Speech recognition had been recently integrated into advanced switches. Switches with voice-button speech recognition accounted for 1993 revenues of $17 million, or less than one percent of the market. Industry experts believed that the market for speech enhanced switches would grow as accuracy levels increased and would represent $300 million in revenues by the year 2000. Many of the OEMs, such as AT&T and Northern Telecom, were working on their own speaker-independent speech recognition programs.

Switch OEMs always looked for new technologies that would add value to their systems. By adding speech recognition, OEMs could spare telephone companies the cost of adding the technology themselves later. Additionally, OEMs were in a strong position to help SR Corp disseminate its technology because their systems were installed in telephone companies' central offices. In fact, if SR Corp decided not to work through the largest switch manufacturers, the switches provided by those OEMs could prove tough barriers to entry to SR Corp's own direct sales.

Through discussions with several switch manufacturers, Hastings concluded that SR Corp could sell its technology at approximately $5,000 per line of recognition and could gain at least three customers during the first two years. The price per line was lower than that for direct sales to Fortune 500 firms ($6,000 per line) or telephone companies ($10,000 per line). This lower price would be required because the switch manufacturers would do all the selling of the final solution to the telephone companies. Also, OEMs would perform the actual manufacturing of the boards containing SR Corp's technology. The speech recognition portion of their equipment would only represent a small percentage (5 to 10 percent) of the overall final sale. Based on his study of their sales volumes, Hastings estimated that an individual switch manufacturer would purchase 6,000 lines of speech recognition, for a total of 18,000 lines if three OEMs became customers in the first two years. He believed that OEMS, like the telephone companies, would pay 10 percent of the contract amount upon signing.

Here again, the best channel for reaching this market niche was to sell directly to the switch manufacturers. Switch OEMs had shown a strong tendency to purchase component technologies from whatever firm had the best technology, be it a large firm or small one. Once an OEM had completed a new type of switch, contacts with component vendors were minimal.

Since SR Corp was seeking to be part of the design of a next-generation system, there would be no significant switching cost for the OEM. SR Corp would become part of a "new design." Of course, the OEM would have to retrain its own engineers so that they would understand how to use SR Corp's development environment and support the system.

SR Corp would have to put a team of six engineers with each switch manufacturer to help integrate its technology into the new switch. Dr. Schall believed that the integration effort would take approximately 10 months. An account manager would also be assigned to each customer to generate additional revenue. Both field engineers and account representatives would be based in a field office near the customer. Labor of $100,000 per person per year and office space costs of 250 square feet at $10 per square foot per person were used for planning purposes.

Hastings reflected on this niche:

OEMs would be a solid way to move SR Corp's technology on a mass scale, while also providing a solid reference base for future customers. In addition, OEMs are always searching for emerging technologies to enhance their offerings, and are willing to take early technological risks if the payoff is there.

However, my concern is that SR Corp runs the risk of not being able to participate in either the way or how fast an OEM decides to market the technology. In addition, although OEMs have a basic working understanding of speech recognition, sales cycles in this niche have been known to approach two years due to integration and standards issues. Furthermore, we may risk getting too close to some of our competitors, such as AT&T, who hold large market shares in this industry and no doubt will do anything to protect their positions—including lawsuits.

THREE RECENT EVENTS

Hastings finished his presentation of the three telephony niches by describing to SR Corp's management team three highly relevant events that had occurred during the last 24 hours.

The first event was a new industry report on the telephone industry, the *Telco Business Report* Hastings handed out copies of the report to his colleagues.[6] It stated that "more than 70 percent of the 1,200 respondents—including RBOCs (regional Bell operating companies), independents, and long distance companies worldwide—said they plan to renew or update their operator

services in the next two years with automation." This report also indicated that telephone companies in the United States wanted more technologically sophisticated software to improve and expedite delivery of regional directory assistance services. Speech recognition systems were a main interest. Technological change in this niche was moving even faster than Hastings, Dr. York, and or Dr. Schall had expected. This carried risks as well as opportunities. Once a telephone company invested in a new speech recognition platform (even if it was an inferior system relative to what SR Corp had to offer), the company's doors would probably be closed to new vendors for at least two or three years because of the need to amortize such a large investment.

Would SR Corp risk losing these customers by pursuing Fortune 500 firms or switch manufacturers? At the same time, could SR Corp afford not to pursue other customers? Hastings knew that selling to a major telephone company might take more than a year because a single speech recognition application would include up to a dozen different departments and each department head would have to agree to contribute budget resources.

The second event was a telephone call from a Fortune 500 airline executive, who had clearly stated that he would purchase SR Corp's systems right away if the accuracy claims could be proven: "We have to handle 200,000 phone calls a day. If this stuff really works, we could cut our operating costs by a substantial amount." Reminding his listeners that the sales cycle for a Fortune 500 customer was typically shorter than that for a telephone company, Hastings pointed out that this executive was someone who could make things happen fast:

Fewer departments, and hence, decision makers would be involved. An airline deal would probably be smaller than a Telco deal. But that's okay because it will be more manageable in terms of scale and scope. I bet we could land the deal in six months. Further, once we did an airline, the other big ones would probably follow soon thereafter because the industry is so price competitive. The big catch in all this is that, from what I have seen, their MIS departments know next to nothing about speech recognition technology. Integration would be painful.

The third event had happened the night before. Hastings had given a guest lecture to engineering managers for a former business school professor. In speaking about market strategies for emerging technologies, Hastings had used his own firm as one of the examples. After Hastings finished speaking, one of the students in the class introduced himself and indicated that he worked for a major telecommunications equipment manufacturer. The student's company was designing a new asynchronous transfer mode switch. Due to customer demand, all the large switch manufacturers were developing state-of-the-art ATM switches. Major telephone and cable companies needed to provide improved commercial data services for businesses and video on demand for home markets. ATM switches seemed the most pragmatic, workable solution to achieve this from a network perspective. The student had said, "If you've got what I think you've got, we need to build it into our next-generation switch." He wanted Hastings to visit his company the following week.

---

[6]"Operator Services Slated as the Next Investment Boom for Telcos." *Telco Business Report*, PC-Plus Group, Munich, Germany, Dec. 5, 1994.

Hastings concluded his remarks to SR Corp's management team by noting the obvious: each market niche exhibited tremendous opportunity, yet each held substantial risk. After listening to Hastings's report and hearing about the three late-breaking developments, the lead investor turned to Dr. Schall and said:

> Engineering better be telling us the truth. If our gun isn't loaded, we're the ones who will end up getting shot!

On a positive note, the investor reiterated that he would provide additional funding once a single major customer showed clear signs of a successful outcome. Any delays in procurement or systems integration would mean that SR Corp would have to wait longer, not only to be paid by the customer but also to get the investment it needed to build a strong sales force. The investor also needed to see a marketing plan that showed the prioritization of the telephony niches and of the key accounts within those niches. Turning to Dr. York, he remarked:

> It all boils down to making sure the technology, is bullet-proof and getting the right customer. You better hurry though. I wouldn't be surprised if there is another 'Hastings' working for a company just like ours trying to make the same decision for his own firm's breakthrough speech technology.

CASE 10
SpainSko

In December 1994, Gonzalo and Pilar Goyes were asking themselves what the future of SpainSko, S.L. might be. They started this small family concern about eight months earlier, and had already invested some seven million pesetas (1), which was about 70 percent of the 10 million total investment they had originally forecasted as funds necessary for their new business venture to reach breakeven.

SpainSko imported Dansko shoes and then distributed them within Spain using direct marketing methods. Dansko shoes followed the new European concept of "comfort shoes"; they were not orthopedic, but simply aimed to allow the feet to work properly. They fitted any shape of healthy foot perfectly and the design sacrificed aesthetic appearance in the interests of greater comfort.

The figures that Gonzalo and Pilar obtained from the calculations they did to work out the cost of identifying new customers seemed excessively high to them. They were still a long way from making each purchase of Dansko shoes a profitable transaction.

In the past, they carried out various promotional activities to reach different potential customer segments, some of which produced results far removed from those obtained in similar exercises in other parts of Europe. They made inserts for magazines, and mailings to various consumer groups (priests and nuns, pharmacists, chiropodists, members of associations of diabetics, etc.).

Gonzalo knew that the key to reaching profitability and self-financing the growth of the business lay in building up a database of existing customers of Dansko shoes, who would be sent a mailing every six months, each of which was expected to yield an 8 percent response.

In December 1994, however, the most important objective was to lower the cost of gaining new customers. If they failed to do so, they would have to give up their attempt to carry out direct sales in Spain, because even greater resources would be needed in order to overcome the lack of response to the advertising campaigns.

Faced with this situation there were several options:

1. Persevere with the system they had been using (inserts and mailings). This was the method used in Germany, the country with the highest sales figures.
2. Set up a retail store.
3. Look for a new distribution channel, such as selling through pharmacists, teachers of physical education, physiotherapists, etc.
4. Publish advertisements like those that Birkenstock (their rival) had been using.
5. Attend trade fairs (as was done in Germany).

BACKGROUND

History

Pilar Cerezo left the labour market at the age of 25 in order to devote herself fulltime to looking after her husband and four children. As they got older, the children took up less and less of her time and Pilar decided to talk to her husband Gonzalo about her wish to make some contribution to the family income, given that she had a few hours a day in which to do so.

Gonzalo Goyes had several years of experience as a manager, consultant, and expert in setting up new business ventures. He had great initiative and imagination. He was the general manager of a company called Interstrategies, S.A., which had a number of shareholders and was a business strategy consultancy and promoter of small companies that were just starting up. In view of Pilar's situation, he realized that he had to come up with an idea for a small business venture that was personal, had flexible working hours, was close to home, did not require regular travel, and called for a maximum investment of 10 million pesetas.

Some 20 years before, Gonzalo had to spend two weeks in Denmark during the month of February. The bad weather, the cold, and the damp ruined his footwear (traditional moccasins) and he found it necessary to buy another pair of shoes that were both hard-wearing and as comfortable as possible. It was his first purchase of Dansko shoes (which in Denmark sold under the brand name of Jacoform). For the next 20 years he remained a loyal consumer of the brand, mainly on account of their comfort and durability. He bought them whenever he went to Denmark or ordered them via any friend or colleague who happened to be going there. Later, he discovered that he could order them by telephone.

Importing Dansko shoes and distributing them in Spain was, on the face of it, the sort of, venture that would suit Pilar. For this reason, on May 25, 1993, Gonzalo got in touch with the manufacturer of Dansko, a Danish company by the name of A/S Jac. Engelbredt which was owned by the family of the same name. Jacob Engelbredt recommended that Gonzalo contact Alfred Frank in Switzerland. He was the person responsible for sales of Dansko worldwide (except in Scandinavian countries), and acted as an independent distributor for Switzerland.

INFORMATION RECEIVED FROM ALFRED FRANK

Jacoform and Dansko Distribution in Europe

A telephone conversation with Alfred Frank helped Gonzalo Goyes begin to understand how the world of Dansko shoes worked.

A/S Jac. Engelbredt was a family company with about 60 workers in its factory near Copenhagen and another 20 or so in a second factory in Poland. The shoes they manufactured were sold in the Scandinavian countries under the name of Jacoform and in the rest of Europe under that of Dansko.

The company started in the 1960s as a designer and manufacturer of children's shoes, prompted by a Danish physiotherapist who was looking for a pair of shoes with the right anatomical shape that would allow his children's feet to develop correctly. From their studies of footwear for children, they realized that it would be possible to apply the same concept to fully developed feet. They started manufacturing shoes for adults: basic, functional, anatomical shoes, with enough room for the toes to spread at each step. In 1994, the leather for the shoes was selected and imported from countries such as Spain, cured in Denmark, then sent to Poland to be hand-sewn, and returned to Denmark, where the soles were stuck on and the shoes were prepared for sale (the laces were fitted, etc.).

At first, A/S Jac. Engelbredt sold in Denmark and exported to Germany using the brand name Jacoform. The shoes were a success, but the distributor registered the Danish brand in his own name and started to manufacture locally. After the subsequent lawsuit, Jacob Engelbredt was allowed to use the Jacoform brand only in the Scandinavian countries. In addition to this, a change in fashion in the Scandinavian countries (one that favoured the sale of Italian-designed shoes) brought serious problems for the manufacturer. It was then that, with the help of Alfred Frank (an expert in consumer marketing who was interested in setting up a small business in Switzerland), the following decisions were made:

1. Change to a new brand name that would be registered internationally: Dansko.
2. Maintain the traditional shape of Jacoform shoes, giving priority to the functionality of the foot over aesthetics, fashion, and price.
3. Dansko would be positioned as a "special" shoe in terms of comfort and functionality.
4. Outside of Scandinavia, the shoes would be distributed by means of direct marketing, since the costs of producing in Denmark and of the raw materials used were incompatible with the demands of traditional shoe retailers.

Product Features

Dansko shoes were authentic moccasins: the leather covering the sides and the sole of the foot was all one piece, thereby guaranteeing that there would be no stitching on the soles. They were shaped anatomically, which made them look strange, but it was this shape which allowed the toes to spread freely when the foot was bent for walking. They were scientifically designed to be adaptable and appropriate to maintaining correct posture. The sole was made of special rubber, the flexibility of which was graduated so that it was softer under the toes than under the heel, which is where practically the whole weight of the body is borne. The high quality leather and the fact that the shoes were hand-sewn ensured their great durability and comfort.

The range of Dansko products was quite wide. There were about 40 different models of shoes and sandals in a variety of basic shoe colours (black, brown, navy blue, beige, etc.).

Sales experience in other European countries showed that one third of the retail price of each pair of shoes went to paying the manufacturer's costs, one third was spent on advertising, and the rest covered the distributor's overhead expenses and profits. (Exhibit 1 has a technical description of the product.)

Distribution of Dansko in Central Europe

The key differentiating features of Dansko's distribution system were that they did not compete on price and they were not sold in traditional shoe shops. Dansko shoes were sold directly to the public using direct marketing methods. They were offered to groups of potential customers, such as religious orders, pharmacists, diabetics, naturist associations, etc., through direct mailings or via inserts in magazines. The mailings included an advertising leaflet about Dansko shoes and an order form (which was printed on thicker card and required no return postage). The customer did not have to pay for the shoes on receipt. The shoes were sent by mail and the customer had a few days to try them out. If the customer finally decided to buy them, he/she went ahead with the payment. If not, the customer was expected to return the shoes, also by mail.

Under this system, 50 percent were returned, half because the customer wanted a different size or style, and the rest because the customer decided not to buy after all, having once seen and tested the product.

The distributor had to bear the risk of dispatching the shoes. Given the particular characteristics of Dansko's customers, there were very few non-payments. The "Group" of importers of Dansko shoes into different countries was very satisfied with this system.

All the importers of Dansko shoes in different countries were considered to form a "group." They shared the design of advertising leaflets, mailings, and other promotional activities in order to reduce costs. Every new distributor had to be accepted by all the members of the group, each of which had exclusive rights in its own country. The group shared their experience and know-how with new members, while new members had to bear in mind that they too would one day be members of "the group" and that they should make financial contributions toward promotion. "The group" met twice a year and participated in product development with Jacob Engelbredt. It also took part in the joint planning of production requirements and would assume the moral obligation of finding a way to get rid of obsolete stock, should it be necessary.

In 1993, "the group" was made up of the exclusive importers of Dansko shoes located in Germany, Switzerland, Holland, and

SpainSko
DESCRIPTION

DANSKO. A really functional shoe.

Shoes are basic requirements which help our feet to work properly for the whole of our life.

The shape and make-up of our feet is closely linked to their function. A thorough understanding of how feet work when we walk or run is the scientific base for good shoe designers.

The manufacture of shoes in natural shapes has increased in Europe over recent decades as fashion preferences have given way to functionality.

Of course, fashion cannot be disregarded altogether, and there are certain limitations with regard to the technology and the materials. This has on occasions prevented knowledge about how feet work being fully applied to the design of shoes.

DANSKO shoes are the result of the most successful attempt to create a shoe that is highly suitable for all modern requirements and has the shape and functions of a good shoe.

The emergence of new materials, better manufacturing techniques, and close collaboration between the manufacturer, the designer and the feet experts have all made it possible to create these shoes (orthopedists, chiropodists, physiotherapists, and kinesiologists).

The following requirements were borne in mind when designing **DANSKO** shoes:

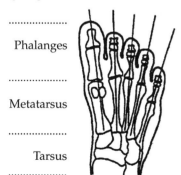

Phalanges

Metatarsus

Tarsus

1. The front part of the shoe is shaped like a fan, so that the natural direction of the toe bones can be kept straight, thereby giving them room to expand a bit.

2. <u>The front profile</u> of the shoe is <u>slightly rounded</u>, not slanted from the big toe to the small toe. In this way, it is suitable for almost all shapes of foot, for example if the second toe is as long as the big toe.

3. Good height internally in the shoe including over the big toe, so that there is enough room for slight movements inside the shoe up or down.

4. The sole has no welts, which assists in the take-off movement over the big toe. With regard to width, as the line of the sole is parallel to the stitching on the moccasin, it makes the shoe look narrower.

5. A relatively small narrow opening to the shoe, and a relatively long area where it does up are combined with a cup-shaped heel and a slightly raised area under the rear of the arch. This ensures firm support in the back half of the shoe and effectively prevents the foot sliding forward.

6. The raised area under the back of the arch mentioned in the previous paragraph, just in front of the heel support, prevents the foot turning inwards when standing (knock-knees). It does not support the arch (which can move freely). Only the rear third of the arch is supported.

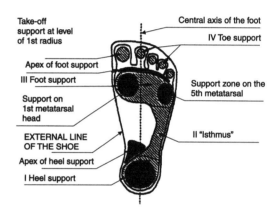

7. Independent of the cup-shaped support that holds the heel in place, the inner sole of the shoe is flat or levelled between the heel support and the forward support of the foot (II: the "isthmus,"). This part of the foot has no external curvature and needs constant contact with the sole.

8. In the part below the toe and foot supports, the sole of the shoe has a malleable layer beneath the leather. Each user shapes this part of the sole individually by compressing it and establishing the greatest area of contact. This leads to the formation of a slight ridge between the foot support and the toes. Together with the support mentioned in points 5 and 6, this prevents the foot from slipping forward.

9. The shoe has a zero heel, in other words, it has no raised heel nor any difference in level. We are born without raised heels and this zero level is the most natural way for the foot to carry out its functions properly. But remember that the shoe has a cup and

Exhibit 1 Technical Description of the Product

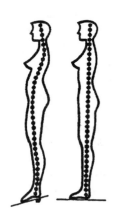

a brake in the heel to prevent knock-knees (see point 6). If shoes with high heels are worn, the foot's natural movements are restricted and the body is forced away from its natural centre of gravity. Even low heels force the toes and arches to support the weight of the body.

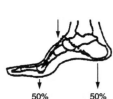

50%   50%   10%   90%

10. The shoe has a flexible sole that is very light and resistant to friction. This helps during the strong, upward twist by the big toe in order to get the foot off the ground.

11. The bottom of the sole is rounded at the front and at the back, over the so-called foot propulsion line. This assists forward movement, carrying the weight from the heel across the isthmus to the front part of the foot, allowing the foot to take off easily and smoothly.

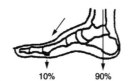

12. The progressively flexible sole and the shank allow the sole and the foot in general to twist lengthwise towards the end of take-off, when the front part of the foot twists anti-clockwise, whilst the back of the foot twists in the opposite direction (right foot).

13. In general, the shoe is designed with a straight axis, that is to say that the heel directs the foot towards the front in such a way that neither the big nor the little toes are squeezed sideways. This is achieved by

having the central axis of the foot in the centre of the heel support and straight down to the second toe, dividing the foot lengthwise in a ratio 3/4.

NATURAL SHAPE OF A FOOT PRINT

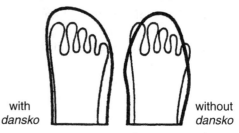

with
dansko

without
dansko

SpainSko

As can be appreciated in the previous thirteen points, the fundamental concept of a **DANSKO** shoe is that the forward part of the foot is free to spread out widthwise whilst holding the rest of the foot and giving maximum support to the arches during the take-off movement. The back area is designed to ensure firm support for the ankle and the heel. In a naturally-shaped shoe, it is not enough for the front part of the foot to be able to move freely, it is also very important that the heel is well supported.

By means of a decreasing angle, the bottom part of the shoe under the sole follows the lengthwise movements of the arch in walking and the rounded edges at the front and back of the sole permit greater surface contact and therefore, a better distribution of weight. Having the foot absolutely level (zero heel) ensures cooperation between the calf muscles and the pressure muscles in the toes.

The leather used is top quality in terms of water proofing, (6 hours water resistance) as well as flexibility and resistance to bending. The leather is dyed gently so as to maintain its porous nature and achieve water resistance and an ability to breathe at the same time. Thick, flexible, hard-wearing leather therefore lasts longer.

DANSKO:
The shoe that lets you walk "barefoot".
The shoe with firm support for your heel.
The shoe to wear standing up, walking and running.

Imported into Spain by
SpainSko, S.L.   **tel. 93.675.51.21**

SPAINSKO. S.L. A. Torreblanca, 2-8, 1° E-08190 S.Cugat del Vallés. Barcelona. Tel: (93) 675.51.21 Fax: (93) 675.51.69 - NIF B 60498250

Exhibit 1 Technical Description of the Product *(continued)*

Austria. Alfred Frank started his importing business in Switzerland very successfully in the same way as Pilar would be doing. He had been a manager at Procter & Gamble and then decided to retire to his farm, at some distance from the centre of Basel, in order to set up his own business. His fine results had led J. Engelbredt to appoint him as "the group's" coordinator.

In 1994, "the group" would sell some 35,000 pairs of shoes and 45,000 were forecast for 1995. Forecasts for the year 2000 were for 120,000 pairs between the whole group.

In the first letter that Alfred Frank wrote to Gonzalo, he talked about various aspects of the distribution and sale of Dansko shoes, and advised the Goyes family:

"Sales prices in the whole of Europe are quite high, higher than Clarks, Ganter, or other brands of comfort shoes that are on sale in shoe shops and other retail stores. This is normal and Dansko customers are not particularly price sensitive.

"The initial problem I had in Switzerland was how to explain to my target audience why Dansko shoes have this peculiar shape, and how to convince women that they could wear these shoes too. It was not an easy task, but the result was brilliant. In 1994, 60–65 percent of Dansko customers in Switzerland were women, whereas in Germany they represented only 40 percent.

"I think that anyone wanting to set up a business importing and distributing Dansko shoes in Spain must do so with a view to reaching reasonable sales levels after three to five years. I ought also to say that I would rather start exporting to France than to Spain.

"Prospective distributors in Spain must believe that the product can be sold directly. In the future, the distributor will be expected to contribute funds to the group of Dansko distributors for the design of advertising leaflets and mailing costs.

"In Switzerland, Germany, and Denmark many different models and colours are currently sold. I would recommend that you start with a limited range of models.

"We are only prepared to collaborate with distributors who we believe really understand the product, have mastered direct sales techniques, able to contribute enough funds to 'the group,' and can reach adequate sales figures in three years."

FIRST STEPS FOR THE GOYES FAMILY

Market Study

During, the summer of 1993, using the sparse information derived from Alfred Frank's letters, Gonzalo asked his daughter Yolanda, who had a diploma in business studies and was about to start the fourth year of her economics degree, to carry out a small market study of the shoe sector in Spain in order to start to get to know their future distribution area. They had to find out if Spain was as difficult a market as Alfred Frank had said.

In broad terms, this was how the Spanish footwear market stood in 1992.

Spain was one of the largest manufacturers of footwear in the EEC, although the average quality of the products was nowhere near as high as Dansko. For this reason, shoes manufactured in Spain were not expensive on average. In spite of this, the figure for the purchase of shoes per capita in Spain (3.2 pairs a year) was one of the lowest in Europe (average of 4.2 pairs a year). This was due to the mild climate in the country (which means that shoes do not have to be replaced so often) and to the lower level of income.

In 1989, 186.3 million pairs had been manufactured in Spain. Shoe manufacturers were small companies and formed a very fragmented sector, with 4 percent of the manufacturers having some international presence. Spain was one of the main footwear exporting countries, particularly in the higher price points. The trade balance in 1989 had been the following:

Exports from Spain	128,738,000,000 ptas.
Imports into Spain	15,001,000,000 ptas.
Balance	113,737,000,000 ptas.

The sector was in difficulty and many manufacturers were going under. With regard to distribution systems, there were no large chains of shops specialized in shoe retail, and the value chain was basically as follows:

- Retailers usually had a gross margin of 50 percent of the retail price.
- Wholesalers and sales representatives had a gross margin of around 13 percent of the retail price.
- Manufacturers got about 37 percent of the retail price.

For example, if the recommended retail price of a pair of shoes in a retail store was 15,000 ptas., 7,500 ptas. was the retailer's gross margin; 1,950 went to the wholesaler or representative; and 5,550 ptas. was the price paid to the manufacturer.

On the other hand, the fashion factor was more important than in other countries that had more functional tendencies. Sports shoes were gaining ground over dress shoes, and the changing seasons were well reflected in sales. Women bought more pairs of shoes per year than men, although at lower unitary values.

Demand in the Spanish market was very seasonal, and was becoming more focused on the medium-high range, with more importance given to comfort and durability. The demand for shoes did not increase with the level of income, and brands were becoming more important (sales through retail stores with exclusive brands were going up).

In Yolanda's opinion, there seemed to have been only one brand of comfort shoe in the Spanish market for two years: Birkenstock, whose head office was in Germany. It was advertised through small advertisements in the magazine *Integral*; anyone interested was invited to send off for further information and a catalogue, prior to placing an order.

In addition to Birkenstock, there were other brands in the Spanish market that, although they were not exactly "comfort shoes," were shoes that were more comfortable than most and were aesthetically more "normal" (such as Mephisto or Clarks). They were sold in retail outlets (pharmacists and shoe shops) at higher than average prices (around 20,000 ptas.). The competition in this category was broadly made up of three groups of brands:

Mephisto: easy to find and similarly priced to Dansko. Their sporty design made them more suitable for use in the mountains, at weekends, etc.

Clarks and Scholl: a little cheaper than Mephisto, but more difficult to find. The design was very classic and not as sporty as Mephisto. The range was wider as it included styles for around the house as well as sandals.

Bally: only sold in top-class shoe shops and at higher prices than Dansko. They were very classical dress shoes.

Selling shoes through distributors and retailers was an option that the Goyes family had not yet rejected until they analyzed the prices and margins: 50 percent of the retail price of each pair of shoes sold was the retailer's margin, which was justified by the high level of stock required because of fluctuations caused by the fashion factor. This margin was too high for a shoe like Dansko, where the cost for the importer-distributor was already higher than the retail price of the majority of shoes sold in Spain.

The immediate conclusion reached by Pilar and Gonzalo Goyes was that they would need to sell the shoes via direct marketing, although it would be difficult to find people interested in the product since this type of shoe was a totally new concept for Spanish consumers. For the time being, they knew that the shoe market had great potential because of its size, and they had the feeling that there was a significant number of people who had problems with their feet.

One of the main problems encountered by the Goyes family was that of introducing the concept of a "comfort shoe." The customers had to be prepared to sacrifice the aesthetic appearance of their shoes and accept comfort as the fundamental feature of Dansko shoes. They would have to get used to the idea of accepting the natural shape of the foot as an aesthetic shape, and likewise the design of Dansko shoes. This seemed to be the most difficult part.

Travel

Before they started buying any shoes from Engelbredt, Gonzalo thought it would be sensible to visit Alfred Frank and the shoe factory in Denmark, thereby making their first serious investment in the potential business.

In October 1993, the Goyes couple traveled first to Switzerland, where their immediate impression was that the business was organized in basically the way that they were looking for: a business run by Frank and his wife, with the help of two girls. They sold enough pairs of shoes to keep the family and cover the cost of two extra salaries.

They went to Denmark a couple of days later, where they familiarized themselves with the manufacturing process of the Dansko shoes and gradually expanded their knowledge of the world of shoes, about which they had never previously known

anything in particular (nor had they ever dreamt they would end up knowing it in such great detail!).

Start of Operations

There were a number of factors that pushed the Goyes family into starting the new business. For example, SpainSko (the name and brand they had chosen for the importing and distribution company in Spain) was able to start operations and share certain costs with other newly created companies that were also supported by Interstrategies (the consulting company of which Gonzalo was a director). In addition to this significant help, they calculated that with a maximum of 10 million pesetas they could set up the business and reach the break-even point.

The business suited Pilar perfectly in terms of day-to-day requirements. She knew that one of the children would be able to answer the telephone and process orders on any occasion when she could not get to the office. For the time being, the costs had been calculated without including any labour costs (Pilar would be paid no salary at the beginning), but Pilar was happy to accept this sacrifice since she knew that "the early bird catches the worm," and being the one to introduce these shoes onto the market could be an important advantage.

Initially, the main aim of the business was to get a database of people who had already bought Dansko shoes, since the chances of them doing so again were very good. Customer loyalty was very high throughout Europe and was the key to success in marketing the product. This was reflected in the fact that they got an 8 percent response to every mailing to past customers, which was done twice a year, whereas mailings to the general public only got a response of two or three per thousand impacts.

In February 1994, once they made the decision to attempt to import and distribute Dansko shoes through Spain by direct marketing, there were two areas where Pilar set to work immediately: the advertising leaflet and the lists of names and addresses to reach the prospective target audience.

The offer from "the group" (the usual way of referring to the group of distributors in Central Europe) regarding the brochures was generous, although it turned out to be unsuitable for the Spanish market. Like the Goyes family, Alfred Frank always tried to save as much as possible on his costs, spending only where absolutely necessary. Therefore, he offered SpainSko the possibility of using the same brochures used in the rest of Europe, which could be obtained at very low cost given the large print runs. This offer was immediately rejected once the samples reached Gonzalo. They were six pages of pale, sad colours, very un-Mediterranean, with a medical air about the recommendations, and graphic explanations of the product. Gonzalo had imagined a much more modern advertising leaflet for the shoes and decided to commission a new design from a small company in Barcelona that specialized in advertising and graphic design and whose work was always very successful. The design and subsequent printing made the leaflet more expensive. In the first print run of 100,000 copies, each leaflet cost 21 pesetas, including the reply coupon that was stuck to it.

The leaflet included explanations about the product and instructions on how the sales system worked. Once it was finished, all they had to do was to send it to people who were particularly sensitive about their footwear.

As for the initial range of products, there were about 40 different possibilities within Dansko (combining the different styles and colours). However, they decided to start in Spain with a much smaller range that would combine the more classic styles with the two-tone styles (considered more sporty). All the styles would be sold at an average price of 18,000 ptas. (VAT and handling and shipping costs included), bearing in mind that the German Mark (the currency used by Engelbredt for invoicing) had an exchange rate of 80 ptas./Deutsche Mark (see Exhibit 1).

The prices were fixed at this level because, according to the information supplied by Alfred Frank, the cost structure for each pair of shoes was as follows: one-third of the retail price covered the cost of buying the shoe from the manufacturer, another third was spent on advertising and sales promotions, and the rest was the contribution margin for the importer/distributor.

Pilar thought it would be useful to have one model with a lower retail price (16,100 ptas., model 5049, Latin brown) in order to find out how sensitive the public was to price. Also, Gonzalo managed to obtain a significant discount on one of the models of which Denmark had a high level of stock. The reason for this excess stock was that the colour of this style was poorly reproduced in the brochure used in Europe (it looked a lot worse in the brochure than in reality), and so it had not sold as well as the rest. Controlling the exact colours was a serious problem when it came to producing advertising material.

Furthermore, in addition to importing shoes with laces or velcro, they also decided to import the model ''Clou,'' which came in a clog design but with the same properties as the other Dansko shoes. Its retail price would be 15,100 ptas. Pilar thought that if Dansko's customers really found the shoes comfortable, they might be interested in having a pair in the same shape as those for outdoors, but for indoor use.

After a few months of operating in Spain, they found that their cost structure would be different: almost 50 percent of the retail price went on import costs (largely owing to the depreciation of the peseta, which in December 1994 reached 88 ptas./DM), while the other 50 percent did not even cover the advertising expenses. The contribution margin was insufficient. At bottom, this was what most worried and frustrated Pilar. ''The shoes may be marvelous, perfect, oh so comfortable . . . but we're never going to make a living from them!''

Features of the Sales System Set Up in Spain

The sales process began by mailing the advertising leaflets to selected names and addresses or by inserting the same leaflets in selected publications. Anybody interested in the product was invited to place his/her order by returning the reply coupon duly completed with their personal details and the size and style required. They also had to send a cheque, VISA number, or proof of a bank transfer. Therefore, payment had to be made in advance, when the order was placed.

The Goyes knew that in Germany the customer paid for the shoes once he/she had tried them on at home and was sure that they fitted. The big disadvantage of this system was that 50 percent of the shoes sent out were returned, although a lot of people tried them on, and this was the main aim: seeing the shoes in a photograph in a brochure was not a great sales tool. In spite of everything, Pilar did not dare to send out hundreds of pairs of shoes in Spain without having any guarantee that they would be either returned or paid for. She had the feeling that the Spanish market was different from the German market in this respect.

Each customer had to choose the style and size. The leaflet included a scale of shoe sizes and foot measurements. There had never been problems with this system in the whole of Europe. The number of changes due to wrong sizes was very low.

SpainSko agreed to change the style, colour, or size as many times as necessary until the customer was satisfied. In some cases, the product could be returned. Payment in advance avoided the problem of non-payment for SpainSko, and was necessary for the dispatch system they were using. The shoes would be sent out to the customer using a courier service and would take less than 24 hours to reach their destination. Dispatch by mail was rejected as they believed the Spanish system was not reliable enough.

Given how difficult it was to try the shoes on, as they were not available in any shops, the option of trying the product at home was offered and could be requested on the order form. The price of this service was the same as the cost of sending the shoes by courier (1,250 ptas. including waiting time for the messenger) and the extra amount was added to the sales price.

Start of the advertising campaign

First shots. In March 1994 SpainSko carried out its first promotional activity by inserting advertising leaflets (printed in Spain but translated into German) into a German-language magazine, *Kontakt,* that was published in Spain. The magazine had 10,000 subscribers, who were basically immigrants from Central and Northern Europe resident in Spain. The idea came about because of the wide acceptance of Dansko shoes in Germany. The insert cost 120,000 ptas. (all the prices of the campaigns are given without the 16 percent VAT), plus the cost of the leaflets that SpainSko gave to the magazine. Only three sales were achieved.

At the same time, an agreement was made with the company, Arex, to do a number of inserts of the same leaflet in Spanish during the months March to June. Arex binds copies of various Spanish magazines into more hardwearing versions for use in waiting-rooms (magazines such as *Hola, Lecturas, Woman, Interviu, Actualidad Económica,* etc., in other words, women's magazines, current affairs, and other non-specialized themes). This cost 102,800 ptas. plus the cost of the leaflets; 8,677 inserts were done. Only one sale was made.

To finish off the promotional effort in this first month, a mailing was done to 500 members of the Goyes family and friends, 550 chiropodists, and 500 religious institutions. A letter presenting SpainSko was sent (see Exhibit 2), with an advertising leaflet and a reply coupon. The cost of each mailing was 64 ptas., which broke down as follows: 21 ptas. for the leaflet and reply coupon; 8 ptas. for the envelope; 28 ptas. for postage; and 7 ptas. for the presentation letter. The results were slightly better: 5 sales to chiropodists, 13 to religious centres and, fortunately, 44 sales to family and friends of the Goyes family.

Sales to family and friends were a great success, which was very comforting for Pilar and Gonzalo, but unfortunately this was not representative of the market. They had not achieved enough sales from the rest, but had gained a lot of experience (bearing in mind that they were starting from scratch).

1st campaign. April/September 1994.   Pilar was not expecting any more replies to the previous inserts, despite the anticipation with which she answered the office telephone, and was looking at alternative means of advertising within the same context. This time, she turned toward inserts in more specialized magazines on nature, health, and dietary matters. She ordered another insert, this time in the magazines *Integral* and *Cuerpomente* (owned by the same publisher), but only in the copies sent out to subscribers (16,900 in *Integral* and 9,000 in *Cuerpomente*). The total cost of the two inserts was 290,000 ptas. plus the cost of the leaflets. This time, Pilar Goyes seemed to be going in the right direction: 7 sales in *Cuerpomente* and 44 in *Integral*.

We have just set up SpainSko, S.A.

We have opened an office in Sant Cugat
Av. Torreblanca, 2-8, 1°, Local E
Tel. 675.51.21 Fax.675.51.69

We will not be having an official inauguration ceremony but we hope you will call in whenever you can to have a glass of cava with us.

You will already be aware how important your help and support can be in these early days. SpainSko imports and directly distributes Dansko shoes.

These Danish shoes have a natural shape which makes them very comfortable. They are not orthopedic or corrective shoes, they are just very comfortable.

They are manufactured to very high quality standards and in spite of seeming quite expensive, their durability makes them very economical. They are anatomical, water-proof, flexible, made of leather, authentic moccasins (like a glove), recyclable, etc.

They are particularly good for people who suffer from aching feet or who appreciate comfort above all else, such as:

- Those of us who are past the stage of wearing sneakers at week-ends.
- For all the football fans who claim to be sufferers (or not) at matches.
- For those who travel, visit trade fairs, or whose hobbies make them abuse their feet (walking, water, cold, standing, etc).
- For older people whose feet ache, diabetics, those who suffer from high levels of uric acid, or who are just up to date in ecology and natural health.

I am sure that you must know a few of these people. They are our target market.

These shoes are not sold in shoeshops, just directly by us, and it is for this reason that your spreading the word about the product is so important to us in helping to get the business going. If you know anyone who might be interested, call us or send us a fax with their address so that we can contact them.

Very many thanks

PILAR y GONZALO GOYES

Exhibit 2 Letter to Friends of Pilar and Gonzalo Goyes, Sent with an Advertising Leaflet (Exhibit 1)

DEAR PHARMACIST: AN OFFER FOR YOU AND YOUR EMPLOYEES.

* You know better than anyone how tired you can feel standing up all day. We would like you to be one of our customers.

* **DANSKO** shoes have the following features:

  ** They are not meant to be corrective, just very comfortable and natural.

  ** They respect the <u>natural shape of the foot</u>. They are good for one's circulation.

  ** They exert <u>no pressure of any kind on the toes</u>, either from the front, from the sides or from the top. (Within normal shapes and sizes).

  ** They are held in place <u>exclusively by the cup-shaped heel and the fastening</u>.

  ** <u>Authentic moccasins</u>, with a single piece of leather enclosing the bottom and the sides of the foot. Like a glove.

  ** <u>Flexible rubber sole</u> that helps the foot to twist. Act as a spring, assisting take-off.

  ** <u>Hand-sewn</u>. Manufactured with <u>very soft top-quality leather</u>, with a minimum thickness of 2.5mm. Water-resistant. Porous, hygienic and totally recyclable.

* <u>We do not sell through any wholesaler</u>, just directly, giving each customer personal and individual service.

* We are writing to you as someone with a professional interest in matters of health.

* *SpainSko* is the <u>exclusive importer and distributor</u> in Spain of **DANSKO shoes**.

* If you are interested in receiving a <u>complete report on the principles behind the design and manufacture</u> of these shoes, or simply more brochures, please call us on:

SpainSko	**Tel. (93) 675.51.21**	**Edificio Torreblanca**
	Fax (93) 675.51.69	**A.Torreblanca, 2-8, 1° E**
		08190 San Cugat del Vallés
		Barcelona

Pharmacies, Sept. 94

Exhibit 2 Letter to Pharmacists, Sent with a Leaflet (Exhibit 1) *(continued)*

News
N°1. Sept. '94

SpainSko

Dear customer,

You are one of the first people in Spain to be wearing Dansko shoes.

Last Spring, our small family company began importing and distributing DANSKO shoes in Spain on an exclusive basis.

I have served nearly all of you or spoken to you on the telephone personally. Many of you have encouraged us to go on with your enthusiasm. It has been a success!

All of those with whom I have spoken after their purchase have commented on how comfortable the shoes are, on the quality of the leather and finishing, and particularly on the prompt delivery thanks to MRW, the courier company used.

We would like to have more or less regular contact with you in order to serve your needs or to contact anyone you pass on to us. We know that there are people who are interested in natural comfort who we cannot reach without your help.

Our objective is quality and comfort, and fashion is moving towards natural, comfortable products.

The Danish manufacturer of these shoes, A/S Jac. Engelbredt, has explained to us how they (a family company), together with Mr Alfred Frank (also a family business), managed to create a group of people in several European countries who distribute and sell these shoes using the same methods as us.

We are so sure of the quality of this product that we have started a sales system in Spain that has no fear of complaints. Up to now, we have had not a single one, except for changes of sizes, which we have done without any quibbles or delays.

We are starting to build a large Dansko Family in Spain.

Thank you for everything.

SPAINSKO. S.L. A. Torreblanca, 2-8, 1° E-08190 S.Cugat del Vallés. Barcelona. Tel: (93) 675.51.21 Fax: (93) 675.51.69 - NIF B 60498250

Exhibit 2 Circular Letter to the First Customers *(continued)*

SpainSko

Many members of <u>religious</u> orders in Northern and Central Europe are loyal users of DANSKO shoes.

* *SpainSko* is the <u>exclusive importer</u> in Spain of **DANSKO** shoes.

* **DANSKO** shoes are very comfortable and natural. <u>They help the circulation and are ergonomic.</u>

  ** They respect the <u>natural shape of the foot</u>.

  ** <u>They exert no pressure of any kind on the toes</u>, either from the front, from the sides or from the top.

  ** <u>They are held in place exclusively by the cup-shaped heel and the fastening</u>.

  ** <u>Authentic moccasins</u>, with a single piece of leather enclosing the bottom and the sides of the foot. Like a glove.

  ** <u>Flexible rubber sole</u> that helps the foot to twist. Act as a spring, assisting take-off.

  ** <u>Hand-sewn</u>. Manufactured with <u>very soft top-quality leather</u>, with a minimum thickness of 2.5mm. Water-resistant (6 hours). Porous, hygienic and totally recyclable.

* *SpainSko* <u>does not sell through any wholesaler</u>, just directly, giving each customer personal and individual service.

* If you are interested in receiving a <u>complete report on the principles behind the design and manufacture</u> of these shoes, or simply more brochures, please call us on:

                     SpainSko   **Tel. (93) 675.51.21**
                                     Fax (93) 675.51.69

                     Edificio Torreblanca
                     A.Torreblanca, 2-8, 1° E
                     08190 San Cugat del Vallés
                     Barcelona

                                       Religious orders, April '94

SPAINSKO. S.L. A. Torreblanca, 2-8, 1° E-08190 S.Cugat del Vallés. Barcelona. Tel: (93) 675.51.21 Fax: (93) 675.51.69 - NIF B 60498250

Exhibit 2 Circular Letter to Religious Centres, Sent Along with an Advertising Leaflet (Exhibit 1) *(continued)*

SpainSko

Some points of interest about *SpainSko*

* *SpainSko* is the <u>exclusive importer</u> in Spain of **DANSKO** shoes.

* **DANSKO** shoes <u>are not meant to be corrective</u>, just very comfortable and natural. <u>They help the circulation and are ergonomic</u>.

* **DANSKO** shoes have the following features:

  ** They respect the <u>natural shape of the foot</u>.

  ** <u>They exert no pressure of any kind on the toes</u>, either from the front, from the sides or from the top.

  ** <u>They are held in place exclusively by the cup-shaped heel and the fastening</u>.

  ** <u>Authentic moccasins</u>, with a single piece of leather enclosing the bottom and the sides of the foot. Like a glove.

  ** <u>Flexible rubber sole</u> that helps the foot to twist. Act as a spring, assisting take-off.

  ** <u>Hand-sewn</u>. Manufactured with <u>very soft top-quality leather</u>, with a minimum thickness of 2.5mm. Water-resistant (6 hours). Porous, hygienic and totally recyclable.

* *SpainSko* <u>does not sell through any wholesaler</u>, just directly, giving each customer personal and individual service.

* If you are interested in receiving a <u>complete report on the principles behind the design and manufacture</u> of these shoes, or simply more brochures, please call us on:

> *SpainSko*   **Tel. (93) 675.51.21**
> **Fax (93) 675.51.69**
>
> **Edificio Torreblanca**
> **A.Torreblanca, 2-8, 1° E**
> **08190 San Cugat del Vallés**
> **Barcelona**

Chiropodists, March '94

Exhibit 2 Circular Letter to Chiropodists, Sent with an Advertising Leaflet (Exhibit 1) *(continued)*

Note on conditions for the ADC

9.3.94

1. Prices include VAT.

2. The prices are set at a level to be used with no extra discounts and are payable in advance. However, the Association's case is special.

3. The Association will pay for its sales in cash on delivery of the shoes, or they will have been paid in advance by the customer and will be sent directly to the customer by courier.

4. If the Association does not invoice but issues a delivery note, SpainSko will send the corresponding invoice to the customer together with the shoes. SpainSko will collect cash on delivery for the shoes and will pay to the Association the corresponding commission at the end of each month:

   1,000 ptas. for each order from a coupon handed out by the Association, and
   2,000 ptas. for each direct sale, whether by messenger or at their premises.

   This commission will be invoiced by the Association with the corresponding VAT for its marketing services.

5. If the Association prefers to invoice directly, it will have to guarantee all payments, and SpainSko will invoice every two weeks with payment by cheque within the following two weeks. The invoice will be made out for the amount shown as RRP minus the 15 percent VAT, which will be added later to the net amount.

Exhibit 2 Note Setting out the Special Sales Conditions for the Association of Diabetics of Catalonia (ADC) *(continued)*

Because it usually obtained good results in other countries in Europe, leaflets were sent to the members of the Association of Diabetics of Catalonia (ADC). In total, 1,550 leaflets were sent out, with mailing costs of 115,000 ptas. including the postage, the envelopes, and the rental of the address list. The addresses were rented as the company did not have a right to the membership list, since it was the ADC that actually did the mailing. They only achieved nine sales, which earned a commission of 2,000 ptas. per pair for the ADC. Also, about 20 leaflets were left in the lobby of the ADC and the International Association of Diabetic Sportsmen (IADS): three sales were made through the IADS. The idea of trying to make contact with members of these associations was that people with diabetes often have problems with their toenails: their toes become painful if their shoes are too tight.

In view of the low response rate achieved in these two activities, the Goyes family reached the conclusion that there were still some illnesses that were socially unacceptable. It was known that in 1994 12 percent of the Spanish population had an excess of sugar in their blood but that only 7 percent were being treated for diabetes.

During the month of May, another sale was made from the Arex campaign, but the arrival of orders came to a complete standstill during the summer. The low level of diversification and the high seasonality of the product range were reflected in SpainSko's income statement.

By September, Pilar was anxious for winter to arrive to get things going in the company again. She thought that the middle of that month would be a good time to restart advertising the shoes. The family wondered whether they ought to go back to one of the target groups to which they had already done mailings and inserts, or whether they should try to get a better response by using different advertising media to target different groups of potential customers.

They opted for the latter course and did a mailing to 3,700 pharmacists all over Spain, addressing the pharmacists as consumers and not as prescribers or retailers of the product, since SpainSko could not yet allow itself the luxury of paying the high margin on each sale that professionals would demand for recommending a product. The cost of buying the list of pharmacists' addresses came to 47,200 ptas. (to which had to be added the cost of the leaflets, the envelopes, the presentation letter, and the postage). The result was four sales.

Conclusion of the first campaign.
Evaluating this first campaign was difficult because sales had been really low (leaving aside the friends) and because cash problems were almost upon them. In spite of this, Gonzalo was aware of the knowledge and experience they had gained, and so did not consider it a failure. They had tried a good number of different means of communication that were appropriate for their budget and product, and only one, the magazine Integral, had brought a slightly hopeful result. The average response rate was decidedly low.

Another important aspect at the end of this first campaign was that of the 134 orders received since the start of operations, 113 were first orders and 21 were repeat orders, or orders of two pairs of shoes.

Just two people sent a cheque with their order form and without calling by phone first, while four telephoned before doing so. The rest placed their orders by telephone. If people were calling by telephone it was because at heart they needed some sort of moral reassurance. ''Are they really as comfortable as the ad says? Are they really as well finished as they look?'' Being able to speak directly to Pilar gave them a sense of security. Therefore, almost 100 percent of telephone calls were converted into sales.

It was also evident that only 5 percent of customers read the information and instructions in the brochure properly.

2nd campaign.
Once again, the Goyes family wondered whether to repeat any of the advertising they had already done, on the assumption that a second impact could increase the response, or whether they should change the focus of the previous campaign. Pilar reluctantly agreed to repeat some mailings while also carrying out some new actions.

Given that the consumer did not seem to be too price sensitive, an increase in price was considered, given how much the peseta had depreciated (it was now standing at 88 ptas./DM). In the end, however, there was no price increase because it would have meant changing all the leaflets and reprinting them.

In September, a second mailing was sent to pharmacists and religious orders, which was where the largest response had been. In total, some 2,500 letters were sent out at a total cost of 160,000 ptas. (including leaflets, envelopes, postage and letters). The result was 17 sales (8 to religious bodies and 9 to pharmacists).

In accordance with the responses, a geographic selection of the provinces with the best response rates were made and an insert was placed in October in copies of Integral and Cuerpomente for subscribers and copies sold at kiosks in those areas (in total, 39,000 copies). The cost was 450,000 ptas. Plus the 21 ptas./unit for the leaflet and reply coupon.

Between October and December, 52 pairs were sold through Integral and 14 through Cuerpomente.

Situation in December 1994.
The Goyes family had invested 7,250,000 ptas. In the business and they were therefore getting close to the limit they had originally set themselves of 10,000,000 ptas. In fact, the most significant investments in stock and advertising had already taken place. A year after the company had been set up and after eight months of activity, breakeven was still a dream in spite of not including any salaries or labour costs in the profit and loss statement. (See Exhibit 3).

Furthermore, the comments reaching Gonzalo about the business were pretty depressing. ''Are you telling me you're trying to sell shoes as ugly as this by direct marketing? You must be mad!'' The income statement showed significant losses.

In spite of everything, the owners of SpainSko knew that in Europe an 8 percent response rate was obtained from mailings to customers if they were carried out twice a year (16 percent annually). Bearing in mind the significance of friends spreading the word and the fact that many potential customers kept the brochures for a long time before deciding to place an order, an annual response of 25 percent might optimistically be reached. If so, the period of amortization of the cost of obtaining clients decreased considerably. Each sale brought the company 7,200 ptas. of gross margin, and it was estimated that each client would buy a further four pairs of shoes in his/her lifetime (on average), in addition to the initial order.

Since each pair of shoes sold generated a gross margin of 7,200 ptas., Gonzalo calculated that the investment made so far in advertising was not greater than the value of the client base they had achieved (187 clients). The gross margin was calculated by subtracting the cost of the imported shoe, the cost of shipping via courier, the cost of collecting the money, and VAT from the price paid by the final consumer. The latter did not affect the company's results for 1994 because during that year the amount of VAT incurred had been much greater than that paid by the customers.

The next problem that SpainSko would encounter was the selection of new promotion media: where to advertise and the best time to advertise.

There were ultimately several options for continuing the business other than letting it die (an option which the Goyes family did consider at times of crisis, but which Gonzalo and Pilar were fairly reluctant to accept):

a. Keep selling their shoes by using essentially the same direct marketing media and systems they had used so far.
b. Set up their own exclusive retail shoe store.

   This was an option that would give the potential customer a chance to try out the product in comfort, although it would require a really high investment, and it would take time to set up. Rent of at least 200,000 ptas. a month would have to be paid, the premises would have to be fitted out and an employee taken on with a minimum salary of 1,200,000 ptas. a year. The high volume of stock needed would make the cost of financing much higher. The Goyes could obtain a bank loan at an annual rate of about 13 percent.
c. Look for new distribution channels.

   They had thought about selling through pharmacies, although the same stock problem occurred as with shops, and they did not want the product to be associated with the idea of treatment or illness. There was yet another significant disadvantage: the margin.
d. Run advertisements in general interest magazines and newspapers.

   This method did not work in Europe and could be too risky to try out in Spain. However, Birkenstock did it.

Assets		Profit and loss statement	
Unexpected capital outlay	0	Income from sales	2,776,915
		Sales of shoes	2,725,481
Fixed assets	1,923,612	Other income	51,434
Set-up costs	830,353		
Fixed assets	1,071,903	Cost of sales	1,292,234
Intangible fixed assets	0	Purchases of materials	1,989,366
Permanent financial investment	84,600	Messengers	165,401
Depreciation	−63,244	Inventory changes	−862,533
Prov. For. Depr. Of perm. Investment	0		
		Contribution margin	1,484,681
Cost to be carried over	0		
Working assets	1,533,425	Other expenses	4,908,516
Stocks	862,533	Office materials, equipment	351,508
Customers	64,150	Administrative agents,...	97,000
Tax accounts receivable	606,742	Maintenance and repairs	11,500
Other debts	0	Advertising and PR	2,841,878
Temporary financial investments	0	Travel costs	443,331
		Various	156,156
Cash	441,575	Salaries and wages	0
		Social security	0
Total assets	3,898,612	Rent	405,600
		Miscellaneous utilities	541,543
Liabilities		Insurance	0
		Tax	60,000
Equity	2,854,819		
Capital	7,250,000	Cash-flow	−3,423,835
Reserves	0		
Profits and losses after tax	−4,395,181	Depreciation	895,831
Long-term creditors	0	Net operating profits	−4,319,666
Short-term creditors	1,043,793	Financial result	−75,515
Bank debts	0		
Accounts payable-suppliers	264,713	*Profits after tax*	*−4,395,181*
Accounts payable-tax	0		
Other creditors	779,080		
Accruals & prepayments	0		
Total liabilities	*3,898,612*		

Notes: Sales in 1994 were 217 pairs, which, multiplied by the average price of the brochure, gives a figure higher than the sales in the profit and loss statement. This is due to the significant discounts given to family and friends.

Note that there are no salaries or wages paid out or charged to this business.

The present balance sheet and profit and loss statement were established before taking into account some tax advantages. For instance, according to Spanish tax law, and having incurred losses in 1994, SpainSko was entitled to a tax credit of 938,181 ptas., which could be used or compensated against future profits generated in the following seven years. Also, it was estimated that some 2,500,000 ptas. of advertising expenses could be offset against future profits.

Exhibit 3 Balance Sheet and Income Statement at 31 December 1994

Type of action	Number of Impacts	Cost (without 16% VAT)		Result No. of pairs of shoes sold
Insert of 10,000 brochures translated into German in the magazine *Kontakt*	10,000	120,000 ptas. + (10,000 × 21 ptas.) =	330,000 ptas.	3
Arex Insert	8,677	102,800 ptas. + (8,677 × 21 ptas.) =	285,017 ptas.	2 (one immediate sale and another in May)
Mailing to friends of the Goyles family	500	500 × 64 (1) =	32,000 ptas.	44
Mailing to chiropodists	550	550 × 64 (list obtained at no cost) =	35,200 ptas.	5
Mailing to religious bodies	500	500 × 64 (list obtained at no cost) =	32,000 ptas.	13
Total first shots	**20,227**		**714,217 ptas.**	**67**
Inserts in magazines *Integral* and *Cuerpomente* (subscribers only)	16,900 + 9,000 = 25,900	290,000 + (25,900 × 21 ptas.) =	833,900 ptas.	*Integral* = 44 *Cuerpomente* = 7
Mailing Association of Diabetics of Catalonia (ADC)	1,550	Mail = 115,000 + (1,550 × 21 ptas.) = ADC commission = 2,000 ptas. × 9 = Total = 147,550 + 18,000 =	147,550 ptas. 18,000 ptas. 165,550 ptas.	9
Brochures left at the International Association of Diabetic Sportsmen (IADS)	20	20 × 21 ptas. =	420 ptas.	3
Mailing to pharmacists	3,700	Cost of the list: Total = 47,200 + 3,700 × 64 ptas.) =	47,200 ptas. 284,000 ptas.	4
Total actions in 1st campaign	**31,170**		**1,283,870 ptas.**	**67 (2)**
2nd mailing to pharmacists and religious bodies	2,500	2,500 × 64 =	160,000 ptas.	Pharmacists = 9 Religious bodies = 8
2nd insert in *Integral* and *Cuerpomente*	39,000	450,000 + (39,000 × 21 ptas.) =	1,269,000 ptas.	*Integral* = 52 *Cuerpomente* = 14
Total actions 2nd campaign	**41,500**		**1,429,000 ptas.**	**83 (3)**
Total actions up to December 1994	**92,897**		**3,427,167 ptas.(4)**	**217 pairs sold to 187 different clients**

(1) The cost of a complete mailing was: 21 ptas. for the brochure with a reply coupon + 8 ptas. for the envelope + 28 ptas. for the stamp + 7 ptas. for the presentation letter.

(2) Of these, only 46 pairs were sold to totally new customers, and 21 were repeat orders, or pairs sold in a two-pair order.

(3) Of these, 74 pairs were sold to new customers, and 9 were repeat orders, or pairs of shoes sold in a two-pair order.

(4) The figure for the total cost of these marketing activities is calculated outside the books, and turns out to be higher than the figure in the column for "advertising and PR" in the income statement because here it includes some costs (envelopes, stamps, letters) which appear under other headings in the profit-and-loss statement.

Exhibit 4 Summary of the Different Marketing Activities Carried out up to December 1994

The cost of an 8 × 11 cm ad in the weekly "Life and Science" supplement of *La Vanguardia*, the most prestigious daily newspaper published in Barcelona with a circulation of 220,000 copies, was 256,000 ptas.; the same size ad in *Cuerpomente* was 60,000 ptas. for a circulation of 40,000 copies, and 60,000 ptas. in *Integral* for some 60,000 copies.

e. Attend large trade shows on different topics.

The aim was to deal directly with people who had tired feet at that precise moment, and ask them to try the shoes. "Who would not enjoy the chance to sit down and try on some new, very comfortable shoes in the middle of a tiring trade fair?" thought Gonzalo.

The cost of exhibiting and selling at a trade fair in Spain was high (500,000 ptas. as a minimum for a small stand, including rental of the space, the decoration, travel and the accommodation costs of the two people to attend the public), and they would not be able to carry enough stock to sell anything. In spite of these disadvantages, the public would be able to get to know the brand better and see and try the product. Birkenstock attended some fairs but with a lot of stock for sale.

Would one of these options be equivalent to throwing themselves off a cliff? Did they have enough capital available?

CASE 11
L'Oréal Netherlands B.V.: Product Introduction

Yolanda van der Zande, director of the Netherlands L'Oréal subsidiary, faced two tough decisions and was discussing them with Mike Rourke, her market manager for cosmetics and toiletries. "We have to decide whether to introduce the Synergie skin care line and Belle Couleur permanent hair colorants." Synergie had recently been successfully introduced in France, the home country for L'Oréal. Belle Couleur had been successfully marketed in France for two decades. Mr. Rourke responded:

> Yes and if we decide to go ahead with an introduction we'll also need to develop marketing programs for the product lines. Fortunately, we only need to think about marketing, since the products will still be manufactured in France.

Ms. van der Zande replied:

> Right, but remember, the marketing decisions on these lines are critical. Both of these lines are part of the Garnier family brand name. Currently Ambre Solaire (a sun-screen) is the only product we distribute with the Garnier name in the Netherlands. But headquarters would like us to introduce more Garnier product lines into our market over the next few years, and it's critical that our first product launches in this line be successful.

Mr. Rourke interjected, "But we already sell other brands of L'Oréal products in our market. If we introduce Garnier what will happen to them?"

After some more discussion, Ms. van der Zande suggested:

> Why don't you review what we know about the Dutch market. We've already done extensive marketing research on consumer reactions to Synergie and Belle Couleur. Why don't you look at it and get back to me with your recommendations in two weeks.

BACKGROUND

In 1992, the L'Oréal Group was the largest cosmetics manufacturer in the world. Headquartered in Paris, it had subsidiaries in over 100 countries. In 1992, its sales were $6.8 billion (a 12 percent increase

This case was prepared by Frederick W. Langrehr, Valparaiso University, Lee Dahringer, Butler University, and Anne Stöcker. This was case written with the cooperation of management, solely for the purpose of stimulating student discussion. All events and individuals are real, but names have been disguised. We appreciate the help of J.B. Wilkinson and V.B. Langrehr on earlier drafts of this case. Copyright © 1994 by the Case Research Journal and the authors. It is reprinted here by permission.

over 1991) and net profits were 417 million dollars (a 14 percent increase). France contributed 24 percent of total worldwide sales, Europe (both western and eastern countries excluding France) provided 42 percent, and the United States and Canada together accounted for 20 percent. The rest of the world accounted for the remaining 14 percent. L'Oréal's European subsidiaries were in one of two groups: (1) major countries (England, France, Germany, and Italy) or (2) minor countries (the Netherlands and nine others).

The company believed that innovation was its critical success factor. It thus invested heavily in research and development and recovered its investment through global introductions of its new products. All research was centered in France. As finished products were developed, they were offered to subsidiaries around the world. Because brand life cycles for cosmetics could be very short, L'Oréal tried to introduce one or two new products per year in each of its worldwide markets. International subsidiaries could make go/no go decisions on products, but they generally did not have direct input into the R&D process. In established markets, such as the Netherlands, any new product line introduction had to be financed by the current operations in that country.

L'Oréal marketed products under its own name as well as under a number of other individual and family brand names. For example, it marketed Anaïs Anaïs perfume, the high-end Lancôme line of cosmetics, and L'Oréal brand hair care products. In the 1970s, it acquired Laboratoires Garnier, and this group was one of L'Oréal's largest divisions. In France, with a population of about 60 million people, Garnier was a completely separate division, and its sales force competed against the L'Oréal division. In the Netherlands, however, the market was much smaller (about 15 million people), and Garnier and L'Oréal products would be marketed by the same sales force.

Dutch consumers had little, if any, awareness or knowledge of Garnier and had not formed a brand image. The Garnier sunscreen was a new product and few Dutch women knew of the brand. It was, therefore, very important that any new Garnier products launched in the Netherlands have a strong concept and high market potential. To accomplish this, the products needed to offer unique, desired, and identifiable differential advantages to Dutch consumers. Products without such an edge were at a competitive disadvantage, and would be likely not only to fail, but to create a negative association with the Garnier name, causing potential problems for future Garnier product introductions.

THE DUTCH MARKET

In the late 1980s, 40 percent of the Dutch population (about the same percentage as in France) was under 23 years old. Consumers in this age group were the heaviest users of cosmetics and toiletries. However, like the rest of Europe, the Dutch population was aging and the fastest-growing population segments were the 25 or older groups.

Other demographic trends included the increasing number of Dutch women working outside of the home. The labor force participation rate of women in the Netherlands was 29 percent. This was much lower than the 50 percent or above in the United Kingdom or United States, but the number of women working outside the home was increasing faster in the Netherlands than it was in the United Kingdom or the United States. Dutch women were also delaying childbirth. As a result of these trends, women in the Netherlands were exhibiting greater self-confidence and independence; women had more disposable income and more of them were using it to buy cosmetics for use on a daily basis.

Despite their rising incomes, Dutch women still shopped for value, especially in cosmetics and toiletries. In the European Union (EU), the Netherlands ranked fourth in per capita income; but it was only sixth in per capita spending on cosmetics and toiletries. Thus, the Dutch per capita spending on personal care products was only 60 percent of the amount spent per capita in France or Germany. As a result of both a small population (13 million Dutch to 350 million EU residents) and lower per capita consumption, the Dutch market accounted for only 4 percent of total EU sales of cosmetics and toiletries.

SYNERGIE

Synergie was a line of facial skin care products consisting of moisturizing cream, antiaging day cream, antiwrinkle cream, cleansing milk, mask, and cleansing gel. It was made with natural ingredients, and its advertising slogan in France was "The alliance of science and nature to prolong the youth of your skin."

Skin Care Market

The skin care market was the second largest sector of the Dutch cosmetics and toiletries market. For the past five quarters, unit volume had been growing at an annual rate of 12 percent and dollar sales at a rate of 16 percent. This category consisted of hand creams, body lotions, all-purpose creams, and facial products. Products within this category were classified by price and product type. Skin care products produced by institutes such as Shisedo or Estée Lauder were targeted at the high end of the market. These lines were expensive and sold through personal service perfumeries that specialized in custom sales of cosmetics and toiletries. At the other end of the price scale were mass market products like Ponds, which were sold in drugstores and supermarkets. In the last couple of years, a number of companies, including L'Oréal, had begun to offer products in the mid-price range. For example, its Plénitude line was promoted as a high-quality, higher-price—but still mass market—product.

Skin care products could also be divided into care and cleansing products. Care products consisted of day and night creams; cleansing products were milks and tonics. The current trend in the industry was to stretch the lines by adding specific products

Table 1. Usage of Skin Care Products by Dutch Women

Product	Percentage of Women Using
Day cream	46
Cleansers	40
Mask	30
Tonic	26
Antiaging cream	3

Table 2. Sales Breakdown for Skin Care Products in Supermarkets and Drugstores

Type of Store	Unit Sales (%)	Dollar Sales (%)
Supermarkets	18	11
Drugstores	82	89
	100	100

Table 3. Sales Breakdown for Skin Care Products by Type of Drugstore

Type of Store	Unit Sales (%)	Dollar Sales (%)
Chains	57	37
Large independent	31	39
Small independent	12	24
	100	100

targeted at skin types such as sensitive, greasy, or dry. An especially fast-growing category consisted of antiaging and antiwrinkling creams. Complementing this trend was the emphasis on scientific development and natural ingredients.

Almost 50 percent of the 5 million Dutch women between the ages of 15 and 65 used traditional skin care products. The newer specialized products had a much lower penetration, as shown in Table 1.

The sales breakdown by type of retailer for the mid- and lower-priced brands is shown in Tables 2 and 3.

COMPETITION

There were numerous competitors. Some product lines, such as Oil of Olaz (Oil of Olay in the United States) by Procter & Gamble and Plénitude by L'Oréal, were offered by large multinational companies; other brands, for example, Dr. vd Hoog and Rocher, were offered by regional companies. Some companies offered a complete line, while others, like Oil of Olaz, offered one or two products. Exhibit 1 lists a few of the available lines along with the price ranges and positioning statements.

The Dutch market was especially competitive for new brands like Oil of Olaz and Plénitude. The rule of thumb in the

	Price Range (Guilders)*	Positioning
Lower end		
Nivea Visage[†]	9.50–11.50	Mild, modest price, complete line
Ponds	5.95–12.95	Anti-wrinkle
Middle		
Dr. vd Hoog	10–11.95	Sober, nonglamorous, no illusions, but real help, natural, efficient, relatively inexpensive
Oil of Olaz (Procter & Gamble)	12 (day cream only)	Moisturizing, antiaging
Plénitude (L'Oréal)	10.95–19.95	Delay the signs of aging
Synergie	11.95–21.95	The alliance of science and nature to prolong the youth of your skin
Upper End		
Yves Rocher	10–26.95	Different products for different skins, natural ingredients
Ellen Betrix (Estée Lauder)	12.95–43.50	Institute line with reasonable prices, luxury products at nonluxury prices

* One dollar = 1.8 guilders; one British pound = 2.8 guilders; 1 deutschmark = 1.1 guilders.
† Although Nivea Visage had a similar price range to Dr. vd Hoog, consumer perceived Nivea as a lower-end product.

Exhibit 1 Competitive Product Lines of Cosmetics

industry was that share of voice for a brand (the percent of total industry advertising spent by the company) should be about the same as its market share. Thus, a company with 10 percent market share should have had advertising expenditures around 10 percent of total industry advertising expenditures. However, there were deviations from this rule. Ponds, an established and well-known company with loyal customers, had about 9 percent share of the market (units) but only accounted for about 2.5 percent of total industry ad expenditures. Alternatively, new brands like Oil of Olaz (10 percent market share, 26 percent share of voice) and Plénitude (5 percent market share, 13 percent share of voice), spent much more. The higher ad spending for these brands was necessary to develop brand awareness and, ideally, brand preference.

Any innovative products or new product variations in a line could be quickly copied. Retailers could develop and introduce their own private labels in 4 months; manufacturers could develop a competing product and advertising campaign in 6 months. Manufacturers looked for new product ideas in other countries and then transferred the product concept or positioning strategy across national borders. They also monitored competitors' test markets. Since a test market typically lasted 9 months, a competitor could introduce a product before a test market was completed.

Consumer Behavior

Consumers tended to be loyal to their current brands. This loyalty resulted from the possible allergic reaction to a new product. Also, facial care products were heavily advertised and sold on the basis of brand image. Thus, users linked self-concept with a brand

image, and this increased the resistance to switching. While all consumers had some loyalty, the strength of this attachment to a brand increased with the age of the user. Finally, establishing a new brand was especially difficult since Dutch women typically purchased facial creams only once or twice a year. Dutch women were showing an increasing interest in products with "natural" ingredients, but they were not as familiar as the French with technical product descriptions and terms.

Market Research Information

Earlier, Mike Rourke had directed his internal research department to conduct some concept and use tests for the Synergie products. The researchers had sampled 200 women between the ages of 18 and 55 who used skin care products three or more times per week. They sampled 55 Plénitude users, 65 Dr. vd Hoog users, and 80 users of other brands.

The participants reacted positively to Synergie concept boards containing the positioning statement and the terminology associated with the total product line. On a 7-point scale with 7 being the most positive, the mean score for the Synergie line for all the women in the sample was 4.94. The evaluations of the women who used the competing brands, Plénitude and Dr. vd Hoog, were similar, at 4.97 and 4.88, respectively.

The researchers then conducted an in-depth analysis of two major products in the line, antiaging day cream and the moisturizing cream. Participants reported their buying intentions after they tried the Synergie product once and again after they used it for a week. Some participants were told the price and others

	All Participants	Plénitude Users	Dr. vd Hoog Users	Other Brand Users
Price Not Known				
Antiaging daycream				
After trial	5.37*	5.63	5.00	5.42
After use	5.26	5.55	5.08	5.17
Moisturizing Cream				
After trial	5.34	5.60	5.38	5.11
After use	5.51	5.74	5.56	5.22
Price Known				
Antiaging daycream				
After trial	3.75	4.13	3.82	3.44
After use	3.60	3.76	3.54	3.54
Certainly buy†	24%	21%	23%	27%
Moisturizing				
After trial	4.08	4.36	4.17	3.77
After use	4.06	4.26	4.13	3.78
Certainly buy	39%	52%	38%	30%

* Seven-point scale with 7 being most likely to buy.
† Response to a separate question asking certainty of buying with certainty buy as the highest choice.

Exhibit 2 Buying Intentions for Synergie Products

did not know the price. The results of this analysis are shown in Exhibit 2.

BELLE COULEUR

Belle Couleur was a line of permanent hair coloring products. It had been sold in France for about two decades and was the market leader. In France the line had 22 shades, comprising mostly natural shades and a few strong red or very bright, light shades. It was positioned as reliably providing natural colors with the advertising line "natural colors, covers all gray."

Hair Coloring Market

There were two types of hair coloring: semipermanent and permanent. Semipermanent colors washed out after five or six shampooings. Permanent colors only disappeared as the hair grew out from the roots. Nearly three-quarters (73 percent) of Dutch women who colored their hair used a permanent colorant. Over the past 4 years, however, the trend had been to semipermanent colorants, with an increase from 12 percent to 27 percent of the market. Growth in unit volume during those years for both types of colorant had been about 15 percent per annum. The majority of unit sales in the category were in chain drugstores (37 percent) with 40 percent equally split between large and small independent drugstores. Food retailers accounted for the remaining 3 percent.

Competition

In the Netherlands, 4 out of 10 total brands accounted for 80 percent of the sales of permanent hair colorants, compared to 2 brands in France. Table 4 gives the market share of the leading permanent color brands in the period 1987–1989. Interestingly, none of them had a clear advertising positioning statement describing customer benefits. By default, then, Belle Couleur could be positioned as "covering gray with natural colors."

Hair salons were indirect competitors in the hair coloring market. The percentage of women who had a hair stylist color their hair was not known, nor were the trends in usage of this method known. It was projected that as more women worked outside the home, home coloring would probably increase because it was more convenient.

L'Oréal's current market entry (Recital) was the leading seller, although its share was declining. Guhl's and Andrelon's increases in shares between 1986 and 1989 reflected the general trend to using warmer shades, and these two brands were perceived as giving quality red tones. In the late 1980s, Guhl had changed its distribution strategy, and started selling the brand through drug chains. In 1987, less than 1 percent of sales were through drug outlets; in the first quarter of 1990, drug-outlet sales had reached nearly 12 percent. Guhl had also become more aggressive in its marketing through large independents, with its share in these outlets climbing from 16 to 24 percent over the same period. Both the increasing shares of the smaller brands and

Table 4. Major Brands of Hair Colorant

	Market Shares %		
	1987	**1988**	**1989**
Upper End (14.95 guilders)			
Recital (L'Oréal Brand)	35	34	33
Guhl	9	12	14
Belle Couleur (12.95 guilders)	—	—	—
Lower-priced (9.95 guilders)			
Andrelon	12	14	17
Poly Couleur	24	23	21
Others	20	17	15
Total	100	100	100

the decreasing shares of the leaders sparked a 60 percent increase in advertising in 1989 for all brands of hair coloring.

CONSUMER BEHAVIOR

Consumers perceived permanent hair color as a technical product and believed its use was very risky. As a result, users had a strong brand loyalty and avoided impulse purchasing. When considering a new brand, both first-time users and current users carefully read package information and asked store personnel for advice.

Traditionally, hair colorants had been used primarily to cover gray hair. Recently, however, coloring hair had become more of a fashion statement. This partially accounted for the increased popularity of semipermanent hair coloring. In one study, the most frequently cited reason (33 percent) for coloring hair was to achieve warm/red tones; another 17 percent reported wanting to lighten their hair color, and covering gray was cited by 29 percent. It was likely that the trend to use colorants more for fashion and less for covering gray reflected the increase in hair coloring by consumers less than 33 years old. In 1989, 46 percent of Dutch women (up from 27 percent in 1986) colored their hair with either semipermanent or permanent hair colorants. Table 5 contains a breakdown of usage by age of user.

Hair coloring was almost exclusively purchased in drugstores; only 3 percent of sales were through supermarkets. The percentage of sales for drug outlets was: chains, 58 percent; large independents, 22 percent; and small independents, 20 percent.

Table 5. Hair Coloring by Age (%)

	1986	**1989**
Less than 25 years	35	50
25–34	24	54
35–49	32	55
50–64	24	33
65 and over	15	19

Market Research

As with Synergie, Mr. Rourke also had the L'Oréal market researchers contact consumers about their reactions to Belle Couleur. Four hundred and twelve Dutch women between the ages of 25 and 64 who had used hair colorant in the past 4 months were part of a concept test, and 265 of these women participated in a use test. A little over 25 percent of the participants colored their hair every 6 weeks or more often while another 47 percent did it every 2 to 3 months. (The average French user colored her hair every 3 weeks.) Nearly 60 percent used hair color to cover gray, while the remainder did it for other reasons.

After being introduced to the concept and shown some sample ads, participants were asked their buying intentions. The question was asked three times—before and after the price was given and after Belle Couleur was used. The results are shown in Exhibit 3.

In most product concept tests (as with the Synergie line) buying intentions *declined* once the price was revealed. For Belle Couleur, buying intentions increased after the price was given, but decreased after actual use. As the exhibit shows, the percentage of participants who would probably or certainly *not* buy the product after using it increased from 13 to 32 percent. In Exhibit 4, only participants who gave negative after-use evaluations of Belle Couleur are included, and they are grouped according to the brands they were using at the time.

To try to determine why some users didn't like the product, the dissatisfied women were asked to state why they disliked Belle Couleur. The results are shown in Table 6.

Many of the women thought that their hair was too dark after using Belle Couleur, and said it "didn't cover gray." Those who thought the Couleur was different from expected were primarily using the blond and chestnut brown shades of colorant. This was expected, since in France Belle Couleur was formulated to give a classical, conservative dark blond color without extra reflections or lightening effects and the product had not been modified for the Dutch test. The competing Dutch-manufactured hair colorant competitors, on the other hand, were formulated to give stronger lightening effects. Thus, some of the negative evaluations of Belle Couleur were due to the fact that Dutch women tended toward naturally lighter hair colors and the French toward darker shades.

	Price Unaware	**Price Aware**	**After Use**
Certainly buy (5)	18%	26%	29%
Probably buy (4)	60	57	30
Don't know (3)	12	5	9
Probably not (2)	7	7	11
Certainly not (1)	3	6	21
Total	100%	100%	100%
Mean score	3.85	3.92	3.35

Exhibit 3 Buying Intentions

	Brand Currently Used				
	Total Sample	Andrelon	Poly Couleur	Guhl	Recital (L'Oréal)
After-use purchase intentions of Belle Couleur					
Probably not (2)	11%	12%	12%	14%	5%
Certainly not (1)	21	24	29	20	5
	32%	36%	41%	34%	10%
Overall mean score	3.35	3.4	3.1	3.4	3.95
Evaluation of final color of Belle Couleur					
Very good (1)	25%	24%	31%	22%	35%
Good (2)	43	40	31	44	49
Neither good or bad (3)	10	10	14	6	8
Bad (4)	12	14	5	18	8
Very Bad (5)	9	12	19	10	—
Mean	2.37	2.5	2.5	2.5	1.89
Comparison to expectations					
Much better (1)	11%	12%	14%	14%	14%
Better (2)	26	12	21	24	38
The same (3)	29	38	26	28	32
Worse (4)	19	24	19	18	11
Much worse (5)	15	14	19	16	5
Mean	3.0	3.17	3.07	2.98	2.57
Compared with own brand	*				
Much better (1)		17%	17%	24%	14%
Better (2)		21	19	24	32
The same (3)		21	31	14	30
Worse (4)		21	12	16	16
Much worse (5)		19	21	22	8
Mean		3.05	3.02	2.88	2.73

* Data for Total Sample Not Available

Exhibit 4 Purchase Intentions and Evaluation of Belle Couleur by Brand Currently Used

Table 6. Reasons for Negative Evaluations of Belle Couleur by Brand Currently Used

	Brand Currently Used				
	Total Sample	Andrelon	Poly Couleur	Guhl	Recital (L'Oréal)
Hair got dark/darker instead of lighter	13%	14%	17%	14%	5%
Irritates skin	8	10	7	2	11
Ammonia smell	5	7	—	2	—
Didn't cover gray	5	12	2	4	3
Color not beautiful	5	7	5	6	3
Color different from expected	5	5	10	4	3

Note: Some of the cell sizes are very small and caution should be used when comparing entries of less than 10 percent.

ROLE OF DISTRIBUTORS

Distributors' acceptance of the two product lines was critical for L'Oréal's successful launch of both Synergie and Belle Couleur. At one time, manufacturers had more control in the channel of distribution than retailers. Retailers, however, had been gaining power as a result of the increasing size of retailers, the development of chains with their central buying offices, and the proliferation of new brands with little differentiation from brands currently on the market. Retailers had also increasingly been offering their own private-label products, since they earned a higher percentage profit margin on their own brands.

Following are the criteria, listed in order of importance (3 being "most important"), that retailers used to evaluate new products.

1. Evidence of consumer acceptance   2.5
2. Manufacturer advertising and promotion   2.2
3. Introductory monetary allowances   2.0
4. Rationale for product development   1.9
5. Merchandising recommendations   1.8

L'Oréal's own goal for developing new products was to introduce only those products that had a differential advantage with evidence of consumer acceptance. It did not want to gain distribution with excessive reliance oil trade deals or higher than normal retail gross margins. L'Oréal also wanted to have its Garnier product lines extensively distributed in as many different types of retailers and outlets as possible. This approach to new product introduction had been effective for L'Oréal, and it currently had a positive image with Dutch retailers. L'Oréal was perceived as offering high-quality, innovative products supported with good in-store merchandising.

For L'Oréal's current products, 35 percent of sales came from independent drugstores, 40 percent from drug chains, and 25 percent from food stores. For all manufacturers, drug chains and supermarkets were increasing in importance. These stores required a brand with high customer awareness and some brand preference. The brands needed to be presold since, unlike independent drugstores, there was no sales assistance.

Introducing a line of products, rather than just a product or two, resulted in a greater need for retail shelf space. Although the number of new products and brands competing for retail shelf space frequently appeared unlimited, the space itself was a limited resource. With Belle Couleur, L'Oréal had already addressed this issue by reducing the number of Belle Couleur colorants it planned to offer in the Netherlands. Although 22 shades were available in France, L'Oréal reduced tile line to 15 variations for the Netherlands. As a result, 1.5 meters (about 5 linear feet) of retail shelf space were needed to display the 15 shades of Belle Couleur. Synergie required about half of this shelf space.

DECISION TIME

After reviewing the information on the market research of the two product lines, Ms. van der Zande summarized the situation. L'Oréal Netherlands could leverage its advertising of the Garnier name by promoting two lines at once. Consumers would hear and see the Garnier name twice, not just once. As a result, Dutch consumers might see Garnier as a major supplier of cosmetics and toiletries. However, she was concerned about the selling effort that would be needed to sell the L'Oréal brands that were already in the Dutch market and at the same time introduce not just one, but two, new brand name product *lines*. The Dutch L'Oréal sales force would have to handle both family brands, since the much lower market potential of the Netherlands market could not support a separate Garnier sales force, as in France. She was also concerned about retailer reaction to a sales pitch for two product lines.

Ms. van der Zande reflected that she was facing three decision areas. First, she had to decide if she should introduce one or both product lines, and she had to make this decision knowing that L'Oréal would not reformulate the products just for the Dutch market. Second, if she decided to introduce either one or both of the product lines, she needed to develop a marketing program. This meant she had to make decisions on the promotion of the product line(s) to both retailers and consumers, as well as the pricing and distribution of the line(s). Third, given that the Garnier product introductions might negatively impact the sales of her current product lines, she needed tactical marketing plans for those products.

CASE 12
Fast-Food Industry Woes

At their quarterly meeting, McDonald's executives were much pleased with the first quarter 2003 results. Although the profits went up only slightly, sales registered a big increase. The executives however, were concerned about a different problem, which in the long run, could become a major headache. It is to do with the obesity suit against the company.

In fall 2002, a New York City attorney Sam Hirsch filed a suit against McDonald's on behalf of a class of obese and over-weight children. He alleged that the fast-food chain negligently, recklessly, carelessly and/or intentionally marketed to children food products that were high in fat, salt, sugar and cholesterol while failing to warn of those ingredients' links to obesity, diabetes, coronary heart disease, high blood pressure strokes, elevated cholesterol intake, related cancers and other conditions.

Although the suit was dismissed, it tapped into something very big. Could years ahead tobacco-like litigation challenge the company and indeed the entire food industry extending beyond fast-foods to snack foods, soft drinks, packaged goods and dietary supplements? The general counsel of the company remarked: "The precedents, the ammo, the missiles are already there and waiting in a silo marked tobacco."

OBESITY PROBLEM

Junk food might not be addictive in the same way that tobacco had been. But weight, once gained, is notoriously hard to lose and childhood weight patterns strongly predict adult ones. Rates of overweight among small children—to whom junk-food companies aggressively market their products—had doubled since 1980; rates among adolescents had tripled.

In 1999 physicians began reporting an alarming rise in children of obesity-linked type 2 diabetes. Once an obese youngster developed diabetes, he or she would never get rid of it. That was a lot more irreversible than a smoking addiction.

Though many people recoiled at the idea of obesity suits—eating habits were a matter of personal responsibility, they protested—the tobacco precedents showed that such qualms could be overcome. Yes, most people knew that eating a Big Mac wasn't the same thing as eating a spinach salad, but most people knew that smoking was bad for them too.

And yes, diet was only one risk factor out of many that contributed to obesity, but smoking was just one risk factor for diseases for which the tobacco companies were forced to fork over reimbursement to Medicaid. (The industry's share of the blame was statistically estimated and then divvied up among companies by market share.) The tobacco companies eventually agreed to pay $246 billion to the states, and juries had been ordering them to pay individual smokers eight-digit verdicts too.

By the Surgeon General's estimate, public-health costs attributable to overweight and obesity came to about $117 billion a year—fast approaching the $140 billion stemming from smoking. Suing Big Food offered allures to contingency-fee lawyers that rivaled those of Big Tobacco, and the implications of that were pretty easy to foresee.

While the food industry was not apt to be socked with anything like the penalties that hit tobacco, companies would face consumer protection suits that might cost them many tens of millions of dollars and force them to significantly change marketing practices.

The triggering event occurred in December 2001. That's when the Surgeon General, observing that about 300,000 deaths per year were now associated with overweight and obesity, warned that those conditions might soon cause as much preventable disease and death as smoking. The report prompted journalists to call John Banzhaf III, an antismoking activist and a law professor at George Washington University School of Law, to see whether tobacco-style litigation might be in the offing.

Banzhaf said it was not the same with fast-food industry since there were important differences between fast-food and tobacco.

But even as he talked, he began to change his mind. Another key academic strategist in the tobacco wars, Northeastern University law professor Richard Daynard, was soon drawn into the foray. At a conference in April 2002 to discuss Marion Nestle's new book, Food Politics, he was asked to talk about possible obesity-related litigation. (Nestle, who chaired the nutrition department at New York University and whose name was pronounced NESSel, was not related to the founders of the food company.)

Daynard, like Banzhaf, at first saw no analogy to tobacco. But as he read Nestle's book, he, too, began to change his mind.

Here is Nestle's argument. For at least the past 50 years public-health authorities had wanted to deliver a simple, urgent message to the American people: Eat less. They had been thwarted from doing so, however, by political pressure from the food industry. The meat industry alone spent millions a year on lobbying, apparently with great success. Instead of forthrightly saying, "Eat less red meat," government health authorities were forced to say, "Eat more lean meat." Food companies compounded the confusion by advertising that their products could be part of a balanced and nutritional diet, even though they knew that their products were not typically consumed that way. Any food could theoretically be part of a balanced diet if you kept the portions tiny enough and ate lots of fruits, vegetables and grains.

As Daynard well knew, advertising claims that were literally true, but misleading when viewed in a real-world context, could violate state consumer-protection laws. In some states, like California, plaintiffs could force companies to disgorge all profits attributable to advertising that employed such statements and the plaintiff could win without having to prove that even a single individual was actually tricked by the statement.

The idea of bringing such suits against the food industry was not unprecedented. In 1983, for instance, the California supreme court green-lighted a suit brought by an advocacy group against General Foods over the way such breakfast cereals as Sugar Crisps and Cocoa Pebbles—which contained 38% to 50% sugar by weight—were being marketed to children. The plaintiffs argued that, although promoted and labeled as "cereals," the products were in fact more accurately described as sugar products, or candies. The court suggested that ads even implicitly claiming that such products were nutritious or healthful were plausible lawsuit targets. (After the ruling, the case settled.)

In July 2002, Daynard attended an informal meeting of lawyers and public-health advocates in Banzhaf's office in Washington. "The first question at the meeting was, 'Is there a there there?'" Daynard recalls. What persuaded them was, in a sense, the media. This thing was so radioactive in terms of media attention that cases would bring in other lawyers and bring in other cases.

In August 2002, a lawyer who'd never heard of Banzhaf or Daynard crashed their party. Sam Hirsch, who ran his small practice in New York City, had become interested in food issues after an overweight associate referred to a burger as a "fat bomb." Though Hirsch, 54, had never brought a class action, he now filed two, one in Brooklyn and another in Bronx. The suits, brought on by classes of obese people, named McDonald's, Burger King, KFC, and Wendy's as defendants.

The press loved the story. The industry was ferocious. The Coalition for Consumer Freedom, a trade group of restaurants and food and beverage suppliers (McDonald's was not a member), promptly took out aggressive full-page ads in newsmagazines. One showed a man's bloated, bare gut spilling over a belted waistline. The copy read: "Did you hear the one about the fat guy suing the restaurants? It's no joke."

For plaintiffs lawyers and nutrition activists, the Hirsch suit was a mixed blessing. Some worried that it was such a laughing stock that it might strengthen the forces pushing for tort reform. As a tool for public education, on the other hand, the Hirsch suit was a landmark. Even if the industry was winning the talk-show shoutfests, its arguments about personal responsibility sent a double edged message: "If you are stupid enough to use our products, you deserve to get diseases our products cause."

In September 2002, Banzhaf invited Hirsch to the second meeting of his group. Afterward Hirsch decided not to pursue his two lawsuits, which had been filed on behalf of adults, and to bring instead a new class-action suit on behalf of obese children. He focused this suit on Mc Donald's alone.

One prospective class member, 400-pound, 15-year-old Gregory Rhymes, who suffered from type 2 diabetes, stated in an affidavit that he had eaten at McDonald's "nearly every day" since he was 6. Neal Barnard, a doctor who headed a vegetarian advocacy group, submitted a declaration asserting that the consumption of McDonald's products had significantly contributed to the development of (Rhymes's) obesity and diabetes.

McDonald's mounted a spirited defense, stating that every reasonable person understands what is in products such as hamburgers and fries. McDonald's lawyers also argued that people understand the consequences to one's waistline and potentially to one's health, of excessively eating those foods over a prolonged period. The lawyers also warned that the plaintiff's theories, if accepted, would usher in an uncontrollable avalanche of litigation against other restaurants and food providers, as well as other industries (such as the pizza, ice cream, cheese and cookie industries). In a statement to *Fortune*, McDonald's said that it had long made nutritional information available to customers upon request. Its nutrition professionals said that McDonald's food could be and was a part of a healthy diet based on sound nutrition principles of balance, variety and moderation. The court has not yet ruled.

Targeting the children was the food industry's Achilles' heel. Fast-food, snack food and soft drink companies focused their marketing on children and adolescents through Saturday morning TV commercials; through cuddly characters like Ronald McDonald (the second most recognized figure among children after Santa Claus); through contracts to advertise and serve soft drinks and fast-food in schools; through ever-changing toys included in Happy Meals.

If misleading advertising could be linked to the childhood disease, the industry could be in big trouble. Food industry insiders came forward to speak to Hirsch about disturbing marketing practices. He claimed that we were not bringing down the fast-food industry next Tuesday, but there were legitimate legal issues here.

Hirsch's case was like the earliest tobacco and asbestos cases, which failed because the damning evidence had not yet come out. But once cases progress into the discovery stage, smoking-gun documents sometimes begin to emerge, showing that the companies knew more than the general public about the impact that their products and advertising were having on children's health. As discovery goes forward, the plaintiffs' lawyers may find documents that, if held up in isolation, make it look like the industry has something to hide. That would give the case heft. According to an expert, it could take about five years to reach that point.

Not everyone on the defense side was worried. Thomas Bezanson of New York's Chadbourne & Parke, who had defended tobacco, alcohol, and pharmaceutical companies, thought that what happened to the tobacco industry was unique. You had a very powerful attack made by plaintiffs bar, the press, the politicians, and the state attorneys general. That only worked since they were able to use all of those in a coordinated way to persuade society that the object of attack was some kind of pariah. It would be difficult to lodge such an attack against food companies. There was another difference between tobacco and food. The tobacco industry could not make a safe cigarette but fast-food companies could do almost everything requested without going broke. They could issue warnings, they could post fat and calorie content on menu boards, and they could put more nutritious things on their menus. In fact, they already were. For instance, McDonald's reduced trans-fatty acids in its fried foods and introduced low-fat yogurt and fruit roll-up desserts.

A McDonald's press release touts the yogurt as a "good source of calcium" and states that the fruit desserts provide 25% of the daily-recommended value of vitamin C. As a mom and registered dietician, a McDonald's staffer said in the release, "I know the importance of having this type of nutrient value in a snack food that kids enjoy."

Such gestures were themselves fraught with legal peril, however. If companies that produced high-calorie and high-fat foods were worried about future lawsuits, they were not saying. PepsiCo, Cadbury Schweppes, and Kraft all declined to comment. Their trade group was less shy and said, "We advocate getting good messages to parents to help children to develop good eating and exercise habits. What we think is counter productive is finger pointing, reckless accusations, and lawsuits that won't make anyone thinner. All the same, prudent food companies might do well to start scrutinizing their advertising and packaging, tweaking product lines, and, yes, squirreling away some reserves for potential judgments."

Meanwhile, the court in New York rejected Hirsch's suit. But it still was not O.K. for McDonald's since new suits might be filed.

CHANGING EATING HABITS

Human diets had been eminently changeable; they changed all the time, and there was nothing inexorable about the national drift toward bloat. There was also nothing immutable about the swill that people bought in supermarkets and restaurants. A generation ago it was almost impossible to get a good cup of coffee in America. Yuppies fixed that. Beer too.

What will it take to transform our diet on a national scale? The problem is huge and depressingly simple: The U.S. food industry provides about 3,900 calories per person per day (the figure is for 2000, the latest available). Allowing for waste and losses in cooking, the USDA estimates that the average American consumes roughly 2,750 calories per day—a full Big Mac beyond its recommendation of 2200 calories for most children, teenage girls, active women, and sedentary men. Of course, diet and exercise are matters of individual choice, but cultural circumstances—car travel, post-industrial jobs, passive entertainment—push us collectively toward eating more calories than we burn. So does the roughly $4.5 billion a year the food industry spends on advertising and the $50 million a year it spends lobbying in Washington D.C.

Successful dieters, like those in the National Weight Control Registry—a database of more than 2000 people who have lost at least 30 pounds and kept them off for at least a year—generally report that their weight loss was triggered by a specific incident or milestone, often painful. Is there some incident that could make us change the way we eat as a nation? Some dietary Sputnik on the horizon that would do for food education what the Soviet satellite launch did for science education? An across-the-board defeat in the Olympics perhaps?

Actually, it might already be here, in the epidemic of obesity and the rise of Type 2 diabetes (which used to be called "adult onset") in children. The Surgeon General's 2001 Call to Action against obesity reported that 13% of young children and 14% of adolescents were overweight, with the number of overweight adolescents having tripled in two decades. That changed the politics of the debate: With children in the picture—children spammed every day with marketing messages for sugar and fat—it was no longer so simple to argue that diet was purely a matter of individual responsibility.

As long ago as the early 1980s, Romans watching American tourists walk by could be overheard muttering, "*Culo Americano*" (American butt). It was about that time, in fact, that the USDA recorded the first big jump in calories in the U.S. diet since it began tracking food consumption in 1909. Today the biological issue is no different than it was then. But since the Centers for Disease Control identified obesity as an "epidemic" in 1999, the politics of girth appear to be changing.

Declaring an epidemic would seem to call for a policy response. Some school districts in California banished soft drinks from vending machines. Activists were pushing for restrictions on the advertising of junk food to children. They were also getting ready to fight for changes in the Food Guide Pyramid, in the USDA's dietary guidelines, and in the federal school lunch program, all of which were up for review in the next few years. And, of course, some Americans were taking the fat fight to the courtroom.

The uproar had only begun. The first thing that's necessary was for the public to be sensitized and even angry about the current situation. The key to getting mad was having victims. And the victims were children. Some experts recommended two things. One, prohibit fast-food and soft drinks in schools. The other would be to create a nutrition superfund to advertise and market healthy food. For example, we could pay Michael Jordan for promoting vegetables rather than McDonald's. Then at least it would be closer to a level playing field.

Healthy food was not just more expensive than unhealthy food but less convenient. Imagine, for instance, that a crazed vegan were to burst into your office with a gun and demand that you produce, within four minutes, some fresh fruit. Could you do it? How about a soft drink?

There's no reason that the food companies should be expected to look out for the nation's health. On the contrary, the market's logic suggested that if food companies were to grow, so must we. In a way, it was a mirror-image of the problem of overfishing: Each restaurant and food company has an incentive to get more stuff on to our plates; an individual company, like an individual fisherman, has no interest in cutting back for the benefit of a species. Only in this case the species that suffered is not swordfish. It's us.

We have national health plans for reducing obesity but no implementation plan. The government could develop an implementation plan and assign an agency to be responsible and accountable for it. We don't have that now.

THE INDUSTRY SITUATION

2002 was a lousy year for burgers and fries. McDonald's stock traded near its seven-year low, its chief executive quit, and in the nine months ended Sept. 30 its global same-store sales were off

2.1%. Burger King, meanwhile, was sold to an investor group at a $700 million discount from the original sale price.

Subway, promoting its (foot-long) sandwiches as a lower-fat alternative to burgers, now had more U.S. franchises than McDonald's. Wendy's had added enough low-fat items to its menu to earn a nice profile in the magazine of the American Diabetes Association.

Something like a backlash was certainly underway in the food business, and it led to curiosities. Seven-Eleven stores in California were selling sushi. Pepsi was pushing organic Tostitos. Whole Foods Markets, the Austin supermarket chain that sold mostly natural and organic groceries, led its sector with profit growth of 20% last year. Heinz and General Mills were waging a premium-priced organic ketchup war.

So far, though, all this was change at the margins. From a health standpoint, America's food supply was still seriously out of whack. According to Department of Agriculture data for 2000, the most recent available, the national food supply (both domestic and imported) provided 280 pounds of fruit per person. Adjusted for losses and waste, that amounted to less than half the person per day minimum for fruit recommended by the Food Guide Pyramid. Yet consumption of added sugars reached 31 teaspoons per person per day, far above the six- to eighteen-teaspoon maximum recommended.

The government wasn't doing too well in its effort to explain what healthy eating involves. Take the Food Pyramid's recommendation to eat six to eleven servings a day from the grain group. What was a serving? The actual size depended on the individual person. In the Food Pyramid, which the USDA developed, a serving of cooked pasta was one-half cup, cooked. In the Nutrition Facts label on a box of pasta, which was regulated by the Food and Drug Administration, it was twice that. No wonder diners were confused.

For the many people who didn't pay especially close attention, a serving was what you were served. Further, restaurants were using larger dinner plates, bakers were selling larger muffin tins, pizzerias were using larger pans, and fast-food companies were using larger drink and French-fry containers.

As a civilization, we had never had huge amounts of food before. Used to be, in the winter you had to eat dried salmon or figs. There had ever been a society that when presented with an endless stream of free cheeseburgers would have said, No.

Abundant food had benefits. People were fatter, but the people who were strong were also stronger. Actors and actresses are really buff now. You go look at an old Elvis movie, and he's supposedly this avatar of masculinity, and he had baby fat all over his torso. Even Leonardo DiCaprio, who is supposedly feminine, is in better shape that Elvis was. DiCaprio could kick Elvis's butt.

Knowledgeable people predict that if the obesity epidemic is ever to be reversed, it will be through some technological fix like a "fat pill" rather than a general expression of national willpower. The very idea of willpower is under attack by some researchers, who argue that the brain might dictate appetite the way it does other sorts of behavior, like drinking and excreting the right amounts of water to maintain a balance in the body.

Of course, cultures do evolve. Perhaps a decade from now this health calamity will have turned us all into mindful epicures. But at the moment we are on our own and we are going to have to pay attention. For lifelong health we must teach people about their own calorie thermometers. But the problem is what tools are available for that.

Actually there is an interesting new one, developed by a Colorado heart-lung transplant surgeon named James Mault. When Mault was working through his way through college in the 1980s, he had a job at a hospital wheeling around a "metabolic cart," a big, cumbersome machine for measuring patients' resting metabolic rates—the daily calories their bodies burned when at rest. Some of the patients were being fed intravenously, with their caloric needs determined by height and weight tables developed in 1919. With his machine, Mault found that some people's actual caloric needs deviated by as much as 1,000 calories a day from what the tables predicted: Despite, the hospital's best efforts, some were being overfed, and others starved. He dreamed of a simple handheld device that would measure the resting metabolic rate (RMR) and indicate precisely how many calories a day that person could take in without gaining weight. "You can't manage what you can't measure," he pointed out.

It took years before Moore's law caught up with Mault's vision, but eventually he found chips and sensors cheap enough to do the job, and in 1998 he founded HealtheTech to market a new RMR meter, called BodyGem. It's being used at fitness and health clubs around the country. A person breathes into the gizmo for a few minutes and it tells you your RMR. It's an interesting breakthrough. Once you know your personal calorie budget, you tend to look differently at the out-of-control national buffet. And that's what it's going to take, for now at least. Big government, big food, big pharma—none of them is going to help us get small. So: Eat like a Frenchman, walk like a New Yorker and hope for new technology to solve the problem.

ANTIFAT PILL

Over the past decade, researchers had made a rush of discoveries about hormones and other molecules that regulated appetite and weight. That had provided a host of targets to tweak with drugs. But given the problems with past obesity drugs—Fen-Phen, the pill combination linked to heart damage—one had to wonder: Would drugs ever deflate the gross national girth without nasty surprises?

Might be, but expect miracles. Consider leptin, the most acclaimed obesity drug candidate in recent years. A naturally occurring hormone whose gene was isolated in 1994 at Rockefeller University by Jeffry Friedman and colleagues, it was thought to convey an "eat less" signal to the brain to the burgeoning fat cells. When it was injected to congenitally obese mice, they quickly lost weight. But leptin performed much less impressively in human trials.

Another hormone, neuropeptide Y, also stirred excitement. It's a potent appetite stimulant, so drugs that blocked it seemed likely to suppress the munchies. Yet when researchers blocked NPY in mice, the rodents continued to show perfectly healthy appetites.

None of that surprises students of Darwin. Redundant mechanisms had evolved to ensure that fuel was conserved as fat to abet survival in lean times. When we push against the fat-conserving system by losing weight, it pushes back in multiple ways: Hormones scream to the hypothalamus, the brain's appetite control center, ''Eat! Eat inch-thick steaks and cheesecake!'' Our metabolisms shift so a higher share of the calories we ingest get socked away instead of burned as fuel. Our muscles even become more efficient, according to some studies, forcing us to work harder to lose weight and keep it off.

Of course, most of us can beat this pushback for a while and shed tons of pounds. Recent data suggested that perhaps one in five who lost 10% or their weight manage to keep it off for at least a year. But that kind of long-term success typically demands Olympic feats of will, such as religiously sticking to a low-calorie diet and exercising for an hour a day.

The thermostat analogy had major implications for research on obesity drugs. For instance, if scientists could unravel the feedback loop that put us in fat-conserving mode when we lose weight, they might be able to interrupt it with medicines, making it a lot easier to keep lost pounds off. Surprisingly, leptin, the apparent dud, may be one such medicine. In a study published in Spring 2002, Leibel and colleagues showed that when leptin was administered to people who had lost 10% of their weight, hormonal signals associated with the body's fat-conserving mode were interrupted. Thus, even though leptin wasn't effective for dropping pounds, it might keep them off.

Amgen, the biotech company that owns rights to leptin, said it had no plans to test it as a weight-loss maintainer. But another medicine in late clinical tests, Axokine, might work in that role. Developed by Regeneron Pharmaceuticals in Tarrytown, N.Y., it activated the same metabolic pathways that leptin did. Unlike leptin, Axokine appeared to help people both lose weight and keep it off. And its effects seemed to linger, helping weight stay down even after doses were stopped. That prolonged efficacy worried some experts, though, for they suggested that the drug could have long-term side effects.

No single drug was likely to block all the mechanisms that kicked in when we lost weight. Instead researchers envisioned treating obesity with combinations of medicines, each of which suppressed a different part of the fat-conserving system. Such cocktails could be tailored to body chemistry, promising long-term weight loss with minimal side effects.

That's still years away. Now we might be able to stimulate some of the desired hormonal effects with lifestyle changes. For instance, obesity apparently causes the brain to become insensitive to leptin's ''eat less'' signal. But some studies indicate the insensitivity could be reversed by losing weight and exercising—so keeping off lost pounds might get easier over time. Indeed, research on weight, hormones, and the brain has made it ever clearer that obesity is basically a state of mind—and we don't necessarily need drugs to change our minds.

CASE 13
Lonetown Press

onetown Press was opened in January 1992 to provide a highly personalized contract printing service to artists and others devoted to hand-printed lithography as a fine art medium. Founded by Randy Folkman, a master printer with eight years of experience, the company was capitalized for about $30,000 of Randy's money, which was used for the purchase of a Griffen Press and printing materials and supplies. Lonetown was located about 40 miles north of New York City in Fairfield County of southwestern Connecticut.

Randy planned to operate as a one-man shop, at least for the first year. As a master printer and occasional artist in his own right, he had worked at Redvale Press, a private printing studio, for the two years prior to founding Lonetown. Before that he was employed for two years at a studio in New York City and for four years at a print shop in Houston, Texas. While in Texas, he completed his hand printing apprenticeship under the supervision of a Tamarind-trained master printer.

Randy wanted to work primarily at his printing and was especially interested in working with up-and-coming artists. Over the long term he wanted Lonetown to become recognized as a quality, highly personalized shop. At the same time, Randy hoped to pay himself fairly and make some profits as well as learn more about how prints are distributed. Otherwise, he did not want to become overly involved in what he saw as the business or "financial" side of Lonetown.

With the founding of Lonetown Press, Randy realized he would need to determine what price to charge and how to quote prices. He contacted an accountant with whom he shared his background and knowledge of the business.

HAND-PRINTED LITHOGRAPHY

Artists are attracted to hand-printed lithography because of its mystique, the quantity of images that are produced, and the technical results the medium offers. Lithographs are created by drawing on a stone or plate with pencils, crayons, or other materials with which artists are familiar. With a variety of surfaces and materials available, the medium is versatile for artists who can easily visualize from the drawing the resulting prints or graphics, as they are called in the trade. The development of hand-printed lithography in the United States is described by Antreasian and Adams:

This case was prepared by Professor Fred W. Kniffin of the University of Connecticut, with the assistance of Amy Erlanger, as a basis for class discussion rather than to illustrate either effective or ineffective handling of an administrative situation. Copyright © 1993 by Professor Fred W. Kniffin.

Although the principles of lithography are in essence simple, the technical processes involved in the printing of fine lithographs are exceptionally complex. For this reason, artists wishing to make lithographs have, since the early years of the nineteenth century, worked in collaboration with master lithographic printers: Gericault with Hullmandel and Villain, Redon with Blanchard and Clot, Picasso and Braque with Mourlot and Desjobert.

Any lithograph printed from a stone or plate conceived and executed by the artist is an original lithograph, whether it is printed by the artist himself or by a collaborating printer. Until late in the nineteenth century, lithographs were rarely signed in pencil, and individual impressions were seldom numbered. Since that time, however, it has become customary for artists to sign and number each impression, attesting in this way both to the authenticity of the print and to its quality. Often, prints made in a lithographic workshop also bear the printer's bindstamp or chop. Like the artist's signature, this mark attests to the quality of the work.

Original lithographs are normally printed in limited editions, although the size of the edition may vary over a wide range. In the United States, artists' editions characteristically range from 10 to 100; in Europe, editions of 200 or more are not uncommon. The limiting of editions is due not so much to technical considerations as to intention. The artist may wish, as a matter of principle, to limit editions of his work, or he may wish to avoid an undue commitment of time or money to a single edition. . . .

By 1960, lithographic workshops had all but disappeared in this country. There were few master printers, and it was only with the greatest difficulty that an artist might engage himself in lithography. As a result, few of the major artists working in the United States made lithographs during the 1940s and 1950s.

In 1960, Tamarind Lithography Workshop was established in Los Angeles under a grant from the Ford Foundation for the primary purpose of providing a new stimulus to the art of the lithograph in the United States. Since 1960, a number of professional lithographic workshops have opened throughout the country, many of them staffed by artisans trained at Tamarind. The lithographic workshops maintained at art schools and university art departments have likewise increased in number and, under the influence of the Tamarind program, have greatly improved in quality. Now, in the United States as well as in Europe, the artist again finds it possible to work in collaboration with skilled printers, and in these circumstances American Lithography has enjoyed a notable renaissance.

Effective 1 January 1992

The total cost of an edition is the *base charge,* plus the *impression charge,* plus *surcharges* (if any), plus the *cost of paper.* Paper will be billed at the most recent price paid by Tamarind with an allowance for care and shipping. The dimensions of a lithograph (paper size) are also a factor in determination of price. Tamarind's prices for printing are established in four groups, according to dimensions, and show the *maximum size* allowed for that price category. Prices for lithographs larger than 30 by 40 inches will be estimated upon request.

Base Charges

The *base charges* (per edition) include the services of Tamarind's professional staff, all costs related to graining of stones or plates, lithographic materials used in making drawings, materials and papers used in proofing, such proofing as is reasonable and necessary to arrive at a *bon à tirer* impression, the printing of the first 10 proofs and/or impressions (however they may be designated), curating services, tissues, and wrapping materials (packing for shipment, if desired, is billed separately).

	Size 15 by 22 in. 38 by 56 cm.	Size 19 by 25 in. 49 by 64 cm.	Size 22 by 30 in. 56 by 76 cm.	Size 30 by 40 in. 76 by 102 cm.
One color	$140.00	$200.00	$240.00	$340.00
Two colors	320.00	390.00	450.00	580.00
Three colors	450.00	530.00	600.00	750.00
Four colors	560.00	640.00	710.00	900.00
Five colors	660.00	740.00	820.00	1,050.00
Six colors	760.00	880.00	930.00	1,200.00

Impression Charges

The first 10 proofs and/or impressions are included in the base charge; no charge is made for proofs and/or impressions rejected because of technical imperfections, or for proofs or impressions that become the property of the collaborating printers or of Tamarind. The following charges apply to all other impressions, however they may be designated:

	Size 15 by 22 in. 38 by 56 cm.	Size 19 by 25 in. 49 by 64 cm.	Size 22 by 30 in. 56 by 76 cm.	Size 30 by 40 in. 76 by 102 cm.
One color	$ 6.00	$ 7.00	$ 8.00	$10.00
Two colors	12.00	14.00	16.00	20.00
Three colors	18.00	21.00	24.00	30.00
Four colors	23.00	25.00	27.00	33.00
Five colors	27.00	29.00	31.00	36.00
Six colors	31.00	33.00	35.00	39.00

Surcharges

Stone charges:	Technical processes: At sizes below 22 by 30, there is no price differential for work on stone. Surcharges for stone begin at 22 by 30 inches ($40.00) and increase proportional to size; the surcharge for use of our largest stone (36 by 52 inches) is $165.00.
Blended inking:	A surcharge will be added for use of blended or split inking. The charge is determined by the complexity of the blend; it will never be less than 10 percent and may be up to double the impression charge.
Curatorial services:	When the design of a print requires special curatorial services (as examples, tearing to a template, cutting to irregular shapes, applying metallic leaf, etc.), surcharges will be added proportional to the time required.
Technical processes:	Use of all standard lithographic drawing materials and processes is included in the base charge, including direct drawing on stones or plates or through transfer methods. For use of photographic processes and such special techniques as image reversal, printing on chine colle, etc., surcharges will be added proportional to the time required.

(Continued)

Examples

The cost of editions of 50 impressions of single-color lithographs at sizes 19 by 25 inches and 22 by 30 inches printed from stone on Rives BFK, would be calculated as follows:

	19 by 25 in.	22 by 30 in.
Base charge	$200.00	$240.00
Surcharge for stone	0	40.00
Impression charge (50%*)	350.00*	400.00*
Paper charges	50.00	50.00
Total:	$600.00	$730.00

* This figure may be adjusted depending upon the number of trial and/or color trial proofs.

Abandoned Projects

On occasion, an artist reaches a decision to abandon a project without printing an edition. In that event, Tamarind will refund a portion of the base charges, as follows:

1. If the project is abandoned prior to processing and proofing of the plates and/or stones, Tamarind's total charge will be the sum of $100.00, plus any surcharges for stone, plus $25 for each metal plate (or small stone) used. The remainder will be refunded or applied to another project.

2. If the project is abandoned during or at the end of a first proofing session (a session in which all of the printing elements are proofed, one upon another), Tamarind's total charge will be the sum of the surcharges for stone, and 75 percent of the base charge. The remainder will be refunded or applied to another project.

3. If a project is abandoned at any point beyond the end of the first proofing session (as defined above), the full base charge will be paid.

PAYMENT OF ONE-HALF THE TOTAL ESTIMATED CHARGES IS DUE BEFORE WORK IS BEGUN.
THE BALANCE IS DUE UPON DELIVERY OF THE EDITION.

Exhibit 1 Typical Prices for Lithographic Printing

While hand-printed graphics drawn by an artist were considered original art, they were priced lower than original canvasses and were therefore generally more affordable. With lower prices than canvasses, the sales of hand-printed lithographs held up well in periods of recession when sales of the total art market were predictably slower.

Prices for hand-printed lithographs varied from $30 to $10,000 for modern prints; older prints of old masters were even higher. An artist whose canvasses commanded $20,000 might sell his hand-printed graphics for $1,000 each. Typical prices for 22 × 30 inch prints ranged anywhere from $150 to $500 depending upon the artist, printer, and where the prints were purchased.

Consumers acquired prints from art galleries, publishing houses, and auctions and from other individuals such as dealers, interior decorators, artists, and printers. Corporate art buyers often purchased graphics for their headquarters and other executive office buildings.

The publisher of a print is anyone who pays for the printing costs of an edition. Publishers may be galleries or publishing houses, or individuals such as dealers, artists, or printers. When not the artist, the publisher pays the artist a flat fee and, after paying the printing costs, owns all the prints except those few retained by the printer and the artist.

In response to an inquiry from Lonetown's accountant, a master printer stated that, in his experience, graphics or print galleries operated on a 50 percent markup from their selling price to the consumer. Of the costs that galleries paid publishers for prints, he estimated that artists' fees accounted for 25 percent and printing costs another 25 percent with the balance going to publishers. On this basis, a print offered by a gallery to retail at $2,000 to the buyer entailed total printing costs of $250.

THE INDUSTRY AND LONETOWN PRESS

The hand-printed lithography business in the United States had, perhaps, a half dozen major print shops that generally did their own publishing. These major shops usually employed four or more printers, while the balance of the industry of 50 or so shops were

Price List
September 1990
Proofing Charges (price including all materials)

Colors/Runs	15 × 22	22 × 30	29 × 41
One	$78.25	$117.20	$156.25
Two	148.50	219.00	281.25
Three	219.00	320.25	406.25
Four	289.00	422.00	531.25
Five	359.00	535.50	656.25
Six	516.00	750.00	937.50
Seven	600.00	872.00	1,087.50
Eight	684.50	828.00	1,237.50
Nine	768.75	1,015.65	1,387.50
Ten	853.00	1,237.50	1,537.50

Printing Charges per Impression

	15 × 22	22 × 30	29 × 41
One	$7.75	$10.25	$13.30
Two	14.50	18.50	23.70
Three	21.00	27.00	34.30
Four	27.75	35.50	44.80
Five	34.50	52.75	55.30
Six	49.00	62.70	79.00
Seven	57.00	72.75	91.50
Eight	65.18	82.80	103.25
Nine	73.20	93.00	116.75
Ten	81.00	103.00	129.50

*Disguised name.

Exhibit 2 Vermont Graphics, Inc.*

Price List
For 22″ × 30″ Size
50 Prints
June 1992
Proofing Charges

Colors/Runs	
One	$120.00
Two	170.00
Three	235.00
Four	285.00
Five	350.00
Six	420.00
Seven	495.00
Eight	575.00
Nine	665.00
Ten	735.00

Printing Charges per Impression

Colors/Runs	
One	$ 7.20
Two	10.80
Three	16.80
Four	21.60
Five	25.20
Six	28.80
Seven	32.40
Eight	36.00
Nine	39.60
Ten	43.20

*Disguised name.

Exhibit 3 Oklahoma Print Shop*

one- or two-printer operations. There were probably fewer than 60 print shops in the U.S. accepting hand-printed lithography work in 1992. Recent price schedules of the Tamarind Institute and two printing companies are shown in Exhibits 1, 2, and 3.

For at least some of their business, most shops co-published. This involved a negotiation of charges in which the printer accepted some number of copies of the artist's edition in exchange for the printer's services. For example, Lonetown Press might retain 10 to 25 copies of a 50-print edition in lieu of the costs for printing services rendered. In this situation, the artist would not incur an outlay for printing and Lonetown would assume responsibility for selling the graphics to compensate for the printing. A variation on co-publishing occurred when printers gave discounts in exchange for a part of the edition. These types of agreements were believed to be particularly appealing to up-and-coming artists to whom Randy wished to cater.

Lonetown's accountant had developed estimates of both annual and per job costs for the shop, since she was thinking of adding a markup to labor and/or material costs as the basis for creating a price schedule. Randy, however, was somewhat skepti-

cal of this approach because he had concerns about pricing too high or too low in relation to competition. He wanted to price high enough to be taken seriously, but low enough to attract initial business. The accountant figured business expenses would run $11,000 annually, not including Randy's salary needs of $30,000 per year.

Lonetown Press Annual Expenses

Public relations (personal entertainment)	$3,000
Advertising	2,000
Travel expenses	2,000
Depreciation	1,300
Lawyer & accountant fees	1,000
Insurance, electricity, heat	1,000
Property taxes	700
Total	$11,000

In addition to the master printer's labor hours, cost estimates that could be directly traced to each job were:

5-Color—50 Print Edition

Item	Cost
Standard paper	$175
Ink	10
Printing plates	95
Various chemicals	20
Total costs per job	$300

The most comfortable edition size for Lonetown Press was 50 prints; and editions over 200 prints were definitely less desirable. With editions of 150 and over, the master printer in a one-person shop often encountered some tedium, which could adversely affect the quality of his work.

At Lonetown, the largest acceptable print was 30 × 40 inches, since this was the maximum size that the Griffen Press could accommodate. Smaller paper sizes presented no problems.

Although four to five colors appealed most to Randy, the number of colors in a print was not of great importance. However, since each color in a print must be printed separately, printing additional colors required additional printing time.

A typical or average job for Lonetown might be a 5-color 22″ × 30″ edition of 50 prints. Randy felt that he could produce 25 such editions per year, or about one such edition every two weeks. Working at this rate would leave him barely sufficient time left over to consult with artists and galleries and do his bookkeeping and purchasing.

Randy felt confident about the long-term success of Lonetown; however, his immediate concern was quoting prices on several pending inquiries. He had decided that his price schedule should have separate prices for proofing and printing, prices for three sizes (18″ × 24″, 22″ × 30″, 30″ × 40″) and prices for one to 10 colors. In addition, he wanted his price schedule to, in some way, reflect his preference for printing smaller editions.

CASE 14
Wal-Mart, Inc.

In spring of 2003, Lee Scott, CEO of Wal-Mart, called his four senior colleagues for the year-end review of results (Wal-Mart's fiscal year starts February 1) and future direction. Wal-Mart had no immediate problem. Not only was it the world's biggest corporation (it replaced Exxon Mobil atop the *Fortune* 500 in 2002), in March 2003, Fortune ranked it as the most admired companies. Yet the company had grown self-conscious about its size. Was someone going to decide that Wal-Mart had too much power? Didn't the government break up companies that get this big?

While Sears and Woolworth once announced their power by erecting the world's tallest skyscrapers, Wal-Mart Strived to be everywhere and nowhere, hidden in plain sight—just your friendly hometown superpower. The reasons for that might be less calculated than cultural. Wal-Mart's founder Sam Walton used the language of service and democracy—customers, he said, "voted with their feet"—to build a republic of fervent consumer advocates. Today the company still saw itself that way—and seemed confounded when the rest of the world did not. However, America's most admired company had also been one of its most maligned, recently attracting headlines about class-action lawsuits alleging that associates were forced to work unpaid overtime. "In the past we were judged by our aspirations," says Scott. "Now we're going to be judged by our exceptions."

WAL-MART STORES

Samuel Moore Walton, the billionaire boy scout of Bentonville, Arkansas, built an empire on a fervid belief in value, pioneered by ideas like empowerment, and revolutionized retailing in the process. Dead at 74 after a long fight with cancer, he did not invent the discount department store, although it hardly seems possible that he didn't. He grabbed hold of the leading edge of retailing in 1962 and never let go, creating a value-powered merchandising machine that seemed certain to outlive his memory.

In 2002, the company earned $9.2 billion on sales of $240 billion. A $1,650 investment in 100 Wal-Mart shares in 1970, when they began trading, was worth $5 million in 2003. He taught American business that the vast amount of American people want value. He saw the future, and he helped make the future. According to a retail executive, while Walton was one of the great showmen of retailing, if he had been a television preacher he'd have become Pope. As a manager he applied such concepts as a flat organization, empowerment, and gain-sharing long before anyone gave them those names. In the 1950s, he shared information and profits with all employees. He ingested as much data as he could to get close to the customer and closer to the competition. He stressed flexibility and action over deliberation.

Wal-Mart was ultimately a monument to consumers: it had saved them billions. Sam Walton truly believed that nothing happens until a customer walks into a store with a purpose, buys something, and walks out. His philosophy was simple: satisfy the customer. Operating nearly 2,800 stores in 47 states, Wal-Mart remained the leader in the discount store industry. In addition, with over 500 Sam's Clubs, Wal-Mart was a major factor in the Warehouse Club industry. Combining general merchandise and groceries, Supercenters represented the company's fastest growing segment.

Walton long ago wanted manufacturers to see themselves, wholesalers, retailers, and consumers as parts of a single customer-focused process rather than as participants in a series of transactions. He personally and permanently altered the relationship between manufacturers and retailer, which had historically been, to put it politely, antagonistic. About fifteen years ago he asked Procter & Gamble executives to view a focus group of Wal-Mart executives talking about their prickly relationship with the packaged-goods company. It was sobering. His strategy clearly was that we ought to be able to work together to lower the costs of both the manufacturer and the distributor and get lower costs for consumers. Walton got both sides to focus on distribution costs and how to cut them. Wal-Mart linked P&G with its computers to allow automatic reordering, thus avoiding bulges in order cycles. With better coordination of buying, P&G could plan more consistent manufacturing runs, passing on some of the savings. This systematic approach was now in broad use throughout the industry. Walton had been described as a visionary, and he clearly was that. His vision was apparent in 1956 as a Ben Franklin variety store owner. To lure one of his first store managers, Bob Bogle, away from the state health department, Walton showed him the books and offered to pay him 25 percent of the store's net profit in addition to salary.

WAL-MART'S COMPETITVE CAPABILITIES

What accounted for Wal-Mart's remarkable success? Most explanations focus on a few familiar and highly visible factors: the genius of founder Sam Walton, who inspired his employees and had molded a culture of service excellence; the "greeters" who welcomed customers at the door; the motivational power of allowing employees to own part of the business; the strategy of "everyday low prices," which offered the customer a better deal and saved on merchandising and advertising costs. Strategists also pointed to Wal-Mart's big stores, which offered economies of scale and a wider choice of merchandise.

Such explanations only redefine the question. *Why* was Wal-Mart able to justify building bigger stores? Why did Wal-Mart alone have a cost structure low enough to accommodate everyday low prices and greeters? What had enabled the company to continue to grow far beyond the direct reach of Sam Walton's magnetic personality? The real secret of Wal-Mart's success was deeper, in a set of strategic business decisions that transformed the company into a capabilities-based competitor.

The starting point was a relentless focus on satisfying customer needs. Wal-Mart's goals were simple to define but hard to execute: to provide customers access to quality goods, to make these goods available when and where customers want them, to develop a cost structure that enables competitive pricing, and to build and maintain a reputation for absolute trustworthiness. The key to achieving these goals was to make the way the company replenished inventory the centerpiece of its competitive strategy.

This strategic vision reached its fullest expression in a largely invisible logistics technique known as "cross-docking." In this system, goods were continuously delivered to Wal-Mart's warehouses, where they were selected, repacked, and then dispatched to stores, often without ever sitting in inventory. Instead of spending valuable time in the warehouse, goods just cross from one loading dock to another in 48 hours or less. Cross-docking enabled Wal-Mart to achieve the economies that come from purchasing full truck-loads of goods while avoiding the usual inventory and handling costs. Wal-Mart ran a full 85 percent of its products through its warehouse system—as opposed to only 50 percent for Kmart. This reduced Wal-Mart's costs of sales by 2 percent to 3 percent compared with the industry average. The cost difference made possible the everyday low prices.

That's not all. Low prices in turn meant that Wal-Mart could save even more by eliminating the expense of frequent promotions. Stable prices also made sales more predictable, thus reducing stock-outs and excess inventory. Finally, everyday low prices brought in customers, which translated into higher sales per retail square foot. These advantages in basic economics made the greeters and the profit sharing easy to afford.

With such obvious benefits, why don't all retailers use cross-docking? The reason: it is extremely difficult to manage. To make cross-docking work, Wal-Mart had to make strategic investments in a variety of interlocking support systems far beyond what could be justified by conventional ROI criteria. For example, cross-docking requires continuous contact among Wal-Mart's distribution centers, suppliers, and every point of sale in every store to ensure that orders can flow in and be consolidated and executed within a matter of hours. Wal-Mart operated a private satellite-communication system that daily sent point-of-sale data directly to Wal-Mart's 5000 vendors.

Another key component of Wal-Mart's logistics infrastructure was the company's fast and responsive transportation system. The company's 24 distribution centers were serviced by nearly 2,800 company-owned trucks. This dedicated truck fleet permitted Wal-Mart to ship goods from warehouse to store in less than 48 hours and to replenish its store shelves twice a week on average. By contrast, the industry norm was once every two weeks.

To gain the full benefits of cross-docking, Wal-Mart had also had to make fundamental changes in its approach to managerial control. Traditionally, in the retail industry, decisions about merchandising, pricing, and promotions had been highly centralized and made at the corporate level. Cross-docking, however, turns this command-and-control logic on its head. Instead of the retailer pushing products into the system, customers "pull" products when and where they need them. This approach placed a premium on frequent, informal cooperation among stores, distribution centers, and suppliers—with far less centralized control.

The job of senior management at Wal-Mart, then, was not to tell individual store managers what to do, but to create an environment where they could learn from the market—and from each other. The company's information systems, for example, provided store managers with details about customer behavior, while a fleet of airplanes regularly ferries store managers to Bentonville, Arkansas headquarters for meetings on market trends and merchandising.

As the company had grown and its stores had multiplied, even Wal-Mart's own private air force hadn't been enough to maintain the necessary contacts among store managers. Therefore, Wal-Mart installed a video link connecting all its stores to corporate headquarters and to each other. Store managers frequently hold videoconferences to exchange information on what's happening in the field, such as which products were selling and which ones weren't, or which promotions worked and which didn't.

The final piece of this capabilities mosaic was Wal-Mart's human resources system. The company realized that its frontline employees played a significant role in satisfying customer needs. Therefore, it attempted to enhance its organizational capability with programs such as stock ownership and profit sharing geared toward making its personnel more responsive to customers. Even the way Wal-Mart stores were organized contributed to this goal. Where Kmart had five separate merchandise departments in each store, Wal-Mart had 36. This meant that training could be more focused and more effective, and employees could be more attuned to customers.

COMPANY'S GROWTH

To understand the company's astonishing development, one needs to grasp the difference between a big company—what Wal-Mart was at the time of Sam Walton's death in 1992, when it was about one-fifth its present size—and a company that created a whole new definition of bigness. If conventional metrics, like Wal-Mart's $240 billion-plus in sales or its 1.3 million "associates," didn't do the trick, these may help:

- Wal-Mart's sales on one day during the fall of 2002—$1.42 billion—were larger than the GDPs of 36 countries.
- It was the biggest employer in 21 states, with more people in uniform then in the U.S. Army.
- It planned to grow in 2003 by the equivalent of—take your pick—one Dow Chemical, one PepsiCo, one Microsoft, or one Lockheed Martin.
- If the estimated $2 billion it loses through theft each year were incorporated as a business, it would rank No. 694 on the Fortune 1,000.

What this meant for Wal-Mart's low-profile CEO, Lee Scott, was that he ran what was arguably the world's most powerful company. What it meant for corporate America was a bit more bracing. It meant for one, that Wal-Mart was not just Disney's biggest customer but also Procter & Gamble's and Kraft's and Revlon's and Gillette's and Campbell Soup's and RJR's and on down the of America's famous branded manufacturers. It meant, further, that the nation's biggest seller of DVDs was also its biggest seller of groceries, toys, guns, diamonds, CDs, apparel, dog food, detergent, jewelry, sporting goods, videogames, socks, bedding, and toothpaste—not to mention its biggest film developer, optician, private truck-fleet operator, energy consumer, and real estate developer. It meant, finally, that the real market clout in many industries no longer rode in Hollywood or Cincinnati or New York, but in the hills of northwestern Arkansas.

If this sounds fanciful, then consider Newell Rubbermaid's new Bentonville office, just a 60-second drive from Wal-Mart headquarters. One of 200 corporate embassies here that form a ring known as "Vendorville," it was home to the 50 members of Newell's Wal-Mart Division. Everything in Bentonville was like Wal-Mart. The carpets mirror those in Wal-Mart headquarters. Same with the cheap cubicles. The first floor had an "exact replica of a Wal-Mart store" showing placement of Newell glassware, Sharpie pens, trashcans, Levelor blinds, and so forth. Upstairs, Sam Walton's image and aphorisms hang on the walls, while even the Gregorian calendar had given way to "Wal-Mart time": Week 9 is understood to mean nine weeks into the company's fiscal year, starting February 1.

Newell's reasoning came down to one number: 15, the percentage of its merchandise that passed through Wal-Mart cash registers. That number helped explain why Newell CEO Joe Galli spent four weeks a year touring Wal-Mart stores, and why Newell seldom designed or launched a new product without Wal-Mart's involvement, and why division president Steven Scheyer gave every new employee a copy of Sam Walton's autobiography. Manufactures lived and breathed with Wal-Mart. They wondered: what's the right Sharpie for Wal-Mart, what's the right closet product for Wal-Mart, what's the right stroller? Little wonder that Stockholm Syndrome—the phenomenon in which hostages come to identify with their captors—had been a problem for some companies.

PHILOSOPHY OF BUSINESS

How Wal-Mart thinks had never been a big mystery: Buy stuff at the lowest cost possible, pass the gains on to the customer through superlow prices, watch stuff fly off the shelves at insane velocity. (Critics who say Wal-Mart was obsessed with its bottom line had one thing wrong: Wal-Mart was obsessed with its top line, which it grows by focusing on the consumer's bottom line.) Suppliers were expected to offer their best price, period. It was not even negotiated anymore. No one would dare come in with a half-ass price. As for a supplier *raising* prices, it did not work. In some cases Wal-Mart had been known simply to keep sending payment for the old amount.

By systematically wresting "pricing power" from the manufacturer and handing it to the consumer, Wal-Mart had begun to generate an economy-wide Wal-Mart Effect. Economists now credit the company's Everyday Low Prices with contribution to Everyday Low Inflation, meaning that all Americans—even members of Whirl-Mart, a "ritual resistance" group that silently pushed empty carts through superstores—unknowingly benefited from the retailer's clout. A 2002 McKinsey study, moreover, found that more than one-eighth of U.S. productivity growth between 1995 and 1999 could be explained "by only two syllables: Wal-Mart." According to a consultant, Wal-Mart had contributed to the financial well-being of American public more than any institution.

PREVAILING OVER COMPETITION

Wal-Mart transformed its competitors, its suppliers, and the industries it dominated. In apparel, for instance, Wal-Mart was moving from staples into cheap-chic fashion, exemplified by its new George line, which offered career basics like skirts and blazers priced between $8.87 and $28.96. That in turn was pressuring everyone from Bloomingdale's to Banana Republic to compete on price as well as image. Wal-Mart had caused the fashion industry to go topsy-turvy.

In Hollywood, Wal-Mart's push for cheap DVDs (as low as $5.88) had exacerbated a schism between studios like Universal, which didn't want to cannibalize the lucrative rental business, and those like Warner, which were pushing a high-volume, low-margin approach. Caught perilously in the middle was Viacom's Blockbuster.

Convenience stores, meanwhile, were threatened by the 700 gas stations now in Wal-Mart parking lots, causing petroleum sellers to lobby vigorously for protective legislation.

The battle of the brands, too, was increasingly played out on Wal-Mart turf. In batteries, perennial third-place Rayovac had used a low-cost "Wal-Mart *uber Alles*" strategy to challenge Energizer and Gillette's Duracell. Tattered Levi Strauss, once too cool for discount stores, had bet its future on sub-$30 jeans to hit Wal-Mart racks this summer. And toy companies anxiously watched the fate—and tried actively to boost the fortunes—of Toys "R" Us, fearing a unipolar world. If Toys "R" Us went under, and then Kmart too, toy would manufactures be selling 60% of toys to Wal-Mart?

Wal-Mart in 2003 was, in short, a lot like America 2003: a sole superpower with a down-home twang. As with Uncle Sam, everyone's position in the world would largely be defined in relation to Mr. Sam. Was your company a "strategic competitor" like China or a "partner" like Britain? Was it a client state like Israel or a supplier to the opposition like Yemen? Was it France, benefiting from the superpower's reach while complaining the whole time? Or was it ... well, a Target? You could admire the superpower or resent it or—most likely—both. But you could not ignore it.

POWER BASE

It is an odd fact that the public face of Wal-Mart continues, after all these years, to be the folksy visage of Sam Walton. Spend enough time inside the company—where nothing backs up a point better than a quotation from Walton scripture—and it's easy to get the impression that the founder is orchestrating his creation from beyond. The explosive growth of the past decade had, of course, actually occurred under the earthly apostleship of David Glass and, since 2000, 53-year-old Lee Scott.

Early power retailers like Sears and A&P started out with the upper hand. A 1930 *Fortune* article noted that A&P's terms become, practically, Economic Law. It was the coming of television, plus laws that prevented stores from selling products below their listed price, that shifted the advantage to mass-marketers like P&G, Coke, and Revlon (which not only sponsored but owned the top-rated '50s TV show *The $64,000 Question*). What Wal-Mart had done was turn that on its head again. The store had a helluva lot of power.

How Wal-Mart used to wield this power was today's $244 Billion Question. Many assumed that the company used it crudely, cracking suppliers' heads and stealing their lunch money. But if that were the case, one would expect to see manufactures' margins shrinking. According to Value Line, operating margins of household product makers actually grew 48% between 1992 and 2001; food processors' went up 30%; soft drink makers' rose 14%. Though horror stories do circulate (some entrepreneurs have accused Wal-Mart of knocking off their product proposals), Wal-Mart also towered as the best retailer with which to do business in a Cannondale Associates survey of 122 manufacturers.

How could that be? It begins to make sense if one considers the byzantine demands that most retailers impose on suppliers. Slotting fees. Display fees. Damage allowances. Handling charges. Late penalties. Special sales and rebates. Super Bowl tickets. Each is a small inefficiency that benefits the retailer at the supplier's expense and, ultimately—since the supplier builds those costs into its prices—the consumer's. Wal-Mart, by contrast, was famous for boiling everything down to a one-number negotiation. "All the funny money—1% for this, 2% for that, 'I need a rebate ... I need a special fund for our annual golf event'—it wasn't there. They'll negotiate hard to get the extra penny, but they'll pass it along to the customers."

While this part of the negotiation was strictly arm's length, Wal-Mart also operated in "partnering" mode, in which both sides swapped information to streamline the flow of goods from raw materials to checkout counter. They would rather extract fat from the process then extract their suppliers' profits. So while Newell Rubbermaid's "We Love Wal-Mart" strategy could seem the ultimate in corporate vassalage, consider what Newell gets out of the deal: not only huge volume but, thanks to Everyday Low Prices, *predictable* volume, which lets it keep its factories running full and steady. There were no advertising costs, no "funny money." And Wal-Mart would even back up its trucks to Newell's factories. Many suppliers, including P&G, like the model so much that they had pushed it on their other customers.

There's more. Newell got product ideas from Wal-Mart. Hundreds of them. A store associate in Arizona mentioned that Hispanic customers were looking for a kind of cookware called a *caldero*. Done. The hardware department saw an opportunity for "light industrial" cleaning products. Time to market: 90 days. Shoppers, in effect, got direct control of the nation's manufacturing facilities—reason to see Wal-Mart as the world's most finely articulated tool for turning customer wants into reality. A win-win-win.

Playing the game, however, required constant hustle. Besides continually cutting your costs, you needed to handle all the data pouring off RetailLink—the system that lets suppliers track their wares through Wal-Mart World—since they wouldn't want to annoy Wal-Mart with excess inventory or, worse yet, not enough. An electronic "vendor scorecard" would let you know how you were doing.

In the meantime, you should also be peppering Wal-Mart with "retail-tainment" ideas about how to make its store more fun. If you were the maker of Power Rangers, that meant creating the world's largest inflatable structure—a 5,000-square-foot moon—for a tour of Wal-Mart parking lots. If you were Coke, it meant routing your L.A.-to-Atlanta Olympic Torch Run past every Wal-Mart possible. You might be "encouraged" to buy time on the in-store TV network. And should you enjoy the privileged position of "category manager," you would be expected to educate Wal-Mart on everything happening in jelly or lingerie or Hulk Hands markets. Above all, you'd better start thinking like a retailer.

"Vendor offenders," as some Wal-Marters jokingly call them, didn't last long. People think they were wired in at the top of the company, but the relationship in itself meant nothing if you didn't perform.

POWER OF THE NATIONAL BRAND

Bentonville wasn't above dropping the occasional bomb. Procter & Gamble's storied partnership with Wal-Mart began on a 1987 canoe trip when Walton and a P&G boss agreed to start sharing information instead of hoarding it. Yet there was little warning when, in 2001, Wal-Mart unveiled its Sam's American Choice detergent at roughly half the price of P&G's family jewel, Tide. Now there were rumors—which Wal-Mart did not confirm—that the retailer was planning to introduce a second, even cheaper detergent under its Great Value label.

Tide still commanded about four times the shelf space of Sam's Choice, but Wal-Mart's private-label assault had turned even its most trusted suppliers into its competitors. With little fanfare and no advertising, Wal-Mart's Ol' Roy dog food (named for Sam Walton's English Setter: 1970-81) had charged past Nestlé's Purina as the world's top-selling brand. Great Value bleach outsold Clorox in some stores.

That raised a tricky question: What, exactly, was the brand here? As Wal-Mart flexed its muscle as a marketer and not just a merchandiser, it could accelerate the demise of weaker brands. Even P&G had refocused on just 12 powerhouses, like Crest and Pampers. Now manufactures worry about losing their direct connection to the consumer. Two decades ago 65% of their ad budgets went to television and other mass media, while today 60% went to retailers for in-store promotions and the like. The worry was that Wal-Mart would become the next Procter & Gamble. The nightmare: Wal-Mart becomes your company's new VP of Marketing.

If the trip on Gulliver's coattails is no joyride, it sure beats being a Lilliputian underfoot. Over the years Wal-Mart thundered its way up the retail food chain, first flattening mom-and-pop stores, then stepping on discounters like Ames, Bradlees, and Kmart, and finally sitting on specialty retailers like Toys "R" Us—threatening, in effect, to kill the category killer. Now no category seemed safe.

Just ask your grocer. The quintessentially low-margin business had benefited from a decade of consolidation and cost cutting by giants like Kroger and Albertsons. Yet most of the gains dropped to the companies' bottom lines, not the consumers. Now, feasting on fat margins in the presence of Wal-Mart was a bit like tucking into a juicy sirloin in the presence of a grizzly: Your dinner won't be there for long, and unless you start running, neither would you. Only ten years after launching its food business amid much guffawing, Wal-Mart was the world's biggest grocer, driving down prices an average of 13% in the markets it entered, according to a UBS Warburg study. The effect had been seismic: Kroger had gone on a cost-cutting drive to narrow the price gap, Albertsons has abandoned some markets entirely, and an army of consultants now advised the grocers on how to grapple with the 800-pound gorilla. When Wal-Mart moved, it adhered to the Powell doctrine of overwhelming force.

SKY IS THE LIMIT

Imagine you were a Wal-Mart strategic planner on the prowl for other high-value targets. Where else were middlemen taking fat profits and stiffing consumers? Consider used cars: the last castle of medieval retailing. Visit the parking lots of several Houston Supercenters, and you would find a dealer quietly testing a no-haggle approach under the Price 1.

What else? Well, what about Microsoft? Its margins were—can this be right?—44%, and it's sitting on $38 billion in cash. Mr. Sam would not approve. Log on to walmart.com and you would find $199 computers powered by a fledgling Windows competitor, Lindows.

Financial services! Regulators had twice thwarted Wal-Mart's attempts to buy a bank, but hey, you didn't need a bank to offer wire transfers and money orders. And get this: Western Union charged $50 to wire $1,000 from Texas to Mexico. How about a flat $12.95 instead, and 46-cent money orders instead of 90 cents charged by the U.S. Postal Service? Available at a store near you. Wal-Mart vacations. Internet access. Flower delivery. Online DVD rentals a la Netflix. All happening.

Wal-Mart stresses that many of these experiments are just that: experiments. But the company had long excelled at using itself as a testing lab, tweaking and refining a concept until—boom!—it's everywhere. That's why even the looniest speculation—Wal-Mart partners with a Korean auto company to make a private-label car, Wal-Mart acquires a drug chain, Wal-Mart becomes a wholesaler to other merchants—can't be dismissed. Just because you're paranoid doesn't mean Bentonville isn't out to get you.

SUCCESS FACTORS

Wal-Mart's zero-to-60 engine was driven by three powerful cylinders: *scale*, *scope*, and *speed*. The scale part was obvious. The scope part allowed Wal-Mart to "flex" its toy section before the holidays and collapse it afterward, while Toys "R" Us was stuck selling toys year-round. (Scope also allowed Wal-Mart use entire categories—gas, soft drinks, whatever—as loss leaders to pull people into the stores.) The speed part might be the most intimidating. Wal-Mart's turnover was so rapid that 70% of its merchandise was rung up at the register before the company had paid for it. Speed was why it routed ships from China through the Suez Canal and across the Atlantic, so that exactly 50% of imports ended up on each coast—more expensive in the short run, but faster in the long. And while the interior of a Wal-Mart distribution center evoked the final scene of *Raiders of the Lost Ark*—42-foot-high corridors of toilet paper stretching toward a vanishing point—many items never hit the warehouse floor, moving directly from truck to truck along 24 miles of conveyor belts.

Competitors' choice was left with two options (surrender not one of them; Bentonville didn't do acquisitions). Option No. 1 was to play Wal-Mart's game. Very risky. In the mid-1990s, Kmart proved it to be ritual suicide. On the other hand, companies already steeped in discounting—Costco, Family Dollar, grocery chain Publix—had more than held their own against Goliath. Option No. 1 should thus carry the warning found atop black-diamond ski runs: EXPERTS ONLY.

Option No. 2: Don't play Wal-Mart's game. Typically a better choice. Grocery folks regularly tromp through H-E-B, a Texas grocery chain that had held Wal-Mart at bay with such "destination products" as ice cream made from Poteet strawberries, a local favorite that H-E-B froze in vast quantities. Not surprisingly, Wal-Mart was already thinking along similar lines, mining its mountains of data to tailor individual stores to local tastes.

FUTURE COURSE

The question on everyone's mind, of course, is, How much more dominant can Wal-Mart get? More than 70 million people already roamed its aisles each week. Its truckers were trained to avoid deluded motorists who dream of a collision and a Wal-Mart-sized settlement. The U.S. Mint chose Wal-Mart, not banks, to introduce its Sacagawea gold dollar in 2000. Target had difficulty finding American flags on Sept. 12, 2001, because guess who had begun buying every flag it could the previous day. Hegemony, it would seem, didn't get any more complete.

Yet a bit of fifth-grade math produced a startling result: If Wal-Mart maintained its annual growth rate of 15%, it would be twice as big in five years. "Could we be two times larger?" asks CEO Lee Scott. "Sure. Could we be three times larger? I think so."

Crazy talk? Maybe not. Roughly half of Wal-Mart's Supercenters (groceries plus general merchandise) are in 11 states of the Old South, leaving plenty of room for expansion in California and the Northeast. And Bentonville is getting creative about overcoming the political and real estate hurdles there. In January it opened its first inner-city Supercenter in the Baldwin Hills neighborhood of Los Angeles, a three-story affair with special escalators for shopping carts. All told, Wal-Mart would open roughly a store a day in 2003.

As it expanded outward, it would be also filling in the gaps. It found that a smaller population than they originally had thought can support a Supercenter, so they put two Supercenters—Rogers (Ark.) and Fayetteville—roughly four miles apart. Same thing is true in Dallas, Houston, Atlanta. Within those four miles Wal-Mart is building new Neighborhood Markets, or "Small-Marts": smartly designed food/drug combos with conveniences like self-checkout, honor-system coffee and pastries, drive-through pharmacies, and half-hour film processing (this is based on a finding that 50% of women shoppers have an undeveloped roll of film in their purse). In Arkansas, Wal-Mart's even dabbling with stand-alone pharmacies. Throw in Sam's Club, with 46 million paid memberships, and walmart.com, with it's mission of "easy access to more Wal-Mart," and you start to wonder: Is there any format Bentonville won't consider on its march to "saturation"?

CASE 15
Mickey Comes to the Rescue! Disneyland in Hong Kong

Disney Company—one of the world leaders in media entertainment, company branded consumer goods, and theme parks and resorts—signed the agreement with Hong Kong concerning the opening of a "Disneyland" amusement park in Hong Kong in the year 2005. The success of Disney Hong Kong will depend on intimate understanding of the regional marketplace and viable marketing strategies.

COMPANY BACKGROUND

In 1928, Walt Disney started as an animator drawing short black-and-white cartoons. Today, Disney's main businesses are television, cinema entertainment, and theme parks. Disney owns national TV channels and radio stations that broadcast all around the USA. Since 1991 Disney cooperates with Pixar, a company specialized in computer animation, and together they produce and publish exclusively animated movies (e.g., "Toy Story").

In 1945 its first theme park "Disneyland" was opened in Anaheim, California, USA, followed by "Walt Disney World" in Orlando, Florida, USA, in 1971. In 1983, the first international Disneyland opened to the public in Tokyo, Japan, and in 1992, the corporation expanded its business to Paris, France. Furthermore, Disney has operated a theme Cruise Ship since 1998. The company has been very successful with its theme park business.

However, Disney was confronted with a major crisis in its past when first operating its "EuroDisney" park near Paris. Insufficient knowledge of the European culture and the buying behavior of potential visitors of the theme park led to an overestimation of the number of visitors and their spending in the park. In addition, operating costs turned out to be higher than expected. The company was able to overcome this crisis. The park now operates under the name "Disneyland Paris," and its operating income contributes to the high success of the theme park business.

In November 1999 the Walt Disney Corporation and Hong Kong signed the first agreements concerning the opening of a "Disneyland" amusement park in Hong Kong in the year 2005. The undertaking will be a joint venture between the Walt Disney Company and the Hong Kong Special Administrative Region Government. Disney will own 43% of the shares and Hong Kong 57%. Both parties are optimistic that this co-operation will result in a win-win situation. Hong Kong is going to invest a high amount of money in the venture both directly and indirectly: Directly by investing in the construction of the park itself, and indirectly by renewing the infrastructure of the city to the park and investing in a new tourism strategy that enhances the city's attractiveness as an international tourist destination. In return, Disney will market the new park effectively. Hong Kong expects this East-meets-West attraction to bring the tourism to a new boom. Especially visitors from the *mainland* of China are predicted to visit Hong Kong and the park.

Disney claims to have enough experience to open another theme park outside the United States. Failures and successes while expanding their amusement park business to Tokyo and Paris helped them to make more accurate predictions on the new project. This win-win situation has led to an agreement about Disneyland Phase I (which will include a Disney theme park, a Disney theme resort hotel complex, and a retail, dining, and entertainment center).

"We will deliver magical and memorable entertainment experiences which create a sense of joy and wonderment for our guests and consistently exceed their expectations. We will continue to be recognized globally as the premier entertainment and hospitality organization by mobilizing our team spirit to perfect our talents and abilities, and to perpetuate our rich Disney legacy. This will be evident to our guests, fellow employees, shareholders, and community and business partners through our words and deeds." It is the company's mission to provide a reasonable return to its shareholders, and to increase the value of their investment. At the same time, Disney must be sure to protect the business and reputation of the company, so that it can meet the expectations of the shareholders, guests, customers, employees and employees.

Disney's idea is to attract more than five million tourists to the park within the first year of business, which is expected to rise to 10 million per year after 15 years. The company intends to provide Hong Kong with a net economic benefit of up to $148 billion over 40 years. Additionally, the park will create thousands of jobs, enrich the quality of life, and enhance Hong Kong's international image.

The company has its own "Disney Culture" consisting of a rich heritage, traditions, quality standards, and values that create a unique environment. A Disney employee needs to commit himself to these characteristics when going to work every day, in order to make the experience of a "magical" vacation possible for the visitors. The company believes that the success in the *family* entertainment business is directly attributed to the individual contributions

---

This case was prepared by a professor of Lingnan University, Hong Kong, and is printed here with his permission.

of the entire team of employees. Other significant aspects are the clean Disney look of its employees, open communication, diversity of its workforce, and good community relationships.

Part of Disney's mission is to expand its market. When going abroad the Disney corporation promises to keep following in mind: "As we expand our operations abroad, we encounter new challenges as a result of cultural differences and unfamiliar practices..., we must recognize that in many cases we are introducing our culture and methods of conducting business into different environments. When conducting business in other countries, it is imperative to be especially sensitive to foreign legal requirements and cultural differences, and make every effort to integrate Disney culture as smoothly as possible."

CURRENT MARKETING POLICIES

The theme park business consists of both providing services and selling consumer goods, including food and beverages, and merchandise. In general, Disney uses the same marketing mix and strategy for both physical goods and services.

Disney's key benefits includes amusement, joy, fun, pleasure, and prestige. Specifically, the theme park provides roller coasters, attractions, shows, Disney characters, food, drinks, toys, and clothes. It intends to provide safety, excellent service, and very high quality. In addition, it strives to exceed guests expectations, for example by having the sections of the parks be consistent with certain themes (e.g., the "Space Mountain" roller-coaster ride is in the "Future Land"), by providing immediate guest service recovery (if a customer receives a product that does not meet his expectations, he can exchange it without problems), or by promising a "magical" experience that the guest will never forget. This experience is supposed to last during the whole voyage to the park. For instance, in Orlando, Disney spends a lot of money on maintenance of the airport of Orlando and of the streets leading to the parks and resorts.

As for pricing, Disney would like to stay being the quality leader in the amusement park business worldwide and therefore chooses for a high price that is perceived to go along with premium quality. In addition, Disney's general policy is not to cut prices. This means that the parks are not offering low-season discounts on the entrance tickets or offering merchandise on sale inside the park. However, Disney decided to make an exception with the park in Paris. Due to a lower-than-expected number of visitors during winter months, the company offers low-season prices and "all-inclusive" packages for a less expensive entrance fee.

In terms of promotion, the company has a high budget to spend on advertisement; therefore Disney can use efficient media tools, such as television, high-quality magazines, newspapers, ads and posters at popular locations (like buses, advertising columns and travel agencies), and they put a lot of emphasis on the quality of their advertising material. Furthermore the company wants to stay in touch with the communities that it operates in (e.g., by sponsoring competitions).

The places of the Disney theme parks are located in Anaheim (California, USA), Orlando (Florida, USA), Tokyo (Japan) and Paris (France). Disney puts a lot of emphasis on easy accessibility to the theme parks. All theme parks can be reached by public transportation, private shuttles, or taxis. The Disney parks have their own highway exits that lead the guest coming by car straight to the Disney-owned parking area. On the Disney property there is a company-owned transportation system, which is free of charge, that brings hotel and resort guests to any location within the Disney property.

FINANCIAL POSITION AND DEVELOPMENT

As can be concluded from the financial statements of Disney, the theme park and resort business counted for USD 1,446 million of operating income in the year 1999. This is about 45% of the total operating income of the company and therefore one of the company's most important sources of income. One reason for the company to be able to keep costs relatively low is the fact that the company has strict salary regulations. In the park in Florida, for instance, a low-educated full-time worker generally earns USD 7.35 per hour, which is the *minimum* wage required by the government. The fact that the company offers a high number of jobs that require no or hardly any education (such as maintenance or attraction host) also has the advantage that there is a low unemployment rate in the area around the theme parks.

DISNEY HONG KONG

Situated at the southeast tip of China, Hong Kong is ideally positioned at the Center of East Asia, one of the worlds most *dynamic* regions. With a land area of only 1.097 square kilometres, Hong Kong is one of the most densely populated places in the world. The population density was 6,330 people per square kilometres at the end of 1998. The annual growth rate in population over the past decade averaged 1.9%. Hong Kong has an industrious population of 6.7 million. A hardworking, flexible and well-educated workforce of 3 million, coupled with entrepreneurial flair, is the bedrock of Hong Kong's productivity and creativity.

Since 1850 Hong Kong has grown into a world-class financial trading and business center. It is the world's eighth largest economy and the ninth largest exporter of services. Hong Kong's economy is supported by a government policy of maximum support and minimum intervention. Its taxes are low and simple.

Hong Kong became a special Administrative Region of the People's Republic of China on July 1, 1997, after a century and a half of British administration. Under Hong Kong's constitutional document the Basic Law, the existing economic, legal and social systems will be maintained for at least 50 years after 1997.

There has been a shift in Hong Kong's economy from manufacturing toward services. The contribution of services to GDP increased from 68% in 1980 to 85% in 1999. Over the years, Hong

Kong has developed an efficient wholesale and retail network to cater for the growing consumption needs for a more affluent population. Financial and business services, including banking, insurance, real estate and a wide range of professional services have developed rapidly. Hong Kong's tax system is simple and relatively inexpensive to administrate. The tax rates are 15% maximum for salary tax, 6% profit tax for corporations, and 15% for unincorporated business.

The Mainland of China is Hong Kong's largest trading partner, accounting for 38% of Hong Kong overall trade value in January–June 1999. China has become the largest supplier and market for Hong Kong's imports, and domestic exports accounting for 43% of total imports and 30% of domestic exports in January–June 1999. Hong Kong is also a major service-center for the Mainland.

According to the Hong Kong Tourist Association, Hong Kong was the most popular tourist destination in Asia in 1998. The total tourism receipts in 1998 (in whole Asia) amounted to 7.1 billion and in the first half of 1999 amounted 3.2 billion. There were 9.57 million visitors arriving to Hong Kong in 1998, an 8% decrease over 1997. From January–end of August 1999 there were 6.9 million visitor arrivals, an 11% increase over the same period in 1998.

There is a contradiction between the official policy of the government and the people's opinion about the Western influence in the country. On the one hand the government is open for free trade with Western nations, including the USA. On the other hand, the influence of the Western society in their Asian country does not like to be seen. The population, however, is more likely to be open about the Western culture and tends to be enthusiastic about American products and the Western way of life.

MARKET DEFINITION

The experience of going to a theme park is non-durable (even though the company claims to offer durable memories). Disney's theme parks are specialty products, and people are willing to travel far and pay a lot of money to experience the "magic."

The potential market for a theme park like the Disney parks are people who are interested in spending time out in an amusement establishment, including all ages and income levels. The available market are the people with an interest in amusement parks who have a level of income that allows them to afford the premium prices Disney charges. This includes people living around the parks as well as people with an income high enough to afford the travel costs to the parks, and still includes people of all ages. The target groups are thus people of all ages, preferably families with children, with an at-least-average income level.

Disney expects visitors from all over the world: mainland of China 27%, Taiwan 19%, Japan 10%, South and Southeast Asia 12%, and the USA 8%. The majority of the expected visitors are families with children. And, as mentioned before, the income level of the expected visitors is at least average. The company has to consider different lifestyles when segmenting the market. There are numerous potential customers that do not like the idea of an "artificial perfect world."

INDUSTRY AND COMPETITION

The Disney park in Hong Kong may face different types of competitive pressures. First, since there is no Western-oriented amusement park in Hong Kong and around, there is no direct competitor for the Disney park in Hong Kong. Indirect competitors include many substitutes. There are many possibilities to spend free time. In Hong Kong there are a lot of museums, parks and restaurants. Besides, one could stay at home, visit friends or relatives, do sports, watch TV, play games, or relax.

There are also potential newcomers. But, a theme park requires high investment. Since the Disney parks are the most popular in the world, a company deciding to open another amusement park in the surrounding of Hong Kong will have a hard time (high entry barriers). However, famous park operators like the "Universal Studios" or "Busch Gardens" have enough financial power to enter the Asian market. At the present, Universal Studios is already talking with the Shanghai city government to establish another major theme park in the city to attract visitors from eastern China and the rest of the country.

Across the border in mainland China, there are also many smaller theme parks in Shenzhen and Guangdong Province, including Windows of the World, Happy Valley, Glorious China, and Country Villages. Knowing of Disney's opening in 2005, these theme parks are investing heavily to upgrade and update their products and services. China is promoting its own tourism industries by establishing and developing more and more tourism destinations to encourage spending on traveling and vacationing by the Chinese people. In addition, many other tourism destinations are not too far away, such as Macao, Thailand, Malaysia, and Singapore.

Naturally the park will depend on Asian suppliers of things like food and beverages and on the prices they are setting. However, brands like Coca Cola are international companies and have been operating with the Disney company for numerous years, and will not ask for a price that will surprise Disney. In the park, Disney will hardly sell any specialty goods, so that the company will not depend on a certain supplier. For the most part Disney will sell company-manufactured merchandise and therefore this will not be a threat.

Disney depends on the people visiting the park. As already experienced with the park opened in Paris, a lot of studies on the buying behavior of the visitors has to be conducted. For example, studies showed that European visitors tended to bring their own food to the parks and did not spend as much money on souvenirs as expected. In addition the Europeans were obviously not as excited about the park itself or more price sensitive as formerly considered, which resulted in a lot lower park attendance than estimated. The park was in high debt and almost had to be closed.

ENTRY AND GROWTH STRATEGIES

Disney would like to expand internationally by targeting new markets. Disney has to find an attractive and feasible market open to the Disney concept and culture. Disney chose to enter the Hong Kong market with a joint venture, although other possibilities exist to enter a foreign market. Disney wants control, good infrastructure, average risk, and knowledge of the local market. A high investment is not that important to Disney, because they are confident that they will be able to cover the costs with their operating income.

After opening the park Phase I (Disney theme park, a Disney-theme resort hotel complex, and a retail, dining and entertainment center) in 2005, the company will continue to develop their property and build new attractions, new resort hotels and other sorts of tourist destinations, depending on the success of the Disneyland in the first years.

Disney will mainly target families with at-least-average income and try to reach children. The company will also aim for the ''young and young at heart'' and appeal to adults' memories of their childhood.

Disney will continue to adopt the premium position for its Hong Kong theme park. There is no need in lowering the perceived quality. Disneyland Hong Kong is supposed to be ''the happiest place on earth,'' as are the already existing parks.

Kortec and Wrenware Architectural Hardware

It was the spring of 1991. Tim McDern was just getting in from his weekly tennis match. The match, a victory, had provided a short but much-needed break from the problem he was facing as Director of International Sales of Kortec and Wrenware Architectural Hardware.

Kortec and Wrenware Architectural Hardware were two separate and distinct companies in the architectural hardware business operating as a single division of a Fortune 100 company (The Lock Company) in central Connecticut. Each company operated separately, each with its own brand names, product lines, and distribution channels. Due to changes in the architectural hardware industry, it was no longer a perceived benefit, nor was it cost-effective, to support two separate brand names.

Reorganizations of sorts had already taken place to combine the separate support areas for the two brand names. Consideration was now focused on creating a new brand name for the two companies. McDern's assignment was to determine the alternate approaches The Lock Company could follow in trying to come up with a new brand name, with the positive and negative factors that should be considered with each approach (specifically, as they related to their international markets) when it came time to actually decide on a new brand name.

COMPANY BACKGROUND

Kortec and Wrenware Architectural Hardware both manufactured commercial locksets, exit devices, closers, and key systems. Each company was started independently in the mid-1800s as a diversified manufacturer of products that ranged from locks to furniture hardware to mailboxes. They were strong competitors with each other in the area of locks. Over time, both of their product lines phased out the furniture hardware and mailboxes and concentrated on commercial locks. The companies went on to expand their product lines to include exit devices and door closers.

As the companies continued to evolve separately, they developed their own unique product lines, distribution channels, and markets.

In the early 1900s, these two staunch competitors took a step that shocked the hardware industry. They decided to merge at the corporate level, but they continued to run their operations separately, with separate product lines, distribution channels, and markets.

This case was prepared as a basis for class discussion rather than to illustrate either effective or ineffective handling of an administrative situation.

In the 1930s and 1940s, the companies experienced some economic gains by using the same screws in the manufacture of the two separate and distinct locks sold by each of the divisions. This marked the first significant step to further economies of scale by the two companies.

In the 1950s and 1960s, the synergy continued. The companies began using the same components in the manufacture of their locksets, with the exception of the key systems. By this time, each company was producing very similar lockset designs, with the primary differences in the key systems used. They also continued to maintain separate brand names, distribution channels, geographic markets (international only), sales forces, and management.

In the late 1960s, a Fortune 500 company acquired both companies and began to operate them as a single division. At this time, the companies were brought under a single roof for the first time—an 800,000 square-foot facility. Because they now shared the same physical location, the companies were able to combine their manufacturing processes, engineering support, and new product development. However, they continued to maintain different brand names, sales organizations, distribution channels, and geographic markets.

In the late 1980s, the Fortune 500 corporation was acquired by a Fortune 100 corporation (The Lock Company). It was at this time that senior management decided to merge its sales and marketing organizations to support the two different brand names. Due to various considerations, which will be discussed in the next several sections, it was felt to be no longer cost-effective, nor were there any perceived benefits, to maintain separate sales and marketing organizations.

Product Description

The product lines of Kortec and Wrenware had evolved so that they were built with identical components except for the key system. The key system is the part of the lockset that is referred to as the *cylinder*. The key system is the major element of the product that keeps the two brands different. Once set up, the key system controls who has access through any particular lock in the system. This is an important concept for two reasons:

1. When an order is received, it is very important to get the precise specifications about the key systems needed (how many and on which doors each system will be installed). An example would be the security needs of a hospital. Each key system in the hospital must be individually set up to provide or restrict access to the locks in the system. In setting up a hospital's key

system, the purchaser (installer) of the system needs to know who should have access to what rooms. The hospital would not want the janitor's key to fit the narcotics room lock, yet the janitor must have access to a number of other rooms for maintenance. Thus, it is very important to identify up front precisely who needs access to what areas to avoid future re-works for the installer and unforseen breaches in security for the customer.

2. Because the key systems of Kortec and Wrenware are designed differently, purchasers must consider these differences carefully before choosing the company from which to purchase key systems. It is probable that, in the lifetime of a key system, additions or changes will be made to the system. Purchasers need assurances that they will be able to acquire locksets compatible with their existing key systems when they are needed.

Market

Kortec and Wrenware's products were primarily sold for new commercial construction and for the aftermarket (i.e., for replacement on buildings such as offices, schools, hospitals, and hotels). Both companies had sales in the U.S., Canada, and 65 countries overseas. Both companies had been selling overseas since the late 1800s and exerting a strong emphasis on international sales over the last 15–20 years. Each brand name had its regional strength. Kortec's strength was largely in North America and Asia, while Wrenware's strength was in Europe and the Middle East.

Distribution Channels

(Manufacturer, Distributor, End User).
Distribution of the products for both Kortec and Wrenware was primarily through small, privately owned family businesses, which would frequently act as subcontractors on new and after-market projects. Distribution through this channel was referred to as *one-step distribution* because the product went to one middleman before going to the end user. For the most part, these distributors supported either the Kortec or Wrenware name. Within a given city, there were as few as one or as many as three distributors.

(Manufacturer, Wholesaler, Distributor, End User).
Wholesalers were also used to some extent. This was referred to as *two-step distribution*. The wholesalers in the architectural hardware industry actually helped bring the two brand names closer together. The distributors and end users gradually become aware that the Kortec and Wrenware products were essentially the same. As a result, the end user would frequently go to a distributor and ask for either brand. For example, if an end user went to a Kortec distributor and asked for a Wrenware product, the distributor was forced to seek out a wholesaler to obtain the product because the distributor was forbidden by agreement with Kortec from going to Wrenware directly.

Distributors had historically been brand loyal, but this had been changing over time. New competition was offering new alternatives. In addition, senior management at The Lock Company no

longer saw any ''perceived benefit'' to having two unique brand names in the marketplace because the end users and people in the architectural hardware industry were aware of the product similarities and differences in the key systems. Experience was showing that distributors were able to get both products from wholesalers. It made sense to reduce the total number of distributors. Therefore, senior management reduced the number of distributors from approximately 900 in the 1970s to approximately 400 in the late 1980s (200 for Kortec and 200 for Wrenware).

Support for Distribution

Operating two separate sales and marketing organizations required The Lock Company to maintain two separate channels of support for their salespeople, literature (catalogues, price books, and technical manuals), promotions (they needed two separate booths at trade shows and any promotional items ordered had to be brand specific), and advertisements (the ads had to be brand specific). Maintaining two separate channels had become very expensive, especially in light of increased competition and the fact that the industry was becoming more and more aware of how similar Kortec and Wrenware products were to each other. The economic benefits of operating these areas separately no longer exceeded the economic costs. Senior managers at The Lock Company decided that the company would be in a better position by combining the monies spent on sales and marketing—they'd get more bang for their buck.

PERCEIVED STRENGTHS AND WEAKNESSES IN THE MARKET

The Lock Company perceived various strengths and weaknesses in Kortec's and Wrenware's positions in the architectural hardware market. This information would be relevant to any decision made regarding changing the individual brand names.

Strengths in the Market

Brand Awareness. Both Kortec's and Wrenware's names were easily recognized by the domestic commercial hardware industry, which consisted of the architects who drew the building designs as well as the end users. This was not the case in the international markets, where each company had a regional presence. In international markets, either the Kortec or Wrenware name was known, but not both.

Market Coverage. Both Kortec and Wrenware had domestic and international sales (North America, Canada, and 65 countries overseas).

Full Line Product Strength. Both companies carried a full assortment of products for commercial doors consisting of locksets, key systems, closers, and exit devices. Because of this, buyers were able to obtain everything they needed from either company (some competitors carried less than a full product line).

Breadth of Product Line.

Both Kortec's and Wrenware's product lines consisted of locksets, key systems, closers, and exit devices in a broad range of price and grade levels.

Regional Sales Office Presence in International Markets.

Between the two companies, the major markets of the world were covered. The international offices were responsible for their own sales and marketing efforts (i.e., they prepared their own brochures). Thus, they were able to "think globally, yet act locally." The international offices were also free to take what they could use from the home office and either use it "as is" or enhance the design to meet their own local needs. In addition, the brochures were designed with an international flavor (e.g., they were written in the local language and included such things as metric conversions).

Weaknesses

Reduction in Distribution Loyalty.

Kortec and Wrenware faced reduction in distributor loyalty due to increased competition. Hardware products were becoming more and more generic.

Reduced Visibility of Brand Names.

Economic constraints, combined with the need to split the advertising and promotion dollars to cover two separate brand names, tended to reduce the overall visibility of each brand.

Delivery and Quality of Products.

Delivery and quality of products, especially in the international markets, had taken a downturn within the past five years. As a result, competitors had picked up some of their markets. Kortec and Wrenware were in the process of addressing these issues through new manufacturing processes; however, the benefits would not be felt immediately.

Promotional and Technical Support Materials in Disrepair.

Both Kortec and Wrenware were in need of new promotional and technical support literature. However, due to the pending brand name decision, managers did not want to develop new materials. A complete product catalogue alone would cost each company $200,000 to develop, design, print, and deliver for worldwide distribution. Managers decided to live with the existing materials for the time being.

New '92 Sales Brochures Needed.

New brochures were needed for the upcoming year at a cost of approximately $80,000 for each company. Management was uncertain about whether or not to combine them.

Expertise in Distribution.

As stated earlier, it is very important for vendors selling key systems to get accurate key-system specifications with each order. In addition, there must be a thorough understanding of the *application of the products*. The purchasers/architects must be careful to comply with various fire codes, handicap codes, UL (Underwriters Laboratory) codes, as well as other laws.

Kortec's and Wrenware's distribution networks, now seen as a strength, could become a weakness due to the recent reduction in distributors around the world.

DECISIONS... DECISIONS...

Tim McDern settled back in his favorite recliner to ponder his assignment. He needed to develop the alternative approaches The Lock Company should consider when determining a new brand name. In addition, he needed to determine the various positive and negative factors that should be considered (specifically, those related to their international markets) when it came time to determine a new brand name.

McDern took a sip of his Gatorade and thought to himself: "In coming up with the various alternative approaches, there will be certain factors that may pertain to more than one alternative." He decided to call these "generic factors." He would list other factors under each alternative approach separately.

So, relying on his knowledge of Kortec's and Wrenware's backgrounds and their perceived strengths and weaknesses, McDern pulled out a notebook and began to write.

GENERIC FACTORS

McDern considered generic factors to be such basic factors as language differences, possibility of brand piracy, and local laws in the markets served by both companies that would affect the new brand name, no matter what approach was followed.

Language

Because Kortec and Wrenware had sales in 65 foreign countries, marketing would take place in a variety of foreign languages. A number of questions had to be answered before a brand name could be chosen. Would the brand name be easily *translatable* to the various languages? Could the brand name be easily *pronounced* in all of the languages? (For example, if *Wrenware* were chosen as the brand name, Asian customers would have difficulty pronouncing the name because of their trouble in pronouncing the 'R' and 'W' sounds of the English language. Could or would this have an effect on sales?) Would the brand name inadvertently insult a particular culture because of what that name might mean when translated to the language of that culture (or even standing on its own untranslated)? McDern realized the need to be sensitive to the various *cultures* in which Kortec and Wrenware operated.

In addition, two other factors that needed to be considered were the length of the name and the image that the name would project. The Lock Company would not want a name that was too long to print when preparing written materials in many different languages. The length might also affect customers' ability to remember the name, especially if a totally new brand name were chosen. Additionally, depending upon the name chosen, certain negative images might be implied in one or more of the various cultures in which the companies did business. An example would be a name that might imply a weak company or a shoddy product in any of the markets, depending upon how the brand name was translated or interpreted. Another example might be that the name chosen is acceptable, but very similar to the name of another company; in any of the markets that has a shoddy reputation. The Lock Company would not want its name inadvertently confused with or associated with the shoddy company or product.

Any one or more of these factors could adversely affect The Lock Company's market in the foreign countries.

Brand Piracy

In selecting a brand name, laws of the various countries regarding brand name piracy must be considered. There are three general forms of piracy:

1. *Imitation*—A company may copy your established brand name or logo.
2. *Faking*—A company may identify its product with a symbol or logo very similar to your established brand/logo.
3. *Pre-emption*—A company may register your brand name in its country before you and then possibly try to sell it back to you to make money.

Between them, Kortec and Wrenware were already established in 65 foreign countries and did not have any piracy problems with their current names.

Local Laws

The names currently used in foreign countries complied with the laws of those countries, but The Lock Company needed to consider the various laws and procedures to register its new brand name when the time came. In addition, The Lock Company needed to be cognizant of the fact that, if it were to choose a new brand name, it would need to ensure that the new name did not infringe upon any other companies already doing business in any of the foreign markets under that name.

Once McDern had finished listing his generic factors, he turned his attention to some alternatives The Lock Company should consider before determining a new brand name. He listed these, with various international factors, both positive and negative, that should also be considered before choosing the brand name.

ALTERNATIVE 1—LITERALLY DO NOTHING

The Lock Company could literally do nothing and continue to do business under the two separate company names. McDern listed this alternative, although he knew it would not be considered. The Lock Company had already made the decision to combine the various parts of the company operations and look for a new brand name. As stated before, there were no more economies of scale operating under separate names.

Still, it was an alternative in the event that no new brand name could be agreed upon. A positive factor in this case was the fact that the Kortec and Wrenware names were already established overseas; on the negative side, The Lock Company would need to maintain two separate sets of support materials (determined as not cost-effective).

ALTERNATIVE 2—KEEP SAME NAMES BUT DIFFERENTIATE THE PRODUCTS

McDern felt that under this alternative The Lock Company could continue to operate the companies under the same two separate names but somehow differentiate the products. By differentiating the products, The Lock Company might substantiate the costs that would be necessary to support two brand names.

The differentiation between the names could come by way of *product quality*. For example, Kortec might be marketed as a high-quality, high-cost product while Wrenware could be the lesser-quality, lower-cost product.

An alternative differentiation could come by way of *product market*. For example, Kortec might be targeted toward the hotel and hospital market, whereas Wrenware would be targeted toward the school and prison market.

A third alternative differentiation could be by *geographic market*. For example, Kortec might be targeted at North America and Asia, whereas Wrenware might be targeted at Europe and the Middle East. Their current regional strengths were already located in these markets.

Several positive and negative factors must be considered in differentiating the products.

Product Quality

Negative. The two companies were in predominantly separate market concentrations overseas. For example, it could potentially cost The Lock Company a great deal of money to introduce the Wrenware name to the Asian market, where it is currently not readily recognized.

Negative. The existing distributors of the Wrenware product might become upset if their product began to be marketed as one of lesser quality. This could affect future sales, as well as relationships with existing customers, to whom distributors had previously marketed Wrenware as a high-quality product. Thus, relationships with distributors, as well as existing and future customers, could be affected.

Negative. The overlap in the markets might create confusion, both on the part of purchasers and those providing the support and necessary technical expertise.

Positive. Differentiating by product quality, if successful, would substantiate the need to continue to support two brand names. It might also help expand the market share of both lines. The Lock Company may be able to pick up some of their competitors' market share by marketing both a high-quality product and one of lesser quality.

Product Market

Positive. Again, if successful, keeping the same names but differentiating the products might cause The Lock Company to focus on more specific types of markets.

Negative. Again, this might have a negative impact on distributors and existing customers. Distributors with contacts in a particular industry (e.g., schools) might suddenly find their product targeted toward hotels, which could affect their sales. Existing customers might also be confused. For example, if school customers needed additional locks that had originally been bought from Kortec, they would be confused to find that Wrenware was now being targeted toward their school—especially since the key systems from the two companies originally were not compatible. McDern made a note that, if this option were to be pursued, The Lock Company would need to be careful how it introduced and promoted the change.

Geographic Market

Positive. The products were already primarily established and concentrated in different geographic markets. The Lock Company would not need to worry about introducing a new brand name. In a sense, the brand name may already be widely recognized in the geographic markets, or it may be the leading seller—no need, then, to interrupt this process.

Negative. This, in a sense, was The Lock Company's current situation, which it hoped to change.

Product Quality and Market

Negative. The architects in the foreign countries were not as familiar with the similarities between the existing brands. This could have an adverse effect on their recommendations if the companies suddenly began to be targeted toward different markets. The architects might be confused or unfamiliar with the specifications of the alternative brand name.

ALTERNATIVE 3—COMBINE THE EXISTING NAMES

Under this alternative, the two company names could be combined in a form such as "Kortec & Wrenware Architectural Hardware."

Positive. This would enable The Lock Company to keep both names. Architects and end users would then not be totally confused by the change. They would still see a name they recognized.

Positive. It would result in fewer costs than having to introduce a "new" or "different" brand name to the markets served.

Negative. The name of the company would become very long. This is important when preparing written literature (catalogues, brochures, advertising—too long is *not good*). For example, the name is put in every "environment" possible, such as letterheads, business cards, and trade show booths, for instance. A longer name would make it more costly and difficult to prepare these materials. A longer name would also be harder for customers to remember.

Negative. Confusion might be created in existing markets. For example, in Hong Kong the name Wrenware means nothing because the product is currently not distributed there.

Major Negative. In those countries where both products were offered, and given the fact that (a) the distribution channels were recently reduced to approximately 200 for each brand name and (b) most distributors were selling either one or the other brand name, The Lock Company is now conceivably going to ask distributors to sell a product that they had considered to be a competitive brand name. These distributors, for example, may have promoted Kortec while criticizing Wrenware because they carried only the Kortec product. The previous separate sales forces selling to the distributors had also promoted in this manner. Now they will be asked to sell a product that includes a name they may have previously "bad-mouthed." This could have an adverse effect on the distributors' existing relationships with their customers.

Negative. The existing names may have meant something special to the architects. The Lock Company wouldn't want to lose their association with the existing brand name.

ALTERNATIVE 4—USE EITHER ONE NAME OR THE OTHER

Positive. Consideration should be given to language, culture, and local brand name laws, as previously discussed. In light of these considerations, The Lock Company would want to choose the name that gave off the stronger image (e.g., Kortec sounds like a stronger company) or be more easily pronounced, (e.g., Kortec may be more easily pronounced, depending on the culture).

Positive. A distribution system is already established in those countries served by the company that would lose its name. Additional work in the form of well-prepared advertising, support, and promotional materials could help overcome the recognition problem faster than if The Lock Company attempted to go in without an established distribution channel and support materials.

Negative. Using one name only, The Lock Company runs the risk of loss of name recognition in the countries served by the company that would lose its name. Additional costs of introduction and promotion would also result. There is a risk of losing sales in these areas, at least until name recognition for the new name is established.

ALTERNATIVE 5—NEW NAME

Alternative 5 would involve coming out with an entirely new brand name.

Positive.   The opportunity would exist here for a clever, descriptive brand name and/or trademark or logo. The name chosen might enable The Lock Company to tie the brand name more closely to the product it is offering.

Positive.   A new name would enable The Lock Company to update its technical manuals, etc., that were in a state of disrepair. In addition, it would offer The Lock Company the opportunity to develop new and better materials.

Positive.   The Lock Company could also continue to sub-label whatever brand name was chosen with ''A Fortune 100 Company: The Lock Company,'' to help maintain the customers' identification with its products. This might help alleviate some anxieties arising from a brand name change.

Positive.   Given that various cultural factors are taken into consideration in arriving at a new name, it will be very important how The Lock Company then uses and effectively markets that name in the future. For example, ''Coke'' doesn't mean anything by itself as a word, but it has been so effectively marketed that it has become synonymous with the soft drink.

Negative.   A new name would require The Lock Company to scrap its existing support materials that contained the old name and develop new materials. This would be more expensive up front. Using any one of the other alternatives would have enabled the company to use its existing materials for a while longer.

Negative.   Finding a new name would most likely require hiring an expert consultant. The consultant would be responsible for determining if the name was already being used, whether it infringed upon existing trademarks or logos, and the impact the new name would have in existing foreign markets with respect to language, culture, and existing local laws, etc.

McDern looked up at the clock as it struck 1 A.M. Before he retired for the night, he reflected on what he had been doing.

In preparing the alternative courses of action that The Lock Company would consider when determining a new brand name for its international markets, he found there was much more to renaming a company than simply coming up with a new name and figuring the associated costs. For instance, the language, culture, and laws of each foreign market had to be considered. Nor could established relationships with distributors and customers be neglected. All in all, there were many associated issues to consider, not just a name change. Arriving at a new brand name would require expert consultants, brand awareness studies (both nationally and internationally), studies on the distribution networks used by both Kortec and Wrenware, and a significant amount of related analysis. The Lock Company would need hard facts to back up any decision it would make.

This was not a short-term but a long-term decision that would affect the long-term positioning of the company. Key strategic decisions would need to be made in order to position The Lock Company to capture a worldwide market share. These decisions should only be made after considering the various international implications and factors.

CASE 17
Capital Insurance Company's Foray into Financial Services

In March of 1997, Albert Posner had just taken over as President and CEO of Capital Insurance Company[1]. His predecessor, Learned Cordoza, had recently retired after successfully running Capital Insurance for 16 years. Cordoza, 71, had taken over Capital Insurance in 1980, and had increased sales revenues over 1000% over his tenure. Cordoza had led the company from having assets under management from $1.0 billion at the beginning of his tenure to $18.4 billion during the year of his retirement. Capital had become the number-one underwriter of commercial insurance, number two in homeowner's insurance, and was rapidly advancing to the top spots in auto insurance and maritime insurance. Cordoza had expanded Capital into the annuities markets, the bond markets, and developed several alternative insurance products, all of which have been fairly successful. At his retirement ceremony, attended by nearly 90% of Capital's 8,000 employees, Cordoza retired by challenging his protege, Posner, to turn Capital Insurance Company into a leading provider of financial services and increase assets under management to the $100 billion mark by 2010. At the ceremony, Posner heartily accepted the challenge.

Now, one week after his succession, Posner contemplated the challenge before him: how to turn a very successful insurance company into a multifaceted financial services firm. Posner's analytic mind began to think of the problem in terms of what relevant resources Capital had now, and what resources and strategies would be needed to enter into the financial services markets. Capital had a very strong brand name, known throughout the United States, but almost unheard of internationally. Capital's reputation was built on a solid foundation of integrity, financial stability, conservatism, and leadership in the insurance industry. Capital's cash reserves, retained earnings, and gain on investments had produced enough capital to declare an annual raise in dividends from $0.50 to $0.80, and still comfortably enter into the bonds and annuities markets several years ago. Capital's financial position had only increased since then. Capital had a solid corporate structure, although somewhat rigid in its underwriting and new product development divisions. Capital had retained several key marketing leaders in the late 1980s who have since built a marketing department known throughout corporate America. Capital had the brand name, reputation, capital reserves and marketing department to enter into almost any market of its choosing - if properly planned, directed and controlled.

[1]Capital Insurance Company is a fictitious corporation made up solely for the this case.

PLANNING

Posner set up weekly meetings with the heads of Capital's product development division, IT department, accounting and finance departments, and requested that they consider what it would take to create, integrate, and successfully manage a multifaceted financial services firm. Posner then recruited several top Vice Presidents of Merrill Lynch, Goldman Sachs, and DLJ Direct to work hand in hand with the V.P.s of the various divisions to develop a plan of setting up the infrastructure necessary to maintain the new business unit. Posner directed the various departments to meet on a weekly basis and present a projected budget and timeline to put the infrastructure in place. Posner then gave the helm to Capital's strategic business manager, David Hamilton, a former officer of McKinsey & Co. Posner's only guideline to Hamilton was to keep intact and fully functional, all of Capital's core values (integrity, professionalism, and conservatism), core competencies (insurance underwriting, risk management, and claims handling), and emerging businesses (annuities, bonds and alternative risk mechanisms).

Hamilton immediately began the strategic formulation of Capitals new foray into the financial services market. Hamilton put the following questions to the team leaders of his marketing department: *What is our primary mission? What are our goals? What should our objectives be? What are our strengths, weaknesses, opportunities, and threats (SWOT)? Should we purchase an existing financial services firm? What specific financial markets should we enter first? What strategic alliances will we need? How will marketing, technology, new product development, and sourcing strategies and teams work together? How will Capital implement the financial services business unit? What will the measures, controls and accountability procedures be?* Over the next several months, the preliminary answers to these questions began to come together.

S.W.O.T

S. W. O. T. Posner and Hamilton defined the core strengths and weaknesses of Capital Insurance Company, and charged the department heads to further define its strengths and weaknesses. The market analysis team defined the primary opportunities and threats of the market. The following are the conclusions of the team:

Mission

What is our primary mission? Several options had been debated, researched, re-debated and finally selected. The V.P. of marketing

S.W.O.T.		
Marketing		
1. Company Reputation	Major Strength	Very High Importance
2. "Capital" Brand Name	Major Strength	Very High Importance
3. Customer Satisfaction	Major Strength	Very High Importance
4. Exist Customer Base Potential	Major Strength	Very High Importance
5. Customer Service	Major Strength	Very High Importance
6. Pricing Effectiveness	Minor Strength	High Importance
7. Promotion Effectiveness	Minor Strength	High Importance
8. Geographic Coverage	Major Strength	Medium Importance
9. Marketing Staff / Leaders	Major Strength	Very High Importance
Finance		
1. Financial Stability	Major Strength	Very High Importance
2. Cash Flow	Major Strength	Medium Importance
3. Cost of Capital	Minor Strength	Low Importance
Products and Distribution		
1. Product Availability	Major Weakness	Very High Importance
2. Infrastructure	Neutral	Very High Importance
3. Capacity	Major Strength	Very High Importance
4. IT Requirements	Neutral	Very High Importance
5. Strategic Alliances	Neutral	High Importance
6. Technical Staffing	Minor Weakness	Very High Importance
7. Existing Distribution Channels	Minor Strength	High Importance
Organization		
1. Senior Leadership Ability	Major Strength	Very High Importance
2. Corporate Structure	Minor Strength	High Importance
3. Corporate Culture	Minor Strength	Medium Importance
4. Existing Workforce	Major Strength	Medium Importance
5. Potential Workforce CASH	Neutral	Very High Importance
Opportunities		
1. Institutional Investors	Neutral	Very High Importance
2. High Net-Worth Individuals	Neutral	Very High Importance
3. Small Corporate Investors	Minor Strength	Medium Importance
4. Small Individual Investors	Minor Strength	Low Importance
5. Discount Investors	Minor Weakness	Low Importance
6. International Markets	Major Weakness	High Importance
Threats		
1. Major Brokerage Firms	Major Weakness	Very High Importance
2. High Capital Barrier to Entry	Major Strength	Medium Importance
3. Discount Brokerage Firms	Neutral	Low Importance
4. Internet Technology	Minor Strength	High Importance
5. Risk Analysis[2]	Major Weakness	Very High Importance

proposed that "The Mission of Capital's Insurance is to provide a full-service brokerage firm with products for institutional investors, individual investors, and international investors, all within the core values of the company, integrity, wisdom, and conservatism." After several consultations with the market segment team, the V.P. of product development proposed that "The Mission of the company was to become a financial services leader among institutional investors and high net worth individuals for the U.S. NYSE and Nasdaq stock and bond markets." Hamilton definitely liked the ambition of the marketing V.P.'s prospect of capturing all aspects

---

[2]Posner and Hamilton both realized the enormity of the undertaking of entering into the financial services market. The initial investment costs, in IT infrastructure, sourcing and staffing, marketing. advertising, research, customer service, and product development and delivery, would be in the range of S250 million to $400 million over the next three years. Given the financial stake involved, the risk of a failed venture would be nearly catastrophic.

of the markets under the reputation of Capital Insurance, but wanted to ensure that the mission was realistic. The market segment team had researched the various financial market segments, polled the newly hired V.P.s from the financial firms, and polled Capital's existing policyholders for input. Succinctly, the market segment team stated that the average individual investor would not be a profitable endeavor because of the high transaction costs associated with minimal dollar transactions. Also, the international markets, while highly lucrative in times, posed a great financial risk as the economics, politics, laws, currency exchanges, and tax structures of foreign countries fluctuated dramatically, and without the solid foreign relationships built over time, the company would assume a great risk in entering this market without a solid U.S. foundation. Hamilton was persuaded. The Mission of the company is to become a financial services leader among institutional investors and high net worth individuals.

Growth Paths

Should Capital purchase an existing, financial services company? Posner and Hamilton had discussed this option at length and put together a financial and market analysis team to report their findings, and to compare the relative costs with the costs of starting the new venture from scratch. The group of analysts reported that the larger financial services firms, such as Merrill Lynch, Morgan Stanley Dean Whitter, and Goldman Sachs, would be too expensive to purchase and too costly to integrate into Capital Insurance. The analysts surveyed several smaller full-service brokers including Fortis Financial Group, Fleet Financial Services Group, or Presidential Financial. All three of these firms were less than 20 years old, had a solid track record of increasing assets under management, and all operated at a 10% earnings increase per year over the past 7 years. Each of the three firms could be acquired at a cost of less that $150 million. The marketing analyst stated that Fortis Financial was the most aggressive in pursuing institutional investors, and had recently gained the business of several major businesses, including Anderson Consulting, Citigroup, and Mass Mutual. Fortis had a solid IT framework, and had a policy of recruiting and retaining top talent. It was Fortis' goal to become a major player in the institutional investor market. Fortis had also recently entered into the international market, and had had a banner first year in its South American and Western Europe operations. Fleet Financial Services Group was an affiliate of Fleet Bank, and was the least profitable of the three. Fleet existed for the convenience of Fleet Bank's largest net worth clients (individuals and institutions). Unfortunately, most of Fleet's business came from its smaller banking clients, as the larger clients preferred to use established financial services firms. Fleet Financial would also require a higher cost to acquire because of its affiliation with Fleet Bank. Presidential seemed an almost perfect fit, with established institutional clients, a sound network and infrastructure, a solid record of increasing assets under management, and a strong management team. The downside to Presidential was that it was being targeted by several other financial services firms as a

potential takeover, and a bidding war would result in a very high cost to Capital Insurance. The financial and marketing analysts agreed that the purchase of an existing financial services company made the most sense because of the existing infrastructure, client base, and strategic alliances in place. Posner and Hamilton agreed that Capital should acquire a financial services group. Further, given the information presented by the analysts, Fortis made the most sense because of the recently gained institutional investors.

Goals

What are the company's primary goals? There was a near consensus that the company's first and foremost primary goal is to gain the highest amount of market share in the institutional and high net-worth NYSE and Nasdaq markets. Capital's second goal was to gain a strong reputation for value and integrity while charging a median premium between the highest cost financial services firm. The company's mission was not to cater to individual investors or bargain hunter companies. Also, the company did not want to charge a premium higher than the top financial services firms, because that would not be in line with firm's first and foremost goal of obtaining market share. Hamilton charged the market positioning group to develop a marketing and pricing strategy that would allow the company to gain as high a market share of clients as possible in the first year, increase prices and increase its market share by 5–7% its second year, and increase prices to a premium rate during the third year, while increasing market share by 3–5% each year thereafter. The market positioning group was to report back to Hamilton with a revised and obtainable marketing and pricing strategy by the end of the quarter. The Company's third goal was to operate at a profit by the end of the 4th quarter of the second year of operations. The fourth goal was to have a positive return on investment by year-end 2004.

MARKET RESEARCH AND FORECASTING

Hamilton's market research team had made huge in-roads in their research. First, the group had hired Boston Consulting group to work with them in ascertaining the financial markets that presented the best opportunity to enter into. The team spent a great deal of time and focus on distinguishing between the institutional investor and high net worth individual markets, and the increasing discount broker market. The barriers to entry to the discount broker market were very small. The main consideration in this market was the lowest cost producer. Small discount brokerages could be acquired at a very low cost, and by being the low-cost producer, Capital could acquire a large market share in a very short time. The team found that no institutional investors and very few high net worth individuals used discount brokerages. Further, the team found that discount brokerages competed on very small profit margins, and clients were likely to defect based on price only: there was very little brand loyalty for consumers in the discount brokerage market. This market segment was becoming saturated with start-up brokers on a weekly basis, and profit margins were becoming increasing smaller. Because of Capital's stated goal of obtaining market share, the discount broker market was a very attractive option. Ultimately, Posner and Hamilton decided that it could not leverage its brand name, reputation, and customer service in the discount broker market. This market segment was rejected.

Next, the research team turned to the international stock markets and currency exchange market. The international stock markets were experiencing unprecedented highs in South America, Japan, and Western Europe. Established firms were reaping 40% annual Returns on Investments in these markets. These same firms were also experiencing losses of 75–80% on their investments in Russia, India, and the Mid-East. Oil commodities were run by cartels and were especially sensitive to political strife internally and internationally. Over an extended *period of* time from 1970 forward, the international markets were an extremely volatile investment. Further, except for the reinsurance market, Capital Insurance did not enjoy the brand loyalty and name recognition that it did in the United States. Posner and Hamilton agreed that the international market was not in line with Capital's conservative nature and its ability to leverage its national name brand recognition.

The team then compared the institutional investor and high net-worth investor markets, in both the commodities market and the stock and bond markets. The team found that the commodities and derivatives market was dominated by a very few investment firms, and that several major companies had experienced catastrophic losses due to the high risk involved in derivative investments and hedging.

The NYSE and Nasdaq stock and bond markets provided the greatest sense of balance between risk and reward. Capital Insurance could leverage its name brand among the institutional and high net-worth investors. The market was a fiercely competitive market, but the majority of the market share was divided among seven major firms. Demand for secure, reputable, and financially stable firms had increased at a steady clip of 15–20% per year from 1992 to 1997. The barriers to entry were extremely high, as only very large firms could enter into this market. Institutional investors, banks, and various government entities required financial services firms to have at least $10 billion of assets under management and cash reserves remaining above $50 million at any given time. Further, profit margins were consistent among the larger firms as the firms would not engage in a price war to the detriment of all. Capital chose this market as the natural choice for its market entry.

The team identified the Midwest and Southwest markets as having the most potential to gain market share without serious competitive opposition. New York City and Los Angeles were by far the prime sites for the clients that Capital sought, but the pushback from the competition would be intense. The team recommended the Midwest and Southwest markets based on the growing affluent populations in Chicago, Phoenix, Dallas, and Minneapolis. The team provided the following forecast to Posner and Hamilton:

Market	Investment	Market Share	Market Share Growth
Chicago	$10,000,000	15%	5% per annum
Phoenix	$25,000,000	7%	12% per annum
Dallas	$15,000,000	12%	10% per annum
Minneapolis	$7,000,000	15%	12% per annum

This forecast was the estimated investment into strategically located central offices, initial staffing and training, advertising budgets, and 20% of required operating costs per year. The team also worked out the following Return on Investment estimates:

Market	Investment	ROI	Time to Positive ROI
Chicago	$10,000,000	20%	2 years
Phoenix	$25,000,000	25%	1.5 years
Dallas	$15,000,000	15%	2.5 years
Minneapolis	$7,000,000	10%	3 years

Posner and Hamilton accepted the team's recommendation to invest in the Midwest and Southwest markets.

Marketing Strategy

Products. Hamilton designated a products team to research the current market for the financial instruments that institutional investors demanded. The products team investigation researched all holdings of the twenty largest institutional investors and found that in New York and Los Angeles, government bonds, growth mutual funds, AAA rated corporate bonds, and technology-heavy mutual funds represented 95% of current holdings. In the geographic locations that Capital was interested, the products team found that institutional investors invested primarily in a mix of government and AAA rated corporate bonds (35–40%), technology mutual funds (25%). commodities[3] (15%), growth mutual funds (15%), and alternative investment vehicles[4] (10%). The products team recommended that Capital offer all of Fortis' existing investments, and begins the research necessary to roll out new "Capital" mutual funds, and other investment vehicles in the near future. The products team further recommended that Capital divest Fortis' international business unit and invest in new product development for the securities market.

Price. The marketing team designated to research pricing provided the following analysis. Prices consisted of commissions, fees and other transaction costs associated with very large trades

---

[3]Although not a stated market that Capital would pursue, because the significant percentage of investment into the Chicago Board of Options Exchange (commodities) come from Chicago and Dallas.

[4]The products team defined Alternative Investment Vehicles as vertical settlements. Offshore captive insurance mechanisms, collateralized asset hacked obligations, and bundled international currency options. The products team did not recommend to Capital that it enter into these specialized markets because of the complexity and risk of these in investment.

and positions taken by institutional investors and high net worth individuals. The major financial services firms set the profit margins from commissions at 2% (+1- 0.25%). Transaction costs made up an additional 0.25%, the cost of which averaged 0.20%. The higher fees and commissions were gained from the financial vehicles actually created by the financial services firms, such as mutual funds and bond packages. The marketing team recommended that Capital stay within the existing market pricing framework, and be the low-cost producer by a very small fraction (1:0.01%) for the first 6 to 8 quarters. The marketing team recommended that Capital invest heavily in new product development and roll out "Capital" mutual funds to obtain the premium fees that the existing firms enjoy. Further, Fortis mutual funds and other financial vehicles were priced well below those of the major financial services firms. The marketing team recommended that Capital slowly integrate these mutual funds into "Capital" products and systematically raise fees in these existing products.

Promotion Avenues.

The promotions and advertising team was charged with constructing the most effective promotion and advertising avenues for the clients Capital was to pursue and to create a realistic budget for these avenues. The team found that institutional investors were the most heavily influenced by high level meetings with the financial teams of financial services firms; further, that institutional investors preferred to be hand-held through large investments project by project, until a cemented relationship was formed. The team recommended that Capital recruit and retain the securities industries top experienced talent to persuade the institutional investors to invest in the Capital reputation and products. The team cautioned that institutional investors primarily retained firms that demonstrated consistent, conservative earnings on their investments. The team researched the cost of the top talent in the leading firms, and estimated that Capital should reserve $20,000,000 to recruit and retain the talent necessary to acquire the institutional investor's business.

Promotion Avenues.

The high net-worth individual market was promoted differently in the securities market. This market was promoted through word of mouth in highly affluent circles, which thrived on advertisement and results. This market could further be segmented by each of the major geographical areas in which Capital chose to pursue. Television, promotional events at country clubs, exclusive vacation resorts, specialized magazines and journals, and political fund-raisers were the most effective promotional avenues for high net worth investors. The team estimated that the annual cost to recruit high net worth individuals would approximate $50,000,000 per year for the first two years, and $20,000,000 for the next two to three years. This recommendation, as well as the institutional investor recommendation, was based on the market share goal given by Hamilton.

Distribution.

The distribution of financial services is largely executed electronically through a complex IT infrastructure. Fortis already had an existing framework for distributing financial products to all major locations. Capital also had an electronic infrastructure in place for insurance vehicles. The distribution problem was the integration of the two companies and possibly of the two distribution networks. The IT department estimated that it would take 2 to 3 years to fully integrate the systems or to roll out a new IT infrastructure capable of distributing both insurance and financial products. The estimated cost of integration: $100 million. The estimated cost of a new IT infrastructure: $175 million. Hamilton directed the IT department to continue to research these estimates and requirements.

CONCLUSION

Posner reflected over the past six months of work that had gone into developing a vision and strategy for Capital Insurance Company's future. Was it really possible to turn Capital Insurance into a premier financial services institution? Was the risk really worth the costs? At the last annual shareholders meeting, Posner presented the proposal to the shareholders and put broad strokes of the plan into the annual report. Within the next three months, Capital would hold a special shareholder's vote on the proposal. Statistical sampling of the shareholders demonstrated that an 80% majority favored the proposal. Capital had carefully chosen its market, set its mission and realistic goals, and retained the leaders necessary to accomplish Capital's goal. Posner was truly following in the footsteps of his predecessor, Cardoza.

CASE 18
Reinventing the Saturn Brand

*T*he 2004 year ended for the Saturn division of General Motors (GM) with sales down again for the third straight year, and it had been more than a decade since it had reached a sales record. In 2004 Saturn was faced with many challenges, one of which was the need to retire its L model sedan after customers rejected it for its stronger competitors, Toyota Camry and Honda Accord. Another unplanned expense and effort was the vast overhauling of their new ION models. The ION Coupe and Sedan had only been released a year earlier; however, the quality of these car was so poor that Saturn was forced to make 600 changes for the second year release. Saturn's unique relationship with labor was severely damaged because of a decline in sales. In order to prevent the immediate closing of the plant, the workers were forced to change their union contract. They agreed to the standard United Auto Workers contract and to giving up the "pull together" contract with its no time clocks, no layoffs, and teamwork. This was end of the cooperative venture between workers and management at Saturn.

Looking ahead to 2005, the company will offer some new models; however, these models will also be available from Chevrolet, Pontiac and Buick. Imitating or offering another company's models will result in Saturn losing its uniqueness; an example of this loss is that their cars will no longer have high polymer dent resistant doors, and this had been one of the company's most prominent trademarks. GM has made even more significant changes to Saturn's management structure by moving its management into GM's. It would have been hard to predict that this could have happened to company whose original motto was:

> "A different kind of car.
> A different kind of company."

Saturn's original strategy had been to distance itself from GM. Now the company has been all but disbanded, has merged into GM's management, and its cars are simply ones using old GM lines posing under new names.

The company had been dealing with some difficult times, but despite this, it still enjoyed some success. For example, the Saturn dealerships were still ranked very high for providing great customer service. The success of the dealerships actually might have been the main reason that GM did not end Saturn the brand, due to high costs associated with buying the dealers out.

THE HISTORY OF SATURN

Saturn started in the 1970's when GM had produced some of the most pitiful performers in the small car field. At the same time the first oil crisis began, this drove up demand for small cars, but GM and the other domestic suppliers were unable to meet this demand because of the pool quality their products. This caused GM's share of the car market to plummet from a high of 46% to a low of 32%, with most of the loss going to foreign competitors. By 1981, GM was experiencing financial losses, a prolonged recession, and was forced to lay off nearly 170,000 workers.

GM understood that it needed to do something quickly to protect itself from foreign competitors, and it started working on building a small car. GM started a project called "Saturn Project" to determine if it had the technology to build a small car, in the United States, that could compete with the foreign imports. The approach it would use was the "clean slate" approach, which would not be bound by "traditional thinking and industry practices." GM was not looking to reinvent the wheel but instead was looking to find new approaches and solutions that it could apply to the building of a car. Its goal was to apply world-class quality, in a cost competitive manner, using an American workforce to build a car that could compete with the foreign automakers.

One of the most historically restrictive parts of the auto industry was its relationship between management and the unions. Both sides were constantly at odds, which created a highly restrictive environment and contracts that were hundred of pages long. This new approach was an opportunity to try a fresh start on both sides; an alliance was formed that brought together a mixed group of 99 GM members of managements and United Automobile Workers of America (UAW). This group contained the knowledge of 55 General Motors Plants and UAW locals. This group was formed to "to identify and recommend the best approaches to integrate people and technology to competitively manufacture a small car in the United States."

The Group of 99 was further split into its areas of expertise: stamping, metal fabrication, power train, hardware, and so on. In the following two months, the teams visited 49 different GM plants and 60 other companies, traveled 2 million miles and put in 50,000 hours. They found many commonalities between the successful companies.

- Quality is a top priority to maintain customer satisfaction.
- The customer is number one, whether your customer is from the parts department (the internal customer) or a driver buying your product at a Saturn Dealership (the external customer).
- Ownership by all. Everyone is responsible.
- Equality is practiced not just preached.
- Barriers to doing a good job must be eliminated.
- Total trust is a must.
- People are the most important asset.
- Union and management are partners and share in the responsibility for assuring success of the enterprise.
- People are given the responsibility and authority to do the job.

In addition to these common threads, several observations were made:

- People will work together toward a common goal under the right atmosphere of mutual trust and respect.
- People can achieve their common goal in a wide variety of cultures.
- People will make personal sacrifices to achieve common goals if they believe their input is important and will be used.

Afterwards, The Group of 99 gave two recommendations to GM's management and the UAW. The first one was to apply a conflict resolution process that they had developed, where central to the process was consensus. All stakeholders must participate in the decision process, and each is given all relevant information in order to reach a conclusion. Each participant must be willing to "buy in" at least at 70% and, combined with a consensus, then demonstrate 100% commitment in implementing that conclusion. Second, group came to the conclusion that GM had the required technology and resources necessary to be more competitive if both were properly integrated. This would require an environment in which partnership on all levels was demanded. Finally, a separate bargaining memorandum of agreement was reached including the aforementioned items.

This created an environment at Saturn in which the unions and management worked hand in hand. This togetherness was apparent at the highest level; the executive suite was shared by the president of Saturn and the U.A.W. coordinator. The two would often travel together and conduct much of the company's business in each other's presence. This practice flowed down to the manufacturing floor, where assembly-line workers had more power than any other factory workers in the United States. They were given wide discretion on deciding how to run their areas. A couple of examples of this freedom are that they were allowed to interview and approve new hires for their teams, and they were given budget responsibility to purchase equipment and supplies. Workers also had the ability to stop the assembly line if they saw a problem.

This new style of operating worked well because of the change in labor agreements. These changes consisted of no job defining shop rules and very flexible guidelines. Instead of working for hourly pay like most auto workers, Saturn's workers earned a salary, 20% of which was at risk. The risk was based on car quality, worker productivity and company profits. Conversely, if workers exceeded these targets they were eligible for a bonus. By implementing this compensation strategy, Saturn was able to recruit and screen members from 38 states. By accepting positions at Saturn, employees gave up their rights to return to any of GM's other plants. The result was a workforce that was much younger. And more entrepreneurial than that of the entire company.

GM knew that simply combining the best people with the best tools did not guarantee the building of a sound product. It decided that it was important to give them the best training possible. Instead of just training its employees on the specific tasks that they would be performing, the company would provide them

a broad training that took anywhere from 250 to 750 hours. This approach to training was modeled on the university style of teaching. Just as a college student who wants to become an engineer takes calculus and physics, he or she must take English, philosophy, history, and other classes. The desired result of this broad based education is to have a student who is well rounded. Saturn's desired result from its "Saturn University" graduates was to have a company full of well-rounded employees; it achieved this by using a clean slate approach. The first topics covered were not specific to the auto industry but ones that could be applied generally. These were Awareness, Conflict Management, Consensus-decision making, Team Dynamics and so on. The goal was to teach the workers to live and thrive in the Saturn environment and to let go of their old GM ideas and philosophies. (Source: Saturn Company)

The next training section continued with the Saturn philosophy but focused more on the team. Workers were required to learn the answers to these questions: How does the team operate? Who are its customers within the plant? How does it relate to the rest of Saturn?

The final part of the initial training process was for the workers to learn their specific jobs. They began by learning how to operate their equipment. They learned how to differentiate between an acceptable part and an unacceptable part. They were also taught how to work with their suppliers and how to maintain their equipment.

When the "Saturn University" phase of the training was completed, each employee received a degree. The focus on training continued on the factory floor, there the workers filled out individual training plans. These plans served as the guides for each employee as he or she made decisions that were relevant in pursuing his or her future goals.

In addition to improving its workforce, Saturn looked at making improvements, from the ground up, in other areas. One business philosophy it applied is known as "Lean Production."

Lean Production is the description given by MIT to a Japanese manufacturing technique that uses half the human effort in the factory, half the manufacturing space, half the investment in tools, and half the engineering time needed to develop a new product. The first step that Saturn took in trying to meet this objective was to reexamine the assembly line. One of the obstacles that GM assembly-line workers faced was that they were forced to move with the assembly line. This meant that they were focusing on two things at one time: moving and installing a part on the car. They felt that this contributed to poor quality. The Saturn plant was to have wooden skillets on which the workers would ride along with car, thus providing them with the freedom to focus on the installation of the car parts.

The new product Saturn developed contained 54 different patents. These included simple items such as electronic controls used for the automatic transmission, allowing smoother shifting, and complex items such as the space frame which gives the structural integrity and provides protection for passengers. One of Saturn's most famous patents was for the plastic polymer side panels; the most noteworthy qualities of these panels are that they were rust proof and were resistant to low-velocity denting.

THE SATURN MARKETING APPROACH

Saturn had successfully overhauled how cars were made in the U.S., but it understood that quality cars alone would not build a strong brand. The first thing that Saturn did was to sever most of its visible ties with GM. It then focused on selling the company, not the car. At the same time it used its dealerships to build strong ties with its customers.

Not only was it important to separate Saturn from GM for labor it reasons, it was also to give it a fresh start for marketing purposes. Early research had made it very clear that the GM name resulted in a perception of substantially lower quality and credibility than that of its competitors. GM's Prism is one example that bore the brunt of that perception. The Prism was actually made by Toyota and was materially the same car as the Toyota Corolla, but after both of these were rolled off their respective lots, the resale value of the Toyota Corolla was 20% higher than that of GM Prism. The main reason for this was that the public perceived GM cars to be of a lesser quality than that of Japanese cars. It was very important that Saturn present itself as a fresh and new American company; linking its efforts to GM would have undercut that concept.

Most car companies use the tactic of conveying to its targeted audience the reason why its car is so good and why its competitors is not. Some examples of the catch phrases used are "the relentless pursuit of perfection" or "as finely tuned under the roof as it is under the hood." The marketing campaigns would usually build on specifics such as safety features, exterior design and finish, fuel economy, acceleration performance, comfort, road-test endorsements by cars magazines, and guarantees.

The weakness with this approach was that every car company used it and the repetitiveness of this practice basically drowned each other out. If Saturn chose this method of marketing it would not distinguish itself from its competitors. Chrysler Corporation's Chairman, Lee Iacocca, had been saying and proving that Chrysler's quality was just as good as that of Japanese cars, but his preaching was ineffective. While Saturn did have many different facts that could be used, it was enough to know that this approach could be easily replicated by its competitors.

Instead of focusing on facts and figures, Saturn decided that it would not even focus on the car. It decided instead to focus the entire marketing campaign on the car company itself. Saturn knew that this approach would be a sure winner since there wasn't another new car company in the United States; therefore, there wasn't a competitor out there with the same edge. One of Saturn's commercials showed the sacrifices and risks of moving to a new area and beginning with a new company. Another showed the pride experienced by one of its workers the first time he stopped the whole production line when he saw that there was a problem with one of the cars. All advertisements were based around the premise of new kind of American Company. Saturn's goal was for its targeted audience upon viewing the commercial was to think of the people who build the car, not the car itself. This novel approach to marketing depicted the innovative and pioneering nature of America and Americans.

Keeping the focus on the company and its products was very important. Saturn again went against the norm of car industry and gave its models simple model names such as L1, L2, SC1. Most car companies gave its models robust sub-brand names such as the Dodge Neon, or a Ford Taurus.

Saturn was a car company that wanted to build a company that would change the car business. Saturn understood that this would not be possible just by building a strong brand; it really had to create a relationship between Saturn and the customer.

Typically manufacturers focus on such attributes as safety, economy, handling, and comfort. For example, Volvo is well known for superior safety, while BMW is known for performance and handling. Such positioning is relatively easy for a competitor to copy and surpass; therefore, it is considered a weak basis for developing brand identity. Strong brands usually surpass product attributes to brand identity based upon brand personality and a relationship with customers. Saturn took the approach that each of its customers was a personal friend and should be treated as such. The hope was that this approach would create a strong relationship leading to an intense, enduring loyalty (Acker, 1996).

The first challenge was to modify the typical behaviors used in the buying and selling of cars. The common haggling over the price, between buyer and seller, did little to create a friendly or trusting relationship. The buyer generally felt that he or she could have gotten a better deal. Saturn implemented a no haggling for price policy, and it demanded strict compliance by all of its dealers. This reduced friction between the buyer and seller. The potential buyer knew exactly how much he or she would have to pay and that if his or her neighbor went to the dealer a few days later, then that neighbor would pay the same price. There were no negotiations.

Another aspect of Saturn's brand-customer relationship is in instilling a sense of customer pride. Saturn believed that the buyer would feel pride in Saturn as a U.S. car company that has beaten the Japanese firms at their own games; pride in the employees for their commitment and achievement and pride in him or herself for buying an American car. This sentiment goes far beyond product center pride felt by many new car buyers because that pride fades as the car ages. This feeling that Saturn was successful at evoking fits in with customers' functional values and personalities. This was not a forced or phony sentiment like that pushed by other car companies that have used mottos such as Chevrolet's (Heartbeat of America) and Oldsmobile (America's Dream). Instead, Saturn allowed its customers to discover this pride for themselves. And the pride associated with owning a Saturn was probably twice what it would have been with another automobile.

THE FIRST SATURN

On July 30, 1990, at exactly 10:57 A.M. CDT, General Motors Chairman Roger B. Smith and UAW President Owen Bieber drove the first Saturn, a red metallic, four-door sedan, off of the final assembly line in Spring Hill. This was the beginning of the first new

American car company in many years. Saturn understood that first impressions could make or break an established car company, so it was extremely critical for a new company to pay close attention to the first impression it was creating. Volkswagen was able to provide to Saturn an example of how damaging the failure to create a good first impression can be for an established company. Volkswagen enjoyed a fine longstanding reputation but was unable to transfer any of the equity that its Beetle had built up to its later model Rabbit, which failed due to mechanical problems. Volkswagen has lived with the tarnished image ever since. Saturn created a no-risk environment for buyers Within the first thirty days or 1500 miles a purchaser could return his or her car for a full refund or for a replacement car.

Saturn's product was strong from the outset. Even the car magazines that had been traditionally very critical of General Motors were giving strong favorable feedback to Saturn. *Road and Track* called the car a major step forward in 1991 and in 1992 JD Power Associates named Saturn the ''Best Domestic Car Line in Customer Satisfact.'' And maybe even more impressive was where Saturn ranked in overall customer satisfaction, beating out all domestic nameplates. The only two companies to exceed Saturn's ranking were Lexus and Infinity, the high-end foreign car makers.

The initial release of the Saturn cars had been quite a success, but then came the first glitch. Saturn learned that a wire on it cars was not properly grounded and could cause electronic malfunctions if not corrected. Saturn chose to recall 350,000 of its cars, even though doing so was not mandated by the federal government. Saturn and car an owners were able to act extremely quickly to fix the problem in part because of the good relationship the dealers had with its customers. After two weeks, 50 percent of the cars had been repaired. In comparing this to a recall by a major competitor in which only 33 percent of the problems were corrected within one year, it is easy to see how well Saturn dealers were connected with its car owners. The Saturn dealers also handled it very differently than most dealerships would have done so and converted the problem to an opportunity to improve its relationships with its customers. Dealerships became very creative in problem solving. One chartered a bus to a minor league baseball game and, by the time the bus returned, the cars had been repaired and washed. Another put on a barbecue that customers could attend while their car were being fixed. Tracking studies of how Saturn handled the recall reported that the Saturn's image ''takes care of customers'' was not affected by the recall and that the brand actually improved on the ''good dealer'' dimension.

As the number of cars that were sold increased, the interest in the company increased. The interactive tours of the factory were selling out weeks in advance. Saturn was building intense and loyal relationships with its customers that was in common with some fellow companies that were an underdog to a larger competitor. These companies include Apple, Harley-Davidson, and Volkswagon (Beetle). Saturn then looked to see what these companies were doing, One item they replicated from Harley-Davidson was an event it hosted in Milwaukee that had drawn over 100,000 bikers. Saturn appropriately named its event Saturn Stock. It was a family get-together that had six stages for music and entertainment

that included country music (Wynonna Judd), rhythm and blues, gospel signers, mimes, clowns, and jugglers. It also had activities that included dancing, barbecues, craft fairs, and celebrities. But the centerpiece was and in-depth tour of the factories. Over 44,000 people attended, and 2,300 employees volunteered to be host for the event. In addition, another 130,000 attended ''Saturn-ites'' picnics and parties organized by local dealers. Overall, one in six owners participated in these events. This created an even stronger user group who encouraged others to buy Saturns (Carlson, 1996).

With in four years of producing its first car, Saturn produced its one-millionth vehicle. It was now ranked at the top for some prestigious awards, including Intelli Choise, Best American Car Value Under $13,000, Best Compact Under $17,000, Best Small Wagon, and Best Subcompact over $12,500. JD Power Associates Ranked the company number one in Sales Satisfaction Index Study and third (behind Lexus and Infinity) in the Customer Satisfaction Study. (Source: Saturn Company).

Saturn did the impossible; it created a car company from the ground up that was able to compete with the Japanese automakers. One of Saturn's biggest strengths was that it was separated from GM, but it turned into a major weakness when it came to getting a budget for new models. Saturn's strongest competitors came from within the company. It was the truck brands, Pontiac and Chevrolet, that were competing with Saturn and winning for the budget needed to develop new products. This left Saturn with out a single new car for almost a decade, causing the no-frill, no-haggle image to grow old (Flint, 2004).

As the 1990's came to an end Saturn's one platform array of coupes, sedans, and station wagons was in a highly competitive part of the market. The problems was increased as gasoline prices dipped to historic lows; consumers focused on larger cars, sportier cars, and sport utility vehicles (SUVs). Saturn did not have any SUVs or Sport Cars in its portfolio, and as a result its sales suffered. Its repeat purchase rates dropped from almost 50% in 1990 to 39% in 2000. Customers were satisfied with their original Saturn purchase, but Saturn was just not offering the model they wanted (usually ''up market'' model.) Originally 70% of customers were new to GM; now Saturn was unable to keep up with the upwardly mobile customer. For example, in 2000 Saturn's entire line up was only made three models, while its competitors like Honda and Toyota were putting together portfolios of cars that included coupes, sedans, sports cars, and sport-utility vehicles in a range of sizes, huge dealer networks, giant marketing budgets and deep stockpiles of customer loyalty.

In 2000, General Motors, in an effort to reduce cost, reorganized Saturn. The Chairman's position of Saturn was eliminated. The Saturn sales, marketing, and manufacturing operations were moved to the same umbrella as other GM brands. The Saturn design team was eliminated, and Saturns will be designed as part of the GM global design team. Due to the management structure change, Saturn will no longer get exclusive engines and components they had in the past.

GM did invest capital to build a new mid-size sedan, but instead of building it in Spring Hill, Tennessee, the new vehicle was built in the Wilmington, Delaware, General Motors plant that was scheduled to close. The workers were not part of Saturn's

United Auto Workers contract; instead they were part of the regular contract. The manufacturing process did not follow Saturn's lean manufacturing that was known for an extremely low number of defects.

Saturn officials have long held that rebates would not be part of the Saturn marketing program because it is unfair to the buyers who previously purchased Saturns and thought they got best deal possible. But in 2002, to regain market share it lost as a result of 9/11, Saturn started offering rebates. Originally the rebate program was to be offered for four months, after which Saturn would drop the policy. But once consumer rebates are offered they become expected. As of April 2005, Saturn was still offering rebates (Chambers, 2002).

Saturn was known for its vehicle polymer dent-resistant body panels, but GM made the decision that some of the Saturns would be built on platforms that it shares with other GM vehicles. This change was made for more efficient design and production, but they were unable include the famous polymer dent-resistant body panels on these new models.

Not long after GM decided to move Saturn production to a non-Saturn plant, GM decided to pressure the Saturn workers to ratify a contract that currently covers all of GM's other United Auto Workers. For the first time Saturn workers would lose the protection of the no-layoff provision that made the original contract unique. The workers signed this because of GM commitment to convert the plant into a flexible facility capable of producing several different vehicles. Without this investment, GM had no plans to build any new cars at the facility in Spring Hill, Tennessee, and probably would have closed the plant in 2007 (Garsten, 2004).

It was not long after these cost savings changes were made that sales began to drop. In the early days it was not uncommon that consumers took numbers and waited for a test drive at Saturn dealerships. It was also not uncommon that there were signs in front of dealerships that said ''Sold out of cars.'' Now the supply of Saturn's cars was not an issue. While the auto industry likes to have no more than a 60-day supply of vehicles, Saturn had three cars with extremely high days of supply. The L series had 177 days, the Vue had 101 days, and the Ion had 144 days of supply.

After all these changes Saturn, was becoming just another nameplate in the GM portfolio, where the GM brands are only positioned slightly may different from each other. For example, Pontiac drivers may want a sporty car and Buick drivers may want a classy car. The difference between these cars are only cosmetic, and many time, the brands did end up competing against each other.

GM was facing two difference choices with its Saturn line of business. It had GM talked about the possibility of closing the Saturn line. The other option that General Motors was discussing was too merge Saturn in with other domestic brands like Buick and Pontiac. But including Saturn as just another nameplate of General Motors destroys all the brand value that Saturn has built up.

GM already has the brand identity problem with its different car brands. This was recently demonstrated when GM ended the production of Oldsmobile. Oldsmobile was the oldest surviving car brand in the U.S. As late as the 1985 it had the most popular car in the U.S., the Olds Cutlass. One of the significant causes of the destruction of Oldsmobile was that it was too tightly positioned between the high-end brands like Cadillac and Buick and the mass-market brands of Chevrolet and Pontiac. Oldsmobile was originally know for having the latest bells and whistles and for typically being driven by individualists. In 1970 Oldsmobile began sharing components and then virtually the entire cars with other GM brands (especially the downstream brands of Chevrolet and Pontiac) to allow them to produce vehicles more efficiently. Stripped of its individual looks, innovation, and personality, it was not long before Oldsmobile began losing customers. In 2001 GM announced that it would not be producing any additional Oldsmobile vehicles, and then in April 29, 2004, the last Oldsmobile rolled off the production line (Sherlock, 2001).

The way GM expects to grow Saturn appears to mirror the cause of the Oldsmobile failure. First they are moving Saturn's car production to regular GM production facilities. Next, in order to save money on development cost, GM is cross-developing similar vehicles that will be shared by Saturn and the other GM lines— Chevrolets, Pontiac and Buick. The first thing to go was to the high polymer dent-resistant body panels because it did not fit well with GM other cars. This will erode the distinctiveness of the brand. First of all, 70% of Saturn buyers did not include a General Motors vehicle in their search for a car. The typical Saturn buyers are new to GM and not looking for the typical General Motors cars. The cross-developing is not only abandoning the values that Saturn was built on; it is going in direct contrast with what Saturn was started for: consumers who wanted a quality American car that was not General Motors. If the cars roll off the same production line as other GM cars, but with only slight cosmetic changes from other cars, it will lose the customers it earned because it was an alternative to General Motors. If Saturn shares production with other GM cars it also might mean that cars are in part produced outside of the United States. One of the significant selling points—that Saturns were 100% American made—may now make some customers angry with GM. Merging Saturn in with other GM brands will lead it down the same path as Oldsmobile. Saturn needs to go back to the brand heritage that Saturn was started on. ''A different type of car, A different type of company.''

CURRENT MARKET OVERVIEW

The year 2005 appears to be the year when there will be a significant shift in the car market. The SUV market is finally beginning to cool off due to the increase in gasoline prices, which is spurring the demand for Hybrid automobiles.

In April 2005, the price of gasoline hit an all-time high of $2.26 per gallon, an increase of 54 cents in just one year. Five years ago, the price was $1.48 per gallon—78 cents less expensive. While the price of gasoline today seems incredibly high, the price of gasoline in 1980, when adjusted for inflation, is even higher: $3.00 a gallon. Overall the 2005 increase is due to the growing economies of and their demand for oil to support their economies. These record prices are not expected to ease anytime soon.

While consumers have yet to rush to trade in their SUVs, there appears to be a weakening of the sales of new SUVs. Two of the three SUVs that showed the largest drop in sales due to climb in gas prices are the Chevrolet Suburban and the Hummer H2, which dropped 20.7% and 21.0%, respectively. This is a great concern to GM because SUV sales is its most profitable sector and one in which it is very competitive against the imports.

In response to the increase in oil prices, a niche that has great potential for growth has been formed; this is the hybrid niche. The demand for hybrids has grown quickly because they use 40% less gas than conventional cars. Hybrid vehicles have a conventional engine combined with a large battery and an electric motor. This combination works so that the wheels of the car are driven by both an internal combustion engine and an electric motor. The main losses of energy in a conventional car occur when it is idling, braking and driving at low speeds. In a hybrid car, the electric motor assists in the acceleration, which allows for a smaller and more efficient internal combustion engine. In addition, the engine does not idle; it is stopped when the car is standing still, and immediately started when required. Furthermore, the electric motor acts in reverse, as a generator, when braking; this recovers the braking energy and feeds it into the battery. When the car is traveling at low speeds, it often uses only the electric motor, which has an efficiency of about 90%. When the car is traveling at medium or high speeds, the internal combustion engine will operate at its most energy-efficient point and produce more power than is needed by the car at that moment. The extra energy is fed into the battery, to be used later when required (Source: International Energy Agency).

The hybrid efficiency can be bought for a price. The sticker price of the hybrid is between $3,000 and $4,000 higher than comparable non-hybrid cars. To determine whether the savings in energy makes sense in the long run, the cost of buying and operating the hybrid must be compared to the cost of buying and operating a comparable conventional car. Using today's vehicles and gasoline at $3.75 a gallon for comparison purposes, compare the Honda Civic Hybrid to a 20-mpg Honda Accord and you will gain a savings of around $983 a year. The total payoff period would be under 4 years. Compare this same Honda Civic hybrid to a 13-mpg SUV and you will save $1893; the payoff period will be 2 1/2 years. Comparing like vehicles such as the Honda Civic to the hybrid Civic results in a savings per year which is less favorable. At $383, it will take almost 10 years to hit the payoff.

The market for hybrid cars has increased 960% since 2000. In 2004 alone, this market increased by 81%. The market still appears to be a niche market with sales of only 84,000; however, it has the potential to mainstream as growth continues. The two automakers that dominate it are Toyota, occupying 64% of the market, and Honda with 31% of the market. The only domestic company with a presence in the hybrid market is Ford, with a small share of 3%. General Motors does not currently produce a hybrid model but it has developed more efficient conventional automobiles. For 2005 Toyota and Honda each plan to produce more than hybrid 100,000 vehicles. If their projections are correct, 2005 hybrid sales growth will be over 100 percent.

The market for hybrid cars is in a growth stage which is marked by its rapid increase in sales. R & L Polk & Co, a firm that collects and interprets data from the automobile industry,

predicts that as early as 2015 hybrids could make up 30% to 35% of the total market. Toyota and Honda appear to be believers; they are using strategies that are consistent with the growth life cycle by adding the hybrid technology across their product lines. Toyota is applying the technology to its Camry and Highlander SUV, both of which are higher end models than the ones currently using the hybrid technology. Honda is applying this technology to its higher end Accord. These products match or exceed the level of styling and the features offered in their traditional counterparts.

Mostly, General Motors has shied away from the hybrid market, calling it a niche market, with limited potential for growth. But with the constantly increasing gas prices it appears that hybrid cars are more than just a fad, and General Motors should consider investing in the technology.

Saturn appears to be the best-positioned GM division for the investment. An investment in hybrids for the Saturn division would bring the brand back to its heritage as "A different type of car. A different type of company." This would be the needed differentiation to keep Saturn from being just another GM nameplate. GM's investing in hybrid technology for Saturn appears to be logical because of its branding position, sales network, and product line.

The Saturn brand has fit well with its customers' core beliefs. Originally it was a point of pride for a Saturn buyer that the U.S. had beaten the Japanese at their own game and that he or she had purchased an American car. In the wake of 9/11 and in the midst of a war that many Americans believe was caused in part by America's dependence on foreign oil, Americans' core beliefs are shifting. Many now believe that driving fuel-efficient cars is important. A recent survey showed that two out of three Americans, including NASCAR fans and conservatives, think buying more fuel-efficient cars is patriotic (Toups, 2005). A Saturn hybrid would be differentiated from its competitors, such as Honda and Toyota, because a Saturn hybrid would be made by an American company in the United States with the same quality as those manufactured in other countries. Although many Hondas and Toyotas are in fact assembled in the U.S., they are perceived to be made in Japan, and therefore neither company enjoys the loyalty that comes with a "Made in the USA" label.

Over the past decade Saturn developed a distribution network that has consistently ranked highest for sales satisfaction index. They built a sales force that understands the product they sell, would not haggle over price, and created a no-risk environment because you could return your vehicle for a refund in the first 30 day. This built a reputation for Saturn's dealers as people you could trust and that were even friends. This is important because the customers who will purchase hybrid cars will need a dealer they can trust, and low-risk environment because they are purchasing such a large new piece of equipment. Saturn's 30-day return policy will allow a customer to purchase a vehicle without feeling like it is such a big risk. If they end up not liking how the hybrid drives, they will have the opportunity to return it free of charge, giving people the ability to adopt this technology without have to risk it all.

Saturn's current product line also provides an opportunity for hybrid cars. Unlike other GM lines, Saturn does not offer many different models. The Saturn line offers only four products, two, which share the same drive train, so only three hybrid systems would be need to be designed to allow Saturn to offer the hybrid option on all its vehicles and build Saturn into an even more distinct brand from GM. Otherwise, spreading this across all divisions would mean mixing the hybrid and gas-guzzling SUV, which could cause brand confusion.

Saturn was originally started to fight the imports and distance itself the General Motors. It accomplished this by revolutionizing the cars built through union management team work and also changed the way cars were sold with no-haggling one price. But most importantly it built a brand that people were proud to own. Just as all the investment in Saturn had begun to pay dividends, General Motors stopped investing money in Saturn to focus on other divisions, and the company was left without an auto for almost a decade. Now GM has a choice to turn Saturn into just another GM name plate and destroy the brand the same way it did to Oldsmobile or go back to Saturn's heritage "different type of company and different type of car." by investing in hybrid technology.

BIBLIOGRAPHY

Acker, David. "How Saturn Built a Strong Brand." Building Strong Brands, 1996, http://groups.haas.berkeley.edu./marketing/PAPERS/AAKER/BOOKS/BUILDING/saturn.html.http

Burns, Scott. "Gas Prices Hitting SUV Sales?" CNN Money, May 13, 2004, http://money.cnn.com/2004.05.13/pf/autos/suv_prices.html

Carlson, James. "Saturn Homecoming." Case Study, June 1996, http://www.cmg.carlson.com/index.cfm?cs_saturn.html

Chambers, William. "Saturns' Vow of No Rebates Gets Broken." *San Antonio Express-News*, December 25, 2002, http://freep.com/money.-business/sat/25_20021225.html

Durbrin, Dee-Ann. "Hybrid Car Sales Sore in U.S. 2004." Associated Press, April 25, 2005, http://news.yahoo.com/s/ap/20050424/hybrid_growth.html

Eldridge, Earle. "Is Beaten-up Saturn GM's Falling Star" *USA Today*, http://www.usatoday.com./money.autos/2003-04-saturnfalling.html

Flint, Jerry. "Saturn: the Forgotten Promise." *Forbes Magazine*, August 17, 2004, http://www.forbes.com/2004/08/17.html

Garsten, Ed. "Saturn Contract Ends Era." *The Detroit News*, April 12, 2004, http://www.usatoday.com/money/autos/2003-12-04-saturn-cover

Hakim, David. "The Endangered Brand List at G.M.," *The New York Times*, April 19, 2005, http://query.nytimes.com/search/restricted/article

Keenan, Tim. "Selling Cars in Saturn Country." *Ward's Dealer*, Sept. 1, 1999, http://wdb.wardsauto.com/ar/auto_selling_cars_saturn.html

Lienert, Paul. "Saturn Would Gain Stature, Appeal by Borrowing from OPEL." Autoinsider http://www.autoinsider.com/newauto/saturnopel

McManus, Walter. "Hybrid and Diesel Markets." Hybridcars.com, March 2005, http://www.hybrid-cars.com/hybrid-versus-diesle.html

Sherlock, Joseph. "The Death of Oldsmobile." Sherlock Strategies Business Management Newsletter, October 2001, http://www.joesherlock.-com/nwstlr19.html

Toups, Des. "Hybrid Cars: Do They Make Sense for You." *MSN Money*, April 2005, http://moneycentral.msn.com/content/savingandebt/saveonacar/p37272.asp

Vanderknyff, Rick. "Why Gas Prices Will Keep on Rising." *MSN Money*, April 2005, http://moneycentral.msn.com/content/savingandebt/saveo-nacar/p98745.asp

Welch, David. "Can Saturn Get off the Ground Again" *BusinessWeek*, October 14, 2002, http://www.businessweek.com.magaziner/content/02_4l/b3803086.html

CASE 19
Excelerite Integrated Systems, Inc. (EIS)

Eloise Moore was elated as she put down the phone. She had been talking with Bob Studz, vice president, data processing at Excelerite Integrated Systems Inc. (EIS), who had just returned from a company-sponsored management development program in late August, 2006. Studz had said:

> Eloise, we had a terrific session on capital budgeting last week. I can now see the utility of projecting operating savings from the Pathrite system as a way of persuading Seattle to provide us with the needed funds. I'm developing tentative savings numbers and will email them to you as soon as I'm finished. Could you take a rough cut at the kind of analysis that will make sense to the Seattle financial mavens?

Moore was a sales representative with Monster Computer Corporation (MCC). A 12-year veteran, she was assigned to large accounts, those whose purchases were expected to exceed $2 million. Working from her office in Phoenix, Arizona, Moore was assigned customers in the western half of the United States. MCC was the largest provider of hardware and software in the data processing field and had recently expanded to provide consulting and data processing services.

Moore saw a golden opportunity. Seattle was the home office for EIS and the source of all EIS corporate capital funds. If she could help Studz sell the system to his top management, she would enhance her standing among the sales staff. Moore sketched out the system that she and Studz had been discussing. It included a supercomputer, data storage and a set of peripherals to allow corporate data to be accessed via the Web and by mobile users in EIS district offices around the country. The total cost for the system was $9 million.

Because of the lead time for assembling components, delivery and payments could be in late 2006, so Moore decided to use a January 1, 2007 operating starting date. She anticipated that the expected marginal tax rate for EIS would be 40 per cent (federal and state

taxes) and that the modified accelerated cost recovery scheme for depreciation would be used for tax purposes (see Exhibit 1).

Moor did not know the target capital structure of EIS or the hurdle rate used by Seattle (i.e. the EIS home office) in evaluating their capital commitments. Accordingly, she decided to estimate them using publicly available financial data (see Exhibit 2). She assumed that EIS management sought to maintain a mix of 30 per cent long-term debt and 70 per cent common equity (book value), which was consistent with industry averages. Furthermore, she knew that EIS management would be reluctant to sell shares at the depressed market price of 80 per cent of book value (see Exhibit 3), and that the average return on large company stocks had exceeded the return on risk-free securities by 6.6 per cent over a

Total Investment	$9,000,000
Guideline life	5 years
Half-year life convention	

Year	Percent	Dollar Amount
1	20.00	1,800,000
2	32.00	2,880,000
3	19.20	1,728,000
4	11.52	1,036,800
5	11.52	1,036,800
6	5.76	518,400

NOTE: EIS could take the full year's depreciation under the half-year convention without regard to the month the Pathrite system was purchased.

Exhibit 1 Modified Accelerated Cost Recovery Calculation (Used by EIS for tax purposes)

Professor Wesley Marple wrote this case solely to provide material for class discussion. The authors do not intend to illustrate either effective or ineffective handling of a managerial situation. The authors may have disguised certain names and other identifying information to protect confidentiality.

Version: (A) 2008-03-07

EIS Debt

In 2004, the company issued 20-year bonds with a coupon rate of 8 per cent. With 18 years until maturity, the A-rated bonds had moved to a premium. They sold for $106.08 in late August 2006, immediately after an interest payment. Interest was paid annually. A typical A-rated bond was yielding seven per cent at the time.

The following chart shows the recent movements of selected long and short-term treasury security rates.

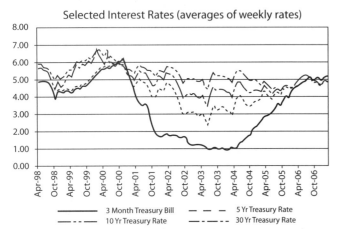

Selected Interest Rates (averages of weekly rates)

Source: Federal Reserve Bank of St. Louis

Exhibit 2 Basic Financial Information

Moore's research disclosed the following earnings per share and dividends paid per EIS share for the previous 10 years.

Year	EPS	Dividends
1997	$1.36	$0.50
1998	1.29	0.50
1999	1.27	0.50
2000	1.33	0.50
2001	1.35	0.50
2002	1.50	0.55
2003	1.75	0.75
2004	2.10	0.90
2005	2.60	0.95
2006	2.71E*	0.95E

* E means expected for the year

Alphamax Investors' Advisory Service issued a "buy" recommendation for EIS stock to its clients. According to the analyst's report, the EIS beta coefficient was 1.25. In September 2006, EIS was heavily traded on a national exchange within the range of $13 5/8 to $14 3/8 per share. Moore knew that at the end of 1996 the price of the stock had dropped to $7.00 per share.

Exhibit 3 Information on EIS Common Stock

To: Eloise Moore
From: Bob Studz, Vice president, data processing
Re: Estimated Savings for Pathrite System
Date: September 1, 2006

As promised, I'm sending you the bottom line of the savings before tax and depreciation that I think we can realize if we purchase the new equipment. As I mentioned, I believe that we can use the new equipment to our competitive advantage. It is impossible to determine precisely how much the system will improve profits, but I think the improvement will be substantial. Can we get together to review the project before I present the figures to Seattle? I would really appreciate your opinion.

My staff estimates net operating savings (before depreciation and taxes) for each year to be roughly $2.5 million. Actual savings could range from 30 percent higher (probability 0.2) to 15 per cent lower (probability 0.1) than this forecast. The current equipment has already been fully depreciated, and now has a zero book value. I also sense that the current market value of the old equipment is virtually nil. This is surprising, inasmuch as I'm sure that it would continue to meet our present needs for another six years at the very least. Given the rate of technological change, I expect that the Pathrite equipment will not have any market value either when it is ultimately replaced. We should assume that its operating life will equal its depreciation life, six years.

I hope you don't mind my sending this to you just before Labor Day. I knew you would want to look at the numbers before I return from the Coast the first week of October. I would like to send your analysis to Seattle so that the Pathrite purchase can be included in our capital expenditure budget. If approved, we could pay MCC upon delivery because we are generating more cash this year than initially expected. Our accountants believe that early payment would facilitate the taking of depreciation for tax purposes in the year of delivery.

Exhibit 4 M-E-M-O-R-A-N-D-U-M

78-year period. She estimated that inflation would average 2.5 per cent each year for the foreseeable future.

A week or so after her conversation with Bob Studz, Moore received a memorandum from him indicating the expected savings from the installation of the equipment (see Exhibit 4). She knew that EIS would expect her analysis to be based on the application of discounted cash flow techniques to determine both a net present value and an internal rate of return. Her next task would be to prepare an analysis for Studz, based on the information available to her.

In China, anything is possible, everything is difficult.

—Anonymous

This is not a destination in China, this is a journey. This is going to be a forever thing.

—Jim O'Mahony Managing Director, Lion Nathan China

A good beginning is half way to winning. The road ahead is long and rough, but step-by-step Lion Nathan will march to success.

—Rheineck launch, Lion Nathan China journal #2

In April 1999, Paul Lockey, chief financial officer of the international brewing company Lion Nathan Limited (LN*), was really quite perplexed as he prepared his midyear report for the board. With responsibility for corporate strategy and finance, Lockey realized that higher losses from their China operations were going to wipe out LN's profits from elsewhere. How would the New Zealand shareholders react? For how long would the board allow these losses to continue? When would the China operations break even? Competition was intensifying in the Chinese beer market, particularly at the higher-margin premium end. Markets were extremely volatile as consumers tried new brands, and the economy was cycling downwards. With overcapacity in the beer industry, consolidation was underway. Was the new deal to brew and market Beck's premium beer under license going to provide the leverage needed to survive the shake-out? How could Jim O'Mahony's China team deliver in the world's most exciting market?

COMPANY HISTORY

In 1999, Lion Nathan Limited was an international brewer with three geographic divisions in New Zealand, Australia, and China. With a portfolio of over 50 brands, the company owned and operated ten breweries in these three countries.[1] To achieve greater international scale, LN also exported beer to 50 countries and licensed three brewers in Europe to produce and distribute Steinlager and Castlemaine XXXX. Through its 45% Japanese equity partner, Kirin Brewing Company, LN was part of the fourth-largest brewing group in the world.

Founded in New Zealand, LN's origins went back 150 years. The company grew by mergers and acquisitions to become the largest brewer in New Zealand and one of the top ten listed companies on the New Zealand stock exchange. From the mid-1980s, leadership of the series of expansion and consolidation strategies

in the brewing company was provided by Douglas Myers, whose family involvement dated back to 1897. Building upon his international experience in the liquor industry, Myers developed Lion Corporation to include a portfolio of businesses in hotels, property, wine, and beer. Myers adopted an overarching strategic view of the New Zealand business and led the company with entrepreneurial drive and enthusiasm.[2]

Lion Nathan Limited was formed in 1988 when Lion Corporation merged with New Zealand's largest retailer, L.D. Nathan & Co. At this time, the chief executives of the two companies, Douglas Myers at Lion and Peter Cooper at Nathan, decided that the best thing to do was to get an outsider who came from neither culture to run the new organization. As a result of an international search, Kevin Roberts was appointed in 1989 to manage the day-to-day operations as chief operating officer. Roberts had significant international experience with consumer product brands from his days with companies such as Procter & Gamble, Gillette, and PepsiCo. Headhunted from Pepsi-Cola in Canada, where he was president, Roberts also had knowledge of the beverage industry and hands-on leadership skills in high-performing organizations. Roberts brought Joe McCollum into the company at this time as human resources director to help build the culture. Also at this stage, LN's corporate strategy was redefined, as Roberts explained:

> It was very evident to me, after being here 10 seconds, that for a consumer products company to be exclusively dependent on New Zealand made no sense, because there were no consumers here. And that was not going to change. We were in a lot of businesses where we had no core competency. Our core competency, I decided, was going to be brand-building. Therefore, that meant the DEKA chain should go; the Woolworths chain should go. We wanted to build our Coke business, but Coke wouldn't give us any more territory, because they wanted to keep it for themselves. So, we sold off all noncore businesses. We decided that we had to go offshore, and the safest place to go was Australia. We also decided that ideally we needed brands that had a pedigree. In the soft drink business, we had to go with an established brand; therefore, go with Pepsi in Australia and New Zealand. We were able to get a deal—the Schweppes franchise for free. And to stay in beer, which was our core business in New Zealand. And buy established regional breweries—that was what we knew how to run. We acquired Alan Bond's breweries and transformed ourselves in a 12-month period from being a top-10 New Zealand conglomerate to the biggest beverage producer in Australasia. We simultaneously brought in a lot of international people to drive the culture, drive performance, and build brands and hired stellar people from offshore and New Zealand who became the core of the management group.

*Reprinted by permission from the *Case Research Journal,* Copyright 2001 by the North American Case Research Association, and the author, Delwyn N. Clark, University of Waikato Management School, Hamilton, New Zealand.

Exhibit 1 China: Yangtze River Delta Region

In 1993, with limited growth in the New Zealand and Australian markets, LN began looking further afield for growth opportunities in America, Europe, and Asia. Like many other multinational consumer product companies at this time, they found the world's largest consumer market—China. According to Roberts, "China represented the single best opportunity for a number of reasons,

including size of market, growth potential, low barriers to entry, and no established big guy in there." Two years and 40 brewery evaluations later, LN entered this market in April 1995 with a 60% joint venture in Wuxi. This initial investment was made in one of the wealthiest cities in the heart of the Yangtze River Delta—China's fastest growing beer market (see Exhibit 1).

Buoyed by success, LN increased its shareholding in this brewery to 80% in 1996 and made a major commitment to build a brand new $178 million[3] brewery 30 kilometers away in the Suzhou Industrial Park. Construction of this 200 million-liter world-class brewery was completed $35.5 million under budget and two months ahead of schedule with "good planning, great people, combined with cooperation and teamwork." Commercial production began in February 1998, and the premium brand Steinlager was launched in September. In April 1999, LN announced a licensing agreement with German brewer Brauerei Beck and Co. to brew and market Beck's international premium beer. The addition of a high-margin brand to its portfolio was important to utilize brewing capacity at Suzhou and to extend its market reach beyond the Yangtze River Delta.

LN's ownership structure changed in April 1998 when Japanese brewing group Kirin Brewery Company acquired a 45% share in the company. The composition of the board was changed at this time to allow participation by Kirin staff in LN's corporate governance. Kirin had its own small brewing and soft drink businesses in China and sold the Kirin lager beer in over 40 countries, particularly in North America, Europe, and Asia.

Gordon Cairns, who became CEO in April 1998 when Douglas Myers stepped up to chairman of the board, described LN's charter as "profitable growth." Business segment results for 1998 are shown in Exhibit 2. With growth of 5.5% in volume, 3.6% in revenue, and 7.5% in earnings, he called 1998 a "watershed year" for LN. Speaking at the company's annual meeting, Cairns reported:

	New Zealand	Australia	China	Soft Drinks	Total
Assets ($M)	781.1	2,524.3	374.4	156.7	3,878.2
Sales Revenue ($M)	414.5	1,106.3	56.2	229.4	1,806.4
Earnings ($M)[b]	100.1	286.0	(29.8)	0.3	346.34
Market Share	6%[e]	41.3%	8.2%[f]		
Staff	600	1,200	1,300		3,100

Notes

a. 1998 financial data in New Zealand dollars.
b. Earnings Before Interest and Tax, EBIT.
c. Total includes property/rental income and unallocated corporate overheads.
d. Total includes property/rental income and unallocated corporate overhead.
e. Share of LN/DB market.
f. Market share in the Yangtze River Delta.

Source: Lion Nathan Limited, *Annual Report*, 1998.

Exhibit 2 Lion Nathan Limited: Business Segments 1998[a]

I believe these results are coming from a simple game plan that sets clear direction for each of our businesses. Australia is the engine of our business, where we expect profits to grow over the next five years, from modest share growth, stable pricing, and further cost reductions. In New Zealand, where our position is more dominant, the market less stable, the economy weaker, and there is a predatory third player, we are less ambitious in wanting to hold our position. In China, we are investing to develop the business, which will be generating profits in the medium term. Finally, provided there is a suitable buyer at a suitable price, we are actively seeking to divest Pepsi.

As a shareholder, you obviously believe in the game plan. But let me draw to your attention five other reasons that differentiate us as a stock. First, we are virtually a pure beer company. Second, everywhere we compete, we are investing to build brands. Third, we believe beer is a regional business, with few truly global brands. Fourth, a key success factor is for us to be the lowest cost producer, everywhere we compete. Finally, we are measured, managed, and motivated by shareholder value, where what we do should earn greater than the cost of capital.

Financial comparisons and statistics for LN from 1994 to 1998 are provided in Exhibits 3 and 4. For the six months to February 1999, LN's profit was $83 million ($0.3 million more than the February 1998 profit figure), with strong results in the Australian business (7.8% EBIT increase). With difficult market conditions in China and prices under pressure, $20.4 million EBIT loss was reported (compared with $17.1 million loss in February 1998).

THE BREWING INDUSTRY IN NEW ZEALAND

Historically, the New Zealand brewing industry was highly concentrated.[4] In 1999, this industry was effectively a duopoly, with the two major competitors, LN and DB Breweries, controlling about 97% of the beer market. Microbreweries accounted for a very small percentage. The two major players displayed a number of similarities. Both operated primarily on a national scale. DB had about 43% of the New Zealand market; LN, some 54%. Both companies had brewing capacities of around 200 million liters per year. Both companies were vertically integrated and enjoyed substantial ownership in companies that supplied their raw materials. In addition, through forward integration they controlled wholesale distribution based on marketing and price differences. Both companies enjoyed shelter from effective competition through the economies of scale and the very considerable capital costs of entering the industry. As both companies battled for leadership and control of a declining market, price competition was eroding profitability. Emerging developments in this industry included maturity of the beer market, proliferation of brands, growth of the premium beer brand, and changes in the location of consumption.

THE BREWING INDUSTRY IN AUSTRALIA

Historically, the Australian brewing industry was fragmented, with a large brewery serving each local market. A gradual change in structure, in part the result of acquisition strategies, led to a situation in the mid-1980s in which two national breweries, Carlton and United Breweries (CUB) and Bond Brewing, controlled almost 90% of the Australian beer market.[5] Government competition policy prevented any further concentration within this industry. Advertising and promotion expenditures increased as the competition between these two companies intensified. The financial difficulties of the Alan Bond empire led to its brewing operations (37.5% of the Australian market) being acquired by LN in 1990. CUB, with 52% market share, responded to this change by increasing investment in product development and marketing. LN's share of the Australian market increased to 46% in August 1993 with the acquisition of South Australian Breweries, after a CUB merger proposal for this company failed. LN's inherited portfolio of local brands provided the basis for its regional strategy and market leadership in Western Australia, South Australia, and Queensland. CUB worked to develop a national brand identity with several key brands including Foster's Lager, Victoria Bitter, Foster's Light Ice, and Carlton Gold. By 1999, as in New Zealand, demand growth was limited, per capita beer consumption was declining, and rising raw material costs were constraining profitability.

THE BREWING INDUSTRY IN CHINA

In 1998, there were over 600 brewers in the highly fragmented Chinese brewing industry, producing 17.8 million metric tons of beer. The sheer size of this beer market, servicing a population of 1.2 billion people, coupled with the growth potential due to increasing per capita consumption, attracted many international brewers to China. However, growth rates had decreased dramatically, from over 20% per year in the 1980s to 12.5% on average between 1992 and 1997, and near 6% growth was projected from 1998 to 2001. Beer consumption had risen to average 14 liters per capita in 1998, but this was still low compared to average consumption of 30–40 liters in the Asian region, 87 liters in New Zealand, and 95 liters in Australia. The demand for beer was influenced by macroeconomic factors such as levels of unemployment and disposable income. Government rulings on items such as entertainment spending were also key to understanding beer consumption in public premises such as restaurants, bars, and hotels. However, this aggregate level of analysis was of limited value in China, because there were quite different patterns of consumption throughout this vast country, particularly between urban and rural communities. For example, per capita beer consumption was 21 liters in the affluent urbanized Yangtze River Delta region and closer to 29 liters within the leading city of Shanghai (the "Golden Chalice"). Therefore, each region in China was

	1998	1997	1996	1995	1994
Total net revenue	**1,806.4**	**1,743.6**	**1,757.0**	**1,771.6**	**1,673.5**
Earnings					
Earnings before					
interest and tax	346.3	333.0	378.3	382.2	378.8
Net interest expense	(102.9)	(105.4)	(131.7)	(151.0)	(169.1)
Earnings from operations	243.4	227.6	246.6	231.2	209.7
Income tax	(90.8)	(85.7)	(75.6)	(1.4)	8.9
Minority interests	(0.8)	0.4	0.2	0.2	1.2
Goodwill amortisation	(15.7)	(15.7)	(15.7)	(15.7)	(15.7)
Earnings after tax & before					
ab. items	136.1	126.6	155.5	214.3	204.1
Abnormal items (net of tax)		(38.5)	(5.1)	(12.0)	17.0
Net earnings	136.1	88.1	150.4	202.3	221.1
Distributions and transfers	(87.6)	(87.6)	(87.0)	(93.5)	(86.8)
Retained profits for the year	48.5	0.5	63.4	108.8	134.3
Financial position					
Current assets	381.1[a]	355.81	353.7	369.3	358.9
Current liabilities	(413.5)	(366.6)	(366.2)	(442.8)	(413.6)
Working capital	(32.4)	(10.8)	(12.5)	(73.5)	(54.7)
Deferred taxation	(52.4)	(83.9)	(44.2)	(6.4)	(15.9)
Investments	124.7	124.8	132.1	106.0	117.7
Fixed assets	1,159.2	1,010.6	937.5	996.3	1,057.9
Brands	1,993.7	1,964.3	2,011.9	2,052.6	2,142.0
Goodwill	220.1	235.8	251.5	267.0	282.0
	3,412.9	3,240.8	3,276.3	3,354.8	3,560.8
Financed by					
Paid in capital	603.6	603.6	603.6	603.6	603.6
Reserves					
(incl. retained earnings)	1,466.8	1,308.6	1,350.8	1,305.6	1,286.4
Minority interests	10.3	10.2	10.2	22.5	1.3
Noncurrent liabilities	1,332.2	1,318.4	1,311.7	1,423.1	1,669.5
	3,412.9	3,240.8	3,276.3	3,354.8	3,560.8

Notes

a. Includes inventories $124.2
b. Includes inventories $116.5

Source: Lion Nathan Limited, *Annual Report,* 1998, p. 62.

Exhibit 3 Lion Nathan Limited: Financial Comparison, Five-Year Review for Year Ended August 31 (dollar amounts in millions)

considered a different market. Beyond the economic factors, provincial government requirements and limited transportation infrastructure for efficient distribution acted as specific constraints for multiregion or national participation. In addition, some uncertainty was created for foreign brewers by the government's signal of possible restriction of the proportion of beer sold by foreign firms to 30%, since it was not clear if, when, or how this would be implemented.

The major segments in the China beer market were linked to the quality and price of the beer. Exhibit 5 shows the key segments with their retail price points, market size in 1998, and market projections for 2001. Market share proportions for each segment in the Yangtze River Delta and Shanghai are shown in Exhibit 6.

There were only 80 breweries in the country with capacity over 50 million liters; 18 of these had over 100 million liters

	1998	1997	1996	1995	1994
Earnings after tax and before abnormal items per share (cents)	24.9	23.1	28.4	39.1	37.3
Net asset backing per share ($)	3.78	3.49	3.57	3.49	3.45
Current assets to current liabilities (ratio)	0.9:1	1:01	1:01	0.8:1	0.9:1
Interest cover (times)	3.2	3.0	2.9	2.5	2.2
Dividend rate (excl supplements)(cents)	16.0	16.0	16.0	16.0	15.0
Dividend cover (pre abnormals)(times)	1.6	1.4	1.8	2.4	2.4
Supplementary dividend (foreign shareholder) (cents)	0.85	0.49	0.99		
Dividend imputation (%)	30.0	17.5	35.0		
Net debt/Net debt & equity (%)	38.7	40.5	40.9	44.1	48.0
Gearing (%)	63.2	68.0	69.1	78.9	92.4
Proprietorship ratio (%)	53.6	52.2	52.5	49.3	47.7
Share price 31 August (cents)	410	395	383	317	340
Highest during year to 31 Aug. (cents)	550	412	389	338	430
Lowest during year to 31 Aug. (cents)	340	322	305	261	295
Number of shareholders	10,268	15,955	17,853	19,298	18,744
Number of employees	4,072	3,741	3,624	3,690	3,140
Total indirect taxes paid to govt's. ($m)	1,069.0	864.4	880.5	869.9	885.5
Australian Dollar					
Period closing exchange rate	0.873	0.873	0.873	0.859	0.809
Period monthly weighted average exchange rate	0.866				
Chinese Renminbi					
Period closing exchange rate	4.093	5.345	5.716	5.399	
Period monthly weighted average exchange rate	4.854				

Source: Lion Nathan Limited, *Annual Report*, 1998, p. 63.

Exhibit 4 Lion Nathan Limited: Financial Comparison, Statistics

	Retail Price Points[a]	China 1998	China 2001	Examples
	(RMB)	(Tons)	(Tons)	
Imported Premium[b]	10.0	40,000	50,000	Heineken[c]
Premium	5.0–6.0	722,000	920,000	Beck's/Budweiser/Carlsberg
Mainstream	2.0–3.50	2,100,000	2,800,000	Reeb/Rheineck
Low End	Under 2.0[d]	14,900,000	14,500,000	GuangMing[e]
	17,762,000	18,270,000		

a. Off-premise retail price points in Chinese reminbi, NZ$1.00 = 4.67 RMB, 30 April 1999.
b. With 0.2% market share, this category was usually included with other premium beer.
c. Retails for 12.50 RMB (NZ$2.67).
d. Most are priced close to 1.0 RMB (NZ$0.214).
e. Retails for 1.90 RMB (NZ$0.406).

Source: Lion Nathan China.

Exhibit 5 China Beer Market Segments

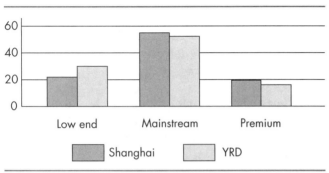

Source: Lion Nathan China.

capacity. The ten largest domestic brewing groups accounted for less than 20% of the total market. Exhibit 7 shows the major international brewers operating in China in 1998 with their origin, type of investment, production capacity, and beer brands. Profiles of the major competitors are provided in Exhibit 8.

The low end of the China beer market was the largest segment, served by several hundred small, state-owned domestic brewers. Many of these breweries suffered from problems of quality, were unable to achieve efficient operations, had insufficient capital for any improvements, and were unable to return a profit. With low-priced products and high distribution costs because of limited transportation networks, these brewers typically served a geographically limited, local market. The situation in this market segment was summarised by media commentator Denise McNabb:

Brewers	Origin	Investment type[a]	Capacity[b]	Premium	Mainstream	Low end
Anheuser-Busch	USA	JV in Wuhan	250	Budweiser		
		5% in Tsingtao				
Asia Pacific	Singapore	JV in Shanghai	200	Tiger	Reeb	
	Holland	Imported		Heineken		
		JV in Hainan	200	Heritage		
		JV in Fuzhou	100			
Asahi	Japan	JV in Hangzhou	600	Asahi		
Beck's	Germany	JV in Fujian	150	Beck's		
Carlsberg	Denmark	JV in Shanghai	180	Carlsberg	Karhu	
Changzhou	Local					Guangyulan
Fosters	Australia	JV in Shanghai	120	Fosters		Guangming
				Haoshun		Pujing
						Shanghai
Interbrew	Belgium	JV in Nanjing	80		Jinling	
		JV in Nanjing	60		YaLi	
Linkman	Local	JV in Guangzhou			Linkman	
Lion Nathan	NZ	WFO in Suzhou	200	Steinlager	Rheineck	
		JV in Wuxi	120	Carbine	Taihushui	
Kirin	Japan	JV in Shenyang	120	Kirin		
Miller	USA	JV in Beijing	200	Miller		
Pabst Blue Ribbon	USA	JV in Guangdong	350		Pabst	
San Miguel	Philippines	JV in Baoding	600	San Miguel		
South African	South Africa	5 breweries—North	950			Snowflake
Suntory	Japan	JV in Shanghai	200	Suntory	Suntory	
Tianmuhu	Jiangsu		50			Tianlun
						Tianmuhu
						Huaguang
Tsingtao[c]	Qingdao	5 breweries	800			Tsingtao
Zhanjiagang	Jiangsu		70	Dongwu		Zhangjiagang

a. International ownership varies for these joint venture (JV) partnerships.
b. Capacity in million liters. Capacity utilization is generally low.
c. Largest local brewery in China.

Source: Lion Nathan China.

Although almost all of the world's major breweries have sought to establish a presence in China, there are significant differences in the competitive position and strategies of the various key players.

Anheuser-Busch

This American company was the world's largest brewer, selling its premium Budweiser brand in 60 countries around the world. The company was aiming for 20 percent of the world's market share. Anheuser-Busch entered the China market with a joint venture (80 percent) in Wuhan (on the Yangtze River for transportation access) in 1994. Anheuser-Busch was 1,160 km. by road and 1,400 km. by rail to Shanghai. Establishing a small stake in Tsingtao, China's largest domestic producer and exporter of beer, provided local connections for Anheuser-Busch and a status partner for Tsingtao. Budweiser was the leading premium beer brand with 30 percent of the China market in 1998. In China, the company built on high levels of ambient awareness of its brand from television, movies, sport, and sponsorship. In addition, Anheuser-Busch invested heavily in marketing to build brand equity; it also used its dominant international brand and resources to establish deals for access to on-premise retailers. By raising the costs to compete, Anheuser-Busch reduced the ability of most competitors to obtain profits from the premium beer segment in China, which lead to industry rationalization.

Asahi

Founded in 1889, 90 percent of the Japanese Asahi Breweries' sales were from its flagship brand, Asahi Super Dry, which was marketed in over 30 countries. Asahi produced specialty beer, including a black draft, Asahi Kuronama, and a low-calorie beer for women, Asahi First Lady. The company also operated about 130 restaurants and sold other beverages, including soft drinks, wines, fruit juices, and whiskey. Growth in international activities through alliances was being developed in Europe and North America. In 1998, Asahi was a major player in the premium segment (estimated at 7 percent share of the China market) with very large scale capacity (600 million liters). The company had joint ventures in Beijing, Quanzhou, and Hangzhou. Asahi was investing heavily in television and media to develop its premium brand; however, its foreign image positioning was not as distinct as the American or European premium brands. Further development of distribution and trade networks was required to further increase sales volume.

Beck's

Founded in 1873 by a master builder with a passion for brewing beer, the German Brauerei Beck & Co. produced and sold its-premium Beck's beer around the world. The

company had a strong international focus with divisions in Finland, Greenland, Great Britain, the United States, Canada, Venezuela, Taiwan, and Puerto Rico. The Beck's brand was differentiated with a distinctive shaped bottle and positioned as a top-quality, world class premium beer. The company had strict quality guidelines for raw materials and the brewing process, to achieve its unique quality and flavor. In China, Beck's beer was brewed under license at Putian [100 km. from Shanghai by road] and sold in over 40 cities, primarily located along the coast from Shenyang to Guangzhou. From mid-1999, the production and marketing of Beck's brand was to be taken over by Lion Nathan China.

Carlsberg

Carlsberg, a Danish company, had global brewing operations in 140 markets, brewing in 40 countries, and 80 percent of sales from overseas markets. The company's brewery construction division entered China in the mid-1980s, renovating 40 breweries. In 1994, Carlsberg established a joint venture brewery (with a Hong Kong trading partner) in Huizhou, Guangdong province, for its premium brand beer [1,600 km. from Shanghai by road]. The company built a new brewery in Shanghai in 1998 and successfully launched a new mainstream brand (Kaihu).

Foster's

This Australian brewer entered China in 1993 with joint ventures in Shanghai and Guangdong, adding a third brewery in Tianjin in 1995. Foster's strategic intent was to become the largest brewer in China with a national network of breweries, selling Foster's premium lager and several mainstream brands. In Shanghai, the company invested heavily in signage - the Foster's signs were in many key central city display areas, but the premium beer was not widely available. To curb continuing losses in Asia, Foster's admitted an "over aggressive" strategy in China and in 1998 announced plans to cut back. Sale of its breweries in Tianjin and Guangdong were announced in 1999, allowing the company to focus on the Shanghai market.

Heineken

Heineken, the largest European brewer, operated in over 170 countries, with shares in over 60 brewing companies. Heineken was a global beer brand with a high level of ambient awareness from television coverage, movies, sport, and sponsorship. In China, Heineken beer was imported and sold as super-premium, working with Asia Pacific Breweries joint ventures in Haikou (Hainan province) and Fuzhou. The company used local mainstream brands to achieve cost-efficient volumes while building its premium brand. Heineken was aiming

Exhibit 8 Key Players in the China Beer Industry

for national coverage of key hotels in China and was prepared to wait while the premium segment grew, but it was not interested in lowering its prices to increase sales volume.

Kirin

Kirin, the fourth largest brewing group in the world, attempted initially to enter the Chinese market through a licensing arrangement, but then formed a joint venture with a local brewer at Zhuhai in Guangdong province. Kirin's premium beer was positioned as a high-quality beer because it was brewed with a single filtration process (and, therefore, had a higher extract loss than standard brewing processes). Kirin targeted Japanese expatriate consumers and their Japanese association. Kirin's beer was also produced under license at Shenyang, in northern China, by South African Breweries. Kirin, with a 45 percent equity stake in Lion Nathan, was planning to have some beer brewed under contract at Lion Nathan's brewery in Suzhou. Apart from its brewing operations, Kirin had joint ventures to produce and sell other beverages (e.g., soft drinks and fruit juices) in China. At home in Japan, Kirin had 15 breweries and captured 40 percent market share; it also sold over 300 beverage products in categories such as soft drinks, tea, coffee, wine, and spirits. Kirin had partnerships in pharmaceutical plants and research laboratories. Other joint venture and subsidiary businesses were in food service and restaurants, transportation, sports and recreation, engineering, building management, and business systems.

San Miguel

The largest brewer in the Philippines, San Miguel began a 5-year overseas expansion into the Asian region in 1998, aiming to brew the most beer in Asia and to be in the top 10 brewers in the world (by volume). The company had four breweries spread across China (including joint ventures in Baoding, Guangzhou, and Shunde) producing its premium beer, plus operations in Indonesia and Vietnam. Following the Asian economic crisis and losses in its China operations, San Miguel's new CEO announced plans (late 1998) to cut back loss-making businesses and focus on regaining market share in its domestic beer market. Talks with four international brewing companies (Anheuser-Busch, Carlsberg, Heineken, and South African Breweries) were underway to find a partner for its China breweries. San Miguel had a portfolio of businesses in food and beverages.

South African Breweries

South African Breweries had 16 brands providing 98 percent of the domestic beer market in South Africa and international operations spread throughout Africa, Asia, and Europe. The company's entry strategy in China involved buying into a local brewery with a joint venture agreement, then upgrading the operations and brands, rationalizing costs, and building distribution infrastructure. This approach was replicated five times in the northern region of China, establishing large-scale capacity for local mainstream and low-end brands. In 1999, the company had two joint ventures in Shenyang and one in each of the following: Dalian, Chengdu, and Jilin. Each area was treated as an independent regional market. Bottled water was also produced and sold by its joint venture on the Hong Kong-Guangzhou border.

Suntory

Suntory was Japan's leading producer and distributor of alcoholic and nonalcoholic beverages. The company was also involved in pharmaceuticals, restaurant operation, sports, music and film, resort development, publishing, and information services. Approximately two-thirds of its annual international sales were from the food and nonalcoholic beverages and 20 percent from alcoholic beverages. In 1984, Suntory established China's first joint venture specializing in beer; in 1994, the company extended its alcoholic beverages to include whiskies and brandies. This company had a large joint venture brewery in Shanghai and a small brewery at Lianyungang (65 million liters). It sold a premium brand with very low volume; however, in the mainstream segment in Shanghai, Suntory was in second place (selling 50,000 tons in 1998), behind Asia Pacific's Reeb beer. The company used extensive market research to develop its positioning and promotion imagery.

Tsingtao

China's largest domestic brewer, Tsingtao was founded in 1903 by British and German businessmen and taken over by the Qingdao Municipal People's Government in 1949. From its head office and five major breweries in Qingdao in Shandong province, plus a few affiliates around the country, Tsingtao provided nearly 3 percent of the total Chinese beer production in 1998. In addition, Tsingtao exported beer to over 30 countries, which provided foreign exchange to import raw materials, packaging, technology, and equipment. The company responded to intensifying competition from foreign brewers by increasing its production capacity and revamping its sales and distribution network. Tsingtao beer was the best-selling domestic brand, sold at a premium to other domestic beer because of its popularity and reputation for award-winning quality taste.

Sources: Company, industry, and media reports.

Exhibit 8 Key Players in the China Beer Industry *(continued)*

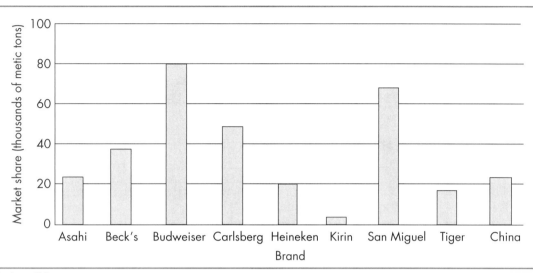

Source: Lion Nathan China.

Exhibit 9 China Premium Segment Market Share

Inefficient and undercapitalised, loss-making breweries are in their death throes as the government stops propping them up in line with cost-cutting reforms, which include the removal of housing and medical subsidies. Ugly price wars are expected to emerge as the tiny state-owned brewers make last-ditch efforts to stay alive by selling below cost on already thin margin prices of 1.9 renminbi (about NZ40 cents) for a 640 ml (quart) bottle.[6]

Brewers in the mainstream segment provided a higher quality beer at a slightly higher price (average 2.5 RMB, NZ$0.53). With higher margins but major executional challenges in sales and distribution, the mainstream segment attracted some of the more adventurous international brewers, including Asia Pacific Breweries with its Reeb (i.e., beer spelt backwards), Carlsberg with Karhu, Lion Nathan with Taihushui and Rheineck, and Suntory from the Japanese brewer Suntory (see Exhibits 7 and 8).

As Exhibit 6 illustrates, the mainstream and premium segments in the Yangtze River Delta and Shanghai were significantly larger than the national average; Exhibit 5 shows that these segments were expected to continue to grow, while the overall market was static. In the coastal cities region, the premium segment was estimated to be 7% of the market. Gross margins from 40% to 60% were needed in the brewing industry to cover marketing (30–100%), freight and warehousing (10–15%), and administration and other overhead expenses (10–40%). Assuming comparable production costs for mainstream and premium beer, the margins for premium beer were significantly higher (50%). However, profitability was elusive in this industry, with marketing expenses running between 30% to 120% of sales.

The premium segment was most attractive for international brewers because of the higher margins and the long-term potential in the China market. Most of the brewers were involved with joint ventures or licensing contracts for domestic brewing with local partners (see Exhibit 7). Exhibit 9 shows the premium market share for the top ten brewers in China. By 1999, with overcapacity intensifying competition and economic growth declining, several of these foreign brewers were cutting back their involvement, putting breweries up for sale (e.g., Foster's), and reconsidering their future options in China (e.g., San Miguel). The imported premium segment was a niche segment for the most expensive beer brands. Rather than take advantage of lower cost production within China, Heineken imported its premium beer and therefore incurred higher transportation and production costs, but it also realized a substantially higher selling price.

Seasonality had a major impact on the beer market in China. As Exhibit 10 shows, consumption of premium beer, primarily on licensed premises such as restaurants, bars, and hotels, did not show as much seasonal variation as sales of mainstream beer. However, to understand these beer consumption patterns, it was necessary to appreciate the perception of beer in China. Steve Mason, who had been LN's business development manager (China) and then marketing director in China for two years before becoming LN's corporate marketing director, explained:

Beer is seen to be a healthy drink, nutritive, low alcohol, no social downsides. Historically, strong alcohol beverages have been drunk, like white spirits or rice wine-based drinks that might be, say, 60 percent or 15 percent to 20 percent alcohol. Central government encouraged breweries as a moderation thing. So beer is seen as a beverage. It's not seen as a liquor or alcohol. So it's seen as a beverage choice. What will I have? A beer or a Pepsi or a cup of tea? With the communal society in China, there is a lot of emphasis put around meal times. Beer in conjunction with food is the habit. So you don't just go out to have a drink. Beer is an auxiliary to food.

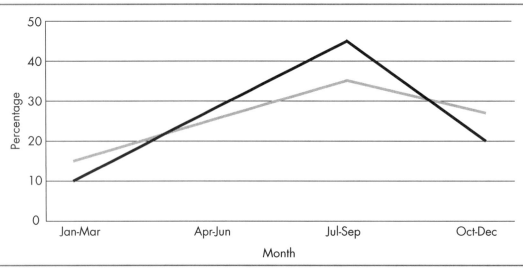

Source: Lion Nathan China.

Exhibit 10 China Beer Market Seasonality

Further, beer was a "cooling" beverage typically consumed warm, on a hot summer day. In winter, a "warming" drink such as rice wine was preferred, so sales of off-premise beer declined dramatically from October. Frank Gibson, who was the company's strategy director within China, elaborated on the nature of Chinese beer:

Chinese beer is clear and lager-like, drunk mainly in the humid summer months. This reflects its German heritage—the main brewery schools are still taught in the German mould. Even though more Chinese households now have refrigerators, it is not drunk cold, as this is considered unhealthy by Chinese.

Mainstream beer was generally purchased in small quantities (one or two bottles) from a nearby street stall and carried to a multistory apartment block home. There was a myriad of small, off-premise retailers in China running kiosks, commonly known as "mom and pop" stores. Mason described the scale of these stores:

The "retail outlet" is often nothing more than a shelving unit stuck to the front of someone's house. There are fewer than a dozen bottles of beer of various brands, some cans of soft drink, chewing gum, washing powder, sweets, and a shelf within a shelf containing packets of cigarettes and cheap lighters. In the doorway, an old lady sits knitting in the winter haze.

LNC sources estimated that there were 350,000–400,000 retailers of beer in the Yangtze River Delta region. Thirty local breweries operated in this region, servicing the population of 70 million via 200–300 distributors and 6,000–8,000 wholesalers. The structure of the Delta beer industry from production to consumers is summarized in Exhibit 11.

Premium beer was primarily consumed in restaurants, bars, and hotels. Status was a major influence on consumption in this segment. Restaurants were prolific in this socialistic society. Steve Mason, who did LN's early research on the Chinese beer market and later became the chief marketing officer, explained, "As face is extremely important in China, you will drink internationally famous high-quality beer when entertaining clients or staff at restaurants." Therefore, the levels of government and corporate entertainment budgets acted as a driver for this segment of the beer market.

Market share statistics for the top brands in each beer segment for the five key cities in the Yangtze River Delta region from 1996 to 1998 are shown in Exhibit 12. Even within this small regional sample, the volatility of the beer market was evident. New brands skyrocketed from obscurity to dominance within a few months with strong advertising, sales promotion, distribution, and support. However, with numerous competing brands and limited brand loyalty, leading brands could also disappear just as quickly. Developing brand equity was therefore a key challenge for competitors in this industry.

THE MACROENVIRONMENT IN CHINA

After record growth for nearly two decades, China's economic growth rate fell below the government's 8% of GDP target in 1998, with slower export growth, falling retail prices, and weaker consumption; the level of per capita GDP was $2,800 at this time. By comparison, Australia's economic growth estimate was 4.7% in 1998, with $23,600 GDP per capita; and New Zealand had −0.4% growth estimate and $18,500 per capita GDP.[7] However, the scale of expansion China offered as a consumer market was exponential. By 2000, there would be 160 cities with a population over one million people; 250 cities with annual income levels high enough to support consumerism; and 260 million people able to

Regional market architecture, highly fragmented

Brewery (local)	Distributors	Wholesalers	Retailers	Consumers
30	200–300	6,000–8,000	350,000–400,000	70 million
Servicing 100–250 distributors/ wholesalers/ retailers	Servicing 50–80 wholesalers	Servicing 50–150 retailers	150–200 consumers	1,500 million liters
Average = 40 m. liters	Average = 300,000 crates	Average = 4,500 crates/ wholesalers	Average = 250 crates/ retailer	Average = 22 liters per capita
= 2,500,000 crates per year	= 1,500 truck loads per year	= 25 truck loads		= 33 bottles p.a.
				China update 4/98 10

Source: Lion Nathan China.

Exhibit 11 Yangtze River Delta Beer Industry Structure

afford packaged consumer products, hence, the world's largest market in many categories including beer and biscuits.[8]

There were still many major challenges ahead for the Chinese government on the road to a free-market economy. The financial system was reported by the *Economist* to be a "mess," but the currency was not considered to be overvalued against a basket of its trading partners:

> There is no doubt that China is stuck with a cluster of financial time-bombs. Its state banks are insolvent, and they have few reliable borrowers. The competence and power of financial supervisors are stretched too thin, while mismanagement and fraud are stripping state assets. The central government has mounting financial liabilities, not least to pay for welfare and for infrastructure meant to sustain growth, but its grip on tax revenue is even shakier.[9]

Reforms were under way, and subsidies were being removed, but there were major performance problems in the state sector, as described in *Fortune* magazine: "The major roadblock: a largely unreformed state manufacturing sector, numbering 300,000 enterprises, that employs 70 percent of the urban workforce (109 million workers), but generates only 30 percent of industrial output. Officially, around 40 percent of these enterprises are losing money; the true figure is certainly much higher.[10]

Reform packages typically included restructuring the state owned enterprise's (SOE's) operating systems and establishing social security systems and reemployment projects. However, allowing loss-making SOE's to continue operating avoided some of the social problems engendered by high unemployment levels. Nevertheless, the gap between rich and poor was increasing. There was an urban drift; according to a World Bank study, 80 million people had moved to the cities in search of work. "China's land-locked hinterland remains, for the most part, an overcrowded world of poor peasants, rapacious officials, and indolent factory managers, with walk-on parts for disaffected ethnic minorities. It's here where foreign investment is thinnest that Premier Zhu Rongji must overcome the toughest resistance to reform."[11]

Improvements were being made to the transportation infrastructure, particularly between key cities in the coastal regions. However, difficulties with interregional and urban distribution were unlikely to be resolved quickly, as demand for transportation was increasing at a faster rate than the new capacity. With limited private ownership of motor vehicles and poor public transportation systems, the number of small-scale stores was increasing. The number of supermarkets was also increasing in the larger cities, but less than 10% of grocery sales were made in these "large format" stores.[12]

Patterns of consumer demand in China were found to vary by age and social activity. Price sensitivity increased with age. Consumers under 30 years of age were least sensitive to price and most responsive to marketing; "they are most likely to be familiar with advertising, especially on television, and to base their purchase decisions on its messages."[13] Within this segment, the majority were socially inactive, sticking close to home and family. The socially active minority group, who spent a lot of time on entertainment and travel, "perceive advertising as truthful, prefer branded products, and put a high value on attractive and comfortable retail environments."[14] The influx of new products to Chinese stores provided these consumers with endless opportunities to experiment with different products and brands. Consumers over 45 years of age, influenced by their experiences in China's Cultural Revolution, were "highly sensitive to price and respond negatively to new products and most forms of marketing."

Shanghai 420,000

Premium 70,000	1996	1997	1998
Budweiser	11,000	16,000	15,000
Beck's	18,600	18,800	10,836
Carlsberg	2,800	2,900	2,800
San Miguel	1,800	1,500	1,400
Tiger	2,335	2,961	3,903
Heineken	650	700	750
Kirin	600	620	600

Mainstream 23,000	1996	1997	1998
Reeb	133,152	88,154	70,182
Suntory	5,800	43,030	50,000
Rheineck	0	10,407	22,000
Karhu	0	0	10,000
Qingdao	26,000	24,200	25,000
Pabst	3,000	2,300	2,400

Low End 120,000	1996	1997	1998
Guangming	37,000	40,000	49,000
Zhonghua	8,000	6,000	7,000
Qianjiang	6,600	4,000	4,500
Shanghai	31,840	31,331	30,000
Donghai	2,320	9,900	10,000
Swan	17,017	14,115	14,000

Suzhou 105,000

Premium 15,000	1996	1997	1998
Budweiser	3,360	6,200	1,000
Beck's	4,200	4,100	800
Carlsberg	840	550	200
San Miguel	240	650	200
Tiger	60	160	100
Heineken	60	220	200
Qingdao*	200	300	600

Mainstream 50,000	1996	1997	1998
Taihushui	10,000	16,050	14,664
Linkman	2,000	1,500	500
Rheineck	0	1,700	10,345
Reeb	1,500	2,200	5,000
Sankong	5,000	4,720	1,000
Wumin	3,000	2,200	800
Pabst	100	100	100

Low End 40,000	1996	1997	1998
Zhangjiagang	30,000	27,696	8,000
Dongwu	7,000	6,200	4,000
White Swan	15,000	12,602	6,000
Shajiabang	14,000	12,200	4,000
Bawang	6,000	4,020	5,000
Weili	4,000	3,700	1,000

Wuxi 92,000

Premium 11,000	1996	1997	1998
Budweiser	1,500	2,200	2,900
Beck's	3,300	3,000	2,000
Carlsberg	500	450	234
San Miguel	650	600	550
Heineken	100	130	156
Qingdao*	400	500	700

Mainstream 54,000	1996	1997	1998
Taihushui	27,000	29,384	30,000
Shanjuan	10,000	10,916	10,000
Rheineck	0	3,550	2,934
Linkman	2,000	1,800	1,000
Guanyulan	1,300	1,200	200
Pabst	350	400	350

Low End 27,000	1996	1997	1998
Zhangjiagang	15,000	13,800	12,000
Fuli	6,000	5,850	4,000

Nanjing 114,000

Premium	1996	1997	1998 26,000
Budweiser	4,300	6,000	11,500
Beck's	3,500	2,500	1,000
Carlsberg	1,200	800	400
San Miguel	1,200	800	400
Heineken	30	40	50
Hansha	450	300	200

Mainstream	1996	1997	1998 70,000
Jinling	33,070	33,613	27,000
Yali	11,860	38,175	25,000
Rheineck	0	1,700	17,000
Qingdao	2,900	2,950	3,000
Pabst	6,400	3,000	1,500

Low End	1996	1997	1998 18,000
Zhangjiagang	800	500	300
Tianmuhu	1,000	700	300
Shenquan	10,000	9,500	9,000
Tiandao	4,000	4,500	5,000
Tianjin	3,000	3,500	4,000

Changzhou 70,000

Premium	1996	1997	1998 4,000
Budweiser	800	1,200	1,000
Beck's	1,500	1,400	1,400
Carlsberg	230	250	200
San Miguel	150	280	250
Heineken	15	25	20

Mainstream	1996	1997	1998 36,000
Guangyulan	2,622	26,214	20,000
Linkman	2,896	2,959	10,000
Taihushui	3,200	3,800	3,939
Rheineck	0	40	1,659
Qingdao	500	350	400
Pabst	400	350	400

Low End	1996	1997	1998 30,000
Tianmuhu	27,000	26,214	27,000
Zhangjiagang	2,400	2,300	2,400

* Qingdao (overseas spelling, Tsingtao) is priced at 3.5 RMB and is categorized as subpremium.
Source: Lion Nathan China.

Exhibit 12 Yangtze River Delta Key Cities: Market Size for Key Brands, 1996–98 (all figures in metric tons)

Lifestyles and culture in China were strongly based upon personal relationships. Stemming from the Confucian view, family relationships were very important. This meant that respect for elders, deference to authority, rank consciousness, modesty, ancestor worship, and harmony (avoidance of direct confrontation) were stressed. There was a cultural focus on team effort and enhancing group harmony. The group process was not just based on authority; it also strongly focused on consensus. For the collectivist Chinese, the family, including extended family and friends, was the prime group toward which allegiance was owed and paid. In the business context, having a good relationship (*guanxi*) network in China was the single most important factor for business success. *Guanxi* was the intricate, pervasive network of personal relationships that Chinese people cultivated with energy and imagination. *Guanxi* was not just a relationship network but one with obligations. In contrast to Western society, where social order and business practices were regulated by law, the Chinese were willing to bend rules in order to get things done. It was regarded as reasonable and acceptable to find ways to avoid the consequences of rules, so that Chinese with *guanxi* connections could circumvent government regulations for their own benefit and for those to whom they owed an obligation.

China was a major player within the broader Asian region. Diplomats and other officials were lobbying actively for China's admission to the World Trade Organization. Media commentators were optimistic that this would occur by 2002. Although rules for market access and tariff levels in many industries would be reviewed, increased uncertainty was expected during the transition period as new regulations and procedures were established. Throughout the Asian region, fluctuations in economic and political stability within specific countries created ripples for neighboring nations, including China. For example, the economic crisis in Korea in 1997 had major impacts on trading partners throughout the region. Similarly, political instability in Indonesia had social and economic consequences extending beyond this country.

LION NATHAN CHINA

LN's research identified the Yangtze River Delta as the best region for its entry to China. Ex-McKinsey consultant Paul Lockey, whose responsibilities included LN's corporate strategy and corporate finance, explained: "With a population of 70 million, the Delta is an area of relative wealth, high growth and above-average beer consumption. It has a rapidly developing infrastructure, including new highways along key corridors, express rail services, and a supply and service industry base suitable for foreign ventures."

LN's entry strategy was to take a small, measured step into an existing brewery with an upgrade path, learn, and then build on the experience. The Taihushui Brewery at Wuxi was a profitable joint venture with good plant and astute management. LN's $50 million investment was used to double capacity to 120 million liters, improve the quality and shelf life of the beer, introduce new packaging, expand distribution, and develop sales capabilities. David Sullivan, who was on LN's managing team for this joint venture and responsible for establishing processes, systems, and controls, explained LN's approach at Wuxi:

We brought in a sales director, who was an expatriate Hong Kong Chinese, out of Coca-Cola to try and build some sales skills into the workforce. We leveraged the expats like Steve Mason [LN's corporate marketing officer] to come in and improve the Taihushui brand, change the packaging a little bit, bring in new advertisements, look at how we communicated with the consumer, and do some research—basically, bringing Western sales and marketing practices into the business.

We had a very good relationship. It started well. We valued the business at a fair price. We immediately doubled the size of it. We retained the workforce. We didn't do anything that created an unfair, unreasonable work environment for the local staff. We very much approached it from "We're here to learn and we're here to teach. You teach us about the local market, and we'll teach you about marketing." In the finance area, for example, we said, "This is what we want you to report, and this is how we want you to do it. Now, let's show you how to do it and teach you why it is important for us," rather than saying "Do this" or "Our guy will do this." We put a lot of trust in them, and they put a lot of trust in us.

Confidence was developed from this first experience in China, the expansion program was successful, sales and profits grew, and LN increased its ownership in this joint venture to 80%.

LN's second step into China was a bold commitment to build a large, world-class brewery in nearby Suzhou. Located within a 70 km^2 special development zone, Suzhou Industrial Park (SIP), established by the Chinese and Singaporean governments in 1994, enabled LN to create a privileged asset. Wholly foreign ownership, which was highly restricted for breweries elsewhere in China, was a unique advantage that SIP offered for early investors. As Steve Mason, LN's chief marketing officer, explained: "To be able to talk about wholly-foreign owned sounds significant, but not particularly awesome. But in China it really, really is awesome. The autonomy to be able to make your own decisions and to be able to act on those decisions—the significance of that autonomy of action is absolutely awesome."

Efficient transportation links were available from Suzhou by air, rail, and canal to Shanghai and other key Delta cities. SIP provided utilities such as water, power, and telecommunications for industrial and residential usage. Other key support services for investors included a one-stop service for company incorporation and construction permits, local customs clearance, and warehousing and distribution.[15] This infrastructure and SIP's services were important for LN's "green field" project. The company also saved $50 million on import duties for plant and equipment; this duty-free policy ceased in 1997. A turnkey approach, driven by performance-based contracts and international sourcing of materials, enabled LN to complete the "single best facility in China" in just sixteen months. Speaking at the official Suzhou opening ceremony in September 1998, Jim O'Mahony, managing director of Lion Nathan China (LNC), said, "We have built the capability to achieve our objective of being the leading brewer in the Yangtze Delta." Production capacity of the state-of-the-art brewery was 470 million bottles of beer per year, or more than one million bottles per day.

STRATEGY

The vision of LNC was "to become the leading brewer in the Yangtze River Delta by 2000 and the market leader in the Shanghai-Nanjing corridor." Three core values were emphasized in the company's formal and informal activities—passion, integrity, and realism. LNC's strategy for competing in China was updated in 1997 with input from the international strategy specialist consultancy firm McKinsey and Co. LNC's five-point strategy involved (1) market leadership in the mainstream beer segment with the Shanghai-Nanjing corridor of the Yangtze River Delta, (2) developing a differentiated brand portfolio including premium and mainstream brands, (3) selling premium beer outside the Delta region, (4) outexecuting the competition, and (5) leading industry consolidation.

Reflecting on LNC's strategic position in February 1999, after eighteen months as managing director for China, O'Mahony said:

We are focusing on five key cities in the Shanghai to Nanjing corridor, south of the Yangtze river. We are number 1 or number 2 in three of those cities already [in mainstream beer] ... but Shanghai is going to be a real battle.

We have four brands now in our portfolio: Taihushui, meaning "water of lake Tai," is a high-quality mainstream beer for blue-collar workers; Rheineck, launched in 1997 with a foreign name and packaging linked to Germany, is positioned as a more outgoing mainstream beer for blue- and white-collar markets; Carbine is a dark, niche beer positioned at restaurants, so it's a beer with food. Then we have Steinlager, launched in September 1998, positioned as a trendy premium beer in a curvy bottle for sale in night venues and upmarket restaurants. The gap in our portfolio is a premium beer in the status segment occupied at the moment by Budweiser, Beck's, Tiger, San Miguel and Carlsberg. Our objective is to forge an alliance with another international player to get access to a major premium brand. We are just about ready to make an announcement. Then we'll have done the portfolio work.

We've been constrained in terms of moving outside the Delta because of lack of a premium brand that can actually do it for us. Apart from 3 million kiwis, nobody's ever heard of Steinlager. But when we announce the deal with the international alliance partner, as it is already a brand that's got presence throughout China, we'll have an immediate volume that we can "piggy back" Steinlager onto.

We started with a zero base, and we are building capabilities and developing infrastructure to compete in this region. This is proving to be as difficult as all the others. We've had a massive recruitment exercise followed by intensive training. We had no systems in place, so we had to build all the basic systems for the business including accounting systems, credit collection, invoicing, and sales reporting. But I think we are in line with plan. I think we are doing as well as anybody else in China.

We believe the long-term success of the beer industry in China is based on consolidation. Our alliance will not only achieve our goal but also lead the way for major consolidation. We are hoping there will be a domino effect to drive industry consolidation.

Adopting a regional strategy in the Yangtze Delta was not only consistent with the company's expertise in its home markets but also aligned closely with understanding of the economic drivers in brewing. CFO Lockey explained that LNC was "a small player in global terms, but we are the biggest where we are." He believed the company was "well positioned with the lowest cost position and amongst the largest capacity." However, continued growth was not without its problems, as Lockey elaborated:

Sustaining growth at 70 percent [as in 1998] is quite extraordinary. A lot of that growth has come from entering new cities. You have to recognise that there are only so many cities you can enter. At that point, you have to compete more aggressively in the cities you are already in. There are some dynamics about just how far you can go. In the mainstream market, for instance, you can only ship the beer about 300 kilometres before the freight costs just kill profits. In the premium market, it is a little bit different. The product is heavy relative to its value, unlike shampoo or microchips. Worldwide, this tends to be a business where local production is a dominant factor.

STRUCTURE AND SYSTEMS

In addition to the two breweries at Wuxi and Suzhou, LNC had a head office and sales team based in Shanghai. The profile of LNC staff in February 1999 is shown in Exhibit 13, and the structure chart in Exhibit 14. Eight of O'Mahony's senior management team were located at the Shanghai office. Many of these key staff were

	Shanghai	Suzhou	Wuxi	Consolidated
Corporate administration	8	2	0	10
Finance	20	21	12	53
Human resources	9	11	5	25
Information technology	1	8	2	11
Marketing	8	0	0	8
Operations	0	181	254	435
Other	3	2	51	56
Sales	174	144	137	455
Total	223	369	461	1,053[a]

a. There are seasonal variations in the total number of staff employed; e.g., extra staff are needed in operations for the peak months from May through August.

Source: Lion Nathan China.

Exhibit 13 Lion Nathan China: Staff Profile, February 1999

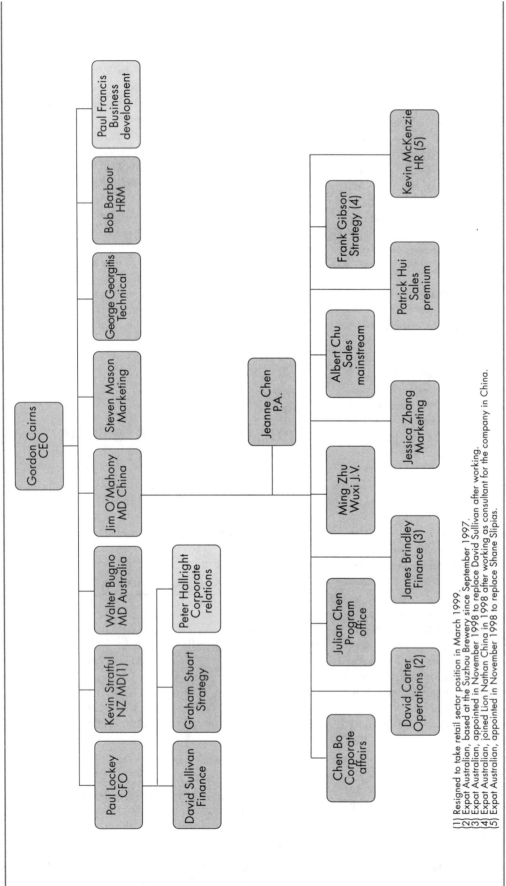

(1) Resigned to take retail sector position in March 1999.
(2) Expat Australian, based at the Suzhou Brewery since September 1997.
(3) Expat Australian, appointed in November 1998 to replace David Sullivan after working.
(4) Expat Australian, joined Lion Nathan China in 1998 after working as consultant for the company in China.
(5) Expat Australian, appointed in November 1998 to replace Shane Slipias.

Source: Lion Nathan Limited Annual Report, 1998, Lion Nathan China.

Exhibit 14 Lion Nathan China: Structure, February 1999

relatively new to these executive positions. However, the company's staff rotation policy meant that expats from Australia or New Zealand had at least five years' experience in two or three breweries before joining the China team. In addition, all of the local Chinese managers had previous experience in the beverage or consumer products industries.

Monthly reporting systems and processes were established in China, leveraging the knowledge and expertise from throughout the company. A consultative team-based approach was used to deal with projects and problems. Corporate staff, including CEO Gordon Cairns, CFO Paul Lockey, and CFO Steve Mason, regularly visited the Shanghai office for performance review and problem-solving meetings. These visits provided invaluable learning opportunities, as well as being directional and driving. To keep track of the many projects that were in process, LNC appointed Julian Chen as program manager in the head office team in 1997.

Computer systems for planning and control were developed and installed in China using expertise and technology from Australia and New Zealand. As David Sullivan, who was on the project team for Wuxi and Suzhou and served as LNC's finance director during 1997 and 1998, explained:

We've got computerised systems in Suzhou. We've put in a full suite of systems that we have in our other breweries. We did it in three months because we want computerised record keeping. We want to be able to report back to our corporate office. Other brewers have gone in and said, "Oh, whatever you give us will be fine; as long as the bank statements are reconciled, that'll do." We've gone in and said, "We want information." So we do the same performance reporting in China that we do in New Zealand or Australia. All our internal standards are exactly the same ... for beer quality, marketing approvals, pricing decisions, human resource policies—everything is using our Lion Nathan standard.

Taking an uncompromising stand on fundamental business practices was a feature of the corporate culture. Motivated by the desire for high performance, the corporate team initiated a project in 1996 to capture best practice and apply it universally across the business. The "Lion Nathan Way" was described by O'Mahony, who joined LN in 1991 and led this development:

The Lion Nathan Way is the "way we do things around here." It says three things—what we do, how we do it, and why we do it. It covers marketing, sales, HR, operations, finance, IT. They're not intended to be big binders that sit on the shelf, they're intended to be live documents. Each of them has a self-paced training module that goes with it. This is something that spans the whole of Lion Nathan.

This resource was particularly useful for LNC with induction and training of new staff, and it also provided guidelines for the full range of core business processes and activities, from financial reporting to developing advertising copy and conducting consumer research.

HUMAN RESOURCES

People were critical for the success of this business in China. Finding staff was not considered a problem by LNC in Shanghai; jobs were highly sought after in this progressive city, since employment provided the work permits needed to relocate into this area. To select new staff, LNC looked for previous retail experience, ambition, and ability of applicants. The company usually preferred recruits who were under 30 years of age and had more than two years' experience in another multinational corporation. Performance targets were established for each person, and a remuneration package including bonuses and rewards was negotiated. Status and loyalty were key elements of the Chinese culture, which influenced employment positions, promotions, and relationships, as Graham Stuart, LN's corporate strategy director (from February 1999) with five years' experience working for LN in China, explained:

Ambitious young staff are prepared to work extremely hard toward long-term personal goals, especially those involving promotion and status. Western distinctions between personal and professional issues are not commonly understood in China. The hierarchical relationship between an employee and his/her boss is also intrinsically personal. Loyalty can be expected from employees as long as promises are kept. However, if they are dissatisfied, then they will feel this "contract" has been broken, and they may leave the company. Typically, they do not complain or ask for any explanation.

According to Stuart, the main reasons for employees leaving jobs in China were (1) being offered more money elsewhere, (2) having pressures at work become too great, and (3) replacing expats with locals. The company had training systems in place to ensure that new staff not only understood their specific tasks but also appreciated key corporate plans. Commenting on staff retention, Stuart said, "Retention of staff is not considered an issue for us in China, as we are still in a rapid growth phase."

Mindful of costs during the early stages of LNC's investment in China, the company leveraged knowledge and skills of key staff from Australia and New Zealand by flying them in for specific projects and then flying them home again. This project-based team approach was successful for introducing new systems and processes as well as transferring and developing new skills within the local companies. This approach was also cost-effective because resident expatriates were significantly more expensive than local staff with their higher salaries, accommodation needs, and transport costs, plus needs for additional English-speaking support staff. Although the number of expatriates increased during the Suzhou construction phase, LNC's commitment to localize and build capabilities continued; by February 1999, LNC had only eight expatriate staff.

Rotating key staff throughout the company had many benefits for the company and the individuals concerned. Sullivan explained:

It transfers skills into the Chinese team, and it continually raises or benchmarks your standard against what we're doing back home. Its also development that the person then takes back home. Every person that we've sent to China from our business in Australia or New Zealand has come back saying they learnt so much. The environment is so different. They are so challenged. They're given a lot of responsibility to actually make things happen, and they've found it invaluable. This is why we've tended to try to use that project-based teamwork approach, rather than having a big bunch of experts.

PRODUCTION

LNC's focus on brewing high-quality beer in Wuxi provided an initial source of differentiation in the mainstream market, since the local breweries did not have the equipment, technology, or the systems to produce a consistent beverage. The addition of a large-scale, technologically advanced, world-class facility at Suzhou enabled LNC to produce at low cost. As LN's board chairman, Douglas Myers, effused at the official opening of the Suzhou brewery in September 1998:

> This brewery is a vital component in our China strategy. Without it, we would not have the capacity we need to continue our rapid growth. Nor would we have the capability to brew and package the high-quality premium brands necessary for profitability. The Suzhou Brewery is also an important asset as the beer market here undergoes very rapid change. It sets us apart as a brewery of the highest quality and lowest costs. Together with our first-class sales force, it gives us a strong position in the Yangtze River Delta.

Capacity at Suzhou was also expandable; the plant design allowed for a mirror operation to be built on the same site. In 1998, LNC utilized one-third of the new plant's capacity (60,000 metric tons), which allowed for 100% volume growth in 1999. Brewing Beck's premium beer under license was expected to contribute a significant proportion of this new volume. LNC was also preparing to use some of this spare capacity for brewing Kirin's premium beer.

The process of brewing beer was well known and documented. With sophisticated technological support, much of the craft of brewing had been routinized into precise scientific processes, which were able to be computer controlled. Fernando Coo, Suzhou's technical department manager, discussed LNC's brewing systems:

> Our production systems are internally accredited with Class A ratings and externally validated by our ISO accreditation. The quality of raw materials is critical for beer attributes such as taste and color. Availability and cost of raw materials have a major impact, too. Beer is made from malted barley, hops, yeast, and water. We get barley from Australia, Taiwan, Hong Kong, and Northern China; rice from Jiangsu province; and three different varieties of hops from New Zealand. Water, which is 90 percent of the beverage, is sourced locally (with assistance from SIP), filtered, and stored in tanks on site. Every beer has its own strain of yeast, which is grown from a 10 ml sample for 8 to 10 generations, and then a fresh batch is started. We are able to use the same suppliers for our breweries

at Wuxi and Suzhou. At the other end of the process, we sell the grain residues that have been extracted as cattle feed.

Quality was monitored at every stage of the brewing process. Further, to ensure that the consumer enjoyed consistent quality, the company worked to improve the shelf life of its beer and enforced strict rules for the product's life: LNC's beer was aged for 30 days before it was released, and it was destroyed if not sold within 84 days.

SALES AND DISTRIBUTION

Producing large volumes of top-quality beer to match local taste palettes was comparatively straightforward for LNC and other international brewers entering the China market. However, developing sales and distribution networks within this environment was significantly more challenging and complex than experiences elsewhere. LNC developed different systems for its two major market segments (see Exhibit 15): (1) selling mainstream brands for off-premise consumption through "mom and pop" stores and supermarkets; and (2) selling premium brands for consumption on-premise in restaurants, cafes, hotels, and bars.

LNC's off-premise system involved selling mainstream brands from five warehouses to 400 wholesalers, who then sold the beer to 70,000 retailers. Sales teams were established for the five Delta target cities, with account managers assigned to each wholesaler and merchandising manager providing the supporting merchandise (e.g., posters, price boards, shelf displays) for the retailers (to create consumer demand). "The primary wholesaler is a man with a truck and a storage shed amid an enclave of houses down a track. He distributes the beer to the next-tier wholesaler, who stacks up a bike or rickshaw with heavy loads for distribution to small openfronted shops (kiosks)."[16]

Although beer sales in supermarkets were increasing (2% of total beer sales in 1998), the vast majority of off-premise beer was sold through "mom and pop" stores. These were typically small kiosks with a few shelves of basic household consumables such as soft drinks, beer, sweets, soap powder, and cigarettes. Located every few meters down many of the narrow streets, these cash-only stores provided a subsistence living. O'Mahony described the context for beer distribution:

> Most people in China go to the store next door, and they buy whatever they need to buy for that day or that half day. They go to the wet markets and buy what they need to buy in the wet market, the fruit market, or whatever. Now, until that changes, we're not going to see much of a change in the distribution infrastructure in China. The people live in very concentrated areas. Public transport is OK, but people don't have cars. They can't afford taxis. So they are not going to carry bag loads of shopping long distances. They are going to buy very small quantities, frequently, and from the closest place to where they live as possible. We'll get in our car and drive 5 or 10 kms to buy whatever we want. These guys won't. They will walk 100 metres. The normal quantity of beer purchased is one or two

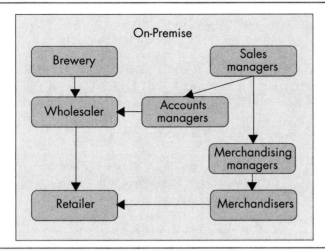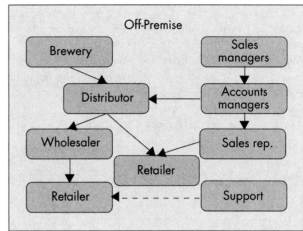

Source: Lion Nathan China.

Exhibit 15 Lion Nathan China Sales Systems

bottles at a time. Carrying one and a half kilos (which is two bottles) more than a short distance, if you are a frail old Chinese woman (the primary off-premise shopper) ... is not something you are going to do.

The physical difficulties of frequent deliveries of crates of beer by tricycle through narrow, congested streets from the wholesaler to the retailer were handled by contractors. LNC negotiated contracts with wholesalers annually but did not do direct store delivery of the returnable bottles and crates of mainstream beer.

Shanghai, a city of 13 million people in 6,340 km², was projected to be the leading consumer market in the twenty-first century. Although it offered a real challenge, LNC had 41,000 retail outlets systematically mapped and allocated to sales teams. Albert Chu, general manager for mainstream beer sales, had 160 permanent sales staff for this dynamic city. Chu outlined his ideas on this challenge as follows:

I was national sales director for Johnson & Johnson before joining LNC. I learned that increasing the proportion of stores stocking a product to 85 percent is needed to provide significant benefits from scale and market share. I am very keen to push the Rheineck brand to that level of coverage. I'd also like to increase our carton sales through supermarkets.

The process of making sales was highly social and time-consuming, requiring continuous communication, camaraderie, and cajoling. Major responsibilities were rested in regional sales managers to achieve aggressive sales targets. For example, Tommy Wang, one of LNC's top-performing regional sales managers, led 71 staff servicing 84 wholesalers and 14,000 retailers in urban Shanghai; in Suzhou, Steven Zhu had a team of 68 staff for sales to 40 wholesalers, 250 secondary wholesalers, and 10,000 retailers. The on-premise system for selling premium brands involved the use of distributors to sell beer to wholesalers, as well as making some direct sales to

large retail accounts (see Exhibit 15). LNC's sales managers had oversight of account managers who worked with the distributors. Sales representatives were employed to interact with wholesalers and retailers. Distributors typically carried a number of premium brands, with the exception of Anheuser-Busch specialists who were "voluntarily" exclusive. Selection of distributors and wholesalers was critical for success, as O'Mahony explained:

There is always a big fight annually to get the best distributors and the best wholesalers. We have a system of annual contracts that run January through December. There is an annual rebate for hitting volume targets. We are in the middle of negotiating the 1999 contracts right now [2 February]. It is a competitive process. Distributors and wholesalers have catchment areas; they have loyal retailers, and then there are floating retailers. Capturing the best distributors and wholesalers is critical. After that, it's brand strength and how much support you are prepared to put into it. Off-premise retailers will stock a much wider range of brands than on-premise. Bars, particularly Western-style bars, may have 50 beers, but the regular restaurant will have only two or three beers.

Higher margins for premium beer attracted many international breweries to China; this gave retailers the power to choose from numerous foreign brands. In addition, consumers typically drank the beer recommended by the restauranteur or bar patron, as Frank Gibson, LNC's strategy director, reported:

People go out to a good restaurant, and they want to impress their friends, so they want to buy a foreign beer. Unfortunately, at this point in time, they really don't care what sort of beer it is, as long as its foreign. They don't care if it's Beck's, or Budweiser, or San Miguel, so the restaurateur has an enormous amount of power over what gets drunk. Research shows that nine out of 10 times the restaurateur can dictate what the consumer will drink. This gives the trade a lot of power. There is an increasing number of competitors, a very fragmented channel, and no brand equity, so the trade can exercise a lot of leverage over the breweries. They don't have to take your beer. You don't have to have every beer in a restaurant. You only have to have two, basically. Most have only two or three. In premium, the vast majority of restaurants will only have two, so they don't have to take your beer. This increases the cost of entry for any foreign players who want to get in. They've got to pay a lot of money below the line.

Higher margins for premium beer extended the distribution zones for these brands. Furthermore, improved intercity transportation infrastructure made it easier to supply beer to a broader region. Marketing Beck's, a top-tier premium brand, with LNC's other brands was expected to significantly improve LNC's access to retail outlets within the Delta region and to springboard distribution well beyond it. Beck's was already sold in over 40 cities along the coast from Shenyang to Guangzhou. Distribution systems were generally a tablestake in most developed markets, but in China mastering logistical difficulties would be advantageous.

MARKETING

Like Procter & Gamble, LN had a portfolio of brands rather than a single brand based on its corporate name. This provided flexibility to select and adapt beer brands for Chinese markets. As O'Mahony noted, "Unlike Budweiser or Carlsberg or Foster's, we don't have to push a particular brand." Launching a new brand, even in just one region of China, was extremely costly. CEO Gordon Cairns reported at the annual general meeting that 37 cents out of every dollar earned in China was being invested in building brands. Steve Mason explained the company's approach to marketing:

We do market research and use very sophisticated psychographic profiling to position and promote our brands in all three countries. We are always measuring the health of our brands and monitoring the effectiveness of our advertising. Our approach has always been to study and learn iteratively about positioning in each market. We really try to build on our experiences.

In the mainstream segment, Taihushui, which was acquired with the Wuxi brewery, was upgraded and relaunched in 1996 as a high-quality local beer for everyday drinking with comfort and affiliation messages. According to Mason, these messages were designed to convey a sense of closeness and belonging—"Because it is from around here, you should feel comfortable drinking it." Taihushui was a market leader in Wuxi and Suzhou and had the second-highest market share in Changzhou (see Exhibit 9). Although a very strong performer, this brand was geographically locked.

Rheineck, which was from the New Zealand portfolio, was adapted and launched very successfully in 1997 as a pan-Delta brand positioned as a beer "you drink with friends." LNC targeted

a younger profile of more upwardly mobile consumers, with images of good times with good friends. Rheineck was an affordable foreign lager beer, brewed locally. In this mainstream segment, the economics of returning bottles and crates constrained geographic expansion. As the market share figures in Exhibit 7 show, Rheineck rocketed into second or third place in these key Delta cities. Building on experience with Taihushui, LNC achieved significant volume growth within 12 months in Nanjing (17,000) and Shanghai (22,000). Sullivan described LNC's mainstream growth:

We said there's growth ... if we bring in a quality product and put in the right relationships with the wholesalers, do the right merchandising, get the brand out in front of the customer, and get consumer awareness, then there's market share available without going beyond price. We actually sell for a higher price than the local brands, and we've got significant growth in those markets.

Rapid turnover in popularity of beers was particularly obvious in the premium segment, where many major international competitors battled for on-premise market share; positioning of these international brands was generally based on status. Mason outlined LNC's promotional strategies for each premium brand:

We launched Steinlager as a progressive premium beer for the "new generation" in Shanghai in September 1998. This was a New Zealand lager with German connections that we adapted for the Chinese palate. To differentiate this beer and position it as trendy, we used a curved green bottle, labeled it as an "international awards winner" and offered it in upmarket Western-style bars, hotels, and restaurants. We also had a dark-colored niche beer, Carbine, which was sold in restaurants and positioned as "a beer with food." This was a mild stout beer, which was named using a brand from Queensland. This premium beer was reformulated and introduced to encourage winter consumption of beer using imagery of energy, warmth, and powerfulness.

The addition of Beck's beer to the portfolio of premium brands LNC brewed and marketed was expected to provide significant leverage in the future. Although Beck's volume and market share in the key Delta cities had declined significantly from 1997, the brand was still ranked number two behind Budweiser in four of these cities and was number one in Changzhou (see Exhibit 9).

Significant investments were involved to promote brands and obtain access to retail outlets. Image-building activities such as advertising, signage, event sponsorship, or merchandising to build brand equity were categorized as "above-the-line" expenditures. There were also "below-the-line" expenses for transactional deals with the trade, which were standard practice to gain access in China. With overcapacity in the on-premise segment, the costs to compete were increasing, as O'Mahony explained:

A restaurant will typically stock two or three premium beers. They know that there are seven or eight producers of premium beer out there. It becomes an auction for which beers will be stocked. It comes down to who pays the most money. Therefore, the costs to compete have risen. You know whether its a listing fee, or whether it's promotional support, whether its paying for new signage, redecoration of the restaurant, whatever it happens to be. The other thing that has happened is the costs of TV advertising have risen as a result of demand. Again, when you've got seven or eight players looking for the same spot on TV, then you have to pay more for it.

Gibson described the below-the-line dealing required for access to restaurants:

You're selling to restaurateurs; you're not selling to consumers. You're trying to convince the restaurateur to stock your beer and push it on to consumers. Its all sales driven. Its all about push. You get in there and you do deals with distributors who've got the best coverage, because you want the distributors who deal with the most restaurants directly. You go in there and do deals with the restaurateur. You give him push girls (who provide information and hand out promotion materials), and you give him so many ashtrays, and so many glasses, and so many beer mats, and uniforms. That's been the focus until now. Increasingly, the focus will be more on above-the-line marketing.

Increasing consumption and driving market share were critical activities for success in this market. LN's ex-COO Kevin Roberts, speaking in his new role as CEO of Saatchi & Saatchi, the worldwide advertising agency, described the status of brands in China:

The Chinese have not been exposed to brands at all, so every brand promise that makes sense to them, hey, they'll try it immediately. They think its cool. They believe it. They are not cynical. A brand to them screams quality so the way to build brand equity is to advertise the living hell out of a property and communicate it. Have consistency of delivery and become part of them. You cannot advertise down to them with Western characters.

Furthermore, Roberts advocated the Coca-Cola strategy to drive consumption: "Make it available everywhere, make it affordable, and make it acceptable."

FINANCIAL CONTROL

In 1998, sales revenue for LNC increased 91% to $56.2 million on volume growth of 73%; this result was impressive in a beer market growing at less than 5%. Performance data for LNC is provided in Exhibit 2, and the corporate financial results and statistics are included in Exhibits 3 and 4. James Brindley moved into LNC's finance director role in November 1998, after six months in Shanghai working as a planning manager for David Sullivan. Brindley's role included oversight of transaction processing, accounts payable, general ledger, and accounts receivable, plus credit control, statu-

tory reporting, tax, funding, corporate reporting (including compliance with "a million" Chinese government regulations), and decision support. Corporate authorization was required for capital expenditure by LNC over $2 million. Having a strong performance ethic in the company created continuous pressure for LNC to deliver on monthly volume and EBIT targets. Brindley was now in the hot seat. He recognized the need to balance shareholders' short-term needs and the company's long-term returns:

We're playing in the premier league now. We've got to realise that its a big game. We've got to act like a big player, not like a small amateur player, and that takes courage. Our NZ$30 million loss is nothing to the likes of Anheuser-Busch and the other big players. You know, beer in China is not a profitable business. Margins are very low and its very competitive. The economy is in a terrible state. Pricing is very hard to maintain. All these things are stacked against us in the short term. But that could turn in two years with a few exits, income growth, the economy turning around … then we could be doing very well. Getting a partner is a great leap forward because it helps share the risk in these early years.

Commenting on the financial dilemma the company faced, CFO Lockey said: "The faster we grow, the more we lose. In the broadest sense, the faster we grow, the more chance we have of winning, but in the short term, the more we would lose. We can improve our financial performance by slowing down."

Because margins for premium beer were 50% higher than mainstream beer, increasing the proportion of premium beer LNC sold was a top priority. Brewing Beck's beer under license in Suzhou would also help to utilize brewing capacity and accelerate breakeven. Geographic expansion to new cities offered volume and sales growth, but there were major setup costs involved in establishing a sales force in a new city. As O'Mahony indicated, "Every time you open a sales office, you could be looking at $1 million loss in year one." This would typically be followed by achieving breakeven in year two and making a profit in year three. Another dynamic factor influencing profitability was the stage of brands in their life cycle; new brands required significantly more investment than older brands. LNC also faced challenges on a daily basis arising from the cash-flow nature of the beer business. Brindley explained: "Most of the cash collection is by hand. Salespeople go to the wholesaler's office and collect a wad of cash, bring it back into the office, and deposit it. It's very high risk. It's very hard work, and it's a real challenge. Paying debts isn't a top priority here. We are really doing quite well on cash collection, but it's very hard work."

Seasonality was another major factor influencing this business. Brindley explained its impact on LNC as follows: "In August [summer], we sold 27 million litres of beer—nearly 1 million litres a day. In December, we sold 1 million litres of beer. So a month's sales equals a day's sales." There was a huge investment in bottles and crates to service peak sales; off-season (from October), the empties were returned and stacked high all around the plant. Bottles typically cost 0.8RMB, and 3% were written off

Volumes

1,000 liters = 1 metric ton

100 liters = 1 hectoliter

Bottles, Cans, and Kegs

The Yangtze River Delta beer market is split approximately 95% bottle, 2% can, and 3% keg.

Standard beer bottle size is 640 ml and costs RMB 1.25; bottles are returnable; each trip averages RMB 0.3.

Standard can holds 300 ml and costs about RMB 1.

Standard keg holds 30 liters.

Most mainstream beer is sold in 24 slot returnable plastic crates, which cost RMB 24 to produce.

Premium beer is sold in nonreturnable bottles of varying size.

Steinlager will be sold in shaped 700 ml bottles and 300 ml bottles.

Beck's also has nonstandard bottle shape.

LNC's Ex-Brewery Gate Prices (in standard 640 ml bottles)

Taihushui	RMB 1.90
Rheineck	RMB 2.08
Carbine	RMB 4.00
Steinlager	RMB 5.50 (300 ml); RMB 5.70 (700 ml)

LNC's Suzhou Packaging Capabilities

3 glass lines @ 36,000 bottles per hour each

1 canning line @ 400 cans per minute

1 kegging line @ 80 kegs per hour

Employee Remuneration in China

Average brewery worker	RMB 2,000–15,000 p.a.
Seasonal contact workers (for peak periods)	RMB 800–1,000 per month
Good sales staff	RMB 24,000 p.a.
Good managers	Over RMB 100,000 p.a.
Skilled local senior managers	Package over RMB 500,000 p.a
Corporate executives (LN)	Up to 60% of pay package depends on individual and company performance.

Exchange Rates

NZ$1 at 30 April 1999

USA	Buy 0.5625	Sell 0.5510
Australia	Buy 0.8499	Sell 0.8366
China	Buy 4.6736	Sell 4.5340

Stock Performance

Stock performance (year ended 31 August 1998)	Return on stock outperformed NZSE40 index by 32% and Australian All Ord index by 11.5%.
LN's Share price (30 April 1999)	Buy NZ$4.55, Sell NZ$4.50 Movement +5, Volume sold 1,712,720

Source: Company and industry sources.

Exhibit 16 Lion Nathan China: Financial Data

annually (see Exhibit 16). Carton beer was more expensive because the bottles were not returned. Brindley was concerned about the financial implications of the government's ruling for beer to be sold only in approved new bottles:

By 1 April, every bottle has to be a B bottle made of safety glass. With the number of bottles in the marketplace and the actual glass-manufacturing capacity in China, it will take 11 years to make that number of bottles. But, they expect it to be done by 1 April. We may have to spend $10 million changing over our bottles. Mainstream beer is sold in returnable 640 ml bottles, but it's impossible to get your own bottles back. Actually, we won't care whose bottle we get back as long as it has a B on it. The old labels are washed off in the washer anyway.

LION NATHAN CHINA: THE FUTURE?

With the partnership deal to brew and market Beck's beer signed on the table, LNC's strategy director, Gibson, reflected on the lengthy process that had been followed to put this international licensing agreement in place. He commented, "The strategy is all set now. We've nailed the final piece of the puzzle. My job is all done." Another key player, Graham Stuart, who had been actively involved in all the developments in China, moved in February 1999 from LNC's general manager sales and marketing to LN's corporate strategy director role. His brief was to look forward: "What's next for LN?" Stuart was excited to be beginning this task of searching for new opportunities and new horizons for LN.

However, the company's financial performance and future depended upon success in China. The competitive landscape was changing, competition was intensifying in the Chinese beer market, and the economy was slowing down. As CFO, Paul Lockey was concerned about the reaction of financial markets to the latest midyear results. In 1998, LNC had achieved record growth in volume and sales in this difficult market. However, Lockey recognized that the challenges in China were far from over. Could O'Mahony and his senior management team continue to deliver on aggressive growth targets? How was LNC going to ensure success in this volatile market? Was it time for another bold move? Could LNC lead consolidation in the Chinese brewing industry? If so, how?

Reflecting upon LNC's future options, Sullivan enthused:

What can we do to drive the industry forward? We can communicate with other brewers. We can talk about how we compete in a profitable way. We can look for alliances with other brewers that don't have competing portfolios. We could license other premium brands and produce them in Suzhou. We can leverage suppliers. We can raise the bar on quality, glass standards, labeling, and packaging. We can acquire other breweries. We can acquire other brands. We can encourage other brewers to acquire other brands. We don't look at Wuxi to grow massively; we look for growth outside of Wuxi. And then expanding out from the traditional base ...

trying to grow seasonality, or extending the shelf life, getting people drinking more beer in winter ... getting premium products into more restaurants, and mainstream into more shops.

NOTES

1. Lion Nathan International Limited website, www.lionnathan.co.nz/companiesbrands.cfm.
2. A. Kukutai, A. Cooper, and D. Gilbertson, *Lion Nathan Ltd. Innovation and Management in New Zealand: A Casebook* (Wellington: Dunmore Press, 1992), p. 167.
3. S. R. H. Jones, and D. R. Paul, *Concentration and Regulation in the New Zealand Brewing Industry: 1870–1970*, University of Auckland Department of Economics Working Papers in Economics Series, No. 33, 1987.
4. G. Lewis, T. Minchev, and A. Lebed, "Foster's Brewing Group." In G. Lewis et al., *Australian and New Zealand Strategic Management: Concepts, Texts and Cases*, 2d ed. (Sydney: Prentice Hall, 1999): pp. 721–745.
5. D. McNabb, "World's Brewers Bleed in China's Beer Wars," *The Dominion* 2, No. 21, August 5, 1998.
6. Anon., "Business: Economic Indicators," *Far Eastern Economic Review* 162, No. 6, 1999, pp. 58–59.
7. J. Ayala, and R. Lai, "China's Consumer Market: A Huge Opportunity to Fail?" *McKinsey Quarterly* 3, 1996, pp. 56–71.
8. Anon., "Economic Dragon Staggers But Will Not Fall," *NZ Herald*, February 17, 1999, p. E2.
9. R. Tomlinson, "China's Reform: Now Comes the Hard Part," *Fortune* 139, No. 1, 1999, pp. 60–65.
10. Ibid.
11. Ayala and Lai, "China's Consumer Market," pp. 56–71.
12. J. T. Landry, "Emerging Markets: Are Chinese Consumers Coming of Age?" *Harvard Business Review* 76, No. 3, 1998, pp. 17–20.
13. Ibid.
14. Suzhou Industrial Park Administrative Committee, Suzhou Industrial Park, p. 18.
15. McNabb, *op. cit.*, p. 21.
16. Ibid.

M ost successful retailers find it hard to go global while remaining true to themselves. Yet Sweden's IKEA succeeded in the United States by carefully adapting its strategies to the unique requirements of the market. Successful though the outcome had been, toward the end of 2000, IKEA's American experience posed wider questions for the whole firm's future. Could it adapt its retailing concept to local peculiarities without compromising the Swedish identity at the heart of its marketing and brand image? Could it continue to control costs if it was forced to dilute the uniformity of its product range? And, as the firm's operations became ever more global, could IKEA retain the intimate corporate culture that had been an important part of its success?

GOING GLOBAL

As store chains struck out beyond their home markets, they often had to change the formula that had previously guaranteed success. This happened to many types of business, but retailers were particularly close to customers. They must, therefore, move especially fast to adapt to local peculiarities. The trick was to do so without destroying the very thing that made them successful in the first place.

As the world's most competitive retail market, the United States had a well-deserved reputation: a graveyard for foreign retailers—and especially for Europe's nonfood retailers. Even Britain's Marks and Spencer had struggled to make a success of its acquisition of Brooks Brothers. In 1995 it looked as if IKEA might suffer a similar fate.

But the Swedish firm had been going from success to success in America. Its secret seemed to be a classic example of the difficult art of "change management": IKEA draped itself in the stars-and-stripes by adapting but not destroying its original formula. Meanwhile, its experience in America persuaded it to remix its recipe elsewhere.

IKEA VENTURING OUT OF SWEDEN

It was not hard to see why IKEA was initially so confident about the United States as a market. In the decade after it opened its first non-Scandinavian outlet, in Switzerland in 1973, the furnishing chain's vast out-of-town warehouse stores decked out in Sweden's blue and yellow colors had marched triumphantly across much of Europe. Its formula was based on reinventing the furniture retailing business. Traditionally, selling furniture was a fragmented affair, shared between department stores and small, family-owned shops. All sold expensive products for delivery up to two months after a customer's order.

IKEA's approach trimmed costs to a minimum while still offering service. It started with a global sourcing network, which in 2005 stretched to 2,300 suppliers in 67 countries. An IKEA supplier gained long-term contracts and received technical advice and leased equipment. In return, IKEA demanded an exclusive contract and low prices. IKEA's designers worked closely with suppliers to build savings into products from the outset.

IKEA displayed its enormous range of more than 10,000 products in cheap out-of-town stores. It sold most of its furniture as knocked-down kits for customers to take home and assemble themselves. The firm reaped huge economies of scale from the size of each store and the big production runs made possible by selling the same furniture all around the world.

This allowed the firm to match rivals on quality while undercutting them by up to 30% on price. An IKEA store, with its free crèche and Scandinavian café, was supposed to be a "complete shopping destination" for value-conscious, car-borne consumers. IKEA had forced both customers and suppliers to think about value in a new way—one in which customers were also suppliers (of time, labor, information, and transportation), suppliers were also customers (of IKEA's business and technical services), and IKEA itself was not so much a retailer as the central star in a constellation of services.

U.S. ENTRY

Initially, IKEA's successful and apparently flexible system hit problems in the United States. In 1995 it opened a 15,700-square-meter (169,000 sq. ft.) warehouse store outside Philadelphia. At first, with the dollar at around 8.6 Swedish kronor, it was quite easy to make money. Six more shops (five on the East Coast and one in Los Angeles) followed in as many years.

But things started to go wrong. By 1999 the American operation looked to be in deep trouble. In each new European country it entered, the company had normally broken into profit after two or three years with its third or fourth store. In America it was still losing money. And this could not be blamed wholly on a slowdown in the economy and a weak furniture market.

Many people visited the stores, looked at the furniture, and left empty-handed. Customers complained of long queues and constantly unavailable stock. Imitators were benefiting from the marketing effort IKEA had made in introducing Americans to Scandinavian design. Worst of all, since it was still making many of its products in Sweden, IKEA's cherished reputation was threatened as the dollar's value dropped to 5.8 kronor by 2001.

Another retailer might at that point have sought a dignified exit. IKEA, it has been claimed, never considered that option. "If you're going to be the world's best furnishing company you have to show you can succeed in America, because there's so much to learn here," remarked Goran Carstedt, who took over North American operations in 2000.

Its perseverance paid off. IKEA's U.S. operation finally turned around. Since 2000, sales tripled, to $480 million in 2004, and the company made a profit beginning in 2005. In December 2001, IKEA purchased Stor, an imitator with four shops in the Los Angeles area. In October it opened its thirteenth American store, a franchised outlet in Seattle.

U.S. MARKETING STRATEGY

To achieve success in the United States, IKEA had to revise several of its central tenets. The most basic was that it could sell the same product in the same way in Houston as it could in Helsingborg. IKEA took this approach to such extremes that its advertising deliberately stressed not only its clean Scandinavian design but its blue-and-yellow Swedishness.

IKEA had cheerfully broken several of the rules of international retailing: Enter a market only after exhaustive study; cater to local tastes as much as possible; gain local expertise through acquisition, joint ventures, or franchising. "We don't spend much money or time on studies. We use our eyes and go out and look, and say it will probably do quite well here. Then we may adapt, but quite often we stick to our opinions," noted Anders Moberg, IKEA's chief executive.

This iconoclasm had paid off in Europe, but it helped to get the firm in trouble in America. In 1999 and 2000, Moberg himself spent much time in the American stores, talking to customers. "We were behaving like all Europeans, as exporters, which meant we were not really in the country," he said. "It took us time to learn this."

Unapologetically, European products clashed with American tastes and sometimes physiques. Swedish beds were narrow and measured in centimeters. IKEA did not sell the matching bedroom suites Americans liked. Its kitchen cupboards were too narrow for the large dinner plates needed for pizza. Its glasses were too small for a nation that piled them high with ice; Carstedt noticed that Americans were buying the firm's flower vases as glasses.

So IKEA's managers decided to adapt. The firm started selling king- and queen-sized beds, measured in inches, as part of complete suites. After noticing that customers were inspecting IKEA's bedroom chests, and then walking away without buying, Carstedt worked out that, because Americans used them to store sweaters, they wanted the drawers in the chests to be an inch or two deeper. Sales of the chests immediately increased by 30–40%. In all, IKEA redesigned around a fifth of its product range for America; its kitchen units were next on the list.

The firm changed its American operations in other ways, too. "When we went in, we hadn't planned a clear strategy of how to supply the American market at low cost," Moberg admitted. That meant, for example, that it was shipping sofas from Europe, adding to costs and problems of stock availability.

In 2005, 45% of the furniture in the American stores was produced locally, up from 15% in 2000. This helped the firm cut prices in its American stores for three years running. And because Americans hated queuing, the firm installed new cash registers that speeded throughput by 20% and altered store layout. It offered a more generous returns policy than in Europe and a next-day delivery service.

MANAGING GROWTH BY CHANGING THE CORPORATE CULTURE

Hard on the heels of its American difficulties, overall sales growth slackened thanks to slower than expected growth in Eastern Europe and recession in Sweden and Germany, IKEA's two largest markets. The firm reacted with intense soul-searching. In 2002/3 it opened only six new stores, compared with 16 the previous year.

One problem was that IKEA had become lax about costs. *Sweden Business* estimated that costs, excluding the purchase of goods, climbed from 30% of sales in the late 1980s to 37.5% by fiscal year 2001/2. Moberg was still trying to return them to 30%. This involved cutting the amount of time it took to develop new products and, over three years, trimming 10% of the workforce at the firm's Swedish product-development and purchasing center.

Another problem imposed by growth was the management of an increasingly complex global supply chain, one that led to glitches in quality control and stock availability. The firm had begun random checks on goods as soon as it received them; it had also taken equity stakes in some East European suppliers to help improve quality.

In making these adjustments, IKEA could draw on an egalitarian culture forged by its founder, Ingvar Kamprad (who remained the chairman of its supervisory board). Fast decision making was helped by a management structure that was as ruthlessly flat as the firm's knocked-down furniture kits, with only four layers separating Moberg from the checkout or warehouse worker. Even senior managers had to share secretaries and travel economy class.

The firm described itself as a learning and problem-solving organization that trusted the intuition of its staff. Insiders were much exercised about how this problem-solving culture could thrive beyond its Swedish roots. In recent years, Kamprad had held annual seminars for managers on the firm's corporate culture. Experience with globalization forced managers to adapt in three important ways in order to maintain the firm's antibureaucratic culture.

One change involved giving more autonomy to Carstedt than his European counterparts enjoyed. "You can't steer America from Europe," noted Moberg. Another decision was characteristically unconventional: In 2002 IKEA abolished internal budgets. "We realized that our business planning system was getting too heavy, we can use the time saved for doing other things better," Moberg said. Now each region must merely keep within a fixed ratio of costs to turnover. Finally, to encourage IKEA to stay lean in the absence of stock market pressures, the firm remained private, with ownership vested in a Dutch charitable foundation. Mr. Kamprad created internal competition: In 2002 he bought Habitat's British and French stores (which were separately managed), and he split off franchise rights into Inter IKEA Systems. Although IKEA itself had first refusal over new markets, the idea was that it must show it could do a better job than franchises would.

LESSONS LEARNED FROM THE U.S. EXPERIENCE

IKEA's contortions should frighten all would-be globalists. They show how even an adaptable system based on what Moberg called "permanent evolution" could not prevent teething troubles in a major market. But unlike many foreign venturers, IKEA started with the advantages of being both unconventional and rich. As Vanessa Cohen, a retailing consultant at Cooper's & Lybrand pointed out, IKEA did comply with at least one of the rules of international retailing: Its strong balance sheet in Europe enabled it to absorb its initial American losses.

So far, the results of IKEA's reorganization are encouraging. At 8.35 billion guilders ($4.5 billion), its sales for the year to August in 2005 grew by 6%. IKEA did not reveal its profits, but outsiders estimated its 2004 net profit margin at 6–7%, a creditable figure given recession in core European markets. Exhibit 1 shows the company sales by country/region. Exhibit 2 identifies its suppliers by country/region. The firm claimed that in the year to August in 2004, 116 million customers—equivalent to 2% of the world's population—visited its 108 wholly owned stores, spread across 18 countries (another 15 stores, mainly in the Middle East, Hong Kong, and Spain, were franchised).

On November 4, 2004, IKEA announced that it planned to move into China, where it would open ten stores in the foreseeable future. In making this move, the firm was sticking to its tradition of jumping into big new markets feet first, as it did in America:

Country/Region	Sales (%)
Germany	29.6
United States	14.2
Belgium, Britain, Denmark, Holland, Norway	21.9
Austria, France, Italy, Switzerland	20.5
Sweden	11.1
Eastern Europe	1.6
Austria	1.1

Source: Company reports.

Exhibit 1 IKEA's Sales by Region, 2004 (Year ending August 31)

Country/Region	Purchases (%)
Nordic countries	33.0
Europe	30.0
Far East	19.5
Eastern Europe	13.0
United States/Canada	4.5

Source: Company reports.

Exhibit 2 IKEA's Purchases by Region, 2004 (Year Ending August 31)

IKEA's managers stressed that it was easier to make changes to the product range once critical volume had been achieved.

But IKEA also would take to China other lessons from America. It had already set up the bones of a supply network in the country. Above all, the firm was tilting toward a more decentralized system of managing. In America, the result was that IKEA's Swedish identity was evolving into "a new alloy," according to Carstedt. "It's still blue and yellow, but mixing in the stars and stripes." Expect a red star to join IKEA's multicolored galaxy.

CASE 22
Bicycles for India*

People tend to treat the poor as idiots or receivers of charity, not as customers! ... There are few companies interested in putting out products to serve poor people's needs. That is what we do. We identify the huge gaps in the market that no one else has worked on, we come up with a product that works, and we work diligently to build market demand through the private sector. And we do it on a shoestring budget! Our first priority is to give the most reliable product employing environmentally friendly appropriate rural technology, at the cheapest price to the consumer. We believe that this is where we have the greatest positive impact ... the economic impact is far greater than the jobs provided in the rural villages."

The speaker, Paul Polak, IDE's president and chairman, was nominated for a prestigious international award for his contributions in two fields—economic development and psychiatry. The mood at the offices of International Development Enterprises (IDE) in Denver, Colorado, was jubilant.

While the staff at headquarters were celebrating the news in spring 1997, a package was delivered. It arrived from Canada and was just in time for the meeting that morning. As Mr. Polak ripped open the package, his excitement rose. The box contained samples of the reinforced polypropylene they had ordered more than a year ago. The samples were finally here! Polak, with no sponsor for the bicycle project and no budget, had to convince the Canadian plastics company to make the samples for a nominal charge. Even though it had been a long wait, they had reached another critical milestone in the bicycle project.

In 1992, Paul set out to take on the challenge of designing a bicycle for the poor living in third-world countries. "Since Joe Montgomery came up with the idea of a solid plastic wheel for a low-cost wheelchair, I have been obsessed with using the same concept as part of the design for a low-cost bicycle," he said as he looked at the ducks swimming in the nearby lake. A group of bicyclists rode on the path close to the park. "If more people walked or rode bicycles to work," he reflected, "the global environment would be improved."

His gaze followed the cyclists as they disappeared around the curve. He then turned and continued, "While in North America and Europe, infrastructure changes, like separate bicycle paths, are needed to increase ridership because of concerns for safety; in poor countries, safety is much less of an issue than cost." There was a twinkle in his eyes! With a passionate tone, he continued. "That's where I was convinced that we could build a low-cost bicycle using Joe Montgomery's solid plastic wheel concept, manufacture, and market it profitably for a retail price as low as $15.

---

*Reprinted by permission from the *Case Research Journal,* copyright 1999 by the North American Case Research Association, and the authors, Vijaya Narapareddy and Nancy Samspon, University of Denver.

At that price, global sales of bicycles would, at least, double to 200 million. Given the criteria we have at IDE of producing a net annual return of a minimum of 100% to our customer, i.e., the poor farmer in third world countries like India, the sale of a hundred million more bicycles a year would increase the global net income of poor people by one and a half billion dollars a year!

"IDE operates in several third-world countries. We have been very successful in selling treadle pumps in Bangladesh, India, and Vietnam. We also sell them in Nepal, and Cambodia. We have set up a coconut processing project in Vietnam, a nut processing plant in Brazil, and a home canning project in the former Soviet Union. The bicycle project, like the others, is one that has the potential to contribute directly to raising the standard of living of our consumers.... We will first develop this $15 bicycle for the rural farmers in India. The potential volumes we can seek in this market would enable us to work with the costs that we want to achieve. Once we are successful there, we can take the bicycle anywhere else. I can see us going to Bangladesh or Africa with the bicycle."

ABOUT IDE

Paul Polak founded IDE with a group of North American entrepreneurs in 1981. IDE espoused the structure and strategies of for-profit multinationals, but its sole purpose was to help poor people improve their lives and to make a contribution to solving world hunger. IDE's mission was well articulated: to improve the social, economic, and environmental conditions of the world's poorest people by identifying and marketing very low-cost, sustainable, appropriate technologies that could be manufactured locally and sold at a fair price.

The corporation's unique approach to product development, manufacturing, and marketing contributed to its quick success in several developing countries. The many countries in which IDE operates can be seen in Exhibit 1. By December 1993, IDE had field offices in five countries, including India. IDE's headquarters in Denver was staffed with five administrative staff members, including Paul Polak, president and chairman of the board; Don Schierling, executive vice president; Beatrice Szadokidrski, vice president of grants; and two staff members. The 13 members of the board of directors had a wide range of expertise and came from diverse backgrounds. The board officially met twice a year; several members were on active committees for various projects.

IDE prided itself in having an administrative structure that was decentralized, according it the flexibility to be highly responsive to the needs of its customers. IDE's main office in India was located in New Delhi. It oversaw ten field offices, each one

| | **TOTAL (US $)** | | | | |
	1990*	1991*	1992*	1993**	1994***
SUPPORT AND REVENUE					
Support:					
Grants	458,654	408,637	779,418	1,335,336	1,216,496
Donations—Cash	12,476	9,268	37,099	42,895	27,100
Donations—Land & Equipment	N/A	N/A	N/A	153,125	N/A
Refund of Project Advances	N/A	N/A	30,000	N/A	N/A
Total Support	471,140	417,905	846,517	1,531,356	1,243,596
Revenue:					
Consulting Fees	24,400	39,407	62,783	59,296	55,941
Interest Income	11,078	4,300	1,756	699	366
Gain on Foreign Exchange	N/A	N/A	8,735	N/A	N/A
Other	11,110	12,828	7,156	19,091	8,371
Total Revenue	46,588	56,535	80,430	79,086	64,678
Total Support and Revenue	517,728	474,440	926,947	1,610,442	1,308,274
EXPENSES					
Program Services:					
Manual Irrigation Pumps:					
Bangladesh Project	243,382	363,896	717,156	979,163	501,758
Nepal Project	44,975	71,181	25,724	N/A	15,010
India Project	N/A	N/A	N/A	138,887	160,226
Miserior India	N/A	N/A	N/A	N/A	49,380
Cambodia Project	N/A	N/A	N/A	N/A	16,413
Vietnam/Am Project	N/A	4,986	49,925	67,846	221,984
Vietnam Coconut Processing	N/A	N/A	N/A	25,000	85,864
Nepal River Transport Project	N/A	19,673	2,774	N/A	N/A
Brazil Village-Level Processing					
Project	112,148	35,198	8,874	N/A	N/A
Russian Home Canning Project	59,750	7,664	924	N/A	N/A
East African Development	N/A	6,234	3,069	N/A	N/A
Pharmacy Project	N/A	5,218	13,741	N/A	N/A
Other Projects	N/A	N/A	N/A	9,156	12,652
Total Program Services	460,255	514,050	822,187	1,220,052	1,063,287
General and Administrative	35,655	34,024	60,131	207,530	204,120
Fundraising	N/A	6,224	751	593	3,049
Total Expenses	495,910	554,298	883,069	1,428,175	1,270,456
Excess (deficiency) of Support and Revenue over Expenses	21,818	(79,858)	43,878	182,267	37,818
FUND BALANCES, beginning of year	96,125	N/A	N/A	N/A	N/A
FUND BALANCES, end of year	117,943	N/A	N/A	N/A	N/A

* This statement year ends October 31.
**This statement is for 14 months ended December 31.
*** This statement year ends October 31.

Exhibit 1 International Development Enterprise Statement of Support, Revenue, and Expenses

responsible for implementing specific projects. For example, the field offices in Orissa and West Bengal managed the treadle pump project, while those in the drought-ridden regions, such as Aurangabad, Bangalore, Indore, Himachal Pradesh, and Udaipur, were responsible for the drip irrigation project (for a map of India, see Exhibit 2). Field testing of the bicycle project was done in Orissa, while the research and development efforts were championed by the New Delhi office. Field testing, marketing, and

INDIA

JAMMU & KASHMIR

JAMACHAL PRADESH

PUNJAB

HARYANA

RAJASTHAN

UTTAR PRADESH

GUJARAT

BIHAR

WEST BENGAL

BHUTAN

ASSAM

NAGALAND

MADHYA PRADESH

ORISSA

Arabian Sea

MAHARASHTRA

ANDHRA PRADESH

Bay of Bengal

GOA

MYSORE

KERALA

TAMIL NADU

Indian Ocean

Exhibit 2 Map of India

distribution efforts at IDE are typically coordinated through field offices. Due to the tremendous success it enjoyed in its irrigation products, by 1998, IDE had a total of 250 staff on its Indian payroll.

IDE was unique in its market approach in seeking funds from international donor organizations. What this meant was that IDE had a clear vision of what it wanted to accomplish, looked for donors who were interested in funding each project, and sent them proposals seeking funding. In contrast, most organizations that compete for funding have used the so-called central planning approach. They typically investigate—through consultants—what the donor organizations want to accomplish and bid for the funding available. The projects undertaken, therefore, are designed to fit the donor organization's funding objectives.

THE DREAM TEAM

The bicycle project was under the leadership of several dedicated volunteers in Denver. Key members of the dream team consisted of Polak, Bill Lincoln, and Rob Carter in the United States. Everyone on the team had full-time occupations and served IDE as a volunteer, donating time as he could.

Rob Carter was involved very early on with the design of the bicycle. Rob was a mechanical engineer with a creative bent and an entrepreneurial spirit. He enjoyed designing special tools and prototypes of machines. He had prior expertise in designing bicycles. In 1993, he had offered to volunteer his time with IDE. As Paul Polak reviewed Rob Carter's resume, he had a feeling that Rob might be the right man for his favorite project.

Rob was fascinated with Polak's concept of "reinventing" the bicycle in order to reach the millions of people who were not being served by existing bicycle companies around the world. He was captivated by Paul's philanthropic mission. Rob was reminded of "Henry Ford, who thought that if he could bring the car to the masses, he would make a lot of money. The only difference here was that Paul was not looking to make money for IDE, but to help people by bringing them an affordable bicycle."

Bill Lincoln, an engineer by training, had recently retired from the executive ranks of Ball Corporation, a major multinational corporation leading in can manufacturing worldwide. With nearly two decades of experience managing Ball's international operations, he was working full-time in the capacity of a consultant. Like Rob Carter, he too was drawn to IDE by Paul Polak's vision and his zealous pursuit to help the poor.

GROUND RULES

From the outset, Paul had communicated the purpose of the project clearly. The bicycle would be sold primarily to the poor farmers living in rural India who needed to take produce to market. These were the people who could not afford to buy a bicycle or have carts drawn by farm animals, such as water buffaloes, to transport the produce.

India has a population of about 952 million people, of which approximately 50% are believed to live below poverty levels. The average annual income in India stands at $270. Census data indicate that 76% of the population live in rural areas where farming is the main occupation. About 10% of the farmers are the so-called landlords, who hold large parcels of land (i.e., 10–50 acres). About 70% of the villagers are small farmers holding less than 10 acres of land, and the rest do not hold any farm land. Of the 71 million rural households holding land, 34% hold on the average less than 0.2 hectares of land each. Family income patterns show that about 50% of rural inhabitants annually earn an income of less than 4,000 rupees (approximately $133). About 30% of the villagers earn 12,000–30,000 rupees ($400–$1,000) a year. Comparative economic and demographic data are shown in Exhibit 3, and population density data are shown in Exhibit 4.

Even though India produced about 7.4 million bicycles (7.3% of world production) in 1994, bicycles available on the market were clearly beyond the reach of the rural farmers. In 1993, retail prices of the Hero models ranged from 930 to 2,500 rupees. Several other lines of bicycles were also produced locally but sold in the market at higher prices. Atlas, Avon, Hero, and Hercules brands were among the more popular ones. Hero was the market leader with approximately 50% of the market, followed by Atlas (25%), and BSA (15%).

The impoverished farmer with a need to take loads of produce to market easily, efficiently, and in a timely manner but who did not own a bicycle was the target customer. From numerous visits to rural India, Polak knew that the farmers needed an economical means of transporting loads of produce or heavy cargo to and from the market.

Because the primary use for the bicycle was hauling loads, the bumpiness of the ride was not an issue. Speed also was not critical for the rural population. Therefore, the bike designed could have limited speed. The IDE bicycle had to:

1. have a simple design that could be manufactured and serviced in a rural industry setting—the goal was to provide employment to the poor people operating small shops, locally;
2. be durable, with ease of maintenance having top priority;
3. have a minimum speed capability of 6 miles an hour, or at least twice the speed of walking;
4. withstand gravel-paved or dirt roads;
5. transport a minimum of 50 kilograms (approximately 110 lbs) of cargo; and, most important,
6. retail (including a profit margin) at no more than $15, half the price of the world's current cheapest bicycle.

The purpose was to provide the most inexpensive means of transportation for the rural farmer who could not afford the conventional bicycles sold. Keeping the bicycle affordable was as important as making it durable and functional. The team knew that this bicycle was going to be the first one poor people could afford. As their incomes rose, it was expected that they would purchase the more expensive bicycles available in the market. Therefore, the project team's goal was to remain focused, at all times, on the ground rules of the project. The boundaries were set: the bicycle had to be the most inexpensive one available on the market, yet it had to be sturdy, hassle-free, and dependable for transporting cargo.

Country (Rank in Human Development Index)	Real GDP per capita (PPP$): Poorest 20% 1980–94	Population below income poverty (%) $1.00 a day (1985 PPP$) 1989–94	% of labor force in agriculture	
			1970	1990
India (rank 139 of 174)	527.0	52.5	72.64	64.02
All developing countries	767.9	32.2	71.80	61.10
Industrial countries	4,811.0	N/A	17.50	10.00
World	1,758.5	N/A	56.00	48.90

Source: Human Development Report, commissioned by the United Nations Development Programme. http://www.undporg/hdro/hpprof.htm.

Exhibit 3 Select Economic and Demographic Data

States	Area in sq.km	Population (1991 census) in millions*	Density per sq.km
Andhra Pradesh	275,045	66.51	261.0
Arunachal Pradesh	83,743	0.87	11.5
Assam	78,438	22.41	308.5
Bihar	173,877	86.38	535.3
Goa	3,702	1.17	333.5
Gujarat	196,024	41.31	225.7
Haryana	44,212	16.46	405.4
Himachal Pradesh	55,763	5.17	99.3
Jammu and Kashmir	100,569	7.72	83.9
Karnataka	191,791	44.98	251.1
Kerala	38,863	29.10	786.3
Madhya Pradesh	443,446	66.18	162.2
Maharashtra	307,713	78.94	278.1
Manipur	22,327	1.84	90.0
Meghalaya	22,429	1.77	87.4
Mizoram	21,081	0.69	36.7
Nagaland	16,579	1.21	85.0
Orissa	155,707	31.66	217.0
Punjab	50,362	20.29	430.8
Rajasthan	342,239	44.00	140.4
Sikkim	7,096	0.41	62.5
Tamil Nadu	130,058	55.86	452.4
Tripura	10,486	2.76	291.4
Uttar Pradesh	294,411	139.11	511.9
West Bengal	88,752	68.08	829.3
Union Territories:			
Andaman & Nicobar	8,249	0.28	39.0
Chandigarh	114	0.64	6,359.7
Dadra & Nagar Haveli	491	0.4	311.9
Daman & Diu	112	0.10	990.7
Delhi	1,483	9.42	7,326.5
Lakshadweep	32	0.11	1,764.2
Pondicherry	492	0.81	1,816.3

* Data is rounded off. Therefore, data in this column may not exactly match figures arrived at by multiplying columns 2 and 4.
Source: The Statesman's Year Book, 1998–99.

Exhibit 4 Area and Population of States and Union Territories in India

TECHNOLOGY DEVELOPMENT

Rob Carter was the manager of a Denver group that designed and built custom automated equipment. His creative designing instincts always came alive under challenging, if not impossible, circumstances.

Rob started designing the bicycle immediately. In order to lower costs, he looked at stripping the bells and whistles off the bike. The design that was found most suitable looked like the bikes of the early days, in the 1840s and 1850s. The chains and sprockets were eliminated, and the drive was placed directly on the front wheel. The bicycle frame was going to be made of sheet metal that could be easily cut and folded for structural strength. This sheet metal could be welded by hand or designed to be spot welded, if mass produced. It was clear from the outset that the conventional wheels could not be used. The multitude of wire spokes, sheet metal rim, and pneumatic tires involved a significant portion of the costs. The cheapest wheel that they could find was in Vietnam; these wheels were available for $5 each; the two wheels together amounted to $10. The frame and front fork, along with the wheels were, therefore, going to cost over $20, which exceeded the ceiling retail price set at $15. The key to the success

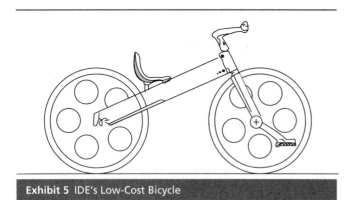

Exhibit 5 IDE's Low-Cost Bicycle

of the project rested on finding a low-cost alternative to the conventional wheel.

Rob Carter started thinking about the design. He decided to go back to the drawing board, build a prototype, field test it and, based on the feedback received, keep building a series of prototypes until the design was perfected. The low-cost product had to be one that did not fall apart as soon as it reached the consumer. He was keenly aware that IDE had a reputation for doing things right. The IDE bicycle designed by Rob Carter is shown in Exhibit 5.

Carter planned to test market the prototype in various phases. The first prototype would be the bicycle without a carrier, but with the wheels of a regular bicycle. It would be front-drive, with no chains or sprockets. The goal was to evaluate customer response to the new design. The second phase would involve sending out prototypes installed with a rear carrier for market testing.

To expedite the process, field testing of the IDE bike would go on independently of the development of the no-nuisance alternative plastic wheel. The team, upon vigorous discussion, decided to explore the possibility of making the alternative wheel with recycled plastics in order to keep costs down. The team was aware that this alternative wheel, if successful, had the potential for far-reaching applications in developed countries, beyond the bicycle project.

FIELD TESTING

Late in 1995, a prototype of the bicycle was developed and shipped to India. The total cost for developing the prototype was $2,000, paid for by Paul Polak and his friends. The IDE board had, at the time, felt that IDE's primary focus should be on irrigation projects alone until it had acquired sufficient expertise in one area, and anything outside of it should not be undertaken until this was accomplished. Because Paul was persuaded that the bicycle project was too worthwhile to be discarded, he started his own nonprofit company under the name Marketplace Village Technologies, Inc. It was through this company that the development was undertaken and funded. Later on, IDE board members changed their stance and brought the bicycle project back to IDE. The first prototype with conventional wheels was painted red.

The IDE office in Bhubaneswar made ten copies of the prototype using local materials and parts, and these were then used for field testing. It turned out to be a flagrant mistake because red was considered by locals to be the color of death. The prototype's weight posed a problem for farmers, who carried their bikes on their heads while crossing streams or rivers during the monsoon season.

A typical village is located about 7 kilometers away from larger townships where produce markets are located. Connecting roads are either dirt roads or gravel-paved roads. Villagers often have to cross two to four rivers or streams before reaching a marketplace. The prototype, when loaded with cargo, was quite problematic. Rob Carter traveled to India for field testing and saw the results firsthand.

Other problems surfaced during market testing of the first prototype. Steel found in the local market was far inferior to the steel used for the U.S.-produced prototypes. IDE found no dearth of shade-tree mechanics in India, but welding techniques were different. Even though the length of the frame in the prototype was adjusted for riders of shorter build than the average American, Indian farmers had difficulty reaching the pedals and steering the bike. Consequently, Rob Carter, who was on-site, had to shorten the frame and reduce the wheel base. Five copies of the corrected prototype were field tested again.

Results from the first round of field tests were very encouraging. First, the concept was proven effective. Second, farmers who tried the prototypes did not want to return the bikes, indicating a favorable response to the prototype from the consumers. It appeared the farmers were drawn to the low price of $15 (approximately 450 Indian rupees), less than half the cost of the lowest priced new bicycle sold by the leading Indian bicycle maker, Hero. IDE placed high emphasis on keeping the price lower than the used bicycles sold in the secondhand market.

In late 1997, IDE installed a rear carrier on the IDE bike and an optional coaster, which prevented the pedals from moving while coasting and carrying loads. Ten prototypes were made in an Indian workshop, and field testing was subcontracted to a local village NGO. This second-phase field testing could not be completed on time. An onslaught of monsoons in Orissa interrupted the activity, with only a few farmers participating.

The handful of detailed market surveys that IDE's Denver offices received contained valuable information. Respondents (age 22–42) cited their primary occupation as farming; some had secondary occupations, such as tailoring. Although each had previously owned a bike, none of them had any other mode of transportation. They used bicycles for personal transportation as well as for carrying produce to market. Reaction to the front-wheel drive was mixed. Farmers found the IDE bicycle with the free-wheel easy to ride, but without the free-wheel they felt that the bike was unstable, difficult to ride, and tiring when carrying cargo over long distances. While finding the handlebar position to be comfortable, they stated the carrier was inferior to the conventional bicycle. They indicated that the IDE bicycle was much stronger than the conventional bicycle, but, overall, the ride on the IDE bike was uncomfortable, especially on unpaved *(kacha)* roads. Though they found the IDE bicycle appealing, they indicated an unwillingness to purchase it at or below the price of a secondhand conventional bicycle.

Polak's personal conversations with a group of farmers during his visit to India in February 1998 revealed deeper insights.

Farmers pointed out that their ability to carry large loads of cargo on the IDE bike was severely limited due to the absence of the front crossbar, which would otherwise allow them to double up cargo. Farmers could carry up to 120 kilograms of cargo on the conventional bike, but only half as much on the IDE bike. The IDE bicycle had a diagonal bar instead of a crossbar. They also indicated a willingness to pay a higher price for the bicycle if additional features, such as brakes and comfortable seats, were added.

THE CHALLENGE

As the design team progressed slowly toward their goal, the problem of the wheel was still unresolved. Prototypes of the IDE bicycle tested in India had used conventional wheels bought locally. The alternative wheel was yet to be developed.

The plastic wheel and the bearings were two parts for which IDE was yet to find satisfactory cost reductions. The alternative to the conventional wheel chosen was a one-piece wheel made from recycled plastic. The team found a plastic wheel that was made out of nylon reinforced with fiberglass, which was extremely strong and durable; it was being used in wheelchairs. The need to reduce costs meant that they could not afford manmade fibers such as rayon, nylon, or fiberglass; these were very expensive and difficult to obtain in developing countries.

Upon investigation, Bill found stockpiles of used plastic available in every country in many forms, including plastic bags—a good source of plastic. Contrary to popular belief, barely 5% of the plastic available in the United States was recycled and put to new uses. Most plastic went into landfills or was burned or buried. The bulk of plastic soft drink bottles, however, were crushed, ground up, and shipped to developing countries where they were recycled into other products.

Bill did extensive research into finding what types of plastics were available around the world and which forms of plastics had the structural abilities needed to make a bicycle wheel. He contacted plastic recyclers, polymer engineers, and environmentalists in North America and, with their input, the team selected a lightweight plastic called polypropylene. Polypropylene had the required structural strengths that the wheel had to have, and it was available in abundance. Therefore, the IDE bicycle team decided to look into adapting that basic design into a polypropylene design.

A major source of polypropylene was twine used for bailing hay or to hold things that were shipped. Bill Lincoln, during his investigation, located a 4-H Club in Alberta, Canada, which collected tons of polypropylene twine (rope) just from local farms. Bill was convinced that this twine was not only available in large quantities but would only cost 4–5 cents a pound.

The design team, then, developed a way to substitute manmade with organic fibers. The popularity and use of natural fibers around the world had declined with the advent of manmade fibers. The team was confident that natural fibers like jute, hemp, flax, and coir (coconut hair) could be found in abundance in developing countries. Bill's research confirmed that there was a good supply of natural fibers in many developing countries, including India, and that there were several natural fiber industries that were declining as a result of competition from manmade fibers. For instance, India was the world's largest producer of organic fibers like jute. While jute was available in India at throwaway prices, Indian jute waste was literally free for anyone willing to take it.

Three samples were made from recycled plastic mixed with each of three indigenous reinforcement fibers—jute, coconut fiber, and flax. Any of these components, if found to have the required strength and durability, would be used to mold the wheel. The engineering department at the University of Colorado at Boulder agreed to perform physical testing free of charge. But the physical laboratories would only be available during the summer when the majority of their students would be away. IDE did not mind the wait. They had to get the plastic mixtures sliced and machined before the test samples could be sent to Boulder. If the values were right for a bicycle wheel, then IDE would use a compression die to mold and make the wheel.

As Bill Lincoln and Rob Carter arrived at the Denver office of IDE for the meeting, they knew that the bicycle was riding a rough road. Paul read the letter from the Canadian firm that made the polypropylene samples, indicating its unwillingness to make any more samples. If they had to redo the polypropylene mixture, the project would be stalled until they found another plastics manufacturer willing to assist them for a nominal charge.

Rob Carter was acutely aware of his inability to raise any corporate support for the prototype despite the fact that he knew he had a winning product in the making. In fact, Cannondale, an American bicycle manufacturer that sold top-of-the-line premium bicycles, was highly impressed with pictures of the IDE prototype shown. One of its star designers, Alex Pong, had come up with a bicycle, the Cannondale V-4000, which closely resembled the IDE bicycle. The Cannondale V-4000 was expected to be sold at $5,000-$7,000. With a budget of $1 million, Cannondale was expecting to attract the attention of top pros in the field. The managers at Cannondale were visibly shocked when they found out that IDE had developed the design of its prototype for very little money while they had spent several hundred thousand dollars to get to the same point.

Paul felt that the project might succeed if they could partner with one of the Indian bicycle manufacturers to manufacture and distribute the bicycles. He saw the best fit in Hero, but he knew that to convince Hero to make and sell the bicycle for $15 could be a Herculean task. Or should they seek one of the larger Indian industrial giants like the Tatas and Birlas as partners in this pursuit to provide affordable bicycles to the poor in their country? The IDE bicycle team was uncompromising in its ideals but was in dire need of resources for ensuring continuity of the project.

REFERENCES

Encyclopedia of World Geography. New York: Marshall Cavendish, 1994.
Statesman's Year Book. New York: St. Martin's Press, 1997–98, 1998–99.

CASE 23
Hewlett-Packard Company in Vietnam*

In September 1995, John Peter (disguised name), a marketing manager of Hewlett-Packard Asia Pacific (HPAP), was evaluating HPAP's long-term strategic investment options for doing business in Vietnam. HPAP was a subsidiary of the Hewlett-Packard Company (HP), and its headquarters was located in Singapore. Vietnam had recently adopted an open-door policy after the United States lifted its embargo on the country in February 1994. The country had a population of over 70 million, and foreign investment in the country had climbed steadily to reach almost US$12 billion by the end of 1994.

An environmental and market analysis revealed that the IT market in Vietnam had potential. However, the market was currently small and market growth was uncertain. Several business units within HP had begun to distribute some HP products in Vietnam. Peter needed to make a recommendation on whether HPAP should enter the Vietnam market in a more strategic fashion, that is, to give serious consideration to Vietnam as a major market for HP. If so, what form should the market entry take, and how should it be done?

VIETNAM AND ITS BUSINESS ENVIRONMENT

Vietnam is situated on the east side of the Indochina peninsula and has a total land area of 330,363 km² (Appendix A). It shares borders with China on the north, Laos on the west, and Cambodia on the southwest. The eastern coastline stretches 3,400 km. The country had 56 provinces. Its major cities include the capital city of Hanoi, Ho Chi Minh City (formerly Saigon), and the port cities of Haiphong and Danang. The official language is Vietnamese.

HISTORY

For over a thousand years, from 111 B.C. to A.D. 939, Vietnam was governed as a Chinese province, Giao Chia. After it liberated itself, Vietnam frequently had to resist Chinese invasions. The country remained free of foreign control until 1885, when the French brought all of Vietnam under its rule. After the Japanese surrender in August 1945, Ho Chi Minh, founder of the Vietminh, proclaimed the independence of the Provisional Democratic Republic of Vietnam.

*Reprinted with permission from the *Case Research Journal,* copyright 2000 by the North American Case Research Association and the author, Geok Theng Lau, National University of Singapore.

France's refusal to give up its colony led to a protracted war. China and the Soviet Union backed the Vietminh, while the United States backed the French. In subsequent years, the U.S.-backed Ngo Dinh Diem took power in the South. A united front organization called the National Front for the Liberation of the South was formed to oppose Diem. The conflict escalated and turned into a U.S. war, with the United States deploying 500,000 troops in Vietnam by 1968. The Southern forces collapsed after U.S. withdrawal; on April 30, 1975, the communists entered Saigon, and Vietnam's 30-year war of independence was over.

After the fall of Saigon, the North proceeded to reunify the country. Vietnam subsequently found itself treated with suspicion and, after its invasion of Cambodia in late 1978, was isolated by the international community. After the final withdrawal of Vietnamese troops from Cambodia in late 1989, the process of normalization of economic ties with ASEAN, Western Europe, Northeast Asia, Australia, and New Zealand began to gather pace. In late 1991, after the Paris Agreement on Cambodia, diplomatic and economic relations with many countries, including China, were fully normalized.

POLITICAL ENVIRONMENT

The supreme organ of state power in Vietnam is the National Assembly, which performs functions such as promulgation of laws; ratification of the annual and long-term plans for economic and social development; budget planning; election of top officials; and selection of the cabinet members. The government is the executive body responsible for the enforcement of the laws of the country issued by the National Assembly.

Until the mid-to-late 1980s, the leadership of the Vietnamese Communist Party held orthodox Marxist-Leninist beliefs, which viewed the world as a mortal struggle between imperialist and revolutionary camps. In the late 1980s to early 1990s, due partly to the fall of the Berlin Wall, the Vietnamese Political Bureau acknowledged the need for Vietnam to participate actively in the global capitalist economy, because the socialist organization for economic cooperation (COMECON) was becoming less relevant. The leadership sought to achieve a breakthrough in trade with the capitalist countries and an expansion of external cooperation, including accepting loans for capital investment and promoting joint venture projects.

Elements of the old worldview, however, continued to coexist with the new one. The aging leadership continued to adopt an autocratic political system, and there was conflict between a closed political system and the economy opening up. This resulted in continuing debates and shifts in emphasis from struggle against imperialism to economic interdependence.

THE PEOPLE AND WORKFORCE

The population of Vietnam in 1995 was approximately 71 million people, 70% of them under 35 years of age. The population growth was 2.2%. The population is basically rural and concentrated in the two main rice growing deltas: the Red River in the north and the Mekong in the south. The river delta population is almost entirely ethnic Vietnamese (Kinh), who make up 87% of the total population. The minority groups (including Khmer, Cham, Muong, and Thai peoples), whose cultures and languages are quite distinct from those of the Kinh Vietnamese, are found in the upland areas. The overseas Chinese community, largely concentrated in the South, has been depleted by the decision of many to leave the country, often as "boat people." This community had partly recouped its position in the economy since the late 1980s, largely on the strength of its links with Hong Kong and Taiwan.

Vietnam is under-urbanized by comparison with many other developing countries in Southeast Asia. The largest city is Ho Chi Minh, with a population of well over 4 million. The capital, Hanoi, has a registered population of 3.1 million. The level of primary education is comparatively high. The population, especially in the north, is basically literate, with a literacy rate of over 90%. The average wages in Vietnam and some neighboring countries are shown in Exhibit 1.

ECONOMIC ENVIRONMENT

Vietnam is the largest of the three Indochinese nations, accounting for about 44% of total land area and 75% of the combined population of the region. The country is endowed with oil reserves and extensive mineral resources. It is an agro-based economy, with the agricultural sector absorbing 70% of the workforce (numbering about 32 million people) and contributing some 40% to the GNP and nearly 40% to total exports. Since 1989, Vietnam has become an important rice exporter and the world's third-largest rice exporter, after Thailand and the United States.

Light industries, including textiles, garments, footwear, paper, food processing, electrical, and electronics, though scattered throughout the country, are more concentrated in the south. Heavy industries, including iron and steel, power generation, cement, mining, chemicals, fertilizers, and machine tools, are mainly concentrated in the north. The number of industrial establishments in Vietnam is shown in Appendix B.

In the past, Vietnam relied mainly on the Soviet Union and Eastern European countries for trade and economic cooperation and assistance. All of its foreign aid and one-half of its export markets vanished with the collapse of the Eastern bloc in 1991. The country, however, survived this crisis, and economic growth rebounded to an official 8.3% in 1992 after a mild slowdown to around 5% in 1990. Inflation eased from about 700% in 1986 to 17.5% in 1992. Foreign investment approvals rose by 73% in 1992 and accounted for 26.2% of total investments. Exports rose by 19% to US$2.5 billion, and imports climbed by 9% during the same year. For the first time in several decades, Vietnam was estimated to have registered a trade and current account surplus in 1992. Exhibit 2 shows some key economic indicators for Vietnam from 1991 to 1994.

The government encouraged greater exports and imports. Exports were encouraged, and only a few items were subject to export duty, which had been kept low. The import of capital goods and materials for domestic production was encouraged; the import of consumer goods that could be produced at home or were considered luxurious was discouraged. The list of items subject to export and import prohibition or quota had been substantially cut down. Greater autonomy was given to companies and enterprises in their export and import business. State subsidies and price controls on exports and imports had ended except for some major items. The country established its first export processing zone, named Tan Thuan, in Ho Chi Minh City in 1991.

Vietnam had diversified its export and import markets to other parts of the world. As a result, about 80% of total trade was now with Asia Pacific countries, with Singapore, Japan, Hong Kong, South Korea, Taiwan, Australia, and Thailand the main trade partners. Meanwhile, widespread tax reforms and improved collection had raised government revenue by 82%. Reflecting

	Monthly Wage Rate (US$)
China	50
Hong Kong	525
Indonesia	80
Malaysia	290
Philippines	95
Singapore	600
Taiwan	650
Thailand	165
Vietnam	35

Source: World Bank, Trends in Developing Countries.

Exhibit 1 Monthly Minimum Wage Rates of Selected Asian Markets

	GDP Growth	Industrial Growth	Services Growth	Agricultural Growth
1991	6.0	10.0	2.2	8.2
1992	8.6	15.0	7.2	8.3
1993	8.1	12.0	4.4	13.0
1994	8.5	13.5	4.5	12.5

Source: General Statistical Office, Vietnam.

Exhibit 2 Key Economic Indicators for Vietnam, 1991–94 (%)

1989	4,000
1990	5,200
1991	9,390
1992	11,181
1993	10,641
1994	11,080

Source: Economic Intelligence Unit, Business in Vietnam.

Exhibit 3 Exchange Rates of the Dong (per US$)

these strengths, the Vietnamese currency, the dong, appreciated almost 5% against the U.S. dollar in 1993, in contrast to 1991 when its value was almost halved (Exhibit 3). Vietnam normalized relations with the World Bank, the IMF, and the ADB and attracted many sources of bilateral and multilateral financial support. Vietnam joined ASEAN in July 1995.

Appendix C shows the distribution of foreign investments by sectors. Appendix D shows the foreign investments from the top ten countries. Joint ventures accounted for about 74% of foreign investments; totally foreign-owned companies accounted for 11.0%, and business cooperation contracts accounted for 15%.

The lifting of the U.S. trade embargo on Vietnam in February 1994 brought benefits such as direct access to U.S. technology and investment and smoother access to soft loans and aids from multi-lateral institutions. A survey of 100 American companies by the U.S.-ASEAN council (reported in *Business Times of Singapore,* February 5, 1994) indicated that trade and investment opportunities in Vietnam were worth US$2.6 billion in the first two years after the lifting of the embargo. Foreign investment had climbed steadily and reached US$11.99 billion (from 1201 projects) as of the beginning of January 1995.

The government set target growth rates of 3.5–4% for the agriculture, aquaculture, and livestock husbandry sectors and 7–8% for the industrial sector. The food processing industry would give priority to the development of the Mekong and Red River Delta regions in order to upgrade the quality of processed agroproducts and aquatic products to export standards. In the production of consumer goods, attention would be paid to the rehabilitation of current equipment and installation of new equipment to improve the quality of manufactured products. Electronics assembling and manufacturing facilities would be established. Oil and gas exploitation on the continental shelf would be carried out, and an oil refinery would be constructed. The mining, cement production, steel, and mechanical industries were also targeted for development.

Despite the positive economic outlook, some economic observers pointed out several problems. A low savings rate and lack of hard currency constrained investment growth. Vietnam had an estimated US$15 billion of foreign debt, and the foreign exchange reserve constituted only about one month of imports. Three-quarters of export revenues were generated from only two sources—unprocessed farm products and crude oil. The inflation rate in Vietnam had ranged from a high of 400% in 1988 to a low of 15% in 1992. The forecast for 1994–98 was 40%. The Vietnam dong was not a fully convertible currency. The official exchange rate had depreciated from 5,200 dong per U.S. dollar to 9,390 dong per U.S. dollar in 1991 (see Exhibit 3). The state-owned enterprises appeared inefficient. They used 85% of the total fixed capital, 80% of total credit volume, 100% of savings, 60% of forestry output, and 90% of trained and high-school-educated people, but they contributed less than 15% of total GDP in 1992.

FOREIGN EXCHANGE AND INVESTMENT REGULATIONS

At one time in Vietnam, all transactions had to pass through the state export and import corporations. Beginning in 1980, however, provinces, cities, and individual enterprises were given some freedom to sign contracts with foreign traders. Exchange control was administered by the State Bank, which had branches in Hanoi and Ho Chi Minh City.

On January 1, 1988, a new foreign investment law was promulgated to supersede the one dating from 1977. The new code allowed foreigners to own up to 100% of a venture, against a previous maximum of 49%. The old requirement that foreign investors should take a minimum 30% stake in joint ventures was retained. Priority areas for investment specified in the code were production for export and import substitution. Investors were expected to meet their own foreign exchange needs. The duration of a venture with foreign capital generally might not exceed 20 years, but it could be extended in special cases.

Corporate income tax had been reduced from 30–50% in the old code to 15–25% in the new one. There was a provision for tax holidays of up to two years after a company made a profit. A statute governing labor relations and remuneration in foreign-invested companies was issued in 1990. Some main provisions in the statute specified the minimum wages, working hours, days of rest and holidays, minimum working age, rights to join a union, and labor arbitration process. The State Committee for Cooperation and Investment was created to manage and administer all foreign direct investment in 1988.

Land in Vietnam could not be purchased, only leased for a period that depended on the duration of investment. The cost of land lease ranged from US$0.50 to $18.00 per m^2 per year in 1995.

INFRASTRUCTURE AND BANKING SYSTEM

The existing telecommunications system in Vietnam was found by many to be expensive and inefficient. The country relied mainly on waterways for transportation. The port facilities were felt to be backward and might hinder the distribution system, especially when volume increased with the expected surge in economic activities. Many observers from the financial sector felt that the banking system, though reformed, was still far from those in capitalist countries and might cause delays and confusion, especially in the handling of foreign exchange remittances.

The Vietnamese government had directed the state to invest in the construction of infrastructures, such as water supply and drainage systems in big cities, in-town traffic projects, highway networks connecting the big cities, a north-south railway network, restoration and improvement of seaports, and upgrading of airports in major cities. There were plans to construct new hydropower plants and thermopower plants, with a target production of 16–17 billion kWh for 1995.

INFORMATION TECHNOLOGY MARKET IN VIETNAM

Market Characteristics

The computer industry in Vietnam was in its infancy. The 18-year-old trade embargo imposed by the United States had effectively prevented computer technology from being transferred into the country by any of the major computer manufacturers and heavily restricted any capital inflow. Because the number of computer installations was small and located mostly in Ho Chi Minh City, many businesspeople viewed the computer industry as an emerging industry with good market potential. There were not many competitors in the market, and there were no clear leaders in the market yet. Distribution channels for the industry were also not fully developed.

An analysis of Vietnam's IT end-user market showed that the government, together with its related agencies and institutions, made up 35% of the market, followed by multinationals (35%), small and medium enterprises (25%), and small home or office users making up the remaining market. The buyers in the foreseeable future would be the public sector and major foreign companies. The deal sizes were forecast to be large as the government departments and foreign companies made initial investments in IT infrastructure.

Different types of computers, such as personal computers, minicomputers, RISC-based workstations, and mainframes, could be used by businesses in their operation in Vietnam. The price differences among them would be an important consideration for these different business customers in their buying decisions. Skilled local expertise in IT in Vietnam was somewhat limited. The Vietnamese workforce, however, was hardworking and well educated and could possibly be trained quickly.

Computer products had limited intrinsic proprietary attributes, and most innovations were easily imitated. Computer products, thus, were increasingly becoming less differentiated. The market, especially the low-end segment, tended to have fierce price competition, and switching costs from one manufacturer to another were low. Vietnamese users tended to favor U.S. computer brands, even though brand loyalty for the product area was currently not strong.

There were problems associated with the lack of normalized ties between the United States and Vietnam, although the trade embargo had been lifted. As a result, U.S. banks were not able to provide credit, although financing for their operation was a necessity for doing business in Vietnam because hard currency was still hard to come by. U.S. IT companies such as UNISYS had invested heavily in at least two large IT bids, only to find that their European and Japanese competitors had an edge over them when it came to extending credit. This problem might be resolved in the near future, for U.S. Secretary of State Warren Christopher had recommended that ties with Vietnam be normalized.

As in other Asian countries, *guanxi* was an important factor in doing business in Vietnam. *Guanxi* is a Chinese term denoting the use of personal connections, relationships, or networks to win business deals, forge business ventures, or get business approvals for government authorities. Local and regional competitors would have a better understanding of such culture and practices, and they would have built up their own networks because they entered the market before the trade embargo was lifted.

VIETNAM'S IT-2000 PROGRAM

In 1993, Vietnam planned to propel itself into the twenty-first century through a billion-dollar program called IT-2000, based on a similar development model created in Singapore. The IT-2000 called for expenditures of up to $2 billion over the next five years to set up the hardware necessary to create a national data communications network, establish a domestic industry in component manufacturing, and educate over 5,000 Vietnamese in the use of computer technology. The government adopted the IT-2000 on August 4, 1993, designating it a national initiative. The Ministry of Science, Technology and Environment was given the formidable task of overseeing the plan.

Part of this plan was to create on-line computer networks for almost all government agencies and the financial sector, build the Vietnam Education Research and Development Network (VERDNet), and provide each secondary school and university student in Vietnam with access to an integrated computer complete with Vietnamese educational software. The IT-2000 also addressed government policies for financial management and support. The State Bank of Vietnam and the Ministry of Finance were desperately in need of an integrated nationwide data processing network to manage the chaos of transactions in banking, financial markets, and tax collection.

The minister of Science, Technology and the Environment and chairman of IT-2000, Dr. Dang Hua, was quoted as saying:

''The purpose of IT-2000 is to build a foundation for basic information demands in the management of government and socio-economic activities, and to develop the IT industry to a level where it can help in national development. We have stated very clearly in the master plan for IT-2000 that an integrated system of different computing networks must be built, with strong enough software and database systems which are able to service the government and other key essential activities. Some domestic services will be integrated with international systems.''

CUSTOMER GROUPS IN THE IT MARKET

Two segmentation approaches, by industry and by benefits, were adopted to examine customer groups in the IT market. The industry segmentation identified the high-growth business segments of the Vietnamese economy which, from HP's experience in other countries, might be heavy and early adopters of IT. The benefit segmentation further defined the characteristics and needs of these segments.

INDUSTRY SEGMENTATION

Financial Services. The Vietnamese government had increasingly liberalized foreign bank participation. Beginning in 1995, investments totaling US$1.77 billion had been made in financial and commercial services. Apart from the lucrative trade finance business, which was forecast to expand rapidly, other financial services, especially venture capital, leasing, and project financing, had potential too. In the short to medium term, this was generally the segment most Vietnam watchers and experts deemed likely to experience explosive growth. Funds from lenders were desperately needed to fuel the growth of the economy. In addition, the government was trying to encourage savings to create a pool of investment money. The financial industry had long viewed IT as a competitive advantage and, thus, IT investment in this segment was expected to pick up strongly. Due to the mission-critical nature of financial applications, financial customers demanded a high level of support services.

Telecommunications. Vietnam's telecommunications infrastructure was still in its infancy. Explosive growth was expected here as well, especially in mobile communications and high-speed data communications links for businesses. The postal and telecommunications sectors were still very much a monopoly, so any investor wanting to offer a public telecommunications service would have to work with VNPT, the Vietnam Post and Telecommunications Department. Sample announcements of foreign joint ventures in the telecommunications sector are shown in Exhibit 4.

Hotel and Tourism. Vietnam had increasingly become a new tourist destination, and business travels continued to surge. This would create demand for hotel facilities and spark the growth of a retail sector. Some international hotel groups, such as the Accor Group and Pullman International Hotels, and some Singapore companies had begun hotel projects in Vietnam. Beginning in 1995, foreign investment projects totaling US$2.23 billion had been made in this sector.

Manufacturing. Vietnam was an attractive location for labor-intensive industries because of its low wages and a relatively skilled and productive workforce. The government encouraged export-oriented and resource- or agriculture-based manufacturing such as assembly operations for electronic goods, garments, and food processing industries.

Utilities. There would be explosive growth in this area as Vietnam sought to build a power infrastructure to cope with the demands of a modern economy. The Phu My thermal power plant project, worth US$900 million, was expected to provide 600 MW of power.

Oil and Gas. There were extensive offshore crude extraction activities going on. The Vietnamese government wished to promote local refining of crude oil. Many joint ventures with the various international and regional oil extraction and refining companies such as BHP, Mobil, Shell, and Petronas were already in

France. Alcatel Alsthom said it had been selected by the Ministry of the Interior to supply the first private national communications network in Vietnam. The contract covered the supply, installation, implementation, and maintenance of a service integration network, which would eventually cover the entire country and represent 50,000 lines. The first part of the network was to be operational in March 1995.

Sweden. Three Swedish companies and Vietnam's Posts and Telecommunications Department had applied for a licence to set up a US$340 million mobile phone network covering the whole of Vietnam. They hoped to install and operate a cellular telephone and paging system connected by hubs in Hanoi in the north, Danang in the center, and Saigon in the south by the end of 1995. The Swedish companies were reported to be Industriforvaltlngs, Kirnevic, and Comvik International, and they said their combined investment would be US$159 million.

Canada. Montreal-based Teleglobe Inc. said its cable systems arm and Telesystem International Wireless Services Inc. had signed a deal to study the feasibility of a multiregional wireless and communication service and coastal submarine fiber optic cable system in Vietnam. The study would cost US$720,000 and the project itself would cost US$1 00 million.

Source: Internal company files, extracted from various sources.

Exhibit 4 Foreign Joint Ventures in the Telecommunications Sector

place. Total foreign investment as of the beginning of 1995 in this sector totaled US$1.3 billion.

Government. The government was expected to play a major role in influencing the use and penetration of IT in the Vietnamese economy. With its IT-2000 plan, the Vietnamese government hoped to follow in Singapore's footsteps and accelerate the country's entry into high technology.

BENEFIT SEGMENTATION

The benefit segmentation of IT customers is shown in Exhibit 5. Benefit segmentation distinguishes customers by choice criteria, technology requirements, and primary needs. Four benefit segments were identified.

Economy Segment. This segment used IT mainly for productivity gains. PCs, simple networks, and off-the-shelf software were generally preferred because of cost reasons. Price-to-performance ratio was an important buying criterion; these customers were extremely cost sensitive and also did not require high-quality, round-the-clock support.

Technology Segment. This segment planned IT implementation so that they could be seen as technology leaders. Customers

Segments	Some customers	Choice criteria	Technology requirements	Primary needs
Economy (low price)	Consumer products; retail sector	Low price; low design content	Simple	Low costs; productivity gains
Technology	Oil and gas utilities	Leading-edge solution	Complex	Technology leadership
Mission-critical, mission-sensitive	Banking and finance; couriers	High reliability; good and fast service	Proven and tested	Maximum uptime; performance
Geographic coverage	MNCs	Regional or worldwide presence	Wide area requirement	Branch connectivity; consistent support

Exhibit 5 Benefit Segments

here generally had deep pockets and were willing to pay for the latest and best technology.

Mission Critical—Mission Sensitive Segment. This segment used IT for competitive advantage. The failure of its information systems would interrupt business operations, sometimes bringing them to a standstill, thus affecting revenue and profit. Hence, these customers looked for high availability, near-zero downtime, round-the-clock support, and reliable solutions. They might also be uncomfortable with new technologies and view them as risky unless they saw a distinct competitive advantage in implementing them.

Geographic Coverage Segment. This segment consisted of multinational corporations that operated worldwide or regionally and had a need to connect their dispersed operations to ensure that information was disseminated quickly and reliably. Consistent, global support was critical when serving this segment.

SOME PLAYERS IN THE VIETNAM IT MARKET

Exhibit 6 shows selected information on some major players in the IT market.

DIGITAL EQUIPMENT CORPORATION

Digital Equipment Corporation (DEC) was a leading supplier of networked computer systems, software, and services. Its areas of differentiation were open systems, client-server knowledge and experiences, and multivendor experiences. Its strategy was to invest in technical research, build up technical capabilities, and focus on training.

Over the past few years, DEC's financial results had been poor, with a net loss of US$2 billion in 1994. This poor performance caused the ouster of DEC's founder and CEO, Ken Olsen. His replacement from within was Robert Palmer, who had since sold off several of DEC's noncore divisions, such as the disk drive

operation, database software, and the consulting unit. He sought to focus on DEC's core hardware business and increase margin by adding value in networking. Palmer had positioned DEC to take advantage of key trends such as mobile computing and video on demand. Palmer had also shifted most sales to indirect distribution channels and sought to slash costs by signing on computer resellers as key partners. Salomon Brothers expected DEC's new Alpha system sales to soar in 1995 by 84% to US$1.7 billion and by another 55% in 1996.

In 1992, DEC had 45% of its turnover in the United States, 40% in Europe, 10% in Asia Pacific (including Japan), and 5% in Canada. Alpha still faced a long-term problem: the chip had not won a single influential convert among computer makers. That could ultimately prove fatal when it came time to fund the mind-boggling cost of succeeding generations of chips. Most industry analysts believed that Palmer's accomplishments of the past year had merely brought DEC to the point where it was ready to compete again. If Palmer could not make DEC stand out with his networking strategy, the company risked following the path of another former industry number two, Unisys Corporation, which now served mostly its old customers, and its revenue was shrinking slowly. DEC had a strong client base in government, banking and finance, insurance, and telecommunications. It had also done projects in health care, transportation, utilities, and retail. DEC currently had a representative office in Hanoi. So far, its main area of activity seemed to be on large, internationally funded tenders. It had appointed three distributors in Vietnam as sales outlets and service providers.

INTERNATIONAL BUSINESS MACHINE

Despite losses amounting to over US$8 billion in 1994, IBM was still the world's largest information systems and services company. In 1995, IBM CEO Lou Gertsner had engineered a turnaround. Recently, IBM had purchased Lotus Corporation for US$3.5 billion. IBM's worldwide revenues had declined since 1990, slipping to US$62.7 billion in 1994. In 1992, IBM had 1,500 consultants

Company	1994 Annual revenue (US$m)	1994 Net income (US$m)	1993 Net income (US$m)	Number of employees	Revenue per Employee (US$)
IBM	62,716.0	−8,101.0	−4,965.0	267,196	234,719
Hewlett-Packard	24,991.0	1,599.0	1,177.0	98,400	253,974
DEC	13,450.8	−2,156.1	−251.0	78,000	172,466
Unisys	7,742.5	565.4	361.2	49,000	158,010
Compaq	7,191.0	462.0	213.0	10,043	716,021

Source: Software Asia Magazine, June/July 1995.

Exhibit 6 Some Players in the IT Market

worldwide. Although these consultants provided support to all industries, their key focus was on finance, retail, and manufacturing.

IBM's key area of differentiation was its ability not only to provide insights, experience, and specialized skills to its customers, but also to deliver results and increase the value of IBM products and services to customers. Its strategy was to focus on customer relationships and develop account presence. Its global organization allowed IBM to bring its best intellectual capabilities to bear on any project. IBM, however, was still encumbered by a mainframe image it might never completely shake. Still in recovery mode and uncertain about its strategic directions, IBM supported more than a half dozen operating systems as well as dual desktop hardware platforms with PowerPC and X86.

IBM had set up ''IBM Vietnam'' in Hanoi in 1995. The operation provided sales and marketing support to distributors and dealers as well as customers. It had also appointed its dealers as service providers for hardware repair and support.

UNISYS

In 1994, Unisys was the ninth-largest systems and PC vendor in the world. Unisys manufactured and marketed computer-based networked information systems and software. The company also offered related services, such as systems integration and IT outsourcing. As such, its strategy was to provide a full spectrum of services and solutions. It sought to develop leading-edge hardware and technology in open systems.

Unisys specialized in providing business-critical solutions based on open information networks for organizations that operated in transaction-intensive environments. In 1992, Unisys generated 49% of its revenue from the United States, 30% from Europe, 9% from Canada, 5% from Asia-Pacific, and 7% from Japan. For international projects, it normally relied upon local resources. Vertically, Unisys focused on airlines, public sectors, financial services, and telecommunications. Horizontally, it focused on networking and on-line transaction processing. Unisys had also established a representative office in Vietnam. With 15 marketing staff based in the country, it appeared that Unisys had adopted an aggressive strategy in Vietnam. In 1995 it installed its equipment for the banking sector in the country for SWIFT (Society for Worldwide Interbank Financial Telecommunications) transactions.

Unisys was targeting to set up an operation (subsidiary) in Vietnam in 1996.

COMPAQ

In 1995, Compaq completed yet another record year, with sales of US$10.9 billion, up 51% from the previous year. Net income grew by a healthy 88% to reach US$867 million. As the leading manufacturer of PC systems (desktops, portables, and servers), Compaq was currently positioned to tackle both the consumer and corporate computing markets and was now a major player in the commercial server market.

The reasons for Compaq's success to date included aggressive expansion of distribution channels, efficient manufacturing, ability to bring new products and technologies into the market early, ability to deliver top-quality products, and ability to include added-value features in its products.

THE HEWLETT-PACKARD COMPANY

In January 1939, in a garage in Palo Alto, California, two graduates from nearby Stanford University, William Hewlett and David Packard, set up the Hewlett-Packard Company with an initial capital of US$538. They marketed their first product (invented by Bill), a resistance capacity audio oscillator. HP's initial emphasis was on instrumentation. It was not until 1972 that the company finally acknowledged that it was in the computer field with the introduction of its first business computer, the HP3000.

By 1995, HP was a sprawling corporate giant with annual sales in excess of US$25 billion and about 90,000 employees worldwide. It was involved principally in the manufacture, supply, marketing, and distribution of computer-based products, test and measurement products, medical and analytical products, electronic components, and IT-related service and support. In 1985, HP was ranked by a *Fortune* survey as one of the two most admired companies in the United States. In 1995, the bulk of the company's business, a good 76.6% of the net revenue, came from computational products and services.

Years ago, Bill Hewlett and Dave Packard developed a set of management objectives for the company. With only slight modification, these became the corporate objectives of HP and were first published in 1957. These objectives gave a clear idea as to how the company viewed itself and its position in society. The HP Statement of Corporate Objectives (October 1986) is shown in Appendix E.

These corporate objectives formed the basis of what was known as the "HP Way," which sought to create a work environment geared to produce capable, innovative, well-trained, and enthusiastic people who could give their best to the company. HP's guiding strategic principle was to provide customers with devices superior to any competitive offering in performance, quality, and overall value. To this day, HP corporate strategy is pursued with three measures in mind: getting the highest return out of the company's most important asset, its people; getting the best output from a given technology; and giving the customer the best performance for price paid.

Around the world, HP was organized broadly into several strategic business units, as shown in Appendix F. Each business unit was represented in HP's top management and was more or less run as an independent entity within HP.

HP MARKET POSITION AND CAPABILITIES

HP had an established presence in Hong Kong, Singapore, Japan, Taiwan, and Korea for more than 25 years. It had extensive experience in entering into emerging Asian markets such as China, Indonesia, and the Philippines. Though a subsidiary of a U.S. company, HP Southeast Asia had a largely Asian management team. They shared similar norms, practices, beliefs, customs, and languages with many local markets. Nevertheless, HP was still a U.S. company with its own stringent code of business and the requirement to comply with U.S. laws.

HP had, over the years, built up many major customer accounts, many of which were multinational corporations with offices worldwide. It had a strong reputation and brand identity. The HP name was often synonymous with high-quality products and high technology, albeit at a premium price. HP could not be as aggressive in product pricing because of its higher cost structure and overheads. HP had, for many years, come up tops in many independent customer satisfaction surveys conducted by organizations such as Datapro and IDC.

HP had a large network of subsidiaries and associated companies in different countries in the Asia-Pacific region. It was thus able to find raw materials and parts in these countries at the cheapest prices, manufacture at locations with the lowest costs, and establish an efficient distribution and warehousing network to transport products from manufacturing sites to markets.

Exhibit 7 shows some information related to the turnover and earnings of HP from 1989 to 1994. In the brutal, fast-paced world of IT, customers looked for financial stability to ensure that vendors would still be around when their projects were completed, especially for large multi-year, infrastructural projects.

HP was a diversified company and had products and services in computation, measurement, and communications. This gave it a breadth that few computer vendors could match. The autonomous units dealing with measurement, communications, and computers in the HP setup, however, often acted as separate companies and thus created functional silos that might not effectively leverage HP's knowledge and diversity.

HP was the industry leader in open systems technology and solutions, and it had a specialized knowledge and extensive experience in this area. The company moved into RISC4 long before DEC, IBM, and other rivals and was now collecting the dividends. HP was strong in client/server computing involving PCs, workstations, and large systems and servers. It opened up its proprietary HP 3000 systems, and it had become a whirlwind of success.

Although HP served a cross section of the IT industry, it had in particular established significant presence in three industry

	1989	1990	1991	1992	1993	1994
Revenue	11,889	13,233	14,494	16,410	20,317	24,991
Cost of Revenue	6,091	6,993	7,858	9,152	12,123	1 5,490
Gross Profit	5,798	6,240	6,636	7,258	8,194	9,501
Research and Development	1,269	1,367	1,463	1,619	1,761	2,027
Marketing, General & Administrative	3,327	3,711	3,963	4,224	4,554	4,925
Operating Income	1,202	1,162	1,210	1,415	1,879	2,549
Other Income/Exp.	(61)	(106)	(83)	(79)	(96)	(126)
Pretax Income	1,141	I,056	1,127	I,336	I,783	2,423
Income Tax	322	317	372	449	606	824
Net Income	819	739	755	887	I,177	I,599

Source: Salomon Brothers.

Exhibit 7 Income and Earnings of HP from 1989 to 1994 (US$ million)

groups: manufacturing, telecommunications, and financial services. In addition, HP also had large installed bases in industries such as retail, hospitality, government, and health services. In manufacturing, HP was the dominant worldwide supplier of UNIX systems, accounting for 45% of this market. HP had a wide range of customers in the manufacturing sector, which remained HP's largest vertical market.

HP sought to use the distribution channel as a means to support its customers. In 1988, HP sold products primarily through a direct sales force. The company foresaw the rapid fall in gross margins as standardization, volumes, and competitiveness increased, and so it developed two distinct sales strategies: one for volume sales, where sales were indirect and took place through sales channels, and the other direct, providing value sales to large HP target accounts around the world. While many high-tech companies viewed distribution channels as their customers, HP had identified end users as its customers. HP recognized that the computer industry had become a demand-driven (pull) environment and sought to create demand for its products among end users. HP tracked very closely consumer buying preferences and responded quickly to changes in the market.

HP BUSINESSES IN SOUTHEAST ASIA

Hewlett-Packard Southeast Asia had its headquarters in Singapore with fully owned subsidiaries in Singapore, Malaysia, and Thailand. In Indonesia, the Philippines, and Brunei, HP appointed distributors. In addition, HP had a joint venture in Indonesia with its distributor, Berca, called HPSI, which was primarily an IT services company.

In Southeast Asia, WCSO was represented by the Southeast Asia (SEA) Customer Support Organization, whose role was to provide services and support in satisfying customer's needs in financing, implementing, and operating their IT operations. The SEA Customer Support Organization managed the following product lines:

PL72-Hardware Support for Computer Systems and Networks
PL3D-Software Support for Computer Systems
PL71-Support for Personal Computers and Peripherals
PL6N-Outsourcing Services
PL6L-Network Integration Services

Product Lines 72, 3D, and 71 were the traditional maintenance services HP had provided for buyers and users of its computer systems and was primarily focused on post-sale maintenance. In recent years, these businesses had experienced a declining growth rate. Prices of computer products continued to drop, even as their performance improved. This trend was especially prevalent in the hardware maintenance business. Support expenditure, typically capped at a percentage of total IT expenditure, was thus greatly affected by this trend.

Product Lines 6N and 6L were the newer businesses WCSO had set up to counter the slower growth of the traditional mainte-

nance businesses. They required higher investment and typically had lower profitability. The selling model for these product lines was also different, requiring more direct selling since it was not always possible to leverage support revenues off computational product sales, as was more often the case in the traditional maintenance businesses.

HP BUSINESS IN VIETNAM

Since the lifting of the U.S. embargo in 1994, different business units in HP had taken initial and ad hoc steps to develop their businesses in Vietnam in response to the current changes taking place in the country. The CSO, CPO, and TMO had signed up distributors in Vietnam to distribute their products. The CSO currently had one main distributor, the High Performance Technology Corporation (HiPT). HiPT was 100% privately owned. One of the owners, Dr. Binh, had good contacts with the Vietnamese government. CSO was ready to appoint a second distributor (the Peregrine Group) for the south of Vietnam. TMO had also appointed a distributor, Systems Interlace, while CPO had appointed several wholesalers and resellers in Vietnam. Projected orders from these product organizations were expected to hit US$10 million at the end of October 1995. HP's computer support business, WCSO, was not represented in Vietnam in 1994.

HP and its CSO distributor in Vietnam, HiPT, officially opened a center for open systems computing expertise in Hanoi on July 1, 1995. Its establishment was part of a formal memorandum of understanding between HP and the Ministry of Science, Technology and the Environment (MOSTE), signed in March 1995. MOSTE was the body responsible for the promotion and development of information technology in Vietnam. The center would assist MOSTE's goal of developing a pool of qualified IT professionals to implement the Vietnam IT-2000 plan, based on the open systems concept.

FIELD TRIP TO VIETNAM

In January 1995, HPAP marketing manager John Peter made a business visit to Vietnam to assess the business climate and investment opportunities firsthand and to provide ideas on how WCSO in Southeast Asia should plan its overall investment strategy in Vietnam, rather than the current ad hoc involvement of its CSO, CPO, and TMO in the Vietnamese market. The first stop was Ho Chi Minh City, a bustling city of 5 million people, 1 hour and 25 minutes from Singapore by air.

Meeting with Dr. Vo Van Mai (Managing Director of HiPT)

Dr. Vo Van Mai was the managing director of HiPT, HP's distributor in Vietnam. He was educated in Hungary. Mai expected the IT market in Vietnam to hit US$300 million by the year 2000. The market size had doubled each year for the past few years, and

Mai expected the IT market to grow even more rapidly in the next two years. Currently, IT took the form of mainly PCs, with some limited local area networks. Vietnam, being an IT greenfield, looked likely to adopt client-server technology in a big way, bypassing legacy and proprietary systems common in most developing and developed countries. The PC brands available in Vietnam included Compaq, HP, ACER, Wearnes, AST, Digital, Unisys, and IBM.

Mai felt that the most attractive segments of the IT market would be finance, utilities, telecommunications, petrochemicals, and airlines. Within Vietnam, the primary means of data transmission were phone lines and modems. Between Hanoi and Ho Chi Minh City, more sophisticated and higher bandwidth transmission methods were available through fiber-optic links and X.25. IBM had representative offices in Hanoi and Ho Chi Minh City, with a staff strength of ten. It had six or seven distributors in Vietnam, and it was known that IBM had applied for a license to operate a service operation in Vietnam.

Mai's conclusions were that it would be three to four years before the Vietnamese market became really significant in IT revenues. He felt that the next two years would be critical in establishing a presence and building relationships and awareness of products and services. Obtaining budgets for IT expenditure was still a problem. The government's IT-2000 plan, however, was a clear indication of the its commitment to IT.

Meeting with Mr. Ross Nicholson (General Manager of DHL Worldwide Express)

Ross Nicholson felt that he had access to good market information because DHL had been operating in Vietnam since 1988. DHL worked through the Vietnam post office, because the Vietnamese government still controlled the provision of mail and postal services tightly. Nicholson was assigned to Vietnam as a technical advisor in April 1994. He told us that things had not boomed as expected since the U.S. embargo was lifted. Some obstacles like chaotic taxation laws and investment risks still plagued potential investors. In the short term, the Mexican peso incident was likely to affect investor outlook, especially in emerging economies like Vietnam. In his opinion, the Asians, especially the Japanese, were moving in very quickly. Hotels in Hanoi were usually full of Japanese.

In Nicholson's opinion, the finance industry had the highest prospects for growth in the immediate future. Currently, agriculture was DHL's biggest customer for the provision of shipping facilities. In time, more technologically advanced production activity would take place. DHL would then have the opportunity to sell logistics services to these new entrants, leveraging their long experience in the Vietnamese market. DHL would like to get itself integrated into these companies, which would be happy to listen because they were in start-up mode.

Nicholson believed that there would not be anything spectacular for two to three years. He cited the lack of skilled IT personnel as one of the obstacles to IT growth. Still, he felt that it was well worth the investment of establishing a presence in Vietnam now,

so that when the boom came companies like DHL would be well positioned to capitalize on the ensuing growth. DHL currently used a standalone PC for its IT needs. This was certainly not suitable for the anticipated growth. Nicholson intended to upgrade to a nationwide system comprising two HP 9000 E45s.

Meeting with Dr. Truene Gia Binh (Managing Director of FPT)

The Corporation for Financing and Promoting Technology (FPT) was a wholly owned government company incorporated under the auspices of MOSTE. Binh, the managing director of FPT and son-in-law of a prominent general in Vietnam, elaborated on the difference in status between a representative office and an operating office. Basically, a representative office could only acquire goods required for the operation of the office. It was not allowed to receive payment for any products or services rendered but could provide marketing and support services as part of its distributor support service. Commenting on the attractiveness of the IT market, Binh felt that the financial sector would be very attractive due to the high growth prospects and the prominence placed on it by the Vietnamese economy in the next three to four years.

Meeting with Mr. Hai Chao Duy (Director of Technical Services and Operations, Vietnam Mobile Telecommunication Services)

Mr. Hai Chao Duy looked forward to a long-term relationship with HP. He mentioned the tremendous opportunities in Vietnam Mobile Telecom Services (VMS) to build networks. VMS supplied cellular services to 9,000 subscribers in Ho Chi Minh City and Hanoi. The IT projects needed to facilitate the provision of cellular services were in operation, transmission, business support, finance, end-user computing, and e-mailing. He also mentioned that the next project would involve some management system software for the telecommunication network.

Meeting with Mr. Nguyen Trang (Chairman of HCMC Computer Association)

Mr. Nguyen Trang was a very influential personality in IT and chairman of the Ho Chi Minh City Computer Association. The Vietnam IT-2000 plan would be driven centrally from Hanoi. The city also had a board that would oversee the implementation of the plan. That plan had been approved, and Nguyen revealed details regarding two other projects.

One was IT applications for municipal and government administration in the areas of transportation and traffic control, financial control, industrial administration, land property, city planning, trade services, and manpower development. The other was governmental IT infrastructure development. This included the setup of units such as the Center for System Analysis and Design and the Center for Manpower Development, and projects such as the feasibility study for Ho Chi Minh EDI, a museum for IT development, and an Internet gateway for Vietnam. In his estimation, the market size of the Vietnamese IT industry would be US$500 million by the year 2000.

MARKET ENTRY DECISIONS

Vietnam represented a promising market with untapped potential. There were, however, risks. Despite all the recent, rapid progress toward a free economy, the basic political structure in Vietnam had not changed. Although Vietnam had recently adopted an open-door policy, economic development in the country was only beginning to take off, and the pace and direction of reform was still uncertain. Although economic growth was robust, the economy had recently suffered from high inflation, and the dong was expected to depreciate against the U.S. dollar. There were gaps in Vietnam's legal framework, with two instances of businesses being subjected to different interpretations of the law by authorities at different government levels, which resulted in different applications of the same law. This had caused uncertainties and delay in the business setup.

Although the IT market in Vietnam had potential, the market was currently small, and market growth was uncertain. HPAP management needed to weigh the positive and negative factors before deciding if the company should enter the Vietnam market in a more strategic manner. The following are some possible entry strategies available to HP to set up its presence in Vietnam if it decides to enter the market.

Majority Joint Venture with Local Partner. HP could use the joint venture strategy to enter the Vietnam market. In Southeast Asia, a HP joint venture existed in Indonesia, where an agreement was entered into with Berca, the distributor, to set up a service company, HPSI. Berca retained the primary responsibility for the sale of HP products, while HPSI was charged with providing HP services to the marketplace. This option required less initial investment compared to the direct presence strategy, thus reducing the risk involved. A local joint venture partner could be a valuable resource where *guanxi* was vital for doing business.

Distribution (Independent Partner). HP could appoint one or more independent organizations as distributors, as well as service and support providers. In the initial years, it was likely that products from each business unit would be sold only through one distributor, although the same distributor might be chosen for the products of more than one business unit.

This strategy offered a quick start-up for HP and was especially suited to the off-the-shelf, mass market, plug-and-play types of product offered by CPO. To be successful, HP needed to commit resources to train and develop the distributor to build up its service capability. The disadvantage of this strategy was that it would result in the cultivation of future competitors for support services. Where services in many other markets were concerned, HP had not found a way to provide support to its mission-sensitive and mission-critical end users through channel members and still maintain the high quality and responsiveness customers required. In addition, the margins on services were high, and services contributed significantly to HP's profit. The profit was likely to drop if HP allowed its channels to sign support contracts directly with the end users.

Distribution (ex-HP Employee Start-up). A modified form of the entry strategy was to appoint a start-up company founded by ex-HP employees as its distributor. These ex-HP employees could be trusted to deliver high-quality service. In the future, this company would probably be more obliged to pay off the goodwill shown by HP in giving it the opportunity to be HP's service provider in Vietnam. When HP decided to establish a direct presence in Vietnam, the former employees could also be rehired as key managers in the new subsidiary.

Cooperative Venture/Franchising. Investment in the form of a cooperative venture was also viable. HP could initially franchise the support services and provide advisory services to a partner on how to establish and manage a support business. HP could act as a supplier of spares to its Vietnamese partner. HP would not have to take the risks incurred in direct investment, and trade ties could still be forged because of the special relationship with a local firm. Singapore firms such as Rothmans of Pall Mall (cigarettes) and Cold Storage (retail supermarkets) had established such ventures with Vietnam firms Agrex Saigon and Saigon-Intershop, respectively.

Direct Presence. HP could have a direct presence in Vietnam by setting up a subsidiary or representative office to provide marketing, sales support, and management services. This strategy required the largest investment and commitment of resources. It also offered maximum control and flexibility and the best payoff. HP's direct presence in the market would allow it to keep in touch with customers. HP would gain invaluable access to markets and customers. To reduce the risk, uncertainty, and investment requirement, it was possible to start off with limited staff on a smaller scale and increase staffing as required.

John Peter knew he had to make a decision soon. Many of HPAP's competitors had already made strategic moves in Vietnam. If HPAP did not act quickly, they might be left behind.

Appendix A. Vietnam

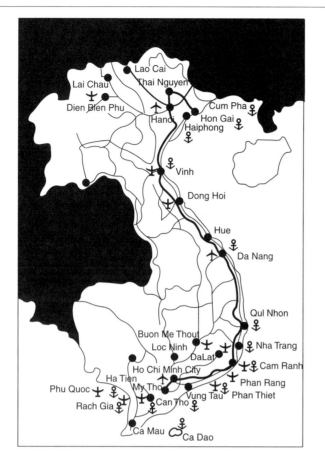

Legend

Railway network	―――
Road network	―
Sea ports	⚓
International airports	✈
Domestic airports	✈

Appendix B. Number of Industrial Establishments

| | State | | | | Non-state private | Private |
Year	Central	Local	Total	Cooperatives	enterprises	household
1985	711	2,339	3,050	35,629	902	
1986	687	2,454	3,141	37,649	567	
1987	682	2,457	3,139	33,962	490	
1988	681	2,430	3,111	32,034	318	318,557
1989	666	2,354	3,020	21,901	1248	333,337
1990	589	2,173	2,762	13,086	770	376,900
1991	546	2,053	2,599	8,829	959	446,771
1992	537	1,731	2,268	5,723	1,114	368,000

Source: General Statistical Office (Vietnam).

Appendix C. Foreign Direct Investments by Economic Activities (as of January 4, 1995)

Activity	Number of projects	Investment Capital (US$ million)
Industry (manufacturing)	548	4,334
Oil and gas	26	1,303
Agriculture and forestry	74	369
Aqua- and mariculture	21	62
Transportation and communication	128	951
Tourism and hotels	113	2,235
Services	134	1,254
Finance and banking	15	177
Housing	14	71
Others	8	14
Export processing zone	29	109
Industrial zone	2	167
TOTAL	1,112	11,046

Source: State Committee for Cooperation and Investment

Appendix D. Foreign Direct Investments In Vietnam; Top Ten Countries (as of January 4, 1995)

Country	Number of projects	Investment capital (US$ million)
Taiwan	179	1,968
Hong Kong	171	1,796
Singapore	76	1,028
Korea, Republic of	98	889
Japan	73	789
Australia	42	861
Malaysia	32	585
France	58	510
Switzerland	14	463
United Kingdom	15	376

Source: State Committee for Cooperation and Investment

Appendix E. Objectives of Hewlett-Packard

a. Profit—To achieve sufficient profit to finance our growth and to achieve corporate objectives through self-generated resources.
b. Customers—To provide products and services of the highest quality and the greatest possible value to customers, thereby gaining and holding their respect and loyalty.
c. Fields of Interest—To participate in those fields of interest that build upon our technology and customer base, that offer opportunities for continuing growth, and that enable us to make a needed and profitable contribution.
d. Growth—To let growth be limited only by our profits and ability to develop and produce innovative products that satisfy real customer needs.
e. People—To help HP people share in the company's success, which they make possible; to provide employment security based on their performance; to ensure them a safe and pleasant work environment; to recognize their individual achievements; and to help them gain a sense of satisfaction and accomplishment from their work.
f. Management—To foster initiative and creativity by allowing the individual great freedom of action in attaining well-defined objectives.
g. Citizenship—To honor our obligations to society by being an economic, intellectual and social asset to each nation and each community in which we operate.

Appendix F. Strategic Business Units of Hewlett-Packard

a. Computer Systems Organization (CSO)—Manufactured and marketed HP minicomputers and workstations.
b. Computer Products Organization (CPO)—Manufactured and marketed PCs, PC peripherals, and networking products.
c. Test and Measurements Organization (TMO)—Manufactured, marketed, and serviced test and measurement products.
d. Analytical Products Group (APO)—Manufactured, marketed, and serviced analytical chemical compound products.
e. Medical Products Group (MPG)—Manufactured, marketed, and serviced products such as defibrillators, ECG, and monitoring equipment used in the medical industry.
f. Components Group—Manufactured and marketed opto-electronic components.
g. Worldwide Customer Support Organization (WCSO)—Provided services for HP's computer-related business, i.e., the CSO and CPO.

CASE 24
Cognex Corporation: Time for a New Vision?*

In March 2002, Dr. Bob Shillman—founder, chairman, and CEO of Cognex Corporation—was wondering about his company's future. Cognex was the global leader in the $600-million market for machine vision systems, or computers that could "see." Such systems were used in manufacturing plants to replace human vision. Highly dependent in the past on the semiconductor and electronics sectors, Cognex had seen its performance rise and fall as those sectors fluctuated.

Cognex had done very well in the 1990s: Revenues and net profits had both grown at an average annual rate of 27%. At the peak of the tech-stock boom in mid-2000, the company's market capitalization exceeded $3 billion. Then, in the last quarter of 2001, following 58 consecutive quarters of profits, Cognex reported a net loss of $20.3 million, after $27 million in special charges for inventory and goodwill write-offs. The company also expected to report a loss for all of 2002. By March 2002, the company's market cap was down to $1.1 billion. Shillman still owned 15% of the company.

In the short run, Shillman worried about restoring the company to profitability. He had already taken several steps to cut costs while preserving the company's core resources. He wondered if he should further cut costs and, if so, in which areas. What should he do if demand did not recover soon enough in the semiconductor and electronics markets, which were in their worst slump in many years?

In the medium to long term, Shillman needed to find a way to grow Cognex's top line and bottom line at rates comparable to those of the 1990s. But that would not be easy. Some observers argued that Cognex's most profitable business—supplying machine vision systems to original equipment manufacturers (OEMs) for the semiconductor and electronics industries—was maturing and that demand was unlikely to return to the levels seen in the late 1990s, even if growth resumed. At the same time, the new business segment that Cognex was targeting—industrial end users—had enormous growth potential, but its profit potential seemed unlikely to be as high as that of the OEM segment. How, then, was Cognex to meet Wall Street's high expectations of future profit growth? Furthermore, what organizational changes would Shillman have to make to ensure that Cognex could meet the differing needs of the industrial end user and OEM markets?

Both the machine vision industry and Cognex had changed dramatically since the company's founding in 1981. Shillman wondered if it was time to craft a new vision for Cognex, or if he should stay the course.

THE MACHINE VISION INDUSTRY

Machine vision systems were a combination of image recognition software and intelligent hardware, consisting of cameras and computers. Manufacturing companies used the systems on production lines where the sophistication, speed, or cost of the process required capabilities beyond those of human vision. The system's cameras captured images, analyzed them, and sent data to other equipment on a manufacturing line, enabling robots to reject defective items or to take other corrective action. Vision systems could be used for diverse purposes, such as checking whether a label was straight on a bottle, whether components were made to specifications, or whether semiconductors met design characteristics (Exhibit 1).

The machine vision market could be segmented along two dimensions: type of customer and type of product produced (Exhibit 2). In turn, customers were either OEMs or end users; the products they manufactured were either discrete/modular (e.g., a computer chip) or continuous (e.g., paper or steel rolls).

OEMs were capital equipment manufacturers who incorporated machine vision systems into their products. Some had "captive" vision system departments (departments that manufactured machine vision for use by other departments of the company and sometimes for external sale); others relied on external suppliers like Cognex for this key component. When Cognex sold machine vision systems to OEMs, it supplied them with the core technology elements in the form of the printed circuit board and software but left it to the OEMs to integrate the technology into their products for eventual use on the factory floor. OEMs did not display their vision system supplier's brand name in their products (a la "Intel inside"), but their customers usually wanted to know which supplier had provided the vision system, and they knew that Cognex was the leading supplier. OEMs worked closely with external vision system suppliers in the product development phase.

End users were manufacturing companies that bought machine vision systems directly from companies like Cognex. They often lacked the OEMs' engineering capabilities to adapt vision systems to their specific needs and, therefore, relied on

*Reprinted by permission from the *Case Research Journal,* copyright 2002 by the North American Case Research Association and the authors, Ravi Ramamurti and Sophie Barratt, Northeastern University. This case was made possible by the cooperation of Dr. Robert Shillman, founder, chairman, and CEO of Cognex Corporation. Susan Conway, Investor Relations Manager, provided valuable facts and data.

Capability	Function	Example
Guidance	Determining the exact physical location of an item	The position of a printed circuit board so that a robot can automatically be guided to insert electronic components
Identification	Determining the identity of an item, either by recognizing its unique shape or reading its serial number	The serial number of a jet engine so that it can be tracked and processed correctly through manufacturing
Inspection	Determining the quality of an item by inspecting it for missing parts or for flaws and defects	The quality of printing on the face of a watch prior to shipment
Gauging	Determining the dimensions of an item	The diameter of a bearing prior to final assembly

Exhibit 1 Capabilities of Machine Vision Technology

Exhibit 2 Segmenting the Machine Vision Market

vision system suppliers or independent system integrators to provide that service. They would buy the core elements like the OEM did and then pay the vision systems vendor or a systems integrator to integrate it into the manufacturing operation. Alternatively, they relied on easy-to-use products that did not require a great deal of application-specific programming or ongoing maintenance. The end-user market was much more fragmented than the OEM market, because it was spread across many more industries, each requiring a slightly different solution.

In a separate category, between OEMs and end users, were system integrators, who created complete, automated inspection solutions for use on the factory floor. For example, they might combine lighting, conveyors, robotics, machine vision, and other components to produce custom inspection systems for examining sneakers or aspirin bottles. Because system integrators encountered a broad range of automation problems, they purchased a variety of machine vision products, from programmable systems to application-specific solutions tailored to particular manufacturing tasks.

Within the OEM segment, the semiconductor and electronics industries were the lead users of vision systems, accounting in the 1980s and 1990s for up to 80% of the total demand. Machine vision systems were attractive for such manufacturers because semiconductor chips, hybrid circuits, and printed circuit boards had high unit costs and were manufactured at extremely high speeds. As devices became smaller, circuit densities increased, and circuit paths became finer, it became increasingly difficult for human vision to detect flaws and increased the necessity for machine vision. Other early adopters of machine vision systems included the automotive and pharmaceutical industries.

From the perspective of vision system suppliers, the hardware and software components for any given industry were largely similar, whether sold to OEMs in the United States, Japan, or Europe. The OEMs made whatever adaptations were necessary for particular applications or countries. The OEMs usually produced all their equipment in one or two factories, typically located in the home country, but sold their products worldwide. Three Asian countries—Japan, South Korea, and Taiwan—accounted for over 40% of the world market for semiconductor capital equipment in 2001, with North America accounting for approximately 25% and Europe for about 15%.[1] Other markets included China and Southeast Asian countries. Semiconductor equipment production was spread in similar proportions across Asia, Europe, and the United States.

The competitive landscape of the machine vision industry was quite varied, ranging from small start-up companies to divisions of giant industrial conglomerates like Matsushita (the latter called "captive" suppliers). However, over the years, independent suppliers like Cognex had been able to use their superior technology to displace captive suppliers.

Standardization of products and high value-to-weight ratios made it easier for firms from one country to sell their products in another, because production and shipping could be done relatively economically. Although local firms enjoyed certain advantages, such as long-standing relationships with customers, leading national firms in the United States, Japan, and Europe were all internationalized to some extent. The main skills required to develop and produce products were software programming and hardware manufacturing, both of which could potentially be done in-house or outsourced. Development of an application could range from a few hundred to several hundred person-years, depending on the level of sophistication of the application.

COGNEX'S ORIGINS

Cognex was founded by Dr. Robert J. Shillman ("Dr. Bob"), who earned his BSEE from Northeastern University, and his MSEE and PhD degrees from MIT. In 1981, while a lecturer in computer science at MIT, he reportedly realized that he really wanted to be an actor or an entrepreneur, not a professor. Therefore, at age 35, Shillman left academia to start Cognex, with life savings of $87,000, earned by renovating apartments and fixing classic cars.[2] He invited two of MIT's top graduate students—Marilyn Matz and Bill Silver—to join the business venture. Together, they gave Cognex its start—and its name, an abbreviation of "cognition experts." In 2002, Matz was senior vice president of engineering and Silver was chief technology officer.

In 1982, Cognex shipped its first product, DataMan, which read numbers, letters, and symbols on product surfaces for identification applications ranging from cardboard shipping cartons to silicon wafers. By 1984, DataMan had become the industry standard for reading laser-etched codes on semiconductor wafers.

At the time, machine vision was a new technology, and the industry was highly fragmented, with more than 100 competitors. Cognex established a leadership position early on, by leveraging its superior technology and translating the technology from the laboratory to the operating environment far more successfully than its competitors. The company was very conscious that technology was the key to its success. Shillman said:

"From day one, I was determined that the shareholders of the company would know that the intellectual assets were owned by the company, not by anyone else. Even today, when we get R&D money from customers, we let them know we will own the technology. We may give them preferential treatment for a certain amount of time, or we may refund their money as they buy product, but we own all of the technology. It doesn't matter if other people wanted us to develop it, or told us to develop it, or gave us the idea to develop it. We still own it—and that's key."

By 2000, Cognex owned 100 patents and had another 140 applications pending.

Until mid-1985, the company focused on developing and selling customized machine vision systems to end users, spending 20% or more of revenues on R&D. However, the company discovered that end users needed a lot of engineering support to integrate machine vision into their processes. Cognex found itself providing such customized services, even for low-volume relationships. After nearly five years of this approach, and start-up losses amounting to $4.7 million that were funded with venture capital ($5 million), Shillman concluded that targeting end users was not a viable strategy.

In 1986, Cognex began to develop products for OEMs, breaking away from the dozens of competitors who continued to target end users. Cognex focused its engineering and programming resources on developing standardized vision components and expanding its proprietary vision technology, leaving it to the OEMs to integrate the technology into their capital equipment. Cognex restructured its sales, marketing, manufacturing, and engineering teams and recruited a new management team to implement the new strategy. The first modular approach to vision systems—the Cognex

Programmable Systems (MVS-8000 Family)
Price: $5,000–$10,000 per system
Description: Product consists of board and software, which are usually built into OEM capital equipment.

Checkpoint Family
Price: Approximately $15,000 per system
Description: Consists of multiple cameras and software constituting a whole system. Broad range of functionality.

Surface Inspection Systems
Price: $300,000–$3 million per system
Description: Entire system used to monitor process manufacturing across a whole web. Includes physical infrastructure supporting camera system.

In-Sight Family
Price: $3,000–$5,000 per unit
Description: Stand-alone product that can be built into production line as user requires. Simple product with limited range of functionality.

Exhibit 3 Cognex Product Family

MVS 2000—was built on a single board and shipped in 1987. The company's gross margin rose from 43% to 70% in one year, and the company turned its first profit in 1987 (Exhibit 3).

In 1989, after eight quarters of profitable operations, Cognex went public, raising $6.9 million and obtaining a listing on NASDAQ. The IPO valued the entire company at $40 million.[3] Shillman owned 33% of the company after the IPO. When the stock tripled in the first year, Shillman made each employee "rich for a night": a chauffeur-driven limousine took each "Cognoid" (as the employees were known) and a guest to one of Boston's most exclusive restaurants for an evening of champagne and fine dining at the company's expense.[4]

INTERNATIONALIZATION

By the time of the IPO, Cognex had already established a presence in Japan and Europe, although the United States still accounted for 80% of revenues. Its first overseas venture began in the early 1980s, when a branch of a Japanese trading company, Marubeni Hytech Co. Ltd., asked to be appointed a distribution agent. At the time, Shillman was more concerned with building the business in the United States than in expanding to Japan. However, he soon recognized that the Japanese semiconductor industry was growing rapidly. Through Marubeni he hoped to sell Cognex's products to such end users as IBM Japan. However, the results did not meet his expectations: Marubeni "was just another link in the chain and not adding value to the chain; they were subtracting price from the chain, as a matter of fact, and complicating things because

Region	1992	1993	1994	1995	1996	1997	1998	1999	2000	2001
United States	51	40	38	41	45	45	37	31	31	37
Japan	40	51	50	46	40	40	40	44	47	37
Europe	8	8	11	12	13	13	21	22	19	22
Rest of the World	1	1	1	1	2	2	2	3	3	4

Exhibit 4 Cognex 10-Year Revenues by Geography (%)

everything had to go through another company. The OEMs said to me that they had to talk to me directly, and to my engineers directly, with no one in the middle.''

Shillman decided to investigate the possibility of establishing a direct presence in Japan, despite the prevailing business wisdom that the market was very difficult to penetrate. He also wanted to adopt in Japan the strategy of targeting OEMs. He realized that Japanese customers were intrigued by Cognex's technology, which was superior to anything available from domestic suppliers. However, it was not easy for them to buy this key component from a foreign, third-party supplier in preference to their captive supplier. Shillman invested a great deal of time listening to prospective customers and adapting his own personality and business habits to fit their style and needs:

> Japanese companies do not view their vendors simply as suppliers of products. Instead, they view them as strategic partners with whom they need to develop an ongoing and trusting relationship. During an introductory meeting, they want to get to know the person and the company they are considering doing business with. The discussion about products comes later.
>
> I very quickly became aware of what it took to succeed in Japan—high quality, delivering things on time, living up to your word, being personable—and began to grow the business. I closed every one of the first deals myself, after bringing engineers over to understand the problem.[5]

Japanese companies' reluctance to displace their captive supplier departments was offset by Shillman's MIT credentials and the reputation of U.S. companies in the software business. Also important was the superiority of Cognex's technology, particularly its ability to work with grey-scale images rather than only black-and-white. In November 1988, Cognex closed its first large Japanese OEM deal, when Tokyo Seimitsu Co., a maker of IC production equipment, agreed to buy at least 50 machine vision systems annually. In May 1989, Cognex signed a $9 million multi-year contract with another OEM, Shinkawa Ltd., a maker of wire bonders.[6] Along the way, Cognex terminated its distribution agreement with Marubeni.

In November 1989, Cognex signed a four-year, multi-million dollar manufacturing and marketing alliance with Komatsu Ltd. of Japan. Although his company had been approached for partnerships by such giants as Matsushita and Fujitsu, Shillman feared those companies could turn into competitors in the future. He preferred instead to ally with a "middle-tech," solid manufacturer like Komatsu that built products around Cognex's hardware and software.

Cognex's business in Japan was profitable from the outset and grew into a major contributor to the company's revenues and profits. Japan's share in Cognex's sales grew from only 11% in 1988, to 20% in 1989, and 40–50% after 1992 (Exhibit 4).

Preferring to staff its Japanese offices with locals, Cognex did not send U.S. expatriates to Japan. The company exhibited at Japanese trade shows, demonstrated its products with Japanese interfaces, and produced all marketing literature in Japanese. It tried to respond promptly to inquiries or requests for help from Japanese customers, usually within 24 hours, flying engineers over to Japan if necessary. Cognex had a policy of only hiring employees who were willing to travel internationally at short notice. For employees who communicated often with Japanese customers, the company provided two-sided business cards—one side in English and the other in Japanese. All employees were offered free, in-house Japanese language classes after work. In 1993, Cognex became the first American firm in 45 years to receive a Vendor Quality Award from Kaijo Corporation.[7]

In the mid-1980s, Cognex also established a network of distributors in Western Europe, supported by a Cognex marketing office in Munich. Later, Cognex scrapped the distributor arrangement and built a dedicated sales force similar to the ones it had in the United States and Japan. Nonetheless, because Europe was not as strong as the United States or Japan in semiconductors and electronics, and the market was more fragmented and protected, it still accounted for only 11% of total sales.

SECOND PASS AT THE END-USER MARKET

By the early 1990s, Cognex had solidified its position as the de facto standard for machine vision technology for OEMs and was the market share leader by a wide margin. This segment accounted for 76% of Cognex's sales even as late as 1995 (Exhibit 5), and Cognex dominated the OEM segment worldwide, with 65% of the market in 2000, excluding captive suppliers (Exhibit 6). It was the leader in the United States, Japan, and Europe. Shillman now turned his attention to other vision segments in which Cognex might grow, and the end user market was once again a target. The technology had matured sufficiently, and end users were beginning to regard vision as a critical component of their manufacturing

	1992	**1993**	**1994**	**1995**	**1996**	**1997**	**1998**	**1999**	**2000**	**2001**
Total Revenue ($000s)	28,642	43,371	62,484	104,543	122,843	155,340	121,844	152,125	250,726	140,729
End User-MVSD	25	23	20	24	24	22	29	32	29	39
End User-SISD	0	0	0	0	11	10	14	7	8	17
OEM-MVSD	75	77	80	76	65	68	57	61	63	44

MVSD, Modular Vision Systems Division; SISD, Surface Inspection Systems Division.

Exhibit 5 Cognex Revenues by Customer Segment (%)

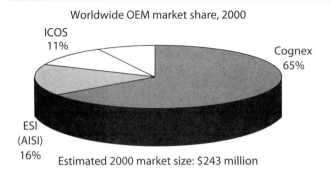

Worldwide OEM market share, 2000

ICOS 11%
Cognex 65%
ESI (AISI) 16%

Estimated 2000 market size: $243 million

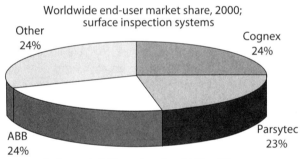

Worldwide end-user market share, 2000; surface inspection systems

Other 24%
Cognex 24%
ABB 24%
Parsytec 23%

Estimated 2000 market size: $110 million

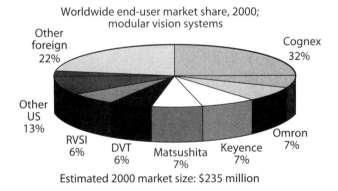

Worldwide end-user market share, 2000; modular vision systems

Other foreign 22%
Cognex 32%
Other US 13%
RVSI 6%
DVT 6%
Matsushita 7%
Keyence 7%
Omron 7%

Estimated 2000 market size: $235 million

Exhibit 6 Cognex Markets and Competitive Position, 2000

operations. Cognex set out to become the machine vision company for all industry.

One of the first steps in targeting the end-user segment was the introduction in 1994 of an internally developed new product called Checkpoint. Checkpoint did not require that its users have either computer programming or machine vision experience to configure and install a vision system on their production lines; it was hoped that it would thus circumvent the problems Cognex had faced earlier in serving end users. Checkpoint was meant for modular vision inspection, that is, to inspect discrete products. Applications served by Checkpoint grew to include ballpoint pens (1995), medical syringes (1995), beer kegs (1996), and checking the number of chocolate chips in chocolate chip cookies (1997).

In the mid-1990s, for the first time in its history, Cognex also began to consider acquisition as a means to enter or strengthen its position in segments of the machine vision market. The company had strict criteria for potential acquisitions. A candidate firm had to be in a related business; be able to leverage Cognex's worldwide sales and marketing resources; be high tech, preferably with a strong software component; be the leader or potential leader in its market; be accretive to earnings in the near future; and have a "work hard, play hard" culture similar to Cognex's. In 1995, one year after a second public offering in which it raised $29.8 million, Cognex acquired Acumen Inc. of Portland, Oregon, a developer of machine vision systems for the semiconductor industry, for $14 million. Cognex paid two-thirds in cash and the rest in stock. In 1998, the company acquired Rockwell Automation's Allen-Bradley machine vision business and became the preferred supplier of machine vision systems to Rockwell's factory automation customers worldwide. This acquisition removed a major competitor in the end-user market and allowed Cognex to penetrate new customer segments.

Cognex also used acquisitions to enter a new segment, the end-user market for continuous process industries, otherwise known as "surface inspection systems." The first big move in that direction was the 1996 acquisition of Isys Controls of Alameda, California, a leading supplier of ultra-high performance surface inspection systems for process industries like paper, steel, and plastics. Isys was acquired in exchange for one million shares of Cognex stock, which placed its value at $12–$14 million. In 1997, Cognex acquired Mayan Automation, a developer of low-cost machine vision systems for surface inspection, for $4.8 million in cash. In 2000, Cognex introduced a flexible, new high-performance surface inspection system, based on internal development and the integration of acquired technologies. Known as Smartview, it was targeted primarily at the paper manufacturing industry.

Unlike the vision systems for the OEM market, surface inspection systems were high-ticket items, costing several million dollars apiece. They included a large number of cameras to scan the full breadth of the paper or steel being produced, housing to protect the vision system in the harsh production environment, and motors and controls to adjust the cameras remotely. Considerable customization of hardware and software was required to adapt the system to the production process and factory in question. Whereas vision systems sold to semiconductor or electronics OEMs almost always ended up in a new factory, surface inspection systems were more likely to be sold to existing paper or steel mills that were being modernized, because few new plants were constructed in these mature industries. For the same reason, surface inspection systems was not a high-growth segment. Cognex estimated that in 2000 it was a $110 million market worldwide.

Surface inspection technology allowed process industries to prevent defects or to pass on to customers, in the form of a CD-ROM or disk, precise details about the nature and location of defects, so that the material could be used optimally during cutting or subsequent processing. With customers demanding higher levels of quality and reliability, surface inspection assumed more and more value to process industries, as machine vision inspection always had in semiconductors or electronics. Despite this importance, Cognex's gross margin in the surface inspection system segment was 10 percentage points lower than in the OEM segment. The company found it hard to raise prices, despite the added costs of customization. Cognex's market share in the surface inspection segment was 24%—roughly equal to that of its two main competitors, ABB of Sweden and Parsytec of Germany. ABB was a giant company which, among other things, sold equipment for industrial process plants; machine vision systems, made by an ABB company, were available as an option and usually priced aggressively. Parsytec was a $20 million company with 170 employees that was trying to use its strong position in serving strip steel makers to also garner share in paper, aluminum, and plastics. Shillman thought Parsytec had excellent marketing skills but that their product was technically inferior to Cognex's. In 2001, Parsytec had a net loss of almost 50% of sales.

THE LAST FRONTIER: MODULAR END-USER MARKET

The modular end-user market was the last frontier that Cognex hoped to conquer. Cognex believed that this segment had the greatest potential for future growth—possibly more than $1 billion in unmet needs, compared to the OEM market of $235 million and the served end-user market of $300 million (Exhibit 7). Serving this market profitably would not be easy, as Cognex's own experience in the 1980s had shown. Demand was fragmented across dozens of industries and firms, and users needed a lot of handholding. However, Shillman believed that circumstances were different in 2002 than they had been in the 1980s. "Back then," he said, "machine vision inspection was a nice thing to have, but for most firms today, it's a *must have.*"

Checkpoint was targeted at this sector, but it had not been a great success. Although simpler to use than the boards and software sold to semiconductor OEMs, the average end user appeared to want something even simpler and cheaper. In 1999 and 2000, Cognex's end-user sales force became aware of a small company

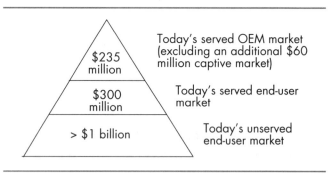

Source: Cognex estimates.

Exhibit 7 Global Machine Vision Market Opportunity, 2001

started out of Georgia Institute of Technology, called DVT Corporation, whose unique business proposition was to "give its software away, give its training away, and continue to drive the price of visual inspection down, while increasing power." Using outsourced production, and distributors who worked with systems integrators, DVT grew by 2000 to a $14 million company. It reportedly lost money in 2001 and received a cash infusion from Saudi Arabian investors.

Another small player in this segment was Robotic Vision Systems Inc. (RVSI) based in Canton, Massachusetts, which regarded machine vision as its core competence. Not considered a serious long-term competitor, RVSI also reportedly lost money in 2001 and sold its material handling business for $11 million so that it could focus its efforts on machine vision and the semiconductor inspection business.

Although Cognex was late to attack the more price-sensitive segment of the end-user market, once it saw what DVT was doing, it reacted very quickly, introducing in 2000 a new product called In-Sight that was cheaper and easier to use than Checkpoint. Shillman justified being the late entrant in this segment as follows:

> I don't think entering the market sooner [with something like In-Sight] would have been any better. As a matter of fact, I'm glad that DVT did it before us because they broke the ground on vision sensors, and they did a lot of advertising that we benefited from. We don't have to be first. Let others experiment. We have the technology after all, in just 9 months we were able to ship a competing product. Once we decided that DVT was worth attacking, it only took us 9 months.

Within months of introducing In-Sight, Cognex acquired a large slice of the U.S. end-user market. It developed a reputation for offering a competitively priced, high-quality product, sold by a dedicated sales force and backed by extensive training, and quickly became the market leader. Unlike OEMs, end users were not necessarily looking for the best technology but rather something that got the job done. For that reason, end users might have been expected to be price sensitive. On the other hand, as in the case of OEMs, Cognex products accounted for a small fraction of the total cost of installing machine vision inspection. Cognex soon

Competitor	Established	2001 Revenues	Products	Notes
Keyence	1974	$750 million	Sensors, optoelectronic equipment and high-technology hobby products, plus support.	Company considered itself a pioneer in the sensor industry. Technologies encompassed lasers, vision, control, optical technology, and ultrasonic technology. Approximately 1,400 employees, with a network of offices and distributors in Europe, Asia, and North America.
Omron	1933	$5 billion	Automation components and systems that used fuzzy logic, open platform, sensing, and life science technologies, including a range of vision sensors, which formed part of the company's industrial automation business.	Company had over 24,000 employees in 1,500 offices and over 35 manufacturing facilities worldwide. Also, more than 7,000 domestic and 11,000 international affiliate companies.
Matsushita Electric Industrial	1935	$62 billion	Premier consumer electronics maker with brands including Panasonic, Quasar, Technics, and JVC. Other products included computers, telephones, industrial equipment, and components.	Company had over 300,000 employees working in 300 operating units in over 45 countries. Consumer products such as VCRs and CD and DVD players accounted for 40% of sales. Products sold worldwide, with Asia accounting for over 70% of sales. Future strategy was focus on digital audiovisual technology and mobile communications. Company regarded its capacity to produce key components and devices for digital networking products as a core strength.

Exhibit 8 Cognex's Competitors in Modular End-User Market in Japan

discovered that there was greater leeway to raise prices. By 2002, Cognex was able to realize prices in the end-user segment that gave it a gross margin as high as, or higher than, in the OEM segment.

At the end of 2001, Cognex had 32% of the end-user market worldwide, most of which was in the United States and Europe, but with only a 2–3% share of the Japanese market. In-Sight customers at the end of 2001 included Avon Products, Bridgestone/Firestone, Ericsson, Hewlett-Packard, Mitsubishi, and Xerox Corporation, among others. The closest end-user competitors, including DVT and RVSI, had 6% each, most of it in the domestic market.

Cognex's poor showing in the Japanese end-user market was a source of some frustration to Cognex. Three strong companies dominated the market there: Omron, Matsushita, and Keyence, all of which had strong relationships with Japanese customers (Exhibit 8). Shillman said: "Omron, Matsushita, and Keyence are extremely well known in Japan. They're like the Allen-Bradley of America or the Siemens of Germany. They are huge conglomerates and sell a broad range of products. Their customers buy

everything else from them, so it's logical that they also buy vision systems from them."

Compared to the OEM market, the end-user market was harder to reach, resulting in higher costs of marketing and selling. The average size of an end-user order was much smaller, because customers bought only a few units at a time rather than the hundreds that an OEM customer might order. As a result, a salesperson serving the end-user market might sell only one-third the volume in a year of a salesperson selling to the OEM segment—$0.7 million per year versus $2.3 million per year. The productivity of the surface inspection system sales force fell between these two extremes, at roughly $1.4 million per year.

Shillman believed that Cognex's end-user products would not become commodities, because they contained a significant amount of unique value-added features. However, they would require a different selling model:

There are challenges in distribution, but it helps that you can order these things over the phone or over the Internet. You clearly can't have salespeople selling products that are $20 or

$50 unless in their bag they have many other things. So that's one of the things we're looking at—acquiring other companies that have other products that our salespeople could carry. Right now, our bag isn't big enough.

Another way is to have someone else carry our products in their bag. But I have to say I'm biased against using someone else's distribution. I like to touch the customer. I like control. I like to control the discount, to hear the ideas from the customers. I don't like middlemen. They're valuable in certain businesses, but I don't want them for my business. I prefer that my account manager do everything—but to do that, I have to have more things in my salespeople's bag.

However, not all industry observers were convinced that Shillman was right. They noted that R&D might also require different emphasis in the end-user market. Although the engineering skills required for the OEM segment involved application development, the end-user segment required building the core technology. In early 2002, the majority of Cognex's research, development,

and engineering resources were focused on serving the OEM segment.

In 2000, Cognex made two acquisitions to strengthen its position in the end-user segment. First, it acquired selected assets of the machine vision business of Komatsu for $11.2 million in cash, plus up to $8 million more if certain performance criteria were met. Because the two companies had been working closely together for some years, and Komatsu was looking to exit the business, the acquisition was a logical fit for Cognex. In a press release, Shillman explained:

> This acquisition is a real coup for Cognex. First, it increases our market share ... and it strengthens our existing position as the leader in that market segment worldwide. Next, we expect the acquisition to accelerate our revenue growth in both the semiconductor and electronics markets in Japan. Finally, by immediately expanding our team by adding more than 20 highly skilled and experienced vision engineers and sales engineers, we expect to be able to increase the rate at

---

Dr. Robert J. Shillman
President, Chief Executive Officer, and Chairman

Dr. Robert Shillman was the founder, president, CEO, and chairman of Cognex Corporation. He was named *Inc. Magazine's* Entrepreneur of the Year in 1990 and received an Achievement Award in Leadership from the Automated Imaging Association in 1992. Dr. Shillman obtained a BSEE from Northeastern University, as well as an MSEE and a PhD from the Massachusetts Institute of Technology.

Patrick Alias
Executive Vice President

Mr. Alias joined Cognex in September of 1991 as executive vice president of sales and marketing. He was a member of Cognex's board of directors. He was responsible for overseeing Cognex K.K., the company's Japanese subsidiary. Mr. Alias came to Cognex with more than 21 years of high-technology management experience, most recently serving as president of Gimeor, Inc., a small software company in France. Mr. Alias obtained master's degrees in electronics, mathematics, and economics from the University of Paris and was a graduate of the Advanced Management Program of the Harvard Business School.

James F. Hoffmaster
Chief Operating Officer and President, MVSD

As Cognex's chief operating officer, Mr. Hoffmaster oversaw the administration and strategic operations of Cognex and its two operating divisions, the Modular

Vision Systems Division and the Surface Inspection Systems Division. He also served as president of the Modular Vision Systems Division. Before joining Cognex, Mr. Hoffmaster was CEO of Fibersense, a Massachusetts-based company specializing in the application of fiber optic technology to gyroscopes and other sensors. Prior to that, he held senior executive positions at a variety of multinational technology companies, most recently serving as president of Fisher-Rosemount Systems, a division of Emerson Electric. He obtained an MS in Computer Science and a BA in Economics from Cleveland State University.

Richard A. Morin
Senior Vice *President of Finance and Administration, Chief Financial Officer, and Treasurer*

Mr. Morin was Cognex's senior vice president of finance and administration, CFO, and treasurer. In this role, he was responsible for the company's finance, investor relations, information technology, facilities, tax, treasury, legal, and corporate employee services departments. Mr. Morin joined Cognex in 1999 after ten years as CFO for C&K Components, Inc., an international manufacturer of electronic components and security systems, where he led the company's growth from $100 million to $200 million in revenue. Mr. Morin also served as corporate controller and vice president of finance for the Jamesbury Corporation. Mr. Morin obtained a BA in economics and accounting from the College of the Holy Cross and was a certified public accountant.

Exhibit 9 Top Management Profile, March 2002

which we can develop and introduce new machine vision products to all of our customers worldwide.[8]

Second, in the United Kingdom Cognex acquired privately owned Image Industries, the leading provider of low-cost vision systems for the end-user market, for $2.7 million. Together, these acquisitions brought to Cognex dozens of new customers and 33 engineers and salespeople steeped in machine vision systems.

COGNEX IN 2002

Cognex's leadership team in March 2002 is profiled in Exhibit 9. The company was organized functionally, with an R&D group, an operations group, and sales divided into the Modular Vision Systems Division and the Surface Inspection Systems Division. Within the modular systems division, there were separate sales forces for OEMs and end users.

The R&D group worked both on enhancing existing products and on developing new ones. It also gained access to new technologies through strategic relationships and acquisitions. With 195 professionals, it spent $30 million, or 21% of sales, in 2001.[9]

The majority of Cognex's machine vision systems were manufactured in Massachusetts using turnkey third-party contractors. Cognex only did the final testing and assembly. Cognex relied on sole suppliers for some components. The surface inspection system, Smartview, was made in Alameda, California. However, plans were afoot in 2002 for the contract manufacturer to shift production to Ireland, where labor was cheaper, taxes lower, and government incentives were available for foreign investors. Cost of goods sold was 25% of sales in 2000 and 44% of sales in 2001.

The company's 225-strong direct sales and service force in December 2000 consisted of sales and application engineers, most with engineering or science degrees. When sales engineers identified opportunities for single-unit sales or turnkey systems, they referred them to independent system integrators who worked with Cognex. OEMs bought products through one-year contracts that

usually included volume discounts. Fuji of America, an OEM customer, had accounted for 10% of the company's sales in 2000; no other single customer had as large a share. SG&A was 25% of revenues in 2000 and 44% in 2001.

Cognex's customer support offerings included vision solutions consulting services, technical support, educational services, and product services. The vision solutions consulting group operated on a fee-for-service basis. The technical support group helped customers who were developing or deploying a Cognex machine vision application. The educational services group offered courses at corporate headquarters, overseas offices, or at the customers' premises. The product services group offered software and hardware maintenance programs.

In 2001, Cognex employed 781 persons, including 375 in sales, marketing, and support activities; 195 in research, development, and engineering; 70 in manufacturing and quality assurance; and 141 in information technology, finance, and administration. Of these, 275 were located outside the United States.

Cognex added 151 people to its headcount in 2000 but laid off 80 in 2001, when sales plummeted. The geographic distribution of Cognex's workforce (excluding administration) in December 2001 is shown in Exhibit 10.

CORPORATE CULTURE AND VALUES

Shillman attributed a good part of Cognex's success to its distinctive culture, which reflected his own style and values. Besides customer-centricity, the company placed high value on innovation and creativity, as seen in its statement of values, ranked from 1 to 10: customer first, excellence, perseverance, enthusiasm, creativity, pride, integrity, recognition, sharing, and fun.

Cognex's values were reflected in its products, in its manner of celebrating achievements and motivating people, and in the production of its annual reports, which were funny and unconventional.

Region	R&D	Sales	Marketing	Field service, customer satisfaction	Total
United States	50	46	52	32	280
Japan	20	34	24	27	105
Europe	151	41	15	21	92
Rest of world	0	7	5	0	12
Total	185	128	96	80	489
(%inU.S.)	81%	36%	54%	40%	57%

*Excludes staff working in the information technology, finance, and administrative areas. This group had 141 people in December 2001.

Exhibit 10 Geographic Distribution of Functional Staff, December 2001*

"If you really want to know what moves our economy, read Bob's Notes."—*Alan Greenspan**

"For my patients, time is short, so I tell them to rely on Bob's Notes."—*Dr. Jack Kevorkian*

"I use Bob's Notes every day. Instead of preparing for hours and speaking for minutes, I can prepare in minutes and speak for hours."—*Fidel Castro*

"The English versions of Bob's Notes are very good, but the Japanese versions are even more concise, less expensive, and have fewer defects."—Takeo *Hiranuma, Japanese Minister* of *International Trade and Industry*

*Mr. Greenspan later sent Shillman a letter objecting to the "quote."

Exhibit 11 Humorous Testimonials in Cognex's 2000 Annual Report ("Bob's Notes")*

Previous editions had included reports that looked like a deck of cards, a software manual, a children's coloring book, and, in 2000, an easy-to-read, yellow-and-black report modeled on the *Cliff's Notes* literature guides (called Bob's Notes). On the back cover of Bob's Notes were hilarious (fake) testimonials from several well-known personalities (Exhibit 11).

Halloween was the company's official celebration day, with everyone at headquarters required to wear a costume, no matter who they were meeting that day. Shillman's previous costumes included that of a court jester, a hotdog, and a peanut (''top Cognut''). On Halloween day, costumed Cognoids were known to parade across Route 9, near the company's headquarters in Natick, Massachusetts, disrupting traffic. One year, Shillman had his executive team dress up in rap outfits and celebrate the company's ''many broken records''; another year, they dressed in tutus to perform the Nutcracker for employees; and when the company

($ Million)	1997	1998	1999	2000	2001
Assets					
Current Assets					
Cash and Investments	178.0	158.5	217.0	128.4	110.2
Accounts Receivable,					
Less Reserves	25.1	21.0	28.7	47.0	17.1
Revenues in Excess of Billings	3.7	4.9	1.0	—	—
Inventories	7.8	10.8	10.9	27.7	23.1
Deferred Income Taxes	3.5	3.9	6.1	7.7	12.2
Prepaid Expenses and Other	5.9	8.1	5.5	8.9	10.1
Total Current Assets	224.0	207.2	268.8	219.7	172.6
Long-Term Investments	0	0	0	149.4	182.5
Property, Plant and Equipment,					
Net	33.0	34.3	31.9	34.0	31.2
Other Assets	3.4	2.2	7.1	26.1	8.6
Deferred Income Taxes	1.4	4.2	7.1	6.9	12.0
Total Assets	261.8	247.9	314.8	436.1	406.9
Liabilities andStockholders' Equity					
Current Liabilities					
Accounts Payable	3.3	2.5	4.2	10.1	4.4
Accrued Expenses	13.7	11.6	18.5	23.0	16.4
Accrued Income Taxes	2.7	0.9	7.5	9.2	2.1
Customer Deposits	3.1	4.9	2.7	3.1	2.9
Deferred Revenue	1.6	3.0	4.5	6.5	3.1
Total Current Liabilities	24.4	22.9	37.5	51.8	28.9
Other Liabilities	1.3	2.1	1.0	0	0
Deferred Income Taxes	0	0	0	0	0
Stockholders' Equity					
Common Stock, $0.002 par Value Authorized: 120,000,000					
Shares, Plus Issued	0	0	0	0	0
Additional Paid-in Capital	91.1	97.6	122.5	163.8	173.7
Cumulative Translation Adjustment	0	0	1.0	(2.5)	(6.3)
Retained Earnings	146.4	166.6	197.0	265.2	254.0
Treasury Stock, at Cost	(1.4)	(41.3)	(43.6)	(42.7)	(43.4)
Total Stockholders' Equity	236.1	222.9	276.7	383.9	378.0
Total Liabilities	261.8	247.9	314.8	436.1	406.9

Exhibit 12 Cognex Corporation 5-Year Balance Sheets ($ Million)

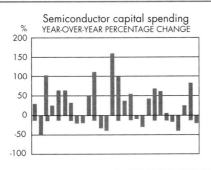

Source: Company reports and Lehman Brothers estimates.

Exhibit 13 Change in Semiconductor Capital Spending

first crossed $100 million in sales, they put on a tap dancing show, for which they secretly took weekly lessons over the previous five months.[10]

Although the company placed a high value on its culture and looked for companies that shared its "work hard, play hard" approach, it did not impose that culture on acquired companies or its foreign offices. For instance, Halloween was not celebrated in Cognex's Japan or European offices. However, the company's Corporate Communications and Culture team encouraged acquired units to embrace Cognex's key values while maintaining their own local identity. This allowed Cognex to be successful in managing remote teams, particularly within the engineering function. The company also recognized the outstanding contributions of teams and individuals in many creative ways.

WHAT NEXT?

In the 1990s, Cognex's growth was driven by strong demand for items containing semiconductor chips, such as cellular phones, personal computers, and televisions. The OEM market had marked

ups and downs in the second half of the 1990s, which were reflected in Cognex's financial results from that period. A stellar year in 2000 had seen Cognex's revenues from semiconductor OEMs increase by 68% over the previous year. However, by the end of 2000, orders from OEMs had begun to slow again, and this continued throughout 2001.

In the OEM segment, Cognex enjoyed a strong position and earned high gross and net margins. The outsourcing of production limited Cognex's investments in physical plant and equipment, as seen in its balance sheet (Exhibit 12). Shillman explained the company's position in the OEM segment:

"If someone else had a comparable product, then our margins wouldn't be value-based margins; they'd be competitive margins. Instead of gross margins of 70 or 80 percent, they might be 50 percent—that's what competition does."

Why do we have so few competitors when we're literally coining money? Well, because it takes an enormous amount of technology, and you have to know how to manage software employees. It's also a very niche business: There is a billion dollars of opportunity, but it's made up of lots of little niches. We did $3 or $4 million dollars in 2000 inspecting cell phones. It's nothing that a huge conglomerate like Mitsubishi or Siemens would care to do. They're used to churning out standard products for big markets, but ours is application specific: When we serve semiconductor customers, we have to learn the semiconductor business. Moreover, we're the standard in the industry. No one else can become a Cognex, because if they did do so, by definition the margins would become depressed. We have the brand name and our products aren't overpriced—they pay for themselves in a few days anyway so why would anyone take a risk on a newcomer? We have worldwide distribution, and we take good care of our customers. We just understand this business better than anyone else and would make it very difficult for anyone to get into the business."

Competition stopped being at the top of my worry list in 1997 or 1998. Today, we worry more about the economics of the industry and about the semiconductor business as a whole.

	2000	2001	2002	2003	2004	2005	2006	CAGR (%) 2000–06
Capital spending (excluding SATS)	62,437	44,407	33,579	43,328	66,843	77,826	62,650	0.1
Growth (%)		*83.8*	*−28.9*	*−24.4*	*29.0*	*54.3*	*16.4*	*−19.5*
Equipment spending (excluding test)	39,919	25,232	20,345	28,609	44,074	50,603	42,195	0.9
Growth (%)		*8.3.7*	*−36.8*	*−19.4*	*40.6*	*54.1*	*14.8*	*−16.6*
Wafer fab equipment	33,170	22,376	18,016	25,168	38,719	44,566	37,306	2.0
Growth (%)		*84.4*	*−32.5*	*−19.5*	*39.7*	*53.8*	*15.1*	*−16.3*
Packaging and assembly equipment	6,794	2,856	2,329	3,411	5,355	6,036	4,889	−5.4
Growth (%)		*80.6*	*−57.7*	*−18.4*	*47.7*	*55.6*	*12.7*	*−19.0*

Source: Gartner Dataquest, *Semiconductor Capital Spending and Equipment Market Outlook 2002: Transition to Recovery,* January 2, 2002.

Exhibit 14 Forecasts for Wafer Fabrication and Other Capital Spending, 2000–2006 ($ million)

Cognex had never lost an OEM customer to a competitor. Many years ago, Sanyo decided to develop its own machine vision system rather than buy it from Cognex for $15,000 apiece, only to return two years later because its internal team could not match Cognex's performance. For OEMs, switching to another vendor to save a little money on a relatively low-ticket item (compared to the cost of the equipment they sold) was not worth the hassle and cost. Shillman noted, "Without our product, which might cost Nikon $10,000, they might be unable to ship a $1 million product."

However, the long-term outlook for growth in semiconductors and electronics was murky, not to mention the challenges of coping with the wild swings in demand (Exhibit 13). In 2001, Cognex's revenues from OEMs had shrunk to 44% of total sales, from 63% the year before. At the end of 2001, there was general agreement that capital spending by OEMs would decline further in 2002, by 5–24%. In addition, Japanese manufacturers that once dominated the industry had lost ground in recent years to more efficient producers like South Korea's Hynix Semiconductor and Samsung Electronics, and Taiwan's TSMC and UMC. (Exhibit 14 shows one analyst's forecast for wafer fabrication and other capital spending.) At the same time, OEM customers, who were being pressured by their customers to keep equipment prices down, were beginning to make the same demand of Cognex.

Another important trend in semiconductors was the transition to producing chips on larger 300 mm wafers, which would create demand for new capital equipment that used machine vision.

Cognex was ready, with the acuReader III, the latest generation of its high-performance wafer-reading system.

Shillman was concerned about whether the demand for semiconductors might not have peaked, as some people argued. He drew parallels to steel: "In semiconductors, it might very well be that the number of chips the world needs has been reached. They're able now, on each chip, to get more die—so you may not have to buy more capital equipment. At some point, the world stopped building steel mills, when there was enough steel capacity. Why should semiconductors be any different?"

The end-user segment raised a different set of questions. Shillman had to decide where to deploy his resources and what the implications would be for the bottom line if end users became a larger part of the revenues. His goal was to earn the 20%+ net income margin that he and Wall Street had come to expect. But what steps were necessary to achieve that? Would Cognex have to rethink the business model that had worked well for OEMs as the end-user market grew in importance, or should it stay the course? Would Cognex's migration to lower-priced, higher-volume systems like In-Sight cannibalize sales of higher margin products aimed at OEMs? Could the company expect to achieve market shares in the end-user market as high as in the OEM segment, and, if not, what were the implications? Why hadn't Cognex done better in the Japanese end-user market, and how might it do better there? What additional steps, if any, should Cognex take to lower its cost structure to make up for the higher costs of selling to the end-user market? Should it use

	1997	1998	1999	2000	2001
Revenue	155.3	121.8	152.1	250.7	140.7
Cost of Revenue	42.3	37.3	45.2	63.8	62.3
Gross Margin	113.1	84.5	106.9	186.9	78.4
Research, Development and Engineering Expenses	22.5	24.7	27.7	33.3	30.1
Selling, General and Administrative Expenses	35.8	38.0	43.7	61.9	61.6
Amortization of Goodwill	0	0	0	2.0	3.1
Charge for Intangible Asset Impairment	0	0	0	0	10.9
Charge for Acquired In-Process Technology	3.1	2.1	0	0	0
Income (Loss) from Operations	51.7	19.8	35.6	89.7	27.3)
Investment and Other Income	6.7	7.5	7.3	10.5	11.7
Income (Loss) Before Provision for Income Taxes	58.3	27.3	42.9	100.2	15.7)
Provision (Benefit) for Income Taxes	17.8	7.1	12.4	32.1	(4.5)
Net Income (Loss)	40.5	20.2	30.4	68.1	(11.1)
Net Income per Share (Diluted)	$0.91	$0.47	$0.69	$1.49	($0.25)
Selected Items as a Percentage of Revenues	1997	1998	1999	2000	2001
Cost of Revenue	27%	31%	30%	25%	44%
Gross Profit	73%	69%	70%	75%	56%
R&D	14%	20%	18%	13%	21%
SG&A	23%	31%	29%	25%	44%
Net Income (Loss)	26%	17%	20%	27%	(8%)

Exhibit 15 Cognex Corporation 5-Year Income Statements ($ million, except share amounts)

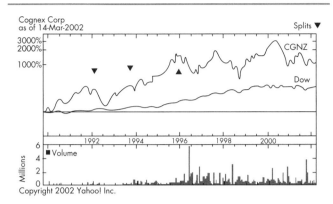

Cognex Corp
as of 14-Mar-2002   Splits ▼

Copyright 2002 Yahoo! Inc.

Stock price (14 March 2002):	$26.95
Volume:	282,100 shares
52-week range:	$17.60—$34.40
Price/sales ratio:	7.97
EPS estimate	-01.4 cents per share
Market capitalization:	$1.18 billion

Source: finance.yahoo.com

Exhibit 16 Cognex's Stock Performance, 1990–2002

the 2002 downturn and its treasure chest to acquire more firms and, if so, which ones?

Then, of course, there was the loss in 2001 (Exhibit 15) and the beating the stock had taken in the last several months. Shillman was confident that, if the company spent and saved wisely, it would weather the current downturn. He had made a conscious decision to lose money in the previous quarter, rather than cut costs too deeply and risk losing the company's key asset—its

software talent. Despite the recession, in 2001, Cognex signed 125 new OEM customers and 954 new end-user customers and introduced several new products. With its core competencies intact, with market share rising, and with a strong balance sheet ($282 million in short-term and long-term financial assets, and no debt), the company seemed well positioned to survive the short-term difficulties.

The long-term outlook was uncertain, with respect to both the OEM and end-user segments. In the 1990s, Cognex's stock had beaten the Dow Jones Industrial Average by a wide margin, even after the tech-stock meltdown in 2001 (Exhibit 16). Could Cognex repeat that performance in the next decade?

NOTES

1. May 2001 data, *Semiconductor Magazine,* August 2001.
2. GinaFarone, ''Mavericks,'' *Electronic Business,* April 1999.
3. Cognex stock was issued at $11 per share. After adjusting for the 8:1 in stock splits since 1989, the issue price represented $1.38 per share, compared to $27 per share on March 14, 2002.
4. Cognex, *Annual Report 2000,* p. 10.
5. Quoted in *Advanced Imaging,* October 1993.
6. ''Breaking into Japan: Small U.S. Companies Show How It's Done,'' *Electronic Business,* November 1989.
7. *Advanced Imaging,* October 1993.
8. Cognex press release, ''Cognex Corporation Acquires the Machine Vision Business of Komatsu Ltd.,'' March 15, 2000.
9. This section draws from Cognex's 10-K report for 2000.
10. Farone, ''Mavericks.''

CASE 25
Kentucky Fried Chicken and the Global Fast-Food Industry*

Kentucky Fried Chicken Corporation (KFC) was the world's largest chicken restaurant chain and third-largest fast-food chain in 2005. It held more than 46% of the U.S. market in terms of sales and operated more than 13,266 restaurants in 89 countries. KFC was one of the first fast-food chains to go international, in the late 1950s, and is one of the world's most recognizable brands. KFC's early international strategy was to grow its company and franchise restaurant base throughout the world. By 2005, however, KFC had refocused its international strategy on several high-growth markets that included China, Canada, the United Kingdom, Australia, South Africa, Malaysia, Thailand, Mexico, Korea, and Indonesia. KFC planned to base much of its growth in these markets on company-owned restaurants, which gave KFC greater control over product quality, service, and restaurant cleanliness. In other international markets, KFC planned to grow primarily through franchises, which were operated by local business-people who understood the local market better than KFC. Franchises enabled KFC to expand more rapidly into smaller countries that could support only a small number of restaurants. KFC planned to expand its company-owned restaurants more aggressively into other major international markets in Europe and Latin America in the future. Latin America was an appealing area for investment because of the size of its markets and geographic proximity to the United States. Mexico was of particular interest because of NAFTA, a free trade agreement among Canada, the United States, and Mexico that went into effect in 1994. McDonald's, Burger King, and Wendy's, however, were rapidly expanding into other countries in Latin America such as Argentina, Chile, Brazil, and Venezuela. KFC's task in Latin America was to develop an effective strategy for further penetrating the Latin American market.

COMPANY HISTORY

Fast-food franchising was still in its infancy in 1952 when Harland Sanders began his travels across the United States to speak with prospective franchisees about his "Colonel Sanders Recipe Kentucky Fried Chicken." By 1960, "Colonel" Sanders had granted KFC franchises to more than 200 take-home retail outlets and restaurants across the United States. He had also established several franchises in Canada. By 1963 the number of KFC franchises had

risen to more than 300 and revenues topped $500 million. The Colonel celebrated his 74th birthday the following year and was eager to lessen the load of running the day-to-day operations of his business, which he sold to two Louisville businessmen—Jack Massey and John Young Brown, Jr.—for $2 million. The Colonel stayed on as a public relations man and goodwill ambassador for the company.

During the next five years, Massey and Brown concentrated on growing KFC's franchise system across the United States. In 1966 they took KFC public and the company was listed on the New York Stock Exchange. By the late 1960s a strong foothold had been established in the United States. Massey and Brown then turned their attention to international markets. In 1969, a joint venture was signed with Mitsuoishi Shoji Kaisha, Ltd., in Japan, and the rights to operate franchises in England were acquired. Subsidiaries were later established in Hong Kong, South Africa, Australia, New Zealand, and Mexico. By 1971, KFC had established 2,450 franchises and 600 company-owned restaurants in 48 countries.

HEUBLEIN, INC.

In 1971, KFC entered into negotiations with Heublein, Inc., to discuss a possible merger. The decision to pursue a merger was partially driven by Brown's desire to pursue other interests that included a political career (he was elected governor of Kentucky in 1977). Several months later, Heublein acquired KFC. Heublein was in the business of producing vodka, mixed cocktails, dry gin, cordials, beer, and other alcoholic beverages. It had little experience, however, in the restaurant business. Conflicts quickly erupted between Colonel Sanders and Heublein management. In particular, Colonel Sanders was distraught over poor quality control and restaurant cleanliness. By 1977 new restaurant openings had slowed to only 20 a year. Few restaurants were being remodeled and service quality had declined. To combat these problems, Heublein sent in a new management team to redirect KFC's strategy. A "back-to-the-basics" strategy was implemented and new restaurant construction was halted until existing restaurants could be upgraded and operating problems eliminated. A program for remodeling existing restaurants was implemented, an emphasis was placed on cleanliness and service, marginal products were eliminated, and product consistency was reestablished. This strategy enabled KFC to gain better control of its operations, and it was soon again aggressively building new restaurants.

---

*This case was prepared by Jeffrey A. Krug of Appalachian State University. It is printed here with his permission.

R. J. REYNOLDS INDUSTRIES, INC.

In 1982, R. J. Reynolds Industries, Inc., (RJR) acquired Heublein and merged it into a wholly owned subsidiary. The acquisition of Heublein was part of RJR's corporate strategy of diversifying into unrelated businesses such as energy, transportation, food, and restaurants to reduce its dependence on tobacco, which had driven its sales since its founding in North Carolina in 1875. Sales of cigarettes and tobacco products, however, were declining as consumption continued to fall in the United States. Reduced consumption was largely the result of increased awareness among Americans of the negative health consequences of smoking.

RJR, however, had little more experience in the restaurant business than Heublein when it acquired KFC 11 years earlier. In contrast to Heublein, which tried to manage KFC actively using its own managers, RJR allowed KFC to operate autonomously. RJR believed that KFC's executives were better qualified to operate the business than its own managers; therefore, KFC's top management team was left largely intact. In this way RJR avoided many of the operating problems that plagued Heublein during its ownership of KFC. In 1985, RJR acquired Nabisco Corporation for $4.9 billion. The acquisition of Nabisco was an attempt to redefine RJR as a world leader in the consumer foods industry. Nabisco sold a variety of well-known food products such as Oreo cookies, Ritz crackers, Planters peanuts, Lifesavers, and Milk-Bone dog biscuits. RJR subsequently divested many of its nonconsumer food businesses. It sold KFC to PepsiCo, Inc., one year later.

PEPSICO, INC.

PepsiCo, Inc., was formed in 1965 with the merger of the Pepsi-Cola Company and Frito-Lay, Inc. The merger created one of the largest consumer products companies in the United States. Pepsi-Cola's traditional business was the sale of soft drink concentrates to licensed independent and company-owned bottlers that manufactured, sold, and distributed Pepsi-Cola soft drinks. Pepsi-Cola's best known trademarks were Pepsi-Cola, Diet Pepsi, and Mountain Dew. Frito-Lay manufactured and sold a variety of leading snack foods such as Lay's Potato Chips, Doritos Tortilla Chips, Tostitos Tortilla Chips, and Ruffles Potato Chips.

PepsiCo believed the restaurant business complemented its consumer product orientation. The marketing of fast food followed many of the same patterns as soft drinks and snack foods. Pepsi-Cola and Lay's Potato Chips, for example, could be marketed in the same television and radio segments, which provided higher returns for each advertising dollar. Restaurant chains also provided an additional outlet for the sale of Pepsi soft drinks. PepsiCo believed it could take advantage of numerous synergies by operating the three businesses under the same corporate umbrella. It also believed that its management skills could be transferred among the three businesses. This practice was compatible with PepsiCo's policy of frequently moving managers among its business units as a means of developing future executives. PepsiCo's acquisition of

KFC in 1986 followed earlier acquisitions of Pizza Hut and Taco Bell. The three restaurant chains were the market leaders in the chicken, pizza, and Mexican categories.

After acquisition of KFC, PepsiCo initiated sweeping changes. It announced that the franchise contract would be changed to give PepsiCo greater control over KFC franchisees and to make it easier to close poorly performing restaurants. Staff at KFC was reduced to cut costs and many KFC managers were replaced with PepsiCo managers. Soon after the acquisition, KFC's new personnel manager, who had just relocated from PepsiCo's New York headquarters, was overheard in the KFC cafeteria saying, "There will be no more home grown tomatoes in this organization." Rumors spread quickly among KFC employees about their opportunities for advancement within KFC and PepsiCo. Harsh comments by PepsiCo managers about KFC, its people, and its traditions, several restructurings that led to layoffs throughout KFC, the replacement of KFC managers with PepsiCo managers, and conflicts between KFC and PepsiCo's corporate cultures created a morale problem within KFC. KFC's culture was built largely on Colonel Sander's laid-back approach to management. Employees enjoyed good job security and stability. A strong loyalty had been created over the years as a result of the Colonel's efforts to provide for his employees' benefits, pension, and other non-income needs. In addition, the Southern environment in Louisville resulted in a friendly, relaxed atmosphere at KFC's corporate offices.

PepsiCo's culture, in contrast, was characterized by a strong emphasis on performance. Top performers expected to move up through the ranks quickly. PepsiCo used its KFC, Pizza Hut, Taco Bell, Frito Lay, and Pepsi-Cola divisions as training grounds for its executives, rotating its best managers through the five divisions on average every two years. This practice created pressure on managers to demonstrate their management skills within short periods to maximize their potential for promotion. This practice reinforced feelings among KFC managers that they had few opportunities for advancement within the new company. One PepsiCo manager commented, "You may have performed well last year, but if you don't perform well this year, you're gone, and there are 100 ambitious guys with Ivy League MBAs at PepsiCo's headquarters in New York who would love to have your job." An unwanted effect of this performance-driven culture was that employee loyalty was lost and turnover was higher than in other companies.

Kyle Craig, president of KFC's U.S. operations, commented on PepsiCo's relationship with KFC:

"The KFC culture is an interesting one because it was dominated by a lot of KFC folks, many who have been around since the days of the Colonel. Many of those people were very intimidated by the PepsiCo culture, which is a very high performance, high accountability, highly driven culture. People were concerned about whether they would succeed in the new culture. Like many companies, we have had a couple of downsizings which further made people nervous. Today, there are fewer old KFC people around and I think to some degree people have seen that the Pepsi-Co culture can drive some pretty positive results. I also think the PepsiCo people who have worked with KFC have modified their cultural values somewhat and they can see that there were a lot of benefits in the old KFC culture.

"PepsiCo pushes its companies to perform strongly, but whenever there is a slip in performance, it increases the culture gap between PepsiCo and KFC. I have been involved in two downsizings over which I have been the chief architect. They have been probably the two most gut-wrenching experiences of my career. Because you know you're dealing with peoples' lives and their families, these changes can be emotional if you care about the people in your organization. However, I do fundamentally believe that your first obligation is to the entire organization."

A second problem for PepsiCo was its poor relationship with KFC franchisees. A month after becoming president and CEO in 1989, John Cranor addressed KFC's franchisees in Louisville to explain the details of the new franchise contract. This was the first contract change in 13 years. It gave PepsiCo greater power to take over weak franchises, relocate restaurants, and make changes in existing restaurants. In addition, restaurants would no longer be protected from competition from new KFC units, and PepsiCo would have the right to raise royalty fees on existing restaurants as contracts came up for renewal. After Cranor finished his address, there was an uproar among the attending franchisees, who jumped to their feet to protest the changes. KFC's franchise association later sued PepsiCo over the new contract. The contract remained unresolved until 1996, when the most objectionable parts of the contract were removed by KFC's new president and CEO, David Novak. A new contract was ratified by KFC's franchisees in 1997.

PEPSICO'S DIVESTITURE OF KFC, PIZZA HUT, AND TACO BELL

PepsiCo's strategy of diversifying into three distinct but related markets—soft drinks, snack foods, and fast-food restaurants—created one of the world's largest food companies and a portfolio of some of the world's most recognizable brands. Between 1990 and 1996, PepsiCo's sales grew at an annual rate of more than 10%, surpassing $31 billion in 1996. PepsiCo's growth, however, masked troubles in its fast-food businesses. Operating margins (profit after tax as a percentage of sales) at Pepsi-Cola and Frito Lay averaged 12% and 17%, respectively. During the same period, margins at KFC, Pizza Hut, and Taco Bell fell from an average of more than 8% in 1990 to a little more than 4% in 1996. Declining margins in the fast-food chains reflected increasing maturity in the U.S. fast-food industry, intense competition, and the aging of KFC and Pizza Hut's restaurant bases. As a result, PepsiCo's restaurant chains absorbed nearly one-half of PepsiCo's annual capital spending during the 1990s but generated less than one-third of its cash flows. This meant that cash had to be diverted from PepsiCo's soft drink and snack food businesses to its restaurant businesses. This reduced PepsiCo's corporate return on assets, made it more difficult to compete effectively with Coca-Cola, and hurt its stock price. In 1997, PepsiCo decided to spin off its restaurant businesses into a new company called Tricon Global Restaurants, Inc.

The new company was based in KFC's headquarters in Louisville, Kentucky.

PepsiCo's objective was to reposition itself as a beverage and snack food company, strengthen its balance sheet, and create more consistent earnings growth. PepsiCo received a one-time distribution from Tricon of $4.7 billion, $3.7 billion of which was used to pay off short-term debt. The balance was earmarked for stock repurchases. In 1998, PepsiCo acquired Tropicana Products, which controlled more than 40% of the U. S. chilled orange juice market. Because of the divestiture of KFC, Pizza Hut, and Taco Bell, PepsiCo sales fell by $11.3 billion and assets fell by $7.0 billion. Profitability, however, soared. Operating margins rose from 11% in 1997 to 14% in 1999 and ROA rose from 11% in 1997 to 16% in 1999. By focusing on high cash-flow market leaders, PepsiCo raised profitability while decreasing its asset base. In 2001, PepsiCo acquired the Quaker Oats Company, which included Gatorade. Gatorade and Tropicana were moved into a separate division to increase efficiencies. By 2005, PepsiCo's sales exceeded $29 billion annually.

YUM! BRANDS, INC.

The spin-off created a new, independent, publicly held company called Tricon Global Restaurants, Inc. The new company managed the KFC, Pizza Hut, and Taco Bell franchise systems. David Novak became Tricon's new CEO and moved quickly to create a new culture within the company. One of his primary objectives was to reverse the long-standing friction between management and franchisees that was created under PepsiCo ownership. Novak announced that PepsiCo's top-down management system would be replaced by a new management emphasis on providing support to the firm's franchise base. Franchises would have greater independence, resources, and technical support. Novak symbolically changed the name on the corporate headquarters building in Louisville to KFC Support Center to drive home his new philosophy.

In 2002, Tricon announced the acquisition of Long John Silver's and A&W All-American Food Restaurants. The acquisition increased Tricon's worldwide system to 32,500 restaurants. The acquisition signaled Tricon's decision to promote aggressively a multibranding strategy that combined two brands in one restaurant and attracted a larger consumer base by offering a broader menu selection in one location. One week after it announced the acquisition, shareholders approved a corporate name change to Yum! Brands, Inc. The new name reflected the company's expanding portfolio of fast-food brands (see Exhibit 1). In 2003, Novak announced the acquisition of Pasta Bravo, a made-to-order pasta and salad concept based in California. The acquisition followed several months of test marketing of the multibranding of Pasta Bravo and Pizza Hut.

Novak also initiated a plan to reduce the company-owned restaurant base by either closing poorly performing restaurants or selling company restaurants to individual franchisees. In 1997, 38% of the restaurant base (KFC, Pizza Hut, and Taco Bell) was company-owned. By early 2005, company-owned restaurants had declined to 25% of the total. The long-term goal was to reduce the

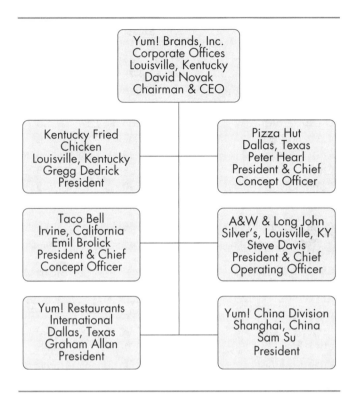

Exhibit 1 Yum! Brands, Inc., Organizational Chart, 2005

company base to 20%. The firm's new emphasis on supporting individual franchisees had an immediate effect on morale. In 1997, the year of the divestiture, the company recorded a loss of $111 million in net income. In 2004, net income was $740 million on sales of $9.0 billion, a return on sales of 8.2%.

THE FAST-FOOD INDUSTRY

The National Restaurant Association estimated that U.S. food service sales increased by 5.5% to $454 billion in 2004. More than 858,000 restaurants made up the U.S. restaurant industry and employed 12 million people. Sales were highest in the full-service, sit-down sector, which grew 5.4% to $157 billion. Fast-food sales grew by 5.9% to $128 billion. Together, the full-service and fast-food segments made up about 63% of all U.S. food service sales.

MAJOR FAST-FOOD SEGMENTS

Eight major segments made up the fast-food segment of the restaurant industry: sandwich chains, pizza chains, family restaurants, grill buffet chains, dinner houses, chicken chains, non-dinner concepts, and other chains. Sales data for the leading chains in each segment are shown in Exhibit 2. Most striking is the dominance of McDonald's, which had sales of more than $24 billion in 2004. Sandwich chains made up the largest segment of the fast-food market. McDonald's controlled 35% of the sandwich segment,

while Burger King ran a distant second with an 11% market share. Sandwich chains, however, were struggling because of continued price discounting that lowered profits. The threat of obesity lawsuits and increased customer demand for more nutritious food items and better service lowered demand for the traditional hamburger, fries, and soft drink combinations. Many chains attempted to attract new customers through price discounting. Instead of drawing in new customers, however, discounting merely lowered profit margins.

By 2005, most chains had abandoned price discounting and began to focus on improved service and product quality. McDonald's, Taco Bell, and Hardee's were particularly successful. They slowed new restaurant development, improved drive-thru service, and introduced a variety of new menu items. To meet health trends, McDonald's introduced premium salads and fruit salads while Burger King introduced a new line of low-fat, grilled chicken sandwiches. In contrast, Hardee's introduced a new "Thickburger" menu that included 1/3-, 1/2-, and 2/3-pound "lean" Angus beef burgers in an attempt to distinguish itself from other hamburger chains. The shift from price discounting to new product introductions increased average ticket sales and helped sandwich chains improve profitability in 2004.

Dinner houses made up the second-largest and fastest-growing fast-food segment. Sales in the dinner house segment increased by 10% in 2004. Much of the growth in dinner houses came from new unit construction in suburban areas and small towns. Applebee's, Chili's, Outback Steakhouse, Red Lobster, and Olive Garden dominated the segment. Each chain generated sales of more than $2 billion in 2004. The fastest-growing dinner houses, however, were newer chains generating less than $700 million in sales, such as Buffalo Wild Wings Grill & Bar, Texas Roadhouse, P. F. Chang's China Bistro, The Cheesecake Factory, and Red Robin Burgers & Spirits Emporium. Each chain was increasing sales at a 25% annual rate. Dinner houses continued to benefit from rising household incomes in the United States. As incomes rose, families were able to move up from quick-service restaurants to more upscale, higher-priced dinner houses. In addition, higher incomes enabled many professionals to purchase higher-priced homes in new suburban developments, thereby providing additional opportunities for dinner houses to build new restaurants in unsaturated areas.

Increased growth among dinner houses came at the expense of sandwich chains, pizza and chicken chains, grilled buffet chains, and family restaurants. "Too many restaurants chasing the same customers" was responsible for much of the slower growth in these other fast-food categories. Sales growth within each segment, however, differed from one chain to another. In the family segment, for example, Denny's (the segment leader), Perkins, and Shoney's shut down poorly performing restaurants while Waffle House, IHOP, Bob Evans, and Cracker Barrel expanded their bases. In the pizza segment, Pizza Hut and Papa John's closed underperforming restaurants while Little Caesars, Chuck E. Cheese's, and CiCi's constructed new restaurants. The hardest-hit segment was grilled buffet chains. Declining sales caused both Sizzlin' and Western Sizzlin' to drop out of the list of top 100 chains, leaving only three chains in the top 100 (Golden Coral,

Sandwich Chains	Sales	Change		Dinner Houses	Sales	Change
McDonald's	24,391	10.3%		Applebee's	3,888	10.5%
Burger King	7,920	3.1		Chili's	2,875	14.8
Wendy's	7,870	5.6		Outback Steakhouse	2,539	6.3
Subway	6,270	10.2		Red Lobster	2,456	3.0
Taco Bell	5,700	6.6		Olive Garden	2,283	5.5
Arby's	2,830	4.4		T.G.I. Friday's	1,862	4.0
Sonic Drive-In	2,666	13.0		Ruby Tuesday	1,560	7.6
Jack in the Box	2,570	8.9		Cheesecake Factory	865	25.5
Dairy Queen	2,360	9.0		Romano's	740	5.9
Hardee's	1,702	2.4		Hooter's	731	9.1
Other Chains	5,530	19.8		Other Chains	9,566	16.8
Total Segment	69,809	8.8%		Total Segment	26,365	10.4%
Pizza Chains	**Sales**	**Change**		**Chicken Chains**	**Sales**	**Change**
Pizza Hut	5,200	3.3%		KFC	5,000	1.3%
Domino's	3,173	5.7		Chick-fil-A	1,746	13.8
Papa John's	1,727	0.5		Popeye's	1,338	5.0
Little Caesars	1,235	2.9		Church's	691	−1.3
Chuck E. Cheese's	521	9.4		Boston Market	675	4.5
CiCi's Pizza	435	14.2		El Pollo Loco	427	7.9
Total Segment	12,291	4.1%		Bojangles'	422	13.5
				Total Segment	10,299	4.5%
Family Restaurants	**Sales**	**Change**		**Other Dinner Chains**	**Sales**	**Change**
Denny's	2,191	2.8%		Panera Bread	1,163	28.1%
IHOP	1,867	11.4		Long John Silver's	800	3.0
Cracker Barrel	1,574	6.3		Disney Theme Parks	756	7.0
Bob Evans	997	4.5		Captain D's Seafood	525	3.8
Waffle House	825	4.6		Old Country Buffet	434	−2.7
Perkins	787	0.0		Total Segment	3,678	10.0%
Other Chains	1,842	4.0		**Non-Dinner Concepts**	**Sales**	**Change**
Total Segment	10,083	5.2%		Starbuck's	4,060	30.9%
Grill Buffet Chains	**Sales**	**Change**		Dunkin' Donuts	3,380	13.6
				7-Eleven	1,505	6.7
Golden Coral	1,340	7.5%		Krispy Kreme	975	1.9
Ryan's	765	−6.0		Baskin-Robbins	535	4.9
Ponderosa	516	−4.0		Total Segment	10,455	16.8%
Total Segment	2,621	0.9%				

Source: Nation's Restaurant News.

Exhibit 2 Top U.S. Fast-Food Restaurants (ranked by 2004 sales, $ thousand)

Ryan's, and Ponderosa). Dinner houses, because of their more upscale atmosphere and higher ticket items, were better positioned to take advantage of the aging and wealthier U.S. population. Even dinner houses, however, faced the prospect of market saturation and increased competition in the near future.

CHICKEN SEGMENT

KFC continued to dominate the chicken segment, with sales of $5.0 billion in 2004, about half of chicken segment sales (Exhibit 3). Its nearest competitor, Chick-fil-A, ran a distant second with sales of

	1998	1999	2000	2001	2002	2003	2004
Sales ($ Millions)							
KFC	4,200	4,300	4,400	4,700	4,800	4,936	5,000
Chick-fil-A	764	943	1,082	1,242	1,373	1,534	1,746
Popeye's	843	986	1,077	1,179	1,215	1,274	1,338
Church's	620	705	699	721	720	700	691
Boston Market	929	855	685	640	641	646	675
El Pollo Loco	245	275	305	339	364	396	427
Bojangles'	250	270	298	333	347	375	422
Total	7,851	8,334	8,546	9,154	9,460	9,861	10,299
U.S. Restaurants							
KFC	5,105	5,231	5,364	5,399	5,472	5,524	5,525
Chick-fil-A	812	897	958	1,014	1,074	1,447	1,472
Popeye's	1,066	1,165	1,248	1,327	1,380	1,235	1,220
Church's	1,105	1,178	1,217	1,242	1,232	1,127	1,191
Boston Market	889	858	712	657	653	630	630
El Pollo Loco	261	270	279	293	306	320	337
Bojangles'	255	265	278	280	292	314	322
Total	9,493	9,864	10,056	10,212	10,409	10,597	10,697
Sales per unit ($ 000s)							
KFC	823	822	820	871	877	898	905
Chick-fil-A	941	1,051	1,130	1,225	1,278	1,394	1,507
Popeye's	790	847	863	889	880	897	917
Church's	561	598	574	581	584	564	563
Boston Market	1,045	997	962	974	982	1,009	1,071
El Pollo Loco	939	1,019	1,094	1,157	1,190	1,277	1,343
Bojangles'	980	1,020	1,072	1,189	1,188	1,215	1,284
Total	827	845	850	896	909	1,038	1,084

Source: Nation's Restaurant News.

Exhibit 3 Top Chicken Chains

$1.7 billion. KFC's leadership in the U.S. market was so extensive that it had fewer opportunities to expand its U.S. restaurant base, which was growing only at about 1% per year. Despite its dominance, KFC was slowly losing market share as other chicken chains increased sales at a faster rate. KFC's share of chicken segment sales fell from 64% in 1993 to less than 49% in 2004, an 11-year drop of 15% (Exhibit 4). During the same period, Chick-fil-A and Boston Market increased their combined market share by 14%. In the 1990s many industry analysts predicted that Boston Market would challenge KFC for market leadership. Boston Market was a new chain that emphasized roasted rather than fried chicken. It successfully created the image of an upscale deli offering healthy, ''home-style'' alternatives to fried chicken. To distinguish itself from more traditional fast food, it refused to construct drive-thrus and established most of its units outside of shopping malls rather than at major city intersections.

On the surface, it appeared that Boston Market and Chick-fil-A's market share gains were achieved by taking customers away from KFC. Another look at the data, however, reveals that KFC's sales grew at a stable rate during the previous ten years. Boston Market, rather than drawing customers away from KFC, appealed to new consumers who did not regularly frequent KFC and wanted non-fried chicken alternatives. After aggressively growing its restaurant base

through 1997, however, Boston Market fell on hard times and was unable to handle mounting debt problems. It soon entered bankruptcy proceedings. McDonald's acquired Boston Market in 2000. The acquisition followed earlier acquisitions of Donatos Pizza in 1999 and Chipotle Mexican Grill in 1998. McDonald's hoped the acquisitions would help it expand its U.S. restaurant base, since there were few opportunities to expand the McDonald's concept.

Chick-fil-A's early strategy was to establish sit-down restaurants in shopping malls. As more malls added food courts, however, malls became less enthusiastic about allocating separate store space to restaurants. As a result, Chick-fil-A began to open smaller units in shopping mall food courts and to build free-standing restaurants that competed head-to-head with existing chicken chains. Despite market share gains by Boston Market and Chick-fil-A, however, KFC's customer base remained loyal to the KFC brand because of its unique taste.

The maturation of the U.S. fast-food industry increased the intensity of competition within the chicken segment. With the exception of Chick-fil-A, most chains were no longer aggressively opening new restaurants. Restaurant profits were also threatened by rising input costs. Chicken prices, which represented about one-half of total food costs, increased dramatically in 2004.

	KFC	Chick-fil-A	Popeyes	Church's	Boston Market	Pollo Loco	Bojangles'	Total
1994	60.7	7.8	10.6	8.0	6.6	3.1	3.2	100.0
1995	56.6	7.7	10.1	7.7	11.6	3.0	3.3	100.0
1996	54.2	7.9	9.3	7.3	15.3	3.0	3.0	100.0
1997	52.5	8.5	9.5	7.6	15.8	3.1	3.0	100.0
1998	53.4	9.7	10.7	7.9	11.8	3.1	3.2	100.0
1999	51.6	11.3	11.8	8.5	10.3	3.3	3.2	100.0
2000	51.4	12.7	12.6	8.2	8.0	3.6	3.5	100.0
2001	51.3	13.6	12.9	7.9	7.0	3.7	3.6	100.0
2002	50.8	14.5	12.8	7.6	6.8	3.8	3.7	100.0
2003	50.1	15.6	12.9	7.1	6.6	4.0	3.8	100.0
2004	48.5	17.0	13.0	6.7	6.6	4.1	4.1	100.0
10-Year Change (%)								
	−12.0%	9.1%	2.4%	−1.3%	−0.1%	1.0%	0.9%	0.0%

Exhibit 4 Top Chicken Chains—Market Share (%, Based on annual sales)

Boneless chicken breast, for example, cost $1.20 per pound in early 2001. By 2004 the price had risen to $2.50 per pound, an increase of more than 100%.

Chicken chains attempted to differentiate themselves based on unique product and customer characteristics. KFC used animated images of the Colonel to drive home its home-style image. It added new menu boards and introduced new products such as Oven Roasted Strips, Roasted Twister Sandwich Wraps, Popcorn Chicken, Honey BBQ Chicken, and Spicy BBQ Wings. Boston Market experimented with home delivery and began to sell through supermarkets. Popeyes continued to reimage its restaurants with its ''Heritage'' design that included a balcony over the drive-thru, Cajun-style murals, and new signage. It introduced a Chicken Strip Po' Boy sandwich to expand its New Orleans–style menu of spicy chicken, jambalaya, etouffée, and gumbo. Bojangles' also promoted a Cajun décor but focused more heavily on core chicken products such as its Cajun Fried Chicken, Cajun Filet Sandwich, and Buffalo Bites. El Pollo Loco served marinated, flame-broiled chicken and other Mexican food entrees such as chicken burritos, tostada salads, and chicken nachos. Church's focused on adding drive-thru service while it also emphasized its ''made-from-scratch,'' Southern-style fried chicken and side dishes such as corn on the cob, fried okra, and macaroni and cheese. Chick-fil-A continued to build free-standing restaurants to expand beyond shopping malls.

TRENDS IN THE RESTAURANT INDUSTRY

Several demographic and societal trends influenced the demand for food eaten outside the home. During the past two decades, rising incomes, greater affluence among a greater percentage of American households, higher divorce rates, and the fact that people married later in life contributed to the rising number of single households and the demand for fast food. More than 50% of women worked outside of the home, a dramatic increase since 1970. This number was expected to rise to 65% by 2010. Double-income households contributed to rising household incomes and increased the number of times families ate out. Less time to prepare meals inside the home added to this trend. Countering these trends, however, was a slower growth rate of the U. S. population and an overpopulation of fast-food chains that increased consumer alternatives and intensified competition.

Baby Boomers 35–50 years of age constituted the largest consumer group for fast-food restaurants. Generation X'ers (ages 25–34) and the Mature category (ages 51–64) made up the second- and third-largest groups. As consumers aged, they became less enamored with fast food and were more likely to trade up to more expensive restaurants such as dinner houses and full-service restaurants. Sales of many Mexican restaurants, which were extremely popular during the 1980s, began to slow as Japanese, Indian, and Vietnamese restaurants became more fashionable. Ethnic foods were rising in popularity as U.S. immigrants, who constituted 12% of the U.S. population in 2005, looked for establishments that sold their native foods.

Labor was the top operational challenge of U.S. restaurant chains. Restaurants relied heavily on teenagers and college-age workers. Twenty percent of all employed teenagers worked in food service, compared to only 4% of all employed men over the age of 18 and 6% of all employed women. As the U.S. population aged, fewer young workers were available to fill food service jobs. The short supply of high school and college students also meant they had greater opportunities outside food service. Turnover rates were notoriously high. The National Restaurant Association estimated that about 96% of all fast-food workers quit within a year, compared to about 84% of employees in full-service restaurants.

Labor costs made up about 30% of the fast-food chain's total costs, second only to food and beverage costs. To deal with the decreased supply of employees in the 16–24 age category, many restaurants were forced to hire lower-quality workers, which affected service and restaurant cleanliness. To improve quality and service, restaurants increasingly hired elderly employees who were interested in returning to the workforce. To attract more workers, especially the elderly, restaurants offered health insurance, non-contributory pension plans, and profit-sharing benefits that were generally not given only ten years before. To combat high turnover rates, restaurants also turned to better training programs and mentoring systems that paired new employees with more experienced ones. Mentoring systems were particularly helpful in increasing the learning curve of new workers and providing better camaraderie among employees.

Intense competition in the mature restaurant industry made it difficult for restaurants to increase prices sufficiently to cover the increased cost of labor. Consumers made decisions about where to eat partially based on price. As a result, profit margins were squeezed. To reduce costs, restaurants eliminated low-margin food items, increased portion sizes, and improved product value to offset price increases. Restaurants also attempted to increase consumer traffic through discounting, by accepting coupons from competitors, by offering two-for-one specials, and by making limited-time offerings.

Technology was increasingly used to lower costs and improve efficiencies. According to the National Restaurant Association, restaurant operators viewed computers as their number-one tool for improving efficiency. Computers were used to improve labor scheduling, accounting, payroll, sales analysis, and inventory control. Most restaurant chains also used point-of-sale systems that recorded the selected menu items and gave the cashier a breakdown of food items and the ticket price. These systems reduced serving times and cashier accuracy. Other chains like McDonald's and Carl's Jr. converted to new food preparation systems that allowed them to prepare food more accurately yet with more variety.

Higher costs and poor availability of prime real estate was another trend that negatively affected profitability. A plot of land suitable for a free-standing restaurant cost between $1.5 and $2.5 million. Leasing was a less costly alternative to buying. Nevertheless, market saturation decreased per store sales as newer units cannibalized sales from existing units. As a result, most food chains began to expand their U.S. restaurant bases into alternative distribution channels in hospitals, airports, colleges, highway rest areas, gas stations, shopping mall food courts, and large retail stores or by dual branding with other fast-food concepts.

THE GLOBAL FAST-FOOD INDUSTRY

Exhibit 5 lists the world's 35 largest restaurant chains in 2004. As the U.S. market matured, more restaurants turned to international markets to expand sales. Foreign markets were attractive because of their large customer bases and comparatively little competition. McDonald's, for example, operated 48 restaurants for every one

million U.S. residents. Outside of the United States, it operated only one restaurant for every five million residents. McDonald's, KFC, Burger King, and Pizza Hut were the earliest and most aggressive chains to expand abroad, beginning in the 1960s. By early 2005, at least 35 chains had expanded into at least one foreign country. McDonald's operated more than 13,000 U.S. units and 17,000 foreign units in 119 countries. With the acquisition of A&W and Long John Silver's, however, Yum! Brands became the world's largest restaurant chain in 2003. It operated more than 21,000 U.S. and close to 33,000 non-U.S. KFC, Pizza Hut, Taco Bell, A&W, and Long John Silver's restaurants in 88 countries. Because of their early expansion abroad, McDonald's, KFC, Burger King, and Pizza Hut had all developed strong brand names and managerial expertise operating in international markets. This made them formidable competitors for fast-food chains investing abroad for the first time. Subway, TCBY, and Domino's were more recent global competitors but were expanding more aggressively than McDonald's or KFC. By 2004, each was operating in more than 65 countries.

The global fast-food industry had a distinctly American flavor. Twenty-eight chains (80% of the total) were headquartered in the United States. U.S. chains had the advantage of a large domestic market and ready acceptance by the American consumer. European firms had less success developing the fast-food concept because Europeans were more inclined to frequent midscale restaurants, where they spent several hours enjoying multicourse meals in a formal setting. KFC had trouble breaking into the German market during the 1970s and 1980s because Germans were not accustomed to buying take-out or ordering food over the counter. McDonald's had greater success penetrating the German market because it made changes to its menu and operating procedures to appeal to German tastes. German beer, for example, was served in all McDonald's restaurants in Germany. In France, McDonald's used a different sauce on its Big Mac sandwich that appealed to the French palate. KFC had more success in Asia and Latin America, where chicken was a traditional dish.

Aside from cultural factors, international business carried risks not present in the domestic market. Long distances between headquarters and foreign franchises made it more difficult to control the quality of individual restaurants. Large distances also caused servicing and support problems. Transportation and other resource costs were higher than in the domestic market. In addition, time, cultural, and language differences increased communication and operational problems. As a result, most restaurant chains limited expansion to their domestic market as long as they were able to meet profit and growth objectives. As companies gained greater expertise abroad, they turned to profitable international markets as a means of expanding restaurant bases and increasing sales, profits, and market share.

Worldwide demand for fast-food was expected to grow rapidly during the next two decades as rising per capita incomes made eating out more affordable for greater numbers of consumers. In addition, the development of the Internet was quickly breaking down communication and language barriers. Greater numbers of children were growing up with computers in their homes and schools. As a result, teenagers in Germany, Brazil, Japan, and the

	Franchise	Corporate Headquarters	Home Country	Countries
1.	McDonald's	Oakbrook, Illinois	U.S.A.	121
2.	KFC	Louisville, Kentucky	U.S.A.	99
3.	Pizza Hut	Dallas, Texas	U.S.A.	92
4.	Subway Sandwiches	Milford, Connecticut	U.S.A.	74
5.	TCBY	Little Rock, Arkansas	U.S.A.	67
6.	Domino's Pizza	Ann Arbor, Michigan	U.S.A.	65
7.	Burger King	Miami, Florida	U.S.A.	58
8.	T.G.I. Friday's	Dallas, Texas	U.S.A.	53
9.	Baskin Robbins	Glendale, California	U.S.A.	52
10.	Dunkin' Donuts	Randolph, Massachusetts	U.S.A.	40
11.	Wendy's	Dublin, Ohio	U.S.A.	34
12.	Chili's Grill & Bar	Dallas, Texas	U.S.A.	22
13.	Dairy Queen	Edina, Minnesota	U.S.A.	22
14.	Little Caesar's Pizza	Detroit, Michigan	U.S.A.	22
15.	Popeye's	Atlanta, Georgia	U.S.A.	22
16.	Outback Steakhouse	Tampa, Florida	U.S.A.	20
17.	A&W Restaurants	Lexington, Kentucky	U.S.A.	17
18.	PizzaExpress	London, England	U.K.	16
19.	Carl's Jr.	Annaheim, California	U.S.A.	14
20.	Church's Chicken	Atlanta, Georgia	U.S.A.	12
21.	Taco Bell	Irvine, California	U.S.A.	12
22.	Hardee's	Rocky Mt., North Carolina	U.S.A.	11
23.	Applebee's	Overland Park, Kansas.	U.S.A.	9
24.	Sizzler	Los Angeles, California	U.S.A.	9
25.	Arby's	Ft. Lauderdale, Florida	U.S.A.	7
26.	Denny's	Spartanburg, South Carolina	U.S.A.	7
27.	Skylark	Tokyo	Japan	7
28.	Lotteria	Seoul	Korea	5
29.	Taco Time	Eugene, Oregon	U.S.A.	5
30.	Mos Burger	Tokyo	Japan	4
31.	Orange Julius	Edina, Minnesota	U.S.A.	4
32.	Yoshinoya	Tokyo	Japan	4
33.	IHOP	Glendale, California	U.S.A.	3
34.	Quick Restaurants	Brussels	Belgium	3
35.	Red Lobster	Orlando, Florida	U.S.A.	3

Source: Case writer research.

Exhibit 5 The World's 35 Largest Fast-Food Chains in 2004

United States were equally likely to be able to converse about the Internet. The Internet also exposed more teenagers to the same companies and products, which enabled firms to develop global brands and a worldwide consumer base quickly.

KENTUCKY FRIED CHICKEN CORPORATION

Marketing Strategy

Many of KFC's problems during the 1980s and 1990s were due to its limited menu and inability to bring new products to market quickly.

The popularity of its Original Recipe Chicken allowed KFC to expand through the 1980s without significant competition from other chicken chains. As a result, new product introductions were not a critical part of KFC's business strategy. KFC suffered one of its most serious setbacks in 1989 as it prepared to introduce a chicken sandwich to its menu. KFC was still experimenting with the chicken sandwich concept when McDonald's rolled out its McChicken sandwich. By beating KFC to the market, McDonald's developed strong consumer awareness for its sandwich. This significantly increased KFC's cost of developing awareness for its own sandwich, which KFC introduced several months later. KFC eventually withdrew the sandwich because of low sales. Today, about 95% of chicken sandwiches are sold through traditional hamburger chains.

KFC's focus on fried chicken ("chicken-on-the-bone") became a serious problem by the 1990s as the U.S. fast-food industry matured. To expand sales, restaurant chains began to diversify their menus to include non-core products, thereby cutting into the business of other fast-food segments. For example, hamburger and pizza chains, family restaurants, and dinner houses all introduced a variety of chicken items such as chicken sandwiches and chicken wings to expand their consumer bases. This made it difficult for KFC to increase per unit sales. By 2003, McDonald's boasted a menu that included hamburgers, chicken sandwiches, fish sandwiches, burritos, a full line of breakfast items, ice cream, and milkshakes. By diversifying its menu, McDonald's was able to raise annual sales to $1.5 million per restaurant. This compared with KFC's average restaurant sales of $883,000. In 2003, Yum! Brands market research showed that customers preferred multiple menu offerings over single-concept menus like chicken or pizza by a six-to-one margin.

KFC's short-term strategy was to diversify its menu. It rolled out a buffet that included over 30 dinner, salad, and dessert items. The buffet was most successful in rural locations and suburbs but less successful in urban areas where restaurant space was limited. It then introduced Colonel's Crispy Strips and a line of chicken sandwiches that complimented its core fried chicken products. More recent product innovations include Popcorn Chicken, Chunky Chicken Pot Pie, and Twisters (a flour tortilla filled with chunks of chicken). To increase brand awareness for these new products, KFC introduced a new television campaign featuring a cartoon caricature of Colonel Sanders stating "I'm a Chicken Genius!" It also featured Jason Alexander from the television sitcom "Seinfeld" promoting Popcorn Chicken with the slogan "There's fast food, then there's KFC." Sandwiches and other non-core items, however, cannibalized sales of KFC's core chicken products. Most important, it did little to address the consumer's desire for greater menu variety beyond chicken.

Multibrand Strategy

By 2000, the company began to open "two-in-one" units that sold both KFC and Taco Bell or Pizza Hut in the same location. Most of KFC's sales (64%) and Pizza Hut's sales (61%) were driven by dinner, while most of Taco Bell's sales (50%) were driven by lunch. The combination of KFC and Taco Bell was a natural success because it increased per unit sales simply by filling up counter space left empty by KFC at lunch or Taco Bell at dinner. It became increasingly apparent, however, that the real value of combining restaurant concepts was in attracting greater numbers of consumers who wanted more menu variety. The acquisition of A&W and Long John Silver's in 2002 provided additional opportunities to create a variety of combinations of five highly differentiated fast-food category leaders. By 2005, Yum! Brands operated nearly 3,000 multibrand restaurants worldwide that included KFC/Taco Bell, KFC/A&W, Taco Bell/Pizza Hut, and A&W/Long John Silver's. The company believed there was potential for opening 13,000 multibrand restaurants in the United States alone. The increase in per unit sales that resulted from multibranding meant that new restaurants could be opened in more expensive locations and lower population areas than were profitable with stand-alone restaurants.

INTERNATIONAL OPERATIONS

KFC's early experience operating abroad put it in a strong position to take advantage of the growing trend toward global expansion. By early 2005, more than 58% of KFC's restaurants were outside the United States. KFC was the most global of the five brands managed by Yum! Brands; the others had a significantly smaller percentage of their restaurant base outside the United States—Pizza Hut (37%), Taco Bell (4%), Long John Silver's (2%), and A&W (22%). Historically, franchises made up a large portion of KFC's international restaurant base because franchises were owned and operated by local entrepreneurs who had a deeper understanding of local language, culture, customs, law, financial markets, and marketing characteristics. Franchising was also a good strategy for establishing a presence in smaller countries like Grenada, Bermuda, and Suriname, whose small populations could only support a single restaurant. The costs of operating company-owned restaurants were prohibitively high in these smaller markets. Of the 7,000 KFC restaurants outside the United States, 77% were franchisees, licensed restaurants, or joint ventures. In larger markets such as Mexico, China, Canada, Australia, Puerto Rico, Korea, Thailand, and the United Kingdom, there was a stronger emphasis on building company-owned restaurants. By coordinating purchasing, recruiting, training, financing, and advertising in these larger markets, fixed costs could be spread over a larger restaurant base. KFC could also maintain tighter control over product quality and customer service.

Latin American Strategy

KFC operated 717 restaurants in Latin America in 2005 (Exhibit 6). Its primary presence was in Mexico, Puerto Rico, and the Caribbean. It established subsidiaries in Mexico and Puerto Rico in the late 1960s and expanded through company-owned restaurants. Franchises were used to penetrate Caribbean countries whose market size prevented KFC from profitably operating company-owned restaurants. Subsidiaries were later established in the Virgin Islands, Venezuela, and Brazil. KFC had planned to expand into these regions using company-owned restaurants. The Venezuelan subsidiary, however, was later closed because of the high costs of operating the small subsidiary. KFC had opened eight restaurants in Brazil but closed them by 2000 because it lacked the cash flow needed to support an expansion program in that market. Franchises were opened in other markets that had good growth potential such as Chile, Ecuador, and Peru. In 2003, KFC signed a joint venture agreement with a Brazilian partner that had a deeper understanding of the Brazilian market. KFC hoped the joint venture would help it reestablish a presence in Brazil.

	McDonald's	Burger King	Wendy's	KFC
Mexico	261	154	16	274
Puerto Rico	112	163	46	97
Caribbean Islands	29	55	20	134
Central America	99	104	38	32
Subtotal	501	476	120	537
% Total	31%	82%	68%	83%
Colombia	25	0	3	9
Ecuador	10	13	0	39
Peru	10	12	0	25
Venezuela	129	20	33	5
Other Andean	45	6	0	5
Andean Region	219	51	36	83
% Total	14%	9%	25%	13%
Argentina	203	25	21	0
Brazil	584	0	0	0
Chile	70	23	0	30
Paraguay + Uruguay	28	6	0	0
Southern Cone	885	54	21	30
% Total	55%	9%	15%	5%
Latin America	1,605	581	143	650
% Total	100%	100%	100%	100%

Source: Case writer research.

Exhibit 6 Latin America Restaurant Count: McDonald's, Burger King, Wendy's, and KFC

KFC's early entry into Latin America gave it a leadership position over McDonald's in Mexico and the Caribbean. It also had an edge in Ecuador and Peru. KFC's Latin America strategy represented a classic internationalization strategy. It first expanded into Mexico and Puerto Rico because of their geographic proximity as well as political and economic ties to the United States. KFC then expanded its franchise system throughout the Caribbean, gradually moving away from its U.S. base as its experience in Latin America grew. Only after it had established a leadership position in Mexico and the Caribbean did it venture into South America. McDonald's pursued a different strategy. It was late to expand into the region. Despite a rapid restaurant construction program in Mexico during the 1990s, McDonald's still lagged behind KFC. Therefore, McDonald's initiated a first mover strategy in Brazil and Argentina, large markets where KFC had no presence. By 2003, 55% of McDonald's restaurants in Latin America were located in these two countries. Wendy's pursued a different strategy. It first expanded into Puerto Rico, the Caribbean, and Central America because of their geographic proximity to the United States. Wendy's late entry into Latin America, however, made it difficult to penetrate Mexico, where KFC, McDonald's, and Burger King had already established strong positions. Wendy's announced plans to build 100 Wendy's restaurants in Mexico by 2010; however, its primary objective was to establish strong positions in Venezuela and Argentina, where most U.S. fast-food chains had not yet been established.

COUNTRY RISK ASSESSMENT IN LATIN AMERICA

Latin America comprises some 50 countries, island states, and principalities that were settled primarily by the Spanish, Portuguese, French, Dutch, and British during the 1500s and 1600s. Spanish is spoken in most countries, the most notable exception being Brazil, where the official language is Portuguese. Catholicism is the major religion, though Methodist missionaries successfully exported Protestantism into many regions of Latin America in the 1800s, most notably on the coast of Brazil. Despite commonalities in language, religion, and history, however, political and economic policies differ significantly from one country to another. Frequent changes in governments and economic instability increase the uncertainty of doing business in the region.

Most U.S. and Canadian companies have realized that they could not overlook the region. Geographic proximity makes communications and travel easier, and NAFTA eliminated tariffs on goods shipped between Canada, Mexico, and the United States. A customs union agreement signed in 1991 (Mercosur) between Argentina, Paraguay, Uruguay, and Brazil eliminated tariffs on trade among those four countries. Other countries such as Chile have also established free trade policies that are stimulating strong growth. The primary task for companies investing in the region is to assess the different risks of doing business in Latin America and to select the proper countries for investment. Kent Miller developed a useful framework for analyzing countries for future investment (*Journal of International Business Studies* 23, no. 2), suggesting examination of country, industry, and firm factors.

Country factors address the risks associated with changes in the country's political and economic environment that potentially affect the firm's ability to conduct business:

- Political risk, such as war, revolution, changes in government, price controls, tariffs and other trade restrictions, appropriation of assets, government regulations, and restrictions on the repatriation of profits
- Economic risk, such as inflation, high interest rates, foreign exchange rate volatility, balance of trade movements, social unrest, riots, and terrorism
- Natural risk, such as rainfall, hurricanes, earthquakes, and volcanic activity

Industry factors address changes in industry structure that inhibit the firm's ability to compete successfully in its industry:

- Supplier risk, such as changes in quality, shifts in supply, and changes in supplier power
- Product market risk, such as consumer tastes and availability of substitute products
- Competitive risk, such as rivalry among competitors, new market entrants, and new product innovations

Firm factors examine the firm's ability to control its internal operations:

- Labor risk, such as labor unrest, absenteeism, employee turnover, and labor strikes
- Supplier risk, such as raw material shortages and unpredictable price changes
- Trade secret risk, such as protection of trade secrets and intangible assets
- Credit risk, such as problems collecting receivables
- Behavioral risk, such as control over franchise operations, product quality and consistency, service quality, and restaurant cleanliness

MEXICO

Many U.S. companies considered Mexico to be one of the most attractive investment locations in Latin America. Mexico's population of 105 million exceeded one-third of that of the United States. It was three times larger than Canada's 32 million. Prior to 1994, Mexico levied high tariffs on many goods imported from the United States. Other goods were regulated by quotas and licensing requirements that made Mexican goods more expensive. As a result, many U.S. consumers purchased less expensive products from Asia or Europe. In 1994, the long-awaited North American Free Trade Agreement among Canada, the United States, and Mexico went into effect. NAFTA eliminated tariffs on goods traded among the three countries and created a trading bloc with a

larger population and gross domestic product than the European Union. The elimination of tariffs led to an immediate increase in trade between Mexico and the United States. In 1995 only one year after NAFTA was signed, Mexico posted its first balance of trade surplus in six years. A large part of that surplus was attributed to greater exports to the United States. By 2003 almost 85% of Mexico's exports were purchased by U.S. consumers. In turn, about 68% of Mexico's total imports came from the United States.

U.S. investment in Mexico also increased significantly after NAFTA was signed, largely in the Maquiladoras located along the U.S.–Mexican border. With the elimination of import tariffs, U.S. firms could produce or assemble goods and transport them back into the United States more quickly and less expensively than they could transport goods from Asia or Europe. Mexico's largest exports to the United States were automobiles, automobile parts, crude oil, petroleum products, and natural gas. A large portion of Mexico's automobiles and auto parts was produced in U.S.-owned plants. The cost of transporting automobiles back into the United States was more than offset by the lower cost of labor in Mexico. In 2005, 2,600 U.S. firms operated in Mexico and accounted for 60% of all foreign direct investment in that country.

Despite the benefits, many Mexican farmers and unskilled workers strongly opposed NAFTA and U.S. investment. The day after NAFTA went into effect, rebels rioted in the southern Mexican province of Chiapas on the Guatemalan border. After four days of fighting, Mexican troops drove the rebels out of several towns the rebels had earlier seized. Around 150 people were killed. The Mexican government negotiated a cease-fire with the rebels; however, armed clashes between rebel groups protesting poverty and lack of land rights continued to be a problem. Another protest followed the signing of NAFTA when 30–40 masked men attacked a McDonald's restaurant in the tourist section of Mexico City. The men threw cash registers to the floor, smashed windows, overturned tables, and spray-painted ''No to Fascism'' and ''Yankee Go Home'' on the walls.

Most Mexicans (70%) lived in urban areas such as Mexico City, Guadalajara, and Monterrey. Mexico City's population of 18 million made it one of the most populated areas in Latin America. Many U.S. firms had operations in or around Mexico City. The fast-food industry was well developed in Mexico's cities. The leading U.S. fast-food chains already had significant restaurant bases in Mexico, most important being KFC (274 restaurants), McDonald's (261), Pizza Hut (174), Burger King (154), and Subway (71). Mexican consumers readily accepted the fast-food concept. Chicken was also a staple product in Mexico and helped explain KFC's wide popularity. Mexico's large population and ready acceptance of fast-food represented a significant opportunity for fast-food chains. Competition, however, was intense.

Despite Mexico's relative economic stability during the late 1990s and early 2000s, Mexico had a history of high inflation, foreign exchange controls, and government regulations. These often affected foreign firms' ability to make a profit. In 1989, President Salinas attempted to reduce high inflation by controlling the peso–dollar exchange rate, allowing the peso to depreciate by only one peso per day against the dollar. He also instituted price and wage controls. Firms like KFC were unable to raise prices and were closely monitored by Mexican authorities. However, smaller firms that supplied KFC and other U.S. firms with raw materials continued to charge higher prices to compensate for inflation. KFC was soon operating at a loss, setting off heated debate in PepsiCo's headquarters. PepsiCo's finance group wanted to halt further restaurant construction in Mexico until economic stability improved. PepsiCo's marketing group wanted to continue expansion despite losses to protect its leading market share in Mexico. PepsiCo's marketing group eventually won the debate and KFC continued to build new restaurants in Mexico during the period.

When Ernesto Zedillo became Mexico's president in December 1994, one of his objectives was to continue the stability of prices, wages, and exchange rates achieved by ex-president Carlos Salinas. This stability, however, was achieved primarily on the basis of price, wage, and foreign exchange controls. While giving the appearance of stability, an overvalued peso continued to encourage imports that exacerbated Mexico's balance of trade deficit. At the same time, Mexican exports became less competitive on world markets. Anticipating a devaluation of the peso, investors began to move capital into U.S. dollar investments. On December 19, 1994, Zedillo announced that the peso would be allowed to depreciate by an additional 15% per year against the dollar. Within two days, continued pressure on the peso forced Zedillo to allow the peso to float freely against the dollar.

By mid-January 1995, the peso had lost 35% of its value against the dollar and the Mexican stock market had plunged 20%. By the end of the year, the peso had depreciated from 3.1 pesos per dollar to 7.6 pesos per dollar. To thwart a possible default by Mexico, the U.S. government, IMF, and World Bank pledged $25 billion in emergency loans. Shortly thereafter, Zedillo announced an emergency economic package called the "pacto" that included lower government spending, the sale of government-run businesses, and a wage freeze. By 2000 there were signs that Mexico's economy had stabilized. Interest rates and inflation, however, remained higher than in the United States, putting continuous pressure on the peso. This led to higher import prices and exacerbated inflation. In sum, optimism about future prospects for trade and investment in Mexico was tempered by concern about continued economic stability.

BRAZIL

Mexico's geographic proximity and membership in NAFTA partially explained why many U.S. firms with little experience in Latin America expanded to Mexico first. Mexico's close proximity minimized travel and communication problems, and NAFTA reduced the complexity of establishing production in Mexico and importing goods back into the United States. Many firms overlooked the potential of Brazil. Brazil, with a population of 182 million, was the largest country in Latin America and fifth-largest country in the world. Its land base was as large as the United States and bordered ten countries. It was the world's largest coffee producer and largest exporter of sugar and tobacco. In addition to its abundant natural resources and strong export position in agriculture, Brazil was a strong industrial power, with major exports

of airplanes, automobiles, and chemicals. Its gross domestic product of $1.3 trillion was larger than Mexico's and the largest in Latin America (see Exhibit 7). Some firms did view Brazil as one of the most important emerging markets, along with China and India.

In 1990, U.S. president George Bush initiated negotiations on a Free Trade Area of the Americas (FTAA) that would eliminate tariffs on trade within North, Central, and South America. The FTAA would create the world's largest free trade area, with a combined gross domestic product of $13 trillion and 800 million consumers. In 1994 the presidents of 33 countries met with President Bush to negotiate details of the free trade agreement to go into effect by 2005. Many Brazilians opposed the FTAA because they feared Brazilian companies could not compete with more efficient U.S. firms. Brazil imposed high tariffs of 10–35% on a variety of goods imported from the United States such as automobiles, automobile parts, computers, computer parts, engines, and soybeans. Other Brazilian firms, however, stood to gain substantially. To protect U.S. producers from lower-cost Brazilian goods, the United States imposed tariffs of 10–35% on imported Brazilian sugar cane, tobacco, orange juice concentrate, soybean oil, and women's leather footwear. FTAA would eliminate these tariffs, giving U.S. consumers the opportunity to buy Brazilian products at significantly lower prices.

Brazil played a leading role in negotiating trade and investment arrangements with other countries in Latin America. In 1991, Brazil, Argentina, Uruguay, and Paraguay signed an agreement to form a common market (Mercosur) that eliminated internal tariffs on goods traded among member countries and established a common external tariff. By 1995, 90% of trade among member countries was free from trade restrictions. Member countries were allowed to impose tariffs on a limited number of products considered to be a threat to sensitive domestic industries. The hope was to expand Mercosur to include other countries in the region. Chile and Bolivia, for example, were offered associate memberships. Chile, however, later withdrew because it wanted to negotiate future membership in NAFTA. Like NAFTA, the signing of Mercosur had a dramatic effect on trade among its members. Argentina quickly became Brazil's second-largest trading partner after the United States, while Brazil became Argentina's largest trading partner. Brazilian officials made it clear that making Mercosur successful was their highest priority and that the FTAA might have to wait. Many believed Brazil was the major stumbling block to establishing FTAA by 2005.

Historically, the Brazilian government used a variety of tariffs and other restrictions on imports to encourage foreign investment in Brazil. The most highly visible example was automobiles taxed at rates up to 100% during the 1980s and 1990s. By 2003 almost all global automobile companies, including General Motors, Mercedes-Benz, Toyota, Volkswagen, Honda, Fiat, and Peugeot, were producing cars in Brazil for the Brazilian market. During the 1980s the Brazilian government attempted to stimulate domestic production in a number of technology industries like computers through an outright prohibition on imports. Texas Instruments (TI), a major computer manufacturer with semiconductor operations in São Paulo, was prohibited from using its own computers in its Brazilian

	U.S.A.	Canada	Mexico	Colombia	Venezuela	Peru	Brazil	Argentina
Population (Millions)	290.3	32.2	104.9	41.7	24.7	28.4	182.0	38.7
Growth Rate	0.9%	0.9%	1.4%	1.6%	1.5%	1.6%	1.5%	1.1%
Population Data: Origin								
European (non-French origin)	65.1%	43.0%	9.0%	20.0%	21.0%	15.0%	55.0%	97.0%
European (French origin)		23.0%						
African	12.9%			4.0%	10.0%		6.0%	
Mixed African & European				14.0%	37.0%		38.0%	
Latin American (Hispanic)	12.0%							
Asian	4.2%	6.0%						
Amerindian or Alaskan native	1.5%	2.0%	30.0%	1.0%	2.0%	45.0%		
Mixed Amerindian & Spanish		60.0%	58.0%	67.0%				
Mixed African & Amerindian				3.0%				
Other	4.3%	26.0%	1.0%			3.0%	1.0%	3.0%
Total	100.0%	100.0%	100.0%	100.0%	100.0%	100.0%	100.0%	100.0%
GDP ($ Billion)	$10,400	$923	$900	$268	$133	$132	$1,340	$391
Per Capital Income ($U.S.)	$37,600	$29,400	$9,000	$6,500	$5,500	$4,800	$7,600	$10,200
Real GDP Growth Rate	2.5%	3.4%	1.0%	2.0%	–8.9%	4.8%	1.0%	–14.7%
Inflation Rate	1.6%	2.2%	6.4%	6.2%	31.2%	0.2%	8.3%	41.0%
Unemployment Rate	5.8%	7.6%	3.0%	17.4%	17.0%	9.4%	6.4%	21.5%
Literacy Rate	97.0%	97.0%	92.2%	92.5%	93.4%	90.9%	86.4%	97.0%

Source: U.S. Central Intelligence Agency, The *World Factbook*. Demographic data is 2003 estimate; economic data as of year-end 2002.

Exhibit 7 Latin American—Selected Economic and Demographic Data

production facilities. Instead, it was forced to use slower, less efficient Brazilian computers. The Brazilian government later eliminated such restrictions after it became clear that Brazilian computer firms were unable to compete head-to-head with global computer firms. Strong government regulations and the tendency of the Brazilian government to change regulations from year to year eventually caused TI to withdraw from Brazil, even though its plant was profitable.

During the 1980s and early 1990s, Brazil battled sustained cycles of high inflation and currency instability. Between 1980 and 1993, inflation averaged more than 400% per year. Brazil's government attempted to reduce inflation through a variety of new currency programs, price and wage controls, and the policy of indexation, which adjusted wages and contracts based on the inflation rate. In 1994, President Cardoso introduced the Real Plan, which restructured Brazil's currency system. The cruzeiro was eliminated and replaced with a new currency called the real. The real was pegged to the U.S. dollar in an attempt to break the practice of indexation. By 1997 inflation had dropped to under 7%. Brazil's ability to peg the real against the dollar was made possible in large part by the large foreign investment flows into Brazil during this period. The inflow of dollars boosted Brazil's dollar reserves, which could be used to buy the real on currency markets, thereby stabilizing the value of the real against the dollar.

By 1998, however, investors began to pull investments out of Brazil. Many investors were increasingly concerned about Brazil's growing budget deficit and pension system crisis. Pension benefits represented almost 10% of Brazil's gross domestic product. Almost half of Brazil's retirement payments went to retired civil servants who made up only 5% of all retired Brazilians. The heavy demand on public funds for pension benefits diminished Brazil's ability to use fiscal and monetary policy to support economic development and promote stability. The Brazilian Central Bank attempted to reduce the outflow of investment capital by raising interest rates; however, dwindling dollar reserves finally reached a crisis in 1999, when Brazil abandoned its policy of pegging the real. The real was subsequently allowed to float against the dollar. The real depreciated by almost 50% against the dollar in 1999.

The fast-food industry in Brazil was less developed than in Mexico or the Caribbean. This was partly the result of the structure of the fast-food industry, which was dominated by U.S. restaurant chains. U.S. chains expanded farther from their home base as they gained experience operating in Latin America. As firms gained a foothold in Mexico and Central America, it was a natural progression to move into South America. McDonald's understood the importance of the Brazilian market and was early to expand there. By 2003 it was operating 584 restaurants. Many restaurant chains such as Burger King, Pizza Hut, and KFC built restaurants in Brazil in the early to mid-1990s but eventually closed them because of poor sales. In one example, Pizza Hut opened a restaurant in a popular restaurant section of Goiânia, a city of more than one million people about a two-hour drive from Brasìlia, Brazil's capital. When the restaurant opened, long lines of Brazilian customers wrapped around the block waiting to try Pizza Hut for the

first time. Within a few weeks, the lines were gone. Pizza Hut had opened a free-standing restaurant identical to those it operated in the United States. U.S. consumers were accustomed to waiting until a table was opened, sitting down and eating their meal, and leaving. Brazilian consumers did not mind waiting. However, they were accustomed to sitting outside with friends, socializing with a drink and hors d'oeuvres until a table was ready. Pizza Hut restaurants didn't accommodate this facet of Brazilian culture. Rather than change the structure of its operations, Pizza Hut sold the restaurant to Habib's, a popular Brazilian restaurant chain that sold Arab food.

Another problem was eating customs. Brazilians normally ate their big meal in the early afternoon. This could last two hours. It normally included salad, meat, rice and beans, dessert, fruit, and coffee. In the evening, it was customary to have a light meal such as a soup or small plate of pasta. Brazilians rarely ate food with their hands, preferring to eat with a knife and fork. This included food like pizza, which Americans typically ate with their hands. They also were not accustomed to eating sandwiches. If they did eat sandwiches, they wrapped the sandwich in a napkin. U.S. fast-food chains catered to a different kind of customer, one who wanted more than soup but less than a full sit-down meal. U.S. fast-food chains such as McDonald's were more popular in larger cities such as São Paulo and Rio de Janeiro, where businesspeople were in a hurry. In smaller cities, however, traditional customs of eating were still popular. Food courts were well developed in Brazil's shopping malls. They included a variety of sit-down restaurants, fast-food restaurants, and kiosks. In the United States, in contrast, food courts consisted primarily of fast-food restaurants. U.S. restaurant chains were therefore faced with a daunting task of changing Brazilians' eating habits—or convincing Brazilians of the attractiveness of fast-food, American style. The risk of not penetrating the Brazilian market, however, was significant given the size of Brazil's economy and McDonald's already significant presence.

RISKS AND OPPORTUNITIES FOR KFC

KFC faced difficult decisions surrounding the design and implementation of an effective Latin American strategy over the next twenty years. It wanted to sustain its leadership position in Mexico and the Caribbean but also looked to strengthen its position in other regions in South America, particularly in Brazil. Limited resources and cash flow prevented KFC from expanding aggressively in all countries simultaneously. KFC also faced the task of adapting its entry strategy to overcome barriers to entry in countries where it had little presence such as Argentina, Paraguay, Uruguay, and Venezuela. In Brazil, KFC hoped a joint venture partner would help overcome cultural barriers that forced it to withdraw in 2000.

How should KFC expand its restaurant base in Latin America given differences in consumer acceptance of the fast-food concept, intensity of competition, and culture? Should it open company-owned restaurants or rely on franchises to grow its restaurant base? In which markets should it approach joint venture partners as a means of more effectively developing the KFC concept? Should it approach markets like Brazil and Argentina cautiously in light of McDonald's and Wendy's aggressive first mover advantages in those countries, or should it proceed more aggressively? In which countries should it establish subsidiaries that actively managed multiple restaurants in order to exploit synergies in purchasing, operations, and advertising? A country subsidiary that was supported by resources from KFC headquarters in Louisville could only be justified if KFC had a large restaurant base in the targeted country. KFC's Latin American strategy required considerable analysis and thought about how to use its resources most efficiently. It also required an in-depth analysis of country risk and selection of the right country portfolio.

REFERENCES

General

Direction of Trade Statistics, International Monetary Fund, Washington, DC.

International Financial Statistics, International Monetary Fund, Washington, DC.

Miller, Kent D., ''A Framework for Integrated Risk Management in International Business,'' *Journal of International Business Studies* 23, no. 2 (1992): pp. 311–331.

Quickservice Restaurant Trends, National Restaurant Association, Washington, DC.

Standard & Poor's Industry Surveys, Standard & Poor's Corporation, New York, NY.

The World Factbook, U.S. Central Intelligence Agency, Washington, DC.

Periodicals

FIU Hospitality Review, FIU Hospitality Review, Inc., Miami, FL.

IFMA Word, International Foodservice Manufacturers Association, Chicago, IL.

Independent Restaurant, EIP, Madison, WI.

Journal of Nutrition in Recipe & Menu Development, Food Product Press, Binghamton, NY.

Nation's Restaurant News, Lebhar-Friedman, Inc., New York, NY (www.nrn.com).

Restaurant Business, Bill Communications, Inc., New York, NY (www.restaurant.biz.com).

Restaurants & Institutions, Cahners Publishing, New York, NY (www.restaurantsandinstitutions.com).

Restaurants USA, National Restaurant Association, Washington, DC. (www.restaurant.org).

Associations

International Franchise Association, 1350 New York Ave. NW, Suite 900, Washington, DC. 20005-4709, (202) 628-8000 (www.franchise.org).

National Restaurant Association, 1200 17th St. NW, Washington, DC 20036-3097, (202) 331-5900 (www.restaurant.org).

Books

Alfino, Mark, John S. Caputo, and Robin Wynyard, eds., *McDonaldization Revisited*, Greenwood Publishing Group, 1998.

Baldwin, Debra Lee, *Taco Titan: The Glen Bell Story*, Summit Publishing Group, 1999.

Cathy, S. Truett (founder of Chick-fil-A), *It's Easier to Succeed Than to Fail*, Oliver-Nelson Books, 1989.

Greising, David, *I'd Like the World to Buy a Coke: The Life and Leadership of Roberto Goizueta*, John Wiley & Sons, 1999.

Hogan, David Gerard, *Selling 'Em by the Sack: White Castle and the Creation of American Food*, New York University Press, 1999.

Kentucky Fried Chicken Japan Ltd.: International Competitive Benchmarks and Financial Gap Analysis, Icon Group Ltd., 2000.

Kentucky Fried Chicken Japan Ltd.: Labor Productivity Benchmarks and International Gap Analysis, Icon Group Ltd., 2000.

Kroc, Ray (founder of McDonald's) and Robert Anderson, *Grinding It Out: The Making of McDonald's*, St. Martins, 1990.

Lechner, Frank, and John Boli, eds., *The Globalization Reader*, Blackwell Publishing, 2000.

Love, John, F., *McDonald's behind the Arches*, Bantam Books, 1986, 1995, 1999.

Ritzer, George, *The McDonald's Thesis: Explorations and Extensions*, Sage Publications, 1998.

Ritzer, George, *The McDonaldization of Society: An Investigation into the Changing Character of Contemporary Social Life*, Pine Forge Press, 1995.

Thomas, R. David (founder of Wendy's), *Dave's Way: A New Approach to Old-Fashioned Success*, Berkley Publishing Group, 1992.

Watson, James L., ed., *Golden Arches East: McDonald's in East Asia*, Stanford University Press, 1998.

Web Pages

Boston Market Corporation: www.bostonmarket.com

Bojangles': www.bojangles.com

Burger King Corporation: www.burgerking.com

Chick-fil-A: www.chickfila.com

Churchs Chicken: www.churchs.com

McDonald's Corporation: www.mcdonalds.com

Popeye's Chicken & Biscuits: www.popeyes.com

Wendy's International Incorporated: www.wendys.com

Yum! Brands, Inc.: www.yum.com

Nestlé (Ghana) Ltd.

I t was January 1995 and Pierre Charles had just taken up his new position of marketing director of Nestlé's subsidiary in Ghana in West Africa. A native of Switzerland, he had never been to Africa. In fact, apart from reports that periodically crossed his desk at headquarters in Vevey, Switzerland, he was not very familiar with developing country environments. His education and work experience had all been in Switzerland. Prior to taking up the appointment, Pierre took the opportunity to review conditions in Ghana and Nestlé's operations in that country. It was important that he do well in the new job since that would enhance his career prospects in the international division.

As he reviewed the available information, he was struck by how different the Ghanaian environment was from what he was used to. Economic and political conditions were like nothing he had experienced. The infrastructure for marketing was totally different. For example, it was impossible to get reliable information on such crucial factors as market shares, market segments, distributor volumes, and other market data. Conducting market research was also a major task primarily because of deficiencies in postal and telephone systems. Yet marketing managers were expected to design effective strategies and maintain profitable positions. It appeared to him that he had to adjust quickly to this environment to maximize his effectiveness. Fortunately he spoke English, the official language of Ghana, so language problems would be minimized. In particular, he had to assess the situation and make decisions about expanding operations, maintaining a competitive position, and above all, maintaining profit margins. He did not have a whole lot of time because competitive pressures were mounting, and the economic and political situation was changing rapidly. Underlying all of this was a need to prioritize possible courses of action.

NESTLÉ (GHANA) OPERATIONS

Nestlé (Ghana) was a joint venture between Nestlé A.S. (a Swiss multinational corporation) and the state-owned National Investment Bank (NIB). The joint venture was established in 1971 with Nestlé S.A. owning 51%. In the mid-1970s, the then ruling military government of Ghana, the National Redemption Council (NRC), pursuing an indigenization strategy, acquired 55% of the shares.

The government of current President Rawlings reverted to a 49% share in 1993, held by the NIB. These changes in ownership structure reflected the country's shift from a nationalistic

This case was prepared by Franklyn A. Manu and Ven Sriram, Morgan State University. It is printed here with permission from the *Case Research Journal* and the authors. Copyright by the North American Case Research Association.

philosophy involving state participation in leading enterprises to a reluctant push towards privatization. Nestlé was very interested in acquiring the shares held by NIB.

The company had stated capital of 1 billion cedis (about US$1.05 million) and 600 employees, 350 more than normal Nestlé standards in its other subsidiaries for that level of capitalization. Annual sales were currently about 25 billion cedis (about US$26.3 million). The company had four main product lines: canned and powered milk, powdered cocoa drinks, coffee, and Maggi spice cubes. It had one factory in the industrial port city of Tema, some 20 miles from the capital Accra, and this was Nestle's only milk-processing plant in West Africa. The subsidiary had been set a growth target of 5% in Swiss francs but had actually averaged a rate of 12% in recent years, compared to 5% for Nestlé worldwide. Exhibit 1 provides performance data for Nestlé (Ghana).

Nestlé (Ghana) was headed by a managing director who oversaw a three-division structure—marketing, production, and finance and administration. The managing director and the plant engineer were typically appointed by Nestlé S.A., which had a management contract to run Nestlé (Ghana). These appointees had usually been white expatriates. As of January 1995, the managing director, director of marketing, sales manager, and plant engineer positions were filled by white expatriates. The remaining positions were mostly filled by Ghanaians. The company had a six-member board of directors, four appointed by Nestlé's S.A. and two appointed by the NIB.

THE REPUBLIC OF GHANA

Political History

The Republic of Ghana is on the western coast of Africa. It has an area of 92,000 square miles and had an estimated population of 15.5 million in 1991. The country had experienced a checkered political history since gaining independence from the British in 1957. Military regimes had run the country for 21 of the years since independence. The current civilian government of President Rawlings, which won the latest elections in 1992, was an offshoot of a military regime, the Provisional National Defence Council (PNDC), which overthrew the previous civilian democratic government of the People's National Party in 1981. The rule of then Flight-Lieutenant Rawlings' PNDC was characterized by suppression of human rights, including imprisonment and execution of alleged opponents. The period was also marked by many attempts to overthrow the PNDC regime. Political and ethnic tensions increased and continue currently, even though Rawlings won the 1992 presidential election with 58% of the vote, a result certified

	1993	1992
Sales	19.3	14.7
Operating profit	2.7	1.9
Net profit	2.5	1.8
Fixed costs	4.9	3.4
Variable costs	11.6	8.4
Total assets	11.8	9.9
Total equity	5.7	4.2
Liabilities (short term)	4.0	2.2
Liabilities (medium term)	1.8	1.7
Dividends	1.7	1.5

1993: US$1 = 699.30 cedis
1992: US$1 = 437.09 cedis

Source: Nestlé 1993 Annual Report.

Exhibit 1 Nestlé Operating Results (Billions of Cedis)

by international observers despite incidents of irregularities. Other political parties refused to accept the results and boycotted the parliamentary elections. This resulted in a situation in which Rawlings and his allies won 199 out of 200 seats in the parliament, with the remaining seat going to a political independent. Independent media consistently attacked government policies and personalities while the state-owned media consistently supported them. Allegations of corruption and ethnic bias had been leveled against the government. Of particular concern were the upcoming 1996 presidential and parliamentary elections. The government and opposition parties had serious disagreements over revision of the voters' register and issuance of identity cards, with the opposition parties threatening violence if the elections were not fair.

Economy

Economically, Ghana was in the lower tier of developing countries and classified as a least developed country (LDC) by international development agencies because its per capita annual income was US$400. Quite prosperous at independence, the country had declined precipitously as a result of economic mismanagement, political instability, brain drain, and corruption. The World Bank and other external donors were currently funding an economic recovery program that appeared to be pulling the economy out of the doldrums. Gross national product was about $7 billion, or $400 per capita, and growing at around 1.2% per annum in real terms. Gross domestic product was growing at about 3.2% in real terms. Consumer prices increased by an average of 10% in 1992 and 16% in 1993. Inflation had averaged 40% per annum since 1985. Exhibit 2 provides selected statistics and information on Ghana.

Agriculture contributed about 49% of GDP and was growing at an annual average of 1.2%. Forty-nine percent of the labor force was employed in this sector. Industry (including mining, manufacturing, construction and power) contributed 17% of GDP and employed 13% of the labor force. Industrial GDP had been

growing at an annual average of 3.7% in recent times. While mining had shown the greatest growth (17.7%) in the industrial sector, manufacturing remained the largest component of the sector. It contributed 10% of national GDP, growing at a rate of 4.1% per annum, and employed 11% of the labor force.

Ghana had merchandise trade and balance-of-payments deficits in the five years prior to 1995. Principal exports were cocoa, gold, and timber, growing at 5% per annum. Major imports were machinery, transport equipment, basic manufactures, and petroleum. External debt was about $4.3 billion, and debt service was equal to 30% of exports of goods and services.

Discussions with other Nestlé managers familiar with Ghana brought out the following additional information:

- Inflation was higher than official estimates.
- Foreign exchange availability was low.
- Cedi would continue to depreciate.
- There was a high level of currency instability.
- Nestlé had very little commitment to exports.
- No price controls existed.
- Interest rates were currently high (around 30%) but were expected to come down to 25%.
- Government regulations were not very burdensome. Sales taxes, for example, had declined from 35% to 15%. Potential problems were expected, though, from current government attempts to implement a value-added tax.
- Money supply was expected to rise dramatically as the government launched its campaign for the 1996 election.
- Nestlé had few labor problems even though there might be general labor unrest.

THE COCOA BEVERAGE MARKET

The size of Ghana's cocoa beverage market was estimated at 4,500 tons and growing slowly. It was forecast to grow at approximately 5% per annum through 1997. Cocoa beverages were primarily a breakfast drink. Information on market segments relating to beverage consumption was unavailable. However, most marketers in Ghana used a classification scheme based on socioeconomic status to segment markets. The scheme and underlying methodology are shown in Exhibit 3. It was not exactly clear how these socioeconomic segments impacted on product consumption or purchase. Other types of segmentation data were nonexistent or were highly proprietary.

The market could, however, be divided into three categories based on the product.

Premium Segment: Brands in this category included malt in addition to the basic cocoa powder, sugar, and milk. Leading brands were Milo, Bournvita, and Ovaltine.

Mass Market: Brands in this category did not contain malt, thus reducing their costs considerably. Leading brands were Chocolim, Drinking Chocolate, Richoco, and Golden Tree.

Institutional Market: Products aimed at this segment contained basic unsweetened cocoa powder supplied to school, hospitals, the armed forces, and so on.

1. Average Exchange Rate (Cedis per US$)

1990	326.33
1991	367.83
1992	437.09
1993	699.30
1994	950.00

2. Money Supply (Billion Cedis at 31 December)

1990	271.64
1991	345.49
1992	525.93
1993	664.67

Average annual growth, 1 980–91: 43%

Sources: International Monetary Fund's International Financial Statistics and World Bank Tables, 1995.

3. Cost of Living (Consumer Price Index. Base: 1980 = 100)

	1990	**1991**	**1992**
Food	2,711	2,955	3,261
Clothing and Footwear	4,371	5,052	5,488
Rent, Fuel, and Light	5,802	8,373	10,097
All Items (incl. others)	3,575	4,219	4,644

Source: United Nations Economic Commission for Africa (UNECA)—*African Statistical Yearbook.*

4. Communications Media

	1989	**1990**	**1,991**
Radios (thousands)	Na	4,000	4,150
TVs (thousands)	211	225	235
Telephones (thousands)	83	84	85

Newspapers	**Circulation**
Daily:	
Daily Graphic	100,000
Ghanaian Times	40,000
Pioneer	100,000
Other Major:	
Chronicle	60,000
Mirror	90,000
Spectator	165,000
Standard	50,000

5. Income Distribution (% Share of Income)

Lowest 20%	2nd Quintile	3rd Quintile	4th Quintile	Highest 20%
7.0	11.3	15.8	21.8	44.1

Highest 10%	
29.0	

6. Education

	Primary	Secondary	Higher Education
1. Population	1.95m	805,000	16,350

2. Government Expenditure: 65 billion cedis (1990), i.e., 26% of total spending.

Sources: (4, 5, and 6): United Nations Economic and Social Council (UNESCO), *Statistical Yearbook,* and UNECA, *African Statistical Yearbook.*

7. Population

	1970–75	**1980–85**	**1990–94**
Urban % of Population	30.1	32.3	35.8
Urban Pop. Growth Rate	2.9	4.3	4.0

Access to Safe Water (% of population)

Total	35	49.2	55.7
Urban	86	72	93
Rural	14	39	39

Source: World Bank—Social Indicators of Development, 1995.

Age Profile of Population:

0–14	=	45%
15–29	=	26.4%
30–44	=	14.6%
45–59	=	8.1%
60–74	=	4.1%
75 plus	=	1.8%

Annual growth rate of population estimated at 3.1% for 1990–95 and 3.04% for 1995–2000.

Source: Encyclopedia of the Third World, 4th ed, Volume 1 (1992). George Thomas Kurian (ed).

Exhibit 2 Selected Information on Ghana

NESTLÉ'S (GHANA) PRODUCTS

Nestlé's powdered cocoa drinks were Milo and Chocolim. Milo came in a 450-gram tin size with 24 tins to a carton. Tin for making the containers was supplied by headquarters and was rapidly becoming a major cost component in the production process. Consideration was being given to the introduction of a 200-gram soft plastic pack. Chocolim was sold in a 500-gram soft plastic pack with 40 packs to a carton. The two products were quite similar, with a cocoa base, added milk, and presweetened. Chocolim did not contain malt and this made it cheaper. Sixty percent of the company's powdered beverage sales came from Milo and 40% from Chocolim. Milo was introduced into Ghana from another Nestlé subsidiary. It was formulated by an Australian, Thomas Maynee, about 60 years earlier and was extremely popular in Africa and Southeast Asia. Annual worldwide sales in 1995 were

The following process was used to determine the socioeconomic status (SES) of respondents

Step 1: Scoring of Variables*

1. Highest Education in Household	Score
None	4
Primary	3
Secondary	2
Post-secondary/University/Higher	1
2. Occupation of Chief Wage Earner	
Professional/Managerial/Large-Scale Entrepreneur	1
Artisan/Skilled/Technician/Civil Servant/Teacher	2
Semi-Skilled/Small Trader/Clerical	2
Manual Labour	3
Agricultural Worker/Farmer/Hunter	3
Not Working/Student/Housewife	4
3. Consumer Durable Ownership	
Telephone	2
Bicycle	1
Television (if any)	2
Video Recorder	2
Refrigerator	2
Car/Truck	2
Kerosene Stove	1
Gas/Electric Stove (Cooker)	2
House	2
Radio	1

Durables Score Range	Recorded Score
0–5	3
6–11	2
12–17	1

Step 2: Importance Weighting of Variable Categories

	Weighting
Education	3
Occupation	2
Consumer Durables	1

Step 3: Application of Formula to Each Respondent Individually

Formula: (Weight ¥ scores)
Total SES score for each respondent = (3 ¥ education score) + (2 ¥ occupation score) + (1 ¥ consumer durables score)

Determination of SES Group	Score Range
Class A/B	6–10
Class C	11–14
Class D	15–20
Class E	21–24
Possible scoring range = 6–24	

* Maximum durables score possible = 17
Source: Market Research International (Ghana)—private communication.

Exhibit 3 An Approach to Market Segmentation: Determining the Socioeconomic Status (SES) of Respondents

90,000 tons, worth about $430 million from the 30 countries where it was marketed. Chocolim was locally developed in 1981–82.

Milo was the premier brand and was targeted to the high end of the market; Chocolim was aimed at rural areas and low-end urban segments. Milo was targeted toward 10- to 18-year-olds but with a focus on mothers as decision makers. The thrust in Nestlé's strategy was to ensure high awareness of its brands and widespread distribution.

COMPETITION

Finding information on competitors' activities was one of the most difficult aspects of designing marketing strategy in Ghana. Industry and brand level data were hard to come by. Nestlé managers estimated their share of the cocoa beverage market at 80% based on research by a firm that tracked sales in a sample of retailers in addition to tracking consumption. Other observers, however, believed Nestlé's share was closer to 55%. Major competitors for Nestlé were Bournvita and Richoco, manufactured by Cadbury (Ghana), with an estimated 20–40% market share, and imported Ovaltine.

Originally known as Cadbury and Fry (England), Cadbury entered Ghana in 1910 to source cocoa beans for its own chocolate-making plants in England. Processing of cocoa beans started in 1963, with a cocoa-based drink introduced soon after. Cadbury (Ghana) was 100% owned by Cadbury Schweppes (U.K.) and had 120 employees. Of estimated 1994 sales of 4 billion cedis, 70% was derived from cocoa beverages and the remainder from sugar confectioneries (e.g., Hacks and Trebor) and Kwench, a fruit-flavored noncarbonated drink. Cocoa beverage capacity of Cadbury averaged 2,000 tons per annum with profit margins of about 35%. In 1990 Cadbury started a major diversification away from cocoa beverages and into sugar confectioneries. The company hoped to have the latter contributing 51% of sales by 1997. Introduction of Richoco in 1990 to exploit a gap in the lower end of the market and good relations with distributors reflected Cadbury's strong marketing skills. For example, Cadbury went to a 1kg package for Richoco, which enabled retailers to repackage, thus increasing the latter's margins by 40%.

Another competitor, though on a much smaller scale, was the state-owned Cocoa Processing Company (CPC), which made Golden Tree Vitaco Instant Drinking Chocolate. CPC was strongest in the institutional market, where it had a cost advantage (estimated 23% lower) because it supplied the basic cocoa powder to other firms. The company also made Golden Tree Chocolates, which had won many awards in European and Japanese competitions.

An additional category of competition came from imports, the most prominent of which was Ovaltine, marketed by NABB Brothers, a leading distributor of supermarket products. Volume of imports was low, about 2% of the market, and there were no statistics on brand volumes. It was believed that these imports were either smuggled or evaded taxes and could therefore be sold at lower prices than domestically produced brands.

The major brands, their composition, packaging, and prices are shown in Exhibit 4. Milo was the leader in the premium category, while Golden Tree was strongest in the institutional market. Richoco was believed to lead Chocolim by about 5–10% market

Company	Brand	Composition	Pack Size	Price (Cedis)
Nestlé	Milo	Malt extract, milk, sugar, cocoa powder, ethyl vanillin	200g soft pack	850
Nestlé	Milo	Malt extract, milk, sugar, cocoa powder, ethyl vanillin	450g can	2,400
Nestlé	Chocolim	Cocoa powder, milk, sugar, vegetable fat, mineral salts, vitamins	500g soft pack	1,300
Cadbury	Bournvita	Malt extract, sugar, glucose syrup, fat reduced cocoa, dried skimmed milk, dried egg	450 plastic jar	2,200
Cadbury	Drinking Chocolate	Sugar, skimmed milk powder, cocoa, flavorings	500g soft pack	1,050
Cadbury	Richoco	Cocoa, sugar, milk, mineral salts	1kg soft pack	2,800
Cocoa Processing Company (CPC)	Golden Tree Vitaco Instant Drinking Chocolate	Cocoa powder, sugar, skimmed milk powder, lecithin, vanillin	350g soft pack	980
NABB Brothers	Ovaltine (Imported)	Barley and malt extract, cocoa skimmed milk powder, whey powder, vegetable fat, sugar, sodium bicarbonate, potassium bicarbonate	200g can	2,700
NABB Brothers	Ovaltine (Imported)	Barley and malt extract, cocoaskimmed milk powder, whey powder, vegetable fat, sugar, sodium bicarbonate, potassium bicarbonate	400g can	4,250
NABB Brothers	Ovaltine (Imported)	Barley and malt extract, cocoa skimmed milk powder, whey powder, vegetable fat, sugar, sodium bicarbonate, potassium bicarbonate	1,200g can	11,500
Unknown (Imported from France)	Petit de Jeuner		400g box	2,800
Unknown (Imported from France)	Instantane		400g plastic jar	2,800

Exhibit 4 Leading Brands and Prices of Selected Powdered Cocoa Beverages at a Leading Supermarket in Accra (January 9, 1995)

share in the mass market. Exhibit 5 indicates available government statistics on imports. Exhibit 6 shows domestic production of cocoa powder.

DISTRIBUTION STRUCTURE

''Ghana is fast becoming a nation of shopkeepers'' was a popular joke in the country as economic liberalization gave the retail industry a very strong boost in urban areas. Most of the retail outlets were small and specialized in merchandise lines such as appliances, food and beverages, and clothing. Competition was intense; however, this had not shown up in price wars at the general retail level. Most outlets were stand-alone, and there were very few retail chains. Stores were usually of the ''mom and pop'' variety found in the Western world. Additional retailing institutions included itinerant street hawkers, wooden kiosks, and ''container'' stores made from metal shipping containers. With no zoning laws,

all the retailing forms were found in business districts as well as residential neighborhoods, making location extremely important. Nestlé had 100 regular distributors nationwide and a few other irregulars. Warehouses in Accra (the capital) and Tamale (in the northern part of the country) supplied these distributors. Some of the large distributors such as supermarkets and department stores were supplied directly from the plant at Tema. The biggest distributor was Unilever's G. B. Ollivant subsidiary. Nestlé also operated its own sales outlets in three of the biggest cities (Kumasi, Takoradi, and Tamale) outside Accra. Margins to distributors were nominally 7.5%, but in reality they made only 2–3% because of serious price undercutting among them to gain sales. Some distributors were also granted a 21-day interest-free credit on supplied goods. The large distributors typically ordered in quantities of 15–20 million cedis (about US$16,000–21,000), while the smaller ones ordered around 5 million cedis (about US$5,500). While officially Nestlé did not place any restriction on its distributors carrying competing lines, unofficially it frowned on the practice.

	Imports (CIF value in cedis)	Cedi/kg
January–May 1991	27,971,505	837.75
January–December 1992	66,379,420	1159.24
January–September 1993	15,559,184	1098.73
January–May 1994	28,920,619	3748.62

*Cocoa powder, containing added sugar or other sweetening matter.
Source: Government of Ghana Central Bureau of Statistics.

Exhibit 5 Imports of Cocoa Powder*

	Production
1986	578,000
1987	665,000
1988	618,000
1989	557,000
1990	830,000
1991	1,078,000
1992	462,000
1993*	467,500

*Provisional.
Source: Government of Ghana Central Bureau of Statistics.

Exhibit 6 Local Production of Cocoa Powder (kg)

PROMOTION

Promotion in Ghanaian industries had become quite intense as the economy was liberalized and consumer goods flooded the market. Most of the promotional wars took the form of contests and advertising in all its forms. What was not so clear were the effects of such promotions. Some argued that different companies' promotions canceled each other out and consumers often postponed their purchases until there was a sales promotion in effect. Others argued that if a company's promotion was unique it would gain an edge. The problem with the latter view was that many of these promotions were easily imitated.

Nestlé used a combination of media advertising and sales promotions targeted at the youth for Milo. In particular, sports-based promotion was emphasized. The company sponsored highly popular youth soccer leagues for ages 10–18 years and for schools and colleges. It also sponsored tennis tournaments and a marathon race for all age groups. Another widely used sales promotion technique was wet sampling (i.e., free drinks) at the Ministry of Education Sports Department's events for school children. Total expenditure for promotion was about 150 million cedis (about US$150,800) and was estimated to grow by 10–15% per annum. Sixty percent of the budget went for nonmedia promotion while 40% covered media expenditures. This was the reverse of other Nestlé products.

Media advertising promoted the themes of good health, growing up, and success as closely related and linked to drinking Milo. Another theme was that Milo contributed to success in sports, and success in sports contributed to success in life. As a policy, Nestlé did not use sports personalities because they switched product endorsements frequently and often had short popularity spans. Rather, Nestlé emphasized the use of ordinary people in its advertisements. This was despite the national and international popularity of Ghanaian stars like Azumah Nelson (world featherweight boxing champion), Abedi Pele (star midfielder in the French soccer league), and Tony Yeboah (star striker in the English soccer league). Advertising development was performed by Media Magique and Market Research Systems (MMRS) and the Advertising Design Agency (ADA), which focused on Milo.

Mass promotion in Ghana was particularly difficult given low levels of television and radio ownership as well as low circulation of print media. This meant that mass promotion was viable primarily in the urban areas, but the majority of people lived in rural areas. Companies had to use the more expensive sponsorship approach in the latter areas. The rural areas were also places where ethnic differences, particularly language, were most pronounced. This required the use of many languages and dialects in local sponsorship programs and activities.

PRICING

Nestlé's brands were sold at premiums of 5–10% over competitors' because of their perceived better quality. With declining real incomes, products were becoming less affordable. There was also increasing price pressure from imports that were flooding the market as a result of import liberalization (see Exhibit 4.) Ghana had a long history of government-controlled prices for consumer goods, and it was only since the late 1980s that companies had been really free to set their own prices. As a result, people were quite sensitive to price changes and were said to have long-term negative perceptions of companies that were perceived to engage in price gouging. Such incidents also attracted negative press coverage. On the other hand, though, rapid increases in inflation and the fast-falling cedi were exerting upward pressure on costs of production and reducing profit margins. Distributors therefore raised their prices frequently in an attempt to keep up with inflation. This often had unintended consequences on the pricing strategy of manufacturers, who often had to reduce their margins to keep their products affordable.

CONCLUSION

As Pierre pondered all this information, he realized the complexity of the task ahead of him and wondered what his focus should be. There was increasing competition in the market, the external economic and political environment was increasingly hostile and risky, and yet there was clearly insufficient information to make decisions in the manner to which he was accustomed. While he could argue that nothing should be done until a marketing information system was put in place, reality indicated that some responses had to be made soon in order to compete effectively and maintain profitability. In the long term, issues relating to new product introductions, further market penetration, market data, diversification, and contingency planning would have to be addressed. Foremost in his mind was the sequence of actions to pursue. Could he put everything on hold while he launched a comprehensive marketing research effort to provide appropriate information? What if, in the meantime, Nestlé's strong position was adversely affected by competition and the political/economic environment?

CASE 27
Planet Starbucks

I n fall 2005, the CEO of Starbucks, Howard Schultz, was concerned about the future growth of his company. The story of how Schultz and his associates transformed a pedestrian commodity into an upscale consumer accessory has a fairytale quality. Starbucks had grown from 17 coffee shops in Seattle 15 years earlier to 5,689 outlets in 28 countries. Sales climbed an average of 29% annually since the company went public in 1995 to 3.1 billion in 2004, while profits bounded ahead an average of 30% per year, hitting $221.5 million in 2004. And the momentum continued.

But how long could that run last? Already, Schultz's team was hard-pressed to grind out new profits in the home market that was quickly becoming saturated. Amazingly, with 4,247 stores scattered across the United States and Canada, there were still eight states in the United States with no Starbucks stores. Frappuccino-free cities included Butte, Montana, and Fargo, North Dakota. But big cities, affluent suburbs, and shopping malls were full to the brim. In coffee-crazed Seattle there was a Starbucks outlet for every 9,400 people, and the company considered that the upper limit of coffee-shop saturation. In Manhattan's 24 square miles, Starbucks had 123 cafes. That was one for every 12,000 people—meaning that there could be more room for even more stores. Given such a concentration, it was likely to take an annual same-store sales increase of 10% or more if the company was going to match its historic overall sales growth. That was a tall order to fill.

STARBUCK'S SUCCESS STORY

The Starbuck's name and image connected with millions of consumers around the globe. It was one of the fastest-growing brands in a *BusinessWeek* survey of the top 100 global brands published in August 2005. At a time when one corporate star after another crashed to earth, brought down by revelations of earnings misstatements, executive greed, or worse, Starbucks did not falter. The company confidently predicted up to 25% annual sales and earnings growth in 2005. On Wall Street, Starbucks was the last great growth story. Its stock, including four splits, had soared more that 2,200% over the previous decade, surpassing Wal-Mart, General Electric, PepsiCo, Coca-Cola, Microsoft, and IBM in total return. Now at $21, it was hovering near its all-time high of $23 in July, before the overall market drop.

And after a slowdown in 2004, Starbucks was rocketing ahead once again. Sales in stores opened at least 13 months grew by 6% in the 43 weeks through July 28, 2005, and the company predicted monthly same-store sales gains as high as 7% through the end of the 2005 fiscal year. That was below the 9% growth rate in 2000, but investors seemed encouraged.

PROMISE OF GLOBAL BUSINESS

To duplicate the staggering returns of its first decade, Starbucks had no choice but to export its concept aggressively. Indeed, some analysts gave Starbucks only two years at most before it saturated the U.S. market. In 2005, the chain operated 1,200 international outlets, from Beijing to Bristol. That left plenty of room to grow. Indeed, about 400 of its planned 1,200 new stores in 2005 would be built overseas, representing a 35% increase in its foreign base. Starbucks expected to double the number of stores worldwide, to 10,000 in three years. During the previous 12 months, the chain had opened stores in Vienna, Zurich, Madrid, Berlin, and even far off Jakarta. Athens would come next. And in 2006, Starbucks planned to move into Mexico and Puerto Rico. But global expansion posed huge risks for Starbucks. For one thing, it made less money on each overseas store because most of them were operated with local partners. While that made it easier to start up on foreign turf, it reduced the company's share of the profits to only 20–50%.

Moreover, Starbucks had to cope with some predictable challenges of becoming a mature company in the United States. After riding the wave of successful baby boomers through the 1990s, the company faced an ominously hostile reception from its future consumers, the 20- or 30-somethings of Generation X. Not only were the activists among them turned off by the power and image of the well-known brand, but many others said that Starbucks' latte-sipping sophisticates felt wanted in a place that sold designer coffee at $3 a cup.

Even the thirst of loyalists for high-price coffee could not be taken for granted. Starbucks' growth over the previous decade coincided with a remarkable surge in the economy. Consumer spending had continued strong in the downturn, but if that changed, those $3 lattes might be an easy place for people on a budget to cut back. Starbucks executives insisted that this would not happen, pointing out that even in the weeks following the terrorist attacks same-store comparisons stayed positive while those of other retailers skidded.

Starbucks also faced slumping morale and employee burnout among its store managers and its once-cheery army of baristas. Stock options for part-timers in the restaurant business were a Starbucks innovation that once commanded awe and respect from its employees. But now, though employees were still paid better than comparable workers elsewhere—about $7 per hour—many regarded the job as just another fast-food gig. Dissatisfaction over odd hours and low pay was affecting the quality of the normally sterling service and even the coffee itself, said some customers and employees. Frustrated store managers among the company's roughly 470 California stores sued Starbucks in 2001 for allegedly refusing to pay legally mandated overtime. Starbucks settled the suit for $18 million in April 2005, shaving $0.03 per share off an otherwise strong second quarter.

However, the heart of the complaint—feeling overworked and under appreciated—did not seem to be going away. To be sure, Starbucks had a lot going for it as it confronted the challenge of maintaining its growth. Nearly free of debt, it fueled expansion with internal cash flow. And Starbucks could maintain a tight grip on its image because stores are company-owned; there were no franchisees to get sloppy about running things. By relying on mystique and word-of-mouth, whether here or overseas, the company saves a bundle on marketing costs. Starbucks spent just $30 million annually on advertising, or roughly 1% of revenues, usually just for new flavors of coffee drinks in the summer and product launches such as its new in-store Web service. Most consumer companies its size shell out upwards of $300 million per year. Moreover, unlike a McDonald's or a Gap Inc., two other retailers that rapidly grew in the United States, Starbucks had no nationwide competitor. Starbucks also had a well-seasoned management team. Schultz, 49, stepped down as chief executive in 2000 to become chairman and chief global strategist. Orin Smith, 60, the company's numbers cruncher, was CEO and in charge of day-to-day operations. The head of North American operations is Howard Behar, 57, a retailing expert who returned two years after retiring. The management trio was known as H2O, for Howard, Howard, and Orin.

Schultz remained the heart and soul of the operation. Raised in a Brooklyn public housing project, he found his way to Starbucks, a tiny chain of Seattle coffee shops, as a marketing executive in the early 1980s. The name came about when the original owners looked to Seattle history for inspiration and chose the moniker of an old mining camp: Starbo. Further refinement led to Starbucks, after the first mate in Moby Dick, which they felt evoked the seafaring romance of the early coffee traders (hence the mermaid logo). Schultz got the idea for the modern Starbucks format while visiting a Milan coffee bar. He bought out his bosses in 1987 and began expanding. In 2005, Schultz had a net worth of about $700 million, including $400 million of company stock.

Starbucks had come light years from those humble beginnings, but Schultz and his team still thought there was room to grow in the United States, even in communities where the chain already had dozens of stores. Clustering stores increased total revenue and market share, Smith argued, even when individual stores poached on each other's sales. The strategy worked, he said, because of Starbucks' size. It was large enough to absorb losses at existing stores as new ones opened up, and soon overall sales grew beyond what they would have with just one store. Meanwhile, it was cheaper to deliver to and manage stores located close together. And by clustering, Starbucks could quickly dominate a local market.

The company could still be capable of designing and opening a store in 16 weeks or less and recouping the initial investment in three years. The stores may be oases of tranquility, but management's expansion tactics were something else. Take what critics called its ''predatory real estate'' strategy—paying more than market-rate rents to keep competitors out of a location. David C. Schomer, owner of Espresso Vivace in Seattle's hip Capitol Hill neighborhood, said Starbucks approached his landlord and offered to pay nearly double the rate to put a coffee shop in the same building. The landlord stuck with Schomer, who said: ''It's a little disconcerting to know that someone is willing to pay twice the going rate.'' Another time, Starbucks and Tully's Coffee, a Seattle-based coffee chain, were competing for a space in the city. Starbucks got the lease but vacated the premises before the term was up. Still, rather than let Tully's get the space, Starbucks decided to pay the rent on the empty store so its competitor could not move in. Schultz made no apologies for the hardball tactics. ''The real estate business in America is a very, very tough game,'' he said. ''It's not for the faint of heart.'' Still, the company's strategy could backfire. Not only will neighborhood activists and local businesses increasingly resent the tactics, but customers could also grow annoyed over having fewer choices. Moreover, analysts contended that Starbucks could maintain about 15% square-footage growth in the United States—equivalent to 550 new stores—for only about two more years. After that, it would have to depend on overseas growth to maintain annual 20% revenue growth.

Starbucks was hoping to make up much of that growth with more sales of food and other non-coffee items, but it stumbled somewhat. In the late 1990s, Schultz thought that offering $8 sandwiches, desserts, and CDs in his stores and selling packaged coffee in supermarkets would significantly boost sales, but growth had been less than expected. A healthy 19% in 2004, it was still far below the 38% growth rate of fiscal 2000. That suggested that, while coffee could command high prices in a slump, food—at least at Starbucks—could not. One of Behar's most important goals was to improve that record. For instance, the company had a test program of serving hot breakfasts in 20 Seattle stores and might move to expand supermarket sales of whole beans. What was more important for the bottom line, though, was that Starbucks had proven to be highly innovative in the way it sold its main course, coffee. In 800 locations it installed automatic espresso machines to speed up service. And in November it began offering prepaid Starbucks cards, priced from $5 to $500, which clerks swipe through a reader to deduct a sale. That, said the company, cuts transaction times in half. Starbucks had sold $70 million of the cards. In early August, Starbucks launched Starbucks Express, its boldest experiment yet, which blended java, Web technology, and faster service. At about 60 stores in the Denver area, customers could preorder and prepay for beverages and pastries via phone or on the Starbucks Express Web site. They just made the call or clicked the mouse before arriving at the store, and their beverage would be waiting, with their name printed on the cup. The company decided on a national launch in January 2006. And Starbucks was bent on even more fundamental store changes. In August it announced expansion of a high-speed wireless Internet service to about 1,200 Starbucks locations in North America and Europe. Partners in the project—which Starbucks called the world's largest Wi-Fi network—include Mobile International, a wireless subsidiary of Deutsche Telekom, and Hewlett-Packard. Customers sit in a store and check e-mail, surf the Web, or download multimedia presentations without looking for connections or tripping over cords. They started with 24 hours of free wireless broadband before choosing from a variety of monthly subscription plans.

Starbucks executives hoped such innovations would help surmount their toughest challenge in the home market: attracting the next generation of customers. Younger coffee drinkers already feel uncomfortable in the stores. The company knows that because it once had a group of 20-somethings hypnotized for a market study. When their defenses were down, out came the bad news. "They either can't afford to buy coffee at Starbucks, or the only peers they see are those working behind the counter," said Mark Barden, who conducted the research for the Hal Riney & Partners ad agency (now part of Publicis Worldwide) in San Francisco. One of the recurring themes the hypnosis brought out was a sense that "people like me aren't welcome here except to serve the yuppies." Then there are those who just find the whole Starbucks scene a bit pretentious. Katie Kelleher, 22, a Chicago paralegal, is put off by Starbucks' Italian terminology of *grande* and *venti* for coffee sizes. She goes to Dunkin' Donuts, saying, "Small, medium, and large is fine for me."

As it expanded, Starbucks faced another big risk, that of becoming a far less special place for its employees. For a company modeled around enthusiastic service, that could have dire consequences for both image and sales. During its growth spurt of the mid- to late 1990s, Starbucks had the lowest employee turnover rate of any restaurant or fast-food company, largely thanks to its then unheard-of policy of giving health insurance and modest stock options to part-timers making barely more than minimum wage.

Such perks are no longer enough to keep all the workers happy. Starbucks' pay does not come close to matching the workload it requires, complain some staff. Said Carrie Shay, a former store manager in West Hollywood, California: "If I were making a decent living, I'd still be there." Shay, one of the plaintiffs in the suit against the company, said she earned $32,000 a year to run a store with 10–15 part-time employees. She hired employees, managed their schedules, and monitored the store's weekly profit-and-loss statement. But she was also expected to put in significant time behind the counter and had to sign an affidavit pledging to work up to 20 hours of overtime a week without extra pay—a requirement the company has dropped since the settlement. Smith said that Starbucks offered better pay, benefits, and training than comparable companies and encouraged promotions from within.

For sure, employee discontent is far from the image Starbucks wants to project of relaxed workers cheerfully making cappuccinos. But perhaps it is inevitable. The business model calls for lots of low-wage workers. And the more people who are hired as Starbucks expands, the less they are apt to feel connected to the original mission of high service—bantering with customers and treating them like family. Robert J. Thompson, a professor of popular culture at Syracuse University, said of Starbucks: "It's turning out to be one of the greatest 21st century American success stories—complete with all the ambiguities."

Overseas, though, the whole Starbucks package seemed new and, to many young people, still very cool. In Vienna, where Starbucks had a gala opening for its first Austrian store in December 2004, Helmut Spudich, a business editor for the paper *Der Standard,* predicted that Starbucks would attract a younger crowd than the established cafes. "The coffeehouses in Vienna are nice, but they are old. Starbucks is considered hip," he said. But if Starbucks could count on its youth appeal to win a welcome in new markets, such enthusiasm could not be counted on indefinitely. In Japan the company beat even its own bullish expectations, growing to 368 stores after opening its first in Tokyo in 1996. Affluent young Japanese women like Anna Kato, a 22-year-old Toyota Motors worker, loved the place. "I don't care if it costs more, as long as it tastes sweet," she said, sitting in the world's busiest Starbucks, in Tokyo's Shibuya district. Yet same-store sales growth had fallen in the past ten months in Japan, Starbucks' top foreign market, as rivals offered similar fare. Add to that the depressed economy, and Starbucks Japan seemed to be losing steam. Although it forecasted a 30% gain in net profit, to $8 million, for the year started in April, on record sales of $516 million, same-store sales were down 14% for the year ended in June. Meanwhile in England, Starbucks' second-biggest overseas market, with 310 stores, imitators were popping up left and right to steal market share.

Entering other big markets might be tougher yet. The French seem to be ready for Starbucks' sweeter taste, said Philippe Bloch, cofounder of Columbus Cafe, a Starbucks-like chain. But he wondered if the company could profitably cope with France's arcane regulations and generous labor benefits. And in Italy, the epicenter of European coffee culture, the notion that the locals will abandon their own 200,000 coffee bars en masse for Starbucks strikes many as ludicrous. For one thing, Italian coffee bars prosper by serving food as well as coffee, an area where Starbucks still struggles. Also, Italian coffee is cheaper than U.S. java and, say Italian purists, much better. Americans paid about $1.50 for an espresso. In northern Italy the price was $0.67; in the south, just $0.55. Schultz insists that Starbucks will eventually come to Italy. It will have a lot to prove when it does. Carlo Petrini, founder of the anti-globalization movement Slow Food, sniffs that Starbucks' "substances served in styrofoam" won't cut it. The cups are paper, of course. But the skepticism is real.

As Starbucks spreads out, Schultz will have to be increasingly sensitive to such cultural challenges. In December, for instance, he flew to Israel to meet with foreign secretary Shimon Peres and other Israeli officials to discuss the Middle East crisis. He did not divulge the nature of his discussions but subsequently, at a Seattle synagogue, Schultz let the Palestinians have it. With Starbucks outlets already in Kuwait, Lebanon, Oman, Qatar, and Saudi Arabia, he created a mild uproar among Palestinian supporters. Schultz quickly backpedaled, saying that his words were taken out of context and asserting that he is "pro-peace" for both sides.

There are plenty more minefields ahead. So far, the Seattle coffee company has compiled an envious record of growth. But the giddy buzz of that initial expansion is wearing off. Now Starbucks is waking up to the grande challenges face by any corporation bent on becoming a global powerhouse.

POSTSCRIPT: THE FATE OF COFFEE GROWERS

Is Starbucks Corporation profiting at the expense of the poor—that is, the poverty-stricken coffee farmers who supply the basic ingredient for the espressos and grande cappuccinos affluent Americans buy?

Consider this: While company profits have tripled since 1997, to $181 million in fiscal 2000, many of the world's coffee farmers have been devastated by historically low prices. Coffee in 2005 was priced around $50 per pound, while production costs were around $80 per pound. "Small farmers are barely able to survive right now," said Guillermo Denaux, who monitors Central American Fair Trade cooperatives from EI Salvador.

Starbucks' role as the world's fifth-largest buyer of coffee—behind the likes of Nestlé and Procter & Gamble—has placed it smack in the center of a controversy over how well-heeled corporations deal with poor farmers. The chain has a lot to lose if consumers, especially young ones, see it as a Third World profiteer. But the plight of the world's financially struggling coffee farmers is a complicated one, and not all the fault of corporate coffee buyers. Farmers are caught up in the harsh world of commodity markets, where prices are based on supply and demand in a highly fragmented industry. A chronic coffee surplus has resulted in years of low prices.

While undeniably benefiting from those cheap beans, Starbucks strives to portray itself as a responsible global citizen. Chief executive Smith points to the company's involvement with various programs aimed at hiking the wages of farmers and improving the local environment. Starbucks recently unveiled guidelines that will pay farmers a premium price if they meet certain environmental, labor, and quality standards. In 2004, the company joined Trans-Fair, an organization that guarantees that farmers will receive most of the $1.26 per pound coffee roasters paid for high-quality beans. "Our longtime suppliers couldn't make it if we weren't doing any of this," Smith said. In 2005, Starbucks bought 150,000 pounds of fair-trade coffee from COOCAFE, the Consortium of Coffee Cooperatives of Guanacaste and Montes de Oro in Costa Rica. That was double what the cooperatives sold Starbucks in 2004 but far below the 1.8 million pounds they had been hoping for. Groups such as Global Exchange and the Organic Consumers Association noted that Starbucks was the only specialty coffee company that would not certify 5% of its coffee as "fair trade."

Critics contend that Starbucks spends more time polishing its image than it does tackling gaping inequities with suppliers. Starbucks makes sure everyone knows about the health clinic it built in Guatemala, said Deborah James, fair-trade director for Global Exchange, a San Francisco-based human rights organization. "Building a clinic is a great thing," she said. "But it doesn't address the underlying poverty that is killing coffee farmers and their families." Starbucks says it is working toward creating a sustainable business model in Guatemala, not trying to change its laws. Still, the company could do more for the people who have a big hand in its success, contends Stephen Coats, executive director for U.S./Labor Education in the Americas Project, another rights group. He would like to see Starbucks move faster to buy more fair-trade coffee. "Starbucks is moving very slowly, given the gravity of the situation, and tends to move only when pushed." It's time, activists suggest, for Starbucks to share the wealth.

Name Index

AACC, 434, 439
ABB company, 600
ABMs, 421, 423
Accor Group, 586
ACER, 591
Acumen Inc., 599
ADB, 584
ADC, 497, 500
Adele Gulfo, 405
Advertising Design Agency (ADA), 629
Agrex Saigon, 592
Airborne, 409
Air France, 467
Alcatel, 482, 586
Allen-Bradley, 601
American Airlines, 476, 477
American butt, 511
American Diabetes Association, 512
Anderson Consulting, 537
Anheuser-Busch, 554–556, 569
Apple, 543
Applebee's, 611, 612, 616
Arby's, 612, 616
Asahi, 554, 555, 557
Asia Pacific Breweries, 554, 557
AST, 591
AstraZeneca, 405
Atlas, 578
AT&T, 471, 472, 474, 475, 478–483
Austin supermarket chain, 512
Australia's Qantas Airlines, 467
Avon, 578
    Products, 601
A&W All-American Food Restaurants, 610,
    615–617

Badalona factory, 450, 451
Ball Corporation, 578
Bank of Montreal, 421, 427
Barnard, Neal, 510
Baskin Robbins, 612, 616
Baycol, 405
Bayer, 405
Beck's, 553–555, 557, 560, 561, 563
Beetle, 543
Beranek & Newman, 474
Berca, 592
Bezanson, Thomas, 510
BHP, 586
Big Brown, 410, 412
Big Tobacco, 509
Blanchard and Clot, 514
BMW, 542
Bob Evans, 611, 612
Bob Studz, 547
BodyGem, 512
Boeing Company, 466, 468

Bojangles', 612–614
Bond Brewing, 551
Boston Market, 612–614
Bournvita, 627
Box-Jenkins, 163
Brauerei Beck and Co., 550
Bridgestone/Firestone, 601
Britain's Marks and Spencer, 572
British Aerospace, 465
British Petroleum (BP), 41
British Telecom, 482,
Brooks Brothers, 572
BSA, 578
Budweiser, 553–555, 557, 560, 561, 563
Buffalo Wild Wings Grill & Bar, 611
Bureaucratic organizations, 475
Burger King, 512, 608, 611, 612, 615, 616,
    618, 619, 622
Busch Gardens, 527

Cadbury, 627, 628
Cadbury Schweppes, 511
Calella, 461
Calella de Palafrugell, 458
Caliber Systems, 410
Camy, 451, 452, 460, 471, 463, 464
Canadian financial services company, 421
Canadian plastics company, 575
Cannondale, 581
Capital Insurance Company, 535–539
CAPS, 434, 439, 477–479
Captain D's Seafood, 612
Carlsberg, 554–557, 560, 561, 563
Carl's Jr., 615, 616
Carlton and United Breweries (CUB), 551
Changzhou, 554
Cheesecake Factory, 612
Chevrolet, 542
Chick-fil-A, 612, 613, 614
Chili's, 611, 612, 616
Chrysler Corporation, 542
Chuck E. Cheese's, 611, 612
CIBC, 421–432
CIBC Contact, 421, 427
CIBC LinkUp, 421, 422, 426
CiCi's Pizza, 611, 612, 615
Cisco, 411–413
Citigroup, 537
C&K Components, Inc., 602
Clorox, 520
CMA, 439
Coca Cola, 527, 562, 569, 610, 624, 631
Cocoa Pebbles, 510
Cocoa Processing Company (CPC), 627,
    628
Cognex Corporation, 595–607
Coke, 405, 522, 534, 549, 623

Cold Storage, 592
Colgate, 416
COMECON, 582
Compaq, 588, 591
COOCAFE, 634
Cooper's & Lybrand, 574
Country Villages. 527
CPC See Cocoa Processing Company
CPO, 590, 592, 594
Cracker Barrel, 611, 612
Crestor, 405
Cruise Ship, 525
CSO, 590, 594
CSWE, 439
Cuerpomente, 492, 498, 500, 501

Dairy Queen, 612, 616
Danish company, 485, 555
Datapro, 589
David Sullivan, 569
Daynard, 509
DB Breweries, 551
DEC See Digital Equipment Corporation
Denny's, 611, 612, 616
Denver group, 579
DHL, 409, 591
Diet Pepsi, 609
Digital Equipment Corporation (DEC), 587,
    589
Disney Culture, 525
Disneyland, 525–528
Disney Theme Parks, 612
Disneyland Paris, 525
Domino's, 612, 615, 616
Donatos Pizza, 613
Douglas Myers, 549
Dow Chemical, 520
Dunkin' Donuts, 612, 616, 633
DVT Corporation, 600, 601

EADS, 465, 467, 469
7-Eleven, 612
El Pollo Loco, 612–614
Elvis movie, 512
Ericsson, 482, 601
Espresso Vivace, 632
Estée Lauder, 503
EuroDisney, 525
Europe's nonfood retailers, 572
Excelerite Integrated Systems, Inc. (EIS),
    547–548

Farga, 450–461
Farggi Corporation, 450
Farggi parlours, 455, 456–458, 460
FedEx, 409–412
Fen-Phen, 512

Fiat, 620
Fibersense, 602
Financial Accounting Standards Board
    (FASB), 219
Fisher-Rosemount Systems, 602
Folkman, Randy, 514–518
Food and Drug Administration, 512
Food Guide Pyramid, 511, 512
Ford Foundation, 514
Fortune 500 niche, 476, 477, 479
Foster's, 554, 555, 557
France's Aerospatiale, 465
Franklin, Ben, 519
French Aerospatiale Matra, 465
Friedman, Jeffry, 512
Frigo, 451, 452, 460, 461
Frito-Lay, Inc., 609, 610
Fujitsu, 598

Gap Inc., 632
Garnier Product, 502, 508
Gatorade, 610
General Electric, 631
General Motors (GM), 540–545, 620
George Washington University School of
    Law, 509
George Weston Ltd., 414
Gericault, 514
German Brauerei Beck & Co., 555
German Dasa, 465
German manufacturer, 417
Gillette, 549
Gillette's Duracell, 521
Gimeor, Inc., 602
GlaxoSmithKline, 408
Glorious China, 527
Golden Coral, 611, 612
Goldman Sachs, 537
Goyes family, 489, 490–492, 497, 498
Great Value, 522
GTE, 478, 480, 482
GuangMing, 553

Häagen Dazs ice cream parlour, 450, 452,
    455, 457
Habib's restaurant, 622
Habitat's British and French stores, 574
Hal Riney & Partners, 633
Happy Valley, 527
Hardee's, 611, 612, 616
Harley-Davidson, 543
Hastings, 471, 472, 474, 475, 484
Haworth Press, 439
4-H Club, 581
HCMC Computer Association See Ho Chi
    Minh City Computer Association
Heineken, 553–557, 560, 561
Heinz and General Mills, 512
Hercules, 578
Hero, 578, 580, 581

Heublein, Inc., 608, 609
Hewlett-Packard Asia Pacific (HPAP), 582,
    592
Hewlett-Packard Company (HP), 411,
    582–594, 601, 632
High Performance Technology Corporation
    (HiPT), 590
Hirsch, 510, 511
Ho Chi Minh City Computer Association,
    591
Home Shopping Network, 479
Honda, 620
    Accord, 540
    Civic, 545
Hong Kong Tourist Association, 527
Hooter's, 612
Houston Supercenters, 523
HP See Hewlett-Packard Company
HPAP See Hewlett-Packard Asia Pacific
HPSI, 590
Hulk Hands markets, 522
Hullmandel, 514
Hynix Semiconductor, 606

IADS, 497, 500
IBM, 479, 481, 587–589, 591, 597, 631
IDC, 589
IDE See International Development
    Enterprises
IHOP, 611, 612, 616
IKEA, 572–574
Industrial organization (IO), 59
Intel Inside, 595
Intelli Choise, 543
Interbrew, 554
International Development Enterprises
    (IDE),
    575–583
International Lease Finance Corporation,
    467
International telephone and telegraph
    corporation (ITT), 50
IPO, 409, 597
Isys Controls, 599

Jamesbury Corporation, 602
Japanese Medium-Priced Single-Lens
    Market, 262
JD Power Associates, 543

Kaijo Corporation, 598
Kellogg's, 419, 420
Kentucky Fried Chicken Corporation,
    608–623
Keyence, 601
KFC See Kentucky Fried Chicken
    Corporation
Kirin Brewing Company, 549, 550, 554,
    556, 557, 560, 566
Komatsu Ltd., 598, 602
Kontakt, 491

Kortec and Wrenware Architectural
    Hardware, 529–534
Kraft, 511
Krispy Kreme, 612
Kroger, 523

Lacrem, 451, 461
La Menorquina, 452, 459, 464
La Vanguardia, 463, 501
L.D. Nathan & Co., 549
Lehman Brothers, 605
Leonardo DiCaprio, 512
Levelor blinds, 521
Lever Brothers, 416
Lexus and Infinity, 543
Linkman, 554
Lion Nathan China (LNC), 549–571
Lion Nathan Limited (LN), 549–571
Lipitor Market, 405–408
Listerine, 406
Little Caesars, 611, 612, 616
L'Illa Diagonal, 457, 460
LN See Lion Nathan Limited
LNC See Lion Nathan China
Loblaw Companies Limited, 414
Loblaws, 414–420
Lockheed Martin, 520
Logistics company, 410, 411, 451, 454, 455,
    459, 520, 591
Lonetown Press, 514–518
Long John Silver's, 610, 612, 615, 617
L'Oréal Group, 502–508
Lotteria, 616
Lotus Corporation, 587

Madrid, 451, 458–461, 631
Malaga, 451, 458, 460, 461
Marketplace Village Technologies, Inc., 580
Marubeni Hytech Co. Ltd., 597
Mass Mutual, 537
Matsushita Electric Industrial, 596, 598, 601
Mayan Automation, 599
McDern, Tim, 529, 531
McDonald's McGriddle, 9
McDonald, 509–511, 608, 611–613,
    615–619, 622, 623, 632
McGriddle, 9
MCI, 478, 480, 481
McKinsey and Co., 562, 563
McKinsey & Co. Posner's, 535
Medicaid, 509
Mercedes-Benz, 620
Merck's Zocor, 405–408
Merrill Lynch, 537
Metropolitan Fiber Services Corp., 479
Mevacor, 405–407
Mickey, 525–528
Microsoft, 520, 523, 631
Miko, 452, 460, 463, 464
Miller, 554
Milwaukee, 543

Miracle Mart, 416
Mitsubishi, 601, 605
Mitsuoishi Shoji Kaisha, Ltd., 608
Mobil, 586
Mobile International, 632
Montgat factory, 451, 453, 456, 457
Montreal-based Teleglobe Inc., 586
Morgan Stanley Dean Whitter, 537
Mos Burger, 616
Mountain Dew, 609
Mourlot and Desjobert, 514

NAACFA, 439
NABB Brothers, 627, 628
Nabisco Corporation, 419, 420, 609
NACSW, 433–440
NACSW's Growth Endeavors, 433–440
NASA, 466
NASW, 434, 439
National Weight Control Registry, 511
Nestlé (Ghana) Ltd., 624–630
Nestlé A.S., 624, 634
New York's Chadbourne & Parke, 510
New York University, 509
Newell glassware, 521
Newell Rubbermaid, 522
North American Entrepreneurs, 575
Northeastern University law, 509
Northern Telecom, 474, 482
Nynex, 474, 480, 481

OEMS, 482, 483, 595–600, 603, 605, 606
Oil of Olaz (Oil of Olay), 503, 504
Old Country Buffet, 612
Olive Garden, 611, 612
Omron, 601
Ontario, 414, 416–418, 420, 421
Orange Julius, 616
Organization of Economic Cooperation and
    Development (OECD), 383
Original Equipment Manufacturers (OEMs),
    595–602, 605–607
Osram, 417, 418
Outback Steakhouse, 611, 612, 616

Pabst Blue Ribbon, 554
Palmolive, 416
Panera Bread, 612
Pans & Company, 459
Papa John's, 611, 612
Parke-Davis, 406
Parsytec, 600
Paseo de Gracia, 457, 459, 460
Pasta Bravo, 610
Pepsi, 405, 511, 512, 520, 549, 551, 557,
    609, 610, 620, 631
PepsiCo, Inc., 511, 520, 549, 609, 610, 620,
    631
Pepsi-Cola Company, 609
Peregrine Group, 590

Perkins, 611, 612
Personal and Commercial Bank, 421
Peter Cooper, 549
Petronas, 586
Peugeot, 620
P. F. Chang's China Bistro, 611
Pfizer, 406–408
Pfizer-Warner-Lambert, 405
Phillips, 417,
Picasso and Braque, 514
Pittsburgh Company, 410
PizzaExpress, 616
Pizza Hut, 609–612, 615–617, 619, 622
Planet Starbucks See Starbucks
Plaza de Cataluña 450, 458, 460
Plénitude line, 503, 504
Pollution Probe, 415, 416
Ponderosa, 612
Ponds, 503, 504
Pontiac, 543
Port Olimpic, 458, 460
Posner and Hamilton, 537, 538
Power Rangers, 522
President's Choice, 414, 418–420
Procter & Gamble, 416, 489, 503, 504, 519,
    522, 523, 549, 568, 634
Publicis Worldwide, 633
Pullman International Hotels, 586

Quaker Oats Company, 610
Quick Restaurants, 616

Rambla de Cataluña, 451, 454, 454, 457,
    459, 460
RBOCs, 483
Red Lobster, 611, 612, 616
Red Robin Burgers & Spirits Emporium,
    611
Redon, 514
Relationship Bankers, 423
RetailLink, 522
Richoco, 627
R & L Polk & Co., 545
R. J. Reynolds Industries, Inc., 609
RJR See R. J. Reynolds Industries, Inc.
Robotic Vision Systems Inc. (RVSI), 600,
    601
Rocher, 503
Rockwell's factory, 599
Rothmans of Pall Mall, 592
Royal Bank, 421, 427, 431
RPS, 409, 410
Ruby Tuesday, 612
Ryan's, 612

Saatchi & Saatchi, 569
Saigon-Intershop, 592
Salou, 458, 461
Samsung Electronics, 606
San Jose, 411, 412
Sankyo, 405, 406

San Miguel, 554, 556, 557, 560, 561, 563
Sanyo, 606
Saturn Brand, 540–546
Saturn University, 541
Scandinavian Café, 572
Schick razors, 406
Scott, Lee, 519, 524
Security and Exchange Commission (SEC),
    219
Seven-Eleven stores, 512
Sharpie pens, 521
Shell, 586
Shinkawa Ltd., 598
Shisedo, 503
Shoney's, 611
Siemens, 601, 605
Singapore Airlines, 467
Sizzler, 616
Skylark, 616
Small- and medium-sized enterprises
    (SMEs), 4
Sonic Drive-In, 612
South African breweries, 554, 556
Spain's CASA, 465
SpainSko, 485–501
Spanish Ice Cream Companies, 451
Speech Recognition Technology, 471, 476,
    482, 483
Sprint Corporation, 472, 480
SR Corp's system, 472, 474, 476, 477,
    479–484
SR Corp's technology, 472, 474, 475,
    477, 482, 483
Starbucks, 612, 631–634
Subway Sandwiches, 612, 615, 616, 619
Sugar Crisps, 510
Suntory, 554, 556, 557
SUV market, 544–545
Suzhou Brewery, 566
SWIFT, 588
S. W. O. T. Posner and Hamilton, 535–536

T.G.I. Friday's, 612, 616
Taco Bell, 609–612, 615, 616, 617
Taco Time, 616
Taihushui Brewery, 562
Taiwan Semiconductor Manufacturing
    Company, Limited, 606
Tamarind Lithography Workshop, 514
Tatas and Birlas, 581
Tattered Levi Strauss, 521
TCBY, 615, 616
Telcos, 478, 482, 483
Teleport Inner Media, 479
Telesystem International Wireless
    Services Inc., 586
Texas Instruments (TI), 472, 474, 620
Texas Roadhouse, 611
The Cheesecake Factory, 611
The Lock Company, 529–534
Tianmuhu, 554

Tiger, 554, 557, 560, 563
TMO, 590, 594
Tokyo Seimitsu Co., 598
Toyota, 210, 540, 544
Tricon Global Restaurants, Inc., 610
Tropicana Products, 610
Tsingtao, 554, 556
TSMC *See* Taiwan Semiconductor
    Manufacturing Company,
    Limited

UBS Warburg, 523
UMC, 606
Unisys Corporation, 587
UNISYS, 585, 588, 591
United American AmEx TRS, 479
United Automobile Workers of America
    (UAW), 540, 542
Universal Studios, 527
UNIX Systems, 590
UPS, 409–413, 605
U.S. Army, 520

USDA, 511, 512
U.S. NYSE and Nasdaq stock, 536

Varbusiness Networking Annual, 472, 474
Vendorville, 521
Verispan, 408
Vietnam Education Research and
    Development Network
    (VERDNet), 585
Vietnam Mobile Telecom Services (VMS),
    591
Villain, 514
Visine, 406
VNPT, 586
Voice Control Systems, 474
Voice Processing Systems, 474
Volkswagen, 543, 620
Volvo, 542

Waffle House, 611, 612
Wal-Mart, Inc., 519–524, 631
    company's growth, 520–521

    goals, 520
    stores, 520
    warehouses, 520
Walt Disney Corporation, 525, 526
Walton, Sam, 519, 522
Warehouse Club industry, 519
Warner-Lambert, 405–408
WCSO, 590
Wearnes, 591
Wendy's, 608, 612, 616, 618, 623
West Germany's Deutsche Airbus, 465
West Hollywood, 633
World Bank, 584
Wuxi brewery, 560, 562, 568

Xerox Corporation, 601

Yangtze River Delta Beer Industry, 558,
    559, 562, 563
Yoshinoya, 616
Yum! Brands, Inc., 610, 611, 615, 617

Zhanjiagang, 554

Subject Index

Ackoff, 7
Acquisition leads, 99
Adaptivizing planning, 8
  philosophy of, 8
Adequate business, 147
  company, 147
  competition, 147
  customer, 147
Advertising, 16, 197
  internet advertising, 364
Advertising objectives, 364
Advertising planning process, 363
Advertising strategies, 363
  balance of argument, 369
  comparison advertising, 371
  cost-per-thousand-contacts comparison, 366
  evaluation criteria, 366
  matching of audience and media characteristics, 366
    three factors, 367
  media-selection procedure, 366
  message repetition, 369
  rational versus emotional appeals, 370
Antitrust division, 228
Appraisal, 38
  factors in, 38
Arbitration, 351
Attitudinal approach, 365
Automatic teller machine (ATM), 86
Average-commitment strategy, 263

Balanced portfolio, 192
Balancing of scale and market responsiveness, 210
Bargaining strategy, 350
Batteries business unit level, 23
Boston Consulting Group, 6
Boundary strategy, 350
Bowmar instruments, 86
Box-Jenkins, 163
Breakdown methods, 356
Breakthrough product, 61
British petroleum (BP), 41
Broad issues, 99
Budget, 6, 16
Budget factors, 361
Bugs Burger Bug Killers (BBBK), 297
Buildup method, 357, 358
Bundling, 324
  pricing strategy, 323
Business, 147
  three measures, 147
Business ecosystem, 12
Business mission, 148
  broader scope, 148
  narrow scope, 148

Business sector prospects, 197, 200
Business strategy, 8

Business-system framework, 74, 78
  use of, 75
Business-unit-level strategy, 170
Business units, 55, 274
  past performance of, 55–56

Capitalism, 40
Cargo ship market, 91
Cash cows, 189
Channel-control strategy, 347
Channel-modification strategy, 342
  communication and control, 346–347
  cost of distribution, 343
  coverage of market, 343
  customer service, 346
Channels, 330
  typical channel structures, 331
Channel-structure strategy, 330
Chesebrough-Ponds, 24
Chief executive officer's (CEO), 5
Classifying competitors, 60
Company's competitive capabilities, 197
Comparative analysis, 70
Competing-brands strategy, 277
Competition, 58–62
  intensity, or degree, of, 61
  meaning of, 58
  sources of, 62
  theory of, 59
Competitive advantage, 11
  seeking, 70
Competitive distinctiveness, 74
Competitive forces, 73
Competitive information, 175
  sources of, 175
Competitive intelligence, 64, 66
  procedure, 66–67
  sources of, 69
  types of, 64
Competitive model, 65
Competitive-parity approach, 357
Competitive segment, 318
Competitive strategic positions, 172
Competitor profiling, 165
Complementary channels, 339
Concept of planning, 4
Concept of stakeholders, 40
Conceptual scheme, 161
  identification of key variables, 165
  issue assessment, 164
Conciliation, 351
Conference board survey, 5
Conflict-management strategy, 350
  kinds of conflict, 350

Conglomerate diversification, 293
Coor's commitment, 44
Core competencies, 13
Core strategy, 167
Corning, 40
Corporate appraisal, 37
  meaning of, 37
  scope of, 38
Corporate culture, 23, 43, 46
Corporate inputs, 23
Corporate publics, 23, 38
  areas of concern, 42
Corporate resources, 23
  factors in appraisal, 50
  finance, 54
  marketing, 54
  miscellaneous, 54
  production, 54
  research and development, 54
Corporate social responsibility (CSR), 39, 43
Corporate strategy, 8
  boundaries, 209
  direction, 140, 142
  planning, 17
Corporate-wide planning, 7
Cost of distribution, 343
Coverage of market, 343
Creating market-responsive organizations, 208
Cross-impact analysis, 112, 237, 238
  example, 112
  use of, 238
Cross-impact matrices, 117
Culture, 389
  five elements of, 389
Customer, 80–81
  focus, 80
  need, 81
Customer factors, 360
Customer segmentation, 90
  bases for, 91
Cyclical change, 236

Darwinian laws, 97
Data mining, 92
Decision-making techniques, 48
Decision support system (DSS), 231
Decline period, 182
Defensive intelligence, 64
Delphi panel, 111
Delphi technique, 118, 234, 235, 236, 241
  salient features of, 236
Demarketing, 264
  strategy, 265
Derived demand, 312
Deutsche mark (DM), 92, 491

Developmental change, 236
Dexter's SBS value planner system, 232
Differentiated strategy, 149
Direct distribution strategy, 330
Dishwashing process, 65
Distribution channel matrix, 335
Distribution-scope strategy, 335, 351
Distribution strategies, 330
    perspectives on, 353
Diversification, 271, 291
    factors, 291
Diversification strategy, 290
Divestment, 283
Docutel Corporation's strategy, 149
Dogs, 190
Dow's direction, 141, 142
Dreft, 16
Duracell batteries, 23

Ebb, 7
Econometric models, 104
Economic trends, 103
    events affecting businesses, 103
Elasticity of demand, 311
Emerging market multinationals (EMMs), 4,
    381
Entry strategies, 386
Environment, 96, 105
    concept of, 98
    diversity of lifestyles, 106
    health, 105
    home, 106
    orientation toward time, 105
    personal finance, 106
    quality, 105
    scanning, 96
        importance of, 96
    types of, 101
Environmental approach, 3
Environmental scanner, 114
    six tasks, 114
        communications, 114
        forecast preparation, 114
        information center, 114
        internal consulting, 114
        trend monitoring, 114
        process improvement, 114
Environmental scanning, 108
    conducting, 111
        example, 111
    on marketing strategy, 108
    procedure, 109
        relationship, 109–110
    systematic approach, 111
Environmental shifts, 346
Exclusive distribution, 336
    disadvantage of, 336
Executive reward systems, 214
Existing demand, 61
Experience curve concept, 225

construction, 245
Exponential smoothing, 163
Extrapolation procedures, 117

FIDO principle, 260
Finance relationship, 23
Financial Accounting Standards Board
    (FASB), 219
Flexible-pricing strategy, 319, 320, 325, 328
    advantage of, 319
    two main characteristics, 320
Focus and flexibility, 13
Forecasting techniques, 163
Formal planning, 5
France's nuclear-testing program, 45
Franchise system, 348, 349
    types of, 349

Game theory, 225, 233–234
Garbage-out syndrome, 201
Generic strategies, 202
    differentiation, 202
    focus, 202
    overall cost leadership, 202
Geopolitical federations, 103
Global business strategy, 394
    marketing in, 394
Global market environment, 389
Global marketing programs, 392
    strategy for, 392
Global market strategies, 380
    developing, 396
    example, 396
Growing globalization, 380
    broad forces, 380
Growth, 152
    reasons, 153
        company reasons, 153
        competitive reasons, 153
        customer reasons, 153
        distributor, dealer, and agent reasons,
        153
Goal, 140

Harnessing information, 14
Harvesting strategy, 283
    conditions, 283
Henderson notes, 26
Hierarchy approach, 365
Higher-price strategy, 316
Horizontal diversification, 293
Hybrid segmentation methods, 92

Iceberg pricing, 323
Identifying markets, 80
Identifying target markets, 381
Imitation strategy, 286, 288
Imitator, 261
Improved product, 61
Incipient demand, 61

Indirect distribution strategy, 330
Individual firm's products, 311
    demand, 311
Industrial organization (IO), 59
Industry
    dynamics of, 71
Industry analysis, 70
Industry demand elasticity business-
    to-business markets, 311
Industry maturity guide, 171
Initiator, 261
Intensive distribution, 336
International account management, 395
International telephone and telegraph
    corporation (ITT), 50
Interpenetration strategy, 351
Intuitive reasoning, 117
Inventory approach, 365
Invest-to-exit strategy, 197
Invest-to-regain strategy, 196

Japanese medium-priced single-lens market,
    262
Joint demand, 311
Joint venture, 388

Key-markets strategy, 265, 270

Laissez-Faire era, 390
Latent demand, 61
Laundry product wisk, 26
Leadership style, 216
Leasing strategy, 322
Lessor, 322
Levitt's thesis, 146
Leyland Mini, 65
Li & Fung's John Wayne structure, 212
Licensing, 387
    advantages of, 387
    disadvantages of, 387
Line-simplification strategy, 284
    implementation of, 284
Long-range plan, 6
Long-term financial goals, 10
Long-term implications, 22
Long-term scanning, 114
Low- and medium-speed machines, 75
Low-price strategy, 317

Macro scanning, 100
Mail-order house, 76
Make-or-buy example, 210
Market boundaries, 83
    customer function, 85
    customer group, 85
    technology, 85
        three different aspects, 101
Market-commitment strategy, 262
Market-dilution strategy, 264
Market emergence, 83

Market-entry strategy, 259
Market factors, 360
Market-geography strategy, 257
Marketing concept approach, 3
Marketing management, 26
  difference, 27
Marketing mix factors, 361
Marketing objectives and goals, 139
  defining objectives, 140
    framework for, 140
  developing, 139
Marketing planning, 145
Marketing strategies, 231
  measuring value of, 231
Marketing strategy formulation, 30
  common problems, 30
Market potential, 83
  measuring, 83
    customer market structure, 83
    market growth, 83
    market size, 83
    profitability, 83
    type of buying decision, 83
Market-responsive organization, 209, 211
  three-phase process, 209
Market-scope strategy, 253, 280
  major alternatives, 253
    singlemarket strategy, multimarket
      strategy, and total-market strategy,
      253
Market segmentation analysis, 164
Market strategies, 253
  dimensions of, 253
  perspectives of, 268
    average-commitment strategy, 269
    demarketing strategy, 269
    early-entry strategy, 269
    first-in strategy, 269
    harvesting strategy, 270
    international-market strategy, 268
    key-markets strategy, 270
    laggard-entry strategy, 269
    light-commitment strategy, 269
    local-market strategy, 268
    multimarket strategy, 268
    national-market strategy, 268
    pruning-of-marginal-markets strategy,
      270
    regional-market strategy, 268
    single-market strategy, 268
    strong-commitment strategy, 269
    total-market strategy, 268
Market tidings, 99
Market transparency, 311
Maslow's hierarchy, 82
Mass market strategy, 255
Matrix quadrants, 188
Maturity, 170, 182
  aging stage of, 170
McDonald's McGriddle, 9

McDonald's, hamburger chain, 8
McGriddle, 9
McKinsey Quarterly survey, 4
Mead corporation, 10
Mead's mix, 10
Measure financial performance, 127
  four standards, 127
Measuring strategic performance, 219
Measuring strengths and weaknesses, 121
Merger, 291
Metpath's strategy, 316
Me-too product, 61, 62, 262, 269
Me-too variable, 306
Micro scanning, 100
Miller's slogan, 276
Missing-link approach, 118
Morphological analysis, 118
Multifactor portfolio matrix, 194
Multimarket strategy, 255
Multinational corporations (MNCs), 4
Multiple brands, 274
Multiple-channel strategy, 338
Multiple-products strategy, 280

National-market strategy, 258
Natural competition, 58
Net plant investment, 232
Network models, 118
New product, 286
New-product development, 286
  implementation of, 286
No-fat sorbet, 45
Nonpulp and paper businesses, 10

Offensive intelligence, 64
One-price strategy, 319
  advantage of, 319
  disadvantage of, 319
Operating decisions, 31
Operations management, 6
Optimal market share, 151
Optimizing planning, 7
Organizational level, 23
Organizational perspectives, 141
Organizational structure, 207
Organization of economic cooperation and
  development (OECD), 383
Over-the-counter (OTC) drug, 29, 134

Passive intelligence, 64
Payoff matrix, 233
Penetration pricing, 314
Perceptual map, 276
Perfect competition, 59
Personal selling strategies, 371, 377
  compensation, 373
  evaluation, 375
  motivation, 373
  objectives, 371
  strategic matters, 372

supervision, 375
P&G's strategy, 29
Policy, 140
Porter's generic strategies framework, 202
  new product portfolio approach, 202
Porter's model, 72
Portfolio analysis, 29, 181
  conclusion, 202
Portfolio matrix, 23, 186
  critical analysis, 198
  product, 188
  properties, 23
Positioning, 271
Positioning strategy, 271
  two types of, 273
Postponement-speculation theory, 333
Post-World War II phenomenon, 281
Prewash-treatment detergent market, 26
Price-flexibility strategy, 319
Price-leadership strategy, 323
  price leaders, 324
Price reduction strategy, 316
Pricing factors, 306
  cost on pricing, 308
  potential pricing objectives, 307
  review of, 306
Pricing game, 233
Pricing guide, 312
Pricing strategies, 306, 313, 324
  competitive information needed
    for, 309
  customer information needed for, 310
  for established products, 315
  for new products, 313
  perspectives of, 327
    flexible-pricing strategy, 328
    increasing price, 328
    maintaining price, 327
    one-price strategy, 328
    penetration pricing, 327
    reducing price, 327
    skimming pricing, 327
  private-label strategy, 278
  to build market share, 324
Product-design strategy, 281, 303
  three strategic alternatives, 281—283
Product-elimination strategy, 283
Product factors, 359
Product life cycle (PLC), 181, 182
  perspectives of,
Product line-pricing strategy, 321
Product-overlap strategy, 277
Products/markets, 23
  roles for, 23
Product/market objectives, 150
  international economic
    development, 154
  social contribution, 154
  strengthening of national security, 154
  technological leadership, 154

Product/market strategy, 161
formulating product/market strategy, 161
step-by-step procedure, 161
framework, 161
Product-positioning strategy, 271
Product-repositioning strategy, 275
Product-scope strategy, 279
Product strategies, 271
dimensions of, 271
implementation of, 271
perspectives of, 302–305
Profit economics analysis, 164
Profit impact of marketing strategy (PIMS),
229
Project-level scanning, 112
Promotion mix, 359
rules, 362
Promotion strategies, 355
strategies for developing, 356
perspectives on, 378
Pruning, 265

Question marks, 189

Responsive advantages, 74
Return on investment (ROI), 230, 357
limitations, 357
Return on total capital (ROTC), 11
Robinson-Patman act, 338
Rostow, 391

Sales compensation alternatives, 374–375
advantages and disadvantages of,
374–375
Sales planning, 145
SBU objectives, 144
and goals, 149
illustrations of, 150
SBU strategy, 170
determining, 170
Scanning techniques, 117
Scenario building, 240
Sears' core business, 13
Security and Exchange Commission (SEC),
219
Selective distribution, 337
Self-evaluating scale, 48
six classes, 48
Served market, 87
Setting objectives, 154
process of, 154
Short-term scanning, 114
Single brand, 274
Single-market strategy, 254
Single-product strategy, 280
Skimming pricing, 313, 327
Skimming strategy, 313
Small- and medium-sized enterprises
(SMEs), 4
Social contract, 39

S-shaped curve, 181
Standard industrial classification (SIC)
manual, 104
Standard-product strategy, 282
Standard strategies
developing, 399
Stars, 189
State-owned enterprises (SOEs), 4
Strategic advantage, 202
Strategically managed organization, 13
Strategic analysis, 35
Strategic business segments (SBS), 231
Strategic business unit (SBU), 14
Strategic competition, 58
basic elements of, 58—59
Strategic decisions, 31
Strategic direction, 140, 141
changing, 141
Strategic effectiveness, 210
organize for, 210
Strategic factors, 52
engineering and production, 52
financial, 52
general managerial, 52
marketing, 52
materials, 53
personnel, 53
products, 53
Strategic marketing, 19
aspects of, 22
concept of, 19
difference, 27
relationship to finance, 23
implementation, 30
process of, 27
example, 27
role for, 24
Strategic performance measurement, 220
Strategic plan, 30
implementation of, 30
Strategic planning, 9, 221
and marketing organization, 221
concept of, 9
effective, 10
achieving, 219
scorecard, 9
Strategic planning institute, 294
step-by-step procedure, 294
Strategic planning process, 3, 10
Strategic sector, 26
Strategic target, 202
Strategic three Cs, 19
how to compete, 21
when to compete, 21
where to compete, 21
Strategic thrust options, 173
perspectives on, 177
attain cost leadership, 178
catch up, 179
defend position, 179

differentiate, 178
divest, 180
find niche, 179
focus, 178
grow fast, 178
grow with industry, 178
hang in, 180
harvest, 179
hold niche, 179
retrench, 180
review, 178
start up, 177
turn around, 180
withdraw, 180
Strategic tools, 225
Strategy, 8
concept of, 8
formulation, 8
two dimensions, 8
quality and attributes, 217
Strategy development, 142
Strategy evaluation, 174
Strategy formulation, 159
Strategy implementation and control, 205
benchmarking, 241
core competencies, 242
customer satisfaction measurement, 242
pay for performance, 243
reengineering, 243
strategic alliances, 243
total quality management, 243
Strategy options, 199
Strategy selection, 161, 166
Strengths and weaknesses, 121
analyzing, 131
meaning of, 121
state of the art, 122
studying, 122
systematic measurement of, 121
Studying current strategy, 125
operational scheme for, 125
Superorganizational strategy, 351
Supporting strategies, 167
Sustaining competitive advantage, 76
Synergy, 136
business synergies, 136
six forms, 136
concept of, 136
quantitative analysis of, 137
Synergy measures, 136
Systems, 213, 281
role of, 213
in implementing strategy, 213
types of, 213
Systems approach, 3
System-of-products strategy, 280

Tear-down process, 64
Technical tidings, 99
Technology, 101

five categories, 101
Technology management matrix, 102
    different technology, 102
        older technology, 102
        newer technology, 102
Thermometers, 147
Tidings, 99
Top fifteen economies
    by GDP, 383
Top management, 45, 53, 376
Top management's value system, 48
Total-market strategy, 255
Total quality management
        (TMQ), 243
    success factors, 243
Traditional organization, 207

Trend-impact analysis (TIA), 111, 236
    example, 112
Turnkey operations, 387

Unbalanced portfolios, 191
    Illustration of, 193
Undifferentiated strategy, 149
Unlicensed mobile access (UMA), 21
Up-market products, 318
Upper crust pizza, 13

Value-added process, 209
Value-added taxes, 103
Value-based planning, 231
Value-marketing strategy, 294
Value system, 27

Vertical marketing systems, 348
    administered vertical marketing system,
        348
    contractual vertical marketing system,
        348
    three types, 348
Viewing information, 99
    conditioned viewing, 99
    informal search, 99
    undirected viewing, 99

Weaknesses, 121
    meaning of, 121
White-space opportunities, 12
Wholesome products, 43
Wisk, 26